Caribbean Islands

The Bahamas
p142

Cuba
p285

Turks &
Caicos
p795

Cayman
Islands
p259

Dominican
Republic
p390

Puerto
Rico
p591

Jamaica p509

Haiti
p489

British Virgin Islands p231

St-Martin/
Sint Maarten
p706

Anguilla p84

St-Barthélemy p648

Saba p623

Antigua & Barbuda
p99

Sint Eustatius p636

US Virgin
Islands
p818

St Kitts &
Nevis p662

Montserrat p582

Guadeloupe
p458

Aruba
p125

Bonaire
p218

Curaçao
p345

See
Enlargement

Dominica p366

Martinique p556

St Lucia p685

St Vincent & the
Grenadines p726

Grenada p433

Barbados p192

Trinidad &
Tobago p750

Mara Vorhees, Paul Clammer, Ashley Harrell,
Liza Prado, Brendan Sainsbury, Alex Egerton, Anna Kaminski,
Catherine Le Nevez, Tom Masters, Carolyn McCarthy,
Hugh McNaughtan, Kevin Raub, Andrea Schulte-Peevers,
Polly Thomas, Luke Waterson, Karla Zimmerman

PLAN YOUR TRIP

ON THE ROAD

VINCENT ST. THOMAS / SHUTTERSTOCK ©

HAVANA P287, CUBA

Contents

ON THE ROAD

CRUZ BAY P829, US VIRGIN
ISLANDS

Contents

Welcome to the Caribbean Islands

From high mountain peaks to shimmering reefs, spicy salsa rhythms to deep rolling reggae, pirate hideouts to sugar-sand beaches, the Caribbean is dizzyingly diverse.

Delicious Diversity

The Caribbean is a joyous mosaic of islands beckoning paradise-hunters, an explosion of color, fringed by beaches and soaked in rum. It's a lively and intoxicating profusion of people and places spread over 7000 islands (fewer than 10% are inhabited). But, for all they share, there's also much that makes them different. Can there be a greater contrast than between bustling Barbados and its neighbor, the seemingly unchanged-since-colonial-times St Vincent? Revolutionary Cuba and its next-door banking capital, the Cayman Islands? Or between booming British-oriented St Kitts and its sleepy, Dutch-affiliated neighbor Sint Eustatius, just across a narrow channel?

Island Colors

Azure seas, white beaches, green forests so vivid they actually hurt the eyes – there is nothing subtle about the landscapes of the Caribbean. Swim below the waters for a color chart of darting fish and corals. Hike into emerald wilderness and spot the accents of red orchids and yellow parrots. Outdoor-adventure enthusiasts make a beeline for unspoilt islands such as nature-lovers' Dominica and St Lucia's iconic lush Piton mountains, which send out a siren call to climbers.

Sunlit Culture

The tropical sunlight is infectious. Like birds shedding dull adolescent plumage, visitors leave their wardrobes of gray and black behind when they step off the plane and don the Caribbean palette. Even the food is colorful, with rainbows of produce brightening up the local markets. You'll also see every hue at intense, costume-filled festivities such as Carnival, celebrated throughout the region but particularly in Trinidad. Glorious crumbling Cuba, reggae-rolling Jamaica and Vodou-loving Haiti top the wish lists for travelers seeking unique cultural experiences and Unesco heritage havens.

Tropical Adventures

You can find any kind of island adventure here. With so many islands, beaches, cultures, flavors and waves to choose from, how could this not be vacation paradise? You can do nothing on the sand, party at a resort, explore a new community, hop between islands, discover wonders under the water or catch a perfect wave above, revel in a centuries-old culture (and sway to some of the world's greatest music while you're at it), and then run off to find your inner pirate... Just about anything is possible in the Caribbean.

Why I Love the Caribbean Islands

By Paul Clammer, Writer

I was on a beach, taking a break from research. Had I been out to the island on the edge of the bay? the fisherman asked. There was a ruin there, stories of pirates. Did I want to see? His boat was beaten up and its sail made from old plastic sheets, but in we got and dipped over the waves, then waded ashore to a tumble of buildings overgrown with roots and lianas. It felt like Treasure Island and I wondered if all guidebooks came with maps telling you 'X marks the spot.' This could only be the Caribbean...

For more about our writers, see p896

Above: Petit Piton and Malgretoute Beach (p696), St Lucia

Caribbean Islands

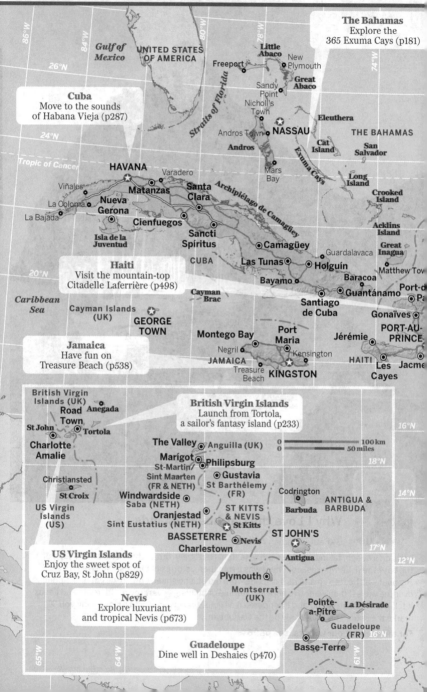

The Bahamas
Explore the
365 Exuma Cays (p181)

Cuba
Move to the sounds
of Habana Vieja (p287)

Haiti
Visit the mountain-top
Citadelle Laferrière (p498)

Jamaica
Have fun on
Treasure Beach (p538)

British Virgin Islands
Launch from Tortola,
a sailor's fantasy island (p233)

US Virgin Islands
Enjoy the sweet spot of
Cruz Bay, St John (p829)

Nevis
Explore luxuriant
and tropical Nevis (p673)

Guadeloupe
Dine well in Deshaies (p470)

Gulf of Mexico
UNITED STATES OF AMERICA
86°W
84°W
80°W
76°W
74°W
26°N
24°N
Tropic of Cancer
20°N
16°N
18°N
14°N
17°N
12°N
16°N
65°W
64°W
19°W

Little Abaco
New Plymouth
Freeport
Great Abaco
Sandy Point
Nicholl's Town
Eleuthera
Andros Town
NASSAU
THE BAHAMAS
Cat Island
San Salvador
Andros
Mars Bay
Exuma Cays
Long Island
Crooked Island
HAVANA
Varadero
Viñales
Matanzas
Santa Clara
Archipiélago de Camagüey
Acklins Island
La Coloma
Nueva Gerona
Cienfuegos
La Bajada
Sancti Spíritus
Great Inagua
Isla de la Juventud
CUBA
Camagüey
Guardalavaca
Las Tunas
Holguín
Matthew Tow
Bayamo
Baracoa
Port-d
Caribbean Sea
Cayman Brac
Santiago de Cuba
Guantánamo
Pa
Cayman Islands (UK)
GEORGE TOWN
Gonaïves
PORT-AU-PRINCE
Montego Bay
Port Maria
Jérémie
Negril
Kensington
Treasure Beach
JAMAICA
KINGSTON
HAITI
Les Cayes
Jacme

British Virgin Islands (UK)
Road Town
Anegada
St John
Tortola
Charlotte Amalie
The Valley
Anguilla (UK)
Marígot
Philipsburg
St-Martin/Sint Maarten (FR & NETH)
Gustavia
St Barthélemy (FR)
Codrington
ANTIGUA & BARBUDA
Christiansted
St Croix
Windwardside
Saba (NETH)
Barbuda
US Virgin Islands (US)
Oranjestad
Sint Eustatius (NETH)
ST KITTS & NEVIS
St Kitts
ST JOHN'S
BASSETERRE
Nevis
Charlestown
Antigua
Plymouth
Montserrat (UK)
Pointe-a-Pitre
La Désirade
Guadeloupe (FR)
Basse-Terre

0   100 km
0   50 miles

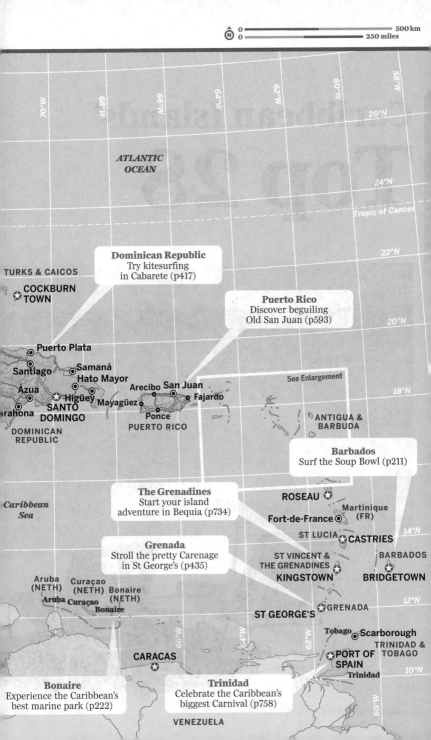

Caribbean Islands

Top 28

N 0 ——— 500 km
0 ——— 250 miles

*ATLANTIC
OCEAN*

Tropic of Cancer

Dominican Republic
Try kitesurfing
in Cabarete (p417)

Puerto Rico
Discover beguiling
Old San Juan (p593)

TURKS & CAICOS

⭐ **COCKBURN
TOWN**

● **Puerto Plata**
● Santiago   ● **Samaná**
● **Hato Mayor**
● Azua   ● Higüey   Arecibo **San Juan**
●rahona ✪ Mayagüez ●   ● Fajardo
SANTO   **Ponce**
DOMINGO   **PUERTO RICO**

**DOMINICAN
REPUBLIC**

See Enlargement

● ANTIGUA &
BARBUDA

Barbados
Surf the Soup Bowl (p211)

*Caribbean
Sea*

The Grenadines
Start your island
adventure in Bequia (p734)

ROSEAU ✪
Martinique
Fort-de-France ◉ (FR)

ST LUCIA ✪ **CASTRIES**

Grenada
Stroll the pretty Carenage
in St George's (p435)

ST VINCENT &   **BARBADOS**
THE GRENADINES
KINGSTOWN   **BRIDGETOWN**

Aruba   Curaçao
(NETH)   (NETH) Bonaire
Aruba **Curaçao** (NETH)
Bonaire

✪**GRENADA**

ST GEORGE'S

Tobago ◉ **Scarborough**
CARACAS   **TRINIDAD &**
✪   **PORT OF** **TOBAGO**
SPAIN
Trinidad

Bonaire
Experience the Caribbean's
best marine park (p222)

Trinidad
Celebrate the Caribbean's
biggest Carnival (p758)

VENEZUELA

Caribbean Islands'
Top 28

Beach Time, Anguilla

1 It's hard to go past the spectacular white sandy coast and glistening turquoise waters of Anguilla (p84). The ultimate way to while away days under the bright tropical sun on the beach is lazing on sun loungers, splashing in the sea and licking your fingers after gorging on ribs grilled over smoky barbecues. On weekends especially, find local artists jammin' at their favorite seaside haunts, such as the world-famous Bankie Banx's Dune Preserve (p92), built from driftwood and old boats.

English Harbour, Antigua

2 Antigua has been blessed with many off-the-charts splendors, including gorgeous beaches, crystalline waters and a deeply indented coastline with natural harbors. There's colonial tradition here too. English Harbour flaunts its heritage at one of the pre-eminent historic sites in the Caribbean: Nelson's Dockyard (p110). Travel back to the 18th century as you wander along cobbled lanes and past meticulously restored old buildings. Still a working marina, it's also one of the world's key yachting centers and attracts an international flotilla to its regattas. Nelson's Dockyard National Park

ALEKSEI POTOV / SHUTTERSTOCK ©

ALAN COPSON / GETTY IMAGES ©

Hot & Sandy Aruba

3 Aruba's two legendary beaches, Eagle (p130) and Palm (p131), stretch for miles and fulfill the sun-drenched fantasies of hordes. Wide, white and powdery, the water has enough surf to be interesting but not so much you'll be lost at sea. The beaches are backed by shady palms, and a long row of resorts just behind. The scene here is pulsing, vibrant and happy, with action that extends well into the night.

Palm Beach

Hidden Coves, the Bahamas

4 With nearly 700 islands spread across 100,000 sq miles of ocean, the Bahamas (p142) has myriad secluded beaches and tempting hidden coves. For ethereal rosy-hued sands, hit up Eleuthera and Harbour Island (p173). The 365 Exuma Cays (p183) are a wonderland of cerulean waters and uninhabited islets, while Grand Bahama offers luscious sands teeming reefs and steaming mangroves.

Exuma Cays

Surfing the Soup, Barbados

5 Although long the haunt of surf-happy locals, only recently has Barbados' east-side surf break, called the Soup Bowl (p211), gone supernova. Sets travel thousands of miles across the rough Atlantic and form into huge waves that challenge the world's best. From September to December, surfing pros stare out to sea from the mellow beach village of Bathsheba. A slight calming from January to May brings out the hopefuls.

PULSONE / SHUTTERSTOCK ©

AMANDA NICHOLLS / SHUTTERSTOCK ©

Shore Diving, Bonaire

6 Almost the entire coast of Bonaire is ringed by some of the healthiest coral reefs in the region. Sometimes it seems like half the population of the island are divers – and why shouldn't they be? The Unesco-recognized shore reefs can be reached right off your room's back deck at oodles of low-key diver-run hotels. All-you-can-breathe-in-a-week tank specials are common. Beyond the exquisite shore diving (more than half of the 90 named sites are right off the beach) are more challenging sites for advanced divers.

Tortola, British Virgin Islands

7 Endowed with steady trade winds, tame currents and hundreds of protected bays, the British Virgin Islands are a sailor's fantasyland. Many visitors come expressly to hoist a jib and dawdle among the multiple isles, trying to determine which one serves the best rum-pineapple-and-coconut Painkiller. Tortola (p233), known as the charter-boat capital of the world, is the launching pad, so it's easy to get geared up. Don't know how to sail? Learn on the job with a sailing school.

USS Kittiwake, Cayman Islands

8 Off the coast of Seven Mile Beach, the 250ft (76m) submarine USS *Kittiwake* (p261) has found her final resting place among the creatures of the sea. Sitting in 60ft of water, the former rescue sub was purposefully sunk to create an artificial reef and a fascinating dive site. The doors and windows were removed, allowing in light and making for easy exploration of the decks and interiors. In fact, when conditions are clear, even snorkelers and free divers can investigate the ship's upper reaches, which are only about 15ft (5m) below the surface.

DELPIXEL / SHUTTERSTOCK ©

Music & Culture, Havana, Cuba

9 Few come to Cuba without visiting Havana (p287), a hauntingly romantic city, ridden with ambiguity and imbued with shabby magnificence. A stroll around atmospheric streets of Habana Vieja reveals rusting American Buicks, kids playing stickball and a mishmash of architecture that mirrors the nation's diverse history. Underlying it all is the musical soundtrack for which Cuba is famous: rumba, salsa, *son*, reggaeton and trova.

Willemstad, Curaçao

10 Colorful Willemstad (p347) feels like an old Dutch city, albeit with sunny skies and Caribbean views. This cosmopolitan capital is a cultural treasure trove, complete with unique museums, street art and vibrant nightlife. The city streets are lined with Dutch-colonial architecture with a citrus-hued, tropical twist. The historic districts are being re-energized, especially Pietermaai, now housing boutique hotels, fine restaurants and funky cafes.

Wild Wonder, Dominica

11 Dominica (p366) is one of the least developed and most unusual islands in the region. Covered almost entirely by thick, virgin rainforest, it's landscape is quilted with innumerable shades of green. See misty waterfalls, chilly and boiling lakes, hot sulfur springs, and valleys and gorges chiseled by time and the elements. It's a natural mosaic that will tug mightily at the hearts of artists, wanderers, romantics and anyone with a green bent. Emerald Pool (p374)

Kitesurfing, Dominican Republic

12 Do your part for the environment: use wind-powered transportation. Year-round strong offshore breezes make Cabarete (p416), on the north coast of the DR, one of the undisputed capitals for the burgeoning sport of kitesurfing. Harnessing the wind's power to propel you over the choppy surface of the Atlantic isn't like another day at the beach. It takes training and muscles, not to mention faith, before you can try the moves of the pros from around the world who ply their trade here.

The Carenage, St George's, Grenada

13 One of the prettiest waterfronts in the Caribbean, this buzzing little horseshoe-shaped harbor (p435) is the perfect place to get a flavor of Grenada, with bobbing boats, busy cafes and a sprinkling of shady spots where you can watch the world go by or admire the lineup of gorgeous old waterside buildings. Spreading up the hillside, brightly colored rooftops and a glowering stone fort get a scenic backdrop courtesy of the green, misty peaks of the Grand Etang National Park.

Deshaies, Guadeloupe

14 This Basse-Terre village strikes just the right balance between working fishing port and sophisticated dining destination to keep its well-heeled visitors happy. The setting is like a colonial-era painting, with wooden houses lining the tidy sand beach and colorful fishing boats bobbing up and down in the turquoise waters. Only the odd yacht in the distance gives you any indication of the smart crowd that flocks to Deshaies (p470) for its great restaurants, lively bars and fabulous nearby beaches.

LASZLO HALASZ / SHUTTERSTOCK ©

AGE FOTOSTOCK / ALAMY STOCK PHOTO ©

Citadelle Laferrière, Haiti

15 In recent years Haiti has been slowly revealing itself as the Caribbean's hidden tourist gem. International hotel chains are starting to catch on, but you can still beat the crowds. Reasons to go? How about the Citadelle Laferrière (p498), the largest fort in the Americas, built on a mountaintop to hold 5000 soldiers and defend the world's first black republic from French invasion. It's one of the Caribbean's most staggering World Heritage sites, and you'll have it almost entirely to yourself.

Treasure Beach, Jamaica

16 Down in Treasure Beach (p538), miles from the urban chaos of Kingston, you'll find a quiet stretch of sand where visitors, expats and Jamaican locals kick back every evening. Beers are passed around, reggae cracks over the air and a supreme sense of chilled-out-ed-ness – oh, let's just say it: 'irie' – descends onto the crowd. Music, food, Red Stripe beer, smiles – it all comes together here to create the laid-back Jamaican scene that many travelers dream of. Come for a day, stay for a week.

Fishing Villages, Martinique

17 The remedy to the often-rampant development that surrounds the busy Martinican capital of Fort-de-France can be found in its many charming fishing villages, where life goes on much as it always has and the tourist dollar has still not made much of an impact. Surrounded by majestic forested hillsides and framed by crescent sand beaches, there's a particularly gorgeous string of these beauties on the island's southwestern corner – don't miss lovely Anse d'Arlet Bourg or stunning Grande Anse (p565).

Grand Anse, Les Anses d'Arlet

CAMERON DAVIDSON / GETTY IMAGES ©

Old San Juan, Puerto Rico

18 Even those limited to a quick visit find it easy to fall under the beguiling spell of the cobblestone streets, pastel-painted colonial buildings and grand fortresses of Old San Juan (p593). Atop the ramparts of El Morro, the allure of this place is evident in every direction – from the labyrinth of crooked lanes to the endless sparkle of the Atlantic. By day, lose yourself in historical stories of blood and drama; by night, tap in (and tap along) to the condensed cluster of bars and clubs constituting the neighborhood's nightlife.

Hiking, Saba

19 Rising dramatically out of the ocean, tiny Saba's volcanic peak Mt Scenery (p624) can only be fully appreciated in person. A photograph can't correctly capture its beauty, especially ethereal when the setting sun casts flickering shadows across the forested terrain. Sign up for a trek with Crocodile James and wend your way through fascinatingly different climate zones as you make your way from the crashing waves up into the lazy clouds. From the top, you can stare out over the island's traditional gingerbread-trimmed, red-roofed white cottages in the valleys below.

Oranjestad Ruins, Sint Eustatius

20 The ruins scattered throughout Sint Eustatius' capital and sole town, Oranjestad (p637), are whispers of a forgotten age, when rum, gold and slaves moved around the world with great alacrity. Sint Eustatius' naturally deep harbor was the doorway to the New World, and during its golden era there were over 25,000 inhabitants representing a diverse spread of cultures and religions. Today, all that's left of this time are the stone skeletons of several imposing forts, mansions, a synagogue and a church.
Fort Oranje (p637)

French-Flavored St-Barthélemy

21 It's easy to dismiss St-Barthélemy (p648) as the Caribbean's capital of jet-setterdom, but there's so much more to this hilly island. Cradled within its craggy coves are small towns that look as though they've been plucked directly from the French countryside. This counterpoint of cultures plays out in the local cuisine as well – scores of world-class restaurants dish out expertly crafted meals that meld the savoir faire and mastery of French cuisine with vivid bursts of bright island flavors.

Spellbinding Views, St Kitts & Nevis

22 Nevis (p673) is tailor-made for trading the beach lounger for the nature trail. Ramble through luxuriant tropical forest, colorful gardens and cane fields clinging to the slopes of volcanic Mt Nevis. Walk along paths shaded by fruit-laden trees while keeping an eye out for the elusive vervet monkey. Panoramic views opening up between the foliage extend to other islands, including neighboring St Kitts, and will have you burning up the bytes in your digicam, fast.

Soufrière, St Lucia

23 Swim-up bars, lavish spas, infinity pools, gourmet restaurants… When it comes to upscale resorts, St Lucia is hard to beat and there's something for everybody. Some venues are straight from the pages of a glossy magazine, with luxurious units that ooze style and class, such as Ladera (p699), Boucan and Jade Mountain (p698), while others specialize in all-inclusive packages. You don't need to remortgage the house to stay in one of them; special rates can be found on the hotels' websites or on booking sites.
Jade Mountain

St-Martin/Sint Maarten

24 Most island-goers would consider huge careening jets and large tracts of concrete runway to be noisy eyesores, but not on St-Martin/Sint Maarten (p706). Clustered around Princess Juliana International Airport you'll find a handful of bumpin' bars that both cling to the sides of the runway and abut the turquoise waters. At Sunset Bar & Grill, arrival times are posted in chalk on a surfboard and aircraft landings are awaited with much anticipation.

Island-Hopping in the St Vincent & the Grenadines

25 It's heard in office cubicles the world over daily: 'I'm chucking it all in and going to tramp around tropical islands!' In a world of package tourism, huge cruise ships and mega-resorts, the very idea seems lost in another, simpler time. Until, that is, you reach the Grenadines. Starting with Bequia (p734), multiple tiny islands stretch south, linked by regular ferries. Jump aboard or hitch a ride on a passing yacht to feel the wind in your face and head off to adventure.

Carnival, Trinidad & Tobago

26 Home to one of the world's biggest and best Carnivals (p758), Trinidad is party central, and its two days of festival fabulousness have inspired the most creative and dynamic music and dance culture in the Caribbean. Visit a panyard and let the rhythmic sweetness of steel pan vibrate through your body, check out the fireworks and drama of a soca concert or, best of all, don a spangly, feathery masquerade band costume and learn to 'wine your waist' like the locals during the two-day street parade.

HAUKE DRESSLER / LOOK-FOTO / GETTY IMAGES ©

Historic Cockburn Town, Turks & Caicos

27 Look no further for the old Caribbean than Cockburn Town (p808), the tiny national capital of the Turks and Caicos, where brightly painted colonial buildings line the roads and life goes on at a wonderfully slow pace miles away from the resorts of Providenciales. Wander down Duke St and Front St and pass whitewashed stone walls, traditional streetlamps and creaking old buildings, some of which have miraculously survived for over two centuries in this charming backwater.

Cruz Bay, US Virgin Islands

28 Nowhere embodies the territory's vibe better than Cruz Bay (p829), St John. As the gateway to Virgin Islands National Park, it has trails right from town that wind by shrub-nibbling wild donkeys and drop onto secluded beaches prime for snorkeling. All the activity can make a visitor thirsty, so it's a good thing Cruz Bay knows how to host a happy hour. Hippies, sea captains, retirees and reggae devotees all clink glasses at daily parties that spill out into the street.

Need to Know

For more information, see Survival Guide (p851)

Main Currencies
US dollar (US$),
Euro (€), Eastern
Caribbean dollar (EC$),

Language
English, Spanish, French

Visas
Requirements vary from
island to island. Citizens
of Canada, the EU and
the US don't need visas
for visits of under 90
days.

Money
US dollars are often
accepted in lieu of local
currency (and in some
cases are the local
currency).

Cell Phones
Most cell phones work
in the Caribbean; avoid
roaming charges with
easily bought local SIM
cards. Puerto Rico and
US Virgin Islands are
included in US plans.

Time
Turks and Caicos, Jamaica, the Cayman Islands,
Dominican Republic:
Eastern Standard Time
(five hours behind GMT/
UTC). All other islands.
Atlantic Standard Time
(four hours behind
GMT/UTC).

When to Go

Dry climate
Warm to hot summers, cold winters
Tropical climate, wet & dry seasons
Tropical climate, rain year-round

The Bahamas
GO Apr-Jun

Cuba
GO Jan-May

Dominican Republic
GO Mar-May

Jamaica
GO Year-round

Guadeloupe
GO Dec-Apr

Grenada
GO Jan-May

Bonaire
GO Feb-Jun

High Season
(Dec–Apr)

➡ People fleeing
the northern winter
arrive in droves and
prices peak.

➡ The region's driest
time.

➡ Can be cold in the
northern Caribbean
from Cuba to the
Bahamas.

Shoulder
(May, Jun & Nov)

➡ The weather
is good, rains are
moderate.

➡ Warm
temperatures
elsewhere reduce
visitor numbers.

➡ Best mix of
affordable rates and
good weather.

Low Season
(Jul–Oct)

➡ Hurricane season;
odds of being caught
are small, but
tropical storms are
like clockwork.

➡ Good for eastern
Caribbean's
surf beaches eg
Barbados.

➡ Room prices can
be half or less than in
high season.

Useful Websites

Lonely Planet (www.lonely planet.com/caribbean) Destination information, hotel bookings, traveler forum and more.

Caribbean Journal (www.carib journal.com) Regional news and travel features.

Daily Costs

Budget:
Less than US$150

➜ Room away from the beach: under US$100

➜ Meal at a locally popular restaurant: US$10

➜ Local buses: US$3

Midrange:
US$150–US$300

➜ Double room in the action: US$200

➜ Bikes or snorkel rental: US$10

➜ Rental car for exploring: US$40–60

Top End:
More than US$300

➜ Beautiful rooms at the best resorts in high season: US$400 and over

➜ Activities in beautiful places: US$100 and up

➜ World-renowned meals: US$100 per person and more

Opening Hours

Opening hours vary across the region, although Sunday remains sacrosanct, with businesses and offices firmly shut throughout the Caribbean. Note that small and family-run businesses may close for a period between August and November.

Top Tips

➜ The US dollar is king. Credit cards are widely accepted in most destinations, but it's always useful to carry some extra in cash.

➜ Hiring a car can be a great way to explore an island.

➜ Islanders tend to dress smartly when they can – keep the beachwear for the beach. Topless/nude swimming is never allowed unless in specially designated areas.

➜ When snorkeling or scuba diving, *never* touch coral, which can be easily damaged.

➜ Book accommodation and car rental in advance to save money. High-season prices particularly apply in December and January.

➜ Much of the Caribbean is poor – use common sense about flashing around expensive smartphones and jewellery.

Arriving in the Caribbean Islands

➜ Every airport will have taxis waiting for flights.

➜ Many hotels and resorts will meet your flight, usually for a modest fee.

➜ Car rental is easily arranged in advance. Don't expect cars to be available for walk-up rental in high season.

➜ Public transit that's convenient for arriving visitors at airports is uncommon.

Getting Around

Air Flying may require long detours and connections.

Rental car Always available; note variations in local road rules. Road conditions are usually bad; travel can be very slow, despite what seems to be short distances.

Public minivan or bus Cheap; can be found in some form on most islands, ask locals for info.

Charter taxi On all islands, taxi drivers give custom tours and arrange for cross-island transfers; agree to a fee in advance.

Ferry Not common, only operating on some routes.

For much more on **getting around**, see p858

Exchange Rates

	US$1	C$1	€1	UK£1
Aruban florin (Afl)	1.79	1.33	1.91	2.18
Barbadian dollar (B$)	2.00	1.49	2.13	2.44
Cayman Islands dollar (CI$)	0.82	0.61	0.87	1.00
Dominican Republic peso (RD$)	47.08	35.01	50.16	57.45
Eastern Caribbean dollar (EC$)	2.70	2.01	2.88	3.29
Jamaican dollar (J$)	128.65	95.69	137.06	157.00
Haitian gourde (HTG)	64.82	48.29	69.05	78.10
Trinidad & Tobago dollar (TT$)	6.74	5.01	7.18	8.23
US dollar (US$)	-	0.74	1.07	1.22

For current exchange rates, see www.xe.com.

If You Like...

White-Sand Beaches

After the color of the water, white-sand beaches may be the second-biggest cliché of the Caribbean. But what a cliché! Almost every island has at least one perfect stretch of powdery sand.

Anse de Gouverneur Wide and blissfully secluded, St-Barthélemy's beautiful beach lines a U-shaped bay with high cliffs at both ends. (p656)

Grace Bay Beach A world-famous long stretch of sand in the Turks and Caicos: you can easily find your own patch of paradise. (p797)

White Bay Bask on the dazzling white sand, sip a cocktail and watch people coming in off yachts in the British Virgin Islands. (p246)

Barbuda There is no such thing as a bad beach on this island. (p117)

Shoal Bay Palm-shaded beach bars in Anguilla fringe this quintessential Caribbean strand's sparkling white sand. (p93)

Good-Vibe Music

Reggae, calypso, salsa, soca and more – the music of the Caribbean is as ingrained in perceptions of the region as beaches and fruity drinks. Vibrant and ever changing, the Caribbean's beat is its soul and reason alone to make the trip.

Jamaica The island that comes with a soundtrack, Jamaica is unbeatable for reggae and dancehall parties. (p543)

Trinidad & Tobago Electrifying, mesmerizing and embodying the creativity of Trinidad and Tobago, steel-pan music here is infectious. (p786)

Santiago de Cuba Cuba's most Caribbean city grinds to its own rhythm in sweaty bars and open-air *trova* and rumba clubs. (p326)

Dominican Republic Test out your merengue moves with seriously talented dancers. (p427)

Puerto Rico Music and dance are part of daily life from the smallest village to the streets of San Juan. (p602)

Romantic Getaways

With 7000 islands, the Caribbean has no shortage of places to get away to and shut out the world. People have been flocking here for steamy, sultry times for decades and everybody's in on it.

Golden Rock Inn, Nevis Fall asleep to a tree frog serenade amid the tropical gardens on the edge of the rainforest. (p677)

Dominica Cuddle and cocoon in an off-grid eco-lodge surrounded by the untamed rainforest of this fairy-tale island. (p378)

Petite Anse, Grenada Has an isolated beach, fragrant with the natural perfumes the island is known for. (p445)

The Grenadines Pick a tiny island like Bequia, Mustique or Canouan and let love blossom. (p734)

Anguilla Many of Anguilla's luxurious villas have amenities such as private butlers and direct beach access. (p95)

Snorkeling

Many of the top dive spots in the region are also rewarding for snorkelers, and there are some sites that are best enjoyed sporting only a mask and fin.

Buck Island Its 29 sq miles (76 sq km) of coral reef system is so impressive it's a National Monument. (p840)

Exuma Cays Land & Sea Park With more than 175 sq miles (453 sq km) of protected land

Top: Windsurfing (p214), Barbados
Bottom: Flamingos (p225), Bonaire

and sea, you won't know which shallows to explore first. (p183)

Curaçao Snorkel with sea turtles at Playa Grandi or explore the unique double reef at Playa Porto Mari. (p357)

Lower Town Beach In Sint Eustatius you can snorkel among the ruins of Oranjestad's Lower Town. (p637)

Réserve Cousteau A marine reserve with big fish schools and shallow reefs that are perfect for snorkeling. (p473)

Colonial Towns

French, British and Spanish ships carrying explorers and colonizers once prowled the Caribbean waters. They established some of the hemisphere's oldest and enduringly charming towns.

Havana A vast and crumbling metropolitan time capsule, the Cuban capital can steal days of your life. (p287)

Willemstad Little changed in a century, this 300 year old Dutch city in Curçao is being beautifully restored. (p347)

Sint Eustatius Once the busiest seaport in the world, it's littered with archaeological sites and ruins. (p636)

Cockburn Town The real old Caribbean, Turks and Caicos' Cockburn Town is undeveloped and absolutely charming. (p808)

Old San Juan Half of Puerto Rico's Old San Juan is in a collapsing shambles – but that only adds to the appeal. (p593)

Santo Domingo The Dominican Republic's capital is home to the Caribbean's biggest and oldest colonial district. (p392)

Outdoor Adventure

The biggest problem with getting outside for an adventure in the Caribbean is choosing a location: you can surf the waves, hike a volcano, mountain bike the trails and more.

Surfing, Puerto Rico Feel the good vibes and ride the near-perfect waves that roll up in the farthest corner of Puerto Rico. (p616)

Windsurfing, Barbados The southern surf isn't too rough, the wind blows well and one of the world's great windsurf shops is here. (p215)

Hiking, Martinique Hike along the base of the still-smoldering Mont Pelée, a volcano that wiped out Martinique's former capital in 1902. (p572)

Mountain biking, St Lucia Ride among the remnants of old plantations and along the sandy shores of Anse Mamin beach. (p695)

Hiking, US Virgin Islands Feral donkeys watch as you hike along St John's trails to petroglyphs, sugar-mill ruins and beaches. (p830)

Rolicking Nightlife

Sipping a glass of wine on a beach with someone special while yachts gently clank offshore, making a hundred new friends at a raucous strip of bars, losing yourself in intoxicating island culture: all ways you'll relish the hours after dark.

Havana A music and culture scene unmatched in the Caribbean – cabarets, rumba, jazz, cutting-edge ballet and more. (p306)

Frigate Bay South, St Kitts Compare the potency of the rum punches poured at the string of funky beach bars making up the 'Strip'. (p667)

Fortaleza, San Juan, Puerto Rico The heart of nightlife in Old San Juan – a lively mix of tourists and locals out for their evening stroll. (p595)

Kingston, Jamaica Check out an all-night dancehall street party or the coolest reggae and dub vibes on the planet. (p515)

Port-au-Prince, Haiti Few Caribbean nights are as memorable as seeing the Vodou rock-and-roots band RAM at iconic Hotel Oloffson. (p494)

Pirates, Forts & Ruins

It could be a movie set. Wait, it was! Old forts and other crumbling ruins date from the days when buccaneers owned the waters.

Brimstone Hill Fortress, St Kitts This rambling hilltop citadel is an outstandingly well preserved example of 18th-century British military architecture. (p671)

Citadelle Laferrière, Haiti A vast mountaintop fortress built to repel French invasions; one of the most inspiring sights in the Caribbean. (p498)

Wallilabou Bay, St Vincent The lush bay here was used as a backdrop for a couple of the Pirates of the Caribbean movies. (p733)

Port Royal, Jamaica Wander the fascinating historic sites of what was once the pirate capital of the Caribbean. (p517)

St-Pierre, Martinique The island's former capital has many ruins from the 1902 eruption of Mt Pelée. (p570)

Watching Wildlife

We don't mean the folks partying one bar over. When it comes to watching wildlife, divers don't have all the fun. There's plenty of wildlife to spot above the water in some of the remote corners of the Caribbean.

Frigate Bird Sanctuary, Barbuda Observe magnificent birds up close in one of the world's largest frigate bird colonies. (p115)

Grand Cayman Frolick with starfish, sea turtles and stingrays on the largest of the Cayman Islands. (p262)

Turks & Caicos Salt Cay is one of the best places on earth to see whales during the annual humpback migration. (p811)

Bonaire Take a break from the underwater thrills to spot pink flamingos across the island. (p226)

Parque Nacional Los Haitises, Dominican Republic Watch birds and manatees from a boat cruising through mangrove forest. (p411)

Month by Month

January

New Year's is celebrated with huge gusto in the Caribbean. Resorts are full, and people are partying. Weather across the region is balmy, although there is the odd cool day in the north.

🎊 Triumph of the Revolution

Cuba celebrates the New Year, the revolution and the nation's birth. Sure there are speeches – often long ones – but this is really an excuse for people to take to the streets with a passion.

🎊 Fiestas de la Calle San Sebastián

Puerto Rico's famous street party, Fiestas de la Calle San Sebastián, draws big crowds to Old San Juan for a week in mid-January. There are parades, dancing and much more.

February

Carnival is a huge event in many Caribbean countries, where it is tied to the Lenten calendar.

🎊 Carnival

It's the biggest party in the Caribbean. Trinidad spends all year gearing up for its legendary, pre-Lent street party, with steel-pan bands, blasting soca and calypso music, and outrageous costumes. Ecstatic revelers indulge their most hedonistic inclinations as they welcome in Carnival. (p758)

Other islands also hold raucous, pre-Lenten Carnival celebrations, including Aruba, Bonaire, Curaçao, Dominica (Roseau), Dominican Republic (Santo Domingo), Haiti (Jacmel), Martinique (Fort-de-France), Puerto Rico (Ponce) and St-Barthélemy.

☆ Bob Marley's Birthday

The love for the sound that plays in beach bars worldwide brings fans to the Bob Marley Museum in Jamaica on Bob Marley's birthday, February 6, and kicks off Jamaica's reggae month.

🎊 Holetown Festival

A week of celebration, the Holetown Festival marks the anniversary of the first English settlers' arrival on Barbados. (p205)

🏃 Master of the Ocean

Called a 'triathlon of the waves,' this thrilling competition has the world's best windsurfers, kitesurfers and surfers going board to board on Playa Encuentro in the Dominican Republic during the last week in February. (p419)

March

It's high season across the Caribbean. On Barbados, American college students invade for spring break. The late-winter influx of visitors is greeted by lovely weather everywhere.

🎊 St Patrick's Week

It's not a day, it's a week on Montserrat. There's a lot of Irish heritage here so the day o' green has always been huge. Costumes, food, drink, dance and concerts by the much-lauded Emerald Community Singers are highlights.

🍷 Maricao Coffee Festival

Puerto Rico's annual Maricao Coffee Festival has demonstrations of traditional coffee-making and local crafting. The mountain backdrop is sublime, and the air fills with the scent of roasting beans.

April

Easter signals more Carnivals. High season continues but the winds of change are blowing. Rates begin to fall at resorts. Temperatures are climbing in the south but the Caribbean is mostly dry.

🎎 Simadan

Bonaire's harvest festival is held in the small town of Rincon in early April. This is only proper as Rincon was the historic home of the slaves who were brought to the island to make salt and harvest food. The celebrations include traditional dance and food.

🏃 Easter Regatta

The Grenadines may be the most boat-friendly region in the Caribbean, with natural moorings throughout. And Bequia is the star of the Grenadines so it makes sense that St Vincent & the Grenadine's top sailing event is here.

🎎 Oistins Fish Festival

On the southern coast of Barbados, the Oistins Fish Festival commemorates the signing of the Charter of Barbados and celebrates the skills of local fishermen. It's held over Easter weekend and features boat races, fish-filleting

Top: Costumed participant in the Crop-Over Festival (p196), Barbados
Bottom: Kiddie Mas parade (p758), Port of Spain, Trinidad

competitions, local foods and dancing. (p202)

⭐ Séu Parade

Curaçao's 'Feast of the Harvest' features parades replete with folk music and dancing on Easter Monday. People in rural areas go a little nuts, and for them it outclasses Carnival.

⭐ Carnival

The Easter Carnival in Kingston brings people into the streets for music and an impressive costume parade (www.jamaicacarnival. com). Huge, as you'd expect. The two-week Sint Maarten Carnival, on the Dutch side, outclasses its counterpart on the French side. Activities begin in the second week after Easter.

🏃 Antigua Sailing Week

The Caribbean's largest regatta, Antigua Sailing Week follows the Antigua Classic Yacht Regatta and involves a range of sailing and social events around Nelson's Dockyard and Falmouth Harbour.

🏃 Family Island Regatta

This regatta draws hundreds of yachts to Elizabeth Harbour, in the Bahamas, during the last week of April.

☆ Carriacou Maroon & String Band Festival

Held late in the month, this music festival draws hordes of partiers from Grenada for big-drum music and dancing, string bands and every other Carriacou tradition at venues around the tiny island.

May

May sees the last of the Caribbean's carnivals, as the temperatures start to get hotter and hotter.

⭐ Cayman Batabano

Cayman Islands' answer to Carnival is a week-long festival of music and masquerade parades – for adults and kids – during the first week in May (www. caymancarnival.com).

June

June remains dry and relatively storm-free. Like May, it's not a peak time for visitors, except the savvy ones who value dry, sunny days and low hotel rates.

☆ St Kitts Music Festival

Top-name calypso, soca, reggae, salsa, jazz and gospel performers from throughout the Caribbean pack into Basseterre's Warner Park during this three-day music festival. Reserve a room way in advance. (p665)

July

A busy month! Summer holiday crowds start arriving, as do the very first tropical storms of the hurricane season. There's another tranche of Carnivals and other special events.

☆ Reggae Sumfest

The big mama of all reggae and dancehall festivals, held in late July in Montego Bay Jamaica, this event

brings top acts together for an unforgettable party. Even if you're not attending, you're attending – the festivities tend to take over MoBay. (p529)

⭐ Saba Summer Festival

Saba's Summer Festival runs for one activity-filled week in late July. (p630)

⭐ Carnivals

St Vincent's Carnival and biggest cultural event for the year, Vincy Mas, is held in late June and early July. (p730) Santiago de Cuba throws Cuba's oldest, biggest and wildest celebration in the last week of July. Sint Eustatius celebrates for 10 days in late July, with music and local food. (p639)

☆ Santo Domingo Merengue Festival

Santo Domingo hosts the Dominican Republic's largest and most raucous merengue festival. For two weeks at the end of July and the beginning of August, the world's top merengue bands play for the world's best merengue dancers all over the city. (p396)

⭐ BVI Emancipation Festival

Held on Tortola, the nation's premier cultural event features beauty pageants, horse racing and 'rise and shine tramps' (3am parades led by reggae bands). The celebration marks the end of slavery in 1834. (p233)

⭐ Crop-Over Festival

Beginning in mid-July and running until early August,

the Crop-Over Festival is Barbados' top event and features fairs, activities and a parade. (p196)

August

The summer high season continues and you can expect the first real storms of the hurricane season, although mostly that means heavy rains as opposed to big blows.

Antigua Carnival

The famous Antigua Carnival celebrates the country's emancipation from slavery during 10 days of merriment starting in late July, culminating with a grand parade on the first Tuesday in August. Calypso music, steel bands, masked merrymakers, floats and street parties all add to the excitement.

Anguilla Summer Festival

Anguilla's 10-day-long Summer Festival takes place around the first week of August and is celebrated with boat races, music, dancing and more. (p93)

Grenada Carnival

Grenada's big annual event may be later than most islands' but that doesn't dim its festivities. The celebration is spirited and includes calypso and steel-pan competitions, costumed revelers, pageants and a big, grand-finale jump-up (nighttime street party).

September

Crowds are down and the weather tends to be wet. This is the low season and it might be a good time to rent a beach house for a month and write that book.

Martinique Heritage Days

Martinique's Journées du Patrimoine (Heritage Days) celebrate local culture and history principally by opening buildings to the public that are normally closed.

October

Dominica comes to the rescue of what is otherwise a quiet month (other than a few passing squalls). Some family-run businesses close all month.

World Creole Music Festival

Dominica's ode to Creole music attracts big-name Caribbean music and dance acts, and food vendors sell much spicy goodness. (p369)

Sea & Learn

For two weeks in October Saba becomes a learning center for scientists and enthusiasts who take part in activities from helping out on a shark research project to learning how to use tropical plants to make medicinal teas. (p630)

November

Hurricane season has mostly blown itself out and Christmas decorations are going up. It's baseball season in the Dominican Republic.

Pirates Week

This wildly popular family-friendly extravaganza on Grand Cayman features a mock pirate invasion, music, dances, costumes, games and controlled mayhem. Book hotels in advance or you'll be out on your booty (www.piratesweekfestival.com).

Livin in the Sun

Some of the world's hottest DJs hit the decks at locations across Anguilla and out on Sandy Island during this three-day beat-filled festival in mid-November (www.livininthesun.com).

St Kitts Carnival

Carnival is the biggest event on St Kitts. It starts in mid-November, kicking into high gear for two weeks of music, dancing and steel pan on December 26. (p665)

December

High season begins mid month and incoming flights are full. Rates are up and everything is open. Down backstreets Carnival prep is reaching fever pitch on many islands.

Rastafari Rootzfest

A three-day gathering near Negril, Jamaica celebrating the best of Rastafari culture, from reggae and I-tal food to the Ganjamaica grower's cup. (p536)

Junkanoo

The Bahamas national festival starts in the twilight hours of Boxing Day (December 26). It's a frenzied party with marching 'shacks,' colorful costumes and music. Crowds prepare much of the year for this. (p161)

Itineraries

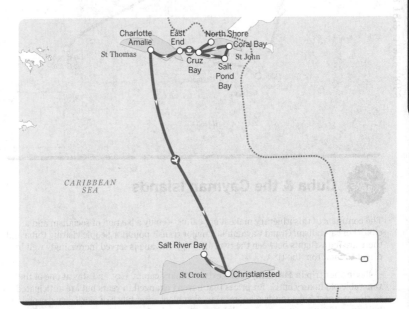

1 WEEK Easy-to-Access Virgin Islands

Scads of nonstop flights put the US Virgin Islands in easy reach of the US and Canada. One week gives the ideal overview of this small but perfectly formed cluster of islands.

Start on **St John**. Spend day one at the **North Shore** beaches: Cinnamon Bay, with windsurfing and trails through mill ruins; Maho Bay, where sea turtles swim; or Leinster Bay/Waterlemon Cay, where snorkelers can jump in amid rays and barracuda. Raise a toast to your beach in rollicking **Cruz Bay**.

Spend day two at **Salt Pond Bay**, where cool hikes and turtle snorkeling await. Drink, dance and dine with the colorful characters in **Coral Bay** afterward.

Devote day three to the Reef Bay Hike, kayaking along coastal reefs or another favorite activity. Hop on a ferry on day four to check out **St Thomas' East End**, with its resorts and marine park.

Spend part of day five in the popular cruise-ship stop of **Charlotte Amalie** on St Thomas, then take the seaplane to **Christiansted**, **St Croix**. Over the next two days drink at old windmills turned gin mills, dive its barrier reef and paddle through the glowing waters of **Salt River Bay**.

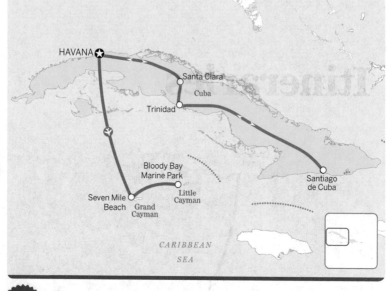

Cuba & the Cayman Islands

2 WEEKS

The contrasts of this itinerary make it appealing – enjoy a bastion of socialism and a citadel of capitalism. Grand Cayman is a major transit point for people visiting Cuba and there are daily flights between the two, although Havana is served increasingly well by direct flights from the USA.

Begin your trip in **Havana**, Cuba's extraordinary capital city, and stay at one of the venerable old luxury hotels for prices that haven't changed in years but are anticipated to rise in a post-Fidel tourism boom. Marvel at block after block of gloriously dissolving buildings, listen to some music and drink with locals. Just wander around: every block holds a surprise and the seawall is world-famous. Head to **Santa Clara** and the venerable monument to Ernesto Che Guevara, the city's adopted son, then plunge into the city's youth-oriented culture. Push on from here to **Trinidad**, a Unesco World Heritage site. You can easily spend a week in this perfectly preserved Spanish-colonial town, hiking in Topes de Collantes or lazing at Playa Ancón. Head east to **Santiago de Cuba** and its many attractions, including the Castillo de San Pedro del Morro, the Cuartel Moncada and, of course, the vibrant music scene.

Return to Havana and fly on to **Grand Cayman**. Head straight to **Seven Mile Beach** and do purely fun things such as snorkeling at Stingray City. Grand Cayman is known for its commercialism, but you can see another side to the islands if you carry on with an excursion to **Little Cayman**, where the 120 or so residents will be happy to see you. Laze on its deserted beaches and consider a world-class wall dive at **Bloody Bay Marine Park**. Choose from its several excellent yet low-key resorts, and have the best ice cream of the trip at the National Trust Visitors Center. There's great birdwatching, and if you're feeling energetic you can cycle around the whole island in a single day.

Top: Stingray Sandbar, Grand Cayman

Bottom: Statue of Che Guevara, Conjunto Escultórico Comandante Ernesto Che Guevara (p315), Santa Clara, Cuba

ANTHONY COLLINS / GETTY IMAGES ©

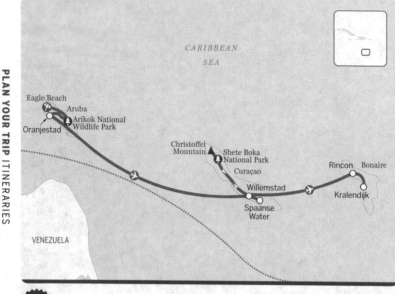

2 WEEKS Aruba, Bonaire & Curaçao

The small size of all three islands, Aruba, Bonaire & Curaçao, mean that even the most peripatetic vacationer will require little time for complete explorations, meaning there'll be plenty of time to simply plop down and relax.

Most places to stay, eat and even play on **Aruba** are in the north. Stay on relaxed **Eagle Beach**, Aruba's best. Assuming you're here for the sand – that's Aruba's real charm – then besides a day to explore the wet and wild northeast coast, **Arikok National Wildlife Park**, which has some nice hiking trails, and interesting **Oranjestad** (which hops when the cruise ships are in port), you should just play on the beach. And given the vast stretches of sand on the island, it won't be too hard to find the ideal plot for your beach blanket.

From Aruba, it's quick hop over to **Curaçao**. This is an island to take your time exploring. Stay in colonial **Willemstad**, which is one of the region's most interesting towns, then wander the coasts to the north, where national parks, restored plantations and a bevy of hidden beaches await. Count on three days at least to enjoy it all at a leisurely pace, including climbing Christoffell Mountain and exploring **Shete Boka National Park**. You might even want to try some snorkeling or head to **Spaanse Water**, where the windsurfing will blow you away.

Fly from Curaçao to **Bonaire**. Once you're there, you may not see much of the island above sea level as you'll be underwater much of the time. One of the world's great diving locations, Bonaire's underwater splendor and 90 named dive sites will keep you busy. Exploring the island, which has stark beauty and flamingo-spotting, and learning about an easily accessed past will take about a day. The island's second city – a village really – **Rincon**, has a slow and inviting pace, while at the horizon-spanning salt flats in the south you can still see evidence of slavery and colonial trade. In the middle of it all, cute little **Kralendijk** combines eating, sleeping and fun.

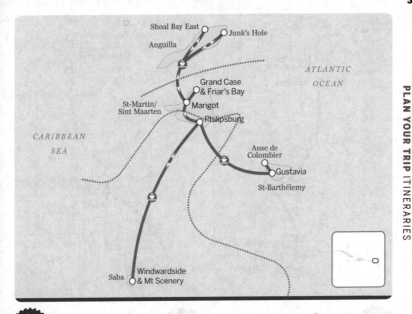

1 WEEK Sint Maarten & Neighboring Islands

Once off the plane in **St-Martin/Sint-Maarten**, you can hop your way around some of the Caribbean's cutest islands by ferry and never see another plane until it's time to go home.

Head to the French side of the island and hang out in **Grand Case**, where your dining choices range from beach-shack casual to fine-French bistro. For beach time try the local favorite **Friar's Bay**, then from Marigot, make the 25-minute ferry run to **Anguilla**. Once there, choose between two beaches: popular **Shoal Bay East** or the quieter, windswept **Junk's Hole**.

Back on St-Martin/Sint Maarten, head down to **Philipsburg** for some retail therapy. Get a ferry to **Saba**, and enjoy views of its splendid volcano. Explore the small town of **Windwardside**, then head out for a hike up **Mt Scenery**. Rent some diving gear – waters here teem with nurse sharks.

Back in Philipsburg, take the ferry to **St-Barthélemy**. Have lunch at the gorgeous French capital of **Gustavia**, and then sun yourself on white-sand **Anse de Colombier**. Although St-Barth is fabled as a playground of the rich and famous, the beauty of the island is that this matters little once everybody's in T-shirts and shorts.

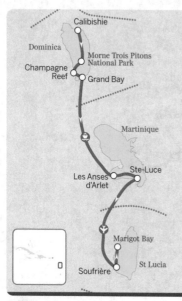

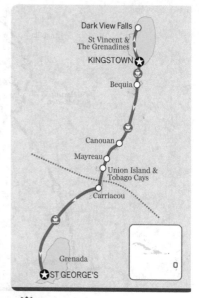

Dominica to St Lucia
1 WEEK

Hopscotch your way south through some of the least visited, least developed Caribbean islands.

Begin in **Dominica**, which many consider the wildest and most natural of the bunch. Start by getting on local time at the comfy properties of **Calibishie** near the airport, then lose yourself in the rainforest at **Morne Trois Pitons National Park**, a Unesco World Heritage site. On an island laced with waterfalls, the half-day walk in the park to Middleham Falls is splendid. Celebrate with a glass of bubbly – or at least the natural bubbles that tickle you while snorkeling at **Champagne Reef**.

It's a quick hop to **Martinique**, where where you should hit the beaches and restaurants of **Les Anses d'Arlet**, followed by diving and drinking in the lively fishing village of **Ste-Luce**.

Take the scenic ferry to **St Lucia** and stay in **Soufrière**, on a bay that's shadowed by the iconic peaks of the Pitons. You can hike these in the morning and dive in the afternoon. For a jaunt, head over to Marigot Bay, with its small beach and beautiful surrounds.

St Vincent to Grenada
1 WEEK

You can join these two itineraries for a real island-hopping adventure. Just get a connecting flight from St Lucia to St Vincent and the Grenadines.

St Vincent is an island of boundless energy. Market days in **Kingstown** are joyfully chaotic as the streets teem with people. Explore some of the island's unexplored lush countryside and enjoy panoramic vistas on a hike to **Dark View Falls**.

Catch a ferry for the one-hour ride to **Bequia**, the center of beach fun and nightlife in the Grenadines and quite possibly the best all-around little island in the Caribbean. Choose between fast and slow ferries and head down the Grenadines, stopping at one of the pretty islands of **Canouan**, **Mayreau** and **Union Island**. Take a day trip to snorkel amazing **Tobago Cays**. Catch a mail boat or hire a fishing boat and cross the aquatic border to **Carriacou**, the pint-sized sister island to **Grenada**, which you will reach by ferry. Once there, immerse yourself in **St George's**, one of the Caribbean's most charming capital cities.

Plan Your Trip
Diving & Snorkeling

Whether you're an experienced diver or slapping on fins for the first time, few places offer such perfect conditions for underwater exploration. The Caribbean Sea is consistently warm and spectacularly clear waters mean great visibility. Professional dive operators are plentiful, helping you get under the waves quickly and safely.

Antigua & Barbuda

Antigua has excellent diving, with coral canyons, wall drops and sea caves hosting a range of marine creatures, including turtles, sharks and barracuda. Popular sites include the 2-mile-long (3km) Cades Reef and Ariadne Shoal. A fun spot for divers and snorkelers is the wreck of the *Jettias,* a 310ft (94m) steamer that sank in 1917 and now provides habitat for fish and coral.

And Barbuda? It's still a secret, word-of-mouth destination, with scores of shipwrecks along its surrounding reef.

Aruba

There is fine diving and snorkeling around the southern shores, with elaborate, shallow reefs and coral gardens ablaze with colorful critters. Wreck fans will love it here too, with a series of plane- and shipwrecks, some of which were sunk intentionally as artificial reefs. Of particular interest is the large German WWII freighter *Antilla.*

Top Sites

Best All-Round Dive Sites
Réserve Cousteau (p473), Guadeloupe

Little Cayman (p278), Cayman Islands

Bonaire (p222)

Saba Marine Park (p633), Saba

St Thomas (p820), US Virgin Islands

Best Snorkeling
Réserve Cousteau (p473), Guadeloupe

Grand Cayman (p281), Cayman Islands

Little Tobago (p784), Trinidad & Tobago

Tobago Cays (p741), St Vincent & the Grenadines

Soufrière (p697), St Lucia

Best for Wreck Diving
Martinique (p556)

Sint Eustatius (p645)

Aruba (p133)

US Virgin Islands (p818)

Grenada (p454)

DIVING IN THE CARIBBEAN

ISLANDS	MAIN DIVE AREAS	WRECK DIVES	FISH LIFE	COSTS
Antigua & Barbuda	Cades Reef, Great Bird Island	YY	YY	US$60-120
Aruba	South coast	YY	YY	US$75-90
The Bahamas	All major islands	YY	YYY	US$90-150
Barbados	West coast	YY	YY	US$60-100
Bonaire	West coast & around Klein Bonaire	Y	YYY	US$25-50
British Virgin Islands	Out Islands, south of Tortola, Virgin Gorda	YY	YY	US$85-120
Cayman Islands	Seven Mile Beach, West Bay, Little Cayman	Y	YYY	US$105-120
Cuba	Bay of Pigs, María la Gorda, Península de Guanahaca-bibes	YY	YYY	US$50-80
Curaçao	Willemstad, Playa Lagún	Y	YY	US$100-110
Dominica	Soufriere-Scott's Head Marine Reserve, Douglas Bay, Salisbury	Y	YY	US$60-80
Dominican Republic	Península de Samaná	Y	YY	US$50-100
Grenada	Southwest coast	YYY	YY	US$80-110
Guadeloupe	Réserve Cousteau, Les Saintes	Y	YY	US$70-110
Haiti	Côte des Arcadins, Môle Saint Nicholas	YY	Y	US$90-110
Jamaica	Ocho Rios, Runaway Bay	Y	YY	US$60-110
Martinique	St-Pierre, Grande Anse, Diamant	YYY	YY	US$70-110
Puerto Rico	Vieques, Culebra, Fajardo, Rincón, La Parguera	Y	YY	US$60-90
Saba	South and west coasts	None	YYY	US$65-135
Sint Eustatius	West and south coasts	YYY	YY	US$60-110
St Kitts & Nevis	West coast	Y	YY	US$70-95
St Lucia	Soufrière, Pigeon Island	Y	YY	US$70-120
St Vincent & the Grenadines	St Vincent, Canouan, Bequia, Tobago Cays	None	YYY	US$80-140
Trinidad & Tobago	Crown Yoint, Speyside, Little Tobago	Y	YYY	US$55-95
Turks & Caicos	Salt Cay, Grand Turk	Y	YYY	US$125-175
US Virgin Islands	St Thomas (south coast, northern cays), St John (south coast), St Croix (north coast)	YYY	YY	US$90-125

Y - good   YY - great   YYY - awesome

The Bahamas

This is Caribbean diving heaven. The Bahamas' great success as a diving hub is due to its unbeatable repertoire of diving adventures. Pristine reefs, shipwrecks, blue holes, vertigo-inducing drop-offs, abundant tropical fish, rays, sharks and dolphins are the reality of diving here. Where else in the world can you join a shark feed, then mingle with dolphins, visit movie-set shipwrecks, descend along bottomless walls and explore a mysterious blue hole – all in the same area? A bonus is state-of-the-art dive operations.

Almost all islands offer diving, from Walker's Cay in the north down to Long Island in the south.

Barbados

Barbados cannot compete with its neighboring heavyweights, but it boasts excellent diving nonetheless. The west coast is blessed with lovely reefs, wreathed with soft corals, gorgonians and colorful sponges. There are also a dozen shipwrecks. The largest and most popular, the 364ft (111m) freighter *Stavronikita,* sits upright off the central west coast in 138ft (42m) of water, with the rigging reaching to within 20ft (6m) of the surface. In Bridgetown's Carlisle Bay, a series of coral-encrusted wrecks lies in only 23ft (7m) of water, making for good snorkeling as well as diving.

Bonaire

Bonaire is one of the most charismatic dive areas in the Caribbean. Since 1979 the crystal-blue canvas that wraps around the island has been a protected haven. Dive boats are required to use permanent moorings and popular dive sites are periodically closed to let the reefs recover. With the exception of Klein Bonaire sites, most dive sites are accessible from shore. Diving is absurdly easy; drive up, wade in, descend, explore. The gently sloping reefs are positively festooned with hard and soft corals, sponges, gorgonians and a dizzying array of tropical fish. A couple of wrecks, including the *Hilma Hooker,* spice up the diving.

British Virgin Islands

The islands huddle to form a sheltered paradise of secluded coves, calm shores and crystal-clear water, which in turn provide outstanding visibility, healthy coral and a wide variety of dive and snorkeling sites. Conservation is taken seriously, and there are lots of permanent mooring buoys.

Salt Island offers one of the Caribbean's best wreck dives: the monster-sized RMS *Rhone* – 310ft (94m) long and 40ft (12m) abeam – sunk in 1867. Amazingly, it's still in good shape and is heavily overgrown with marine life.

Another drawcard is the seascape – expect giant boulders, canyons, tunnels, caverns and grottoes.

Cayman Islands

With more than 250 moored sites, and plenty of shore diving and snorkeling possibilities, diving is the most popular activity in the Cayman Islands. Little Cayman has the finest Caribbean wall diving – along Bloody and Jackson's Bays, sheer cliffs drop so vertically they'll make you gasp in your regulator. The snorkeling here can be fantastic. Coral and sponges of all types, colors and sizes cascade downward as you slowly descend along the wall.

Grand Cayman has plenty of shallow dives suitable for novices and snorkelers, including the legendary Stingray City, where stingrays can be approached on a sandy seafloor in less than 12ft (4m) of water.

Cuba

Improving diving facilities and abundant coral make Cuba a great destination for divers The best diving can be found at the Bay of Pigs, María la Gorda, the Península de Guanahacabibes and the Isla de la Juventud. For snorkelers, there are several fine swim-out reefs.

Curaçao

Curaçao was once a secret escape for savvy divers, but the news has spread, so the island now ranks among the best diving destinations in the region. There's a slew of rewarding dive sites along the southern lee coast. Some of the most popular sites are accessible from the beach, including Alice in Wonderland at Playa Kalki, Mushroom Forest near Boka Pretu and the double reef at Playa Portomari. South of Mambo Beach, the coast and reefs have been protected as part of the National Underwater Park. *Tugboat* is a popular wreck dive east of the Spaanse Water.

Dominica

The strength of Dominica is its underwater topography. The island's rugged scenery continues below the surface, where it forms sheer drop-offs, volcanic arches, massive pinnacles, chasms, gullies and caves.

Many top dive sites are in the Soufriere Bay marine reserve. Scotts Head Drop-Off, the Pinnacle and the Soufriere Pinnacle are favorites. Champagne Reef, popular with beginners and snorkelers, is a subaquatic hot spring off Pointe Guignard where crystal bubbles rise from underwater vents. The central west coast is another premier diving area. The topography is not as unique as in the southwest, making the dives less challenging.

Dominican Republic

The Dominican Republic is mostly famous for its kitesurfing and windsurfing, but the diving is nothing to sneeze at. There's a wide choice of easy dives lurking off the Península de Samaná on the northeastern coast, including near Las Galeras and Las Terrenas. Facing the Atlantic, the water there is cooler and visibility is somewhat reduced but the terrain is varied and you'll find a few shipwrecks to keep you happy. All the main dive spots have shallow reefs where nondivers can snorkel, but Las Terrenas and Playa Frontón are probably the best.

Grenada

With extensive reefs and a wide variety of marine life, the waters around Grenada offer excellent diving. The southwest coast has the majority of dive sites, with the wreck of the *Bianca C* ocean liner one of the most popular. Other good log entries for wreck buffs include the *King Mitch,* the *Rum Runner* and the *Hema 1.*

Molinière Bay, north of St George's, has some of Grenada's best snorkeling and is also an access point for the underwater sculpture park, a swim-through gallery of sunken monuments.

Guadeloupe

Guadeloupe's top diving site is the Réserve Cousteau, at Pigeon Island off the west coast of Basse-Terre. This is a protected area, so you can expect myriad tropical fish, turtles and sponges, and a vibrant assemblage of hard- and soft-coral formations. There are also two superb wrecks in the vicinity. The Réserve Cousteau is also a magnet for snorkelers, with scenic spots in shallow, turquoise waters.

For those willing to venture away from the tourist areas, there's Les Saintes. This area is a true gem with numerous untouched sites, striking underwater scenery and a diverse fish population – not to mention the phenomenal Sec Pâté, which consists of two giant pitons in the channel between Basse-Terre and Les Saintes.

Haiti

Haiti has a number sites where divers and snorkelers will encounter a variety of hard, soft and even rare black coral, along with an abundance of fish. The best are located in the northeast near the Dominican border and around the Côte des Arcadins and La Gonave. Dive shops based in resorts along the Côte des Arcadins offer wreck dives, reef dives, shallow dives and wall dives.

Top: Diver inspecting a giant sponge, Bloody Bay Wall, Little Cayman (p278)

Bottom: Diving at the wreck of the *Hema 1*, Grenada

WOLFGANG POELZER / GETTY IMAGES ©

RESPONSIBLE DIVING

➡ Never use anchors on the reef and take care not to ground boats on coral.

➡ Avoid touching or standing on living marine organisms, or dragging equipment across the reef. Polyps can be damaged by even the gentlest contact. If you must hold on to the reef, only touch exposed rock or dead coral.

➡ Be conscious of your fins. Even without contact, the surge from fin strokes near the reef can damage delicate organisms. Take care not to kick up clouds of sand, which can smother organisms.

➡ Practice and maintain proper buoyancy control. Major damage can be done by divers descending too fast and colliding with the reef.

➡ Take great care in underwater caves. Spend as little time within them as possible as your air bubbles may be caught within the roof and thereby leave organisms high and dry. Take turns to inspect the interior of a small cave.

➡ Resist the temptation to collect or buy corals or shells or to loot marine archaeological sites (mainly shipwrecks).

➡ Ensure that you take home all your rubbish and any litter you may find. Plastics, in particular, are a serious threat to marine life.

➡ Do not feed fish.

➡ Minimize your disturbance of marine animals. Never touch, chase or otherwise harass sea turtles.

Jamaica

So, you want variety? Jamaica's your answer. Sure, nothing is really world-class, but Jamaica offers an assortment of diving experiences. Treasures here include shallow reefs, caverns and trenches, walls, drop-offs and wrecks just a few hundred meters offshore. This is especially true on the north coast from around Ocho Rios, where diving and snorkeling conditions are exceptional.

Martinique

Wrecks galore! St-Pierre is a must for wreck enthusiasts. Picture this: more than a dozen ships that were anchored in the harbor when the 1902 volcanic eruption hit now lie on the seabed, at depths ranging from around 30ft to 280ft (10m to 85m).

To the southwest, Grande Anse and Diamant also deserve attention, with a good balance of scenic seascapes, elaborate reef structures and dense marine life.

Puerto Rico

You will find good snorkeling reefs off the coasts of Vieques and Culebra. The cays off the south and east coasts also have good shallow reefs. The best diving is from Rincón and Culebra, as well as the Escambrón Marine Park near San Juan.

Saba

This stunning volcanic island might even be more scenic below the ocean's surface. Divers and snorkelers can find a bit of everything (except wrecks): steep wall dives just offshore, submerged pinnacles and prolific marine life, including nurse sharks, stingrays and turtles. The Saba Marine Park has protected the area since 1987 and offers many untouched, buoy-designated diving spots.

Diving at Anchor Point, St Eustatius

Sint Eustatius

The island's last volcanic eruption was in AD 400 but you can still see evidence of the lava flow on the seabed, in its deep trenches and fissures. Vestiges of 18th-century colonial Sint Eustatius are also found beneath the surface, such as portions of quay wall that have slipped into the sea. Old ballast stones, anchors, cannons and ship remains have become vibrant coral reefs, protected by the Statia Marine Park. A collection of ships has also been purposefully sunk in recent years.

St-Barthélemy

St-Barth has healthy, expansive reefs and varied marine line that includes barracuda, gropers, turtles, rays, sea fans, giant barrel sponges and black coral. The best sites lie just off the various islets that are scattered off the island. St-Barth also features a handful of wrecks, adding diving variety.

St Lucia

If you think the above-ground scenery is spectacular in St Lucia, you should see it under the sea. The area near Soufrière boasts spectacular, near-shore reefs, with a wide variety of corals, sponges, fans and reef fish. It's excellent for both diving and snorkeling. Wreck enthusiasts will enjoy *Lesleen*, a 165ft (50m) freighter that was deliberately sunk in 1986.

St Vincent & the Grenadines

The sparsely inhabited islands and bays shelter thriving offshore reefs. You'll find steep walls decorated with black coral around St Vincent, giant schools of fish around Bequia, and a coral wonderland around Canouan. There's also pure bliss in the Tobago Cays: these five palm-studded, deserted islands surrounded by shallow reefs are part of a protected marine sanctuary and offer some of the most pristine reef diving in the Caribbean. Snorkeling is also superlative.

Trinidad & Tobago

Tobago is most definitely a diving destination. Situated on the South American continental shelf between the Caribbean and Atlantic, the island is massaged by the Guyana and North Equatorial Currents. Also injected with periodic pulses of nutrient-rich water from the Orinoco River, Tobago's waters teem with marine life, including pelagics (read: hammerhead sharks). The variety of corals, sponges and ancient sea fans make this a top destination.

Speyside is the launching pad for Little Tobago island, which is famous for its large brain corals and is also a mecca for snorkelers.

Turks & Caicos

Salt Cay is a diving highlight, where you can dive with humpback whales during their annual migration. Grand Turk has pristine reefs and spectacular wall diving, while the exceptional diving on rarely

> **BEST DIVING BOOKS**
>
> ➡ *Best Dives of the Caribbean* (1994) by Joyce Huber
>
> ➡ *The Complete Diving Guide: The Caribbean* (1998) series by Colleen Ryan and Brian Savage
>
> ➡ *Reef Fish Identification: Tropical Pacific* and *Reef Creature Identification: Florida, Caribbean Bahamas* (2010) by Paul Humann

visited South Caicos is worth the hassle of getting there. There is also diving off Provo, where you can get the chance to see dolphins and numerous reef species.

US Virgin Islands

The sister islands of St Thomas and St John offer top-notch diving and snorkeling conditions, with a combination of fringing reefs and a contoured topography (arches, caves, pinnacles, tunnels and vertical walls). St Croix features a fascinating mix of wreck (Butler Bay shelters no fewer than five wrecks) and wall dives; the Cane Bay Wall is the most spectacular, dropping from 40ft (12m) to more than 3200ft (975m).

Plan Your Trip
Outdoors

The Caribbean has plenty to get you active, and with water everywhere it's no wonder aquatic sports are a big draw for many vacationers. But you'll also be seduced by fun on land, such as hikes through rainforests and up volcanoes.

Boating & Sailing

The Caribbean is a first-rate sailing destination – boats and rum-sipping, salty-skinned sailors are everywhere. On many public beaches and at resorts, water-sports huts rent out Hobie Cats or other small sailboats for near-shore exploring. Many sailboat-charter companies run day trips to other islands and offer party trips aboard tall ships or sunset cruises on catamarans (usually complete with Champagne or rum cocktails).

The region is one of the world's prime yachting locales, offering diversity, warm weather and fine scenery. The many small islands grouped closely together are not only fun to explore but also form a barrier, providing relatively calm sailing waters.

Highlights include the following:

Antigua & Barbuda Yachting base. Dickenson Bay is a popular anchorage with resorts ashore and a good beach, while English Harbour is a historic and premier yacht harbor.

The Bahamas Yachting base. The Abacos is the self-proclaimed 'Sailing Capital of the World' so take time to tool around the Loyalist Cays with a rental boat. Explore the 365 Exuma Cays at your leisure with a rental boat.

British Virgin Islands Sailing here is a top Caribbean activity thanks to steady trade winds, hundreds of protected bays and an abundance of charter boats. Tortola is the charter-boat capital of the Caribbean.

Best Outdoor Activities

Boating & Sailing A top activity on almost every island, the purpose of many trips.

Diving & Snorkeling This is the Caribbean's top activity.

Fishing Hemingway made it famous and fishing the blue waters continues to challenge many.

Hiking Myriad possibilities on almost every island.

Kayaking The best way to see hidden coves and beaches or wildlife-rich mangroves.

Surfing The Beach Boys sang about Rincón and pros rave about Barbados.

Windsurfing & Kitesurfing It blows a lot in the islands and there's plenty of ways to catch the wind.

FLAVIO VALLENARI / GETTY IMAGES ©

Above: Stingrays, Grand Cayman (p261)

Left: Hiker on the Lighthouse Footpath (p275), Cayman Brac

Dominican Republic Parque Nacional Los Haitises operates boat trips. Take a whale-watching tour around Bahía de Samaná to see 30-tonne humpbacks or visit Bahía de Las Águilas, best reached by boat. Catamaran sailing trips frequently travel between Cabarete and Sosúa.

Haiti Boat trips from Grand Goâve to remote and pristine beaches on the southwest peninsula.

Jamaica Montego Bay, Kingston, Ocho Rios and Port Antonio are all major ports for yachts. Catamaran charters are available from northern resorts.

St Kitts Has a new superyacht harbour at Christophe Harbour in southern St Kitts.

St Lucia Yachting base. Popular ports and anchorages are Rodney Bay, Marigot Bay and Soufrière. Take a day trip by boat up the beautiful west coast of the island.

St-Martin/Sint Maarten Yachting base. Popular ports include Marigot, Anse Marcel and Philipsburg.

St Vincent & the Grenadines Yachting base. Sailing the Grenadines is a top Caribbean activity. Bequia is one of the Caribbean's best small islands and a lovely anchorage for yachts. Union Island is a popular anchorage with a busy harbor.

Trinidad & Tobago Trinidad's Chaguaramas peninsula is lined with yacht harbors and full-service marinas that are popular refuges during hurricane season.

US Virgin Islands Sailing here is a top Caribbean activity.

Fishing

There's good deep-sea fishing in the Caribbean, with marlin, tuna, wahoo and barracuda among the prime catches. Charter fishing-boat rentals are available on most islands. Expect a half-day of fishing for four to six people to run to about US$400. Boats are usually individually owned and, consequently, the list of available skippers tends to fluctuate.

Highlights include the following:

The Bahamas The Biminis were good enough for Hemingway!

Cayman Islands There are many charter-boat operators on Grand Cayman; blue marlin is a big catch.

Jamaica Montego Bay, Negril and Ocho Rios resorts organize trips and cook the catch.

St Lucia Billfish, marlin and yellowfin tuna can be caught from November to January, and wahoo and dorado from February to May. A good place to get on a boat is Vigie or Soufrière.

Trinidad & Tobago Charter boats offer deep-sea fishing from Tobago's Crown Point or Buccoo.

Turks & Caicos The country's biggest fishing competition, the Grand Turk Game Fishing Tournament, gets underway at the end of July. Providenciales is the center for sport fishing.

US Virgin Islands Deep-sea fishing charters depart from the St Thomas port of Red Hook.

Hiking

Verdant peaks rise high above dramatic valleys, volcanoes simmer, waterfalls rumble in the distance and rainforests resonate to a chorus of birdsong. Most people come to the Caribbean for the beaches, but many islands draw hikers seeking rugged terrain and stunning mountain vistas. Of course some just hike the beautiful beaches.

Highlights include the following:

Antigua & Barbuda Hikes around Shirley Heights on Antigua, including Carpenters Trail, have beautiful views of English Harbour. Mt Obama and Signal Hill also offer great views.

Aruba Roam around Arikok National Wildlife Park for fabulous views of the windswept coast, desolate beaches and wild goats, not to mention the refreshing Natural Pool.

The Bahamas Search for blue holes while avoiding the mythical chickcharnies on hikes in the pristine Androsian forests.

Barbados The Barbados National Trust leads guided hikes. Hike through botanic gardens in central Barbados.

Bonaire Washington-Slagbaai National Park has hiking trails through its desert landscape, with a good chance to spot pink flamingos congregating in the salt marshes.

British Virgin Islands Take watery hikes at the aptly named Baths, wading around boulders and through grottoes at sunrise.

Cayman Islands On Cayman Brac, the Lighthouse Footpath offers fabulous Caribbean vistas and glimpses of nesting booby birds, while Bight Rd bisects the National Trust Parrot Reserve. On Grand Cayman, the Mastic Trail is also rich with birdlife.

Cuba The best hikes are to be found at Topes de Collantes near Trinidad and Valle de Viñales near Viñales.

Curaçao Near the island's west end, Christoffel National Park has eight different hiking trails, including one to the island's highest point at Christoffel Mountain.

Dominica The hiking king of the Caribbean. Take an easy rainforest loop trail or hire a guide for an arduous trek. Morne Trois Pitons National Park has trails to Boiling Lake through ancient rainforest, and Waitukubuli National Trail is a challenging long-distance hike.

Dominican Republic Cabarete has canyoning trips. At Jarabacoa, climb Pico Duarte and navigate its trek-filled parks or take canyoning trips at Rancho Baiguate.

Grenada Grand Etang National Park has a volcanic lake and plenty of hiking trails, or hike around the island microparadise of Petit Martinique.

Guadeloupe Hike well-marked rainforest trails to Chutes du Carbet. Rainforest hikes to Grand Étang offer views of a smoldering volcano, or hike to the misty summit of the active volcano, La Soufrière. Walk the tiny island of Terre-de-Haut, with its soaring central peak and multiple excellent hikes.

Haiti Parc National La Visite offers excellent hiking southeast of Port-au-Prince, down toward the Caribbean coastline near Jacmel.

Jamaica Hike past coffee plantations to climb Blue Mountain peak, or go deep off-trail into remote Cockpit Country.

Martinique Walk the foothills of the volcano Mont Pelée, exploring the soaring interior. Hike the dramatic and pristine 12.4-mile (20km) trail along the northern coast, from Grand-Rivière to Anse Couleuvre.

Puerto Rico Hike the dry forest in Bosque Estatal de Guánica to experience one of the most unique climates in the Caribbean. At Culebra, there's a 2.5-mile (4km) hike from Dewey to idyllic Playa Flamenco, then explore the rainforest trails and misty waterfalls of El Yunque.

Saba Has an expanding network of steep hiking trails, including the 2017-established Elfin Forest Trail, which branches off from the Sandy Cruz Trail close to Hell's Gate, and provides an alternative summit route to the Mt Scenery Stairway Trail.

Sint Eustatius Hike the Quill, climbing the extinct volcano, then winding your way down to the bottom through rainforest.

St Kitts & Nevis Hire a guide for the strenuous volcano hike to the crater rim of Mt Liamuiga on St Kitts or of Mt Nevis on, yes, Nevis, or opt for a less demanding walk through gorgeous foothills.

St Lucia Gros Piton is an amazing climb. Hike to see parrots around inland park Millet Bird Sanctuary. Don't miss the Tet Paul Nature Trail at Soufrière.

St Vincent & the Grenadines The Vermont Nature Trail (St Vincent) takes you through thick rainforest. There's also a cross-island route around volcanic La Soufrière.

Trinidad & Tobago Hike to waterfalls big and small from Brasso Seco or Salybia.

US Virgin Islands Virgin Islands National Park on St John is a regional hiking highlight with 20 cool trails, including ones that lead to petroglyphs, sugar-mill ruins and isolated beaches rich with marine life.

Kayaking

You can rent kayaks across the Caribbean. Explore beach-dotted islands, wildlife-filled mangroves and more. Many tour companies now offer kayak adventures, some at night in bioluminescent waters.

Highlights include:

Aruba Kayak through mangroves and old pirate sites with Aruba Kayak Adventure.

The Bahamas The Exuma Cays offer endless exploration for kayakers. Lucayan National Park on Grand Bahama has mangrove swamps and blue holes.

Bonaire The Mangrove Info & Kayak Center offers highly recommended tours through mangroves.

British Virgin Islands Foxy's Charters rents clear-bottom kayaks on Jost Van Dyke and offers night tours.

Cayman Islands Kayak tours depart from the North Side to explore the mangrove swamps, Starfish Point, and/or the magically luminescent Bio Bay.

Grenada Conservation Kayak explores Grenada's shores and mangroves.

Montserrat The only white-sand beach, at Rendezvous Bay, is best reached by kayak.

Puerto Rico Abe's Snorkeling & Bio-Bay Tours offers family-friendly kayak trips in Vieques; Vieques Adventure Company has totally transparent canoes that let you see the action.

Trinidad & Tobago Explore Trinidad's Caroni or Nariva Wetlands by kayak or SUP with Paria Springs or Caribbean Discovery Tours. The Kayak Center in Chaguaramas offers tours of Williams Bay.

US Virgin Islands Night tours through the bioluminescent Salt River Bay on St Croix.

Surfing

Except for Barbados, which is further out into the open Atlantic, the islands of the Eastern Caribbean aren't really great for surfing. Once you head north and west, however, you can find surfable swells.

In late summer swells made by tropical storms off the African coast begin to race toward Barbados, creating the Caribbean's highest waves and finest surfing conditions. The most reliable time for catching good, high breaks is September to November.

Among the highlights:

Barbados At Silver Sands there are good south-coast breaks and a fine surf school. Soup Bowl is a legendary east-coast break at Bathsheba.

British Virgin Islands Apple Bay has good surfing on Tortola's north coast.

Dominican Republic The best waves – up to 13ft (4m) – are to be found at Cabarete, breaking over reefs on Playa Encuentro.

Guadeloupe Surf's up in St-François, where you can take a class, rent gear or just stay at a cool surf camp.

Jamaica Boston Bay boasts the best surfing in Jamaica.

Martinique Presqu'île du Caravelle has several excellent beaches for surfing and a small but growing surfer presence on its north coast.

Puerto Rico Rincón is well known for perfect tubes and a Beach Boys song.

Trinidad & Tobago Trinidad's Sans Souci and Blanchisseuse are popular with local surfers.

US Virgin Islands Hull Bay is St Thomas' most popular break.

Windsurfing & Kitesurfing

The favorable winds and good water conditions found throughout the Caribbean have boosted the popularity of windsurfing and kitesurfing.

Highlights include:

Antigua & Barbuda Antigua's Jabberwock Beach and Nonsuch Bay for kitesurfing.

Aruba Hadicurari Beach, better known as the Fisherman Huts, is the island's top spot for windsurfing and kitesurfing, but those in the know escape the crowds at Boca Grandi.

Barbados Set on one of the hemisphere's premier spots, deAction Beach Shop at Silver Sands is run by windsurfing legend Brian Talma.

Bonaire Lac Bay has fabulous windsurfing year-round, while kitesurfers ride the wind at Atlantis Kite Beach.

British Virgin Islands Anegada hosts a kitesurfing school for novices and experienced enthusiasts alike.

Cayman Islands Kitesurf Cayman sets up its operation near Barkers Beach on Grand Cayman.

Curaçao The island's top spot for windsurfing is the smooth and breezy waters of the Spaanse Water, a large inland bay.

Dominican Republic Cabarete and Las Terrenas are both excellent areas.

Haiti The Boukan Guinguette kitesurfing camp in Môle Saint-Nicolas is remote but tremendous.

Martinique The village of Ste-Anne draws adventurers to the windy beach at Anse Michel.

St-Barthélemy Grand Cul-de-Sac's sandy beach is one of the island's top spots for water sports including windsurfing and kitesurfing.

Trinidad & Tobago Radical Watersports at Pigeon Point are Tobago's kitesurf experts.

Turks & Caicos Long Bay Beach is a prime kitesurfing destination.

US Virgin Islands The North Shore beaches on St John, especially Cinnamon Bay.

Plan Your Trip
Island-Hopping

It's quite easy to island-hop really. Planes and/or boats link all the main Caribbean islands with their neighbors. Because tickets are priced for the local market, with advance planning you can find airline tickets for about US$150 to US$200 or less.

Getting Around the Islands

Best Ways to Island-Hop

Airplane Airlines link every island with an airport to its neighbors.

Ferry Not comprehensive but, where they exist, the most scenic links.

Sailboat Aboard a rental yacht, you have the ultimate freedom to island-hop.

What You Need

Time With two weeks you can see a lot of a region; with a month you'll live the fantasy.

Sense of adventure Unexpected experiences will be the most memorable.

Money Perhaps not as much as you think, as you'll be traveling like a local.

The Ultimate Itinerary

It's possible to get from Aruba in the far south to the Bahamas in the north, stopping at every major island on the way (p53)

Getting Around

Air

Regional airlines, large and small, travel around the Caribbean. A certain level of patience and understanding is required when you island-hop. Schedules can change at a moment's notice or there may be delays without explanation. Your best bet is to embrace island time, relax and enjoy the ride.

Regional planes are sometimes like old buses, seemingly stopping at every possible corner to pick up passengers – a boon for island-hoppers! You'll sometimes get stuck on what you could call the 'LIAT shuffle,' where your plane touches down and takes off again from several different airports. For example, if you're flying from St Thomas to Trinidad, you might stop in Antigua, St Lucia and St Vincent before arriving.

There are many airlines operating within the Caribbean. There are some good local carriers with dozens of connections, which will give you ideas for itinerary building:

Caribbean Airlines (www.caribbean-airlines.com)

Intercaribbean (www.intercaribbean.com)

LIAT (www.liat.com)

Seaborn Airlines (www.seaborneairlines.com)

Sunrise Airways (www.sunriseairways.net)

WinAir (www.fly-winair.sx)

CARIBBEAN GEOGRAPHY 101

You will hear the Caribbean islands referred to in numerous ways – the Leewards, the Windwards, the West Indies etc. It can get confusing, so here's a quick primer in Caribbean geography.

Caribbean islands An archipelago of thousands of islands that stretch from the southeast coast of Florida in the USA to the northern coast of Venezuela. The largest island within the Caribbean Sea is Cuba, followed by the island of Hispaniola (shared by the nations of Haiti and the Dominican Republic), then Jamaica and Puerto Rico. The Bahamas, to the north, are technically outside of the Caribbean archipelago.

Greater Antilles Consists of the large islands, such as Hispaniola, Cuba and Jamaica at the top of the Caribbean and extends east as far as Puerto Rico. It also includes the Cayman Islands, due to their western location.

Lesser Antilles The archipelago that extends east and southeastward from the Virgin Islands down to Trinidad and Tobago, just off the northern coast of Venezuela. Also called the Eastern Caribbean Islands, the Lesser Antilles are further divided into the Leeward Islands and the Windward Islands.

Leeward Islands From north to south: the US Virgin Islands (USVI), the British Virgin Islands (BVI), Anguilla, St-Martin/Sint Maarten, St-Barthélemy, Saba, Sint Eustatius (Statia), St Kitts and Nevis, Antigua and Barbuda, Montserrat, and Guadeloupe.

Windward Islands From north to south: Dominica, Martinique, St Lucia, St Vincent and the Grenadines, and Grenada. Barbados, and Trinidad and Tobago are often geographically considered part of the Windwards, but do not belong to the Windward Islands geopolitical group.

Ferry

For a place surrounded by water, the Caribbean doesn't have as many ferries as you'd think. However, there are regional ferries, which travel between several island groups. These can be a nice change of pace after cramped airplanes, smelly buses and dodgy rental cars.

When available, ferries tend to be reasonably modern and a great travel option.

Yacht

The Caribbean is a prime locale for yachting. The many small islands grouped closely together are not only fun to explore but also provide calm sailing waters.

It's easiest to sail down-island, from north to south, as on the reverse trip boats must beat back into the wind. Because of this, several yacht-charter companies only allow sailors to take the boats in one direction, arranging for their own crews to bring the boats back to home base later.

Yacht charters are the ultimate Caribbean fantasy, sailing in a large boat from idyllic island to idyllic island. And it's a surprisingly achievable – albeit not cheap – fantasy.

Start by choosing from two basic types of yacht charter: bareboat or crewed.

On a bareboat charter, you skipper a fully equipped sailboat after you've proved your qualifications; sail where you want, when you want. With a crewed charter, you sip a drink on deck while the rental boat's crew swabs the poop deck and does everything else (usually including cooking, and bringing you that drink). You can either make your own detailed itinerary or provide a vague idea of the kind of places you'd like to visit and let the captain decide where to anchor.

The cost of a bareboat charter for a week for four people begins at about US$3000 and goes up from there. Crewed options are much more and all prices vary hugely by season, type of boat, crew etc. The British Virgin Islands are the top destination for renters.

The following charter companies offer both bareboat and crewed yacht charters in the Caribbean: **Catamaran Company** (www.catamarans.com), **Horizon Yacht Charters** (www.horizonyachtcharters.com),

Moorings (www.moorings.com) and **Sunsail** (www.sunsail.com).

For those who don't want to be bothered shopping around, charter-yacht brokers work on commission, like travel agents, and they match you to a rental boat. Better-known charter-yacht brokers include **Ed Hamilton & Co** (www.ed-hamilton.com) and **Nicholson Yacht Charters** (www.yacht vacations.com).

Island Links

The following list shows direct links between neighboring islands.

Anguilla Air: Puerto Rico, St-Barthélemy, St-Martin/Sint Maarten; Sea: St-Martin/Sint Maarten

Antigua and Barbuda Air: Dominica, Guadeloupe, Montserrat, St Kitts & Nevis, Trinidad; Sea: Montserrat

Aruba Air: Curaçao

The Bahamas Air: Cayman Islands, Cuba, Jamaica, Turks & Caicos

Barbados Air: Dominica, Grenada, St Lucia, St Vincent & the Grenadines, Trinidad & Tobago

Bonaire Air: Curaçao

British Virgin Islands Air: Puerto Rico, US Virgin Islands

Cayman Islands Air: The Bahamas, Cuba, Jamaica

Cuba Air: The Bahamas, Cayman Islands, Dominican Republic, Haiti, Turks & Caicos

Curaçao Air: Aruba, Bonaire, Dominican Republic, Haiti, Trinidad & Tobago

Dominica Air: Antigua, Barbados, Guadeloupe, Martinique, Puerto Rico; Sea: Guadeloupe, Martinique, St Lucia

Dominican Republic Air: Cuba, Curaçao, Guadeloupe, Haiti, Puerto Rico, Turks & Caicos; Land: Haiti

Grenada Air: Barbados, Martinique, St Vincent & the Grenadines, Trinidad & Tobago; Sea: St Vincent & the Grenadines

Guadeloupe Air: Antigua, Dominica, Dominican Republic, Martinique, St-Barthélemy, St-Martin/Sint Maarten; Sea: Dominica, Martinique, St Lucia

Haiti Air: Cuba, Curaçao, Dominican Republic, Jamaica, Turks & Caicos; Land: Dominican Republic

Jamaica Air: The Bahamas, Cayman Islands, Haiti, Trinidad, Turks & Caicos

Martinique Air: Dominica, Grenada, Guadeloupe, St Lucia; Sea: Dominica, Guadeloupe, St Lucia.

Montserrat Air: Antigua; Sea: Antigua

Puerto Rico Air: Anguilla, British Virgin Islands, Dominica, Dominican Republic, Turks & Caicos, US Virgin Islands

Saba Air: St-Barthélemy, St-Martin/Sint Maarten

Sint Eustatius Air: St-Martin/Sint Maarten; Sea: St-Martin/Sint Maarten

St-Barthélemy Air: St-Martin/Sint Maarten, Anguilla, Guadeloupe, Saba; Sea: St-Martin/Sint Maarten

St Kitts & Nevis Air: Antigua, St-Martin/Sint Maarten

St Lucia Air: Barbados, Martinique, St Vincent & the Grenadines, Trinidad & Tobago; Sea: Dominica, Guadeloupe, Martinique

St-Martin/Sint Maarten Air: Anguilla, Guadeloupe, Saba, Sint Eustatius, St-Barthélemy, St Kitts & Nevis, Trinidad; Sea: Anguilla, Sint Eustatius, St-Barthélemy

St Vincent & the Grenadines Air: Barbados, Grenada, St Lucia, Trinidad & Tobago; Sea: Grenada

Trinidad & Tobago Air: Antigua, Barbados, Curaçao, Grenada, Jamaica, St Lucia, St-Martin/Sint Maarten, St Vincent & the Grenadines

Turks & Caicos Air: The Bahamas, Cuba, Jamaica, Dominican Republic, Haiti, Puerto Rico

US Virgin Islands Air: British Virgin Islands, Puerto Rico

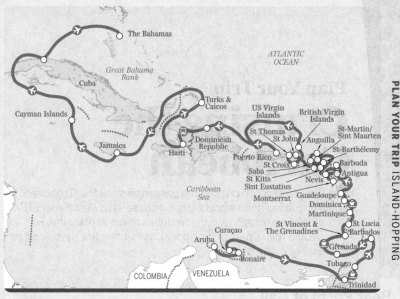

Ultimate Island-Hopping

4 WEEKS

This trip lets you see all the main regions, starting in the south. Ferries are used when possible, supplemented by planes. If you don't have the time or cash for this mammoth adventure just do just one part. A full tour could take from three weeks to one month.

Start in the resorts of **Aruba**, then fly to **Bonaire** for diving and then to **Curaçao** for old Willemstad. Now it's a flight to Port of Spain, **Trinidad**, followed by a ferry trip to the natural beauty of **Tobago**. From here fly to lovely beaches and even better surfing in **Barbados**, then take a flight to surprising **Grenada**. Here you can take boats (ferries and mail boats) island-hopping up through **St Vincent & the Grenadines**. Don't miss Bequia.

A quick flight to **St Lucia** and you are again island-hopping. Going north, make the ferry voyages to *très* Française **Martinique** and on to the waterfalls and wilds of **Dominica** and then the twin cones of **Guadeloupe**. You are back on a plane to **Antigua**, from where you can take a boat round-trip to beautiful **Barbuda** before making the 20-minute flights round-trip for plucky **Montserrat** and its active volcano.

Leave the Antigua hub by plane for **Nevis**, followed by a chance to get spray in your face on a ferry to **St Kitts**. From here it's 30 minutes by air to the transport hub of **St-Martin/Sint Maarten**, with its awesome runway beach and bar.

Do round-trip ferry visits to upscale **Anguilla**, tiny **Saba** and very French **St-Barthélemy**, and a hop by air to volcanic **Sint Eustatius** and its ruins. Now fly to St Thomas in the **US Virgin Islands** and escape by boat to lovely St Croix. Get a ferry to the **British Virgin Islands** and then a flight to **Puerto Rico** and beautiful Old San Juan. Fly to the **Dominican Republic** and then go for a bus adventure to **Haiti** (or fly). Another plane takes you to the **Turks & Caicos,** where you can continue by air to reggae-licious **Jamaica**. In the **Cayman Islands**, stroke a stingray, and continue on to amazing, intoxicating and confounding **Cuba**. From here it is a short flight from Havana across to Nassau in the **Bahamas**, where you can lose yourself amid hundreds of islands.

Plan Your Trip

Cruising the Caribbean

More than two million cruise-ship passengers sail the Caribbean annually, making it the world's largest cruise-ship destination. This is the ultimate package tour that requires minimal planning. For many people this is part of the appeal, as in just a few days you can get a taste of many islands.

Best Ports of Call

Bridgetown, Barbados

A vibrant, modern Caribbean capital with loads of shops popular with locals and cruisers alike. Plus you can walk to a great beach.

Tortola, British Virgin Islands

Port of fancy for yachties, this lovely spot handles visitors with aplomb, never hitting a false note.

Havana, Cuba

Begin exploring the endlessly fascinating old parts of the city as soon as you step off the gangplank.

St George's, Grenada

A beautiful old port town with interesting shops and top-notch strolling.

Old San Juan, Puerto Rico

Cruisers blend right into this ever-surprising, vast and historic neighborhood of tiny bars, cafes, shops and ancient buildings.

Main Routes

Ports of Departure

Main departure ports for Caribbean cruises are Fort Lauderdale and Miami, Florida; and San Juan, Puerto Rico. All three cities are well equipped to deal with vast numbers of departing and arriving cruise-ship passengers and are closest to the Caribbean.

Secondary departure ports are typically set up for local markets and won't see the line's biggest or flashiest ships (though some veteran cruisers like that). These include Galveston, Texas; New Orleans, Louisiana; Port Canaveral and Tampa, Florida and even as far north as Baltimore, Maryland and New York City. Cruises from these ports need more time at sea to travel to and from the Caribbean.

Eastern Caribbean

Cruises can last three to seven days; the profusion of port calls means that there are few days during which you're at sea all day . Some itineraries may venture south to Barbados or even to Aruba, Bonaire and Curaçao; there is much overlap between the eastern and southern itineraries. Islands in the eastern area: Antigua, Bahamas, British Virgin Islands, Dominican Republic, Guadeloupe, Puerto

Rico, St Kitts and Nevis, St-Martin/Sint Maarten, Turks and Caicos, US Virgin Islands.

Southern Caribbean

Itineraries are usually at least seven days due to the distance from the main departure ports. There is often some overlap with the Eastern Caribbean islands, with stops at the US Virgin Islands common. Islands in the southern area: Aruba, Barbados, Bonaire, Curaçao, Dominica, Grenada, Martinique, St Lucia, St Vincent and the Grenadines, Trinidad and Tobago.

Western Caribbean

Often only five days in length, the western itineraries usually also include Mexican ports, such as Cancun. There are often stops at Puerto Rico and other eastern ports, though Cuba is really stepping up cruises with a handful of major cruise lines adding stops here. Longer itineraries may include southern stops. Islands in the western area: Cayman Islands, Jamaica and Dominican Republic.

Costs

The cost of a cruise can vary widely, depending on the season and vacancies. While it will save you money to book early, keep in mind that cruise lines want to sail full, so many will offer excellent last-minute discounts – sometimes up to 50% off the full fare.

You'll pay less for an inside room deep within the ship, but be aware that the really cheap rooms are often claustrophobic and poorly located (be sure to study deck plans). Some packages provide free or discounted airfares to and from the port of embarkation (or will provide a rebate if you make your own transportation arrangements).

Most cruises end up costing US$200 to US$600 per person, per day, including airfare from a major US gateway city. Port charges and government taxes typically add on another US$150 per cruise. Be sure to check the fine print about deposits, cancellation and refund policies, and travel insurance.

Shore Excursions

Numerous guided tours and activities are offered at each port of call, each generally costing US$40 to US$100 or more. These tours are also a major profit earner for the cruise lines so there is great pressure for passengers to join – some reported heavy-handed tactics include people who booked tours with third parties being left behind in port.

Note the following:

➡ There is no requirement to book tours via the cruise lines.

➡ By going outside of the cruise line's shore excursions, travelers can set their own itinerary, avoid less-appealing mandatory stops (for shopping) and save money.

➡ Find activities and tours in advance and book over the web.

➡ Local drivers waiting at cruise-ship ports offer their services to popular and offbeat sights and activities. Cruise forums are often filled with recommendations of locals with great reputations.

Tipping

Tipping is usually expected and can add 20% or more to your shipboard account. Many lines have gotten around the discretionary nature of tips (which are the primary wages for the crew) by automatically putting them on your bill in the form of 18% to 20% gratuity fees.

Note, however, that there's often no transparency about how much of these 'gratuities' actually reach the crews, many of whom work 12-hour days, seven days a week.

Extras

Alcoholic drinks Usually not included in the price of the cruise; a profit center for the lines.

Meals You can still get free and abundant food but ships now have a range of extra-cost restaurants where for, say, US$20 you can get a steak dinner in an exclusive setting. But even fancy coffees now often come with a fee.

Activities Spas, adventure sports, classes; the lines are always looking for new things they can sell to passengers.

Above: Brownes Beach (p197), Barbados

Left: St George's Harbour (p435), Grenada

Above: Soper's Hole (p236), British Virgin Islands

Right: Paseo de la Princesa (p593), San Juan, Puerto Rico

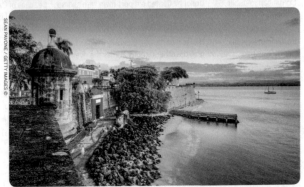

POPULAR PORTS OF CALL

Unless otherwise noted, ships dock at ports located in or very near town.

PORT	DESCRIPTION	EXCURSIONS
Antigua: St John's	Busy, vibrant capital with lots of daily life & shopping at markets	Rainforest canopy tours, catamaran sail, English Harbour, beaches, market, kayaking
Aruba: Oranjestad	Commercial hub divided between a zone of malls (some quite tired) serving cruisers, & a regular shopping area	Natural sites on the east coast, beaches
The Bahamas: Nassau	The country's busy, main cruise-ship port; passengers can walk to the sights of downtown, which revolves around cruisers	Aquaventure Waterpark, diving & snorkeling at Stuart Cove
The Bahamas: Lucaya	The Lucayan Harbour cruise port is a few miles from Freeport & Lucaya – cruise-ship passengers have to take a bus or taxi to town	Trips to Garden of the Groves, hanging out on Lucaya Beach
Barbados: Bridgetown	Attractive capital with plenty of locally owned shops; it's big so absorbs crowds easily	Beaches, rum distilleries, nature & wildlife
Bonaire: Kralendijk	Tiny with only a few shops so large ships bring a tsunami of people; it's best to get a driver and leave	Diving, windsurfing, sightseeing, flamingo spotting
British Virgin Islands: Road Town	Vibrant place that accepts cruisers with aplomb, but gets crowded	Taxi to Cane Garden Bay, ferry to Virgin Gorda
Cayman Islands: George Town	Has a busy, compact center with a mix of local- and tourist-oriented businesses; ships don't dock, tenders are used	Seven Mile Beach, Stingray City, Cayman Turtle Center
Cuba: Havana	This is one place you don't need an excursion. It's a fascinating city perfect for wandering, especially the old Habana Vieja area near the port	Exploring the old city, shopping, museums
Curaçao: Willemstad	The harbor cleaves the city in two – it's a spectacular place to arrive by ship; most central shops are geared toward cruisers	Tours of historic Willemstad, museums, beaches, snorkeling
Dominica: Roseau	Scruffy but charismatic city center with busy markets, bars & historic sights	Boiling Lake, Morne Trois Piton National Park, Titou Gorge, snorkeling
Dominican Republic: Samaná	Unsophisticated old port town with sparse waterside restaurants; hops during whale season; ships don't dock, tenders are used	Beaches of Cayo Levantado, Cascada El Limón waterfall, whale-watching (in season)
Dominican Republic: Santo Domingo	Has two ports: one basically in Zona Colonial, the other directly across the river	Walking tour of the remarkable Zona Colonial to absorb its culture
Grenada: St George's	One of the Caribbean's most beautiful old cities – a mini San Francisco; it has interesting local shops hidden about	Touring the town, Grand Anse Beach, Grand Etang hikes
Guadeloupe: Pointe-à-Pitre	Slowly growing as a cruise stop, Pointe-à-Pitre may be rather dilapidated, but it has the excellent Mémorial ACTe museum, which rightly attracts crowds	Hiking in Parc National de la Guadeloupe is worth the effort

PORT	DESCRIPTION	EXCURSIONS
Jamaica: Montego Bay	Bustling city that many cruisers miss; the trendy areas get packed when many ships arrive; dock is 2.5 miles (4km) south of town	Doctor's Cave Beach (walkable from town), exploring downtown Montego, shopping, diving
Jamaica: Ocho Rios	Very sleepy place when cruise ships aren't in port; doesn't get crowded	Dunn's River Falls, Turtle Beach, Nine Mile
Martinique: Fort-de-France	Following a massive cleanup, Fort-de-France is a popular destination & now has two cruise terminals within easy walking distance of the center	Take a ferry from the port to the beaches at Pointe du Bout or explore colonial Fort Louis, which also has its own beach
Nevis: Charlestown	A small, historic & lovely capital; tenders are used to bring passengers to the port in town	Touring the plantation inns, rainforest hiking, beach time
Puerto Rico: Old San Juan	Has the region's best combination of historic, cultural, drinking & shopping spots; gets crowded with cruisers	El Morro, El Yunque, beaches and casinos of Isla Verde
St Kitts: Basseterre	Compact, working Caribbean port town interesting for about an hour's wander beyond the non-alluring port shops	Cockleshell Bay, Brimstone Hill Fortress, Mt Liamuiga volcano, St Kitts Scenic Railway
St Lucia: Castries	Has two ports; feel the modern Creole vibe while taking a stroll through the large covered market	Reduit Beach (Rodney Bay), Pigeon Island National Landmark, zip-lining
St-Martin/Sint Maarten: Philipsburg	Has a large duty-free shopping area near the dock on Front St in Philipsburg, & boisterous daytime beach bars; gets crowded with cruisers	Catching a cab to remote beaches, island-wide food tours, shopping
St Vincent: Kingstown	Seems little changed in 150 years; the streets teem with locals out shopping for staples while socializing	Visit Dark View Falls or the Montreal Gardens, ferry to beautiful Bequia
Tobago: Scarborough	An interesting small town where you can browse stores and markets – most quite authentic	Pigeon Point Beach, Tobago Forest Reserve, Argyle Falls
Trinidad: Port of Spain	Pulsing city that moves to the beat of beloved local music; port is in a lively part of town	Asa Wright Nature Centre, Caroni Bird Sanctuary, Maracas Bay
Turks & Caicos: Grand Turk	Small Grand Turk has a cruise center with beaches & a range of facilities; port is 3 miles south of town	Snorkeling and diving trips, wandering charming Cockburn Town, whale-watching (in season)
US Virgin Islands: Charlotte Amalie	An old town filled with new duty-free megastores and good local food; there are two ports, each is 1.4 miles (2.3km) from town; it gets crowded with cruisers	Magens Bay beach, strolling downtown Charlotte Amalie, ferry to St John's beaches
US Virgin Islands: Frederiksted	A tiny, uncrowded place that seems empty with no cruise ships visiting	Cruzan Rum Distillery, Estate Whim Plantation Museum, Christiansted

Choosing a Cruise

So many options! So many decisions! Things to consider:

Budget How much can you spend? Can you trade a cabin with a balcony (the most common kind now) for a cheaper, windowless room on a nicer ship for a longer voyage?

Style A mass-market, upscale or specialist cruise? Consider your budget; whether you prefer numerous formal evenings, or to keep things casual; and any special interests you have.

Itinerary Where do you want to go and what ports of call appeal? Do you like the idea of days spent just at sea?

Size matters The megaships are geared for various budgets, so the important decision is how many people you want to sail with. On large ships, you can have 5000 potential new friends and also have the greatest range of shipboard diversions. Small ships, while sometimes exclusive and luxurious, are not always so, and usually lack the flashier amenities (such as climbing walls). Smaller ships will also call at smaller ports on less-visited islands.

Season High season for Caribbean cruising is the same as at resorts in the islands: mid-December to April. The largest number of ships sail at this time and prices are at their highest. At other times there are much fewer voyages but prices drop. Storms are more likely to cause itineraries to suddenly change during hurricane season June to November.

Demographics Different cruise lines, and even ships within cruise lines, tend to appeal to different groups. Although cruisers in general tend to be slightly older, some ships have quite a party reputation; others are known for their art auctions and oldies music in the lounges. Also consider if

---

SUSTAINABLE CRUISING?

Although all travel comes with an environmental cost, by their very size, cruise ships have an outsize effect. Among the main issues:

➡ **Air pollution** According to UK-based Climate Care, a carbon-offsetting company, cruise ships emit more carbon per passenger than airplanes – nearly twice as much – and that's not including the flights that most passengers take to get to their point of departure. Most ships burn low-grade bunker fuel, which contains more sulfur and particulates than higher-quality fuel. The US and Canada are phasing in new regulations to require ships to burn cleaner fuel when they are close to land; however, the industry is fighting this. Small nations in the Caribbean are also being pressured into not adopting these regulations.

➡ **Water pollution** Cruise ships generate enormous amounts of sewage, solid waste and gray water. While some countries and states have imposed regulations on sewage treatment (with which the cruise lines comply), there's little regulation in the Caribbean. In 2016 Princess Cruises was fined US$40 million for illegal sewage dumping.

➡ **Cultural impact** Although cruise lines generate money for their ports of call, thousands of people arriving at once can change the character of a town and seem overwhelming to locals and noncruising travelers. In Bonaire, for example, 7000 cruisers can arrive in one day – half the country's population.

What You Can Do

If you're planning a cruise, it's worth doing some research. Email the cruise lines and ask them about their environmental policies: wastewater treatment, recycling initiatives and whether they use alternative energy sources. Knowing that customers care about these things has an impact. There are also organizations that review lines and ships on their environmental records. These include the following:

Friends of the Earth (www.foe.org/cruisereportcard) Letter grades given to cruise lines and ships for environmental and human health impacts.

World Travel Awards (www.worldtravelawards.com) Annual awards for the 'World's Leading Green Cruise Line.'

you're looking for a family- or singles-oriented cruise.

Theme Cruises

Old TV shows, science fiction, computers, musicians, (very) minor celebrities, soap operas, sports teams, nudism... What these all have in common is that they're all themes for cruises.

Cruise lines sell group space to promoters of theme cruises but typically no theme is enough to fill an entire ship. Rather, a critical mass of people will occupy a block of cabins and have activities day and night just for them, including lectures, autograph sessions, costume balls and performances.

No theme or interest is too obscure or improbable. To find one, simply search your phrase with 'cruise'.

GLBT Cruises

One of the largest segments of special-interest cruises are those aimed at lesbian, bisexual, gay and transgender people. So popular are these cruises that often an entire ship will be devoted to catering for LBGT passengers. Start by checking out the following operators:

Olivia (www.olivia.com) Organizes lesbian-only cruises.

RSVP Vacations (www.rsvpvacations.com) Good for active travelers, RSVP has trips on both large cruise ships and smaller yachts.

Booking a Cruise

There are several options for researching and booking a cruise. A cruise line's own website will offer deals or upgrades not found elsewhere and there are big discounts for booking with them up to a year in advance. Large travel-booking sites often have last-minute discounts.

Cruise Lines

Cruising is huge business and the major players earn billions of dollars a year. Many lines are actually brands owned by one of the two big players: Carnival and

---

Royal Caribbean control 90% of the market in the Caribbean.

There are also nontraditional cruises, where you can feel the wind at your back on large sailing ships equipped with modern technology.

Popular Cruise Lines

The following cruise lines sail large vessels on numerous itineraries in the Caribbean:

Carnival Cruise Lines (www.carnival.com) The largest cruise line in the world. Its enormous ships offer cruising on myriad Caribbean itineraries.

Celebrity Cruises (www.celebritycruises.com) An important brand of Royal Caribbean, it has huge ships that offer a more upscale experience than many other lines.

Costa Cruises (www.costacruises.com) Owned by Carnival, Costa is aimed at European travelers: bigger spas, smaller cabins and better coffee. Ships are huge, similar to Carnival's megaships.

Crystal Cruises (www.crystalcruises.com) Luxury cruise line with ships carrying about 800 passengers – small by modern standards. Attracts affluent, older clients who enjoy a wide range of cultural activities and formal evenings.

Cunard Line (www.cunard.co.uk) Owned by Carnival, Cunard Line operates the huge *Queen Elizabeth*, *Queen Mary II* and *Queen Victoria*. The focus is on 'classic luxury' and the ships have limited Caribbean sailings.

Disney Cruise Line (www.disneycruise.com) Disney's large ships are like floating theme parks, with children's programs and large staterooms that appeal to families.

Holland America (www.hollandamerica.com) Owned by Carnival, Holland America offers a traditional cruising experience, generally to older passengers.

Norwegian Cruise Line (NCL; www.ncl.com) Offers 'freestyle cruising' on large cruise ships, which means that dress codes are relaxed and dining options more flexible than on other lines. There are lots of extra-fee dining choices.

Princess Cruises (www.princess.com) Owned by Carnival, Princess has large ships that ply the Caribbean and offer a slightly older crowd a range of pampering activities while aboard.

Regent Seven Seas Cruises (www.rssc.com) Smaller ships (maximum 750 passengers) with a focus on luxury cabins and excellent food. All shore excursions are included in the price.

Royal Caribbean International (RCI; www.royalcaribbean.com) The archrival to Carnival has a huge fleet of megaships (some carry over 5600 people), aimed right at the middle of the market. It has itineraries everywhere in the Caribbean all the time and offers lots of activities for kids.

Nontraditional Cruise Lines

Sail Windjammer (www.sailwindjammer.com) Cruises around the Leeward Islands under sail on the three-masted S/V Mandalay, a 236ft (72m) sailing yacht built in 1923.

Sea Cloud Cruises (www.seacloud.com) This German-American company operates luxury cruises in the eastern Caribbean. The fleet includes a four-masted, 360ft (110m) ship dating from 1931 and a modern sibling. On both, the sails are set by hand.

Star Clippers (www.starclippers.com) These modern four-masted clipper ships have tall-ship designs and carry 180 passengers. Itineraries take in smaller islands of the eastern Caribbean.

Windstar Cruises (www.windstarcruises.com) Windstar's luxury four-masted, 440ft (134m) vessels have high-tech, computer-operated sails and carry under 400 passengers. Note that the sails aren't the main means of propulsion most of the time.

Plan Your Trip

Weddings & Honeymoons

The Caribbean is a world-class destination for love. If you're getting married, you'll join the numerous couples who've exchanged vows in one of these beautiful places. Because the region is so popular for weddings, most hotels and resorts can offer plenty of planning advice, from arranging the event to getting your license.

Wedding Destinations

Adventure

These islands are great for weddings with a touch of the great outdoors as only the Caribbean can provide.

Bonaire Perfect for outdoor nuptials with a twist: get married at a small waterfront resort, then go diving with the bridal party. Or, get married underwater.

British Virgin Islands Tortola is the center of Caribbean yachting; great for boat-based weddings or for honeymoons. Get a few of your favorite couples and laze your way through the islands on a chartered yacht.

Dominica With so much outdoors action you might be too pooped to…no, of course not. Hike wild trails in the morning, get hitched in the afternoon. Lots of isolated wilderness-retreat getaways.

Grenada Small, secluded lodges with warm hospitality make good choices for smaller events. Choose Anse La Roche for splendid isolation or Calabash Hotel (p442) for waterside luxury.

St Vincent & the Grenadines From chartering a yacht to finding a small, intimate setting on a small, intimate island such as Bequia, SVG is good for adding a dash of adventure to your event.

The Perfect Caribbean Wedding

Caribbean weddings come in all flavours and sizes. Try on these different options while picking out your dress and suit:

Big Adventure

Enjoy one of the Caribbean's off-the-beaten-path locations where you can hike, kayak or dive. These are good choices for couples who want a nontraditional ceremony.

Intimate Luxe

Live large in a small exclusive resort. These can be expensive, so it could limit the number of guests. Luxury boutique resorts will usually handle all details and customize anything according to your needs.

Grand Event

Group rates at a large resort mean that you can send out invitations far and wide for an event that isn't out of reach. Resorts can be expert in organizing a traditional ceremony and reception.

ROMANCE NEEDS NO EXCUSE

ISLANDS	BEST FOR	DESCRIPTION	RECOMMENDATIONS
Anguilla	Intimate luxe, big adventure	Exclusive and expensive for something exquisite and exotic	Rent your own villa with a butler
Antigua & Barbuda	Intimate luxe, big adventure	A popular destination for Brits thanks to good air links and colonial history	Rendezvous Bay, Antigua; Barbuda Cottages (p118), Barbuda
Aruba	Grand event	Plenty of resorts specializing in weddings	Any of the resorts at Palm Beach
The Bahamas	Big adventure, intimate luxe, grand event	Private islands where you can indulge in almost anything	Kamalame Cay, Andros; The Cove, Atlantis; Harbour Island, Eleuthera
Barbados	Big adventure, intimate luxe, grand event	A full array of services for any style of wedding; good UK connections make this popular with Brits	Coral Reef Club (p205); Crane Beach Hotel (p204); Sea-U! Guest House (p211)
Bonaire	Big adventure	Perfect for outdoor nuptials with a twist	Get married at a small waterfront resort, then go diving with the bridal party
British Virgin Islands	Big adventure	Tortola is the center of Caribbean yachting; great for boat-based weddings or for honeymoons	Get a few of your favorite couples and laze your way through the islands on a chartered yacht
Cayman Islands	Grand event	Plenty of resorts that offer good group rates	Seven Mile Beach
Cuba	Big adventure	A great adventure; don't count on legally recognized marriage certificates	Post-nuptials drive in a classic convertible past clapping throngs on the streets of Havana
Dominica	Big adventure	Great for outdoors activities alongside your ceremony	Cloud 9 Dominica (p380); Manicou River Resort (p378)
Dominican Republic	Big adventure, grand event	Big resorts or more intimate options	Resorts at Punta Cana or secluded coves such as Playas Madama & Frontón
Grenada	Big adventure	Small, secluded lodges with warm hospitality	Anse la Roche; Green Roof Inn (p447)

Intimate

Boutique hotels and resorts can create an intimate setting for the perfect day.

Anguilla One of the Caribbean's poshest islands is bound to offer everything you'd want for an exclusive and expensive event. Go ahead, rent your own villa with a butler.

Antigua & Barbuda A big range of upscale resorts means this is the place for an exquisite event. It's a popular destination for Brits thanks to good air links and its colonial history. Isolated Barbuda is great for honeymoons.

Barbados A full array of top-end services for any style of wedding; good UK connections make this popular with Brits. The many long-time-open resorts and hotels mean they know just what to do, although the smaller sizes favor more intimate affairs.

St-Barthélemy Excels at small, top-end weddings. Rent a villa with staff for your special day. Also the place to go for a top-end honeymoon.

St Kitts & Nevis Bliss-inducing pampering on Nevis plus the island's own intimate beauty make this a natural for a small and special event.

ISLANDS	BEST FOR	DESCRIPTION	RECOMMENDATIONS
Jamaica	Big adventure, intimate luxe, grand event	One of the top Caribbean wedding destinations. Some major resorts offer free ceremonies if you book enough rooms	Treasure Beach; Negril
Puerto Rico	Big adventure, grand event	Large resorts or hidden retreats; marriage legalities simple for Americans	Vieques; Culebra; Isla Culebrita
Saba	Big adventure	An island so small that a wedding party would almost take it over	No beaches but plenty of outdoorsy fun
St-Barthélemy	Intimate luxe	Excels at small, top-end weddings	Rent a villa with staff for your special day
St Kitts & Nevis	Intimate luxe, grand event	Bliss-inducing pampering on Nevis and a resort vibe on St Kitts	Four Seasons (p676) or Golden Rock Inn (p677), Nevis; Belle Mont Farm (p672), St Kitts
St Lucia	Big adventure, intimate luxe	Boutique options with a French accent	Fond Doux Holiday Plantation (p696); Ladera (p699); Pink Plantation House (p688)
St-Martin/Sint Maarten	Grand event	Dutch and French resorts that host fabulous weddings	Get a group together and take over a resort
St Vincent & the Grenadines	Big adventure, intimate luxe	Plenty of accommodations options for groups; also offers top-end luxury hidden away from the paparazzi	Palm Island Resort (p744); Petit St Vincent Resort (p745)
Trinidad & Tobago	Big adventure	Relaxed hideaways – a quirky, offbeat option	Tobago's Pigeon Point Beach has a purpose-built wedding gazebo
Turks & Caicos	Intimate luxe	Small resorts and one of the longest and most beautiful beaches in the Caribbean	Parrot Cay; the resorts at Grace Bay
US Virgin Islands	Big adventure, intimate luxe, grand event	Everything from lavish resorts to secluded eco-escapes	Take your pick of Honeymoon Beaches – one by St Thomas, the other on St John

St Lucia A score of small, luxurious boutique hotels in the gorgeous south are naturals, both for the wedding and the honeymoon.

Grand

Go big with a wedding party to remember hosted by a resort that can handle a lot of guests

Aruba There are plenty of resorts specializing in big weddings. In fact any of the resorts at Palm Beach will easily handle affairs with hundreds of guests. Good airlinks make access easy.

Cayman Islands There are plenty of resorts that offer good group rates on Seven Mile Beach. Lots of flights make it easy to invite people from all over.

Dominican Republic Big resorts by the dozen mean you have lots of choices for planning a big event. Try Punta Cana; flights can be cheap, easing the fiscal pain on guests.

Jamaica One of the top Caribbean wedding destinations. Some major resorts offer free ceremonies if you book enough rooms, so invite everyone you know. Lots of flights make getting there easy. Consider Treasure Beach or Negril.

GLBT-FRIENDLY WEDDING DESTINATIONS

Not all Caribbean islands are created equal when it comes to recognizing gay marriage. Homosexuality is still illegal in some countries, including Jamaica and Barbados. Destinations where you can get married and that are known for their gay-friendly resorts include the US Virgin Islands, Saint Barthélemy, St-Martin/Sint Maarten, Aruba, Bonaire, Sint Eustatius and Saba.

Puerto Rico All those huge resorts right on the beach in San Juan are perfect for large ceremonies. Americans will find the marriage legalities are extra simple plus there are lots of good venues for subsidiary events such as rehearsal parties.

St-Martin/Sint Maarten Dutch and French resorts are well versed in hosting fabulous weddings. You can literally choose the kind of accent you want.

Turks & Caicos The large resorts on Grace Bay beach will easily absorb scores of friends and family, yet the scale is not so vast that everyone will get lost. The smaller islands offer complete honeymoon escapes.

US Virgin Islands A good place for Americans wary of red tape, or requiring that all their guests have passports. Large resorts have decades of experience with nuptials, yet you can find tiny, intimate places for the honeymoon.

Paperwork

It is vital that you confirm in advance what you'll need for a marriage license. It varies greatly by country. Get info from the national tourism authority or a resort that specializes in weddings and then double-check it all.

Here are just some of the bureaucratic hoops you may need to bound through:

➡ original birth certificates

➡ legal proof of divorce or death of previous spouse

➡ legal proof of the marriage officiant's status

➡ a local marriage license (up to US$300 or more in some places)

➡ blood tests.

There can also be delays in processing: some islands need 48 hours or more to process a license request; others require that you be on the island 48 hours or more in advance of the ceremony

If the red tape proves too much, you can always have the unofficial ceremony of your dreams in the Caribbean while saving the legal ceremony for your home country.

Plan Your Trip
Budget Caribbean

The Caribbean isn't cheap, but there are ways to get the most bang for your buck with a little forward planning and some savvy choices. All islands are not created equal in the budget department – some can be much more affordable than others.

Great-Value Islands

These islands are least likely to break the bank.

Bonaire Excellent budget choice. Small resorts on the water cater to divers who are value-conscious.

Dominica One of the Caribbean's best bargains: everything is much cheaper than the region's averages, especially lodging and eating; public transportation is comprehensive.

Montserrat Definitely a budget island: great value and high standards, even at guesthouses. Local eateries are cheap and excellent. Limited public transportation; taxis are not too expensive.

Puerto Rico In San Juan there's an abundance of hotels: look for internet deals and good rates for apartment rentals. Culebra and Vieques have fine budget options. Good public transportation.

Saba A tiny island with few accommodations choices but some nice ones for around US$100.

Sint Eustatius Although choices are few, limited tourism except for value-conscious divers means accommodations choices are good value, even January to March.

Trinidad Not particularly tourist-oriented, so many good-value options. Inexpensive in comparison to other islands. Public transportation and street food are cheap and good.

Tobago As in Trinidad, there are many good-value options. Crown Point has the majority of places to stay, and competition keeps prices low.

Best Budget Tips

Here are some of the best ways to save money:

Travel in groups
Bring your friends along with you and rent a villa.

Book far in advance
For high-season deals.

Book at the last minute
For incredible deals as hotels dump empty rooms.

Follow the divers
They demand great value near beautiful waters.

Ride buses and ferries
You meet folks and may have an adventure.

Live like a local
Save money while having a more authentic visit.

Travel sustainably
It's the right thing to do and it saves you money.

Travel in low season
Prices can drop 40% or more.

Eagle Beach (p130), Aru

Islands for All Budgets

You can spend a lot or, well, less on these islands.

Antigua Expensive island: mostly higher-end resorts; few guesthouses and those are not appealing. Rent an apartment and self-cater.

QUICK & EASY GETAWAYS

With competitive airfares from the US and Canada and resorts offering great deals online, several Caribbean islands are well suited to a quick, affordable getaway. Consider the following:

➡ **Montego Bay, Jamaica** Famous resort town with a huge range of beachside accommodations.

➡ **Old San Juan, Puerto Rico** Explore forts and beaches by day; wander lively streets by night.

➡ **St-Martin/Sint Maarten** The choice of a French frolic or Dutch treat.

Vacation rentals have become more prevalent – try along the southwest coast near Cades Bay. Public transportation is OK in developed areas but rare to the remote east and southeast.

Aruba The beaches are lined with mostly top-end resorts but Eagle Beach – our favorite – does have some good midrange options. Stay 10 minutes' walk from the beach and you can get a good room with a kitchen for about US$100 a night. Public transportation is excellent.

Barbados The west coast with its old-money resorts and mansions can be pricey, although there are good-value apartments 10 minutes from the beaches. The south is filled with budget and midrange choices close to the sand. Good public transportation.

British Virgin Islands Tortola is the secret to budget travel in the BVI. It has a good range of guesthouses and moderate resorts.

Curaçao Budget accommodations in beautiful Willemstad are often not worth the cheap prices, but some better midrange options are opening. Holiday apartments on north-coast beaches are good value. Public transportation is OK.

Dominican Republic The central highlands are better value than elsewhere.

Grenada Generally affordable. There are some modest resorts in and around George Town plus excellent local restaurants. A car will be good for a couple days' exploration. Carriacou has a few good budget options.

The Grenadines Some islands are quite expensive (eg Mustique) but others such as Bequia have excellent good-value choices. You can walk where you want to go.

Guadeloupe Good budget and midrange options are available throughout the country – think US$70 per night. Good buses; ferries to the tiny offshore islands are cheap and fun.

Jamaica Treasure Beach, Port Antonio and Kingston are all good for backpackers, while the resorts on the north coast offer plenty of opportunities for a blowout.

Martinique Budget and cheap midrange options are available throughout the country for around US$70 per night. Ferries and buses provide good links.

St Lucia Consider staying in midrange places such as inns and guesthouses that are not directly on the beach. Travel in low season.

St-Martin/Sint Maarten Consider staying in the island's towns, such as Philipsburg or Marigot. Shop at local markets (ask the locals where they buy their groceries). Public transportation is just OK.

St Vincent There are some good modest resorts near Kingstown, which also has a good inn in town. Public transportation just OK.

Turks & Caicos Expensive beachfront resorts; the best value is at diving resorts in Providenciales and Grand Turk.

US Virgin Islands Rates are very seasonal, falling 40% or more in slack times. Resorts tend to be pricey; look for holiday apartments online.

LIVE LIKE A LOCAL

Take time to meet the locals by doing what they do – you'll enjoy a more affordable and authentic experience. Some simple, common-sense tips:

➡ Eat at lunch wagons or stalls. The local fare is cheap and often incredibly good.

➡ Drop by a local bar – often the de facto community center. Besides a drink, you'll get all sorts of useful – or wonderfully frivolous – advice.

➡ Look for community fish fries or barbecues in the Eastern Caribbean.

Top-End Islands

These are the posh islands of the Caribbean; still, there are ways even these can fit a budget.

Anguilla One of the most exclusive and expensive islands in the Caribbean; not a budget option.

Barbuda At least 50% more expensive than Antigua. Only way to save money is by staying in guesthouses but these are very basic. Getting around is ridiculously expensive.

Cayman Islands Most of the accommodations are on beautiful Seven Mile Beach and are quite expensive. There are more-affordable options off-beach. Public transportation is excellent.

Nevis Stay in Charlestown, which has some reasonably priced eateries. The rest of the island is very expensive but actually good value given the high standards.

St-Barthélemy Prohibitively expensive in high season; other times you might find an affordable villa rental online. Splurge at the luxury restaurants with their €29 'value' meals.

St Kitts Expensive island. Look for online specials at the resorts. Use the decent public transportation and get a room with a kitchen.

Plan Your Trip
Traveling Sustainably

Tourism pays the bills in most of the Caribbean, and the impact on the environment and the culture is huge. Most islands are still putting economic development ahead of the environment because poverty is so widespread, but luckily there are some 'green' trailblazers worth supporting.

Sustainable Seafood

Many fish and shellfish species in the Caribbean are at risk due to overfishing. Where you can, try to order dishes that use sustainable catches – preferably wild-caught from managed stocks of local fish, rather than imported, farmed fish. Many fish and crustaceans also have a 'closed' season to allow them to breed and maintain stock levels.

Good Seafood Choices

Farm-raised barramundi, conch and tilapia

Lionfish (an invasive species)

Shrimp

Yellowtail snapper

Mahi-mahi

Crab

Seafood to Avoid

Atlantic salmon

Conch (wild-caught)

Florida pompano

Grouper

Spiny lobster

Swordfish

Wild turtle

Steps for Sustainable Travelers

You can do your part and make a difference. Here are a few pointers for minimizing your impact on the environment.

➡ **Turn off the tap** Fresh water is an extremely precious commodity on all of the islands, where desalination plants work overtime converting saltwater to fresh. Many islanders depend only on rainwater collected in cisterns. Keep in mind that winter – peak tourism time – is the driest time of year.

➡ **Skip bottled water** If the water is safe to drink, use it to fill containers so you can skip bottled water and its transport and refuse costs.

➡ **Turn off the air-con** Rarely is it so hot in the Caribbean that you need air-con at night; turn it off and let the breezes in.

➡ **Ride the bus** Instead of renting a car, immerse yourself in local culture while you save gas. Islands such as Aruba, Barbados and Grand Cayman have excellent bus networks.

➡ **Return the car early** Decide if you need a rental car for your entire stay. You might only need it for a day or two of exploration.

➡ **Say no to plastic** On Barbados and some other islands, stores will ask you if you want a plastic bag rather than just giving you one. Straws are also best avoided because they float around for years.

➡ **Go green** Look for hotels and resorts that carry an audited green certification. A good place to start your search is at Eco-Index Sustainable Tourism (www.eco-indextourism.org), which features businesses that have been recognized as environmentally and socially responsible.

➡ **Ask questions** Ask your hotel or tour operator about its green practices. Even if they have none, it'll tell them it matters to customers.

➡ **Travel globally, shop locally** Not only will buying local products infuse the local economy, it will also help to save you money. Local beer is always fresher than imported.

➡ **Avoid coral** Don't touch it in the wild and don't buy it in shops or from vendors. Also avoid any souvenirs made of seashell or turtle shell. Buying goods made with any of these only encourages environmental destruction and hunting.

➡ **Don't litter** Sure, you'll see many locals do it (especially with KFC boxes), but don't do it yourself. Almost everything discarded on land makes its way to the sea, where it can wreak havoc on marine life. Carry your trash off beaches, trails and campsites.

➡ **Consider the dolphins** Be aware that wild dolphins are often captured to be used in enclosed swim-with-dolphins tourist attractions, a practice that has been condemned by wildlife conservationists.

Patronizing Eco-Conscious Establishments

Green awareness is growing in the Caribbean, especially as visitors make this a priority.

Aruba

Manchebo Beach Resort (p132) Despite being in a built-up tourist area, this resort wears its green credentials proudly.

The Bahamas

On islands where golf carts are a popular mode of transport (Loyalist Cays, Harbour Island), choose an electric cart rather than a gas-powered one.

Small Hope Bay Lodge (p179) This laid-back ecoresort takes a genuine interest in sustainabil-

ity, composting food and making drinking glasses from old wine bottles.

Barbados

Sea-U! Guest House (p211) Excellent green cred not far from the most natural beach in Barbados.

Barbuda

The small population of Barbuda is quite environmentally aware.

Barbuda Cottages (p118) A new, solar-powered villa on stilts.

Bonaire

The entire coast of the island is a marine reserve and conservation is taken seriously.

Captain Don's Habitat (p221) Leads the way in local environmental causes.

Cuba

Staying in a casa particular (private home that lets rooms to foreigners) is more 'eco' as the food is always locally produced and you're putting money into the pockets of Cubans.

Dominica

Cocoa Cottage (p372) A cluster of eco-cottages; serves organic meals around communal tables.

Zandoli Inn (p376) Set in a remote corner of the island is this quiet, arty ecolodge.

Manicou River Resort (p378) Octagonal cottages built from recycled materials.

Hotel The Champ (p378) A small hotel with superb hilltop views and solar panels.

Dominican Republic

Explora Eco Tours (p401) Customized tours of national parks, nature preserves and rural communities.

NaturaPark Beach Ecoresort & Spa (p406) A beach resort with abundant birdlife.

Tubagua Plantation Eco-Village (p417) Simple, low-impact wooden cabins on a mountaintop.

Sonido del Yaque (p422) Basic jungle cabins run by a collective of local women.

DREW MCARPHUR / SHUTTERSTOCK ©

Top: Conch shell

Bottom: Nassau grouper, Little Cayman (p277)

SAVE THE GROUPER (& THE CONCH)!

Grouper graces many a menu but it may not for long. The big and slow fish is a slow breeder and overfishing may doom this dinner favorite to extinction. It's a similar situation with the conch, as numbers in the wild fall fast.

One solution that visitors can help with is to eat less of both species. If you've got the taste for conch, make sure you opt for farm-raised versions. There are many good alternatives to endangered Caribbean-ocean species.

Lionfish, an invasive species that is causing damage to ecosystems in much of the Caribbean, increasingly pops up on restaurant menus. Eating one for dinner is a particularly delicious way of playing a part in controlling numbers.

Grenada

Maca Bana (p441) Luxury ecovillas scattered along a hillside.

St Lucia

Ladera (p699) A solid green ethos and one of the island's best-located resorts.

Boucan (p698) Set in a cocoa planation, this resort prides itself on the contribution it makes to the local community.

Turks & Caicos

Greenbean Cafe (p802) A cafe in Providenciales setting a great example for the region. It uses organic produce, compostable packaging and, where possible, locally sourced ingredients.

US Virgin Islands

The USVI has several extra-green camp-grounds.

Virgin Islands Campground (p821) Self-contained 'tent-cottages' on Water Island.

Mt Victory Campground (p844) Located on a small working farm, this campground uses no electricity; guests share the solar-heated bath-house.

Northside Valley (p844) Eight villas with ocean views; green initiatives include the use of ecofriendly cleaning supplies.

Plan Your Trip

Travel with Children

Taking the kids on their first-ever boat ride, building sandcastles, wandering rainforest trails or meeting local children – it's simple adventures like these that make the Caribbean such a great region for families, with islands offering attractions and facilities to cater from tinies to teenagers.

Best Islands for Kids

Aruba
Plenty of family-friendly resorts with great beaches and soft waves, with lots of organised activities and water sports.

Barbados
Head to the south and west for the best beaches and resorts; the east-coast surf is too powerful for novice swimmers of any age.

Cayman Islands
Seven Mile Beach is ideal for families, as it's lined with resorts offering child-friendly activities, and the water is calm.

Puerto Rico
An island hosting brilliant resorts, while its old colonial forts and historic parks bring out the inner pirate.

US Virgin Islands
The islands offer a mix of kid-friendly beaches, shallow water, minimal waves and water-sports centres, plus a host of old cannon-clad forts.

Children's Highlights

Little Critters

➡ **Stingray City, Grand Cayman** (p264) Get up close in the water with these semi-wild (but harmless) creatures.

➡ **Maho Bay, St John** (p833) Lots of seagrass means lots of enormous sea turtles nibbling close to shore.

➡ **Donkey Sanctuary, Aruba** (p135) Befriend these former beasts of burden at this child-friendly centre.

Amazing Adventures

➡ **Antigua Rainforest Zip Line Tours** (p110) Make like mini Tarzans and Janes while roaring on a wire through the treetops.

➡ **Dunn's River Falls, Jamaica** (p519) Popular child-friendly attraction that has you swimming and climbing up a series of beautiful waterfalls.

➡ **Crystal Caves, Grand Cayman** (p272) Explore the seemingly endless network of limestone caves, deep in the island's interior.

KIDS IN THE CARIBBEAN

The following islands all offer something for children. Kids will never want to leave islands rated 1, while those rated 2 have some interesting diversions.

Antigua & Barbuda	2	Good beaches for playing plus several fun activities: Antigua Rainforest Zip Line Tours, Antigua Donkey Sanctuary
Aruba	1	Large resorts with kids activities, excellent beaches, mostly calm seas & lots of adventure activities, including water sports
The Bahamas	1	Grand Bahama is clean & easy to get around, but the Abacos is laid-back, with endless beaches, reefs & activities by the bucketload
Barbados	2	Lots of family-friendly beaches in the south & west, & popular surfing lessons for kids, but few large resorts with kids programs
Bonaire	2	Good for older kids who want to learn how to dive & windsurf, but limited beaches
British Virgin Islands	2	Many islands have no special kiddie allure but at the Bitter End Yacht Club & Resort, on Virgin Gorda, youngsters learn to sail, windsurf, kayak & more
Cayman Islands	1	Seven Mile Beach is great for families; large resorts have kids programs; Stingray City is always a hit, as is spotting sea stars at Starfish Point, snorkeling with sea turtles at Spotts Beach & exploring Crystal Caves
Dominican Republic	2	The resorts of Punta Cana & Bávaro cater to kids, who can make friends with other young holidaymakers from around the world
Jamaica	2	Montego Bay & Ocho Rios have resorts good for families, but some resorts are aimed at adults-only partying. Dunn's River Falls is the stand-out family-friendly attraction
Puerto Rico	1	Old San Juan has resorts nearby that are good for kids; top attractions include the Museo del Niño de Carolina, amazing forts with pirate history & the Observatorio de Arecibo; Playa Flamenco in Culebra is one of the world's best beaches & has lifeguards
St-Barthélemy	2	Water sports galore & gourmet children's menus
St Lucia	2	Many resorts cater to families, plus there are lots of kid-friendly activities, such as zip-lining, hiking & horseback riding
US Virgin Islands	1	One of the best destinations for kids; Highlights are abundant & include resort fun, tourist towns with child-friendly allure on all three islands, lifeguard-patrolled Magens Bay beach, & Maho Bay's sea turtles

Pirates!

➡ **Pirates of Nassau museum, Bahamas** (p146) Explore a full-scale replica pirate ship at this brilliant interactive museum.

➡ **Pirates Week, Grand Cayman** (p30) Mock pirate invasions and more keep scurvy dogs entertained in this popular festival.

➡ **Blackbeard's Castle, St Thomas** (p821) Legend has it that this tall tower was the famous pirate's lookout back in the day.

Planning
Where to Stay

Resorts offer scores of kid-friendly amenities, but some families prefer staying in simpler places closer to island life. Before booking any lodging, ask for details to assess its appropriateness. For example:

➡ Does it welcome kids or accept them grudgingly?

➡ If it's a resort, what sort of kids activities does it offer?

➡ Does the room have a DVD player and wi-fi?

➡ Is there a kitchen or at least a refrigerator, so you can avoid the expense of always eating out?

➡ Are there safe places where kids can play?

➡ Even if the beach is nearby, is it across a heavily trafficked street?

➡ Does it provide cribs, change tables and other baby supplies?

➡ Does it offer on-site babysitting?

Staying Safe

To help kids acclimatize to the Caribbean heat, take it easy at first and make sure they drink plenty of water. Children should wear a high-protection sunscreen and cover up whenever they're outside to avoid sunburn and heatstroke.

Bring insect repellent formulated for children and whatever medication you normally use to treat insect bites.

What to Pack

Be prepared for lots of time in the sun and sea. Most lodgings provide beach towels, chairs and umbrellas. You can buy sand pails, snorkel masks and anything else you forget at beach shops in resort areas. Elsewhere you'll need to bring what you want in the diversions department. Bring the following:

➡ snorkel gear (especially masks) that you've tested for leaks and proper fit

➡ water wings and other flotation devices

➡ pails and shovels

➡ sturdy reef shoes

➡ underwater camera

➡ car seat if driving a lot.

Islands at a Glance

Part of the Caribbean's allure is its diversity. Sure, you'll find great climate and fab beaches across the region, but there are plenty of local characteristics that set each island apart from the next – you can zero in on the islands that best suit you. Whether your interests are history, music, food or diving, there are islands that will meet your travel needs. If your idea of pleasure is a night dancing to local rhythms, or simply taking time to smell the flowers, you can find that here too.

Anguilla

Beaches
Food
Water Sports

This scrubby limestone bump may not be as visually striking as its neighbors, but Anguilla's ethereal beaches make up for it. Neon-blue waves crash against powder-white shores where you'll find locals barbecuing succulent local fare.

p84

Antigua & Barbuda

Beaches
History
Activities

Antigua is the place to frolic on the beach, play golf, indulge in a fancy meal or explore Britain's naval history, whereas Barbuda, with its pearly-white beaches, is a remote, unspoiled place where creatures outnumber people.

p99

Aruba

Resorts
Beaches
Parties

Choose from beachside resorts great and small, from flashy to funky, from high-rise to low-rise. Hit the beaches by day, then hit bars, restaurants and clubs, as you would at home if it was warmer.

p125

The Bahamas

Diving
Beaches
Fishing

This watery wonderland, with its 700 islands, hundreds of miles of white sand and innumerable hidden coves, is paradise for beach bums, history buffs, diving enthusiasts, sailors, anglers and, well, pretty much everybody else.

p142

Barbados

Water Sports
Resorts
Nature

From surfing the waves to windsurfing the shallows to snorkeling the reefs, you may never dry off. But if you do, this genteel island's verdant interior might lure you for a tropical hike.

p192

Bonaire

Diving
Outdoor Adventure
History

Bonaire is a diver's paradise, with dozens of easily accessible dive sites. The adventure continues above the surface, with kayaking in the mangroves, windsurfing on Lac Bay, miles of mountain-biking trails, and a fascinating history to discover.

p218

British Virgin Islands

Sailing
Islands
Beaches

Tortola lets its hair down with sailing, surfing and full-moon parties, while Virgin Gorda offers boulder-studded beaches and billionaires' yachts. Jost Van Dyke is the 'barefoot island,' where Main St is a hammock-lined beach.

p231

Cayman Islands

Beaches
Diving
Islands

Seven Mile Beach is the most famous and fabulous beach in the Cayman Islands, but these islands are lined with stunning stretches of sand. Underwater, the reef is rich with sealife and dotted with shipwrecks, inviting exploration by divers.

p259

Cuba

Music
Architecture
Beaches

Cuba's musical prowess is no secret – the whole archipelago rocks to an eclectic pot of live sounds – and the nation's 50-year political time warp has unwittingly led to benefits such as period architecture and unblemished beaches.

p285

Curaçao

History
Nightlife
Beaches

The Dutch-colonial legacy is hundreds of beautiful old buildings in Willemstad neighborhoods dripping with character. Join the raucous music culture that practices for Carnival year-round or explore the coast and discover a hidden beach.

p345

Dominica

Nature
Adventure
Hiking

With thundering waterfalls, a boiling lake, bushy jungle, hot sulfur springs, secret swimming holes, sprightly rivers, teeming reefs and dramatic coastline, this untamed and mass-tourism-free 'nature island' promises unusual experiences and adventures.

p366

Dominican Republic

History
Beaches
Outdoor Adventure

The country's coastline – a mix of postcard-perfect beaches and isolated coves – offers windswept conditions for water sports. Roaring rivers and mountain peaks draw active travelers, while Santo Domingo's Zona Colonial takes you back in time.

p390

Grenada

Beaches
Nature
Diving

White sand, turquoise sea, palm trees and no crowds make Grenada's beaches truly sublime. If you've had too much sun, go for a hike on the island's interior shaded by lush rainforest or dive among shipwrecks and the underwater sculpture park just offshore.

p433

Guadeloupe

Hiking
Beaches
Diving

Guadeloupe offers world-class hiking in Basse-Terre, superb beaches with some of the Caribbean's best diving on Grande-Terre, and a selection of remote and virtually pristine islands perfect for the ultimate getaway.

p458

Haiti

History
Art
Adventure

Home to the world's only successful slave revolution, Haiti has the richest visual-arts tradition in the Caribbean and its most spectacular fortress. It's also the most rugged destination in the region – somewhere for pioneering travelers.

p489

Jamaica

Music
Food
Outdoors

Jamaica and music are inseparable concepts, and its cuisine pits spice rub against delicious Jamaican Jerk. Raft Black River to find Jamaica's jungly interior or dance all night at a Kingston street party.

p509

Martinique

Beaches
Hiking
Eating

Southern Martinique has great beaches, friendly fishing villages and lots of activities to keep you busy, while the north, with its mountains and botanical gardens, is perfect for hikers and nature lovers.

p556

Montserrat

Novelty
Nature
Wildlife

Stand in awe of nature's destructive power when surveying the damage done by the mean-but-majestic Soufrière Hills Volcano, the key attraction of this tranquil and charming island. Exhilarating diving, birdwatching and nature walks also beckon.

p582

Puerto Rico

Nightlife
History
Nature

Atop the ramparts of El Morro, visitors look over the cobblestone labyrinth of Old San Juan and the Atlantic's endless sparkle. Soak up sunshine and hike the rainforest before grooving to libidinous late-night rhythms.

p591

Saba

Diving
Hiking
Crafts

Dive deep to cavort with sharks in the colorful playground of reefs that encircles Saba's skyscraping volcano. On land, wander through six unique ecosystems that wind up the jagged granite spire.

p623

Sint Eustatius

Diving
Hiking
History

Crowned by a lonely volcano, this forgotten islet was once a hub of activity as goods were passed between Old and New Worlds. Signs of former greatness dot the landscape amid quaint clapboard shacks.

p636

St-Barthélemy

Beaches
Food
Water Sports

A brilliant tapestry of arid, cactus-clad cliffs and ebbing azure waters sets the scene on this idyllic isle, which lures celebrities and other discerning travelers with top-notch fusion cuisine and acres of silky sand.

p648

St Kitts & Nevis

History
Party
Beaches

Wander in the footsteps of Nelson, Hamilton and African slaves while exploring these verdant twin islands, which are dotted with romantic sugar-plantation inns, ringed by beautiful beaches and lorded over by a cloud-fringed (dormant) volcano.

p662

St Lucia

Outdoors
Village Life
Beaches

Take an enticing coastline, add rainforest and mountains, then sprinkle in attractive coastal towns. Next, pepper this island with history and culture, spike it with an array of outdoor activities, and there you have St Lucia.

p685

St-Martin/Sint Maarten

Beaches
Food
Nightlife

St-Martin/Sint Maarten is a kaleidoscope of Caribbean clichés: postcard-worthy beaches, superb local restaurants and roaring bars that spill over every crevice – even right up to the airport's main runway.

p706

St Vincent & the Grenadines

Island-Hopping
Adventure
Beauty

Hike the impossibly green jungles of St Vincent and then set off by slow boat to the beautiful beach-ringed islands of the Grenadines, starting with perfect little Bequia. Take time to explore wonders underwater.

p726

Trinidad & Tobago

Music & Nightlife
Birdwatching
Hiking

Trinidad and Tobago's party mentality leaks into every walk of life, and there's tip-top birdwatching, too. Trinidad's wild Northern Range and Tobago's ancient protected rainforest are laced with trails and swimmable waterfalls.

p750

Turks & Caicos

Diving
Beaches
Wildlife

With some of the whitest beaches, the clearest waters and the most varied marine life in the Caribbean, Turks and Caicos will thrill anyone who likes to spend time in or by the water.

p795

US Virgin Islands

Food
Parks
Diving

St Thomas sets the table with fungi, callaloo (spicy soup) and West Indian fare. St John goes green with hiking, snorkeling and kayaking in Virgin Islands National Park. St Croix offers divers the 'wall' and drinkers the rum factories.

p818

On the Road

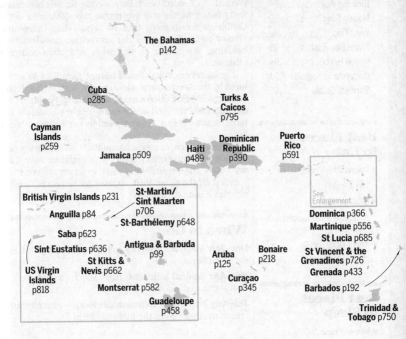

Anguilla

POP 13,550 / ☎ 264

Best Places to Eat

➡ Barrel Stay (p88)

➡ Veya (p88)

➡ B&D's (p90)

➡ Artisan Pizza Napoletana (p94)

➡ Ken's BBQ (p86)

➡ Roti Hut (p86)

Best Places to Sleep

➡ Malliouhana (p90)

➡ Zemi Beach House (p93)

➡ Cap Juluca (p92)

➡ Fountain Residences (p93)

➡ Lloyd's (p86)

Why Go?

Fringed by shimmering white-sand beaches shaded by coconut palms and sea-grape trees, and filled with colorfully painted, open-sided beach bars serving sizzling barbecues, feisty rum punches and live reggae tunes, Anguilla is the Caribbean dream come true. Its crystal-clear waters and vibrant reefs offer spectacular snorkeling, glass-bottomed kayaking, and sailing to tiny islets and atolls scattered offshore.

The island's rich and varied history dates back to settlement by the Amerindians and Arawaks, with extraordinary rock art still being discovered in sites such as Fountain Cavern National Park. And unlike many nearby islands, the flat terrain makes it easy to get around by car, bicycle or quad bike.

There's a catch, of course. Anguilla is no shoestring destination and authenticity comes at a premium here. Luxury hotels and private villas cater to jet-setters craving a vacation off the radar. Visit outside high season for a more affordable taste of paradise.

When to Go

Dec–Jan Anguilla's celebrity roll call gives St-Barth a run for its money.

Feb–Apr Rainfall is lightest; from March the holiday rush starts to die down.

Jul–Aug Prices drop to reasonable levels – capitalize on breezy weather before the humidity kicks in.

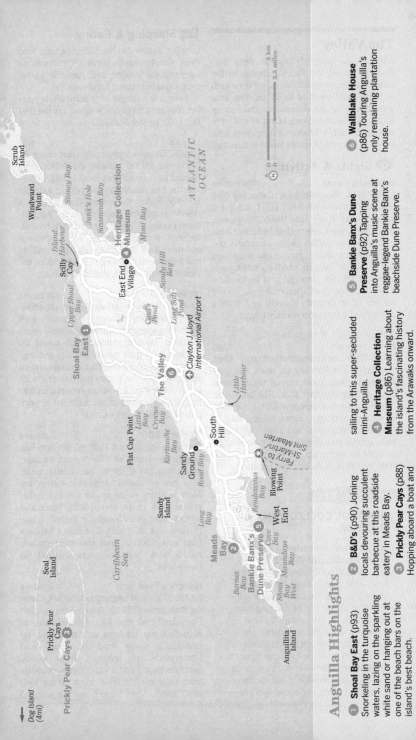

Anguilla Highlights

1 Shoal Bay East (p93) Snorkeling in the turquoise waters, lazing on the sparkling white sand or hanging out at one of the beach bars on the island's best beach.

2 B&D's (p90) Joining locals devouring succulent barbecue at this roadside eatery in Meads Bay.

3 Prickly Pear Cays (p88) Hopping aboard a boat and sailing to this super-secluded mini-Anguilla.

4 Heritage Collection Museum (p86) Learning about the island's fascinating history from the Arawaks onward.

5 Bankie Banx's Dune Preserve (p92) Tapping into Anguilla's music scene at reggae-legend Bankie Banx's beachside Dune Preserve.

6 Wallblake House (p86) Touring Anguilla's only remaining plantation house.

The Valley

Although no part of Anguilla feels particularly urban, the Valley is home to the island's government buildings, services such as banks, and most of its shops. The area was chosen as the colonial capital largely because of the abundance of arable soil – the island is mostly a limestone formation with only tiny pockets of viable land for farming.

◉ Sights & Activities

Wallblake House   HISTORIC BUILDING
(☑ 497-2944; www.wallblake.ai; Carter Rey Blvd; ☺ tours 10am-noon Tue & Fri) **FREE** Behind a white picket fence lies Wallblake House, the Valley's most interesting building. Built in 1787, it's Anguilla's oldest structure and the only remaining plantation house on the island, having survived the French invasion of 1796, fire, drought and hurricanes. Now owned by the Catholic Church, it's the rectory of St Gerard's church, and is only accessible by free twice-weekly tours.

National Trust of Anguilla
Heritage Tours   TOURS
(☑ 497-5297; www.axanationaltrust.com; Albert Lake Dr; ☺ 8am-4pm Mon-Fri, hours may vary) Various heritage tours run by the National Trust of Anguilla start at its HQ, housed in Anguilla's former customs house. Options include a Heritage Town walking tour, a Flora and Fauna walk and a Heritage Island tour; prices and durations vary depending on your requirements. It's essential to book your tour at least 48 hours in advance.

> **WORTH A TRIP**
>
> ### HERITAGE COLLECTION MUSEUM
>
> Anguilla's only **museum** (☑ 497-4092; Liberty Rd; adult/child US$5/3; ☺ 10am-5pm Mon-Sat) occupies a quaint bungalow next to East End Salt Pond. Anguilla's flag, bearing the Union Jack and the Anguillan coat of arms (featuring three dolphins above blue water), flies out front. Inside, the museum details the island's history through an impressive assortment of artifacts. A wander through the different rooms lets you experience a well-curated timeline of events, from the settling of the ancient Arawaks to Queen Elizabeth II's 1994 visit.

🛏 Sleeping & Eating

Low-key eateries in the Valley include food vans, simple shacks serving Caribbean or international cuisine and roadside barbecues, especially along Landsome Rd.

There are a couple of supermarkets here, but they're often poorly stocked; try the Best Buy (p91) in Meads Bay.

Lloyd's   B&B $
(☑ 497-2351; www.lloyds.ai; Old Court House Rd, Crocus Hill; s/d incl breakfast US$99/145; ☀ 🤝) Owned by a prominent local family, Lloyd's was the first guesthouse to open on Anguilla in 1959. Today, the vintage-flair B&B in a yellow clapboard building is a bargain-hunter's dream. Mornings start with cooked-to-order breakfast served in a spacious common area that gives way to smallish, low-frills rooms splashed in bright colors; the pick is Harmony, with a small kitchenette.

★ Roti Hut   CARIBBEAN $
(☑ 497-5030; Edwin Wallace Rey Dr; roti US$8-12; ☺ 11am-8pm) Heavenly aromas waft from this adorable mustard-colored, mint-trimmed wooden shack, which cooks up chicken, beef, goat, conch, shrimp and vegetarian rotis, plus a bull-foot soup special on Fridays. From the communal tables on its small covered deck, you can spot planes taking off and landing at the adjacent airport. Expect to wait at peak times.

★ Ken's BBQ   BARBECUE $
(Landsome Rd; dishes US$5-9; ☺ 11am-11pm Thu-Sun) Across from the Valley's open-air marketplace, Ken's is by far the most popular of a row of smoky street-side barbecues. Most regulars swing by for the delectable grilled pork chops served with limes and johnnycakes; other highlights include crispy chicken and juicy ribs. Ken raises his own hogs and chickens, and also masterminds mild-to-wild barbecue sauces used as marinades.

Hungry's Food Van   CARIBBEAN $
(☑ 235-8907; www.hungrysgoodfood.com; Carter Rey Blvd; dishes US$4-16; ☺ noon-10pm Mon-Sat) Chefs Irad and Papi have helmed some of Anguilla's top kitchens and now dish up homemade soups (bull-foot, conch and lobster-and-corn included), fresh salads, delicious pastas and a variety of quesadillas from their colorful food truck, along with fresh juices. Most ingredients are sourced

from the island; there's also a nearby sit-down restaurant and fish depot.

Da'Vida
FUSION $$$

(☑498-5433; www.davidaanguilla.com; Crocus Bay Rd, Crocus Bay; tapas US$12-20, mains US$30-50, Bayside Grill mains US$10-22; ⊙5-10pm Tue-Sat, Bayside Grill 10am-5pm daily; ☎) Locally owned Da'Vida is an island of sophistication in the humble Valley. From the deck a few feet above the water, you can enjoy tapas from 5pm and stunning Asian-Caribbean creations (Anguillan crab cake with pineapple sauce, crayfish tails in green curry) from 6pm. On the nearby small beach, the **Bayside Grill** is a casual daytime alternative.

Sandy Ground

Sandy Ground's quaint cluster of bars and restaurants sits between the impossibly clear waters of Road Bay and a shallow salt pond out back, which was commercially harvested until the 1970s.

◎ Sights & Activities

Sandy Ground
BEACH

(Sandy Ground Rd) Fronting bobbing yachts and a pier, this white-sand beach is shallow and free from coral, making it a good spot to splash about. Snorkeling is best at the rocky northern end. The beach bars and restaurants here draw plenty of punters, especially on weekends, when live bands often play.

Scuba Shack
DIVING

(Shoal Bay Scuba; ☑235-1482; www.scubashackaxa.com; 2-tank boat dive US$100, gear extra US$20; ⊙8am-5pm Mon-Sat) Anguilla's only PADI-affiliated diving operation has high-quality equipment, good boats and professional divemasters familiar with every underwater crack and crevice, and can take you out to seven wrecks and over 30 reefs. An introductory dive course costs US$110; PADI Open Water Certification starts from US$300. Snorkeling equipment rental rates begin at US$15.

🛏 Sleeping

Sea View
GUESTHOUSE $

(☑497-2427; www.inns.ai/seaview; Sandy Ground Rd; 1-/2-bedroom apt US$87/170; ☎) A hop, skip and jump from the beach, bars and restaurants, these apartments make a fine, if basic, base for longer stays. Each has a well-equipped kitchen, cable TV and ceiling fans. A cleaner swings by regularly. You'll be

downstairs from a local family who can help arrange diving and sightseeing adventures.

La Vue Boutique Inn
INN $$

(☑497-6623; www.lavueanguilla.com; Back St, South Hill; 1-/2-bedroom ste from US$160/310; ⊙Nov-Aug; P✳🛜🏊) Owned and run by a helpful family, this good-value hilltop spot lets you enjoy sweeping beach or garden views from your private balcony, perhaps with a drink and snack prepared in your kitchenette. Its seasonally opening restaurant, **Flavours** (5pm to 9pm Monday to Saturday; mains US$16 to US$26), has Caribbean fare and live jazz on Thursdays from 7pm to 9:30pm.

Ambia
VILLA $$$

(☑498-2741; www.ambiavilla.com; South Hill Rd; villa US$333-550; P✳🛜🏊) Perched on a scrubby hillside, this Zen-like villa flanked by smooth wooden balusters and bursts of bamboo sleeps up to eight people and is only rented in its entirety, so privacy is guaranteed. Asian-inspired rooms incorporate shoji screens and offer views of Sandy Ground's distant moorings. Amenities include a gas barbecue, a beautiful pool, and a washing machine and dryer.

✗ Eating

Geraud's Patisserie
BAKERY $

(☑497-5559; www.anguillacakesandcatering.com; South Hill Plaza, Rendezvous Rd, South Hill; dishes US$2-8; ⊙5:30am-1pm Tue-Fri, to noon Sat, 8am-noon Sun; ☎) In a contemporary white-washed building, Geraud's bakes delectable breads including crunchy baguettes, cakes such as carrot, choc-raspberry or lime cheesecake, and flaky croissants and *pains au chocolat*. There's a handful of tables, either inside or out on the terrace, where you can dine on sandwiches, bagels, savory English muffins, pies and quiches.

Meze
TAPAS $$

(☑498-8392; www.meze-axa.com; off Sir Emile Gumbs Dr; tapas US$4-16, sharing platters US$20-24; ⊙6-11pm Mon-Sat) Situated below gourmet restaurant Veya (p88), this globetrotting sister establishment has a Moroccan-themed tent strewn with cushions and low tables, and tapas inspired by the Caribbean (conch fritters with plantain chips, johnnycakes and spiced jicama spears) and the Mediterranean (white anchovies with blistered peppers, hummus and pigeon-pea dip). Live jazz, reggae and blues plays from 8pm to 10pm.

WORTH A TRIP

WHAT'S ON THE OFFSHORE ISLANDS

Prickly Pear Cays (www.pricklypearanguilla.com; ⊙Nov-Jul) For the best diving on Anguilla, head out to this underwater cavern some 6 miles (9.6km) northwest of the mainland, where nurse sharks and barracuda swim through rock formations not far from several sunken shipwrecks. On land, there's a **restaurant** (mains US$18 to $25, whole lobster US$49) serving food from noon to 2:30pm, and a **bar** (10am to 4pm). Snorkeling, diving and day-trip tour operators such as **Gotcha Garfield's Sea Tours** (☑235-7902; www.gotcha-garfields-sea-tours-anguilla.com; half-day cruises from US$40, charters from US$125) or **Sail Chocolat** (☑497-3394; www.sailinganguilla.com; adult/child US$80/60) usually leave out of Sandy Ground.

Sandy Island (☑476-4104; www.mysandyisland.com; shuttle boat return US$10; ⊙shuttle boat 10am-4pm Nov-Jul) Just 1.6 miles (2.5km) northwest of Sandy Ground, this tiny islet has a pure white-sand beach fringed by palm trees, translucent waters for snorkeling amid the turtle- and grouper-filled colored coral, and a daily **seafood barbecue** (mains US$24 to US$38) with a bar serving island-inspired cocktails including potent JoJo rum punch. The island's own tender runs a shuttle-boat service on demand; journey time is 10 minutes. Tour operators making the trip out here include **Sail Chocolat**.

Livin in the Sun (www.livininthesun.com; ⊙mid-Nov) Some of the hottest DJs from around the planet hit the decks at locations across Anguilla and out on Sandy Island during this three-day beat-filled festival.

SandBar
TAPAS **$$**

(☑498-0171; www.facebook.com/sandbaranguilla; Sandy Ground Rd; tapas US$7-15; ⊙5:30-9:30pm Mon-Sat) Exquisite tapas treats at this chic beachside restaurant span the continents, from feta and watermelon microsalad, yellowfin tuna wantons and sticky baby back ribs with orange and tamarind glaze to pulled-pork sliders with pickles. Equally inspired cocktails include jalapeno and pineapple mojitos and homemade thyme lemonade with Cointreau. Sunsets are magnificent.

Roy's Bayside Grill
INTERNATIONAL **$$**

(☑497-2470; www.roysbaysidegrill.com; Sandy Ground Rd; mains lunch US$12-22, dinner US$18-34; ⊙8am-10pm, bar to late; 🐾) Six different burgers are served at this easygoing seaside shack, along with island-style dishes such as Creole mahi-mahi and lobster sautéed in garlic butter, but the standout is the prime Angus beef, which Roy grills on the smoky barbecue. From Monday to Friday there are bargain US$10 lunch specials.

E's Oven
CARIBBEAN **$$**

(☑498-8258; www.facebook.com/EsOven; South Hill Rd, South Hill; mains US$10-28; ⊙11:30am-10:30pm Wed-Mon Nov-Aug; 🐾) In a wooden cottage painted bright red and yellow, E's is a sure bet for Caribbean specialties at competitive prices. Insiders phone ahead to preorder the famous roast chicken, but even if it's all gone, coconut-encrusted grouper, curried goat or creole conch are tasty alternatives.

★ Barrel Stay
FUSION **$$$**

(☑497-2831; www.barrelstay.com; Sandy Ground Rd; mains US$28-44; ⊙6-10pm Thu-Tue) Blackened snapper with crushed sweet potatoes, pan-seared pork in rum-and-raisin jus, lobster ravioli and oriental seaweed, maple-leaf-wrapped duck leg, and rich dark-chocolate tart with lime and chili sauce are among the wild flavor combinations at this gastronomic extravaganza in a polished-timber open-sided dining room right on Sandy Ground beach.

★ Veya
FUSION **$$$**

(☑498-8392; www.veya-axa.com; off Sir Emile Gumbs Dr; mains US$32-52; ⊙6:30-10pm Mon-Sat Nov-May, Mon-Fri Jun-Oct) Hidden amid tropical gardens with a koi pond and waterfalls, this gastronomic outpost is one of Anguilla's top tables. The menu changes regularly, but might feature conch carpaccio, local lobster with mustard-passion fruit sauce or jerk-spiced tuna with rum-coffee glaze, and incredible desserts such as choc-hazelnut mousse with malted chocolate ice cream.

Tasty's Restaurant
CARIBBEAN **$$$**

(☑497-2737; www.facebook.com/tastysrestauranguilla; South Hill Rd, South Hill; tapas US$4-14, mains US$18-46; ⊙10:30am-10:30pm Mon-Sat, 8:30am-10:30pm Sun, closed Thu Apr-Nov; 🐾)

Chef Dale Carty puts an upscale spin on Caribbean classics amid a cheerful setting of shells and tropical paraphernalia. Standout dishes include coconut fish with spicy banana rum sauce, while grazers can put together an evening meal from a dozen creative tapas. Live music plays on Tuesday and Saturday nights.

🍷 Drinking & Nightlife

★ **Johnno's**   BAR

(📞497-2728; www.facebook.com/johnnosbeach stop; Sandy Ground Rd; ⊙11am-midnight Tue-Sun; 🛜) No shirt and no shoes still gets you service at this funky wooden beach shack where Johnno's 'famous rum punch,' piña coladas, fresh-fruit daiquiris and classic cocktails are served amid photos of Miles Davis and other jazz greats. Live jazz and reggae bands play 8pm to midnight Friday and Saturday and 1pm to 4pm Sunday.

Pumphouse   PUB

(📞497-5154; www.facebook.com/thepumphouse axa; Sandy Ground Rd; ⊙5pm-2am Mon-Sat, 10am-2pm Sun; 🛜) Facing the salt pond, this historic former salt plant – where salt was cleaned and packed for shipping – is now one of Anguilla's liveliest venues. Bands, trivia quizzes, DJ nights, karaoke and drinks specials, including beer by the bucket, draw a big party crowd.

Elvis' Beach Bar   BAR

(www.elvisbeachbar.org; Sandy Ground Rd; ⊙11am-1am Tue-Sat, to midnight Sun) The beer is ice-cold, the margaritas are strong and the rum punch is laced with amaretto at Elvis' salty beach bar, which also has a feisty menu of Mexican food (dishes US$5 to US$16). Hang out at the 16ft-boat-turned-bar or rock out to live bands during high-octane weekend beach parties. Times can vary; the party often stretches into the wee hours.

🛍 Shopping

**SeaSpray Boutique and Ice
& Easy Smoothies**   ARTS & CRAFTS

(South Hill Rd, South Hill; ⊙10am-5pm Mon-Sat) Ice-cream-colored shades of pink, yellow and blue adorn the facade of this charming shop, where artist Pamela Miller sells handmade jewelry, clothing, handicrafts, pottery and local art and prints from around the island – including her own works, which you'll often see her crafting on the porch. Her attached smoothie bar is a great stop for fresh-fruit concoctions.

Blowing Point

If you're coming to Anguilla by ferry, Blowing Point will be the first community you encounter. Centered on the tiny pier, this little village consists of a smattering of shops and services.

🏃 Activities

Freedom Rentals   ADVENTURE SPORTS

(📞498-2830; www.freedomrentalsaxa.com; Blowing Point Rd; ATV quad-bike rental per half-/full day US$75/120; ⊙8am-6pm Nov-Sep) For an intrepid exploration of the island, rent an ATV quad bike accommodating up to two people, or sign up for a two-hour guided quad-bike tour taking in historic and cultural sights via mainly off-road tracks (US$150 per vehicle).

🛏 Sleeping & Eating

Ferryboat Inn   HOTEL $$

(📞497-6613; www.ferryboatinn.ai; Cul De Sac Dr; apt from US$286; P❄🛜) Situated 150m west of the ferry pier, the Ferryboat Inn's seven old-fashioned apartment-style rooms with basic kitchens look out over the jagged volcanic peaks of St-Martin/Sint Maarten nearby. Views of the water are partially obscured by the four-person beach house (from US$375), the in-house restaurant and its car park (meaning balconies or ground-level terraces don't offer any privacy).

Good Korma   INDIAN $

(📞581-7226; Blowing Point Rd; mains US$8-13; ⊙11am-3pm & 6-9pm Mon-Sat; 🍴) An aqua-painted, gold-trimmed wooden shack capped by a red roof houses this excellent little Indian restaurant. There's a handful of picnic tables outside, otherwise pick up takeout dishes such as fish tikka masala, goat balti, shrimp korma and West Indian vegetable curry. All sauces are meat-free, offering good mix-and-match options for vegetarians.

Ferryboat Inn Restaurant   INTERNATIONAL $$

(📞497-6613; www.ferryboatinn.ai; Cul De Sac Dr; mains US$12-30; ⊙noon-3pm & 5:30-8:30pm) Next to the hotel of the same name near the ferry pier, this waterfront restaurant has uninterrupted views across to mountainous St-Martin/Sint Maarten. The house-speciality Dutty's Burger is loaded with a half-pound beef patty, sautéed mushrooms, cheese, bacon and a fried egg.

Meads Bay

Meads Bay's majestic beach gets busy around the big resorts but has plenty of quiet spots further east to unwind.

⊙ Sights

Meads Bay   BEACH
Facing the Caribbean to the northwest, this wide white-sand beach is a lovely spot to swim and an ideal place to catch a spectacular sunset.

🛏 Sleeping

Most accommodations in this coveted part of the island are luxury hotels, resorts and villas with matching price tags.

★ Malliouhana   LUXURY HOTEL **$$$**
(🖉in USA 786-261-0800, in USA (toll free) 877-733-3611; https://malliouhana.aubergeresorts.com; John Hodge Rd; d from US$850; P❋@🛜🌊) On a low cliff at the eastern end of Meads Bay, Malliouhana is one of the island's most iconic luxury hotels, built in 1984 and reopened in 2014 following a US$36-million renovation. Starting from 720 sq ft, the stunning rooms have Italian-tile floors, marble baths, oversized black-and-white Caribbean landscape photographs, tropical watercolor murals and wraparound terraces with hammocks.

Meads Bay Beach Villas   LUXURY HOTEL **$$$**
(🖉497-0271; www.meadsbaybeachvillas.com; John Hodge Rd; villas US$800-2200; P❋🛜🌊) Each of the four villas here has two bedrooms, 2.5 bathrooms, a full kitchen, a spacious living area, wooden cathedral ceilings, West Indian tiling and a private pool, making them a favorite with honeymooners, though anyone with enough cash will feel like they've found their own pocket of paradise.

Frangipani Beach Resort   HOTEL **$$$**
(🖉497-6442, in USA 877-593-8988; www.frangipaniresort.com; John Hodge Rd; d/ste incl breakfast from US$400/650; P❋🛜🌊) With its pale-pink-painted exterior, red-tile roofs and Juliet balconies, this family-owned and run 19-room boutique resort evokes an Italian palazzo-by-the-sea. Rooms, though, have Caribbean flair, with wicker furniture, tiled floors and floral-print bedspreads. Even the cheapest rooms facing the gravel car park have cool 'cave showers' with massage jets. Rates include all water sports (SUP, wakeboarding and snorkeling).

Anacaona   HOTEL **$$$**
(🖉497-6827; www.anacaonahotel.com; Albert Hughes Dr, West End Village; d from US$370, 2-/3-bedroom ste from US$650/800; P❋@🛜🌊) Surrounded by flourishing gardens, this locally run boutique hotel is only a 200m walk south of dreamy Meads Bay beach. Accommodating staff look after the 20 rooms and four suites and also host Thursday's popular 'Antillean Night,' featuring a local Mayoumba folklore troupe, starting at 7:45pm (free; nonguests welcome). There are two pools, a Balinese spa and a hydrotherapy clinic.

Carimar Beach Club   HOTEL **$$$**
(🖉497-6881, in USA 866-270-3764; www.carimar.com; John Hodge Rd; 1-/2-bedroom ste from US$470/605; ◷mid-Oct–Aug; P❋@🛜) On the quiet eastern end of Meads Bay, these two-story Spanish-style haciendas framed by bougainvillea-draped balconies harbor 24 units with tropical rattan furnishings, fully equipped modern kitchens, and dining rooms seating up to six, all overlooking the lovely beach. Only the bedrooms have air-con, other rooms have ceiling fans. Extras include private tennis courts and a laundry room.

🍴 Eating

★ B&D's   BARBECUE **$**
(John Hodge Rd, Long Bay Village; mains US$10-12, lobster US$30; ◷6-9pm Fri & Sat) An Anguilla institution, this family-run roadside barbecue dishes up finger-lickin' platters of chicken, ribs, fish and lobster accompanied by sides such as rice, pasta salad, fries or coleslaw to a cult following of islanders and clued-in visitors under an open tent. The johnnycakes are the biggest and flakiest around. Arrive early before the lobster sells out.

Blanchard's Beach Shack   INTERNATIONAL **$**
(🖉498-6100; www.blanchardsrestaurant.com; John Hodge Rd; snacks & mains US$4-20; ◷11:30am-8:30pm mid-Dec–mid-Jan, 11:30am-8:30pm Mon-Sat mid-Jan–Aug & mid-Oct–mid-Dec; 🛜) Along a flowery garden path, this charismatic barefoot beach bar painted in vibrant primary colors is an island budget favorite. Dining is right on the beach beneath shady palms; wriggle your toes in the sand while devouring snacks such as tacos, burgers, salads, sandwiches and hot dogs, or mains such as grilled steaks and seafood, all made to order with fresh ingredients.

Straw Hat
INTERNATIONAL **$$**

(📞497-8300; www.strawhat.com; Frangipani Beach Resort, John Hodge Rd; mains lunch US$8-26, dinner US$16-36, lobster US$46; ⊙7-11am, noon-3pm & 6-9pm; 🛜🎏) This breezy charmer pairs a feet-in-the-sand atmosphere with high-end cooking. Straw hats filled with homemade bread precede sophisticated evening meals such as a half-lobster surf-and-turf or jerk mahi-mahi; lunch is a more casual affair (New York bagels, pastrami Reuben sandwiches, West Indian veggie burgers).

Best Buy Supermarket
SUPERMARKET

(Albert Hughes Dr; ⊙7:30am-9pm Mon-Fri, 8am-10pm Sat, 8am-9pm Sun) If you're self-catering, you absolutely need to know about this supermarket, which is the best stocked on the island (you'll often see Anguilla's top chefs shopping here), with fresh meats, fruits, vegetables, premade meals and salads, and artisan bread from its own ovens, along with homewares and pharmacy items.

West End

Stunning beaches at Anguilla's rugged west end include Rendezvous Bay, which is home to a major golf course and is within easy walking distance of Cove Bay, where you can canter along the sands on horseback. Further along, Shoal Bay West has fabulous snorkeling and nearby dive sites.

⊙ Sights

Rendezvous Bay
BEACH

(Willow Lane) Lapped by calm, crystal-clear waters, this pearly white crescent is idyllic for an extended stroll with a rum-punch stop or live music gig at Bankie Banx's Dune Preserve.

Cove Bay
BEACH

(off Anderson Fleming Dr) Cove Bay has shallow, clear and mostly calm water, but limited amenities other than a rollicking beach bar, Smokey's at the Cove (p92), and the kid-friendly Anguilla Aqua Park. Seaside Stables offers horseback rides along the beach.

Shoal Bay West
BEACH

(Rupert Carty Dr) The island road ends at this divine well-worn deserted sweep of white powdery sand with views of St-Martin/Sint Maarten and fabulous offshore snorkeling. Bring snorkeling gear with you as there are no rental outlets.

PRACTICALITIES

Smoking Smoking is banned inside enclosed spaces including hotel rooms and restaurants. Outdoor areas, including some open-air dining areas, are often not smoke-free.

Weights & Measures Anguilla uses the imperial system.

🏃 Activities

Anguilla Aqua Park
WATER PARK

(📞584-1204; www.anguillawatersports.com; off Anderson Fleming Dr, Cove Bay; half-/full day US$40/50; ⊙10am-6pm Nov-Sep) Kids adore splashing around on this interconnected island of trampolines, slides and climbing structures. Floating on Cove Bay's warm, clear waters, it sports Anguilla's national colors (orange, white and sky-blue) and is monitored by lifeguards. Anguilla's only kitesurfing academy is based here (US$175 per hour). SUP and glass-bottomed kayak rentals cost US$80/100 per three hours/day.

CuisinArt Golf Club
GOLF

(📞498-5602; www.cuisinartresort.com; Sisal Rd, Rendezvous Bay; 9/18 holes US$200/299, club rental from US$60) Tee off with breathtaking views of St-Martin/at this par 72, 7063yd course designed by Greg Norman. Shoes cost US$20; practice range prices start from US$15. Brush up on your game with lessons (US$55/115 per 30 minutes/one hour). Wear a collared shirt.

Seaside Stables
HORSEBACK RIDING

(📞235-3667; www.seasidestablesanguilla.com; Paradise Dr; 30min/1hr private beach ride US$50/90, minimum 2 people; ⊙9am-7pm, hours may vary) Seaside Stables offers horseback rides along the beach as well as kids' pony rides (US$20 per 15 minutes) and full-moon beach rides (US$150 per hour).

🎉 Festivals & Events

Moonsplash
MUSIC

(⊙Mar) Legendary musician Bankie Banx invites his old reggae friends along with emerging artists to the Dune Preserve (p92) under a March full moon for late-night jamming. Guests have included Third World, the Wailers, and Toots and the Maytals.

🛏 Sleeping

This secluded part of the island is largely the domain of wealthy and/or famous vacationers who drop thousands of dollars per night on luxurious suites. Several more major resorts are planned in the area.

Anguilla Great House   HOTEL **$**
(☑497-6061, in USA 800-583-9247; www.anguilla greathouse.com; Willow Lane, Rendezvous Bay; d from US$150; P☎) Dwarfed by vast surrounding resort properties, this cluster of West Indian–style cottages has simply furnished rooms with fridges, including some connecting rooms that are handy for groups.

Paradise Cove Resort   HOTEL **$$**
(☑497-6603; www.paradisecoveanguilla.com; Paradise Dr, Cove Bay; ste from US$265; P☀☎☀) Set amid flowering gardens, Paradise Cove is a comfy, well-priced enclave of spacious rooms with private terraces and light, bright Caribbean furnishings. In-room kitchenettes can be stocked prior to arrival, but there's also a good on-site restaurant and bar. The only downside is its inland location, although the ocean is only a 500m walk southwest.

★ Cap Juluca   LUXURY HOTEL **$$$**
(☑497-6666, in USA 888-858-5822; www.capjuluca.com; off Samuel Fleming Rd, Maundays Bay; d from US$1066; P☀☎☀) With its domed Greco-Moorish villas and three on-site restaurants stretching along a white sandy arc, Cap Juluca is easily one of Anguilla's most seductive, exclusive resorts. Each beachfront room has direct access to the sand, and comes with marble bathroom, extensively stocked minibar and private terrace; some have a second private terrace on the rooftop.

CuisinArt Golf Resort & Spa   RESORT **$$$**
(☑498-2000; www.cuisinartresort.com; Sisal Rd, Rendezvous Bay; ste/villa from US$666/2886; P☀☎☀) This top-notch whitewashed golf resort sits on a divine stretch of beach and features a trio of restaurants supplied with produce grown in the huge on-site hydroponic greenhouse (tours available). As well as 91 suites with marble bathrooms, terraces and state-of-the-art interiors, there are seven villas with private pools and Jacuzzis.

Covecastles   LUXURY HOTEL **$$$**
(☑497-6801, in USA 800-223-1108; www.covec astles.com; Rupert Carty Dr, Shoal Bay West; villas US$895-6395; ☺Nov-Aug; P☀☎☀) Designed by statement-making American architect Myron Goldfinger in the 1980s, Covecastles' space-age curvilinear white villas, sleeping four to 10 people, have soaring floor-to-ceiling sliding-glass windows, snazzy kitchens, flowing lounges, stucco floors, chic wicker furniture with raw silk cushions, and brilliant absolute beachfront locations.

🍴 Eating

High-end restaurants are located in the resorts, with more casual eateries dotted along beaches.

Picante   MEXICAN **$$**
(☑498-1616; www.picante-restaurant-anguilla. com; Albert Hughes Dr; mains US$11-21; ☺6:30-9:15pm Wed-Mon Nov–mid-Aug) In a romantically lit, open-air, tin-roofed space, this long-standing spot run by a Californian couple turns out sophisticated Mexican fare: chili tuna tacos, grilled chipotle shrimp burritos, lime-marinated steak quesadillas. The house margarita, by the glass or pitcher, is a must; there are also 13 different tequilas and five Mexican beers.

🍷 Drinking & Nightlife

★ Bankie Banx's Dune Preserve   BAR
(www.bankiebanx.net/dunepreserve; Botanic Rd, Rendezvous Bay; ☺11:30am-11:30pm Thu-Tue, hours may vary) Legendary reggae star Bankie Banx transformed huge piles of driftwood and old boats into what's essentially a giant tree house on the beach. Phenomenal live music plays regularly; with luck, you'll catch Bankie or his musician/cricketer son Omari Banks performing. After knocking back a signature Dune Shine (ginger, pineapple juice, white rum and bitters), you'll never want to leave.

Smokey's at the Cove   BAR
(☑497-6582; www.smokeysatthecove.com; Anderson Fleming Dr, Cove Bay; ☺11.30am-9pm; ☎) Break up a day of swimming in Cove Bay with a Frisky Parrot cocktail (Malibu rum, pineapple juice, passion-fruit and mango puree and spices) and some grilled lobster or ribs with smoky BBQ sauce. Local bands play on Tuesday, Friday, Saturday and Sunday evenings, with an additional performance from 1pm to 4pm on Sunday afternoons.

🔒 Shopping

Cheddie's Carving Studio   ARTS & CRAFTS
(📞497-6027; www.cheddieart.ai; Driftwood Ave;
🕙9am-5pm Mon-Fri, 10am-3pm Sat, hours may
vary) Master wood-carver Cheddie displays
his inspired artworks at his studio. Stop by
to witness the transformation as pieces of
forgotten driftwood are turned into striking
sculptures. It's at the end of a narrow dirt
road off Albert Hughes Dr. Call ahead to
confirm Cheddie is around.

Shoal Bay East

A quintessential Caribbean stretch of white
sand, glorious Shoal Bay East is a 2-mile-
long beach with swaying coconut palms and
sea grape trees, reefs ideal for snorkeling,
and luminous turquoise water.

Just inland is the Fountain Cavern
National Park, with fascinating rock art by
the Arawaks dating back over two millennia.

◉ Sights

★Shoal Bay East   BEACH
Idyllic Shoal Bay East – a shimmering,
nearly deserted stretch of brilliant white
sand strewn with tiny crushed shells – is
still miraculously blight-free. There's a handful of small-scale resorts and villas as well
as a string of laid-back beach bars along the
sand, but it's surprisingly quiet, even in high
season. Bring your snorkeling gear (or rent
some on-site), as the glassy turquoise waters
are perfect for underwater observation.

Fountain Cavern National Park   NATIONAL PARK
(Brimegin Dr) Designated a national park in
1985, this 14.5-acre site's limestone terraces
rise up from the sea. Its cavern is home to
numerous petroglyph rock-art works created by the Arawaks around AD 300, which
provide an extraordinary glimpse into their
life on the island. The most spectacular is
a head of Jocahu, the Arawak God of Creation, carved from a stalagmite. While the
park remains open, the cavern is currently
closed pending Unesco-listing status; check
with the National Trust (p86) for updates.

🛏 Sleeping

Fountain Residences   APARTMENT $$
(📞216-5600, in USA 866-376-7077; www.fountain
anguilla.com; off Brimegin Dr; studio/1-/2-bed-
room apt US$250/275/445; 🅿✹🛜❄) Stylishly

ANGUILLA SUMMER FESTIVAL

Anguilla's Carnival (www.anguillasummer
festival.com; 🕙late Jul–early Aug) is its
main festival. The 10-day celebration
starts on the weekend preceding August
Monday (the first Monday in August) and
continues until the following weekend.
High-spirited events include traditional
boat racing, costumed parades, a beauty
pageant and calypso competitions with
continuous music and dancing.

designed apartments at this welcoming,
well-kept complex have oversized bathrooms
with rain showers, cable TV, and kitchens
kitted out with everything you need to whip
up a gourmet meal. The best have private
terraces overlooking Shoal Bay East beach
a 100m stroll away; garden apartments fan
around the landscaped pool.

★Zemi Beach House   RESORT $$$
(📞584-0001; www.zemibeach.com; Brimegin Dr;
d/ste from US$795/2650; 🅿✹@🛜❄) Sprawl-
ing over 6 acres of beachfront, this 2016-built
ultra-contemporary property has a spectacular infinity pool, a dramatically floodlit bar,
two restaurants (one casual, one gourmet),
54 rooms and nine two- and three-bedroom
suites. Top-floor luxury rooms have rooftop
terraces and plunge pools; suites have full
kitchens and private pools. The kids' club
keeps youngsters entertained.

🍴 Eating

Beach bars serving food – from smoky barbecue fare to Caribbean staples such as fish
soup as well as burgers and sandwiches –
scatter along the length of the beach. High-
end hotels here also have excellent restaurants open to the public.

Gwen's Reggae Bar & Grill   BARBECUE $$
(Brimegin Dr; mains US$12-30; 🕙10am-5pm Mon-
Sat, to 7pm Sun; 🛜) A vibrant red-and-yellow
beach shack with palm trees painted on the
side is home to Gwen's famous barbecue,
char-grilling fish, chicken, ribs and lobster.
Eat on the deck or head to a picnic table
on the sand. It's jumping on Sundays when
Anguilla's famous Scratch Band performs
reggae favorites and barefoot dancing takes
place fueled by *super*-strong rum punch.

Island Harbour

Anguilla's quiet eastern seascape is a narrowing strip of breezy coves dotted by casbah-like villas and hidden eateries. Island Harbour is a working fishing community, not a resort area, and its beach is lined with brightly colored fishing boats rather than umbrella-shaded sun loungers.

According to local lore, Island Harbour got its name from Irish settlers who were shipwrecked off Anguilla's northeastern tip in the early 17th century and made it ashore here. They named it Ireland Harbour, but the local population had difficulty pronouncing 'Ireland' and it was transmuted over time to Island Harbour. Although no official documentation exists, to this day about 100 inhabitants of the area have the surnames Harrigan and Webster, and are thought to be of Irish descent.

🏃 Activities

Anchor Miniature Golf   MINIGOLF
(☑498-7258;   www.anchorminiaturegolf.com; Nashville Webster Rd; minigolf per round before/after 5pm US$5/7; ☺10am-8pm Mon-Thu, to 6pm Fri, 6-11pm Sat, 1-8pm Sun) Flowering magnolias, bougainvilleas and palms line this superbly landscaped 18-hole minigolf course, interspersed with ponds, waterfalls and fountains. You can also rent sports equipment here, including snorkeling gear (US$8 per day); bikes (US$15/20 per half-/full day); and SUPs, 'zayaks' (glass-bottomed flotation devices for lounging on while you peer underwater) and kayaks (all US$25/60 per hour/day).

🍴 Eating

⭐ Artisan Pizza Napoletana   PIZZA $$
(☑235-6116; www.pizzanapoletana.org; Webster's Yard, Nashville Webster Rd; pizza & pasta US$14-25; ☺6-10pm Mon, Tue & Thu-Sat) An enchanting wooden shack with a candlelit terrace and outdoor lounge is home to the Caribbean's only establishment certified by the Associazione Verace Pizza Napoletana, Italy's standard-bearer for authentic Neapolitan-style pizzas. Soft-crust pizzas are topped with imported Italian ingredients from approved suppliers and fired up in the mosaic-tiled 1650°F wood-fired oven. It also hand-makes its own pastas and seasonal gelato.

Elite Italian   ITALIAN $$
(☑476-5178; Nashville Webster Rd; panini US$12-18, mains US$16-32, lobster US$32-45; ☺noon-8:30pm, bar to late Oct-Aug) Beneath sea grape trees and coconut palms, this open-sided beachfront restaurant overlooks traditional fishing boats and Scilly Cay beyond. Pastas – such as spinach and ricotta ravioli or spaghetti *vongole* – and panini sandwiches are lunchtime highlights. Mains such as calamari with caper sauce or lobster with truffle Parmesan star at dinner, when the space is lit by flickering candles.

Hibernia Restaurant   FUSION $$$
(☑497-4290; www.hiberniarestaurant.com; Harbour Ridge Dr; mains US$35-47; ☺noon-1:30pm & 6-8:30pm Tue-Sat Nov–mid-Jul) Raoul and Mary hail from France and Ireland and travel regularly throughout Asia. Their Caribbean-Zen culinary retreat harmonizes these influences in the fusion cooking – chilled almond and melon soup, vanilla and lemongrass sautéed crayfish, eggplant and shiitake mushroom stir-fry – and in the decor, with a tranquil Balinese-style reflection pool and attached Asian art gallery. Reservations required.

🔒 Shopping

Anguilla Sea Salt Company   FOOD
(www.anguillaseasalt.com; Nashville Webster Rd; ☺8am-5pm Mon-Fri, 9am-4pm Sat) 🌿 Historically renowned for its salt, by the mid-20th century, Anguilla's industry had shut down. In 2013 salt production was resurrected by this enterprising company, which pumps seawater into greenhouses, where salt is collected after evaporation to produce coarse, semi-coarse and fine grades.

UNDERSTAND ANGUILLA

History

First settled by the Amerindian peoples from South America about 4000 years ago, then by a succession of tribes and cultures, including the Arawaks, Anguilla was called 'Malliouhana,' meaning arrow-shaped sea serpent. The Arawaks remained on the island for millennia, as evidenced by many cave sites with petroglyphs and artifacts such as shell axes, flint blades and conch-shell drinking receptacles still visible today and studied by archaeologists.

Columbus sailed by in 1493, but didn't land on the island (probably because he didn't notice it since it's extremely flat compared with St-Martin/Sint Maarten next door). Britain sent a colony in 1650 to take advantage of soil that was hospitable to growing corn and tobacco. However, it wasn't hospitable to much else, and the plantation colonies that bloomed on nearby Caribbean islands, such as St Kitts and Nevis, never defined Anguilla.

When the sugar plantations were abandoned due to a lack of viable soil and insufficient rain, small-scale industries, such as sailing, fishing and private farming, began to crop up on the island. In 1834 Britain abolished slavery in its colonies, and many Anguillan ex-slaves took up positions as farmers, sailors and fishers.

In 1958, Anguilla formed a federation with St Kitts and Nevis, which was disliked by most of the ex-slave population. Anguilla was allowed only one freeholder representative to the House of Assembly on St Kitts and was largely ignored, eventually culminating in the Anguilla Revolution in 1967. Anguilla Day marks May 30, 1967, the day Anguillans forced the Royal St Kitts Police Force off the island for good.

As a result of its revolt against St Kitts, Anguilla returned to Britain and once again became an overseas territory. Under the Anguilla constitution, which came into effect in 1982, one queen-appointed representative acts as the British governor and presides over the Executive Council and an elected Anguilla House of Assembly.

People & Culture

Anguillan culture is a blend of West Indian, British and African influences. Anguilla's local population is almost entirely descended from African slaves brought to the Caribbean several centuries ago. Since 2006, many Chinese, Mexican and Indian workers have been employed on the island to build Anguilla's surge of new resorts.

Sailboat racing is the national sport and a vital part of everyday life. Races are a common occurrence and are a great way to hang out with the community. Cricket is also popular, and a rugby team formed in 2006.

Upscale tourism drives the economy and today almost three-quarters of the island's inhabitants work in hospitality or commerce. Anguillans take pride in maintaining the balance between tourist development and the preservation of local society.

For a small island, Anguilla has an impressive arts-and-crafts scene that mostly focuses on inventive local artists rather than a rich textile history. There are currently about two dozen resident artists and several galleries displaying their work.

Landscape & Wildlife

Anguilla, an arid island shaped like an eel (its namesake), lies 5 miles north of St-Martin/Sint Maarten. Its 33 white-sand beaches have prompted countless imaginations to linger over whether one could subsist on a diet of coconuts to take an early retirement here.

Throughout the island, 159 bird species have been recorded, including the Antillean crested hummingbird, frigate, brown pelican, snow egret and black-necked stilt. Endangered sea turtles, such as the hawksbill, can be spotted offshore in seven protected marine parks: Dog Island, Little Bay, Prickly Pear, Sandy Island, Seal Island Reef System, Shoal Bay-Island Harbour Reef System and Stoney Bay. The most commonplace creatures on the island are the many roaming goats and sheep. (If you see a slightly fuzzier-looking goat with its tail down, not up, it's actually a Caribbean sheep.)

Like many Caribbean islands, Anguilla desalinates much of its water. Be mindful of letting the water run needlessly.

SURVIVAL GUIDE

❶ Directory A–Z

ACCOMMODATIONS

There's no getting around it: Anguilla is an expensive destination. While high-season rates usually run December 15 to April 15, it's around Christmas and New Year's when prices rise

SLEEPING PRICE RANGES

The following price ranges refer to a double room with bathroom in high season (mid-December to mid-April).

$	less than US$200
$$	US$200–US$400
$$$	more than US$400

astronomically. Most hotels and villas charge significantly less in the low season.

Accommodations charge a 10% government tax, a 10% service charge and a daily US$1 per person tourism fee. These are not included in rates unless otherwise stated.

Booking Services

Island Dream Properties (☎ 498-3200; www.islanddreamproperties.com) Offers villa rental (per week from around US$3000 for a one-bedroom property); can also organize private chefs, provisioning, car rental, babysitting and boat charters.

Ricketts Luxury Properties (☎ 497-6049; www.rickettsluxury.com) Rents everything from one-bedroom villas to fully staffed three-villa compounds with 22 bedrooms. Rates per week for a one-bedroom villa start at around US$3000.

ELECTRICITY

110-120V; North American–style sockets are common.

EMBASSIES & CONSULATES

There are no official embassies on the island. Those seeking consular services, however, can contact the Anguilla Tourist Board, which has a list of local contacts representing foreign nations.

EMERGENCY NUMBERS

Ambulance, Fire, Police	☎ 911

FOOD

Global flavors abound on Anguilla, along with some exquisite fusion creations, while local specialties include seafood, barbecue and Creole cuisine. Beach bars are popular dining spots throughout the day; many higher-end restaurants only open at night.

If you're self-catering in an apartment or villa, be aware that supermarkets are often poorly stocked. Anguilla's best supermarket is Best Buy Supermarket (p91) in Meads Bay.

GLBT TRAVELERS

In general, Anguilla does not have an open-minded approach to gay and lesbian travelers, so it's best to avoid public displays of affection. While homosexuality has been legal on Anguilla since 2000, same-sex marriage is not, and there are no nondiscrimination laws. Hotels, however – especially larger and/or high-end establishments – tend to be more tolerant, so booking a double room shouldn't pose any problems.

HEALTH

Princess Alexandra Hospital (☎ 497-2551; Queen Elizabeth Ave) Located in the Valley; has a 24-hour emergency room.

MONEY

The Eastern Caribbean dollar (EC$) is the local currency, but the US dollar is preferred and often required. Many smaller establishments don't accept credit cards.

ATMs

Banks with ATMs are located in the Valley and dispense both US and EC dollars. Keep cash on hand, as ATMs won't work for all foreign cards.

First Caribbean International Bank (www.cibc.com; Albert Lake Dr; ☉8am-2pm Mon-Thu, to 4pm Fri)

Scotiabank Anguilla (www.scotiabank.com; Cosely Dr; ☉8am-5pm Mon-Fri) In the Fairplay Commercial Complex.

Exchange Rates

AUSTRALIA	A$1	US$0.72
CANADA	C$1	US$0.74
EURO ZONE	€1	US$1.05
JAPAN	¥100	US$0.85
NEW ZEALAND	NZ$1	US$0.69
UK	UK£1	US$1.23

For current exchange rates, see www.xe.com.

Tipping

Most restaurant bills include a 15% service charge, while hotels add a 10% service charge; no further tipping is necessary.

POST

Post office (www.aps.ai; Carter Rey Blvd; ☉8am-3:30pm Mon-Fri)

PUBLIC HOLIDAYS

New Year's Day January 1
James Ronald Webster Day March 2
Good Friday March/April
Easter Monday March/April
Labor Day May 1
Whit Monday mid-May
Anguilla Day May 30
Queen's Birthday Mid-June

EATING PRICE RANGES

The following price ranges refer to a main course.

$	less than US$15
$$	US$15–US$35
$$$	more than US$35

August Monday (Emancipation Day) First Monday in August

August Thursday first Thursday in August

Constitution Day early August

National Heroes and Heroines Day December 19

Christmas Day December 25

Boxing Day December 26

TAXES & REFUNDS

At the time of writing, Anguilla was preparing to implement a 10% goods and services tax (GST).

TELEPHONE

➜ Anguilla's country code is 🖉1-264, which is followed by a seven-digit local number.

➜ To call the island from North America, dial 🖉1 + 264 + the local number.

➜ From elsewhere, dial your country's international access code + 1 + 264 + the local number.

➜ If you are calling internationally from Anguilla, unless you are dialing a landline within the North American Numbering Plan (NANP), you need to dial the international exit code 🖉011.

TIME

Anguilla is on Atlantic Time (GMT/UTC minus four hours). Daylight saving time is not observed.

TOURIST INFORMATION

Anguilla doesn't have a tourist office open to the public, but brochures and maps are available at most hotels. Alternatively, you can contact the **Anguilla Tourist Board** (🖉497-2759, in USA 🖉800-553-4939; www.ivisitanguilla.com) by phone or via its comprehensive website for information about the island.

TRAVELERS WITH DISABILITIES

Anguilla's flat terrain makes things easier for travelers with disabilities or limited mobility compared to many Caribbean islands. In addition, many hotels and villas have rooms equipped for wheelchair users. Wheelchair-friendly bathroom facilities at bars and restaurants are rare, however – confirm when booking.

Download Lonely Planet's free Accessible Travel guide from http://lptravel.to/Accessible Travel.

❶ Getting There & Away

Anguilla has regular regional flights, particularly to St-Martin/Sint Maarten's Princess Juliana International Airport, and frequent ferries to St-Martin/Sint Maarten.

No cruise ships dock in Anguilla.

❶ DRINKING WATER

Most of the island's water is collected in cisterns, so it's advisable to drink bottled water.

AIR

Anguilla's **Clayton J Lloyd International Airport** (AXA; 🖉497-2514) accepts mostly smaller aircraft and will require a transfer before arriving from most international destinations (unless you're using your private jet).

Anguilla Air (🖉498-5922; www.anguillaair services.com) serves St-Martin/Sint Maarten's Princess Juliana International Airport (Dutch side) and St-Barthélemy, while **Seaborne Airlines** (🖉Puerto Rico 787-946-7800; www. seaborneairlines.com) and **Tradewind Aviation** (🖉Puerto Rico 203-267-3305; www. flytradewind.com) serve San Juan (Puerto Rico). There are also various high-season services.

SEA

Ferry

The **ferry terminal** (Blowing Point Rd) is in Blowing Point.

Public ferries (⏲ one-way US$20) make the 25-minute run between Anguilla and Marigot in St-Martin/Sint Maarten (French side) an average of once every 45 minutes, departing Anguilla from 7:30am to 6:15pm, and departing St-Martin/Sint Maarten from 8:15am to 7pm, with an additional departure at 10pm. There's a US$3 security fee and a US$20 departure tax (US$5 for day trips).

GB Ferries (🖉235-6205; www.anguillaferry andcharter.com; one-way day/night US$65/80) is a reliable operator running to Princess Juliana International Airport in Simpson Bay, St-Martin/Sint Maarten (20 to 30 minutes). It departs Anguilla from 8:45am to 5:30pm, and from St-Martin/Sint Maarten between 10am and 6:30pm. In addition, it runs a high-season evening ferry between 10pm and 1am to connect with Princess Juliana International Airport's late-night flights. It saves considerable time compared with taking a taxi from Marigot to the airport. There's a US$20 departure tax (US$5 for day trips).

Yacht

The port of entry for yachts is at Sandy Ground. Before arriving, contact the **immigration and customs office** (🖉497-2451; Sandy Ground Rd; ⏲8:30am-noon & 1-4pm) on VHF channel 16.

ⓘ DEPARTURE TAX

Departure tax is US$20 plus a US$3 security fee (US$5 for St-Martin/Sint Maarten day trips).

ⓘ Getting Around

Anguilla has no public transport. The island is very petite – you can easily drive from one end to the other in around an hour.

BICYCLE

Anguilla's flat terrain makes cycling easy, but be aware that roads can be narrow and rough.

Rentals cost around US$25 per day. Bike-rental outlets include Anchor Miniature Golf (p94) and Boo's Cars & Cycle Rentals (p98).

Freedom Rentals (p89) rents ATV quad bikes.

CAR & MOTORCYCLE

Driving is on the left-hand side of the road, but steering wheels can confusingly be on either the left or the right side of the car. The speed limit is 30mph unless signposted otherwise.

Petrol prices are around US$3.80 for 1 gallon of gas. The island is very flat and there is rarely traffic.

CAR HIRE

Car-rental companies issue the compulsory local driving permit for US$20 cash. Compact cars start from US$45 per day (usually US$5 cheaper in summer).

Most companies don't have physical offices open to the public; book in advance to arrange pickup and drop-off.

Andy's Auto Rentals (☑ 584-7010; www. andyrentals.com; Ferry Terminal, Blowing Point Rd; per day from US$35) Has a handy location right next to the ferry terminal, a good range of vehicles, and offers welcome drinks on arrival. Cars can be picked up and/or dropped off at the airport or delivered to accommodations.

Apex/Avis (☑ 497-2642; www.avisanguilla. com; per day from US$40)

Boo's Cars & Cycle Rentals (☑ 497-8523; oboo@anguillanet.com; bike/car rental per day from US$12/40)

Carib Rent A Car (☑ 497-6020; caribcar rental@anguillanet.com; per day from US$40)

Connor's Car Rental (☑ 497-6433; mauricec@ caribserve.net; per day from US$35)

Island Car Rental (☑ 497-2723; www.island car.ai; per day from US$35)

Romcan Car Rental (☑ 497-6265; www. romcan.co; per day from US$35)

Triple K Car/Hertz Rental (☑ 497-2934; hertz triplek@anguillanet.com; per day from US$35)

TAXI

Anguilla is divided into 10 taxi zones with fares depending on how many zones you travel through (ie one zone US$10, 10 zones US$36). Surcharges apply for rides after 6pm or for more than two people. Two-hour island tours for two people cost US$55. Drivers only accept US dollars.

Antigua & Barbuda

POP 93,000 / ☎ 268

Best Places to Eat

➡ Le Bistro (p107)

➡ Cecilia's High Point Cafe (p107)

➡ C&C Wine Bar (p104)

➡ Sun Ra (p113)

Best Places to Sleep

➡ Admiral's Inn (p112)

➡ South Point Hotel (p112)

➡ Buccaneer Beach Club (p106)

➡ Waterfront Hostel (p112)

Why Go?

On Antigua, life is a beach. Its corrugated coasts cradle hundreds of perfect little strands lapped by beguiling enamel-blue water, while the sheltered bays have provided refuge for everyone from Admiral Nelson to buccaneers and yachties. If you can tear yourself away from that towel, you'll discover that there's a distinct English accent to this island. You'll find it in the bustling capital of St John's, in salty-glamorous English Harbour, and in the historic forts and other vestiges of the colonial past. Yet, Antigua is also quintessential Caribbean, full of candy-coloured villages, a rum-infused mellowness and bright-eyed locals that greet you with wide smiles.

If life on Antigua is a beach, Barbuda *is* a beach: one smooth, pink-tinged strand hemming the reef-filled waters. Birds, especially the huffing and puffing frigates, greatly outnumber residents on this Caribbean dream island.

When to Go

Dec–Apr Peak travel season when daily highs average 81°F (27°C), while nighttime temperatures drop to a balmy 72°F (22°C).

Jul & Aug Only slightly hotter (86°F/30°C high and 77°F/25°C low) but can get humid. July is also the start of hurricane season, which runs into November.

May–Nov Prices drop and crowds thin.

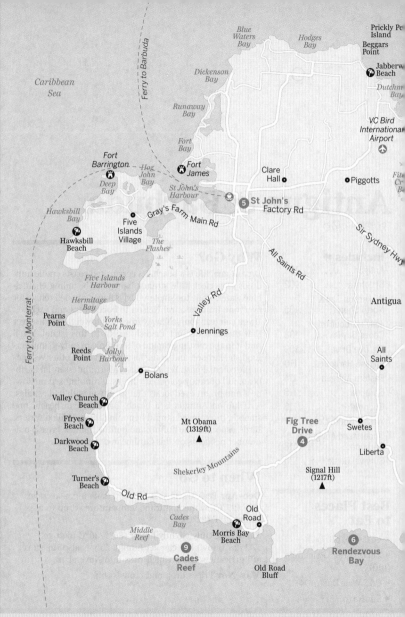

Antigua & Barbuda Highlights

1 Half Moon Bay (p114)
Playing in the waves of
Antigua's most beautiful beach.

2 Frigate Bird Sanctuary
(p115) Marveling at
the magnificent winged

denizens off Barbuda's
northwest coast.

**3 Shirley Heights Lookout
Restaurant** (p113) Swaying
to reggae during the Sunday-

afternoon barbecue at English
Harbour.

4 Fig Tree Drive (p109)
Tasting a sweet black pineapple
at a roadside fruit stand.

ATLANTIC
OCEAN

Long
Island

Maiden
Island

Great Bird
Island

**North Sound
National Park**

Guiana
Island

*Parham
Harbour*

*Guiana
Bay*

Crump
Island

Pelican
Island

Parham

Mercers Creek
Bay

*Long
Bay*

Indian
Town
Point

Devil's Bridge

Seatons

Pares

Willikies

Betty's
Hope

*Nonsuch
Bay*

Green
Island

Potworks
Dam

Great Deep Bay

York
Island

Bethesda

1 **Half Moon Bay**

*Willoughby
Bay*

Hudson
Point

Falmouth

mouth
arbour
on Point
Beach

English
Harbour

3 **Shirley
Heights**

*Mamora
Bay*

8 **Nelson's
Dockyard**

Galleon
Beach

*English
Harbour*

7 **Pillars of
Hercules**

Antigua & Barbuda

2 **Frigate
Bird
Sanctuary**

Barbuda

CODRINGTON

ST JOHN'S

Antigua

0   20 km
0   10 miles

0   4 km
0   2 miles

5 **St John's Public Market**
(p102) Putting together an
exotic tropical beach picnic.

6 **Rendezvous Bay** (p111)
Traipsing through thick
rainforest to shimmering sands.

7 **Pillars of Hercules**
(p111) Exploring these
whimsically eroded cliffs.

8 **Nelson's Dockyard**
(p110) Flashing back to
colonial times at this restored

18th-century naval base at
English Harbour.

9 **Cades Reef** (p111)
Exploring Antigua's watery
underbelly on a diving
excursion.

ANTIGUA

Antigua's capital, St John's, is tucked into a sheltered bay, about 5 miles west of the airport. Most hotels and resorts cluster north of here along Dickenson Bay and south in historic English Harbour. The best beaches hem the west coast between Jolly Harbour and Old Road village. The wind-swept east is sparsely settled and has only a few beaches.

ⓘ Getting There & Away

Flights arrive at the spanking new terminal at VC Bird International Airport, about 5 miles east of St John's. It has two ATMs, a currency-exchange office, a few duty-free shops and several food outlets, including a Big Banana branch past security. Buses and taxis leave from outside the terminal, while car-rental companies are based in an old building up the ramp to the left as you exit the terminal.

ⓘ Getting Around

Privately operated minivans ply pretty much all corners of the island. All routes begin and end in St John's, either at the West bus station (destinations north, west and south) or the East bus station (points east and southeast). There's no set timetable. Buses depart St John's when full and generally run from about 6am until 7pm, stopping at regular and requested stops along the way. It's also possible to flag down a bus. There are very few buses on Sunday.

Fares cost EC$2.25 to EC$4. **Bus Stop Antigua** (www.busstopanu.com) has details.

St John's

Intriguingly shabby, Antigua's capital and commercial center is worth a spin for its cafes, restaurants, shops, cute museum and bustling market lining its compact town. There's a melange of buildings from restored colonial survivors to modern horrors. St John's all but shuts down at night and on Sundays.

◉ Sights

Fort James   FORT
(Fort Rd; 🅿; 🚌17) **FREE** Fort James, a small stronghold at the north side of St John's Harbour, dates back to 1706, but most of what you see today was built in 1739. Still sporting a few of its 36 cannons, a powder magazine and wall remnants, the site drips with atmosphere: it's moodily rundown and is rarely the scene of crowds.

Public Market   MARKET
(Market St; ⊙6am-6pm Mon-Sat) Forage for exotic local produce such as sorrel, black pineapple and sugar apple alongside more familiar bananas, limes, mangoes and eggplant at St John's vibrant market, which spills out into surrounding streets on Friday and Saturday mornings. It's a fun place for a browse, snack or people-watching. For fresh fish, follow your nose to the stalls next to the bus station where vendors are happy to fillet your purchase.

Museum of Antigua & Barbuda   MUSEUM
(☎268-462-1469; www.antiguamuseums.net; cnr Market & Long Sts; adult/child under 12yr EC$8/free; ⊙8:30am-4pm Mon-Fri, 10am-2pm Sat) In the stately 1750 courthouse, this modest museum traces the history of Antigua from its geological origins to its political independence in 1981. The hodgepodge of objects includes Arawak pottery, models of sugar plantations and the cricket bat of hometown hero Viv Richards. On display outside are four narrow-gauge locomotives from the early 20th century once used to transport sugarcane.

🏃 Activities

Bike Plus   CYCLING
(☎268-462-2453; cnr Independence Ave & St Mary's St; bike rental per day from US$17.50) Well-respected bike shop has a sizeable fleet of bicycles for rent and is close to the East bus station.

Fort Bay Beach   BEACH
This narrow beach north of Fort James is backed by trees and has toilets, showers and a few beach bars that also rent sun loungers and umbrellas. It's popular with locals, but is also popular with cruise-ship visitors because of its proximity to the pier.

👉 Tours

★ Adventure Antigua   ADVENTURE
(☎268-726-6355; www.adventureantigua.com) Eli Fuller, a former Olympian and third-generation Antiguan, offers educational and fun tours. His signature trip is the all-day Eco-Tour (US$115), which involves boating, swimming and snorkeling amid the pristine waters of North Sound National Park. The Xtreme Circumnav (US$170) aboard a 45ft speedboat includes a snorkel trip, a stop at a stingray marine park and a swim at remote Rendezvous Bay. Book online for a 10% discount.

St John's

ANTIGUA & BARBUDA ST JOHN'S

Treasure Island Cruises BOATING
(☑ 268-461-8675; www.facebook.com/Treasure
IslandCruises) Denzil and Brian take small
groups of people out on boat trips aboard
a 70ft catamaran that combine sailing,
snorkeling, entertainment and a barbecue.
Options include the Circumnavigation tour
(US$120), the Cades Reef tour (US$120) and
the Bird Island tour (US$100).

✖ Eating

St John's has several excellent restaurants
as well as plenty of street food in the downtown area and near the market, which is
busiest on Saturday mornings.

Big Banana PIZZA $
(☑ 268-480-6985; www.bigbanana-antigua.com;
Redcliffe Quay; pizzas EC$25-81; ⊙ 10am-midnight
Mon-Sat; 🛜) Some patrons have been coming
to this buzzy former rum warehouse (locally
known simply as 'Pizzas') for more than 30

---

years, so irresistible are its pizzas that come
in four sizes, on regular or thin crusts and

with classic toppings. On weekends you may have to elbow your way inside.

Roti King
CARIBBEAN $

(☑ 268-462-2328; cnr St Mary's St & Corn Alley; roti EC$18-26; ◷ 10am-midnight Sun-Thu, to 2:30am Fri & Sat) This little sibling-owned cottage does brisk business all day long with its mouth-watering roti – chicken, shrimp, pork, beef, veggies or conch swimming in a mildly spicy curry sauce and wrapped into a soft flatbread. Try them with a homemade passionfruit or sorrel juice or ginger beer.

Epicurean
SUPERMARKET $

(☑ 268-484-5400; www.epicureanantigua.com; Friars Hill Rd; ◷ 7am-11pm; P 🛜) This upscale market has a big selection of fresh local foods, imported international foods (especially from the UK and the US), as well as a pharmacy, a hot-food counter and ATMs.

First Choice Foods
SUPERMARKET $

(☑ 268-463-3663; Anchorage Rd; ◷ 8am-10pm; P) Medium-priced supermarket with many local products; en route to Dickenson Bay.

★ Papa Zouk
SEAFOOD $$

(☑ 268-464-6044; www.facebook.com/Papazouk; Hilda Davis Dr; mains EC$55-90; ◷ 7pm-midnight Mon-Sat; ☺) This high-energy joint is a local institution, famous for its Antiguan-style bouillabaisse and fresh fish – mahi-mahi to butterfish – served grilled or fried. With zouk on the sound system, crazy murals, Christmas lights and a nautical decor, it's the kind of place that's downright trippy even before you've started sampling the vast rum selection. Reservations essential.

C&C Wine Bar
INTERNATIONAL $$

(☑ 268-460-7025; www.ccwinehouse.com; Redcliffe Quay, Redcliffe St; dishes EC$25-68; ◷ noon-5pm Mon, to 10:30pm Tue-Sat) 'Eat, drink, socialise' is the tantalizing motto of this locally adored courtyard cafe where South African wines complement tasty pastas, burgers, paninis and mains such as fragrant shrimp coconut curry. Tables spill from the pint-sized wine shop–bar onto a romantic courtyard, and fill to capacity crowd during 'Lasagne Thursdays' and 'Karaoke Saturdays' – book ahead.

Hemingways
CARIBBEAN $$

(☑ 268-462-2763; www.hemingwaysantigua.com; Lower St Mary's St; mains lunch EC$24-65, dinner EC$50-85; ◷ 9:30am-10pm Mon-Sat) No matter where the hands of the clock are, you can have a fine meal upstairs at this breezy 1820s Creole cottage with gingerbread trim. Skip the international choices and go for local flavors such as spicy chicken curry, coconut rum-flambéed lobster and the off-menu blueberry bread pudding with rum-butter sauce.

Russell's
SEAFOOD $$

(☑ 268-462-5479; www.facebook.com/russellsbarandrestaurant; Fort James; mains EC$45-60; ◷ 10am-8pm Tue-Sat; P 🛜) In the reconstructed officers' quarters of Fort James, one of Antigua's main citadels, bluff-top Russell's offers drinks and sea-to-table fish with awesome eyefuls of the ocean and passing boats from its wide verandas. Sunsets can be achingly beautiful and there's live music on some nights, usually Fridays.

🛍 Shopping

Duty-free shops cluster in Heritage Quay just off the cruise-ship pier, but don't expect major bargains except on booze and cigarettes. It segues into the Vendors' Mall, a cacophonous maze of trinkets and T-shirts (bargaining advised). Adjacent Redcliffe Quay (the former site of St John's slave market) has more upscale galleries and boutiques. For local color, skip over a block or two to Market, Thames and St Mary's Sts.

Natura
COSMETICS

(☑ 268-725-6402; www.facebook.com/pg/naturahealthandhealing; Lower Mary's St; ◷ 9am-4pm Mon-Sat) This pretty store is the domain of Silvana and Jennifer, two local women who produce an entire range of herbal remedies and healing balms from organic ingredients grown on the island. Bestsellers include the Mosquito Cream, the Sunburn Soothe and the Bye Bye Bumps Acne Cream. There's also a line of edibles including honeys, jams and chutneys.

ℹ Information

EMERGENCY & IMPORTANT NUMBERS

Police (☑ 268-462-0045; cnr Newgate & Market Sts) Main downtown police station.

INTERNET ACCESS

Best of Books (☑ 268-562-3198; bestofbooks@yahoo.com; Lower St Mary's St; ◷ 8:30am-5:30pm Mon-Sat; 🛜) Bookstore with PCs for internet access at EC$25 per hour.

Public Library (☑ 268-462-0229; www.antiguapublib.org; Woodland Dr; ◷ 9:30am-5pm Mon-Thu, to 3:30pm Fri) Free wi-fi.

Rituals Coffee House (☑ 268-562-7870; Lower St Mary's St; ◷ 8am-7pm; 🛜) Free wi-fi.

ℹ Getting There & Around

BUS

West bus station (p124) Minivans headed to points north, west and south (eg Jolly Harbour, the beaches and English Harbour) leave from this station next to the public market.

East bus station (p124) For destinations east and southeast of town (eg Betty's Hope, Long Bay).

Buses depart when full and stop at regular and request stops en route. Fares cost EC$2.25 to EC$4.

TAXI

There's a taxi stand adjacent to the West bus station, and taxi drivers also hang around Heritage Quay.

United Taxi Association (☏268-562-0262; www.unitedtaxiassociation.com; ⊙8:30am-6pm)

Dickenson Bay & North Shore

North of St John's, the middle market of Antigua's holidaymakers finds fun and refuge in the resorts along Dickenson Bay, a long but partly very narrow crescent of yellow sand on the northwest coast. The swimming is good and there's no shortage of aquatic activities to lure punters off their loungers.

The beach can get crowded, what with the vendors peddling wares, women hoping to braid hair and the hordes of fun seekers from the massive Sandals resort. Still, the pervasive strains of reggae set the mood for a quintessential Caribbean beach vacation.

East of here, all the way to the airport, are some of Antigua's poshest residential areas, with a golf course, fancy restaurants and surf sports off Jabberwock Beach. Nearby, a catamaran shuttles anyone with villa or restaurant reservations to the private Jumby Bay Resort on offshore Long Island.

◉ Sights

Dickenson Bay   BEACH
(☐50) Antigua's busiest beach is jammed with low-rise hotels and resorts, most notably the sprawling all-inclusive Sandals resort. Naturally, there's no shortage of beach bars and water-sports facilities. The calm waters are good for kids and the beach is wide except toward the southern end, where storms have eroded the sands into a narrow strip.

Runaway Bay   BEACH
If you're keen on escaping the holiday hubbub of busy Dickenson Bay, head south beyond a small bluff to Runaway Bay, whose beach is just as white but tranquil and facility-free.

Jabberwock Beach   BEACH
(Hodges Bay) This long white sandy beach is largely the domain of windsurfers and kite-surfers thanks to its excellent cross-onshore winds and shallow waters. Conditions are generally best between January and June.

🏃 Activities

Tony's Water Sports   WATER SPORTS
(☑268-462-6326; www.tonyswatersports.com; next to Sandal's resort, Dickenson Bay; ⊙8am-5pm; ☏; ☐50) Run by the son of local calypso great King Short Shirt, well-respected Tony's gets you waterborne with Hobie Cats, jet skis, banana boats and water skis (about US$50 each per session). If you're a landlubber, order a burger and a local Wadadli beer and hang out in the bar.

Kite Antigua   KITESURFING
(☑268-720-5483; www.kitesurfantigua.com; Jabberwock Rd) This pro outfit has taught kite-surfing to the curious in a vibe that's convivial and supportive since 2001. It's right on northeast-facing Jabberwock Beach, which has ideal wind conditions for the sport.

Windsurf Antigua   WINDSURFING
(☑268-461-9463; www.windsurfantigua.net; Jabberwock Beach, Hodges Bay; rental per hr/day US$30/80) Local windsurfing guru Patrick Scales guarantees to get beginners up and onto the water in one session (US$90 for two hours). Boards can be delivered island-wide. Prebooking advised.

Cedar Valley Golf Club   GOLF
(☑268-462-0161; www.cvgolfantigua.com; Cedar Valley Rd; 9/18 holes US$31/60, clubs US$30/20; ⊙tee times 8am-4pm; ☏) Opened in 1970 and expanded to 18 holes in 1977, this is a par 70 course with a 300yd driving range set amid hilly terrain and mature tropical trees.

🛏 Sleeping

The Dickenson Bay area has the largest concentration of properties on Antigua, from cute apartments to the mega-sized Sandals resort. The more affordable places are often just a short walk away from the beach.

OBSESSED WITH CRICKET

To Antiguans, cricket is not a sport but a religion. The tiny island state has produced some of the world's best cricketers, including Andy Roberts, Curtley Ambrose and, most famously, Sir Vivian Richards, aka King Viv or the 'Master-Blaster.' Known for his aggressive style of batting, he became captain of the West Indies team and captained 27 wins in 50 tests between 1980 and 1991.

Not surprisingly, when it came time to build a new stadium for the 2007 World Cup (with major financing courtesy of mainland China), it was named after Antigua's most famous son. About 4 miles east of St John's, the 10,000-seat **Sir Vivian Richards Stadium** (☑ 268-481-2450; www.windiescricket.com; Sir Sydney Walling Hwy) ranks among the region's top cricket facilities yet has been dogged by difficulties from the start. The worst blow came in 2009 when the International Cricket Council imposed a one-year ban after a Test match between West Indies and England had to be called off for unhealthy playing conditions. Play resumed in February 2010 and these days the new and improved stadium again hosts regional and international matches.

The cricket season runs from January to July with official matches usually played on Thursdays, Saturdays and Sundays. If you want to see local passion in action, check www.windiescricket.com or www.antigua-barbuda.org for the schedule.

Wind Chimes Inn
B&B $

(☑ 268-728-2917; www.windchimesinnantigua.com; Sir George Walter Hwy; s/d incl breakfast US$85/95; P ✳ 🛜; 📶42) Plane-spotters will cherish the runway views at this modern inn 2 miles from the airport, but anyone can enjoy the spotless, spacious rooms whose pillow-top mattresses, small kitchenettes and patio belie the modest price. Rates include continental breakfast brought to your room.

Ocean Point Resort & Spa
HOTEL $$

(☑ 268-562-8330; www.oceanpointantigua.com; Hodges Bay Main Rd, Hodges Bay; d all-inclusive from US$242; P ✳ 🛜 ❄) This rambling north-shore property has been recast as an all-inclusive resort and is very popular with Italian tourists. Pastel-coloured rooms come with a balcony, preferably one overlooking the huge pool and the two lovely secluded beaches that rarely get busy. The breezy Italian restaurant serves buffet-style meals. No children under 16 years.

Dickenson Bay Cottages
APARTMENT $$

(☑ 268-462-4940; www.dickensonbaycottages.com; Trade Winds Dr; 1-/2-bedroom apt US$160/200; P ✳ @ ❄; 📶50) A good option if you want to be close to the beach without paying beachfront prices, this hillside charmer gets our thumbs up for its friendly staff, good-sized kitchens, tropical gardens and well-maintained pool. There's a supermarket nearby. Small units are priced for two; large ones for up to four people.

★ Buccaneer Beach Club
VILLAS $$$

(☑ 268-562-6785; www.buccaneerbeach.com; Marina Bay Rd; villas US$245-550; ✳ 🛜 ❄; 📶50) This serene cluster of cottages with full kitchens alongside a large pool is perfect for families and self-caterers. It sits amid a lovely palm-and-orchid garden on a tiny sugary beach on the quiet end of Dickenson Bay with easy access to the restaurants and water-sports facilities of the adjacent resorts.

Jumby Bay Resort
RESORT $$$

(☑ 268-462-6000; www.rosewoodhotels.com/en/jumby-bay-antigua; ste all-inclusive from US$2850; ✳ 🛜 ❄) There's a virtual 'Do Not Disturb' sign attached to this ultra-exclusive luxury resort set on its own private island reached by shuttle boat from Dutchman's Bay. You need a reservation for one of the 40 guest rooms to be taken here.

Siboney Beach Club
HOTEL $$$

(☑ 268-462-0806; www.siboneybeachantigua.com; Marina Bay Rd, Dickenson Bay; ste US$315-335; P ✳ 🛜 ❄; 📶50) This low-key, 12-unit beachfront retreat on busy Dickenson Bay has newly upgraded suites with kitchenettes dressed in shades of beige that offset the riot of color of the tropical garden and the intense blue of the ocean. Watch hummingbirds flutter among the frangipani trees from your patio or let massage therapist Barbara work out your kinks beneath the swaying palm trees.

✖ Eating

From a food truck to fine French dining, there's some excellent eating in this area. The nicest places are right on the beach.

Chippy Antigua　　　　　SEAFOOD $
(☑268-724-1166; www.caribya.com/antigua/chippy.antigua; Marina Bay Rd; mains EC$25-40; ◷4-9pm Wed & Fri; P; 🚌50) Dave and Jane's food truck enjoys cult status among local British-style fish-and-chips devotees, but the succulent shrimp, spicy sausages and Indian curries also deserve a mention. There's a full bar and you can enjoy it all at plastic tables under the stars. The truck parks on the road next to Buccaneer Beach Club. Cash only.

Ana's on the Beach　　　　ITALIAN $$
(☑268-562 8562; www.anas.ag; Marina Bay Rd; mains EC$50-100; ◷10am-11pm Tue-Sun; 🛜; 🚌50) With its hot-pink, white and black color scheme, wispy cabanas and attached art gallery, Ana's mixes urban sophistication with a relaxed vibe that matches its beachfront setting. The menu is big on Mediterranean staples including Caprese salad, *risotto di mare* (seafood risotto) and salmon tagliatelle, but also does convincing curries.

★ Cecilia's High Point Cafe
　　　　　　　　　MEDITERRANEAN $$$
(☑268-562-7070; www.highpointantigua.com; Texaco Dock Rd, Dutchman's Bay; mains EC$55-110; ◷noon-9pm Mon & Thu, to 4pm Fri-Sun; P🛜; 🚌42) With chill-out music playing softly in the background and unimpeded views of the azure seas, this shabby-chic beachfront cottage is presided over by a former Swedish model and is a popular lunch spot en route to or from the airport. Perennial top menu picks include the lobster ravioli and the beef tenderloin, although the blackboard specials also beckon mightily.

★ Le Bistro
　　　　　　　　　　　FRENCH $$$
(☑268-462-3881; www.antigualebistro.com; Hodges Bay; mains EC$80-160; ◷6:30-10:30pm Tue-Sun; P🛜; 🚌42) To put it plainly, Le Bistro is out of a foodie's daydream with a kitchen that has consistently wowed diners with meticulously prepared classic French cuisine. No matter if you fancy *escargots* (snails), *langoustes* (lobster) or *canard* (duck), you'll find the ingredients top flight, the presentation exquisite and the service immaculate. Reservations are essential.

Coconut Grove　　　　　CARIBBEAN $$$
(☑268-462-1538; www.coconutgroveantigua.com; Marina Bay Rd; mains EC$65-125; ◷7:30am-11pm or later; P🛜; 🚌50) This beachy daytime hangout beneath the palm trees at Siboney Beach Club morphs into an elegant candle-lit affair for dinner. The lobster thermidor medallions in mustard-brandy sauce is a top menu pick among regulars who also invade for beers and rum punch, and not only during daily happy hour (5pm to 7pm).

ⓘ Getting There & Away

Bus 50 leaves St John's West bus station for Dickenson Bay, while bus 55 heads to Hodges Bay from the East bus station. A one-way taxi ride from St John's costs US$12 to anywhere in the area. From the airport, the fare costs US$13 to US$16.

Five Islands Peninsula

A single road connects the peninsula with St John's. Five Islands Village itself is a fairly scruffy place giving way to a string of lovely and unhurried turquoise coves and white-sand beaches, dotted with mostly all-inclusive resorts. One of the beaches is clothing optional – it's the only one on Antigua. The sole sightseeing attraction is colonial-era Fort Barrington.

◉ Sights

Deep Bay　　　　　　　BEACH
Lorded over by the ruins of Fort Barrington, this curvy little – and often deserted – bay is backed by a large salt pond and has a shadeless beach with grey-yellow sand and calm and protected turquoise waters. As an added bonus, the coral-encrusted **Andes wreck**, a cargo boat from Trinidad that sank in the middle of the bay some 100 years ago, is just a short swim away and great for snorkeling.

Hawksbill Bay　　　　　　BEACH
(Gray's Farm Rd, Five Islands Village; 🚌61) Named for a landmark rock formation, this bay has a string of four blissful beaches that are rarely crowded. The turnoff for the first one is before you get to Hawksbill by Rex Resort, but the other three must be accessed through the property. The furthest one (Eden Beach) is Antigua's only official clothing-optional beach.

① Getting There & Away

Bus 61 travels to the peninsula from St John's West bus station as far as Five Islands Village. A taxi to the hotels or beaches costs US$14 from St John's.

Jolly Harbour to Cades Bay

Jolly Harbour is a busy marina and dockside condominium village with a big supermarket, an ATM, a pharmacy, and a few restaurants and bars. South of here, the coastal road wears a necklace of some of Antigua's best beaches, which are popular with cruise-ship passengers and, on weekends, with locals but otherwise often deserted. Down in Cades Bay, the road passes a pineapple farm before turning inland and cutting through rainforest and Fig Tree Dr, which culminates in Swetes. From here, you're back in St John's in a 20-minute drive.

◉ Sights

★ Hermitage Bay   BEACH

(off Valley Rd, Jennings; P) This dreamy secluded arc punctuates the end of a 2½-mile-long road (the last two are graded dirt road). Wave-tossed shells litter the white sand that remains largely crowd-free despite being next to the ultra-posh Hermitage Bay resort.

Valley Church Beach   BEACH

(Valley Rd, Valley Church village; P; 🖫22) This pretty palm-lined beach has calm and shallow aquamarine waters and powdery white sand and is a popular excursion for cruise-ship guests. Most gather around the popular beach restaurant called the Nest, so if you're looking for a quiet spot, head to the south end of the beach. The gate to the beach is open from dawn to sunset. If it's closed, park and walk in.

Ffryes Beach   BEACH

(Valley Rd, Bolans; P🛜; 🖫22) This long, sea-grape-shaded sandy ribbon has barbecue facilities, showers and toilets, and is popular with local families on weekends. Grab a cocktail in time for sunset from Dennis Cocktail Bar & Restaurant. Behind it is the gentle arc of Little Ffryes Beach, overlooked by the all-inclusive Cocobay Resort.

Darkwood Beach   BEACH

(Valley Rd; ⊙cafe 10am-sunset; 🖫22) This road-adjacent swath of beige sand makes for a convenient swimming and snorkeling spot. The eponymous cafe has a shower (US$1), changing rooms and also rents beach chairs. It's popular with locals on weekends.

Mt Obama   MOUNTAIN

(Mt Obama Rd, off Old Rd; 🖫22) Antigua's 'Everest' rises a modest 1319ft in the island's southwestern corner as part of the Sherkeley mountain range. Until renamed in honor of US President Barack Obama in 2009, it was known as Boggy Peak. It's crowned by dense trees and (usually locked) telecommunications structures, including a large radio tower. This makes views only so-so unless you can get inside the compound.

🏃 Activities

Jolly Dive   DIVING

(📞268-462-8305; www.jollydiveantigua.com; Jolly Harbour Dr; 2-tank dive incl equipment & wetsuit US$140; ⊙8am-4pm Mon-Fri, to 2pm Sat; 🖫22) This dive shop has been in business for more than 30 years and enjoys a fine reputation. Boat dives hit nearby reefs, wrecks and dropoffs, bringing you close to corals, sharks, rays and lobsters. Also does PADI certifications. It's on the beach next to Castaways Beach Bar and the Tranquility Bay resort.

🛏 Sleeping

This part of the island has some of the best places to stay with exclusive all-inclusives scattered among the hillsides to Caribbean-chic boutique hotels and self-catering apartment buildings. No matter where you stay, you'll never be far from a superb beach.

South Coast Ocean View
Apartments   APARTMENT $$

(📞268-560-4933; www.scova-antigua.com; Cades Bay; apt US$139-155; ⊙closed Jun & Jul; ❄🛜; 🖫22) A steep road deposits you at Rudi and Wilma's four spanking, one-bedroom apartments with subdued tropical decor, tranquil vibe and breezy terraces.

Cocobay Resort   RESORT $$$

(📞268-562-2400; www.cocobayresort.com; Little Ffryes Beach, Bolans; all-inclusive per person cottage US$570-810; P❄@🛜🏊; 🖫22) This stylish, 49-unit, all-inclusive resort eschews the usual resort paradigms. After a day by the infinity pool or on nearby Valley Church Beach, retire to Creole garden cottages sheathed in pale Mediterranean colors.

Sugar Ridge Resort BOUTIQUE HOTEL **$$$**
(🕿268-562-7700; www.sugarridgeantigua.com; Valley Rd, Jolly Harbour; r incl breakfast US$336-550; 🟥🗦🗨; 🖵22) This sophisticated yet relaxed hilltop charmer has stunning views from its 60 colonial-meets-contemporary rooms, the nicest of which have a big veranda, four-poster beds and a private plunge pool. Several pools, two restaurants and a posh Aveda spa provide ample diversion, and a stellar beach is only a short ride away on a free shuttle (or bicycle).

🍴 Eating

Jolly Harbour itself has a few pleasant eateries but there are plenty more interesting and atmospheric spots along the highway and on the beaches.

Dennis Cocktail Bar
& Restaurant CARIBBEAN **$$**
(🕿268-462-6740; www.dennisantigua.com; Valley Rd, Ffryes Beach; mains EC$52-109; ⊙10:30am-late, closed Mon Apr-Oct; 🅿🗦🛍; 🖵22) Local boy Dennis Thomas creates magic on the plate with his mom's recipes and produce from his own garden. Tuck into such soulful dishes as creamy conch curry or pungent shrimp-and-chicken medley while taking in the sublime beach views from the breezy terrace. Insiders invade Fridays for the reggae barbecue or Sundays for the suckling pig roast.

Miracle's CARIBBEAN **$$**
(🕿268-732-1682; www.miraclessouthcoast.com; Valley Rd, Jolly Harbour; mains EC$30-100; ⊙11am-10pm; 🗦; 🖵22) What was once a humble roadside cottage has evolved into a cozy restaurant with linen-bedecked tables and a sophisticated island vibe. Chicken, fish, prawns or lobster can be ordered grilled, jerked, curried, barbecued, sautéed or fried and are served with a choice of two sides, such as spinach rice or rice and peas.

OJ's Beach Bar & Restaurant CARIBBEAN **$$**
(🕿268-460-0184; www.facebook.com/OJs-Beach-Bar-Restaurant-192486710801636; Valley Rd, Crabbe Hill Village; sandwiches EC$22-30, mains EC$40-100; ⊙10am-11pm; 🅿🗦; 🖵22) Driftwood, conch shells, fishing nets and whatever else the sea washes up gets worked into the salty decor of this sun- and rum-soaked, beach-bum hangout and Antigua institution. Top menu picks include the grilled snapper and lobster salad, but it's also worth stopping by for a swim and the cinnamon-scented rum punch.

Epicurean SUPERMARKET **$$**
(🕿268-481-5480; www.epicureanantigua.com; Jolly Harbour; ⊙7am-9pm; 🅿🗦; 🖵22) Big, high-end supermarket with local and international groceries, cold and hot meals to go, a good liquor selection and international newspapers.

Carmichael's FUSION **$$$**
(🕿268-562-7700; www.sugarridgeantigua.com/eat/fine; Sugar Ridge Resort, Valley Rd, Jolly Harbour; mains EC$72-130; ⊙6-10pm; 🟥🗦; 🖵22) This fine-dining outpost, whose chefs whip up a creative blend of Carib-continental cuisine, boasts a dramatic setting in its eyrie above the Sugar Ridge Resort. Bring a swimsuit for a sunset dip and cocktail in the infinity pool, then settle into a stylish rattan chair on the wooden deck and take in the breezes.

✈ Getting There & Away

From St John's West bus station, bus 22 travels south along Valley Rd via Jolly Harbour and the beaches as far as Old Road Village. A taxi costs US$18 to Jolly Harbour, about US$22 to the beaches and US$26 to Old Road village.

Fig Tree Drive

Old Road, a village that juxtaposes scruffiness with two swank resorts, marks the southern start of 5-mile-long Fig Tree Dr, which winds through rainforest teeming with big old mango and giant-leaved banana trees (called 'figs' locally). Roadside stands sell fruit, jam, juices and the local black pineapple. A number of trails start at the historic Wallings Dam, including one to Signal Hill and another to Rendezvous Bay.

◉ Sights & Activities

Wallings Dam & Reservoir HISTORIC SITE
(off Fig Tree Dr; ⊙24hr) FREE Built by the British around 1900, the Victorian-style dam originally created a reservoir holding 13 million gallons and supplying to the surrounding villages. In 1912, after three years of drought, it was drained and the area was reforested and is now teeming with mahoe, ironwood, locust, mango, white cedar and other tree species.

Birdwatchers might be able to spot banana quits, broadwinged hawks and redstars, among others. The reservoir is also the starting point for hikes up Signal Hill and to secluded Rendezvous Bay.

★ Footsteps Rainforest Hiking Tours HIKING

(☑268-773-2345, 268-460-1234; www.hiking antigua.com; Fig Tree Dr; adult/under 16yr US$45/25, minimum 2 people; ☺tours 9am Tue, Thu & by arrangement; ☎) Charismatic local guide Dassa shares his extensive knowledge of the island's flora, fauna and history on fun and educational hikes. His signature two- to 2½-hour Signal Hill loop trail goes through the rainforest and past the historic Wallings Reservoir to the top for 360-degree island views. Other routes, including treks to secluded Rendezvous Bay, can be customised. Tours depart from the Fig Tree Studio Art Gallery.

Antigua Rainforest Zip Line Tours ZIP LINING

(☑268-562-6363; www.antiguarainforest.com; Fig Tree Dr, Wallings; adult/child from US$79/59; ☺tours hourly 9am-noon Mon-Sat) Channel your inner Tarzan (or Jane) while roaring through the treetops suspended on zip lines. The 2½-hour 'Full Course' includes 12 zips, short hikes between suspension bridges and a challenge course. Note that the park is usually only open when a cruise ship is in port and that reservations are a must.

🛏 Sleeping & Eating

Aside from the restaurants at the Curtain Bluff and Carlisle Bay resorts in Old Road, the only places to pick up sustenance along Fig Tree Dr are from roadside vendors selling juices and fruit. One of the best known is Clemie's, who grows most of her produce right across the street, including the supersweet local Antigua Black, a pineapple with flesh that is more golden than the usual variety.

Carlisle Bay HOTEL $$$

(☑268-484-0000; www.carlisle-bay.com; Old Road; ste incl breakfast from US$1163; P❉☎❄; ☲22) Ultra-posh and contemporary, the Carlisle courts style-conscious global nomads who like to trade the beach lounger for the tennis court, the gym, the trail or the yoga mat. All rooms face the calm bay, where you can engage in the gamut of water sports. The kids club keep little ones from six months to 12 years old entertained.

🛍 Shopping

Fig Tree Studio Art Gallery ART

(☑268-460-1234; www.figtreestudioart.com; Fig Tree Dr; ☺9am-5pm Mon-Sat Nov-Jun; ☎) For quality regional art and crafts, drop by this lovely gallery in a cottage cradled by rainforest and run by local artist Sallie Harker. The British expat handpicks an ever-changing roster that might showcase boldly pigmented Caribbean scenes by Bruce Smith, engraved calabash by Ezekiel Jno Baptiste, and Harker's own woodcuts, oils and watercolors.

❶ Getting There & Away

If you're driving, be careful on Fig Tree Dr. It isn't nearly as cratered with potholes as it used to be, but because of its winding nature it should still be negotiated slowly and with care.

There is no bus service right along Fig Tree Dr. You can get close by taking either bus 13 from St John's West bus station to Swetes near the northern end, or bus 22 to Old Road on the southern end. From there you'll have to either walk, call a cab (eg at ☑268-460-5353) or hitch a ride.

English Harbour

Nowhere does Antigua flaunt its maritime heritage more than in English Harbour. It sits on two sheltered bays, Falmouth Bay and English Harbour, where salty boats and ritzy yachts bob in the water. The era when the British Navy was based here is still encapsulated in the beautifully restored Nelson's Dockyards, the island's top historical attraction. For superb views, make your way up to the top of Shirley Heights.

◉ Sights

★ Nelson's Dockyard National Park HISTORIC SITE

(☑268-481-5021; www.nationalparksantigua.com; Dockyard Dr, English Harbour; adult/child under 12yr US$8/free; ☺8am-6pm; P; ☲17) Continuously in operation since 1745, this extensively restored Georgian-era marina is Antigua's top sightseeing draw and was made a Unesco World Heritage site in 2016. Today its restored buildings house restaurants, hotels and businesses.

The Dockyard Museum relates tidbits about Antigua history, the dockyard and life at the forts. Among the many trinkets on display is a telescope once used by Nelson himself. Admission to the Dockyard area is also good for Shirley Heights and the Dow's Hill Interpretation Centre.

Pillars of Hercules · ROCK FORMATION
(off Galleon Beach; 🖳17) **FREE** The entrance to English Harbour is guarded by this stunning phalanx of rock soldiers eroded by the relentless wind, rain and crashing waves. The formation is best appreciated from a boat but it's also possible to get close-ups by hiking to the end of Galleon Beach and then scrambling over large boulders. They're slippery, so watch your footing and don't go during high tide.

Shirley Heights · HISTORIC SITE
(📞 268-481-5028; www.nationalparksantigua.com; Shirley Heights Rd, English Harbour; adult/child under 12yr $8/free) This restored military lookout and gun battery was named after St Thomas Shirley (1727–1800), who became the first Governor of the Leeward Islands in 1781. Get some historical background at the small interpretive center, then head uphill to explore the grounds for crumbling ruins and enjoy sweeping views. Admission includes entry to Nelson's Dockyard.

★ Rendezvous Bay · BEACH
After a 90-miute walk through the rainforest, you'll have earned bragging rights for making it to one of Antigua's loveliest beaches. Because of its remoteness, it usually delivers footprint-free solitude. The path starts near the Wallings Reservoir off Fig Tree Dr but is not signposted, so either ask for detailed directions locally or sign up with a guide. Alternatively, you can pick up the shorter trail past the Springhill Riding Stables off Falmouth Rd.

Follow the signs to the stables and either park here or continue to the end of the road and park just outside a gated compound, then follow the dirt road on your left down to the beach.

🏃 Activities

Springhill Riding Stables · HORSEBACK RIDING
(📞 268-773-3139; www.antiguaequestrian.com; 1hr lesson & ride US$65; ⏱ tours 8:30am) Offers riding lessons as well as a variety of morning tours, including a two-hour ride to Rendezvous Bay (US$125). If you want to swim with your horse, it's an extra US$45.

Middle Ground Trail · HIKING
(Pigeon Beach; 🖳17) This popular 1-mile trail connects Pigeon Beach with Nelson's Dock-

FUN FACTS FROM THE DOCKYARD MUSEUM

➡ The museum's plank floor is painted red, the same color as the decks of warships to disguise the bloodshed during battle.

➡ Antigua was first called Wadadli; centuries later the name inspired that of the local beer Wadadli.

➡ When Nelson left Antigua as a sick man in 1787, he carried a barrel of rum to preserve his body in case he died en route.

yard and is popular with joggers in the morning and evening hours. From the trailhead near Bumpkins beach bar, it climbs steeply at first, then levels out and follows the ridge of Windward Bay before descending down toward Fort Berkeley and the dockyards.

Desmond Trail · HIKING
(off Galleon Beach Rd; 🖳17) This short moderate walk starts just before Galleon Beach and culminates near the Shirley Heights Lookout Restaurant and offers nice views of English Harbour in the course of the half-hour climb.

Carpenters Trail · HIKING
(Galleon Beach; 🖳17) This moderate 1.5-mile-long trail up Shirley Heights starts at the far end of Galleon Beach, skirts ruined Fort Charlotte, and treats you to breezy views of the rugged coastline and rock formations. It's easily combined into a loop route with the Desmond Trail.

Soul Immersions Dive Centre · DIVING
(📞 268-720-8314; www.soulimmersions.ag; Dockyard Dr, Falmouth Harbour; 2-tank dive with full equipment US$125; 🖳17) This well-respected dive center offers PADI certification as well as one- and two-tanks dives for certified divers (bring proof) to sites in the southern part of the island. You'll get to poke around coral-covered boulders and reefs teeming with rays, sharks and other creatures

Dockyard Divers · DIVING
(📞 268-729-3040; www.dockyard-divers.com; Nelson's Dockyard, English Harbour; 2-tank dive US$99, snorkeling trip US$45; 🖳17) This well-established outfit offers diving and snorkeling trips to caves, reefs and sunken wrecks. Snorkeling gear rents for US$13 per day.

🛏 Sleeping

English Harbour is a justifiably popular place to hang your hat. Instead of big resorts, options range from a convivial waterfront hostel to genteel colonial gems and smart boutique hotels.

Waterfront Hostel   HOSTEL $
(📞268-460-6575; www.caribbean-hostels.com; Compton Bldg, Dockyard Dr; dm/s/d/tr US$25/45/65/85; 🛜; 🖥17) Quality budget lodging in English Harbour is as rare as hen's teeth, making this cheerful hostel a great find. Each of the 10 rooms sleeps up to three people and comes with sink and shower; shared toilets are down the hall. Make new friends at the harbor-view bar over home-cooked breakfast or cold beers. Restaurants and a supermarket are nearby.

Lodge Antigua   HOTEL $
(📞268-562-8060; www.thelodgeantigua.com; Dockyard Dr, English Harbour; d/apt/cottage US$95/120/140; 🅿❄🛜; 🖥17) This perky budget pick at the National Sailing Academy comes with a restaurant-bar overlooking the harbor and a clutch of compact and simply but nicely furnished units surrounded by leafy grounds. Apartments and cottages sleep up to four and come with cooking facilities. Gracious hosts Peter and Elizabeth also rent sailing dinghies, kayaks and SUP boards.

Ocean Inn   B&B $$
(📞268-463-7950; www.theoceaninn.com; English Harbour; d incl breakfast US$147-270; ❄🛜❄; 🖥17) For reasonably priced five-star views of English Harbour, secure a room at Robert's hillside hideout with 12 units cradled by flowery, terraced grounds. The nicest are the cottages with private veranda; the cheapest, the breezy 'ocean view budget' rooms with shared bathroom. Avoid the windowless room 5.

★ Admiral's Inn   HISTORIC HOTEL $$$
(📞460-1027; www.admiralsantigua.com; Dockyard Dr, English Harbour; r US$175-275, ste US$320-350; 🅿❄🛜❄) This intimate inn with 23 rooms spread over four Georgian stone buildings is charmingly old-school and romantic with lots of design touches and service that lend character and a deep sense of place. The nicest rooms are the 'Gunpowder Suites' with four-poster beds, modern bathrooms, and views of the harbor and the infinity pool. There are two restaurants on-site.

Inn at English Harbour   BOUTIQUE HOTEL $$$
(📞268-460-1014; www.theinnantigua.com; Freeman's Bay, English Harbour; ste incl tax & service from US$940, 3-night minimum; ❄@🛜❄) Enjoy sublime sunsets, cold Carib in hand, from the private terrace of your lusciously furnished suite or beach cabana at this peaceful and romantic retreat from reality. Though it has a colonial style in looks and flair, all the expected 21st-century amenities are accounted for, both in rooms and the public areas.

South Point Hotel   DESIGN HOTEL $$$
(📞268-562-9600; www.southpointantigua.com; English Harbour; ste incl breakfast US$495; 🅿❄🛜❄; 🖥17) Urban cool meets Caribbean chic at this classy port of call where you can enjoy front-row views of the sailing yachts from your sleek one- or two-bedroom suites, with kitchens, big terraces, and walk-in showers and closets. Fresh flowers add bright accents to the subdued white-and-gray color scheme.

Copper & Lumber Store Hotel   HOTEL $$$
(📞268-460-1058; www.copperandlumberhotel.com; Nelson's Dockyard, English Harbour; ste US$235-400; 🅿❄🛜; 🖥17) Dripping with colonial character, this gracious hotel was built in the 1780s to store the copper and lumber needed for ship repairs. It now has 14 studios and suites, each named after one of Nelson's ships. All open onto a flowery courtyard and burst with vintage flair courtesy of four-poster beds, brick walls, wooden beams and mock gas lamps.

🍴 Eating

English Harbour has some great eats down by the waterfront and along the main highway. Sunday-afternoon barbecues at Shirley Heights Lookout Restaurant are legendary.

Grace Before Meals   CARIBBEAN $
(📞268-460-1298; Dockyard Dr, English Harbour; mains EC$15-20; ⏱8am-4pm Mon-Fri; 🖥17) Owned by local lady Grace Piper, this brightly painted bungalow dishes up divine home-cooked fare at blessedly low prices. The roti is a specialty alongside other soul-sustaining West Indian staples, such as chicken curry and pepper pot. Cash only.

Dockyard Bakery   BAKERY $
(📞268-460-1474; Nelson's Dockyard; baked goods EC$5-10; ⏱8am-4pm Mon-Sat; 🖥17) Behind the museum at Nelson's Dockyard, the fresh bread and delectable baked goods such as

cinnamon rolls and chocolate cake will draw you in like a sailor to rum.

Sun Ra
MEDITERRANEAN $$

(☑268-720-3826; www.facebook.com/pg/sunra antigua; Dockyard Dr, Falmouth; mains lunch EC$35-65, dinner EC$60-90; ⊗noon-2:30pm Wed-Fri, 6-10pm Mon-Sat; ℗ 🕾; 🖳17) Named for an American jazz composer, this upscale but laid-back lair is great for a chill lunch or a romantic dinner. Mellow jazz goes appropriately well with candlelit tables on a wooden waterfront deck, a good glass of wine and a menu revolving around the day's catch.

Flatties Flame Grill
PORTUGUESE $$

(☑268-726-6899; www.facebook.com/Flatties-Flame-Grill-1628770127393263; Dockyard Dr, English Harbour; mains EC$30-70; ⊗3pm-midnight Tue-Sun; 🕾; 🖳17) At Mark and Amanda's roadside grill, quality meats and spices get orchestrated into culinary symphonies, mostly of Portuguese origin. The signature dish is the Peri-Peri chicken, a succulent half or whole bird bathed in a marinade before getting just the right tan on the grill. Look for South African specials such as *boerewors* (sausage) or biltong (dried meat).

Ristorante Paparazzi
ITALIAN $$

(☑268-720-3201; www.ristorantepaparazzi.net; Dockyard Dr, Antigua Slipway, English Harbour; pizza & pasta EC$35-65, mains EC$65-180; ⊗6:30-10:30pm Tue-Sun; ℗🕾; 🖳22) Walk through the Antigua Slipway to this salty-chic eatery whose sprawling terrace treats you to romantic views of Fort Berkeley and Nelson's Dockyard. Conversation flows as freely as the wine and rum among eclectic patrons tucking into wood-fired pizzas, pungent pastas and rustic trattoria classics.

Shirley Heights Lookout Restaurant
CARIBBEAN $$

(☑268-728-0636; www.shirleyheightslookout.com; Shirley Heights Rd, English Harbour; mains EC$20-75; ⊗9am-10pm; ℗🕾) Feast on jerk chicken, Creole fish or lobster salad while taking in splendid views of English Harbour from this hilltop restaurant in the restored stone guardhouse of this colonial military lookout and gun battery. On clear days, Guadeloupe and Montserrat loom in the misty distance.

Trappas
INTERNATIONAL $$

(☑268-562-3534; www.facebook.com/Trappas; Dockyard Dr, English Harbour; mains EC$52; ⊗6-10pm Mon-Sat; 🕾; 🖳17) It's often standing-room only in this dining room with tropical murals and a big bar. Expats, locals

SHIRLEY HEIGHTS SUNDAY BARBECUE

For more than three decades, the place to be in Antigua on a Sunday afternoon has been the **Shirley Heights Lookout Restaurant** with free killer views of English Harbour. A steel band gets everyone in the mood from around 4pm during the afternoon barbecue before a reggae band hits the stage at 7pm and the wicked rum punches flow ever more freely. Admission is US$10, and so is the one-way cab ride to or from English Harbour.

and yachties descend upon this long-time hangout for upscale comfort food such as breaded calamari with garlic dip, the burger with blue cheese and creative curries bathed in an aromatic balm of local spices.

Abracadabra
ITALIAN $$

(☑268-460-2701; www.facebook.com/abracadabra. antigua; Dockyard Dr, English Harbour; mains US$13-33; ⊗dinner Mon-Sat; ℗🍴; 🖳17) Fondly known as 'Abra,' Salvatore's outpost has been all things to all people since 1984: a little slice of Italy where you can devour homemade pastas or the signature suckling pig, a chilled bar and lounge, and, on weekends, an energetic open-air club with a white-sand dance floor in a tropical garden setting. Pure magic!

Caribbean Taste
CARIBBEAN $$

(☑268-562-3049; off Dockyard Dr, English Harbour; mains US$9-25; ⊗11am-8pm Mon-Sat) For authentic local food cooked with 'soul,' point your compass to this cheerily painted cottage just off the main road to Nelson's Dockyard. The chalkboard menu lists such flavor-packed staples as conch stew and goat curry along with changing specials that might include octopus ceviche or Creole snapper.

★ Catherine's Cafe Plage
FRENCH $$$

(☑268-460-5050; www.facebook.com/Catherines-Cafe; south end, Pigeon Beach; mains EC$75-95; ⊗11:30am-sunset Wed-Mon, 6-10pm Wed & Fri; ℗🕾🍴; 🖳17) After relocating to Pigeon Beach, hosts and Brittany transplants Claudine and Guillaume now regale expats, yachties and locals with mouthwatering French fare from a stylish-casual cottage with a long bar and lounge chairs in the sand. It's a great lunch spot and especially busy for Sunday brunch. Reservations recommended.

ANTIGUA & BARBUDA ENGLISH HARBOUR

South Point Restaurant INTERNATIONAL $$$
(☑ 268-562-9600; www.southpointantigua.
com; English Harbour; mains EC$52-125; ⊙7am-
10:30pm; P🐾; 🚪17) The contempo-styled
above-water deck with yacht views is just
as enticing to the chic-but-sensible crowd
as the eclectic menu that hopscotches from
Asia (sushi bar!) to the Med and the Middle
East without missing a step. The bar draws
cocktail connoisseurs with ginger margari-
tas and other clever concoctions.

ⓘ Information

Eastern Caribbean Amalgamated Bank
(☑ 268-480-5300; www.ecabank.com; Nel-
son's Dockyard; ⊙8:30am-1:30pm Mon-Thu, to
3:30pm Fri; 🚪17) Has an ATM.

Nelson's Dockyard Post Office (☑ 268-460-
1379; Dockyard Dr; ⊙8:15am-3pm Mon-Thu, to
1pm Fri; 🚪17)

ⓘ Getting There & Aroung

English Harbour is about 13 miles south of St
John's via All Saints Rd. Bus 17 make the trip
from the West bus station (EC$3.75). A taxi costs
US$24 from St John's and US$31 from the airport.
Water taxis (one way EC$10; ⊙9am-6pm) to
Galleon Beach or other points in the harbour can
be hired near the Copper & Lumber Store Hotel
in Nelson's Dockyard. Most rides are EC$15.

Eastern Antigua

Flat and windswept, Antigua's eastern side
is dotted with a few sleepy villages and gets
fewer vacationers than other parts of the
island. Those that stay are drawn to the
Atlantic-side beaches at Long Bay and Non-
such Bay, which have great conditions for
windsurfing and kitesurfing. Most people,
though, come on day trips to explore his-
toric sites including Betty's Hope, the rugged
splendor of Devil's Bridge or the ethereal
beauty of remote Half Moon Bay.

⊙ Sights

Antigua's Donkey Sanctuary ZOO
(☑ 268-461-4957; www.antiguaanimals.com/
donkey; near Bethesda; donations appreciated;
⊙10am-4pm Mon-Sat; P🖈) FREE Meet Char-
ley, Chrissy, blind Stevie or any of the other
150 or so stray donkeys that have found a
loving home in this sanctuary operated by
the Antigua & Barbuda Humane Society.
Dedicated staff are happy to introduce vis-
itors to the friendly animals and let them
brush and take pictures with them.

★**Half Moon Bay** BEACH
(near Freetown; P) Water the color of Blue
Curacao laps this undeveloped white cres-
cent in the remote southeast. Bodysurfers
head to the north end, snorkelers to the
calm waters south, and everyone meets at
the two beach bars for grilled-fish lunches
and rum cocktails. For shade, unfold your
towel beneath the shrub and sea grapes.

Scrambling over the bluff at the far end
takes you to another beach backed by an
exclusive villa resort with views of uninhab-
ited offshore Smith Island.

Betty's Hope HISTORIC SITE
(off Pares Village Main Rd, Pares; ⊙site 24hr, inter-
pretive centre 9am-4pm Mon-Sat; 🚌33 from East
bus station) FREE Ponder Antigua's colonial
past while poking around a restored stone
windmill, as well as remnants of the Great
House, the distillery and other buildings
of the island's first sugar plantation, estab-
lished in 1674 by Christopher Codrington
and named for his daughter. An interpretive
center demystifies the sugar-making process
and provides glimpses into the hardship
of daily life on the plantation, which had
around 400 slaves at its peak.

Devil's Bridge NATURAL FEATURE
(Pares Village Main Rd, past Willikies, Long Bay;
⊙24hr; P) Just before reaching Long Bay, a
rough 1-mile dirt road (better with a 4WD)
veers off the main highway toward this wind-
swept bluff ringed by rugged cliffs shaped by
the relentless crashing of powerful waves.
Views are fabulous and especially rewarding
at sunset. If the tide is right, you can see the
powerful blowhole at the far end in action,
while Devil's Bridge itself is a rather small
natural bridge on your right near the sign.

Long Bay BEACH
A favorite beach with locals, Long Bay has
clear-blue, kid-friendly waters and
a gorgeous white-sand beach that's reef-
protected and good for snorkeling. Two
resorts bookend the beach, which is lined
with souvenir shops, a water-sports conces-
sion and a couple of bars.

🏃 Activities & Tours

**40 Knots Kitesurfing
& Windsurfing School** KITESURFING
(☑ 268-788-9504; www.40knots.net; Nonsuch
Bay Resort, near Freetown; kite-flying lessons 1hr/
half-day/2 half-days US$89/225/550; ⊙Oct-Aug)
If you've always wanted to 'fly' over water,

this friendly and dedicated international team will get you up and going with individual lessons or in groups of up to three. The reef-enclosed bay offers ideal learning conditions for kite-flying, windsurfing and SUP. Experienced surfers can rent equipment and catch a lift to nearby idyllic Green Island.

Antigua Paddles KAYAKING
(✍ 268-720-4322; www.antiguapaddles.com; Mercers Creek, Seatons; adult/child US$55/45) British couple Conrad and Jennie have offered kayak and snorkeling trips off Antigua's eastern shore since 2001. Their signature half-day trip to the North Sound National Park off Antigua's eastern coast involves a motorboat shuttle to a lagoon, kayaking around mangroves, another boat ride to a deserted island, a short nature walk, plus snorkeling and time on the beach.

✕ Eating

★ Road House CARIBBEAN $
(✍ 268-764-8090; roadhouserest@hotmail.com; Main Rd, New Field Village; mains EC$10-35; ☺ 6:30am-3pm Mon-Thu, 6:30am-late Fri & Sun) A popular stop for a cold beer and local lunch (goat water, seafood chowder, grilled fish) en route to Half Moon Bay, this place kicks into high gear on Fridays when all dishes cost just EC$5 after 5pm, and even more so on Sunday afternoons when villagers arrive in droves to ring out the weekend with barbecue and the jamming Reggae Band.

Smiling Harry's CARIBBEAN $
(✍ 268-460-4084; www.facebook.com/smiling harrys; Half Moon Bay, near Freetown; mains EC$20-40; ☺ 11am-sunset Sat & Sun, sometimes on other days) The eponymous owner, Harry Thomas, has passed on, but his smiling spirit still hovers over this rustic beach shack famous for its 'Thirst Quenchers' and unfussy Antiguan fare. There's no set menu, so just ask what's cooking. Gets busy with local families at Sunday lunchtime.

It's on your left as you drive toward Half Moon Bay.

❶ Getting There & Away

This sprawling area is best explored by vehicle, either your own rental car or by taxi. Gas stations are scarce, so be sure to have plenty in the tank. The drive from English Harbour to Half Moon Bay takes about 30 to 45 minutes and presents you with spectacular views of Willoughby Bay. A taxi from the capital costs US$17 to

FRIGATE BIRD SANCTUARY

Off Barbuda's northwest coast, Codrington Lagoon National Park protects a vast estuary that supports one of the world's largest **colonies** of frigate birds (sea taxi US$50, 4 people maximum, national park US$2). More than 2500 of these black-feathered critters roost amid the scrubby mangroves. The birds' nesting sites are all abuzz with squawking, and the sight of all those blood-red inflating throat pouches is mesmerizing. The lagoon can only be visited by licensed sea taxi from the Codrington jetty. Make arrangements at least a day in advance through your hotel or the tourist office. **Foster Hopkins** (✍ 268-785-2742) is a local boat operator offering tours of the Frigate Bird Sanctuary.

Betty's Hope, US$26 to Long Bay and Devil's Bridge, and US$28 to Half Moon Bay.

From St John's East bus station, bus 33 runs east past Betty's Hope as far as Willikies (close to Long Bay and Devil's Bridge).

BARBUDA

When Gertrude Stein famously opined, 'There is no there there,' she might have meant Barbuda. Antigua's tiny sister island is where you go when you want to get away from it all. And we mean all: the internet, TV, phones, water sports, nightlife and so on. But don't worry, the stunning beaches and crystalline turquoise sea provide plenty of soul candy to make you forget the trappings of civilization in no time.

❶ Getting There & Around

At the time of writing, Barbuda could only be reached by the **Barbuda Express** (p123) ferry and by private plane and helicopter charter.

Barbuda has no public transportation. There are only a few private rental cars available, making taxis your main four-wheel option. **Bicycle and kayak rentals** (p117) are also available.

Codrington

Barbuda's only village, sleepy Codrington is home to most residents and the minuscule airstrip. It's about 3.5 miles north of

Barbuda

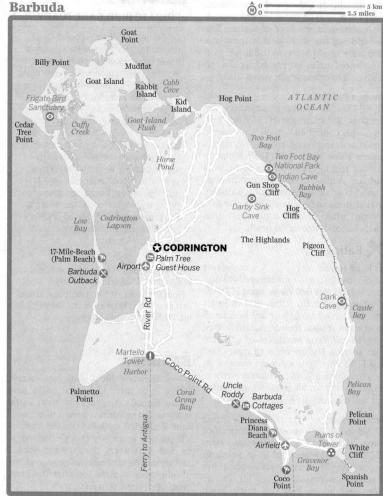

the ferry landing on the eastern edge of the lagoon with its famous frigate bird colony.

🛏 Sleeping

Palm Tree Guest House   GUESTHOUSE **$**
(☎268-784-4331, 268-560-0517; Codrington; d/ste US$80/130; 🌢🤖) Cerene's no-nonsense guesthouse is about a 15-minute walk from central Codrington and has eight spacious doubles, each with a small fridge and cable TV, as well as a two-bedroom suite with kitchen.

Bus Stop Guest House   GUESTHOUSE **$**
(☎268-721-2796; lyntonthomas@ymail.com; Codrington; s/d incl tax US$86/96; 🅿🤖) This little guesthouse is a good budget pick in the heart of Codrington. Lynton Thomas rents three basic yet comfortable rooms with fridge, TV and private bathroom, and can also provide meals and tours upon request. His bar below is rarely noisy at night. Rates include transfer from the ferry landing or airport.

🍴 Eating & Drinking

Codrington is a great place to try home-cooked specialties such as crab, conch and, of course, lobster and fish served in snack-ettes and bars, and from roadside kitchens. In fact, the street-food scene is excellent, especially on Friday and Saturday. Note that food often sells out by 2pm.

Green Door Tavern BAR
(📞 268-783-7243; Madison Sq; ⊙ 7am-late) Byron Askie's long-running joint is the perfect place to party with friendly locals. If you've had one rum punch too many, come back in the morning for goat water or pepperpot to chase away the hangover.

❶ Information

Barbuda Tourist Office (📞 268-562-7066; barbudacouncil@act.net; Lagoon St; ⊙ 8am-4:30pm Mon-Thu, to 3pm Fri) Near the Codrington jetty, this office has maps and brochures, and friendly staff who can set you up with a local guide.

❶ Getting Around

Andrea Car Rentals (📞 268-560-2826, 268-775-0168; per day US$45)
Barbuda Bike & Kayak Rental (📞 268-773-9599, 268-784-5717; www.facebook.com/Barbuda-Bike-Tours-Kayak-Rentals-288537511168135; Codrington) Jonathan Pereira rents bicycles and kayaks from his place in central Codrington and also does guided tours. Contact him directly for availability and prices.
C and J Car Rentals (📞 268-725-4970, 268-734-2509; per day US$46-61) Has five Toyota Rav 4s with 4WD for rent. Rates include insurance.

West & South Coasts

Just when you think beaches can't get any better, turn your compass to Barbuda's southern shores to find a sublime strand sure to inspire comparison to the Garden of Eden. It was a favorite getaway of the late Princess Diana, which inspired the island to name a beach in her honor. In 2014 Robert de Niro and an Australian investor announced plans to restore the K-Club Resort where Diana used to stay and which has been closed since 2004. The project has met with opposition from the local community.

◉ Sights

17-Mile-Beach (Palm Beach) BEACH
This epic stretch of silky smooth, unblemished sands separates the ocean from the Codrington Lagoon. It's possible to walk for hours but note that there's no shade and no vendors, so bring everything you need.

Martello Tower TOWER
(south coast) FREE Barbuda's most important colonial vestige sits just a short walk northwest of the ferry harbor, near River Beach. The 56ft-high mini-fort was built by the British in the early 1800s and looks just like an old sugar mill from afar. It stands on the site of an earlier, probably Spanish, fort. Today, it's a popular place to get hitched.

BARBUDA ISLAND TOURS

Caribbean Helicopters (📞 268-562-8687; www.caribbeanhelicopters.com; US$385, 4-passenger minimum, 6-passenger maximum; ⊙ tours 9am, 9:45am & 10:30am) See Barbuda like a frigate bird on these airborne tours that depart from Antigua and include the flight as well as a beachside lobster lunch at Low Bay. The entire trip takes 4½ hours and includes time to swim and explore the bird sanctuary. Note that these tours target the cruise-ship market. Private tours can also be arranged (US$1315 for up to six people).

John Taxi Service (📞 268-788-5378, 268-779-4652; www.facebook.com/JohnTaxiServiceTours; per person US$75; ⊙ tours 11am-3pm Tue-Fri) Levi John specializes in guided minibus tours targeted at day-trippers arriving by ferry. In four hours, he'll take you to the caves, the bird sanctuary and to a lobster lunch at his own restaurant called River Beach and Grill.

Barbuda Outback Tours (📞 268-721-1972, 268-721-3280) Local guides Jala and Calvin can arrange customized tours of Barbuda by boat, car or a combination thereof.

Barbuda Day Tour (📞 268-560-7989; www.barbudaexpress.com; adult/child 3-12yr US$159/100; ⊙ office 9am-6pm, tours 9am-4pm Tue-Sat) This day trip, operated by Barbuda Express, includes the 90-minute ferry ride and visits to the bird sanctuary, the caves, as well as a lobster lunch and a beach-splashing session. Another day trip lets you feel like a royal on the south coast's Princess Diana Beach (US$129/100). Barbuda was a favorite getaway of the late princess.

TWO FOOT BAY

Two Foot Bay National Park (east coast) This nature area on the northeastern coast consists of coastal scrub forest hemming in the cliff-lined waterfront. It's famous for its caves, most importantly the Indian Cave with the only known petroglyphs on Barbuda.

Indian Cave (Highland Rd) Barbuda is riddled with mysterious caves, some of which are so well hidden you'll need a guide to locate them. Not so with Indian Cave in the Two Bay National Park on the northeastern coast. The three-chambered hole-in-the-ground features Arawak petroglyphs and a bat chamber. Look for the entrance atop a small bluff opposite a stone ruin.

Darby Sink Cave (northeast coast) Darby is not a true cave but a 300ft wide and 70ft deep sinkhole with tall palm trees growing out of it and mighty ferns and lianas dangling down from the rim, creating a miniature rainforest ecosystem. Look for lizards, hermit crabs, iguanas and other critters among the dense foliage.

Princess Diana Beach BEACH
(southeastern coast) This sublime southwest-facing beach is home to the famous all-inclusive Coco Point Lodge, but anyone is free to enjoy the often footprint-free sands lapped by the crystal-clear sea. Previously known as Coco Point Beach, it was renamed in honor of Princess Diana, who loved vacationing here, to mark what would have been her 50th birthday in 2011.

Gravenor Bay BAY
(southeast coast; 🖈) The pristine waters of Gravenor Bay between Coco Point and Spanish Point are a popular yacht anchorage and have reefs offering excellent snorkeling. Near the heart of the bay is an old, dilapidated pier, while the ruins of a small tower lie about a half-mile away to the east.

🛏 Sleeping & Eating

⭐ **Barbuda Cottages** APARTMENT $$$
(☑268-722-3050; www.barbudacottages. com; Coral Group Bay; 1-/3-bedroom cottage US$300/450, 3-night minimum; ⊘closed Aug-Oct; 🐾) 🐾 At this little slice of paradise you'll fall asleep to the ocean breezes in a solar-powered villa within a Frisbee toss of pearly Coral Group Bay beach. Each of the four cottages has a kitchenette with fridge and microwave, but the adjacent restaurant-bar (Uncle Roddy's) makes tempting culinary treats.

Uncle Roddy Beach Bar & Grill CARIBBEAN $$
(☑268-722-3050; info@uncleroddys.com; next to Barbuda Cottages, Coral Group Bay; mains EC$30-100; ⊘11am-10pm Mon-Sat) 🐾 This newly expanded but still solar-powered beach bar is perfect for spending a relaxing day with grilled lobster and the signature Barbuda Smash. Make reservations 24 hours in advance as Roddy only buys supplies as needed. Bring bug spray to combat pesky sand flies.

Barbuda Outback CARIBBEAN $$
(☑268-721-3280; Palm Beach, Low Bay; mains EC$35-80; ⊘noon-3pm) This casual hangout on gorgeous Palm Beach doles out such finger-lickin' proteins as chicken, fish and lobster tickled to perfection on the open grill. It's only accessible by boat. If you don't have your own, call Jala or Calvin to arrange for a free pick-up from the Codrington jetty.

ℹ Getting There & Away

If you happen to have your own yacht, you can drop anchor for easy access. Everyone else will have to get here by taxi or rental car, on foot or by bike or kayak.

UNDERSTAND ANTIGUA & BARBUDA

History

Wadadli

The first permanent settlers were an Amerindian tribe called Siboney who came to the area around 2900 BC. They were followed by the Arawaks who arrived around the 1st century AD and called Antigua 'Wadadli,' a name still used today. Around AD 1200 the Arawaks were forced out by invading Caribs, who used the islands as bases for their forays in the region, but apparently didn't settle them.

Columbus sighted Antigua in 1493 and named it after a church in Seville, Spain. In 1632 the British colonized Antigua, establishing a settlement at Parham, on the east side of the island. The settlers started planting indigo and tobacco, but a glut in the supply of those crops sent drove down prices, leaving growers looking for something new.

Colonialism & Sugarcane

In 1674 Sir Christopher Codrington arrived on Antigua and established the first sugar plantation, Betty's Hope. By the end of the century, a plantation economy had developed, huge numbers of slaves were imported, and the central valleys were deforested and planted with cane. Britain had annexed Barbuda in 1628 and granted it to the Codrington family in 1680. After the slave trade was abolished in 1807, the Codringtons established a 'slave breeding farm' on Barbuda, which remained in operation until slavery as such was abolished in 1834. In 1860 Barbuda reverted back to the Crown and became a dependency of Antigua.

As Antigua prospered, the British built numerous fortifications around the island, turning it into one of their most secure bases in the Caribbean. The most heavily fortified area was English Harbour, where the Caribbean fleet of the British Royal Navy was based from 1725 until 1854. What is today's Nelson's Dockyard was continually expanded and improved throughout the 18th century. Other forts were Fort James and Fort Barrington who protected the harbor of St John's.

With the abolition of slavery, the plantations went into a steady decline. Unlike on some other Caribbean islands, the land was not turned over to former slaves when the plantations went under, but was instead consolidated under the ownership of a few landowners. Many former slaves moved off the plantations and into shantytowns, while others crowded onto properties held by the church.

Road to Independence

A military-related construction boom during WWII, and the development of a tourist industry during the postwar period, helped spur economic growth. A first step in Antigua's road to independence was the West Indies Act of 1967 in which Britain granted the island control over domestic issues while retaining responsibility for external issues and defense. Finally, on November 1, 1981, Antigua and Barbuda became an independent state within the

ANTIGUA & BARBUDA HISTORY

A NEST OF BIRDS

Vere Cornwall (VC) Bird, founder of the Antigua Labour Party in 1951, became the nation's first prime minister, and despite leading a government marred by political scandals and corruption, he held that position through four consecutive terms. He stepped down in 1994 to be succeeded by his son Lester.

Another son, Vere Bird Jr, received international attention in 1991 as the subject of a judicial inquiry that investigated his involvement in smuggling Israeli weapons to the Medellín drug cartel. As a consequence of the inquiry, Vere Bird Jr was pressured into resigning his cabinet post, but was allowed to keep his parliamentary position. A third son of VC Bird, Ivor, was convicted of cocaine smuggling in 1995.

Throughout the five terms that the family had a hold on government, controversy continued to surround the Birds. In 1997 Prime Minister Lester Bird announced that a group of eco-sensitive islands, including Guiana Island, was being sold to Malaysian developers, who planned to build a 1000-room hotel, an 18-hole golf course and a casino. The highly controversial project stalled when the Malaysian developers failed to pay up, but was revived when Bird's old ally, Texas billionaire Allen Stanford, agreed to step in instead.

In March 2004, the Birds' reign of the 'aviary' (as Antigua had become known) ended when the United Progressive Party won a landslide victory and Baldwin Spencer became prime minister. He was re-elected in 2009, the same year that the FBI arrested Stanford for running a massively fraudulent Ponzi scheme. He was convicted in March 2012 and is now serving a 110-year prison sentence. Spencer resoundingly lost the 2014 election, which returned the Antigua Labour Party to power under Prime Minister Gaston Browne.

British Commonwealth with Vere Cornwall Bird as its first prime minister.

Culture

Away from the resorts, Antigua retains its traditional West Indian character. It's manifested in the gingerbread architecture found around the capital, the popularity of steelpan (steel-band), calypso and reggae music, and in festivities, such as Carnival. Still, English traditions also play an important role, as is evident in the national sport of cricket.

Many Barbudans originally come from or have spent time living on their sister island, Antigua, and favor the quieter pace of life on the more isolated Barbuda. In fact, many Barbudans working in tourism are happy with the trickle of tourists that the remote island attracts, and have been reluctant to court the kind of development Antigua has seen.

Approximately 90% of Antiguans are of African descent. There are also small minority populations of British, Portuguese and Lebanese ancestry. The population of Barbuda is approximately 1600, with most of African descent.

Beside the Anglican Church, Antiguans belong to a host of religious denominations, which include Roman Catholic, Moravian, Methodist, Seventh Day Adventist, Lutheran and Jehovah's Witness. On Sundays, services at the more fundamentalist churches draw such crowds that roads are blocked and drivers pray for divine intervention.

Landscape & Wildlife

Unlike Montserrat, its (at times) smoking neighbor to the southwest, Antigua is not dominated by a dramatic volcano. However, the southwest corner is volcanic in origin and quite hilly, rising to 1319ft at Mt Obama (known as Boggy Peak until 2009), the island's highest point. The rest of the island, which is predominantly of limestone and coral formation, is given to a more gently undulating terrain of open plains and scrubland.

Antigua's land area is 108 sq miles. The island is vaguely rounded in shape, averaging about 11 miles across. The coastline is cut by numerous coves and bays, many lined with white-sand beaches.

Barbuda, 25 miles north of Antigua, is nearly as flat as the surrounding ocean. A low-lying coral island, Barbuda's highest point is a mere 145ft above sea level. The west side of Barbuda encompasses the expansive Codrington Lagoon, which is bound by a long, undeveloped barrier beach of blindingly white sand.

As a consequence of colonial-era deforestation for sugar production, most of Antigua's vegetation is dryland scrub. The island's marshes and salt ponds attract a fair number of stilts, egrets, ducks and pelicans, while hummingbirds are found in garden settings. Codrington Lagoon has one of the largest frigate-bird colonies in the world.

SURVIVAL GUIDE

ⓘ Directory A–Z

ACCOMMODATIONS

Antigua and Barbuda are expensive and besides a few locally run guesthouses in the inland villages, older hotels and moderately priced apartments, the market is dominated by high-end (usually all-inclusive) resorts. On Antigua, properties cluster on Dickenson Bay, around Jolly Harbour and in English Harbour. Many close for a few weeks between August and October.

CHILDREN

The Antigua and Barbuda tourism industry generally caters more to grown-up visitors, with

---

FRIGATE BIRDS: AERIAL PIRATES

Frigate birds skim the water's surface for fish, but because their feathers lack the water-resistant oils common to other seabirds, they cannot dive into water. Also known as the man-of-war bird, the frigate bird has evolved into an aerial pirate that supplements its own fishing efforts by harassing other seabirds until they release their catch, which the frigate bird then swoops up in mid-flight.

While awkward on the ground, the frigate bird, with its distinctive forked tail and 6ft wingspan, is beautifully graceful in flight. It has the lightest weight-to-wingspan ratio of any bird and can soar at great heights for hours on end – making it possible for the bird to feed along the coast of distant islands and return home to roost at sunset without having landed anywhere other than its nesting site.

some resorts even being restricted to 'adults only'. If traveling with children, check if your resort has a children's pool, organized activities or day-care/babysitting services.

West-coast beaches tend to be calmer. Watersports activity is best on Dickenson Bay.

A great place to visit with animal-loving tots is Antigua's Donkey Sanctuary. Older children will enjoy the Antigua Rainforest Zip Line Tours.

ELECTRICITY

220V, 60 cycles. Some places provide 110V, 60 cycles, some provide both. American two-pin sockets dominate, UK sockets are rare.

EMBASSIES & CONSULATES

Consular affairs for US citizens are handled by the **US Consular Agent** (☑ 268-726-6531, mobile 268-463-6531; Jasmine Crt, Ste 2, Friars Hill Rd) in St John's. The **UK** (☑ 268-561-5046; ukinantigua@fco.gov.uk; c/o Price Waterhouse Coopers, 11 Old Parham Rd) and **Germany** (☑ 268-462-3174; st-johns-ant@hk-diplo.de) are represented by honorary consulates on Antigua.

FOOD

From roadside barbecues to rustic beach bars and gourmet temples, feeding your tummy is no tall order in Antigua, although on Barbuda the selection is more limited. Opening hours are erratic and subject to change at any time; some places close from August to October. Menu prices may not include tax (15%) and a service charge (10%). This should be noted on the menu itself or on the check.

Essential Food & Drink

Black pineapple The local pineapple was first introduced by the Arawaks and is smaller than your garden variety. It's known as 'black' because it's at its sweetest when kind of dark green. It grows primarily on the southwest coast, near Cades Bay.

Cavalier and **English Harbour** Locally produced rums best mixed with fruit juice.

Pepperpot Antigua's national dish is a hearty stew blending meat and vegetables, such as okra, spinach, eggplant, squash and potatoes. It's often served with fungi, which are not mushrooms but cornmeal patties or dumplings.

Rock lobster This hulking crustacean has a succulent tail but no claws and is best served grilled. (And you'll be forgiven if after a few rum punches you're humming a tune by the B-52s while digging in.)

Wadadli Antigua Brewery makes this local brew, a fresh pale lager, with desalinated seawater.

GLBT TRAVELERS

There is no real gay scene on Antigua and Barbuda but no overt discrimination either. How-

ever, homosexuality is on the books as illegal and is theoretically punishable with jail time, although enforcement is practically nonexistent. Just be discreet and avoid public displays of affection, especially outside the international resorts, and you're unlikely to run into any problems.

HEALTH

For minor illnesses, hotels and resorts will be able to help you find medical assistance. Healthcare is expensive and the standard of the care and equipment not as high, modern or comprehensive as you might be used to. The nearest hyperbaric chambers are in Saba, St Thomas and Guadeloupe.

Hannah Thomas Hospital (☑ 268-460-0076; River Rd) Tiny outpatient facility on Barbuda.

Mt St John's Medical Centre (☑ 268-484-2700; Michael's Mount, off Queen Elizabeth Hwy; ⊙ 24hr) Main hospital with 185 beds and 24-hour emergency room; on Antigua.

LEGAL MATTERS

Antigua and Barbuda's legal system is based on British common law. In case of legal difficulties, you have the right to legal representation and are eligible for legal aid if you can't afford to pay for private services. Foreign nationals should receive the same legal protections as local citizens.

Drunk driving, drug or gun possession, cross-dressing, prostitution, public cursing and wearing camouflage clothing are among the offenses that can get you in trouble on Antigua and Barbuda.

The police have the right to arrest anyone suspected of committing a crime without a warrant. Suspects must be brought before a court within 48 hours of arrest or detention.

MONEY

ATMs are scarce but credit cards are widely accepted.

Exchange Rates

AUSTRALIA	A$1	EC$1.93
CANADA	C$1	EC$1.98
EURO ZONE	€1	EC$2.81
JAPAN	¥100	EC$2.30
NEW ZEALAND	NZ$1	EC$1.86
UK	UK£1	EC$3.29
US	US$1	EC$2.68

For current exchange rates, see www.xe.com.

Tipping

Hotels US$0.50 to US$1 per bag is standard; gratuity for cleaning staff is at your discretion.

Restaurants If the service charge is not automatically added to the bill, tip 10% to 15%; if it is, it's up to you to leave a little extra tip.

Taxis Tip 10% to 15% of the fare.

POST

When mailing a letter to the islands, follow the addressee's name with the town and 'Antigua, West Indies' or 'Barbuda, West Indies.'

Post Office English Harbour (p114)

Post Office St John's (cnr High St & Heritage Quay; ☉8:15am-3:30pm Mon-Thu, to 2pm Fri)

PUBLIC HOLIDAYS

New Year's Day January 1

Good Friday/Easter Monday March/April

Labor Day First Monday in May

Pentecost/Whit Monday 40 days after Easter

Carnival Late July to first Tuesday in August

Independence Day November 1

VC Bird Day December 9

Christmas/Boxing Day December 25/26

TELEPHONE

➸ The country code for Antigua and Barbuda is ☑268.

➸ To place a call to Antigua and Barbuda, dial your country's international access code + ☑268 + local number.

➸ To call abroad, dial ☑011 + country code + area code + local number.

EATING PRICE RANGES

The following price ranges refer to a main course.

$ less than US$10

$$ US$10–25

$$$ more than US$25

➸ If making a call within or between Antigua and Barbuda, you only need to dial the seven-digit local number if dialing from a landline.

➸ For directory assistance, dial ☑411.

➸ In hotels, local calls are often free but international ones are charged at exorbitant rates.

TIME

Clocks in Antigua and Barbuda are set to Eastern Caribbean Time (Atlantic Time), which is four hours behind GMT. The islands do not observe daylight saving time, but as other countries do, the following times are indicative only:

TOURIST INFORMATION

For advance planning, check www.antigua-barbuda.org, www.visitantiguabarbuda.com or www.barbudaful.net.

Antigua Tourist Office (☑268-562-7600; www.visitantiguabarbuda.com; ACB Financial Centre, High St; ☉8am-4pm Mon-Fri) Maintains an information kiosk at Heritage Quay on cruise-ship days.

Barbuda Tourist Office (p117)

TRAVELERS WITH DISABILITIES

Generally speaking, Antigua and Barbuda are not very progressive when it comes to meeting the needs of the disabled. The big resorts usually have rooms that can accommodate the mobility-impaired; some provide beach wheelchairs.

In most villages, sidewalks are in poor condition or nonexistent. In St John's, many of the shops and toilets adjacent to the cruise-ship terminal (ie at Heritage Quay and Redcliffe Quay) are accessible.

Neither buses nor taxis are equipped to transport wheelchair-bound travelers. The nonprofit Antigua & Barbuda Association of Persons with Disabilities is working toward improving the situation.

VOLUNTEERING

Antigua's Donkey Sanctuary (p114) Operated by the Antigua Humane Society, this outfit needs volunteer help to take care of stray donkeys.

Environmental Awareness Group of Antigua & Barbuda (www.eagantigua.org) Needs help with a wide variety of programs, from turtle protection to bird censuses and fern conservation.

Volunteer Global (www.volunteerglobal.com) Platform with occasional volunteer opportunities in Antigua and Barbuda.

ⓘ Getting There & Away

AIR

VC Bird International Airport (www.vcbia.com; Sir George Walter Hwy, Antigua; ☎), about 5 miles east of St John's, opened a shiny new, state-of-the-art terminal in August 2015.

Delta, US Airways, United Airlines, WestJet, JetBlue, CanJet and Air Canada have direct flights from various North American gateway cities to Antigua.

British Airways and Virgin Atlantic operate direct flights from the UK, while Alitalia has a direct flight from Milan, and Condor from Frankfurt.

LIAT (☎268-480-5582; www.liat.com) and **Caribbean Airlines** (☎800 744 2225; www.caribbean-airlines.com; ◷8am-4pm Mon-Fri) are the main regional carriers. **Fly Montserrat** (☎664-491-3434; www.flymontserrat.com) and **ABM Air** (☎268-562-7183; www.anti-gua-flights.com) fly to Montserrat.

Getting to Neighboring Islands

At the time of writing, scheduled flights to Barbuda had been suspended, so the ferry is your only option.

Montserrat is served by air (Fly Montserrat, ABM Air) and sometimes by ferry.

Antigua is the hub of regional airline LIAT, and has frequent flights to St Kitts, Nevis, St-Martin/Sint Maarten and other islands. Winair has connections to its base in St-Martin/Sint Maarten as well as to St Kitts and Dominica. Caribbean Airlines flies to Antigua from Jamaica and Trinidad via Barbados, and Seabourne Airline operates flights from San Juan, Puerto Rico.

SEA
Cruise Ship

Antigua is a major port of call for cruise ships. The cruise-ship pier, at Heritage Quay in St John's Harbour, segues into a duty-free shopping mall, and is within easy walking distance of St John's main sights.

When several behemoths are docked on the same day, beaches and other attractions can get very busy. Independent travelers might want to check the cruise-ship schedule (eg www.cruise timetables.com/cruises-to-st-johns-antigua.html) if they wish to avoid the crowds.

Ferry

There is on-and-off-again ferry service with **Montserrat Ferry** (☎268-778-9786; return adult/child 2-12yr EC$300/150; ◷hours vary) between Antigua and Montserrat. Call to inquire if it's running. Montserrat's tourist office site (www.visitmontserrat.com) also posts the latest schedule. The round-trip fare is EC$300 (EC$150 for children aged two to 12).

Yacht

Antigua's many fine, protected ports make it one of the major yachting centers of the Caribbean. Full-service marinas are at English Harbour, Falmouth Harbour, Jolly Harbour and Parham Harbour. If you're going on to Barbuda, ask for a cruising permit, which will allow you to visit

that island without further formalities. Bring everything you'll need, because there are no yachting facilities on Barbuda.

❶ Getting Around

AIR

Scheduled air service between Antigua and Barbuda is erratic. Airlines that may offer flights during your stay are **ABM Air** and **Fly Montserrat**. Transfers and tours may also be arranged through **Caribbean Helicopters** (☎268-460-5900; www.caribbeanhelicopters.com).

BICYCLE

Check with your hotel, as many have a small fleet of bikes available for their guests. A reliable bike shop with rentals is **Bike Plus** (p102) in St John's. On Barbuda, rentals are available from **Barbuda Bike & Kayak Rental** (p117) in Codrington.

BOAT

Bumpy 90-minute catamaran rides operated by **Barbuda Express** (☎268-560-7989; www.barbudaexpress.com; return adult/child 7-12yr/child 3-6yr/child 0-2yr US$85/75/45/15; ◷office 9am-6pm daily, ferry daily except Mon) link St John's with the **River Wharf Landing** in southern Barbuda. Boats leave at 9am (noon on Sundays) and return from Barbuda at 4pm. There is no service on Mondays.

In peak season, it's best to make reservations or buy tickets in advance. Inclement weather may cancel service, so call ahead to confirm departure times and take precautions if you're prone to seasickness.

The company also operates guided day tours to Barbuda (from US$129).

RENTAL CAR WARNING

Because of the poor road conditions, most vehicles have dents and scratches. Make sure that the car-rental agent records all damages and hands you a copy before taking over the car. In addition, take photographs of all existing damages.

If the agent is not present when you return the car, take another set of photographs before leaving it. Some companies, including presumably reputable international ones, may claim that you added additional damage and charge your credit card for bogus repairs. With your photographs, you should be able to prove the scam.

BUS

Antigua has a decent network of private minivans traveling along the main roads. Buses to the south, northwest and west leave from the **West bus station** (Market St) opposite the Public Market in St John's; buses to the northeast, the east and southeast leave from the **East bus station** (Independence Ave) on Independence Ave. Fares cost EC$2.25 to EC$4, with a small surcharge between 10pm and 5am. Bus Stop Antigua (www.busstopanu.com) has details.

Buses don't leave until full and generally run from about 6am until 7pm; there are very few buses at night and on Sunday. Buses to English Harbour may run as late as midnight, but do confirm this with the driver.

CAR & MOTORCYCLE

Driving is on the left, the steering wheel is on the right. The speed limit is generally 20mph in built-up areas and 40mph on highways.

If you have an accident, call the police and don't move the vehicle.

Driving Licence

A local driving permit, available from car-rental agencies, is required for driving on Antigua or Barbuda. It costs US$20 or EC$50 and is valid on both islands for three months.

Car Hire

International car-rental companies with outlets at the Antigua airport include Avis, Dollar and Hertz. **Big's Car Rental** (📞 268-562-4901; www.bigscarrental.net; English Harbour; vehicles per day from US$40) is a local outfit in English Harbour. Car rentals on Barbuda are all local and

very limited as most visitors prefer to get around by taxi. Ask at your hotel for a referral.

Most agencies will deliver cars to your hotel free of charge. Daily rates start at about US$40 for a compact. Gas stations are scattered around the island, including a handy one for refueling just outside the airport.

Road Conditions

Antigua's roads range from smooth to rough to deadly. You'll be cruising along when suddenly a hubcap-popping pothole or a speed bump appears. Smaller roads are often narrow with poor visibility, particularly on curves. If you plan to get off the beaten track (especially in the remote eastern part of Antigua), it's best to hire an SUV or 4WD.

Driving at night is even more dangerous since roads are narrow, street lights or reflector posts are nonexistent and most people use their blinding brights. Also be aware of people, donkeys, dogs, goats and other animals by the side – or on – the road.

Finding your way around Antigua can prove difficult at times. The island is randomly dotted with green road signs, but they peter out the further away you get from the main centers. Private signs pointing the way to restaurants, hotels and a few other tourist spots are far more frequent. Beyond that, locals are always happy to offer advice – at times an adventure in itself.

Navigating by Google Maps generally works but can be erratic in rural areas where you may also occasionally lose the GPS signal.

TAXI
Antigua

Taxis on Antigua have number plates beginning with 'TX.' On both Antigua and Barbuda, fares are government regulated with one tariff applying to up to four passengers. However, it's best to confirm the price before riding away.

Private island tours are charged at US$24 per hour with a two-hour minimum. Waiting times cost US$5 per 30 minutes. See www.antigua-barbuda.org for a full list of official rates (link to 'Transportation').

Barbuda

Taxis wait at the airport or the ferry dock, but you may prefer to prearrange a transfer or an island tour through your hotel, the Barbuda tourist office or by contacting a driver directly. See www.barbudaful.net for a list, or try Lynton Thomas at 📞 268-721-2796, John Taxi Service at 📞 268-788-5378 or D&D Taxi at 📞 268-724-2829. There is usually a minimum charge of US$20, no matter where you're going.

Aruba

POP 103,000 / ☏ 297

Best Places to Eat

➡ Fred (p129)

➡ Pinchos (p128)

➡ Madame Janette (p132)

➡ Wacky Wahoo (p133)

➡ Yemanja Woodfired Grill (p129)

➡ Gasparito (p133)

Best Places to Sleep

➡ Beach House Aruba (p134)

➡ OceanZ (p134)

➡ Bucuti & Tara Beach Resort (p132)

➡ Club Arias (p137)

➡ Bananas Resort (p134)

Why Go?

North Americans fleeing winter make Aruba the most touristed island in the southern Caribbean. The draws are obvious: miles of glorious white-sand beaches, plenty of all-inclusive resorts, and a cute, compact capital, Oranjestad, which is well suited for the two-hour strolls favored by cruise-ship passengers. It's all about sun, fun and spending money.

Venture away from the resorts and you're in for a real treat. At the island's extreme ends are rugged, windswept vistas and uncrowded beaches – perfect for hiking and horseback riding. Crystal-clear waters are bursting with sea life and shipwrecks (and an airplane wreck or two), providing incredible opportunities for snorkeling and diving. And nonstop breezes create near-perfect conditions for wind-surfing and kiteboarding.

So whether you're longing to lounge on a beach or to delve into the great outdoors, Aruba has got you covered. One happy island, indeed!

When to Go

Dec–Apr High season, where accommodations fill up and prices are significantly higher.

Jan & Feb Carnival is Aruba's biggest celebration – a month of music and costumes, parades and parties. It starts just after New Year and culminates the weekend before Ash Wednesday.

Sep–Dec Although Aruba is below the hurricane belt, the island does experience an increase in rain.

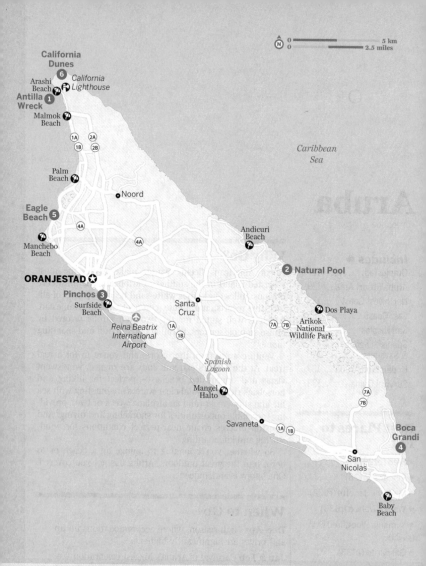

Aruba Highlights

1 Antilla Wreck (p133) Discovering the amazing underwater world at dive and snorkel sites around the island.

2 Natural Pool (p135) Hiking or horseback riding through the wilds of Arikok National Wildlife Park, then cooling off in this geological wonder.

3 Pinchos (p128) Sitting under the twinkling stars, listening to the lapping waves and feasting on creatures of the sea.

4 Boca Grandi (p136) Riding the wind on Aruba's best kitesurfing beach.

5 Eagle Beach (p130) Lounging on the long ribbon of powdery sand at the most beautiful beach of the bunch.

6 California Dunes (p134) Catching a glorious sunset from the dunes at the island's desolate northern tip.

Oranjestad

Oranjestad is a bustling island town that mingles a respectable amount of local life with the breathless pursuit of tourist dollars. The main drag, aka Caya GF Betico Croes, is lined with a charming mix of mom-and-pops and international chains. In the surrounding blocks, the colorful colonial buildings are sprinkled in among shiny new shopping malls. A lovely linear park follows the waterfront, from the airport, past the city's finest beaches, and all the way to the cruise-ship terminal in downtown Oranjestad.

Speaking of which, Oranjestad maintains a pleasant low-key buzz – except when a cruise ship is in port. Then, thousands of passengers descend on the capital, invading the shops and restaurants, transforming the vibe into a high-pitched frenzy.

Sights & Activities

Aruba Archaeological Museum MUSEUM
(Map p128; 582-8979; www.namaruba.org; Schelpstraat 42; 10am-5pm Tue-Fri, to 2pm Sat & Sun) FREE The capital's newest museum is housed in the beautifully restored colonial-era Ecury Complex, home to a successful merchant family throughout the 20th century. The engaging exhibits focus on Arawak life in the precolonial period, with a reproduction of a traditional home and multimedia presentations. Actual artifacts are few, though there are some stone tools and other artifacts dating from 4000 BC.

Fort Zoutman FORT
(Map p128) It's not much to look at, but it is an 18th-century fort built to defend the port against pirates. The attached Willem III Tower was added later, serving as both lighthouse and clock tower until 1963. The complex now houses the small **Aruba Historical Museum** (582-6099; admission $5; 8:30am-4pm Mon-Fri) and the weekly **Bonbini Festival** (admission US$5; 6:30-8:30pm Tue).

SE Aruba Fly 'n' Dive DIVING
(588-1150; www.se-aruba.com; Lloyd G Smith Blvd 1a; 2-tank dive from US$90) This highly recommended dive shop is located just north of the airport, which explains the name. Trips to local dive sites depart every morning at 9am, with transportation available from area hotels or the cruise-ship terminal. Fly 'n' Dive is unique in that they cater to divers and snorkelers, so there's no need to leave your nondiving friends behind.

Festivals & Events

Carnival CARNIVAL
(www.arubacarnival.com; Jan or Feb) Carnival is a big deal on the islands, where a packed schedule of fun begins shortly after New Year's Day.

Sleeping

Aruba Surfside Marina HOTEL $$
(583-0300; www.arubasurfsidemarina.com; Lloyd G Smith Blvd 7; d from US$170;) This gem has only five suites, each with plenty of living space, plus kitchenette, private balcony and fabulous ocean view. A spacious private garden overlooks the waves or, upon request, staff will kindly set up chairs on the sand at nearby Surfside Beach. It's a 20-minute walk to Oranjestad center. Great value.

Wonders Boutique Hotel B&B $$
(593-4032; www.wondersaruba.com; Emmastraat 63; r US$120-150;) It calls itself a boutique hotel, but it's really more of a B&B, with its warm welcome and intimate atmosphere (adults only). The 10 stylish rooms are decorated with understated elegance and stocked with local aloe-vera products. They overlook a lush garden and swimming pool fed by natural springs. It's a 15-minute walk south to downtown Oranjestad.

Eating

Some of Aruba's finest dining is in Oranjestad. Take a break from predictable resort restaurants and sample the city's excellent, eclectic local dining scene.

In addition to the brick-and-mortar restaurants, snack trucks are an island institution, serving up a wide range of street food from sunset into the wee hours. Look for them in the parking lots near the Yacht Basin.

Baby Back Grill BARBECUE $
(Map p128; 582-4410; Caya GF Betico Croes; mains US$6-8; 11am-11pm;) Like a snack truck but it doesn't go anywhere. This completely open-air restaurant grills up tender ribs, steaks, chicken and more for appreciative local masses. There are shady picnic tables where you can eat your barbecue.

Qué Pasa INTERNATIONAL $$
(Map p128; 583-4888; www.quepasaaruba.com; Wilhelminastraat 18; mains US$17-27; 5-11pm;) The accent is Spanish but the language is global at this effusive spot. The vibrant, sunshine-yellow cafe is just the place to settle in for cocktails, conversation

Central Oranjestad

Central Oranjestad

and flavors from the world around. The on-site art gallery is similarly internationally inspired.

Italy in the World   ITALIAN $$
(Map p128; ☎585-7958; Oranjestraat 2; mains US$17-25; ☺1-10pm; ✐) At first appearance this looks like a well-stocked Italian deli and wine shop. Slip in to the back to discover the secret stash of wine, plus a handful of tables and a daily changing menu scrawled on a blackboard. A tantalizing selection of handmade pastas is paired with Chef Mauro's favorite wine selections and served to a lucky few.

The West Deck   CARIBBEAN $$
(Map p128; www.thewestdeck.com; Lloyd G Smith Blvd; mains $8-20; ☺10:30am-11pm; 🐾) At the water's edge, the West Deck is a casual, open-air beach bar with a friendly atmosphere and terrific food. Look for conch fritters, steak and plantain pinchos, fish sliders and barbecued ribs. Order up a tropical fruity cocktail and you'll know for sure that you're on vacation.

★ Pinchos   SEAFOOD $$$
(☎583-2666; www.pinchosaruba.com; Lloyd G Smith Blvd 7; mains US$24-36; ☺5pm-midnight) Pincho's is surely one of Aruba's most romantic spots. Set on a pier jutting into the ocean,

the restaurant is surrounded by twinkling stars and lapping waves. Local fish and hearty steaks show off a fusion of flavors, such as the pan-seared grouper with apricot-ginger dipping sauce, or the maple bourbon barbecue skewer. Reservations recommended. The restaurant is located behind the Aruba Surfside Marina.

Fred FUSION $$$
(Map p128; www.fredaruba.com; 2nd fl, Wilhelminastraat 18; 5-course dinner per person $100, wines by the glass US$10-20; ⊙7pm Mon-Fri; ⍟) The evening starts at 7pm with a sundown drink on the terrace. Then Fred invites you into his kitchen to watch him work magic, as he prepares a unique, custom, five-course meal. His partner Tom does the drink pairings. The duo are perfect hosts, as they wine and dine their guest with the utmost charm and warm hospitality. Reservations are essential.

Yemanja Woodfired Grill FUSION $$$
(Map p128; ⍟ 588-4711; www.yemanja-aruba.com; Wilhelminastraat 2; mains US$24-38; ⊙5:30-10:30pm Mon-Sat; ⍟) Two colorful, colonial-era buildings have been transformed into one of Aruba's most stylish eateries, which grills most of its menu items over a fire of wood from the local Watapana tree, adding a rich, natural flavor to the seafood, steaks and veggies. While meats and seafood are the specialty, folks with dietary restrictions (including vegetarians) will not go hungry.

⍟ Drinking & Nightlife

Oranjestad is pretty quiet after dark. There are a few respectable drinking establishments with live music on weekends and there's always some action around the **Renaissance Marketplace** (Map p128; www.shoprenaissancearuba.com; Lloyd G Smith Blvd 82; ⊙10am-late; ⍟). If you're looking for a beach party, you're likely to find one further north, in the high-rise resort area, especially on weekends.

⍟ Shopping

Aruba Aloe COSMETICS
(Map p128; www.arubaaloe.com; Caya GF Betico Croes 78; ⊙9am-6pm Mon-Sat) Did you get too much sun? Swing by this little boutique to pick up some 'After Sun', made from the gel of the revered aloe plant, which grows prolifically on this island. There's a wide range of high-quality skin-care products – all made from local plants at the Aruba Aloe factory on the island.

Cosecha ARTS & CRAFTS
(Map p128; www.arubacosecha.com; Zoutmanstraat 1; ⊙noon-6pm Mon, 10am-6pm Tue-Sat) If you're looking for a unique, locally made souvenir, look no further. Cosecha is the local artists' cooperative stocking a range of wonderful creations, from sea-glass jewellery to handwoven tote bags to driftwood and ceramic sculpture to fine arts and paintings. Look for the Seyo seal, which certifies authentic, local, handmade products.

ⓘ Getting There & Away

Reina Beatrix International Airport (p141) is located just south of Oranjestad. Most hotels and car rental agencies offer airport transfers. Or you can catch **Arubus** (⍟ 297-520-2300; www.arubus.com; single/day ticket US$2.60/5), which operates several routes from the **main bus depot** (p141) in Oranjestad to the airport and on to San Nicolas, with additional routes to the resort area (20 minutes), as well as Malmok and Arashi Beaches (30 minutes).

ⓘ Getting Around

The easiest way to get around Oranjestad is to walk, as most of the sights and attractions are within an area of a few square miles. There is also a free, single-track, electric **trolley** (⊙10am-5pm) that runs from the cruise-ship terminal, through downtown Oranjestad and along Caya GF Betico Croes, before looping back to the port. It runs every 20 to 30 minutes.

Note that if you drive into Oranjestad, there is plenty of parking around town but you'll need Aruban florins to pay for it.

Aruba Resort Area

Here is the Aruba that you see in the tourist brochures. Beginning just north of Oranjestad, the western coastline is a 10km chain of wide, wonderful, fine-sand beaches, fronted by gorgeous turquoise waters. The vast majority of island accommodations are located along this coast – mostly clustered in two areas known as the low-rise resort area and the high-rise resort area – which gives you a good idea about the backdrop.

The resorts provide the lush landscaping, which fools many a tourist into forgetting that this is a desert, along with the lounge chairs, the towel service, the beach bars and the water aerobics. And if there's anything the resorts don't provide, many tour operators do: from snorkel tours to sunset cruises,

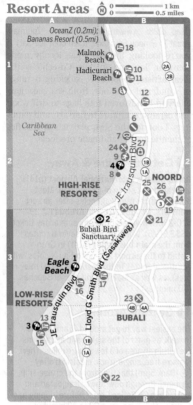

there is no shortage of ways to experience the Caribbean blue.

◉ Sights

Manchebo Beach　　　　　　BEACH
(Map p130) Just south of Eagle, this large beach reaches out to a point. It is something of a destination for topless sunbathers (an activity frowned on elsewhere) and offers the best chance on the strip to get away from the crowds.

★ Eagle Beach　　　　　　BEACH
(Map p130) Fronting a stretch of the low-rise resorts just northwest of Oranjestad, Eagle is a long stretch of white sand that regularly makes lists of the best in the world. There are shade trees in some areas and you can obtain every service you need here, from a lounger to a cold drink.

Butterfly Farm　　　　　　GARDENS
(Map p130; www.thebutterflyfarm.com; JE Irausquin Blvd; adult/child US$15/8; ⊗8:30am-4:30pm) Tucked in between the low-rise and high-rise resort areas, this place will make your heart go aflutter, as the gorgeous gardens are teeming with butterflies and moths of all sizes and colors. Guided tours walk you through the lepidoptera life cycle. If you ever wanted to see butterflies mating or emerging from their pupa, here is your chance. The habitat includes tropical dry forest and rain forest species, so the variety is impressive.

Palm Beach
BEACH

(Map p130) A classic white-sand beauty, but only for those who enjoy the company of lots of people, as it fronts the high-rise resorts. During high season the sands can get jammed, but for some that's part of the scene.

🎿 Activities & Tours

Tour operators are lined up along Palm Beach, offering scores of tours by land and by sea. The most popular boat trips are sail and snorkel tours, which often include breakfast or a beach-barbecue lunch. Sunset cruises are another standard offering.

Most tour operators also offer sightseeing by land (often by 4WD). Note, though, that it's easy enough to see most of the island independently, which is less expensive and more adventurous.

Spa del Sol
SPA

(Map p130; www.spadelsol.com; Palm Beach; ⊙9am-6:30pm Mon-Sat) Ocean breezes and rolling waves are integral to any treatment at Spa del Sol, which is located on the beach at Playa Linda Resort. The open-air facilities are clean and quiet enough, and take advantage of the resort's gorgeous gardens and marvelous ocean view. Bring a bathing suit if you want to soak in the hot tub. There is another location at Manchebo Beach Resort (p132).

Native Divers Aruba
DIVING

(Map p130; ☑586-4763; www.nativedivers.com; Palm Beach; 2-tank dive US$80) This is one of the smaller dive operations on the island, which makes for a more personal experience. The beachfront place offers custom trips and certification training. Located on the beach in front of the Marriott Surf Club.

Roberto's
SNORKELING

(Map p130; ☑592-2850; www.robertoswatersports.com; Palm Beach; per person US$40) Climb aboard Roberto's trimaran for a three-hour sail and snorkel tour. The two snorkel stops usually include the *Antilla* wreck, a local favorite. Sandwiches, snacks and drinks are included.

🎉 Festivals & Events

Soul Beach Music Festival
MUSIC

(www.soulbeach.net) On Memorial Day weekend, Aruba becomes a hot spot (even more than usual) for music, comedy and beach parties. This three-day event attracts an

NATURE SENSITIVE TOURS

Join the former top ranger at Arikok National Wildlife Park who now runs **Aruba Nature Sensitive Tours** (☑594-5017; www.naturesensitivetours.com; tours from US$80), leading tours through seldom explored parts of the island. The most popular choice is an all-day 4WD tour, which covers from the northern tip – California Lighthouse – to the southern tip – Baby Beach – and many things in between. There are also half-day hikes and monthly moonlight walks.

impressive line-up of artists, in the past featuring the likes of Alicia Keys, Boyz II Men, Chaka Khan, Estelle, Lauryn Hill, MJ Blige, Robin Thicke and more.

🛏 Sleeping

The vast majority of accommodations are lined up along the beach, north of Oranjestad. The low-rise resorts front Eagle and Manchebo Beaches. Further north, the high-rise resort area runs the length of Palm Beach, which is lined with huge hotels run by international chains. Inland, especially in the district of Bubali, you'll find some smaller lodgings that cater to travelers on a more restrained budget.

Coconut Inn
HOTEL $

(Map p130; ☑586-6288; www.coconutinn.com; Noord 31, Riberostraat; r US$90-95, apt US$110; ⊙reception 9am-5pm; ❄@❄) You'll want a car if you stay at this budget-friendly place, which has 40 dated rooms surrounding a large rectangle of aqua joy. It's not much more than a place to sleep, but the guest rooms do have private balconies and kitchenettes. A hearty homemade breakfast is included in the price.

MVC Eagle Beach Aruba
HOTEL $$

(Map p130; ☑587-0110; www.mvceaglebeach.com; JE Irausquin Blvd 240, Eagle Beach; d/q US$175/245; ❄@❄🐾) 🌿 Thank Dutch taxpayers for this excellent deal right across from Eagle Beach. Owned by the Dutch Navy, it's a basic two-story block with 19 small, bright rooms facing a postage-stamp-sized pool. Although beefy sailor-types do stay here, it's open to the masses, who enjoy the best value on Aruba for the location.

Sasaki Apartments HOTEL $$
(Map p130; ☎587-7482; www.sasaki-apartments.com; Bubali 143; r US$135; ✳@🎧🐾) The price is right for these studio apartments, located just a couple of busy roads away (400m) from Eagle Beach. The 24 spiffy apartments are spare in decor but have kitchenettes and other standard amenities. Conveniently, a giant supermarket is right across the road.

★**Boardwalk Hotel** BOUTIQUE HOTEL $$$
(Map p130; ☎586-6654; www.boardwalkaruba.com; Bakval 20; d from US$305; ☺reception 9am-5pm Mon-Sat; ✳🎧🐾🔥) 🏄 Located on a former coconut plantation, this delightful boutique hotel is just a short block from Palm Beach (where beach service is available) but miles from the tourist madness. A dozen delightful casitas feature well-equipped kitchens, spacious living areas hung with local artwork, and private terraces decked with hammocks and grills. Five-night minimum.

★**Bucuti & Tara Beach Resort** RESORT $$$
(Map p130; ☎583-1100; www.bucuti.com; Lloyd G Smith Blvd 55B, Manchebo Beach; r US$510-640, ste US$750; ✳🎧🐾) 🏄 With its white stucco edifice and red-tile roofs, Bucuti & Tara is among the classiest of the low-rise resorts. The adult-only facility is all about the romance: massive rooms have chic contemporary interiors and sunset-view balconies. Other perks include movies under the stars and private dining on the beach.

Manchebo Beach Resort RESORT $$$
(Map p130; ☎582-3444; www.manchebo.com; JE Irausquin Blvd 55, Manchebo Beach; r US$360-420, ste from US$560; ✳@🎧🐾) 🏄 Facing the eponymous beach, this crescent-shaped boutique resort makes you feel like you're being pampered. It's all understated luxury here, where recently renovated rooms feature cherry wood furniture, new marble bathrooms and a color palette to match the sea and sand. There's an explicit focus on wellness, with daily yoga classes, special fruit smoothie menus and the glorious Spa del Sol.

✕ **Eating**

Close to the high-rise resorts there is a plethora of development that is thick with international chains and other tourist-oriented restaurants. A short walk or drive inland, in Noord, there's a range of privately owned places, serving local fare, international cuisine and, of course, tons of seafood.

Ling & Sons SUPERMARKET $
(Map p130; Schotlandstraat 41, Bushiri; ☺8am-8pm Mon-Sat, to 1pm Sun) All those kitchenettes demand a good supermarket, and this is it. It has a large deli, salad bar and fresh-made fruit smoothies.

Diana's Pancakes Place BREAKFAST, DUTCH $
(Map p130; ☎586-7003; JE Irausquin Blvd 330; mains US$6-12; ☺8am-3pm Tue-Sun) Here's a great spot for breakfast or brunch, serving traditional Dutch pancakes, as well as scrummy sandwiches, fresh juices and rich dark coffee. Look for the restaurant next to the Old Dutch Windmill. And don't forget to leave your mark on the 'Wall of Fame.'

Pelican Nest SEAFOOD $$
(Map p130; ☎587-2302; www.pelican-aruba.com; Pelican Pier, Palm Beach; mains US$15-25; ☺11am-10pm Tue-Sun) Pelican Pier juts out into the Caribbean Sea, offering sea breezes, salty air and – if you time it right – gorgeous sunset views. The full menu of seafood includes such delicacies as local seafood ceviche (a specialty of the Peruvian chef) and perfectly grilled shrimp. A reservation (or an early arrival) is essential if you want to catch that sunset.

Bingo CAFE $$
(Map p130; www.bingoaruba.com; Rte 3, Noord 6b; mains US$15-25; ☺5-11pm, bar to 1am; 🎧) This popular Dutch-run cafe is both a genial bar and a good place for a casual meal. Sit at the bar and enjoy the popular pub fare such as burgers, brochette and shawarma, or opt for more ambitious meat and seafood mains. All menu items come in small and large portions – great option for light eaters and penny pinchers.

★**Madame Janette** INTERNATIONAL $$$
(Map p130; ☎587-0184; www.madamejanette.info; Cunucu Abou 37; mains US$18-28; ☺5:30-10pm Mon-Sat) An 'international restaurant with a Caribbean touch,' Madame Janette offers an enticing menu of seafood, steaks and schnitzels, such as sweet and spicy 'Big-Bang Shrimp,' a popular grouper amandine, and the decadent 'Gianni Versace' – filet mignon topped with spinach, portobello mushrooms and lobster medallions. Twinkling with lights, the lush garden makes for a delightful dining room.

Madame Janette also promises the biggest selection of craft beers in the Caribbean (which is about 70, if anybody is counting).

Wacky Wahoo SEAFOOD **$$$**
(Map p130; ☑586-7333; Palm Beach 33b, Rte 3; mains US$22-35; ⊙5:30-10pm Mon-Sat) You'll find some of the freshest seafood on the island at this crowded, colorful joint. The food comes in enormous portions – usually with a side of sass from the server. The strip-mall location is odd: don't mind the XXX shop next door.

Gasparito Restaurant CARIBBEAN **$$$**
(Map p130; ☑594-2550; www.gasparito.com; Gasparito 3, Noord; mains US$22-40; ⊙5:30-9pm Mon-Sat, by reservation Sun; ☑) If you can find it, you're in for a treat: at this family-run favorite, you'll get a taste of delectable, down-home Aurban cuisine. Old family recipes include goat stew and *keshi yena* (a melted-cheese wonder, filled with chicken or seafood). Dine inside the *cunucu* (country house) or outside on the candlelit patio. Book for one of three nightly seatings.

⬤ Drinking & Nightlife

In the high-rise resort area, nightlife centers on several high-concept malls, which have many restaurants, bars, bowling alleys, cinemas, and live entertainment and souvenir kiosks cramming the outdoor areas. By contrast, nightlife in the low-rise resort area is blissfully sedate.

Almost every high-rise resort has a casino, with slot machines taking up the most real estate.

Local Store BAR
(Map p130; ☑586-5544; www.localstorearuba. com; Palm Beach 13a, Rte 3; ⊙5-11pm Tue-Sun) Do you love a local dive bar? Then you'll love the Local Store, with its beer-keg bar stools, bare light bulbs and tin ceiling. This is the place for excellent burgers, wings and beer (with a surprising selection of North American craft brews).

❶ Getting There & Away

To reach the resort area from Oranjestad or from the airport, drive north on Lloyd G Smith Blvd (Rte 1). About 3km north of the city, turn left at JE Irausquin Blvd to reach the low-rise resorts. Or continue north to the high-rise resort area and watch for the turnoff to your destination.

Taxi fare from the airport to the low-rise and high-rise resort areas is US$22 and US$25

respectively. The resort area is also accessible by **Arubus** (p129), which runs every 10 to 15 minutes from Oranjestad.

Northwest Coast

If high-rise hotels and crowded casinos are not your thing, that's OK. Just take the coastal road north – all the way north – where it's lined with gracious homes and small but stellar beaches. This stretch is perfect for snorkeling, bodysurfing and sunset viewing, giving way eventually to a magnificent and foreboding landscape of sand dunes and wild waves.

These stunning natural surroundings are your destination for windsurfing at the Fisherman Huts, snorkeling at Malmok Beach, swimming at Arashi Beach or hiking in the California Dunes. Yet, it's only a few miles north of Palm Beach – so when you get bored or tired or hungry or thirsty, it's a quick trip to the comforts and conveniences of civilization.

⦿ Sights

Arashi Beach BEACH
Near the island's northwestern tip, this is a favorite with locals and popular with families. There's good bodysurfing, some shade and just a few rocks right offshore.

California Lighthouse LIGHTHOUSE
Up the hill from Arashi Beach, this tall sentinel is named for an old shipwreck named *California,* which is *not* the ship of the same name that stood by ineffectually while the

DON'T MISS

ANTILLA WRECK

The USS *Antilla* is a US Navy ship from WWII that was sunk near Malmok Beach, much to the delight of snorkelers and divers. The 400ft wreck is lying on its side in about 60ft of water. What's unique about the *Antilla* is that the masts, bow and forward deck are shallow enough that they are mostly visible to snorkelers.

The ship is turning into an artificial reef, so it's covered with coral and home to ample sea life. It's a cool site, but be aware that the water is often choppy and currents are strong. Do not try to swim out to the wreck; book with **Roberto's** (p131) or another boat tour.

Titanic sank (despite much local lore to the contrary). The views are great and the wind is strong, especially at the top. This is a popular spot to catch the sunset.

🏃 Activities

Fisherman Huts
WINDSURFING, KITESURFING

(Hadicurari Beach; Map p130) Hadicurari is easy to recognize from the old fishing shanties that line the shore. Sandy beach, shallow water and strong trade winds make this a prime spot for boarding. The windsurfers set up at the northern end of the beach, while kitesurfers take over the southern part. There are several operators that give lessons and rent gear, including **Aruba Active Vacations** (Map p130; ☑741-2991; www.aruba-active-vacations.com; Hadicurari Beach; rentals per hr/day US$25/60, lessons from US$50).

Malmok Beach
SNORKELING

North of Fishermen Huts, this is a narrow rocky beach that's close to the road. The coral shoreline attracts ample sea life, making it an excellent snorkel site. The water is clear and calm, with an easy entry from the beach. Many snorkel tours come here, so arrive early in the morning or late in the afternoon to avoid the crowds.

★ California Dunes
HIKING

The northern tip of Aruba is wild. Wind and waves relentlessly pound the landscape, which consists of endless sand dunes, enormous boulders and little else. A network of trails crisscrosses the area, eventually arriving at the sea. This is a ridiculously romantic sunset spot – but don't linger, as darkness comes quickly. Water and sunblock are essential during the day.

🛏 Sleeping & Eating

Practically speaking, there is no place to eat in the north of the island, which is why all hotel rooms have kitchenettes. That said, it's less than 2 miles to Palm Beach – in some cases, much less – so you don't have to cook if you don't want to.

★ Beach House Aruba
HOTEL $$

(Map p130; ☑593-3991; www.beach-house-aruba.com; Lloyd G Smith Blvd 450; garden view r US$115-160, ocean view r/ste US$220/250; ❋@☎☒) This charming collection of beach huts is the perfect antidote to the generic resorts that dominate the island. The eight apartments and surrounding gardens are littered with conch

shells, driftwood, handmade furniture and unusual artwork, creating an atmosphere of intimacy and eclecticism. A tiny plunge pool and shady gardens face the ocean, so everyone can enjoy the breeze.

Bananas Resort
APARTMENTS $$

(www.bananas-resort.com; Malmokweg 19; apt US$110-120; ❋@☎☒🚣) Here's one of the island's best bargains: the apartments are spacious and comfortable, with tile floors, wicker furniture, well-equipped kitchens and private terraces. They surround a large pool with lush gardens. Your gracious hosts (including dog and cat) are always on hand. The residential location is delightfully peaceful, but it's only a half-mile to Malmok Beach. What's not to love?

Sunset Beach Studios
HOTEL $$

(Map p130; ☑586-3940; www.aruba-sunset-beach.com; Lloyd G Smith Blvd 486; studio US$140-240; ❋@☎☒) Right across the coast road from rocky Malmok Beach, this 10-room property has an excellent location and an easygoing atmosphere. The studios are modern and comfortable, with cool tile floors, dark-wood furniture, private terraces and well-equipped kitchenettes. Swimming pool, hot tub and blooming gardens are on-site, and snorkel gear, beach chairs and barbecue grills are available for guest use.

Aruba Beach Villas
HOTEL $$

(Map p130; ☑586-1072; www.arubabeachvillas.com; Lloyd G Smith Blvd 462; r without/with ocean view from US$180/210; ⊘reception 9am-5pm; ❋@☎☒) Nicely located near Hadicurari Beach, the 31 units here are basic but bright, with kitchenettes and private patios. The ocean units have wide decks with comfy lounge chairs and lovely views. Kayaks and snorkel and windsurfing gear are available for guest use. This place is ideal for the self-sufficient traveler who prefers independence to indulgence.

OceanZ
BOUTIQUE HOTEL $$$

(www.oceanzaruba.com; Lloyd G Smith Blvd 526; r US$300-350, ste US$525-625; ❋☎☒) Venezuelan architect Óscar Enrique Bracho Malpica can take credit for this minimalist stunner facing Malmok Beach. Thirteen guest rooms exude understated luxury, with plush white linens, open-air showers and enormous windows. Rates include airport transfers and champagne on arrival, plus a gourmet breakfast served in the oceanfront dining

ARIKOK NATIONAL WILDLIFE PARK

Arid and rugged, Arikok National Wildlife Park is a vast, desolate stretch of desert wilderness, covering much of the east coast (and 20% the island's total area). It's a fascinating contrast to the heavily developed and lushly landscaped west coast. Even the ocean is different over here. Midnight blue, it smashes against the rocky shore with a fury not evident on the west coast.

As you explore the park, you'll notice the peculiar flora: the iconic and bizarrely twisted divi-divi; the *kwihi*, with its tasty sweet-sour long yellow beans; and the *hubada*, which has sharp, tough thorns. Spiky aloe plants abound, as do some 70 varieties of cactus. Also keep your eyes peeled for wild donkeys and goats, electric-blue whiptail lizards, and a few dozen species of birds.

Stop at the **visitors center** (☑585-1234; www.arubanationalpark.org; adult/child US$11/free; ⊙ticket sales 8am-4pm) to pay your park admission fee, pick up a map and browse the displays on the park's flora and fauna. There is also a small cafe on-site.

At the **Natural Pool** (Conchi) powerful wave action has worn a natural depression into the limestone coastal ridge. The surrounding rocks break the surf so – with waves crashing all around – you can take a peaceful, cooling dip. Bring your mask and snorkel and commune with the fish who are hiding out in there. You'll want water shoes for the sharp rocks.

The principal road is about 5-miles long and links the west entrance with the southern one near San Nicolas, allowing a circular tour. With the exception of the Natural Pool, it's doable in a budget rental car.

room. Service is exceptional, so prepare to be pampered.

ⓘ Getting There & Away

The best way to reach the north island from the resort area is to walk or cycle along the coastal road (it's about 2 miles from Palm Beach to Arashi Beach). **Arubus** (p129) also plies this route: line 10 goes to Malmok, line 10A all the way to Arashi and line 10B to the Fisherman Huts.

East Coast

Aruba may be small but you'll feel like you've left the island behind on its remote and wild east coast, where wind and wave add atmosphere to the desolation. Geology is the star attraction here, with fantastic cliffs, beaches and pools carved out of the rocky coastline, and mysterious rock formations studding the desert further inland. It's worth taking a day or two to marvel at the geological wonders, relax on desolate beaches, explore the remains of the gold-mining industry and discover the surprising life inhabiting the island's biggest national park.

⊙ Sights & Activities

★ **Andicuri Beach** BEACH
Cliffs, crystal blue waters and crashing waves make this beach experience different from all others on the island. This east-coast beauty is popular with surfers and boogie boarders. Otherwise, you might have the place to yourself (swimming is treacherous).

Donkey Sanctuary WILDLIFE RESERVE
(www.arubandonkey.org; Bringamosa; donations appreciated; ⊙9am-4pm) **FREE** Make an ass out of yourself doting on these winsome critters, who will follow you around for attention and snacks. Originally brought to Aruba by the Spaniards, many donkeys went rogue when they were no longer needed on farms. Unfortunately they didn't fare well with the increase in automobile traffic on the island. The donkeys at the sanctuary are well taken care of: they are named, treated, fed, protected and loved. You won't be able to resist them!

Gold Mine Ranch HORSEBACK RIDING
(☑586-4954; www.thegoldmineranch.com; Rte 6, Matividiri 60; per person US$75; ⊙tours 9am & 4pm) Explore the eastern side of Aruba on horseback, visiting the island's most remote beaches and most spectacular countryside, as well as the Natural Bridge and the Bushiribana Ruins. The two-hour tour is billed not as a trail ride, but as a 'horseback adventure.' Confident riders have the chance to run the horses on the beach and in the water.

Action Tours Aruba HORSEBACK RIDING
(Rancho Daimari; ☎ 592-7514; www.actiontours aruba.com; tours from US$105) Highly recommended for riding through the waves on the wild east coast. Departing from Rancho Daimari, the three-hour tour goes to Daimari Beach, Moro Beach and the Natural Pool. Certainly, riding a fertilizer-producing critter to these attractions is better than tearing across the landscape in a 4WD – which is also on offer.

San Nicolas

A small town near the island's southern tip, San Nicolas preserves Aruba's former rough-and-ready character long since banished from Oranjestad. The centerpiece of the town is the Valero oil refinery, which does not make for the most picturesque scenery. But this is an authentically Aruban town, where locals abound, the beaches are blissful and tourists are few.

Kitesurfers will certainly want to spend some time here, as nearby Boca Grandi offers the most consistent wind on the island.

⊙ Sights & Activities

Baby Beach BEACH
At the island's far southern tip, Baby Beach is a nice curve of sand with gentle waters. It's popular with locals, but not nearly as crowded as the west-coast beaches. The beach bar at the eastern end is a hoot for Flintstones fans. Nearby, Rodger's Beach is also quite lovely, if you don't mind the oil refinery towering above.

Boca Grandi KITESURFING
Boca Grandi is the island's top destination for experienced kitesurfers, as the winds are more consistent and the beach less crowded than at the Fishermen's Huts. As is typical of windward beaches, conditions here are hazardous for swimming. The beach is accessible from San Nicolas or Arikok.

✗ Eating & Drinking

San Nicolas is not packed with eateries, as the more touristy parts of Aruba are. But it's not difficult to find a bite to eat. In addition to the beach bars around Baby Beach, there are some worthwhile restaurants in town – not to mention Charlie's Bar which should be a required stop for all visitors.

Charlie's Bar BAR
(www.facebook.com/charliesbararuba; Zeppenfeld-straat 56; ⊙ 11:30am-7pm Mon-Sat) Charlie's is an island institution, serving up cold beers and good times to tourists and locals alike since 1941. The walls are plastered with old photos, flags, pennants, posters, newspaper clippings and license plates – recounting a colorful, characterful history of the restaurant, town and island. The food is pretty good and service is tops.

❶ Getting There & Away

At the southern tip of the island, San Nicolas is a straight shot 20km south from Oranjestad on Rte 1. **Arubus** (p129) runs regular buses into town and all the way to Baby Beach.

Spanish Lagoon & Savaneta

About 10km south of Oranjestad, Savaneta is an old Aruban town, settled in 1816 and since forgotten. Compared to the northwest coast, the beaches are not as wide and glorious; the attractions and amenities are fewer and further between; and tourists are scarce. And that's precisely what makes this area so appealing. Besides its yet to be discovered status, Savaneta boasts excellent onshore snorkeling and a few restaurants that defy comparison.

Just north of here, Spanish Lagoon is a narrow inlet fringed by mudflats and mangroves, providing an atmospheric spot for kayaking and snorkeling. Although you're unlikely to encounter one now, this was one of the few spots on the island that pirates were known to visit. What's a pirate's favorite island? Aaarrrrrrrrr-ruba.

✗ Activities & Tours

Mangel Halto SNORKELING
(Pos Chiquito) Just south of Spanish Lagoon, Mangel Halto is a small sandy beach with clear, calm waters and a few palm umbrellas for shade. The beach is unique for its cluster of mangroves at the southern end. The beachfront is protected by a reef, which makes Mangel Halto an excellent and accessible snorkel spot.

Aruba Bob's Snorkel Tours SNORKELING
(☎ 745-7459; www.arubabob.com; Savaneta 123k, Club Arias; per person US$90) Not your typical snorkel tour. Aruba Bob provides each client with an underwater scooter, which allows

you to cover a lot more ground (nearly a mile of reef in a 1½-hour tour), and also makes it easier to dive down for an up-close look at the sea creatures. Tours enter the water from the beach at Mangel Halto.

Aruba Kayak Adventure KAYAKING
(☑582-5520; www.arubakayak.com; tours from US$83; ⊗tours depart 8:30am) Both novices and pros enjoy a fascinating circuit of the mangroves and shoreline near Spanish Lagoon on the south coast. Transportation, gear and lunch are included in the tour price. Both tour options also include a snorkel stop – either at Mangel Halto or De Palm Island.

🛏 Sleeping & Eating

⭐**Club Arias** B&B $$
(☑593-3408; www.clubarias.com; Savaneta 123k; r US$135, ste US$200-250; ❄🛜🏊🅿) This small resort is a sweet retreat well off the beaten tourist track. The place has 10 enormous suites surrounding a fantastic Bedrock-style swimming pool. Other perks include outdoor showers and fabulous breakfast prepared by the famous Chef Gabriel (who also operates the pizza joint on-site). It's a 15-minute walk to the beach.

Zeerover SEAFOOD $
(☑584-8401; www.facebook.com/zeerovers; Savaneta 270a; mains US$6-15; ⊗11am-9pm Tue-Sun) Folks come from all around the island to dine at this fisherfolk cooperative by the water. The menu is short and sweet, featuring the catch of the day (whatever that may be) and shrimp – all of it fresh caught and deep fried. Wait in line to place your order, then grab a drink from the side window. Cash only.

Flying Fishbone INTERNATIONAL $$$
(☑584-2506; www.flyingfishbone.com; Savaneta 344; mains US$25-42; ⊗5-10pm) The ultimate romantic beach dining experience. Kick off your shoes and sink your toes into the sand – or dip them in the water – as you feast on fresh seafood and prime-cut steaks. The setting is spectacular, and only enhanced by sunset or starlight, but the food presentations are also inspired. Reservations are essential.

❶ Getting There & Away

Savaneta is 10km south of Oranjestad along Rte 1. **Arubus** (p129) runs north to the capital and south to San Nicolas and Baby Beach.

UNDERSTAND ARUBA

History

Caquetío History

Aruba's earliest inhabitants were the Caquetíos – a branch of the Arawak – who were hunter-gatherers (and fishers) along the northwest coast, as early as 2500 BC. Evidence of their civilization is still visible today in the piles of conch shells that were discarded around the salina near Malmok Beach. From AD 1000 to 1500, these natives settled in five different villages around the island, where they crafted pottery and practiced agriculture, growing corn and yucca. Artifacts from this so-called Ceramic Period are on display at the Aruba Archaeological Museum (p127). The cave paintings in Fontein Cave also date to this period.

Spain claimed the island in 1499, but its inhospitable arid landscape provoked little colonial enthusiasm, even earning Aruba its status as *una isla inútil*, or 'a useless island.' Eventually, most of the native population was enslaved and taken to work on the plantations in Hispaniola.

Politics: From Colony to Autonomy

In 1636, the Netherlands claimed Aruba to ameliorate its other nearby acquisitions: Curaçao (base of the West India Trading Co) and Bonaire (center of its salt industry). The colony of Aruba served a strategic purpose with the establishment of a naval base. Aruba would remain in Dutch hands for most of the next three centuries. In 1954, the islands formed the autonomous Netherlands Antilles.

The ABC islands (Aruba, Bonaire and Curaçao) have never been chums, and Aruba was able to leverage its affluence to break away from the rest of the Netherlands Antilles and become an autonomous entity within the Netherlands in 1986. Talk of achieving full independence has not become anything more than that: talk.

Economics: From Crude Oil to Suntan Oil

Prosperity came to the island in the form of the huge oil refinery built to refine

PRACTICALITIES

Newspaper The main English-language newspaper is *Aruba Today* (www.arubatoday.com), which focuses on international news.

Radio Listen to the cheery boosterisms of the *Dick Miller Show* (www.dickmiller.com) every night at 7pm on 89.9 FM.

Television Local television channels generally broadcast in Dutch and/or Papiamentu.

Smoking All restaurants, bars and casinos allow smoking, although they usually have nonsmoking sections too. Hotels usually have specific smoking and nonsmoking rooms.

Weights & Measures The metric system is used.

Venezuelan crude oil in the 1920s. This large complex occupies the southeastern end of Aruba and still dominates the blue-collar town of San Nicolas. Jobs at the plant contributed to the development of a local middle class, and the island thrived.

Mid-century, the industry began to modernize and many oil workers lost their jobs. The Dutch government established a tourist commission to promote the nascent holiday sector as an alternate source of employment. In 1959, the first multistory hotel, the Caribbean Hotel, opened on the island and tourism has been booming ever since.

Culture

The population of Aruba hovers around 100,000, which includes some 90 different nationalities. Most islanders have mixed ancestry, with Caquetío, African and European roots. About 20% of the population are Dutch and American expats.

Most Arubans speak Dutch, English and Spanish, but the native language is Papiamento, which is an Afro-Portuguese Creole. The predominant religion is Catholicism.

This melange of peoples has created a colorful fusion of cultures that blends the best of Caribbean, African and European influences. It is on full display during Carnival, a month-long, pre-Lenten celebration. Dancers don extravagant costumes; steel and brass bands play; and the city streets are alive with parades, music and lights.

Landscapes & Wildlife

Despite the lush landscaping that surrounds the resorts, Aruba has an arid climate, with less than 20 inches of rainfall per year. Its indigenous plants are hardy desert species, including some 70 kinds of cactus, as well as the ubiquitous aloe plant and the iconic divi-divi tree. Native animals are mostly reptiles, including a large variety of iguanas and lizards. Bird life abounds, including the ubiquitous banana quit and the striking troupial. Donkeys and goats run wild on the island's eastern side.

Aruba's most visible environmental woe is the puffing stacks of the oil refinery in San Nicolas. Smog also comes from the world's second-largest desalination plant, south of the airport, which roars away 24/7. (In fairness, water on the island is safe and delicious to drink.)

Meanwhile, the island has set a goal of utilizing 100% renewable energy resources by the year 2020. Toward this goal, the Vader Piet Windmill Farm was constructed on the southeast coast, with a second wind farm in the works.

The need to balance the island's healthy economy with its limited water and energy resources has been a major point of discussion on the island, as locals have pressed for growth controls. This has slowed – but certainly not stopped – the rampant development of hotels and condos on the long strip to the north.

SURVIVAL GUIDE

❶ Directory A–Z

ACCOMMODATIONS

Most of Aruba's sleeping options are among the so-called 'high-rise resorts' and the 'low-rise resorts' along Palm Bach and Eagle Beach, respectively. On a smaller scale, there's a new breed of classy boutique hotels and a few B&Bs in the less touristy areas. You'll also find more modest-priced places off the main strip, both to the east (inland) and to the north.

High-season prices usually run mid-December to mid-April. Prices do not include taxes, which are a 9.5% hotel tax and a US$3 per day environmental levy. Many resorts also tack on an 11% (or more) service fee.

CHILDREN

Aruba is an ideal destination for families, as there are sights and activities for kids of all ages. Many resorts, shopping malls and other facilities cater especially to families.

All of Aruba's west-coast beaches are protected from the strongest surf, making them ideal for kids to frolic, swim and build sand castles. There are some waves at Arashi Beach (p133), where older children will enjoy bodysurfing. Mangel Halto (p136) is a perfectly calm, protected place for snorkeling. Aruba Bob's (p136) can teach kids as young as five years old to snorkel.

Even if they are not ready for snorkeling, children can get a peek at the underwater world with **Atlantis Adventures** (Map p128; ☎ 522-4500; LG Smith Blvd 82; adult/child US$105/80; ⊙ departs 11am, noon & 1pm) and **Seaworld Explorer** (Map p130; ☎ 522-4500; www.depalmtours.com; Palm Beach; adult/child US$44/30) boat tours.

When they need a break from the beach, kids will be delighted by the Donkey Sanctuary (p135), where they can befriend these beasts of burden, and the Butterfly Farm (p130), for up-close looks at these beauties. **De Palm Island** (☎ 522-4400; www.depalmisland.com; adult/child US$100/70; ⊙ 9am-5pm) has activities of all kinds, including a zip line and a water park.

Some resorts are adults only, but most are very, very family-friendly. Swimming pools are often designed with kids in mind, and most larger resorts offer kids clubs, game rooms and other kinds of programming to keep the little ones busy. Family-style rooms and suites are common, as are kitchenettes.

Public restrooms are few and far between and practically nonexistent at beaches (with the exception of some portable toilets). Changing tables are not common. Sidewalks are super in some dedicated areas, such as the high-rise resort area (JE Irausquin Blvd) and the coastal road (Lloyd G Smith Blvd) along the northwest shore, but once you leave these specific stretches, sidewalks are practically nonexistent, making it dangerous to walk with children or push a stroller.

ELECTRICITY

110V, 60Hz; US-style two- and three-pin plugs are used.

FOOD

Eating is one of the joys of Aruba, although it is pricey. If you are on a budget, take advantage of your kitchenette. Generally, the most creative

cooking takes place outside the resort area. Look for interesting, innovative cuisine in inland Noord and in Oranjestad. That is not to say that you won't eat well on Palm Beach, which is lined with seafood restaurants, beach bars and snack shacks – some very tasty indeed.

GLBT TRAVELERS

As of 2016, the civil code allows for 'registered partnerships' for both same-sex and opposite-sex unions.

For visitors, Aruba is an open and welcoming island, no matter what your sexual orientation. Resorts and hotels welcome all comers. That said, there is not much of a GLBT 'scene' – with the exception of **Jimmy's Place** (Map p128; www.jimmysaruba.com; Windstraat 32; ⊙ 5pm-1am Tue-Thu, to 3am Fri & Sat), the one gay bar in Oranjestad.

HEALTH

Dr Horacio Oduber Hospital (☎ 527-4000; www.arubahospital.com; off Lloyd G Smith Blvd) is a large and well-equipped hospital, near the low-rise resorts. Emergency care is available.

LEGAL MATTERS

The police do not maintain a particularly visible presence in Aruba, but they are here. And they stringently enforce the island's laws:
➡ Unlike in the Netherlands proper, all drugs are illegal. Violating these laws can lead to arrest and imprisonment.
➡ Prostitution, on the other hand, is legal and regulated by the government. There is an active red light district in San Nicolas.

→ Littering laws are strictly enforced, so pick up after yourself on the beach and do not leave your cigarette butts around.

→ As always, if you get arrested, your embassy can help you contact an attorney, but not much else.

MONEY

ATMs are widely available, dispensing US dollars (US$) and Aruban florins (Afl). Credit cards are accepted at most hotels and restaurants.

Currency

Although Aruba's official currency is the florin (Afl), prices are often quoted in US dollars and you can pay for just about everything in US currency. Sometimes you will get change back in US currency, other times you will receive it in Aruban florins.

Exchange Rates

AUSTRALIA	A$1	Afl1.34
CANADA	C$	Afl1.36
CURAÇAO	Nafl	Afl1.0
EURO ZONE	€1	Afl2.0
JAPAN	¥100	Afl1.75
NEW ZEALAND	NZ$1	Afl1.30
UK	£1	Afl2.37
US	US$	Afl1.80
VENEZUELA	BsF1	Afl0.18

For current exchange rates, see www.xe.com.

Tipping

Bars & restaurants For good service, tip 15% to 20% (minus the service charge that is sometimes included in the bill).

Resorts Often include a 15% service charge on the bill. If not, tip US$1 to US$3 per day for housekeeping.

Taxis A 10% tip is usual.

Tour guides Tip US$10 for a half-day outing.

POST

Post Aruba provides reliable international service. Expect mail to reach the US or Canada in a week or two and Europe in two or three weeks. The main post office is located in downtown Oranjestad, but there is also an outlet in the Palm Beach Plaza.

PUBLIC HOLIDAYS

New Years Day January 1
GF (Betico) Croes Day January 25
Carnival Monday Monday before Ash Wednesday
National Day March 18
Good Friday Friday before Easter
Easter Monday Monday after Easter
King's Birthday April 27
Labour Day May 1
Ascension Day Sixth Thursday after Easter
Christmas Day December 25
Boxing Day December 26

TELEPHONE

Aruba's country code is ☑ 297.

To call locally, just dial the seven-digit number with no area code. To call internationally, dial the international access code ☑ 00 + country code + number.

TIME

Aruba is in the Atlantic time zone (AST), which is four hours behind Greenwich Mean Time. Daylight saving time is not observed.

TOURIST INFORMATION

Aruba Tourism Authority (☑ 800-862-7822; www.aruba.com; Lloyd G Smith Blvd 8; ⊙ 7:30am-noon & 1-4:30pm Mon-Fri) is a well-funded entity, with a comprehensive and useful website. It has an Oranjestad office, part of a trio of buildings that comprise the Aruban tourism-industrial complex, with helpful staff.

TRAVELERS WITH DISABILITIES

It's not perfect, but Aruba is a relatively friendly destination for travelers with disabilities.

Many resorts offer accessible rooms and beach *palapas* (an open-sided structure with a thatch roof). Many restaurants and casinos around the island are also wheelchair accessible.

Other services such as beach wheelchair rental and medical transportation can be arranged through specialty suppliers such as **Essential Health Supplies** (www.essentialaruba.com) and **Lite Life Medicab** (www.litelifemedicab.com).

Accessible Caribbean Vacations (www.accessiblecaribbeanvacations.com) offers sightseeing tours and beach excursions for wheelchair-bound travelers.

De Palm Tours (Map p130; ☑ 582-4400; www.depalm.com; Palm Beach; adult/child from US$40/30) has one wheelchair-accessible bus, which may be requested for airport transportation or sightseeing tours. Wheelchair-accessible sights include the Aruba Archaeological Museum (p127) and the Butterfly Farm (p130).

The downside is that there are no wheelchair-accessible boats or taxis, which makes transportation and boat tours a challenge.

In Oranjestad, the cruise-ship pier has a wheelchair ramp, as do many sidewalks around town. But once you leave Oranjestad or the immediate resort area, sidewalks are practically nonexistent.

Download Lonely Planet's free Accessible Travel guide from http://lptravel.to/Accessible Travel.

VOLUNTEERING

Aruba is one of the more prosperous islands in the Caribbean, and volunteer opportunities are scarce. That said, there are a few organizations that depend on the efforts of dedicated volunteers:

Aruba Animal Shelter (www.arubaanimalshelter.com; Plantenrust, Oranjestad) Give some love to the island's homeless dogs and cats.

Aruba Reef Care Foundation (☑ 740-0797; castroeperez@gmail.com) For 20-plus years, this group has sponsored an annual clean-up of the island's beaches and dive and snorkel sites.

Donkey Sanctuary (p135) Entirely volunteer-run sanctuary caring for donkeys without a home.

Special Olympics Aruba (www.special olympicsaruba.org) Volunteers help with coaching, event planning, publicity and more.

ⓘ Getting There & Away

You can reach Aruba by air or sea (cruise ships). Flights, cars and tours can be booked online at lonelyplanet.com/bookings.

AIR

Reina Beatrix International Airport (AUA; ☑ 524-2424; www.airportaruba.com) is a busy, modern airport with plenty of service to North and South America, as well as daily flights to Amsterdam and weekly flights to the UK. It is located just south of Oranjestad.

Regional carriers:

Aruba Airlines (www.arubaairlines.com) Daily flights to Miami, Florida, as well as Maracaibo and Valencia, Venezuela.

Avianca (www.avianca.com) Services South and Central America, via Bogotá.

Insel Air (☑ 582-1200; www.fly-inselair.com) Frequent flights to Curaçao, with connections to Bonaire.

Pawa Dominicana (www.pawadominicana.com) The Dominican airline operates two daily flights between Aruba and Curaçao.

Tiara Air (www.tiara-air.com) An on-again, off-again Aruban airline servicing Curaçao and Venezuela.

ⓘ FLYING TO THE US

Passengers flying to the US absolutely must check-in at least three hours before flight time. This is not your typical international departure. US-bound passengers clear US customs and immigration *before* leaving Aruba, so don't underestimate the time required.

Most flights to the US leave around the same time, and the US-staffed immigration facilities are often mobbed. If possible, try to avoid going on a weekend, when things are at their worst. In any case, allow plenty of time: three hours is the minimum.

SEA

The ABCs are part of cruise-ship itineraries that cover the southern Caribbean, often on longer 10-day and two-week trips. When the biggest ships are in port, it's not unusual to have more than 10,000 passengers descend on the island in a day. Boats dock at the port in the middle of Oranjestad.

ⓘ Getting Around

BUS

Arubus (p129) operates several routes running from the **main bus depot** (Map p128; Lloyd G Smith Blvd) in Oranjestad south to the airport and on to San Nicolas, with additional routes to the Fisherman Huts, Malmok Beach and Arashi Beach (all via the resort areas). Buses run every 10 to 15 minutes.

CAR & MOTORCYCLE

Driving is on the right-hand side, seat belts are required and motorcyclists must use helmets.

You'll know the tourists not only by the V-registrations of their rental cars but also by their actual use of turn signals. All the major car-rental companies have offices at the airport, including **Economy Car Rental** (☑ 583-0200; www.economyaruba.com). It's worth comparing prices with local outfits, including **Optima Rent-A-Car** (☑ 582-4828; www.optimarentacar.com; Camacuri 8; ⊙ 8am-5pm Mon & Tue, 6am-7pm Wed-Sun) and **Wheels 2 Go** (☑ 586-8632; www.wheels2goaruba.com; ⊙ 8am-5pm Mon-Sat, 10am-4pm Sun).

The Bahamas

POP 369,670 / 🗹 242

Best Places to Eat

➡ Tropic Breeze (p183)

➡ Fish Fry (p152)

➡ Café Matisse (p153)

Best Places to Sleep

➡ Pineville Motel (p179)

➡ Graycliff Hotel (p151)

➡ Hope Town Harbour Lodge (p169)

Why Go?

Renowned as a maritime playground for sun-starved Americans, this stunning string of subtropical islands is so much more than a cruise-ship stopover. Stretched between the depths of the North Atlantic and Florida's eastern coast, the Bahamas comprises more than 700 islands and 2400 cays, most uninhabited, and all fringed by spectacular coral and fathomless ocean trenches. From the grit and bustle of funky Nassau to the vast mangroves of Andros, there's an astonishing array of beaches, reefs, forests and historic towns to be discovered, all within the compass of an hour's flight.

There's sailing around the Abacos' history-filled Loyalist Cays. Partying til dawn at Paradise Island's over-the-top Atlantis resort. Diving the spooky blue holes of Andros. Kayaking the 365 Exuma Cays. Lounging on Eleuthera's pink-sand beaches. Pondering pirates in Nassau. There's a Bahamian island to match most every water- and sand-based compulsion, each framed by a backdrop of gorgeous, mesmerizing blue.

When to Go

Jun–Sep Daytime temperatures average a perfect 80°F (26°C) June to September.

mid-Dec–mid-Apr High season, when hotel prices are highest.

Mar Spring break means Nassau and Grand Bahama crawl with rum-fueled revelers.

NEW PROVIDENCE

What New Providence lacks in size, it more than makes up for in energy, attitude and devil-may-care spirit. In fact, this 34km-long powerhouse of an island is a perfect fit for the extroverted tourist with money to burn. Plummet down a 15m waterslide, puff on a hand-rolled stogie, place your bets on a high-stakes hand and carouse like a pirate into the wee hours – it's all there for the grabbing.

But all is not lost for quieter types, who can escape the beach-bar and cruise-ship scene with minimal effort. Behind Nassau's eager touristic facade are engaging museums, historic buildings and locally owned restaurants that are crowd-free and full of personality. The western end of the island is set aside as a handsome heritage park, and there are some good snorkeling and diving sites a little way offshore.

ⓘ Getting Around

BOAT

Water taxis (p191) Run between Woodes Rogers Walk in Nassau and the Paradise Island Ferry Terminal for BS$8, round-trip.

BUS

New Providence's public transport consists of private fleets of minibuses called jitneys, which follow government-prescribed routes from roughly 6am to 8pm. However, there are no fixed schedules and many routes stop running earlier, once the demand from local workers dries up. No jitneys run all the way to Paradise Island or the airport, although some routes can drop you within easy walking distance. All routes go to downtown Nassau at some point.

Destinations are clearly painted on the front of the jitneys, which can be waved down at any point. To request a stop, simply call out, 'Bus stop!' when you want to get off, paying the driver as you leave. Fares start at BS$1.25 for downtown Nassau and rise to BS$2.50 for the airport. Some useful routes:

10 & 10A Running through Cable Beach, Sandyport Bay and Lyford Cay, this is the busiest route, and the cheapest way to get a tour of the island.

1, 7 & 7A Paradise Island bridges.

12b Love Beach and the airport.

CAR & SCOOTER

You don't need a car to explore downtown Nassau or to get to the beaches, but you will if you intend to explore New Providence (taxi fares would quickly outweigh rental costs). The major car-rental companies have booths at the airport; local companies rent more cheaply. Ask your hotel to recommend a company or try **Virgo Car Rental** (☑ airport 242-377-1275, main office 242-393-7900; www.virgocarrental.com; Kemp Rd, Nassau; ☺ 9am-5pm).

Scooters are widely available for around BS$75 per day, and can be found outside most major hotels or at the Prince George Wharf. Bear in mind that New Providence roads can be dangerous, especially in busy Nassau.

TAXI

Taxis can be hailed on any busy road (they'll often hail you, if you seem in need of transport) and await fares on Woodes Rodgers Walk, near the cruise-ship dock. If you need to call one, try ☑ 242-323-7900 or ☑ 242-323-4323.

Nassau

Nassau is the gritty, vivacious alter ego to the relaxed character of most of the Bahamas. The country's only city, it teems with haring jitneys, bawling straw-goods vendors, rum-happy locals and endless waves of cruise-ship passengers.

It's appropriate that Nassau has some hustle to it – it's been a redoubt of hustlers for centuries. From the 18th-century pirates who blew their doubloons on women and wine to the Confederate steamers smuggling cargo past the Union blockade during the American Civil War, the city has long sheltered daring dodgers on the make. The make-a-buck spirit of this global tax haven animates the duty-free shops and cigar salesmen of Bay St, while the historic wealth of the ruling classes finds tangible expression in grand, Georgian government buildings and homes. Whether you come to shop, eat, party or sightsee, Nassau is *the* place for a dose of urban excitement.

◉ Sights

Downtown Nassau and Bay St largely consist of modern commercial buildings dedicated to the cruise-ship market, although some historic buildings remain. Other sights are dotted throughout Nassau, in walkable proximity to each other, especially to the landward side of Bay St.

Junkanoo Beach   BEACH
(Map p152) Between downtown Nassau and Araway Cay, Junkanoo is popular with locals and visitors alike, with beach-shack bars, volleyball nets, sky-juice vendors and friendly Bahamians in ample supply.

The Bahamas Highlights

1 Diving (p157)
Plunging into one of the world's great underwater playgrounds.

2 Fish Fry (p152)
Chowing down at Nassau's premiere spot for conch salad, blackened grouper and sky-juice-fueled parties.

3 Bimini Road (p172) Snorkeling this uncannily geometric undersea highway.

4 RumBahamas (p151) Getting nice and easy at this annual festival of cane spirit, food and culture.

5 Harbour Island (p173) Losing yourself in the ramshackle streets and top-drawer resorts of this perfect Bahamian microcosm.

6 Elbow Cay (p167) Slipping into a lower gear in this impossibly photogenic redoubt of Bahamian Loyalist culture.

7 Lucayan National Park (p165) 'Hunting' hummingbirds through Grand Bahama's lush forests.

8 Sailing the Exuma Cays (p181) Setting sail for these tiny paradises.

9 Blue Holes National Park (p179) Dodging the mythical chickcharnies in Andros's vast virgin Caribbean pine forest.

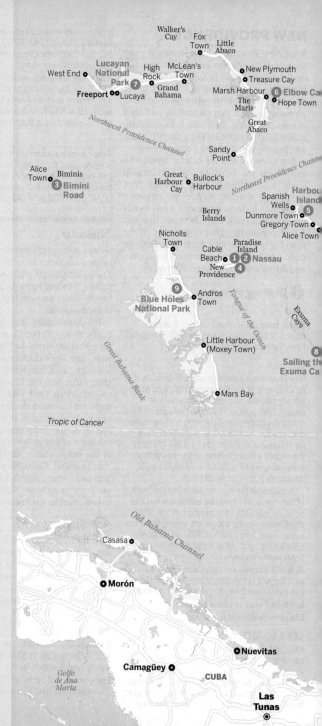

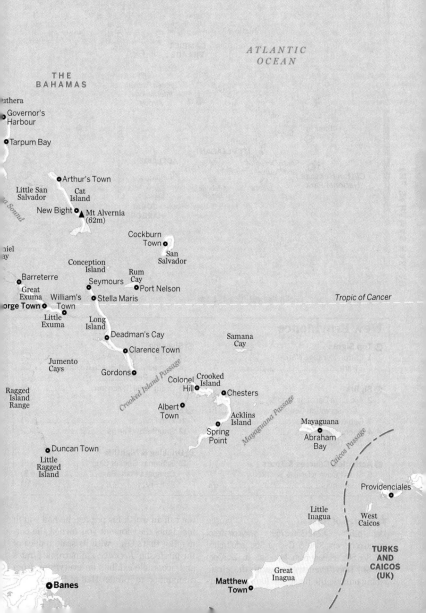

New Providence

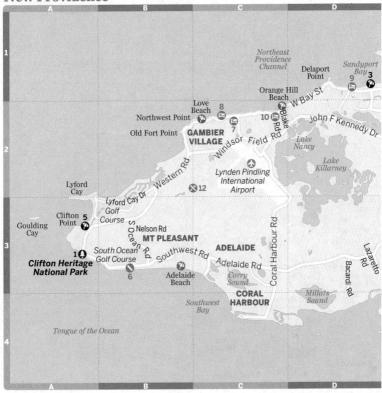

New Providence

★ **Pirates of Nassau** MUSEUM
(Map p152; ☏242-356-3759; www.piratesof
nassau.com; cnr King & George Sts; adult/child
BS$13/6.50; ☺9am-6pm Mon-Sat, to 12:30pm
Sun; ⓘ) Don't even try to ignore the pirate
pacing outside the museum: like any seafaring ruffian worth his peg leg, he had you in
his sights the moment you turned the corner. But that's OK – with its scale replica of
the pirate ship *Revenge,* animatronic pirates
and accessible exhibits on everything from
marooning to pirate Hall-of-Famers, this

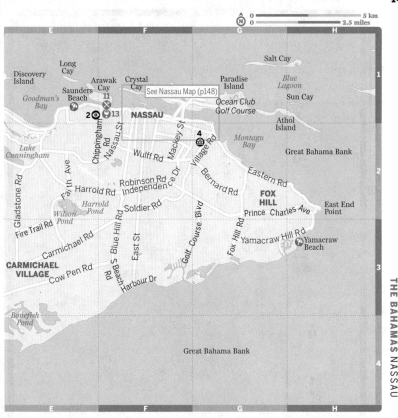

0 — 5 km
0 — 2.5 miles

Salt Cay
Long Cay
Discovery Island
Arawak Cay
Crystal Cay
Paradise Island
Blue Lagoon
Goodman's Bay
Saunders Beach
11
See Nassau Map (p148)
Sun Cay
Ocean Club Golf Course
2 13
NASSAU
Athol Island
Lake Cunningham
Chippingham Rd
Nassau St
Wulff Rd
Mackey St
4
Village Rd
Montagu Bay
Great Bahama Bank
Faith Ave
Robinson Rd
Independence Dr
Bernard Rd
Eastern Rd
Gladstone Rd
Harrold Rd
Harrold Pond
Soldier Rd
FOX HILL
East End Point
Wilson Pond
Blue Hill Rd
East St
Golf Course Blvd
Prince Charles Ave
Fire Trail Rd
S Beach Rd
Fox Hill Rd
Yamacraw Hill Rd
Carmichael Rd
Yamacraw Beach
CARMICHAEL VILLAGE
Cow Pen Rd
Harbour Dr
Bonefish Pond
Great Bahama Bank

THE BAHAMAS NASSAU

museum provides the right mix of entertainment and history for kids and parents alike. There's a great gift shop, Plunder (p154), next door.

★ **National Art Gallery of the Bahamas** MUSEUM

(Map p152; ☑242-358-5800; www.nagb.org.bs; cnr West & West Hill Sts; adult/child BS$5/free; ⊙10am-4pm Tue-Sat, from noon Sun) If you're jangled by the chaos of Bay St, you'll find a welcome oasis inside the stately 1860s-era Villa Doyle: a grand art museum that's one of the gems in the Bahamian crown. The permanent collection focuses on modern and contemporary Bahamian artists, from renowned sculptor Antonius Roberts to folk painter Wellington Bridgewater. There are also pieces by artists of the wider Caribbean, and temporary exhibits on ecological, cultural and historical themes relevant to the islands.

★ **Graycliff Cigar Co** FACTORY

(Map p152; ☑242-302-9150; www.graycliff.com; Graycliff Hotel & Restaurant, West Hill St; ⊙9am-5pm) **FREE** Wandering into this cigar factory is like falling into 1920s Cuba. In a narrow, smoke-yellowed room with old-fashioned mosaic floors, up to 16 *torcedores* (cigar rollers) are busy at work, their fingers a blur as they roll hand-dried tobacco leaves into premium stogies. Cigar-rolling lessons (BS$75) and demonstrations paired with rum tastings (BS$150) are available Monday to Saturday.

John Watling's Distillery DISTILLERY

(Map p152; ☑242-322-2811; www.johnwatlings. com; 17 Delancy St; ⊙10am-6pm; P☎) Watling's, new to the Bahamian rum-distilling game, has draped itself in the antique vestments of the beautifully restored 18th-century Buena Vista Estate, its extensive tiki-lit gardens patrolled by fluffy-legged

THE BAHAMAS NASSAU

Nassau

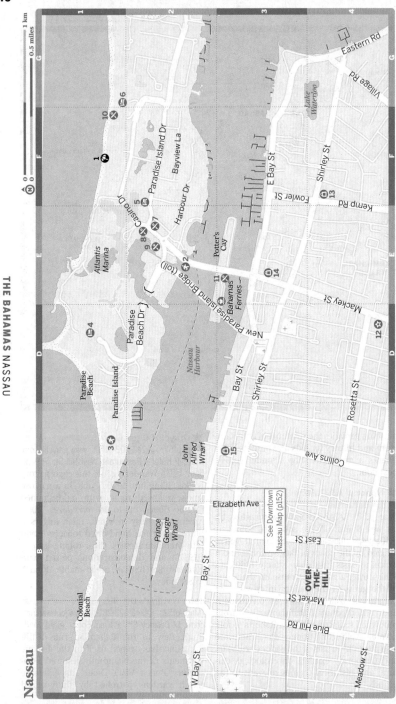

Nassau

bantams and staff in colonial-era costumes. You can take a free 15-minute tour of the house and distillery – named for a 17th-century pirate – or head straight to the stylish bar. Locals gather here on Friday nights, when happy hour runs to 9pm, and rum cocktails go for BS$15.

Government House
NOTABLE BUILDING

(Map p152; ☑242-322-1875; Duke St; ⊙9am-5pm Mon-Fri) This splendid Georgian mansion, residence of the governor-general, tops Mount Fitzwilliam (central Nassau's low hill) like a particularly festive pink cake. Sitting on the site of a predecessor built in 1737, the 1803 structure was badly damaged by a hurricane in 1929, leading to extensive repairs and remodeling (1932), and lavish redecoration during the Duke of Windsor's time as governor (1940–45). Below, the statue of Christopher Columbus has maintained a jaunty pose on the steps overlooking Duke St since 1830.

Fort Fincastle & the Queen's Staircase
FORT

(Map p152; ☑242-322-7500; Elizabeth Ave; BS$1; ⊙8am-4pm) Shaped like a digital-map pinpoint, this hilltop fort was built by Lord Dunmore in 1793 to guard the harbor against invaders. Never used, it was eventually converted into a lighthouse. The fort itself is not particularly fascinating, but it's worth the trip for the sweeping panoramic views from the top. Leading up is the Queen's Staircase: built from solid limestone carved by slaves, it's one of the island's most enduring landmarks.

Ardastra Gardens, Zoo & Conservation Center
GARDENS

(☑242-323-5806; www.ardastra.com; Chippingham Rd; adult/child/under 4yr BS$18/9/free; ⊙9am-5pm, last admission 4pm; ⊞) This lush 4 acre tropical garden contains a small zoo, home to around 180 animals of 60 different species. Crowd-pleasers include the Madagascan lemurs and three endangered Bahamian boa constrictors, but the undisputed highlight is the small regiment of marching West Indian flamingos, which strut their stuff at 10:30am, 2:15pm and 4pm daily. Pint-sized visitors will also thrill at feeding the lory parrots by hand, even as they're used for convenient perches.

Doongalik Studios
GALLERY

(☑242-394-1886; www.doongalik.com; 18 Village Rd; ⊙10am-4pm Mon-Wed, 9am-1pm Sat) Offering an eclectic window into modern Bahamian art, Doongalik runs exhibitions on solo artists' work, and everything from quilts to island life. Book launches, musical performances and other events are also frequent. It's set in the lovely two-storied building and the surrounding gardens, and there's a farmers market every Saturday morning.

Cable Beach
BEACH

New Providence's biggest and most popular beach is three curving miles of white sand and sparkling turquoise sea, just west of downtown Nassau. Named for the undersea telegraphic cable that came ashore here in 1892, Cable Beach is lined with resorts, hotels and casinos. It's often packed with vacationing families, spring breakers, water-sports operators and roving souvenir vendors. If you want a beach chair, pay a day-use fee at one of the hotels for use of its facilities.

🏃 Activities & Tours

Tru Bahamian Food Tours   FOOD
(Map p152; ☑242-601-1725; www.trubahamian foodtours.com; cnr George & Bay Sts; adult/child BS\$75/53; ☺8am-9pm Mon-Sat, to 6pm Sun) This outfit's Bites of Nassau tour is a 3½-hour excursion around the best of Bahamian food, stopping off at six local kitchens to meet the chefs and sample the good stuff. Tours meet near George and Bay Sts, or you can book a customized cooking class.

Boating

There's a jaunt for every type of adventurer in New Providence. Dozens of operators run fishing charters, island excursions, party boats and sunset cruises. Most depart from the Woodes Rogers Walk area or the Paradise Island Ferry Terminal, between the Paradise Island bridges.

Powerboat Adventures   BOATING
(Map p148; ☑242-363-1466; www.powerboat adventures.com; Atlantic Bridge; adult/child BS\$214/151; 🚸) Flying over the brine in a jet-powered boat must be one of the most exciting ways to reach the remote Exuma Cays. Powerboat trips leave at 9am from the Paradise Island Ferry Terminal, returning at 5pm after making landfall at privately owned Ship Channel Cay, with snorkeling, stingray feeding, shark-spotting and lunch provided along the way.

Seaworld Explorer   BOATING
(Map p152; ☑242-356-2548; www.seaworldtours.com; Bay St; adult/child BS\$45/25; 🚸) A connecting boat whisks passengers out to this window-lined, 45-passenger semisub-

---

OFF THE BEATEN TRACK

BIRDING IN THE BAHAMAS

A lovely antidote to the cruise ships and beach vendors, **Bahamas Outdoors** (Map p152; ☑242-457-0329; www. bahamasoutdoors.com) takes birding trips around New Providence (BS\$129/79 per day/half-day), or to Andros, Eleuthera or Abaco by arrangement. Binoculars are provided, as is a picnic lunch (on full-day tours), and nature tours are also offered. Pick-up is at most hotels or the cruise-ship dock.

---

marine beyond Nassau Harbour. From there it takes a diverting 90-minute excursion through the fish-filled coral reefs of the **Sea Gardens Marine Park**, off the north shore of Paradise Island.

Fishing

Nassau is a great base for fishing, with superb deepwater sites just 20 minutes away. Game species include blue marlin, sailfish, yellowfin tuna, mahi-mahi and wahoo. Charters can be arranged at most major hotels or by calling a charter company, which typically charge two to six people BS\$500 to BS\$700 per half-day, or BS\$900 to BS\$1400 per full day.

★Chubasco Charters   FISHING
(Map p148; ☑242-324-3474; www.chubasco charters.com; Paradise Island Ferry Terminal; half-/full-day charter from BS\$580/1160; ☺departures 8am & 1pm) Chubasco swaggeringly offers a 'no splash, no cash' guarantee: if you book a full-day fishing charter and don't catch a thing, your trip is free. Chubasco runs four boats, from 11m to 14.5m long, taking its fleet into the deep waters just 15 to 30 minutes out of Nassau Harbour to chase down tuna, marlin, wahoo and mahi-mahi.

Born Free Charter Service   FISHING
(Map p152; ☑242-393-4144; www.bornfreefish ing.com; ☺departures 8am & 1pm) Captain Pinder has uncanny knowledge of Bahamian waters, taking anglers to where the big game – sailfish, tuna, marlin – are most likely to bite. Chartering one of his five vessels, together with all that know-how, will set you back at least BS\$650/1300 (half-/full day). Pick-ups are from behind the Straw Market or by the toll booth on Paradise Island.

Hunter Charters   FISHING
(☑242-364-1546; www.huntercharters.com; ☺7am-9pm) With a five-strong fleet ranging from a 5.5-meter fishing boat to a 13-meter Hatteras, Hunter is well equipped for reef and deep-sea fishing. Half-day charters range from BS\$490 to BS\$730; call to arrange pick-up.

Diving & Snorkeling
Flying Cloud Catamaran Cruises & Snorkeling Tours   CRUISE
(Map p148; ☑242-394-5067; www.flyingcloud. info) These fast-flying 17-meter catamarans whisk you away for half- and full-day snorkel adventures (BS\$70/95), or for sunset dinner cruises (BS\$70). Departures are from the

NASSAU FOR CHILDREN

From pirate-history museums to big days out on the water, there's plenty to keep kids occupied in Nassau. It's also one of the best places in the country for parents of small children: you're more likely to find changing facilities (in modern restaurants), pharmacies, supermarkets and stroller-friendly sidewalks here than anywhere else. As for distractions, try one (or all) of these:

➡ Ride a horse-drawn surrey through downtown.

➡ Salute a marching flamingo, yawn at a dozing iguana, cluck at a Bahama parrot and smile at a big cat at **Ardastra Gardens, Zoo & Conservation Center** (p149).

➡ Walk past a bunch of wicked buccaneers and their pirate ship at the brilliant interactive **Pirates of Nassau museum** (p146).

➡ Ride in a glass-hulled semisubmarine with **Seaworld Ex** (p150)plorer.

➡ Get wet. **Cable Beach** (p149) is lined with operators offering water-sports activities and equipment for hire. Beachside resorts usually have their own facilities, which are open to nonguests upon the purchase of a day ticket.

Paradise Island ferry terminal, and free transport can be provided to and from your hotel.

🎉 Festivals & Events

RumBahamas   FOOD & DRINK
(www.festivalrumbahamas.com; Fort Charlotte, West Bay St; ⊙late Feb) Rum producers from across the Caribbean and Latin America descend on Nassau each February for this three-day celebration of food, culture and cane spirit. Held behind the doughty ramparts of 18th-century Fort Charlotte, it features rum tastings and classes, competitive cocktail mixing, live music, fire dancing, a Junkanoo party and, naturally, Bahamian food aplenty.

🛏 Sleeping

El Greco   HOTEL $
(Map p152; ☑242-325-1121; West Bay St; d/ste BS$120/190; ❄🛜🏊) Central location and price are the chief advantages of this 'Spanish-style' hotel, in which some of the (interior) rooms can be a bit gloomy. Ask for a sunny end room with gracefully arched entranceways and a view over the bougainvillea-draped balconies, and you'll be happy with your bargain.

Orange Hill Beach Inn   GUESTHOUSE $$
(☑242-327-7157; www.orangehill.com; West Bay St; d/tr BS$170/181; ❄🛜🏊) Divers and international backpackers adore this homey hillside guesthouse, with its Fawlty Towers sign and just-like-family staff. The sprawling property has a wide range of rooms, from basic motel units (upper rooms are nicer) to full apartments. At night, everyone congregates

in the funky main house, with its self-serve bar and shelves full of used books. Close to the airport.

⭐**Graycliff Hotel**   BOUTIQUE HOTEL $$$
(Map p152; ☑242-302-9150; www.graycliff.com; West Hill St; r from BS$475; ❄🛜🏊) Nassau's most characterful hotel is this slightly spooky 260-year-old home, built by a wealthy pirate. Hidden above town on West Hill St, the Georgian main house is filled with high-ceilinged rooms, musty antiques, mismatched oriental rugs and intriguing nooks and corners begging further exploration. Huge gardenside cottages, arrayed around an extraordinary Spanish-tiled pool, are equally alluring.

The astonishing wine cellar (250,000-plus bottles!) and a library redolent of the rich aroma of Cuban cigars have kept guests such as Winston Churchill and The Beatles happy. There are two main buildings on the grounds: one is the hotel itself, which includes the Graycliff Restaurant, and the other contains the steakhouse Humidor Churrascaria and the Graycliff Cigar Co.

British Colonial Hilton   HOTEL $$$
(Map p152; ☑242-322-3301; www.hiltoncaribbean.com; 1 Bay St; d from BS$367; ❄🛜🏊) Built in 1922, this seven-story grand dame is a downtown Nassau institution. The hotel was a location for two James Bond movies, and it's easy to see why – with its gleaming marble lobby, private beach and sleek graphite-and-mahogany common spaces, it has the timeless international elegance of 007 himself.

Downtown Nassau

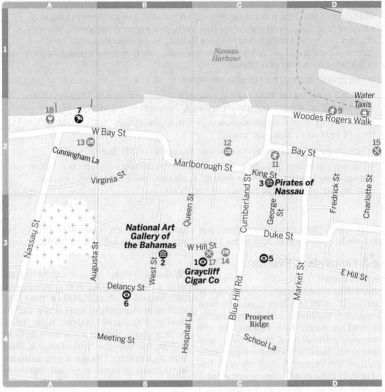

Marley Resort
BOUTIQUE HOTEL **$$$**
(☎242-702-2800; www.marleyresort.com; West Bay St, Cable Beach; ste from BS$538; ❋🖥🏊) Formerly the governor's house, then Bob Marley's Bahamian bolt hole, this shaded coastal retreat is now a boutique hotel, run by Rita Marley and her daughters. Rooms, each named after a Marley song, are spare-no-expense luxurious, with hand-carved mahogany furniture, rich linens and original Africana art. There's also the full range of treatments at the 'Natural Mystic' Spa.

✖ Eating

★ Fish Fry
BAHAMIAN **$**
(☎242-425-7275; Arawak Cay, off West Bay St; mains BS$12-22; ⏱7am-midnight) The colorful village of conch stands, bars, jerk joints and seafood restaurants at Arawak Cay, known collectively as the 'Fish Fry', is one of Nassau's great experiences. Come for conch salad, fried chicken wings, fritters, black-ened snapper, 'sky juice' (a high-octane libation of coconut water and gin), rake 'n' scrape bands, reggae DJs, Junkanoo dances and friendly chatter.

Potter's Cay
BAHAMIAN **$**
(Map p148; ☎242-466-6895; East Bay St; mains BS$12-15; ⏱6am-11pm) Less popular than the Fish Fry, but just as good for a conch salad or sheep's-tongue souse, this lively market sits beneath the Paradise Island Exit Bridge. Fishing boats from the Out Islands arrive daily, carrying the sea's harvest, as well as fruit, herbs, pepper sauces and vegetables.

Athena Cafe
GREEK **$$**
(Map p152; ☎242-326-1296; cnr Bay & Charlotte Sts; mains BS$28-32; ⏱8:30am-6pm Mon-Sat, to 4pm Sun) This family-run Greek taverna above a Bay St jewelry store does very solid renditions of the Hellenic classics, such as dolmades, grilled seafood, moussaka and gyro (the pork is particularly good). It can be

THE BAHAMAS NASSAU

very pleasant to eat on the veranda, watching the duty-free shoppers mill around below.

★ **Café Matisse**   ITALIAN $$$
(Map p152; ☑ 242-356-7012; www.cafe-matisse.com; Bank Lane; mains BS$38-42; ☺noon-3pm & 6-10pm Tue-Sat; 🛜) Hidden among downtown Nassau's historic government buildings, this dignified Italian is a delightful alternative to the nearby cruise-ship and duty-free scene. Grab a patio table in good weather and let professional, crisp-shirted waiters serve you rack of wild boar with red-wine sauce, oregano-grilled mahi-mahi or orecchiette with broccoli rabe (rapini), anchovies and capers. If you don't feel like wine, try the ginger lemonade.

Graycliff Restaurant   INTERNATIONAL $$$
(Map p152; ☑ 242-302-9150; www.graycliff.com; Graycliff Hotel, West Hill St; mains BS$45-57; ☺noon-2:30pm Mon-Fri, 6:30-10:30pm daily; 🛜) Make like a colonial-era dignitary at this atmospheric fine-diner in the 18th-century Graycliff Hotel (p151). The predominantly European menu deploys a lot of imported ingredients (French chèvre, Russian caviar) but also makes use of Bahamian lobster and other local treasures. The wine cellar is legendary, with precious vintages such as an 1865 Château Lafite among its 250,000 bottles.

Humidor Churrascaria   BRAZILIAN $$$
(Map p152; ☑ 242-302-9150; www.graycliff.com; Graycliff Hotel, West Hill St; prix fixe BS$48; ☺6:30-10:30pm Mon-Sat; 🛜) Machismo hangs in the smoky air at this Brazilian steakhouse attached to the Graycliff Hotel complex. Hunks of dripping pork loin, lamb, beef and spicy sausages are carved tableside from wicked-looking metal skewers, and the prix fixe includes a salad bar stuffed with seafood appetizers, veggies and pastas. Conclude with a fine stogie, hand-rolled at the on-site Graycliff Cigar Co (p147).

🍷 Drinking & Nightlife

Nassau is the undisputed nightlife capital of the Bahamas. Downtown Nassau's bars cater mainly to tourists, but the farther you move from the cruise-ship dock toward Junkanoo Beach and Arawak Cay (for instance), the more local places and sociable Bahamians you'll find.

★ Khyla's Island Philosophy   BAR
(Map p152; ☑ 242-544-0721; Junkanoo Beach, West Bay Dr; ⊕ 11am-6pm) This tiny charismatic beach bar exemplifies all that is convivial and distinctive about Nassau, with an ebullient proprietress (Khyla), ever-welcoming locals and good tunes. Sadly gutted by fire in 2016, Island Philosophy still opened the next day, dispensing beers and basic mixes along with life wisdom from its small beachside deck. Try the signature ginger switcher (BS$10).

★ Fish Fry   BAR
(West Bay St; ⊕ 5pm-midnight) The unmissable nightly Fish Fry is not the only reason to spend a night or two in Arawak Cay. Sky-juice trailers, wooden beer shacks and more substantial establishments keep everyone oiled and easy, as multiple DJs compete for the most bowel-shuddering bass line. Many of the Fish Fry joints are restaurants that serve drinks; others are bars with food.

Bahamas Cricket Club   PUB
(☑ 242-326-4720; http://bahamascricket.com; West Bay St; ⊕ 8am-11pm) Ravaged by Hurricane Matthew in 2016, this historic cricket pavilion-pub immediately got back on its feet, a sign of how much it means to those who water and wield the willow here. Welcoming visitors with warmth and interest, its a great place to eat Bahamian (or British) food and knock back a beer while watching a game from the 1st floor veranda.

Compass Point Bar   BAR
(www.compasspointbeachresort.com; Compass Point Beach Resort, West Bay St; ⊕ 8am-midnight; 🛜) A stylish crowd sips potent cocktails on the pool deck with the deep blue sea as a backdrop. There's live music on Tuesday, Thursday and Saturday nights, from 10pm.

☆ Entertainment

Dundas Centre for the Performing Arts   PERFORMING ARTS
(Map p148; ☑ 242-393-3728; 103 Mackey St; ⊕ office 10am-4pm Mon-Fri) Comedy, drama, dance, live music, kids' shows, spoken word: the Dundas Centre is a haven for many forms of expression under-represented in the Bahamas. Ticket prices depend on the show, but generally start at around BS$10; check their Facebook page for what's coming up.

🛍 Shopping

Visitors flock to Bay St for duty-free liquor, jewelry, perfume and cigars, but savings are not guaranteed; check prices at home before your trip. Most stores close at night and on Sunday, even when the cruise ships are in port. Bahamian-made products are sold at booths throughout Festival Place at Prince George Wharf.

Bahama Handprints   CLOTHING
(Map p148; ☑ 242-394-4111; www.bahamahandprints.com; Island Traders' Bldg, Ernest St; ⊕ 10am-4pm Mon-Fri, 9am-2pm Sat) Actually on Ernest St, just behind the main Island Traders' Building, this boutique and factory outlet sells lovely, handmade interior-design fabric, clothes, accessories and furnishings. It's possible to tour the factory by arrangement.

Bahama Art & Handicraft   ARTS & CRAFTS
(Map p148; ☑ 242-394-7892; East Shirley St; ⊕ 8:30am-4:30pm Tue-Sat) If you're interested in picking up traditional Bahamian handicrafts from around the islands, this shop makes it easy. The paintings, jewelry, driftwood sculptures, handmade baskets and other pieces are the work of many different producers from across the archipelago.

Plunder!   GIFTS & SOUVENIRS
(Map p152; ☑ 242-356-3759; www.piratesofnassau.com; cnr King & George Sts; ⊕ 9am-6pm Mon-Sat, to 12:30pm Sun) Eye patches, black flags, pirate tees and a good selection of pirate lit for buccaneering bookworms are to be had for the taking in this gift shop within the Pirates of Nassau (p146) museum.

Bahamas Rum Cake Factory   FOOD
(Map p148; ☑ 242-328-3750; https://thebahamasrumcakefactory.com; 602 East Bay St; ⊕ 10am-5pm Mon-Sat, to 3pm Sun) Thoroughly marinated in Ole Nassau Bahamian rum, these buttery little bundt cakes sell for BS$6.50, and up to about BS$18 for large ones in decorative tins. Pineapple, pecan and pina colada vie with the original, but they're all dependably moist, delicious and a tiny bit boozy.

CAT ISLAND

The heart of traditional Bahamian culture still beats on Cat Island, one of the islands least touched by tourism. Obeah and bush medicine are still practiced. Cat has several interesting historic sites, including plantation ruins and the Mt Alvernia Hermitage.

The island's second-largest settlement is Arthur's Town, 48km north of New Bight, the governmental administrative center. The hamlet's main claim to fame is that it was the boyhood home of Sir Sidney Poitier, the Academy Award–winning actor. Sadly, his childhood home is now derelict.

On top of Mt Alvernia (62m), or Como Hill as it is called by locals, is a blanched-stone church, built by the hermit Father Jerome, with a bell tower that looks like something Merlin might have conjured up in the days of King Arthur. You can enter the small chapel, tiny cloister and a guest cell the size of a large kennel. It's reached by a rock staircase hewn into the side of the hill. From the top, there's a spiritually reviving 360-degree view. Try to make it at sunrise or sunset. Although it's close to Eleuthera, you may have to take the mail boat or a **Southern Air** (p178) charter from Nassau to get here.

ⓘ Information

INTERNET ACCESS

There's free wi-fi along downtown Woodes Rogers Walk.

MEDICAL SERVICES

Pharmacies can be found in all shopping malls, but mainly keep standard shop hours. For medical attention, visit **Princess Margaret Hospital** (☏ 242-322-2861; www.pmh.phabahamas.org; Shirley St; ⊘ emergencies 24hr) or the **Doctor's Hospital** (☏ 242-302-4600; www.doctorshosp.com; 1 Collins Ave; ⊘ emergencies 24hr).

MONEY

Banks are clustered around Rawson Sq and Bay St; ATMs dispensing US and Bahamian dollars are found throughout Nassau and at banks such as the **Royal Bank of Canada** and **Scotiabank**.

POST

Main **post office** (Map p152; ☏ 242-556-6966; East Hill St; ⊘ 8:30am-5:30pm Mon-Fri).

TOURIST INFORMATION

Tourist Office (Map p152; ☏ 242-323-3182, 242-322-7680; www.bahamas.com; Welcome Centre, Festival Pl, Prince George Wharf; ⊘ 8am-11pm)

ⓘ Getting There & Away

Taxis to and from the airport and downtown Nassau cost BS$30 plus tip. The 12b jitney, running along Bay St between downtown Nassau and Lyford Cay, can drop you just outside the airport, on JFK Boulevard, for BS$2.50 between 7am and 3pm to 4pm. **Ferries** (Map p148; ☏ 242-323-2166, 242-394-9700; http://bahamasferries.com) embark/disembark at Potter's Cay Dock, under the bridges linking Paradise Island with downtown Nassau.

ⓘ Getting Around

Minibuses, known locally as 'jitneys,' are Nassau's only public transport. The route number and principal stops are painted on the front of each bus, and a single fare within Nassau, paid as you get off, is only BS$1.25 (BS$2 will get you to Love Beach, or BS$2.50 to just outside the airport). To catch one, flag it down from the roadside, then simply sing out 'bus stop' when you want to get off.

Water taxis (p191) connect Prince George Wharf and Paradise Island every 30 minutes from 8am to 6pm. One-way/return fares are BS$4/8.

Paradise Island

Privileged Paradise Island – linked to Nassau by two great arcs that may as well be bridges to another world – is unashamedly built for profit and pleasure. Its landscape is mostly artificial: vast hotels straight from the covers of fantasy paperbacks, hangar-sized casinos, ersatz 'villages' in which to shop and eat, and the lushest lawns you'll see anywhere in the Bahamas.

Before the 1960s, PI was 'Hog Island' – flat and undistinguished. A&P supermarket heir Huntington Hartford II renamed it in 1959, resolving to build the next Monte Carlo here. He clearly had some success: over the years it became a bolt-hole for Howard Hughes, Richard Nixon and the deposed shah of Iran. But it was the 1998 opening of the vast resort, casino and shopping complex Atlantis that did the most to realize Hartford's dream. It's now synonymous with Bahamian luxury for families, honeymooners, high-stakes gamblers and bachelor partiers.

⊙ Sights

Atlantis' central hotel, the Royal Towers, is a sight in and of itself, with shops, a casino and faux archaeological excavation and giant aquarium windows in its lower lobby. The adjacent Marina Village is a popular shopping and eating destination.

Cabbage Beach   BEACH
(Map p148) While the west end of this stretch of sand – one of the more popular in New Providence – is obscured by the Atlantis resort, there is a public access to the east. When the Atlantic isn't kicking up a fuss, it can be a pleasant place to swim, snorkel or just stretch out. Water sports including banana boats, Jet-Ski rental, parasailing and more are available, but you must be careful of the strong undercurrents.

🏃 Activities & Tours

★ Aquaventure Water Park   WATER PARK
(Map p148; ☑ 242-363-3000; www.atlantis bahamas.com; Suite 42, 1 Casino Dr, Atlantis Resort; adult/child/hotel guests BS$135/99/free; ⊘ 9am-5pm) Kids and adults alike will hyperventilate at the sight of this astonishing 141-acre water park, an Indiana Jones–style vision of the ruins of the Lost City of Atlantis. The vast park – one of the largest in the hemisphere – is centered on a five-story Mayan temple, with multiple waterslides shooting guests into a variety of grottoes and caves.

Discover Atlantis Tour   AQUARIUM
(Map p148; ☑ 242-363-3000; www.atlantis bahamas.com; Atlantis, 1 Casino Dr; adult/child/ hotel guest BS$49/35/free; ⊘ 9am-5pm; 🖲) Strolling through a glass tunnel while sharks glide overhead is, simply put, awesome. This thrill is found in the Predator's Lagoon, one of the exhibits on this walking tour of Atlantis' aquariums and faux-archaeological sites. Look for manta rays, spiny lobsters, striped Nemos, translucent jellyfish and thousands of other sea creatures in the underground Great Hall of Waters.

Sivananda Yoga Ashram   YOGA
(Map p148; ☑ 242-363-2902; www.sivananda. org; programs per day incl accommodation BS$109-206) The backyard of the Atlantis megaresort is perhaps not the place you'd expect to find a yoga ashram. On a heavily forested 5½-acre patch of Paradise Island, Sivananda Yoga Ashram has been attracting both hardcore yoga devotees and spandex-clad chippers since 1967. Expect programs such as 'Full Lotus Detox and Cellular Regeneration' and 'You Are the Universe'.

🛏 Sleeping

The number of visitors that flock to the big resorts of Paradise Island easily outweighs those staying in Nassau proper. But staying within PI's magic bubble comes at a price – rooms are at least 50% more here than in downtown Nassau or Cable Beach.

Comfort Suites   HOTEL $$
(Map p148; ☑ 242-363-3680; www.comfort suitespi.com; Paradise Island Dr; d from $350; ❄ 🛜 🌊) Though this above-average hotel is not part of Atlantis, guests here get full pool and water-park privileges at the neighboring megaresort. The 200-plus rooms are clean and modern, with bright tropical appeal, and the on-site restaurant (Crusoe's) and bar (Bamboo Lounge) are good for lazy days.

★ Atlantis   RESORT $$$
(Map p148; ☑ 242-363-3000; www.atlantis bahamas.com; 1 Casino Dr; d from $300; ❄ 🛜 🌊) If Disneyland, Vegas and Sea World birthed a love child, this watery wonderland would be its pricey but irresistible spawn. The Lost World of Atlantis–themed megaresort has a number of separate hotels, all within walking distance of one another. The mothership is the Royal Towers – 23-story conch-pink towers linked by the enormous central arch featured on all the brochures.

One & Only Ocean Club   RESORT $$$
(Map p148; ☑ 242-363-2501; www.ocean club.oneandonlyresorts.com; 1 Casino Dr; r from BS$1026; ❄ 🛜 🌊) Paradise Island's most elite hotel, this is the kind of place where people with marquee names come to get away from it all, in lush gardens surrounded by high walls and gates. Rooms come with personal butlers, who will sprinkle rose petals on your bed or bring you your afternoon champagne. Minimum stays sometimes apply.

🍴 Eating

Some of the best and priciest dining in the Bahamas is to be found on Paradise Island; much of it in the Atlantis complex.

Anthony's Grill   INTERNATIONAL $$
(Map p148; ☑ 242-363-3152; www.anthonys grillparadiseisland.com; Paradise Island Shopping Center, Paradise Dr; mains BS$29-35; ⊘ 8am-10pm; 🛜 🖲) One of Paradise Island's few non-hotel restaurants, this Caribbean-bright

diner is a favorite with families for its big menu of burgers, pizzas, pastas and big American-style breakfasts. There's a BS$9 kids' menu and happy hour every day from 4pm to 6pm (BS$7 appetizers and two-for-one drinks).

★**Dune** FUSION $$$
(Map p148; 242-363-2501; www.oceanclub. oneandonlyresorts.com; One & Only Ocean Club, 1 Casino Dr, Paradise Island; mains BS$52-55; ⊗7-11am, noon-3pm, 6-10:30pm) French-American celebrity chef Jean-Georges Vongerichten created the menu at this ultrapopular (and ultrapricey) fusion restaurant, floating atop a dune in front of the genteel Ocean Club hotel. The menu globe hops with agility: Asian fish dishes, Australian lamb, local lobster in a light curry sauce.

★**Nobu** JAPANESE $$$
(Map p148; 242-363-3000; www.atlantis bahamas.com; Royal Towers, Atlantis, 1 Casino Dr; mains BS$39-52; ⊗sushi bar 5:30-10pm, dinner to 11pm Fri & Sat; ❋⊛) Like every outpost of Nobu Matsuhisa's empire, this restaurant deals exclusively in immaculately sourced and prepared Japanese food with judicious modern twists. Sushi and noodles are impeccable, but why not create enduring memories, with Matsuhisa's signature miso black cod, or Bahamian lobster in truffled panko? The decor is very 'Lost in Translation': a wistful, stylish collision of Japanese and Western ideas.

Café Martinique MODERN FRENCH $$$
(Map p148; 242-363-3000; www.atlantis bahamas.com; Atlantis, 1 Casino Dr; mains BS$47-52; ⊗6-10pm; ⊛) A homage to the long-gone original featured in the 1965 Bond flick *Thunderball*, this upscale French-fusion restaurant in Atlantis bears the imprimatur of French-American celebrity chef Jean-Georges Vongerichten. Alongside Gallic classics such as *sole meunière* and *steak au poivre* you'll find classy renditions of more Bahamian fare, such as local lobster roasted with plantain, oregano and chili.

Carmine's ITALIAN $$$
(Map p148; 242-363-3000; www.atlantis bahamas.com; Suite 2, 1 Paradise Dr, Atlantis Marina; mains BS$46-51; ⊗5:30-10pm; ⊛⊞) Waiting time for dinner at this subtropical outpost of the famous New York original can top an hour or more, such is its popularity among vacationing families. All the classics

are here – spaghetti with meatballs or clam sauce, veal parmigiana, tiramisu – and all in heartily indulgent (if indulgently priced) proportions.

ⓘ Getting There & Away

Water taxis leave every half-hour, on the hour, from Nassau's cruise-ship terminal to Paradise Island. A round-trip is BS$8, one way is BS$4.

West of Nassau

🏃 Activities

**Stuart Cove's Dive
& Snorkel Bahamas** DIVING
(242-362-4171; www.stuartcove.com; Southwest Rd; ⊗8am-8pm) Stuart Cove's Dive & Snorkel Bahamas is one of the Bahamas' best and largest dive operators. It offers a range of diving, PADI certification and snorkeling choices, including a buttock-clenching shark wall and shark-feeding dive (BS$182); a two-tank dive trip (BS$134); and a three-dive 'Seafari' trip to the blue holes and plunging walls of Andros island (by prior arrangement).

🛏 Sleeping & Eating

★**A Stone's Throw Away** B&B $$
(242-327-7030; www.astonesthrowaway. com; Tropical Gardens Rd, Gambier Village; d from BS$242; ❋⊛⊞) Talk about dramatic entrances: getting to this extraordinary B&B requires climbing steep stone stairs through a cliffside tunnel, after which you emerge in a tropical garden that's like something out of a Merchant Ivory film. Burnished wood, worn oriental rugs, a rock grotto swimming pool: just lovely.

Compass Point Beach Resort RESORT $$$
(242-327-4500; www.compasspointbeach resort.com; West Bay St, Gambier Village; hut from BS$315; ❋⊛⊞) Founded by Island Records supremo Chris Blackwell, this jumble of crayon-bright, 'Junkanoo-inspired' luxury huts is an automatic mood enhancer. They're on the small side, but hip furniture, surround-sound systems, cute porches and astounding views make up for that. There's a sweet poolside bar on the premises and monthly house parties draw the revelers, as does the daily happy hour.

CLIFTON HERITAGE NATIONAL PARK

Only narrowly saved from the developers' bulldozers in 2000, coastal **Clifton Heritage National Park** (☎242-362-4368; www.cliftonheritage.org; Southwest Rd; adult/child BS$10/3; ⊘9am-5pm; ⚑) bears witness to the whole spectrum of human habitation in the Bahamas. Comprising coppice wood, wetlands, beaches, Loyalist and slave-era remains, a replica Lucayan hut and an underwater sculpture garden centered on a giant underwater Atlas, the park is great for birdwatching, history buffing, picnicking, swimming or just dallying. Snorkeling here costs BS$20 (or BS$40 if you need to hire gear) and tours are BS$10/5 for adults/kids. **Jaws Beach** – so named for its role in a climactic scene in the eponymous movie franchise – is also part of the Clifton Heritage Park area, and thus protected, onshore and off. It's pretty, low-key and ideal for small kids to splash about.

Goodfellow Farms CAFE **$**
(☎242-377-5000; www.goodfellowfarms.com; Nelson Rd, Mt Pleasant; mains BS$12-15; ⊘8am-4pm Mon-Sat, from 10am Sun) Far from the fast-food joints of Nassau, this farm stand and cafe is a favorite of yachties, picnickers and Lyford-Cay locals looking for wholesome grub. Grab a cranberry-almond chicken salad or some grilled salmon and relax on the patio overlooking the fields, where the greens and herbs grow before your eyes.

GRAND BAHAMA

Despite the name, Grand Bahama has always run second to bigger, more glamorous Nassau. Yet if you're looking for a laid-back, affordable getaway with a minimum of fuss, this is your place. The streets of Freeport, its main city, and Lucaya are wide and calm. Its golden beaches and aquamarine waters are rarely overcrowded, even in high season. The frequent cruise-ship arrivals ensure that all the amenities of a perfect vacation – dive shops, restaurants, pubs, boutiques – are all within a few blocks. No wonder Grand Bahama has become so popular with cruise-ship tourists and families on quick weekend breaks.

Outside the city, the 85-mile-long island is an unexplored playground of mangrove swamps, sea caves and sandy cays. There's world-class diving and snorkeling, great kayaking and fishing. All this just a hop, skip and 55-mile jump from the US.

ⓘ Getting There & Away

The 35-minute flight from Nassau is easily the most convenient way to reach Grand Bahama; there are multiple flights every day. There's also the mail boat and **Pinder's Ferry** runs two small daily boats – maximum 20 people – from McLean's Town, Grand Bahama, to Crown Haven, Little Abaco.

ⓘ Getting Around

BUS

A handful of private minibuses operate as 'public buses' on assigned routes from the bus depot at Winn Dixie Plaza in Freeport, traveling as far afield as West End and McLean's Town. Buses are frequent and depart when the driver decides he has enough passengers. In Lucaya, the main bus stop is on Seahorse Dr, 400m west of the Port Lucaya Marketplace.

Fares from Freetown include Port Lucaya Marketplace (BS$1.25), East End (BS$8, twice daily) and West End (BS$4, twice daily). Though drivers are meant to stick to their circuit, they'll often function as impromptu taxis, taking you wherever you want for a fee. Just ask.

Free shuttles also run between most downtown hotels, the beach and town.

CAR & SCOOTER

You'll need your own wheels on Grand Bahama, and need to be vigilant avoiding potholes. There are a number of car-rental agencies at the airport. The local companies are cheaper than the international chains, with daily hire from BS$75. Collision waiver insurance is about BS$15 a day.

You can rent a scooter in the parking lot of the Port Lucaya Marketplace for about BS$50 to BS$70 per day, plus a deposit.

Rental agencies:

Avis (☎ 242-352-8144; www.avis.com; cnr Queen's Hwy & Airport Rd; ⊘ 6:30am-7pm)

Brad's (☎242-352-7930; www.bradscarrental. com; Grand Bahama International Airport)

Island Jeep and Car Rental (☎ airport 242-351-4810, cell 242-727-2207; www.islandjeep carrental.com; Freeport International Airport)

Millie's (☎242-351-3486; www.millies-cars.com)

TAXI

You'll find taxis at the airport and major hotels. Fares are fixed by the government for short distances. You can call for a radio-dispatched taxi from **Buddy's Mobile Transportation Service** (☑ 242-646-7287) or **Grand Bahama Taxi Union** (☑ 242-352-7101, 242-352-7859; Old Airport Rd).

Freeport & Lucaya

Freeport, Grand Bahama's only urban settlement, was built seemingly overnight in the 1950s to serve as a duty-free tourist destination for Rat Pack–era pleasure-seekers. Half a century and several major hurricanes later, it's now an uninspiring grid of banks, strip malls and government buildings, with little appeal for travelers.

Lucaya, a modern coastal suburb of Freeport, is where most of the vacation action takes place. Its tidy – some might say antiseptic – strip of shops and restaurants appeals to a largely cruise-ship-based tourist contingent, who appreciate its safety and walkability. On warm nights, when the music is thumping at the Port Lucaya Marketplace bandstand, this is the place to be.

⊙ Sights

Perfume Factory   FACTORY
(Map p162; ☑ 242-352-9391; www.perfume factory.com; International Bazaar, East Mall Dr; ⊙ 9am-5pm Mon-Fri, 11am-3pm Sat) FREE Also known as Fragrance of the Bahamas, this company occupies a three-story pink Baha-mian house at the rear of the **International Bazaar** (Map p162; Freeport; ⊙ some shops daily, others only for cruise-ship tours). Free tours (during the week) reveal some secrets of production, and you can pick up a bottle of the ever-popular Pink Pearl (frangipani-based, with a pink conch-shell 'pearl' inside) or blend your own signature sniff.

Taino Beach   BEACH
(Map p163) The island's second most popular beach, this postcard-perfect stretch of white sand has ample parking and a handful of **seafood shacks**. Drive or take the ferry behind Pelican Bay Hotel.

Churchill Beach & Fortune Beach   BEACH
(🚹) East of Taino Beach, Churchill and Fortune Beaches are equally glorious and even less crowded.

★**Garden of the Groves**   GARDENS
(☑ 242-373-5668; www.thegardenofthegroves.com; cnr Midshipman Rd & Magellan Dr, Freeport; adult/child B$16.50/11; ⊙ 9am-4pm) This 12-acre botanical garden is a lush tropical refuge on an island that's otherwise mostly scrub pine and asphalt. A walking trail meanders through groves of tamarind and java plum trees, past cascading (artificial) waterfalls, a placid lagoon and a tiny 19th-century hilltop chapel. The spiritually minded will enjoy a meditative stroll through the limestone labyrinth, a replica of the one at Chartres Cathedral in France. Kids will dig the raccoon habitat, where trapped specimens of the invasive critter come to retire.

MCLEAN'S TOWN

This East End village, technically on another cay from Grand Bahama, is a popular jumping-off point for fishing in the shallows. It's also possible to connect with Crown Haven on Little Abaco by ferry, twice a day.

Phil & Mel's Bonefishing Guide Service (☑ 242-353-3086; www.bahamasbonefishing. net; McLean's Town; half-/full day B$350/450) This experienced fishing outfit runs charters out of McLean's Town (with free transport from Freeport) delving deep into the mangroves in pursuit of this wily fish.

EJ's Bayside Cafe (☑ 242-353-3676; Rev Davis Way; mains B$12-15; ⊙ 9am-5pm Mon-Sat) This is how it feels Bahamian food should be: whatever's fresh from the ocean, served with generosity in a pastel clapboard-shack, in a tiny settlement among the cays. Lobster, snapper, fritters, chicken wings: it's all good.

Pinder's Ferry (p166) At 7am and 2:30pm daily, Pinder's 20-person boat makes the 45-minute trip from McLean's Town to Crown Haven on Little Abaco. Returns are at 8:30am and 4:30pm and tickets are B$90/45 return/one way (child half-price).

The only other way to get here is to drive from Freeport. Watch for potholes on long stretches of empty road.

Grand Bahama

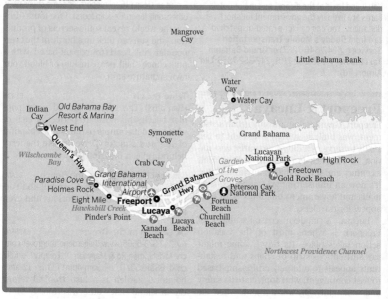

The gardens are several miles east of Freeport on Midshipman Rd; a minibus will take you there for about $5 if you ask.

🏃 Activities

Diving is excellent here. One prime site is the *Theo* wreck, a 70m-long sunken freighter with safe swim-through areas. East End Paradise, an underwater coral range, and Deadman's Reef, off Paradise Cove, are other good spots.

Golf is a popular pastime on the island, which is home to four championship courses.

The area is also superb for fishing.

Water Sports

Ocean Motion   WATER SPORTS
(Map p163; 242-373-9603; www.oceanmotion-watersportsbahamas.com; Lucaya Beach) On the beach in front of Our Lucaya Beach & Golf Resort, this large outfit offers parasailing (BS$80 per person), snorkeling (adult/child BS$55/25), boat tours (BS$30 per person) and nearly every other conceivable water-based distraction.

Junkanoo Beach Club   WATER SPORTS
(Map p163; 242-373-8018; www.junkanoo beachfreeport.com; Jolly Roger Dr, Taino Beach; BS$3; 10am-6pm; 🛜🛥) This beach club offers snorkeling, kayaking, jet-skiing and paddleboarding, and has a restaurant, changing facilities and (free) beach chairs, wi-fi and paddleboats.

Snorkeling & Diving

Sunn Odyssey   DIVING
(242-373-4014; www.sunnodysseydivers.com; 30 Beachway Dr, Freeport; 8am-5pm Mon-Sat, from 1pm Sun) Sunn Odyssey offers personalized dive tours, taking small groups on the kind of adventures they're most interested in. Two-tank dives are BS$110 with tax and night dives are BS$91; there's a surcharge of 4% if paying by card.

Pat & Diane Fantasia Tours   SNORKELING
(Map p163; 242-373-6706; www.snorkeling-bahamas.com; Port Lucaya Marketplace; adult/child from BS$50/33) This experienced outfit puts together imaginative snorkeling and fish-feeding tours to the reefs and beaches around Grand Bahama. Tours last from two to five hours, aboard the *Fantasia*, a 72ft custom-built catamaran with a bar, restaurant, waterslide and climbing wall (honestly) onboard. Tours leave from Port Lucaya Marketplace.

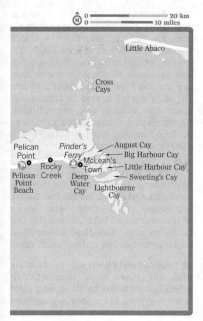

N 0 ———— 20 km
0 ———— 10 miles

Little Abaco

Cross
Cays

Pelican   Pinder's   August Cay
Point   Ferry   Big Harbour Cay
              Rocky McLean's Little Harbour Cay
Pelican Creek   Town   Sweeting's Cay
Point   Deep
Beach   Water   Lightbourne
              Cay   Cay

Golf

Lucaya Golf & Country Club   GOLF

(Map p163; ☑242-373-2004; Balao Rd) The island's first golf course features 18 holes and 6488 yards of tight doglegs and elevated greens. Green fees are BS$75.

Reef Course & Country Club   GOLF

(Map p163; ☑242-350-5466; www.grandlucayan. com; Tarrytown St; 18 holes BS$99; ⊘7am-6pm Dec-Apr, to 7pm May-Nov) Run by the Grand Lucayan, this 6909-yard championship course is conveniently tucked close to the beach, marketplace and hotels.

☞ Tours

Reef Tours   WATER SPORTS

(Map p163; ☑242-373-5880; www.reeftours-freeport.com; Port Lucaya Marketplace, Lucaya; ⚓) Introducing visitors to the delights of the Grand Bahamas since 1978, Reef Tours offers a wine-and-cheese-fueled Enchanted Evening Sail (BS$40), a glass-bottomed-boat tour (adult/child BS$30/18), a snorkel and fish-feeding trip (adult/child BS$40/20) and more. It's great value compared to many Bahamian tourist operations.

Exotic Adventures   BOATING

(☑242-374-2278; www.exoticadventuresbahamas. com; half-/full day BS$95/139, child under 12yr

half-price; ⊘10am-5pm) Captain AJ runs rum-fueled deep-sea and bottom-fishing trips, as well as reef-snorkeling excursions, dolphin encounters and other watery diversions. Call to organize collection, and to arrange overnight trips to the Biminis and Abacos.

Paradise Watersports   CRUISE

(☑242-373-4001; http://the-bahamas-watersports. com/paradisewatersports; adult/child BS$30/18) Paradise runs 1½-hour tours on its glass-bottomed boat, taking in the reef, shipwrecks and more. It also takes deep-sea fishing and snokeling tours (BS$130/65 per person) and rents out wave-runners (BS$70 per 30 minutes). Just call to arrange your fun.

✹ Festivals & Events

New Year's Day Junkanoo Parade   PARADE

(⊘Jan 1) A highlight of the social calendar, the parade takes over East Mall in Freeport, with extravagant costumes, music, dancing and rum.

Boxing Day Junkanoo Parade   PARADE

(⊘5pm-midnight Dec 26) The flamboyant music, dancing and costumes of Junkanoo are publicly judged and awarded, with much crowd support and hollering. This parade follows West Sunrise Highway.

⚏ Sleeping

Grand Bahama has some of the best budget options in the country – check online, but watch out for hidden fees. The majority of the appealing options are in Lucaya or its adjacent beaches; downtown Freeport has little to offer tourists.

Bell Channel Inn   MOTEL $

(Map p163; ☑242-373-1053; www.bellchannel inn.com; King's Rd, Port Lucaya Marina; d BS$107; P❄🕸☀) On the far side of Bell Channel from the Port Lucaya Marketplace, this slightly faded pink hotel is popular with divers, who can book very reasonable room-and-scuba packages with the on-site dive center.

★ Grand Lucayan Beach

& Golf Resort   RESORT $$

(Map p163; ☑242-373-1333; www.grandlucayan. com; 1 Sea Horse Rd, Lucaya; Radisson r from BS$195, Grand Lucayan r from BS$175; P❄🕸☀) Incorporating two hotels, the Radisson and the Grand Lucayan, this perfectly coiffed beachfront complex hogs the best views of stunning Lucaya Beach. The resort sits on

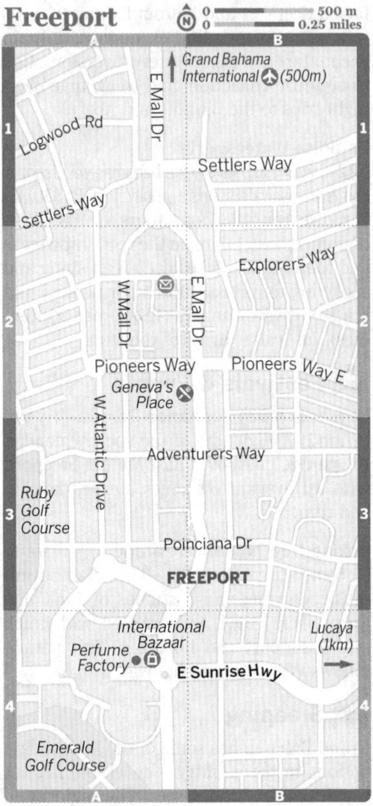

7.5 acres and incorporates numerous restaurants, bars, spas, a casino and multiple swimming pools of every style and variety, all a short stroll from the Reef Golf Course and Port Lucaya Marketplace.

The ambience at the pricier Radisson is a bit more sophisticated, while the Lucayan's playgrounds and wading pools are unabashedly family-friendly.

Pelican Bay Hotel HOTEL **$$**

(Map p163; ☎242-373-9550; www.pelicanbayhotel.com; Sea Horse Rd, Port Lucaya Marina; d from BS$159; P❄📶🏊) Pelican Bay's retro-Bahamian colonial exterior contains 186 marina-side suites with private balconies. The interiors continue the theme, with lots of dark wood, canopy beds and 'exotic' art. Though the hotel isn't oceanfront, the views of Bell Channel from the pool deck are lovely at sunset.

Taino Beach Resort & Club HOTEL **$$**

(Map p163; ☎242-350-2200; www.tainobeach.com; Jolly Roger Dr, Taino Beach; r BS$175; ❄📶🏊) On the far end of Taino Beach, this low-key complex encompasses three buildings: the upscale Marlin, the midrange Coral and the dated but budget-friendly Ocean. The all-suite setup is good for families and longer-term visitors, with one-bedrooms, efficiencies and studios. Activities such as bonfires, Bahamian Night and bingo lend a cheery communal touch.

Eating

As with accommodations, most of the eateries worth visiting are in Lucaya. Port Lucaya Marketplace draws crowds with dozens of restaurants and bars, as does the Our Lucaya resort complex. Head further afield for authentic fish fries and Bahamian cafes.

★Smith's Point Fish Fry BAHAMIAN **$**

(Map p163; Taino Beach; mains BS$13-15; ⏲5pm-2am Wed, to 11pm Sat) Wednesday night at the Fish Fry is like a giant neighborhood party. Several beachfront shacks fire up oil-drum cookers and fry turbot, lobster and conch fritters for crowds of locals, who gossip the night away eating and drinking cold Kaliks and rum punch. The scene heats up after 9pm, when the live music gets rolling.

Billy Joe's on the Beach BAHAMIAN **$**

(Map p163; ☎305-735-8267; Lucaya Beach; mains BS$13-15; ⏲10am-5:30pm) Tucking into a bowl of Billy Joe's conch salad as you wiggle your bare feet in the sand is a quintessential Grand Bahama experience. This venerable waterfront conch shack was here long before the Grand Lucaya complex took over the beach, and it's still the place to go for cold Kalik and conch cooked any way you like it.

Geneva's Place BAHAMIAN **$**

(Map p162; ☎242-352-5085; cnr East Mall Dr & Kipling La, Freeport; mains BS$14-16; ⏲7am-10pm) You'll hardly spot a non-Bahamian face in this huge, fluorescent-lit dining room, popular with locals for traditional breakfasts such as pig's feet souse and sardines and grits. Lunch means cracked conch or minced turbot, while dinner features massive portions of fish, chicken or steak.

Tony Macaroni's Conch Experience BAHAMIAN **$**

(Map p163; ☎242-533-6766; Taino Beach; mains BS$14-20; ⏲noon-11pm Wed-Sun) Tony Mac-

Lucaya

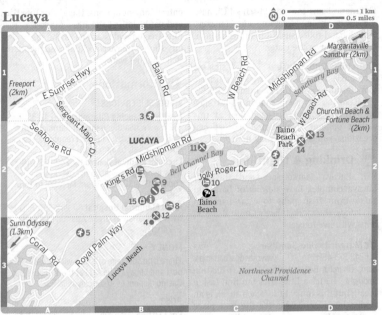

Lucaya

◎ Sights

◎ Activities, Courses & Tours

◎ Sleeping

◎ Eating

◎ Shopping

aroni, the self-proclaimed 'most unique man in the Bahamas' and proprietor of this famed Taino Beach conch shack, is a bit of an acquired taste. Get ready for nonstop teasing and (if you're female) flirting along with your roast conch or conch salad. It's all part of the 'experience'; thankfully the conch is worth it.

Zorba's GREEK **$$**
(Map p163; ☎242-373-6137; Port Lucaya Marketplace; mains BS$16-22; ☺7am-11pm; 🛜🖶)
Locals know the food at Zorba's is some of the best on Grand Bahama, and will fre-

quently recommend it to visitors. There's a smattering of Bahamian and American dishes (conch chowder, hamburgers) but the menu's mostly straight-shooting Hellenic classics: saganaki, gyro, moussaka, Greek salad and the like.

China Beach ASIAN **$$**
(Map p163; ☎242-373-1333; www.grandlucayan. com; Grand Lucayan, Lucaya; mains BS$20-28; ☺6-10pm Tue-Thu & Sat) One of Our Lucaya's more popular dinner spots, this mod Asian bistro is heavy on the atmosphere: pagoda-style bar, Buddha statues and stone lions.

The menu leans toward old-school Chinese classics such as sweet-and-sour chicken, though hand-rolled sushi adds a fresh touch. Killer views over the water.

Churchill's Chophouse STEAK $$$
(Map p163; ☑ 242-373-1333; www.grandlucayan.com; Grand Lucayan, Lucaya; mains BS$25-68; ☺6-10pm Thu-Sat) Swill martinis and slice into truly excellent dry-aged beef at this clubby, opulent steak house. For special occasions, you can't go wrong here.

Drinking & Nightlife

Port Lucaya Marketplace and the Our Lucaya complex have dozens of bars and cafes, from Irish pubs to cigar bars. On weekends, the marketplace's Count Basie Sq hops with live music.

★**Margaritaville Sandbar** BAR
(☑ 242-373-4525; www.sandbarbahamas.com; Churchill Beach, Mather Town; ☺11:30am-midnight; ☎) It's a little tricky to find (ask a local), but this funky little beach shack is an under-the-radar classic. It's the best place on Grand Bahama for NFL addicts to get their Sunday fix, and closing time depends entirely on how lively things get.

Shopping

Port Lucaya Marketplace MARKET
(Map p163; ☑ 242-373-8446; www.portlucaya.com; Sea Horse Rd; ☺9am-midnight) At Lucaya's heart, this tidied-up pastel version of a traditional Bahamian marketplace has the majority of the area's shopping, dining and

entertainment options. Haggle for tote bags and batik cloth at the straw market, peruse duty-free emeralds at one of the many jewelry shops or have a cocktail overlooking the Bell Channel waterway.

ℹ Information

MEDICAL SERVICES
Health Enhancing Pharmacy (☑ 242-352-7327; www.healthenhancingpharmacy.com; LMR Mini-Mall, 1 W Mall Dr, Freeport; ☺8am-8pm Mon-Sat, to 3pm Sun)

Lucayan Medical Centre (☑ 242-373-7400; www.lucayanmedical.com; East Sunrise Hwy, Lucaya; ☺8:30am-5:30pm Mon-Fri, to 1pm Sat)

Rand Memorial Hospital (☑ 242-350-6700; www.phabahamas.org; E Atlantic Dr, Freeport; ☺24hr)

MONEY
There's no shortage of banks with ATMs in Freeport and Lucaya. The ATM at the Treasure Bay Casino dispenses American dollars.

POST
Post Office (Map p162; ☑ 242-352-9371; Explorers Way, Freeport; ☺8:30am-5pm Mon-Fri)

TOURIST INFORMATION
Grand Bahama International Airport (☑ 242-352-6020)

Grand Bahama Island Tourism Board (☑ 242-352-8356; www.grandbahamavacations.com)

Port Lucaya Marketplace (Map p163; ☑ 242-373-8988; www.bahamas.com; Port Lucaya Marketplace, Sea Horse Rd; ☺9am-5pm)

WEST OF FREEPORT
....

Head west out of Freeport, over the Freeport Harbour Channel and past the docks, and the island narrows into a slender, scrub- and mangrove-covered peninsula. Two resorts attract snorkelers, sailors and sunseekers, but there's not much beyond those, and a few workaday settlements, to see.

Paradise Cove (☑ 242-349-2677; www.deadmansreef.com; Deadman's Reef; 1-/2-bedroom cottages BS$188/242; ❈☎) This friendly beach club has blooms of psychedelic coral head just offshore, so rent snorkel gear (BS$20) and wade right in. Not a snorkeler? You can always lounge on the beach, kayak, play volleyball or just enjoy a grouper sandwich and a draught Kalik at the resort's Red Bar. Overnighters can snag one of two modern, beachy cottages on stilts.

Old Bahama Bay Resort & Marina (☑ 242-346-6500; www.oldbahamabay.com; Bayshore Rd, West End; ste from BS$269; P❈☎☀) Just 90km from Florida, this candy-colored resort and marina on Grand Bahama's western extremity is a favorite with the American yachting fraternity. Facilities include walking and snorkeling trails, a 4000-sq-ft heated swimming pool with massage jets, a gym, spa, restaurant, bar and helipad. Tennis, massages, deep-sea fishing and other activities await.

LUCAYAN NATIONAL PARK

The 40-acre **Lucayan National Park** (☑242-352-5438; http://bnt.bs/lucayan-national-park; BS$3; ☺8:30am-4:30pm) is Grand Bahama's finest treasure. About 25 miles east of Ranfurly Circle, the park is known for its underwater cave system, which is one of the longest in the world. Visitors can easily check out two of the caves – Ben's Cave and Burial Mound Cave – via a short footpath. Bones of the island's earliest inhabitants, the Lucayans, were discovered in Burial Mound Cave in 1986. The park is also unique because it's home to all six of the Bahamas' vegetation zones.

Mangrove trails spill out onto the secluded and beautiful Gold Rock Beach, definitely worth a stop if you're out this way. You'll see more raccoons and seabirds than people, but watch your food at the picnic area near the beach – the raccoons are unabashed (but harmless) beggars.

Bahamas EcoVentures (☑242-352-9323; www.bahamasecoventures.com; ☺Wed, Fri & Sun) organizes fascinating 40-minute walks through the pristine mangroves of Lucayan National Park (BS$15 per person). If you don't fancy the stroll, there's a four-hour airboat tour to Hawksbill Creek, with a guide to point out blue holes (underwater sea caves), turtles, sharks and bonefish.

ⓘ Getting There & Away

Grand Bahama International Airport (p164) Has multiple daily connections with Nassau, and more sporadic ones with some American cities.

OUT ISLANDS

The slightly twee sobriquet of 'Family Islands', coined by Bahamas Tourism to make them seem more inviting, has only caught on to a degree. The older name, 'Out Islands,' is still very much in currency, and you'll hear both used interchangeably. While not many objected to the rebranding, it was largely unnecessary: the 'Out Islands' – everywhere in the Bahamas beyond New Providence and Grand Bahama – include hundreds of stunning islands and cays, already have an enviable reputation for peace, beauty and natural splendor. And families.

It's trite to say this is the 'real' Bahamas, but if you're seeking solitude, world-class diving, beaches of rare magnificence and a laid-back, welcoming culture then you'll probably say it anyway, about any number of these gorgeous specks of land.

The Out Islands Promotion Board (www.myoutislands.com) is the place to begin planning.

The Abacos

The Abacos – Great and Little Abaco, and their offshore cays – are one of the jewels of the Bahamas: a 320km crescent of sand that's a sailor's paradise, a history-buff's delight, a seafood-lover's dream and a bold entry in any diver's wish list.

Most Abaconians live in Marsh Harbour, capital of Great Abaco and the only urban area of any size. This bustling 'metropolis' boasts the Out Islands' only stoplight, and its marinas are the launching pad for exploring the surrounding area: the 'Loyalist Cays' – Elbow, Great Guana, Man O' War and Green Turtle – are all just a short ferry ride away. Named after the 18th-century settlers who came here after backing the wrong side in the American Revolution, they're special places graced by clapboard homes, historic lighthouses, lush mangroves and a unique culture. Offshore, the warm and bounteous Sea of Abaco is studded with stunning coral, and overflowing with marine life.

✳ Festivals & Events

Regatta Time in Abaco   SAILING (www.regattatimeinabaco.com; ☺early Jul) The first week of July sees the biggest celebration of all things wind-powered and wave-washed sail into town. Small races among the islands and cays are interspersed with parties and feasts.

ℹ Getting There & Away

There are multiple flights between Nassau and Marsh Harbour. The 35-minute flight costs a little over BS$100.

Bahamas Ferries (p190) Runs several weekly services between Nassau and the South Abaco Terminal at Sandy Point, Great Abaco (BS$71, four hours). A taxi from here to Marsh Harbour will cost around BS$150.

Pinder's Ferry (☑ 242-365-2356) Sets off twice daily from Grand Bahama (McLean's Town) for (Little Abaco) Crown Haven (BS$45, one hour).

There's also a mail boat between Nassau and Abaco.

ℹ Getting Around

Schedules for the regular ferries between Great Abaco and the Cays can be found on maps, in the *Abaconian* (the island's weekly newspaper) or on the websites for **Albury's Ferries** (p169). You can set your watch by the latter – get to the departure dock on time.

Marsh Harbour

Believe it or not, this one-stoplight town is the third-largest city in the Bahamas. Situated on a peninsula, quiet Marsh Harbour has worked to establish itself as a small tourism and boating center for visitors to the Abacos. It's a pleasant enough place, with most of the hotels and restaurants lining a small strip of road alongside the marina. Most visitors stop here to refuel, shop for groceries, replenish their cash or rest for a night or two before sailing on or hopping a ferry to the cays.

Treasure Cay is the pin-up girl of the Abacos. The white sand and turquoise shallows routinely land Top 10 Most Beautiful Beaches lists. Follow the SC Bootle Hwy 17 miles north from Marsh Harbour.

🏃 Activities

Boating

Sailboats and motorboats can be rented at most marinas. Demand often exceeds supply, so reserve early. See the Visitors' Guide in the weekly *Abaconian* for a full listing of rental companies.

Most outfitters in Marsh Harbour are clustered on Bay St, east of Don McKay Blvd. A few sights and tour companies are based in Treasure Cay.

Blue Wave Boat Rentals BOATING
(☑ 242-367-3910; www.bluewaverentals.com; Harbour View Marina; ⊙ 9am-4pm Mon-Sat, 11am-3pm Sun) This well-set-up operation charges BS$285/595/1185 per day/three days/week for a 6½m Dusky, and has boats of up to 10m too.

Diving & Snorkeling

There are some tremendous and easy snorkeling sites to enjoy in the Abacos. **Sandy Cay Reef** and **Pelican Park** in Pelican Cays Land & Sea Park are renowned for their populations of spotted eagle rays, huge stingrays and sea turtles. **Fowl Cay Reef** in Fowl Cay Preserve is the place to swim with friendly groupers.

A huge variety of dive sites take in wrecks, walls, caverns and coral kingdoms, including the *Bonita*, a WWII wreck populated by groupers that like to be hand-fed; **Cathedral**, a swim-through cavern with rays and parrotfish; and **Tarpon Cave**, a 50ft drop-off with smiling moray eels.

Dive Abaco DIVING
(☑ 242-367-2787; www.diveabaco.com; Conch Inn Hotel & Marina, East Bay St; ⊙ 8:30am-4pm Nov-Aug) This long-established dive shop offers two-tank dives (BS$145) in the vibrant reef of Fowl Cay, night dives (BS$160) and NAUI and PADI certification courses (BS$730). Specialties include a shark-observation dive (BS$160) and inland blue-hole dive (BS$160).

🛏 Sleeping

Marsh Harbour is a good central base for day-tripping to the various cays.

★**Lofty Fig Villas** VILLA $$
(☑ 242-367-2681; http://loftyfig.com; East Bay St; apt from BS$198; ❈ 🛜 ⛱) This minivillage of retro lemon-yellow duplexes works well for budget-minded travelers wanting to be close to the harborside action. Each of the airy villas has a small kitchen, flat-screen TV and an open porch, set among lawns and flowering gardens. Don't doubt any helpful tips provided by the Fig's friendly owner, Sid: he knows the Abacos.

Abaco Beach Resort and Boat Harbour RESORT $$
(☑ 242-367-2158; www.abacobeachresort.com; East Bay St; d from BS$297; ❈ 🛜 ⛱) Down a gated drive, set among manicured gardens of hibiscus, casuarina and palm, Marsh Har-

bour's only resort is an appealing retreat fronted by a private beach and marina with views to the distant cays. There are also two pools (one with swim-up bar) kayaks, paddleboards, tennis courts and plenty of opportunities for boating and diving.

✖ Eating

East Bay St and the marinas are the most obvious and densely served dining precinct, but downtown Marsh Harbour has plenty of options too.

Jamie's Place   DINER $

(☑ 242-367-2880; East Bay St; mains BS$15-17; ⊙ 7am-9pm Mon-Sat) A real fixture in the local community, this friendly but unceremonious Bahamian-American diner serves up piping-hot plates of eggs and grits at breakfast, cracked conch at lunchtime, buffalo wings as the day dwindles, and ice cream at any time.

★ Colors By The Sea   BAHAMIAN $$

(☑ 242-699-3294; East Bay St; mains BS$22-26; ⊙ noon-11pm; 🐾) This brightly painted open-sided shack over the water is a contender for the most atmospheric restaurant-bar in Marsh Harbour. Some may be here to argue good-naturedly over football and a few Kaliks, but most take advantage of the deft hands in the kitchen, savoring blackened grouper, excellent conch and lobster (in season).

Jib Room Restaurant & Bar   AMERICAN $$

(☑ 242-367-2700; www.jibroom.com; Johnny Cake Ln; mains BS$20-30; ⊙ noon-2:30pm Wed-Sat, dinner by reservation Wed & Sat; 🐾🅿) Beloved by those in the know (who tend to return as often as they can), this convivial restaurant-pub has its own marina, handy for ending a day's sailing with grilled fish, ribs, steak and other Bahamian-American favorites on the outdoor patio. Expect music and dancing on Wednesday and Saturday. Book ahead.

Snappa's   PUB FOOD $$

(☑ 242-367-3378; www.snappasbar.com; East Bay St; mains BS$16-26; ⊙ 11am-midnight, to 2am Sat; 🐾) Snappa's is one of Bay Streets favorite places to congregate after a day on the water: it has lovely marina views, plenty of wooden tables spread out for socialization, and a decent bar menu of grilled fish, burgers and the like. Happy hours are daily, from 5pm to 7:30pm; there's live music on Wednesday and Saturday.

ABACO NATIONAL PARK

This 20,500-acre **national park** (☑ 242-393-1317; http://bnt.bs/abaco-national-park) in South Abaco is the last remaining holdout of the iconic Abaco Parrot, a bird once so numerous that Columbus reported flocks that 'darkened the sun.' Wild and undeveloped, it's now managed by the Bahamas National Trust, with pine forest, isolated beaches and broad mangroves offering excellent fishing.

Maxwell's Supermarket   SUPERMARKET

(☑ 242-367-2601; Stratton Dr; ⊙ 8am-7pm Mon-Thu, to 8pm Fri & Sat, to 4pm Sun; 🅿) Stock up for off-island trips at this supermarket, the most complete in the Abacos.

ℹ Information

Abaco Island Pharmacy (☑ 242-367-2544; www.abacoislandpharmacy.com; Fire Rd; ⊙ 8:30am-6pm Mon-Sat, 9am-4pm Sun)

Marsh Harbour Government Clinic (☑ 242-367-0412; Don McKay Blvd; ⊙ 9am-5pm Mon-Fri)

There are plenty of ATMs in Marsh Harbour – hit one up before heading to the Loyalist Cays.

Police Station (☑ 242-367-2560; Dundas Town Rd)

Post Office (Don McKay Blvd; ⊙ 9am-5pm Mon-Fri)

Tourist Office (☑ 242-699-0152; www.bahamas.com; Queen Elizabeth Dr; ⊙ 9am-5pm Mon-Fri)

ℹ Getting There & Away

Leonard M. Thompson International Airport (☑ 242-367-5500) – formerly Marsh Harbour Airport – is a short BS$15 taxi ride south of town. It has daily connections with Nassau, Miami, Fort Lauderdale and several other US cities. A taxi from **Treasure Cay Airport** to Marsh Harbour is BS$85.

Elbow Cay

Separated from Marsh Harbour by 10km of clear, shallow sea, Elbow Cay is just lovely. Greeted on arrival by the most photogenic lighthouse in the Bahamas, visitors glide into a broad sheltered harbor flanked by sturdy timber cottages, studded with sails and framed by low greenery. This is **Hope Town**, founded in 1785 by Loyalists fleeing the fledgling United States, and still housing their descendants today. Strict building controls and a ban on cars make it a delightful village to perambulate, admiring tiny gardens full of bougainvillea and flowering shrubs that spill blossoms over picket fences, and ducking into diverting little museums and convivial inns. The reefs off the Atlantic side of the cay are excellent for diving and snorkeling. The waters near Hope Town and the northern tip of the cay are calmer and easily reached by swimming from shore. Staghorn, elkhorn, star and brain coral are abundant.

⊙ Sights

★ **Wyannie Malone Museum**   MUSEUM
(☑242-366-0293; www.hopetownmuseum.com; Back St; adult/child BS$5/2; ⊙10am-4pm Mon-Sat, closed Sep & Oct) Wyannie Malone, a South Carolina Loyalist whose husband was killed during the American Revolution, fled to Elbow Cay with her four children and helped found Hope Town. Today, the Malone name is spread across the Bahamas, and Wyannie is considered the spiritual matriarch of Hope Town. Her story, and that of Elbow Cay, is told at this small but engaging museum.

Elbow Reef Lighthouse   LIGHTHOUSE
(☑242-367-3067; www.elbowreeflighthousesociety.com; ⊙9am-5pm Mon-Sat) Lit by a hand-pumped kerosene burner (the last of its kind still in operation), this candy-striped lighthouse was erected in 1863, despite the attempts of local wreckers to sabotage its construction. Featured on the Bahamian $10 bill, it's now a much-loved icon. You can check out views from the top, if you fancy the 101-step climb, but will need to ask the ferry to drop you at (and collect you from) the lighthouse marina.

Tahiti Beach   BEACH
This small sand bar disappears at high tide and is surrounded by exquisitely clear, warm and peaceful waters. At the sheltered southern end of Elbow Cay, it's ideal for kids, and is reached by a road through private property that the locals routinely use without issue. For the best views, go round the peninsula on foot.

🏃 Activities

There are several good surfing breaks on Elbow Cay's south Atlantic shore, especially in winter. Try **Rush Reef** or the reef off **Garbanzo Beach** for some of the Bahamas' best surfing. **Sundried T's** (☑242-366-0616; ⊙9am-5pm Mon-Sat), located beside the Government Dock, rents boards.

Froggies Out Island Adventures   DIVING
(☑242-366-0431; www.froggiesabaco.com; Front St) This husband-and-wife outfit runs three boats, offering one-/two-tank dives for BS$140/150 and snorkeling excursions (BS$90/55 per adult/child) in the coral wonderlands of Fowl Cay Preserve and Sandy Cay Reef, as well as day-trip excursions.

FLYFISHING THE ABACOS

Blackfly Lodge (☑1-904-997-2220; www.blackflylodge.com; off Great Abaco Hwy, Schooner Bay, South Abaco; 3-night trip BS$2925; ⊙mid-Sep–mid-Aug; 🅿🤖) Only for serious (and seriously well-heeled) fly-fishing enthusiasts, Black Fly is an all-inclusive fishing lodge that takes guests into the Marls – the vast mangroves that cloak the western shore of the Abacos. Equipment, booze, expert guidance and excellent food are all laid on to make the experience of fighting the prehistoric fish in the shallows as pleasurable as possible.

The Marls This vast expanse of saltwater shallow, mudflats and mangroves west of Marsh Harbour is fishing Valhalla. It's not recommended that you attempt to negotiate the Marls without the services of someone who knows the area well: guided fishing will cost you around BS$500/700 per half-/full-day excursion.

JR's Bonefish (☑242-475-1892; www.jrsbonefishabaco.com; Casuarina Point) JR and his guides know the best secluded flats for spotting the elusive 'gray ghosts.' They can also take you wild-boar hunting.

Justin Sands Bonefishing (☑242-367-3526; www.bahamasvacationguide.com/justfish.html; Marsh Harbour) Run by Captain Justin Sands, a past Abaco Bonefish Champion, which means he knows where to find the slippery critters you desire. Pick up by arrangement.

🛏 Sleeping & Eating

There are some lovely sleeps on Elbow, and the number of second-home owners who've bought themselves a patch of this special place means many houses double as holiday villas, usually rented by the week. See **Elbow Cay Properties** (📞242-366-0569; http://elbowcayproperties.com; Front St, Hope Town; houses per week from BS$700; ⊗8am-4pm Mon-Fri, 9am-1pm Sat) for listings.

The hotels generally house the island's restaurants, although there are a few alternatives on Front St. Some places have a seasonal closure, around September to early November.

★**Hope Town Harbour Lodge**   HOTEL $$
(📞242-366-0095; www.hopeownlodge.com; Queen's Hwy; r & cottage BS$129-366; 🅿 ❄ 🛜 🏊) With a white-picket fence and frosting-blue balconies, this seaside seductress will enchant you at first sight. Main-house rooms are compact and bluff-top cottages more spacious, but all have lovely palm-framed harbor views. The Great Harbour Room, the attached restaurant, serves delightful food from 6:30pm to 9:30pm daily.

Abaco Inn   HOTEL $$
(📞242-366-0133; www.abacoinn.net; Old White Sound Rd; d from BS$253; ❄ 🛜 🏊) Talk about location! Straddling the bluff that forms the island's narrowest point, the Abaco Inn has killer views of two gorgeous, but very different, beaches. The 20 rustic cottages have painted wood paneling, postage-stamp-sized bathrooms and private hammocks. A lively tiki bar, dramatically situated oceanfront pool and generous touches such as kayaks and snorkel gear tie things together.

ℹ Information

Public restrooms and a tourist information board are across from the main public dock in Hope Town.

FirstCaribbean (Fig Tree Ln; ⊗10am-2pm Tue) No ATM; only open Tuesdays.

Police Station (📞242-366-0667, emergency 911 or 919; Front St)

Post Office (📞242-366-0098; Front St; ⊗9am-5pm Mon-Fri)

ℹ Getting There & Around

Albury's Ferry (📞242-367-3147; www.alburysferry.com; one-way/round-trip BS$19/30) Runs up to nine services a day from Marsh Harbour to Hope Town on Elbow Cay. The 20-minute

GREEN TURTLE BEACHES

On the island's northern tip, **Coco Bay** is a sugar-white wedge of sand with calm turquoise waters protected by a horseshoe-shaped bay. Half a mile east of town, handsome **Gillam Bay Beach** is heaven for shell collectors. On the island's west side, **White Sound** is a deep bay protected by a bluff-faced peninsula. Half an hour north of Green Turtle, uninhabited **Manjack Cay** is a desert island straight out of central casting. If you don't have your own boat, ask around at the docks about charters.

ride is BS$30/17 return for adults/kids, and BS$19/11 one way.

Island Cart Rentals (📞242-366-0448; www.islandcartrentals.com; per day BS$50; ⊗Mon-Sat) Can sort you out with wheels if you don't fancy walking.

Green Turtle Cay

The northernmost of the Loyalist Cays, Green Turtle takes a little more organization to get to, but is well worth the effort. Rich with tangible Loyalist history, harboring dense emerald mangroves and surrounded by exceptional diving and sailing opportunities, it's also a delightfully friendly place where slipping into conversation with the locals is the most natural thing in the world. Compact, orderly New Plymouth, the only town, is easily explored on foot, but golf carts can be hired from several operators near the docks: try **Kool Karts** (📞242-365-4176; www.koolkartrentals.com; day/overnight BS$35/50). Note that many shops and businesses close for lunch.

⦿ Sights & Activities

New Plymouth's small grid of streets is worth wandering for a short spell: on Victoria St you'll find the pink ruins of Ye Olde Jail and, nearby, a small, windswept cemetery where the headstones have spectacular views of Great Abaco. On Parliament St is the strangely touching Loyalist Memorial Sculpture Garden.

★**Albert Lowe Museum**   MUSEUM
(📞242-365-4094; https://albertlowemuseum.com; Parliament St; BS$5; ⊗9am-noon & 1-4pm Mon-Sat; ♿) Every small town needs a musty, knickknack-filled repository, and this 1825

house has served this purpose admirably since 1976, when local Alton Lowe opened it as a museum in honor of his father. Once home to former British prime minister Neville Chamberlain, and numbering Richard Nixon among its visitors, the museum now boasts a fine collection of locally crafted model ships (Mr Lowe was himself a model-ship builder), Lucayan artifacts and black-and-white photographs highlighting the cay's history.

No Name Cay
ISLAND

Just off Green Turtle's southern tip is this gorgeous, uninhabited cay, a dedicated nature reserve and home to swimming pigs and curious stingrays. It's a great spot for a day trip with a picnic and snorkel gear, but you'll need to charter a boat or join a tour from Treasure Cay to get here.

Brendal's Dive Center
DIVING

(☑ 242-365-4411; www.brendal.com; White Sound) This well-established and highly regarded diving outfit offers two-tank dives (BS$112), night dives (BS$95), open-water certification courses (BS$650) and snorkel trips (BS$70). Ask about meeting the divers' wild 'pets': groupers Junkanoo and Calypso, who cuddle up like dogs, and Goombay the grinning green moray eel. Specialty trips include diving and hand-feeding a family of wild stingrays (BS$105, including fresh seafood picnic).

🛏 Sleeping

The Cay's best accommodations lie outside of New Plymouth, where hotels and resorts occupy their own little mangrove-fringed inlets and shorefronts.

★ Green Turtle Club & Marina
RESORT $$

(☑ 242-365-4271; www.greenturtleclub.com; White Sound; r from BS$285; ❄ 🛜 🏊) This peaceful cluster of cottages exudes good taste and attention to detail. Sage-green linens and British colonial–style dark wood furniture are common touches in the villas and waterfront rooms. The lobby has a kind of tropical-ski-lodge feel, with a fireplace and charmingly dim pub, and its Caribbean-flavored restaurant, The Club, is one of the island's top dining spots.

🍴 Eating & Drinking

McIntosh Restaurant & Bakery
BAHAMIAN $

(☑ 242-365-4625; Parliament St; mains BS$14-15; ❂ 8am-4pm & 5-9pm) It could be 1955 inside

this humble New Plymouth cafe, with plastic-covered tables, carpeted floors and delectable Bahamian dishes such as coconut-crusted lobster and fried plantain. It's worth saving room for the Key lime pie and other homemade cakes and desserts.

★ Miss Emily's Blue Bee Bar
BAR

(Victoria St; ❂ 11am-10pm) From the walls layered with business cards, photographs and personal messages to the devoted customers who've been coming since it opened in the '60s, it's clear that this bar is truly loved. A portrait of the original owner, Miss Emily, perches high above the front counter, watching over the happy hordes enjoying her signature drink, the goombay smash.

❶ Getting There & Away

The only scheduled service to the cay is the **Green Turtle Ferry** (☑ 242-365-4166; Treasure Cay Airport dock, SC Bootle Hwy; adult/child return BS$19/12, one-way BS$13/8; ❂ 8am-4:30pm), which leaves from the Treasure Cay Airport dock, around 6 miles north of Treasure Cay. There are eight trips per day.

Great Guana Cay

Surrounded by shallow, coral-filled seas, ringed with gorgeous beaches and home to some of the most convivial bars and resorts in the country, Great Guana is a fortunate little stretch of sand. A short hop from Marsh Harbour, it's quiet and only modestly populated: the only thing you need to watch out for are wandering its streets are the golf carts that zip hither and thither on hushed tires.

🏃 Activities

Abaco Scuba Center
DIVING

(☑ 242-365-5021; Front St; ❂ 8am-5pm, closed Sep) This super-friendly dive outfit has top-notch equipment and is in easy striking distance of Fowl Cay and other top diving spots. A two-tank dive is BS$160, and they also rent SUBs (personal submersibles, BS$160 for a three-hour excursion), run snorkeling trips (adults/kids BS$90/45) and can organize boat rental for those who prefer to sail under their own steam.

🛏 Sleeping

Grabbers Bed, Bar & Grill
RESORT

(☑ 242-365-5133; www.grabbersatsunset.com; r from $220; ❄ 🛜) Descended from the first resort on Guana Cay, Grabbers is a charmingly relaxed little pleasure compound that sprawls in gay primary colors along its own small slice of beach. If fishing, diving, swimming and other active diversions don't appeal, you could always just laze in a hammock sipping an eponymous Guana Grabber, first mixed here in the 1960s. Two-night minimum.

Eating & Drinking

Nipper's Beach Bar & Grill   BAHAMIAN $$$
(242-365-5111; www.nippersbar.com; mains BS$28-35; 7am-10pm;) This candy-bright beachside Shangri-la can rock like a spring-break party in Cancún, which may not be everyone's cup of tea, but it is undeniably Great Guana's most famous destination. The Sunday-afternoon pig roast is legendary, drawing locals and tourists from across the Abacos, and it's backed by 9km of stunning white sand, for those itching to slip the crowds.

Kidd's Cove   BAR
(242-475-3701; Front St) The outdoor bar at this charismatic little beachside joint is what first attracts you, but as the night deepens and liquid friendships are forged, you'll also be glad of the cracked conch, grilled fish and other delicious food on offer.

Getting There & Away

Albury's Ferry (p169) Runs up to five services a day to/from Great Guana and Scotland Cays. The 30-minute ride costs BS$30/19 return for adults/kids and BS$17/11 one way, and leaves from Marsh Harbour's **Conch Inn marina** (242-367-4000; www.conchinn. com; East Bay St; r BS$193;) – not the main Albury dock on the eastern end of the island.

Man O' War Cay

This tiny ribbon of an island is home to a proud and insular Loyalist culture, the origins of which are audible in peoples' archaic British-tinged accents. Almost as powerful is the 200-year-old boatbuilding industry that still thrives today.

The island is undoubtedly one of the most conservative parts of the Bahamas. The village, with its tidy New England–style cottages, is clean and quiet, its residents polite but highly reserved – no bikinis, no booze. As there are no hotels, few restaurants and

only a handful of shops, it's best visited on a day trip.

The beach, a short walk over the hill from the ferry dock, is empty and lovely, though sometimes rough.

Eating & Drinking

Dock & Dine   BAHAMIAN $$
(242-365-6139; Man O'War Marina, Sea Rd; mains BS$24-32; 11:30am-2:30pm Mon-Sat & 5:30-8:30pm Mon, Tue, Thu & Fri Nov-Jul;) Either a much-needed reform or the vanguard of the devil, depending on your perspective, Dock & Dine campaigned long and hard to be the first (and only) place in Man O'War where you can get a drink. Beer and wine only, but it's more than adequate to accompany the zingy blackened mahi-mahi tacos on this breezy white-washed terrace.

Shopping

Albury's Sail Shop   FASHION & ACCESSORIES
(242-365-6014; Sea Rd; 7am-5pm Mon-Sat) The granddaughter of the original woman who began sewing bags and purses from canvas leftover from her husband's sailmaking business is still behind the needle at this island institution. Annie and her fellow seamstresses churn out a bewildering variety of bright canvas luggage and personal effects, dissecting the world over the constant whir of their machines.

Getting There & Away

Albury's Ferry (p169) Runs five services a day connecting Marsh Harbour and Man O'War. The 20-minute ride costs BS$30/19 return for adults/kids and BS$17/11 one way.

The Biminis

On the edge of the Gulf Stream, closer to Miami than Nassau, this postage-stamp paradise comprises North, South and East Bimini and a scattering of private and uninhabited islets. Naturally stunning, culturally relaxed and boasting excellent diving and unsurpassed deep-sea fishing, Bimini is well worth the 30-minute flight from Nassau. Once home to Prohibition-era rum-runners and one of Papa Hemingway's legendary haunts, it's now a favorite destination of serious fisherfolk and sunseekers from the States and beyond. The arrival of the slick Resorts World complex on North Bimini has

DON'T MISS

BIMINI ROAD

Eighteen feet below the waves and stretching for half a mile, this bizarrely symmetrical limestone formation was discovered off North Bimini's western coast in 1968. Its precision seems unnatural, giving rise to the perhaps inevitable interpretation that Plato's mythical city of Atlantis had finally been located. Nothing else of the 'city' remains, but it's an evocative dive site, often blessed with abundant sea life.

deprived Alice Town and other settlements of a good deal of the tourist trade they once enjoyed.

👁 Sights & Activities

★ Dolphin House   HOUSE
(☑242-347-3201; http://inmyrighthand.home stead.com/dolphinhouseindex.html; Saunders St, Alice Town, North Bimini; donation BS$5; ☉10am-6pm) Looking like Gaudí's tropical hobby, this astonishing house is the lifelong labor of Bimini historian and poet Ashley Saunders. Born on the site (all the surrounding houses belong to the Bimini Saunders), Ashley was touched after swimming with wild dolphins, and has been building this 'tribute' piece by piece since 1993. Plastered with dolphin mosaics, sea glass, shells, Lucayan artifacts, coconut rum bottles, pickled sausage jars and every conceivable type of flotsam and jetsam, it's absolutely unique and arrestingly beautiful.

Downstairs you'll find a museum filled with salvaged ephemera such as a brass naval cannon from an 18th-century British wreck, photos of Hemingway having his hair cut, copper from a pirate ship and countless other random pieces. There's also a gift shop, where you can get both volumes of Ashley's history of Bimini.

Neal Watson's Bimini Scuba Center   DIVING
(☑242-473-8816; www.biminiscubacenter.com; Bimini Big Game Club, King's Hwy; 9am-5pm) Operating out of the Bimini Big Game Club, Neal Watson's has an 18m glass-bottomed boat that serves divers, snorkelers and plain old sightseers equally well. Destinations include Bimini Road, Hawksbill Reef and various wrecks. A two-tank dive with tax is BS$128, a snorkel safari with wild

dolphins is BS$139 and a PADI open-water referral course is BS$538.

🛏 Sleeping

Resorts World, north of Porgy Bay, has sucked much of the business away from Alice Town, although a few lower-budget locally run hotels are still hanging on.

Bimini Big Game Club   RESORT $$
(☑242-347-3391; http://biggameclubbimini.com; Kings Highway, Alice Town, North Bimini; r from BS$210; ❈🛜🏊) If you want to indulge your inner Hemingway, then the Big Game Club is where it's at. But it's not only about deep-sea fishing: there's also reef fishing, diving, snorkeling, and the usual resort pastimes of massage, wining and dining. Dating back to 1954, the resort nonetheless has modern, cheerfully decorated and thoroughly comfortable rooms.

🍴 Eating

Bahamian bakeries, conch shacks and clapboard kitchens by the beach are the mainstays of Alice Town and other North Bimini settlements. If you want more, the resorts have broader (and pricier) options.

My Three Daughters   BAHAMIAN $
(☑242-347-2119; Queen's Hwy, Bailey Town, North Bimini; mains BS$13-16; ☉9am-midnight Mon-Sat) Perhaps the best Bahamian joint on the island, this welcoming little family affair does great things with lobster and conch, and the sweet Bimini bread is very moreish.

Stuart's Conch Stand   BAHAMIAN $
(☑242-347-2474; King's Hwy, Bailey Town; mains BS$12; ☉4pm-midnight) Chopping up superfresh and tangy examples of the Bahamas' favorite sea-snail snack, this renowned conch stand stands by Porgy Bay, in Bailey Town in the center of North Bimini. Conch salad is all Fabian (Stuart) does, and he does it very well.

CJ's Deli   BAHAMIAN $$
(☑242-347-3295; Queen's Hwy, Alice Town; mains $15-20; ☉7am-7pm daily) This simple clapboard shack by the beach in Alice Town is a local favorite for eggs and grits, souse, stew fish, conch and other Bahamian comfort foods. Go inside to order and collect, then eat on the wooden tables overlooking the Atlantic.

ⓘ Information

Bimini Medical Clinic (☑242-347-2210; Government Offices, Queen's Hwy; ⊙9am-4pm Mon-Fri)

Police Station (☑242-347-3144, emergency 911 or 919; Queen's Hwy) The police station, post office and government medical clinic are all housed in a low pink complex on Queen's Hwy in Alice Town.

Post Office (☑242-347-3546; Government Offices, Queen's Hwy; ⊙9am-5pm Mon-Fri)

Tourist Office (☑242-347-3528; www.bahamas.com; King's Hwy; ⊙9am-5pm Mon-Fri) In Alice Town.

ⓘ Getting There & Away

Several daily flights connect South Bimini International Airport with Nassau, Miami and Fort Lauderdale. From the airport a bus and ferry combination (BS$5) whisks you to Alice Town on North Bimini.

Eleuthera

A painfully skinny 175km-long crescent of pink-sand beaches, Atlantic-battered reefs, weather-warped rock and dense subtropical scrub, lovely Eleuthera also harbors boutique hotels, revered surf breaks and some fabulous restaurants. Depending on where you wander, whom you meet and (in some cases) how fat your wallet is, this is a place you're sure to extemporize one of the most diverse and memorable experiences possible on any Bahamian island.

ⓘ Getting There & Away

AIR

There are three airports spaced along skinny Eleuthera:

North Eleuthera International Airport (☑242-335-1242) The busiest, convenient for Harbour Island.

Governor's Harbour Airport (☑242-332-2321; Queen's Hwy) Halfway down the island near the capital.

Rock Sound Airport (☑242-334-2177; ☎) Some also fly down south.

BOAT

Bahamas Ferries fast boats (BS$81 one way, two hours) and (slow) **mail boats** (BS$30, five hours) run to Harbour Island and Governor's Harbour from Nassau. One-day vacation packages are also available on various private boats from Nassau (BS$30, five hours). From Harbour Island, **water taxis** run between the Government Dock and North Eleuthera (BS$5).

Harbour Island

'Briland', as locals and repeat visitors call it, is renowned as one of the loveliest, most stylish and enjoyable islands in the Bahamas, if not the Caribbean. Just 5km long and 2km wide, it's a photogenic bric-a-brac of pink-sand beaches and colonial houses that once served as the national capital. Now it's a tourist-brochure-designer's delight: humble pastel cottages abut BS$800-a-night boutique hotels, chickens peck the dust in front of sleek French bistros, and local fishermen wave to millionaire businessmen as they speed past each other in identical golf carts.

Quaint Dunmore Town, on the harbor side, harks back 300 years: it was laid out in 1791 by Lord Dunmore, governor of the Bahamas (1787–96), who had a summer residence here. The clip-clop of hooves may have been replaced with the whir of golf carts, but the daily pace since Dunmore's time hasn't changed all that much.

⊙ Sights & Activities

Pink Sands Beach BEACH
The powdery sand here shimmers with a pink glow – a result of finely pulverized coral – that's a faint blush by day and a rosy red when fired by the dawn or sunset. It's been called the world's most beautiful beach by a slew of international glossies, and we won't argue. Follow Chapel St or Court St to public access paths to the Atlantic side shores.

Valentine's Dive Center DIVING
(☑242-333-2080; www.valentinesdive.com; Bay St; ⊙8am-7pm Mon-Sat, shorter hours Sun) This professional dive school takes you to the reefs around Eleuthera for one- and two-tank dives (BS$106/149), PADI open-water referral (BS$450 in a group) and other certification courses, and snorkeling tours to Cistern Rock (adults/kids BS$89/40).

Michael's Cycles CYCLING
(☑242-464-0994; www.michaelscyclesbriland.com; Colebrook St; ⊙8am-5pm Mon-Sat, to 4pm Sun) Michael's has been renting bikes, kayaks, boats and golf carts to Harbour Island visitors for decades. Bikes are BS$15 per day, and golf carts BS$50.

⨭ Sleeping

Tingum Village HOTEL $$
(☑242-333-2161; Colebrook St; r BS$185; ❋☎) Keeping on since 1969, Tingum Village is pleasingly low-key and low-priced,

compared to much of Briland's accommodation. Spick-and-span suites are arranged around a tranquil picket-fenced garden; the cheaper ones are simple, tiled and dim, while the fancier have stylish touches such as stone accent walls and in-room tubs. All have patios and basic kitchens.

★ Pink Sands Resort
RESORT $$$

(☑242-333-2030; www.pinksandsresort.com; Chapel St; cottages from BS$837; ✳🛜⊠) This delightful resort, rambling over 20 acres of landscaped foliage behind the impossibly photogenic Pink Sands Beach, may be Harbour Island's loveliest accommodations. Arriving in the impeccably tasteful lobby under the shade of ancient fig trees, where koi and turtles swim through an ornamental pool, you realize why this place is beloved by celebrities, models and the super-rich.

The 25 sleek cottages are their own private small kingdoms, with sitting areas, porches and minibars stocked with everything from champagne to popcorn snacks. There's also a restaurant, Malcolm 51 (p174), and a superbly situated beach bar, the Blue Bar.

Rock House
BOUTIQUE HOTEL $$$

(☑242-333-2053; www.rockhousebahamas.com; cnr Bay & Hill Street Sts; r from BS$460; ✳🛜⊠) This lovely 1940s home has been skilfully redeveloped as an upmarket hotel. The 10 rooms are smallish but luxe, with top-notch king-size beds, private cabanas and crisp white decor broken up with designer touches such as vintage birdcages and orchids. There's also a small gym, umbrellas, chairs and snorkeling gear for the beach, and one of Briland's best restaurants (p175).

Runaway Hill
BOUTIQUE HOTEL $$$

(☑242-333-2150; www.runawayhill.com; cnr Colebrook St & Love Lane; r from BS$486; ⊙Dec-Jul; ✳🛜⊠) A Harbour Island icon, this 1940s private estate is now a hotel on an unimprovable setting on a bluff overlooking the Atlantic, and is lavishly blessed with WWII-era features such as the checkerboard lobby and dark-wood library. Rooms are distinguished by subtle whites, Cuban tiles and vintage woods, and the pool deck dramatically overlooks the ceaseless sea. Surprisingly, children are welcome.

✗ Eating

Harbour Island probably has more fine-dining options than all the other Out Islands combined. And if you're not hankering for haute cuisine, some of the island's best meals are served at the shacks lining Bay St.

Arthur's Bakery & Café
BAKERY $

(☑242-333-2285; cnr Crown & Dunmore Sts; mains BS$9-12; ⊙8am-2pm Mon-Sat; 🖫) One of the friendliest spots in town, this cornerside nook is the place to catch up on gossip, gather travel advice and relax over coffee, banana pancakes and croissants. Lunch means salads, sandwiches and lazy people-watching. Owner Robert Arthur is a one-time screenwriter and well-known man-about-town; his baker wife, Anna, makes a mean Key lime pie.

Angela's Starfish Restaurant
BAHAMIAN $

(☑242-333-2253; Nesbit St; mains BS$15; ⊙9am-8:30pm) Grandmotherly Angela will cook you a heaping plate of conch with peas and rice at this cozy local joint, decorated in beachy kitsch including old street signs and tiki dancer dolls. Never refuse a slice of her homemade pineapple cake.

Sip Sip
INTERNATIONAL $$

(☑242-333-3316; www.sipsiprestaurant.com; Court St; mains BS$18-24; ⊙11:30am-4pm Mon-Thu; 🛜🖫) The cosmopolitan Bahamian menu at this convivial lime-green cafe behind the dunes ranges from lobster quesadillas to curried chicken salad. It's a blissfully sited place to linger over a plate, enjoy pink-sand views and indulge in a little 'sip sip' – the local term for gossip.

Ma Ruby's
BAHAMIAN $$

(☑242-333-2161; Tingum Village, Colebrook St; mains BS$15-30; ⊙8am-midnight; 🛜🖫) Ma Ruby MBE sadly passed away in 2016, but the secret to her 'cheeseburger in paradise' has been passed on to Michael, the new chef at this family-run patio restaurant. Cooked to order and served smothered with gooey cheese on thick slices of toasted brioche, it has earned legions of fans from across the globe.

★ Malcolm 51
INTERNATIONAL $$$

(☑242-333-2030; www.pinksandsresort.com; Pink Sands Resort, Chapel St; mains BS$39-45; ⊙6:30-9pm; 🛜) This serious, grown-up's restaurant brings the luxury that Pink Sands' pampered guests expect. The menu shows plenty of Mediterranean touches (such as charred octopus with tabbouleh and salsa verde) alongside 'island cuisine' (pumpkin and crab soup with curry spices and coconut rum cream). The terraced gardens and wooden exotica create an atmosphere commensurate with the food.

★ Rock House Restaurant
INTERNATIONAL $$$

(242-333-2053; www.rockhousebahamas.com; cnr Bay & Hill Sts; mains BS$40-45; ⊗noon-2pm & 6:30-9pm; 🐾) With a cracking view overlooking Dunmore Town's harbor, this two-storied colonial building serves some of Harbour Town's most upmarket fare. Expect lavish use of ingredients such as lobster, New Zealand lamb and grass-fed beef on a menu that throws some Bahamian touches into its generally French-inspired international dishes.

The Landing
EUROPEAN $$$

(242-333-2707; www.harbourislandlanding.com; Bay St; mains BS$44-47; ⊗8-11am & 6-10pm Thu-Tue; 🐾) Another of HI's higher-end diners, the Landing wins friends in some quarters for including a kids' menu alongside more adult temptations such as spicy capellini of local crab and lobster with risotto cake and asparagus. The chef, Madelene Pedican, has been here for over 15 years, suggesting something's working well at this establishment.

🍷 Drinking & Nightlife

Vic-Hum Club
CLUB

(242-333-2161; cnr Barrack & Colebrook Sts; ⊗8pm-3am) For ramshackle good times, park your putter at this late-night party shack (pronounced 'viccum') and abandon all reserve at the door. From kick-back natives to Aussie kiteboarders and yacht crews on shore leave, it's a funky, rum-fueled bazaar where a basketball court doubles as a dance floor. Miss it and forever rue the day.

Gusty's Bar
BAR

(242-333-2342; Coconut Grove Ave; ⊗9:30pm-1am) Jimmy Buffet has been known to jam at this ramshackle north-end cottage, with its pink-sand dance floor. No singlets (tank tops) or political attire allowed.

🛍 Shopping

Harbour Island's not kidding around when it comes to boutiques, even earning kudos from *Travel + Leisure* as the best Caribbean island for shopping.

There's a waterfront straw market facing Sugar Mill Trading Company. Most stores are closed Sundays. Most shops are in Dunmore Town.

Sugar Mill Trading Company
FASHION & ACCESSORIES

(242-333-3558; Bay St; ⊗9am-5pm Mon-Fri, from 10am Sat) Owned by India Hicks, socialite designer and cousin to Prince Charles, this upscale boutique has an impeccably edited selection of men's and women's clothes and island-inspired gifts.

ℹ Information

Harbour Island Community Clinic (242-333-2227; Colebrook St; ⊗8:30am-4pm Mon-Fri, to noon Sat)

Harbour Pharmacy (242-363-2514; Bay St; ⊗9am-5pm Mon-Fri)

Police Station (242-332-2111, 919; Gaol St)

Post Office (242-332-2215; Gaol St; ⊗9am-5pm Mon-Fri)

Royal Bank of Canada (242-333-2230; Dunmore St; ⊗9am-4pm Mon-Fri)

Tourist Office (242-333-2621; www.bahamas.com; Bay St; ⊗9am-5pm Mon-Fri)

ℹ Getting There & Away

Most visitors fly to **North Eleuthera Airport** (p173), which connects with Nassau, Atlanta, Miami, Orlando and Fort Lauderdale. From the airport, it's a short taxi ride (BS$4 per person) to Three Island Dock, then another five minutes by water taxi (BS$5) to Dunmore Town.

ℹ Getting Around

While distances are negligible, Briland is a mini-LA – no one walks if they can help it. You can rent golf carts from taxi drivers and rental agencies who are based at the dock, beginning at $50 per day. Try **Johnson's Rentals** (242-332-2376; Bay St) or **Michael's Cycles** (p173), which also rents bikes.

Taxis on Harbour Island are slightly pricier than elsewhere in Eleuthera. Try **Danny 'The Minister' Major** (242-333-2166).

Gregory Town

Quiet six nights out of the week, this low-key village is 40km north of Governor's Harbour and 8km south of the Glass Window Bridge. Once famous for its thriving pineapple industry, it sits on a compact, deep harbor in a cove once used by pirates.

◉ Sights & Activities

Surfer's Beach
BEACH

The long left-hand break at this secluded Atlantic-facing beach has been popular with surfers since the 1970s. It's a little difficult to access (the 'road' is deeply pitted rock) but

THE BAHAMAS ELEUTHERA

DON'T MISS

GLASS WINDOW BRIDGE

Here Eleuthera narrows dramatically to a thin span straddling the divide between pounding Atlantic waves and the tranquil green shoals of the Bight of Eleuthera. A hurricane destroyed the natural bridge that was once there, so a narrow built substitute is now the only thing connecting north and south Eleuthera. It's one of the island's premier photo ops.

that only makes it more likely you'll have it largely to yourself.

Gaulding Cay BEACH
(Queen's Hwy) This beautiful yet often-empty beach just south of Glass Window Bridge has shallow, gin-clear water and great snorkeling around a small rocky island in the middle of the bay. Lovely for a picnic or unscheduled nap, too.

Hatchet Bay Cave CAVE
The rough-stone entrance to this mile-long cave is between Gregory Town and Alice Town, on the southwestern side of the Queen's Hwy. Several chambers bear charcoal signatures dating back to the mid-19th century, and there are some impressive stalagmites and stalactites. If exploring beyond the first few chambers, you'll need a headlamp, long pants and local guide.

**Bahamas Out-Island
Adventures** WATER SPORTS
(☑ 242-335-0349; www.bahamasadventures.com; Surfer's Beach; half-/full day BS$79/109) Tom Glucksmann (owner of Surfer's Haven guesthouse) runs eco-minded kayaking, snorkeling and nature trips. The man knows his birds and is a passionate advocate for preserving lonely **Lighthouse Point** at the southern tip of the island. Surf lessons are BS$75 per person in a group, or BS$100 for one or two people. Board hire is BS$25 per day.

🛏 Sleeping & Eating

The few places to stay are located a kilometer or two outside of town.

Surfer's Haven GUESTHOUSE $
(☑ 242-333-3282; Surfer's Beach; r/ste BS$60/80; 🛜) A laid-back, hostel-style guesthouse only 10 minutes' walk from Surfer's Beach, the Haven has rooms attached to the owners' house and a private apartment on the top floor. There's a wooden deck with lovely sea views, a covered outdoor kitchen and tiki hut, and boards and other gear for hire (BS$25). The owner, Tom, also runs Bahamas Out-Island Adventures (p176).

Rainbow Inn INTERNATIONAL $$
(☑ 242-335-0294; www.rainbowinn.com; Queen's Hwy, Rainbow Bay; mains BS$25-28; ⊙ 11am-10m; 🛜 ♿) Seafood (local) and black Angus steak (imported) are two of the menu mainstays at this ever-popular octagonal timber restaurant overlooking Rainbow Bay, 15km south of Gregory Town. Monday's wood-fired pizzas are incredibly popular, while live music lands on Mondays, Wednesdays and Saturdays. The Rainbow's a bit of a community hub for Eleuthera's middle section, and the bonhomie can be infectious.

🍷 Drinking & Nightlife

Sadly, the eponymous founder of Elvina's, the legendary bar whose jam sessions were known to draw Lenny Kravitz and other famous musos, has passed on, and another venue occupies the space. This, plus a few shacks dealing Kalik and a booming dance hall on Friday nights, comprise the nightlife.

🛍 Shopping

Rebecca's Beach Shop GIFTS & SOUVENIRS
(☑ 242-335-5436; Queen's Hwy; ⊙ 9am-10pm) Set back from the bend in the main road in central Gregory Town, and surrounded by foliage and cars in various states of repair, Rebecca's is an eccentric gem. Proprietor Pete, an American expat with a ponytail and feisty opinions, regales visitors who come for handicrafts and souvenirs, exceptional hot sauce ('Pirate's Revenge) and surf lessons led by Pete himself (BS$80).

ℹ Getting There & Around

There's no public transport to Gregory Town: you'll need your own wheels.

Governor's Harbour

Eleuthera's sleepy island 'capital' overlooks a broad and handsome harbor that runs west to **Cupid's Cay**, apparently the original settlement of the Eleutheran Adventurers, English Puritans who emigrated here in 1648. It has some faded architectural reminders of its official stature, and is an ideal base for exploring Eleuthera in either direction.

◎ Sights

French Leave Beach
BEACH

This winsome crescent of soft pink sand, just north of town, was once occupied by Club Med, before Hurricane Floyd ripped it apart in 1999. Relieved of development, its softly curving shore is once again one of the prettiest beaches in the Bahamas, with generally gentle waves in spite of the Atlantic behind it.

⊨ Sleeping

A decent range of hotels, guesthouses, villas and resorts can be found in the Governor's Harbour area, particularly up the hill to the east and toward the Atlantic coast.

Quality Inn Cigatoo
HOTEL $

(☑ 242-332-3060; Haynes Ave; d from BS$130; P ✳ 🛜 ⌧) This no-frills hotel offers clean, basic rooms just up a leafy hill from the center of Governor's Harbour. It's well located and reasonably priced.

Cocodimama Charming Resort
RESORT $$$

(☑ 242-332-3150; Queen's Hwy; villa BS$1900; P ✳ 🛜) Ideal for large groups or families celebrating milestones in style, this resort on Alabaster Bay is beautifully put together and blissfully relaxing. There's a main house decorated in wealthy Italian style – think whitewashed walls, mosaic floors, avant-garde driftwood chandeliers – and sunny villas set on a private beach lined with palm-thatch umbrellas.

✕ Eating

Anchor Bay Fish Fry
BAHAMIAN $

(☑ 242-332-2467; Anchor Bay; BS$12-15; ☺ 6pm-midnight Fri) Music, singing, dancing, conch, lobster, Kalik: this has all the pre-requisites of a classic Bahamian fish fry.

New Sunset Inn
BAHAMIAN $

(☑ 242-332-2487; Queen's Hwy; mains BS$12-16; ☺ noon-11pm Fri-Wed) The ample patio of this friendly, unhurried seaside bar and grill is the place to down a cold Kalik at sunset while nibbling cracked conch and Christine's famous coconut pie.

★ Tippy's Bar & Beach Restaurant
INTERNATIONAL $$

(☑ 242-332-3331; Banks Rd, North Palmetto Point Beach; mains BS$25-31; ☺ 11am-midnight Tue-Sun; 🛜) This platonic model of the beach bar has a delightful ocean-facing deck and eclectic, welcoming timber decor inside. The restaurant specializes in globally influenced seafood dishes – coconut shrimp, Bahamian bouillabaisse – presented on a giant chalkboard menu that's carried to your table with a flourish. Jam-packed even in low season, it gets totally wild on busy weekend nights.

Buccaneer Club
INTERNATIONAL $$

(☑ 242-332-2000; cnr Haynes Ave & New Bourne St; mains BS$15-20; 🛜) With an inviting deck beneath a spreading Lebbek tree, a whitewashed interior lit by radiantly colorful local art and subtle tunes piped throughout, this is the most relaxing place in Governor's to kick back for a drink or meal. The Jamaican chef is equally at home with Bahamian, American and pan-Asian flavors.

ℹ Information

First Caribbean International Bank (Queen's Hwy; ☺ 9:30am-3:30pm Mon-Thu, to 4:30pm Fri)

Police Station (☑ 242-332-2117; Queen's Hwy)

Post Office (Administrator's Office, Haynes Ave; ☺ 9am-4pm Mon-Fri)

Tourist Office (☑ 242-332-2142; www.bahamas.com; Queen's Hwy; ☺ 9am-5pm)

ℹ Getting There & Around

Governor's Harbour Airport (p173) has connections to Nassau and Fort Lauderdale; 15km north of town.

To hire a taxi or rent a car, call **Cecil Cooper's Taxi Service** (☑ 242-332-1620) or **Clement Cooper Car Rental** (☑ 242-332-1726).

Andros

Known as 'the Big Yard,' Andros is the country's largest and wildest major island – 5960 sq km of mangroves, palm savannas and eerie pine forests full of wild boar and (as legend has it) an evil man-bird known as the chickcharnie. It's also largely uninhabited – considerable distances separate tiny settlements dotting the east coast, while the entire western side is an uninhabited patchwork of swampland known, appropriately, as 'the Mud.' Bonefishing here is world renowned.

Off the east shore lies a 225km-long coral reef, and beyond that the 3000m-deep Tongue of the Ocean, making diving and fishing equally exceptional. Then there are the many blue holes: vast, water-filled caves found both on- and offshore.

Public transport is nonexistent: to get around, it's just you, your rental car and some long expanses of empty, potholed road. Hitching is extremely common: someone will quickly pick you up, if you'll accept the risk.

ⓘ Getting There & Away

AIR

Of Andros's four airports, you're most likely to use either **San Andros** (☏242-329-4224; Queen's Hwy, North Andros), near Nicholls Town, or **South Andros Airport** (☏242-369-2640; Queen's Hwy, Congo Town), near Congo Town on the island of the same name. **Western Air** (☏242-329-4000; www.westernairbahamas. com) runs scheduled flights between these airports and Lynden Pindling in Nassau, but low demand can see you decanted into a nine-seater charter plane flown by **Southern Air** (☏242-323-7217, 242-323-6833; www.southernair charter.com), who also fly to **Andros Town Airport** (☏242-368-2030; Queen's Hwy) in Central Andros. **Flamingo Air** (☏242-351-4963; www. flamingoairbah.com) can get you to **Mangrove Cay Airport** (Clarence A Bain Airport; ☏242-369-0083).

BOAT

Bahamas Ferries (p190) runs a 7am Friday service from the Potter' Cay dock in Nassau to Fresh Creek on Central Andros. It's a three-hour journey, returning the same day at 12:30pm and costing BS$107/59 return/one way for adults, and BS$68/37 for children.

ⓘ Getting Around

Andros is divided into three discrete islands: North and Central Andros (connected by road bridge) and South Andros, which is estranged from its northern brethren by a maze of mangroves, channels and cays. The largest of these, Mangrove Cay, connects to South Andros via a twice-daily government **ferry** (p181), but that's it for interisland transport. To get from the southern extremity of Central Andros to Mangrove Cay (and then on to South Andros by ferry), you'd need to pay a willing Behring Point local to boat you across. Or you could fly back to Nassau, and double back to South Andros by plane.

North & Central Andros

Technically one island, North and Central Andros are two separate administrative districts. Sleepy Nicholls Town (population 645) is the closest settlement to San Andros

Airport and the center of activity for much of North Andros. Outside of town are some extraordinary hidden beaches and coves – ask a local. Northeast of here, poor settlements such as Lowe Sound were hit hard by Hurricane Matthew in 2016 and need a great deal to rebuild their lives. Heading south across Stafford Creek and into Central Andros, the mostly empty roads are bordered by whispering forests of Caribbean pine and the glorious Blue Holes National Park (p179). Settlements begin to emerge as you veer toward the coast, eventually reaching the largest center on these islands: Fresh Creek/Andros Town.

◉ Sights

Androsia Ltd   FACTORY
(☏242-376-9339; www.androsia.com; Adrosia St, Andros Town; ⊙9:30am-4pm Mon-Fri, to 2:30pm Sat) This factory has been hand-producing the gorgeous batiks sold throughout the Bahamas since 1973. Watch workers create fabric with age-old wax techniques, then buy some for yourself at the adjacent outlet. Turn east off the Queen's Hwy immediately after taking the Fresh Creek Bridge south into Andros Town, and you'll see the sign on your right.

🏃 Activities

Fishing is huge here, especially around the Cargill Creek area of Central Andros. Ask at your hotel about a guide, or book into a dedicated bonefishing lodge, where your days and nights will be devoted to outwitting the elusive silvery prey. Diving, snorkeling, hiking and birdwatching are also ideal pursuits in this vast natural playground.

Andros Island Bonefish Club   FISHING
(☏242-368-5167; www.androsbonefishing.com; Queen's Hwy, Behring Point; ☏) Fly-fishing devotees will be in clover at this dedicated bonefishing club, offering all-inclusive packages bundling bed and board in its 29-room lodge with guided trips to the vast mudflats of Western Andros, one of the meccas of the sport. Three nights, with two days' fishing, is BS$1452 per person, on a twin-share basis.

Small Hope Bay Lodge   DIVING
(☏242-368-2014; www.smallhope.com; Small Hope Bay; ⊙departures 9:30am, 2pm & 8:45pm) This highly acclaimed dive outfit, based in a lovely, laid-back resort, offers one-/two-tank dives (BS$90/110), night dives (BS$100) and shark dives (BS$100), as well as snorkeling

DON'T MISS

NATIONAL PARKS ON ANDROS ISLAND

The national parks are some of Andros' gems: the flats and channels of the west are protected by the **West Side National Park**, while inland Caribbean pine forest pitted with limestone karst holes make up the **Blue Holes National Park**.

West Side National Park (☏ 242-393-1317; http://bnt.bs/west-side-national-park) Covering the entire western side of Andros, this 1.5-million acre expanse of pristine mangrove is a precious breeding ground for many marine and bird species, and is protected by the Bahamas National Trust. It's wild and lovely, but very difficult to access, unless you're taken there by a local fishing guide.

Blue Holes National Park (http://bnt.bs/blue-hole-national-park) Blue Holes – deep vertical 'caves' formed by karst limestone subsidence that fill with rain and seawater, forming unique ecosystems – are more abundant on Andros than anywhere else. This 40,000-acre national park comprises vast tracts of Caribbean pine and coppice forest pitted with these phenomena. Trails and info boards introduce you to the flora, fauna and geology, while picnic benches encourage lingering. Don't forget your swimming gear, if you fancy a plunge into Captain Bill's hole.

The access road for the park heads west off the Queen's Hwy from the settlement of Love Hill.

safaris (BS$40). Ask about specialty trips, including blue-hole dives and wall dives to 56m. Rates fall when you dive for three or more days.

🛏 Sleeping

Nicholls Town and Fresh Creek both have a handful of accommodations. Small Hope is about 6 miles north of Fresh Creek on the Queen's Hwy. Further south, the Stafford Creek and Staniard Creek areas have a handful of accommodations.

★ Pineville Motel
MOTEL $

(☏ 242-329-2788; www.pinevillemotel.com; Nicholls Town; r from BS$70; ❈🔊) The Pineville, and its ebullient creator, Eugene, are an absolute joy. Creativity, imagination, community-mindedness and inspirational industriousness shine everywhere. A very small sample of what Eugene has created includes a petting zoo (with wild boar and goat mazes), outdoor performance marquee, fish-fry shacks, ornate garden, and a disco and cinema. There's always something happening, and the rooms are cheap and comfy, too!

★ Small Hope Bay Lodge
RESORT $$$

(☏ 242-368-2014; www.smallhope.com; Small Hope Bay; d from BS$677; ⊖🔊≋) These 21 luxurious yet unfussy units on a quiet, mangrove-backed stretch of Small Hope Bay are a lovely place to linger. Ravaged by Hurricane Matthew, it has since gotten back on its feet and resumed what it does best.

Always convivial and beloved by divers, it's a barefoot holiday-mode kind of place that continues to lead the way for ecotourism in the Bahamas.

The Lodge is so intimate that the guests really get to know each other – stay a week, and you're sure to come away with new friends. Most are here on dive packages, though it's also popular with anglers. Packages often include everything from bikes to kayaks to dinners, but will be happily tailored to your interests.

★ Kamalame Cay
RESORT $$$

(☏ 242-368-6281; www.kamalame.com; villas from BS$704; ❈🔊≋) A ferry whisks lucky guests across the water to a 96-acre private island, home to this exquisite luxury resort. Discrete, delightful villas are tucked away down paths lined with kamalame trees, wild dilly, casuarina and love vine, inland from miles of perfect beach. Don't miss a massage at the spa on stilts above the sea. Access near Staniard Creek.

🍴 Eating & Drinking

If you like fresh fish and straightforward Bahamian cooking, you'll do very well in these parts. There are no fancy establishments, but clean, welcoming shacks serving souse, conch, wings and fish to the locals are present in every settlement.

Taste & See
BAHAMIAN $

(☏ 242-368-2240; Love Hill; mains BS$13-17; ⊙noon-10pm Tue-Sat) Expect to be embraced when you walk into this homey cafe – literally! Owner Cinderella Hinsey hugs all her guests, whether or not she's met them before. Her love overflows into the food – delectable cracked conch, sautéed lobster and barbecue turkey.

Hank's Place BAR

(242-368-2447; east of Fresh Creek Bridge, Fresh Creek; ⊙ 3-10pm Tue-Fri, to 2am Sat; 🛜) With a cabana stretching out over Fresh Creek, a chicken-wire-sided bar that lets in the afternoon breezes and setting sun, a welcoming local clientele and good Bahamian food, Hank's is a great place to unwind after a day's diving, exploring or fishing. Things get late and louche on Saturdays, when a DJ cranks up the fun.

ⓘ Information

Government Medical Clinic (242-368-2038, after hours 242-471-8360; Fresh Creek; ⊙ 8:30am-4pm Mon-Fri)

Police Station (242-368-2626, 919; www.royalbahamaspolice.org; Fresh Creek) In the pink government complex on the east side of the Queen's Hwy as you head north out of Fresh Creek, into Coakley Town.

Post Office (242-368-2012; www.bahamas.gov.bs; Fresh Creek; ⊙ 9am-4pm Mon-Fri) Also in the pink government complex.

Royal Bank of Canada (Fresh Creek; ⊙ 9am-4pm Mon-Fri)

Tourist Office (242-368-2286; www.bahamas.com; Mayeu Plaza, Queen's Hwy, Andros Town; ⊙ 9am-5pm Mon-Fri)

ⓘ Getting There & Away

You'll arrive either at **San Andros International Airport** (p178) for North Andros or **Andros Town Airport** (p178) for Central Andros; both are just a 15-minute joy-flight from Nassau. **Western Air** (p178) schedules a few services a day to San Andros, but jumping on one of **Southern Air's** (p178) nine-seat charters is more likely. There's also **Bahamas Ferries'** (p190) Friday-morning service from Nassau to Fish Creek.

ⓘ Getting Around

Whether you fly or get the ferry, you'll need to hire a car to get anywhere once you're in the Big Yard. If arriving in Fresh Creek, try Adderley's (242-357-2149); in San Andros, give the Nicholls Town–based A&H Car Rental a go (242-329-2685 or 242-329-2131). Rentals start from around BS\$75 per day, with discounts for three or more days.

Mangrove Cay & South Andros

Mangrove Cay and South Andros are pretty much the wildest and most isolated areas of one of the Bahamas' wildest and most isolated islands. Virgin Caribbean-pine forests, vibrant reefs, uncluttered beaches of pink-and-silver sand, eerie blue holes and abundant, lush mangroves make it a nature-lover's dream. Add to that its inaccessibility, sparse population and minimal development, and it could hardly be a better place to drop off the grid.

🛏 Sleeping & Eating

The paucity of options is more than outweighed by how blissful many of those options are, from all-inclusive resorts to fishing lodges. And once you're happily accommodated, that paucity means peace.

★ Seascape Inn RESORT \$\$

(242-369-0342; www.seascapeinn.com; Mangrove Cay; cabanas from BS\$180; ⊜🛜) New Yorkers Mickey and Joan McGowan escaped the city life to run this Swiss Family Robinson–like colony of beach cabanas, and their friendliness has earned them a loyal following. Snorkel, kayak, fish, borrow a bike, commune with the dogs on the beach, or just shoot the breeze with other guests in the small on-site restaurant and pub.

Tiamo RESORT \$\$\$

(242-225-6871; www.tiamoresorts.com; South Andros; villa from BS\$850; ⊙ 7am-8pm; ❄🛜) Accessible only by water, this all-inclusive resort caters to couples seeking intimacy and exclusivity. Ten cottages have a luxe ecochic vibe – all pale wood, slate tiles and textured linens. Guests lounge on private porches, swim in the placid, protected beach or sip cocktails on the poolside terrace. Everything but liquor is included, and the minimum guest age is 14.

ⓘ Getting There & Away

Flights from Nassau to South Andros (Congo Town) and Mangrove Cay (Clarence A. Bain Airport) aren't scarce, but may require a charter with either **Southern Air** or **Flamingo Air** (p178). That sounds extravagant, but these little nine-seaters wait until they have a full load (which rarely takes long) and sharing the cost of the 15- to 20-minute flight translates to a reasonable fee (perhaps BS\$80, one way).

Regular ferries don't serve South Andros, and there's no way to get the car you've been driving on North and Central Andros onto the southern parts of Andros. There's a daily government passenger ferry between Lisbon Creek (Mangrove Cay) and Driggs Hill (South Andros). To get to Mangrove Cay from the southern end of the Middle Caicos road at Behring Point, you'll need to ask (and probably pay) a local with a boat.

Government Ferry (🕿 242-357-2926; Lisbon Creek, Mangrove Cay) This free service departs every day from Lisbon Creek in Mangrove Cay at 8:30am and 4pm, hopping across to Driggs Hill on South Andros. The return service leaves Driggs Hill at 4:30pm.

The Exumas

More than 300 islands and cays scattered across the central Bahamas, the Exumas are renowned for blissfully isolated beaches, world-class diving, and serene resorts that effortlessly dissolve anyone's troubles away. There's Great Exuma and Little Exuma, wonderful in their own right, and then there's the stunning Exuma Cays: a string of mostly uninhabited ocean outposts surrounded by blooming reefs and astonishing ecological bounty. The jewel in that crown is the Exuma Cays Land and Sea Park, a huge expanse of islands, water and reef founded as the world's first land-and-sea reserve in 1958.

Dry land, especially that of Great and Little Exuma, supports historic ruins, lively settlements, blissful beaches and some exceptional hotels, resorts and restaurants. Whether you visit just the principal islands, sail through the gorgeous reef-fringed Cays, or are lucky enough to combine the two, your time in the Exumas will be a highlight of your Bahamian adventure.

ⓘ Getting There & Away

There are regular flights connecting Nassau and Exuma. Or you can take the ferry or mailboat.

ⓘ Getting Around

BOAT

Two services leave from George Town Government Dock for various points on Stocking Island: **Elvis Water Taxi** (🕿 242-464-1558; return BS$12) and Martin Ferry. They're basically doing the same thing, and will charge you BS$15 to BS$20 return, depending on which part of Stocking Island you're headed to. They operate from roughly 10am to 5pm daily, leave hourly (or when full) and will collect you for the return trip at your preferred time.

CAR

Airport Car Rental (🕿 242-345-0090; www.exumacarrental.com; Exuma International Airport; ⊙7am-7pm) rents cars from BS$75 per day.

TAXI

Exuma Transit Services (🕿 242-345-0232) and **Leslie Dames** (🕿 242-357-0015) both run taxi services around the island.

George Town

Great Exuma's major center, the capital of the island group, is where you'll find the sugar-pink-and-white neoclassical Government Administration Building, housing the post office (p182) and jail. Just south, the small **straw market** (🕿 242-336-2584; Queen's Hwy, George Town; ⊙8am-6pm Mon-Sat) sells Bahamian-made straw goods, while to the north is the white-stoned Georgian St Andrew's Anglican Church, straddling a bluff above Lake Victoria, the circular saltwater lagoon in the middle of town.

🏃 Activities

Out Island Explorers   BOATING
(🕿 242-336-2246; www.outislandexplorers.com; George Town; per person BS$1895) Out Island Explorers' guided sailing trips are one of the loveliest ways to see the Exuma Cays. From George Town you'll wend your way north through the cays for six days and five nights, with snorkeling gear, food and everything else you might need onboard. At Staniel Cay the trip ends, and a charter flight carries you back. Four-person minimum.

Off Island Adventures   TOUR
(🕿 242-524-0524; www.offislandadventures.com; George Town) Off Island specializes in exploring the sights and sites close to George Town and Elizabeth Harbour. Tours start from BS$300 for three hours' snorkeling and exploring Stocking Island's blue hole and beaches, and go all the way to an eight-hour, BS$900 trip to White Cay, the most remote of the cays and yet another Exuman *Pirates of the Caribbean* location.

Starfish   WATER SPORTS
(🕿 242-524-1104; www.starfishexuma.com; 👪) Starfish offers a variety of watery pursuits, including renting sea kayaks by the day/week (BS$60/240), snorkeling at Mystery Cave and Fowl Cay, and guided trips to visit Thunderball Grotto, Staniel Cay and the famous swimming pigs of Major Cay. They'll

pick you up from most hotels within a reasonable distance of George Town.

Minn's Water Sports
BOATING

(🖂 242-336-3483; www.mwsboats.com; Queen's Hwy, George Town) Rents out boats from BS$125/155 per half-/full day, with reduced rates for bookings over two days. The boats, which aren't licensed for waters beyond Elizabeth Harbour, vary in size from 4½m to 6½m. A BS$200 to BS$300 cash deposit is required.

Dive Exuma
DIVING

(🖂 242-357-0313; www.dive-exuma.com; Government Dock, George Town; ⊙ 9am-3pm Mon-Fri, or by appointment) The most highly recommended (and only PADI) operation in town, Dive Exuma offers two-tank dives for BS$145, shark-dives on Long Island for BS$180, PADI courses from BS$450 and half-day snorkeling trips for BS$75.

🎆 Festivals & Events

Bahamian Music & Heritage Festival
CULTURAL

(🖂 242-336-2430; Regatta Point, Georgetown; per night adult/6-12yr/2-5yr BS$20/7/5; ⊙ noon-midnight Fri-Sun early Mar) This annual celebration of Bahamian food, music, crafts and other cultural traditions turns Regatta Point into a night party from Friday to Sunday. Watch out for competitive conch cracking and sugarcane peeling.

🛏 Sleeping

Coral Gardens
B&B $

(🖂 242-336-2206; www.coralgardensbahamas. com; George Town; r/apt from BS$99/125; ❋ 🛜) Run by retired Brits Peter and Betty, this charming house is located a few hundred meters inland from lovely Hooper's Bay, and is one of the best deals on the island. The three bedrooms all have private bathrooms, and two small apartments are equally pleasant and good value. Peter is a mine of local information.

Regatta Point
GUESTHOUSE $$

(🖂 242-336-2206; www.regattapointbahamas.com; Regatta Point, George Town; d from BS$211; 🅿) Perfectly located on the peninsula sheltering Kidd Cove, these guesthouses manage to be both tucked away and close to the center of George Town. All six enjoy full kitchens and casuarina-shaded gardens leading to a rocky private beach. TV and wi-fi are deliberately absent, rooms are fan-cooled, hot water is

solar-powered and the welcome is genuinely warm.

Club Peace & Plenty
HOTEL $$

(🖂 242-336-2551; www.peaceandplenty.com; Queen's Hwy, George Town; r from BS$222; ❋ 🛜 ≋) Built on the location of an old slave market and plantation, this friendly hotel in the middle of George Town has 32 bright rooms, a small pool, a bar (the former plantation cookhouse) and a seaside deck with views to Stocking Island. There's also rake 'n' scrape barbecues on Thursdays, and snorkel gear available for rent.

🍴 Eating

Eddie's Edgewater Club
CAFE $

(🖂 242-336-2050; Queen's Hwy, George Town; mains BS$12-17; ⊙ 7am-10pm Mon-Thu, to midnight Fri & Sat) This very reliable, friendly and informal restaurant serves up three tasty Bahamian meals a day, including changing daily specials. There's a pleasant terrace with views over Lake Victoria, a more formal dining room at the back and a large bar that's always packed on Mondays for the island's most popular rake 'n' scrape music evening.

ℹ Information

Police (🖂 242-336-2666; George Town)

Post Office (🖂 242-336-2636; George Town; ⊙ 9am-4pm Mon-Fri)

Royal Bank of Canada (Queen's Hwy, George Town; ⊙ 9am-4pm Mon-Fri) Has an ATM.

Tourist Office (🖂 242-336-2430; www.bahamas.com; Queen's Hwy, George Town; ⊙ 9am-5pm Mon-Fri)

South of George Town

The first major settlement south of George Town is Rolle Town, recalling the Loyalist planter who lends his name to the estimated 60% of native Exumans descended from his emancipated slaves. For panoramic views, follow the main road, Queen's Hwy, to the town's hilltop crossroads. A keep-you-on-your-toes one-lane bridge links Great and Little Exuma at the town of Ferry.

Further on down the Queen's Hwy, past the town of Forbes Hill, two stunning beaches await. (Look for the beach access signs.) On one of them, Tropic of Cancer Beach, has the namesake line of latitude marked by a faded blue line. Further down the Queen's Hwy, lonely William's Town is home to the overgrown ruins of the Hermitage Estate, a cotton plantation once run by local bigwigs the Rolles.

Exuma Kitesurfing   KITESURFING

(☑ 242-524-7099; www.exumakitesurfing.com; Beach Access Rd, Rolle Town; ☺ 9am-5pm) Offers a dizzying array of packages, including 2½-hour beginner lessons from BS$250 and four-hour 'kiteventures' from BS$190. Also offers stand-up paddleboarding (three hours, with gear and instruction, from BS$160) and accommodation (cottages and bungalows from BS$259 per night).

Santanna's Grill   BAHAMIAN $$

(☑ 242-345-4102; Queen's Hwy, William's Town; mains BS$18-22; ☺ 10:30am-5pm Mon-Sat) Run by the formidable Denise Rolle, this friendly grill offers the best-value fresh lobster in the Exumas, and its many regulars often entertain diners with increasingly tall stories from the *Pirates of the Caribbean* shoot, part of which took place at nearby Sandy Point. There's also a great (if rocky) beach just a few feet from the bar.

★ Tropic Breeze   BAHAMIAN $$

(☑ 242-345-4100; Queen's Hwy, William's Town; mains BS$16-25; ☺ 11am-7pm Tue-Sat) The sandy extremes of Great Exuma aren't the first place you'd look to find a Cordon Bleu–trained chef pumping out lobster poppers and other must-have favorites, but this relaxed shack perched above the pounding waves serves some of the country's best Bahamian food.

Stocking Island

This 240-hectare (600-acre) slip of an island beckons about 1½km off the coast, separated from George Town by the turquoise beauty of Elizabeth Harbour. For a day trip appealing to adventurers and beach bums alike, grab a water taxi to from the Government Dock in George Town to the island (BS$15 to BS$20), where you can snorkel, stroll over talcum-fine sand or bushwhack up a nature 'trail' to the island's highest point. Don't miss the short hike across the island to the Atlantic for more deep-blue views. The Chat & Chill's (p183) Sunday-afternoon pig roast (BS$20) is a don't-miss affair.

Chat & Chill Bar & Grill   BAHAMIAN $$

(☑ 242-336-2700; www.chatnchill.com; Stocking Island; mains BS$20-23; ☺ 11am-7pm; ☑) Located on the low sand spit bordering Stocking Island's shallow 'harbor', Chat & Chill combines a bar, broad casuarina-shaded beaches, volleyball court, gift shop, conch shack and more into one beachside pleasure complex. Sunday's pig-roast (BS$20) is an Exuma institution, and you should make sure to bring swimwear to fraternize with the friendly stingrays beneath the conch shack.

Exuma Cays

The Exuma Cays are a world unto themselves and the stuff of Caribbean fantasy. Tantalizingly inaccessible (you'll need to have your own boat or charter one to make it to most places), they begin at the barren Sail Rocks, nearly 60km southeast of New Providence, and continue in a long line of some 360 islets to Great Exuma. Most are uninhabited, and all are part of the same oceanic mountain range, yet each is distinct, and many are privately owned.

If you're in your own boat and island-hopping at your leisure, visiting picturesque Staniel Cay is recommended. Here you can explore wonderful Thunderball Grotto (appearing in the eponymous 1965 Bond flick), and snorkel around pristine reefs for an unbeatable Bahamas experience.

The first marine 'replenishment nursery' in the world, created in 1958, the **Exuma Cays Land & Sea Park** (☑ 242-225-6402; www.exumapark.org; ☺ office 9am-noon & 1-4pm Mon-Sat, 9am-noon Sun) boasts 283 sq km of protected islands and surrounding seas. All fishing and collecting is banned – including plants and shells – and the diving is accordingly out of this world.

Staniel Cay Yacht Club   RESORT $$

(☑ 242-355-2024; www.stanielcay.com; Staniel Cay; r from BS$291; ❋ ☞ ☲) On tiny picturesque Staniel Cay, this resort offers waterfront bungalows, smaller double rooms and all-inclusive packages including sailing, meals, snorkeling, kayaks and more. Spacious verandas make soaking in the sensational views a pleasure, and the cool and comfortable rooms are available at reduced weekly rates. Book ahead.

Long Island

Straddling the Tropic of Cancer, Long Island is one of the most scenic Out Islands, a slender 130km north–south expanse of sand with stunning white-and-sky-blue churches, lush greenery, elaborate cave systems and bougainvillea-draped villages. The lone highway leads to magnificent bays, blue holes and kilometers of empty beaches, and some delightful resorts help you make the most of this Eden, without sacrificing comfort.

🏃 Sights & Activities

Dean's Blue Hole
CAVE
The second-deepest blue hole in the world, at 203m, this remarkable vertical cave teems with sea life and is globally renowned as a free-diving location.

Conception Island Wall
DIVE SITE
Some 20km northeast of Long Island lies the Conception Island, an uninhabited land-and-sea nature reserve. The lavish coral heads, warm currents and unmolested marine life to be found in the waters off its leeward shore offer some of the most spectacular diving in the Bahamas.

Love Beaches
BEACH
This beautiful string of pink-sand beaches near Stella Maris includes a sheltered 'swimming pool' (a calm stretch of water protected by rocks) for wee ones to paddle in safety.

🛏 Sleeping & Eating

Long Island's beaches, reefs and unspoiled space are natural territory for resorts, and there's a wide range of these throughout the island, alongside more basic hotels (which are most plentiful in Clarence Town).

⭐ Cape Santa Maria
RESORT $$
(☑ 1-800-663-7090; www.capesantamaria.com; 1327 Beach Dr, Stella Maris; bungalow from BS$366; 🛜) A string of bungalows and villas along the gleaming-white Cape Santa Maria Beach, this resort brings to life what many have in mind when seeking untrammeled coastal relaxation. There are gazebos and daybeds for enjoying the island air, the usual suite of sea-based activities on offer, and half- and full-board packages available.

Stella Maris Resort
RESORT $$
(☑ 242-338-2050; www.stellamarisresort.com; s/d from BS$187/233; @🛜🏊) Hotel-style rooms and beach cottages at this delightfully situated resort invite relaxed satisfaction, with patios or verandas, quality bedding, and unspoiled Atlantic views throughout. Activities on offer are mainly marine and the on-site beach bar and restaurant are

no afterthoughts (full-board packages are BS$102 extra).

Chez Pierre
INTERNATIONAL $$
(☑ 242-338-8809; www.chezpierrebahamas.com; Queen's Hwy, Miller's Bay; mains BS$22-26; ⏰ 7-8:30am, noon-1:30pm, 5-8pm; 🛜) The eponymous French-Canadian Pierre produces food that treats good produce with love and skill, all in a delightfully scenic setting by the sea. Global crowd-pleasers such as pizza and pasta are augmented by more refined French and European fare.

ℹ Information

Tourist Office (☑ 242-338-8668; Queen's Hwy, Salt Pond; ⏰ 9am-5pm Mon-Fri)

ℹ Getting There & Away

Long Isand has two airports: **Stella Maris** (☑ 242-338-2006; Queen's Hwy) in the north, with three scheduled flights per week from Nassau, and **Deadman's Cay** (☑ 242-337-7077; Queen's Hwy), north of Clarence Town, with daily flights to the capital.

UNDERSTAND THE BAHAMAS

History
The original inhabitants of the Bahamas were a tribe of Arawaks, the peaceful Lucayans, who arrived near the turn of the 9th century. Christopher Columbus arrived in 1492, and shortly thereafter the Spanish began shipping out the Lucayans as slaves.

Infamous pirates such as Blackbeard and Calico Jack took over New Providence in the 1600s, establishing a pirates' paradise lined with brothels and taverns for 'common cheats, thieves and lewd persons.' With the aid of Woodes Rogers, the Bahamas' first Royal Governor and a former privateer, the British finally established order, and an administration answerable to the English Crown, in 1718. The Bahamas' new motto was *Expulsis Piratis – Restituta Commercia* (Pirates Expelled – Commerce Restored).

Following the American Revolution, Loyalist refugees – many quite rich or entrepreneurial – began arriving, giving new vigor to the city. These wealthy landowners lived well and kept slaves until the British Empire abolished the slave trade. During the American Civil War the islands were an exchange center for blockade runners transferring munitions and supplies for Southern cotton.

While Nassauvians illicitly supplied liquor to the US during Prohibition, Yankees flocked to Nassau and its new casinos. When Fidel Castro spun Cuba into Soviet orbit in 1961, the subsequent US embargo forced revelers to seek their pleasures elsewhere; Nassau became *the* new hot spot.

Tourism and finance bloomed together. The government promoted the nascent banking industry, encouraging British investors escaping onerous taxes.

This upturn in fortunes coincided with the evolution of party politics and festering ethnic tensions, as the white elite and a growing black middle class reaped profits from the boom. Middle-class blacks' aspirations for representation coalesced with the pent-up frustrations of their impoverished brothers, leading to the victory of the black-led Progressive Liberal party and leader Sir Lynden Pindling in 1967. On July 10, 1973, the Bahamas officially became a new nation – the Independent Commonwealth of the Bahamas – ending 325 years of British rule.

Devastating hurricanes ravaged various islands between 1999 and 2016, wreaking havoc on tourism. Despite these storms, the tourism juggernaut continues and massive resorts on New Providence, Grand Bahama and several Out Islands are chugging toward completion.

People & Culture

Contemporary Bahamian culture still revolves around family, church and the sea, but the proximity of North America and the arrival of cable TV has had a profound influence on contemporary life and material values.

In Nassau and Freeport, most working people are employed in banking, tourism or government work and live a nine-to-five lifestyle.

The citizens inhabiting the islands outside of New Providence and Grand Bahama, called the Out Islands or Family Islands, are a bit more neighborly and traditional. Thus the practice of Obeah (a form of African-based ritual magic), bush medicine, and folkloric songs and tales still infuse their daily lives. Though tourism is bringing change to the Out Islands, many people still live simple lives centered on fishing, catching conch and lobster, and raising corn, bananas and other crops.

The Bahamas rock to the soul-riveting sounds of calypso, soca, reggae and its own distinctive music, which echoes African rhythms and synthesizes Caribbean calypso, soca and English folk songs into its own goombay beat.

Goombay – the name comes from an African word for 'rhythm' – derives its melody from a guitar, piano or horn instrument, accompanied by any combination of goatskin goombay drums, maracas, rhythm sticks, rattles, conch-shell horns, fifes, flutes and cowbells, to add a *kalik-kalik-kalik* sound.

Rake 'n' scrape is the Bahamas' downhome, working-class music, usually featuring a guitar, an accordion, shakers made from the pods of poinciana trees, and other makeshift instruments, such as a saw played with a screwdriver.

Landscape & Wildlife

Wildlife

The islands are a birdwatcher's paradise, with about 300 recorded species of birds. Only a few are endemic, including the Bahama swallow, the endangered Bahama parrot, and the Bahama woodstar hummingbird, a pugnacious bird weighing less than a US nickel. The West Indian (Caribbean) flamingo – the national bird – inhabits Crooked Island, Long Cay and the sanctuary of Great Inagua.

Iguanas inhabit some outlying isles and cays, and are protected. The archipelago's largest native land animal, they can reach 1.2m in length.

The region's marine life is as varied as its islands and coral reefs. Depending on who you believe, the Bahamas have between 2330 sq km and 6992 sq km of coral reef, and countless species of fish, such as bonito, stingrays, sharks, kingfish, jewelfish and deep-blue Creole wrasse.

Humpback whales pass through the waters windward of the Bahamas and blue whales are also frequently sighted.

The Land

The Bahamian islands are strewn in a linear fashion from northwest to southeast.

Several of them – Great Abaco, Eleuthera, Long Island and Andros – are more than 160km in length. Few, however, are more than a few miles wide. All are low-lying, and the highest point in the Bahamas – Mt Alvernia on Cat Island – is only 62m above sea level.

Virtually the entire length of these shores is lined by white- or pinkish-sand beaches – about 3540km in all – shelving into turquoise shallows. The interiors are generally marked by scrub-filled forests and, on some of the more remote islands, the plants found here are still used in bush medicine.

The islands are pocked by blue holes – water-filled circular pits that open to underground and submarine caves and descend as far as 182m.

Environmental Issues

The Bahamas National Trust maintains 26 national parks and reserves, including large sections of the barrier reef, but outside of the national park system, inappropriate development, pollution and overexploitation increasingly threaten wildlife and marine resources. Although the Bahamas was the first Caribbean nation to outlaw long-line fishing, the islands' stocks of grouper, spiny lobster and conch all face the consequences of overfishing.

Today, local groups are leading the eco-charge. The Abacos' Friends of the Environment (www.friendsoftheenvironment. org) organizes community-wide projects and passes the message along in schools. In Eleuthera, the Eleuthera School (www. islandschool.org) is earning kudos as an environmental learning center, drawing US high schoolers as well as adult 'students' looking to become environmentally engaged global citizens.

The Bahamas banned hunting and eating of sea turtles, an endangered species, in 2009.

SURVIVAL GUIDE

ℹ Directory A–Z

ACCOMMODATIONS

The Bahamas are known for their resorts, from basic family places to no-expense-spared enclaves of extreme privilege. But there are alternatives: most inhabited islands offer villas and hotels and (with a little more effort) a few hostels and campsites can be found. Bear in mind that some places close annually around September and October, and that booking ahead is strongly advised in peak periods (US summer and college holidays).

ACTIVITIES

The Bahamas are an outdoor-lover's paradise: swimming, snorkeling, diving, kitesurfing, sailing, hiking and birdwatching are just some of the activities most islands have on tap.

Fishing Seasons

Bahamian waters are famed for their aquatic life, but of course it pays to know when the fish are biting. The months in which the main species are are most common:

Amberjack March to August
Blackfin tuna & bonito June & July
Blue marlin June
Bonefish Perennial, especially March and April
Grouper & snapper March to August
Mahi-mahi ('dolphin') April
Swordfish June to September
Wahoo November to March

Naturally, there's not an inexhaustible supply of fish, and strict limits and (in some cases) seasons are enforced. The primary considerations:
➤ All boats engaged in fishing must have a permit, available from customs officials at ports

of entry. Naturally, chartered fishing boats will be licensed.

⇒ Only hooks and lines may be used (no nets or spear-guns) and no more than six rods at once.

⇒ Lobsters may only be caught from August to March, and only 10 tails (of more than 6 inches each; no egg-bearing females) at a time are allowed.

⇒ Conch must have a well-formed lip, and no more than six per vessel may be harvested.

⇒ No more than 60lb of (or 20 individual) demersal fish (such as grouper and snapper) of more than 3lb each are allowed per vessel.

⇒ No more than 18 migratory species (tuna, kingfish, wahoo etc) are allowed per vessel.

CHILDREN

With endless acres of beach, a tourist industry that avidly pursues the family dollar and a naturally kid-friendly culture, the Bahamas are an ideal place to vacation with wee ones. The larger hotels provide good facilities, including babysitting, pools and activities, and resorts such as Atlantis (p156) are such kid-friendly wonderlands that families could feasibly never leave their pleasure compounds (and many don't). Children under 12 years often room with their parents for free.

From the colossal Aquaventure Waterpark (p156) on Paradise Island to the eccentric petting zoo at Andros's Pineville Motel (p179), there's a full spectrum of attractions for kids of all ages. Dive outfits like Stuart Cove (p157) offer discounted snorkeling rates to kids between four and 11, for whom the personal submersibles (SUBs) rented by Abaco Scuba Center (p170) are also a sure bet. For the very small (or less confident), companies such as Reef Tours (p161) run glass-bottomed boats that make getting face-to-face with the reef and its critters a cinch.

Sightseeing with a stroller is easiest in the built-up centers of Nassau, Paradise Island and Port Lucaya. Outside these areas, sidewalks get rougher, and often disappear altogether, obliging you to walk on the shoulder of the road. Dedicated change facilities are scarce to non-existent in public, so prepare to improvise.

Well-behaved kids are generally welcome in all restaurants, barring a few top-end places that explicitly advertise a minimum age.

ELECTRICITY

Electrical outlets are 120 volts/60 cycles, which is compatible with US appliances. Plug sockets are two- or three-prong US standard: appliances may require an adapter and 220-volt converter.

FOOD

Bahamian food reflects the bounty of the seas and the islands' mixed European, African and

South American heritage. Chilies, bay leaves, allspice and lime are common spices. The islands aren't especially fertile, and many staples must be imported. If it grows in sandy tropical soils (coconut), or it swims in the surrounding seas (lobster, grouper), it's usually the best thing on the menu.

Essential Food & Drink

Conch Roasted, cracked (fried), chopped into salads or dipped in dough and fried into fritters, this chewy sea snail is ubiquitous in the Bahamas. Think calamari. Starchy side dishes like peas 'n' rice (rice with beans), mac 'n' cheese and potato salad round out the menu.

Boil fish A breakfast dish of grouper stewed with lime juice, onions and potatoes. Usually served with johnnycake, a sweetish type of flat cornbread.

Spiny Caribbean lobster The Bahamas' native lobster, often served sautéed with onions and pepper, minced and even curried.

Souse A thick stew of chicken, sheep's head, pig's trotter or other 'leftover' meats.

Guava duff Boiled pastry filled with sweet guava paste and topped off with rum or cream sauce.

Beer Wash everything down with a cold Kalik or Sands beer.

Rum cocktails Try goombay smash or a Bahama mama.

Switcher A refreshing lime-based drink, sometimes available as an alcoholic version.

Sky juice Gin and coconut milk.

THE BAHAMAS DIRECTORY A–Z

EMBASSIES & CONSULATES

Most countries are represented by honorary consuls and most consulates are located in Nassau, New Providence. These include the following:

Australian Consulate (🗹 242-327-8301; http://dfat.gov.au; Lyford Manor, Lyford Cay; ⊙ 9am-5pm Mon-Fri)

Canadian Consulate (🗹 242-393-2123; Shirley St Plaza; ⊙ 9:30am-noon Mon-Thu)

Dutch Consulate (🗹 242-359-3322; Virginia St)

French Consulate (🗹 242-302-5001; Lyford Cay House, Western Rd; ⊙ 8am-4pm Mon-Fri)

German Consulate (🗹 242-357-3633; Suite 115, Lagoon Ct, Olde Towne Sandyport)

UK Consulate (🗹 242-225-6033)

US Embassy (🗹 242-322-1181; https://bs.usembassy.gov; Mosmar Bldg, Queen Street; ⊙ 8:30am-5:30pm Mon-Thu, to 1pm Fri)

GLBT TRAVELERS

Homosexuality is legal in the Bahamas (for those 18 and over), though the pink dollar isn't particularly welcome. There's not much public support for gay and lesbian populations across the islands, and discretion is the better part of affection here. Gay bars and clubs are very subterranean.

The Facebook page of the gay-rights group Rainbow Alliance of the Bahamas is a good place for information and contacts.

HEALTH

Nassau and Grand Bahama have modern hospitals with emergency rooms open 24/7, but free care is only provided to legal residents. The Out Islands are serviced by small government clinics, usually found off the Queen's Hwy in the major settlements and open 9am to 5pm Monday to Friday. All will have 24-hour emergency numbers posted outside, although serious conditions will have to be treated in one of the major centers.

LEGAL MATTERS

The Bahamian legal system bears traces of UK common law and the US constitutional model. Innocence is presumed, and arrests must follow prescribed legal limits.

Recreational drugs are strictly prohibited in The Bahamas. There are reports of cruise-ship passengers in possession of small amounts of marijuana and cocaine being faced with either paying a BS$500 to BS$800 on-the-spot fine, or being sent to jail for three months.

The legal limit for blood alcohol content when driving is 0.06%; breaching this can attract penalties of up to BS$3000, or time in jail.

If you are arrested, authorities are obliged to contact your embassy or consulate on request.

There is no automatic public-defense provision for foreigners in lower courts, and any representation must be self-funded.

MONEY

Bahamian (BS$) and US (US$) are equal and interchangeable throughout the country.

ATMs

There are plenty of banks with ATMs in the major tourist centers, though they can be rare to nonexistent on the Out Islands. ATMs near the Nassau cruise-ship dock offer either BS$ or US$.

Exchange Rates

AUSTRALIA	A$1	BS$0.74
CANADA	C$1	BS$0.76
EURO ZONE	€1	BS$1.07
JAPAN	¥100	BS$0.88
NEW ZEALAND	NZ$1	BS$0.72
UK	UK£1	BS$1.26

For current exchange rates, see www.xe.com.

Tipping

A tip of 15% or so is standard for restaurants, but it's often added to your bill automatically – check before you pay. About 15% is the norm for taxis, while BS$2 per bag is routine for porters.

PUBLIC HOLIDAYS

Bahamian national holidays that fall on Saturday or Sunday are usually observed on the previous Friday or following Monday.

New Year's Day January 1

Majority Rule Day January 10

Good Friday March/April

Easter Monday March/April

Whit Monday Seventh Monday after Easter

Labour Day First Friday in June

Independence Day July 10

Emancipation Day First Monday in August

National Heroes Day Second Monday in October

Christmas Day December 25

Boxing Day December 26

TAXES & REFUNDS

Value-added tax (VAT) of 7.5% is imposed on all goods and services in the Bahamas. Some businesses list the pretax price, some the final price, and some both prices. Hotels and restaurants usually list just the pretax price.

The introduction of a VAT Free Shopping Scheme in 2016 has enabled participating merchants to sell goods tax-free to tourists.

TELEPHONE

Hotel phones Rates are expensive across the region and should be avoided when possible. Many hotels also charge for an unanswered call after the receiving phone has rung five times.

Phone codes The Bahamian country code is ☑242. You need to dial this when making inter-island calls from landlines, but not from cell phones. To call the Bahamas from the US and Canada, dial ☑1-242. From elsewhere, dial your country's international access code + 242 + the local number. Most US toll-free numbers can't be accessed from the Bahamas. Usually you must dial ☑1-880, plus the last seven digits of the number.

Public phones The government-owned Bahamas **Telecommunications Corporation** (☑242-302-7000; www.btcbahamas.com), or BTC, has an office on most Bahamian islands. Even the smallest settlement usually has at least one public phone.

TIME

All of the Bahamas falls within the Eastern Standard Time Zone. It switches to Daylight Saving Time (DST) at the same time as the USA and Canada.

TRAVELERS WITH DISABILITIES

Disabled travelers will need to plan their vacation carefully, as few allowances have been made for them in the Bahamas. The larger hotels and resorts are generally well set up for accessibility, but beyond their gates, things get tough. Tourism boards can provide a list of hotels with wheelchair ramps, as can the **Bahamas National Council for Disability** (☑242-323-8533; www.bncdbahamas.org) and the **Bahamas Association for the Physically Disabled** (☑242-322-2393). While these organizations don't have offices open to the public, you can call them or contact them online for help hiring equipment and organizing accessible holiday options.

For more ideas, download Lonely Planet's free Accessible Travel guide from http://lptravel.to/AccessibleTravel.

VOLUNTEERING

Volunteering options aren't rich in the Bahamas, outside of missionary organizations. Hurricane season does bring its opportunities, sadly, as there can be huge cleanup and reconstruction efforts to be undertaken. Organizations such as Volunteer Match (www.volunteermatch.org) can help you find a way to make a difference in the wake of a particularly violent storm.

Marine monitoring and conservation is, however, an area in which volunteer programs are well established in the Bahamas. Programs lasting several weeks to several months and involving volunteers in reef monitoring, turtle tagging and similar activities can be found through Earthwatch Institute (www.earthwatch.org). The Bahamas National Trust (http://bnt.bs) also invites volunteers for conservation programs in the 2 million acres of habitat it manages throughout the islands.

🛈 Getting There & Away

The Bahamas have six international airports, with major hubs at Nassau and Freeport. The two cities are also popular stopovers for cruise ships.

AIR

The Bahamas' proximity to Florida means regular, relatively inexpensive flights from Miami, Fort Lauderdale and Orlando, as well as other East Coast gateways. A few airlines fly directly to airports on the larger Out Islands, but the majority of flights arrive in Nassau or Freeport where passengers will connect to another flight before continuing to the Out Islands. For a brief summary of airlines and flight schedules by island, check www.bahamas.com.

The national airline **Bahamasair** (☑242-702-4140; https://bahamasair.com) has an unblemished safety record and its pilots have an excellent reputation (see www.airsafe.com for details). Delays, however, are regular occurrences and flights are canceled without warning. Bahamians like to say, 'If you have time to spare, fly Bahamasair.'

Lynden Pindling International Airport (Nassau; http://nassaulpia.com) The Bahamas' number-one entry point, with direct services to the USA, Canada, the UK, the Cayman Islands, Cuba, Jamaica, Panama and Turks and Caicos.

Grand Bahama International Airport (Freeport) Direct flights to the US and Canada.

SEA

Numerous cruise ships dock in Nassau and Grand Bahama, most originating in Florida. Among the most prominent are **Carnival** (☑US 1-800-764-7419; www.carnival.com), **Bahamas Paradise** (☑US 1-800-995-3201; www.grandcelebration.com), **Costa** (☑US 1-800-462-6782; www.costacruise.com), **Norwegian** (☑UK 020-8834-9019; www.ncl.com) and **Royal Caribbean** (☑UK 0844-493-4005; www.royalcaribbean.com).

The sheltered waters of the archipelago attract thousands of yachters each year. Winds and currents favor the passage south, and sailing conditions are at their best in summer, though hurricanes can be a threat throughout the season (June to November).

Private boats arriving in the Bahamas must clear customs and immigration at an official port of entry, of which there are around 50 across the islands. Until clearance is given, the yellow quarantine flag must be flown, and only the captain can come ashore. All aboard must fill out immigration forms, and there's an entry fee for each vessel (BS$150 for vessels of less than 35ft, BS$300 for anything larger), which includes cruising and fishing permits and departure tax for three people.

ⓘ Getting Around

Perusing a map, it's tempting to think that island-hopping down the chain is easy. Unfortunately, it's not – that is, unless you have your own boat or plane. Interisland air is centered on Nassau, and getting between the islands without constantly backtracking is a bit of a feat. Even the mail boats are Nassau-centric.

AIR

Airlines

Interisland airlines include:

Bahamasair (☑ 242-702-4140; https://bahamasair.com)

Pineapple Air (☑ 242-702-7133; www.pineappleair.com)

SkyBahamas (☑ 242-702-2600; www.skybahamas.net)

Southern Air (☑ 242-323-7217, 242-323-6833; www.southernaircharter.com)

Western Air (☑ 242-329-4000; www.westernairbahamas.com)

Charter Service

In the Bahamas, charter services fill the gaps that scheduled flights can't profitably address. Islands served and the services that can connect to them:

DESTINATION	AIRLINE
Andros	Southern Air
Cat Island	Southern Air
Exuma Cays	Flamingo Air
Inagua	Flamingo Air
San Salvador	Flamingo Air, Southern Air

BOAT

Ferry

The only major interisland ferry operator in the Bahamas is **Bahamas Ferries** (☑ 242-323-2166, 242-394-9700; www.bahamasferries.com), which runs high-speed services between Nassa and Andros, the Abacos, Eleuthera, the Exumas, Grand Bahama and Long Island.

Services (one-way fares, tax included) from Nassau:

.....

INTERISLAND FLIGHTS

Interisland flights offer the only quick and convenient way to travel within the Bahamas; islanders ride airplanes like Londoners use buses. Private charter flights can be an economical option for those traveling in a group – or they might be the only option for some more remote destinations.

Regular scheduled flights from Nassau (one-way prices with taxes are given):

.....

DESTINATION	AIRLINE	COST, TRAVEL TIME & DEPARTURES
Abaco (Marsh Harbour)	Bahamasair, SkyBahamas	BS$103, 30 min, 5 daily
Andros (South Andros)	Western Air	BS$95, 20 min, 2 daily
Biminis (South Bimini)	Western Air	BS$101, 35 min, 2 daily
Crooked Island	Bahamasair	BS$148, 75 min, once weekly
Eleuthera (North Eleuthera)	Pineapple Air	BS$99, 20 min, 6 daily
Exuma (George Town)	Bahamasair, SkyBahamas	BS$111, 40 min, 4 daily
Grand Bahama (Freeport)	Bahamasair, SkyBahamas, Western Air	BS$113, 40 min, frequent
Inagua	Bahamasair	BS$154, 1½hr, 2 weekly
Long Island (Upper Channel Cay)	Bahamasair, Southern Air	BS$135, 45 min, 1-2 daily
San Salvador	Bahamasair, Southern Air	BS$116, 1hr, 2-4 daily

DESTINATION	COST, TRAVEL TIME & DEPARTURES
Fresh Creek (Andros)	BS$59, 3hr, 7am Fri
Freeport (Grand Bahama)	BS$71, 15½hr, 4 weekly
George Town (Exuma)	BS$71, 13-14hr, 4 weekly
Governor's Harbour (Eleuthera)	BS$59, 5-6½hr, Mon & Thu
Simms (Long Island)	BS$71, 17½hr, 1 weekly
South Abaco Terminal	BS$71, 6½hr, Mon & Wed
Harbour Island (Eleuthera)	BS$81, 2¾hr, 6 weekly

Ferries leave from the Potter's Cay Dock in Nassau.

Mail Boat & Water Taxi

Mail boats sail under government contract to most inhabited islands, delivering post, freight and passengers. They regularly depart Potter's Cay for Grand Bahama and all the Out Islands. Traditionally sailing overnight, mail-boat journeys last between five and 24 hours; comforts are minimal, and fares between BS$30 and BS$45. Always call the **Dockmaster's Office** (☏ 242-393-1064) and check with the **Bahamas Ministry of Tourism** (☏ 242-302-2000; www.bahamas.com) for the latest schedules and prices.

In New Providence, water taxis (Map p152; ☏ 242-363-1030; h9am-6pm) zip back and forth between Prince George Wharf, Nassau and Paradise Island every half-hour between 9am and 6pm. Other offshore islands and their neighboring cays are served by private water taxis, such as the services between George Town and Stocking Island, Exuma.

Government-run water taxis link islands that are a short distance apart, such as North and South Bimini, Mangrove Cay and South Andros, and Crooked and Acklins Islands.

CAR & MOTORCYCLE

Road conditions Driving in busy downtown Nassau can be a pain, but nothing citizens of busy cities aren't accustomed to. A real danger in the Out Islands are potholes: you can be cruising for ages on smooth road, then suddenly encounter an axle-cracking crater. Stay vigilant.

Rental Major international car-rental companies have outlets in Nassau, Freeport and other tourist centers, and there are a host of local firms and individuals to choose from. It can be as casual as arriving at the airport and asking around for someone who knows someone, especially In the Out Islands. Ask your hotel or look for display boards at the airport. Renters must be 21 (some companies rent only to those 25 or older), and collision damage waiver insurance is around BS$15 per day (smaller local companies may not offer insurance). Rates start at around BS$75 per day. Golf carts are popular on the smaller islands and cays, and rent for about BS$50 to BS$70 per day.

Road rules In order to drive you must have a current license from your home country or state. A visitor can drive on their home license for three months. Drive on the left-hand side. At traffic circles (roundabouts), remember to circle in a clockwise direction, entering to the left. You must give way to traffic already in the circle. It's compulsory to wear a helmet when riding a motorcycle or scooter.

Barbados

POP 285,000 / ☎ 246

Best Places to Eat

➡ Champers (p199)

➡ Waterfront Cafe (p196)

➡ India Grill (p198)

➡ Nishi (p206)

Best Places to Sleep

➡ Little Arches Hotel (p201)

➡ Surfer's Point Guest House (p203)

➡ Sea-U! Guest House (p211)

➡ Coral Reef Club (p205)

Why Go?

While it's justifiably famed for its fantastic beaches, Barbados is an island that has it all. In addition to fine powdery sand and brilliant turquoise bays, you'll find smashing nightlife, a Unesco World Heritage–listed capital, a beautiful interior dotted with gardens, and wild surf on the lonely east coast, all inhabited by a proud and welcoming populace.

No matter your budget or style, you'll find a place to stay, especially on the popular south and west coasts. Elsewhere, however, is where you'll find what makes the island special. Barbados has lush scenery among rolling hills dotted with fascinating survivors of the colonial past. Vast plantation homes show the wealth of European settlers, while several botanical gardens exploit the beauty possible from the perfect growing conditions.

The wild Atlantic-battered east coast is a legend with surfers; those looking for action will also find windsurfing, hiking, diving and more. Away from the glitz, it's still a civilized place (with a 98% literacy rate) of classic calypso rhythms, an island-time vibe and world-famous rums.

When to Go

Apr Dry weather, and crowds start to dissipate.

Jun–Oct Wet season brings smaller crowds and lower prices, though you may get a storm.

Aug Crop-Over Festival reaches its climax.

Barbados Highlights

1 Rockley Beach (p199)
Unwinding on one of the island's most blissful beaches.

2 Oistins Fish Fry (p202)
Dancing the night away at one of the Caribbean's great parties.

3 Paynes Bay (p204)
Snorkeling with majestic sea turtles in warm tranquil waters.

4 West Coast (p204)
Exploring the region in style aboard a sailing boat.

5 Speightstown (p206)
Strolling the streets of this charismatic old port town.

6 Welchman Hall Gully (p209)
Enjoying the lush beauty of the island's rich floral wonders.

7 Bridgetown (p195)
Sampling Barbados' most popular meal, a flying-fish dish at a cafe in Bridgetown.

8 St Nicholas Abbey (p209) Experiencing the beautiful present and ugly past at grand plantation homes.

Bridgetown

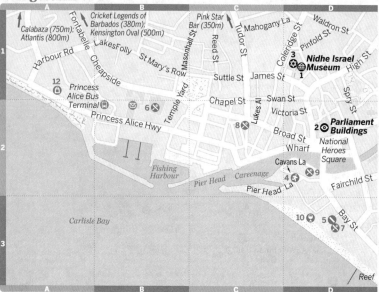

BRIDGETOWN

Wandering bustling Bridgetown, with its many sights and old colonial buildings, can easily occupy a day. There is good shopping, especially along Broad St and on pedestrian-only Swan St, which buzzes with the rhythms of local culture. The entire downtown area and south to the Garrison was named a Unesco World Heritage site in 2012 for its historical significance.

⊙ Sights

Bridgetown is a compact city and all the main sights in town are located within walking distance.

★ Parliament Buildings   NOTABLE BUILDING
(museum B$10; ⊙ museum 9am-4pm Mon & Wed-Sat) On the north side of National Heroes Sq are two stone-block, neo-Gothic-style buildings constructed in 1871. The western building with the clock tower contains public offices; the building on the east side houses the Senate and House of Assembly. At the museum learn about the island's proud democratic heritage.

Barbados Synagogue   SYNAGOGUE
(Synagogue Lane; ⊙ 9am-4pm Mon-Fri) Built in 1833 this small synagogue between James St

and Magazine Lane, near National Heroes Sq, was abandoned in 1929 and beautifully restored in 1986. The entire block around the synagogue is undergoing a major redevelopment to restore its colonial heritage, but you can still visit.

★ Nidhe Israel Museum   MUSEUM
(☑ 822-5421; Synagogue Lane; adult/child B$25/12.50; ⊙ 9am-4pm Mon-Fri) Housed in a restored 1750 Jewish community center, this museum documents the fascinating story of the Barbados Jewish community.

🏃 Activities

Day cruises are a popular way to explore the island, especially the west coast, from a pirate's vantage point. Many of the larger boats are floating parties, while the smaller operations tend to be more tranquil. For those who want the scuba experience without getting wet, there are submarine cruises. Most boats dock near Bridgetown, but take passengers from across the island; ask about transportation options when you book.

Calabaza   BOATING
(☑ 826-4048; www.sailcalabaza.com; Shallow Draught; adult/child from US$90/75; ⊙ 9:30am-2:30pm & 3-6:30pm) Professionally run sailing cruises with snorkeling stops at reefs and

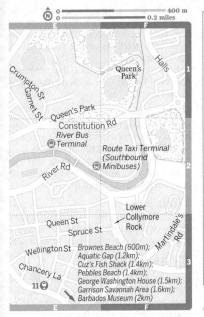

wrecks as well as turtle-watching. Groups are limited to 12 guests to ensure a more tranquil experience.

Barbados National Trust   HIKING
(☑ 426-2421, 436-9033; Wildey House, St Michael) Organizes regular Sunday hikes on different routes around the island. There are usually 6am and 3:30pm departures and they vary in difficulty, covering from 10km to 20km. Most take about three hours to complete. The hikes are a great way to see parts of the country you might not otherwise get to know.

El Tigre   BOATING
(☑ 417-7245; www.eltigrecruises.com; Cavans Lane; adult/child from US$70/35) Offers a variety of cruises, including a three-hour option with snorkeling at a shipwreck and turtle-watching.

The Dive Shop Barbados   DIVING
(☑ 422-3133; www.thediveshopbarbados.com; Ameys Alley, Upper Bay St; 1-/2-tank dive US$70/120) Well-established and reputable shop offering reef- and wreck-dive excursions to sites all over the island.

Atlantis   BOATING
(☑ 436-8929; http://barbados.atlantissubmarines.com; Shallow Draught; adult/child US$104/52;

⊙8am-4pm) The Atlantis is a 28-seat submarine lined with portholes. It departs from Bridgetown and tours the coral reef and shipwrecks off the island's west coast. Also runs evening and night tours.

✖ Eating

Bridgetown is the best place to enjoy genuine local food and genuine local prices. You can find cheap eats at any of the markets around town, which are generally open from 7am to late afternoon Monday to Saturday.

★ Mustor's Restaurant   CARIBBEAN $
(McGregor St; lunch from B$14; ⊙10am-4pm Mon-Sat) Climb the stairs to a large, plain dining room. Choose from staples such as baked pork chops and flying fish. Then select the sides – we love the macaroni pie. Finally, hope for an open balcony table.

Pink Star Bar   CARIBBEAN $
(Baxters Rd; cutters B$5; ⊙7pm-6am) Located on rough-and-ready Baxters Rd, Pink Star is famous among locals for being the cheapest place in town to fill your stomach. It opens in the evenings and runs through to dawn serving liver cutters, fried chicken necks and steppers (chicken feet) to the drunk and hungry masses. It's the Caribbean version of an all-night greasy-kebab spot.

DON'T MISS

CROP-OVER FESTIVAL

The island's top event, this **festival** (www.barbadoscropoverfestival.com; ⊘ Jul & Aug) originated in colonial times as a celebration to mark the end of the sugar cane harvest. Festivities stretch over a three-week period, beginning in mid-July with spirited calypso competitions, fairs and other activities. The festival culminates with a Carnival-like costume parade and fireworks on Kadooment Day, a national holiday, in August.

Cheapside Market MARKET $

(Cheapside; ⊘ 7am-3pm Mon-Sat) Even if you're not intending to buy, this is a fascinating place to browse local produce in a grand old market hall recently restored by the Chinese government. It has some nice snack stands on the 2nd floor. The best times to visit are Friday and Saturday mornings.

★ Waterfront Cafe CAFE $$

(✉ 427-0093; www.waterfrontcafe.com.bb; Careenage; sandwiches B$30-35, mains B$42-78; ⊘ 9am-6pm Mon-Wed, to 10pm Thu-Sat) Always packed, especially the breezy tables on the river. Lunches include a fine version of a flying-fish sandwich; dinners are more elaborate and have Mediterranean color and flair. There's live music ranging from steel pan to jazz – call to find out what's on.

Lobster Alive SEAFOOD $$$

(✉ 435-0305; www.lobsteralive.net; Bay St; lobster mains B$100-130; ⊘ noon-4pm & 6-9pm Mon-Sat, noon-5pm Sun) The name is only true until you order. Lobster bisque and grilled lobster are just some of the choices on the crustacean-heavy menu at this cute joint on the beach. A huge tank holds hundreds of the namesake critters at any given time – all flown in from the Grenadines. Smooth jazz (Tuesday, Thursday and Sunday nights) is also a trademark.

🍷 Drinking & Nightlife

Bridgetown's many rum shops are patronized by local regulars, though visitors are not unwelcome. Along Baxters Rd, just north of the center, you'll find a concentration of these bars, where alcohol flows and fish is fried until late at night. Although women will not be turned away, be warned that rum shops are a macho haunt.

On the south side of town, along Bay St, there is another collection of rum shops and bars, but stick to the main drag because one block back you'll be among shady Nelson St's brothels.

For a daylight drink, check out the beach bars right on the sand at the northern end of Carlisle Bay.

Pirate's Cove BAR

(✉ 832-7413; Lower Bay St, Carlisle Bay) On the closest stretch of sand to Bridgetown, this beach bar is less than a 10-minute walk from downtown but feels far from the bustle. The sand is soft and white, the water brilliantly blue and the drinks are cold.

Smith Corner Pub BAR

(Bay St; ⊘ 5pm-late) For an accessible rum-shop-style experience, check out this classic place, which is one of several on the stretch.

🔒 Shopping

Broad St, in the city center, is the place for higher-end shopping, while Swan St, one block back, is more blue collar with plenty of shops hawking cheap products.

Pelican Craft Village ARTS & CRAFTS

(Princess Alice Hwy; ⊘ 10am-5pm Mon-Sat) This ever-evolving complex of galleries and workshops, between downtown and the cruise-ship terminal, features the works of many local artists.

ℹ Information

Computer Knowledge Institute (✉ 430-6255; internet per hr B$10; ⊘ 9am-5pm) Downtown internet access and printing.

Post Office (Cheapside; ⊘ 7:30am-5pm Mon-Fri) Next to the Cheapside Market.

Queen Elizabeth Hospital (✉ 436-6450; www.qehconnect.com; Martindale's Rd; ⊘ 24hr)

ℹ Getting There & Away

The main bus stations are inconveniently located on opposite sides of town and there's no service between them, so if you're traveling from north to south, or vice versa, you'll either need to cross town on foot (15 minutes) or take a taxi (B$10).

ℹ Getting Around

Bridgetown is easily covered on foot, although taxis can be flagged on the street if necessary, or hailed from the waiting area. The set taxi fare from one end of town to the other is B$10.

AROUND BRIDGETOWN

There are many worthwhile sights within 5km of Bridgetown's center, especially to the south where you'll find the Garrison Savannah Unesco World Heritage site.

You don't have to travel far to reach good beaches either. Carlisle Bay, just a 10-minute walk from town, has a couple of fine stretches of sand.

◉ Sights

Cricket Legends of Barbados   MUSEUM
(✆ 227-2651; www.cricketlegendsbarbados.com; Herbert House, Fontabelle; ⊘ 10am-4pm Mon-Fri) A must for cricket fans, this museum is the best of its kind in the Caribbean. The walls are plastered with press clippings and there are many interesting artifacts from the game. The rear wall downstairs features an impressive roll call of Barbados' many great cricketers. Large groups can even get one of the legends to show them around.

Brownes Beach   BEACH
(Hwy 7) A fine beach close to downtown Bridgetown (a 10-minute walk) that makes a good break before and after lunch and shopping. A long white crescent of sand bends along with the brilliant waters of Carlisle Bay. Lots of parking and shade trees plus shacks selling drinks.

Pebbles Beach   BEACH
Running between two high-end hotels, this lovely stretch of sand is really just an extension of Browne's Beach. It has soft sands and calm waters and is home to water-sports outfitters. It offers a lively ambience rather than island tranquility and can get a bit crowded, but is a fine place to hang out.

There are several shacks selling snacks, including great fish cutters. If you're walking down from Bridgetown you have to either get wet by paddling beneath the Sheraton restaurant, or take a long road around.

Garrison Savannah Area   HISTORIC SITE
(www.barbadosgarrison.org) About 2km south of central Bridgetown and inland from Carlisle Bay, the Garrison is part of the World Heritage area and was the home of the British command in the 1800s. A focal point is the oval-shaped Savannah, which was once parade grounds and is now used for cricket games, jogging and Saturday horse races.

Standing along the west side of the Savannah are some of the Garrison's more ornate colonial buildings, where you'll find the world's largest collection of 17th-century cannons. It's now possible to visit some of the networks of tunnels built to link colonial buildings. The garrison administration runs a number of interesting tours – check the website for details.

George Washington House   MUSEUM
(Bush Hill, Garrison; adult/child B$20/5; ⊘ 9am-4:30pm Mon-Fri) Just west of the Barbados Museum is a place that can truly claim that the great man slept here. After decades of research and debate, it was finally shown that this 18th-century estate had been the home of the future US president and his brother Lawrence during their stay in 1751. The beautifully restored home shows what it must have looked like during their stay. A large museum brings 1750s Barbados to life for visitors.

Tours of the Garrison's tunnels begin here.

Barbados Museum   MUSEUM
(✆ 427-0201; www.barbmuse.org.bb; Garrison; adult/child B$20/10; ⊘ 9am-5pm Mon-Sat, 2-6pm Sun) This excellent museum is housed in an early-19th-century military prison. It has engaging displays on all aspects of the island's history, beginning with its indigenous residents.

🏃 Activities & Tours

Carlisle Bay Marine Reserve   SNORKELING
Protects an area of calm and shallow water full of marine life just offshore from Bridgetown. Both fishing and anchoring are prohibited within the reserve. In addition to marine turtles and schools of reef and predatory fish, there are five shipwrecks within the reserve boundaries.

GEORGE WASHINGTON SLEPT HERE

In 1751, at 19 years ago – 38 years before he would become the first US president – George Washington visited Barbados as a companion to his half-brother Lawrence, who suffered from tuberculosis. It was hoped that the tropical climate would prove therapeutic.

The pair rented a house in the Garrison area and stayed on the island for six weeks. The restored **George Washington House** gives a fascinating glimpse of the trip and the time. As it was, Lawrence never recovered and died the next year.

Mount Gay Rum Visitors Centre TOURS

(☑425-8757; www.mountgayrum.com; Spring Garden Hwy; tours B$30; ⊙hourly tours 9:30am-3:30pm Mon-Fri) The aged rums here are some of Barbados' best. At the visitors centre, about 1km north of Bridgetown Harbour, you can learn about the process and then taste them to find your favorite.

🛌 Sleeping

There are a couple of good hotels and midrange resorts on the southern edge of the Garrison, particularly around Aquatic Gap and on the road towards Hastings. A number of big-chain hotels can be found at Needhams Point.

Island Inn Hotel RESORT $$$

(☑436-6393; www.islandinnbarbados.com; Aquatic Gap; s/d US$350/425; ❈@🛜🏊) This 24-room, all-inclusive hotel is partially built in a restored 1804 garrison building that was originally a military rum store. It is near the beach off Bay St and close to town. It was given a complete renovation in 2009 and has muted island-chic motifs.

🍴 Eating

⭐India Grill CARIBBEAN $

(☑436-2361; Bay St; roti B$10-20; ⊙11am-3:45pm Mon-Sat) Ask serious roti connoisseurs the best place on the island to indulge and they'll point you to this simple hole-in-the-wall restaurant at the entrance to Aquatic Gap. It also does curry and rice, but the rotis are where it's at.

Eddie's Rib Van RIBS $

(UWI Hill; ribs B$20-30; ⊙from 6pm) The empty car park looks like the kind of place where you'd go to buy weed, but parked in the middle is a large industrial truck with the sides cut out serving the island's best ribs. Eddie also serves chicken and fish, but the crowds come for the huge servings of barbecue ribs, which come on a bed of fries.

There are no tables, chairs or even bathrooms – folks either take their meal home or chow down right there in their cars. Come early – once the van sells everything, it goes home.

Cuz's Fish Shack SEAFOOD $

(Pebbles Beach; sandwiches B$8; ⊙10am-4pm Mon-Fri) Doles out stupendously juicy fish cutters (sandwiches) from a beachside food truck.

Brown Sugar CARIBBEAN $$

(☑426-7684; www.brownsugarbarbados.net; Aquatic Gap; lunch buffet B$59, mains B$39-89; ⊙noon-2:30pm Sun-Fri, 6-9:30pm daily) The much-loved Brown Sugar, next to the Island Inn Hotel at Aquatic Gap, is a lush paradise inside and out. The excellent West Indian buffet is popular, while dinner is off a menu that includes shrimp Creole, lobster, flying fish and much more. The Bajan bread pudding is a rummy delight. Book for dinner.

☆ Entertainment

Cricket matches are played throughout the year at the Kensington Oval (☑274-1200; www.kensingtonoval.org; President Kennedy Dr) near Bridgetown. While there is no longer a guaranteed Test match here every season, if you're lucky enough to be in town when the West Indies do play here you're in for a treat.

Barbados Cricket Association CRICKET

(www.bcacricket.org) Distributes tickets for local cricket matches. Check the website for schedules.

❶ Getting There & Away

You can walk from downtown Bridgetown to the Garrisson Savannah area; walking along Browne's Beach is far nicer than along the busy road. Alternatively, hop on any Oistins-bound van or bus.

The Kensington Oval is also walking distance, but its not the prettiest stroll. Minivans from the Princess Alice terminal will drop you close by.

SOUTH COAST

The south coast is the island's mid-range-tourism epicenter. This virtually uninterrupted stretch of development – and beach – runs from the outskirts of Bridgetown all the way to the airport.

Hastings, Rockley and Worthing are part of one long commercial strip. St Lawrence Gap and Dover Beach is a surprisingly appealing area off the main road. Next up is the more relaxed pace of Maxwell and the fishing community of Oistins. East of here, development begins to thin out until the end of the road at Silver Sands, a residential area popular for wind sports. The entire area is within Christ Church Parish.

❶ Getting There & Away

All of the south-coast towns are linked by the main road along the coast, which, while designated Hwy 7, is never actually called that, rather taking on a variety of names depending on the town it is passing through.

Frequent minibuses from the Route Taxi Terminal in Bridgetown run along Hwy 7 down to Silver Sands and link all the south-coast villages. Less frequent large blue buses leave from the Fairchild St Terminal and run the same route before continuing on to the southeast coast, ending at Sam Lord's Castle. There's also a blue bus service from the south coast all the way up to Speightstown that bypasses Bridgetown.

Private taxis are fairly easy to find throughout this area. Expect to pay B$20 to B$25 to travel between south-coast villages.

Hastings & Rockley

Hastings and Rockley are home to some attractive, popular beaches. Commercialism rules here, although there's an attractive new boardwalk on the waterfront east of Hastings. There are plenty of shops, banks and ATMs along the main road, Hwy 7.

◉ Sights

★ **Rockley Beach** BEACH
(Accra Beach; Rockley Main Rd) The largest beach in the area, Rockley is a picture-perfect crescent of sand. Backed by shade trees, there's moderate surf. The new boardwalk allows you to walk west for more than 3km to Hastings.

✕ Eating

★ **Punchline** CARIBBEAN, VEGETARIAN $
(Hastings main road; mains B$12-25, smoothies B$10-12; ⊙11am-8pm Mon-Thu, to 9pm Fri & Sat) Vegetarians, vegans and pescatarians can all get their fill at this awesome little eatery on the main road in Hastings that serves a variety of delicious light meals. There are many varieties of veggie burger as well as wraps, salads and awesome smoothies. On the fish front there are great cutters alongside fish and salad plates.

Wok Up SOUTHEAST ASIAN $
(☏271-0051; Lanterns Mall, Hwy 7; mains B$20-25; ⊙11am-9pm) Pop in for some fast food done well at this bright, contemporary Asian spot. Choose fish, chicken or veggies in a variety of sauces served over rice or noodles.

★ **Champers** SEAFOOD $$$
(☏435-6644; www.champersbarbados.com; Skeetes Hill, Rockley; dinner mains B$52-95; ⊙11:30am-3pm Sun-Fri, 6-9:30pm daily) This longtime favorite has a dreamy location overlooking Rockley Beach. Elegant meals include the usual range of grilled seafood plus fresh pasta. Brits will understand the name means 'Champagne' – drink some in the lower-level lounge. At lunch there's a three-course menu for B$79.

Worthing

Worthing is a good base if you're on a tight budget but still want to be near the action. It has a pretty, uncrowded beach and good transportation links.

◉ Sights

Sandy Beach BEACH
A nice strip of white powder without a clever name that's well off the main road. The water defines 'turquoise'.

⊨ Sleeping

The small, quiet streets between Worthing Main Rd and Sandy Beach shelter several cheap guesthouses that are popular with budget travelers.

House Cleverdale GUESTHOUSE $
(☏826-0772; info@barbados-rentals.com; 4th Ave; s with shared bathroom US$40, r US$45-60, apt US$80; @⊜) Set back just a bit from Sandy Beach and away from the main road, this large wooden home is a popular budget spot. The three rooms and two apartments have mosquito nets, fans and wi-fi. Some rooms have shared bathrooms and there's a large kitchen.

It's rustic, but if you want to meet other travelers in the common rooms and never, ever wear shoes, you'll love it. The owner has other cheap places nearby.

Maraval Guesthouse & Apartments GUESTHOUSE $
(☏435-7437; www.maravalbarbados.com; 3rd Ave; r from US$40, apt US$100-150; ⊜) On a tiny lane near Sandy Beach, Maraval is a fantastic budget choice with simple but spotless rooms in a vintage beach house. There's a spacious kitchen, a pleasant common room and an appealing communal vibe. Nearby are several apartments that are right on the beach. All are bargain-priced for Barbados.

Cyrstal Waters GUESTHOUSE $
(☏435-7514; http://crystalwatersbds.wixsite. com; 1st Ave; s/d US$61/76; ⊜) With a fantastic location right on Sandy Beach, this

traditional guesthouse has plenty of character. The simple but elegant rooms have polished hardwood floors and classic furniture, while the breezy common room opens onto a fantastic veranda overlooking the turquoise Caribbean. The shared breakfast downstairs is a social affair that is a great place to meet partners for sightseeing trips.

Palm Garden
HOTEL $$

(☑ 621-7256; www.palmgardenbarbados.com; Worthing Main Rd; r US$75-95, ste US$125-135; ✳ 🛜 🛋) Set just far enough off the highway to escape the worst of the noise, but close enough for optimum convenience, this welcoming hotel is a good-value choice if you don't need to be right on the water. The accommodation block doesn't look like much, but inside, the rooms are spacious, comfortable and tastefully decorated.

★ Coral Mist Beach Hotel
HOTEL $$$

(☑ 435-7712; www.coralmistbarbados.com; Worthing Main Rd; r US$205-340; ✳ 🛜 🛋) This small and traditional beachfront hotel wins plaudits for its ideal beachfront location. All 32 rooms have kitchen facilities, balconies and views of the blinding-white beach. You can walk to much nearby.

✗ Eating & Drinking

Graeme Hall Nature Sanctuary Cafe
CAFE $

(www.graemehall.com; Hwy 7; mains B$20-35; ☉ 9am-5pm Tue-Sat) While the Graeme Hall Nature Sanctuary remains closed to visitors, you can still get a view of the mangroves from the excellent attached cafe on a little knoll. The food and fine coffee alone are reason enough to stop. Excellent sandwiches, pastas and baked goods are served all day.

Massy Stores
SUPERMARKET $

(☑ 435-9588; Rendezvouz Rd; ☉ 8am-8pm Mon-Thu, to 9pm Fri & Sat, 9am-7pm Sun) The biggest supermarket in the area has everything for self-caterers, including a good range of imported products.

Coast Beach Cafe
ITALIAN $$

(☑ 622-1858; www.coastbarbados.com; 2nd Ave; mains B$22-38; ☉ 10am-11pm) Formerly the Carib Beach Bar, this open-air cafe right on Sandy Beach has been given a makeover, but remains a local hot spot. The menu mostly features Italian classics. It hosts a beach barbecue (B$35) on Sundays with local DJs that draws a good mixed crowd and goes on until late.

Mojo
BAR

(Hwy 7; ☉ 11am-late) A big old house by the side of the road, Mojo has a wide open-air veranda plus all sorts of nooks inside for nuzzling your companion or listening to the excellent music. Monday is open-mic night. Good burgers.

St Lawrence Gap & Dover Beach

Blink and you'll miss the tiny village of St Lawrence, which pretty much gets lost among the urban development on Hwy 7 south of Worthing. The real action here lies along a 1.6km-long spur road that runs close to the beach and is lined with hotels, bars, restaurants and shops. The west end is known as St Lawrence Gap; the east end carries the Dover Beach moniker.

It's Barbados' most famed nightlife zone and is mostly free of traffic, allowing nighttime strolling.

Dover Beach itself is worth a visit while the sun is out. It has a nice, broad ribbon of white sand that attracts swimmers, bodysurfers and windsurfers.

✗ Activities

Barry's Surf Barbados
SURFING

(☑ 256-3906; www.surfing-barbados.com; Salt Ash Apartments, Dover) A long-running outfit that transports beginners and experienced surfers to the breaks that best suit their needs. Beginners classes cost US$75 for two hours and include free rental for the rest of the day to practice. Also rents boards.

🛏 Sleeping

★ Dover Woods Guest House
GUESTHOUSE $

(☑ 624-5150; www.doverwoodsguesthouse.com; St Lawrence Gap; r US$65-75; 🛜) Huge trees keep this large house shaded and cool. Located on estate-sized grounds at the east end of the strip, it has four spacious and elegant air-conditioned rooms that share a kitchen and TV lounge. It is the ideal place for those looking to be close to the action while enjoying peaceful and homely surroundings.

Dover Beach Hotel
HOTEL $$

(☑ 428-8076; www.doverbeach.com; St Lawrence Gap; r $175-200; ✳ @ 🛜 🛋) You go down a tiny lane to reach this gracious, secluded and older beach hotel, tucked into a corner at the east end of the Gap. The main three-story building surrounds a good-sized pool and large oceanfront terrace with access to a stretch of white sand that lies to the side.

Southern Palms Beach Club
RESORT $$$

(☑ 428-7171; www.southernpalms.net; St Lawrence Gap; r US$300-550; ❄@🛜🌊) A traditional beach resort that stays in the pink, literally – most of the various three-story blocks are decked out in a cheery pink tone. It is a large place, but still has plenty of character and is fronted by a fine stretch of white sand.

Yellow Bird Hotel
HOTEL $$$

(☑ 418-8444; www.yellowbirdbarbados.com; St Lawrence Gap; r US$210, 2-bedroom apt US$350; ❄🛜🌊) This modern, four-story block sits right at the west entrance to the Gap. Excellent modern studios have kitchens and all the mod cons, but the best part is the sunset views from the balconies. It's across a narrow street from the water and there's a small pool in front. Larger apartments are also available.

✖ Eating & Drinking

Harlequin
INTERNATIONAL $$

(☑ 420-7677; www.harlequinrestaurant.com; St Lawrence Gap; mains B$38-85; ⏲6-10pm; 🖋) The deck at this relaxed open-air bistro doesn't back onto the water like some of its neighbors, but it makes up for the lack of view with an excellent varied menu of carefully prepared dishes and professional service. In addition to Bajan classics you'll also find pastas, Thai-spiced dishes and imported steaks and lamb. Reservations recommended.

Castaway
CARIBBEAN $$

(☑ 420-7587; www.castawaybarbados.com; St Lawrence Gap; mains B$44-86; ⏲5pm-1am Tue-Fri, 11am-1am Sat & Sun) Set right on the water at the entrance to the Gap, this fantastic open-air bistro has great meals and service. The fun, relaxed atmosphere makes it an excellent place to stick around for drinks after the plates are cleared away. Good cocktails.

Old Jamm Inn
BAR

(☑ 428-3919; St Lawrence Gap; ⏲6pm-3am) This spacious bar is popular with both locals and visitors and plays a somewhat frustrating mix of good dancehall and bad pop. There's an air-con dance floor out the back where plenty of simulated loving goes on, but the best seats in the house are the bar stools on the deck at the front overlooking the Gap's comings and goings.

Oistins

This decidedly local yet modern town, a few kilometers east of St Lawrence, is best known as the center of the island's fishing industry. Oistins' heart is the large, bustling seaside fish market, which on Friday and Saturday hosts the island's best party.

⊙ Sights

★ Miami Beach
BEACH

(Enterprise Beach; Oistins Bay) A somewhat hidden gem that is the antithesis of its American namesake. Small, shady and intimate, it's well removed from the often frenetic south-coast pace. The beach is divided into two sections by a rock breakwater. The west side is one of the premier swimming spots on the island, with deep, calm and crystal-clear waters, while the east side has a wide recreation area featuring picnic tables under shady evergreen pines and almond trees.

🛏 Sleeping

There are few hotels in Oistins town itself but just to the north in Maxwell, or to the south in the Enterprise area, there's a variety of options.

★ Little Arches Hotel
BOUTIQUE HOTEL $$$

(☑ 420-4689; www.littlearches.com; Enterprise Beach Rd, Miami Beach; r US$325-550; ❄@🛜🌊) Possibly the best boutique hotel on the south coast. Once a Mediterranean-style mansion, the hotel now has 10 rooms in a variety of shapes and sizes, some with private whirlpool baths. The decor combines bright Caribbean colors with restrained luxury, such as deeply comfortable wicker chairs. It's on the quiet Miami Beach access road.

Privacy is at a maximum and there are lots of artful touches throughout, but the undoubted star of the show is the spacious terrace shaded by white linen that features an appealing swimming pool that affords panoramic views of the calm Caribbean below. There are free bicycles available for guest use.

✖ Eating

Golden Sands
CARIBBEAN $

(☑ 428-8051; Maxwell main road; pudding & souse from B$10; ⏲6:30am-10pm) This unassuming restaurant out the back of a midrange hotel is a great place to try some traditional Bajan dishes, especially on Saturday when it serves souse – pickled pieces of pork served cold

BARBADOS OISTINS

LOCAL KNOWLEDGE

OISTINS FISH FRY

This legendary spot for fresh fish meals (meals B$25-35; ⊗food 6-10:30pm Fri & Sat) attracts roughly 60% locals, 40% tourists, and there's a joyous electricity in the air on Friday night, which is just a tad more fun than the fish fry's other main night, Saturday. It's held in a complex of low-rise modern buildings right on the sand next to the fish market.

Most of the stalls serve the same menu: grilled fish and shellfish, pork chops, ribs and chicken. Sides include macaroni pie, chips, plaintains, grilled breadfruit, garlic bread and more. Unless you specify, you'll get a bit of each side with your main. Just because there are more than 30 vendors serving the same menu doesn't mean all are created equal, however. Go with the crowds; they know. Buy a cheap and icy bottle of Banks and plunge in.

There's a large stage in the middle of the complex where DJs belt out high-volume sets while dancers show off their moves to the crowd – don't expect much conversation during your meal.

While most of the action is on the weekends, even during off-peak moments there are usually a couple of places serving meals and snacks, including tasty fish cakes.

with steamed potato and blood pudding. It includes all parts of the animal (ears and feet are highly prized), but if you're feeling squeamish you can order 'steam and lean', the all-meat version.

Massey Stores　　　　　SUPERMARKET $
(Oistins main road; ⊗ 8am-8pm Mon-Thu, to 9pm Fri & Sat, to 2pm Sun) The biggest grocery store in the area has a good selection of packaged goods and offers a free shuttle to get them back to your apartment or hotel. For good fresh produce, there is a small fruit-and-vegetable store on the road just east of the entrance.

🍷 Drinking & Nightlife

The bars around the fish fry never close, and get a genial mix of fishing types, locals and visitors.

Lexie's　　　　　　　　　　　BAR
(Fish Market, Oistins Beach; ⊗24hr) With ballroom dancing on a literally hot open-air dance floor, this combo of beach and fishing bar stands out from its nearby contemporaries. There is no longer a sign, so just look for the big green place in the corner with the crowds outside.

ℹ Information

First Caribbean International Bank (☏367-2300; Oistins main road; ⊗ 8am-3pm Mon-Thu, to 5pm Fri) Has two ATMs.

ℹ Getting There & Away

Minivans running along the south coast from Bridgetown stop right in the heart of Oistins village, in front of the fish fry. Vans get fairly crowded on Fridays so you might have to squeeze in by the doorway or hop on another passenger's lap.

If you want to go further south to the airport, or beyond to the southeast, blue-and-yellow buses pass through on their way to Sam Lord's Castle.

You'll find plenty of taxis circulating on the main road.

Silver Sands

At the southernmost tip of the island, between Oistins and the airport, is the sleepy suburban area of Silver Sands. It's a sun-baked corner of the island that gets comparatively few visitors. The real action here is out on the water, where the regular winds attract serious kitesurfers.

🏃 Activities

Surfing, whether powered by waves, kite or sail, is the huge draw here.

★deAction Beach Shop　　　KITESURFING
(☏428-2027; www.briantalma.com; 6hr course US$450, 2hr rentals US$60; ⊗ 8am-dusk) Run by board legend Brian Talma, this shop is set on one of the hemisphere's premier spots for windsurfing and kitesurfing. Watch huge kites twirl about the sky while riders hop the waves below with a cold Banks at the cafe. It also rents surf and SUP boards.

The whole colorful wooden compound is plastered with articles and photos covering both the host and wind-sport culture in Barbados. Worth a trip even for those that don't fancy getting in the water.

Endless Kiteboarding
KITESURFING

(☑420-3253; www.endlesskiteboarding.com; Round the Rock) Run by an enthusiastic young Bajan, this recommended kite school offers lessons on good equipment with patient instructors.

Zed's Surfing Adventures
SURFING

(☑428-7873; www.zedssurftravel.com; Surfer's Point; board rental per day US$25-40, lessons from US$80; ◷9am-5pm Mon-Sat) An experienced outfit offering tours and classes island-wide.

🛏 Sleeping & Eating

Many kitesurfers and windsurfers stay a night or two in a hotel and then, through word of mouth, find a shared house or apartment nearby (simple doubles for around US$50 a night can be found in high season – ask at the activity shops).

There are not many places to dine in the Silver Sands area, although most bigger hotels have their own restaurants. Many accommodations here are self-catering and there are a couple of small supermarkets in the village. The closest big supermarket is in Oistins.

★Surfer's Point
Guest House
GUESTHOUSE $$

(☑428-7873; www.barbadossurfholidays.com; Surfer's Point; apt US$150-250; ❄@⑤) The HQ of Zed's Surfing Adventures is on a little point just steps from the sand and a very good break. The seven comfortable units here come in various sizes; some have balconies with views, all have kitchens and wi-fi.

Peach & Quiet Hotel
HOTEL $$

(☑428-5682; www.peachandquiet.com; Inch Marlow; r from US$120; ⊠) Like mushrooms after the rain, organic shapes abound at this private, laid-back retreat on a breezy headland. The 22 airy rooms come with sea-view patios and are set around a secluded pool. Among the rocks below there is a natural pool that is good for snorkeling. Interesting meals are served in the oceanside bar restaurant.

Ocean Spray
Beach Apartments
APARTMENT $$

(☑428-5426; www.oceansprayapartments.com; Inch Marlow; r US$135-175; ⑤) Salt spray from the pounding surf mists the air at this attractive and modern 25-unit apartment complex. Balconies on rooms with views offer a captivating spectacle of the famous local surf. Relax with a cranberry juice and vodka.

❶ Getting There & Away

Silver Sands is the end of the line for minivans running along Hwy 7 from Bridgetown. Service is frequent, but they don't all go all the way down to the water's edge, so you may have to walk a couple of blocks up to the main road.

St Philip & Crane Beach

St Philip, the diamond-shaped parish east of the airport, is sparsely populated, with a scattering of small villages. Along the coast are a couple of resort hotels and fine beaches.

❍ Sights

Crane Beach
BEACH

Crane Beach, 7km northeast of the airport, is a hidden beach cove backed by cliffs and fronted by aqua-blue waters. An adventurous trail over rocks along the water provides access to the beach from the end of a small road about 700m east of the Crane Beach Hotel. Parking is competitive, but the sands are simply wonderful. Bring a picnic and make a day of it.

★Shark Hole
BEACH

Well off the beaten track, the pint-sized Shark Hole is one of those special places for which your selfie will not do justice. Down a short flight of steps, a small stretch of delicate white sand is totally enclosed by rocks that wrap around 300 degrees, forming a perfect secluded cove. A reef just offshore calms the water, creating a perfect natural saltwater swimming pool.

Local kids like to perform backflips off the rocks – emulate at your own risk. If you come during the week you might get the whole place to yourself – magical!

★Bottom Bay
BEACH

On an island blessed with beautiful stretches of sand, Bottom Bay is up there with the best. With translucent turquoise waters framed by rocks and windswept palms, it's a remote piece of paradise where you won't have to share the sands with hordes of visitors. The only downside is the strong currents that make swimming tricky.

🛏 Sleeping

There's one large resort in St Philip and another one on the way. For a more intimate experience check out the many villa rentals in the region.

Crane Beach Hotel   RESORT $$$

(☑ 423-6220; www.thecrane.com; r from US$715; ❄ @ 🛜 🛋) Dating to 1887, the roots of this gracious resort can still be found in the lovely restaurants set in classic buildings that overlook the beach and ocean. Much of the complex is quite modern, with hundreds of luxurious condos decked out with high-end furnishings and mod cons. Some have fantastic views and all have access to the lavish resort facilities.

ℹ Getting There & Away

Large blue buses and midsized yellow buses from the Fairchild St Bus Terminal in Bridgetown run through St Philip to Sam Lord's Castle, dropping visitors within walking distance of many of the area's beaches.

WEST COAST

Barbados' west coast has lovely tranquil beaches that are largely hidden by the majority of the island's luxury hotels and walled estates. It's known to some as the Platinum Coast, a moniker earned either from the color of the sand or the color of the credit cards.

In colonial times, the area was a popular holiday retreat for the upper crust of British society. These days the villas that haven't been converted to resorts are owned by the wealthy and famous. That's on the water side, of course. On the *other* side of Hwy 1 are modest huts and simple vacation retreats. Although the beaches are all public, the near-constant development means you only get a few coastal glimpses.

ℹ Getting There & Away

The west coast is served by both the large blue buses and midsized yellow vehicles that depart from the Princess Alice Terminal in Bridgetown, running up to Speightstown. Minivans do not run along this route.

If you're coming or going to the south coast there are direct blue buses that run between Oistins and the west coast without entering Bridgetown.

For points further north, buses and minibuses run up the west coast from the Speightstown terminal, passing through Weston, Mt Standfast, Shermans and Moon Town.

Paynes Bay

Chic Paynes Bay in St James boasts one of the best beaches on the island. The village itself is little more than a collection of high-end hotels and luxury homes, along with a couple of places to eat and a fish market at the southern end.

◉ Sights

★ Paynes Bay Beach   BEACH

Fringed by a fine stretch of sand, gently curving Paynes Bay is endlessly popular and its calm waters make it one of the west coast's best spots for swimming and snorkeling (if you're patient enough there's a very good chance of seeing sea turtles).

There are three public access points. The easiest is next to the fish market on the south side, where there are a couple of parking spots, but the bay is more picturesque further north.

The middle access is a narrow alley between houses about 200m north of the Tamarind Hotel – blink and you'll miss it, there's no sign.

The northernmost access is just alongside the north wall of the ultra-exclusive Sandy Lane hotel and resort – right next to Rhianna's villa.

🛏 Sleeping

Luxurious hotels line the beach here, but there are also some cheaper options on the other side of Hwy 1 just a short walk from the sand.

Angler Apartments   APARTMENT $$

(☑ 432-0817; www.anglerapartments.com; Clarke's Rd 1, Derricks; r US$125-135; ❄ 🛜) An unpretentious place with 12 older, basic apartments. Studios in an adjacent old plantation house are similar but smaller. There's a little patio bar. It's at the south end of Paynes Bay, off a road east of the main road. Good value for the area.

Tamarind Hotel   RESORT $$$

(☑ 432-1332; www.tamarindbarbados.com; Hwy 1; r from US$493; ❄ @ 🛜 🛋) Everything is discreet about this understated luxury resort, right on the beach at Paynes Bay. The 110 units are decked out in a restful palette of beachy pastels. All have balconies or patios and views of either one of the three pools or the ocean. The lushly landscaped grounds boast many fountains.

Sandy Lane
RESORT $$$

(☑ 444-2000; www.sandylane.com; Hwy 1; r from US$1300; ✸ ☎ ☀) Situated right on the best part of Paynes Bay, the ultra-luxurious Sandy Lane is the most prestigious resort on the island. As you'd expect for the price tag, everything is top of the line. You even get access to an exclusive guest-only golf course carved out of an old quarry.

✗ Eating

Roti Den
CARIBBEAN $

(Hwy 1; rotis B$13-28; ☉ 10am-8pm) Step inside the bright-yellow house right by the road to find a full selection of great rotis – take your pick from vegetable, chicken, pork, shrimp, lamb or beef, or mix it up. They are filled to bursting, so it's easier to eat in on a plate than try to keep it in one piece outside.

Daphne's
ITALIAN $$$

(☑ 432-2731; www.daphnesbarbados.com; Hwy 1; mains B$48-98; ☉ 6:30-10pm Tue-Sun) In an elegant open-air dining room right next to one of the island's best stretches of sand, Daphne's serves good contemporary Italian dishes in a semi-formal environment.

Holetown

The first English settlers to Barbados landed at Holetown in 1627. Long a bastion of understated luxury, Holetown has exclusive shops and a charming little nightlife area near the beach. There's lots of good snorkeling in the mellow waters and reefs here.

Holetown is the center for all services north of Bridgetown, with banks, ATMs and a large supermarket.

◉ Sights & Activities

Mt Standfast Beach
BEACH

A narrow but pretty stretch of sand just north of Holetown with good swimming. The real reason to come here is the marine life. The waters are inhabited by hawksbill turtles, which come to feed on sea grasses just offshore. Many snorkeling tours stop here, but you can also rent snorkel gear along the beach and go it alone.

Like many spots along this stretch, beach access is becoming increasingly blocked off by large hotels and private properties. Parking is nigh on impossible.

Hightide Watersports
DIVING

(☑ 432-0931; www.divehightide.com; Coral Reef Club; 1-/2-tank dive US$72/128) One of the better dive shops on the west coast.

Folkestone Marine Park
SNORKELING

(Folkestone Beach) Spanning several kilometres along the mid-west coast, this marine reserve was set up to preserve coral and shallow areas inhabited by turtles. There are four reserve zones: two areas where motorized aquatic sports are permitted, a scientific zone and a recreation zone where you can snorkel in peace free of Jet Skis and speedboats.

There is no entry fee or permit required to enter the reserve and if you're staying in the area there's a good chance that the waters in front of your hotel are part of it. In front of the reserve office (p206) there's a large area protected by buoys that's good for snorkeling.

⚡ Festivals & Events

Holetown Festival
CULTURAL

(www.holetownfestivalbarbados.org) This festival celebrates February 17, 1627 – the date of the arrival of the first English settlers on Barbados. Holetown's weeklong festivities include street fairs, a music festival, a road race and even a tattoo show.

🛏 Sleeping

The Holetown area has some of the island's most vaunted resorts, many in former mansions of the fabulously wealthy.

★ Coral Reef Club
RESORT $$$

(☑ 422-2372; www.coralreefbarbados.com; Hwy 1; r US$540-1680; ☗ ✸ @ ☎ ☀) This family-owned 88-unit luxury hotel has 12 acres of gorgeous landscaped grounds surrounding an elegant gingerbread fantasy of a main building. Unlike some other top-end accommodations in the area, this place oozes character. Rooms are spacious and elegant, especially the suites, which have private porches overlooking the sea.

Lone Star Hotel
BOUTIQUE HOTEL $$$

(☑ 629-0599; www.thelonestar.com; Hwy 1, Mt Standfast; r from US$695) Built right on the sands, this new low-rise boutique hotel has supremely comfortable rooms with stained wooden floors, vaulted ceilings and full-length sliding glass doors that afford tremendous sea views. It doesn't have the spacious grounds, and hence the privacy, that some of the nearby resorts offer, but you'll hear the waves from bed.

Tropical Sunset Hotel
HOTEL $$$

(📞432-2715; www.tropicalsunsetbarbados.com; Hwy 1; r US$215; 🅿️❄️🛜🏊) Right on the water in the center of Holetown, this popular hotel has clean and spacious rooms all offering views over the pool to the Caribbean. The attached waterfront bar-restaurant serves decent meals and is a fine place for a drink at sunset. Good value for this area.

✖️ Eating

Just Grillin'
CARIBBEAN $

(Hwy 1; mains B$20-39; ⏲11am-10:30pm Mon-Sat, 5:30-10:30pm Sun) For a reasonably priced meal, head to this unpretentious place next to the Chatel village. It serves up good sandwiches and grilled plates of everything from catch of the day to jerk chicken. Portions aren't huge, but it's all tasty. There is another branch in Rockley.

Millie Ifill Fish Market
MARKET $

(Hwy 1, Weston; ⏲7am-7pm) Organized and clean small market that is the best place in the area to pick up fish fresh from the boat.

Massy Stores
SUPERMARKET $

(Hwy 1; ⏲9am-8pm Mon-Fri, to 9pm Sat, to 2pm Sun) Best supermarket on the west coast, with a full range of imported products and a decent selection of fruit and veg.

Lemongrass
THAI $$

(📞271-8265; www.lemongrassbarbados.com; Limegrove Mall; mains B$32-45; ⏲11:30am-9:30pm) OK, so the atmosphere is far removed from a dingy alley in Bangkok, but this Thai restaurant in an upmarket mall knocks out some tasty dishes and is great value for Holetown.

Nishi
BURGERS, SUSHI $$$

(📞432-8287; www.nishi-restaurant.com; 2nd St; mains B$50-98) Holetown's hippest eatery doesn't feel particularly Caribbean: there's a gold Buddha in the garden and a house-music soundtrack, but locals love it, giving it a lively atmosphere. The food, which spans the gamut from burgers and curries to sushi, is all carefully prepared and full of flavor.

Beach House
INTERNATIONAL $$$

(📞432-1163; www.thebeachhousebarbados.com; dinner mains B$55-95; ⏲11am-10pm) Anchored by a vast terrace right on the water, the Beach House fulfills all your holiday dining fantasies. The drinks and wine list is encyclopedic. The menu segues from comfy lunch food (burgers, salads) to steak and seafood at night.

🍷 Drinking & Nightlife

John Moore Bar
BAR

(Hwy 1, Weston; ⏲4:30am-late) One of the most atmospheric bars on this coast, John Moore is a fantastic place to escape the confines of your hotel and meet some Bajan characters. You could take a seat at one of the stools inside, but you're better off at the picnic tables outside, where locals chew the fat over cold Banks.

Come early for a bargain fried-fish breakfast – you won't find a fresher plate anywhere. It opens early to serve the crowd from the fish market next door.

Red Door Lounge
LOUNGE

(2nd St) A hip cocktail bar that's popular among both visitors and the island's young movers and shakers. It has a rather warm, urban vibe that is far removed from the rest of Holetown. On weekends top local DJs play here.

ℹ️ Information

Folkestone Marine Park Visitor Centre
(📞422-2314; Folkestone Park; B$5; ⏲9am-5pm Mon-Fri) At Folkestone Park at the north end of Holetown, the Folkestone Marine Park's visitor center includes a small museum with displays on the reserve, which extends a few kilometers north and south from here. You can rent snorkeling gear (from B$25) and there are lockers. From here you can walk along the water to Holetown.

Speightstown

Easily the most evocative small town on Barbados, Speightstown combines old colonial charms with a vibe that has more rough edges than the endlessly upscale precincts to the south. The settlement was once dubbed 'Little Bristol' as, thanks to its maritime connection to that English town, many of the first settlers originated from there, and it still has a classic nautical vibe.

Since the main road was moved to the charmless bypass east, traffic is modest, so take time strolling to look up at the battered old wooden facades.

⊙ Sights & Activities

Arlington House
HISTORIC BUILDING

(☑422-4064; arlington@caribsurf.com; Queen St; adult/child B$25/12.50; ⊙9am-5pm Mon-Fri, 10am-3pm Sat) A radiant vision in white stucco, this 18th-century colonial house now has an engaging museum run by the National Trust. It's divided into various sections, including the old stores of the area, plantations and nautical trade.

Mullins Beach
BEACH

A popular and family-friendly beach along Hwy 1 between Holetown and Speightstown with waters that are usually calm and good for swimming and snorkeling. Drinks from the boisterous cafe are delivered to your beach chair. Just around the corner, **Gibbs Beach** is less crowded but not quite as attractive.

Heywoods Beach
BEACH

One of the best strands on the west coast for day-trippers from elsewhere on the island, Heywoods Beach offers good parking, a location well off Hwy 1 and lots of uncrowded sand (especially on weekdays). It's about 500m north of the road into Speightstown.

Reefers & Wreckers
DIVING

(☑422-5450; www.scubadiving.bb; Sand St; 1-/2-tank dive US$70/125; ⊙9am-5pm) A highly rated family-owned dive shop in the heart of Speightstown.

🛏 Sleeping

Legend Garden Condos
INN $$

(☑422-8369; www.legendcondos.com; Mullins Beach; s/d US$150/160, 3-night minimum; ❈🐾🛜🌊) Fabulous value for the location, across the road and just 200m from the beach. The units have kitchens, are lovingly decorated by the owners and spread out across the spacious grounds of a former plantation.

Little Good Harbour
BOUTIQUE HOTEL $$$

(☑439-3000; www.littlegoodharbourbarbados.com; Shermans; villas from US$446; ❈@🛜🌊) This fine hotel has 21 one- to three-bedroom villas in a little compound near the water. The decor combines wicker with linens in units that open completely to the outside and flowering trees.

✗ Eating

★ Fisherman's Pub
CARIBBEAN $

(☑422-2703; Queen St; meals from B$15; ⊙11am-late Mon-Sat, noon-4pm Sun) This waterfront cafe is a local institution that serves up fish from the boats floating off the side deck. On Wednesdays there is steel-pan music and a buffet. As the evening wears on, the scene gets more Bajan. Line up for the ever-changing and excellent fare.

PRC Bakery
BAKERY $

(Sand St; items B$2.50-5.50; ⊙8am-8pm) One of the best traditional Caribbean bakeries on the island. Take your pick from sweet and savory delights. We love the unadvertised currant rolls – delicious layers of buttery pastry filled with sweet currants – but everything is good. Best time to come is between 2pm and 4pm when most things come out hot from the ovens.

★ Orange Street Grocer
CAFE $$

(Sand St; mains B$20-49; ⊙8am-6pm Mon-Thu, to 10pm Fri & Sat) A bright, modern cafe that opens out onto a lovely shaded deck right by the water. It offers a wide variety of scrumptious dishes with Caribbean and Mediterranean flavors featuring prominently. There's also great wood-fired pizzas, bruschetta, baguette sandwiches and tasty breakfast options. Finish up with real coffee from the Italian machine.

Fish Pot Restaurant
SEAFOOD $$$

(www.littlegoodharbourbarbados.com; Shermans; mains B$45-95; ⊙8am-10pm) The Fish Pot Restaurant at the Little Good Harbour hotel is renowned for its views and seafood. It has a good wine list.

Juma's
CARIBBEAN $$$

(☑432-0232; www.jumasrestaurant.com; Queen St; mains B$55-95; ⊙8am-8pm) An atmospheric 2nd-floor eatery under a thatched roof right by the water serving good modern Caribbean cuisine, including Bajan chicken, rotis and a variety of fish plates. There is a lighter lunch menu (B$12 to B$40) that offers subs, salads curries and burgers. Also a fine place for breakfast out on the deck.

🍷 Drinking & Nightlife

Braddie's Bar
BAR

(Six Men Bay) Hang out with a bunch of charming old gents at Mr Bradshaw's no-nonsense waterside bar in the small village of Six Men Bay. It's little more than a zinc shed with some picnic tables around the side, but it serves cheap beers and fried fish (B$16 to B$18) and you'll hear plenty of good stories from the regulars.

ℹ Getting There & Away

Speightstown is the main transport hub for the west coast, with regular bus services running south to Bridgetown, through the interior to Bathsheba and north to St Lucy via the villages of the northern west coast. Buses leave from the terminal just off Hwy 1.

Minivans to St Lucy depart from outside the small market near the entrance to town on Hwy 1.

NORTH BARBADOS

The remote parish of St Lucy covers the northern tip of the island. While it was once considered a backwater, the wilderness here is slowly being tamed as new housing projects go up on cheap land. However, it still remains a wonderfully raw and rarely visited destination, with a rugged coastline that boasts towering cliffs that shelter tiny bays.

◉ Sights

Archer's Bay   BEACH

Fierce waves pummel stone cliffs, eroding them into giant mushroom-shaped oddities at Archer's Bay, a desolate and ruggedly gorgeous bit of the north coast. To get there, follow the signs off Hwys 1B and 1C to Grape Hall, then keep driving north 500m and follow the 'Public Beach Access' sign that directs you to a parking area near the cliff.

The views are stunning, and a short but steep trail leads down to a tiny pocket of beach. Swimming is unsafe.

Animal Flower Cave   CAVE

(☑ 439-8797; www.animalflowercave.com; adult/child B$20/10; ☉ 9am-4:30pm) At the northern tip of the island, near where the Caribbean and Atlantic meet, you'll find this large waterside cave carved into a cliff face. It is accessed by a set of stairs that have been carved into a blowhole – there's no other way down the cliffs – and there's a pool inside for paddling.

You'll be accompanied by a guide into the cave. Bring reef shoes if possible, but any old tennis shoes will also do the trick.

A visit here is appealing even for those who don't fancy a spot of spelunking. The sheer cliffs either side of the site are spectacular and the restaurant meals (B$30 to B$60) take full advantage of the location, with tables spread along the edge protected by a rope barrier.

River Bay   BAY

You can drive right up to this beautiful little bay, where a tiny river has carved its way through imposing cliffs to the Atlantic. Waves wash into the narrow inlet, which stretches back to a tiny little beach area backed by trees. You can wade in the shallows, but swimming here is dangerous.

North Point   SURFING, DIVING

Drive in past the ruins of a once-grand resort to find one of the best surf breaks on the north side. The eerie shells of buildings on the clifftop add to the epic end-of-the-world atmosphere. It's a complicated wave – not for beginners.

The area is also known for its sharks (rumor has it that local chicken farmers throw their dead birds off the cliffs here), and many dive operators make trips up this way to see various species in a challenging swim-through.

The road in is full of crater-sized potholes – go slow, especially if you're in a rental.

✗ Eating

Most of the bays in the area are undeveloped and you won't find anywhere nearby selling food, so bring some snacks. For a meal with a view, check out the fine restaurant at Animal Flower Cave.

Merton's Place   CARIBBEAN $$

(Moon Town Fish Fry; Half Moon Fort, St Lucy; meals B$30; ☉ 6pm-midnight Thu-Sat) Pull up a table on the elevated wooden platform overlooking the water in this local hangout in the tiny village of Half Moon Fort and take your pick of a variety of market fresh fish – you can have it grilled or fried – and various sides. It also serves chicken and pork, but the fish is the popular choice.

ℹ Getting There & Away

There are a few direct buses to St Lucy each day from the Princess Alice Terminal in Bridgetown, but they depart in the evening and are not convenient. The best way to access the island's northern reaches is to make your way to Speightstown, from where regular buses and minivans ply the roads of St Lucy.

CENTRAL BARBADOS

Several roads cross the rolling green hills of the island's interior. There's a wealth of historic and natural sights here and you can spend days winding around small roads far from the crowds.

Surprises abound – you'll round a corner and discover a huge 19th-century stone church or a fascinating plantation-era signal tower, which was how the colonials once communicated. The rolling hills in the interior are also home to the island's best gardens and some wonderful old mansions.

◉ Sights & Activities

Farley Hill National Park PARK

(☑ 422-3555; Hwy 2; per car B$6; ⊙ 7am-6pm) A tree-covered hillside set around the ruins of an old estate home. Climb to the top and sit on one of the benches in front of the pagoda for a fresh breeze and phenomenal views down to the Atlantic. Bring a book and a picnic lunch. If you arrive in a vehicle you pay admission, but if you walk up from the public bus it's free.

Cherry Tree Hill HILL

A historic avenue lined with mahogany trees that leads from St Nicholas Abbey down to the Atlantic. The view from the top is spectacular.

★ St Nicholas Abbey HISTORIC SITE

(www.stnicholasabbey.com; adult/child B$40/20; ⊙ 10am-3:30pm Sun-Fri) St Nicholas Abbey is a Jacobean-style mansion that is one of the oldest plantation houses in the Caribbean and a must-see stop on any island itinerary. The grounds include the Great House, various gardens and a very traditional rum distillery. An on-site cafe serves light lunches (B$24 to B$42) on a platform overlooking a lush valley full of trees.

★ Welchman Hall Gully NATURE RESERVE

(☑ 438-6671; www.welchmanhallgullybarbados. com; Hwy 2, Welchman Hall; adult/child B$24/12; ⊙ 9am-4pm) Once part of a large estate that covered the area, this National Trust property contains some rare tracts of original Barbados tropical rainforest, although there are also several introduced species present. A trail leads from the car park through a narrow canyon lined with diverse tree species and rocks covered in moss past some wonderful shallow caves draped in vines.

Flower Forest GARDENS

(☑ 433-8152; www.flowerforestbarbados.com; off Hwy 2, Richmond; adult/child B$25/12.50; ⊙ 8am-4pm) A 20-hectare botanic garden on the site of a former sugar estate that has many stately, mature citrus and breadfruit trees as well as a fine range of heliconias. Don't expect to see fields and fields of flowers – it's more an enchanted forest – but it's a peaceful place to take a break from the white sands and get close to nature.

Harrison's Cave CAVE

This cave is promoted as one of the island's premier attractions, but how much you enjoy it will depend on which tour you choose. The main 'tram tour' involves sitting on a vehicle and being driven through the interior, but the one you really want is the rather pricey 'adventure tour' where you'll crawl, swim and duck through the cave's smaller passageways.

Huntes Gardens GARDENS

(☑ 433-3333; Castle Grant St, St Joseph; ⊙ 9am-5pm) Although a relatively new project, these gardens at the home of famed local horticulturalist Anthony Hunte already have a magical aura. All kinds of plants and shrubs line crisscrossing paths beneath majestic cabbage palms, while hummingbirds, lizards and monkeys frolic around. Make use of the benches at key points on the trail to sit back and take in the beauty.

Gun Hill HISTORIC SITE

(☑ 429-1358; Fusilier Rd, Salisbury; adult/child B$12/6; ⊙ 9am-5pm Mon-Sat) This 1818 hilltop signal tower has impressive views of the surrounding valleys and the southwest coast. The island was once connected by six such signal towers that used flags and lanterns to relay messages. The official function was to keep watch for approaching enemy ships, but they also signaled colonial authorities in the event of a slave revolt. There's a cute cafe here.

To reach the tower, take Hwy 3 – 3km east of the Clyde Wolcott Roundabout on the bypass, look for signs for Gun Hill on a small road turning south. There's a couple of twists and turns as you travel 1.5km to the site.

Ride Barbados HORSE RIDING

(☑ 422-7433; Cleland Plantation; rides B$180-230; ⊙ 8am-4pm) Organizes rides through the forest and down to the beach from its stables near Farley Hill.

✗ Eating

Many of the major sights in the interior have their own restaurants that are usually only open for lunch and morning and afternoon tea. If you're driving, bring a picnic or a couple or rotis to enjoy in one of the many scenic spots along the way.

Brighton Farmers Market   MARKET **$**
(☑ 262-1901; ☺ 6-10am Sat) Early on Saturdays, foodies, chefs, artisans and more converge on the Brighton Farmers Market in the heart of the fertile St George Valley on Hwy 4B. It's a festival of the finest produce, prepared foods and crafts and is a good place to get off the traveler trail and mingle with the locals.

❶ Getting There & Away

There are numerous roads crisscrossing the interior of the island. Public buses run on the main interior highways, but many of the attractions are off spur roads and you'll lose plenty of time waiting for a passing service.

In order to maximise your experience, it's highly recommended to hire a vehicle to explore the region. A good map is essential or, even better, work with a GPS.

BATHSHEBA

The wild Atlantic waters of the east coast are far removed from the rest of the island – the population is small, the coast craggy and the

waves incessant. Bathsheba is prime surfing country, and it's also good for long beach walks that leave you feeling like you've reached the end of the world. It's an idyllic image of sand, sea and palm trees.

If you're not a great swimmer, this is not really the place to go into the water; rather, enjoy the wave-tossed scenery on long beach walks.

◉ Sights & Activities

Andromeda Botanic Gardens   GARDENS
(☑ 433-9384; www.andromedabarbados.com; Hwy 3; adult/child B$30/15; ☺ 9am-5pm, last admission 4:30pm) The island's original botanic gardens, this lovely spot has two exploratory paths that wind their way through a wide collection of tropical plants, including orchids, ferns, water lilies, bougainvillea, cacti and palms.

Bathsheba Beach   BEACH
A wild stretch of golden sand that's framed by rough headlands and punctuated by magnificent rock formations standing defiant in the shallows against the constant pounding of the waves. The waters here are not suitable for swimming.

DRIVING ROUTES IN CENTRAL BARBADOS

Highway 2

Running a loop from the Caribbean near Speightstown through the northern center of the island and back out near Bridgetown, Hwy 2 takes visitors through some of Barbados' most marvelous landscapes and past some of the islands best natural attractions.

Going into the hills east of Speightstown, the road steadily climbs through historic sugarcane fields. The ruins of mills dot the landscape. At Portland there's a turnoff on a narrow road that winds under a cathedral of huge mahogany trees arching overhead to **St Nicholas Abbey** (p209). About 700m southeast of the abbey, the road passes **Cherry Tree Hill** (p209), which has grand views right across the Atlantic coast.

Rejoining Hwy 2 the road heads toward the coast, passing through the little town of Belleplaine, before curling back around and up into the hills where you'll find a pair of inviting botanical gardens. It continues west, passing close to **Harrison's Cave** (p209) and **Welchman Hall Gully** (p209) before sloping back down the hill to Bridgetown.

Highway 3

This lovely road goes up and over the middle of Barbados on a 16km route that links the west and east coasts. Along the way there are some historic sights and bucolic scenery.

Three kilometers east of the Clyde Wolcott Roundabout on the bypass, you'll pass the turnoff to **Gun Hill** on a small road heading south. Hwy 3B runs northeast of Gun Hill through gorgeous valleys and plains. It's worthwhile to literally lose yourself here amid pretty farms punctuated with the odd colonial-era building. Turn north on one of the many small roads any time you want to rejoin Hwy 3.

Back on Hwy 3, about 8km after the Gun Hill turn, you'll see squat little St Joseph's Church on the left. From here it's a short drive downhill to Bathsheba.

Soup Bowl
SURFING

The world-famous reef break known as the Soup Bowl is right off the beach and is one of the best waves in the Caribbean islands. Don't underestimate the break just because the region is not known for powerful surf – Soup Bowl gets big. The best months are August to March.

🛏 Sleeping

There are a couple of great hotels on the outskirts of Bathsheba, but there's not a lot of quality options for budget travelers.

★ Sea-U! Guest House
BOUTIQUE HOTEL $$

(🖉 433-9450; www.seaubarbados.com; Tent Bay, Bathsheba; r US$192-278; @🛜) A wonderful wooden guesthouse with comfortable rooms and a very appealing porch looking out to sea from the hillside location. Cottages and a restaurant pavilion round out the verdant site. The higher-end rooms have air-con and kitchens.

Atlantis Hotel
HOTEL $$$

(🖉 433-9445; www.atlantishotelbarbados.com; Tent Bay, Bathsheba; r from US$455-520; ❄🛜🏊) One cove south of Bathsheba, Atlantis was the original hotel in the area. It has 10 units in a solid old wooden building facing the sea. The views are sweeping and you have a choice of one-bedroom suites in the original building, or apartments in a new wing by the small pool.

🍴 Eating & Drinking

You can get local-style meals at some of the bars around town.

Along the waterfront you'll find a couple of lively bars where locals and visitors mix. They open from quite early in the morning.

Roundhouse Restaurant
CARIBBEAN $$

(🖉433-9678; meals from B$40; ⊘breakfast, lunch & dinner) Set in a dramatic stone building up on the hillside at the north end of town, this popular restaurant has customers throughout the day who sit around, sip cocktails and savor the views south over Soup Bowl. You can enjoy banana bread with your breakfast, sandwiches and salads at lunch, and specials such as breadfruit soup at dinner.

Sea Side Bar
CARIBBEAN

(⊘10am-late) More bar than cafe (though local stews and the like are served on the deck at lunch), this joint hums with energy through the day as locals and surfers do their best to out-shout each other.

ℹ Getting There & Away

A taxi can be negotiated for about B$80 to B$100 from Bridgetown or the south coast. Alternatively take bus 6 from the Fairchild St Terminal in Bridgetown, or catch one of the regular vans from the River Bus Terminal. The trip takes about 45 minutes.

Bus 1E travels from Bathsheba to Speightstown along Hwy 2, passing by Farley Hill.

BATHSHEBA SOUTH TO CHRIST CHURCH PARISH

Few people take the time to follow the coast south of Bathsheba. They should. The road curves around hillsides above the rugged Atlantic, passing tiny villages populated by friendly locals who eke out a living from the sea. This is another Barbados, far removed from the glitzy resorts of the west, a place where tradition is still strong and nature remains wild.

The road runs south from Bathsheba along the Atlantic past Martin's Bay and Bath before turning inland through cane fields. Look for the iconic Anglican St Philip Church from where, if you turn south, you'll reach the historic Sunbury Plantation House. Continuing south will take you to the busy village of Six Cross Roads, where your route options live up to the promise of the name. You can head southeast to Crane Beach, southwest to Oistins or west to Bridgetown.

⊙ Sights

Martin's Bay
VILLAGE

Fronted by a sliver of sand, this little village is about as local as you get. It has a sweet little rum shop, a shop-restaurant and some picnic tables – that's it. Like elsewhere around here, this isn't swimming country, but watching the fishing boats bobbing up and down in the ceaseless surf is captivating.

Bath
BEACH

This wonderful long and remote stretch of golden sand is usually totally empty. It is one of the few places on this coast where it's safe to swim, thanks to the offshore reef that tames the wild currents. There are picnic tables, but you'll need to bring your own meal because the cafe-shop has gone out of business.

Sunbury Plantation House   NOTABLE BUILDING
(☑ 423-6270;   www.barbadosgreathouse.com;
Sunbury, St Philip; tours adult/child B$20/10;
⊙ 9:30am-4:30pm) Built between 1660 and
1670, the handsome Sunbury Plantation
House was painstakingly restored after a
1995 fire. The house has 60cm-thick walls
built of local coral blocks and ballast stones,
the latter coming from the ships that set sail
from England to pick up Barbadian sugar.
It's the only one of Barbados' great houses
where visitors are able to get inside all the
rooms.

✖ Eating

Martin's Bay Fish Fry   CARIBBEAN $
(mains B$16-20) Like a country version of the
Oistins fry, but with lower prices and wilder
scenery, the Martin's Bay fish fry is a low-
key affair where visitors dig into plates of
fresh-from-the-boat marlin or snapper and
macaroni pie at the many picnic tables on
the water's edge.

❶ Getting There & Away

Public transport is very thin on the ground south
of Bathsheba. The best way to explore this area
is in a rental vehicle.

UNDERSTAND BARBADOS

History

The original inhabitants of Barbados were
Arawaks, who were driven off the island
around AD 1200 by Caribs from South
America. The Caribs, in turn, abandoned
(or fled) Barbados close to the arrival of
the first Europeans. The Portuguese visited
the island in 1536, but Barbados was uninhabited by the time Captain John Powell
claimed it for England in 1625. Two years
later, a group of settlers established the
island's first European settlement, James-
town, in present-day Holetown. Within a
few years, the colonists had cleared much
of the forest, planting tobacco and cotton
fields. In the 1640s they switched to sugarcane. The new sugar plantations were
labor intensive, and the landowners began
to import large numbers of African slaves.
These large sugar plantations – some of the
first in the Caribbean – proved immensely
profitable, and gave rise to a wealthy colo-

nial class. A visit to a plantation estate, like
the one at St Nicholas Abbey, will give some
idea of the money involved.

The sugar industry boomed during the
next century, and continued to prosper
after the abolition of slavery in 1834. As the
planters owned all of the best land, there
was little choice for the freed slaves other
than to stay on at the cane fields for a pit-
tance.

Social tensions flared during the 1930s,
and Barbados' black majority gradually
gained more access to the political process.
The economy diversified through international tourism and gave more islanders
the opportunity for economic success and
self-determination. England granted Barbados internal self-government in 1961 and it
became an independent nation on November 30, 1966, with Errol Barrow as its first
prime minister. While not flawless, Barbados has remained a stable democracy.

Owen Arthur and the Barbados Labour
Party were in power from 1993 to 2008.
In a campaign that saw 'change' as the
popular theme, David Thompson and the
left-leaning Democratic Labour Party won
election in 2008. But in late 2010 Thompson died suddenly, which was a traumatic
event for a nation used to political stability.
He was succeeded by Deputy Prime Minister
Freundel Stuart.

Unlike other Caribbean islands, Barbados
maintains its sugar industry, although the
majority of the economy is now based on
tourism and offshore banking. Condos are
being built as fast as the concrete dries.

Culture

Bajan culture displays some trappings of
English life: cricket, polo and horse racing
are popular pastimes, business is performed
in a highly organized fashion, gardens are
lovingly tended, older women often wear
prim little hats and special events are carried out with a great deal of pomp and
ceremony.

However, on closer examination, Barbados is very deeply rooted in Afro-Caribbean
tradition. Family life, art, food, music, architecture, religion and dress have more in
common with the Windward Islands than
with London. The African and East Indian
influences are especially apparent in the
spicy cuisine, rhythmic music and pulsating
festivals.

Like other Caribbean cultures, Bajans are relatively conservative and the men are macho, but the ongoing bond with a cosmopolitan center such as London has made Barbados slightly more socially progressive than its neighbors.

Bajan youth are fully within the media orbit of North America. The NBA and New York hip-hop fashion are as popular in Bridgetown as in Brooklyn.

Another similarity to the US is the suburban sprawl around Bridgetown. Traffic is often a problem and you can join the masses at a growing number of air-conditioned malls.

Sports

The national sport, if not national obsession, is cricket. Per capita, Bajans boast more world-class cricket players than any other nation. One of the world's top all-rounders, Bajan native Sir Garfield Sobers, was knighted by Queen Elizabeth II during her 1975 visit to Barbados, while another cricket hero, Sir Frank Worrell, appears on the B$5 bill.

In Barbados you can catch an international Test match, a heated local First Division match, or even just a friendly game on the beach or grassy field. Although international matches are less common here now that they are being spread more widely around the Caribbean, when it is Barbados' turn, thousands of Bajans and other West Indians pour into matches at Kensington Oval. For schedules and tickets, contact the Barbados Cricket Association (p198).

Horse races and polo are at their peak during the tourist season.

Music

Bajan contributions to West Indian music are renowned in the region, having produced such greats as the Mighty Gabby, a calypso artist whose songs on cultural identity and political protest speak for emerging black pride throughout the Caribbean. These days Bajan music leans toward the faster beats of soca (an energetic offspring of calypso), *rapso* (a fusion of soca and hip-hop) and dancehall (a contemporary offshoot of reggae with faster, digital beats and an MC). Hugely popular Bajan soca artist Rupee brings the sound of the island to audiences worldwide.

BARBADOS READING LIST

Numerous books cover Bajan history and culture:

➡ *The History of Barbados* by Robert H Schomburg is a thorough study of the island's past.

➡ *To Hell or Barbados: the Ethnic Cleansing of Ireland* by Sean O'Callaghan traces the scores of Irish sent by Cromwell to work as slaves on sugar plantations.

➡ *Treasures of Barbados* by Henry Fraser, a past president of the Barbados National Trust, surveys island architecture.

➡ *The Barbadian Rum Shop: the Other Watering Hole* by Peter Laurie is an overview of the history of the rum shop and the role it has played in Bajan life.

➡ *In the Castle of My Skin* by George Lamming is a much-acclaimed 1953 novel about growing up black in colonial Barbados.

The massively popular singer Rihanna has achieved worldwide fame while being idolized at home. Her reggae-style rap has won many Grammy awards, including best rap song and best dance recording.

Landscape & Wildlife

The Land

Barbados lies 160km east of the Windward Islands. It is somewhat pear-shaped, measuring 34km from north to south and 22km at its widest. The island is composed largely of coral accumulations built on sedimentary rocks. Water permeates the soft coral cap, creating underground streams, springs and limestone caverns.

Most of the island's terrain is relatively flat, rising to low, gentle hills in the interior. However, the northeastern part of the island, known as the Scotland District, rises to a relatively lofty 340m at Barbados' highest point, Mt Hillaby. The west coast has white-sand beaches and calm turquoise waters, while the east side of the island has turbulent Atlantic waters and a coastline punctuated with cliffs. Coral reefs surround most of the island and contribute

PRACTICALITIES

Newspapers Barbados has two daily newspapers, the *Barbados Advocate* and the *Daily Nation*. Some UK papers are sold in touristy areas for those who need a dose of Middle England.

TV The government-owned TV station CBC broadcasts on Channel 8.

Radio Local radio is on FM 92.9, 94.7 and 98.1 or AM 900. There's soca music on FM 95.3, gospel on FM 102.1 and the BBC on FM 92.1.

Smoking Smoking is prohibited in public places. In effect this means in enclosed spaces. It's permitted to smoke in non-enclosed spaces, including beaches and parks.

Weights & Measures Barbados uses the metric system, though many islanders still give directions in feet and miles and sell produce by the pound.

to the fine white sands on the western and southern beaches.

Two good places to enjoy the island's lush natural beauty are Andromeda Botanic Gardens (p210), in a gorgeous setting above Bathsheba with a huge range of beautifully displayed local flora; and Welchman Hall Gully (p209), off the highway from Bridgetown to Belleplaine, which has examples of the island's ancient forests.

Environmental Issues

The forests that once covered Barbados were long ago felled by British planters. One of the knock-on effects is that the country now has a problem with soil erosion. This loose dirt, along with pollution from ships and illegally dumped solid wastes, threatens to contaminate the aquifers that supply the island's drinking water.

Wildlife

The majority of Barbados' indigenous wildlife was overwhelmed by agriculture and competition with introduced species. Found only on Barbados is the harmless and elusive grass snake. The island also shelters a species of small, nonpoisonous, blind snake, plus whistling frogs, lizards, red-footed tortoises and eight species of bats.

Hawksbill turtles regularly come ashore to lay their eggs, as does the occasional leatherback turtle. As elsewhere, the turtles face numerous threats from pollution and human interference. The **Barbados Sea Turtle Project** (www.barbadosseaturtles.org; UWI, Bridgetown) is working to restore habitat and populations. Most, if not all, mammals found in the wild on Barbados have been introduced. They include wild green monkeys, mongooses, European hares, mice and rats. More than 180 species of birds have been sighted on Barbados. Most of them are migrating shorebirds and waders that breed in North America and stop over on Barbados en route to winter feeding grounds in South America.

SURVIVAL GUIDE

🛈 Directory A–Z

ACCOMMODATIONS

You can find some place to stay at every price point on Barbados, although there are quite a few more places at the top end than at the budget end.

Camping is generally not allowed on any public lands.

Most hotels add a 7.5% government tax plus a 10% service charge, and many have a minimum high-season stay. As elsewhere in the Caribbean, rates decline by as much as 40% outside of high season.

ACTIVITIES

Hiking

The **Barbados National Trust** (p195) leads guided hikes in the countryside. Hike leaders share insights into local history, geology and wildlife.

A nice hike to do on your own is along the old railroad bed that runs along the east coast from Belleplaine to Martin's Bay. The whole walk is about 20km, but it can be broken into shorter stretches.

Kitesurfing & Windsurfing

Barbados has good windsurfing and kitesurfing, with the best winds from December to June. Silver Sands, at the southern tip of the island, has excellent conditions for advanced practitioners, while Maxwell, just to the west, is better for intermediates. There are also good breaks for surfers in the area.

Surfing

Barbados has gained international fame for its east-coast breaks. Ground zero is the **Soup**

Bowl (p211), off Bathsheba, and another spot called **Duppies**, up the coast. **South Point**, **Silver Sands** and **Rockley Beach** (p199) on the south coast are sometimes good, as is **Brandon's**, which is next to the Hilton Hotel at Needham's Point. There are some 30 other named breaks.

There are local guys renting out boards on the beach at most of the popular surf spots. Prices are negotiable depending on the quality of the board, but even the nicest board shouldn't be much more than B$20 per hour, or B$60 for daily rental. It's worth noting that the locals are generally nice and welcoming to outsiders.

There are two good surf schools of note: **Zed's Surfing Adventures** (p203), based at Silver Sands, and **Barry's Surf Barbados** (p200) at Dover, which transports clients to various spots, depending on conditions.

CHILDREN

Barbados is generally a family-friendly destination. A number of resorts have organized children's activities or in-house day care and babysitting.

Most beaches are safe for children to play on and many of the southern and western beaches are calm enough for younger swimmers. The east-coast surf is too powerful for novice swimmers of any age.

Older kids enjoy surfing lessons.

ELECTRICITY

110V, 50Hz. US-style two-pin plugs are used; you may find the occasional UK-style three-pin sockets as well.

EMERGENCY & IMPORTANT NUMBERS

Ambulance	☎ 511
Fire	☎ 311
Hyperbaric chamber	☎ 436-5483
Police	☎ 211

FOOD

Eating in Barbados is a rewarding experience at all budget levels. Whether you're hitting up humble waterside fry shacks or fine-dining restaurants, you'll find plenty of outstanding fresh seafood. But Bajan cuisine is about more than just fried fish and there are many richly spiced local specialties to try out. Most restaurants in areas popular with travelers offer menus featuring both traditional plates and international cuisine.

Essential Food & Drink

Bananas Local varieties are green even when ripe (look for them in markets).

Banks The island's crisp lager is refreshing after a day in the hot sun.

Barbadian rum Considered some of the finest in the Caribbean, with Mount Gay being the best-known label.

Conkies A mixture of cornmeal, coconut, pumpkin, sweet potato, raisins and spices, steamed in a plantain leaf.

Cou-cou A creamy cornmeal-and-okra mash.

Cutters Meat or fish sandwiches in a salt-bread roll.

Fish cakes There are myriad Bajan recipes, made from salt cod and deep-fried.

Flying fish Served fried in delicious sandwiches all over the country. It's a mild white fish that is great sautéed or deep-fried.

Jug-jug A mixture of cornmeal, green peas and salted meat.

Roti A curry filling rolled inside flat bread.

GLBT TRAVELERS

Barbados is a conservative and religious place that is generally opposed to homosexuality. That said, there are a few openly gay Bajan couples, although they still tend to be discreet.

Gay visitors to Barbados will need to be judicious outside of international resorts, and especially in smaller, more traditional towns, but are unlikely to run into any major problems.

HEALTH

There are excellent medical facilities in Barbados. For minor illnesses, nearly all hotels will have a doctor on call or will be able to help you find assistance. Be sure to have travel insurance that covers medical care.

The country's main hospital is in Bridgetown.

LEGAL MATTERS

Barbados is an ordered place and the local police force is friendly but professional. It is highly unlikely that you'll be shaken down or approached for a bribe by law enforcement.

The island has a British legal system. If you find yourself in legal difficulties you have the right to legal representation and are eligible for legal aid if you can't afford to pay for private services.

MONEY

You'll certainly want some Barbadian dollars on hand, but larger payments can be made in US dollars, frequently with a major credit card. Hotels and guesthouses quote rates in US dollars (as do many dive shops and some restaurants), although you can use either US or Bajan currency to settle the account.

Exchange Rates

The exchange rate is fixed at B$2 to US$1.

AUSTRALIA	A$1	B$1.49
CANADA	C$1	B$1.52
EASTERN CARIBBEAN	EC$1	B$0.74
EUROPE	€1	B$2.11
JAPAN	¥100	B$1.73
NEW ZEALAND	NZ$	B$1.42
UK	£1	B$2.51
US	US$1	B$2.00

Tipping

A tip of 10% to 15% is standard in restaurants (often added to the bill), and 10% in hotels (usually added to the bill). A 10% tip is the norm in taxis.

PUBLIC HOLIDAYS

In addition to those observed throughout the region, Barbados has the following public holidays:

Errol Barrow Day January 21
Heroes' Day April 28
Labor Day May 1
Emancipation Day August 1
Kadooment Day First Monday in August
UN Day First Monday in October
Independence Day November 30

TAXES & REFUNDS

Barbados applies a VAT of 17.5% on most goods. The rate is 7.5% for hotel rooms.

Visitors are not eligible to reclaim VAT paid during their trip to Barbados.

TELEPHONE

Barbados' country code is 1; the area code is 246. To call any other country with a country code of 1 (most of North America and the Caribbean), just dial 1 and the 10-digit number. For other countries, dial the international access code 011 + country code + number.

TIME

Atlantic Standard Time (GMT/UTC minus four hours).

TOURIST INFORMATION

Barbados Tourism Marketing Inc (BTMI; 467-3600; www.visitbarbados.org; Warrens Office Complex, St Michael) Government tourism promotion office. Has information desks at Grantley Adams International Airport and the cruise-ship terminal.

TRAVELERS WITH DISABILITIES

Barbados is one of the better-equipped destinations in the eastern Caribbean for travelers with disabilities, though it still has some way to go.

Many areas still have uneven sidewalks, or don't have any at all. Furthermore, public transport is generally not conditioned for wheelchair access.

The excellent **Barbados Council for the Disabled** (http://barbadosdisabled.org.bb) is working with local businesses to make them accessible through the 'Fully Accessible Barbados' program. They provide a number of services to travelers, including beach wheelchairs, accessible transportation and travel-planning assistance.

VOLUNTEERING

Barbados has quite a large charity and nongovernmental sector, some of which accept volunteers. Many are local organizations that don't arrange placements from overseas – you'll have to organize your own trip and accommodations.

The two main sectors for volunteers are community and environmental projects, particularly in marine conservation.

One organization that regularly needs volunteers is the Hope Sanctuary animal shelter (www.thehopesanctuarybarbados.com) in St John.

Getting There & Away

AIR

Grantley Adams International Airport (BGI; www.gaia.bb) is on the island's southeast corner, about 16km from Bridgetown. It's the largest airport in the Eastern Caribbean and the major point of entry for the region.

Barbados is served by major airlines flying from North America and the UK.

SEA
Cruise Ship

About 450,000 cruise-ship passengers arrive in Barbados each year as part of Eastern Caribbean itineraries. Ships dock at Bridgetown

Harbour, about 1km west of the city center. The harbour has the usual duty-free shops and a branch office of the **Barbados Tourism Authority** (Cruise Ship Terminal; ◷ when ships are in port).

Yacht

The Windward Islands are among the most popular places to sail in the world. Yacht harbors and charters abound. Barbados, however, is the one exception – its easterly position and challenging sailing conditions keep it well off the main track for most sailors.

ⓘ Getting Around

BICYCLE

Barbados offers good riding for the adventurous. It's hilly, but roads are not usually steep (except-ing parts of the east). However, most roads are quite narrow, so traffic is a constant bother in the west and south.

Most shops require a credit card or B$100 deposit for rentals. Your hotel can hook you up with a rental.

BOAT

With its good networks of roads, water taxis are not common in Barbados (unlike some other parts of the Caribbean), although on the west coast there are a couple of operators running between local businesses.

BUS

It's possible to get to virtually any place on the island by public bus. There are three kinds of bus:

Government-operated public buses Large and blue with a yellow stripe.
Privately operated minibuses Midsized buses painted yellow with a blue stripe.
Route taxis Individually owned minivans that have 'ZR' on their license plates and are painted white.

All types of bus charge the same fare: B$2 to any place on the island. You should have exact change when you board the government bus, but minibuses and route taxis will make change.

Most buses transit through Bridgetown, although a few north–south buses bypass the city. Buses to the southeast part of the island generally transit through Oistins.

Bus stops around the island are marked with red-and-white signs printed with the direction in which the bus is heading ('To City' or 'Out of City'). Buses usually have their destinations posted on or above the front windshield.

Buses along the main routes, such as Bridge-town to Oistins or Speightstown, are frequent, running from 6am to around midnight. You can get complete schedule information for public

buses on any route from the **Transport Board.** (☏ 436-6820; www.transportboard.com)

CAR & MOTORCYCLE

In Barbados, you drive on the left. At intersec-tions and narrow passages, drivers may flash their lights to indicate that you should proceed.

Driving Licence

Visitors must obtain a temporary driving permit (US$5) from their car-rental agency; you'll need to show a valid driving license from your home country.

Car Rental

Barbados doesn't have many car-rental agents affiliated with major international rental chains. There are, instead, scores of independent car-rental companies, some so small that they're based out of private homes.

Despite the number of companies, prices don't seem to vary much. The going rate for a small car is about B$130 to B$150 a day, including unlimited mileage and insurance.

Previously it was common for companies to rent out strange, small convertible cars called 'mokes' (they look like the odd car in *Fantasy Island*), which don't have doors. These are an acquired taste and small economy cars are more common now. Rental cars are marked with an 'H' on the license plate.

While most car-rental companies don't have booths at the airport, they will often deliver your car there or to your hotel.

Road Conditions

Highways are not very well marked, although landmarks are clearly labeled, as are some roundabouts (traffic circles) and major intersec-tions. The most consistent highway markings are often the low cement posts at the side of the road showing the highway number and, below that, the number of kilometers from Bridgetown.

All primary and main secondary roads are paved, although some are a bit narrow. There are plenty of gas stations around the island, except on the east coast. Some stations in the Bridge-town area are open 24 hours.

Expect rush-hour traffic on the roads around booming Bridgetown.

TAXI

Taxis have a 'Z' on the license plate and usually a 'taxi' sign on the roof. They're easy to find and often wait at the side of the road in popular tourist areas.

Although fares are fixed by the government, taxis are not metered and you will have to haggle for a fair price. The rate per kilometer is around B$3, but short trips cost more. Sample fares from Bridgetown include Bathsheba (B$76), Oistins (B$40) and Speightstown (B$60).

Bonaire

POP 17,400 / ☎599

Best Places to Eat

➡ Wil's Tropical Grill (p222)

➡ Bobbejan's Take-Away (p222)

➡ Capriccio Ristorante (p222)

Best Places to Sleep

➡ Bellafonte (p227)

➡ Carib Inn (p221)

➡ Captain Don's Habitat (p221)

➡ Coco Palm Garden & Casa Oleander (p226)

Why Go?

A small island with a desert landscape, Bonaire is not for everyone – but it *is* for divers and snorkelers who want to immerse themselves in that vibrant world under the sea. The beauty of Bonaire is that the coral reef, designated a national park, is just a few feet from the shoreline. Dozens of exceptional dive sites are easily accessible from the shore and teeming with life, making this island an independent diver's (and snorkeler's) paradise.

Above the surface, there is world-class windsurfing on Lac Bay and excellent kayaking among the mangroves. Biking trails wind through the arid hills, while driving routes show off the island's historical and natural sights. Classy but low-key resorts and restaurants complete the picture – perfect for travelers who prefer their adventure with some amenities.

When to Go

Dec–Apr High season, where accommodations fill up and prices are significantly higher.

Jan & Feb Carnival (*Karnaval*) is Bonaire's biggest celebration – a week or more of music and costumes, parades and parties. It culminates the weekend before Ash Wednesday, with the final parade and effigy-burning taking place on the Tuesday.

Sep–Dec Although Bonaire is below the hurricane belt, the island does experience an increase in rain and cooler temperatures.

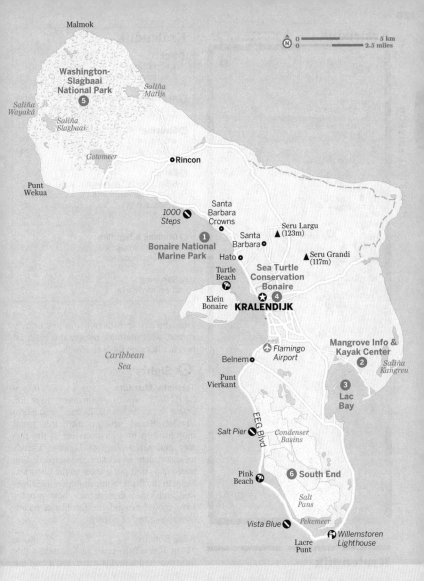

Bonaire Highlights

1 **Bonaire National Marine Park** (p222) Donning a mask and discovering the incredible underwater world that lies right offshore.

2 **Mangrove Info & Kayak Center** (p226) Kayaking and snorkeling in the ecologically rich 'reef nursery.'

3 **Lac Bay** (p226) Windsurfing at one of the world's premier destinations for beginners and pros alike.

4 **Sea Turtle Conservation Bonaire** (p221) Keeping the beaches safe for sea turtles – and maybe even ushering some newborn *tortuguitas* to the safety of the sea.

5 **Washington-Slagbaai National Park** (p224) Exploring the island's remote northern tip.

6 **South End** (p225) Seeing pink (flamingos!) while driving or cycling through the salt pans.

Kralendijk

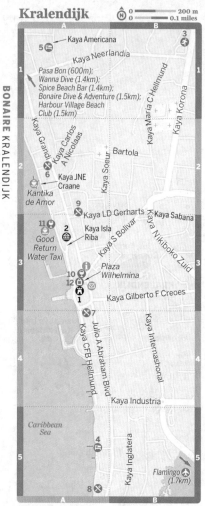

Kralendijk

◎ Sights
1 Fort Oranje...A3
2 Terramar Museum................................A3

◉ Activities, Courses & Tours
3 Sea Turtle Conservation Bonaire.......B1

◉ Sleeping
4 Carib Inn...A5
5 Lizard Inn A1

◉ Eating
6 Bobbejan's Take-Away A2
7 Capriccio Ristorante A4
8 Sebastian's...A5
9 Wil's Tropical Grill.................................A2

◉ Drinking & Nightlife
10 Cuba Compagnie A3
11 Karel's Beach Bar A3

◉ Shopping
12 Artisan Market A3

area, the city spreads out in a less orderly sprawl, with marinas, resorts and artificial beaches hogging the waterfront.

◎ Sights

Terramar Museum MUSEUM
(☐717-0423; www.terramarmuseum; Kaya JNE Craane 6; adult/child US$10/free; ☺9am-6pm Mon-Sat) Brand new in 2016, this small museum provides an overview of the history and archaeology of Bonaire. There's an assortment of artifacts, accompanied by audio clips that put a voice to the historical facts. In the front room, an impressive timeline and video demonstrate how peoples have moved around the Caribbean region over the course of history.

Klein Bonaire ISLAND
About 1km off the coast of Kralendijk, this little deserted island is where you'll find the the region's most attractive beach, aka No Name Beach. There are no facilities, aside from the marked dive sites. But this is a popular spot for cruisers and other beach bums who come over to snorkel the turquoise waters and lounge on the white sands. **Good Return Water Taxi** (Karel's Water Taxi; ☐788-8501; www.goodreturnbonaire.com; adult/child US$15/10; ☺departs 10am, noon & 2pm Mon-Sat) or **Kantika de Amor** (☐796-5399; www.water-taxikleinbonaire.com; round-trip US$20; ☺departs

Kralendijk

Kralendijk is a small island capital, with a long, strollable seafront and a smattering of colorful, colonial architecture. It lacks historic sites or beautiful beaches, but it's a pleasant place to stop, shop, lunch, dine or drink – with a few prime spots for catching the sunset.

Right around the cruise-ship terminal, the compact 'downtown' area is lined with shops and restaurants and shady plazas, all of which lend their tropical charm to the capital. Outside of this three-square-block

10am, noon & 2pm) can give you a lift across the sea.

🏃 Activities

⭐ Sea Turtle Conservation Bonaire
WILDLIFE-WATCHING

(STCB; ☎717-2225; www.bonaireturtles.org; Kaya Korona 53; turtle tour US$40) Three mornings a week, travelers can accompany the STCB workers on their rounds monitoring the sea-turtle nests on Klein Bonaire. The organization maintains careful records of all new and existing nests, including counting the egg shells and looking for stragglers from any newly hatched nest. For travelers who can make a longer-term commitment, there are several cool volunteer opportunities.

Wanna Dive
DIVING

(☎717-8884; www.wannadive.com; Kaya Gobernador N Debrot 73, Eden Beach Resort; boat dive US$42, night diving US$65; ⊙9am-5pm) Wanna dive? Of course you do! In addition to the regular range of equipment and air, this low-key operation also offers full-day boat trips (US$150), east-coast diving (US$45) and night diving.

Sea Cow Snorkeling
SNORKELING

(☎785-7727; www.seacow-bonaire.com; adult/child US$44/22; ⊙8:30am & 1:30pm Dec-Apr) You don't really need anybody to take you snorkeling in Bonaire, as you can just put on a mask and walk into the water. But if you want somebody to take care of you – picking the best sites and pointing out the creatures – you can't go wrong with Henk and Gea and their Holstein-patterned boat. Prices include snacks and gear.

🎉 Festivals & Events

Carnival
STREET CARNIVAL

(Karnaval) Carnival is Bonaire's biggest celebration – a week or more of music and costumes, parades and parties. It culminates the weekend before Ash Wednesday, with the final parade and effigy-burning taking place on the Tuesday.

🛏 Sleeping

Unlike many other Caribbean islands, Bonaire has few large resorts. Instead, you'll find rental units, guesthouses and midsized resorts, most located along the coast in Kralendijk and its northern outskirts.

CAPTAIN DON

In 1962, Captain Don Stewart arrived in Bonaire from California aboard the *Valerie Queen* with just 63 cents to his name. He fell in love with the island, and devoted the next 50-plus years to protecting the reef and making it more accessible to divers and snorkelers. Although the good captain passed in 2014, his legacy lives on at the so-called 'home of diving freedom,' Captain Don's Habitat, and at the island's 90 dive sites, many of which he marked and named himself.

⭐ Captain Don's Habitat
RESORT $$

(☎717-8290; www.habitatbonaire.com; Kaya Gobernador N Debrot 103; s/d US$160/210, ste US$185-245; ❄@🛜🏊) 🍴 Captain Don's Habitat is set on lushly landscaped grounds 3km north of town, with 85 units surrounding a large swimming pool. The rooms are spacious, clean and comfortable, without too many frills. Always at the forefront of environmental technologies, the place uses solar water heaters and a state-of-the-art water treatment system. The on-site restaurant, Rum Runners, is an obligatory stop.

⭐ Carib Inn
GUESTHOUSE $$

(☎717-8819; www.caribinn.com; Julio A Abraham Blvd; r/apt from US$120/140; ❄🛜🏊) Long-time resident Bruce Bowker extends a warm and personable welcome to his waterside compound on the southern side of town. Surrounding a small pool, the rooms are quirky, cozy and comfortable. The on-site dive shop offers daily trips to Klein Bonaire, as well as equipment rental, guided shore dives and various training programs.

Buddy Dive Resort
RESORT $$

(☎717-5080; www.buddydive.com; Kaya Gobernador N Debrot 85; studio US$230, 1-/2-bedroom apt US$260/425; ❄@🏊) North of town, this place is a diver's delight. With more than 70 studios and apartments in 10 sunny yellow buildings, this is one of the larger resorts on the island. All the facilities are here, including two restaurants, two swimming pools, truck rental, a dive shop and – for your convenience – a drive-through filling station.

Lizard Inn
B&B $$

(☑717-6877; www.lizardinnbonaire.com; Kaya Americana 14; r/studio US$80/100; ❋🐾🔊🏊) This tidy compound has 12 basic but comfortable rooms in white stucco buildings, clustered around a hammock-strung courtyard and small swimming pool. The place is simple and sweet, with perks such as storage for your dive gear and breakfast served in the gazebo. Guaranteed on arrival: a warm welcome and cold drink.

Harbour Village Beach Club
RESORT $$$

(☑717-7500; www.harbourvillage.com; Kaya Gobernador N Debrot 71; r from US$400; ❋@🔊🏊) Bonaire's most lavish resort is still a relatively low-key affair. Set on a beautiful beach and yacht harbor 2km north of town, it has sedately decorated lodgings in wide two-story blocks. Amenities include large balconies and luxury foam mattresses. Climb the rate card and you gain kitchenettes and more.

🍴 Eating

Between 2 Buns
SANDWICHES $

(www.facebook.com/between2bunsbonaire; Kaya Gobernador N Debrot; sandwiches US$8-12; ⊙7am-5pm Mon-Fri, 8am-4pm Sat; 🔊) The go-to spot for a hearty and wholesome breakfast or lunch. A wide variety of sandwiches are served on fresh bread. It's a perfect lunch stop between dives.

BONAIRE NATIONAL MARINE PARK

The island's star attraction, **Bonaire National Marine Park** (☑717-8444; www.stinapabonaire.org; Park Headquarters, Barcadera 10; diving/snorkeling US$25/10), is a unique and precious resource that attracts divers and snorkelers to explore miles of pristine coral reef. The protected area covers the entire coast of the island, including Klein Bonaire, to a depth of 200ft (60m). Between the two islands, there are about 90 named dive sites, many of which are accessible from the shore. Look for the painted yellow rocks.

Conservation is taken seriously. Divers new to Bonaire must do an orientation and check-out dive at a local dive shop, to get comfortable with weights, conditions and park rules.

Pasa Bon
PIZZA $

(☑780-1111; Kaya Gobernador N Debrot; pizza US$5-20; ⊙5-10pm Wed-Sun) You can't miss Pasa Bon, located at the only stoplight on the island. Besides its location, it's famous for its pizza topped with lionfish. Do good by eating well! Even without the specialty topping, the pizza is tasty and the atmosphere is fun.

★ Wil's Tropical Grill
CARIBBEAN $$

(Kaya LD Gerharts 9; mains US$18-25; ⊙5:30-9:30pm Mon-Sat) With contemporary art inside and a blooming garden outside, this contemporary Caribbean bistro exudes the colors and flavors of the region. The menu changes daily, but look for favorites such as Thai coconut shrimp and a house-smoked marlin. Start things off with a signature cocktail and you're in for a good night.

★ Bobbejan's Take-Away
BARBECUE $$

(☑717-4783; Kaya Albert Engelhardt 2; mains US$10-12; ⊙6-10pm Fri & Sat, noon-2pm & 6-10pm Sun) Don't let the name fool you: there are tables here out back under a nice tree. But getting one is a challenge as *everybody* comes here for the super-tender ribs and the velvety peanut sauce on the plate of Indonesian-style chicken satay.

Spice Beach Bar
CARIBBEAN $$

(www.spicebonaire.com; Kaya Gobernador N Debrot, Eden Beach Resort; mains US$15-25, prix fixe US$35; ⊙7am-11pm Sun-Thu, to midnight Fri & Sat) On the sand at Eden Beach Resort, this is a recommended spot for classic, casual fare, such as barbecue, burgers, satay or steaks. If you're looking for something fancier, the more formal restaurant offers a set menu.

★ Capriccio Ristorante
ITALIAN $$$

(☑717-7230; www.capricciobonaire.com; Kaya CEB Hellmund 5; pasta US$18-25, mains US$25-30; ⊙6-10pm) Direct from Italy, this *ristorante* and boutique is sophisticated, stylish and delicious. Tempting *cicchetti* (small bites), handmade pizza and pasta, and classic main dishes are accompanied by a thoughtful wine list and lots of love.

Ingridiënts
MODERN EUROPEAN $$$

(www.ingridientsrestaurant.com; Kaya Gobernador N Debrot 85; mains US$20-30; ⊙6-10pm) This cool and contemporary spot is an excellent place to spend an evening, sampling the unusual fare and watching the night divers. Tantalizing offerings include several different options for tarte flambée, local seafood specialties such as sea bream, and a delectable Parmesan truffle pasta, prepared at the table in a cheese wheel. Located on the grounds of Buddy Dive.

Sebastian's SEAFOOD $$$
(☑ 717-5263; www.sebastiansrestaurantbonaire.com; Julio A Abraham Blvd 60; mains US$15-40; ☺6-10pm Tue-Sun) Sebastian's gets top marks for its romantic waterfront location, especially if you manage to snag the solitary table for two that's out at the end of the pier (book way in advance). The menu changes frequently, but there's always plenty of seafood; the octopus quesadilla is a favorite.

🍷 Drinking & Nightlife

★Cuba Compagnie BAR
(www.cubacompagniebonaire.nl; Kaya Grandi 1; ☺5pm-late) The island's hottest spot is this sultry Cuban cafe, especially on Thursday night, when salsa dancers show their stuff. Any night of the week, the place is packed with happy patrons sipping mojitos and feasting on fusion fare. The atmospheric interior is adorned with eclectic artwork and old photographs, but the outdoor seating area is the place to be.

Karel's Beach Bar BAR
(www.karelsbeachbar.com; Kaya JNE Craane 12; ☺9am-1am Sun-Thu, to 3am Fri & Sat) It's not technically a beach bar, but it is set on a pier that juts into the water and promises happy-hour specials, sunset views and good vibes all around.

🛍 Shopping

The city's shopping area is crammed into a few blocks on Kaya Grandi, just one block in from the cruise-ship terminal. It's a short strip, but there are plenty of interesting local shops (and no international chains). An **artisan market** (www.bonaireartandcraftmarket.com; Plaza Wilhelmina; ☺hour vary) sets up when there's a cruise ship in port.

ℹ Information

Post Office (www.fxdc-post.com; Plaza Wilhelmina 11; ☺8am-4pm Mon-Fri) Reliable postal service is provided by Flamingo Express Dutch Caribbean.
Bonaire Tourist Office (☑ 717-8322; www.tourismbonaire.com; Kaya Grandi 2; ☺8am-noon & 1:30-5pm Mon-Fri) Staff can answer questions about accommodations, tours

and more, as well as offer a good selection of brochures.

ℹ Getting There & Away

Flamingo Airport (p230) is just south of town, about 3km from the center of Kralendijk. Although most resorts do not offer airport transfers, it's easy enough to arrange a taxi to your hotel (destinations in and around Kralendijk cost between US$10 and US$20). Car rentals can be arranged at or near the airport.

ℹ Getting Around

The city is small enough that you can explore most of it on foot, though you'll want a vehicle (or at least a bicycle) to get around the island. Boats to Klein Bonaire depart from Karel's Beach Bar or from the small marina across from It Rains Fishes.

North End

You'll likely make your way to the North End on a quest to dive at one site or another. Even so, it's also worth spending a day or more on land – exploring the national park and hiking in the hills, visiting Rincon, the island's oldest town, and discovering some of the small-scale grassroots ecological and agricultural initiatives in the area.

Bonaire's second town, Rincon, is rather sleepy and very old – even older than Kralendijk. More than 500 years ago, Spaniards chose this valley to establish their settlement because it was relatively fertile, and because it was hidden from passing pirates. Rincon became the home base of the slaves who worked the farms and made the long trek to labor in the salt flats in the south.

Nowadays, most of the residents are descended from slaves, and the village maintains an authentic island atmosphere, celebrating true Bonairean culture with classic Caribbean architecture, lively cultural markets, tantalizing local cuisine, and a rousing annual harvest festival.

⊙ Sights

Gotomeer LAGOON
(Kaminda Goto) On the edge of Washington-Slagbaai National Park, this large, inland saltwater lagoon attracts flocks of flamingos, especially during nesting season (January to June). You can't get too close to these shy feathered friends, but you can usually spot some from the observation area.

BEYOND DIVING

Outdoor Bonaire (☑791-6272; www.outdoorbonaire.com; tours from US$50) Caters to adventurers of all kinds, with active tours that include rock climbing, kayaking, caving, hiking and birding. Note that this eco-forward operation does not offer tours for cruise-ship passengers.

Bonaire Dive & Adventure (☑717-2229; www.bonairediveandadventure.com; Kaya Gobernador N Debrot 77a; shore/boat dive $33/52, 6 days unlimited air or nitrox US$195; ☺8:30am-4:30pm) Offers a full menu of dive packages, including boat and shore dives, air and nitrox etc. Orientation and check-out dive take place every day. The 'adventure' part of Dive & Adventure refers to mountain biking, kayaking and cave explorations.

Take the paved road heading due west from Rincon for about 4km.

★**Washington-Slagbaai National Park** NATIONAL PARK
(www.stinapabonaire.org; entry incl with purchase of national marine park tag, US$25 per calendar year; ☺8am-5pm, last entry 2:45pm) Comprising almost 20% of the island's area, this vast, desert landscape is a fantastic place to explore on foot, by bike or by vehicle (preferably a 4WD). Stop at the visitors center, at the entrance, to pick up a map and check out exhibits on the park's ecology and history. From here, two driving routes and two hiking trails show off the park's diversity, including salt ponds, seascapes, remote beaches, mangroves, volcanic hills and amazing desert vistas. And cacti, lots of cacti.

Mangazina di Rei MUSEUM
(☑786-2101; www.bonaireculturetours.com; Blvd Miguel A Pourier; adult/child US$10/5; ☺9am-4pm Mon-Fri) About 1.5km east of Rincon, the second-oldest stone building on Bonaire used to be the storehouse. Every week, the slaves made the arduous 10-hour journey from the salt pans in the south to this village in the north, to see their families and to get their provisions from the storehouse. Now it contains a small museum about the nature, geology and history of Bonaire, as well as island culture and how it evolved during and after slavery.

Cadushy Distillery DISTILLERY
(www.cadushy.com; Kaya Cornelis D Crestian; ☺10am-5pm Mon, Wed & Fri, plus any day cruise ships are in port) FREE Drinking a cactus sounds like a prickly affair, but it's not as scary as it sounds. Pay a visit to this small-scale island distillery in Rincon village to see how the prickly green plant gets turned into the delicious 'Spirit of Bonaire' known as Cadushy. Sample it in the shady courtyard, surrounded by blooming gardens and squawking parrots.

Bonaire Botanical Garden GARDENS
(Kaminda Tras di Montagne; adult/child US$10/5; ☺10am-6pm Wed-Sat) Everything you ever wanted to know (and more!) about organic gardening, permaculture and medicinal plants. Manuel Vargas' gardens are a delightful maze of lush greenery, flowing fountains and whimsical artwork. The 1½-hour tour is followed by a complimentary cup of herbal tea. Located about 7km southeast of Rincon.

✹✹ Festivals & Events

Dia di Rincon FESTIVAL
(Rincon Day) The island's traditional harvest festival, Simadan, culminates with Rincon Day, celebrated on April 30. The day starts with Mass and a flag-raising at the Catholic church, followed by eating, drinking, singing and dancing. The highlight is the traditional Simadan parade, which takes place late in the afternoon.

✕ Eating

Rincon is the place to come to sample authentic, delicious local fare, whether you get it at the monthly **cultural market** (Mangazina di Rei; ☺8am-1pm last Sat of the month) or at one of the charming restaurants in the village.

Le-Ma-Se CARIBBEAN $
(www.lemase.info; Kaya Rincon 34; mains US$4-7; ☺hours vary) There are two reasons to stop at this roadside shack in Rincon village: pumpkin soup and milkshakes, both made with an extra dose of love from Norman (the 'Ma' of Le-Ma-Se). This is what you want for lunch after you spend a morning diving 1000 Steps or hiking around Washington-Slagbaai National Park.

Posada Para Mira CARIBBEAN $$
(Kaya Para Mira; mains US$10-18; ☺11am-6pm Fri-Mon & Wed) On the western outskirts of Rincon, this colorful house has a wide front

porch that is a delightful place to sample local specialties such as *sopi di yuana* (iguana soup) and *stoba di kabritu* (goat stew), as well as some less intimidating options.

Rose Inn CARIBBEAN $$
(Kaya Guyaba 4; mains from US$10; ☺11am-3pm Thu-Tue) A local institution run by Rose herself. A genial mix of folks enjoy plate lunches of local fare (fish stew, goat, fried chicken etc) at mismatched tables scattered under trees. Service can be erratic, but that's part of the charm. Located in the heart of Rincon village.

ⓘ Getting There & Away

There are two different routes to the northern end of the island – both reasonably maintained roads with wonderful vistas and little else. The wider, faster and more direct route cuts through the center of the island and approaches Rincon from the east.

The road along the west coast winds around the ins and outs of the shoreline, with spectacular vistas of the rocky seashore and frequent pullouts for the marked dive sites. About 5km north of Kralendijk the road becomes one way, northbound, so you are committed at this point. After another 5km, you reach a T-junction, with the left fork continuing along the coast (and further to Gotomeer) and the right fork turning inland toward Rincon.

South End

The southern end of Bonaire is flat and arid, with vistas that extend for many miles in all directions. The horizon is broken only by the massive mounds of sparkling white salt. Yes, salt. This is the product of the Cargill solar salt works, and further south you'll see the acres and acres of salt pans, where the ocean water sits and eventually evaporates, leaving the salty residue. The landscape is oddly – startlingly – beautiful, especially as the water evaporates, and with increasing salinity, the pans turn 50 shades of pink. Speaking of pink, look out for flamingos flocking in the salt pans.

Aside from the salt works, the South End is nearly deserted. But the coast is punctuated by stunning beaches, colonial-era landmarks, and the lovely windsurfer-dotted Lac Bay, making the perimeter a fascinating driving or cycling route.

WORTH A TRIP

MAIKY SNACK

This food-serving shack (Kaminda Nieuw Amsterdam; meals from US$10; ☺lunch Fri-Wed) – rustic to say the least – is a much-loved spot for traditional local fare (read: goat). Yes, the goat dishes incorporate all parts of the animal, served in stew and on skewers. Sides include a long list of old favorites such as *funchi* (cornmeal cakes), *yambo* (okra soup) and papaya.

Maiky Snack is (sort of) on the way to Lac Bay. From Kaminda Sorobon, watch for the turnoff onto a dirt road heading east, and follow the signs.

◉ Sights

Donkey Sanctuary Bonaire WILDLIFE RESERVE
(☏9560-7607; www.donkeysanctuary.com; Kaya lr Randolph Statius; adult/child US$7/3; ☺10am-4pm) Do you ever feel like you're surrounded by jackasses? You will in Bonaire, because the animals live free and wild on the island. The vast Donkey Sanctuary offers safe haven for these gentle creatures. Visitors can meet the newborns and survivors in the special-care unit, observe the droves from the watchtower, and drive the circuit to meet all the resident jack and jennies. Bring some carrots and you'll make some friends, for sure!

Slave Huts HISTORIC SITE
Along the coast you will see the legacy of a vile chapter in Bonaire's past. The dwarf-sized stone huts were built in the mid-19th century, as residences for the slaves who worked in the salt mines. The slaves' permanent homes (and families) were in Rincon, so every Friday afternoon, they would take a seven-hour hike to the other end of the island to spend a day at home, returning on Sunday to their arduous work.

🏃 Activities

Horse Ranch Bonaire HORSEBACK RIDING
(Kunuku Warhama; ☏786-2094; www.horseranchbonaire.com; Kaya Warahama 40; per person US$125; ☺tours depart 8am) The signature tour here is the 'Ride & Swim', a half-day tour that takes you riding over forested trails and along deserted beaches. The tour stops halfway at Lac Bay so both riders and horses can cool down in the water. If you love horses, you'll love the thrill of swimming with them.

LAC BAY

On the island's southeastern side, Lac is a large inland bay that provides a critical habitat for green turtles, queen conchs – and windsurfers. Indeed, this is one of the world's premier destinations for riding the wind, thanks to steady trade winds and warm, shallow waters.

The northern side of Lac Bay is sheltered by mangrove forests, where wetland birds breed and reef creatures mature (which explains why the mangrove is sometimes called a 'coral reef nursery'). It's a gem for paddlers and snorkelers, who can spot young fish, sea stars and sponges in the crystal clear waters. The Kaminda Lac – around the northern side of the bay – is a picturesque drive (and a popular cycling route) with views of dense mangroves and flocks of flamingos.

★**Mangrove Info & Kayak Center** KAYAKING
(☑ 780-5353; www.mangrovecenter.com; Kaminda Lac 140; 30min tour US$27/46; ☺from 8:30am Mon-Sat) ✐ Set in the middle of the Lac Bay mangrove forest, this operation offers guided kayak trips, as well as excursions in a solar-powered boat. Stop by the information center (completely powered by wind and solar, by the way) for some informative displays about this unique ecosystem.

Snorkeling & Diving

East Coast Diving DIVING
(☑ 717-5211; www.bonaireeastcoastdiving.com; Fishermens Pier, Sorobon; 2-tank dive US$120) This unique dive operation specializes in dives on the windward side of the island. Conditions can be tricky but this is where the big guys hang out. You're likely to see southern stingrays, spotted eagle rays, green morays and sea turtles, not to mention amazing coral formations. The rigid inflatable boat makes it easier to tolerate the rough seas.

Pink Beach SNORKELING, DIVING
Just north of the slave huts, Pink Beach is a long sliver of sand that takes its color from pink coral washed ashore. It's pretty rough for sunbathing, but the swimming and snorkeling (and diving) are prime. The beach is even better to the south at the Vista Blue dive site.

Windsurfing & Kitesurfing

Kiteboarding Bonaire KITESURFING
(☑ 701-5483; www.kiteboardingbonaire.com; Atlantis Beach; intro lesson US$150-225, 3-lesson package US$610; ☺lessons 10am-1pm & 2-5pm) Learn to fly on Atlantis Kite Beach, where the wind blows between 17 and 22 knots almost every day of the year. The school operates out of a colorful kite bus, with bean bags, hammocks and cold drinks on the beach for when it's time to take a break.

Jibe City WINDSURFING
(www.jibecity.com; Kaminda Sorobon 12; rental per hr/day/week US$35/80/385, kayak/SUP per hr US$15/20; ☺10am-6pm) Located on Lac Bay along 'windsurfing row'. Lessons, clinics and gear are all available, as are stand-up paddle boards and kayaks for rent. The on-site Hang Out Beachbar is a great place to, well, hang out. The view and the vibe (and the food) are good enough to attract nonsurfers too.

Bonaire Windsurf Place WINDSURFING
(☑ 717-2288; www.bonairewindsurfplace.com; Kaminda Sorobon; lessons from US$50, 2-day rental from US$145; ☺10am-6pm) This locally owned place could be your windsurfing home, offering lessons and gear rental. The rental boards are 'twin-fin Fire-ride' boards, which were specially designed for Lac Bay's shallow waters. Refuel at the cafe, with a shady veranda for watching the action on the water.

🛏 Sleeping

Your options for sleeping in the South End are slim. There is one resort near Lac Bay, as well as some vacation rentals in Belnem, a residential area just south of the airport.

★**Coco Palm Garden
& Casa Oleander** APARTMENTS $
(☑ 717-2108; www.cocopalmgarden.com; Kaya van Eps 9, Belnem; d US$65-85; ❋@☎☀) Coco Palm rents a variety of rooms and apartments in various brightly painted houses in the residential neighborhood of Belnem, just south of the airport. Beds and layouts vary, as do amenities, but you can always count on a kitchen and a hammock-strung

garden. Bachelor Beach is just down the road.

Surf Hostel
HOSTEL $

(🖉 701-1982; www.surfhostelbonaire.com; Kaminda Lac 101; s/d US$35/45; 🛜 🆒) 🏊 Located north of Lac Bay, this place is surely one of the cheapest – if not *the* cheapest – place to stay on the island. Guests are mostly local and international windsurfers who are here for one thing only. Rooms are basic, clean and cheap, with necessities such as kitchen and laundry facilities on-site – though no potable water, which is not cool.

The hostel is 8km from the windsurfing beach and 4km from the city – in other words, it's not close to anything. You'll need to rent a bicycle or a scooter or get used to hitching.

★ Bellafonte
APARTMENTS $$

(🖉 717-3333; www.bellafontebonaire.com; 10 EEG Blvd, Belnem; studio/ste US$180/275; ❄ 🛜 🆒) This ocean front property offers a collection of spacious, sparkling studios and suites, all equipped with private balconies, well-stocked kitchens and luxurious linens. Staff are on hand to ensure all needs are met (including dining recommendations, since there is no restaurant on-site). A private pier juts into the Caribbean blue, offering a perfect spot for sunbathing, swimming and snorkeling.

ⓘ Getting There & Away

EEG Blvd hugs the southern coast, starting just below the airport and continuing around the tip and all the way up to Lac Bay. If you're headed to Lac Bay, however, it's quicker to take the main road, Kaminda Sorobon, which comes directly from Kralendijk. It takes about 15 minutes to drive directly from Kralendijk to Lac Bay, but the longer route around the tip takes about 40 minutes.

The third and final road on the island's southern end is Kaya Van Eps, which bisects the tip, from Belnem to Lac Bay, passing the Donkey Sanctuary on the way.

UNDERSTAND BONAIRE

History

The Arawaks lived on Bonaire for thousands of years before Spain laid claim to it in 1499. A mere 20 years later there were none left, as the Spanish sent all the natives to work in mines elsewhere in the empire. The only remains of the Arawak civilization on Bonaire are a few inscriptions in remote caves – although there are some artifacts from around the region at the Terramar Museum (p220).

The depopulated Bonaire stayed pretty quiet until 1634, when the Dutch took control, building Fort Oranje to protect the harbor. The Dutch looked to the flat land in the south and saw a future in salt production. Thousands of slaves were imported to work in horrific conditions. You can see a few surviving slave huts (p225) at the southern end of the island, and the Mangazina di Rei (p224), where the slaves had to travel to get their provisions, in Rincon.

When slavery was abolished in the 19th century, the salt factories closed. The population – former slaves, Dutch landowners and South American transplants – lived pretty simple lives until after WWII, when the salt ponds reopened (this time with machines doing the hard work). The revived industry, coupled with the postwar booms in tourism and diving, gave a real boost to the economy.

Meanwhile relations with Curaçao, capital of the Netherlands Antilles (NA), slowly turned frosty. Locals felt ignored by their wealthier neighbor and lobbied for change. In 2008 Bonaire returned to direct Dutch rule as a rather far-flung special municipality within the Netherlands, a designation it shares with Saba and Sint Eustatius. The NA was formally dissolved in 2010.

Landscape & Wildlife

Bonaire's landscape is arid and mostly flat, with a few notable hills and valleys in the northern part of the island. Vegetation consists of cactus and scrubby trees – nothing else can really grow due to the lack of water and the onslaught of goats, donkeys and other nibblers. The southern part of the island is characterized by its vast salt flats and the lush mangrove swamps around Lac Bay.

Despite the seeming desolation, the island is rich with bird life, including the iconic pink flamingo and the endangered yellow-shouldered Amazon parrot. Other species you're sure to spot include the banana quit, brown-throated parakeet, caracara, tropical mockingbird and troupial, not to mention many water birds.

Speaking of water, this is where Bonaire is truly rich in life. Coral reefs grow in profusion along the lee coast, often just a few meters from the shore. Hundreds of species of fish and dozens of corals thrive in the clear, warm waters. Sea turtles, dolphins and rays are among the larger creatures swimming about.

Bonaire has few major environmental problems, thanks to a lack of industry, but there are always concerns. Development and overgrazing have caused deforestation in much of the island – a problem that has been exacerbated in recent years by extended drought. The reef along the coastline is protected by the marine park, but the degree of independence granted to divers makes the regulations difficult to enforce.

SURVIVAL GUIDE

❶ Directory A–Z

ACCOMMODATIONS
Bonaire has small guesthouses and resorts geared mostly toward divers: most have in-house dive operations and some dive sites right offshore. Most accommodations are located in the northern outskirts of Kralendijk, with a few places south of the airport in Belnem. The high season is from December to April, but the island does not see a huge spike in visitors (or prices).

The tax on accommodation is US$5.50 to US$6.50 per person per night, plus 10% to 15% service charge.

ELECTRICITY
110V, 60Hz; US-style two- and three-pin plugs are used.

EMERGENCY NUMBERS

Ambulance	☎ 114
Fire	☎ 191
Police	☎ 911

SLEEPING PRICE RANGES

The following price ranges refer to a double room with private bathroom, not including taxes.

$ less than US$75

$$ US$75–US$200

$$$ more than US$200

FOOD
Eat. Sleep. Dive. So goes the mantra of many a Bonaire visitor. As such, the island boasts some excellent places to eat (in addition to the places to sleep and dive). The major resorts all have excellent restaurants, but downtown Kralendijk is also peppered with recommended eateries, offering Caribbean, American and European cuisine with plenty of innovation. For local fare, head to Rincon.

GLBT TRAVELERS
Bonaire is a 'special municipality' of the Netherlands, and as such, observes the same laws regarding GLBT equality. Same-sex marriage is legal (though rare) on the island.

That said, gay populations are not out or active on the island. There are no gay bars (and few bars of any type). There is no official Pride celebration and there are no gay activist groups. GLBT travelers are unlikely to encounter any discrimination, but they are also unlikely to encounter other gay folks, except by sheer coincidence.

HEALTH
Foundation Recompression Chamber (www.bonairehyperbaric.com; Kaya Soeur Barola 7; ☉24hr) Provides treatment for diving accidents and is staffed by diving medical professionals.

St Franciscus Hospital (Fundashon Mariadal; ☎715-8900; Kaya Soeur Bartola 2; ☉24hr) Provides emergency care.

MONEY
ATMs are widely available, dispensing US dollars (US$). Credit cards are accepted at most hotels and restaurants.

Exchange Rates

ARUBA	Afl1	US$0.55
AUSTRALIA	A$1	US$0.77
CANADA	C$1	US$0.76
CURAÇAO	Naf1	US$0.56
EUROPE	€1	US$1.12
JAPAN	¥100	US$0.98
NEW ZEALAND	NZ$1	US$0.73
UK	£1	US$1.30
VENEZUELA	BsF1	US$0.10

For current exchange rates, see www.xe.com.

Tipping

Bars & restaurants For good service, tip 15% to 20% (minus the service charge that is sometimes included in the bill).

Dive guides Tip US$10 for a half-day outing.

Resorts Often include a 15% service charge on the bill. If not, tip US$1 to US$3 per day for housekeeping.

Taxis A 10% tip is usual.

PUBLIC HOLIDAYS

New Years Day January 1

Carnival Monday Monday before Ash Wednesday

Good Friday Friday before Easter

Easter Monday Monday after Easter

King's Birthday April 27

Labour Day May 1

Ascension Day Sixth Thursday after Easter

Bonaire Day September 6

Christmas Day December 25

Boxing Day December 26

TAXES & REFUNDS

A 6% sales tax is levied on the purchase of all goods and services in Bonaire. There is an additional per night per person charge – ranging from US$5.50 to US$6.50 – on accommodations.

TELEPHONE

Bonaire's country code is is 599.

To call within Bonaire, dial the seven-digit number without the code. For other countries, dial the international access code 011 + country code + number.

TIME

Bonaire is in the Atlantic time zone (AST), which is four hours behind Greenwich Mean Time. Daylight saving time (DST) is not observed.

TRAVELERS WITH DISABILITIES

It's not perfect, but Bonaire is a relatively friendly destination for travelers with disabilities.

Many resorts offer accessible rooms, restaurants and docks. Several resorts – including **Captain Don's Habitat** (p221) – have staff trained in assisting disabled divers, with extensive experience training and guiding groups of disabled US Vets.

In Kralendijk, the cruise-ship terminal has a wheelchair ramp, as do many sidewalks around town. **Roro Services** (717-6787; www.roro bonaire.com) offers wheelchair-accessible transportation and tours.

Download Lonely Planet's free Accessible Travel guide from http://lptravel.to/Accessible Travel.

VOLUNTEERING

Bonaire is one of the more prosperous islands in the Caribbean, and volunteer opportunities are scarce. That said, there are a few organizations that depend on the efforts of dedicated volunteers:

Animal Shelter Bonaire (www.animalshelter bonaire.org) This beloved place depends on volunteers to help out with maintenance and working the markets, as well as showering some loving kindness on the resident dogs and cats.

Coral Restoration Foundation (CRF; www.crf-bonaire.org) This inspiring organization works hard to preserve and produce endangered species of staghorn and elkhorn corals around Bonaire's reef. After undergoing specialized PADI training to be a coral restoration diver, volunteers can help maintain CRF's offshore coral nurseries and transplant healthy specimens to degraded areas.

Donkey Sanctuary ((9560-7607; www. donkeysanctuary.com) Dote on the donkeys and make them feel at home.

Echo Parrot Sanctuary (Kunuku Dos Pos; www.echobonaire.org; Kaminda Goto; by donation; tours 4:30pm Wed) This bird sanctuary – working to protect the yellow-shouldered Amazon parrot – depends on volunteers for all

---

EATING PRICE RANGES

The following price ranges refer to the cost of a main meal.

$ less than US$10

$$ US$10–US$25

$$$ more than US$25

PRACTICALITIES

Newspaper *Bonaire Reporter* (www. bonairereporter.com) is a free biweekly newspaper that actually covers controversial issues on the island.

Television Tourist TV Bonaire (Telbo MiTV channel 1 and Flamingo TV channel 60) shows short documentaries on the island's history, culture and nature.

Smoking Smoking is not usually restricted in bars or casinos, though restaurants usually designate smoking and nonsmoking areas. The airport and other public buildings also have designated smoking areas. Most hotels and resorts prohibit smoking in rooms, but allow it on the grounds.

Weights & Measures The metric system is used.

> ### ⓘ DEPARTURE TAX
>
> Departure tax for international flights is US$35, while it's just US$9 for flights to Aruba and Curaçao US$9. The tax is normally included in the ticket price.

manner of support, including population monitoring, bird care, trail maintenance and more.

Sea Turtle Conservation Bonaire (☏ 717-2225; www.bonaireturtles.org) Long-term volunteers undergo training to become independent 'beachkeepers' – monitoring beaches all around the island. From January to April, STCB recruits snorkelers to help out with its in-water survey to count, identify and record sea-turtle species.

ⓘ Getting There & Away

You can arrive in Bonaire by air or by sea (cruise ship). Flights, cars and tours can be booked online at lonelyplanet.com/bookings.

AIR

Flamingo Airport (www.flamingoairport.com) is immediately south of Kralendijk. There are weekly flights from North America on Delta and United, while KLM flies more often from New York and Amsterdam. **Insel Air** (www.fly-insel air.com) and **Divi Divi Air** (www.flydivi.com) offer frequent service to/from Curaçao, as well as charters to Aruba.

SEA

Many cruise ships call at Bonaire, docking at the port in the middle of Kralendijk. On days when there is more than one ship at port, the center of town is closed and thousands of visitors swarm the island. See **Info Bonaire** (www.infobonaire. com) for the schedule of ships and cruises arriving in the port of Bonaire.

ⓘ Getting Around

BICYCLE

Although there are no bike lanes on Bonaire, plenty of people ride along the flat roads, especially in the south. Traffic is usually light and roads are in decent conditions. There are also mountain-biking routes in Washington-Slagbaai National Park and other off-road destinations in the north.

Bicycles are available at many resorts, bike shops and tour companies such as **Bonaire Dive & Adventure** (p224). **Bike Rental Delivery** (☏ 701-1441; www.bikerentalbonaire.com; cruiser/mountain bike per day US$14/16) operates out of a van, which explains the name.

CAR & MOTORCYCLE

Most international car-rental firms are at the airport, while local agencies are located nearby.

➡ Main roads are mostly in good condition; however, you'll want a 4WD for the rough roads in the national park and some remote spots on the east coast.

➡ Gasoline can only be found in Kralendijk.

➡ Road signs are sporadic, so you'll need a map or a GPS.

➡ Driving is on the right-hand side, seat belts are required and motorcyclists must use helmets.

British Virgin Islands

POP 28,000 / ☏ 284

Best Places to Eat

➜ Hog Heaven (p244)

➜ CocoMaya (p243)

➜ Hendo's Hideout (p247)

➜ Cruzin Bar & Grille (p239)

➜ Wonky Dog (p250)

Best Places to Sleep

➜ Anegada Beach Club (p249)

➜ Guavaberry Spring Bay Homes (p242)

➜ Ke Villas (p238)

➜ Evening Star Villas (p247)

Why Go?

The British Virgin Islands (BVI) are territories of Her Majesty's land, but aside from scattered offerings of fish and chips, there's little that's overtly British. Most travelers come to hoist a jib and dawdle among the 50-plus isles. With steady trade winds, calm currents, protected bays and pirate-ship bars, this is one of the world's sailing hot spots.

Main island Tortola is known for its full-moon parties and sailing prowess. Billionaires and yachties swoon over Virgin Gorda and its magical rocks. Anegada floats in a remote reef and has a hammock waiting for those serious about unplugging. And who can resist little Jost Van Dyke, the 'barefoot island' where Main St is a calypso-wafting beach?

The islands have a quirky edge, and despite all the fancy boats and celebrity visitors, they remain relatively undeveloped.

When to Go

Mid-Dec–Apr Peak season when the weather is at its best, everything is open, and the sailing scene is in full swing.

May & Jun Good for those who like the ambience dialed down a notch. Everything is still open, but crowds are less, lodging rates decrease, and winds are more mild for sailors.

Nov–Jul Lobster season when the famed crustaceans are at their juiciest and widely available.

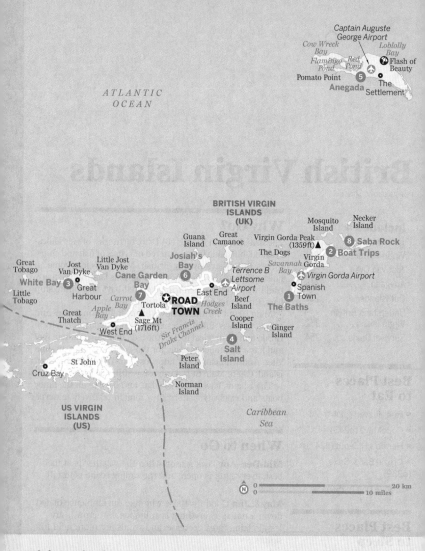

British Virgin Islands Highlights

1 The Baths (p241)
Wading around megaboulders and sloshing through grottoes.

2 Boat trips (p244)
Sailing around the islands in a DIY charter boat or a glass-bottomed day-tour boat.

3 White Bay (p246)
Drinking a rum-soaked Painkiller on the dazzling sand.

4 Wreck of the Rhone (p251) Snorkeling or diving at the 1867 shipwreck by Salt Island.

5 Anegada (p248)
Leaving the world behind on the far-flung island.

6 Josiah's Bay (p240)
Kicking back on the dramatic

strand of sand after a day of perfecting your surfing skills.

7 Cane Garden Bay (p237) Dancing to reggae at the beach bars.

8 Saba Rock (p244)
Joining the yachties for happy hour at this fleck of island off Virgin Gorda.

TORTOLA

Among Tortola's sharp peaks and bougainvillea-clad hillsides you'll find a mash-up of play places. Take surfing lessons, join fire jugglers at a full-moon party, dive on shipwrecks, and by all means go sailing amid the festive surrounding isles.

More than 80% of the BVI's 28,000 citizens live and work on Tortola. It's the BVI's governmental and commercial center, plus its air and ferry hub. It's also the Caribbean's charter-boat capital. Beyond the busy capital of Road Town, groovy beaches and West Indian settlements full of local flavor await.

❶ Getting There & Away

AIR
Modern **Terrence B Lettsome Airport** (p256) is located on the island's east end. It is a 25-minute drive between the airport and Road Town; a taxi costs US$27.

SEA
Tortola is the hub for ferries to the rest of the Virgin Islands. The two main marine terminals are at Road Town (ferries to Virgin Gorda, Anegada and St Thomas' Charlotte Amalie) and West End (ferries to Jost Van Dyke, St John and St Thomas' Red Hook). A smaller dock at Trellis Bay/Beef Island has boats to Virgin Gorda.

Road Town

Let's be honest: the BVI's capital is nothing special – no mega sights to see or scenery to drop your jaw. But there's nothing wrong with Road Town either (perhaps excepting all the traffic). It's a perfectly decent place to spend a day or night, and most visitors do exactly that when they charter their own boat or take the ferries to the outlying islands.

◎ Sights

Tortola Pier Park   AREA
(www.tortolapier.com; ⊘9am-6pm; 🛜) Located right by the cruise-ship dock, the area holds lanes of brightly painted, purple-roofed buildings filled with souvenir shops, clothing and jewelry boutiques, bars, restaurants and tour operators.

JR O'Neal Botanic Gardens   GARDENS
(☑284-494-2069; cnr Botanic Rd & Main St; adult/child US$3/2; ⊘8am-4pm) The elegantly dilapidated, 4-acre gardens provide a shady refuge from Road Town's hullabaloo and heat. Benches are set amid indigenous and exotic tropical plants and there is also an orchid house, lily pond, small rainforest, cactus grove and herb garden. It's about two blocks north of the town's main roundabout.

1780 Lower Estate Sugar Works Museum   MUSEUM
(☑284-494-9206; Station Rd; ⊘9am-3pm Mon-Fri) FREE There are no bells and whistles here, but if you're keen to take time and read about the area's history, this museum in an old sugar mill is a worthy stop. A group of friendly volunteers runs it. You'll learn how the McClevery slaves built the dwelling in 1780, and how molasses, sugar and rum were produced until the 1940s. Rooms hold a hodgepodge of exhibits on local shipwrecks, fauna and flora, and paintings by area artists.

⊂ᗧ Tours

Day-sail boats are rife. Most go to the Baths, Cooper Island, Salt Island and Norman Island.

Kuralu Charters   BOATING
(☑284-499-1313; www.kuralu.com; Village Cay Marina; day tours US$120) Climb aboard *Day Dream*, a 43ft catamaran, for a day of snorkeling and bopping around Salt, Peter and Cooper Islands or Norman Island and the Caves.

Aristocat Charters   BOATING
(☑284-499-1249; www.aristocatcharters.com; Village Cay Marina; day tours US$120) Glide out in *Lionheart*, a 48ft catamaran, for a day of island hopping and snorkeling.

🎇 Festivals & Events

BVI Emancipation Festival   CULTURAL
(www.bvitourism.com; ⊘late Jul–early Aug) This marks the 1834 Emancipation Act that abolished slavery in the BVI. Activities include everything from a beauty pageant to 'rise and shine tramps' (noisy parades led by reggae bands in the back of a truck that start at 3am). Events take place at various locations.

BVI Spring Regatta   SAILING
(www.bvispringregatta.org; ⊘late Mar–early Apr) One of the Caribbean's biggest parties, with seven days of bands, boats and beer.

Road Town

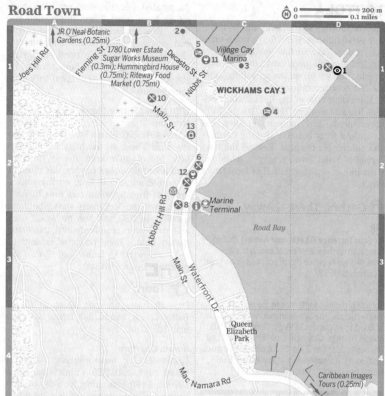

BRITISH VIRGIN ISLANDS ROAD TOWN

Sleeping

Village Cay Hotel & Marina   HOTEL **$$**
(📞 284-494-2771; www.villagecaybvi.com; Wickhams Cay 1; r US$135-250; ❄@🛜🏊) Located in the middle of Road Town overlooking the bay's yacht slips, Village Cay is a swell place to rest your head, especially if you want to schmooze with fellow boaters. The 23 rooms, suites and condos have first-class amenities for less than you'll find elsewhere in town. It fills fast. If nothing else, come for a drink at the pier-side bar-restaurant.

Maria's by the Sea   HOTEL **$$**
(📞 284-494-2595; www.mariasbythesea.com; Wickhams Cay 1; r US$170-260; ❄@🛜🏊) Maria's is on the harbor (no beach). The expansive property has a nice pool and sundeck for watching boat traffic, but otherwise is unremarkable. People typically stay here because of its convenient location. Most rooms have a balcony and kitchenette.

Rooms in the original wing have tropical but plain-Jane decor. Rooms in the new wing have modern, business-like furnishings.

Hummingbird House   B&B **$$**
(📞 284-494-0039; www.hummingbirdbvi.com; Pasea; r US$150-160; ❄@🛜🏊) Tile floors, batik decor and thick towels fill the four breezy rooms run by long-time UK transplant Yvonne. Breakfast is a fully cooked affair served poolside. There's a surcharge to use the air-con (per night US$10). Hummingbird is located in the leafy Pasea neighborhood, a 25-minute walk or US$5 cab ride northeast from town. It's near the Moorings, so many boaters stay here.

Eating

Ruby Roti Queen Restaurant   INDIAN **$**
(📞 284-441-0770; Main St; mains US$6-11; ⏰10am-9pm Mon-Sat) Ruby may well cook the best roti on the islands at her cute little

Road Town

six-table restaurant above Serendipity Bookshop. Fiery hot sauce sets off the chicken-, goat-, shrimp- or chickpea-filled rolls. Flowery garlands hang from the entrance, Bollywood videos blare on TV, and pots of dhal (spiced lentils), pumpkin and eggplant waft from the kitchen for additional sustenance.

Mac's Live Well Cafe   CAFE **$**

(☑284-346-6227; www.facebook.com/macslivewellcafe; Tortola Pier Park; mains US$6-10; ⊙7:30am-5pm Mon-Sat) Even though Mac's is located by the cruise-ship dock, it still draws heaps of locals grabbing island dishes (saltfish, rotis, macaroni pie, lentil rice) for lunchtime takeaway. The soups and sandwiches are dandy, but it's the raisin-studded sweet rolls, carrot bread and fat slices of cake that will set you free.

Riteway Food Market   SUPERMARKET **$**

(☑284-340-2263; www.rtwbvi.com; Pasea; ⊙7am-10pm Mon-Sat, to 9pm Sun) This is the main supermarket, located east of downtown, just beyond Wickhams Cay 2.

Cabernet Bar & Grill   INTERNATIONAL **$$**

(☑284-494-8660; Waterfront Dr; mains US$24-32; ⊙11am-10pm Mon-Sat; 🐾) The breezy Cabernet cooks a mishmash of meaty dishes – ribeye steak, grilled pork, lamb gyros, grilled fish – all reasonably priced. The open-air terrace, carved from a classic West Indian house, becomes a happenin' scene at night with DJs and live music.

Capriccio di Mare   ITALIAN **$$**

(☑284-494-5369; Waterfront Dr; mains US$12-19; ⊙8am-9pm Mon-Sat) Set on the porch of a classic West Indian house across from the ferry dock, this Italian cafe draws both locals and travelers. Breakfast includes pastries and cappuccino. Lunch and dinner feature salads, pasta dishes and pizza, with plenty of wines to wash it all down.

⭐ **Dove**   FRENCH **$$$**

(☑284-494-0313; 67 Main St; mains US$26-33; ⊙5-9:30pm Tue-Sat) The cozy, French-flaired Dove, set in a historic house, is pretty much the top address in town. The menu changes but you might see pan-roasted duck, dry-aged steaks, charcuterie platters, even some sushi. For something lighter, head upstairs to the wine bar for tapas. Oh, did we mention the wine? The list at the Dove is supposedly the BVI's largest.

◉ Drinking & Nightlife

Dockside Bar   BAR

(☑284-494-2771; www.villagecaybvi.com; Village Cay Marina; ⊙7am-10pm) The expansive, open-air bar-restaurant at Village Cay Marina is an amiable spot for a drink among charterboat crews and networking local business people. There is live music on Wednesday and Saturday nights.

Pusser's Pub   PUB

(☑284-494-3897; www.pussers.com; Waterfront Dr; mains US$12-24; ⊙11am-10pm) Pusser's English-style, nautical-themed pub gets lively with travelers swilling European beers and whooping it up at brass-ringed tables. The menu of burgers, sandwiches and fish and chips helps soak up the alcohol.

🛍 Shopping

Sunny Caribbee Spice Shop   GIFTS & SOUVENIRS

(☑284-494-2178; www.sunnycaribbee.com; Main St; ⊙10am-5pm Mon-Sat) It's a favorite for its colorful array of island-made seasonings such as 'rum peppers' and 'mango magic.' Spices are also packaged as hangover cures and bad-spirit repellents.

Pusser's Company Store · GIFTS & SOUVENIRS

(☑284-494-3897; www.pussers.com; Waterfront Dr; ⊙11am-6pm) Adjoining Pusser's Pub, this shop sells logo clothing and accessories, as well as bottles of Pusser's Rum – the blend served on Her Majesty's Royal Navy ships for more than 300 years.

❶ Information

Branches of Scotiabank, FirstBank and First Caribbean are all found on Wickhams Cay 1 near Decastro and Nibbs Sts. All have ATMs.

Bits 'n' Pieces (☑284-494-5954; Wickhams Cay 1; per 30min US$5; ⊙9am-4pm Mon-Sat) Has four computer terminals and a printer.

Peebles Hospital (☑284-494-3497; Main St; ⊙24hr) Has complete emergency services.

Post Office (☑284-468-5160; ⊙8:30am-4:30pm Mon-Fri, 9am-noon Sat)

Tourist Office (www.bvitourism.com; Main St; ⊙8:30am-4:30pm Mon-Fri) Drop by the tiny office at the ferry terminal for a free road map and *BVI Welcome Guide*.

❶ Getting There & Away

BOAT

Road Town's marine terminal is a busy hub for ferries to/from:

Virgin Gorda Roughly every hour (30 minutes, one way US$20), via Smith's (p257) and Speedy's (p257).

St Thomas' Charlotte Amalie direct Three times daily (45 minutes, one way US$35), via Road Town Fast Ferry (p257).

St Thomas' (Charlotte Amalie) via West End Several daily (60 minutes, one way US$35), via Native Son (p257) and Smith's (p257).

Anegada Monday, Wednesday and Friday (75 minutes, round trip US$55), via Smith's (p257).

CAR

Rates start at US$70 per day. **Itgo Car Rental** (☑284-494-5150; www.itgobvi.com; Wickhams Cay 1) is a well-used independent company, located at Wickhams Cay 1. Avis, Hertz and National also have branches around town.

TAXI

Taxis queue at the marine terminal and by the Crafts Alive Market. Or call the **BVI Taxi Association** (☑284-494-3942). The following are set, per-person rates from downtown:

Apple Bay US$27
Cane Garden Bay US$24
Nanny Cay US$15
Wickhams Cay 2 US$5

Around Road Town

Just west of Road Town the highway hugs the shoreline, dipping past marinas and resorts that tuck into the bays, offering several wet and wild activities.

🏃 Activities

Caribbean Images Tours · SNORKELING

(☑284-496-7935; www.snorkelbvi.com; Prospect Reef Marina; price varies) Fun trips aboard a 27ft catamaran. Adventurous types can go via a seven-person, rigid-hull, inflatable boat for further-flung jaunts.

Blue Water Divers · DIVING

(☑284-494-2847; www.bluewaterdiversbvi.com; Nanny Cay Marina; 1-/2-tank dives US$90/120) It is PADI-certified with four boats to get you to the good spots. It has another branch at Sopers Hole.

🛏 Sleeping

Nanny Cay Resort & Marina · HOTEL **$$**

(☑284-394-2512; www.nannycay.com; r US$155-200; ❈@❷❢❄) Despite the 'resort' title, Nanny Cay is used more by boaters and business people than pleasure-seeking holidaymakers. The 40-room hotel has serviceable chambers with kitchenettes and balconies, as well as two restaurants, a marina, beach, dive shop and a minimarket on-site – all good since the property is isolated 3 miles west of Road Town.

❶ Getting There & Away

Waterfront Dr heads southwest from Road Town and eventually turns into Sir Francis Drake Hwy. A taxi between town and Nanny Cay costs US$15.

West End

The West End is known mostly for its busy little ferry terminal for vessels going to and from Jost Van Dyke, as well as the US Virgin Islands' St Thomas and St John. The action centers on Soper's Hole, the former site of a 16th-century pirates' den. It's now a major anchorage, with a marina and pastel-colored complex of buildings holding convivial pubs and shops.

👁 Sights & Activities

Smuggler's Cove   BEACH

Near the island's northwestern tip, Smuggler's is a gorgeous patch of sand that is lightly trod compared to its neighbors, as access is via a crazy-narrow, pothole-cratered road. That said, cruise-ship groups do make their way here on occasion. Nigel's snack stand sells beer and rents beach chairs. The only other amenity is a portable bathroom. Snorkeling is fair.

Island Surf & Sail   WATER SPORTS

(☑ 284-494-0123; www.bviwatertoys.com; Soper's Hole Marina; ⊙ 9am-4pm) It rents all kinds of boards (surf, windsurf, stand-up paddle-boards), fishing gear and snorkeling equipment. It also has an outlet on the beach at Brewers Bay.

✖ Eating & Drinking

Fish 'n Lime Inn   PUB FOOD $$

(☑ 284-495-4276; www.fishnlime.com; Soper's Hole; mains US$20-30; ⊙ 11am-9pm) On the north side of Soper's Hole next to the ferry dock, Fish 'n Lime is a festive waterfront pub. Sit on the wood dock and watch the boats while forking into fresh seafood catches. Burgers, sandwiches and yummy fries hit the tables, too. The sunsets are glorious.

Six simple rooms above the restaurant comprise the inn (useful if you have an early ferry to catch).

Scaramouche   ITALIAN $$$

(☑ 284-495-3443;   www.facebook.com/scaramouchetortola; Soper's Hole Marina; mains US$34-42; ⊙ 11:30am-3pm & 5:30-9pm Tue-Sun) An Italian couple owns Scaramouche. She is the chef, he is the mixologist, and their specialty is artistically prepared Italian dishes, such as grilled octopus or freshly made pasta with shrimp (the menu changes). The funky setting features wine-glass chandeliers, white-wood decor and nautical touches like starfish dangling from the ceiling. Make reservations.

Pusser's Landing   PUB

(☑ 284-495-4603; www.pussers.com; Soper's Hole Marina; ⊙ 11am-9:30pm; 🐾) This outpost of the local chain offers outdoor harborside seating and a fun, Margaritaville ambience. The seafood-based dinners are a bit pricey for their quality. It's best to stick to snacks and booze (happy hour is 5pm to 6:30pm) while watching the boats drift in.

ℹ Getting There & Away

The ferry dock at Soper's Hole bustles. Main companies and routes:

Inter Island (p257) To St John, one-way US$40, 30 minutes, four daily

Native Son (p257) To St Thomas (Red Hook), one-way US$35, 60 minutes, four daily

New Horizon Ferry (p257) To Jost Van Dyke, one-way US$15 (cash only), 25 minutes, five daily

Smith's Ferry/Tortola Fast Ferry (p257) To St Thomas (Charlotte Amalie), one-way US$35, 45 minutes, four daily

Taxis wait at the ferry terminal, or call the **West End Taxi Association** (☑ 284-495-4934). **Denzil Clyne Jeep & Car Rentals** (☑ 284-495-4900; www.denzilclynerentals.com) is nearby for DIY drivers.

Cane Garden Bay Area

A turquoise cove ringed by steep green hills, Cane Garden Bay is exactly the kind of place Jimmy Buffett would immortalize in song – which he did in the 1978 tune 'Mañana'. The area's perfect 1-mile beach and throngs of rum-serving bars and restaurants make it Tortola's most popular party zone.

South of Cane Garden Bay is a series of picturesque bays. Speckled amid clumps of shoreside holiday villas are small West Indian settlements. When you stay out here you're living among locals.

👁 Sights

Brewers Bay   BEACH

Palm-fringed Brewers has decent snorkeling and a more tranquil scene than you'll find at nearby Cane Garden Bay – possibly because getting here involves a brake-smoking drive down steep switchbacks. Nicole's Beach Bar has restrooms, rents chairs and sells snacks at one end of the sand, while Bamboo Bar offers food and drinks, and Island Surf & Sail rents kayaks, paddleboards and snorkel gear at the other end. Brewers gets moderately crowded with families if a cruise ship is in; otherwise it's quiet.

★ Cane Garden Bay   BEACH

Cane Garden Bay is probably on the postcard that drew you to the British Virgin Islands. The gently sloping crescent of sand hosts plenty of beachside bars and watersports vendors renting kayaks and paddleboards. It's a popular yacht anchorage, and becomes a full-on madhouse when cruise ships arrive in Road Town and shuttle passengers over for the day. It's the island's most party-hearty beach, but you can't deny its beauty and good-time vibe. Live bands often rock the bars.

Callwood Rum Distillery
DISTILLERY
(284-495-9383; Cane Garden Bay; 7:30am-5pm) FREE Just off the North Coast Rd at the west end of Cane Garden Bay, this is the oldest continuously operated distillery in the Eastern Caribbean. The Callwood family has been producing Arundel rum here for more than 300 years, using copper vats and wooden aging casks. A small store sells the delicious local liquor and pours samples (four shots US$1). There's a small fee to take photos inside the atmospheric structure.

Apple Bay
BEACH
Apple Bay is long and narrow, and is known as the 'surfing beach,' especially from late December to March when the consistent swells roll in. It's not a traditional beach with lounge chairs, swimming and people lolling on the sand. Rather it's a spot to watch ripped folks catch waves, while relaxing over a drink at one of the reggae wafting bars.

North Shore Shell Museum
MUSEUM
(284-495-4714; Carrot Bay; by donation; hours vary) It's more of a folk-art gallery and junk shop than museum, but it's funky by whatever name you call it. A hodgepodge of shells and signs painted with cryptic local sayings fill the shelves. The hours vary depending on when the proprietor, Egbert Donovan, is around to show you through. He'll also encourage you to buy something.

Sage Mountain National Park
PARK
(Ridge Rd; sunrise-sunset) At 1716ft, Sage Mountain rises higher than any other peak in the Virgin Islands. Seven trails crisscross the 92-acre surrounding park, including the main path that leaves from the car lot and moseys up through the greenery. A sign showing all the routes is at the trailhead. Be prepared for mud.

Long Bay
BEACH
Long Bay is an attractive 1-mile stretch of white sand well used by joggers and walkers. A top-end resort sits on the eastern portion, where you can get food and drinks.

✦ Festivals & Events

Bomba's Full Moon Party
CULTURAL
(284-495-4148; Cappoons Bay; 9pm-late) The monthly full-moon parties at Bomba's Shack (p239) have achieved mythic status. They feature live reggae and plenty of dancing and drinking, but they're most famous for serving psychoactive mushroom tea (mushrooms grow wild on Tortola and are legal); Bomba himself brings it out at midnight. It's best to partake gently. The party goes on until the wee hours.

🛏 Sleeping

Cane Garden Bay has the mother lode of options. You could feasibly stay at its beachside digs without a car, but you'll need wheels to stay at any of the lodgings at Brewers Bay, Carrot Bay or Apple Bay.

Rhymer's Beach Hotel
HOTEL $
(284-495-4639; Cane Garden Bay; r from US$90; ❄) Smack on the beach and right in the center of the action, Rhymer's was one of the area's first inns. The big pink concrete building with its restaurant and laundry shows serious signs of hard use, but the price and energy of the place can work for those on a budget. Rooms are mostly studios with kitchenettes and patios.

★ Ke Villas
HOTEL $$
(284-496-8991; www.kevillasbvi.com; Carrot Bay; r US$155-215; ❄ 🛜) It's pronounced 'key,' and has 12 great-value recently built, spick-and-span, waterfront rooms. Each offers wi-fi, a comfy bed, kitchenette with dishware and a big walk-in rainshower. First-floor rooms have a patio and 2nd-floor rooms have a balcony, both prime for watching pelicans dive-bomb for fish out front. Ke's hospitable owners are a font of island information.

Some rooms have an adjoining door that can be used to make a larger, two-bedroom suite for families. Ke's location between Cane Garden Bay and Apple Bay is ideal: it's a quiet spot, yet near all the popular restaurants and bars.

Mongoose Apartments
APARTMENT $$
(284-495-4421; www.mongooseapartments.com; Cane Garden Bay; apt US$200-240; ❄) Each of the six large units has a living room, full kitchen (including a blender for frosty drinks), bathroom and bedroom, as well as a private balcony. The common area has books and board games, and the beach – where lounge chairs and rafts await guests – is a

two-minute walk through a coconut-palm grove. There's a US$20 surcharge to use the air-conditioning.

Icis Villas
HOTEL $$

(📞 284-494-6979; www.icisvillas.com; Brewers Bay; 1-/2-bedroom ste US$180/290; ❄️ ☀️) Icis' one- to three-bedroom units aren't villas in the luxury sense. It's more like a small hotel with a shady courtyard and pool, conveniently located a five-minute walk from Brewers Bay beach. Most units have a kitchen. A fresh fruit and muffin-laden continental breakfast is included.

Heritage Inn
HOTEL $$

(📞 284-495-5842; www.heritageinnbvi.com; Windy Hill; 1-/2-bedroom ste US$225/360; ❄️ 🛜 ☀️) High on Windy Hill between Cane Garden Bay and Carrot Bay, this property has nine spacious rooms that seem to hang out in thin air. If you like the feel of a self-contained oasis with a pool, sundeck, and bar-restaurant with awesome views, Heritage Inn is for you. Each unit has a full kitchen.

Quito's Inn
HOTEL $$

(📞 284-495-4837; www.quitosltd.com; Cane Garden Bay; r from US$125; ❄️ ☀️) Reggae master Quito Rymer built his 21-room inn within the walls of a centuries-old rum factory. The property has been recently revamped (and changed its name from Ole Works Inn).

Sugar Mill Hotel
BOUTIQUE HOTEL $$$

(📞 284-495-4355; www.sugarmillhotel.com; Apple Bay; r US$395-495; ❄️ 🛜 ☀️) In a league of its own for ambience, intimacy and customer service, this boutique hotel rises from the ruins of the Appleby Plantation that gave Apple Bay its name. Guests stay in the 24 studios and suites that hide on the steep hillside among mahogany trees, bougainvillea and palms. All rooms have balconies and sea views. Breakfast is included.

✕ Eating

★ Cruzin Bar & Grille
CARIBBEAN $$

(📞 284-443-7724; Carrot Bay; mains US$14-33; ⏰ 11am-2:30pm & 5-9pm Tue-Sat, 5-9pm Sun) Take a seat in the courtyard, listen to waves lap the shore, and fork into whatever home-cooked dishes are on for the day: maybe fish in a jerk-lime sauce, a side of sautéed squash and a guava tart for dessert. It's real local flavor, made with local ingredients. The husband and wife owners foster a welcoming, laid-back ambience.

D' Coalpot
CARIBBEAN $$

(📞 284-495-4998; www.dcoalpotbvi.com; Zion Hill; mains US$18-29; ⏰ 5-10pm) The casual outdoor tables under strings of lights are a local favorite. Spicy jerk meats, curries, rotis, grilled fish and other West Indian staples emerge from the kitchen in heaping portions. Staff are friendly, prices are reasonable, what's not to love?

Sugar Mill Restaurant
CARIBBEAN $$$

(📞 284-495-4355; www.sugarmillhotel.com; Apple Bay; mains US$30-42; ⏰ 7-8:30pm) Mod Caribbean concoctions such as creamy lobster ravioli and coconut-crusted chicken with lime chutney hit the Sugar Mill's polished tables. It's hard to beat for romance, served in the restored, candlelit boiling house of the plantation's rum distillery. Wines, fizzy cocktails and decadent desserts complete the sensory experience. Reservations are a must.

🍷 Drinking & Nightlife

★ Bomba's Shack
BAR

(📞 284-495-4148; Cappoons Bay; ⏰ noon-late) Bomba started his bar some 40 years ago to fuel the surfers who still ride the waves curling out front. Today the spot is famous for its monthly full-moon parties, but moon or not, it's worth a stop for a cold brew and look-see. Bomba's truly is a shack, built from a wild mishmash of license plates, surfboards, bras and graffiti-covered signposts.

Quito's Gazebo
BAR

(📞 284-495-4837; www.facebook.com/quitos-gazebo; Cane Garden Bay; ⏰ 10am-11pm) This beachside bar-restaurant almost always has a crowd of boozy revelers. It takes its name from owner Quito Rymer, whose band has toured with Ziggy Marley. You can dance up a storm to Quito's reggae rhythms, and people flock in to do just that. Check Facebook for when he's playing. Live music often fills the air at lunchtime and happy hour, too.

Elm Beach Bar
BAR

(📞 284-494-2888; www.elmbvi.com; ⏰ 11am-10pm Tue-Sun) The Elm is the smallest and perhaps the most welcoming of all the beachfront joints on Cane Garden Bay, great for kicking back with a beer and chatting with friendly Tortolians. The Elm serves better than usual Caribbean bar food, and puts on a big ol' barbecue on Friday and Sunday nights.

ℹ️ Getting There & Away

Cane Garden Bay is a 25-minute drive over the mountainous road from Road Town; a taxi costs US$24. It's the same price from Road Town to Brewers Bay, and a few dollars more to Apple Bay and Cappoons Bay (US$27). Cane Garden Bay has a taxi stand, but otherwise you'll need a car to get around.

East End

Tortola's eastern end is a mix of steep mountains, remote bays and thickly settled West Indian communities. Art and surfing take pride of place. The BVI's main airport welcomes travelers here.

◉ Sights & Activities

★ Josiah's Bay
BEACH

An undeveloped gem on the north shore near the East End, Josiah's Bay is a dramatic strand at the foot of a valley that has excellent surf with a point break in winter. Many say it offers Tortola's best surfing. Lifeguards patrol the water, and a couple of beach bars serve cold beers and snacks. Surf School BVI (p240) has a facility on-site from which they rent boards and offer lessons.

Aragorn's Studio
ARTS CENTER

(☑ 284-495-1849; www.aragornsstudio.com; Trellis Bay; ☉ 9am-6pm) Local metal sculptor Aragorn Dick-Read started his studio under the sea-grape trees fronting Trellis Bay, the broad beach just east of the airport. It grew to include space for potters, coconut carvers and batik makers, many of whom you can see at work in the now-sprawling arts center. Aragorn also hosts family-friendly full-moon parties.

Surf School BVI
SURFING

(☑ 284-343-0002; www.surfschoolbvi.com; Josiah's Bay; 1½hr lessons from US$60; 👪) Excellent instructors teach you how to hang ten at Josiah's Bay. Beginners and children welcome. Board rentals for experienced surfers are available too.

✦ Festivals & Events

★ Fireball Full Moon Party
CULTURAL

(Trellis Bay; 👪) Aragorn's Studio and the surrounding businesses combine to put on the Fireball Full Moon Party each month, which is an artsy, family-friendly event (unlike the island's other moon bashes). The party kicks off around 8pm with calypso music, stilt walkers and fire jugglers. At midnight Aragorn sets his steel 'fireball sculpture' ablaze on the ocean – a must-see.

🛌 Sleeping

The area holds its fair share of economical lodgings to keep the surfers happy. Most are near the airport or on the road to Josiah's Bay.

Tamarind Club Hotel
HOTEL $$

(☑ 284-495-2477; www.tamarindclub.com; Josiah's Hill; r US$139-199; ☉ Oct-Jul; ❋ ⊛ ⊠) The eight rooms at this red-roofed, West Indian–style building surround a central garden and pool. The units have quirky, mismatched decor, and are a bit dark and worn. No matter. You'll be mingling at the on-site restaurant that teems with locals, or at the swim-up bar, or at Josiah's Bay beach (a 10-minute walk away). Rates include continental breakfast.

Beef Island Guest House
GUESTHOUSE $$

(☑ 284-495-2303; www.deloosemongoosebvi.com; Trellis Bay; r US$150; ❋ 🛜) Located on Trellis Bay, the guesthouse is a five-minute walk to the airport and therefore an excellent choice for anyone with a late arrival or early departure. The four basic rooms have unexpected character, with beam ceilings and whirring ceiling fans; all come with a private bathroom. The on-site cafe has live music some nights that can be noisy.

🍴 Eating

Jeremy's Kitchen
CAFE $$

(☑ 284-343 3075; www.jeremyskitchen.com; Trellis Bay; mains US$15-29; ☉ 7:30am-3:30pm Mon & Thu, to 9:30pm Fri-Sun; 🛜) Stop in for all-day breakfasts, such as pancakes, omelets, porridge or English-style, baked-bean-laden plates; or for West Indian dishes, including curried goat, crab cakes, steamed mahimahi and rotis. It's a superfriendly place to hang out, sip a cocktail and use the free wi-fi while waiting for a flight at the nearby airport.

De Loose Mongoose
CAFE $$

(☑ 284-495-2303; www.deloosemongoosebvi.com; Trellis Bay; mains US$12-23; ☉ 3-11pm Mon, from 11am Tue-Sat, from 9:30am Sun) Next to the Beef Island Guest House, this boater hangout is a great place to eat lunch, hoist a happy-hour cocktail or watch the sunset over dinner. Try the conch fritters; they're among the BVI's best. Bands play a few nights a week.

ⓘ Getting There & Around

Terrence B Lettsome Airport (p256) is technically on Beef Island, connected via bridge to Tortola. It is a 25-minute drive to Road Town. A small dock lies within walking distance of the airport at Trellis Bay, where ferries depart for Virgin Gorda. Josiah's Bay is a good 15-minute drive (US$20 taxi ride) from the airport.

For a taxi try **Beef Island Taxi Association** (☑ 284-495-1982).

VIRGIN GORDA

Virgin Gorda is the BVI's rich, plump beauty. The otherworldly, granite megaliths at the Baths put on the main show, but gorgeous beaches unfurl all around the island. Movie stars live here (oh hey, Morgan Freeman), and billionaires own the isles floating just offshore (lookin' at you, Richard Branson). Somehow, Virgin Gorda keeps a level head and remains a slowpoke, chicken-dotted destination sans rampant commercialism.

ⓘ Getting There & Away

AIR

Taddy Bay Airport (VIJ; ☑ 284-495-5621; www.bviaa.com) is on the Valley's east side, about 1 mile from Spanish Town. A taxi into town costs US$5. The airport is teeny, though well used by small regional airlines.

BOAT

The main dock is in Spanish Town. Ferries sail between here and Road Town in Tortola almost every hour during the daytime (one way US$20, 30 minutes) via two companies:

➧ **Smith's Ferry/Tortola Fast Ferry** (p257)

➧ **Speedy's** (p257)

Speedy's also provides direct service between Spanish Town and Charlotte Amalie, St Thomas (in the US Virgin Islands), on Tuesday, Thursday and Saturday (one way US$40, 90 minutes) and to Beef Island, Tortola (by the airport), several times daily (one way US$20, 20 minutes).

ⓘ Getting Around

CAR

You'll pay US$70 to US$90 per day for a 4WD vehicle. Companies that will pick you up at the ferry or airport:

Mahogany Car Rentals (☑ 284-495-5469; www.mahoganycarrentalsbvi.com)

Speedy's Car Rental (☑ 284-495-5235; www.bviferries.com)

TAXI

Taxi fares are set. The rate from the ferry dock to the Baths is US$6 per person, to Gun Creek on the island's north side is US$30. Reliable companies:

Mahogany Taxi Service (☑ 284-495-5469)

Virgin Gorda Tours Association (☑ 284-495-5252)

Spanish Town & The Valley

Spanish Town isn't a town so much as a long road with businesses strung along it. It's the commercial center of Virgin Gorda, with its hub at the boat-bobbing Yacht Harbour. Overall the settlement is a sleepy place, but the mix of islanders, yachties and land travelers eating and drinking together creates a festive vibe.

'The Valley' is the long rolling plain that covers the island's southern half, including Spanish Town.

⊙ Sights

★**The Baths**   PARK
(US$3; ⊙sunrise-sunset; ♿) This collection of sky-high boulders marks a national park and the BVI's most popular attraction. The rocks – volcanic lava leftovers from some 70 million years ago – form a series of grottoes that flood with seawater. The area makes for unique swimming and snorkeling, but the coolest part is the trail through the 'Caves' to Devil's Bay. During the 20-minute trek, you'll clamber over boulders, slosh through tidal pools, squeeze into impossibly narrow passages, then drop on to a sugar-sand beach.

While the Baths and environs stir the imagination, the places are often overrun with tourists. By 9am each morning fleets of yachts have moored off the coast, and visitors have been shuttled in from resorts and cruise ships. All you have to do, though, is come at sunrise or late in the afternoon, and you'll get a lot more elbow room.

The Baths' beach has bathrooms with showers, a snack shack and snorkel-gear rental (US$10). Taxis run constantly between the park and ferry dock.

Spring Bay   BEACH
FREE An excellent beach with national-park designation, Spring Bay abuts the Baths to the north. The beauty here is having a Baths-like setting but without the crowds. Hulking

boulders dot the fine white sand. There's clear water and good snorkeling off the area called 'the Crawl' (a large pool enclosed by boulders and protected from the sea). Seagrape trees shade a scattering of picnic tables, but that's the extent of the facilities.

Copper Mine National Park PARK

(⊙ sunrise-sunset) FREE You'll drive a heck of a winding road to reach this forlorn bluff at Virgin Gorda's southwest tip, but it's worth it to see the impressive stone ruins (including a chimney, cistern and mine-shaft house) that comprise the park. Cornish miners worked the area between 1838 and 1867 and extracted as much as 10,000 tons of copper, then abandoned the mine to the elements. A couple of trails meander through the ruins while the blue sea pounds below.

🏃 Activities & Tours

Dive BVI DIVING

(☑ 284-495-5513; www.divebvi.com; Yacht Harbour; 1-/2-tank dives US$85/120) This shop, with outlets at both Yacht Harbour and Leverick Bay, has several fast boats that take you diving at any of the BVI sites. It also offers full-day boating/snorkeling trips (from US$100 per person) aboard a catamaran.

Double 'D' BOATING

(☑ 284-499-2479; www.doubledbvi.com; Yacht Harbour; day trips US$125) Glide to Jost, Anegada, Cooper or Norman islands aboard a 40ft yacht or trimaran. Trips include time for snorkeling, hiking and general island shenanigans.

🎉 Festivals & Events

Virgin Gorda Easter Festival CARNIVAL

(www.facebook.com/virgingordaeasterfestival; ⊙ late Mar–Apr) Spanish Town around the yacht harbor fills with mocko jumbies (costumed stilt walkers representing spirits of the dead), a calypso competition, a food fair and parades for the Easter Fest, held Friday through Sunday during the Christian holiday (usually late March or April).

🛏 Sleeping

⭐ Guavaberry Spring Bay Homes COTTAGE $$

(☑ 284-495-5227; www.guavaberryspringbay.com; apt US$270-340; @ 🛜) A short walk from the Baths and plopped amid similar hulking boulders, Guavaberry's circular cottages have one or two bedrooms, full kitchen, din-

ing area and sun porch. The setting amazes. There's a common area with wi-fi (for a small fee), games, books and cable TV, and a commissary stocked with alcohol, snacks and meals to cook in your cottage.

Fischer's Cove Beach Hotel HOTEL $$

(☑ 284-495-5252; www.fischerscove.com; d/cottage from US$165/245) Surrounded by gardens and just a few steps from the beach, Fischer's Cove has eight triangular-shaped cottages and a main hotel building with 12 no-frills studios. The cottages have full kitchens, but most do not have TV or air-conditioning (they're also located by a drainage ditch). The hotel rooms do have TV and some also have air-con.

Bayview Vacation Apartments APARTMENT $$

(☑ 284-495-5329; www.bayviewbvi.com; apt US$140-165; ✳🛜) Each of these apartments, behind Chez Bamboo restaurant, has two bedrooms, a full kitchen, dining facilities and an airy living room. It has a plain-Jane ambience, with faded rattan furnishings, but it can be a good deal, especially if you have three or four people.

Little Dix Bay HOTEL $$$

(☑ 284-495-5555; www.littledixbay.com; r from US$850; ✳🛜🖼) This is the resort that rocketed Virgin Gorda to glory, and it remains the island's swankiest, most celebrity-filled digs. An army of staff keeps the grounds and 90-plus rooms perfectly coiffed. The property closed for extensive renovations through much of 2016 and 2017, emerging in fresh, modern luxury. Free use of watersports gear (Hobie Cats, kayaks, snorkel gear) is included.

🍴 Eating

Mad Dog SANDWICHES $

(☑ 284-495-5830; mains US$7-12; ⊙ 11am-6pm; 🛜) Expatriates and tourists alike gather at this airy little pavilion set among the rocks where the road ends at the Baths. They can't resist the toasted sandwiches – turkey and bacon wins particular plaudits – to help take the edge off the killer, secret-recipe piña coladas.

Buck's SUPERMARKET $

(☑ 284-495-5423; ⊙ 7am-7:45pm Mon-Sat, to 6:45pm Sun) The island's main grocery store recently moved from the Yacht Harbour to a two-story building on the road to the Baths. Groceries on the 1st floor; wholesale items on the 2nd floor.

Rock Cafe
ITALIAN $$

(☑ 284-495-5482; www.therockcafebvi.com; mains US$24-36; ⊘ 5pm-midnight) The romantic cafe features outdoor dining amid fountains and Virgin Gorda's famous boulders, or indoor dining in a cozy, air-conditioned room with a piano bar. The cuisine is mostly Italian, with pizzas, pastas and fish. Many locals think the chef bakes the best lobster on the island.

Island Pot
CARIBBEAN $$

(☑ 284-346-3569; mains US$10-18; ⊘ 11am-2:30pm & 6-10pm Tue-Sat) Follow the locals to Island Pot. They know great home-cooked West Indian food when they lay lips on it. Barbecue chicken and ribs are the house specialty, but daily dishes such as bull-foot soup, salt fish, chicken curry and rotis also impress – especially at such reasonable prices. Eat in at the open-air tables, or take away (as most locals do).

Mermaid's Dockside Bar & Grill
CARIBBEAN $$

(☑ 284-495-6663; mains US$19-32; ⊘ 11am-11pm) Mermaid's is indeed dockside, on a breezy pier over the true-blue water where fish swim up for a look-see. The menu spans four or five West Indian mains – maybe jerk chicken or grilled snapper or barbecue ribs – plated alongside rice and pigeon peas and lots of veggies. Sunset vistas complement the casual, open-air vibe. DJs rock the house on occasion.

Top of the Baths
INTERNATIONAL $$

(☑ 284-495-5497; www.topofthebaths.com; mains US$16-25; ⊘ 8am-10pm Mon-Sat, to 5pm Sun) Yes, it sits above the Baths and yes, it's touristy. But the hilltop view kills and the comfort food (say, Amaretto French toast for breakfast and chicken-noodle soup for lunch) is decent. Plus there's a little swimming pool to dip into.

★ CocoMaya
INTERNATIONAL $$$

(☑ 284-495-6344; www.cocomayarestaurant.com; mains US$30-38; ⊘ noon-3pm & 5-10pm Mon-Sat; ♪) Slick, loungey Cocomaya seems more apt for the big city than the beach. But on the sand it is, creating dishes with an Asian and Latin twist. Small plates include hoisin-sauced duck tacos and lobster gyoza (dumplings), while large plates bring snapper red curry and pad thai. There are more vegetarian and gluten-free choices than usual. Inventive, gingery cocktails add pizzazz.

❶ Information

The Yacht Harbour mall, near the ferry dock, holds most of the island's services, including banks.

❶ Getting There & Away

The ferry dock sits next to the Yacht Harbour, both abuzz with boats. **Smith's Ferry/Tortola Fast Ferry** (p257) runs ferries to Road Town, Tortola (30 minutes). **Speedy's** (p257) runs ferries to Road Town as well as to Beef Island, Tortola (20 minutes), and to Charlotte Amalie, St Thomas (90 minutes). Taxis queue outside the terminal. Rental-car companies usually will meet you here.

North Sound

Steep mountain slopes rise on Virgin Gorda's midsection, culminating at hike-worthy Gorda Peak. Beyond lies North Sound, a little settlement whose job is to serve the resorts and myriad yachts anchored in the surrounding bays. A mini-armada of ferries tootle back and forth from the Sound's Gun Creek dock to Bitter End Yacht Club and Saba Rock Resort, both excellent for a happy-hour drink and sea views at their bars, even if you're not staying there. Kiteboarding, glass-bottomed-boat tours and long beach walks are also on tap.

◉ Sights

★ Savannah Bay
BEACH

A short distance north of the Valley, Savannah Bay features more than a mile of white sand. Except for the beaches of Anegada, no other shore provides such opportunities for long, solitary walks. Sunsets here can be fabulous. The water is calm and typically very few people are here. There are no facilities and not much shade, so come prepared. A small sign off North Sound Rd points the way to a little parking area.

Gorda Peak National Park
PARK

(⊘ sunrise-sunset) `FREE` At 1359ft, Gorda Peak is the island's highest point. Two well-marked trails lead to the summit off North Sound Rd, and make a sweet hike. If you are coming from the Valley, the first trail-head you see marks the start of the longer trail (about 1.5 miles). It's easier to begin at the higher-up trailhead, from where it's a 30-minute, half-mile walk to the crest. The lookout tower at the top provides vistas of the entire archipelago.

SABA ROCK

On the teeny islet of Saba Rock, **Saba Rock Lounge** (☑284-495-9966; www.sabarock.com; ⊙11am-9pm) is a very cool place for a drink. Lots of yachties drift in, especially during happy hour. Wander around and examine the shipwreck booty on-site, and take in views of all the gleaming boats. Also keep an eye out for big fish lurking nearby; there's quite a splash at 5pm when they get fed.

A small ferry zips here from Gun Creek. The 10-minute jaunt is free, though the driver expects a tip; call ☑284-495-7711 to arrange pickup. The lounge is part of wee Saba Rock Resort. It also serves a seafood-laden menu that's decent.

Activities & Tours

★Sea It Clear Tours   BOATING

(☑284-343-9537; www.seaitcleartours.com; Gun Creek dock; price varies) Also know as Gumption's Tours (after amiable owner Gumption Creque). Gumption takes you out in his glass-bottom boat to see shipwrecks and creatures swimming on the local reef. He also runs nature tours to Sir Richard Branson's Necker Island; Branson is the one who loaned Gumption the money to start his company. See the website for the changing schedule. Cash only.

Carib Kiteboarding   SURFING

(☑284-495-7740; www.caribkiteboarding.com; 1hr class per person US$75) Take advantage of the trade winds and get airborne with Carib Kiteboarding. It provides gear and lessons for all levels of experience; located at Bitter End Yacht Club (p244).

Sleeping

Most North Sound lodgings are resorts that are fairly isolated, accessible by car or ferry only. They're great places for active couples or families who like to spend their days on the water.

Leverick Bay Resort   RESORT $$

(☑284-495-7421; www.leverickbay.com; r from US$149; ❄ 🛜 🌊) When you see the purple, green and turquoise buildings splashed up the hillside, you'll know you've arrived. The 14 no-fuss rooms each have two double beds, rattan furnishings, free wi-fi and a private balcony. They're pretty worn, but hey, the price is right and there's a beach, marina, dive shop, spa, market...oh, and the popular bar-restaurant, too.

Saba Rock Resort   BOUTIQUE HOTEL $$$

(☑284-495-7711; www.sabarock.com; r US$195-795; ❄ 🛜) On a fleck of island just offshore, this charismatic hotel has seven stylish rooms. They range from a couple of small, functional ones with a queen bed and TV to large, airy chambers with a vaulted ceiling and sea-view balcony. The real selling point is being on your own little isle, with its own beach, helicopter pad and festive bar-restaurant.

Continental breakfast is included. The hotel operates a ferry from Gun Creek to the island. Call to arrange pickup; it's a 10-minute trip.

Bitter End Yacht Club & Resort   RESORT $$$

(☑284-393-2745; www.beyc.com; r from US$600; ❄ @ 🛜 🌊) This resort at the east end of North Sound has 85 hillside villas adorned with batik bedspreads and teak floors. Villas have hammocks, wrap-around verandas and are open to the trade winds; they have air-conditioning and wi-fi, but no TV. Rates include unlimited use of the resort's bountiful equipment for sailing, windsurfing, kayaking and much more.

Mango Bay Resort   RESORT $$$

(☑284-495-5672; www.mangobayresort.com; apt from US$300; ❄ 🛜) Located on the tranquil beach at Mahoe Bay, this lush and quiet resort is a compound of 12 Italian-style duplex villas. The most expensive are at the water's edge, with one or two bedrooms and a full kitchen. Lower-priced studios with kitchenettes are a short walk from the action. Kayaks, rafts and snorkeling gear are free for guest use.

Eating

The majority of the area's far-flung restaurants are located at resorts, though a couple of nifty exceptions pop up.

★Hog Heaven   BARBECUE $$

(☑284-547-5964; mains US$16-27; ⊙10am-10pm) Off-the-beaten-path Hog Heaven is located way up on a hill that unfurls spectacular views. Tender, tangy, ginger-touched barbecue ribs are the house specialty, and the crunchy fried chicken, potato salad and conch chowder are terrific. There are banquet-hall-like indoor tables, but most people throng around the outdoor bar and deck from where you see Moskito, Necker and other islands glimmering offshore.

Fat Virgin's Cafe
CARIBBEAN $$

(☑284-495-7052; www.fatvirgin.com; mains $12-22; ☺10am-10pm) Travelers must come by boat to the little bistro that rises from the Biras Creek Resort's dock. The reward is delicious comfort food for (relatively) bargain prices. The curried-chicken-stuffed roti rocks the palate, or opt for a good ol' burger, thick hand-cut fries or fresh fish to go with your beer, all served at color-splashed picnic tables right on the water.

ⓘ Getting There & Away

Bitter End and Saba Rock resorts have their own ferries (more like water taxis) that depart from **Gun Creek**.

You can also reach Bitter End from Tortola: **North Sound Express** (p257) runs five ferries a day between the resort and Trellis Bay on Tortola's east end (a stone's throw from the airport); it's a 30-minute trip. Call to reserve.

JOST VAN DYKE

Jost (pronounced 'yoast') is a little island with a big personality. It may only take up 4 sq miles of teal-blue sea, but its reputation has spread thousands of miles beyond. A lot of that is due to calypsonian and philosopher Foxy Callwood, the island's main man.

In the late 1960s, free-spirited boaters found Jost's shores, and Foxy built a bar to greet them. Soon folks such as Jimmy Buffett and Keith Richards were dropping by for a drink.

Despite its fame, Jost remains an unspoiled oasis of green hills fringed by blinding white sand. There's a small clutch of restaurants, beach bars and guesthouses, but little else.

ⓘ Getting There & Away

Most visitors arrive by yacht. Landlubbers can get here by ferry from Tortola's West End via:
New Horizon Ferry (p257) or from St John and St Thomas via **Inter Island** (p257). Ferries arrive at the pier by Great Harbour.
Dohm's Water Taxi (☑340-775-6501; www.dohmswatertaxi.com) A customized, much pricier way to get between Jost and St John or St Thomas.

ⓘ Getting Around

Taxis wait by the ferry dock. Fares are set. They charge per person, and fares go down considerably the more passengers there are.

A car is more of a luxury than a necessity on Jost. Expect to pay US$70 to US$80 per day for a 4WD. Companies will meet you at the ferry dock.
Abe's Jeep Rental (☑284-495-9329)
Paradise Jeep Rental (☑284-495-9477)

Great Harbour

In Jost's foremost settlement, Main St is a beach lined with hammocks and open-air bar-restaurants – which might give you a hint as to the vibe here. Most folks just hang out, though active types can arrange kayaking, snorkeling and boating trips.

🏃 Activities & Tours

Endeavor II
BOATING

(☑284-540-0861; www.jvdps.org; per person US$125) Head out for a day sail to remote cays for snorkeling and an education about Jost's ecology. Locals (led by Foxy Callwood) built the 32ft wooden sloop by hand. The JVD Preservation Society sponsored the project to teach the island's youth traditional boat-building skills. Tour proceeds fund the nonprofit group.

JVD Scuba
OUTDOORS

(☑284-495-0271; www.jostvandykescuba.com; ☺8am-6pm Sun-Fri) The one-stop shop for activities on Jost. It can set you up for hiking and snorkeling ecotours, paddleboard rentals, and diving and fishing trips.

Foxy's Charters
KAYAKING

(☑284-546-1905; www.foxyscharters.com; per hr/half-day US$20/50) Rent a clear-bottom kayak in front of Foxy's bar and see what the fish are up to. Guided paddles of the bay take place at night. You can also arrange day sails and water taxis here.

🛏 Sleeping

Great Harbour has a smattering of simple rooms. White Bay offers more choices.

Ali Baba's
GUESTHOUSE $$

(☑284-495-9280; r US$140-160; ✳) This popular restaurant offers three 'heavenly rooms' on its 2nd floor. The compact, whitewashed, wicker-furnished units face the beach and have a wind-cooled balcony from which to view the action. Given the location, noise

BRITISH VIRGIN ISLANDS GREAT HARBOUR

can sometimes be an issue. Patrons flock to the lazy, open-air restaurant (mains US$22 to US$37, open 8am to 11pm) for fresh fish and barbecue.

✖ Eating & Drinking

Christine's Bakery
BAKERY $

(☑ 284-495-9281; mains US$3-11; ⊙ 8am-3pm) The scent of banana bread, coconut bread and coffee waft out of Christine's and fill the settlement by 8am. It's the local breakfast hangout.

Corsairs
MEDITERRANEAN $$

(☑ 284-495-9294; www.corsairsbvi.com; mains US$25-45; ⊙ 8:30am-11pm) Corsairs provides a variation on the usual theme by featuring lots of pizzas, pastas and calzones on its menu. Most incorporate seafood in some fashion, including shrimp fettuccine, scallop risotto and lobster mac and cheese.

★ Foxy's
BAR

(☑ 284-495-9258; www.foxysbar.com; ⊙ 9:30am-11pm) Calypso signer Foxy Callwood single-handedly put Jost on the map with this legendary beach bar. He has his own micro-brewery and rum distillery on-site, so fresh booze fills the glasses. Rotis, seafood dishes and darn good burgers help soak it up. The best time to catch Foxy crooning is around 10am. Bands rock the stage on weekend nights.

❶ Getting There & Away

Ferries land at the pier on the west side of town. It's about a 10-minute walk to Great Harbour's center, or a steep 15-minute walk to White Bay. Taxis linger by the dock. It costs US$10 per person to White Bay, US$12 to Little Harbour.

White Bay

With Jost's most striking beach – and the jovial birthplace of the rum-soaked Pain-killer cocktail – you'll find yourself at White Bay at some point during your visit. It's a primo place to hang out thanks to its highly entertaining beach bars.

White Bay is a hilly, 1-mile walk from Great Harbour, or a US$10 taxi ride.

◉ Sights

★ White Bay
BEACH

The gorgeous long white crescent lies pressed to the sea by steep hills. A barrier reef shelters the water from swells and waves, which makes for good swimming and a protected anchorage. Lots of day-trippers arrive by charter boat. The beach's main activities are drinking, wriggling your toes in the sand and people watching.

🛏 Sleeping

White Bay has the island's largest range of options, from low-cost camping to exclusive waterfront villas.

White Bay Campground
CAMPGROUND $

(☑ 284-495-9358; www.ivanswhitebay.com; campsites US$30, equipped tents US$55, cabins US$75-90) It's one of the Virgin Islands' most popular stops for backpackers. Ivan, the owner, mixes it up by offering bare sites (the best, right on the beach, where you can string your hammock between sea-grape trees), equipped platform tents (with beds and linens) and cabins (electricity plus beds and linens). Everyone shares the communal kitchen and cold-water bathhouse.

Perfect Pineapple
GUESTHOUSE $$

(☑ 284-495-9401; www.perfectpineapple.com; ste from US$170; ✲) Foxy Callwood's son Greg owns this property set on a steep hill back from the beach. The three one-bedroom suites each have a full kitchen and private porch with ocean views. There are also a couple of larger cottages on-site. The family owns Gertrude's seafood restaurant down on the beach if you don't want to cook your own meals.

White Bay Villas & Seaside Cottages
VILLA $$$

(☑ 410-349-1851; www.jostvandyke.com; per week from US$2100; ✲ 🤶) It rents out view-tastic beachfront villas, ranging from one-bedroom cottages to three-bedroom spreads. All units have a kitchen and wi-fi. Rentals typically are for weekly stays, but you might snag a three- or five-night opening. Reserve far in advance, as the well-run property has loads of repeat guests. Prepare to walk up a big hill to get here.

Sandcastle Hotel
HOTEL $$$

(☑ 284-495-9888; www.soggydollar.com; r US$285-310) Situated smack on the beach, the Sandcastle offers four cottages and two hotel rooms, all sans phone and TV (and only the hotel rooms have air-con). The grounds host the infamous Soggy Dollar Bar (p247), which is the most popular of the strip's venues, so there's always an active scene here. Three-night minimum stay required.

Eating

★Hendo's Hideout
CARIBBEAN $$

(☎284-340-0074; www.hendoshideout.com; mains US$20-35; ⊙10am-6pm; 🛜) Hendo's is one of Jost's newer spots and a bit more refined than its competitors, starting with its handsome, reclaimed wood decor. Bite into rum-and-Coke-marinated pulled-pork sandwiches, tender mahi tacos and lobster eggrolls. Sip a Delirious Donkey (lemongrass-infused vodka and ginger beer). Heck, stay all day playing bean bags or lazing in the hammock on the beach out front.

One Love Bar & Grill
CARIBBEAN $$

(☎284-495-9829; mains US$17-26; ⊙11am-11pm) Foxy's son Seddy owns this reggae-blasting beach bar. He'll wow you with his magic tricks, and certainly magic is how he gets the place to hold together – old buoys, life preservers and other beach junk form its 'walls.' Lobster quesadillas and curry-sauced fish are the house specialties.

Drinking & Nightlife

Soggy Dollar Bar
BAR

(☎284-495-9888; www.soggydollar.com; ⊙9am-11pm) The infamous Soggy Dollar takes its name from the sailors swimming ashore to spend wet bills. It's also the bar that invented the Painkiller, the BVIs' delicious-yet-lethal cocktail of rum, coconut, pineapple, orange juice and nutmeg. This place is always hopping. Be sure to play the ring game, and find out how addictive swinging a metal circle onto a hook can be.

Ivan's Stress Free Bar & Restaurant
BAR

(☎284-495-9358; www.ivanswhitebay.com; ⊙8am-11pm) Ivan's is a Jost institution, especially among younger travelers. If no one is around you simply grab your own drinks at the shell-strewn bar using the honor system. The food is average burgers, kabobs and pizzas (assuming you can find someone to take your order!). Hours can be erratic. Ivan's is located at White Bay Campground (p246).

Little Harbour

This is Jost's quieter side, with just a few businesses. Most visitors arrive by yacht to hike, swim and soak up the wild, sage-dotted landscape.

A taxi from Great Harbour to Little Harbour costs US$12; it costs US$20 to Bubbly Pool.

Activities

Bubbly Pool
SWIMMING

This natural whirlpool is formed by odd rock outcrops. When waves crash in, swimmers experience bubbling water like that of a Jacuzzi. Conditions vary: sometimes it's so calm there are no bubbles (still worth hopping in for a soak); other times it can be too rough to go in (though this is rare).

Reach the site via a goat trail from Foxy's Taboo restaurant (about a 20-minute walk). Many visitors bring a picnic and stay a while.

Sleeping

There aren't many options here. You'll have to head to Great Harbour or White Bay for more.

★Evening Star Villas
APARTMENT $$

(☎800-524-2063; www.eveningstarvilla.com; apt per week US$1400; ❄🛜) The seven pink apartments cluster in two buildings high on a hill amid lush fruit trees. The one-bedroom units are modern, with clean white walls, a large kitchen (though no stove, just two hot plates), wi-fi and a patio. The sea views are stunning. An honor bar, hammock and games fill the gazebo, where continental breakfast is served (US$5 extra).

Eating

The handful of restaurants that dot the area are similar open-air, casual, weather-beaten, waterside spots with a penchant for lobster.

Jewel's Snack Shack
BURGERS $

(☎284-495-9286; mains US$5-10; ⊙11am-4pm) Saucy Jewel cooks fine burgers, hot dogs and fries, and pours a mean rum punch. The little shack makes a great stop to or from Bubbly Pool. Prepare to chat!

Foxy's Taboo
CARIBBEAN $$

(☎284-340-9258; www.foxysbar.com; mains US$16-35; ⊙11am-8pm Tue-Sun, to 3:30pm Mon) Foxy teams up with daughter Justine at Foxy's Taboo to serve breezy dishes such as pizza, lamb kebabs and pepper-jack cheeseburgers for lunch, and more sophisticated fare (say lobster-stuffed tilapia) for dinner, all accompanied by candy-like cocktails. Taboo sits in a scenic dockside building under a thatch of palms, overlooking the turquoise sea.

Sidney's Peace & Love
CARIBBEAN $$

(☎284-495-9271; mains US$22-42; ⊙10am-8pm) The specialty here is lobster, but Sidney's serves up plenty of West Indian fish dishes, along with burgers and barbecue. Pour your own drinks to go with the goods at the honor bar. T-shirts left behind by visiting revelers decorate the rafters.

ANEGADA

The easternmost Virgin floats just 12 miles away from its brethren, but you'll think you've landed on another planet. Anegada's pancake-flat, desert landscape looks that different, and its wee clutch of restaurants and guesthouses are that baked-in-the-sun mellow. Flamingos ripple the salt ponds, and ridiculously blue water laps at beaches with whimsical names such as Loblolly Bay and Flash of Beauty.

You've probably seen 'Anegada lobster' on menus throughout the islands. Indeed, this is where it's sourced. Dinners consist of huge crustaceans plucked from the water in front of your eyes and grilled on the beach in converted oil drums.

Some travelers find Anegada to be too sleepy. But if listening to waves and walking solitary beaches rank high on your list, this is your island. It's a mysterious, magical and lonesome place to hang your hammock for a stretch.

ℹ Getting There & Away

AIR

Tiny **Auguste George Airport** (NGD) lies in the island's center. There is no commercial service, only charter planes from Tortola and Virgin Gorda. **Fly BVI** (p257) and **Island Birds** (p257) offer day-trip packages for around US$235.

BOAT

Smith's Ferry/Tortola Fast Ferry (p257) sails from Road Town, Tortola, on Monday, Wednesday and Friday at 7am and 3:30pm; it departs Anegada at 8:30am and 5pm. The boat makes a quick stop at Spanish Town, Virgin Gorda, en route. Many travelers use this public ferry to do a day trip. It costs US$55 round-trip and takes 75 minutes.

ℹ Getting Around

BICYCLE & SCOOTER

Scooters are a cool way to get around the island. Various businesses rent them by the ferry dock. Try **Scooth Tooth** (p248), which also offers tours.

CAR

A 4WD rental costs about US$75 per day at the **Anegada Reef Hotel** (p249) by the ferry dock. Roads are unpaved sand, other than a short stretch between the dock and the Settlement.

TAXI

Taxis wait by the ferry dock. A one-hour island tour costs US$55. Open-air shuttles (per person round-trip US$8) run to the beaches from the **Anegada Reef Hotel** (p249).

West End

Setting Point anchors the island's west end. It contains the ferry dock and a small cluster of restaurants, hotels and supply shops. To the north lies Cow Wreck Bay, one of the Caribbean's most breathtaking beaches, and the waterfront glamping tents at the Anegada Beach Club.

The Anegada Reef Hotel, by the ferry dock, serves as the island's unofficial information center. Inquire at the hotel office about fishing, car rental or transport to the beaches.

◉ Sights

★ Cow Wreck Bay   BEACH

Here's what you'll find on dazzling, secluded Cow Wreck beach: the most sea-green water you've even seen, colorful wood beach chairs under rustling palms, roaming cows, conch shells, a delicious bar-restaurant, bathrooms and maybe even Sir Richard Branson on a kiteboard. The best way to spend the afternoon here is to swim, lounge and then lounge some more.

Flamingo Pond   NATURE RESERVE

The large salt pond at the island's west end hosts a flock of flamingos. These birds were once plentiful on Anegada and other cays in the BVI, until hunters seeking their tender meat and feathers decimated the population. Since being reintroduced in 1992 they've been making a comeback. You can't get close, but you often can see the birds (as pink blobs) wading on the far north side of the pond, or sometimes in the pond near Neptune's Treasure hotel.

⚐ Activities & Tours

Scooth Tooth   OUTDOORS

(☑ 284-543-8308; www.scoothtooth.com; rentals per half/full day US$35/45) Owner Kenny rents groovy scooters, which are a fine way to explore the island. Even better, he gives guided tours by scooter. If you prefer pedaling by bicycle, he also can hook you up. Reserve in advance.

Tommy Gaunt Kitesurfing SURFING
(☑ 284-541-7876; www.tommygauntkitesurfing.com; kite & board per half/full day US$50/70; ☉ Nov-Aug) Get your kite on at this facility located at the Anegada Beach Club. Lessons available for all skill levels.

Danny's Bonefishing FISHING
(☑ 284-441-6334; www.dannysbonefishing.com; per half/full day US$400/600) There is world-class bonefishing year-round on the flats around Setting Point and Salt Heap Point on the south shore. Danny Vanterpool's family has been guiding in the area for decades. Gear is included in the price. Reserve in advance.

🛏 Sleeping

A couple of simple hotels are walkable from the ferry dock. More exotic options pop up along the water on the north shore.

★ Cow Wreck Beach Resort COTTAGE $$
(☑ 284-495-8047; www.cowwreckbeachbvi.com; apt US$200-300; ❄) You want peace and quiet? It'll just be you and the wandering bovines who share the grounds at Cow Wreck. Three sunny yellow-and-green cottages front the perfect, hammock-strewn beach. The festive, open-air **bar-restaurant** (mains US$25 to US$50, open 9am to 8pm) features lobster and shellfish cooked on the outdoor grill. Owner Bell's hospitality (and her conch fritters) are something special.

Anegada Reef Hotel HOTEL $$
(☑ 284-495-8002; www.anegadareef.com; d US$175-310; ❄@🅢) The island's first and largest hotel, this seaside lodge by the ferry dock has the feel of a classic out-island fishing camp. The property's 20 rooms are quite basic, but the fishing dock, **restaurant** (mains US$25 to US$50, open 8:30am to 9pm) and beach bar here are Anegada's social epicenter.

Neptune's Treasure HOTEL $$
(☑ 284-495-9439; www.neptunestreasure.com; r US$170; ❄🅢) The nine simple, color-washed rooms sit right on the sand and garner lots of loyal patrons. For those needing more space and a kitchen, there are also a couple of cottages (US$250 to US$300). The Soares family, originally fisherfolk from the Azores, has run Neptune's and its adjoining restaurant for more than 35 years. It's a 15-minute walk from the ferry dock.

★ Anegada Beach Club HOTEL $$$
(☑ 284-340-4455; www.anegadabeachclub.com; r US$265, tent US$320-375; ❄🅢❄) Anegada's most modern property has two options: beachfront glamping tents (canvas-sided structures on stilts with a canopy bed, solar-heated shower, deck with hammock and romantic views of the water); and 16 regular hotel rooms in soothing pastel blues and blond wood decor, with air-conditioning and TV. A kitesurfing school is on-site, and you can rent kayaks, paddleboards and bicycles.

ABC's restaurant – open for breakfast, lunch and dinner – makes fab food, including its BLLT (bacon, lettuce, lobster and tomato) sandwich. A free shuttle picks up at the airport and ferry dock.

🍴 Eating

Several open-air restaurants await along the water by Setting Point. Follow your nose toward the lobster and other meats sizzling on the grill. The restaurants also have bars if you just want a beverage.

Pam's Kitchen BAKERY $$
(☑ 284-495-9237; mains US$12-20; ☉7am-5pm) Pam cranks out loaves of herb bread, key-lime pies, cinnamon rolls and brownies. It's a terrific breakfast stop for egg-stuffed sandwiches or coconut-rum French toast, or for lunchtime savory snacks such as a burger or fish *pate*. The bakery attaches to Neptune's Treasure, the restaurant at the same-named hotel, which serves fish freshly caught from Pam's family's fishing boat.

LOBSTER LOWDOWN

Cracking an Anegada lobster is a tourist rite of passage. Every restaurant serves the massive crustaceans, usually grilled on the beach in a converted oil drum and spiced with the chef's secret seasonings. Because the critters are plucked fresh from the surrounding waters, you must call ahead by 4pm to place your order so each restaurant knows how many to stock. Most places charge around US$55 to indulge. Note that lobster fishing is prohibited from August 1 through November 1 so stocks can replenish, thus they're not on menus (nor is conch) during that time.

★ **Wonky Dog** SEAFOOD $$$
(☑284-547-0539; www.thewonkydog.com; mains US$25-55; ⊙8am-11pm) The Wonky Dog is a class act, with candlelit tables on the sand, bartenders who know how to mix, and a beyond-the-norm menu that ranges from Thai red-curry mussels to Mediterranean vegetable stew to all sorts of lobster (ie jerk mango coconut lobster, lobster Rockefeller, creamy lobster Thermidore and more). Open mic nights and DJs entertain most nights.

★ **Lobster Trap** CARIBBEAN $$$
(☑284-495-9468; mains US$25-55; ⊙11am-9pm) Lobster Trap's grilled version of the namesake crustacean approaches perfection on a menu that includes the usual seafood suspects. The chef pulls the spiny critters straight from the sea, out of a dockside snare. The twinkly garden setting on the main anchorage's waterfront adds to the pleasure. The Anegada Beach Hotel runs the Trap and offers shuttles between the two properties.

Potter's by the Sea CARIBBEAN $$$
(☑284-495-9182; www.pottersbythesea.com; mains US$25-55; ⊙10am-2pm & 7:30-9pm; ☎) Potter's is the first place you stumble into when departing the ferry dock. Potter lived in Queens, New York, and worked in the restaurant biz there for years, so he knows how to make customers feel at home while serving them ribs, fettuccine, curried shrimp and lobster. Graffiti and T-shirts cover the open-air walls; live bands occasionally play.

Pomato Point Restaurant CARIBBEAN $$$
(☑284-495-9466; mains US$25-55; ⊙11am-7pm) It's one of Anegada's many open-air options for fish and shellfish, typically served with West Indian rice, salad and dessert. The sunsets here can't be beat and you can browse the room of shipwreck relics while waiting for your food.

❶ Getting There & Away

The ferry runs between Road Town, Tortola, and Setting Point on Monday, Wednesday and Friday. **Lil Bit** (☑284-495-9932; rental per half/full day US$35/45) offers scooter rental by the dock and this is a great way to get around the island. A taxi to Cow Wreck costs US$11.

East End

The Settlement, Anegada's only town, is a wee village of boxy houses, laundry flapping in the breeze and folks feeding goats and chickens. There are a couple of teensy shops where you can buy food and supplies. The iguanas and beaches a few miles north are the draws.

Open-air shuttles (per person US$8) make frequent runs to Loblolly from the Anegada Reef Hotel (p249).

⊙ Sights

Loblolly Bay Beach BEACH
Loblolly is an idyllic stretch of sand with a few bars, palm-thatched umbrellas for shade, a shower (requires a small fee) and a shop for snorkel-gear rental (per hour US$5). You can swim over a widespread area with spotted eagle rays and barracudas. The water might be rough between November and March.

Flash of Beauty BEACH
Flash of Beauty is just east of Loblolly beach. It lives up to its name, with perfect white sand and deep turquoise water. There's a bar-restaurant and nifty snorkeling over a compact area of big coral and bright-hued fish.

Rock Iguana Headstart Facility WILDLIFE RESERVE
(⊙8:30am-4:30pm) **FREE** The Parks Trust started the facility because feral cats were eating the island's baby iguanas, endangering the rare species. So workers now bring the babies to the nursery's cages to grow safely. After two years, they're big enough to be released back into the wild, where they'll sprout to around 5ft from tip to tail. The hatchery sits behind the government administration building; just let yourself in.

✖ Eating

Flash of Beauty Restaurant CARIBBEAN $$
(☑284-495-8014, 284-543-7050; mains US$20-45; ⊙11am-6pm) After you finish snorkeling the waters out front, climb up to shore to Flash of Beauty's bar-restaurant, where owner Monica awaits with spicy rotis, curried conch and lobster (it's usually a bit cheaper here than elsewhere on the island). The staff also makes a mean 'bushwhacker' – a milkshake-drink using seven liquors.

Big Bamboo
CARIBBEAN $$

(☑ 284-499-1680; www.bigbambooanegada.com; mains US$20-44; ⊙10am-6pm) Aubrey Levons' tiki-esque restaurant-bar is on the beach at Loblolly Bay's west end and always packs a crowd. It specializes in island recipes for lobster, fish and chicken.

OUT ISLANDS

The BVI's 'Out Islands' (a Creole expression for remote or undeveloped cays) are a wonderful mix of uninhabited wildlife sanctuaries, luxurious hideaways for the rich and famous, and provisioning stops for sailors. Most are reachable only by charter or private boat. If you don't have your own vessel, hook up with a Tortola or Virgin Gorda daysail tour.

⦿ Sights

Necker Island
ISLAND

(www.virginlimitededition.com) Private Necker Island belongs to Richard Branson, famous adventurer and scion of Virgin Atlantic Airways and Virgin Records. About 1 mile north of Virgin Gorda, Necker is one of the world's most luxurious retreats. If you have US$80,000 you can rent it for the night (Branson not included, though your own DJ is).

Sea It Clear Tours (p244), departing from Virgin Gorda's North Sound, offers a less costly way to set foot on the island.

The Dogs
ISLAND

This clutch of five little islands lies halfway between Tortola and Virgin Gorda. Protected by the BVI National Parks Trust, the Dogs are sanctuaries for birds and marine animals. The diving and snorkeling here are excellent.

Cooper Island
ISLAND

Lying about 4 miles south of Tortola, Cooper Island is a moderately hilly cay and is virtually undeveloped except for the Cooper Island Beach Club (p251), whose restaurant (p252), rum bar and brewery make it a popular anchorage for cruising yachts. Snorkelers and divers also swarm to the island's surrounding sites.

Peter Island
ISLAND

This lofty L-shaped island, about 4 miles south of Tortola, is the BVI's fifth-largest and home to the luxurious Peter Island Resort

(p252). The island remains lush and wild for the most part. There are five pristine beaches, plus excellent snorkeling sites and hiking paths.

Anyone with reservations can come to the resort's Tradewinds Restaurant (p252) for gourmet international cuisine, or Deadman's Bar & Grill (p252) for wood-fired pizzas. The resort's ferry (round-trip US$25) sails from Road Town; call ☑ 284-495-2000 for times and exact location.

★ Salt Island
ISLAND

This T-shaped island is a forlorn place. The salt making (which gave the island its name) still goes on here, but the RMS *Rhone* is the big attraction. The *Rhone* crashed against the rocks off the southwest coast during a hurricane in 1867. Now a national park, the steamer's remains are extensive, making it one of the Caribbean's best wreck dives. The stern lies in shallower water, so snorkelers can get in on the action, too.

Norman Island
ISLAND

Since 1843, writers have alleged that treasure is buried on Norman Island, supposedly the prototype for Robert Louis Stevenson's book *Treasure Island*. It fits the bill: Norman is the BVI's largest uninhabited landmass.

Today adventurers come for two raucous beach bars. The William Thornton (p252), aka Willy T, is a schooner converted into a bar-restaurant and moored in the bight. Pirate's Bight (p252) is an open-air pavilion on the beach. Both have loud music and a party-hearty crowd.

If you don't have your own boat, call Pirate's Bight and ask about the ferry (round-trip US$20).

🛏 Sleeping

While most of the Out Islands are uninhabited, a few have their own resort, for which you'll typically pay big bucks for the exclusivity.

Cooper Island Beach Club
RESORT $$

(☑ 284-495-9324; www.cooperislandbeachclub.com; Cooper Island; r US$290; ⊙closed Sep; 🛜) It's not really a 'club' at all, but a casual property where it's just fine to be barefoot. The 10 teak-furnished rooms each have one king bed or two twin beds, a minifridge, balcony and rain shower. Solar panels provide 70% of the electricity and heat the water. Ceiling fans keep you cool at night.

Peter Island Resort
RESORT $$$

(☑ 284-495-2000; www.peterisland.com; Peter Island; r from US$900; ❉@🌐❉) It offers rooms in a variety of configurations, ranging from four-bedroom villas to the original A-frame cottages built in the 1960s. All have balconies. The rooms aren't exceptional, but the amenities – including water sports, gorgeous beaches, tennis courts, yoga classes, a fitness center and Ayurvedic spa – are. Staff is at your service, and can arrange private, candlelit dinners on the beach.

✕ Eating

Cooper Island Beach Club Restaurant
CARIBBEAN $$

(☑ 284-495-9084; www.cooperislandbeachclub. com; Cooper Island; mains US$20-32; ⊘ noon-3pm & 5:30-9pm, closed Sep) This casual restaurant is a premier gathering spot for boaters. Curried chicken rotis, jerk pork tenderloin and basil-butter-drizzled mahimahi have exceptional flavor. The rum bar and on-site, solar-powered brewery add to the pleasure. The bar stools made from recycled fishing boats are a nice touch. Make reservations for dinner.

Tradewinds Restaurant
INTERNATIONAL $$$

(☑ 284-495-2000; www.peterisland.com; Peter Island; mains US$34-45; ⊘ 8-10am & 5-9pm) Tradewinds is Peter Island Resort's main restaurant, featuring gourmet international cuisine served on German china alongside fine wines (some 300 types are available) in Italian crystal. Breakfast brings out the omelets, French toast and banana pancakes. There's a dress code for dinner: no coats and ties, but trousers and collared shirts are required.

Deadman's Bar & Grill
INTERNATIONAL $$$

(☑ 284-495-2000; www.peterisland.com; Peter Island; pizzas US$22-32, mains US$37-45; ⊘ 11am-9pm) This is Peter Island Resort's more casual eatery, set right on the beach. Wood-fired pizzas are the house specialty, along with a changing array of mains such as curried shrimp and rice, and eggplant and pasta. A steel-drum band plays Sunday afternoons and Wednesday evenings (when there's a Caribbean buffet).

🍷 Drinking & Nightlife

William Thornton
BAR

(☑ 284-340-8603; www.willy-t.com; Norman Island; ⊘ 11:30am-10pm) The Willy T, as it's known, is a 100ft schooner converted into a bar-restaurant. Conch fritters, barbecue ribs, fish and chips and burgers are really just side dishes for all the booze that goes down the hatch. Body shots are de rigueur, and many a patron has been known to jump off the deck nude after a few too many.

Pirate's Bight
BAR

(☑ 284-443-1305; www.piratesbight.com; Norman Island; ⊘ 11am-9pm) This open-air pavilion on the beach at the bight pours an awful lot of rum (and gin, and tequila, and vodka). Chicken rotis, conch fritters and grilled mahimahi sandwiches help soak it up. Kick back in the waterside hammocks and beach chairs and enjoy. If you don't have your own boat, call and ask about the ferry (round-trip US$20).

ℹ Getting There & Away

The majority of Out Islands are reachable only if you have your own boat, but there are a few exceptions: Peter Island (call ☑ 284-495-2000) and Norman Island (call ☑ 284-443-1305) will send a boat to pick you up if you call ahead. Both docks are on the outskirts of Road Town, Tortola.

UNDERSTAND THE BRITISH VIRGIN ISLANDS

History

Columbus & the Pirates

On Christopher Columbus' second trip to the Caribbean in 1493, Caribs led him to an archipelago of pristine islands that he dubbed Santa Ursula y Las Once Mil Vírgenes (St Ursula and the 11,000 Virgins), in honor of a 4th-century princess who was raped and murdered, along with 11,000 maidens, in Cologne by marauding Huns.

By 1595 the famous English privateers Sir Francis Drake and Jack Hawkins were using the Virgin Islands as a staging ground for attacks on Spanish shipping. In the wake of Drake and Hawkins came French corsairs and Dutch freebooters. All knew that the Virgin Islands had some of the most secure and unattended harbors in the West Indies. Places such as Sopers Hole at Tortola's West End and the Bight at Norman Island were legendary pirates' dens.

While the Danes settled on what is now the US Virgin Islands, the English had a firm hold on today's BVI. The middle island of St John remained disputed territory until 1717, when the Danish side claimed it for good. The Narrows between St John and Tortola has divided the eastern Virgins (BVI) from the western Virgins (USVI) for more than 250 years.

Queen Elizabeth & the Offshore Companies

Following WWII, British citizens in the islands clamored for more independence. In 1949 BVI citizens demonstrated for a representative government and got a presidential legislature the next year. By 1967 the BVI had become an independent colony of Britain, with its own political parties, a legislative council and an elected premier (with elections every four years). Queen Elizabeth II also made her first royal visit to the BVI in 1967, casting a glow of celebrity on the islands. Royal family members still cruise through every few years.

In the mid-1980s the government had the shrewd idea of offering offshore registration to companies wishing to incorporate in the islands. Incorporation fees – along with tourism – now prop up the economy. Whether you call the territory an 'international financial center' or a tax haven, you have to admit it's odd that this population of 28,000 people hosts more than 450,000 active registered companies. It has created an unusual island workforce infused with foreign accountants, trust lawyers and investment brokers.

Culture

Despite the name, apart from little touches such as Cadbury chocolate, the culture of the British Virgin Islands is West Indian to the core. The population is a mix of professional people working in financial services, folks working the tourist trade or raising livestock, and adventurers whose biochemistry is intricately tied to the seas. The ethnic breakdown is 77% black, 5% white, 5% Latino and the remainder mixed, East Indian or other.

The BVI have one of the Caribbean's most stable economies. The per-capita GDP is US$42,300. In general, most people live comfortably.

FUNGI MUSIC

Fungi (*foon*-ghee, also an island food made of cornmeal) is the BVI's local folk music. It uses homemade percussion such as washboards, ribbed gourds and conch shells to accompany a singer. You'll hear lots of it at the **BVI Emancipation Festival** (p233). The Lashing Dogs are popular players around the territory.

Some visitors complain that the locals (particularly on Tortola) are unfriendly. The demeanor is not rude so much as reserved.

Landscape & Wildlife

The Land

The BVI consist of some 50 islands and cays. On most, steep mountains dominate the island interiors. The one exception is easternmost Anegada, which is a flat coral atoll. Sage Mountain on Tortola is the highest point on the islands, at 1716ft.

Thousands of tropical plant varieties grow on the islands, and a short drive can transport a nature lover between entirely different ecosystems. Mangrove swamps, coconut groves and sea-grape trees dominate the coast, while mountain peaks support wet forest with mahogany, lignum vitae, palmetto and more than 30 varieties of wild orchid.

Islanders also grow and collect hundreds of different roots and herbs as ingredients for 'bush medicine.' Psychoactive mushrooms grow wild (and are consumed) on the islands, particularly on Tortola.

Wildlife

Few land mammals are natives; most were accidentally or intentionally introduced. Virtually every island has a feral population of goats, donkeys, cats and dogs.

More than 200 species of birds inhabit the islands, adding bright colors and a symphony of sound to the tropical environment. A few snake species (none of which are poisonous) slither around, along with a host of small and not-so-small lizards, including the 5ft-long rock iguanas of Anegada and the common green iguana found throughout

BEST DIVING & SNORKELING

Dive Sites

RMS Rhone The famous 1867 shipwreck sits in 20ft to 80ft of water off Salt Island, making it an accessible wreck dive for all levels.

Alice in Wonderland This spot off Ginger Island has some of the best deep-water coral formations in the BVI.

The Indians Just off Pelican Island, three cone-shaped rock formations rise from 36ft underwater to 30ft above water. Lots of fish and dramatic scenery.

Chikuzen The 250ft wreck is remote and for experienced divers only. Big swimmers such as reef, bull and lemon sharks are the payoff.

Snorkel Sites

The Caves Three large caves on Norman Island feature shallow waters and many small fish, which in turn attract larger predators. Good for newbie snorkelers as the water is usually calm.

The Indians Loads of colorful fish dart around these rock pinnacles that rise up from the water near Norman Island. It's a great spot for experienced snorkelers.

RMS Rhone Although most of the Salt Island shipwreck is in deep water, the stern section is shallow – you can see the bronze propeller, rudder and aft mast from the surface. Best for experienced snorkelers.

Cooper Island Beginners fare well here, as you can swim in from the beach, it's shallow, and you'll see lots of small fish.

---

the islands. Anoles and gecko lizards are ubiquitous, and numerous species of toad and frog populate the islands.

Environmental Concerns

Environmental concerns have resulted in the formation of the BVI National Parks Trust, which protects 21 natural and cultural areas, including the *Rhone* shipwreck, Jost Van Dyke's Bubbly Pool and the giant boulder formations at the Baths on Virgin Gorda.

Prior years of overfishing have put conch and lobster in a precarious situation. Currently, fishing for these creatures is not allowed from August through October so stocks can replenish. Other issues that environmentalists keep an eye on are deforestation, soil erosion and mangrove destruction. Mangrove replanting projects are underway.

SURVIVAL GUIDE

ⓘ Directory A–Z

ACCOMMODATIONS

Guesthouses, hotels, apartment-like villas and resorts are common on all the islands. High season is mid-December through April, when rooms are costly and advance reservations essential. Three-night minimum stay requirements are common. Some lodgings close in September and into October, the heart of low season.

Be aware that while air-conditioning is widely available, it is not a standard amenity, even at top-end places.

Booking Services

Companies that rent properties in the BVI:

Purple Pineapple (☑ 284-343-8186; www. purplepineapple.com)

Villas Virgin Gorda (☑ 284-495-6493; www. villasvirgingorda.com)

Virgin Gorda Villa Rentals (☑ 284-495-7421; www.virgingordabvi.com)

Also check **Vacation Rental by Owner** (www. vrbo.com). Many BVI visitors say it provides the best results since you work out all the details with the property owners themselves.

ACTIVITIES

Sailing is the BVI's main claim to fame. Clear water, secluded coves and shipwrecks make for primo diving and snorkeling. Surfing is popular at Josiah's Bay on Tortola, while kitesurfing is big on Anegada and Virgin Gorda.

CHILDREN

The islands are fairly child-friendly. While baby-changing facilities and smooth pavements for prams are not ubiquitous, resorts with kids' programs and a welcoming attitude toward families are.

Virgin Gorda offers a couple of top attractions. The **Bitter End Yacht Club & Resort** (p244) has a full slate of activities for kids each week where they hike, learn to sail and have cupcake and pizza parties. It's best for youngsters aged eight and older. **The Baths** (p241) are a splash-worthy national park, where kids can tromp around enormous boulders, climb up rope ladders and explore sea-filled grottoes.

Tortola's East End features **Surf School BVI** (p240), which teaches all ages to hang ten but is especially good for teens. Not far away, Aragorn's **Full Moon Party** (p240) at Trellis Bay thrills families with fire jugglers and stilt walkers.

All the islands offer villa and apartment rentals, which have lots of space and kitchens for DIY meals. Virgin Gorda and Tortola's Cane Garden Bay Area (p237) are laden with such properties.

Most restaurants do not have a children's menu, but they often serve burgers and pizza as part of their line-up. The ambience tends to be informal and relaxed wherever you go.

On Virgin Gorda, Tropical Nannies (www.tropicalnannies.com) provides babysitting services by trained, professional nannies. They'll come to your hotel or take the kids off your hands starting at US$20 per hour. The company also rents cribs and high chairs.

EMERGENCY NUMBERS

Ambulance, Fire, Police	☑ 999

FOOD

Restaurants are pretty similar in their fare – mostly Caribbean dishes such as spicy barbecue and curries, along with grilled fish and lobster (the latter being the famed, strapping crustaceans from Anegada). Virgin Gorda and Tortola's Cane Garden Bay area have concentrations of excellent eateries. Meals usually are expensive.

Essential Food & Drink

Anegada lobster Hulking crustaceans plucked from the water in front of your eyes and grilled on the beach in converted oil drums.

Roti Spicy chutney sets off the curried chicken, beef, conch (a local shellfish) or vegetable fillings in these burrito-like flat-bread wraps.

Fungi (*foon*-ghee) A polenta-like cornmeal cooked with okra, topped by fish and gravy.

Pate (pah-*tay*) Flaky fried dough pockets stuffed with spiced chicken, fish or other meat.

Painkiller Jost Van Dyke's Soggy Dollar Bar supposedly invented this sweet mix of rum, coconut, pineapple, orange juice and nutmeg.

SLEEPING PRICE RANGES

The following price ranges refer to a double room with bathroom in peak season. Unless otherwise stated, breakfast is not included in the price, nor is tax (10%) or other service charges (often 8% or so).

$ less than US$100

$$ US$100–300

$$$ more than US$300

GLBT TRAVELERS

Religious taboos on the gay and lesbian lifestyle are slow to crumble. You're not likely to meet many islanders who are 'out,' nor are you likely to see public displays of affection among gay couples. GLBT discrimination is illegal. Same-sex marriage is not recognized here.

MONEY

Currency is the US dollar (US$). ATMs are in main towns on Tortola and Virgin Gorda, but not elsewhere. Credit cards accepted in most hotels and restaurants.

Exchange Rates

AUSTRALIA	A$1	US$0.77
CANADA	C$1	US$0.76
EURO ZONE	€1	US$1.06
JAPAN	¥100	US$0.88
NZ	NZ$1	US$0.72
UK	UK£1	US$1.24

For current exchange rates, see www.xe.com.

Tipping

Dive/tour boat operators 15% of fee is reasonable.

Hotels US$1 to US$2 per bag for bellhop; US$2 to US$5 per night for cleaning staff.

Restaurants 15% to 20% of bill.

Taxis 10% to 15% of fare.

EATING PRICE RANGES

The following price indicators denote the cost of a dinner main dish.

$ less than US$15

$$ US$15–35

$$$ more than US$35

PRACTICALITIES

Newspapers The *BVI Beacon* is the main newspaper; it is published weekly. BVI News (www.bvinews.com) offers free daily content online. The free, weekly *Limin' Times* has entertainment listings.

Radio ZBVI (780AM) airs talk and music from Tortola, including BBC broadcasts.

Smoking Banned in all restaurants, bars and other public venues.

Weights & Measurements The islands use imperial measurements. Distances are in feet and miles; gasoline is measured in gallons.

PUBLIC HOLIDAYS

New Year's Day January 1
HL Stoutt's Birthday First Monday in March
Commonwealth Day Second Monday in March
Good Friday & Easter Monday (in March or April)
Whit Monday May or June (date varies)
Sovereign's Birthday Mid-June (date varies)
Territory Day July 1
BVI Festival Days First Monday to Wednesday in August
St Ursula's Day October 21
Christmas Day & Boxing Day December 25 and 26

TAXES & REFUNDS

The BVI has no sales tax on goods or services. The stated price on restaurant menus and in shops is what you pay.

TELEPHONE

Country code ☑1
Area code ☑284

Dialing BVI phone numbers consist of the area code, followed by a seven-digit local number. If you are calling from abroad, dial ☑1 + 284 + seven-digit number. If you are calling locally, just dial the seven-digit number.

TIME

The islands are on Atlantic Standard Time (GMT/UTC minus 4 hours). Relative to New York, Miami and the eastern time zone: the Virgins are one hour ahead in winter, and in the same time zone in summer (due to daylight saving time).

TOURIST INFORMATION

BVI Tourist Board (www.bvitourism.com) Official site with comprehensive lodging and activity info.

TRAVELERS WITH DISABILITIES

The BVI is not particularly accessible and does not have any specific services geared toward travelers with disabilities.

ⓘ Getting There & Away

AIR

Tortola's **Terrence B Lettsome Airport** (EIS; ☑284-494-3701; www.bviaa.com; ☎) is the gateway. It's a modern facility with an ATM, car-rental agencies, free wi-fi and food concessions. The tiny airports on Virgin Gorda and Anegada are mostly for charter planes (though a couple of small commercial airlines do go to Virgin Gorda daily).

Many visitors opt to fly to Cyril E King Airport on St Thomas in the US Virgin Islands, as it is the region's largest airport and has more flights. Visitors then complete the journey by ferry. **BVI Airways** (www.gobvi.com) is slated to launch direct flights from Miami to Tortola by late 2017. Otherwise, flights from the US mainland, Canada and Europe usually connect via Puerto Rico, St Thomas or St-Martin/Sint Maarten. The following airlines are the main carriers:

Air Sunshine (☑954-434-8900; www.air sunshine.com)
Cape Air (☑800-227-3247; www.flycapeair. com)
LIAT (www.liat.com)
Seaborne Airlines (☑787-946-7800; www. seaborneairlines.com)
Winair (☑866-466-0410; www.fly-winair.sx)

SEA
Cruise Ship

A big ship or two calls at Road Town almost daily during peak season. The dock is downtown, so no tenders are needed (except in rare cases when the dock is particularly busy) – passengers disembark and they're in the heart of the action.

Ferry

Excellent ferry connections link Tortola, Virgin Gorda and Jost Van Dyke with the US Virgin Islands' St Thomas and St John. BVI Tourism (www.bvitourism.com) has schedules. For trips between the USVI and BVI, a passport is required.

Ferries between the two territories run until about 5pm only. Check schedules if you're trying to get from one to the other at night. Taxes are not included in the fees below. There is a US$20 departure tax to leave the BVI, and US$10 port fee to leave the USVI. Checked luggage costs US$3 per bag. Arrive at least 30 minutes before departure time to buy tickets at the terminal.

Main companies and routes:

Inter Island (☑ 284-495-4166; www.inter islandboatservices.com)

Native Son (☑ 284-495-4617; www.nativesonferry.com)

Road Town Fast Ferry (☑ 284-494-2323; www.roadtownfastferry.com)

Smith's Ferry/Tortola Fast Ferry (☑ 284-494-4454; www.bviferryservices.com)

Speedy's (☑ 284-495-5240; www.bviferries.com)

Ferries to/from Tortola (Road Town):

St Thomas (Charlotte Amalie) direct 45 minutes, three daily, one way US$35; Road Town Fast Ferry

St Thomas (Charlotte Amalie) via West End 60 minutes, several daily, one way US$35; Native Son and Smith's

Ferries to/from Tortola (West End):

St Thomas (Red Hook) 60 minutes, four daily, one way US$35; Native Son

St Thomas (Charlotte Amalie) 45 minutes, four daily, one way US$35; Smith's

St John (Cruz Bay) 30 minutes, four daily, one way US$40; Inter Island

Ferries to/from Virgin Gorda:

St Thomas (Charlotte Amalie) 90 minutes, three weekly (Tuesday, Thursday, Saturday), one way US$40; Speedy's

Ferries to/from Jost Van Dyke:

St Thomas (Red Hook) via St John 45 to 75 minutes, two daily (except none Thursday), one way US$60; Inter Island

Yacht

If arriving by yacht – as many do! – it must be at one of the following ports, which have customs and immigration facilities:

Jost Van Dyke Great Harbour

Tortola Road Town or West End

Virgin Gorda Spanish Town or Gun Creek

ⓘ Getting Around

AIR

Charter planes fly between islands. Companies making the rounds (including day trips to Anegada for roughly US$235 round-trip):

Fly BVI (☑ 284-340-5661; www.bviaircharters.com)

Island Birds (☑ 284-495-2002; www.islandbirds.com)

VI Airlink (☑ 284-495-2271; www.viairlink.com)

> **ⓘ DEPARTURE TAX**
>
> You must pay a US$20 departure tax to leave the BVI. This is not included in the ticket price, and must be paid separately at the airport or ferry terminal (usually at a window by the departure lounge).

BOAT

Frequent ferries glide between the islands. Getting around on your own by chartering a boat is also possible.

Ferry

Tortola is the BVI ferry hub, and all boats route through its various docks. The BVI Welcome Guide (www.bviwelcome.com) prints the timetables. In most cases, you can buy tickets on the spot at the ferry terminal. Sometimes credit-card machines don't work, so it's good to have cash as a backup.

Main companies:

New Horizon Ferry (☑ 284-495-9278; www.newhorizonferry.com)

North Sound Express (☑ 284-495-2138)

Smith's Ferry/Tortola Fast Ferry (p257)

Speedy's (p257)

Main routes:

Tortola (Road Town) to Virgin Gorda (Spanish Town) 30 minutes, roughly every hour, one way US$20; Speedy's and Smith's

Tortola (Road Town) to Anegada 75 minutes, Monday, Wednesday and Friday, round trip US$55; Smith's

Tortola (West End) to Jost Van Dyke 25 minutes, five daily, one way US$15; New Horizon Ferry

Tortola (Beef Island/Trellis Bay) to Virgin Gorda (Spanish Town) 20 minutes, several daily, one way US$20; Speedy's

Tortola (Beef Island/Trellis Bay) to Virgin Gorda (North Sound) 30 minutes, five daily, one way US$40; North Sound Express

Boat Charter Basics

The British Virgin Islands provide it all: a year-round balmy climate, steady trade winds, little to worry about in the way of tides or currents, a protected thoroughfare in the 35-mile-long Sir Francis Drake Channel, and hundreds of anchorages, each within sight of one another. These factors make the islands one of the easiest places to sail, which explains why more than a third of all visitors come to do just that.

If you want to sail, there are three basic options: a crewed boat, with skipper and cook; a 'bareboat' sans staff that you operate on your own; or a sailing-school vessel.

A typical week-long itinerary involves sampling the islands, while partially circumnavigating Tortola. The attraction of a sailing vacation is that you can sail or stay put as long as you want, look for quiet anchorages or head for the party spots and add on diving, hiking or shopping trips at will.

The cost of chartering a boat depends on the vessel's size and age and the time of year. It is a misconception that sailing is too expensive; once you do a little research you might be pleasantly surprised.

Charter Companies

Charter companies depend on their reputations. Ask for references and spend time talking with the company's representatives. Most companies sail out of the Moorings at Wickhams Cay 2 in Road Town.

The following is a list of respected charter services based in the BVI. Each can arrange bareboat charters, as well as a variety of crew options.

Barecat Charters (www.barecat.com) Smaller company specializing in catamarans.

BVI Yacht Charters (www.bviyachtcharters. com) Long-standing company.

Catamaran Company (www.catamarans.com) Another catamaran specialist.

Horizon Yacht Charters (www.horizon yachtcharters.com) Smaller company.

Moorings (www.moorings.com) It started the BVI bareboat business and remains the islands' largest yacht company.

Sunsail Yacht Charters (www.sunsail.com) The BVI's second-largest company.

TMM Yacht Charters (www.sailtmm.com) Smaller company with reasonable prices.

Sailing School

Offshore Sailing School (www.offshoresailing. com) Venerable company offering courses out of the Moorings in Road Town.

Rob Swain Sailing School (www.swainsailing. com) Well-rated, smaller school operating out of Nanny Cay, Tortola.

CAR & MOTORCYCLE

Driving is undoubtedly the most convenient way to get around, as there is no public transport system and taxi fares add up in a hurry.

You can drive in the BVI using a valid license from your home country. A temporary license is required if you're staying longer than 30 days; any car-rental agency can provide the paperwork.

Rental

To rent a car in the BVI you generally need to be at least 25 years old, hold a valid driver's license and have a major credit card.

Cars cost between US$70 and US$90 per day. If you're traveling in peak season, it's wise to reserve a couple of months in advance, as supplies are limited.

Road Conditions

Be prepared for challenging road conditions. Steep, winding roads are often the same width as your car, and the potholes can be outrageous.

Chickens, cows, goats and donkeys dart in and out of the roadway. Keep your eyes peeled for critters.

Road Rules

➡ Rule number one: drive on the left-hand side of the road!

➡ The steering wheel is on the left side.

➡ Seat-belt use is compulsory; children under five years must be in a car seat.

➡ Driving while using a handheld cell phone is illegal (but earpieces are permitted).

➡ Proceed clockwise at traffic roundabouts.

TAXI

All the islands have taxis that are easily accessible in the main tourist areas. Most vehicles are vans that carry up to 12 passengers; sometimes they're open-air pickup trucks with bench seats and awnings. Rates are set. They are usually charged on a per-person basis, and they go down a bit if more than one person takes the taxi. You can access rate sheets from the BVI Tourist Board (www.bvitourism.com).

Reliable companies:

Beef Island Taxi Association (☎ 284-495-1982)

BVI Taxi Association (☎ 284-494-3942)

West End Taxi Association (☎ 284-495-4934)

Cayman Islands

POP 60,400 / 📞 345

Best Places to Eat

➡ Vivo (p270)

➡ Barry's Golden Jerk (p276)

➡ Kaibo Beach (p273)

➡ Catch (p270)

➡ Big Tree BBQ (p274)

Best Places to Sleep

➡ Lighthouse Point (p270)

➡ Turtle Nest Inn (p271)

➡ Shangri-La (p270)

➡ Southern Cross Club (p279)

Why Go?

Some two million tourists visit the Cayman Islands each year. Most of them are cruise-ship passengers, who spend a few hours shopping, sunbathing or swimming with stingrays, before pulling out of port. Others hunker down near Seven Mile Beach, enjoying their all-inclusive resort on one of the Caribbean's most beautiful stretches of sand. And a lucky few venture further.

Cayman is an undeniably cosmopolitan place – nearly half the population is from somewhere else – but its rich local culture is alive and well, especially in Bodden Town, East End and Cayman Brac. Explore the North Side and the Sister Islands to discover lush forests, diverse birdlife, mysterious caves and untrammeled beaches. Under the waves lie amazing underwater walls and accessible shipwrecks.

Dive in. It takes only a small sense of adventure to uncover Cayman's greatest treasures – the warm hospitality and the fantastic natural phenomena above and below the sea.

When to Go

Dec–Apr High season, temperatures average a pleasant 75°F (24°C) and humidity is at its lowest. Accommodations fill up and prices are significantly higher.

Sep–Oct Rainfall is highest, with frequent afternoon showers that clear as quickly as they arrive. Some venues close during these months (especially on Little Cayman and Cayman Brac).

Nov Pirates Week is a super fun, island-wide event that takes place in early November.

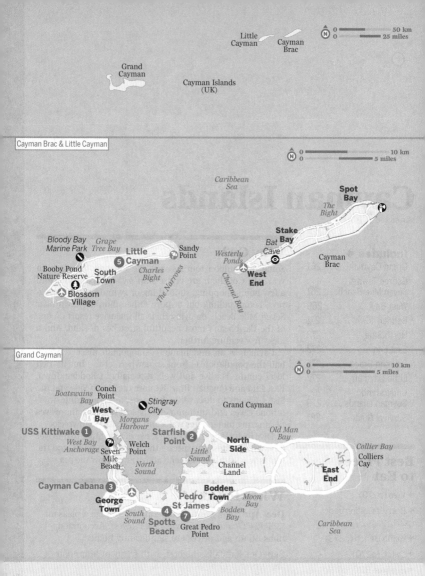

Cayman Islands Highlights

1 USS Kittiwake (p261) Discovering the ins and outs of this US Navy ship, 60ft below the surface of the sea.

2 Starfish Point (p272) Counting the sea stars on an otherwise deserted beach.

3 Cayman Cabana (p265) Making new foodie friends and sharing a delectable locavore dinner under the stars.

4 Spotts Beach (p271) Snorkeling with sea turtles at this little-known public beach.

5 Little Cayman (p277) Marveling at pristine coral reefs, spying on birds and swinging in hammocks on the smallest Cayman Island.

6 Cycling (p281) Enjoying smooth roads, little traffic and gorgeous seaside scenery while exploring Grand Cayman on two wheels.

7 Pedro St James (p271) Learning about the history of an island through the history of a house.

GRAND CAYMAN

To most of the world, Grand Cayman *is* the Cayman Islands, a glitzy shopping mecca and global financial center where resorts line the fabulous white-sand Seven Mile Beach and the wealthy from around the world spend time sipping cocktails and discreetly playing with their millions.

It does have another side – literally. If you head east, you can escape the cruise-ship crowds, experience local culture, discover underwater marvels and explore the undeveloped interior.

George Town & Seven Mile Beach

George Town is the supremely wealthy but surprisingly modest capital of the Cayman Islands. While undoubtedly cosmopolitan, it is tiny, tidy and pleasantly tropical – though it can feel overrun by tourists when there are multiple cruise ships in port. George Town is a draw for dining, shopping and a few historic sights, but you'll likely spend most of your time somewhere north of here.

The focal point of Cayman's tourism industry is Seven Mile Beach, a gorgeous stretch of unbroken white sand, which offers unlimited opportunities for swimming, sunbathing and sunset viewing. The beach is lined with resorts and vacation properties, but there is plenty of public access to this paradise – whether you're looking for a peaceful patch of sand or a full-blown beach party.

◉ Sights

Cayman National Museum   MUSEUM
(www.museum.ky; cnr Harbour Dr & Shedden Rd, George Town; adult/child US$8/3; ⊙9am-5pm Mon-Fri, 10am-2pm Sat) The centerpiece of this small museum is the engaging audiovisual presentation that offers an overview of the island's heritage. Natural and cultural history are the focus of exhibits, including one on animals that have become extinct. Housed in George Town's oldest building, the museum also displays two rooms of the Old Gaol (jail), with recently discovered prisoners' graffiti on the walls.

National Gallery
of the Cayman Islands   GALLERY
(www.nationalgallery.org.ky; Esterley Tibbetts Hwy, George Town; ⊙10am-5pm Mon-Sat) FREE This

small but delightful museum offers a wonderful break from the sand and sun. The ground floor houses rotating exhibits, while the 2nd floor shows off the national collection of Caribbean and Caymanian works. The impressive quarters include a lovely sculpture garden and a small gift shop.

Seven Mile Beach   BEACH
Although it's really only about 5½ miles long, this gorgeous strand of beach has flawless white sand and crystal blue waters – just as pretty as a postcard. It is lined with resorts and vacation properties, but the beach itself is public. The main public beach access point – just south of the Kimpton – has a big parking lot, a playground, beach volleyball and lounge chair rental, with beach bars and plenty of other diversions nearby. Crowded but fun.

Governor's Beach   BEACH
FREE Tucked in between resorts, the tree-shaded parking lot opens onto a sweet section of Seven Mile Beach that is rarely crowded. There's a reason they call it Governor's Beach: this quiet stretch of sand fronts the Governor's mansion.

★ Cemetery Beach   BEACH
FREE Ask a local where they like to spend a sunny day, and they will likely direct you to this gorgeous strip of sand at the northern end of Seven Mile Beach. It's rarely crowded – not because it's haunted, but because there

TOP DIVE SITES

USS Kittiwake (www.facebook.com/kittiwakecayman) Cayman's top requested dive site, this is a 76m US Navy submarine rescue ship. The wreck was sunk deliberately to create an artificial reef and dive site: ample entries and exits allow divers to swim through and explore the many rooms, peek through windows, sit at a table in the mess hall or take a turn at the steering wheel.

North Wall Grand Cayman's most famous diving destination is this magnificent underwater wall, which drops off some 6000ft into the great blue. The many dive sites offer opportunities to spot eagle rays, reef sharks and sea turtles, as well as myriad fish and coral formations. Babylon is a favorite dive site along this wall.

Grand Cayman

are no big resorts in the area. You can park on the street or in the lot across from West Bay Cemetery.

🏃 Activities

Off the Wall Divers DIVING
(☎916-0303; www.offthewalldiverscayman.com; 245 N Church St, George Town; 2-tank dive US$115) Located in the Lobster Pot Dive Center, this operation has two things going for it: small groups, allowing for personalized service, and early departures, promising the pick of the dive sites. You can also rent a tank and dive at the house reef, best known as Cheeseburger Reef (named after the nearby Burger King).

Wall to Wall Diving DIVING
(☎916-6408; www.walltowalldiving.com; 245 N Church St, George Town; 2-tank dive US$105, Cayman Rover US$165) Praised for its high level of service, Wall to Wall is based at the Lobster

Pot Dive Center. They have a full menu of dive training and trips, including a special all-day trip on the Cayman Rover, which visits three different dive sites in the island's most remote and unspoiled corners.

Eden Rock Diving Center DIVING
(☎949-7243; www.edenrockdive.com; 124 S Church St, George Town; guided 1-/2-tank dives US$70/110; ⏲ guided dives 9am, 11am & 2pm) Overlooking the George Town harbor, this outfit is above two favorite shore-dive spots: Eden Rocks and Devil's Grotto. Dive or snorkel with or without a guide; but be sure to bring a light to explore the underwater caves.

Divers Down DIVING
(☎945-1611; www.diversdown.net; 69 N Church St, George Town; 2-tank dive US$105) Caters to cruise-ship passengers, with three boat dives per day. Also offers trips to USS *Kittiwake* and Stingray City, as well as various training packages.

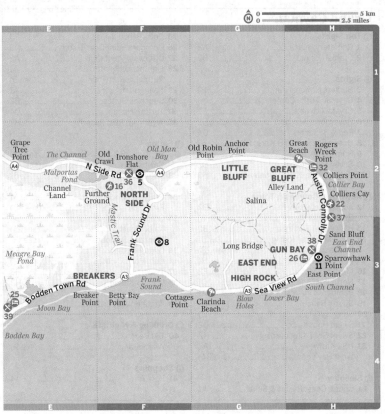

Red Sail Sports
WATER SPORTS, DIVING

(📞945-0178; www.redsailcayman.com; ⏰8am-6pm) This large water-sports center has a whole list of activities on offer, including diving, sailing, snorkeling, stand-up paddling, wave-running, wake-boarding, windsurfing and more. There are outlets at several resorts along Seven Mile Beach – the Marriott, the Westin, the Kimpton Seafire – as well as at Rum Point (p272).

👉 Tours

Sea Elements
BOATING, KAYAKING

(📞936-8687; www.caymanseaelements.com; tours adult/child from US$35/25) Excellent, informative tours focus on the island's natural wonders, including Bio Bay swimming (among the bioluminescence), mangrove tours by boat or kayak, and custom trips to Stingray City. Tours depart from the Cayman Island Yacht Club in Governor's Bay. Transportation is provided.

Atlantis Adventures
SUBMARINE TOURS

(📞949-7700; www.caymanislandssubmarines.com; 30 S Church St, George Town; adult/child Seaworld Observatory US$39/19, Atlantis submarine US$89/59) It's possible to visit the underwater world without even mussing up your hair. The Seaworld Observatory was specially designed for the shallow reefs around Grand Cayman, offering a front-row view of two shipwrecks and one fish feeding. The *Atlantis XI* submarine descends to depths up to 100ft, with options to go by day or by night.

Blue Water Excursions
FISHING, SNORKELING

(📞925-8738; www.bluewaterexcursions.com; Yacht Dr, Cayman Islands Yacht Club; ⏰half-day excursion US$550-700) Local fisherman Captain Richard Orr is at the helm of his 32ft vessel, *Trouble Maker*. Private snorkeling excursions make two snorkel stops, plus Stingray City. Alternatively, spend some time in the deep sea, reeling in your dinner.

Grand Cayman

Top Sights		
1	Cemetery Beach	A2
2	Starfish Point	D2
Sights		
3	Barkers National Park	B1
4	Cayman Turtle Center	A1
5	Crystal Caves	F2
6	Governor's Beach	B2
7	Pedro St James	D4
8	Queen Elizabeth II Botanic Park	F3
9	Rum Point	D1
10	Seven Mile Beach	B2
11	Wreck of the 10 Sail Monument	H3
Activities, Courses & Tours		
12	Action Watersports	B2
	Blue Iguana Safari	(see 8)
13	Blue Water Excursions	B2
14	Cayman Horse Riding	B1
	Divetech	(see 28)
15	Kitesurf Cayman	B1
16	Mastic Trail	F2
17	North Wall	C1
18	Pampered Ponies	A1
19	Spotts Beach	C4
20	Stingray City	B1
21	Sweet Spot Kaibo	D2
22	Sweet Spot Kiteboarding	H2
23	USS Kittiwake	A2
	West Bay Loop	(see 34)
Sleeping		
24	Cobalt Coast Resort & Suites	A1
25	Coco Beach Villas	E3
26	Compass Point Dive Resort	H3
27	Discovery Point Club	A2
28	Lighthouse Point	A1
	Retreat at Rum Point	(see 9)
29	Shangri-La	A1
30	Sunshine Suites	B2
31	Turtle Nest Inn	D4
32	Wyndham Reef Resort	H2
Eating		
	Big Tree BBQ	(see 38)
	Calypso Grill	(see 33)
33	Catch	B1
	Chester's	(see 25)
34	Cracked Conch	A1
	Eats Cafe	(see 30)
35	Grape Tree Cafe	D4
	Kaibo Beach	(see 21)
	Morgan's Seafood	(see 13)
36	Over the Edge	F2
	Rum Point Club	(see 9)
37	Tukka	H3
38	Vivine's Kitchen	H3
	Vivo	(see 28)
39	White House	E3
Drinking & Nightlife		
40	Tiki Beach	B2
	Wreck Bar	(see 9)
Shopping		
41	Pure Art	A4

Captain Marvin's Watersports SNORKELING
(☎945-6975; www.captainmarvins.com; N Church St, George Town; tours adult/child US$45/30; ⊙tours 10am & 2:30pm Mon-Fri, 9am & 1pm Sat & Sun) Apparently, Captain Marvin originated this now standard tour to Stingray City, which includes two or three snorkel stops after the main attraction. Price includes transportation from Seven Mile Beach.

Stingray City WILDLIFE-WATCHING, DIVING
This stretch of sandy seafloor in the North Sound is a meeting place for southern stingrays. As soon as you enter the water, you'll be swarmed by these prehistoric creatures, who glide over in search of squid. Boat tours have pretty standardized itineraries – feed, stroke and photograph. The tours usually make one or two snorkel stops afterwards.

Lots of tour operators take clients here, including Captain Marvin's Watersports. Dive shops lead trips to a nearby, slightly deeper site (14ft), so divers are underwater while stroking and feeding the animals.

Studies have shown that the stingrays have both unusual growth (since they have an unbalanced diet) and have oddball schedules (normally they are nocturnal). It's not the wildest wildlife you'll ever meet, but it's a rare opportunity to get up-close and personal with a stingray. To avoid crowds, visit on a day when there's no cruise ship in port.

Sleeping

Eldemire's Tropical Island Inn B&B $
(☎916-8369; www.eldemire.com; 18 Pebbles Way, George Town; r from US$120, apt US$144-160;) Here is a friendly, affordable alternative to the island's typical resorts and condos. For your money, you get clean, comfy quarters, with weekly housecleaning and minimal interference from your host. Laundry service and communal kitchen are at your disposal; bicycles are available for rental. The quiet residential location is

a short walk from the beautiful beach at Smith Cove.

Sunshine Suites
HOTEL $$

(949-3000; www.sunshinesuites.com; 1465 Esterley Tibbetts Hwy, Seven Mile Beach; r from US$170; ❋@🛜⛱) This sunny, yellow all-suite resort is a short walk away from the beach. You'll pay less for the off-beach location, but the place does not skimp on service. Value-conscious travelers will also appreciate the well-stocked kitchens and complimentary continental breakfast.

Grandview
CONDO $$$

(945-4511; www.grandviewcondos.com; 95 Snooze Ln, Seven Mile Beach; 2-bedroom condo US$350-550; ❋@🛜⛱) At the secluded, southern end of the beach, this gracious condo complex is set back from the water on wide, grassy grounds. The three-story units have either balconies or terraces and all units either face the ocean or are right on the beach. Each condo has a full kitchen plus laundry facilities. You may not wish to leave.

Sunset House
HOTEL $$$

(949-7111; www.sunsethouse.com; 390 S Church St, George Town; r US$265-325; ❋@🛜⛱) 'For divers, by divers.' What this means, is that there's terrific shore diving, morning and afternoon boat dives, and various training programs – all just a few steps from your doorstep. The rooms are spacious, clean and comfortable, some with ocean views from the balcony. The price includes a full, hearty breakfast.

The open-air, thatch-roof cabana is the perfect spot to recover from your day under the sea. Important to know (even if you're not staying here): Sunset House serves the island's best curries. Don't miss!

Discovery Point Club
CONDO $$$

(945-4724; www.discoverypointclub.com; 2043 West Bay Rd, Seven Mile Beach; r from US$260, 1-/2-bedroom ste from US$540/585; ❋@🛜⛱) This excellent condo complex is recommended for a comfortable family beach holiday. At the far north end of Seven Mile Beach (in front of a good snorkeling area), all the suites have superb views, balconies or patios, and kitchens. The studios are much more basic, with no view.

🍴 Eating

There are worthwhile restaurants clustered around downtown George Town and strung out along West Bay Rd. Day-trippers will want to move beyond the immediate zone of the cruise-ship tender dock. Within walking distance, there's a range of restaurants serving excellent local fare.

Bread & Chocolate
VEGAN $

(www.cafe.ky; cnr Dr Roys Dr & Edward St, George Town; mains US$10-16; 8am-4pm Mon-Fri, 9am-2pm Sat & Sun;) 'Bread & Chocolate' refers to the signature French toast, which is stuffed with chocolate hazelnut butter and bananas, dipped in coconut batter and topped with fresh fruit. If you can resist that, you might be tempted by the other breakfast and lunch offerings, which range from delicious to decadent. The entire menu is animal-free from beet burger to BLT.

Singh's Roti Shop & Bar
CARIBBEAN $

(www.singhsroti.ky; cnr Doctor Roy's Dr & Shedden Rd, George Town; mains US$8-10.50; 9am-10pm Sun-Thu, to midnight Fri & Sat) In a city where dinner often means a three-figure check, this cheerful hole-in-the-wall is a great place for some tongue-searing roti (curry filling, often potatoes and chicken, rolled inside flat bread). Definitely one of George Town's best bargains.

Greenhouse
VEGETARIAN $

(www.greenhousecayman.com; 72 N Church St, George Town; mains US$12-15; 8am-4pm Mon-Sat;) Here's your perfect downtown lunch stop, with fresh, creative combinations of toppings and stuffings for sandwiches, salads and pizzas. Health-conscious eaters will be in heaven. Dietary restrictions pose no challenge here, as the menu is rife with gluten-free, paleo and veg-friendly options.

⭐ Cayman Cabana
CARIBBEAN $$

(949-3080; www.caymancabanarestaurant.com; 53 N Church St, George Town; mains US$16-25, farm-to-table dinner US$75; 9am-10pm Mon-Sat) Anytime is a good time to sit on the seaside deck, sip cocktails and dine on burgers, sandwiches and Caymanian specialties. You'll find out what they mean when they promise to 'love ya like cook food.' On Thursday nights, Cabana takes the concept of 'local cuisine' to a whole new level, offering a farm-to-table feast that will delight your senses (reservations required).

Eats Cafe
DINER $$

(www.eats.ky; Cayman Falls Center, West Bay Rd, Seven Mile Beach; breakfast US$8-12, sandwiches

George Town

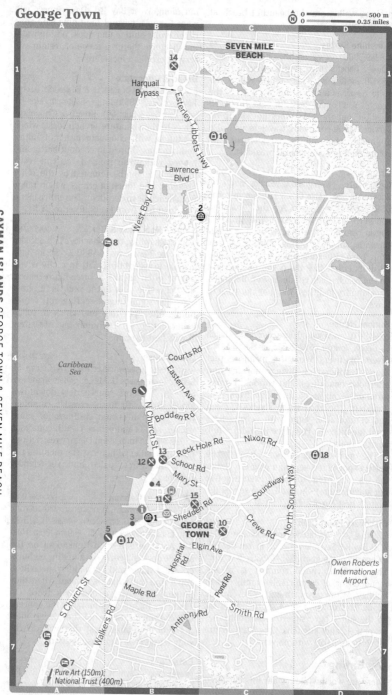

George Town

US$12-16, mains US$16-30; ⊙ 6:30am-11pm) No matter what you're in the mood for, you're likely to find it on the mile-long menu at Eats Cafe. The old-fashioned diner has seating in big booths, nostalgic posters on the wall and sports on the multiple screens. Also on-site: Legendz sports bar and Yoshi sushi bar.

Ragazzi
ITALIAN $$

(☑ 945-3484; www.ragazzi.ky; Buckingham Sq, West Bay Rd, Seven Mile Beach; pizza US$15-20, pasta US$22-30, mains US$30-50; ⊙ 11:30am-11pm) This much-loved Italian place has a sort of oddball location in a small strip mall, but the casual interior offers a warm, welcoming atmosphere. Keep it simple with crispy-crust pizza or delectable pasta dishes, or take it upscale with adeptly prepared steaks and seafood.

Casanova by the Sea
ITALIAN $$

(www.casanova.ky; 65 N Church St, George Town; mains lunch US$12-20, dinner US$23-42; ⊙ 11am-11pm) Romantic and relatively affordable, this seaside spot is an excellent option for Italian favorites. Service is charming and the view from the veranda is a perfect place to catch the sunset.

Brasserie
SEAFOOD $$$

(☑ 945-1815; www.brasseriecayman.com; 171 Elgin Ave, Cricket Sq, George Town; cafe US$12-16, mains US$20-24, 5-course tasting menu US$80; ⊙ restaurant 11:30am-10pm Mon-Fri, cafe 7am-5pm Mon-Fri) The Brasserie can guarantee the freshest of seafood, because they have their own fishing boat that goes out daily to catch it. There's also a thriving garden that supplies the produce. The result is an eclectic, innovative menu that changes frequently but is always delectable. For lighter fare including sandwiches, salads and breakfast, grab something at the on-site Market Cafe.

Morgan's Seafood
SEAFOOD $$$

(www.morganscayman.com; Cayman Island Yacht Club, Governor's Creek; mains lunch US$23-30, dinner US$30-44; ⊙ 11am-10pm) This popular seafood restaurant has gone all fancy on us, with a new location at the local yacht club and a new upscale attitude. The waterfront setting is absolutely lovely – a delightful place to feast on favorites such as seafood crepes and Thai seafood curry.

🍷 Drinking & Nightlife

Nightlife is not one of Cayman's main attractions, but the island does know how to do beach bars; you're never far from a tropical cocktail and a sunset view. The scene often gets grooving after dark, especially on Thursday and Friday nights. As a result of draconian laws, all clubs and bars close at midnight on Saturday (so folks can get up and go to church on Sunday).

Calico Jack's
BEACH BAR

(West Bay Rd, Seven Mile Beach; ⊙ 9am-1am Sun-Fri, to midnight Sat) 'Calico Jack' Rackham was an English pirate who marauded around these parts in the 18th century. Nowadays, he lends his name (not to mention his mug) to this classic beach bar – a place for locals, tourists, and everybody who likes to dance, drink and let loose on the sand. It's high-energy fun, especially during infamous full-moon parties.

CAYMAN, PLEASE

If there's one thing that gets the dander up of locals (in a polite way of course), it's hearing their nation referred to as 'the Caymans'. Don't ask why: they don't know any more than a resident of San Francisco shudders at hearing 'Frisco' – it's nails on a chalkboard. Preferred terms for the entire country are 'Cayman' or 'Cayman Islands'. As a pair, Cayman Brac and Little Cayman are known as the 'Sister Islands' and the individual islands are called by their correct names.

Tiki Beach   BEACH BAR
(www.tikibeachcayman.net; West Bay Rd, Seven Mile Beach; ⊙11am-10pm) There are lots of good times to be had at Tiki Beach. Rent snorkel gear, ride a waverunner or challenge your friends to a game of beach volleyball. Or sidle up to the bar for cocktails, dinner or dancing under the stars. Or...all of the above. This place gets packed when there are cruise ships in port.

Shopping

Tortuga Rum Co   FOOD
(www.tortugarumcakes.com; North Sound Way, George Town; ⊙10am-5pm Mon-Fri) Some 10,000 addictive rum cakes are made here daily. Sure, you can buy them all over the island – and the region – but those at the factory are freshest and the samples the most generous.

Pure Art   ARTS & CRAFTS
(www.pureart.ky; cnr S Church St & Denham Thompson Way, George Town; ⊙9am-6pm Mon-Thu, to 5pm Fri & Sat) About 1.5 miles south of the center, this traditional Caymanian house is packed with arts and crafts – a perfect stop for creative souvenirs, most of which are locally made.

Cayman Craft Market   ARTS & CRAFTS
(www.craftmarket.ky; cnr S Church St & Boilers Rd, George Town; ⊙8:30am-3pm Mon-Fri) This local handicraft market caters to the cruise-ship crowd, but it's not a bad place to pick up conch shells, caymanite jewelry and other handmade products. Local food products are also on sale.

Camana Bay   MALL
(www.camanabay.com; 10 Market St, Camana Bay; ⊙10am-5:30pm Mon-Fri, 10am-2pm Sat) Cour-tesy of the ubiquitous Dart development group, this vast upscale mall and multi-use development has transformed the North Sound side of Seven Mile Beach. There's plenty of shops, restaurants, fountains and movie theaters – plus a 75ft observation tower to see where Dart might place its next development.

ℹ Information

EMERGENCY NUMBERS
Police (RCIP; ☑911, 949-4222; www.rcips.ky; 69 Elgin Ave, George Town)

INTERNET ACCESS
Most resorts and condos offer internet access on-site, as do many restaurants and bars.
Cafe del Sol (The Paseo, Camana Bay; ⊙7am-9pm Mon-Thu, to 10pm Fri & Sat, to 8pm Sun;)
Cafe del Sol (cnr West Bay Rd & Lawrence Blvd, Seven Mile Beach; ⊙7am-7pm Mon-Sat, 8am-7pm Sun)
Camana Bay Mall (10 Market St, Camana Bay; ⊙10am-5:30pm Mon-Fri, 10am-2pm Sat)

POST
Main Post Office (www.caymanpost.gov.ky; 14 Edward St; ⊙8:15am-5pm Mon-Fri & 9am-12:30pm Sat)

TOURIST INFORMATION
Cayman Islands Tourism Association (www.cita.ky; 1320 West Bay Rd, Seven Mile Beach; ⊙9am-4pm Mon-Fri) Operates a useful office near Seven Mile Beach.
Department of Tourism (www.caymanislands.ky; Harbour Dr) Located at the North Terminal cruise-ship dock at George Town harbor; open when cruise ships are in port.
Department of Tourism (Owen Roberts International Airport) Booth at the airport; open when flights arrive.
National Trust (www.nationaltrust.org.ky; 558 S Church St; ⊙9am-5pm Mon-Fri & 10am-4pm Sat) The main office; has a wealth of information.

ℹ Getting There & Away

Owen Roberts International Airport (p284) is the transportation hub for all three Cayman Islands, with regular flights to the US, Canada and the UK, as well as the Sister Islands.

There's a taxi stand just outside the airport exit. Fares are set by the government: the dispatcher will give you a receipt, though you pay the driver. Expect to pay US$15 to George Town, US$25 to Seven Mile Beach, US$70 to East End and US$80 to Rum Point.

Hotels are not permitted to collect guests at the airport, though some hotels will pay your taxi fare upon arrival.

Several car-rental agencies, including **Andy's Rent-a-Car** (☑ 949-8111; www.andys.ky; ⊘ 6am-10pm), **Avis** (☑ 949-2468; www.aviscayman.com; ⊘ 7am-11pm), **Budget** (☑ 949-5605; www.budgetcayman.com; ⊘ 7:30am-11pm) and **Economy Car Rental** (☑ 949-9550; www.economycarrental.com.ky), have offices across the road from the terminal (exit the terminal and cross the road to the left); some also have outlets across the island.

There is no bus service to the airport.

❶ Getting Around

BICYCLE

With its flat terrain and always stunning views of the sea, Grand Cayman is a pleasure for cyclists. Renting a scooter will enable you to easily access the far reaches of the island. Many hotels have bikes available to guests; or you can rent from **Cayman Auto Rentals** (☑ 949-1013; www.caymanautorentals.com.ky; N Church St; bike rental per day US$19-25).

BUS

The George Town **bus depot** (p284) serves as the dispatch point for color-coded minibuses to all districts of Grand Cayman. Buses run every day from 6am to 11pm and to 1am on Friday. Bus stops are few and far between: flag down a bus from any point along the route.

West Bay

West Bay is on the itinerary for almost every visitor to Cayman, most of whom shuttle through, making obligatory stops at a few over-hyped attractions. Fewer visitors experience the true highlights of the district – running horses on deserted beaches, diving the incredible North Wall, or exploring the country roads and beach trails by bicycle.

Surrounded by the sea on three sides, West Bay offers spectacular sunrises and sunsets – not to mention excellent eating and drinking venues to enjoy the sea views.

❍ Sights

Cayman Turtle Center   AQUARIUM
(www.turtle.ky; 786 Northwest Point Rd; turtle center US$18, adventure tour US$45; ⊘ 8am-5pm) This is essentially a petting zoo for sea turtles. There are lots of turtles swimming in tanks, and guests are invited to handle the young turtles (who are clearly distressed by the experience). If you pay for the 'adven-

ture tour', there is an enclosed lagoon for swimming with the turtles, with a few additional attractions. It's not much of a 'wildlife encounter,' as it's touted: you're better off snorkeling with sea turtles in the wild at Spotts Beach (p271).

Barkers National Park   BEACH, NATIONAL PARK
FREE The first national park in the Caymans, Barkers combines low scrub, dense mangroves and long, sandy beaches. There are no amenities here, but it's a beautiful spot for cycling, horseback riding and kitesurfing. The beach is often deserted. Unfortunately, beach clean-up crews have a hard time keeping up with the trash that the tide brings in, so it's far from pristine.

⚑ Activities

Cayman Horse Riding   HORSEBACK RIDING
(☑ 916-3530; www.caymanhorseriding.com; Conch Point Rd; tours US$90-130) Nicki takes small groups (not more than five people) horseback riding on the beautiful beaches of Barkers National Park. If you're willing to pay for it, you can even take the horses swimming. Prices include transportation from Seven Mile Beach and photographs.

Divetech   DIVING
(☑ 946-5658; www.divetech.com; 571 Northwest Point Rd; 2-tank dive from US$108) In addition to daily boat dives, Divetech offers some pretty excellent shore diving, which features a mini-wall, canyons and swim-throughs, as well as an underwater statue known as the Guardian of the Reef. This is one of the few dive shops on the island that offers lessons in free diving.

West Bay Loop   CYCLING
(☑ 939-0911; www.westbayloop.com; Northwest Point Rd; tour US$70, rental per day US$40-60) The West Bay Loop is a 9-mile cycling trail that circles the peninsula, following the spectacular coastline through Barkers National Park, through the residential areas along Spanish Bay, and around the Northwest Point. Sign up for the three-hour guided tour; or rent a bike, grab a map and follow the route on your own. Located at the Cracked Conch (p270).

Kitesurf Cayman   KITESURFING
(☑ 916-5483; www.kitesurfcayman.com; Barkers Beach; 2hr lesson from US$150; ⊘ 10am-5:30pm Nov-Jul) Walter, Neil and John have been offering private and group kitesurfing lessons on Cayman for nearly a decade. They

use radio helmets, so they can coach you (and you can actually hear them) while you are on the board. For days when there is not quite enough wind, they also offer hydrofoil rental and lessons.

Pampered Ponies HORSEBACK RIDING
(📞 916-2540; www.ponies.ky; Conch Point Rd) Take these pampered ponies riding on the beach in Barkers National Park, with an option for cooling off in the ocean with your horse. There is also a monthly full-moon ride; book in advance.

🛏 Sleeping

West Bay is a mostly residential neighborhood with plenty of rental properties, as well as a few full-service resorts. It's a peaceful, pleasant place to stay that's still within striking distance of Seven Mile Beach.

★ Shangri-La B&B $$
(📞 526-1170; www.shangrilabandb.com; 29 B Sticky Toffee Ln; r US$165-219, ste US$319; ❄ 🛜 🏊) Overlooking a little lake in residential West Bay, this B&B (a rarity in Cayman) is quite the find. Its eight refreshing rooms and one luxurious suite are individually decorated in a soothing palette, with an absence of frills but an abundance of natural light. The place is renowned for its satisfying breakfasts and exceptional attention to detail.

★ Lighthouse Point CONDOS $$$
(📞 945-5658; www.lighthouse-point-cayman. com; 571 Northwest Point Rd; condo from US$450; ❄ 🛜) 🌿 This gorgeous, green facility features nine two-bedroom condos, with balconies that face the setting sun. Cayman's first ecoresort utilizes solar and wind power, a zero-discharge water-management system and custom wood interiors from repurposed wood. The condos are fully equipped and quite lovely – with top-notch vegetarian dining and dive operation on-site.

Cobalt Coast Resort & Suites RESORT $$$
(📞 946-5656; www.cobaltcoast.com; 18a Sea Fan Dr; d/ste from US$290/330, per week from US$1700; ❄ @ 🛜 🏊) This small but classy all-inclusive resort does its best to facilitate an amazing dive vacation. The rooms are modern and bright, the setting is dramatically beautiful, and the shore diving is phenomenal, with the North Wall (p261) located just 125ft off the dock. Reef Divers is the on-site 'valet' dive operator, which will take care of all your diving needs.

🍴 Eating

Some of the island's best restaurants are sprinkled around the West Bay. They are pretty pricey, but you can't beat the delicious seafood and beautiful seaside settings.

★ Vivo VEGETARIAN $$
(www.vivo.ky; 571 Northwest Point Rd; mains US$15-22; ⏰ 7:30am-8:30pm; 🍴) 🌿 At the forefront of Cayman's farm-to-table movement, Vivo is all about sustainability. Sit on the breezy porch and sample sandwiches, salads and other delectable innovations made with locally grown produce, farm-fresh eggs, and lots of love. This place does amazing things with coconut, including irresistible coconut 'ceviche' and smoked spiced coconut 'bacon'.

Although the menu is mostly vegan and vegetarian, Vivo is doing its part to rid the reef of its most dangerous invasive species. You can help by ordering a seared lionfish sandwich or a coconut lionfish curry. Good for the body, good for the soul, good for the earth!

★ Catch SEAFOOD $$$
(📞 949-4321; www.catch.ky; Morgan's Ln; mains lunch US$18-25, dinner US$32-50; ⏰ 11am-1am Mon-Fri, to 11pm Fri & Sat) A delightful addition to dining in West Bay, Catch offers a tantalizing menu of seafood, including a daily local crudo and a daily fresh ceviche, in addition to other land and sea delicacies. The shady deck is rivaled only by the cool, contemporary decor inside. Service is utterly charming.

Calypso Grill SEAFOOD $$$
(www.calypsogrillcayman.com; Morgan's Ln; mains lunch US$18-27, dinner US$35-50; ⏰ 11:30am-10pm Tue-Sun) Tucked away on Morgan's Harbour, Calypso Grill is a boldly colorful and wonderfully eclectic venue. The menu is mostly seafood, but there are preparations you won't find anywhere else, such as crispy mango shrimp and – the ultimate in decadence – lobster in champagne cream sauce. Sticky toffee pudding is the signature dessert: don't miss it.

Cracked Conch SEAFOOD $$$
(📞 945-5217; www.crackedconch.com.ky; 857 Northwest Point Rd; mains lunch US$18-30, dinner US$33-55; ⏰ 11am-3pm & 5-10:30pm Dec-May, 5-10:30pm only Jun-Nov) This oceanfront stunner has been delighting discerning diners for some three decades. Although it sounds like the name of a beach bar, this high-

concept restaurant and lounge is all white tablecloths and sublime service. There's a more informal venue on the vast open-air deck. Perfect spot for a sunset dinner.

❶ Getting There & Away

The sights of West Bay are about 12km north of the cruise-ship terminal in George Town. The yellow-line minibus runs from the George Town **bus depot** (p284) to the Cayman Turtle Center and Batabano Rd, running every 15 minutes from 6am to 11pm.

Bodden Town

Historic Bodden Town was the capital of the Cayman Islands until George Town scooped that honor in the mid-19th century. It's far removed from the bustle of the west – in atmosphere if not in distance – and maintains the appealing vibe of an authentic locals' town. A couple of historical sites and some unique dining experiences make Bodden Town a worthy stop on any drive around the island.

◉ Sights & Activities

★ Pedro St James   HISTORIC BUILDING
(Pedro Castle; www.pedrostjames.ky; Pedro Castle Rd, Savannah; guided/self-guided/child US$18/12.50/free; ⊙9am-5pm) The island's oldest building, this Caribbean great house was built in 1780 by one of Cayman's founding families (with slaves doing the heavy lifting). Over the years, the house served as jailhouse, courthouse and parliament building. It was here in 1831 that the decision was made in favor of a public vote for elected representatives. And here, in 1835, the Slavery Abolition Act was announced. Nowadays, the house is fitted with antiques and reproductions to evoke the era.

★ Spotts Beach   SNORKELING
(Shamrock Rd, Savannah) This pretty little public beach is the favorite feeding spot for sea turtles, who come to chow down on sea grass. Don your mask and snorkel and swim with them, but please don't touch, chase or otherwise harass these gentle creatures. Even if you don't feel like getting wet, you can usually spot them from the pier.

Snorkeling with sea turtles in the wild is a wonderful alternative to the contrived turtle encounters at the Turtle Center. The beach is about 7km west of Bodden Town.

🛏 Sleeping

With Bodden Town as your base, you might feel you're on a quiet, traditional Caribbean island, even as the bright lights of George Town shine 20 minutes to the west.

★ Turtle Nest Inn   GUESTHOUSE $$
(☑947-8665; www.turtlenestinn.com; Bodden Town Rd; r US$199, apt US$239-279; ❄ 🖥 ≋) Not a resort person? Located way off the tourist track, this lovely Spanish-style guesthouse offers the intimacy and authenticity that you're craving. In addition to the comfy quarters (all with kitchen facilities), there are two swimming pools, a sweet, sandy beach and an onshore reef for snorkeling.

Coco Beach Villas   COTTAGES $$
(☑926-0102; www.caymanbeachvillas.com; Bodden Town Rd; garden/ocean view from US$179/299; ❄ 🖥 ≋) Here's a collection of cozy cottages facing the crystal blue. The five units – complete with modern kitchens and one or two bedrooms – sit on a private beach, strung with hammocks and kissed by Caribbean breezes. The location near the center of Bodden Town offers easy access to the island's sights.

🍴 Eating

Your eating options are limited, but there are a few gems in town – definitely worth stopping for lunch if you are passing through.

Grape Tree Cafe   SEAFOOD $
(Bodden Town Rd; mains US$10-15; ⊙Sat & Sun) Right on Bodden Town beach, this simple thatch-roof shack is the hottest spot in town during its weekend fish fry. Besides the fresh fish, there's conch fritters and fried plantains, not to mention fresh tropical fruit juices. Dine at picnic tables in the sand, with unbeatable sea views. Save room for dessert.

Chester's   CARIBBEAN $
(563 Bodden Town Rd; mains US$10-16; ⊙10am-10pm Nov-Apr) The aromas of barbecue will lure you into this simple roadside house, just east of Bodden Town center. Take your pick from pan-fried seafood and tasty jerk chicken and pork. The menu is scrawled on a white board; seating is at picnic tables in the parking lot; and the welcome is warm as can be.

White House   INTERNATIONAL $$$
(www.thewhitehousecayman.com; Bodden Town Rd; lunch US$16-30, dinner US$26-34;

☺11am-9pm) Here's a fabulous seaside mansion that has been converted into a classy fine-dining venue. Get fancy in the chandelier-decked dining hall, or enjoy the sea breeze on the long, shaded dock. Either way, the food is expertly prepared, with burgers and curries for lunch, and steaks and seafood for dinner.

❶ Getting There & Away

Bodden Town is about 15km east of George Town, along the south shore of the island. Both orange-line and purple-line minibuses stop in Bodden Town (en route to North Side or East End), running every 30 minutes between 6am and 11pm.

North Side

Windswept and uncrowded, the North Side is a region of lush greenery, secluded beaches and watery inlets, all lined with pastel-colored vacation homes with too-cute names. Here, you can wander among wonderfully landscaped gardens, spot the rare blue iguana, explore mysterious caves and make a wish upon a starfish.

The only way to get here (unless you come by boat) is to drive east along the south coast and cut through the center of the island – a long, meandering journey through the heart of the island – making the North Side feel even more remote than it really is. But then again, that's part of the appeal.

◉ Sights

Queen Elizabeth II Botanic Park GARDENS
(www.botanic-park.ky; Frank Sound Dr; adult/child US$12.50/free; ☺9am-5:30pm) A veritable treasure trove of the island's native species. A series of walking trails traverse the lovely landscaped gardens, which include a rainbow-themed Color Garden, the historical Heritage Garden with a traditional Caymanian house as its centerpiece, an orchid garden (in bloom in late May and June) and the longer woodland trail. The botanic park is also an excellent birding destination.

Crystal Caves CAVE
(www.caymancrystalcaves.com; 69 North Side Rd; adult/child US$40/30; ☺tours 9am, 11am, 1pm & 3pm) Grand Cayman's newest attraction is this network of mysterious limestone caves, located deep in the island's interior. There are actually some 105 caves located on this property, though only three are open to the public (so far). Look for impressive stalactite and stalagmite formations, lots of hidden rooms and connecting passageways, and a gorgeous interior lake. And, of course, bats. The excursion is pricey, but cool.

Rum Point BEACH
(www.rumpointclub.com) Swinging in hammocks and snorkeling are the main activities at this quiet beach, although Red Sail Sports (p263) also has an outlet here. Take some time to explore the trails along the reef-protected shore and mangroves, then enjoy a beachside burger at the fun-filled Wreck Bar (p273).

★ Starfish Point BEACH
(Water Cay Rd) Crystalline waters protect countless red cushion sea stars along this wonderful little stretch of sand. Soaking in a foot of water all along the beach, the starfish are easy to spot from above the surface, so you don't need snorkel gear. To get there, drive past Rum Point and take Water Cay Rd as far as it goes.

🏃 Activities & Tours

Blue Iguana Safari WILDLIFE
(www.blueiguana.ky; Queen Elizabeth II Botanic Park; tours adult/child incl park US$30/20; ☺tours 11am Mon-Sat) Knowledgeable guides lead a daily, 90-minute tour of the Blue Iguana Recovery Center, where naturalists are working to restore the population of this critically endangered species. Visitors get a tour of the breeding facility, as well as a guided walk around the woodland trail, where some iguanas have been released.

Sweet Spot Kaibo KAYAKING, BOATING
(www.sweetspotwatersports.com; 585 Water Cay Dr; adult/child US$55/45) The two-hour kayak tour stops at Starfish Point – to see the sun set and starfish awake – and Bio Bay – to experience the magic of bioluminescence. If you don't care to paddle the 3 miles round-trip, you can take the same tour in a purpose-designed 'bio boat.'

Cayman Kayaks KAYAKING
(☑926-4467; www.caymankayaks.com; adult/child from US$49/39) 🌿 By day, paddle through the bio-rich mangrove swamps; by night, explore the bioluminescent Bio Bay. If you don't care to paddle, this operation also has an ecofriendly electric catamaran. Tours

depart from Rum Point or from Water Cay Public Beach, which is 2km further south.

Mastic Trail
HIKING

(☑ 749-1121; www.nationaltrust.org.ky; Further Rd; tours adult/child US$30/15; ☺ tours 8am Tue-Sat) This surprisingly lush 2-mile-long trail meanders through the old-growth forest that once supplied early settlers with timber. Hikers can explore deep into the old-growth forest of Grand Cayman's wild interior, with wooden walkways traversing some of the marshy portions. Expect to see wild jasmine, wild coffee, myriad birds, land crabs and much more. The National Trust (p268) offers excellent guided hiking and birding tours.

The northern trail head – on Further Rd (off North Side Rd) – is the drier, more accessible starting point, but you can also start at the southern trail head on Mastic Rd (near the botanical garden).

⌷ Sleeping

Rum Point and the surrounding areas are sprinkled with condominium complexes and other vacation rentals, although there is a dearth of full-service hotels and resorts and more traditional places to stay.

Retreat at Rum Point
CONDO $$$

(☑ 947-9135; www.grandcaymanretreat.com; Rum Point; condos from $300; ✳@☎≋) A fantastic beach and an exclusive atmosphere are the draws at this waterfront complex. Amenities include a tennis court, gym, luscious swimming pool and sauna. The 28 condo units – which are out rented by various individual owners – all have modern kitchens, laundry facilities and screened-in porches to foil the 'skeeters.

✗ Eating & Drinking

★ Kaibo Beach
INTERNATIONAL $$

(☑ 947-9975; www.kaibo.ky; 585 Water Cay Rd; mains US$16-25, Upstairs from US$35; ☺ 11am-late daily, Upstairs from 6pm Thu-Sun) Here's a near-perfect beach bar, with tables in the sand, creative cocktails, and scrumptious food – ranging from conch fritters to coconut curry fish. For a rollicking good time, come for the Tuesday-night beach barbecue, with live music, Caymanian cooking and dancing on the sand. (Need a lift? Catch the water taxi from Camana Bay.)

Upstairs (that's the name, as well as the location) is a highly lauded and high-priced fine-dining restaurant by Michelin-starred chef Laurence Tham. The six-course tasting menu is a culinary extravaganza.

Over the Edge
WEST INDIAN $$

(www.overtheedgecayman.com; 312 North Side Rd; breakfast US$6-20, mains US$13-30; ☺ 8am-10:45pm) This place is not much to look at, but you can't beat it for friendly service and tasty food, served on a breezy deck facing the water. Ingredients are grown in local gardens and fished in local waters, so this is fresh, flavorful and authentic West Indian cuisine. Try cod and ackee (Caribbean fruit often served with saltfish), quiche callallou (a leafy green similar to okra), or spiny-tail lobster, sautéed Cayman style.

Rum Point Club
SEAFOOD $$$

(☑ 947-9412; www.rumpointclub.com; Rum Point; mains US$28-48; ☺ 5:30-11pm Tue-Sun) Rum Point Club is a locally famous foodie destination that specializes in elaborate creations of seafood, as well as rare rums. The signature dish is a seafood hotpot, no less than five *fruits de mer*. Reservations recommended: book a table on the screened porch for maximum sea breezes.

An exceedingly pleasant way to get here is to take the catamaran ferry (US$5, Tuesday to Friday), which Red Sail Sports (p263) runs from Seven Mile Beach.

Wreck Bar
BAR

(www.rumpointclub.com; Rum Point; mains US$9-20; ☺ 10am-5pm) Beach bars don't come much more friendly than this boozy refuge, which sets up chairs on the sand. Burgers, sandwiches and cocktails are on the menu for lunch, which you can devour at a picnic table in the shade. Here's your perfect spot to sample the famous mudslide (a cocktail, which was apparently invented here).

❶ Getting There & Away

It takes about 45 minutes to drive the 40km around the island to the North Side. The orange-line minibuses go as far as Old Man Bay (6am to 9pm) but you'll need a private vehicle to get to Rum Point.

Rum Point Club and Kaibo Beach both offer a sort of water taxi for guests coming to dine at their establishments.

East End

A world away from the rest of the island, the East End is a place where life goes slowly – and where the rampant development has not yet reached. Here's your chance to catch a last glimpse of traditional Caymanian living (and a taste of traditional Caymanian cooking). There's not a ton to do here, but the folks are friendly and the scenery is dramatic and beautiful, with avian-rich marshlands, hidden beaches and ironshore coastline. And, there are plenty of hammocks.

⊙ Sights & Activities

Wreck of the 10 Sail Monument MEMORIAL
(Austin Connolly Dr) In 1794, a convoy of 10 British merchant ships wrecked on the reef off the East End. Local residents came to the aid of the convoy, rescuing all but eight of the passengers and crew. Legend has it that a royal prince was among the rescued, and King George was so grateful that he rewarded the islanders' bravery by forever exempting them from paying taxes and from being conscripted. (Good story, but there's no documentary evidence.)

Dedicated by Queen Elizabeth on the bicentennial of the wreck, the memorial overlooking the wreck site remembers the victims and honors the rescuers. North of here (on the opposite side of the street), you can see a couple of cannons that were salvaged from the wreck.

Eco Rides CYCLING
(www.ecoridescayman.ky; per person US$70-100; ⊙7:30am Tue-Sun) A lifelong East Ender, Shane Edwards is passionate about showing off his end of the island – preferably on two wheels. Ranging from two to five hours, the cycling tours stop at landmarks such as the Wreck of the 10 Sail monument, the East End lighthouse and the blowholes, with a rest stop at Shane's own cozy home at Grapetree Cove.

Sweet Spot Kiteboarding KITESURFING
(www.sweetspotwatersports.com; Austin Connolly Rd; lessons from US$149) The uncrowded East End offers ideal conditions for kiteboarding, with strong, steady winds and reef-protected waters. There is instruction for all levels, as well as SUP rental when water is calm enough.

🛏 Sleeping

For the moment, the East End feels gloriously remote, with just a few small and medium-sized resorts dotting the main drag. Enjoy it while it lasts, as the tireless developer Dart Realty has recently acquired

seaside property in these parts, including beloved Barefoot Beach.

Compass Point Dive Resort RESORT $$
(☑640-4444; www.compasspointdiveresort.com; Austin Connolly Rd; ste from US$255; P❄🔊🏊)
🛥 Catering to discerning divers, Compass Point offers 28 spacious and stylish units, all with balconies overlooking the beach or the pool. Dive boats dock on-site, promising a quick, easy commute to the world-class dive sites around the East End. Snorkel gear, bicycles and kayaks are also available for guest use.

Wyndham Reef Resort RESORT $$$
(☑947-3100; www.wyndhamcayman.com; Queen's Hwy; r US$200-400; ❄@🔊🏊) All 110 rooms in cheery, yellow-hued, three-story blocks face the sea along the long, gorgeous beach. The rooms are quite luxurious, and service is top-notch, with good snorkeling right off the beach. Until its recent sale, the Reef was celebrated as one of the island's few locally owned resorts; hopefully, Wyndham will be able to maintain the resort's personal service and intimate atmosphere.

🍴 Eating

Come to the East End for old-fashioned Caymanian cooking. The best restaurants operate out of somebody's kitchen (or open-air grill), so you know it's pure homemade goodness.

Vivine's Kitchen CARIBBEAN $
(Austin Connolly Dr; mains US$8-20; ⊙11am-8pm) There really is a Miss Vivine and she really does live in this roadside home with stellar views of the ocean. Local treats such as red-bean soup, fish balls on rice, fish fritters and much more are served up home-style. Eat at a picnic table under a tree on the terrace and enjoy the scene.

★Big Tree BBQ BARBECUE $$
(Austin Connolly Dr; mains US$12-18; ⊙11am-6pm Sun, Wed & Fri) Three days a week, Henry fires up the grills in his front yard and prepares an authentic island feast for anyone who cares to sit down in the shade of the big tree. Come for tender ribs, barbecue chicken and authentic local specialties.

Tukka FUSION $$$
(www.tukka.ky; 898 Queen's Hwy; lunch US$12-20, dinner US$28-40; ⊙11:30am-10pm Mon-Sat, from 8:30am Sun) Tukka is Australian for 'food'. At this fun and funky seaside restaurant,

Aussie native Ron Hargrave will show you exactly what that means, with an eclectic assortment of Caribbean and Australian eats. Specialties include lionfish ceviche, conch and croc fritters, and kangaroo sausage 'lollipops.' The Wednesday night walkabout is a highlight.

ℹ Getting There & Away

The East End is about 30km east of George Town. The purple-line bus runs from the George Town **bus depot** (p284) to the East End terminal every hour or so, from 6am to 9pm (midnight on Friday night).

CAYMAN BRAC

Named after the 'brac' or 'bluff' that dominates this cheese wedge of an island, the most easterly of the Cayman Islands is also the most authentically Caymanian. Tourism is not the name of the game here. Instead, residents work in the quarries, on fishing boats, and in other enterprises, as well as for the local government. While the island has (almost) all the conveniences of the modern era, it also has a laid-back, small-island atmosphere that is pretty irresistible. Come here for a visit for top-notch diving, a scenic hike along the Brac and little else.

⊙ Sights

Bluff   LANDMARK
The limestone cliff – 140ft high at its eastern end – stretches almost the entire length of this little island and dominates the landscape. Along the north side, there are several access points for hikers, including the National Trust Parrot Reserve and Lighthouse Footpath. By car, drive up Ashton Reid Dr to Major Donald Dr, which runs west to east across the top of the bluff.

Great Cave   CAVE
(South Side Rd, East End) The largest, most enticing cave as at the eastern end of South Side Rd. Ascend with ladders and ropes to enter a massive cavern that begs exploration.

🏃 Activities

Most people come to Cayman Brac for the diving, which is pristine and amazing. The island also has a few excellent hiking trails, some caves to explore and plenty of birds to watch.

Hiking & Birdwatching

★Lighthouse Footpath   BIRDWATCHING, HIKING
(Major Donald Dr) With stunning vistas all around, this 2.5-mile walking trail (one way) runs along the edge of the bluff. It starts at the lighthouse, which – at 140ft – is the highest point in Cayman. The scenery is spectacular, and the bluff is an excellent vantage point for spotting the varied birdlife, including brown boobies and frigate birds gliding in the updrafts. To reach the trailhead, drive to the far eastern end of Major Donald Dr.

National Trust
Parrot Reserve   BIRDWATCHING, HIKING
(Bight Rd; www.nationaltrust.org.ky; Major Donald Dr) Come here to spot one of the 400 remaining Cayman Brac parrots. Access to the reserve is on a hiker-only trail, Bight Rd, which crosses the Brac from north to south. The hiking is mostly on ironshore, which can be challenging. The trail includes a 200m boardwalk through the dense forest that echoes with songbirds.

The northern trailhead is at the staircase leading up the bluff from North East Bay Rd, or start at the midpoint on Major Donald Dr.

Westerly Ponds   BIRDWATCHING
Birdwatchers should head for the Westerly Ponds at the western tip of the island, where there are more than 100 species of birds nesting around the wetlands, with viewing platforms For your birdwatching pleasure.

Diving

With crystal waters affording superb visibility and more than 40 permanent dive moorings, Cayman Brac attracts its share of diving and snorkeling enthusiasts. An artificial reef, a 315ft Russian frigate now named the *Captain Keith Tibbetts,* is popular.

Brac Scuba Shack   DIVING
(www.bracscubashack.com; West End; 2-tank dive US$110) An independent dive shop that specializes in small groups and custom trips.

Reef Divers   DIVING
(☑ 948-1642; www.reefdiverscaymanbrac.com; West End; 2-tank dives US$108) Long-established dive operator, based at Cayman Brac Beach Resort.

🛏 Sleeping

The small selection of accommodations includes private condos as well as the main

Little Cayman & Cayman Brac

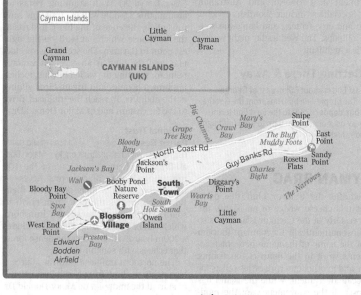

resort, Cayman Brac Beach Resort, which caters to diving enthusiasts.

Brac Caribbean
CONDO $$

(☑ 948-2265; www.866thebrac.com; West End; 1-/2-bedroom condo from US$225/265; ❋ ❀) Like its sibling the **Carib Sands** (☑ 948-1121; www.caribsands.com; West End; 1-/2-/3-bedroom from US$190/243/320; ❋ ❀ ❀), this condo complex offers understated luxury and top-notch service. The demure, three-story buildings feature 16 apartments with ocean-view balconies, tropically colored interiors and easy access to the on-site **restaurant** (www.facebook.com/Captains-Table-Bar-Restaurant-137029733010563; West End; mains US$12-35; ⊙ 11am-midnight).

Cayman Brac Beach Resort
RESORT $$$

(☑ 948-1323; www.caymanbracbeachresort.com; West End; 7-day package incl meals & diving per person from US$1490; ❋ @ ❀ ❀) Cayman Brac Beach Resort is a relaxed and friendly diving hotel on a charming stretch of beach. The 40 rooms, each with either a small patio or balcony, are spread around a gorgeous pool. Bicycles and kayaks are available for guests, as are the nature trails, dotted with hammocks, through the grounds.

✕ Eating

★ Barry's Golden Jerk
JAMAICAN $

(Cross Rd; meals US$12; ⊙ from 3pm Thu-Sat) Barry's roadside shack will sate your craving for jerk chicken and pork, served with fresh baked bread. He's only here three days a week, but if you time it right, you'll see (and smell) the spicy goodness being cooked up in the oil-drum smoker in the yard.

Star Island Restaurant
CAYMANIAN $

(137 West End Rd; sandwiches US$5-8, mains US$10-15; ⊙ 8am-8pm Mon-Sat) The definitive local favorite. The menu is extensive, with well-stuffed omelets, burgers and sandwiches. But the highlight is the old-fashioned Caymanian cooking, including fish stew and shrimp curry.

❶ Information

Cayman National Bank (West End Cross Rd; ⊙ 9am-4pm Mon-Fri) Has a 24-hour ATM and currency exchange.

Faith Hospital (p282) This modern hospital serves both the Brac and Little Cayman.

Post Office (West End; ⊙ 8:30am-5pm Mon-Fri)

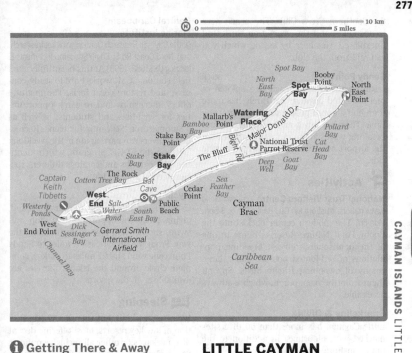

ⓘ Getting There & Away

Gerrard Smith International Airport is located at the west end of the island. **Cayman Airways Express** (www.caymanairways.com) operates several daily flights to Grand Cayman (US$130, 40 minutes) and Little Cayman (US$40, 10 minutes).

ⓘ Getting Around

There's no public transportation on Cayman Brac, but it's not that difficult to get around without a car. Lodging providers will pick you up by prior arrangement. Bikes may be rented or borrowed from the resorts. The negligible crime rate – and the amiability of the locals – makes hitchhiking safe and easy. The mere sight of a visitor marching down the roadway often results in ride offers by passing motorists.

All that said, if you intend to do extensive exploring of the island, the best way to do it is to rent a car from **B&S Motor Ventures Ltd** (☑ 948-1646; www.bandsmv.com; 126 Channel Rd SW; ☺ 8am-5pm) or **CB Rent-A-Car** (☑ 948-2424; www.cbrentacar.com; Gerrard Smith International Airport; ☺ 8am-6:30pm). You can also catch a lift from **Elo's Taxi** (☑ 948-0220) or **Hill's Taxi** (☑ 948-0540).

LITTLE CAYMAN

The clue is in the name. Little Cayman is tiny indeed, but it abounds with birdlife, marine life and glorious natural scenery. With more resident iguanas than humans, this delightful island is the place to head for solitude, tranquility and the odd spot of extraordinary diving.

⊙ Sights

The sights of Little Cayman are almost entirely natural, whether they be the birds that nest in the wetlands, the marine life lurking on the reef or the iguanas basking by the road.

Little Cayman Museum   MUSEUM
(www.littlecaymanmuseum.org; Guy Banks Rd, Blossom Village; ☺1:30-3pm Mon-Thu, 2-5pm Fri, 10:30am-noon Sat) **FREE** Housed in new quarters, this is an impressive museum for a little island. Stop by to peruse exhibits on the history of Cayman, as well as a display of wonderful underwater photography.

Owen Island   ISLAND
Stroke your inner pirate at this tiny deserted island that's a quarter-mile offshore from

the Southern Cross Club. The beach here is unspoiled and the vegetation thick and unexplored. Get here by kayak, which you can rent from the club.

Sandy Point   BEACH

Little Cayman's best beach is a splotch of reef-protected powder that rarely has more than half a dozen people visiting at any one time. There's a tiny pier, limited shade and breaking waves 200m out. It's 8 miles from the airport, which makes for a nice bicycle ride.

🏃 Activities

National Trust Visitors Centre   BIRDWATCHING

(www.nationaltrust.org.ky; Guy Banks Rd; ⏱ 3-5pm Mon-Fri) The modern center backs onto the Booby Pond Nature Reserve, home to one of the hemisphere's largest breeding populations of red-footed boobies and a large colony of swooping frigate birds. Spy on them from the back porch, which is always accessible.

Snorkeling & Diving

Little Cayman has more than 60 dive sites marked with moorings, in addition to the many onshore sites that are accessible for snorkelers and shore divers. Almost all of the hotels and resorts have diving operations.

★ Bloody Bay Marine Park   DIVING

At a depth of only 18ft, Bloody Bay Wall plummets vertically into aquamarine infinity as the divers hovering over the abyss wonder whether they are hallucinating. Located on the north side of the island, Bloody Bay includes some two dozen spectacular named dive sites.

Conch Club Divers   DIVING

(☑ 948-1026; www.conchclubdivers.com; Guy Banks Rd; 2-tank dive US$95-110) This independent dive operation is located at the Conch Club condos, but they offer their top-notch valet service to anyone on the island. The 42ft *Sea-Esta* takes divers and snorkelers to the Bloody Bay Wall and other excellent sites around the island.

Jackson's Point   SNORKELING

Just about 50m from the narrow beach on the shore, there is a mini-wall under the waves. If the water is not too rough, there are some nice spots for snorkeling, making Jackson's Point a perfect stop on a round-island bike ride. Look for the entrance opposite the turn-off to Olivine Kirk Dr.

Central Caribbean Marine Institute   DIVING

(Little Cayman Research Center; www.reefresearch.org; Nord Coast Rd E; Edge/Seacamp incl meals & lodging US$1688/1999) At this beautifully sited field station, CCMI works hard to study, conserve and restore coral reefs. The institute offers internships and research opportunities for scientists and students, as well as a summertime 'Seacamp' for teens. Recreational divers can participate in the weeklong 'Dive on the EDGE' program, which identifies, photographs and catalogs different species of coral and sea life.

Cycling

Cycling is a fantastic way to tour the island, giving plenty of opportunity to stop and swim, snorkel and spy on birds along the way. From the airport, it's 8 miles to Sandy Point (one way) and 22 miles to make a complete circle around the island. Bicycles are available at all the resorts.

🛏 Sleeping

It's a small island, but there's a good selection of low-key resorts, most offering decent dive packages or other all-inclusive options. Some close in September and/or October. Most prefer weeklong bookings.

★ Pirates Point Resort   RESORT $$

(☑ 948-1010; www.piratespointresort.com; Guy Banks Rd; r per person incl meals from US$240; ❄@🤖🏊) This rustic resort in a fantastic location was founded by the legendary Gladys Howard, an avid conservationist and supporter of all things Caymanian, who sadly passed away in 2015. Now run by Gladys's daughter, the place is known for comfortable rooms, warm hospitality and amazing food – worth a visit even if you're not staying here. The dive packages offer excellent value.

Paradise Villas   VILLA $$

(☑ 948-0001; www.paradisevillas.com; Blossom Village; s/d/tr US$200/225/245; ❄@🤖🏊) Just a few steps from the airport, this friendly property is a longtime favorite for its unpretentious charm and oceanfront setting. Twelve smart cottages are right on the beach, with private verandas and swinging hammocks to catch the breeze. The property was recently purchased by new owners, so changes may be in store.

Southern Cross Club   RESORT $$$

(☎ 948-1099; www.southerncrossclub.com; Guy Banks Rd; all-incl 5 nights per person US$1638-1919; ❄ @ 🛜 ⛵) ⟋ Definitely the classiest place on the island, Southern Cross is a gorgeous, boutique operation with an ecoconscious approach. There are 14 pastel-colored bungalows, most with private porches and outdoor showers, all with glorious views. Guests rave about the meals provided by Chef Anu and his team.

Little Cayman Beach Resort   RESORT $$$

(☎ 948-1033; www.littlecayman.com; Guy Banks Rd; d incl meals from US$350, 2-tank dive US$108; ❄ @ 🛜 ⛵) The largest resort on the island (which is not saying much) is a perfect base for your diving vacation. Some 28 stylishly tropical rooms surround the pool, while an additional dozen have private balconies facing the ocean. The property is dreamy, with hammocks swaying and the friendly, fun Beach Nuts bar keeping folks happy.

✖ Eating

There are only a handful of restaurants on Little Cayman, almost all of which are located at the resorts. You may want to take advantage of that all-inclusive option. Otherwise, you'll appreciate a kitchen in your rental unit.

Village Square Store   MARKET $

(Guy Banks Rd, Blossom Village; ⊘ 9am-5pm) Groceries, beer and other basic necessities, such as phone cards and insect repellent.

ℹ Information

Cayman National Bank (Village Sq, Guy Banks Rd; ⊘ 10am-4:30pm Mon-Fri) Has an ATM.

Post Office (Blossom Village; ⊘ 9:30am-noon, & 1:30-3pm Mon-Fri, 10:30am-1:30pm Sat)

ℹ Getting There & Away

Tiny Edward Bodden Airfield is a short walk from town. **Cayman Airways Express** (www.caymanairways.com) runs several daily flights to Grand Cayman (US$130, 35 minutes) and Cayman Brac (US$40, 10 minutes).

ℹ Getting Around

Cycling is the preferred mode of transportation on the island, and nearly every hotel makes bicycles available for guests. Be sure to take plenty of water, as the Village Square Store is your main source.

Scooters are also available from **Scooten Scooters** (☎ 916-4971; www.scootenscooters.

HURRICANE IVAN

In September 2004, Hurricane Ivan gave Grand Cayman a body blow, causing such widespread destruction that tourism was halted and a curfew enforced for several months to prevent looting. Fortunately, Cayman Brac and Little Cayman did not receive a direct hit and damage to the smaller islands was limited, but much of Grand Cayman was devastated. While the damage has been repaired and the island has been rebuilt (and then some), the hurricane remains fresh in the memories of many islanders.

com; 3hr/24hr from US$35/55; ⊘ Nov-Jun). You'll need a Cayman Islands driving permit, but then you'll have free access to the whole island on scooter. Pick-up and drop-off are included in the price.

UNDERSTAND THE CAYMAN ISLANDS

History

Las Tortugas

For the first century after Christopher Columbus happened upon the Cayman Islands in 1503, the islands remained uninhabited by people – which may explain why the place was overrun with sea turtles, giving the islands their original Spanish name, Las Tortugas. The sun-bleached landscape languished in a near-pristine state, undisturbed but for the occasional intrusion of sailors stopping in to swipe some turtles and fill up on fresh water. No permanent settlers set up house until well after the 1670 acquisition of the islands by the British Crown, which has held dominion over the three islands ever since.

Settlement & Growth

Once settlers started trickling in from Jamaica in the early 18th century, Caymanians quickly established their reputation as world-class seafarers. From the 1780s the Caymanian shipbuilding industry produced schooners and other seacraft used for trade and turtling. According to local legend, the islands' status as a tax haven dates back to 1794, when local residents lent assistance at the Wreck of the 10 Sail (p274).

By 1800 the population still numbered fewer than 1000 – of whom half were slaves. Originally dependencies of Jamaica, the islands eventually established their own local legislature, with a capital at Bodden Town. Here, at Pedro St James (p271), the Slavery Abolition Act was first read in 1835.

The population continued to grow – quintupling by the turn of the 20th century – while the economy remained tied to the sea, with fishing, turtling and shipbuilding as the main industries.

Tourism & Development

The Cayman Islands appeared on the international tourist map as early as the 1950s, when the islands were discovered by divers and fishers. Initially, islanders were understandably protective of their little slice of paradise and slow to relinquish their isolation. By the next decade, however, Caymanians had begun fashioning the tax structure that's made Grand Cayman an economic powerhouse – and designing an infrastructure that's made it a capital of Caribbean tourism.

People & Culture

For centuries, the Cayman Islands had been left to simmer undisturbed in their own juices as the rest of the world rushed headlong into modernity. As recently as 50 years ago (aside from a few adventurers and fishing nuts) there were few tourists. Electric power was provided solely by noisy generators, and most islanders did without it. What has occurred between then and now constitutes a Caymanian cultural revolution, with the advent of large-scale tourism and big-business banking.

Historically, the population is an amalgamation of British, Jamaican and African peoples, but contemporary Cayman has become even more multifaceted. Nowadays, North America is well represented, as are Europe, South America and Southeast Asia. This large influx of expatriate workers – representing more than 80 countries – means that native-born Caymanians make up just half of the population in their own country.

Landscape & Wildlife

The Land

Located approximately 150 miles south of Cuba and 180 miles west of Jamaica, the Cayman Islands consist of Grand Cayman and two smaller islands – Cayman Brac and Little Cayman – 75 miles to the northeast and 5 miles apart. All three islands are low-lying, flat-topped landmasses, although Cayman Brac does have a 140ft cliff, by far the most dramatic scenery in the country. In fact, the Cayman Islands are the tips of massive submarine mountains that barely emerge from the awesome Cayman Trench, an area with the deepest water in the Caribbean.

Encircling all three of the islands are shallow waters and a reef system harboring one of the world's richest accumulations of marine life. At Bloody Bay Wall, on the north shore of Little Cayman, the seafloor ends abruptly at a depth of only 18ft to 25ft, dropping off into a 6000ft vertical cliff. Along its sheer face grows an astonishing variety of corals, sponges and sea fans and thousands of marine creatures.

Flora & Fauna

With nearly 200 native winged species, the islands offer outstanding birdwatching. Keep your eyes open and you'll spot parrots, boobies, yellow-bellied sapsuckers, herons and egrets. Reptiles include celebrities such as green sea turtles and blue and rock iguanas, and plenty of common geckos and lizards (the latter sometimes making an appearance in the baths of luxury hotels). Cayman tries to balance protecting the environment with development – driving on beaches is against the law due to the harm this can do to turtle habitats, iguanas have the right of way and there are plentiful marine replenishment zones where fishing is not permitted.

The islands' landscape is dry and scrubby. Poisonous species include maiden plum (a weed with rash-causing sap), lady's hair or cowitch (a vine with fiberglass-like barbs) and the vicious manchineel tree, which produces a skin-blistering sap. Take care not to shelter under a manchineel in the rain! Other indigenous plants are cochineel, used as a shampoo as well as eaten, and pingwing, whose barbed branches were once fashioned into natural fences.

SURVIVAL GUIDE

ⓘ Directory A–Z

ACCOMMODATIONS

Upscale resorts and vacation condominiums line the beaches of the Cayman Islands, especially Seven Mile Beach, but independent hotels and guesthouses are few and far between. Prices are high, but so are standards.

Booking Services

Cayman Villas (☏ 800-235-5888; www. caymanvillas.com; ☉ 9am-5pm Mon-Fri) This long-standing service offers vacation properties for rental by the night or for longer stays. There is a wide variety of sizes, styles and locations, but each property is carefully inspected to guarantee high standards of quality and comfort.

ACTIVITIES

Cycling

Cycling is always a fantastic way to explore a new place, and the Cayman Islands are no exception.

On Grand Cayman, **West Bay Loop** (p269) is a popular route and tour, while **Eco Rides** (p274) offers informative tours of the East End. Alternatively, rent a bike from **Cayman Auto Rentals** (p269) and go it alone.

Little Cayman is also ideal for independent exploration by bicycle, and all the resorts offer bikes for their guests.

Diving & Snorkeling

Warm temperatures, amazing visibility and robust reefs make Grand Cayman a top choice for divers. Arguably, there are better, more pristine sites on Cayman Brac and Little Cayman, but the diving around Grand Cayman is also fantastic – and unlikely to disappoint.

Several excellent resorts cater almost exclusively to divers, including **Sunset House** (p265), **Cobalt Coast** (p270), **Compass Point** (p274) and **Lighthouse Point** (p270). These resorts offer discounts on dive packages, gear rental and storage and excellent shore diving on-site.

There are a slew of other dive shops around the island, especially in George Town and along Seven Mile Beach. Many offer easy shore access to a 'house reef', in addition to boat dives and gear rental. Two-tank dives usually run US$105 to US$115.

The resorts on Little Cayman and Cayman Brac cater almost exclusively to divers and have easy access to numerous good dive sites.

Fishing

The clear, warm waters of the Cayman Islands are teeming with blue marlin, wahoo, tuna and mahi-mahi. Charter a boat (half-day charters about US$600, full-day charters US$900 to US$1200) with an experienced Caymanian captain and hook some real action. Fishing charters include **Blue Water Excursions** (p263) and **Red Sail Sports** (p263).

Kayaking

Several operators offer kayak rental and tours, including trips through the mangroves and to luminescent Bio Bay:

➧ **Action Watersports** (☏ 548-3147; www.ci actionmarine.com; 278 Crighton Dr, Safe Haven; kayak per hr US$20, waverunner per 30min US$75, tour per person from US$60; ☉ 8am-6pm Mon-Sat)

➧ **Cayman Kayaks** (p272)

➧ **Sea Elements** (p263)

➧ **Sweet Spot Kaibo** (p272)

CHILDREN

Cayman is a fantastic destination for families, with countless sights and activities to entertain the kiddies, and plenty of facilities to make life easier for their parents.

Sights & Activities for Kids

The beaches of Grand Cayman are perfect for children, with warm, gentle water and sparkling, white sand. **Seven Mile Beach** (p261) has the most facilities, including a playground, but any beach will do. **Starfish Point** (p272) is a giant touch tank, with countless sea stars just waiting to be discovered.

When your family needs a break from the sun, the **Cayman National Museum** (p261) features a multimedia presentation and kid-friendly exhibits on the islands' history. **Crystal Caves** (p272) is an awesome place for kids (and adults) to explore.

The Sister Islands are geared more to divers and less to families, although kids will get a thrill out of exploring the **caves** (p275) on Cayman Brac or investigating **Owen Island** (p277) near Little Cayman.

The array of aquatic activities for kids is seemingly endless:

Stingray City (p264) Up-close interactions with stingrays, followed by a few stops for easy snorkeling.

Spotts Beach (p271) Snorkeling with sea turtles is a treat, but beware of currents.

Kayaking (p261) Kids will get a kick out of paddling around Bio Bay in Grand Cayman.

Atlantis Adventure (p263) Explore under the sea without getting wet!

Back on dry land, landlubber children will enjoy:

Barkers National Park (p269) Where they can go horseback riding.

West Bay Loop (p269) Excellent for children who can ride.

Need to Know

Condominiums are ubiquitous on Grand Cayman, so families can make themselves comfortable with multiple bedrooms, living space and kitchens. Alternatively, most resorts have plenty of rooms that sleep four people or more. Resorts and hotels also offer babysitting services or programmed activities for kids.

ELECTRICITY

110V, 60Hz; US-style two- and three-pin plugs are used.

EMBASSIES & CONSULATES

Citizens of the US should contact the embassy in Kingston, Jamaica.

UK Governor's Office (☑ 244-2434; www. gov.uk/government/world/cayman-islands; ☺ 8:30am-5pm Mon-Fri)

EMERGENCY & IMPORTANT NUMBERS

Police, fire, ambulance	☑ 911
Hurricane emergency operations	☑ 949-6555
Hyperbaric chamber	☑ 911

FOOD

You'll eat superbly almost anywhere in the Cayman Islands (though it won't be cheap). The combination of a large international community and plenty of cash sloshing about means that no effort is spared to import excellent fresh food and specialties from around the world. Plus, there's a rocketing interest in farm-to-table dining, or sea-to-table as the case may be. See www.nationaltrust.org.ky/seasense for sustainable seafood choices.

Essential Food & Drink

Caymanian cuisine centers mostly on what can be caught in the sea, but look out for all of these local specialties.

Conch A popular item on restaurant menus – look for farm-raised versions as conch in the wild are endangered. This large pink mollusk is cooked with onion and spices in a stew, fried up as fritters, or sliced raw and served with a lime marinade.

Jelly ice Chilled coconut water sucked from the shell.

Mannish water Stewy mixture of yams plus the head and foot of a goat; it may cure impotency, and it may not.

Mudslide A delightfully creamy cocktail combining Kahlua, Baileys and vodka – invented at Rum Point.

Tortuga rum cake A heavy, moist cake available in a number of addictive flavors; makes a great gift to take home.

GLBT TRAVELERS

Homosexuality is legal in Cayman, but the islands remain very conservative and discretion is advised. Same-sex unions are recognized for immigration purposes, thanks to a 2016 ruling by the European Court of Human Rights. Most hotels accommodate same-sex couples but any kind of public display of affection is taboo. There are no gay bars or clubs in the Cayman Islands.

HEALTH

Healthcare in Cayman is not free, though UK nationals may receive medical treatments for reduced cost or, in some cases, for free. Health insurance is required for all Cayman residents and recommended for all visitors.There are excellent medical facilities in the Cayman Islands:

Cayman Islands Hospital (☑ 949-2489, 949-8600; www.hsa.ky; 95 Smith Rd, George Town; ☺ 24hr) Grand Cayman's medical facility has a state-of-the-art recompression chamber.

Faith Hospital (☑ 948-2243; 215 Dennis Foster Rd, Stake Bay) This modern hospital serves both the Brac and Little Cayman.

LEGAL MATTERS

The Royal Cayman Islands Police Service maintains a visible presence in Cayman, though the service has been the target of criticism for a lack of responsiveness to tourist concerns.

All drugs are illegal in the Cayman Islands, and drug laws are strictly enforced. Littering is also a crime that is punishable by fines (up to CI$500) and even jail time.

EATING PRICE RANGES

The following price categories are for the cost of a main course.

$	less than US$15
$$	US$15–US$25
$$$	more than US$25

MONEY

ATMs are widely available, dispensing both US dollars (US$) and Cayman Island dollars (CI$). Credit cards are accepted by most hotels and restaurants.

Exchange Rates

AUSTRALIA	A$1	CI$0.63
CANADA	C$1	CI$0.61
EUROPE	€1	CI$0.91
JAPAN	¥100	CI$0.79
NEW ZEALAND	NZ$1	CI$0.57
UK	£1	CI$1.00
US	US$1	CI$0.82

For more exchange rates, see www.xe.com

Tipping

Restaurants A tip of 15% is usually included in the bill. If not, tip to that amount (or more, for exceptional service).

Resorts Often include a 15% service charge on the bill. Otherwise, tip $1 to $3 a day for housekeeping.

Taxis 10%

Tour Guides US$10 for half-day outing.

PUBLIC HOLIDAYS

New Year's Day January 1

National Heroes' Day Fourth Monday in January

Ash Wednesday First Wednesday of Lent (usually late February)

Good Friday Friday before Easter

Easter Monday Monday after Easter

Discovery Day Third Monday in May

Queen's Birthday Second Monday in June

Constitution Day First Monday in July

Remembrance Day Second Monday in November

Christmas December 25

Boxing Day December 26

TAXES & REFUNDS

There is no sales tax on the Cayman Islands (of course not, it's a tax haven!). There is, however, a 13% accommodation tax. You will also pay a vehicle environmental fee (US$4 to US$8 per day) and a licensing fee (about $2 per day) on vehicle rentals.

TELEPHONE

To call locally, just dial the seven-digit number with no area code or country code.

Country code	☑ 1
Area code	☑ 345

PRACTICALITIES

Newspapers The Cayman Islands has a number of news outlets: *The Cayman Compass* (www.caymancompass.com), *The Cayman Reporter* (www.cayman-reporter.com) and *The Cayman News Service* (https://caymannewsservice.com). Some UK papers are sold in touristy areas.

TV The government-owned TV station CIGTV broadcasts on channel 23 and Logic TV.

Smoking Smoking is prohibited in all public places, including bars, restaurants, hotels, parks and public transportation.

Weights & Measures The imperial system is used.

TIME

The Cayman Islands are in the Eastern time zone (EST) which is five hours behind Greenwich Mean Time. Daylight saving time is not observed.

TRAVELERS WITH DISABILITIES

Grand Cayman is a relatively friendly destination for travelers with disabilities:

➡ Many resorts offer accessible rooms, including **Sunshine Suites** (p265). Many restaurants and shopping malls around the island are also wheelchair accessible.

➡ Other services are available such as beach wheelchair rental.

➡ **Accessible Caribbean Vacations** (www.accessiblecaribbeanvacations.com) offers sightseeing tours and snorkel excursions (including Stingray City) for wheelchair-bound travelers.

➡ Wheelchair-accessible activities include **Queen Elizabeth II Botanic Park** (p272) and **Cayman Turtle Center** (p269).

➡ Wheelchair-accessible boats and vans facilitate transportation and boat tours.

➡ George Town and Seven Mile Beach have well-maintained sidewalks, most of which have ramps. (Outside the capital, sidewalks are not common.)

There is one major challenge that wheelchair-bound travelers may face. The cruise ships do not dock at a pier, but rather shuttle passengers to shore on tenders. These smaller boats have ramps that allow wheelchairs on and off, but access may be prohibited by bad weather or other factors.

Download Lonely Planet's free Accessible Travel guide from http://lptravel.to/Accessible Travel.

VOLUNTEERING

In addition to the following options, **Volunteer Me** (www.volunteerme.ky) maintains a database of volunteer opportunities.

Blue Iguana Recovery Program (p272) Volunteers do hard labor at the Salina Reserve and Colliers Wilderness Reserve, including trail maintenance, fence building, nest digging and iguana counting.

Cayman Islands Humane Society (www. caymanislandshumanesociety.com) This organization depends on volunteers to help out with dog walking, cat care, administrative support, event planning, fundraising and more.

Central Caribbean Marine Institute (p278) Sign up to the weeklong Dive on the EDGE, which involves identifying, photographing and cataloging different species of coral and sea life around Little Cayman.

National Gallery (p261) Support Cayman's most distinguished cultural institution.

Reef Environmental Education Foundation (REEF; www.reef.org) Divers and snorkelers can help protect the reef by participating in sea life surveys, including the Great Annual Fish Count (www.fishcount.org).

❶ Getting There & Away

Back in the day, adventurers would arrive in the Cayman Islands by pirate ship or, later, by sea plane. Nowadays, sea and air are still your only options, though the vehicles usually take the form of a cruise ship or a jet airplane.

AIR

Owen Roberts International Airport (GCM; www.caymanairports.ky) is Cayman's main portal to the outside world, with flights from North America and the UK.

In addition to major international carriers such as American Airlines and British Airways, the local **Cayman Airways** (www.caymanairways. com) operates flights to Cuba, Jamaica and Honduras, as well as the US (Chicago, Dallas, Miami, New York, Tampa).

SEA

Scores of cruise ships drop anchor in George Town. There are no deep-water port facilities so passengers shuttle ship to shore using frequent tenders. Visit Cayman Port Authority (www. caymanport.com) to determine what cruise ships will be in port when.

❶ Getting Around

There is no ferry service within the Cayman Islands, but there is public transportation around Grand Cayman.

AIR

Each island has a small airport. **Cayman Airways Express** (www.caymanairways.com), a subsidiary of Cayman Airways, provides near-monopoly service between the three islands.

BICYCLE

Bikes are readily available on all three islands and are often included as part of an accommodations package. Flat terrain, relatively light traffic and near-constant sea access make cycling a pleasure.

BUS

Minibuses run from the depot in **George Town** (cnr Fort St & Edward St) to other parts of Grand Cayman.

CAR & MOTORCYCLE

Driving is an essential part of life on the islands, with limited public transportation but plenty of parking. While traffic on the islands is light compared with big cities, it can still be surprisingly heavy in and around George Town and Seven Mile Beach, especially during rush hour.

➸ Driving is on the left-hand side (as you will be frequently reminded by signs all over the islands).

➸ Visitors must obtain a temporary driver's license from their car-rental agency (CI$16).

Car Rental

Most rentals are automatics, although 4WDs may have manual transmissions. A variety of models at competitive rates are available in Grand Cayman and fewer options on Cayman Brac. Scooter rentals are available on all three islands.

You must be aged at least 21 to rent a car in the Cayman Islands, and some rental agencies' insurance will not cover renters under 25; check with your rental company in advance.

While quoted rates can be surprisingly low, look out for the variable environmental recovery fee (US$4 to US$8 per day) and licensing fee (around US$2 per day) which are tacked on to the daily rate.

Road Rules

➸ Driving is on the left-hand side of the road.

➸ Seat-belt use is mandatory.

➸ Speed limits are very low; 25mph is common.

➸ Iguanas have right of way, which simply means don't hit the endangered critters.

Cuba

POP 11.2 MILLION / ☎53

Best Places to Eat

➡ Lamparilla 361 Tapas & Cervezas (p303)

➡ Doña Eutimia (p303)

➡ Tres Jotas (p313)

➡ La Redaccion Cuba (p320)

Best Places to Sleep

➡ Hotel Ordoño (p333)

➡ Roy's Terrace Inn (p331)

➡ Hostal Peregrino Consulado (p300)

➡ Hotel Iberostar Parque Central (p301)

Why Go?

Cuba is like a prince in a poor man's coat; behind the sometimes shabby facades, gold dust lingers. It's these rich dichotomies that make travel here the exciting, exhilarating roller-coaster ride it is. And, as a country on the cusp of change, there's rarely been a better time to visit. Private enterprise is displaying the first buds of a creative spring, while the big-name brands from that well-known frenemy in the north have yet to dilute the cultural magic. As a result, the country is rife with experimentation. Here a free-spirited cafe where earnest students sit around debating Che Guevara's contribution to world revolution; there an avant-garde art studio where the furniture is as outlandish as the exhibits. From rural Viñales to urban Havana, it's as if the whole country is slowly awakening from a deep slumber. Come now and ride the wave.

When to Go

Nov-Mar Peak season, with cooler weather, prices 30% higher and advance booking of hotels required.

Apr & Oct Look out for special deals, but prices and crowds increase with the onset of Easter.

May, Jun & Sep Smaller crowds, but some resort hotels offer fewer facilities or shut altogether.

Cuba Highlights

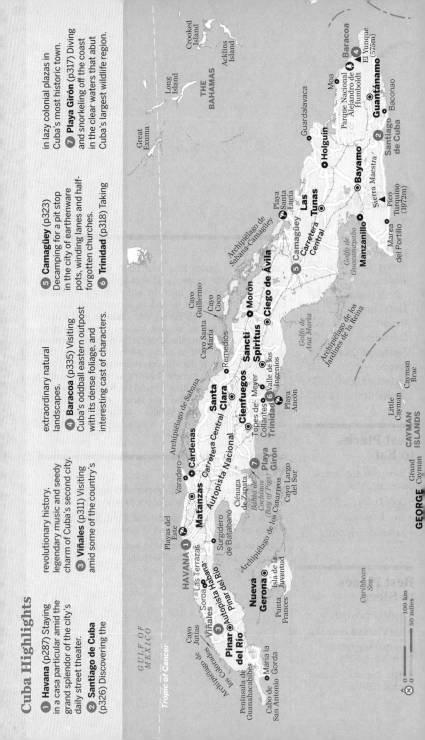

❶ **Havana** (p287) Staying in a casa particular amid the grand splendor of the city's daily street theater.

❷ **Santiago de Cuba** (p326) Discovering the revolutionary history, legendary music and seedy charm of Cuba's second city.

❸ **Viñales** (p311) Visiting amid some of the country's extraordinary natural landscapes.

❹ **Baracoa** (p335) Visiting Cuba's oddball eastern outpost with its dense foliage, and interesting cast of characters.

❺ **Camagüey** (p323) Decamping for a pit stop in the city of earthenware pots, winding lanes and half-forgotten churches.

❻ **Trinidad** (p318) Taking in lazy colonial plazas in Cuba's most historic town.

❼ **Playa Girón** (p317) Diving and snorkeling off the coast in the clear waters that abut Cuba's largest wildlife region.

HAVANA

📋 7 / POP 2.1 MILLION

No one could have invented Havana. It's too audacious, too contradictory, and – despite 50 years of withering neglect – too damned beautiful. How it does it is anyone's guess. Maybe it's the swashbuckling history still almost perceptible in atmospheric colonial streets; the survivalist spirit of a populace scarred by two independence wars, a revolution and a US trade embargo; or the indefatigable salsa energy that ricochets off walls and emanates most emphatically from the people. Don't come here with a long list of questions. Just arrive with an open mind and prepare for a long, slow seduction. Awaiting you lies history piled up like wrecked treasure on a palm-fringed beach; an art culture threatening to out-create Paris or New York; cool new cafes full of denizens plotting the next cultural revolution; and old-fashioned neighborhoods alive with aromas, rhythms, gossip and candid snippets of Cuban life.

⊙ Sights

Havana is like a museum of museums, so numerous are its collection of artifacts, from one of the best art galleries in the Caribbean to museums dedicated to coins, old playing cards and chocolate. Equally worth getting excited about are some magnificent forts, an eerily beautiful cemetery and enough provocative street art to fill a whole neighborhood – and beyond.

⊙ Habana Vieja

★ Plaza Vieja   SQUARE

(Old Square; Map p288) Laid out in 1559, Plaza Vieja is Havana's most architecturally eclectic square, where Cuban baroque nestles seamlessly next to Gaudí-inspired art nouveau. Originally called Plaza Nueva (New Square), it was initially used for military exercises and later served as an open-air marketplace.

During the Batista regime an ugly underground parking lot was constructed here, but this monstrosity was demolished in 1996 to make way for a massive renovation project. Sprinkled liberally with bars, restaurants and cafes, Plaza Vieja today has its own microbrewery, the Angela Landa primary school, a beautiful fenced-in fountain and, on its west side, some of Havana's finest *vitrales* (stained-glass windows). Several new bars and cafes give it a sociable buzz in the evenings.

★ Plaza de la Catedral   SQUARE

(Map p288) Habana Vieja's most uniform square is a museum to Cuban baroque, with all the surrounding buildings, including the city's beguiling asymmetrical cathedral, Catedral de la Habana, dating from the 1700s. Despite this homogeneity, it is actually the newest of the four squares in the Old Town, with its present layout dating from the 18th century.

★ Fortaleza de San Carlos de la Cabaña   FORT

(before/after 6pm CUC$6/8; ⊙10am-10pm) This 18th-century colossus was built between 1763 and 1774 on a long, exposed ridge on the east side of Havana harbor to fill a weakness in the city's defenses. In 1762 the British had taken Havana by gaining control of this strategically important ridge, and it was from here that they shelled the city mercilessly into submission. In order to prevent a repeat performance, the Spanish King Carlos III ordered the construction of a massive fort that would repel future invaders.

Measuring 700m from end to end and covering a whopping 10 hectares, it is the largest Spanish colonial fortress in the Americas. The impregnability of the fort meant that no invader ever stormed it, though during the 19th century, Cuban patriots faced firing squads here. Dictators Machado and Batista used the fortress as a military prison, and immediately after the revolution, Che Guevara set up his headquarters inside the ramparts to preside over another catalog of grisly executions (this time of Batista's officers).

These days the fort has been restored for visitors, and you can spend at least half a day checking out its wealth of attractions. As well as bars, restaurants, souvenir stalls and a cigar shop (containing the world's longest cigar), La Cabaña hosts the **Museo de Fortificaciones y Armas** (entry incl in La Cabaña ticket; ⊙10am-10pm) and the engrossing **Museo de Comandancia del Che** (entry incl in La Cabaña ticket; ⊙10am-10pm). The nightly 9pm *cañonazo* ceremony is a popular evening excursion in which actors dressed in full 18th-century military regalia re-enact the firing of a cannon over the harbor. You can visit the ceremony independently or as part of an organized excursion.

CUBA HAVANA

Habana Vieja

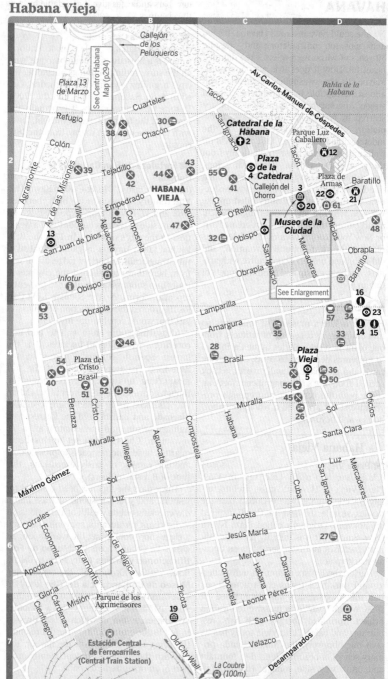

★ **Castillo de los Tres Santos Reyes Magnos del Morro** FORT

(El Morro; CUC$6; ☉10am-6pm) This wave-lashed fort with its emblematic lighthouse was erected between 1589 and 1630 to protect the entrance to Havana harbor from pirates and foreign invaders (French corsair Jacques de Sores had sacked the city in 1555). Perched high on a rocky bluff above the Atlantic, the fort has an irregular polygonal shape, 3m-thick walls and a deep protective moat, and is a classic example of Renaissance military architecture.

★ **Calle Mercaderes** AREA

(Map p288) Cobbled, car-free Calle Merca-deres (Merchant's Street) has been exten-sively restored by the City Historian's Office and is an almost complete replica of its splendid 18th-century high-water mark. Interspersed with the museums, shops and restaurants are some real-life working social projects, such as a maternity home and a needle-craft cooperative.

Most of the myriad museums are free, including the **Casa de Asia** (Map p288; Calle Mercaderes No 111; ☉10am-6pm Tue-Sat, 9am-1pm Sun) **FREE**, with paintings and sculpture from China and Japan; the **Armería 9 de Abril** (Map p288; Calle Mercaderes No 157; ☉9am-5pm Tue-Sat, 1-5pm Mon) **FREE**, an old gun shop (now museum) stormed by revo-lutionaries on the said date in 1958; and the **Museo de Bomberos** (Map p288; cnr Merca-deres & Lamparilla; ☉10am-6pm Mon-Sat) **FREE**, which has antediluvian fire equipment ded-icated to 19 Havana firefighters who lost their lives in an 1890 railway fire.

Just off Mercaderes down Obrapía, it's worth slinking into the **Casa de África** (Map p288; Obrapía No 157; ☉9:30am-5pm Tue-Sat, 9:30am-1pm Sun) **FREE**, which houses sacred objects relating to Santería and the secret Abakuá fraternity collected by ethnographer Fernando Ortíz.

The corner of Mercaderes and Obrapía has an international flavor, with a bronze statue of Simón Bolívar, the Latin Amer-ica liberator, and across the street you'll find the **Museo de Simón Bolívar** (Map p288; Calle Mercaderes No 160; donations accepted; ☉9am-5pm Tue-Sat, 9am-1pm Sun) dedicated to Bolívar's life. The **Casa de México Ben-ito Juárez** (Map p288; Obrapía No 116; CUC$1; ☉10:15am-5:45pm Tue-Sat, 9am-1pm Sun) exhib-its Mexican folk art and plenty of books, but not a lot on Señor Juárez (Mexico's first indigenous president) himself. Just east

CUBA HAVANA

Habana Vieja

is the **Casa Oswaldo Guayasamín** (Map p288; Obrapía No 111; ⊙9am-4:30pm Tue-Sun) FREE, now a museum, but once the studio of the great Ecuadorian artist who painted Fidel in numerous poses.

Mercaderes is also characterized by its restored shops, including a perfume store and a spice shop. Wander at will.

★ **Museo de la Ciudad**   MUSEUM
(Map p288; Tacón No 1; CUC$3; ⊙9:30am-6pm) Even with no artifacts, Havana's city museum would be a tour de force, courtesy of the opulent palace in which it resides. Fill-

ing the whole west side of Plaza de Armas, the **Palacio de los Capitanes Generales** (Map p288) dates from the 1770s and is a textbook example of Cuban baroque architecture, hewn out of rock from the nearby San Lázaro quarries. A museum has resided here since 1968.

★ **Catedral de la Habana**   CATHEDRAL
(Map p288; cnr San Ignacio & Empedrado; ⊙9am-4:30pm Mon-Fri, 9am-noon Sat & Sun) FREE 'Music set in stone' was how Cuban novelist Alejo Carpentier once described Havana's incredible cathedral, which is dominated by

two unequal towers and framed by a theatrical baroque facade designed by Italian architect Francesco Borromini. Construction of the church was begun by Jesuits in 1748 and work continued despite their expulsion in 1767. When the building was finished in 1787, the diocese of Havana was created and the church became a cathedral – it's one of the oldest in the Americas.

The remains of Columbus were brought here from Santo Domingo in 1795 and interred until 1898, when they were moved to Seville Cathedral in Spain.

A curiosity of the cathedral is its interior, which is neoclassical rather than baroque and relatively austere. Frescoes above the altar date from the late 1700s but the paintings that adorn the side walls are copies of originals by Murillo and Rubens. You can climb the smaller of the two towers for CUC$1.

Plaza de San Francisco de Asís   SQUARE

(Map p288) Facing Havana harbor, the breezy Plaza de San Francisco de Asís first grew up in the 16th century when Spanish galleons stopped by at the quayside on their passage through the Indies to Spain. A market took root in the 1500s, followed by a church in 1608, though when the pious monks complained of too much noise, the market was moved a few blocks south to Plaza Vieja.

The plaza underwent a full restoration in the late 1990s and is most notable for its uneven cobblestones and the white marble **Fuente de los Leones** (Fountain of Lions; Map p288), carved by the Italian sculptor Giuseppe Gaggini in 1836. A more modern statue outside the square's famous church depicts **El Caballero de París** (Map p288), a well-known street person who roamed Havana during the 1950s, engaging passersby with his philosophies on life, religion, politics and current events. The square's newest sculpture (added in 2012) is **La Conversación** (Map p288) by French artist Etienne, a modernist bronze rendition of two seated people talking.

Castillo de la Real Fuerza   FORT

(Map p288; Plaza de Armas; CUC$3; ⊙9am-5pm Tue-Sun) On the seaward side of Plaza de Armas is one of the oldest existing forts in the Americas, built between 1558 and 1577 on the site of an earlier fort destroyed by French privateers in 1555. Imposing and indomitable, the castle is ringed by an impressive moat and shelters the **Museo de Navegación**, which covers the history of the fort and Old Town, and its connections with the erstwhile Spanish Empire. Look out for the huge scale model of the *Santíssima Trinidad* galleon.

Edificio Bacardí   LANDMARK

(Bacardí Bldg; Map p288; Av de las Misiones, btwn Empedrado & San Juan de Dios; ⊙hours vary) Finished in 1929, the magnificent Edificio Bacardí is a triumph of art-deco architecture with a whole host of lavish finishes that somehow manage to make kitsch look cool. Hemmed in by other buildings, it's hard to get a full kaleidoscopic view of the structure from street level, though the opulent bell tower can be glimpsed from all over Havana.

Plaza de Armas   SQUARE

(Map p288) Havana's oldest square was laid out in the early 1520s, soon after the city's foundation, and was originally known as Plaza de Iglesia after a church – the Parroquial Mayor – that once stood on the site of the present-day Palacio de los Capitanes Generales.

The name Plaza de Armas (Square of Arms) wasn't adopted until the late 16th century, when the colonial governor, then housed in the Castillo de la Real Fuerza, used the site to conduct military exercises. Today's plaza, along with most of the buildings around it, dates from the late 1700s.

In the center of the square, which is lined with royal palms and hosts a daily (except Sundays) secondhand book market, is a marble **statue of Carlos Manuel de Céspedes**, the man who set Cuba on the road to independence in 1868. The statue replaced one of unpopular Spanish king Ferdinand VII in 1955.

Also of note, on the square's eastern aspect is the late-18th-century **Palacio de los Condes de Santovenia** today the five-star **Hotel Santa Isabel** (Map p288; ☑7-860-8201; www.habaguanexhotels.com; Baratillo No 9; r incl breakfast CUC$360; ❊@☎).

Calle Obispo   AREA

(Map p288) Narrow, chock-a-block Calle Obispo (Bishop's Street), Habana Vieja's main interconnecting artery, is packed with art galleries, shops, music bars and people. Four- and five-story buildings block out most of the sunlight, and the swaying throng of people seems to move in time to the beautiful din of competing live music that wafts out of every bar.

Museo-Casa Natal de José Martí MUSEUM
(Map p288; Leonor Pérez No 314; CUC$2; ⊙9:30am-5pm Tue-Sat, 9:30am-1pm Sun) Opened in 1925, this tiny museum, set in the house where the apostle of Cuban independence was born on January 28, 1853, is considered to be the oldest in Havana. The City Historian's Office took over the house in 1994, and its succinct stash of exhibits devoted to Cuba's national hero continues to impress.

⊙ Centro Habana

★**Museo Nacional de Bellas Artes** MUSEUM
(Map p294; www.bellasartes.cult.cu; each gallery CUC$5, combined entry to both CUC$8, under 14yr free; ⊙9am-5pm Tue-Sat, 10am-2pm Sun) Spread over two campuses, the Bellas Artes is arguably the finest art gallery in the Caribbean. The 'Arte Cubano' building contains the most comprehensive collection of Cuban art in the world, while the 'Arte Universal' section is laid out in a grand eclectic palace overlooking Parque Central, with exterior flourishes that are just as impressive as the art within.

The **Museo Nacional de Bellas Artes** (Arte Cubano; Map p294; www.bellasartes. cult.cu; Trocadero, btwn Agramonte & Av de las Misiones; CUC$5, under 14yr free; ⊙9am-5pm Tue-Sat, 10am-2pm Sun) displays purely Cuban art and, if you're pressed for time, is the better of the duo. Works are displayed in chronological order starting on the 3rd floor and are surprisingly varied. Artists to look out for are Guillermo Collazo, considered to be the first truly great Cuban artist; Rafael Blanco, with his cartoonlike paintings and sketches; Raúl Martínez, a master of 1960s Cuban pop art; and the Picasso-like Wifredo Lam.

Two blocks away, arranged inside the fabulously eclectic Centro Asturianos (a work of art in its own right), the **Museo Nacional de Bellas Artes** (Arte Universal; Map p294; www.bellasartes.cult.cu; San Rafael, btwn Agramonte & Av de las Misiones; CUC$5, under 14yr free; ⊙9am-5pm Tue-Sat, 10am-2pm Sun) exhibits international art from 500 BC to the present day on three separate floors. Its undisputed highlight is its Spanish collection with some canvases by Zurburián, Murillo, de Ribera and a tiny Velázquez. Also worth perusing are the 2000-year-old Roman mosaics, Greek pots from the 5th century BC and a suitably refined Gainsborough canvas (in the British room).

★**Malecón** WATERFRONT
(Map p294) The Malecón, Havana's evocative 7km-long sea drive, is one of the city's most soulful and quintessentially Cuban thoroughfares, and long a favored meeting place for assorted lovers, philosophers, poets, traveling minstrels, fishers and wistful Florida-gazers. The Malecón's atmosphere is most potent at sunset when the weak yellow light from creamy Vedado filters like a dim torch onto the buildings of Centro Habana, lending their dilapidated facades a distinctly ethereal quality.

★**Museo de la Revolución** MUSEUM
(Map p294; Refugio No 1; CUC$8, guided tours CUC$2; ⊙9:30am-4pm) This emblematic museum resides in the former **Presidential Palace**, constructed between 1913 and 1920 and used by a string of Cuban presidents, culminating in Fulgencio Batista. The world-famous Tiffany's of New York decorated the interior, and the shimmering Salón de los Espejos (Hall of Mirrors) was designed to resemble the eponymous room at the Palace of Versailles.

The museum itself descends chronologically from the top floor, focusing primarily on the events leading up to, during, and immediately after the Cuban revolution. It presents a sometimes scruffy but always compelling story told in English and Spanish, and tinted with *mucho* propaganda.

The palace's sweeping central staircase, guarded by a bust of José Martí, still retains the bullet holes made during an unsuccessful attack on the palace in March 1957 by a revolutionary student group intent on assassinating President Fulgencio Batista.

The stairs take you up to the 2nd floor and several important exhibit-free rooms, including the **Salón Dorado** (decorated in Louis VI style and once used for banquets), the **Despacho Presidencial** (president's office where Fidel Castro was sworn in, in 1959), and the **capilla** (chapel, with a Tiffany chandelier).

In front of the building is a fragment of the former city wall, as well as an SAU-100 tank used by Castro during the 1961 Bay of Pigs battle. In the space behind you'll find the **Pavillón Granma**, containing a replica of the 18m yacht that carried Fidel Castro and 81 other revolutionaries from Tuxpán, Mexico, to Cuba in December 1956. The boat is encased in glass and guarded 24/7, presumably to stop anyone from breaking in and sailing off to Florida in it. The pavilion is surrounded by other vehicles associated with the revolution, including planes, rockets and an old postal van used as a getaway car during the 1957 attack.

Paseo de Martí — HISTORIC SITE
(El Prado; Map p294) Construction of this stately European-style boulevard – the first street outside the old city walls – began in 1770, and the work was completed in the mid-1830s during the term of Captain General Miguel Tacón (1834–38). The original idea was to create a boulevard as splendid as any found in Paris or Barcelona (Prado owes more than a passing nod to Las Ramblas). The famous bronze lions that guard the central promenade at either end were added in 1928.

Capitolio Nacional — LANDMARK
(Map p294; cnr Dragones & Paseo de Martí) The incomparable Capitolio Nacional is Havana's most ambitious and grandiose building, constructed after the post-WWI sugar boom ('Dance of the Millions') gifted the Cuban government a seemingly bottomless bank vault of sugar money. Similar to the Washington, DC, Capitol building, but actually modeled on the Panthéon in Paris, the building was initiated by Cuba's US-backed dictator Gerardo Machado in 1926 and took 5000 workers three years, two months and 20 days to construct at a cost of US$17 million.

El Barrio Chino — AREA
(Map p294) One of the world's more surreal Chinatowns, Havana's Barrio Chino is notable for its gaping lack of Chinese people, most of whom left as soon as a newly inaugurated Fidel Castro uttered the word 'socialismo.' Nevertheless, it's worth a wander on the basis of its novelty and handful of decent restaurants.

Parque Central — PARK
(Map p294) Diminutive Parque Central is a verdant haven from the belching buses and roaring taxis that ply their way along the Paseo de Martí (Prado). The park, long a microcosm of daily Havana life, was expanded to its present size in the late 19th century after the city walls were knocked down. The 1905 marble statue of José Martí (Map p294) at its center was the first of thousands to be erected in Cuba.

☉ Vedado

★ Necrópolis Cristóbal Colón — CEMETERY
(Map p298; CUC$5; ☉8am-6pm, last entry 5pm) Havana's main cemetery (a national monument), one of the largest in the Americas, is renowned for its striking religious iconography and elaborate marble statues. Far from being eerie, a walk through these 57 hallowed hectares can be an educational and emotional stroll through the annals of Cuban history. A map (CUC$1) showing the graves of assorted artists, sportspeople, politicians, writers, scientists and revolutionaries is for sale at the entrance.

★ Museo Napoleónico — MUSEUM
(Map p298; San Miguel No 1159; CUC$3; ☉9:30am-5pm Tue-Sat, 9:30am-12:30pm Sun) Without a doubt one of the best museums in Havana and, by definition, Cuba, this magnificently laid-out collection of 7000 objects associated with the life of Napoleon Bonaparte was amassed by Cuban sugar baron Julio Lobo and politician Orestes Ferrara.

Hotel Nacional — HISTORIC BUILDING
(Map p298; cnr Calles O & 21; ☉free tours 10am & 3pm Mon-Fri, 10am Sat) Built in 1930 as a copy of the Breakers Hotel in Palm Beach, Florida, the eclectic art-deco/neoclassical Hotel Nacional is a national monument and one of Havana's architectural emblems.

The hotel's notoriety was cemented in October 1933 when, following a sergeants' coup by Fulgencio Batista that toppled the regime of Gerardo Machado, 300 aggrieved army officers took refuge in the building hoping to curry favor with resident US ambassador Sumner Welles, who was staying here. Much to the officers' chagrin, Welles promptly left, allowing Batista's troops to open fire on the hotel, killing 14 of them and injuring seven. More were executed later, after they had surrendered.

In December 1946 the hotel gained infamy of a different kind when US mobsters Meyer Lansky and Lucky Luciano used it to host the largest ever get-together of the North American Mafia, who gathered here under the guise of a Frank Sinatra concert.

These days the hotel maintains a more reputable face and the once famous casino is long gone, though the spectacular Parisian cabaret is still a popular draw. Nonguests can admire the Moorish lobby, stroll the breezy grounds overlooking the Malecón or

Centro Habana

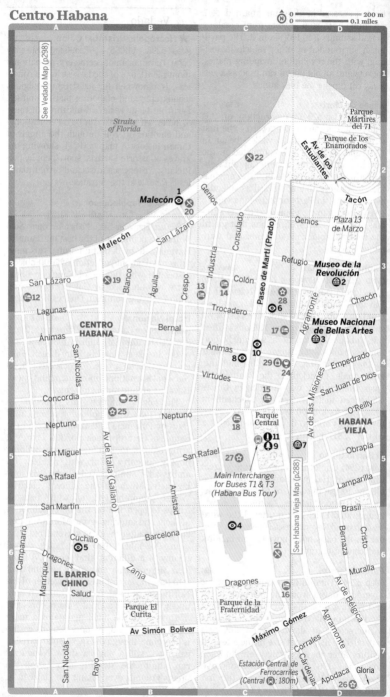

N

0 — 200 m
0 — 0.1 miles

See Vedado Map (p298)

Straits of Florida

Parque Mártires del 71

Parque de los Enamorados

Av de los Estudiantes

Tacón

Plaza 13 de Marzo

Genios

Malecón 1 ⊗20

Genios

Malecón

San Lázaro

Consulado

Paseo de Martí (Prado)

Refugio

Museo de la Revolución 2

Chacón

San Lázaro ⊗19

12

Lagunas

Blanco

Águila

Crespo

Industria

Colón

13 14

Trocadero

28 ⊙6

CENTRO HABANA

Bernal

Ánimas

8⊙ 10

17

Museo Nacional de Bellas Artes 3

Ánimas

San Nicolás

Virtudes

29 24

Empedrado

San Juan de Dios

O'Reilly

Concordia

Neptuno

25

Neptuno

15

18

Parque Central

Av de las Misiones

HABANA VIEJA

Obrapía

San Miguel

Av de Italia (Galiano)

23

San Rafael

San Rafael

27

11
9

7

Main Interchange for Buses T1 & T3 (Habana Bus Tour)

Lamparilla

Brasil

San Martín

Amistad

Barcelona

4

Bernaza

Cristo

Campanario

Manrique

Dragones

Cuchillo

5

Zanja

EL BARRIO CHINO

Salud

21

Muralla

Av de Bélgica

Dragones

16

See Habana Vieja Map (p288)

Agramonte

Parque El Curita

Parque de la Fraternidad

San Nicolás

Rayo

Av Simón Bolívar

Máximo Gómez

Corrales

Agramonte

Estación Central de Ferrocarriles (Central ☒: 180m)

Cárdenas

Apodaca

Gloria

26

Centro Habana

partake in a free guided hotel tour that runs at 10am every day except Sunday.

Plaza de la Revolución   SQUARE
(Map p298) Conceived by French urbanist Jean Claude Forestier in the 1920s, the gigantic Plaza de la Revolución (known as Plaza Cívica until 1959) was part of Havana's 'new city,' which grew up between 1920 and 1959. As the nexus of Forestier's ambitious plan, the square was built on a small hill (the Loma de los Catalanes) in the manner of Paris' Place de l'Étoile, with various avenues fanning out toward the Río Almendares, Vedado and the Parque de la Fraternidad in Centro Habana.

Surrounded by gray, utilitarian buildings constructed in the late 1950s, the square today is the base of the Cuban government and a place where large-scale political rallies are held. In January 1998, one million people (nearly one-tenth of the Cuban population) crammed into the square to hear Pope John Paul II say Mass.

The ugly concrete block on the northern side of the plaza is the **Ministerio del Interior**, well known for its huge mural of Che Guevara (a copy of Alberto Korda's famous 1960 photograph) with the words *Hasta la Victoria Siempre* (Always Toward Victory) emblazoned underneath. In 2009 a similarly designed image of Cuba's other heroic *guerrillero,* Camilo Cienfuegos, was added on the adjacent telecommunications building. Its wording reads: *Vas Bien Fidel* (You're going well Fidel).

On the eastern side is the 1957 **Biblioteca Nacional José Martí** FREE, which sometimes has a photo exhibit in the lobby, while on the west is the Teatro Nacional de Cuba (p308).

Tucked behind the **Memorial a José Martí** are the governmental offices housed in the heavily guarded **Comité Central del Partido Comunista de Cuba**.

Universidad de la Habana   UNIVERSITY
(Map p298; cnr Calles L & San Lázaro) Founded by Dominican monks in 1728 and secularized in 1842, Havana University began life in Habana Vieja before moving to its present site in 1902. The existing neoclassical complex dates from the second quarter of the 20th century, and today some 30,000 students here take courses in social sciences, humanities, natural sciences, mathematics and economics.

⮞ Tours

★**CubaRuta Bikes**   CYCLING
(☑ 52-47-66-33; www.cubarutabikes.com; Calle 16 No 152; city tour CUC$29) ✎ This was Havana first decent bicycle-hire and tour company

FUSTERLANDIA

Where does art go after Gaudí? For a hint, head west from central Havana to the seemingly low-key district of Jaimanitas, where Cuban artist José Fuster has turned his home neighborhood into a masterpiece of intricate tilework and kaleidoscopic colors – a street-art extravaganza that makes Barcelona's Park Güell look positively sedate. Imagine Gaudí on steroids relocated to a tropical setting.

The result is what is unofficially known as **Fusterlandia** (cnr Calle 226 & Av 3) `FREE`, an ongoing project first hatched around 20 years ago that has covered several suburban blocks with whimsical but highly stylized public art. The centerpiece is Fuster's own house, **Taller-Estudio José Fuster** (🕘 9am-4pm Wed-Sun) `FREE`, a sizable residence decorated from roof to foundations by art, sculpture and – above all – mosaic tiles of every color and description. The overall impression defies written description (just GO!), a fantastical mishmash of spiraling walkways, rippling pools and sunburst fountains. The work mixes homages to Picasso and Gaudí with snippets of Gauguin and Wifredo Lam, elements of magic realism, strong maritime influences, Santería, the curvaceous lines of *modernisme*, plus a large dose of Fuster's own Cubanness, which runs through almost everything. Look for the Cuban flags, a mural of the Granma yacht, and the words 'Viva Cuba' emblazoned across eight chimney pots.

Fusterlandia stretches way beyond Fuster's own residence. More than half the neighborhood has been given similar artistic treatment, from street signs to bus stops to the local doctor's house. Wandering around its quiet streets is a surreal and psychedelic experience.

Jaimanitas is located just off Quinta Avenida (Av 5) in the far west of Playa, sandwiched between Club Havana and Marina Hemingway. A taxi from central Havana will cost CUC$12 to CUC$15.

when it started in 2013. Their guided cycling tours have proved to be consistently popular, particularly the three-hour classic city tour, which takes in the Bosque de la Habana, Plaza Vieja, Plaza de la Revolución, the Malecón and more. Book via phone or email at least a day in advance.

★ **Havana Super Tour** TOURS
(Map p294; ☎ 52-65-71-01; www.campanario63.com; Campanario No 63, btwn San Lázaro & Lagunas; tours CUC$35) One of Havana's first private tour companies, Super Tour runs all its trips in classic American cars. The two most popular are the art-deco architectural tour and the 'Mob tour,' uncovering the city's pre-revolution Mafia haunts. If you're short on time, the full-blown Havana day tour (CUC$150) will whip you around all of the city's key sights.

🎒 Courses

★ **La Casa del Son** DANCING, LANGUAGE
(Map p288; ☎ 7-861-6179; www.bailarencuba.com; Empedrado No 411, btwn Compostela & Aguacate; per hr from CUC$10) A highly popular private dance school based in an attractive 18th-century house. It also offers lessons in Spanish language and percussion. Very flexible with class times.

🛏 Sleeping

With literally thousands of casas particulares (private houses) letting out rooms, you'll never struggle to find accommodation in Havana. Rock-bottom budget hotels can match casas for price, but not comfort. There's a dearth of decent hotels in the midrange price bracket, while Havana's top-end hotels are plentiful and offer oodles of atmosphere, even if the overall standards can't always match facilities elsewhere in the Caribbean.

🛏 Habana Vieja

★ **Greenhouse** CASA PARTICULAR $
(Map p288; ☎ 7-862-9877; fabio.quintana@infomed.sld.cu; San Ignacio No 656, btwn Merced & Jesús María; r CUC$30-40; ❄) A fabulous Old Town casa run by Eugenio and Fabio, who have added superb design features to their huge colonial home. Check out the terrace fountain and the backlit model of Havana on the stairway. There are seven rooms in this virtual hotel packed with precious

period furnishings and gorgeous wooden beds; two of them share a bathroom.

Hostal Calle Habana
CASA PARTICULAR $

(Map p288; ☑ 7-867-4081; www.hostalcalle habana.com; Habana No 559, btwn Brasil & Amargura; r CUC$30-40; ✻) This is one of a new wave of private casas that realistically qualify as small hotels. It's well managed and beautifully maintained with a small cafe (guests only) out front, and a profusion of art, plants and tiles throughout. The four rooms are clean and uncluttered, but punctuated with tasteful lamps and bright paintings.

Hostal El Encinar
CASA PARTICULAR $

(Map p288; ☑ 7-860-1257; www.hostalperegrino. com; Chacón No 60/Altos, btwn Cuba & Aguiar; r incl breakfast CUC$35-50; ✻) This outpost of Centro Habana's popular Hostal Peregrino is like a little hotel for independent travelers. Eight rooms all with private bathrooms are approaching boutique standard with classy tilework, hairdryers, TVs and minibars. There's a comfortable lounge area and a delightful roof terrace overlooking the bay and La Cabaña fort.

Penthouse Plaza Vieja
CASA PARTICULAR $

(Map p288; ☑ 7-861-0084; Mercaderes No 315-317; r CUC$60; ✻) A private penthouse in a historic central square – this place would cost thousands anywhere else, but in Havana you can still bag it for CUC$60. Fidel and Bertha's two rooms high above Plaza Vieja share a leafy terrace guarded by a Santería shrine.

Conde de Ricla Hostal
HOTEL $$

(Map p288; ☑ 52-91-63-23; www.condedericla hostal.com; San Ignacio No 402, btwn Sol & Muralla; d/ste CUC$100/150; ✻) It might not be obvious to first-timers in Cuba, but this place is rather unique; it's an early attempt at a truly *private* hotel as opposed to a casa particular (up until now all Cuban hotels have been government-owned). The five rooms pass the test – all are large, clean and equipped with minimalist boutique touches despite the colonial setting.

★ Hotel Los Frailes
HISTORIC HOTEL $$$

(Map p288; ☑ 7-862-9383; www.habaguanex hotels.com; Brasil No 8, btwn Oficios & Mercaderes; d/ste CUC$200/230; ✻@☎) There's nothing austere about Los Frailes (The Friars), despite the monastic theme (staff wear hooded robes), inspired by the nearby San Francisco de Asís convent. Instead, this is the kind of hotel you'll look forward to coming back to after a long day, to recline in large, historical rooms in your monkish dressing gown, with candlelight flickering on the walls.

Hostal Conde de Villanueva
HOTEL $$$

(Map p288; ☑ 7-862-9293; www.habaguanex hotels.com; Mercaderes No 202; s/d CUC$235/305; ✻@☎) If you want to splash out on one night of luxury in Havana, check out this highly lauded colonial hotel. Restored under the watchful eye of the City Historian in the late 1990s, the Villanueva has been converted from a grandiose city mansion into a thoughtfully decorated hotel with nine bedrooms spread around an attractive inner courtyard (complete with resident peacock).

Hotel Florida
HOTEL $$$

(Map p288; ☑ 7-862-4127; www.habaguanex hotels.com; Obispo No 252; d/ste CUC$245/305 incl breakfast; ✻@☎) They don't make them like this anymore. The Florida is an architectural extravaganza built in the purest colonial style, with arches and pillars clustered around an atmospheric central courtyard. Habaguanex has restored the 1836 building with loving attention to detail: the amply furnished rooms retain their original high ceilings and wonderfully luxurious finishes.

Hotel Raquel
HOTEL $$$

(Map p288; ☑ 7-860-8280; www.habaguanex hotels.com; cnr Amargura & San Ignacio; d/ste CUC$280/330; ✻@☎) Encased in a dazzling 1908 palace (that was once a bank), the Hotel Raquel gives you historical hallucinations with its grandiose columns, sleek marble statues and intricate stained-glass ceiling. Behind its impressive architecture, the Raquel offers well-presented if noisy rooms, a small gym and sauna, friendly staff and a great central location.

Hotel Armadores de Santander
HISTORIC HOTEL $$$

(Map p288; ☑ 7-862-8000; www.habaguanex hotels.com; Luz No 4, cnr San Pedro; d/ste CUC$235/305; ✻@☎) The Santander down by the harbor has a tangible nautical feel. You almost expect some old Spanish sailor to come strolling into the thin mahogany bar and start singing a sea shanty. The 32 rooms are variable. The split-level suites with their stained glass and spiral staircases are well worth the investment. The sundeck overlooking the harbor is another highlight.

Vedado

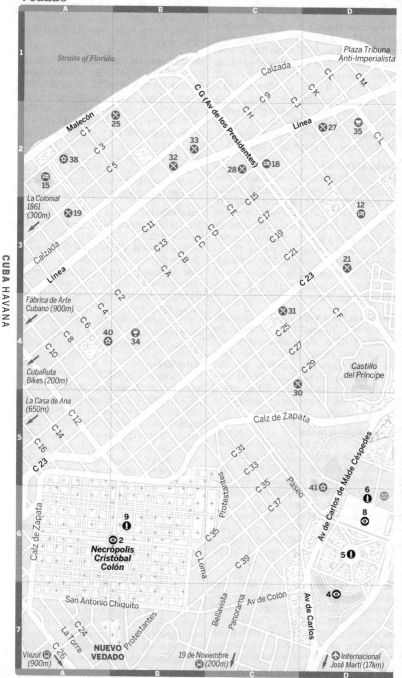

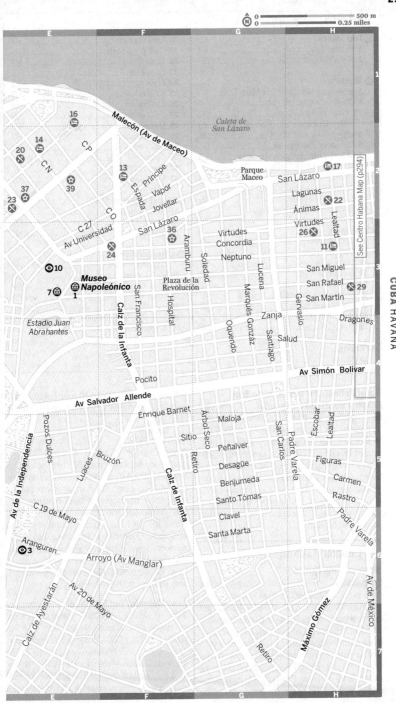

N

0 ——————— 500 m
0 ——————— 0.25 miles

See Centro Habana Map (p294)

CUBA HAVANA

Caleta de San Lázaro

Malecón (Av de Maceo)

16

14

20

C N

C P

37

23

13

39

C O

C 27

Av Universidad

Espada

Príncipe

Vapor

Jovellar

San Lázaro

36

24

10

Museo Napoleónico

7   1

Aramburu

Soledad

Hospital

Plaza de la Revolución

San Francisco

Calz de la Infanta

Estadio Juan Abrahantes

Parque Maceo

17

San Lázaro

Lagunas   22

Ánimas

Virtudes   26

11

Virtudes

Concordia

Neptuno

Lucena

Marqués González

Oquendo

Zanja

Salud

Santiago

Lealtad

San Miguel

San Rafael

San Martín

Gervasio

29

Dragones

Av Simón Bolívar

Pocito

Av Salvador Allende

Enrique Barnet

Árbol Seco

Maloja

Sitio

Retiro

Peñalver

Desagüe

Benjumeda

Santo Tómas

Clavel

Santa Marta

San Carlos

Padre Varela

Escobar

Lealtad

Figuras

Carmen

Rastro

Padre Varela

Av de la Independencia

Pozos Dulces

Luaces

Bruzón

C 19 de Mayo

Aranguren

3

Arroyo (Av Manglar)

Calz de Infanta

Av 20 de Mayo

Calz de Ayestarán

Máximo Gómez

Retiro

Av de México

Vedado

Hotel Palacio del Marqués de San Felipe y Santiago de Bejucal   HOTEL **$$$**
(Map p288; ☎7-864-9191; www.habaguanex hotels.com; cnr Oficios & Amargura; d CUC$360; ❉@❧) Cuban baroque meets modern minimalist in one of Habaguanex's more expensive offerings, and the results are something to behold. Spreading 27 rooms over six floors in the blustery Plaza de San Francisco de Asís, this place is living proof that Habana Vieja's delicate restoration work is getting better and better.

🛏 Centro Habana

★Hostal Peregrino

Consulado   CASA PARTICULAR **$**
(Map p294; ☎7-861-8027; www.hostalperegrino. com; Consulado No 152, btwn Colón & Trocadero; r incl breakfast CUC$35-50; ❉@) Julio Roque is a pediatrician who, along with his wife Elsa, has expanded his former two-room casa particular into a growing web of accommodations. His HQ, Hostal Peregrino, offers three rooms a block from Paseo de Martí (Prado) and is one of the most professionally run private houses in Cuba. Super-helpful Julio and Elsa are fluent in English and a mine of local information.

★Casa 1932   CASA PARTICULAR **$**
(Map p294; ☎7-863-6203, 52-64-38-58; www. casahabana.net; Campanario 63, btwn San Lázaro & Lagunas; r CUC$30-40; ❉@) The charismatic owner, Luis Miguel, is an art-deco fanatic who offers his house as both boutique private homestay and museum to the 1930s, when his preferred architectural style was in vogue. Collectibles, including old signs, mirrors, toys, furniture and stained glass, will make you feel like you've walked into a Clark Gable movie. There are three comfortable rooms and huge breakfasts.

Casa Colonial Yadilis & Yoel   CASA PARTICULAR **$**
(Map p294; ☎7-863-0565; www.casacolonial yadilisyyoel.com; Industria No 120/Altos, btwn Trocadero & Colón; r CUC$30-35; ❉) A magic formula: take a solid-pink colonial house in the thick of Centro Habana's street life, throw in four well-maintained, spacious rooms, an ample terrace and lavish breakfasts, then

add charming English-speaking hosts Yoel and Yadilis, who go above and beyond with tips and local information. The result: a casa that's highly professional and refreshingly down-to-earth.

Casa Amada
CASA PARTICULAR $

(Map p298; ☑ 7-862-3924; www.casaamada.net; Lealtad No 26/Altos, btwn Neptuno & Concordia; r CUC$30-40; ❄) A huge house with gracious hosts that offers five rooms (all with private bathrooms) and a communal roof terrace. An enclosed balcony out front overlooks the gritty cinematic street life that is Centro Habana.

Duplex Cervantes
APARTMENT $$

(Map p298; ☑ 52-54-36-29, 7-879-5486; duplex cervantes@gmail.com; Espada No 7 Apt 312, btwn Calle 25 & Calzada de Infanta; apt CUC$100-150; ⓟ❄) You won't find many of these in Havana – yet. A fully renovated, tastefully minimalist duplex apartment with three bedrooms, two bathrooms, lounge-dining room, kitchen and balcony. And you don't have to sacrifice on location either: you're still deep in the heart of the 'hood. English, French and Italian are spoken by the friendly owners and large breakfasts go for CUC$5 extra.

★Hotel Iberostar Parque Central
HOTEL $$$

(Map p294; ☑ 7-860-6627; www.iberostar.com; Neptuno, btwn Agramonte & Paseo de Martí; r from CUC$450; ⓟ❄@ 🖙 🏊) With the exception of perhaps the Hotel Saratoga, the Iberostar is Havana's best international-standard hotel, with service and business facilities on par with top-ranking five-star facilities elsewhere in the Caribbean. Although the fancy lobby and classily furnished rooms may lack the historical riches of Habana Vieja establishments, the ambience here is far from antiseptic.

★Hotel Saratoga
HOTEL $$$

(Map p294; ☑ 7-868-1000; www.saratogahotel-cuba.com; Paseo de Martí No 603; r CUC$506-1204; ⓟ❄@ 🖙 🏊) The glittering Saratoga is an architectural work of art that stands imposingly at the intersection of Paseo de Martí (Prado) and Dragones, with fantastic views over toward the Capitolio. Sharp, if officious, service is a feature here, as are the extra-comfortable beds, power showers, a truly decadent rooftop swimming pool and an exquisite hotel bar.

Hotel Terral
BOUTIQUE HOTEL $$$

(Map p298; ☑ 7-860-2100; www.habaguanex hotels.com; Malecón, cnr Lealtad; s/d CUC$235/305; ❄@ 🖙) A boutique hotel on Havana's semi-ruined sea drive that looks out across the water at Florida and compares notes. Despite being built (and run) by the City Historian's Office, Terral is not historic. On the contrary, the 14 ocean-facing rooms are chic, clean-lined and minimalist. A sinuous glass-fronted cafe-bar downstairs offers inviting sofas and great coffee.

Hotel Sevilla
HOTEL $$$

(Map p294; ☑ 7-860-8560; www.hotelsevilla-cuba.com; Trocadero No 55, btwn Paseo de Martí & Agramonte; s/d incl breakfast CUC$260/340; ⓟ❄@ 🖙 🏊) Al Capone once hired out the whole 6th floor, Graham Greene used room 501 as a setting for his novel *Our Man in Havana*, and the Mafia requisitioned it as operations center for their pre-revolutionary North American drugs racket. Nowadays the Moorish Sevilla still packs a punch, with its ostentatious lobby that could have been ripped straight out of Granada's Alhambra.

Hotel Telégrafo
HOTEL $$$

(Map p294; ☑ 7-861-4741, 7-861-1010; www.hoteltelegrafo-cuba.com; Paseo de Martí No 408; d/ste CUC$235/305; ❄@ 🖙) This bold royal-blue beauty on the northwest corner of Parque Central juxtaposes old-style architectural features (the original building hails from 1888) with futuristic design flourishes; these include big, luxurious sofas, a huge winding central staircase and an intricate tile mosaic emblazoned on the wall of the downstairs bar. The rooms are large and elegant.

🛏 Vedado

★Central Yard Inn
CASA PARTICULAR $

(Map p298; ☑ 7-832-2927; centralyardinn@ gmail.com; Calle I, btwn Calles 21 & 23; r CUC$30-40; ⓟ❄) Some of Havana's state-run hotels could learn a lot from this highly professional casa particular located in the middle of Vedado's nightlife zone. The yard in question is a stunner, beautified with plenty of greenery and a fountain, and surrounded by four hotel-standard rooms.

★La Colonial 1861
CASA PARTICULAR $

(☑ 7-830-1861; www.lacolonial1861.com; Calle 10 No 60, btwn Calles 3 & 5; d/f CUC$55/80; ❄) It's unusual to find a house this old in western Vedado, so make the most of the 1861, whose five private rooms (one is family-sized) are a riot of wrought iron, stained glass and mosaic floor tiles. The house is self-contained, with its own patio, common areas and antique furniture, and the owner is very knowledgeable about Havana's brilliant art scene.

La Casa de Ana
CASA PARTICULAR $

(☑7-833-5128; www.anahavana.com; Calle 17 1422, btwn Calles 26 & 28; CUC$30-35; ❄@) Don't be put off by the out-of-the-way location (western Vedado); there's plenty going on in this neck of the woods and the highly professional Casa de Ana will put you straight on everything from cheap transportation to where to find the best mojitos. Rooms are modern and clean, and service goes well beyond the call of duty. Book well in advance.

Marta Vitorte
CASA PARTICULAR $

(Map p298; ☑7-832-6475; www.casamartainhavana.com; Calle G No 301 Apt 14, btwn Calles 13 & 15; r CUC$40-60; P❄) Marta has lived in this craning apartment block on Av de los Presidentes since the 1960s. One look at the view and you'll see why – the glass-fronted wraparound terrace that soaks up 270 degrees of Havana's pockmarked panorama makes it seem as if you're standing atop the Martí monument. Not surprisingly, her four rooms are deluxe, with lovely furnishings, minibars and safes.

★ Casavana Cuba
CASA PARTICULAR $$

(Map p298; ☑58-04-92-58; www.casavanacuba.com; Calle G No 301, 5th fl, btwn Calles 13 & 15; r CUC$50-90; ❄) When casas particulares start to look like four-star hotels you know you're onto something. Encased in a *rascacielo* (skyscraper) in Vedado, Casavana's huge rooms are positively luxurious, with precious furniture and floors so polished you can virtually see your face in them. Behold the carved wooden beds and then drink in the wondrous views from your personal balcony.

★ Hotel Nacional
HOTEL $$$

(Map p298; ☑7-836-3564; www.hotelnacionaldecuba.com; cnr Calles O & 21; s/d CUC$338/468; P❄@📶≋) The cherry on the cake of Cuban hotels and a flagship of the government-run Gran Caribe chain, the neoclassical/neocolonial/art-deco (let's call it eclectic) Hotel Nacional is as much a city monument as it is an international accommodation option. Even if you haven't got the money to stay

here, find time to sip at least one minty mojito in its exquisite oceanside bar.

Hotel Meliá Cohiba
HOTEL $$$

(Map p298; ☑7-833-3636; www.meliacuba.com; Paseo, btwn Calles 1 & 3; s/d CUC$527/600; P❄@📶≋) Cuba's most business-like city hotel is an oceanside concrete giant built in 1994 (it's the only building from this era on the Malecón) that will satisfy the highest of international expectations with its knowledgeable, consistent staff and modern, well-polished facilities. After a few weeks in the Cuban outback you'll feel like you're on a different planet here.

Hotel Capri
HOTEL $$$

(Map p298; ☑7-839 7200; cnr Calles 21 & N; s/d CUC$290/350; P❄@📶≋) After spending more than a decade as a rotting ruin, one of Havana's most famous hotels was reborn as a quieter, less notorious version of its former self in 2014. And, rather like *The Godfather,* the sequel is better. The 19-story Capri has a sharp minimalist lobby and a rooftop pool. The rooms are slick and modern but not ostentatious.

✖ Eating

Havana's eating scene has progressed exponentially in recent years thanks to new laws governing private enterprise. The most condensed scene is in Habana Vieja. Playa, thanks to its diplomatic heritage, has traditionally harbored the city's most exclusive restaurants. Culinary experimentation has also proliferated. You can now find specialist Russian, Korean, Chinese, Iranian and Italian restaurants.

✖ Habana Vieja

Helad'oro
ICE CREAM $

(Map p288; ☑53-05-91-31; Aguiar No 206, btwn Empredrado & Tejadillo; ice cream CUC$2-4; ☺11am-10pm) Back when Fidel was 'king,' the government had a monopoly on many things, including ice cream, which was controlled by the legendary Coppelia and the flavors rarely strayed beyond *fresa y chocolate.* Then along came the economic defrosting of the 2010s, ushering in Helad'oro with its artisan ice cream dispensed in 30-plus different flavors, including mamey. Viva the ice-cream revolution!

Café Bohemia
TAPAS, CAFE $

(Map p288; ☑7-836-6567; www.havanabohemia.com; San Ignacio No 364; tapas CUC$6-10;

⊙10:30am-9:30pm) Inhabiting a beautifully curated mansion on Plaza Vieja, Café Bohemia – named for a Cuban culture and arts magazine – manages to feel appropriately bohemian, but also serves great cocktails, tapas and extremely addictive cakes.

D'Next
CAFETERIA $

(Map p288; ☎7-860-5519; Brasil No 512, btwn Av de las Misiones & Bernaza; snacks CUC$3-6; ⊙8:30am-midnight) The plastic black and red diner seats of D'Next provide a welcome pew for knackered travelers who've over-dosed on Che Guevara. One chunky chicken sandwich and guava fruit shake later and you'll be back on the revolutionary band-wagon, probably relieved to escape from the cafe's ear-splitting reggaeton music.

Café del Ángel Fumero Jacqueline
CAFE $

(Map p288; ☎7-862-6562; Compostela No 1, cnr Cuarteles; breakfast CUC$4-6; ⊙8am-11pm) Guarding the heavenly small square behind the Iglesia del Santo Ángel Custodio (the result of a foresighted community project), the highly minimalist Fumero is part cocktail bar, part ladies clothing boutique, and also one of the best breakfast spots in Habana Vieja. Pull up an alfresco chair for eggs, waffles and super-hot coffee.

★El Rum Rum de la Habana
SEAFOOD, SPANISH $$

(Map p288; ☎7-861-0806; Empedrado No 256, btwn Cuba & Aguiar; mains CUC$7-13; ⊙noon-mid-night) In Cuba, eating establishments are full of rum (the vital ingredient for mojitos) and *rum rum* (local term for gossip). And gossip we must, because El Rum Rum is the talk of Habana Vieja – an ambitious new restaurant run by a cigar sommelier that pays homage to seafood, Spanish gastronomy, cigars and throat-warming shots of the hard stuff.

★Lamparilla 361 Tapas & Cervezas
TAPAS $$

(Map p288; ☎52-89-53-24; Lamparilla No 361, btwn Aguacate & Villegas; tapas CUC$3-12; ⊙noon-midnight) What makes a new restaurant just...click? Come to this nascent place on Lamparilla (never really a happening street – until now) and try to work out the secret. Maybe it's the perfect tapa-sized lasagna, the crisp sautéed vegetables served in ceramic dishes, the rich espresso-flavored crème brûlée, or the table menus written on dried palm leaves.

★Doña Eutimia
CUBAN $$

(Map p288; Callejón del Chorro 60c; mains CUC$9-12; ⊙noon-10pm) Keep it simple. The secret at Doña Eutimia is that there *is* no secret. Just serve decent-sized portions of incredibly tasty Cuban food. The *ropa vieja* – shredded beef – and minced beef *pica-dillo* both deserve mentions. Doña Eutimia was the first private restaurant to grace this small cul-de-sac near the cathedral.

★Trattoria 5esquinas
ITALIAN $$

(Map p288; ☎7-860-6295; Habana No 104, cnr Cuarteles; mains CUC$5-11; ⊙11am-11pm) Best Italian restaurant in Havana? There are a few contenders, but 5esquinas is making a strong claim. It has the full trattoria vibe right down to the open glow of the pizza oven and the aroma of roasted garlic. Visiting Italians won't be disappointed with the seafood pasta (generous on the lobster) or the crab and spinach cannelloni. Round it off with tiramisu.

ChaChaChá
INTERNATIONAL $$

(Map p288; ☎7-867-2450; Av de las Misiones No 159, btwn Tejadillo & Chacón; mains CUC$7.50-14; ⊙noon-2am) Spanking new in 2016, ChaChaChá has presented a good opening dance. The food is a smattering of international fare, with early kudos to the sizzling fajitas and the well-executed pasta dishes. There's an attractive interior with a mezzanine, retro-50s Mob-era decor, vinyl records serving as place mats and a bistro-style open-fronted location luring people fresh out of the Museo de la Revolución and Bellas Artes.

Donde Lis
CUBAN $$

(Map p288; ☎7-860-0922; www.dondelis.com; Tejadillo No 163, btwn Habana & Compostela; mains CUC$5-12; ⊙noon-midnight) The Lis' interior is like a modern love letter to Havana; iconography from the Rat Pack era of the 1950s, reproduced 20th-century tropical art and bright colors are splashed onto old colonial walls. The menu is a carefully cultivated mélange of different flavors presenting Cuban staples with modern twists – octopus with guacamole, lobster enchilados – along with some Italian and Spanish cameos.

O'Reilly 304
INTERNATIONAL $$

(Map p288; ☎52-64-47-25; O'Reilly No 304; meals CUC$8-13; ⊙noon-midnight) Thinking up the name (the restaurant's address) can't have taken much imagination, so it is perhaps a little ironic that O'Reilly 304 serves up some of the most imaginative cuisine in Havana. Exquisite seafood with crispy veg is presented on metal pans set into wooden trays, while the cocktails and tacos are fast becoming legendary.

La Vitrola
BREAKFAST, INTERNATIONAL $$

(Map p288; ☑ 52-85-71-11; Muralla No 151, cnr San Ignacio; breakfast CUC$4-7; ⊙ 8:30am-midnight) A retro '50s place with live music on the corner of Plaza Vieja that routinely gets swamped by tourists in the evening. Unbeknown to many, La Vitrola is actually far better for its quieter alfresco breakfasts of fruit, coffee, toast and generous omelets.

Restaurante el Templete
SEAFOOD $$$

(Map p288; Av Carlos Manuel de Céspedes No 12; mains CUC$15-30; ⊙ noon-11pm) Welcome to a rare Cuban breed: a state-run restaurant that can compete with the nascent private sector. The Templete's specialty is fish, and special it is: fresh, succulent and cooked simply without the pretensions of celebrity-chef-producing nations.

✕ Centro Habana

Nazdarovie
RUSSIAN $$

(Map p294; ☑ 7-860-2947; www.nazdarovie-havana.com; Malecón No 25, btwn Prado & Cárcel; mains CUC$10-12; ⊙ noon-midnight) Cuba's 31-year dalliance with bolshevism is relived in this new and highly popular restaurant in prime digs overlooking the Malecón. Upstairs, the decor is awash with old Soviet propaganda posters, brotherly photos of Fidel and Khrushchev and slightly less bombastic Russian dolls. The menu is in three languages (to get in the real spirit, try ordering in Russian).

Castas y Tal
CUBAN $$

(Map p294; ☑ 7-864-2177; Av de Italia No 51, cnr San Lázaro; mains CUC$6-9; ⊙ noon-midnight) In its short life the C & T has gone from old-school paladar (ensconced in someone's 11th-floor apartment) to trendy bistro-style restaurant. High-quality and adventurous food, such as lamb with Indian masala, or chicken in orange sauce, comes backed up with Cuban classics (lashings of rice and beans are served on the side). It's all beautifully presented, too.

Castropol
SPANISH $$

(Map p294; ☑ 7-861-4864; Malecón 107, btwn Genios & Crespo; mains CUC$9-20; ⊙ 6pm-midnight) Castropol is run by the local Spanish Asturianas society, and its reputation has expanded in line with its restaurant space over the last few years. Word is now out that the venerable two-story establishment with its upstairs balcony overlooking Havana's dreamy sea drive serves some of the best Spanish and Caribbean food in Havana.

Casa Miglis
SWEDISH $$

(Map p298; ☑ 7-864-1486; www.casamiglis.com; Lealtad No 120, btwn Ánimas & Lagunas; mains CUC$6-12; ⊙ noon-1am) There's a place for everything in Havana these days, even Swedish-Cuban fusion food. Emerging improbably from a kitchen in the battle-scarred tenements of Centro Habana, comes toast *skagen*, ceviche, couscous, and the *crème de la crème:* melt-in-your-mouth meatballs with mashed potato.

Los Nardos
SPANISH $$

(Map p294; ☑ 7-863-2985; Paseo de Martí No 563; mains CUC$4-10; ⊙ noon-midnight) An open secret opposite the Capitolio, but easy to miss (look out for the queue), Los Nardos is a semi-private restaurant operated by the Spanish Asturianas society. The dilapidated exterior promises little, but the leather and mahogany decor and generous-sized dishes inside suggest otherwise – Los Nardos is touted in some quarters as one of the best cheap eateries in the city.

★ San Cristóbal
CUBAN $$$

(Map p298; ☑ 7-867-9109; San Rafael, btwn Campanario & Lealtad; meals CUC$9-18; ⊙ noon-midnight Mon-Sat) San Cristóbal was knocking out fine food long before the leader of the free world dropped by in March 2016, although the publicity garnered from President Obama's visit probably helped. Crammed into one of Centro Habana's grubbier streets, the restaurant has a museum-worthy interior crowded with old photos, animal skins, and a Santería altar flanked by pictures of Maceo and Martí.

La Guarida
INTERNATIONAL $$$

(Map p298; ☑ 7-866-9047; www.laguarida.com; Concordia No 418, btwn Gervasio & Escobar; mains CUC$15-22; ⊙ noon-3pm & 7pm-midnight) Only in Havana! The entrance to the city's most legendary private restaurant greets you like a scene out of a 1940s film noir. A decapitated statue at the bottom of a grand but dilapidated staircase leads up past drying lines of clothes to a wooden door, behind which lie multiple culinary surprises.

✕ Vedado

El Biky
CAFETERIA $

(Map p298; ☑7-870-6515; cnr Calzada de la Infanta & San Lázaro; sandwiches & burgers CUC$2-5; ☻8am-11pm) Havana needs more places like El Biky, a kind of upscale diner with quick service, cozy booths, walls covered in retro 1950s photos and the option to choose either a snack or a full meal. There's an affiliated bakery next door selling the best chocolate croissants in Havana (which you can have brought in to your table).

Café Presidente
INTERNATIONAL $

(Map p298; ☑7-832-3091; cnr Av de los Presidentes & Calle 25; breakfast CUC$4-6.50; ☻9am-midnight) With its red awnings and huge glass windows doing a good impersonation of a Champs-Élysées bistro, the Presidente delivers the goods on Havana's very own Champs-Élysées, Av de los Presidentes. It's the kind of place where you won't feel awkward popping in for a quick milk shake or plate of pasta, but it also does killer breakfasts and coffee.

Topoly
IRANIAN $

(Map p298; ☑7-832-3224; www.topoly.fr; Calle 23 No 669, cnr Calle D; small plates CUC$4-7; ☻10am-midnight) Cuba finds solidarity with Iran in Havana's first Iranian restaurant, corralled in a lovely collonaded mansion on arterial Calle 23. Sit on the wraparound porch beneath iconic prints of Gandhi, José Martí and Che Guevara, and enjoy pureed eggplant, lamb *brochetas*, fantastic coffee, and tea in ornate silver pots.

La Chucheria
AMERICAN $

(Map p298; Calle 1, btwn Calles C & D; snacks CUC$2-7; ☻7am-midnight) Clinging to its perch close to the Malecón, this sleek sports bar looks as if it floated mockingly across the straits from Florida like a returning exile. But you can forget about politics momentarily as you contemplate pizza toppings, sandwich fillings and the best ice-cream and fruit milkshakes in Havana.

Coppelia
ICE CREAM $

(Map p298; cnr Calles 23 & L; ice cream from MN$40; ☻10am-9:30pm Tue-Sat) The Coppelia, Havana's celebrated ice-cream parlor housed in a flying-saucer-like structure in a park in Vedado, is as celebrated for its massive queues as much as it is for its ice cream. Insanely popular since opening in 1966 (through some very rough economic times), this state-run institution is about far more than mere ice cream.

★ Starbien
INTERNATIONAL $$

(Map p298; ☑7-830-0711; Calle 29 No 205, btwn Calles B & C; lunch CUC$12; ☻noon-5pm & 7pm-midnight) The ingredients: an elegant tucked-away Vedado mansion, an authentic Cuban welcome, complimentary bites to start you off, a great wine list, never-miss-a-beat service, and chicken in pineapple sauce. And it's all yours for CUC$12 if you bag the lunchtime special four-course menu. So get over to Calle 29 near the Plaza de la Revolución.

★ Café Laurent
INTERNATIONAL $$

(Map p298; ☑7-832-6890; Calle M No 257, 5th fl, btwn Calles 19 & 21; meals CUC$10-15; ☻noon-midnight) Talk about a hidden gem. The unsigned Café Laurent is a sophisticated fine-dining restaurant encased, incongruously, in a glaringly ugly 1950s apartment block next to the Focsa building. Starched white tablecloths, polished glasses and lacy drapes furnish the bright modernist interior, while sautéed pork with dried fruit and red wine, and seafood risotto headline the menu.

Mediterraneo Havana
MEDITERRANEAN $$

(Map p298; ☑7-832-4894; www.medhavana.com; Calle 13 No 406, btwn Calles F & G; mains CUC$9-18; ☻noon-midnight) 🍴 Allying themselves with the *granja a la mesa* (farm-to-table) movement and utilizing a couple of agricultural co-ops in Guanabacoa, the Med serves primarily Italian food with a few nods to Spain in a pleasant Vedado residence. Run by two Cuban-Sardinian friends, it hits most of the right notes, with pasta dishes that aren't afraid to go out of the box.

Versus 1900
INTERNATIONAL $$$

(Map p298; ☑7-835-1852; www.versus1900.com; Línea No 504, btwn Calles D & E; mains CUC$7-24; ☻noon-midnight) Opened in late 2015, Versus 1900 shows how Cuban restaurants are moving the yardstick ever forward. Set inside a large detached house and making good use of the multifarious space including interior rooms, front terrace and rooftop, the place is exquisitely decorated (antique, but uncluttered) and delivers an interesting menu that includes rabbit, duck and Peruvian soup.

Atelier
CUBAN $$$

(Map p298; ☑7-836-2025; Calle 5 No 511/Altos, btwn Paseo & Calle 2; meals CUC$12-25; ☻noon-midnight) The first thing that hits you here is the stupendous wall art – huge, thought-provoking, religious-tinged paintings. You'll also notice the antique wooden ceiling, Moorish-style roof terrace and old-school elegance – even the plates are interesting. At some point you'll get around to the food – Cuban with a French influence – scribbled onto an ever-changing menu. Try the duck (the specialty) if it's on, or the rabbit.

Le Chansonnier
FRENCH $$$

(Map p298; ☏7-832-1576; www.lechansonnier habana.com; Calle J No 257, btwn Calles 13 & 15; meals CUC$12-20; ☺12:30pm-12:30am) A great place to dine if you can find it (there's no sign), hidden away in a faded mansion whose revamped interior is dramatically more modern than the front facade. French wine and French flavors shine in house specialties such as rabbit with mustard, eggplant gratin and spare ribs. Opening times vary and it's often busy; phone ahead.

VIP Havana
MEDITERRANEAN $$$

(Map p298; ☏7-832-0178; Calle 9 No 454, btwn Calles E & F; mains CUC$15-21; ☺noon-3am) You don't have to be a very important person to eat at VIP Havana, but it probably helps. This is Havana posing as Miami, with a large central bar on the restaurant floor, drink shelves backlit with neon strip-lights, and old black-and-white movies showing (silently) on a massive cinema screen.

🍷 Drinking & Nightlife

Havana's cafe scene has entered an interesting stage. Bland international franchises have yet to gain a foothold but, with more freedom to engage in private business, local entrepreneurs are directing their artistic creativity into a growing number of bohemian bars and cafes.

🍷 Habana Vieja

★ El Dandy
BAR, CAFE

(Map p288; ☏7-867-6463; www.bareldandy. com; cnr Brasil & Villegas; ☺8am-1am) The jury's still out on Havana's trendiest bar-cafe, but there's little doubt that it's the dandiest. Proving itself to be 'unduly devoted to style, neatness, and fashion in dress and appearance,' El Dandy is a vortex of strong coffee, powerful cocktails and (something not always included in the hipster rule book) warm, unpretentious service.

★ Azúcar Lounge
LOUNGE

(Map p288; ☏7-860-6563; Mercaderes No 315; ☺11am-midnight) How to make an old square trendy: stick a low-lit, chill-out bar with IKEA-style couches on the upper floor of one of its oldest houses. Sprinkle said bar with avant-garde art and weird light fixtures. Offer lavish cocktails and hypnotic trance music. Call it Azúcar (sugar).

★ El Chanchullero
BAR

(Map p288; www.el-chanchullero.com; Brasil, btwn Bernaza & Christo; ☺1pm-midnight) *Aqui jamás estuvo Hemingway* (Hemingway was never here) reads the sign outside roguish Chanchullero, expressing more than a hint of irony. It had to happen. While rich tourists toast Hemingway in La Bodeguita del Medio, hip Cubans and foreigners who think they're hip pay far less for better cocktails in their own boho alternative.

El Patchanka
BAR

(Map p288; ☏7-860-4161; Bernaza No 162; ☺1pm-1am) Live bands rock the rafters, locals knock back powerful CUC$2 mojitos, and earnest travelers banter about Che Guevara's contribution to modern poster art in this new dive bar in Plaza del Cristo that already looks comfortably lived in. Cultural interaction is the key here. By keeping the prices low (lobster for CUC$6!), Patchanka attracts everyone.

Museo del Chocolate
CAFE

(Map p288; cnr Amargura & Mercaderes; ☺9am-9pm) Chocolate addicts beware, this unmissable place in Habana Vieja's heart is a lethal dose of chocolate, truffles and yet more chocolate (all made on the premises). Situated – with no irony intended – in Calle Amargura (literally, Bitterness Street), it's more a cafe than a museum, with a small cluster of marble tables set amid a sugary mélange of chocolate paraphernalia.

La Bodeguita del Medio
BAR

(Map p288; Empedrado No 207; ☺11am-midnight) Made famous thanks to the rum-swilling exploits of Ernest Hemingway (who by association instantly sends the prices soaring), this is Havana's most celebrated bar. A visit here has become de rigueur for tourists who haven't yet cottoned on to the fact that the mojitos are better and (far) cheaper elsewhere.

El Floridita
BAR

(Map p288; Obispo No 557; ⊙11am-midnight) El Floridita was a favorite of expat Americans long before Hemingway dropped by in the 1930s, hence the name (which means 'Little Florida'). Bartender Constante Ribalaigua invented the daiquiri soon after WWI, but it was Hemingway who popularized it and ultimately the bar christened a drink in his honor: the Papa Hemingway Special (a grapefruit-flavored daiquiri).

La Factoria Plaza Vieja
BAR

(Map p288; cnr San Ignacio & Muralla; ⊙11am-midnight) Havana's original microbrewery occupies a boisterous corner of Plaza Vieja and sells smooth, cold, homemade beer at sturdy wooden benches set up outside on the cobbles or indoors in a bright, noisy beer hall. Gather a group together and you'll get the amber nectar in a tall plastic tube drawn from a tap at the bottom. There's also an outside grill.

☕ Centro Habana

★Café Arcangel
CAFE

(Map p294; ☑5-268-5451; Concordia No 57; ⊙8:30am-6:30pm Mon-Sat, 8:15am-1pm Sun) Excellent coffee, fine *tortas* (cakes), suave non-reggaeton music and Charlie Chaplin movies playing on loop in a scarred Centro Habana apartment – what more could you want?

Sloppy Joe's
BAR

(Map p294; cnr Agramonte & Ánimas; ⊙noon-3am) This bar, opened by young Spanish immigrant José García (aka 'Joe') in 1919, earned its name due to (1) its dodgy sanitation and (2) a soggy *ropa vieja* (shredded-beef) sandwich. Legendary among expats before the revolution, it closed in the '60s after a fire, but was reincarnated in 2013 beneath the same noble neoclassical facade. And it's still serving decent cocktails and soggy sandwiches.

☕ Vedado

★Café Mamainé
CAFE, BAR

(Map p298; ☑7-832-8328; Calle L No 206, btwn Calles 15 & 17; ⊙8am-midnight Mon-Thu, 8am-3am Fri-Sun) ✐ Art and coffee go together like Fidel and Che in this wonderfully reimagined eclectic mansion with an interior decked out with revolving local art, much of it made from recycled 'junk.' Flop down on a cushion on the wooden mezzanine, order a strong coffee or cocktail and chat with the person next to you (probably an artist).

★Café Madrigal
BAR

(Map p298; Calle 17 No 302, btwn Calles 2 & 4; ⊙6pm-2am Tue-Sun) Vedado flirts with bohemia in this dimly lit romantic bar that might have materialized serendipitously from Paris' Latin Quarter in the days of Joyce and Hemingway. Order a *tapita* (small tapa) and a cocktail, and retire to the atmospheric art-nouveau terrace where the buzz of nighttime conversation competes with the racket of vintage American cars rattling past below.

Chill Out
BAR

(Map p298; Línea No 504, btwn Calles D & E; ⊙7pm-3am) Chill Out doesn't need much more explanation beyond its name. It's the trance-y, super-cool rooftop bar at Versus 1900 (p305), with sofas, poufs and four-poster recliners. The ideal after-party haunt in Vedado.

☆ Entertainment

Although it may have lost is pre-revolutionary reputation as a dazzling casino quarter, Vedado is still *the* place for nightlife in Havana. Cabaret, jazz, classical music, dance and cinema are offered in abundance and it's invariably of a high standard. Entertainment in Habana Vieja is emerging from a Rip Van Winkle–like slumber and becoming increasingly hip. Centro's nightlife is edgier and more local.

★Fábrica de Arte Cubano
LIVE PERFORMANCE

(☑7-838-2260; www.fabricadeartecubano.com; cnr Calle 26 & 11; CUC$2; ⊙8pm-3am Thu-Sun) The brainchild of Afro-Cuban fusion musician X-Alfonso, this is one Havana's finest new art projects. At this converted cooking-oil factory in Vedado, an intellectual nexus for live music, art expos, fashion shows and invigorating debate over coffee and cocktails, there isn't a pecking order or surly bouncers.

Instead you can mingle with the artists, musicians and mainly Cuban clientele for electrifying 'happenings' that kick off at 8pm Thursday to Sunday in the Bauhaus-like interior. Check the website for upcoming acts.

★Cabaret Parisién
CABARET

(Map p298; ☑7-836-3564; Hotel Nacional, cnr Calles 21 & O; entry CUC$35; ⊙9pm) One rung down from Marianao's world-famous

Tropicana, but cheaper and closer to the city center, the nightly Cabaret Parisién in the Hotel Nacional is well worth a look, especially if you're staying in or around Vedado. It's the usual mix of frills, feathers and semi-naked women (and men), but the choreography is first class and the costumes wonderfully flamboyant.

★ **Gran Teatro de la Habana Alicia Alonso**   THEATER
(Map p294; ✆7-861-3077; cnr Paseo Martí & San Rafael; per person CUC$20; ⊗box office 9am-6pm Mon-Sat, to 3pm Sun) Havana's fabulously renovated 'great' theater is open again and offering up the best in Cuban dance and music. It's specialty is ballet (it's the HQ of the Cuban National Ballet), but it also stages musicals, plays and opera. Check the noticeboard for upcoming events.

Callejón de Hamel   LIVE MUSIC
(Map p298; ⊗from noon Sun) Aside from its funky street murals and psychedelic art shops, the main reason to come to Havana's high temple of Afro-Cuban culture in Centro Habana is the frenetic rumba music that kicks off every Sunday at around noon.

Tropicana Nightclub   CABARET
(✆7-267-1871; Calle 72 No 4504, Marianao; tickets from CUC$75; ⊗from 10pm) A city institution since its 1939 opening, the world-famous Tropicana was one of the few bastions of Havana's Las Vegas–style nightlife to survive the revolution. Immortalized in Graham Greene's 1958 classic *Our Man in Havana,* the open-air cabaret show here has changed little since its 1950s heyday, with scantily clad *señoritas* descending from palm trees to dance Latin salsa amid bright lights.

Jazz Café   LIVE MUSIC
(Map p298; ✆7-838-3302; top fl, Galerías de Paseo, cnr Calle 1 & Paseo; cover after 8pm CUC$10; ⊗noon-2am) This upscale joint, located improbably in a shopping mall overlooking the Malecón, is a kind of jazz supper club, with dinner tables and a decent menu. At night, the club swings into action with live jazz, *timba* and, occasionally, straight-up salsa. It's definitey the suavest of Havana's jazz venues.

Basílica Menor de San Francisco de Asís   CLASSICAL MUSIC
(Map p288; Plaza de San Francisco de Asís; tickets CUC$3-8; ⊗from 6pm Thu-Sat) Plaza de San Francisco de Asís' glorious church, which

dates from 1738, has been reincarnated as a 21st-century museum and concert hall. The old nave hosts choral and chamber music two to three times a week (check the schedule at the door) and the acoustics inside are famously good. It's best to bag your ticket at least a day in advance.

Jazz Club la Zorra y El Cuervo   LIVE MUSIC
(Map p298; ✆7-833-2402; cnr Calles 23 & O; CUC$5-10; ⊗from 10pm) Havana's most famous jazz club (The Vixen and the Crow) opens its doors nightly at 10pm to long lines of committed music fiends. Enter through a red British phonebox and descend into a diminutive and dark basement. The scene here is hot and clamorous and leans toward freestyle jazz.

El Guajirito   LIVE MUSIC
(Map p294; ✆7-863-3009; Agramonte No 660, btwn Gloria & Apodeca; show CUC$30; ⊗9:30pm) Some label it a tourist trap but this restaurant-cum-entertainment-space bivouacked upstairs in a deceptively dilapidated Havana tenement plays some of the most professional Buena Vista Social Club music you'll ever hear. Indeed, this *is* a Buena Vista Social Club of sorts.

Casa de la Música   LIVE MUSIC
(Map p294; Av de Italia, btwn Concordia & Neptuno; CUC$5-25; ⊗5pm-3am) One of Cuba's best and most popular nightclubs and live-music venues. All the big names play here, from Bamboleo to Los Van Van – and you'll pay peanuts to see them. Of the city's two Casas de la Música, this Centro Habana version is a little edgier than its Miramar counterpart (some say it's too edgy), with big salsa bands and not much space.

Submarino Amarillo   LIVE MUSIC
(Map p298; cnr Calles 17 & 6; ⊗2-7:30pm & 9pm-2am Tue-Sat, 2-10pm Sun, 9pm-2am Mon) You can't escape The Beatles in Cuba; their iconic status is epitomized in clubs such as this one, which abuts Parque Lennon and hosts all types of live music as long as it's in 4/4 time and a subgenre of 'rock.' Look out for top Cuban band Los Kents. Afternoons are more laid-back, when you can nibble tapas while watching surreal '60s videos.

Teatro Nacional de Cuba   THEATER
(Map p298; ✆7-879-6011; cnr Paseo & Calle 39; per person CUC$10; ⊗box office 10am-5pm & before performances) One of the twin pillars of Havana's cultural life, the Teatro Nacional

de Cuba on Plaza de la Revolución is the modern rival to the Gran Teatro in Centro Habana. Built in the 1950s as part of Jean Forestier's grand city expansion, the complex hosts landmark concerts, foreign theater troupes and La Colmenita children's company.

🛍 Shopping

Sixty years of *socialismo* didn't do much for Havana's shopping scene. That said, there are some decent outlets for travelers and tourists, particularly for those after the standard Cuban shopping triumvirate of rum, cigars and coffee. Art is another lucrative field. Havana's art scene is cutting edge and ever changing, and browsers will find many galleries in which to while away hours.

★**Clandestina**   CLOTHING
(Map p288; ☑ 53-81-48-02; Villegas No 403; ⊙10am-8pm) Progressive private shops are still in their infancy in Havana, but this is one of the best, set up by a Cuban artist in the mid-2010s and selling its clothes (many of them recycled), bags and accessories under the banner *99% Cuban design*. Viva the private boutique.

★**Memorias Librería**   BOOKS
(Map p294; ☑ 7-862-3153; Ánimas No 57, btwn Paseo de Martí & Agramonte; ⊙9am-5pm) A shop full of beautiful old artifacts, the Memorias Librería opened in 2014 as Havana's first genuine antique bookstore. Delve into its gathered piles and you'll find wonderful rare collectibles including old coins, postcards, posters, magazines and art-deco signs from the 1930s. Priceless!

★**Centro Cultural Antiguos Almacenes de Deposito San José**   ARTS & CRAFTS
(Map p288; cnr Desamparados & San Ignacio; ⊙10am-6pm Mon-Sat) Havana's open-air handicraft market sits under the cover of an old shipping warehouse in Desamparados. Check your socialist ideals at the door. Herein lies a hive of free enterprise and (unusually for Cuba) haggling. Possible souvenirs include paintings, *guayabera* shirts, woodwork, leather items, jewelry and numerous apparitions of the highly marketable El Che.

Librería Venecia   BOOKS
(Map p288; Obispo No 502; ⊙10am-10pm) A nice little private secondhand bookshop in Obispo where you might uncover all number of mysteries. It's particularly good for its old Cuban posters, which steer clear of the clichéd Che Guevara poses.

Casa del Habano – Hostal Conde de Villanueva   CIGARS
(Map p288; Mercaderes No 202; ⊙10am-6pm) One of Havana's best cigar shops, with its own roller, smoking room and expert sales staff.

Plaza de Armas Secondhand Book Market   BOOKS
(Map p288; cnr Obispo & Tacón; ⊙9am-7pm) This long-standing book market convenes under the leafy boughs in Plaza de Armas. It stocks old, new and rare books, including Hemingway, some weighty poetry and plenty of written pontifications from Fidel. There's no market if it rains or on important holidays.

ℹ Information

INTERNET ACCESS

Cuba's internet service provider is national phone company **Etecsa**. Etecsa runs various *telepuntos* (internet cafe and telephone center) in Habana: the main ones are in **Centro Habana** (Águila No 565, cnr Dragones; ⊙8:30am-7pm) and **Habana Vieja** (Habana No 406, cnr Obispo; ⊙9am-7pm).

The drill is to buy a one-hour user card (CUC$2) with a scratch-off user code and *contraseña* (password), and either help yourself to a free computer or use it on your own device in one of the city's 30-plus wi-fi hot spots

Most Havana hotels that are rated three stars and up also have wi-fi. You don't generally have to be a guest to use it.

Popular wi-fi hot spots in Havana include La Rampa (Calle 23 between Calle L and Malecón) in Vedado, the corner of Av de Italia and San Rafael in Centro Habana, and the Miramar Trade Center in Playa.

MEDICAL SERVICES

Pharmacy (☑ 7-838-4593; Calle L, btwn Calles 23 & 25, Vedado; ⊙8:30am-8:30pm) Pharmacy located at the Hotel Habana Libre.

MONEY

The quickest and most hassle-free places to exchange money are in Cadecas. There are dozens of them across Havana and they usually have much longer opening hours and quicker service than banks.

Banco de Crédito y Comercio Two branches in Vedado; one on **Línea & Paseo** (cnr Línea & Paseo, Vedado; ⊙9am-3pm Mon-Fri) and one on **Calle 23** (🗹 7-870-2684; Airline Bldg, Calle 23, Vedado; ⊙ 9am-3pm Mon-Fri)

Banco Financiero Internacional Branches at **Habana Vieja** (🗹 7-860-9369; cnr Oficios & Brasil; ⊙ 9am-3pm Mon-Fri) and **Vedado** (Hotel Habana Libre, Calle L, btwn Calles 23 & 25, Vedado; ⊙ 9am-3pm Mon-Fri)

Banco Metropolitano Branches at **Centro Habana,** (🗹 7-862-6523; Av de Italia No 452, cnr San Martín; ⊙ 9am-3pm Mon-Fri) **Vedado** (🗹 7-832-2006; cnr Línea & Calle M, Vedado; ⊙ 9am-3pm Mon-Fri) and **Habana Vieja** (cnr Cuba & O'Reilly; ⊙ 9am-3pm Mon-Fri)

Cadeca Branches at **Centro Habana** (cnr Neptuno & Consulado; ⊙ 8am-12:30pm, 1-3pm, 4-6:30pm & 7-10pm) and **Habana Vieja** (cnr Oficios & Lamparilla; ⊙ 8am-7pm Mon-Sat, to 1pm Sun), and two in **Vedado** (cnr Calles 23 & J; ⊙ 7am-2:30pm & 3:30-10pm); one on **Calle 23** (cnr Calles 23 & J; ⊙ 7am-2:30pm & 3:30-10pm) and one in the **Hotel Meliá Cohiba** (Hotel Meliá Cohiba, Paseo, btwn Calles 1 & 3; ⊙ 8am-8pm) on Paseo.

POST

Post Office branches include those in **Habana Vieja** (Map p288; Plaza de San Francisco de Asís, Oficios No 102; ⊙ 8am-5pm Mon-Sat) and **Vedado** (Map p298; Av de la Independencia, Vedado; ⊙ 8:30am-5pm Mon-Fri, stamp sales 24hr). The Vedado branch has many services, including photo developing, a bank and a Cadeca.

TOURIST INFORMATION

State-run Infotur books tours and has maps, phonecards and useful free brochures.

Pretty much every hotel in Havana has some type of state-run tourist information desk.

Infotur (Map p288; 🗹 7-866-4153; Obispo No 524, btwn Bernaza & Villegas; ⊙ 9:30am-5:30pm) Infotur's main Habana Vieja office.

Infotur (🗹 7-642-6101; Terminal 3, Aeropuerto Internacional José Martí; ⊙ 24hr) The airport Infotur branch.

🛈 Getting There & Away

AIR

Aeropuerto Internacional José Martí (p344) is at Rancho Boyeros, 25km southwest of Havana via Av de la Independencia. There are four terminals, the main one being Terminal 3.

BOAT

There are currently no international ferries calling at Havana.

Cruise ships dock at the **Terminal Sierra Maestra (Cruise Terminal)** (Map p288), adjacent to Plaza de San Francisco de Asís on the cusp of Habana Vieja.

BUS

Víazul (🗹 7-881-5652, 7-881-1413; www.viazul. com; Calle 26, cnr Zoológica, Nuevo Vedado; ⊙ 7am-9:30pm) covers most destinations of interest to travelers, in safe, air-conditioned coaches. Most buses are direct except those to Guantánamo, Baracoa, Remedios and Cayo Santa María. You board all Víazul buses at their inconveniently located terminal 3km southwest of Plaza de la Revolución. This is where you'll also have to come to buy tickets from the Venta de Boletines office. Buses get busy particularly in peak season (November through March), so it's wise to book up to a week in advance. You can also book online. Full bus schedules are available on the website. Some casa particular owners may offer help with prearranging bus tickets.

The Víazul bus terminal is in the suburb of Nuevo Vedado, and taxis will charge between CUC$5 and CUC$10 for the ride to central Havana. There are no direct metro buses from central Havana.

TAXI

Full buses are the norm in Cuba these days, as public transportation hasn't yet caught up with the increase in tourist numbers. To counter the shortfall, many travelers are turning to *colectivos* (shared taxis). Taxis charge approximately CUC$0.50 to CUC$0.60 per kilometer. This translates to around CUC$90 to Varadero, CUC$90 to Viñales, CUC$150 to Santa Clara, CUC$120 to Cienfuegos and CUC$160 to Trinidad. A *colectivo* can take up to four people, meaning you can share the cost. Colectivos can usually be organized through your casa particular, at an Infotur office or by negotiating at a standard pickup point. It's also usually pretty easy to arrange a *collectivo* at the **Víazul bus terminal**.

TRAIN

Trains to most parts of Cuba depart from **La Coubre station** (Túnel de la Habana) while the **Estación Central de Ferrocarriles** (Central Train Station; 🗹 7-861-8540, 7-862-1920; cnr Av de Bélgica & Arsenal) is being refurbished until 2018 or later.

At the time of research, Cuba's main train (No 11), the *Tren Francés* (still using its increasingly dilapidated French SNCF carriages), was running every fourth day between Havana and Santiago, stopping in Santa Clara and Camagüey.

🛈 Getting Around

TO/FROM THE AIRPORT

Public transportation from the airport into central Havana is practically nonexistent. A standard taxi will cost you approximately CUC$20 to CUC$25 (30 to 40 minutes).

VÍAZUL BUS DEPARTURES FROM HAVANA

DESTINATION	COST (CUC$)	DURATION (HR)	DEPARTURES
Camagüey	33	9	12:30am, 6:30am, 9:30am, 3pm, 7:45pm
Santa Clara	18	3¾	12:30am, 6:30am, 9:30am, 3pm, 7:45pm
Santiago de Cuba	51	15	12:30am, 6:30am, 3pm
Trinidad	25	5-6	7am, 10:45am, 2:15pm
Viñales	12	4	8:40am, 11:25am, 2pm

BUS

The handy hop-on, hop-off **Habana Bus Tour** (Map p294) runs on two routes, numbers T1 and T3. The main stop is in Parque Central opposite the Hotel Inglaterra. This is the pickup point for bus T1, which runs from Habana Vieja via Centro Habana, the Malecón, Calle 23 and Plaza de la Revolución to La Cecilia at the west end of Playa; and bus T3, which runs from Centro Habana to Playas del Este (via Parque Histórico Militar Morro-Cabaña).

All-day tickets for T1/T3 are CUC$10/5. Services run from 9am to 7pm and routes and stops are clearly marked on all bus stops.

Havana's metro bus service calls on a relatively modern fleet of Chinese-made 'bendy' buses and is far less dilapidated than it used to be. These buses run regularly along 17 different routes, connecting most parts of the city with the suburbs. Fares are 40 centavos (five centavos if you're using convertibles).

TAXI

Taxis hang around outside all the major tourist hotels, outside the two main bus stations and at various city-center nexus points such as Parque Central and Parque de la Fraternidad. You're never far from a taxi in Havana.

The most common taxis are the yellow cabs of **Cubataxi** (📞7-796-6666; Calle 478, btwn Av 7 & 7B). Other taxis might be Ladas, old American cars or modern Toyotas.

WESTERN CUBA

Viñales

📞 48 / POP 27,806

When Pinar del Río's greenery starts to erupt into craggy *mogotes* (limestone monoliths) and you spy a cigar-chewing *guajiro* driving his oxen and plow through a rust-colored tobacco field, you know you've arrived in Viñales. Despite its long-standing love affair with tourism, this slow, relaxed, wonderfully traditional settlement is a place that steadfastly refuses to put on a show. What you see here is what you get – an agricultural town where front doors are left wide open, everyone knows everyone else, and a night out on the tiles involves sitting on a *sillón* (rocking chair) on a rustic porch analyzing the Milky Way.

People don't come to Viñales for the music or the mojitos, they come to dip indulgently into the natural world, hiking, horse riding or cycling through some of the most wonderful landscapes in Cuba. Join them.

◉ Sights

Finca Raúl Reyes FARM

(⏰dawn-dusk) FREE Finca Raúl Reyes, 1km north of the town center, is a tobacco plantation where you can enjoy fruit, coffee, *puros* (cigars) and a dose of throat-warming rum. From here, you can also hike up to Cueva de la Vaca, a cave that carves a tunnel through the *mogotes:* from the cave mouth, unforgettable valley vistas roll out before you.

🏃 Activities

While most activities in Viñales are located outside town, there's a handful – including some climbing routes – within easy walking distance. Even if you're staying in a casa, it's worth strolling the 2km uphill to the lovely La Ermita (p312) where you can swim (CUC$8, including bar cover) in the gorgeous pool or book amassage (CUC$20 to CUC$35). Hotel los Jazmines (p312) has an equally amazing pool (CUC$8, including bar cover), though the ubiquitous tour buses can sometimes kill the tranquility.

CUBA VIÑALES

🏃 Tours

Cubanacán TOURS
(📋 48-79-63-93; Salvador Cisneros No 63c; ⏰ 9am-7pm Mon-Sat) Cubanacán organizes perennially popular day trips to Cayo Levisa (CUC$39), Cayo Jutías (CUC$15), Gran Caverna de Santo Tomás (CUC$20) and María la Gorda (CUC$35). Official park hikes leave from here daily (CUC$8).

🛏 Sleeping

Viñales is like a giant hotel. Practically every house rents private rooms giving you at least 400 to choose from. Most are of a decent standard offering family-style lodging in a large village-like setting with breakfast available for CUC$5 extra. The settlement's two hotels are situated on higher ground between 2km and 3km outside Viñales village. Both have views to die for.

★ Casa Daniela CASA PARTICULAR $
(📋 48-69-55-01; casadaniela@nauta.cu; Carretera a Pinar del Rio; r CUC$25; 🅿 ❄ 🛜 ♨) Run by a former doctor and his wife, who must have had formidable bedside manners if their hospitality in this surgically clean casa is anything to judge by, this orange house has expanded into a sizeable residence without losing its local intimacy. There are six rooms, a pool, a roof terrace and a shady outside yard for the obligatory Viñales relaxation.

Villa Los Reyes CASA PARTICULAR $
(📋 48-79-33-17; http://villalosreyes.com; Salvador Cisneros No 206c; r CUC$25-30; 🅿 ❄ @) A great modern house with five rooms (including a new block out back), all amenities, a secluded patio where a restaurant serves some original Cuban-fusion food, and one of the town's best roof terraces. Hostess, Yarelis, was a biologist at the national park and host, Yoan, has Viñales running through his veins.

The couple are known for their excellent tours, including a popular sunrise tour to Los Aquáticos and a sunset tour to the Valle del Silencio.

La Auténtica CASA PARTICULAR $
(📋 48-69-58-38; Salvador Cisneros No 125; r CUC$30) Giving a plush new brush-stroke to Viñales' main drag, La Auténtica is like a mini-hotel with four new rooms encased in a large one-story house that adds modern adornments to a traditional base. Unlike other Viñales casas, the owners don't live on-site, meaning you're free to roam between the various common areas, including a spacious back patio equipped with comfy chairs.

Casa Haydée Chiroles CASA PARTICULAR $
(📋 52-54-89-21; casahaydee@nauta.cu; Rafael Trejo No 139; r CUC$25) With six rooms split between two adjacent houses and a lovely lush communal back patio where you can rock beneath the stars on your *sillón* (rocking chair), this house reflects all the best attributes of Viñales. Even better, the daughter of the owner works at the Infotur office, meaning English and French are spoken and recommendations are well informed.

Casa Nenita CASA PARTICULAR $
(📋 48-79-60-04; emiliadiaz2000@yahoo.es; Salvador Cisneros Internal No 1; r CUC$35-40; 🅿 ❄ ♨) Nenita's has quietly become one of Cuba's top casas particulares. While its out-of-center location might deter some, the eight rooms are above par and, when augmented by the amazing restaurant, pool and roof terrace, give you a luxurious launchpad from which to go *mogote*-hopping. Nenita's battered fish has even featured in recipe books. Finding the place can be tricky, however – it's behind the *policlinico* (hospital).

Villa Cafetal CASA PARTICULAR $
(📋 53-31-17-52; edgar21@nauta.cu; Adela Azcuy Final; r CUC$20-25; 🅿 ❄) The owners of this quiet house on the edge of town are experts on climbing and have a shed stacked with equipment – appropriately, given the best climbs in Viñales are on their doorstep. Ensconced in a resplendent garden that cultivates its own coffee (yes, you get it for breakfast), you can practically taste the mountain air as you swing on the hammock.

★ Hotel los Jazmines HOTEL $$$
(📋 48-79-64-11; Carretera a Pinar del Río; s/d incl breakfast CUC$88/138; 🅿 ❄ ♨) Prepare yourself: the vista from this pastel-pink colonial-style hotel is one of the best in Cuba. Open the shutters of your classic valley-facing room and drink in the shimmering sight of magnificent *mogotes*, oxen-ploughed red fields and palm-frond-covered tobacco-drying houses. While no five-star palace, Los Jazmines benefits from its unrivaled location and a gloriously inviting swimming pool.

La Ermita HOTEL $$$
(📋 48-79-64-11; Carretera de La Ermita Km 1.5; s/d incl breakfast CUC$88/138; 🅿 ❄ ♨) La Ermita

takes Viñales' top honors for architecture, interior furnishings and all-round services and quality. Notably peaceful for its absence of tour buses, the rooms with views here are housed in handsome two-story colonial edifices and the restaurant is an ideal breakfast perch. Extracurricular attractions include an excellent pool, skilfully mixed cocktails, tennis courts, a shop, horseback riding and massage.

✗ Eating

El Olivo
MEDITERRANEAN $

(Salvador Cisneros No 89; pasta CUC$4-6; ☺noon-11pm) Viñales' most popular restaurant, as the perennial queue outside will testify, serves tremendous lasagna and pasta dishes, backed up by other Med classics such as duck *à l'orange*. The joker in the pack is rabbit with herbs in a dark chocolate sauce.

Restaurant La Berenjena
VEGETARIAN $

(☏52-54-92-69; Mariana Grajales, btwn Salvador Cisneros & Rafael Trejo; mains CUC$4-7; ☺10am-10pm; ☏) ⌁ A commendable attempt to fill a void in Cuba's food market – ie vegetarianism – La Berenjena (meaning 'aubergine' or 'eggplant') inhabits a lovely blue and white house with an awning-covered terrace out front. This is a genuine eco-restaurant plying fruit shakes, vegetable lasagna, crepes, soups, aubergines (of course), and a few meat dishes for those who can't be swayed.

★Tres Jotas
TAPAS $$

(☏53-31-16-58; Salvador Cisneros No 45; tapas CUC$2-6; ☺8am-2am) Who knew that Viñales, long a bastion of *cerdo asado* (whole roast pig), also produces huge crayfish fresh from the Ancón River? For a reminder pop into 3J's, a tapas bar, restaurant, cocktail lounge and breakfast cafe run by the affable Jean-Pierre, who tirelessly welcomes guests at the door.

★Balcón del Valle
CUBAN $$

(Carretera a Pinar del Río; mains CUC$8; ☺noon-midnight) With three deftly constructed wooden decks overhanging a panorama of tobacco fields, drying houses and craggy *mogotes*, this aptly named restaurant (translation: Balcony of the Valley) has food that stands up to its sensational views. The unwritten menu gives a three-way choice between chicken, pork and fish, all prepared country-style with copious trimmings. It's 3km outside Viñales towards Hotel los Jazmines.

La Cuenca
INTERNATIONAL $$

(☏48-69-69-68; Salvador Cisneros No 97, cnr Adela Azcuy; mains CUC$5-12; ☺11am-10:30pm) Looking less rustic than some of its Viñales brethren, La Cuenca's narrow covered terrace and funky black-and-white interior are rather tempting. The food is all over the map, from Spanish tapas to rack of lamb, although some dishes (rabbit with chocolate) seem to mimic nearby culinary king, El Olivo. If you're not lingering long, the coffee and cocktails are famously good.

☆ Entertainment

Centro Cultural Polo Montañez
LIVE MUSIC

(cnr Salvador Cisneros & Joaquin Pérez; after 9pm CUC$1; ☺music from 9pm-2am) Named for the late Pinar del Río resident, *guajiro* hero and legendary folk singer, Polo Montañez, this open-air patio off the main plaza is a bar-restaurant with a full-blown stage that comes alive after 9pm.

ⓘ Information

INTERNET ACCESS

Etecsa Telepunto (Ceferino Fernández No 3; internet per hr CUC$1.50; ☺8:30am-7pm Mon-Sat, to 5pm Sun) Three terminals in a tiny office; it also sells cards for wi-fi. The main square has good wi-fi reception.

MONEY

Banks in Viñales have long queues. Arrive early or consider changing money in Pinar del Río

Banco de Crédito y Comercio (Salvador Cisneros No 58; ☺8am-noon & 1:30-3pm Mon-Fri, 8-11am Sat) Has two ATMs.

Cadeca (cnr Salvador Cisneros & Adela Azcuy; ☺8:30am-4pm Mon-Sat) Quickest service.

TOURIST INFORMATION

Infotur (Salvador Cisneros No 63b; ☺8:15am-4:45pm)

ⓘ Getting There & Around

BUS

The well-ordered **Víazul ticket office** (Salvador Cisneros No 63a; ☺8am-noon & 1-3pm) is opposite the main square in the same building as Cubataxi. Daily Víazul buses depart from here for Havana at 8am and 2pm (CUC$12, 3¼ hours). At 6:45am another bus heads to Cienfuegos (CUC$32, eight hours) and Trinidad (CUC$37, 9½ hours). All buses stop at Pinar del Río (CUC$6, 30 minutes)

TAXI

Víazul buses are often fully booked days in advance. The solution? A *collectivo* (shared) taxi. These can be booked at the office that **Cubataxi** (☑ 48-79-31-95; Salvador Cisneros No 63a) shares with Víazul. Prices per person, if taxis are full (four people), are Havana (CUC$20), Varadero (CUC$30), Cienfuegos (CUC$35) and Trinidad (CUC$40).

VIÑALES BUS TOUR

The Viñales Bus Tour is a hop-on, hop-off minibus that runs nine times a day between the valley's spread-out sites. There are 18 stops along the route. All-day tickets cost CUC$5 and can be purchased on the bus.

Valle de Viñales

Embellished by soaring pine trees and bulbous limestone cliffs that teeter like top-heavy haystacks above placid tobacco plantations, Parque Nacional Viñales is one of Cuba's most magnificent natural settings. Wedged spectacularly into the Sierra de los Órganos mountain range, this 11km-by-5km valley was recognized as a national monument in 1979, with Unesco World Heritage status following in 1999 for its dramatic steep-sided limestone outcrops (known as *mogotes*), coupled with the vernacular architecture of its traditional farms and villages.

Viñales offers opportunities for fine hiking, rock climbing and horseback trekking. On the accommodations front, it boasts first-class hotels and some of the best casas particulares in Cuba. Despite drawing in day-trippers by the busload, the area's well-protected and spread-out natural attractions have somehow managed to escape the frenzied tourist circus of other less well-managed places, while the atmosphere in and around the town remains refreshingly hassle-free.

◉ Sights

Gran Caverna de Santo Tomás   CAVE
(CUC$10; ⊙9am-3pm) Welcome to Cuba's largest cave system and the second largest on the American continent. There are more than 46km of galleries on eight levels, with a 1km section accessible to visitors. There's no artificial lighting, but headlamps are provided for the 90-minute guided tour. Highlights include bats, stalagmites and stalactites, underground pools, interesting rock formations and a replica of an ancient native Indian mural.

᚛ Activities

Hiking

The Parque Nacional Viñales has added a considerable number of new hikes to its repertoire in recent years. There are now around 15 routes and maps are displayed at the visitor center. It is best to go with a guide as signposting is terrible. Prices for guides are around CUC$10 per person but depend on distance and group size.

Aside from the park guides, almost every casa particular in Viñales will be able to hook you up with a private guide who can pretty much custom-build any trip you want. Eternally popular is the loop around the **Valle de Palmarito**, which starts and ends in the village and takes in a coffee plantation, tobacco house and the Cueva de Palmarito where swimming by torchlight is possible.

Other favorites are the hikes to Los Aquáticos and the Valle del Silencio.

Horseback Riding

The lush hills and valleys (and the *guajiros*, indeed) around town lend themselves to horseback riding, particularly the Valle de Palmarito and the route to Los Aquáticos. Most casas particulares can hook you up with a guide. Riding a horse will mean you see more in a shorter space of time. It's particularly useful in the wet season (April to October) when the trails can be muddy.

ℹ Information

Parque Nacional Viñales Visitors Center
(☑ 48-79-61-44; Carretera a Pinar del Río Km 22; ⊙8am-6pm) Located 3km south of Viñales, the visitor center is equipped with a good set of maps, trail information and natural history pertaining to the park. Park wardens are always on hand and hikes and other activities can be arranged here.

CENTRAL CUBA

Santa Clara
☑42 / POP 239,000

Sorry Havana. Santa Clara is Cuba's most revolutionary city – and not just because of its historical obsession with Argentine doctor turned *guerrillero* Che Guevara. Smack bang in the geographic center of Cuba, this is a city of new trends and insatiable creativity, where an edgy youth culture has been

REMEDIOS

A small, tranquil town that goes berserk every Christmas Eve in a cacophonous firework festival known as Las Parrandas, Remedios is one of Cuba's lesser-glimpsed colonial highlights. Some historical sources claim it is Cuba's second-oldest settlement (founded in 1513), although it is officially listed at number eight after Santiago and proudly celebrated its quincentennial in 2015. The anniversary has transformed Remedios from a slightly scruffy stopover on the way to Cayo Santa María into a mini-Trinidad replete with handsome boutique hotels, a beautifully restored central square and several decent eating joints. However, the bulk of Cuba's culture-seeking tourists have yet to cotton on to Remedios' glorious rebirth. Come now before they find out.

Remedios is the only city in Cuba with two churches on its main square, Plaza Martí. Well worth a look is the **Parroquia de San Juan Bautista de Remedios** (Camilo Cienfuegos No 20; donations accepted; ⊙9am-noon & 2-5pm Mon-Sat), one of the island's most interesting and oldest ecclesiastical buildings, dating from around 1550.

The town also has a quartet of boutique hotels set in rejuvenated historical buildings. **Hostal Camino del Príncipe** (☑42-39-51-44; Camilo Cienfuegos No 9, btwn Montaiván & Alejandro del Río; s/d CUC$98/144; ❋) merits a splurge.

Remedios is accessible from Santa Clara on a daily Víazul bus (CUC$7, 1¼ hours) or by taxi (CUC$30).

testing the boundaries of Cuba's censorship police for years. Unique Santa Clara offerings include Cuba's only official drag show, a graphic artists' collective that produces satirical political cartoons, and the best rock festival in the country: Ciudad Metal. The city's fiery personality has been shaped over time by the presence of the nation's most prestigious university outside Havana, and a long association with Che Guevara, whose liberation of Santa Clara in December 1958 marked the end of the Batista regime. Little cultural revolutions have been erupting here ever since.

◉ Sights

Santa Clara's sights are liberally distributed to the north, east and west of Parque Vidal. All are within walking distance, with the big Che sight, Conjunto Escultórico Comandante Ernesto Che Guevara, 2km from the center.

★ Conjunto Escultórico Comandante Ernesto Che Guevara   MONUMENT

(Plaza de la Revolución; ⊙mausoleum & museum 9:30am-4pm Tue-Sun) **FREE** The end point of many a Che pilgrimage, this monument, mausoleum and museum complex is 2km west of Parque Vidal (via Rafael Tristá on Av de los Desfiles), near the Víazul bus station. Even if you can't stand the Argentine guerrilla for whom many reserve an almost religious reverence, there's poignancy in the

vast square that spans both sides of a wide avenue, guarded by a bronze statue of El Che atop a 16m-high pedestal.

Parque Vidal   SQUARE

A veritable alfresco theater named for Colonel Leoncio Vidal y Caro, who was killed here on March 23, 1896, Parque Vidal was encircled by twin sidewalks during the colonial era, with a fence separating blacks and whites. Scars of more recent division are evident on the facade of mint-green **Hotel Santa Clara Libre** on the park's west side: it's pockmarked by bullet holes from the 1958 battle for the city between Guevara and Batista's government troops.

Monumento a la Toma del Tren Blindado   MONUMENT

(boxcar museum CUC$1; ⊙boxcar museum 8:30am-5pm Mon-Sat) History was made at the site of this small boxcar museum on December 29, 1958, when Ernesto 'Che' Guevara and a band of 18 rifle-wielding revolutionaries barely out of their teens derailed an armored train using a borrowed bulldozer and homemade Molotov cocktails.

Fábrica de Tabacos Constantino Pérez Carrodegua   FACTORY

(Maceo No 181, btwn Julio Jover & Berenguer; CUC$4; ⊙9-11am & 1-3pm) Santa Clara's tobacco factory, one of Cuba's best, makes a quality range of Montecristos, Partagás and Romeo y Julieta cigars. Tours here are lo-fi compared to those in Havana, and so the experience is a lot more interesting and less rushed. Buy tickets in advance at the **Hotel Santa Clara Libre** (📞 42-20-75-48; Parque Vidal).

Across the street is **La Veguita** (📞 42-20-89-52; Maceo No 176a, btwn Julio Jover & Berenguer; ☺ 9am-7pm Mon-Sat, 11am-4pm Sun), the factory's diminutive but comprehensively stocked sales outlet, staffed by a friendly, ultra-professional team of cigar experts. You can buy cheap rum here, and the bar brews exquisite coffee.

Teatro la Caridad THEATER, HISTORIC BUILDING
(cnr Marta Abreu & Máximo Gómez) Many are deceived by the relatively austere neoclassical facade. But toss CUC$1 to whoever is on the door and you'll serendipitously discover why the 1885 Teatro la Caridad is one of the three great provincial theaters of the colonial era.

Museo de Artes Decorativas MUSEUM
(Parque Vidal No 27; CUC$2; ☺ 9am-6pm Sun-Thu, 1-10pm Fri & Sat) Something of a sleeping beauty on Parque Vidal, this 18th-century mansion turned museum is packed with period furniture from a whole gamut of styles that seem to ape Cuba's architectural heritage. Look for baroque desks, art-nouveau mirrors, art-deco furniture and Veláquez's epic *Rendición de Brega*, reproduced on a china plate. Live chamber music adds to the romanticism in the evenings.

🛏 Sleeping

It's not always obvious from street level, but Santa Clara has some of the best casas particulares in Cuba, many of them hidden away in rambling colonial abodes.

The half-a-dozen hotels (two of which are several kilometers outside the city) are less alluring.

★**Hostal Florida Terrace** CASA PARTICULAR $
(📞 42-22-15-80; florida.terrace59@gmail.com; Maestra Nicolasa No 59, btwn Maceo & Colón; r CUC$30-35; 🅿✳🌐) This finely decorated hotel-like place is affiliated with Restaurant Florida Center across the road and has more floors (four) than most casas particulares have rooms. The smart colonial decor has art-deco echoes, offering plenty to admire, and the six rooms with antique beds are top drawer. It has an upstairs bar and *mirador* (viewpoint) with some of Santa Clara's best views.

★**Hostal Familia Sarmiento** CASA PARTICULAR $
(📞 42-20-35-10; www.santaclarahostel.com; Lorda No 56, btwn Martí & Independencia; r CUC$25-35; ✳🌐) The Sarmiento offers two options directly opposite each other: a traditional family-run casa particular and a smart new boutique-style hotel. The latter has its own reception, 24-hour bar and room service amid minimalist design features. Between the properties there are eight rooms, all with private bathrooms.

Casa Mercy 1938 CASA PARTICULAR $
(📞 42-21-69-41; casamercy@gmail.com; Independencia No 253, btwn Estévez & Gutiérrez; r CUC$30-35; ✳🌐) The name might hark back to another age, but this wonderful neocolonial house only opened recently after a restoration. The details are spectacular; check out the Seville-style fountain that sets off the central patio. The house is self-contained (the owners live elsewhere) but diligently staffed and comes with two large rooms and plenty of communal space – including that patio.

Authentica Pérgola CASA PARTICULAR $
(📞 42-20-86-86; carmen64@yahoo.es; Luis Estévez No 61, btwn Independencia & Martí; r CUC$30; ✳) The Pérgola is set around an Alhambra-esque patio draped in greenery and crowned by a fountain, from where several large rooms lead off. Pretty much everything here is antique, including in the bedrooms. There's a beautiful roof-terrace restaurant open to all called La Aldaba.

Hotel América HOTEL $$$
(📞 42-20-15-85; Mujica, btwn Colón & Maceo; r CUC$156; ✳@🌐) The first hotel in the city center that you'd recommend to your friends rather than your enemies, the 27-room América, which opened in 2012, can't quite claim a 'boutique' moniker. But it's relatively new, keen to please and has some interesting details (check out the metal staircase balustrades). It has a decent bar (open to nonguests) and a small outdoor pool.

🍴 Eating

★**Restaurant Florida Center** CUBAN, FUSION $$
(📞 42-20-81-61; Maestra Nicolasa No 56, btwn Colón & Maceo; mains CUC$10-15; ☺ 6-8:30pm) The Florida has been Santa Clara's best restaurant for at least a decade. The food is as good as the experience. Diners eat in a colo-

DIVING IN PLAYA GIRÓN

The sandy arc of Playa Girón nestles peacefully on the eastern side of the infamous Bahía de Cochinos (Bay of Pigs), backed by one of those gloriously old-fashioned Cuban villages where everyone knows everyone else. Notorious as the place where the Cold War almost got hot, the beach is actually named for a French pirate, Gilbert Girón, who met his end here by decapitation in the early 1600s at the hands of embittered locals. In April 1961 it was the scene of another botched raid, the ill-fated, CIA-sponsored invasion that tried to land on these remote sandy beaches in one of modern history's classic David-and-Goliath struggles. Lest we forget, there are still plenty of propaganda-spouting billboards dotted around rehashing past glories.

These days Girón, with its clear Caribbean waters, precipitous offshore drop-off and multitude of private homestays, is one of the best places in Cuba to go diving and snorkeling. The reasons? Well, a) it's relatively close to Havana; b) most of the dives are directly offshore and don't need boat transfers; c) at CUC$25 an immersion, the diving is cheap; d) water clarity is excellent; and e) there's a plenitude of good diving instructors, many of whom also rent rooms.

The **International Scuba Center** (☎45-98-41-10, 45-98-41-18; Villa Playa Girón) is the main diving headquarters. This is the best place for coordinating dives in the area. It's well run and offers dives from CUC$25 per immersion.

Additionally, some of the village's casa-particular owners also double up as dive instructors and can organize trips. Recommended is **Casa Julio y Lidia** (☎45-98-41-35; lidia.aguero@nauta.cu; r CUC$30; P❄) , the second house on the left as you're entering the settlement from the west.

Playa Girón is close to the protected Zapata swamps and its many trails and excursions. Close to the village and popular is the Sendero Enigma de las Rocas that leads to a *cenote* (flooded tectonic fault) where you can swim.

Daily Víazul (www.viazul.com) buses connect Playa Girón with Havana (CUC$13, 3¼ hours) leaving at 5:35pm. There are also two departures to Trinidad (CUC$13, three hours).

nial, plant-festooned, candlelit courtyard full of interesting antiques. Owner Ángel is as active as his waitstaff, advising on the profusion of dishes in French, English, Italian and Spanish. The highlight: lobster with prawns in a tangy tomato sauce.

Restaurante Casona Jover   INTERNATIONAL **$$**
(☎42-20-44-58; Colón No 167, btwn 9 de Abril & Serafín García; mains CUC$8; ⊙noon-10pm) A long-standing casa particular owner has decided to give it a go in the culinary sphere. The Jover is encased in a lovely 1867 colonial house with a patio and specializes in honey chicken. Give it a try!

🍷 Drinking & Nightlife

Thanks to its large student population, Santa Clara has some of Cuba's best nightlife outside Havana – and it's not just the usual suspects. The city has an established gay scene and a strong contingent of *roqueros* (rock musicians). Most of the nightlife is on or around Parque Vidal, although there are

a couple of outlying strongholds, including a new cabaret venue.

★**La Marquesina**   BAR
(Parque Vidal, btwn Máximo Gómez & Lorda; ⊙9am-1am) You can chin-wag and neck a cold bottled beer with locals of all types in this legendary dive bar under the porches of the equally legendary Teatro la Caridad on the corner of Parque Vidal. The clientele is a potpourri of Santa Clara life – students, bohemians, cigar-factory workers and the odd off-duty bici-taxi rider. Live music erupts regularly.

Cafe-Museo Revolución   CAFE
(Independencai No 313; ⊙11am-11pm) You say you want a revolution... Well, Santa Clara's a good place to start. It's already had one, successfully ignited by Che Geuvara in 1958. This new cafe pays homage to Santa Clara's (and Cuba's) revolutionary past with photos, old uniforms and other ephemera lovingly curated by the owner. The coffee and milk shakes are pretty revolutionary too.

BUS DEPARTURES FROM SANTA CLARA

DESTINATION	COST (CUC$)	DURATION (HR)	DEPARTURES
Cayo Santa María	13	2½	11:30am
Havana	18	4	3:35am, 8:40am, 4:50pm
Santiago de Cuba	33	12½	12:10am, 1:45am, 9:50am, 7pm
Trinidad	8	3½	10:30am, 5:15pm
Varadero	11	3¼	7:50am, 4:55pm

☆ Entertainment

★ Club Mejunje
LIVE MUSIC

(Marta Abreu No 107; ⊘4pm-1am Tue-Sun; ⏺) Urban graffiti, children's theater, transvestites, old crooners belting out boleros, tourists dancing salsa. You've heard about 'something for everyone,' but this is ridiculous. Welcome to Club Mejunje, set in the ruins of an old roofless building given over to sprouting greenery. It's a local – nay, national – institution, famous for many things, not least Cuba's first official drag show (every Saturday night).

ⓘ Information

INTERNET ACCESS

Etecsa Telepunto (Marta Abreu No 55, btwn Máximo Gómez & Villuendas; internet per hour CUC$1.50; ⊘8:30am-7pm) Eight internet terminals and three phone cabins.

Parque Vidal Wi-fi hotspot.

MONEY

Banco Financiero Internacional (Cuba No 6, cnr Rafael Tristá; ⊘9am-3pm Mon-Fri) Has an ATM.

Cadeca (cnr Rafael Tristá & Cuba; ⊘8:30am-8pm Mon-Sat, to 11:30am Sun) On the corner of the main square, this is the best place to change money. Long opening hours.

TOURIST INFORMATION

Infotur (⌨42-20-13-52; Cuba No 68, btwn Machado & Maestra Nicolasa; ⊘8:30am-5pm) Handy maps and brochures in multiple languages.

ⓘ Getting There & Away

AIR

Santa Clara's **Abel Santamaría Airport** (⌨42-22-75-25; off Rte 311) receives several weekly flights from Montreal, Toronto and Calgary, plus a Copa Airlines flight to Panama City on Tuesday and Sunday, and is now the country's third-most-important airport. There are no flights to Havana.

BUS

The **Terminal de Ómnibus Nacionales** (⌨42-20-34-70), which is also the Víazul bus station, is 2.5km west of the center, out on the Carretera Central toward Matanzas, or 500m north of the Che monument. Tickets for air-conditioned Víazul buses are sold at a special 'foreigners' ticket window at the station entrance.

ⓘ Getting Around

Horse carriages congregate outside the cathedral on Marta Abreu and will angle for CUC$1 per ride. Bici-taxis (from the northwest of the park) cost the same. Taxis from the center to the Terminal de Ómnibus Nacionales/airport cost CUC$3/15.

Trinidad

⌨ 41 / POP 73,500

Trinidad is one-of-a-kind, a perfectly preserved Spanish colonial settlement where the clocks stopped in 1850 and – apart from a zombie invasion of tourists – have yet to restart. Huge sugar fortunes amassed in nearby Valle de los Ingenios during the early 19th century created the illustrious colonial-style mansions bedecked with Italian frescoes, Wedgwood china and French chandeliers.

Declared a World Heritage Site by Unesco in 1988, Cuba's oldest and most enchanting 'outdoor museum' attracts busloads of visitors. Yet the cobblestone streets, replete with leather-faced *guajiros* (country folk), snorting donkeys and melodic troubadours, retain a quiet air. Come nightfall, the live-music scene is particularly good.

It's also ringed by sparkling natural attractions. Twelve kilometers south lies platinum-blond Playa Ancón, the best beach of Cuba's south coast. Looming 18km to the north, the purple-hued shadows of the

Sierra del Escambray (Escambray Mountains) offer a lush adventure playground with hiking trails and waterfalls.

◉ Sights

★ Museo Histórico Municipal   MUSEUM
(☑ 41-99-44-60; Simón Bolívar 423; CUC$2; ⊙ 9am-5pm Sat-Thu) Trinidad's main museum, this grandiose mansion just off Plaza Mayor belonged to the Borrell family from 1827 to 1830. Later it passed to a German planter named Kanter, or Cantero, for whom it's now named. The rundown exhibits could use a full makeover but the city panoramas from the tower, reached by rickety stairs, is alone worth the price of admission.

Plaza Mayor   SQUARE
(☎) Trinidad's remarkably peaceful main square is located in the heart of the *casco histórico* and is the town's most photographed spot.

Iglesia Parroquial de la Santísima Trinidad   CHURCH
(⊙ 11am-12:30pm Mon-Sat) Despite its unremarkable facade, this church on the northeastern side of Plaza Mayor graces countless Trinidad postcards. Rebuilt in 1892 on the site of a church destroyed in a storm, it mixes 20th-century touch-ups with artifacts dating to the 18th century, such as the venerated Christ of the True Cross (1713), second altar from the front to the left.

Museo Nacional de la Lucha Contra Bandidos   MUSEUM
(☑ 41-99-41-21; Echerri 59; CUC$1; ⊙ 9am-5pm Tue-Sun) The most recognizable building in Trinidad, the dilapidated pastel-yellow bell tower occupies the former convent of San Francisco de Asís. Since 1986, it has been a museum with photos, maps, weapons and objects relating to the struggle against the various counter-revolutionary bands that took a leaf out of Fidel's book and operated illicitly out of the Sierra del Escambray between 1960 and 1965.

Museo Romántico   MUSEUM
(☑ 41-99-43-63; Echerri 52; CUC$2; ⊙ 9am-5pm Tue-Sun) Across Calle Simón Bolívar is the glittering Palacio Brunet. The ground floor was built in 1740, and the upstairs was added in 1808. In 1974 the mansion was converted into a museum with 19th-century furnishings, a fine collection of china and various other period pieces. Pushy museum staff may materialize out of the shadows for a tip.

⚡ Activities

Centro Ecuestre Diana   HORSEBACK RIDING
(☑ 41-99-36-73; www.trinidadphoto.com; riding CUC$26-30) 🐎 This unique equestrian center offers nature excursions and riding lessons with helmets on a *finca* (farm) on the edge of town. It's not set up for walkins, inquire first with Julio at Casa Muñoz (p319). Visits include huge country-style meals that are a hit. It's also a rescue center promoting better equine care and humane horse-training techniques.

Parque el Cubano   HIKING
(CUC$10) This pleasant spot within a protected park consists of a *ranchón* (farmstyle restaurant) serving *pez gato* (catfish) from the on-site fish farm. Take the Huellas de la História trail (3.6km) to the refreshing Javira Waterfall. With a stop for lunch in the *ranchón* (thatched-roof restaurant) it can make an excellent day trip.

☞ Tours

Trinidad Travels   HIKING, HORSEBACK RIDING
(☑ 52-82-37-26; www.trinidadtravels.com; Antonio Maceo No 613a) One of the best private guides is English- and Italian-speaking Reinier at Trinidad Travels. He leads all kinds of excursions, including hiking in the Sierra del Escambray and horseback riding in the nearby countryside. Spanish lessons are also offered. He's based at Casa de Victor (☑ 41-99-64-44; hostalsandra@yahoo.es).

🛏 Sleeping

★ Casa El Suizo   CASA PARTICULAR $
(☑ 53-77-28-12; P Pichs Girón No 22; r CUC$40; P ❄) Away from the hustle of the center and handily located for excursions by the Trinidad–Cienfuegos road, this spacious lodging feels more like an inn, with five large rooms each featuring private terraces. Installations are new, with a safe, hair dryer and wi-fi on the way. English and German are spoken. The only downside is longer walking distances from central attractions.

★ Casa Muñoz – Julio & Rosa   CASA PARTICULAR $
(☑ 41-99-36-73; www.trinidadphoto.com; José Martí No 401, cnr Escobar; d/tr/apt CUC$40/45/50, photography tour CUC$25; P ❄) A stunning colonial home with outstanding warmth, English-speaking assistance and a few gentle dogs on-site. There are three huge rooms and a two-level apartment. Delicious food is

served on the patio. Book early. It's insanely popular with licensed US people-to-people groups. Julio is an accomplished photographer offering courses on documentary photography, religion and life in Cuba's new economic reality.

Nelson Fernández Rodríguez
CASA PARTICULAR $

(☑41-99-38-49; www.hostalcasanelsontrinidad.com; Piro Guinart No 226, btwn Maceo & Gustavo Izquierdo; r CUC$30; ❋) Nelson's place above the lovely **Restaurant El Dorado** (meals CUC$6-12; ⊙noon-midnight) bears all the hallmarks of a fine Trinidadian homestay – lush patio, romantic terrace and Unesco-standard colonial splendor. Four rooms are available, as well as two across the street (run by the same family).

El Rústico
CASA PARTICULAR $

(☑41-99-30-24; Juan Manuel Márquez No 54a, btwn Piro Guinart & Simón Bolívar; s/d/tr CUC$25/30/35; ❋) These upstairs rooms above the El Criollo restaurant (guests get discounts) are a pleasant, breezy surprise, with attractive, immaculate spaces and hair dryers in the bathrooms. The roof terrace is a nice bonus. It's one cobbled block from Plaza Mayor.

Hostal José & Fatima
CASA PARTICULAR $

(☑41-99-66-82; hostaljoseyfatima@gmail.com; Zerquera No 159, btwn Frank País & Pettersen; r CUC$30-35; ❋🛜) Highly popular casa with five rooms and colonial trimmings, including a terrace. The helpful hosts can hook you up with many local activities. There's also an adorable dachshund keen on dog lovers.

★ Iberostar Grand Hotel
BOUTIQUE HOTEL $$$

(☑41-99-60-70; www.iberostar.com; cnr José Martí & General Lino Pérez; d incl breakfast from CUC$400; ❋@🛜) Start in the fern-filled tiled lobby and browse the courtyard surrounded by three floors of rooms in a remodeled 19th-century colonial. The five-star Grand oozes luxury. Forget the standard all-inclusive tourist formula. Instead there's privacy, refinement and an appreciation for local history. Details shine from a cool cigar bar to 36 rooms with designer toiletries, in-room minibars, safes and coffee makers.

✖ Eating

★ Vista Gourmet
CUBAN, INTERNATIONAL $$

(☑41-99-67-00; Callejón de Galdos; mains CUC$13; ⊙noon-midnight; ✈) A slick private option perched on a lovely terrace above Trinidad's red-tiled rooftops. Run by the charismatic sommelier Bolo, its novelties include free rooftop sunset cocktails. Hungry diners will love the appetizer and dessert buffet. Tender *lechón asado* (roast pork) and fresh lobster are both recommended. Wines have climatized storage, choose your bottle from an extensive selection. It has vegetarian options.

Restaurante San José
CUBAN $$

(☑41-99-47-02; Maceo No 382; mains CUC$6-15) Word is out on this handsome restaurant serving fresh grilled snapper, sweet-potato fries and frozen limeade. It's among the town's best. Servers weave between gleaming furniture and crowded tables. Come early if you don't want to wait.

Cubita Restaurant
INTERNATIONAL $$

(☑54-30-63-76; Antonio Maceo No 471; mains CUC$8-15; ⊙11am-midnight) When good food and fine service conspire, it can be a highly pleasurable experience – and one which, until recently, had been hard to find in Trinidad. Fighting hard in a highly competitive field, La Cubita has inventive starters, complimentary salads, some wonderfully marinated *brochetas* and highly discreet service. It's run by Trinidad's famous ceramicmakers.

★ La Redaccion Cuba
INTERNATIONAL $$$

(☑41-99-45-93; www.laredaccioncuba.com; Maceo No 463; mains CUC$8-17) With bare-bones brickwork more Brooklyn than Cuba, this new French-run offering provides a dose of comfort for travelers with culinary homesickness. Think huge lamb burgers with yam chips, pasta tossed with lobster and herbs, and stone-oven cooked meals. For solo travelers, there's a huge shared table in the center conducive to making friends. Otherwise, reserve ahead as it's popular.

Esquerra
CUBAN $$$

(☑41-99-34-34; Rosario No 464; mains CUC$8-18; ⊙noon-11pm) With a prime location on the cobblestone plaza, this elegant restaurant serves well-prepared Cuban fare. It differs from the competition with specialty flavors – spicy *criollo* tomato sauce, meunière and Catalan sauces that give a boost to fish or pork. Shrimp cocktail is a standout, as is service. There's also a nice intimate courtyard option.

🍷 Drinking & Nightlife

⭐ Taberna La Botija   BAR
(cnr Juan Manuel Márquez & Piro Guinart; ⊘24hr)
While other restaurants send their waitstaff
out into the street to fish for customers, La
Botija crams half the town into its lively corner bar without even trying. The key: a warm
talk-to-your-neighbor atmosphere, cold beer
served in ceramic mugs and the best house
band in Trinidad (think jazz meets soul over
a violin). The food ain't bad either.

Café Don Pepe   CAFE
(☑41-99-35-73; cnr Piro Guinart & Martínez Villena;
⊘8am-11pm) In an adorable colonial courtyard decorated with modern graffiti, the
best coffee in Trinidad is served in ceramic
mugs with a square of Baracoan chocolate.

Taberna la Canchánchara   BAR
(cnr Rubén Martínez Villena & Ciro Redondo;
⊘10am-midnight) This place is famous for
its eponymous house cocktail made from
rum, honey, lemon and water. Local musicians regularly drop by for off-the-cuff jam
sessions, and it's not unusual for the *can-
chánchara*-inebriated crowd to break into
spontaneous dancing. Note that hours can
be sporadic.

☆ Entertainment

⭐ Casa de la Música   CLUB
(Cristo; cover CUC$2) One of Trinidad's
(and Cuba's) classic venues, this casa is
an alfresco affair that congregates on the
sweeping staircase beside the Iglesia Parroquial off Plaza Mayor. A good mix of tourists
and locals take in the 10pm salsa show here.
Alternatively, full-on salsa concerts are held
in the casa's rear courtyard (also accessible
from Juan Manuel Márquez).

⭐ Casa de la Trova   LIVE MUSIC
(Echerri No 29; CUC$1; ⊘9pm-2am) Trinidad's
spirited casa retains its earthy essence
despite the high ratio of package tourists
to Cubans. Local musicians to look out for
here are Semillas del Son, Santa Palabra and
the town's best *trovador* (traditional singer/
songwriter), Israel Moreno.

Rincon de la Salsa   CLUB
(☑53-91-02-45; Zerquera, btwn Martínez Villena &
Ernesto; ⊘10pm-2am) A fun live-music venue
aimed at those practicing their salsa steps. It
can also connect travelers to dance teachers
for private lessons during the daytime.

Palenque de los Congos Reales   LIVE MUSIC
(cnr Echerri & Av Jesús Menéndez) A must for
rumba fans, this open patio on Trinidad's
music alley has an eclectic menu incorporating salsa, *son* (Cuban popular music) and
trova (traditional poetic singing). The highlight, however, is the 10pm rumba drumming with soulful African rhythms and
energetic fire-eating dancers.

🛍 Shopping

Arts & Crafts Market   CRAFTS, SOUVENIRS
(Av Jesús Menéndez; ⊘9am-6pm) This open-air
market in front of the Casa de la Trova is
the place to buy souvenirs, especially textiles
and crochet work. Avoid buying black coral
or turtle-shell items, made from endangered
species. Many countries forbid travelers
from bringing them in.

Taller Alfarero   CERAMICS
(☑41-99-31-46; Andrés Berro No 51, btwn Pepito
Tey & Abel Santamaría; ⊘8am-noon & 2-5pm Mon-
Fri) 𝗙𝗥𝗘𝗘 Trinidad is known for its pottery.
In this large factory, teams of workers make
trademark Trinidad ceramics from local clay
using a traditional potter's wheel. You can
watch them at work and buy the finished
product.

ℹ Information

INTERNET ACCESS
There's public wi-fi in Plaza Mayor and on the
steps leading to the Casa de la Musica.

Dulcinea (Antonio Maceo No 473; internet per
hr CUC$4.50; ⊘9am-8:30pm) Half a dozen
terminals on the corner of Simón Bolívar.
Crowded.

Etecsa Telepunto (cnr General Lino Pérez &
Francisco Pettersen; internet per hr CUC$1.50;
⊘8:30am-7pm) Modern, if slow, computer
terminals. Not too crowded.

MEDICAL SERVICES
Trinidad has a hospital and pharmacy services.
General Hospital (☑41-99-32-01; Antonio
Maceo No 6) Southeast of the city center.
Servimed Clínica Internacional Cubanacán
(☑41-99-62-40; General Lino Pérez No 103,
cnr Anastasio Cárdenas; ⊘24hr) There is
an on-site pharmacy selling products in
convertibles.

MONEY
There are banking services and a currency-exchange house.
Banco de Crédito y Comercio (José Martí No
264; ⊘9am-3pm Mon-Fri) Has an ATM.

VIAZUL BUS DEPARTURES FROM TRINIDAD

DESTINATION	COST (CUC$)	DURATION	DEPARTURES
Cienfuegos	6	1½hr	7:30am, 8:15am, 3pm, 4pm
Havana	25	6hr 20min	8:15am, 4pm
Santa Clara	8	3hr	7:30am
Santiago de Cuba	33	12hr	8am
Varadero	20	6hr	7:30am, 3pm

Cadeca (Maceo, btwn Camilo Cienfuegos & Lino Perez; ⊘8:30am-5pm) Money changers.

TOURIST INFORMATION

The agencies in Trinidad usually have a line – try to go early.

Cubatur (☑41-99-63-14; Antonio Maceo No 447; ⊘8am-8pm) Good for general tourist information, plus hotel bookings and excursions. Goes to Valle los Ingenios (CUC$35) and Salto de Caburni in Topes de Collante (CUC$30). Snorkeling excursions go to Cayo Las Iguanas (CUC$45) and Cayo Blanco (CUC$50). State taxis congregate outside.

Infotur (☑42-99-82-58; Gustavo Izquierdo No 112; ⊘9am-5pm) Useful for general information on the town, its surroundings and Sancti Spíritus province.

ⓘ Getting There & Away

BUS

The centrally located **bus station** (Piro Guinart No 224) has buses for nationals and the more reliable Víazul service aimed at foreign travelers. The **Víazul ticket office** (☑41-99-44-48; ⊘8:30am-4pm) is further back in the station.

The Cubanacán **Conectando** tourist shuttle service has direct links daily with Havana (CUC$25). There's no office. Inquire at **Infotur** (p322).

ⓘ Getting Around

BICYCLE

Casas particulares can help organize bike rentals with a local. Just don't expect the latest Shimano gears. Trinidad to Playa Ancón is a pleasant and flat 30-minute ride; Trinidad to Topes de Collantes is akin to a tough stage in the Tour de France.

TRINIDAD BUS TOUR

Trinidad has a handy hop-on, hop-off tourist-oriented minibus, **Bus Turístico** (all-day ticket CUC$5), similar to Havana's and Viñales', linking its outlying sights.

Around Trinidad

Topes de Collantes

The Sierra del Escambray is Cuba's second-largest mountain range. The beautiful crenellated hills are rich in flora and surprisingly isolated. With the best network of hiking trails in Cuba, these jungle-clad forests harbor vines, ferns and eye-catching epiphytes.

⊙ Sights

Museo de Arte Cubano Contemporáneo   MUSEUM
(CUC$2; ⊘8am-8pm) Believe it or not, Topes de Collantes' monstrous sanatorium once harbored a veritable Louvre of Cuban art, containing works by Cuban masters such as Tomás Sánchez and Rubén Torres Llorca. Raiding the old collection in 2008 inspired provincial officials to open this infinitely more attractive museum, which displays more than 70 works in six *salas* (rooms) spread over three floors. The museum is on the main approach road from Trinidad, just before the hotels.

🏃 Activities

★**Sendero 'Centinelas del Río Melodioso'**   HIKING
(entry CUC$10, tour incl lunch CUC$47) The least accessible but the most rewarding hike by far from Topes de Collantes is this 6km round-trip hike in Parque Guanayara. The trail begins in cool, moist coffee plantations and descends steeply to **El Rocio** waterfall, where you can enjoy a bracing shower. Following the course of the Río Melodioso, pass another inviting waterfall and swimming pool, **Poza del Venado**, before emerging into the gardens of **Casa la Gallega**, a traditional rural hacienda.

★ Salto del Caburní   HIKING, SWIMMING

(CUC$10) The classic Topes hike, easily accessed on foot from the hotels, goes to this 62m waterfall that cascades over rocks into cool swimming holes before plunging into a chasm where macho locals dare each other to jump. Be warned: at the height of the dry season (March to May) there may be low water levels.

Hacienda Codina   HIKING

(CUC$10) At the hacienda, the **Sendero de Alfombra Mágica** is a 1.2km circular trail through orchid and bamboo gardens and past the Cueva del Altar. There are also mud baths, a restaurant and a scenic viewpoint. It's 8km from Topes by a rough road (the 4km 4WD track begins on a hilltop 3km down the road toward Cienfuegos and Manicaragua).

ℹ Information

Centro de Visitantes (⊘8am-5pm) Near the sundial at the entrance to the hotel complexes; it's the best place to procure maps, guides and trail info.

ℹ Getting There & Away

Without a car, it's very difficult to get to Topes de Collantes and harder still to get around to the various trailheads. Your best bet is a taxi (CUC$40 to CUC$60 return with a wait), an excursion from Trinidad (from CUC$35) or a hire car.

Camagüey

🗹 32 / POP 301,000

Cuba's third-largest city is easily the suavest and most sophisticated after Havana. The arts shine brightly here and it's also the bastion of the Catholic Church on the island. Well known for going their own way in times of crisis, its resilient citizens are called *agramontinos* by other Cubans, after local First War of Independence hero Ignacio Agramonte, coauthor of the Guáimaro constitution and courageous leader of Cuba's finest cavalry brigade.

Camagüey's pastel colonials and warren-like streets are inspiring. Get lost for a day or two exploring hidden plazas, baroque churches, riveting galleries and congenial bars and restaurants. The flip side is that there is a higher-than-average number of *jineteros* (touts) who can dog you as you stroll.

WORTH A TRIP

PLAYA ANCÓN

A ribbon of white beach on Sancti Spíritus' iridescent Caribbean shoreline Playa Ancón is often considered the finest arc of sand on Cuba's south coast. The beach has three all-inclusive hotels and a well-equipped marina with catamaran trips to nearby coral keys. While it can't compete with the north-coast giants of Varadero, Cayo Coco and Guardalavaca, Ancón has one trump card: Trinidad, Latin America's sparkling colonial diamond, lies just 12km to the north.

◉ Sights

Camagüey's peculiar street pattern was designed to confuse pillaging invaders and provide cover for its long-suffering residents (or so legend has it). As a result, Camagüey's sinuous streets and narrow, winding alleys are more reminiscent of a Moroccan medina than the geometric grids of Lima or Mexico City.

★ Plaza del Carmen   SQUARE

(Hermanos Agüero, btwn Honda & Carmen) Around 600m west of the frenzy of República sits another sublimely beautiful square, one less visited than the central plazas. It's backed on the eastern side by the masterful Iglesia de Nuestra Señora del Carmen, one of the prettiest city churches.

★ Casa de Arte Jover   GALLERY

(🗹32-29-23-05; Martí No 154, btwn Independencia & Cisneros; ⊘9am-noon & 3-5pm Mon-Sat) **FREE** Camagüey is home to two of Cuba's most creative and prodigious contemporary painters, Joel Jover and his wife Ileana Sánchez. Their magnificent home in Plaza Agramonte functions as a gallery and piece of art in its own right, with a slew of original pieces, resident chihuahuas and delightfully kitschy antiques on show. Guests can browse and purchase high-quality original art.

The artists also keep a studio and showroom, the **Estudio-Galería Jover** (Calle Ramón Pinto 109; ⊘9am-noon & 3-5pm Mon-Sat) **FREE**, in Plaza San Juan de Dios.

★ Museo Provincial Ignacio Agramonte   MUSEUM

(🗹32-28-24-25; Av de los Mártires No 2; CUC$2; ⊘9am-5pm Tue-Fri, 9am-4pm Sat, to 1pm Sun) Named (like half of Camagüey) after the exalted local War of Independence hero, this cavernous museum, just north of the train station, is in a Spanish cavalry barracks dating from 1848. There's some impressive artwork upstairs, including much by Camagüey natives, as well as antique furniture and old family heirlooms.

Museo Casa Natal de Ignacio Agramonte
MUSEUM

(📞 32-28-24-25; Av Agramonte No 459; CUC$2; ⏰9am-5pm Tue-Fri, 9am-4pm Sat, to 1pm Sun) The birthplace of independence hero Ignacio Agramonte (1841-73), the cattle rancher who led the Camagüey area's revolt against Spain. The house – an elegant colonial building in its own right – tells of the often-overlooked role of Camagüey and Agramonte in the First War of Independence. The hero's gun is one of his few personal possessions displayed.

Plaza San Juan de Dios
SQUARE

(cnr Hurtado & Calle Ramón Pinto) Looking more Mexican than Cuban (Mexico was capital of New Spain so the colonial architecture was often superior), Plaza San Juan de Dios is Camagüey's most picturesque and beautifully preserved corner. Its eastern aspect is dominated by the Museo de San Juan de Dios, formerly a hospital. Behind the square's arresting blue, yellow and pink building facades lurk worthwhile restaurants.

Parque Ignacio Agramonte
SQUARE

(cnr Martí & Independencia) Camagüey's most dazzling square in the heart of the city invites relaxation with rings of marble benches and an equestrian statue (c 1950) of Camagüey's precocious War of Independence hero, Agramonte.

Iglesia de Nuestra Señora de la Merced
CHURCH

(Plaza de los Trabajadores) Dating from 1748, this is arguably Camagüey's most impressive colonial church. Its history is imbued with legend. Local myth tells of a miraculous figure that floated from the watery depths here in 1601 and it has been a spot of worship ever since. The active convent in the attached cloister is distinguished by its two-level arched interior, spooky catacombs (where the church faithful were buried until 1814) and the dazzling Santo Sepulcro, a solid silver coffin.

Catedral de Nuestra Señora de la Candelaria
CHURCH

(Cisneros 168) Any exploration of Camagüey's religious history should begin at its most important church, named for the city's patron saint. Rebuilt in the 19th century on the site of an earlier chapel dating from 1530, the cathedral was fully restored with funds raised from Pope John Paul II's 1998 visit. While not Camagüey's most eye-catching church, it is noted for its noble Christ statue that sits atop a craning bell tower. You can climb the tower for CUC$1.

👉 Tours

★ Camaguax Tours
TOURS

(📞 32-28-73-64, 58-64-23-28; www.camaguax.com/en; República 155 No 7; ⏰8:30am-5:30pm) A private agency with English- and French-speaking guides and myriad quality offerings throughout the province with a cultural or adventure focus. Hits include a city tour, sugarcane-farm visits, hiking and caving. There's excursions to Sierra del Chorrillo, Reserva Nacional Limones Tubaquey and Río Maximo. Uses 4WD vehicles for rough roads and has overnight options.

🛏 Sleeping

The city is undergoing a boom in boutique hotel accommodations, with two more planned to open in the near future.

★ Los Vitrales
CASA PARTICULAR $

(Emma Barreto & Rafael Requejo; 📞 32-29-58-66, 52-94-25-22; requejobarreto@gmail.com; Avellaneda No 3, btwn General Gómez & Martí; r CUC$30; 🅿❄) A former convent, this enormous, painstakingly restored colonial house sports broad arches, high ceilings and dozens of antiques. The helpful owner Rafael is an architect and it shows. Three rooms with good water pressure are arranged around a shady patio draped in lush gardens that are a highlight. There's over-the-top breakfasts and dinners with special orders available (vegetarians welcome).

La China House
CASA PARTICULAR $

(📞 32-28-30-28, 54-65-92-40; houselachina@gmail.com; Padre Valencia No 57; r $25; ❄) In front of the Teatro Principal, this impeccably kept 2nd-story apartment features modern art and colonial style. There are two rooms with leather headboards, TV and electric showers. Friendly host Misleydi offers dinner and can arrange massage, salsa and guitar classes. With some English.

Casa Láncara CASA PARTICULAR $
(☑32-28-31-87; aledino@nauta.cu; Avellaneda No 160; r CUC$30; ❄🛜) A dose of Seville with beautiful blue and yellow *azulejos* (tiles), this welcoming colonial is overseen by Andalucian fanatic Alejandro and his wife, Dinorah. The two rooms are hung with original local art and there's a roof terrace all within spitting distance of the Soledad church. They are in the process of building a gorgeous lodging across the street.

★**El Marqués** BOUTIQUE HOTEL $$$
(☑32-24-49-37; ventas@ehoteles.cmg.tur.cu; Cisneros No 222; s/d incl breakfast CUC$120/160; ❄@🛜) Simply lovely, this six-room colonial is a treasure trove of character. Rooms shoot off a central courtyard with rod-iron furniture, each door guarded by a Marta Jimenez sculpture on a pedestal. Bedrooms feature satellite TV, safe and air-conditioning. There's period furniture and quiet throughout. Also features a small bar with 24-hour service and hot tub. It's part of the exclusive E hotel brand managed by Cubanacan.

★**Hotel Camino de Hierro** BOUTIQUE HOTEL $$$
(☑32-28-42-64; ventas@ehoteles.cmg.tur.cu; Plaza de la Solidaridad; s/d CUC$115/140; ❄@) Among the best of Camagüey's boutique hotels, it occupies an attractive city center building that was once an office for the Cuban *ferrocarril* (railway). So goes the railway theme. There's also lovely colonial furniture and romantic balconies. Guests enjoy a 24-hour bar and a pleasant patio privy to all the downtown action. It's also part of the exclusive E hotel brand.

✖ Eating

Restaurante Carmen CUBAN $
(☑32-28-79-02; Maceo No 6; mains CUC$2-12; ⊙11am-11pm; ❄) With a Siberian chill thanks to hyperactive air-conditioning, this popular restaurant on the pedestrian stretch of Maceo brims with locals at midday. Most come for the cheap lunch specials – get yours early because they usually run out. It's consistent, with a diverse menu that ranges from sandwiches to stewed meat with rice.

★**Casa Austria** EUROPEAN $$
(☑32-28-55-80; Lugareño No 121, btwn San Rafael & San Clemente; meals CUC$5-14; ⊙7:30am-11:30pm; ❄) Locals line up for strudel and decadent cakes at this Austrian-run cafe. After so much *comida criolla* (Creole food), travelers embrace the international menu featuring chicken cordon bleu, schnitzel and garbanzos stewed in tomato sauce with bacon. It's all good. The setting, stuffed with heavy colonial furniture, is a bit claustrophobic, but there's patio dining as well.

★**El Paso** INTERNATIONAL $$
(☑32-27-43-21; Hermanos Agüero No 261, btwn Carmen & Honda; meals CUC$5-10; ⊙9am-11pm) Finally, a private restaurant with all-day hours, plus a funky interior and an enviable Plaza del Carmen location. There's flavorful *ropa vieja* (spiced shredded beef) and heaping bowls of *arroz con pollo a la chorillana* (chicken, rice prunes and peppers in a ceramic bowl). Try *pan patato* for dessert – consisting of cassava and coconut. With lovely patio and 2nd-floor terrace seating.

☆ Entertainment

★**Teatro Principal** THEATER
(☑32-29-30-48; Padre Valencia No 64; tickets CUC$5-10; ⊙shows 8:30pm Fri & Sat, 5pm Sun) If a show's on, GO! Second only to Havana in its ballet credentials, the Camagüey Ballet Company, founded in 1971 by Fernando Alonso (ex-husband of the number-one Cuban dancing diva, Alicia Alonso), is internationally renowned and performances are the talk of the town. Also of interest is the wonderful theater building of 1850 vintage, bedizened with majestic chandeliers and stained glass.

Casa de la Trova Patricio Ballagas LIVE MUSIC
(☑32-29-13-57; Cisneros No 171, btwn Martí & Cristo; CUC$3; ⊙7pm-1am) An ornate entrance hall gives way to an atmospheric patio where old crooners sing and young couples *chachachá*. One of Cuba's best *trova* (traditional singing) houses, where regular tourist traffic doesn't detract from the old-world authenticity. Tuesday's a good night for traditional music. Cover includes one drink.

❶ Information

INTERNET ACCESS

There's public wi-fi (with scratchcard-code access) at Parque Ignacio Agramonte and between Plaza los Trabajadores and Iglesia de Nuestra Señora de la Soledad.

Etecsa Telepunto (☑32-25-15-59; República, btwn San Martín & José Ramón Silva; internet per hr CUC$1.50; ⊙8:30am-7pm) Camagüey is light on wi-fi, so grab one of the dozen

VÍAZUL BUS DEPARTURES FROM CAMAGÜEY

DESTINATION	COST (CUC$)	DURATION (HR)	DAILY DEPARTURES
Havana	33	9	12:35am, 6:30am, 11:05am, 2:25pm, 11:45pm
Holguín	11	3	12:30am, 4:30am, 6:25am, 1:20pm, 6:40pm
Santiago de Cuba	18	6	12:30am, 6:25am, 9:30am, 1:20pm, 4pm
Trinidad	15	4½	2:45am
Varadero	24	8¼	3:10am

terminals here. Visitors can buy a scratch card for wi-fi.

MEDICAL SERVICES

Policlínico Integral Rodolfo Ramirez Esquival (☑ 32-28-14-81; cnr Ignacio Sánchez & Joaquín de Agüero) North of the level crossing from the Hotel Plaza; it will treat foreigners in an emergency.

MONEY

Banco de Crédito y Comercio (☑ 32-29-25-31; cnr Av Agramonte & Cisneros; ☉ 9am-3pm Mon-Fri) Has an ATM.

POST

Post Office (☑ 32-29-39-58; Av Agramonte No 461, btwn Independencia & Cisneros; ☉ 9am-6pm Mon-Sat)

TOURIST INFORMATION

Infotur (☑ 32-25-67-94; www.facebook.com/camaguey.travel; Ignacio Agramonte; ☉ 8:30am-5:30pm) Very helpful information office hidden in a gallery near Casablanca cinema.

❶ Getting There & Away

AIR

Ignacio Agramonte International Airport (☑ 32-26-72-02; Carretera Nuevitas Km 7) Ignacio Agramonte International Airport is 9km northeast of town on the road to Nuevitas and Playa Santa Lucía.

Air connections to the United States continue to grow. **Air Transat** (www.airtransat.com) and **Sunwing** (www.sunwing.ca) fly in the all-inclusive crowd from Toronto, who are hastily bussed off to Playa Santa Lucía.

BUS

The **Estacion Ferro Omnibus** (regional bus station) near the train station, has trucks to regional destinations (CUC$2) including Playa Santa Lucía, paid in Cuban pesos. Arrive at 5am to be secure a spot for beach-bound trucks.

Long-distance **Víazul** (☑ 32-27-03-96; www.viazul.com) buses depart from the **Estacion Interprovincial** (Bus Station; Carretera Central), 3km southeast of the center.

TRAIN

The **train station** (☑ tickets 32-28-47-66; cnr Avellaneda & Av Carlos J Finlay; to Santiago/Havana CUC$11/19) is more conveniently located than the bus station – though its service isn't as convenient. Every fourth day the Tren Francés leaves for Santiago at around 3:19am and for Havana, stopping in Santa Clara, at around 1:47am.

❶ Getting Around

Bicycle taxis are found around most of the city's squares, with the main contingent in Plaza de los Trabajadores. They should cost five pesos, but drivers will probably ask for payment in convertibles.

EASTERN CUBA

Santiago de Cuba

☑ 22 / POP 431,500

Cuba's cultural capital, Santiago is a frenetic, passionate and noisy beauty. Situated closer to Haiti and the Dominican Republic than to Havana, it leans east rather than west, a crucial factor shaping this city's unique identity, steeped in Afro-Carribean, entrepreneurial and rebel influences.

Trailblazing characters and a resounding sense of historical destiny define it. Diego Velázquez de Cuéllar made Santiago his second capital, Fidel Castro used it to launch his embryonic revolution, Don Facundo Bacardí based his first-ever rum factory here, and nearly every Cuban music genre from salsa to *son* first emanated from these dusty, rhythmic and sensuous streets.

Caught dramatically between the indomitable Sierra Maestra and the azure Caribbean, the colonial *casco histórico* (historical center) retains a time-worn air reminiscent of Salvador in Brazil or forgotten New Orleans. So don't let the hustlers, the speeding Chevys or the clawing heat defeat you. There's untold magic here too.

◉ Sights

★ Castillo de San Pedro de la Roca del Morro   FORT

(El Morro; ☏22-69-15-69; CUC$5; ⏰9am-7pm; ♿) A Unesco World Heritage site since 1997, the San Pedro fort sits impregnably atop a 60m-high promontory at the entrance to Santiago harbor, 10km southwest of the city. The stupendous views from the upper terrace take in the wild western ribbon of Santiago's coastline backed by the velvety Sierra Maestra.

The fort was designed in 1587 by famous Italian military engineer Juan Bautista Antonelli (who also designed La Punta and El Morro forts in Havana) to protect Santiago from pillaging pirates who had successfully sacked the city in 1554. Due to financial constraints, the building work didn't start until 1633 (17 years after Antonelli's death) and it carried on sporadically for the next 60 years. In the interim British privateer Henry Morgan sacked and partially destroyed it.

Finally finished in the early 1700s, El Morro's massive batteries, bastions, magazines and walls got little opportunity to serve their true purpose. With the era of piracy in decline, the fort was converted into a prison in the 1800s and it stayed that way – bar a brief interlude during the 1898 Spanish-Cuban-American War – until Cuban architect Francisco Prat Puig mustered up a restoration plan in the late 1960s.

Today, the fort hosts the swashbuckling Museo de Piratería, with another room given over to the US-Spanish naval battle that took place in the bay in 1898.

The fort, like Havana has a cañonazo ceremony (firing of the cannon) each day at sunset when actors dress up in Mambises regalia.

To get to El Morro from the city center, take bus 212 to Ciudamar and walk the final 20 minutes. Alternatively, a round-trip taxi ride from Parque Céspedes with wait time should cost no more than CUC$25.

★ Cementerio Santa Ifigenia   CEMETERY

(Av Crombet; CUC$3; ⏰8am-6pm) Nestled peacefully on the city's western extremity, the Cementerio Santa Ifigenia is second only to Havana's Necrópolis Cristóbal Colón in its importance and grandiosity. Created in 1868 to accommodate the victims of the War of Independence and a simultaneous yellow-fever outbreak, the Santa Ifigenia includes many great historical figures among its 8000-plus tombs, notably the mausoleum of José Martí and final resting place of Fidel Castro.

★ Cuartel Moncada   MUSEUM

(Moncada Barracks; ☏22-66-11-57; Av Moncada) Santiago's famous Moncada Barracks, a crenellated art-deco building completed in 1938, is now synonymous with one of history's greatest failed putsches. Moncada earned immortality on July 26, 1953, when more than 100 revolutionaries led by then little-known Fidel Castro stormed Batista's troops at what was then Cuba's second-most important military garrison.

After the Revolution, the barracks, like all others in Cuba, was converted into a school called Ciudad Escolar 26 de Julio, and in 1967 a museum (CUC$2; ⏰9am-5pm Mon-Sat, to 1pm Sun) was installed near gate 3, where the main attack took place. As Batista's soldiers had cemented over the original bullet holes from the attack, the Castro government remade them (this time without guns) years later as a poignant reminder. The museum (one of Cuba's best) contains a scale model of the barracks plus interesting and sometimes grisly artifacts, diagrams and models of the attack, its planning and its aftermath. Most moving, perhaps, are the photographs of the 61 fallen at the end.

The first barracks on this site was constructed by the Spanish in 1859, and actually takes its name from Guillermón Moncada, a War of Independence fighter who was held prisoner here in 1874.

CUBA SANTIAGO DE CUBA

Santiago de Cuba

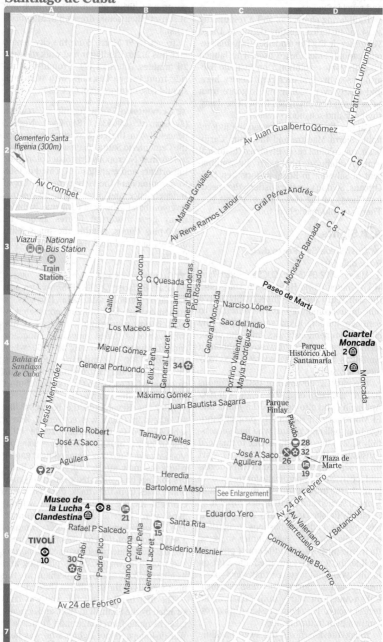

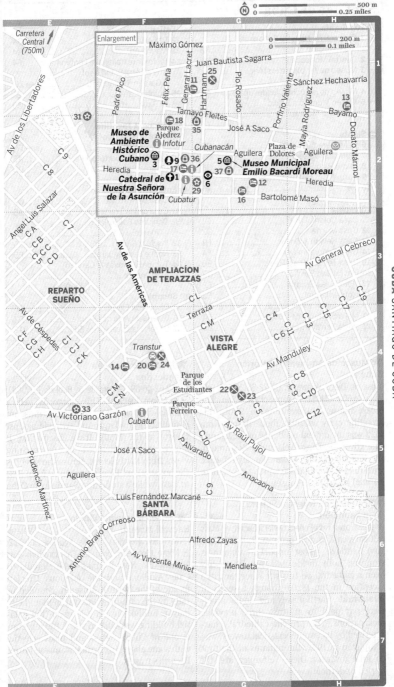

0 — 500 m
0 — 0.25 miles

Carretera Central (750m)

Enlargement

0 — 200 m
0 — 0.1 miles

Máximo Gómez

Juan Bautista Sagarra

Padre Pico

Félix Peña

General Lacret

Hartmann

Pío Rosado

Sánchez Hechavarría

Porfirio Valiente

Mayía Rodríguez

Donato Mármol

Bayamo

13

25

11

Tamayo Fleites

José A Saco

18

35

Parque Ajedrez
Infotur

Aguilera

Plaza de Dolores

Aguilera

Museo de Ambiente Histórico Cubano

Cubanacán

9

36

5

Museo Municipal Emilio Bacardí Moreau

Heredia

3

17

37

Heredia

Catedral de Nuestra Señora de la Asunción

1

6

29

12

16

Cubatur

Bartolomé Masó

Av de los Libertadores

31

C 9

C 8

Angel Luis Salazar

C A

C B

C C

C 5

C D

C 7

REPARTO SUEÑO

Av de las Américas

AMPLIACIÓN DE TERAZZAS

Av General Cebreco

C L

Terraza

C M

VISTA ALEGRE

C 4

C 6

C 11

C 13

C 15

C 17

C 19

Av de Céspedes

C F

C G

C I

C H

C J

C K

Transtur

14

20

24

C M

C N

Parque de los Estudiantes

22

23

C 5

Av Manduley

C 8

C 9

C 10

33

Av Victoriano Garzón

Cubatur

Parque Ferreiro

C 3

C 10

Av Raúl Pujol

C 12

José A Saco

P Alvarado

Aguilera

Prudencio Martínez

C 9

Anacaona

SANTA BÁRBARA

Luis Fernández Marcané

Antonio Bravo Correoso

Alfredo Zayas

Av Vincente Miniet

Mendieta

Santiago de Cuba

★ Museo de Ambiente Histórico Cubano   MUSEUM

(Casa de Diego Velázquez; ☎ 22-65-26-52; Felix Peña No 602; CUC$2; ⊙9am-5pm Mon-Sun) The oldest house still standing in Cuba, this arresting early colonial abode dating from 1522 was the official residence of the island's first governor, Diego Velázquez. Restored in the late 1960s, the Andalusian-style facade with fine, wooden lattice windows was inaugurated in 1970 as a museum.

★ Catedral de Nuestra Señora de la Asunción   CHURCH

(Heredia, btwn Felix Peña & General Lacret; ⊙Mass 6:30pm Mon & Wed-Fri, 5pm Sat, 9am & 6:30pm Sun) Santiago's most important church is stunning both inside and out. There has been a cathedral on this site since the city's inception in the 1520s, though a series of pirate raids, earthquakes and dodgy architects put paid to at least three previous incarnations. The present cathedral, characterized by its two neoclassical towers, was completed in 1922; the remains of the first colonial governor, Diego Velázquez, are still buried underneath.

★ Museo de la Lucha Clandestina   MUSEUM

(☎22-62-46-89; General Jesús Rabí No 1; CUC$1; ⊙9am-5pm Tue-Sun) This gorgeous yellow colonial-style building houses a museum detailing the underground struggle against Batista in the 1950s. It's a fascinating, if bloody, story enhanced by far-reaching views from the balcony. Across the street is the house where Fidel Castro lived from 1931 to 1933, while a student in Santiago de Cuba (not open for visits).

★ Museo Municipal Emilio Bacardí Moreau   MUSEUM

(btwn Calle Heredia & Calle Aguilera; CUC$2; ⊙1-5pm Mon, 9am-5pm Tue-Fri, 9am-1pm Sat) Narrow Pío Rosado links Calle Heredia to Calle Aguilera and the fabulous Grecian facade of the Bacardí Museum. Founded in 1899 by the rum-magnate war hero and city mayor, Emilio Bacardí y Moreau (the palatial building was built to spec), the museum is one of Cuba's oldest and most eclectic, with some absorbing artifacts amassed from Bacardí's travels.

Calle Heredia STREET

The music never stops on Calle Heredia, Santiago's most sensuous street and also one of its oldest. Melodies waft from the paint-peeled **Casa de Cultura Josue País García**, where *danzón*-strutting pensioners mix with svelte teen rap artists. One door up is Cuba's original **Casa de la Trova**, a beautiful balconied townhouse redolent of New Orleans' French Quarter.

Tivolí AREA

Santiago's old French quarter was first settled by colonists from Haiti in the late 18th and early 19th centuries. Set on a south-facing hillside overlooking the shimmering harbor, its red-tiled roofs and hidden patios are a tranquil haven these days, with old men pushing around dominoes and ebullient kids playing stickball amid pink splashes of bougainvillea.

The century-old **Padre Pico steps** (cnr Padre Pico & Diego Palacios), cut into the steepest part of Calle Padre Pico, stand at the neighborhood's gateway.

Parque Céspedes PARK

(🛜) Archetype for romantic Cuban street life, Parque Céspedes is a throbbing kaleidoscope of walking, talking, hustling, flirting, guitar-strumming humanity. Surrounded by colonial architecture, this most ebullient of city squares is a sight to behold day or night. See the bronze bust of **Carlos Manuel de Céspedes**, who kick-started Cuban independence in 1868, and Cubans enjoying the open wi-fi signal.

🛌 Sleeping

⭐ Roy's Terrace Inn CASA PARTICULAR $

(📲 22-62-05-22; roysterraceinn@gmail.com; Diego Palacios No 177, btwn Padre Pico & Mariano Corona; r CUC$35; 🅿 ❄ 🛜) From the hanging rooftop garden to wall murals and impeccable rooms, every fiber gleams. Run by an enthusiastic team of well-traveled Cubans and local mamas who woo you with their warmth and cooking, this spot is tops. Rooms are filled with modern amenities, including TV, hair dryers and information packets. Service – in English, Spanish, French and some German – is a highlight.

Casa Colonial 1893 CASA PARTICULAR $

(📲 22-62-24-70; casacolonial1893@gmail.com; Hechavarría No 301; r CUC$25-30; ❄) In a lovely, well-preserved colonial, this home features seven rooms gathered around a huge inte-

rior patio with original tiles. Rooms feature bright satin bedcovers. Not unusual for casas where renting is important to the household, but still unsettling, the family congregates off to the side, beyond a partial wall in the front room.

Casa Señora Inalvis CASA PARTICULAR $

(📲 22-65-11-13, 53-08-80-20; nalviscasado@nauta.cu; Calle 6ta No 660; r CUC$25-30; ❄) Located on a convenient corner near Melia hotel, this cute suburban home has just a couple of rooms and a shady back patio. Your host Sra Inalvis is a gem, a former journalist who is unusually helpful and quick to offer fresh juice or coffee.

Casa Milena CASA PARTICULAR $

(📲 22-62-88-22, 53-19-58-14; penelope1212@nauta.cu; Heredia No 306; r CUC$25-30; ❄) Smack in the heart of the street renowned for live music, this welcoming family colonial home features three huge rooms. It's very clean and central.

Casa Terraza Pavo Real CASA PARTICULAR $

(📲 22-65-85-89; juanmarti13@yahoo.es; Santa Rita No 302, cnr San Félix; r CUC$25-30; ❄ 🛜) The meticulously maintained family home of Juan Martí has a palatial quality, with a riot of antique furniture, light-filtering *vitrales* and coiled spiral staircases. The crowning glory is a huge Alhambra-esque patio with a sleep-invoking fountain and an expansive roof terrace with exotic orchids. Yet many might feel at odds with the tropical birds and peacocks in cages.

Casa Nelson & Deisy CASA PARTICULAR $

(📲 22-65-63-72, 33-65-81-33; casanelsonydeysi@yahoo.es; Donato Marmol No 476 1/2; r CUC$20-25; ❄) Decked in white, this thoroughly modern casa sits in a renovated building in the colonial core. There are three smart rooms and a private terrace. Nelson and Deisy are famous for their cooking, with good vegetarian fare and cocktails to boot. Has very cordial service.

Hotel Libertad HOTEL $

(📲 22-62-77-10; reserva@libertad.tur.cu; Aguilera No 658; s/d CUC$61/66; ❄ @ 🛜) Cheap Cuban hotel chain Islazul breaks out of its Soviet-themed concrete-block obsession and goes colonial in this venerable beauty on Plaza de Marte. It has positive staff and 17 clean (if sometimes dark) high-ceilinged rooms featuring narrow singles. It's quirky in novelesque ways – don't be surprised if a

Chinese salesperson is selling clothes out of suitcases in the hall.

Hotel Casa Granda
HOTEL $$

(☑ 22-65-30-24; Heredia No 201; s/d CUC$92/128; ✻@🖥) This elegant 1914 hotel, artfully described by Graham Greene in his book *Our Man in Havana*, has 58 rooms and classic atmosphere. Greene stayed here in the late 1950s when he enjoyed relaxing on the streetside terrace while his famous pen captured the nocturnal essence of the city. Half a century later, rooms are serviceable but the atmosphere remains potent.

Hostal San Basilio
BOUTIQUE HOTEL $$

(☑ 22-65-17-02; www.cubatravelnetwork.com; Bartolomé Masó No 403, btwn Pío Rosado & Porfirio Valiente; d incl breakfast CUC$100; ✻@) The lovely eight-room San Basilio (named for the original name of the street on which it lies) is cozy and refreshingly contemporary – with a romantic colonial setting including a petite patio dripping with ferns. Rooms come with DVD players, umbrellas, bathroom scales and mini bottles of rum. Alas, some mattresses need replacing. A small restaurant serves breakfast and lunch.

★ Hotel Imperial
HISTORIC HOTEL $$$

(☑ 22-62-82-30; José A Saco, btwn Felix Peña & General Lacret; s/d CUC$97/138; ✻🖥) The return of a Santiago landmark, the eclectic-style 1915 Hotel Imperial has been refurbished to sparkling condition with some welcome concessions to modernity. The 39 rooms are smartly furnished and spanking new, with flat-screen TVs, tall windows and glass showers. Features an elevator to an elegant roof-terrace bar with great city views and live music on weekends.

Meliá Santiago de Cuba
HOTEL $$$

(☑ 22-68-70-70; www.meliacuba.com/cuba-hotels/hotel-melia-santiagodecuba; cnr Av de las Américas & Calle M; s/d incl breakfast CUC$174/224; P✻@🖥≋) Sleek on the inside, a blue-mirrored monster on the outside, the 1990s-designed Meliá is Santiago's only 'international' hotel with a laundry list of amenities hard to find elsewhere. Count on real bathtubs in every room, three pools, four restaurants, various shopping facilities and an elegant 15th-floor bar. The downsides are its location on the outskirts and lack of genuine Cuban charm.

✖ Eating

Despite having more than one million inhabitants and a medley of culture, Santiago has a somewhat lean restaurant scene. The outlook is mediocre with the odd get-out-of-jail card, though the situation has improved slightly in the last few years.

In the *casco histórico*, Calle José A Saco is a pedestrian-only street with mobile food units selling *comida ligera* (light food).

Rumba Café
CAFE $

(☑ 58-02-21-53; Hartmann No 455; sandwiches CUC$3-7; ⏰ 9:30am-10:30pm Mon-Sat; 🖋) You can escape the frenetic pace of downtown Santiago by ducking into this sleek, air-conditioned cafe that seems an alternate reality. Lattes? Vegetarian sandwiches? It's real. There are inviting spaces, satisfying grilled sandwiches and beautiful omelets.

La Fortaleza
CUBAN $

(☑ 22-64-62-96; cnr Av Manduley & Calle 3; meals CUC$3-7; ⏰noon-11:30pm) In a conducive setting amid Vista Alegre's mansions, a spacious, inviting shady patio serving above-average food (pay in pesos) alongside live music at lunchtime. But? A big fat zero for the quality of service.

★ Roy's Terrace Inn Roof Garden Restaurant
CUBAN $$

(☑ 22-62-05-22; roysterraceinn@gmail.com; meals CUC$10-15; ⏰7-9:30pm; 🖥🖋) If only the rest of Cuba could harness this formula: quality homemade food, caring service and excellent atmosphere. Reserve one day ahead for one of only six rooftop tables surrounded by tumbling flowers in candlelight. Cocktails deliver and family-style servings come overflowing. Fish, chicken and pork are served with sides such as crispy *tamal* or sautéed eggplant. Vegans and vegetarians welcome.

★ St Pauli
INTERNATIONAL $$

(☑ 22-65-22-92; José A Saco No 605; meals CUC$4-15; ⏰noon-11pm Mon-Thu, noon-midnight Fri-Sun) In a city of no great culinary tradition, St Pauli arrived like a hurricane. Walk the long mural-decorated corridor off Calle Saco to a bright room featuring blackboard menus and a glass-wall kitchen. Everything is consistently good, particularly the cocktail-glass gazpacho, *pulpo al ajillo* (octopus with garlic) and pineapple chicken fajitas. If you've come behind a group: patience!

GIBARA

Matched only by Baracoa for its wild coastal setting, half-forgotten Gibara, with its faded pastel facades and surging ocean rollers, conspires to seduce you. Close to Holguín, there's a cultural life here that seems big for a small town. In 2008, Hurricane Ike almost wiped the town off the map.

Situated 33km from Holguín via a scenic road that undulates through villages, Gibara is a small, intimate place receiving a lift from much-needed investment. Unlike nearby Guardalavaca, development here is low-key and focused on renovating the town's beautiful but dilapidated architecture. The saddle-shaped Silla de Gibara that so captivated Columbus creates a wild, scenic backdrop.

As Gibara's specific attractions are few, rather like Baracoa, this is more a town to stroll the streets and absorb the local flavor. There are a couple of decent beaches within striking distance, including lovely **Playa Caletones** 17m to the west.

Gibara has some of the province's best options for bedding down, from regal casas particulares to the wonderful **Hotel Ordoño** (24-84-44-48; recepcion@hotelordono.tur. cu; J Peralta, cnr Donato Mámol & Independencia; s/d/ste incl breakfast CUC$100/130/160; ⚙ @), a contender for the best hotel in Cuba.

There are no reliable buses to Gibara. Travelers will need their own wheels or a taxi. Cars from Guardalavaca or Holguín cost around CUC$40.

Madrileño CUBAN $$

(22-64-41-38; Calle 8 No 105; meals CUC$4-15; ⊙noon-11pm) A well-respected, good-quality option, Madrileño occupies a classy colonial abode in Vista Alegre with interior patio dining with chirping birds. Contrary to the name, this is Cuban *comida criolla* (creole food). Succulent odors waft from the kitchen. There's an extensive menu with an emphasis on grilled meats. Forgo the seafood skewers, which are on the dry side.

El Palenquito PARRILLA $$

(22-64-52-20; Av del Río No 28, btwn Calle 6 & Carretera de Caney; mains CUC$6-12) Barbecue is the specialty of this casual backyard restaurant on the outskirts of Santiago. Grilled pork and chicken are served with the typical sides, but the real star is dessert. Try rich zapote or coconut ice cream in the shells of the original fruit – portions are huge, but you suddenly might not want to share. With good service.

Ristorante Italiano la Fontana ITALIAN $$$

(cnr Av de las Américas & Calle M, Meliá Santiago de Cuba; mains CUC$6-18; ⊙noon-11pm) Pizza *deliciosa* and lasagna *formidable,* ravioli and garlic bread; *mamma mía,* this has to be the number-one option for breaking away from all that chicken and pork! Prices are jacked up on Chilean wines, but it might be worth it anyway.

🍷 Drinking & Nightlife

★**Casa Granda Roof Garden Bar** BAR

(top fl, Heredia No 201; cover CUC$3-10; ⊙11am-1am) Slip up to the 5th-floor roof of Casa Granda for the most breathtaking sunset in Cuba. Views of the scene in Parque Céspedes and the dramatically lit cathedral are well worth the minimum consumption charge for nonguests (it increases after 7pm), which credits toward your first drink. So what if drinks are twice what you'd pay elsewhere? You're well above the fray.

Cervecería Puerto del Rey MICROBREWERY

(22-68-60-48; Paseo Alameda & Aguilera; ⊙noon-midnight) You know Cuba is changing when you find an actual warehouse-style brewpub filled with locals quaffing pints brewed on-site. If your taste runs stronger and darker than Buccanero, come to this noisy, fun spot. Flavors aren't yet perfected, but who cares? There's decent pub food, including popular *caldo del rey* (a broth with a pork-rib base).

La Gran Sofía CAFE

(Paraíso; snacks CUC$1-2; ⊙24hr) A local hangout where the coffee is good and *bocaditos* (sandwiches) won't set you back.

☆ Entertainment

'Spoiled for choice' would be an understatement in Santiago. For what's happening, look for the biweekly *Cartelera Cultural*.

The reception desk at Hotel Casa Granda usually has copies.

★ **Casa de las Tradiciones** LIVE MUSIC
(☑ 22-65-38-92; General J Rabí No 154; CUC$1; ☺ 5pm-midnight) The most discovered 'undiscovered' spot in Santiago still retains its smoke-filled, foot-stomping, front-room feel. Hidden in the genteel Tivolí district, some of Santiago de Cuba's most exciting ensembles, singers and soloists take turns improvising. Friday nights are reserved for straight-up classic *trova*, à la Ñico Saquito and the like. There's a gritty bar and some colourful artwork.

★ **Iris Jazz Club** JAZZ
(General Serafín Sánchez, btwn José A Saco & Bayamo; CUC$5; ☺ shows 9:30pm-2am) When Santiago gets too hot, noisy and agitated, you need a dose of Iris, one of Cuba's suavest and best jazz clubs where you can sit in a comfy booth surrounded by pictures of puffing jazz greats and watch some incredibly intuitive exponents of Santiago's small but significant jazz scene.

Noche Santiagüera LIVE PERFORMANCE
(Av Victoriano Garzón, btwn Moncada & Parque los Estudiantes; ☺ 6pm-midnight Sat) FREE Every Saturday night, the side streets branching off this main thoroughfare teem with street food, music and crowds for a city-wide outdoor party.

Conjunto Folklórico de Oriente DANCE
(☑ 22-64-31-78; Teatro José María Heredia, cnr Avs de las Américas & de los Desfiles) Santiago's oldest *folklórico* group was formed in 1959; they are currently bivouacked at the Teatro Heredia. They perform a huge range of Afro-Cuban dance genres from *gagá* and *bembé* to *tumba francesa*.

Casa de la Trova LIVE MUSIC
(☑ 22-65-38-92; Heredia No 208; ☺ hours vary) Santiago's shrine to the power of traditional music is still going strong five decades on, continuing to attract big names such as Buena Vista Social Club singer Eliades Ochoa. Warming up on the ground floor in the late afternoon, the action slowly gravitates upstairs where, come 10pm, everything starts to get a shade more *caliente*.

Tumba Francesa la Caridad de Oriente DANCE
(Pio Rosado No 268) For pure *tumba francesa* dancing, check out the Tumba Francesa la Caridad de Oriente, one of only three of these French-Haitian groups left in Cuba. They can be seen in their rehearsal rooms on Tuesdays and Thursdays at 9pm.

🛍 Shopping

Galería de Arte de Oriente ARTS & CRAFTS
(☑ 22-65-38-57; General Lacret No 656; ☺ 9:30am-6pm Mon-Fri, 9:30am-noon Sat, 10am-10pm Sun) Probably the best gallery in Santiago de Cuba, the art here is consistently good.

Librería la Escalera de Edy BOOKS
(Heredia No 265; ☺ 10am-10pm) A veritable museum of old and rare books stacked ceiling high, plus vinyl records. Sombrero-clad *trovadores* often sit on the stairway and strum.

Discoteca Egrem MUSIC
(☑ 22-62-61-91; José A Saco No 309; ☺ 9am-6pm Mon-Sat, to 2pm Sun) The definitive Cuban specialist-music store; this retail outlet of Egrem Studios has a good selection from local musicians.

ℹ Information

INTERNET ACCESS

There's wi-fi in public plazas, major hotels and a few casas particulares. Buy wi-fi credit on scratchcards at Etecsa Telepunto centers, where there's usually a line out the door, or hotel lobbies, though the latter frequently run out.

Etecsa Multiservicios (☑ 22-62-47-84; cnr Heredia & Félix Peña; internet per hr CUC$1.50; ☺ 8:30am-7:30pm) Internet terminals and wi-fi scratchcards in a small office on Plaza Céspedes.

Etecsa Telepunto (☑ 22-65-75-21; cnr Hartmann & Tamayo Fleites; internet per hr CUC$1.50; ☺ 8:30am-7:30pm) Internet terminals, and sells wi-fi scratchcards.

MEDICAL SERVICES

Santiago has the best access to medicine and related services in the region.

Clínica Internacional Cubanacán Servimed (☑ 22-64-25-89; cnr Av Raúl Pujol & Calle 10, Vista Alegre; ☺ 24hr) Capable staff speak some English. A dentist is also present.

Farmacia Clínica Internacional (☑ 22-64-25-89; cnr Av Raúl Pujol & Calle 10; ☺ 24hr) Best pharmacy in town, selling products in convertibles.

MONEY

The city has plenty of banks and currency-exchange centers.

VÍAZUL BUS DEPARTURES FROM SANTIAGO DE CUBA

DESTINATION	COST (CUC$)	DURATION (HR)	DAILY DEPARTURES
Baracoa	15	4¾	1:50am, 8am
Havana	51	13-14½	12:30am, 6:30am, 4pm
Trinidad	33	11½	7:30pm
Varadero	49	15	8pm

Banco de Crédito y Comercio (☎22-62-80-06; Felix Peña No 614; ☺9am-3pm Mon-Fri) In the jarring modern building in Plaza Céspedes.

Banco Financiero Internacional (☎22-68-62-52; cnr Av de las Américas & Calle I; ☺9am-3pm Mon-Fri) Has an ATM.

Cadeca (☎22-65-13-83; Aguilera No 508; ☺8:30am-4pm Mon-Fri, to 11:30am Sat) Long lines for currency exchange; there's also a branch at **José A Saco.** (José A Saco No 409; ☺8:30am-4pm Mon-Fri, to 11:30am Sat)

POST

Post Office (☎22-62-21-08; Aguilera No 519; ☺9am-5pm Mon-Fri) Has telephones too.

TOURIST INFORMATION

As all tour agencies are government-run, they offer overlapping services and consistent prices.

Cubanacán (☎22-68-64-12; Heredia No 201; ☺8am-6pm) Very helpful; sells tours in the Hotel Casa Granda.

Cubatur (☎22-65-25-60; Av Victoriano Garzón No 364, cnr Calle 4; ☺8am-8pm) Sells all number of excursions, for everything from La Gran Piedra to El Cobre. There's another branch at Heredia No 701.

Infotur (☎22-68-60-68; Felix Peña 562; ☺8am-8pm) Helpful location and staff. There's also a branch in Antonio Maceo International Airport.

ⓘ Getting There & Away

AIR

Antonio Maceo International Airport (SCU; ☎22-69-10-53) is 7km south of Santiago de Cuba, off the Carretera del Morro. International flights arrive from Santo Domingo (Dominican Republic), Toronto, Montreal and Miami.

Internally, Cubana flies nonstop from Havana to Santiago de Cuba two or three times a day (about CUC$136 one way, 1½ hours). There are also services to Holguín with Aerogaviota.

BUS

The **National Bus Station** (Paseo de Martí s/n, behind train station), opposite the Heredia Monument, is 3km northeast of Parque Céspedes.

Víazul (☎22-62-84-84; www.viazul.cu) buses leave from the same station.

TRAIN

The modern French-style **train station** (☎22-62-28-36; cnr Av Jesús Menéndez & Martí) is situated near the rum factory northwest of the center. The *Tren Francés* leaves every fourth day for Havana (CUC$30 minimum 16 hours) stopping at Camagüey and Santa Clara en route. Check ahead regarding departure times.

ⓘ Getting Around

TO/FROM THE AIRPORT

A taxi to or from the airport should cost CUC$10, but drivers will often try to charge you more. Haggle hard before you get in.

You can also get to the airport on bus 212, which leaves from Av de los Libertadores opposite the Hospital de Maternidad.

CAR

Santiago de Cuba suffers from a chronic shortage of rental cars (especially in peak season). You might find there are none available; though the locals have an indefatigable Cuban ability to *conseguir* (manage or get) and *resolver* (resolve or work out). The airport offices usually have better availability than those in town.

TAXI

There's a **Transtur** (☎22-68-71-60) taxi stand in front of Meliá Santiago de Cuba. Taxis also wait on Parque Céspedes near the cathedral and hiss at you expectantly as you pass. Hammer out a price beforehand. To the airport, costs range between CUC$8 and CUC$10 depending on the state of the car.

Baracoa

☎21 / POP 82,000

Beguiling, outlandish and surreal, Baracoa's essence is addictive. On the wet and windy side of the Cuchillos del Toa Mountains, Cuba's oldest and most isolated town exudes original atmosphere.

Feast your eyes upon deep green foliage that's wonderfully abundant after the stark aridity of Guantánamo's south coast. Delve into fantastical legends, and acquaint yourself with an unorthodox cast of local characters. There's Cayamba, the self-styled 'Guerrilla troubadour' who once claimed he was 'the man with the ugliest voice in the world'; La Rusa, an aristocratic Russian émigré who inspired a novel by magic-realist author Alejo Carpentier; and Enriqueta Faber, a French woman who passed herself off as a man to practice as a doctor and marry a local heiress in Baracoa's cathedral in 1819 – likely Cuba's first same-sex marriage. Baracoa – what would Cuba be without you?

While 2016's Hurricane Matthew hit Baracoa hard, the town is already on the rebound.

☉ Sights

★ Museo Arqueológico 'La Cueva del Paraíso'
MUSEUM

(Moncada; CUC$3; ☉8am-5pm) Baracoa's most impressive museum, Las Cuevas del Paraíso is a series of caves that were once Taíno burial chambers. Among nearly 2000 authentic Taíno pieces are unearthed skeletons, ceramics, 3000-year-old petroglyphs and a replica of the *Ídolo de Tabaco*, a sculpture found in Maisí in 1903 and considered to be one of the most important Taíno finds in the Caribbean.

Casa del Cacao
MUSEUM

(☑21-64-21-25; Antonio Maceo, btwn Maraví & Frank País; ☉7am-11pm) FREE Baracoa, you will quickly ascertain (via your nose), is the center of Cuba's chocolate industry; cacao beans are grown hereabouts and subsequently chocolate-ized in a local factory. Thus this museum with cafe chronicles the history of cacao and its importance in eastern Cuba as well as offering cups full of the pure, thick stuff (hot or cold) in a pleasant indoor cafe. They also sell bars of dark, agreeably bitter Baracoan chocolate.

Parque Natural Majayara
PARK

(CUC$2, lookout CUC$5) 🏊 Southeast of town in the Parque Natural Majayara are a couple of magical hikes and swimming opportunities plus an archaeological trail in the grounds of a lush family farm. It's a very low-key, DIY diversion. Alternatively, **Ecotur** (☑21-64-24-78) leads trips here (CUC$20).

Fuerte Matachín
FORT

(Museo Municipal; ☑21-64-21-22; cnr José Martí & Malecón; CUC$1; ☉8am-noon & 2-6pm) Baracoa is protected by a trio of muscular Spanish forts. This one, built in 1802 at the southern entrance to town, houses the Museo Municipal. The small but beautiful building showcases an engaging chronology of Cuba's oldest settlement including *polymita* snail shells, the story of Che Guevara and the chocolate factory, and the particular strand of music Baracoa gave birth to: *kiribá*, a forefather of *son*.

Catedral de Nuestra Señora de la Asunción
CHURCH

(☑21-64-30-05; Antonio Maceo No 152; ☉7-11am & 4-9pm Tue-Sun) After years of neglect, Baracoa's hurricane-battered historic cathedral has been lovingly restored using primarily Italian funding. There's been a building on this site since the 16th century, though this present, much altered incarnation dates from 1833.

☞ Tours

★ José Ángel Delfino Pérez
TOURS

(☑21-64-13-67, 54-25-58-19; joseguia@nauta.cu; day tours CUC$25-27) Walking plant encyclopedia and enthusiastic geological expert, José has to be Baracoa's best private guide. His professional tours visit El Yunque, Punta de Maisi, Humboldt and – best of all – Boca de Yumurí, a trip that takes in cacao plantations, chocolate tastings and visits to isolated beaches. Prices drop for larger groups.

Ask to see José's ID, as he has some unwelcome local impersonators. You can contact him by phone, email or at the casa particular of Nilson Abad Guilaré.

🛏 Sleeping

Baracoa has a good assortment of lodgings ranging from private homes to hotels.

Casa Colonial Ykira Mahiquez
CASA PARTICULAR $

(☑21-64-38-81; ykiram@nauta.cu; Antonio Maceo No 168A, btwn Ciro Frías & Céspedes; r CUC$25; ❋) Welcoming and hospitable, Ykira is Baracoa's premier hostess. She also serves a mean dinner made with homegrown herbs. With a lovely mural lining the entrance walk, there are two rooms set in the bosom of family life but with plenty of personal space. Guests enjoy terraces and a *mirador* (viewpoint) with sea views.

Isabel Castro Vilato   CASA PARTICULAR $
(☑ 53-55-36-34, 21-64-22-67; rosellocastro@gmail.
com; Mariana Grajales No 35; r CUC$25; P ❄)
You can't tell from the busy street outside,
but this elegant green clapboard-and-stone
house has lovely country style and a tranquil
atmosphere. There are four massive rooms
with minibars and a beautiful backyard garden growing breakfast provisions for your
table. The hosts are helpful and wonderful.
Unusually for Baracoa, there's a secure car
park.

Casa Yamicel   CASA PARTICULAR $
(☑ 21-64-11-18; ncc.gtm@infomed.sld.cu; Martí No
145A, btwn Pelayo & Ciro Frias; r CUC$25; mains
CUC$6-12; ❄) Doctor-proprietors that make
killer mojitos? You'd better believe it. This
colonial house offers four pleasant rooms
with gorgeous wooden window bars (the
best are on the top floor). There's wonderful hospitality, good meals (mains CUC$6 to
CUC$12) and a roof terrace with reviving sea
breezes.

La Casona   CASA PARTICULAR $
(☑ 21-64-21-33; Félix Ruenes No 1 Altos; r CUC$20-
25; ❄) Rarely is a city's most central casa
among its best, but thus have the young
hosts made this place: two spotless 2nd-floor
rooms and a knockout terrace where you
can enjoy a cocktail or two.

Hostal 1511   HOTEL $$
(☑ 21-64-57-00; reservas@gavbcoa.co.cu; Ciro
Frías, btwn Rubert López & Maceo; s/d CUC$59/64;
❄🛜) The year 1511 is Baracoa's foundation
date, and this diminutive place is a land-
mark, too, for offering dead-central accom-
modations with an abundant colonial vibe.
The model ship in the lobby sets the tone for
an overtly nautical decor that works best in
the more charming upstairs rooms.

Hostal la Habanera   HOTEL $$
(☑ 21-64-52-73; Antonio Maceo No 126; s/d
CUC$59/64; ❄🛜) Atmospheric and invit-
ing in a way only Baracoa can muster, La
Habanera sits in a restored and regularly
repainted colonial mansion. The four front
bedrooms share a street-facing balcony
replete with tiled floor and rocking chairs:
perfect for imbibing that quintessential
Baracoa ambience (street-hawkers, hip-
gyrating music, and seafood a-frying in the
restaurants).

Hotel El Castillo   HOTEL $$
(☑ 21-64-52-24; reservas@gavbcoa.co.cu; Loma
del Paraíso; s/d CUC$59/80; P ❄🛜🏊) Recline
like a colonial-era conquistador in this his-
toric fort-turned-hotel in the hilltop Castillo
de Seboruco. Choose your room well, there's
some wear and tear, though conquistadors
never boasted the privilege of a swimming
pool or housekeeping fashioning towels into
ships and swans. The 28 newer rooms in a
separate block offer jaw-dropping El Yunque
views.

✕ Eating

After the dull monotony of just about every-
where else, eating in Baracoa is a full-on
sensory experience. Cooking here is creative,
tasty and – above all – different. To experi-
ence the real deal, eat in your casa particular.

Cafetería el Parque   FAST FOOD $
(☑ 21-64-12-06; Antonio Maceo No 142; snacks
CUC$1-3; ⊙24hr; 🕿) The favored meeting
place of just about everyone in town, you're
bound to end up at this open terrace at some
point, if only to crack open a Bucanero beer
and tune into the wi-fi.

**★Restaurante Las Terrazas
Casa Nilson**   CUBAN $$
(☑ 21-64-31-23; Flor Crombet No 143, btwn Ciro
Frías & Pelayo Cuervo; meals CUC$6-15; ⊙noon-
3pm & 6:30-11pm) Up above his house on a
spectacular two-level terrace decorated in
quirky Afro-Caribbean style, owner Nilson
serves some of the best authentic Baracoan
food in town, and hence Cuba. You can't
miss with wonderfully rich *pescado con
leche de coco* (fish fillet in coconut milk) or
the melt-in-your-mouth octopus with basil
ink with homemade *patacon guisado,* a
plantain dish. Unforgettable!

El Buen Sabor   CUBAN $$
(☑ 21-64-14-00; Calixto García No 134 Altos; meals
CUC$6-15; ⊙noon-midnight) Served on a spot-
less and breezy upstairs terrace, meals come
with salad, soup and side included. You can
expect the best of Baracoan cuisine at this
private restaurant, including swordfish in a
coconut sauce, *bacán* (raw green plantain
melded with crabmeat and wrapped in a
banana leaf) and chocolate-y deserts. Ser-
vice is attentive.

☆ Entertainment

**★Casa de la Trova
Victorino Rodríguez**   TRADITIONAL MUSIC
(Antonio Maceo No 149A; CUC$1; ⊙matinee
5:30pm, 9pm-midnight) Cuba's smallest, zani-
est, wildest and most atmospheric *casa de*

la trova (*trova* house) rocks nightly to the voodoo-like rhythms of *changüí-son*. One night the average age of the band is 85, the next it's 22. The common denominator? It's all good. Matinees are usually free. Order a mojito in a jam jar and join in the show.

🛍 Shopping

Taller Mirate   ART
(Antonio Maceo; ☺10am-8pm) An artist's co-op where you'll always find one of the young creative painters sitting at a palette in the window. The very local painting style is best described as Gauguin meets Van Gogh in the pages of a Gabriel García Márquez novel.

ℹ Information

INTERNET ACCESS
Etecsa Telepunto (☎21-64-31-82; Antonio Maceo No 182; internet per hr CUC$1.50; ☺9am-7pm) Sells wi-fi internet scratchcards and offers internet on computer terminals.

MONEY
Banco Popular de Ahorro (☎21-64-52-09; José Martí No 166; ☺8-11:30am & 2-4:30pm Mon-Fri) Has an ATM.

Cadeca (☎21-64-53-45; José Martí No 241; ☺8:15am-4pm Mon-Fri, 8:15am-11:30am Sat & Sun) Short queues for currency exchange.

TOURIST INFORMATION
Infotur (☎21-64-17-81; Antonio Maceo No 129a, btwn Frank País & Maraví; ☺8:30am-noon & 1-4:45pm Mon-Sat) Very helpful.

ℹ Getting There & Away

AIR
Gustavo Rizo Airport is 4km northwest of the town, just behind the Hotel Porto Santo. Book flights to Havana with one of the travel agencies.

The planes (and buses) out of Baracoa can be fully booked, so don't arrive on a tight schedule without outbound reservations.

BUS
The **National Bus Station** (☎21-64-38-80; cnr Av Los Mártires & José Martí) has services by Víazul to Guantánamo and Santiago de Cuba. Reserve your tickets a day in advance (more in high season).

ℹ Getting Around

The best way to get to and from the airport is by taxi (CUC$8 to CUC$10), or bici-taxi (CUC$5) if you're traveling light.

There's a helpful **Via Gaviota** (☎21-64-16-65) car-rental office at the airport. If you're driving to Havana, note that the northern route through Moa and Holguín is the most direct but the road disintegrates rapidly after Playa Maguana – for this reason taxi prices can be astronomical. Most locals prefer the La Farola route.

Bici-taxis around Baracoa charge foreigners CUC$2 to CUC$5.

UNDERSTAND CUBA

History

Columbus & Colonization

Columbus neared Cuba on October 27, 1492, describing it as 'the most beautiful land human eyes had ever seen.' He named it 'Juana' in honor of a Spanish heiress. But deluded in his search for the kingdom of the Great Khan, and finding little gold in Cuba's lush and heavily forested interior, Columbus quickly abandoned the territory in favor of Hispaniola (modern-day Haiti and the Dominican Republic).

The colonization of Cuba didn't begin until nearly 20 years later in 1511, when Diego Velázquez de Cuéllar led a flotilla of four ships and 400 men from Hispaniola to conquer the island for the Spanish Crown. Docking near present-day Baracoa, the conquistadors promptly set about establishing seven *villas* (towns) on the main island – Havana, Trinidad, Baracoa, Bayamo, Camagüey, Santiago de Cuba and Sancti Spíritus – in a bid to bring their new colony under strong central rule. Watching nervously from the safety of their *bohíos* (thatched huts), a scattered population of Taínos looked on with a mixture of fascination and fear.

Despite Velázquez' attempts to protect the local Taínos from the gross excesses of the Spanish swordsmen, things quickly got out of hand and the invaders soon found that they had a full-scale rebellion on their hands. Leader of the embittered and short-lived Taíno insurgency was the feisty Hatuey, an influential *cacique* (chief) and archetype of the Cuban resistance, who was eventually captured and burned at the stake, Inquisition-style, for daring to challenge the iron fist of Spanish rule.

With the resistance decapitated, the Spaniards set about emptying Cuba of its relatively meager gold and mineral reserves, using the beleaguered natives as forced labor. As slavery was nominally banned under a papal edict, the Spanish got around the various legal loopholes by introducing a ruthless *encomienda* system, whereby thousands of natives were rounded up and forced to work for Spanish landowners on the pretext that they were receiving free 'lessons' in Christianity.

The brutal system lasted 20 years before the 'Apostle of the Indians,' Fray Bartolomé de Las Casas, appealed to the Spanish Crown for more humane treatment, and in 1542 the *encomiendas* were abolished for the indigenous people. For the unfortunate Taínos, the call came too late. Those who had not already been worked to death in the gold mines quickly succumbed to fatal European diseases such as smallpox, and by 1550 only about 5000 scattered survivors remained.

The Independence Wars

With its brutal slave system established, the Spanish ruled their largest Caribbean colony with an iron fist for the next 200 years, despite a brief occupation by the British in 1792. Cuba's Creole landowners, worried about a repetition of Haiti's brutal 1791 slave rebellion, held back when the rest of Latin America took up arms against the Spanish in the 1810s and 1820s. As a result, the nation's independence wars came more than half a century after the rest of Latin America had broken away from Spain. But when they arrived, they were no less impassioned – or bloody.

Independence or Dependence?

On May 20, 1902, Cuba became an independent republic – or did it? Despite three years of blood, sweat and sacrifice during the Spanish–Cuban–American War, no Cuban representatives were invited to the historic peace treaty held in Paris in 1898 that had promised Cuban independence *with conditions*.

The conditions were contained in the infamous Platt Amendment, a sly addition to the US 1901 Army Appropriations Bill that gave the US the right to intervene militarily in Cuba whenever it saw fit. The US also used its significant leverage to secure itself a naval base in Guantánamo Bay in order to protect its strategic interests in the Panama Canal region.

Despite some opposition in the US and a great deal more in Cuba, the Platt Amendment was passed by Congress and was written into Cuba's 1902 constitution. For Cuban patriots, the US had merely replaced Spain as the new colonizer and enemy. The repercussions have been causing bitter feuds for more than a century and still continue today.

The Batista Era

Fulgencio Batista, a *holguiñero* of mixed race from the town of Banes, was a wily and shrewd negotiator who presided over Cuba's best and worst attempts to establish an embryonic democracy in the 1940s and '50s. After an army officers' coup in 1933, he had taken power almost by default, gradually worming his way into the political vacuum it left amid the corrupt factions of a dying government. From 1934 onwards, Batista served as the army's chief of staff and, in 1940 in a relatively free and fair election, he was duly elected president.

Given an official mandate, Batista began to enact a wide variety of social reforms and set about drafting Cuba's most liberal and democratic constitution to date. But neither the liberal honeymoon nor Batista's good humor were to last. Stepping down after the 1944 election, the former army sergeant handed power over to the politically inept President Ramón Grau San Martín, and corruption and inefficiency soon reigned like never before.

The Revolutionary Spark Is Lit

On March 10, 1952, Batista, hedging his bets, staged another coup. With discontent brewing, a revolutionary circle formed in Havana, with Fidel Castro and many others at its core. On July 26, 1953, Castro led 119 rebels in an attack on the Moncada army barracks in Santiago de Cuba. The assault failed when a 4WD patrol encountered Castro's motorcade, costing the attackers the element of surprise. Castro and a few others escaped into the nearby mountains, where they planned their guerrilla campaign. Soon after, Castro was captured and stood trial; he received a 15-year sentence on Isla de Pinos (now Isla de la Juventud).

In February 1955 Batista won the presidency and freed all political prisoners, including Castro, who went to Mexico and trained a revolutionary force called the 26th of July Movement ('M-26-7'). On December 2, 1956, Castro and 81 companions alighted from the Granma at Playa Las Coloradas in the Oriente. The group was quickly routed by Batista's army, but Castro and 11 others

CUBA HISTORY

(including Argentine doctor Ernesto 'Che' Guevara, Fidel's brother Raúl, and Camilo Cienfuegos) escaped into the Sierra Maestra. In May of the next year, Batista sent 10,000 troops into the mountains to liquidate Castro's 300 guerrillas. By August, the rebels had defeated this advance and captured a great quantity of arms. Che Guevara and Camilo Cienfuegos opened additional fronts in Las Villas Province, with Che capturing Santa Clara. Batista's troops finally surrendered on December 31, 1958.

In the small hours of January 1, 1959, Batista fled by private plane to the Dominican Republic. Meanwhile, materializing in Santiago de Cuba the same day, Fidel made a rousing victory speech from the town hall in Parque Céspedes before jumping into a 4WD and traveling across the breadth of the country to Havana in a Caesar-like cavalcade. The triumph of the revolution was seemingly complete.

Post-Revolution Realities

Cuba's history since the Revolution has been a David and Goliath tale of confrontation, rhetoric, Cold War stand-offs and an omnipresent US trade embargo that has featured 11 US presidents and two infamous Cuban leaders – both called Castro. For the first 30 years, Cuba allied itself with the Soviet Union as the US used various retaliatory tactics (all unsuccessful) to bring Fidel Castro to heel, including a botched invasion, 600-plus assassination attempts and one of the longest economic blockades in modern history.

When the Soviet bloc fell in 1989–91, Cuba stood alone behind an increasingly defiant and stubborn leader surviving, against all odds, through a decade of severe economic austerity known as the Special Period. GDP fell by more than half, luxuries went out the window, and a wartime spirit of rationing and sacrifice took hold among a populace that, ironically, had prized itself free from foreign (neo)colonial influences for the first time in its history.

Enter Raúl

In July 2006, the unimaginable happened. Fidel Castro, rather than dying in office and paving the way for an American-led capitalistic reopening (as had long been predicted), retired from day-to-day governing due to poor health and passed power quietly onto his younger brother, Raúl. Inheriting the country's highest office on the cusp of a major worldwide recession, Raúl began a slow package of reforms.

It kicked off modestly in 2008 when Cubans were permitted access to tourist hotels, and allowed to purchase mobile phones and myriad electronic goods, rights taken for granted in most democratic countries, but long out of reach to the average Cuban. These moves were followed in January 2011 by the biggest economic and ideological shake-up since the country waved *adiós* to Batista. Radical new laws laid off half a million government workers and tried to stimulate the private sector by granting business licenses to 178 state-recognized professions – everything from hairdressers to disposable-lighter refillers. By 2013, Cuba had witnessed its most dramatic economic shift in decades with nearly 400,000 people working in the private sector, 250,000 more than in 2010, though it was still far from anything like Western-style capitalism.

The Passing of Fidel

Fidel's omnipresence for the past half-century made the man seem invincible, yet on November 25th, 2016, Raúl Castro announced his brother's passing at the age of 90. His cremated remains were laid to rest in Santiago de Cuba after a cross-island procession that recalled the march of his revolutionary triumph, done in reverse. Throughout Cuba, crowds lined the streets to pay homage to their longtime leader as exiles celebrated in Miami.

Culture

Just try to understand life on this ever-contradictory island. Your first impression may be that it is solid and immutable. But the truth is that Cuba is a moving target that evades easy definition.

For starters, it's like nowhere else. For those familiar with Latin America, there's close-knit families and an ease with unpredictability. But there are differences too. Cuba's strong education system has created erudite citizens more likely to quote the classics than pop songs. They are playful, even raucous, but also intimate with hardship and austerity, skilled but as languorous as any Caribbean outpost.

The best way to get to know Cuba is to reserve comment and watch it unfold before you. While long lines and poor service infuriate tourists, Cubans remain unflappable. Rushing doesn't make things happen any faster. But there are richer ways to pass the time: shooting the breeze in rocking chairs, spending Sundays with families or inviting their cousins, friends and neighbors over when a bottle of rum comes their way.

Music

Rich, vibrant, layered and soulful, Cuban music has long acted as a standard-bearer for the sounds and rhythms emanating out of Latin America. This is the birthplace of salsa, where elegant European dances adopted edgy black rhythms, and where the African drum first courted the Spanish guitar. From the down-at-heel docks of Matanzas to the bucolic villages of the Sierra Maestra, the amorous musical fusion went on to fuel everything from *son*, rumba, mambo, *chachachá*, *charanga*, *changüí*, *danzón* and more.

Aside from the obvious Spanish and African roots, Cuban music has drawn upon a number of other influences. Mixed into an already exotic melting pot are genres from France, the US, Haiti and Jamaica.

Landscape & Wildlife

Landscape

Formed by a volatile mixture of volcanic activity, plate tectonics and erosion, Cuba's landscape is a lush, varied concoction of mountains, caves, plains and *mogotes* (flat-topped hills). The highest point, Pico Turquino (1972m), is situated in the east among the Sierra Maestra's lofty triangular peaks. Further west, in the Sierra del Escambray, ruffled hilltops and gushing waterfalls straddle the borders of Cienfuegos, Villa Clara and Sancti Spíritus provinces. Rising like purple shadows in the far west, the 175km-long Cordillera de Guanaguanico is a more diminutive range that includes the protected Sierra del Rosario Biosphere Reserve and the distinctive pincushion hills of the Valle de Viñales. Lapped by the warm turquoise waters of the Caribbean Sea in the south, and the chop of the Atlantic Ocean in the north, Cuba's 5746km of coastline shelters more than 300 natural beaches and features one of the world's largest tracts of coral reef. Home to approximately 900 reported species of fish and more than 410 varieties of sponge and coral, the country's unspoiled coastline is a marine wonderland and a major reason why Cuba is renowned as a diving destination.

As a sprawling archipelago, Cuba contains thousands of islands and keys (most uninhabited) in four major offshore groups: the Archipiélago de los Colorados, off northern Pinar del Río; the Archipiélago de Sabana-Camagüey (or Jardines del Rey), off northern Villa Clara and Ciego de Ávila; the Archipiélago de los Jardines de la Reina, off southern Ciego de Ávila; and the Archipiélago de los Canarreos, around Isla de la Juventud. Most visitors will experience one or more of these island idylls, as the majority of resorts, scuba diving and beaches are found in these regions.

Lying in the Caribbean's main hurricane region, Cuba has been hit by some blinders in recent years, notably 2012's Sandy, which more than US$2 billion in damage, and Hurricane Matthew, which touched down in Baracoa in 2016.

Wildlife

Cuba has an unusual share of indigenous fauna to draw serious animal-watchers. Birds are the biggest draw and Cuba has more than 350 different varieties, two dozen endemic. Head to the mangroves of Ciénaga de Zapata in Matanzas province or to the Península de Guanahacabibes in Pinar del Río for the best sightings of *zunzuncito* (bee hummingbird), the world's smallest bird. At 6.5cm, it's not much longer than a toothpick. These areas are also home to the *tocororo* (Cuban trogon), Cuba's national bird. Other popular bird species include *cartacubas* (indigenous to Cuba), herons, spoonbills, parakeets and rarely seen Cuban pygmy owls.

Flamingos are abundant in Cuba's northern keys, though the largest nesting ground in the western hemisphere located in Camagüey province's Río Máximo delta has been compromised by contamination.

Land mammals have been hunted almost to extinction with the largest indigenous survivor the friendly *jutía* (tree rat), a 4kg edible rodent that scavenges on isolated keys living in relative harmony with armies of inquisitive iguanas. The vast majority of Cuba's other 38 species of mammal are from the bat family.

Cuba harbors a species of frog so small and elusive that it wasn't discovered until 1996 in what is now Parque Nacional Alejandro de Humboldt near Baracoa. Still lacking a common name, the endemic amphibian is known as *Eleutherodactylus iberia*; it measures less than 1cm in length, and has a range of only 100 sq km.

Other odd species include the *mariposa de cristal* (Cuban clear-winged butterfly), one of only two clear-winged butterflies in the world; the rare *manjuarí* (Cuban alligator gar), an ancient fish considered a living fossil; the *polimita*, a unique land snail distinguished by its yellow, red and brown bands; and, discovered only in 2011, the endemic *Lucifuga*, a blind troglodyte fish.

Reptiles are well represented in Cuba. Aside from iguanas and lizards, there are 15 species of snake, none poisonous. Cuba's largest snake is the *majá*, a constrictor related to the anaconda that grows up to 4m in length; it's nocturnal and doesn't usually mess with humans. The endemic Cuban crocodile (*Crocodylus rhombifer*) is relatively small but agile on land and in water. Its 68 sharp teeth are specially adapted for crushing turtle shells. Crocs have suffered from major habitat loss in the last century though greater protection since the 1990s has seen numbers increase. Cuba has established a number of successful crocodile breeding farms (*criaderos*), the largest of which is at Guamá near the Bay of Pigs. Living in tandem with the Cuban croc is the larger American crocodile (*Crocodylus acutus*) found in the Zapata Swamps and in marshy territories on Cuba's southern coast.

Cuba's marine life compensates for what it lacks in land fauna. The manatee, the world's only herbivorous aquatic mammal, is found in the Bahía de Taco and the Península de Zapata, and whale sharks frequent the María la Gorda area at Cuba's eastern tip from November to February. Leatherback, loggerhead, green and hawksbill turtles are found in Cuban waters and they nest annually in isolated keys or protected beaches in Península de Guanahacabibes.

SURVIVAL GUIDE

ⓘ Directory A–Z

ACCOMMODATION

Cuba's tourist numbers continue to climb, but hotel provision has lagged behind. It is thus advisable to book all accommodation well in advance.

Casas particulares Cuban homes that rent rooms to foreigners; an authentic and economic form of cultural immersion.

Campismos Cheap, rustic accommodations in rural areas, usually in bungalows or cabins.

Hotels All Cuban hotels are government-owned. Prices and quality range from cheap Soviet-era to high-flying colonial chic.

Resorts Large international-standard hotels in resort areas that sell all-inclusive packages.

Cuban accommodations run the gamut from CUC$10 beach cabins to five-star resorts. Solo travelers are penalized price-wise, paying 75% of the price of a double room.

BUSINESS HOURS

Banks 9am to 3pm Monday to Friday

Cadeca Money Exchanges 9am to 7pm Monday to Saturday, 9am to noon Sunday. Many top-end city hotels offer money exchange late into the evening.

Pharmacies 8am to 8pm

Post Offices 8am to 5pm Monday to Saturday

Restaurants 10:30am to 11pm

Shops 9am to 5pm Monday to Saturday, 9am to noon Sunday

FOOD

Private Restaurants Although slightly pricier than their state-run equivalents, private restaurants nearly always offer the best, freshest food and the highest quality service.

Casas Particulares Cuban homestays invariably serve a massive breakfast for around CUC$5; some also offer an equally large and tasty dinner made from the freshest ingredients.

Hotels & Resorts The all-inclusives offer buffet food of an international standard but after a week it can get a bit bland.

State-run Restaurants Varying food and service from top-notch places in Havana to unimaginative rations in the provinces. Prices often lower than private places.

GLBT TRAVELERS

While Cuba isn't a queer destination (yet), it's more tolerant than many other Latin American countries. The hit movie *Fresa y Chocolate* (Strawberry and Chocolate, 1994) sparked a national dialogue about homosexuality. Activist Mariela Castro, the daughter of Raúl, has led the way in much-needed GLBT reforms and changing social perceptions. Today Cuba is pretty tolerant, all things considered.

People from more accepting societies may find this tolerance too 'don't ask, don't tell' or tokenistic, but Cuba remains ahead of most of Latin America in this respect.

Lesbianism is less tolerated and seldom discussed and you'll see very little open displays of gay pride between female lovers. There are occasional *fiestas para chicas* (not necessarily all-girl parties but close); ask around at the **Cine Yara** (Map p298; cnr Calles 23 & L) in Havana's gay cruising zone.

Cubans are physical with each other and you'll see men hugging, women holding hands and lots of friendly caressing. This type of casual, non-sensual touching shouldn't be a problem.

MONEY

Cuba has two currencies though the government is in the process of unifying them. At the time of writing, convertibles (CUC$) and pesos (*moneda nacional*; MN$) were both still in circulation. One convertible is worth 25 pesos. Non-Cubans deal almost exclusively in convertibles.

ATMs & Credit Cards

→ Cuba is primarily a cash economy. Credit cards are accepted in resort hotels and some city hotels. There are a growing number of ATMs.

→ US residents must note: debit and credit cards from the USA cannot be used.

→ The acceptance of credit cards has become more widespread in Cuba in recent years and was aided by the legalization of US and US-linked credit and debit cards in early 2015. However, change is still a work in process.

→ While services can still be booked with credit cards from the USA on the internet, in country it's another story. Residents of the US can wire money via Western Union, though this requires help from a third party and hefty fees.

→ Cash advances can be drawn from credit cards, but the commission is the same. Check with your home bank before you leave, as many banks won't authorize large withdrawals in foreign countries unless you notify them of your travel plans first.

→ ATMs are becoming more common. This being Cuba, it is wise to only use ATMs when the bank is open, in case any problems occur.

SAFE TRAVEL

Cuba is generally safer than most countries, with violent attacks extremely rare. Petty theft (eg rifled luggage in hotel rooms or unattended shoes disappearing from the beach) is common, but preventative measures work wonders. Pickpocketing is preventable: wear your bag in front of you on crowded buses and at busy markets, and only take the money you will need when you head out at night.

Hustlers are called *jineteros/jineteras* (male/female touts), and can be a real nuisance.

SLEEPING PRICE RANGES

The following price ranges refer to a double room with bathroom in high season.

Havana

$ less than CUC$70

$$ CUC$70–150

$$$ more than CUC$150

Rest of Cuba

$ less than CUC$50

$$ CUC$50–120

$$$ more than CUC$120

TELEPHONE
Cell Phones

→ Check with your service provider to see if your phone will work (GSM or TDMA networks only). International calls are expensive. You can buy services from the state-run phone company, Cubacel.

→ You can use your own GSM or TDMA phones in Cuba, though you'll have to get a local chip and pay an activation fee (approximately CUC$30) at Etecsa Telepunto. Bring your passport.

Phone Codes

→ To call Cuba from abroad, dial your international access code, Cuba's country code (53), the city or area code (minus the 0, which is used when dialing domestically between provinces), and the local number.

→ To call internationally from Cuba, dial Cuba's international access code (119), the country code, the area code and the number. To the US, you just dial 119, then 1, the area code and the number.

→ To call cell phone to cell phone, just dial the eight-digit number (which always starts with a 5).

→ To call cell phone to landline (or landline to landline), dial the provincial code plus the local number.

EATING PRICE RANGES

It will be a very rare meal in Cuba that costs over CUC$25. Restaurant listings use the following price brackets for main dishes.

$ less than CUC$7

$$ CUC$7–15

$$$ more than CUC$15

LICENSES FOR US VISITORS

The US government issues two sorts of licenses for travel to Cuba: 'specific' and 'general.' Specific licenses require a lengthy and sometimes complicated application process and are considered on a case-by-case basis; their application should start at least 45 days before your intended date of departure.

Most visitors will travel under general licenses. General licenses are self-qualifying. Persons traveling under a general license do not need to notify OFAC (Office of Foreign Assets Control) of their travel plans. Travelers sign an affidavit stating the purpose of travel and purchase a Cuban Visa at check-in when departing the United States via airplane. Visas average US$50, purchased through airlines or established third parties.

You might need supporting documentation to back up your claim when you book your flight ticket. Check with the US Department of the Treasury (www.treasury.gov/resource-center/sanctions/Programs/pages/cuba.aspx) to see if you qualify for a license.

➡ To call landline to cell phone dial 01 (or 0 if in Havana) followed by the eight-digit cell phone number.

VISAS

➡ Regular tourists who plan to spend up to two months in Cuba do not need visas. Instead, you get a *tarjeta de turista* (tourist card) valid for 30 days, which can be extended once you're in Cuba (Canadians get 90 days plus the option of a 90-day extension).

➡ Package tourists receive their card with their other travel documents. Those going 'air only' usually buy the tourist card from the travel agency or airline office that sells them the plane ticket, but policies vary (eg Canadian airlines give out tourist cards on their airplanes), so you'll need to check ahead with the airline office via phone or email.

➡ In some cases, you may be required to buy and/or pick up the card at your departure airport, sometimes at the flight gate itself some minutes before departure.

➡ Once in Havana, tourist-card extensions or replacements cost another CUC$25. You cannot leave Cuba without presenting your tourist card.

➡ You are not permitted entry to Cuba without an onward ticket.

🛈 Getting There

AIR

Cuba has 10 international airports. The largest by far is **Aeropuerto Internacional José Martí** (www.havana-airport.org; Av Rancho Boyeros) in Havana. The only other sizeable airport is **Juan Gualberto Gómez International Airport** (☑ 45-61-30-16, 45-24-70-15) in Varadero.

Cubana (www.cubana.cu), the national carrier, operates regular flights to Bogotá, Buenos Aires, Mexico City, Cancún, Caracas, Madrid, Paris, Toronto, Montreal, São Paulo, San José

(Costa Rica) and Santo Domingo (Dominican Republic). Its airfares are usually among the cheapest, though overbooking and delays are nagging problems.

SEA

There are no scheduled ferries between Cuba and other countries.

With US–Cuban relations evolving, many more cruise ships are calling at Cuban ports. **Oceania Cruises** (www.oceaniacruises.com), **Norweigan Cruise Line** (www.ncl.com), **Pearl Seas Cruises** (www.pearlseascruises.com) and **Royal Caribbean** (www.royalcaribbean.com) are all adding Cuba itineraries.

Canadian compan **Celestyal** (www.yourcubacruise.com) circumnavigates the island calling in at Havana, Holguín, Santiago, Montego Bay (Jamaica), Cienfuegos and La Isla de la Juventud.

Another option is with British-based **Thomson** (www.thomson.co.uk) whose seven-night *Cuban Fusion* trip runs out of Montego Bay, Jamaica.

🛈 Getting Around

Buses are the most efficient and practical way of getting around.

Bus The state-run Víazul network links most places of interest to tourists on a regular daily schedule. Cubanacán runs a less comprehensive *conectando* service. Local buses are crowded and have no printed schedules.

Car Rental cars are quite expensive and driving can be a challenge due to the lack of signposts and ambiguous road rules.

Taxi Taxis are an option over longer distances if you are traveling in a small group. Rates are approximately CUC$0.55 per kilometer.

Train Despite its large train network, Cuban trains are slow, unreliable and lacking in comfort. For stoics only!

Curaçao

POP 158,600 / ☎ 5999

Best Places to Eat

➡ Rozendaels (p350)

➡ Mundo Bizzarro (p351)

➡ Old Market (p350)

➡ Seaside Terrace (p353)

➡ Kome (p351)

➡ Jaanchie's (p355)

Best Places to Sleep

➡ Scuba Lodge (p349)

➡ Sonesta Kura Hulanda Village (p350)

➡ Kura Hulanda Lodge (p355)

➡ Floris Suite Hotel (p349)

Why Go?

With its delightful Dutch colonial architecture, bustling commercial capital and excellent history museums, go-go Curaçao feels like a little piece of Europe on the edge of the Caribbean. That is, a little piece of Europe with glorious hidden beaches, amazing onshore snorkeling and diving, and a wild undeveloped windward coast.

Curaçao has a surging economy beyond tourism, which means that Willemstad has factories, humdrum neighborhoods and sometimes bad traffic. Catering to visitors is not the primary aim here. But if you're looking for a Caribbean island that is busy setting its own pace, Curaçao is for you.

When to Go

Dec–Apr High season, where accommodations fill up and prices are significantly higher.

Jan & Feb Carnival is Curaçao's biggest celebration – a month of music and costumes, parades and parties. It starts just after New Year and culminates the weekend before Ash Wednesday.

Sep–Dec Although Curaçao is below the hurricane belt, the island does experience an increase in rain.

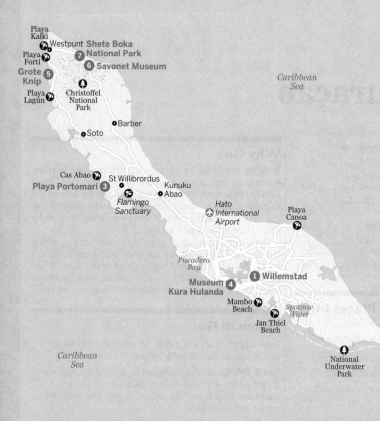

Curaçao Highlights

1 **Willemstad** (p347)
Discovering the Dutch colonial
architecture and rich local
culture in this busy port town.

2 **Snorkeling & Diving**
(p357) Going straight from
the beach to the reef (no boat
required!).

3 **Playa Portomari** (p354)
Following two underwater

snorkel trails to discover the
beach's unique double reef.

4 **Museum Kura Hulanda**
(p347) Bearing witness to
the horrible legacy of slavery
in Curaçao.

5 **Grote Knip** (p354)
Finding your place in the sand
on the island's most scenic
beach.

6 **Savonet Museum**
(p354) Learning the history
of an island nation through the
story of one plantation and its
residents.

7 **Shete Boka National
Park** (p354) Feeling the
power of nature on the
windblown and wave-tossed
east coast.

Willemstad

Gazing across Sint Annabaai at the colorful townhouses lined up on the shore, you might think that you're in the Old Country. Until you remember that the sun is shining, it's 28°C (82°F), and you're on your way to the beach. Despite the flawless weather, Willemstad feels like a Dutch city, complete with waterways and street cafes.

Residents live in the hills surrounding Schottegat, the deep inland harbor. Much of the sprawling city is traffic-clogged and rather mundane. But the crowded streets of Punda are packed with galleries and shops, while nearby Pietermaai is coming alive with restaurants, bars and clubs. Throughout the old town, the architecture is rich, with stunning examples of 17th- and 18th-century fortifications, Dutch colonial planning and diverse building styles, all of which earned this city its Unesco-protected status.

⊙ Sights

Fort Amsterdam   FORT
(Map p348; www.fortchurchcuracao.com; Gouvernementsplein, Punda; ⊙ grounds 8am-5pm Mon-Fri, church 10am-1:30pm Mon-Fri) FREE Dating from the 17th century, this much-modified fort is now home to government offices. Inside the large courtyard (enter through the gate on the western side), the rich colors of Dutch colonial architecture are on full display. The only building that's open to the public is the 1769 church, **Fortkirche**, which is the oldest church on the island. It contains the original pulpit and Governor's pew, with other historic items on display in the small museum.

★ Queen Emma Bridge   BRIDGE
(Map p348) Spanning the Sint Annabaai, this local landmark is sometimes called Our Swinging Old Lady. It's a pontoon bridge that swings open to make way for ocean-going ships. When the bridge is open, two free public ferries shuttle passengers back and forth between Punta and Otrobanda.

Jewish Cultural-Historical
Museum   MUSEUM
(Map p348; ☑461-1067; www.snoa.com; Hanchi Snoa 29, Punda; US$10; ⊙9am-4:30pm Mon-Fri) Since 1651, the Mikvé Israel Emanuel Synagogue is the oldest continuously operating Jewish congregation in the western hemisphere. Its small but fascinating museum occupies two 18th-century buildings, which originally housed the rabbi's residence and bathhouse. The museum's centerpiece is the original *mikveh* (bath), which was found during renovation. Also on display is a Torah scroll that was brought to Curaçao by the first Jewish settlers.

Floating Market   MARKET
(Map p348; Sha Caprileskade; dawn-dusk) A colorful place to see piles of papayas, melons, tomatoes and much more. The vendors sail 70km from Venezuela to set up shop here.

Curaçao Maritime Museum   MUSEUM
(Map p348; ☑465-2327; www.curacaomaritime. com; Van den Brandhofstraat 7, Scharloo; adult/child US$6.50/3, harbor tours adult/child US$10/5; ⊙9am-4pm Tue-Sat, harbor tours 2pm Wed & Sat) Engaging displays trace the island's history, including exhibits on the Dutch West Indian Co, the growth of Willemstad, the slave trade and more. A highlight is **Steam for Oil** (Map p348; www.curacaomaritime.com; guided tour adult/child US$6.50/3, unguided US$2.50/free; ⊙9am-4pm Tue-Sat, tour 1pm Wed & Sat), a working model of the oil refinery that has been a centerpiece of the island's economy throughout the 20th century. The museum also runs informative biweekly harbor tours. Combination tickets are available.

★ Museum Kura Hulanda   MUSEUM
(Map p348; ☑434-7701; www.kurahulanda. com; Klipstraat 9, Otrobanda; adult/child US$10/7; ⊙9am-4:30pm Mon-Sat) Located in a 19th-century merchant's house and slave quarters, this excellent museum documents the brutal history of slavery in the New World, including the slave trade, slave culture and abolition. There is also a fantastic collection of art and artifacts from West Africa – including a cool sculpture garden – showcasing the significant African influences on Caribbean culture.

Gallery Alma Blou   ART GALLERY
(Map p350; ☑462-8896; www.galleryalmablou. com; Frater Radulphusweg 4; ⊙9:30am-5:30pm Mon-Fri, 9am-2pm Sat) FREE Housed in the 17th-century plantation house Landhuis Habaai, this cooperative gallery has the city's largest collection of works by local artists. The rotating exhibits usually feature one or two artists with local connections, but there's always a great variety of works on display, including whimsical sculptures in the courtyard and gardens. Located about 3km northwest of Otrobanda.

CURAÇAO WILLEMSTAD

Willemstad

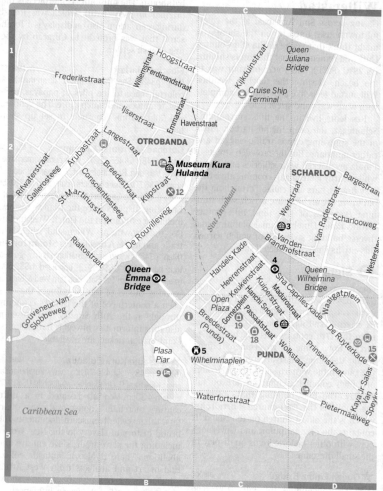

Marshe di Artesania (Handicraft Market; Frater Radulphusweg 4; ⏱10am-2pm 2nd Sat of the month) is the island's only handicraft market.

Curaçao Museum   MUSEUM
(Map p350; www.thecuracaomuseum.com; Van Leeuwenhoekstraat; adult/child US$6/3; ⏱8:30am-4:30pm Tue-Fri, 10am-4pm Sat & Sun) Small but worthwhile, this museum touches on art, history and society in its eclectic collections. Located in an unlikely residential location 1.6km west of the Otrabanda center, it's housed in a beautifully renovated military hospital. Highlights include the cockpit of the Snip (the first airplane to cross the ocean from Holland to Curaçao) and the impressive collection of contemporary sculptures in the garden.

🛏 Sleeping

The transformation of Pietermaai has produced a handful of lovely new hotels, most of them occupying beautifully restored colonial-era buildings. If you want to see what these buildings looked like before, just look across the street or next door, where neighboring edifices are still crumbling and decrepit.

Willemstad

◉ Top Sights
1	Museum Kura Hulanda	B2
2	Queen Emma Bridge	B3

◉ Sights
3	Curaçao Maritime Museum	C3
4	Floating Market	C3
5	Fort Amsterdam	C4
6	Jewish Cultural-Historical Museum	C4
	Steam for Oil	(see 3)

🛏 Sleeping
7	City Suites	D4
8	Pietermaai Boutique Hotel	E5
9	Plaza Hotel Curaçao	B4
10	Scuba Lodge	F5
11	Sonesta Kura Hulanda Village	B2

✖ Eating
12	Gouverneur De Rouville	B2
13	Kome	F5
14	Mundo Bizzaro	E5
15	Old Market	D4

🍷 Drinking & Nightlife
16	Miles Jazz Cafe	E5

✦ Entertainment
17	27	F5

🛍 Shopping
18	Nena Sanchez Gallery	C4
19	Serena's Art Factory Store	C4

welcome drink. The on-site dive shop is also recommended.

Floris Suite Hotel & Spa   BOUTIQUE HOTEL **$$**
(Map p350; ☑ 462-6111; www.florissuitehotel.com; John F Kennedy Blvd, Piscadera Bay; ste US$140-160; ❋ @ 🛜 ≋) The Floris is not right on the beach, but guests have access to Moomba Beach, across the street. The place has a striking, minimalist design, a gorgeous pool, and a brand new spa that's perfect for pampering. The 70-plus suites look out over lush grounds, with Piscadera Bay beyond. There's also a free shuttle into downtown Willemstad. Adults only.

Pietermaai Boutique Hotel   BOUTIQUE HOTEL **$$**
(Map p348; ☑ 465-0478; www.pietermaaihotel.com; Pietermaaiweg 51, Pietermaai; ste US$130; ❋ 🛜 ≋) Here is an old colonial Pietermaai building that has been beautifully restored, preserving historical quirks such as wooden shutters, narrow hallways, wood floors and high ceilings. The result is lovely

In Punda and Otrobanda the accommodation options are quite dated, though perhaps more affordable.

★ Scuba Lodge   HOTEL **$$**
(Map p348; ☑ 465-2575; www.scubalodge.com; Pietermaaiweg 104, Petermaai; r from US$180, ste US$320-390; ❋ 🛜 ≋) Occupying a rainbow-colored row of colonial houses in Petermaai, this hotel exemplifies the exuberant blend of fashion and funk of this district. Enormous rooms have luxe touches and mod design features. Service is super-friendly from the moment you walk in and receive a

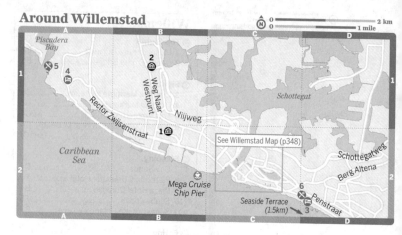

Around Willemstad

See Willemstad Map (p348)

and atmospheric, although the rooms vary widely. All have kitchenettes and a small seating area; some have open bathrooms. The rooms surround a lush tropical garden with a plunge pool.

City Suites HOTEL **$$**
(Map p348; ☑ 465-1551; www.citysuitescuracao. com; Pietermaai Plein 8; r from US$100; P✳☎) This stylish all-suite hotel is on the edge between Pietermaai and Punda, giving easy access to both. The light-filled guest rooms feature polished tile floors, fully equipped kitchenettes and sleek lines. Staff gets A+ for friendly and accommodating service.

Sonesta Kura Hulanda
Village HISTORIC HOTEL **$$$**
(Map p348; ☑ 434-7700; www.kurahulanda.com; Langstraat 8, Otrobanda; d/ste from US$320/400; P✳@☎≋) *Kura Hulanda* is Papiamentu for 'Dutch courtyard,' which gives an idea of the atmosphere of this colonial village, where restored buildings are clustered along cobblestone pathways and shady courtyards are littered with sculptures. The rooms are uniquely decorated, featuring hand-carved furnishings and original art, along with plenty of modern amenities. The Museum Kura Hulanda (p347) is on the grounds.

Avila Beach Hotel BOUTIQUE HOTEL **$$$**
(Map p350; ☑ 461-4377; www.avilabeachhotel.com; Penstraat 130; r from US$250; P✳@☎≋) 🌱 The Avila Beach Hotel occupies the magnificently restored 18th-century home of a Dutch governor, along with several modern wings of luxurious accommodation. The ele-

gant grounds include two private beaches and a gorgeous infinity pool. It's a short walk to Pietermaai, or you can catch the free shuttle bus to the city center.

🍴 Eating

The most innovative cooking is happening in the kitchens of Pietermaai, where inviting restaurants and bars line the main streets. In Punda, keep your eyes open for humble backstreet eateries serving good traditional fare, but keep your wallet closed for most of the touristy places lining the Sint Annabaai.

Old Market CARIBBEAN **$**
(Plasa Bieu; Map p348; Sha Caprileskade, Punda; mains US$8-12; ⊙7am-2pm Mon-Sat) A local favorite. Folks of all stripes crowd into the vast barn-like structure to snag seats at the picnic tables and feast on down-home Curaçao cooking. The specialty here is local dishes such as goat stew, pumpkin pancakes, cactus stew and whole red snapper. It's tasty, cheap and absolutely authentic.

★Rozendaels CARIBBEAN **$$**
(Map p350; ☑ 461-8806; www.rozendaels. com; Penstraat 47, Pietermaai; meals US$15-25; ⊙5-10pm Sun-Fri; 🍴) Rozendaels will be a highlight of your trip. The secret garden setting and the personable service are a good start, but the food is near perfection. It's a fantastic place to try local delicacies such as *keshi yena* (cheese and chicken casserole) and grilled mahi-mahi, but the varied menu features international fare as well.

CURAÇAO WILLEMSTAD

Around Willemstad

★ Mundo Bizzarro · CUBAN $$

(Map p348; ☑ 461-6767; www.mundobizarro curacao.com; Nieuwestraat 12, Pietermaai; mains US$8-20; ⊙8am-10pm, bar til late; 🔊) The anchor of Pietermaai, this place evokes old Havana. The ground floor opens to the streets and alleys around; inside it's got a faux look of urban decay, countered by the fine food. Upstairs there's a bar with fab mojitos and live music on Saturday night.

Pirate Bay · CARIBBEAN $$

(Map p350; www.piratebaycuracao.com; Piscad-erabaai; mains lunch US$8-20, dinner US$15-30; ⊙8:30am-midnight) Make a reservation if you want to watch the sunset with a drink in hand and toes in the sand. This is a super-popular spot for its chilled-out atmosphere and excellent Caribbean fare, including jerk chicken, beef and plantain stew, and red snapper with mango chutney. Piscadera-baai is 4km west of Otrobanda.

Gouverneur De Rouville · DUTCH $$

(Map p348; ☑ 462-5999; www.de-gouverneur. com; De Rouvilleweg 9, Otrobanda; lunch/dinner mains US$15/25; ⊙10am-10pm, bar to 1am; 🔊) The Dutch and Caribbean food served in this restored colonial building is good, but the views of Sint Annabaai are magic, especially when a huge freighter passes at night with a carnival of colored lights. Avoid the cute but viewless courtyard; the classy bar has a terrace.

Kome · INTERNATIONAL $$$

(Map p348; ☑ 465-0413; www.komecuracao. com; Johan van Walbeeckplein 6, Pietermaai; lunch US$18-29, dinner US$42-49; ⊙noon-2:30pm Mon-

Fri & 6-10pm Tue-Sat) There's a buzz around town about this new place in Pietermaai, which effortlessly blends artful innovation with casual comfort. The interior is sleek, but not snooty; the menu highlights sophisticated presentations of old favorites, ranging from tasty sandwiches to spicy curries to fresh-baked goodness, straight from the oven. Signature cocktails feature fresh fruit juices: that's a treat but you'll pay for it.

🍷 Drinking & Nightlife

Miles Jazz Cafe · BAR

(Map p348; www.facebook.com/milescuracao; Nieuwestraat 48, Pietermaai; ⊙4pm-2am) That's Miles as in Davis, one of the inspirations for this stylishly divey night spot in Pietermaai. This place is old-school, as in jazz music from vinyl. Live music on Saturday night.

Rainbow Lounge · GAY & LESBIAN

(Map p350; www.facebook.com/rainbowlounge curacao; Floris Suite Hotel, Piscadera Bay; ⊙6pm-midnight) The Floris Suite Hotel bar is a gathering spot for gay and lesbian folks – and their friends – as well as anyone who wants to relax and drink in a welcoming, open atmosphere. Friday happy hours are a draw (free drinks between 6pm and 7pm!).

☆ Entertainment

Willemstad has several clubs catering to the local passion for music and dancing. For details on the latest, check out K-Pasa (www.k-pasa.com), which lists entertainment around the island. Otherwise, head out of town to Mambo Beach (p352) or Jan Thiel Beach (p352), where several beach clubs keep the party going late into the night.

WORTH A TRIP

LANDHUIS CHOBOLOBO

Did you ever wonder why Blue Curaçao is blue? Find out at the **Landhuis Cho-bolobo** (☑ 461-3526; www.curacaoliqueur. com; Elias RA Moreno Blvd; ⊙8am-noon & 1-5pm Mon-Fri), where the liqueur is produced (in five different colors, actually) from the peels of Valencia oranges. Walk yourself through an informative tour of the history and production process, then hit the gift shop to sample the goods. Landhuis Chobolobo is located on the eastern side of the Schottegat.

CURAÇAO WILLEMSTAD

FESTIVALS & EVENTS

Carnival (www.curacaocarnivalinfo. com; ☺ Jan & Feb) This is a big deal on the islands, especially Curaçao, where a packed schedule of fun begins right after New Year's Day.

Séu Parade (☺ Easter Mon) Curaçao's 'Feast of the Harvest' features parades replete with lots of folk music and dancing. People in rural areas go a little nuts.

27 LIVE MUSIC

(Map p348; http://27curacao.com; De Ruyterkade, Pietermaai; ☺ 11am-1am Mon-Thu, to 3am Fri, 4pm-3am Sat) Check out the island's music scene at this happening club overlooking Waaigaat. Rockers crowd in to hear rock 'n' roll, reggaeton and everything in between. There's at least five different burgers on the menu, which is always a good thing.

🔒 Shopping

Serena's Art Factory Store ARTS & CRAFTS

(Map p348; www.chichi-curacao.com; cnr Windstraat & Gomezplein, Punda; ☺ 10am-5pm Mon-Sat) Serena Janet Israel is the creative mind (and hands) behind Chichi, the vibrantly painted, big-bosomed lady sculptures that decorate the island's courtyards and alleyways. Chichi comes in many sizes and designs, and you can pick your favorite – or opt for another colorful creature – at Serena's Art Factory Store.

Nena Sanchez Gallery ART

(Map p348; Windstraat 15, Punda; ☺ 10am-6pm Mon-Sat) Displays the vibrant and colorful works of the longtime local artist. Ms Sanchez has another, larger outlet (Landhuis Jan Kok; ☏ 864-0965; www.nenasanchez.com; Willibrordus) across from the flamingo lookout.

ℹ Information

Punda Post Office (Map p348; Waaigatplein 1, Punda; ☺ 7:30am-noon & 1:30-5pm Mon-Fri)
Tourist Information Kiosk (Map p348; www. curacao.com; Breedestraat, Punda; ☺ 8am-4pm Mon-Sat) Has a wealth of information. It's by the Queen Emma Bridge on the Punda side.

ℹ Getting There & Away

The **Hato International Airport** (p359) is on the outskirts of Willemstad, on the island's otherwise undeveloped northeast coast. It's a 20-minute drive into town. Most hotels and resorts can help make arrangements for airport transfers (US$40 to US$50 to Willemstad). Otherwise, taxis and buses pick up at the plaza just outside the arrival hall.

Public buses (NAf1.60 to NAf2.10) depart every two hours from **Otrobanda Bus Station** (p359) for the West End (stopping in Willibrordus en route) and from **Punda Bus Station** (p359) for the southeast (including Mambo Beach or Caracasbaai).

Southeast of Willemstad

Southeast of Willemstad, much of the coast has been transformed into somebody's version of paradise. Artificial beaches Mambo Beach and Jan Thiel Beach are lined with resorts, shopping malls and private beach clubs. Artificial islands are surrounded by big ocean tanks, keeping captive the creatures of the sea. And beautiful people lounge on beach chairs and sip cocktails and stare out to sea.

It's not all bad of course. The beaches are lovely, with calm, refreshing water that is an eerily perfect shade of blue. The clubs are fun, offering some of the island's best places to dine, drink, dance and shop. And there's certainly nothing wrong with beautiful people lounging on beach chairs, sipping cocktails and staring out to sea. But it does feel a bit surreal.

👁 Sights

Mambo Beach BEACH

(Bapor Kibra; US$3.50; ☺ 9am-late; 🅿) By day this ribbon of white sand is a family-friendly beach with a full range of beach activities. By night it transforms into a beach club and disco branded 'Wet & Wild,' with DJs and dancing. The action gets frenetic after midnight from Thursday onward.

Jan Thiel Beach BEACH

(Jan Thiel; US$3.50; ☺ 9am-midnight) The beach at Jan Thiel was literally carved out of the coast – by humans. The whole thing is artificial, which explains why the swimming area is actually a saltwater infinity pool. The sand is brilliant white, the water is perfectly azure. Everything you might want is here: restaurants, bars, shopping, dive shop, beach tennis, gear rental etc. It's all lovely (fake, but lovely).

🏃 Activities

Windsurfing Curaçao WINDSURFING
(☑524-4974; www.windsurfingcuracao.com;
Caracasbaaiweg; rental per hr US$20, lesson from
US$49; ☺10am-6pm) The island's top spot
for windsurfing is the smooth and breezy
waters of the Spaanse Water, a large inland
bay. The experts at Windsurfing Curaçao are
excellent teachers: the course is four lessons,
but they promise you'll be surfing after the
first one! If you already know your stuff, you
can just rent equipment here too.

Bounty Adventures BOATING, BUS
(www.bountyadventures.com; Caracasbaaiweg;
adult/child bus tour US$65/48, snorkel US$75/38,
Klein Curaçao US$108/54, pick-up service per per-
son US$9) Bounty Adventures has a whole
menu of boat trips, including deep-sea fishing, sail and snorkel tours, sunset sails and
trips to Klein Curaçao. In addition to the
boat tours, there is also a bus tour, which
takes guests to the West End parks and
beaches. Prices generally include lunch and/
or drinks.

Mermaid Boat Trips BOATING
(☑560-1530; www.mermaidboattrips.com; Caracasbaaiweg; adult/child US$105/52.50; ☺departs
6:45am Tue-Fri & Sun) Five days a week, the
Mermaid takes passengers to Klein Curaçao
(p355) for a day of sunbathing, swimming
and snorkeling. Mermaid is the only company that has facilities on the island (eg picnic tables, shade umbrellas and restrooms).
The price includes breakfast and lunch,
snorkel gear and beach chairs.

🍴 Eating

There are dozens of restaurants and bars at
Mambo Beach and Jan Thiel Beach – juice
bars and snack shacks to upscale dining on
the beach. To see where the locals eat, drop
by the places on the public beaches – Pop's
Place (p353) or Seaside Terrace (p353).

★Seaside Terrace SEAFOOD $$
(461-8361; Goetoeweg, Marie Pompoen Beach;
mains US$8-20; ☺noon-10pm Tue-Sun) Red
snapper, mahi-mahi and other *fruits de mer*
get pan-fried and served with a super-tasty
secret Creole sauce. The furniture doesn't
match. The forks bend. And the service is
endearingly gruff. Yet this place is an island
institution, serving what many say is the
island's best seafood. Located just north of
Mambo Beach.

By the way, here's your chance to do your
part to save the reef: sample the lionfish;
you won't regret it.

Pop's Place PUB FOOD $$
(Caracasbaai; sandwiches US$6, mains US$10-
22; ☺11am-9pm, bar to 11pm) Here's a local
favorite. Right on the beach at Caracas Bay,
there's a wooden shack on the sand where
you can get people-pleasers such as goat
stew, burgers and cold drinks. On many
weekends, the live music at Pop's inspires a
beach party.

❶ Getting There & Away

You can take a bus (NAf1.60, departs hourly)
from **Punda Bus Station** (p359) in Willemstad
to Mambo Beach (bus no 6A) or Caracas Bay
(5A, 6A or 6B), but you'll need a car to reach Jan
Thiel Beach.

Willibrordus & Around

Even before you get to the West End, there
are scores of beautiful beaches hidden in
coves along this coastline. They are private
beaches, which means you'll pay to use
them; but the trade-off is that the facilities
are generally better and they don't get as
crowded on weekends.

The village of Sint Willibrordus is not
exactly a destination, but you'll surely find
yourself stopping here, whether to snap pics
of the photogenic flamingos or peruse the
masterpieces of local artist Nena Sanchez.
While in town, don't miss the most famous
landmark: the white block-letter 'Williwood'
sign on a wooded hillside.

◉ Sights & Activities

Flamingo Sanctuary BIRD SANCTUARY
(Sint Willibrordrus) **FREE** For an island that's
lacking in lawns, there is no shortage of
pink flamingos. You'll see them congregating in the Saliña Sint Marie, the salt flats
on the southern side of the road heading
toward Playa Portomari. There are several
places to pull off the road, but be sure to
lock your car when you go to get a better
look at the wading beauties (whose numbers
can vary greatly, anywhere from a dozen to
hundreds).

Cas Abao BEACH
(www.casabaobeach.com; per car NAf10-12.50;
☺8am-6pm) This mid-coast beach (sometimes spelled Cas Abou) is an island favorite
for its soft white sand, crystal-clear waters

and surrounding scenery. It's a private beach with good facilities, including guarded parking lot, lockers, restaurant and massage hut. You can also rent snorkel gear, though you'll see more sea life further up the coast.

Playa Portomari SNORKELING, DIVING
(www.playaportomari.com; adult/child US$3.50/ free; ⊙ 9:30am-6:30pm) There's a lot to love about Playa Portomari, including the white coral sand and clear waters that shelter a unique double reef – excellent for snorkelers and divers alike. Look for the artificial 'reef balls' that were constructed to encourage new coral growth. Facilities at this private beach include a dive shop and a restaurant.

Onshore, there are three hiking trails (also popular for mountain biking), providing a diversion from the water sports.

❶ Getting There & Away

The easiest way to explore the area around Sint Willibrordus is by private vehicle. In fact, the west coast beaches are *only* accessible by car. Buses do go through Sint Willibrordus (NAf2.10; departing from Otrobanda Bus Station in Willemstad), but it's a small place and you'll be stuck there until the next bus comes trundling through, which could be two hours later.

To get here by car, take the main road Weg Naar Westpunt (literally, 'road to Westpunt') to Kunuku Abao, where you turn west onto Weg Naar St Willibrordus. For 18km you drive through some of the most lush countryside in the southern Caribbean.

West End

Welcome to the wild, wild west. Curaçao's West End – also called Banda'bou – is where you'll find the island's most stunning beaches, most striking natural landscapes and most spectacular sea life. Here, two national parks give access to the rugged windward coast, allowing adventurers to witness the ferocity and artistry of the surf on the rocky cliffs.

On the more sedate west coast, the same cliffs are punctuated by fishing villages and sandy beaches, providing easy entries into tranquil turquoise waters. Dive and snorkel sites are almost too numerous to count – and most are accessible from the shore. So don your mask and fins and prepare to frolic with sea turtles and reef fish. The underwater world is even more enticing than the top side!

◉ Sights

Grote Knip BEACH
(Kenepa Grande) `FREE` This west-end beach is a stunner. In fact, you've probably seen it on the cover of a Curaçao tourist brochure. A perfect crescent of brilliant white sand is framed by azure waters and verdant hills. There are a few snack shacks and places to rent snorkel gear, but it's much less cluttered than the island's private beaches.

Shete Boka National Park PARK
(www.shetebokapark.org; Weg Naar Westpunt; US$6; ⊙ 9am-5pm) Shete Boka means 'seven inlets,' named for a series of picturesque coves that are carved out of the limestone along this 10km stretch of coastline. Park your car near **Boka Tabla**, where the powerful surf thunders into a cave in the cliffs. It's impressive from the bluff above, and even more so from inside the cave. From here, you can walk or drive north along the coast to the other smaller inlets, which are sea-turtle nesting grounds.

Heading south from Boka Tabla, a second road leads to **Boka Pistol**, a very narrow inlet which produces a stunning – and startling – explosion when the waves roll in. You can also reach Boka Pistol by following a circular hiking trail, taking about an hour.

★ Christoffel National Park PARK
(📞 864-0363; www.christoffelpark.org; Weg Naar Westpunt; adult/child US$12/5; ⊙ 7:30am-4pm Mon-Sat, 6am-3pm Sun, last entrance 1½hr before closing) This 1800-hectare preserve is formed from three old plantations, including the Savonet Plantation (now the excellent Savonet Museum; combination ticket available). The park has two driving routes and eight hiking trails, which provide a variety of perspectives on the island's landscape, flora and fauna. It takes two to three hours to hike to the summit of **Christoffel Mountain** (375m), the island's highest point. You'll want to bring plenty of water and get an early start – 11am at the latest.

Savonet Museum MUSEUM
(www.savonetmuseum.org; Christoffel Park; adult/child US$7/5; ⊙ 8am-3pm) Set in the old *landhuis* (plantation house), this is a fascinating museum that recounts the history of Curaçao through the story of the Savonet Plantation. Visitors learn about the plantation owners and slaves, and witness how their society and customs evolved after emancipation. There's also a small

room focusing on archaeology and the pre-colonial cultures. Exhibits include some historical artifacts, but what's really special here is the oral history that is shared in the audiovisual presentations.

🏃 Activities

Playa Forti   SWIMMING

(Westpunt) **FREE** There is really only one reason to stop at Playa Forti, but it's a good one. Behind the restaurant, the sheer cliff walls and deep water create perfect conditions for some epic cliff jumping. It's about a 40ft drop into crystal-clear coolness, where you might just find yourself swimming with sea turtles. The beach itself is small and dirty, and the restaurant is not recommended. But the thrill of the jump...

Playa Grandi   SNORKELING, DIVING

FREE This is not the prettiest beach on the island – nor the cleanest – but it is a top-notch snorkel and dive site. You're almost guaranteed to spot sea turtles swimming in the bay. (Please, look, but don't touch, chase or otherwise harass these gentle creatures.)

Go West Diving   DIVING

(☏864-0102; www.gowestdiving.com; Playa Kalki, Westpunt; tank/equipment rental US$10/50, 2-tank boat dive US$97) The top dive shop on the west end. Go West offers a few things that other dive shops do not, such as boat dives (including Klein Curaçao) and snorkel trips. It's also next to an excellent shore diving site, Alice in Wonderland, which is a destination in itself. All divers do a 'welcome dive' to test equipment and weights (and competence, presumably).

🛏 Sleeping & Eating

Nos Krusero Apartments   APARTMENT **$$**

(☏524-9454; www.noskrusero-apartments.com; Playa Kalki, Westpunt; apt US$90-150; ✽ 🛜 ⛱) Attentive service is the hallmark of this tropical-colored complex near Playa Kalki. The five apartments (with one or two bedrooms) are simply decorated with tile floors, wood furniture and hammock-strung balconies, not to mention well-equipped kitchens. Our favorite perk: coolers provided for your beach-lounging convenience.

Bahia Apartments & Diving   APARTMENT **$$**

(☏864-1000; www.bahia-apartments.com; Playa Lagún; 1-bedroom apt per week €560-590; ✽ @ 🛜) Here are eight simple, spacious apartments on the cliff overlooking Playa Lagún. They're

KLEIN CURAÇAO
....

Remember all those plans you made about the one book/song/food/friend you would bring when you're stuck on a deserted island? They'll come in handy when you take a trip to **Klein Curaçao**, an uninhabited island, about 15 miles off the coast of Curaçao. Spend the day lounging on the sand, exploring the lighthouse, frolicking in the waters and swimming with sea turtles (as well as reading that book, listening to the song, eating the food and hanging out with your BFF).

not too fancy, but the welcome is warm and the location is prime. There's a dive shop on-site, making this a perfect home base for a good-value dive vacation.

Kura Hulanda Lodge   RESORT **$$$**

(☏839-3600; www.kurahulanda.com; Playa Kalki 1, Westpunt; r US$290-310, ste US$340-390; ✽ @ 🛜 ⛱) Once you settle into this boutique resort overlooking Playa Kalki, you may never want to leave. Tasteful lodgings surround tropical gardens, along with two pools and a private beach. The restaurant is recommended, especially for amazing sunset views. Kayaks and SUP boards are available, plus there is a dive shop on-site and a reef just offshore. What more do you need?

Jaanchie's   CURAÇAOAN **$$**

(☏864-0126; Weg Naar Westpunt; mains US$7-20; ☉noon-8pm) Jaanchie himself often visits the tables in his restaurant near Playa Grandi, chatting up customers and explaining the menu. And it does require some explanation, as it usually features island delicacies such as iguana soup and goat stew. Guests sit in the festive, open-air dining room and watch the colorful birds flocking to the nearby feeders.

ℹ Getting There & Away

Buses (NAf2.10) go to the West End (including Playa Lagún, Knip and Westpunt), departing from the **Otrobanda Bus Station** (p359) in Willemstad every two hours or so. Take the Banda'bou bus (via Barber) to reach Shete Boka or Christoffel.

You'll obviously have much more flexibility and freedom if you rent a vehicle. Aside from dive trips, there is a dearth of organized tours to this side of the island.

CURAÇAO WEST END

UNDERSTAND CURAÇAO

History

Caquetío History

The earliest inhabitants of Curaçao were the Caquetío peoples, a branch of the Arawaks who inhabited the island as early as 2500 BC. Archaeological evidence from these peoples include the petroglyphs at **Hato Caves** (www.curacaohatocaves.com; FD Rooseveltweg; adult/child US$8/6; ☺9am-4pm) and some artifacts on display at the Savonet Museum (p354). After the arrival of the Spanish in 1499, most of the indigenous population were killed by disease or sent to work elsewhere in the empire.

Dutch West India Co

The Dutch West India Co arrived in 1634, and so did commerce, agriculture and slavery. The island was divided into plantations for small-scale agriculture. Nowadays, many of the old *landhuis* (plantation houses) have been restored. The most vivid history of plantation life is on display at the Savonet Museum (p354), formerly the Landhuis Savonet.

Half the slaves destined for the Caribbean passed through the markets of Curaçao. The Museum Kura Hulanda (p347) examines this horrible institution in-depth, while **Museo Tula** (Landhuis Kenepa; Knip; admission US$5.50; ☺9am-4pm Mon-Fri) remembers one tragic slave revolt.

Emancipation & Modernization

The collapse of the Dutch West India Co in 1792 and the end of slavery in 1863 sent Curaçao into economic decline. Small-scale farming (aloe and oranges) provided a meager living for most.

In the early 20th century, oil refineries were built to process Venezuelan oil. This development jump-started the economy and the island flourished once again. See the refinery work at the Steam for Oil (p347) exhibit at the Maritime Museum.

Relative affluence and Dutch political stability have made Curaçao a regional center for commerce and banking. Tourism provides additional income, as does the growing expat population. In 2010, with the dissolution of the Netherlands Antilles, Curaçao became an independent entity within the Netherlands.

Peoples & Cultures

Historians do not believe that there are descendants of the island's original Caquetío inhabitants still living on the island. But the population of Curaçao is a rich mix of peoples. The majority have Afro-Caribbean roots (descended from the slaves who worked the plantations), but there is a sizable Dutch minority, as well as Latinos, Southeast Asians and other Europeans. Some 73% of the population are Roman Catholic, usually practiced with a healthy dose of Santería. Many other religions are represented, including a significant and long-standing Jewish presence.

Landscape & Wildlife

Curaçao is a mix of lush areas near the coasts and more arid regions inland. (The contrast is on full display at Christoffel National Park.) Human development has meant that land-based wildlife is limited, though birdlife is rich. The National Underwater Park protects a 20km stretch of coastline along the island's southern tip, but the reef is rich with marine life all along the west coast, where there are dozens of dive and snorkel sites.

The main environmental threat in Curaçao is air and water pollution from the Venezuelan-run oil refinery and other industry on the inner harbor (Schottegat) of Willemstad. Given the importance of these installations to the local economy, efforts to control their negative effects are modest at best. The growing traffic problem (and exhaust-spewing diesels) means that getting stuck in a traffic jam is an unpleasant possibility.

SURVIVAL GUIDE

❶ Directory A-Z

ACCOMMODATIONS

Curaçao offers a wide variety of accommodations. There are resorts and rental units up and down the coast, giving easy access to the beach, but Willemstad also has some interesting urban hotels.

Although there are not many budget options, prices are definitely lower the further inland you go. Camping is uncommon.

High-season prices usually run mid-December to mid-April. A 7% sales tax applies to hotel rooms, while some resorts may tack on a service charge of 12% or higher.

ACTIVITIES

Curaçao is an excellent destination for diving and snorkeling, not least because so many sites are located onshore. Dive shops do offer guided shore dives, but you and your dive buddy can just as easily go diving on your own (though the dive shops are still useful for recommendations and air). There are dive shops at almost every beach; good ones include **Go West Diving** (p355) and **Scuba Lodge** (p349).

The main areas for diving are along the west coast, from St Michiel out to Westpunt, and from Mambo Beach south to the tip. The latter coast and reefs have been protected as part of the **National Underwater Park**.

CHILDREN

Curaçao is an ideal destination for families, as there are sights and activities for kids of all ages. Many resorts, shopping malls and other facilities cater especially to families.

All of the beaches are along the tranquil west coast, which means they are protected from the strongest surf, making them ideal for kids to frolic, swim and build sand castles. The private beaches such as **Mambo Beach** (p352) and **Jan Thiel Beach** (p352) offer some kid-friendly beach activities, including an island of inflatable toys for kids to play on. Also, children as young as five can learn to snorkel, especially in calm, comfortable waters such as these. **Playa Grandi** (p355) is a surefire hit, with practically guaranteed sightings of sea turtles.

When they tire of sun and sand, take your kids to admire the power of the wind and waves at **Shete Boka National Park** (p354). The **Museum Kura Hulanda** (p347) and the **Savonet Museum** (p354) do not have a lot of flash, but they are both interesting and educational for older children.

Some resorts are adults-only, but most are very family-friendly. Swimming pools are often designed with kids in mind. And most larger resorts offer kids clubs, game rooms and other kinds of programming to keep the little ones busy. Family-style rooms and suites are common, as are kitchenettes.

Many private developments are designed with families in mind, so you'll find that facilities are up to snuff in resorts, shopping malls and the like. The public facilities are a different story.

Public restrooms are few and far between and practically nonexistent on public beaches. Changing tables are not common. Willemstad is an old city with narrow streets and some hills. Sidewalks are not always present, making it dangerous to walk with children or push a stroller.

ELECTRICITY

110V, 60Hz. Generally, US-style two- and three-pin plugs are used; but some resorts have 220V EU-style sockets, so you may want to bring an adapter just in case.

EMERGENCY NUMBERS

Ambulance	☎ 912
Fire & police	☎ 911

FOOD

Curaçao has a surprisingly sophisticated dining scene, if you know where to look, that is, in the streets and alleyways of Pietermaai, in Willemstad. The main tourist beaches are also packed with restaurants and bars. On the remote West End, the choices are mostly limited to resort restaurants and snack shacks on the beach.

GLBT TRAVELERS

'We live and let live!' claims the official Gay Curaçao website (www.gaycuracao.com). The fact that this website exists proves the point. While gay and lesbians tourists will likely receive a warm welcome on the island, the GLBT 'scene' is rather limited outside of the **Floris Suite Hotel** (p349) – sometimes called a 'straight-friendly hotel' – and its hotel bar, the **Rainbow Lounge** (p351).

CURAÇAO DIRECTORY A–Z

CURAÇAO DIRECTORY A–Z

ⓘ DEPARTURE TAX

The departure tax varies according to your destination.

International	US$39
Aruba	US$20
Bonaire	US$10
Transfer	US$5

Most of the larger international airlines include the departure tax in the price of the ticket. If you're flying on a smaller regional airline, you will need to pay the tax at the designated window prior to going through security.

Some other resources for gay travelers:

Curaçao Pride (www.curacaopride.com) A weeklong celebration held in late September or early October.

Pink Curaçao (www.pinkcuracao.com) A gay-friendly travel website.

HEALTH

St Elisabeth Hospital (☎ 462-4900; www.sehos.cw; Breedestraat 193, Otrobanda; ⊙ 24hr) is a large and well-equipped medical facility in Willemstad. Emergency care is available.

LEGAL MATTERS

Unlike in the Netherlands proper, all drugs are illegal. Violating these laws can lead to arrest and imprisonment.

Prostitution, on the other hand, is legal – but only at one designated adult-only resort. Outside this resort, prostitution is illegal and unsafe.

As always, if you get arrested, your embassy can help you notify your family and contact an attorney, but not much else.

MONEY

ATMs are widely available, dispensing US dollars (US$) and Netherlands Antillean guilders (NAf). Credit cards are accepted at most hotels and restaurants.

Cash

Although the island's official currency is the Netherland Antillean guilder (NAf), prices are often quoted in US dollars and you can pay for just about everything in US currency. You might get change back in guilders.

Exchange Rates

ARUBA	Afl1	NAf1.0
AUSTRALIA	A$1	NAf1.34
CANADA	C$	NAf1.36
EUROPE	€1	NAf2.0
JAPAN	¥100	NAf1.75
NEW ZEALAND	NZ$1	NAf1.30
UK	£1	NAf2.37
US	US$	NAf1.80
VENEZUELA	BsF1	NAf0.18

Tipping

Bars & restaurants For good service, tip 15% to 20% (sometimes included in the bill).

Resorts Usually includes a 12% service charge on the bill.

Taxis A 10% tip is usual.

Tour Guides Tip US$10 for a half-day outing.

PUBLIC HOLIDAYS

New Years Day January 1

Carnival Monday Monday before Ash Wednesday

Good Friday Friday before Easter

Easter Monday Monday after Easter

King's Birthday April 27

Labour Day May 1

Ascension Day Sixth Thursday after Easter

Flag Day July 2

Curaçao Day October 10

Christmas December 25

Boxing Day December 26

TAXES & REFUNDS

The Curaçao sales tax (OB) ranges from 6% to 9%, depending on the purchase. Unfortunately, most things you pay for while on holiday – restaurants, tours, rental cars – are taxed at 9%. Hotel rooms are taxed at 7%.

TELEPHONE

Curaçao's country code is ☎ 599; the area code is ☎ 9.

To call out from Curaçao to any country with a country code of ☎ 1, just dial 1 and the local number. To reach other countries, dial the international access code 00 + country code + the number.

To dial Curaçao from another country, dial the country's international access code + 599 + 9 + the local number. Within Curaçao there is no need to dial any code.

TIME

Curaçao is in the Atlantic time zone (AST), which is four hours behind Greenwich Mean Time. Daylight saving time is not observed.

TRAVELERS WITH DISABILITIES

Curaçao has made strides in catering to travelers with disabilities, and it's getting better. Many resorts and rental units offer accessible rooms and zero-entry swimming pools, including the **Avila Beach Hotel** (p350). Many restaurants and casinos around the island are also wheelchair accessible. Wheelchair-accessible sights include the **Maritime Museum** (p347), the **Savonet Museum** (p354), **Landhuis Chobolobo** (p351) and **Jan Thiel Beach** (p352).

Some other companies catering specifically to travelers with disabilities:

Dushi Taxi (☑ 516-8863; www.dushitaxi.wee bly.com) Natasja Gibbs caters to cruise-ship passengers, offering tours and transportation in a wheelchair-accessible van.

Joseph Cares (www.josephcares.com) Joseph Cares is a company that specializes in taking care of travelers with special needs – particularly providing tours, transportation and other services for disabled travelers. It offers tours of some of the islands most remote spots, as well as airport transfers and rental of medical equipment.

Download Lonely Planet's free Accessible Travel guide from http://lptravel.to/Accessible Travel.

ⓘ Getting There & Away

You can reach Curaçao by air or sea (on a cruise ship). Flights, cars and tours can be booked online at lonelyplanet.com/bookings.

AIR

Hato International Airport (CUR; www. curacao-airport.com), 10km from Willemstad on the northern side of the island, receives international flights from North and South America, as well as twice-daily flights from Amsterdam.

Regional carriers:

Avianca (www.avianca.com) The Colombian national airline runs daily flights between Curaçao and Bogotá.

Divi Divi Air (www.flydivi.com) Ten or 12 daily flights between Curaçao and Bonaire, as well as charters to Aruba. The airplanes are tiny so they book out well in advance.

Insel Air (www.fly-inselair.com) Frequent flights to Aruba and Bonaire.

Pawa Dominicana (www.pawadominicana. com) The Dominican airlines has twice-daily flights to Santo Domingo, as well as daily flights to Aruba.

Tiara Air (www.tiara-air.com) An on-again, off-again Aruban airline servicing Curaçao and Venezuela.

SEA

Curaçao is part of cruise-ship itineraries that cover the southern Caribbean, often on longer 10-day and two-week trips.

Many cruise ships call in Curaçao. The really big ones dock at the **Mega Cruise Ship Pier**, which is just outside the capital's natural harbor. Smaller ships dock at the **Cruise Ship Terminal** (Map p348) in the harbor.

ⓘ Getting Around

One highlight of a Curaçao visit is exploring the island, which is easiest to do with your own vehicle.

Car You won't need 4WD. Driving is on the right-hand side.

Bus Public buses run every two hours on major routes.

BUS

There is a public bus network on Curaçao, with buses to the West End departing from **Otrobanda Bus Station** (Map p348; Sebastopolstraat, Otrobanda) and buses to the southeast departing from **Punda Bus Station** (Map p348; Waaigatplein, Punda), both in Willemstad. Most routes run buses every one or two hours.

CAR & MOTORCYCLE

Driving is on the right-hand side, seat belts are required and motorcyclists must wear helmets.

All of the major international rental firms have affiliates at the airport, but there are many reliable local outfits, such as **Prins Car Rental** (www.prinscarrental.com). Note that off-site agencies (the local ones) charge an additional $20 fee for the airport transfer.

1. Grace Bay (p797), Turks & Caicos **2.** Marigot Bay (p694), St Lucia **3.** Seven Mile Beach (p261), Grand Cayman **4.** Grande Anse des Salines (p568), Martinique

Beaches

Like Paris and art or Arizona and canyons, when you think of the Caribbean, you think beaches. Alluring beaches in Jamaica, perfect beaches in Grand Cayman, lost beaches in the Bahamas and unspoiled beaches in the Grenadines all await.

Grace Bay, Caicos Islands

This stretch of snow-white sand is perfect for relaxing, swimming and forgetting about home. Though it's dotted with resorts, its sheer size means that finding your own square of paradise is a snap.

Marigot Bay, St Lucia

Marigot Bay is a stunning example of natural architecture. Sheltered by towering palms and surrounding hills, the narrow inlet hid the British fleet from French pursuers. Today it hides a fabulous beach.

Seven Mile Beach, Grand Cayman

Walk the length of this beach, straight out of central casting, and see if it measures up – literally. Enjoy swimming, sunbathing and water sports galore on Grand Cayman's superb stretch of white sand.

Shoal Bay East, Anguilla

Got a fantasy of an idyllic white-sand beach? You've just pictured Shoal Bay East, a 2-mile-long beach with pristine sand, reefs ideal for snorkeling, and glassy turquoise water.

Grande Anse des Salines, Martinique

Les Salines is probably Martinique's finest beach. The gorgeous long stretch of golden sand lures French tourists and local families alike, but it never seems crowded.

BRENT HOFACKER / SHUTTERSTOCK ©

1. Jerk chicken **2.** Sugar apples **3.** Mofongo **4.** Mojito

Food & Drink

GWENGOAT / GETTY IMAGES ©

Seafood

A fish still dripping with saltwater, thrown on the grill and spritzed with lime, has made many a Caribbean travel memory. So too has a tasty lobster, grilled over coals then drenched in garlic butter.

Meat & Poultry

As for meat, chicken rules the roost. Mixed with rice, it's called *arroz con pollo* in the Spanish-speaking islands and *pelau* in Trinidad and St Kitts. Other favorites are roast pork (*lechón asado*), which features in Cuban and Puerto Rican sandwiches; and goat (*cabrito*).

Fruits

Tropical fruits are Caribbean icons. There are the usual suspects, like papaya, but be sure to sample sugar apple – a custardy fruit shot through with black pits – in the Bahamas (*anon* in Cuba); or *guinep*, a small lychee-like fruit, in Jamaica.

Drinks

Minty mojitos and lemony daiquiris in Cuba, sugary ti-punch in Martinique and the smooth and fruity goombay smash in the Bahamas are just some of the drinks on offer. It's no surprise that all of these contain rum: the Caribbean makes the world's best, and while some people venture no further than a regular old Cuba libre (rum and cola) or piña colada, a highball of exquisite seven-year-old *añejo* over ice is liquid heaven.

FOODIE FAVORITES

➡ **Jerk** Jamaica's classic barbeque of spice-rubbed meat served with a fiery side sauce is found in many variations across the region.

➡ **Roti** A tasty and ubiquitous South Asian–derived flat bread filled with curried meats, vegetables and more.

➡ **Mofongo** A plantain crust encases seafood or steak in this Puerto Rican classic.

➡ **Callaloo** Spicy soup with okra, meats, greens and hot peppers.

1. Angelfish, parrotfish and blue tang with sponges, Bonaire
2. Dolphins, Bahamas **3.** Iguana, Bonaire **4.** Flamingo

GEORGETTE DOUWMA / GETTY IMAGES ©

Wildlife

RODRIGO FRISCIONE / GETTY IMAGES ©

Reef Creatures

If you're anxious to behold the Caribbean's richest fauna, you're going to get wet and you're going to see coral. Fish pecking away at nutritious tidbits or hiding out in coral reefs include the iridescent Creole wrasse, groupers, kingfish, sergeant majors and angelfish. Hang – or float – around and you might see inflatable porcupine fish, barracuda, nurse sharks, octopus, moray eels and manta rays.

Sea Mammals

Other species to seek out include pilot, sperm, blue and humpback whales, famous for their acrobatic breaching from January to March. Spinner, spotted and bottle-nosed dolphins, and loggerhead, green, hawksbill and leatherback turtles are common sights for divers. Manatees or sea cows – herbivorous marine mammals so ugly they're cute – are found in waters around Cuba, the Dominican Republic, Haiti, Jamaica and Puerto Rico.

Iguanas & Other Land Animals

Apart from iguanas – especially Grand Cayman's spectacular blue variety – native land animals have largely vanished from Caribbean islands. Responsibility is shared between humans and other introduced species, including goats, cats, dogs and monkeys. Trinidad, home to 100 types of mammal, is the big exception.

Birds

Hundreds of bird species, both endemic and migratory, frequent scores of islands. Look for iconic pink flamingos in the Bahamas and Bonaire. Rainforests on islands such as Dominica and St Vincent are home to all manner of colorful native birds. Parrots in a profusion of colors are found on almost any island with forests. From jade green to iridescent yellow, they are always crowd-pleasers and the focus of many a daytime jungle hike. Spotting Dominica's two indigenous species is popular. While exploring Dominica's dense rainforests you'll likely see many other species in what is the region's best island for watching wildlife.

Dominica

POP 74,870 / ♪767

Best Places to Eat

➡ Poz Restaurant & Bar (p381)

➡ Rainbow Beach Bar & Restaurant (p381)

➡ Sisters Beach Bar & Restaurant (p379)

Best Places to Sleep

➡ Jacoway Inn (p380)

➡ Pagua Bay House (p382)

➡ Cloud 9 Dominica (p380)

➡ Aywasi Kalinago Retreat (p383)

Why Go?

Dominica defies the Caribbean cliché on many levels. No mass tourism, no white powdery beaches, no rum-fueled pool parties. Nicknamed 'nature island' for a reason, the island lures largely individualists and ecoadventurers with its Boiling Lake, Champagne Reef, rainforest-shrouded volcano, sulfurous hot springs, superb diving and the Caribbean's first long-distance hiking trail.

Halfway between Guadaloupe and Martinique, Dominica is the only place in the Eastern Caribbean that's still home to a sizeable population of indigenous people, the Kalinago, who've lived on the island since the 13th century. Owing to the Kalinago's fierce resistance, Dominica was the last Caribbean island to be colonized – by the British in 1763.

Mother Nature may have been especially generous with Dominica, but it also deals it the occasional hardship in the form of hurricanes and tropical storms. Most recently, in August 2015, Tropical Storm Erika wreaked major havoc from which the island is still recovering.

When to Go

Feb–Jun The island's driest months, are the most popular.

Jul–Oct The rainy season, coinciding with the Caribbean's hurricane season, which peaks in August and September.Dominica's Carnival celebrations run for two weeks prior to Ash Wednesday.

Oct & Nov Roseau hosts the World Creole Music Festival in November. The week leading up to Independence Day (November 3), or Creole Day, is a vibrant celebration of local heritage.

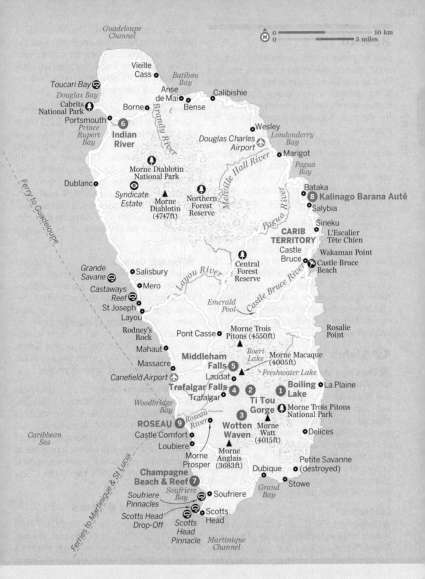

Dominica Highlights

1 **Boiling Lake** (p373) Trekking through spectacular scenery to the world's second-largest hot lake.

2 **Ti Tou Gorge** (p373) Swimming through a narrow canyon to a gushing waterfall.

3 **Wotten Waven** (p373) Relaxing in hot sulfur springs in this valley outside Roseau.

4 **Trafalgar Falls** (p372) Taking a stroll to these easily accessible twin waterfalls.

5 **Middleham Falls** (p374) Counting the shades of green en route to this 200ft-high waterfall.

6 **Indian River** (p378) Experiencing the watery side of the jungle on a glide down this placid west-coast river.

7 **Champagne Beach & Reef** (p375) Being tickled by the volcanic bubbles of this underwater attraction.

8 **Kalinago Barana Autê** (p382) Connecting with ancient traditions at this east-coast heritage village.

9 **Roseau** (p368) Plunging into the baffling bustle and history of Dominica's capital.

Roseau

Roseau (*rose*-oh) is Dominica's compact, noisy, chaotic but vibrant capital, situated on the southwest coast along the Roseau River. Reggae music blares through the narrow streets while people zip around in the daytime, but at night the town all but empties.

Roseau's streets are lined with historic stone-and-wood buildings in states ranging from ramshackle to elegant. Look closely and you'll spot a blend of French, Spanish and English architectural elements such as porticoes, louvers, hurricane shutters and verandas.

Roseau is best explored on foot, especially since many sights are clustered around the cruise-ship dock along Dame Eugenia Charles Blvd (also known as Bayfront). The most historic section is the French Quarter, south of King George V St. A bit further south are the coastal suburbs of Newtown, Citronier and Castle Comfort. The latter especially has a number of dive operators and dive lodges.

◎ Sights

★ Dominica Museum   MUSEUM
(✆767-448-8923; Dame Mary Eugenia Charles Blvd (Bayfront); adult/child EC$3/1; ◷9am-4pm Mon-Fri, to noon Sat) This small but interesting museum above the tourist office right near the cruise-ship pier provides an overview of the history of Dominica and its people. Maintained by the island's top historian, Lennox Honychurch, it has informative displays and objects on Kalinago and Creole culture as well as the slave trade.

Old Market   SQUARE
(off King George V St; ◷9am-4pm) This cobblestone plaza has been the center of action in Roseau for more than 300 years. It's been the site of political meetings, farmers markets and, more ominously, public executions and a slave market. Nowadays it's got craft and souvenir stalls that get plenty of attention from cruise-ship passengers.

Roseau Cathedral   CHURCH
(✆767-448-2766; www.dioceseofroseau.org/ our-lady-of-fairhaven; Virgin Lane; ◷closed for renovation) Gothic meets Caribbean at this landmark cathedral which evolved from simple wooden hut to the majestic 1916 volcanic stone pile you see today. The upper windows are stained glass, but much like a typical Creole home, the lower windows are wooden shutters that open for natural ventilation. Alas, time and hurricanes have left their mark and it's been undergoing restoration for quite some time.

Morne Bruce   VIEWPOINT
(above Botanic Gardens; ◷24hr; P) FREE Dominica's president is among the residents of this rather exclusive hillside enclave above the Botanic Gardens. The main reason to venture up here is for the panoramic vista of Roseau. Pick up either the short but strenuous half-mile **Jack's Walk trail** starting behind the aviaries in the Botanic Gardens (free admission) or drive up the steep road off Bath Rd just north of the Anglican cemetery.

★ Botanic Gardens   GARDENS
(www.dominicagardens.com; Valley Rd; ◷6am-7pm; 🖭) FREE Tucked beneath Morne Bruce hill, Roseau's beautiful 40-acre botanic gardens teem with mature banyan, century palms and ficus trees along with flowering tropical shrubs. It's a great place for a wander and a picnic on the expansive lawns. Definitely stop by the parrot aviaries housing endemic Jaco and Sisserou parrots.

Old Mill Cultural Center   CULTURAL CENTER
(✆767-449-1804; http://divisionofculture.gov. dm; Canefield) FREE A short drive north of Roseau, near Canefield Airport, this old sugar mill used to produce sugar, rum and molasses, and now has taken on new life as a community center and venue for cultural events. A gallery displays the work of local artists.

🏃 Activities & Tours

The diving is superb in the Soufriere-Scotts Head Marine Park just south of Roseau. Many dive shops also run whale-watching tours. Humpback, sperm and pilot whales, as well as schools of bottlenose dolphins, can be spotted year-round but are most common between November and March.

Dive Dominica   DIVING
(✆767-448-2188; www.divedominica.com; Loubiere Rd, Castle Comfort; 1-/2-tank dive US$55/90) This well-established shop is based at diver-geared Caste Comfort Lodge south of Roseau with a reef right on-site and within easy access of Scotts Head Marine Reserve.

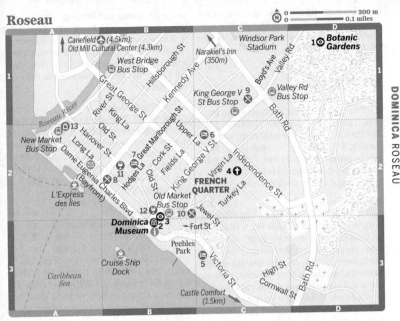

Roseau

Top Sights
1 Botanic Gardens D1
2 Dominica Museum B3

Sights
3 Old Market B2
4 Roseau Cathedral C2

Activities, Courses & Tours
Ken's Hinterland Adventure
   Tours .... (see 5)

Sleeping
5 Fort Young Hotel C3
6 Ma Bass Guest House C2

7 Sutton Place Hotel B2

Eating
8 Cocorico Café B2
9 J Astaphan & Co C1
10 Old Stone Grill & Bar B2
   Pearl's Cuisine .... (see 7)

Drinking & Nightlife
11 Garage Bar & Grill B2
12 Ruins Rock Cafe B2
   Warner's Bar .... (see 5)

Shopping
13 New Market A2

Anchorage Dive Center   DIVING
(☎767-448-2638; www.anchoragehotel.dm; Victoria St, Castle Comfort; 1-/2-tank dive US$55/75)
Based at the Anchorage Hotel, this well-established outfit offers boat dives, a snorkeling trip to Champagne Reef (US$30), 'Discover Scuba' courses (US$95) and whale-watching trips (US$60).

Ken's Hinterland Adventure Tours   TOURS
(KHATTS; ☎767-448-1660; www.khattstours.com; Fort Young Hotel, Victoria St; hikes US$40-85, 4-person minimum) This pro outfit based at the Fort Young Hotel offers a large selection of standard and unusual tours, including hikes to Boiling Lake (US$60), a day trip to the Kalinago Territory (US$75) and birdwatching in the Syndicate rainforest (US$65).

✯✯ Festivals & Events

★ **World Creole Music Festival**   MUSIC
(Windsor Park Sports Stadium, Roseau; ⊙late Oct) For three days, Roseau gets swept up in the head-rushing, feet-stomping beats of zouk, compa, soca, bouyon, afro beat, calypso and reggae during this famous annual festival. The rum-fueled party kicks off in the

daytime, with bands, food and exuberant dancing and singing taking over the narrow streets of downtown Roseau before the lucky ticket holders boogie on down to Windsor Park Stadium.

🛏 Sleeping

Hotels in downtown Roseau cater to everyone from penny-saving backpackers to business travelers with expense accounts. Note that the town is pretty dead at night and that parking is a nightmare in the daytime. Most people prefer to stay in one of the convivial if somewhat ramshackle oceanfront dive lodges about 1 mile south in Castle Comfort.

Narakiel's Inn   GUESTHOUSE $
(✆877-281-4529, 718-941-6220; http://narakiels inn.com; riverside, off Goodwill Rd; r US$68-88, apt US$130, 2-night minimum; ❇🔊) This six-room property in a converted apartment on the Roseau River is an excellent-value pick. Newly redone rooms have pleasant, modern decor and, despite being petite, pack in loads of amenities, including a microwave and a fridge that can be prestocked upon request. Rates include local cell-phone rental. Extra kudos for the ultra-comfy mattresses.

Ma Bass Guest House   GUESTHOUSE $
(✆767-448-2999; www.mabassdominica.com; 44 Fields Lane; s US$44-75, d US$80-118; ❇🔊) The friendly owner, Theresa Emanuel (better known as Ma Bass), offers true hospitality that's like staying with your auntie. Her guesthouse on a quiet side street in the heart of Roseau has 10 low-frills but clean and well-kept rooms with old-school furnishings. Most have private bathroom and air-con.

Castle Comfort Lodge   HOTEL $$
(✆767-448-2188; www.castlecomfortdivelodge. com; Loubiere Rd, Castle Comfort; r US$100; ❇🔊) One of a trio of diver-geared guesthouses side-by-side in Castle Comfort, this oceanfront lodge has an on-site dive center (Dive Dominica) and 12 basic but good-sized, contemporary rooms dressed in bold colors, some with ocean views. The alfresco restaurant-bar is perfect for post-dive chilling. Breakfast is good but pricey (US$15 to US$25).

Evergreen Hotel   HOTEL $$
(✆767-448-3288; www.evergreenhoteldominica. com; Loubiere Rd, Castle Comfort; d incl breakfast US$101-164; ❇🔊⛱) This family-run hotel has spacious grounds, a nice pool and a

to-die-for oceanfront location. Some of the nicest rooms feature four-poster beds, natural stone walls and sea-facing balconies. A teensy beach gives access to a snorkeling reef. The fine-dining restaurant and Cafe Sol lounge bar are well regarded in the local community.

Sutton Place Hotel   HOTEL $$
(✆767-449-8700; www.suttonplacehoteldominica. com; 25 Old St; r from US$96; ❇@🔊) Catering mainly to the business brigade, this charmer in a historic building has been put through a refurb but preserved its homey, old-timey flair. The on-site restaurant (Pearl's) is a local institution.

⭐Fort Young Hotel   HOTEL $$$
(✆767-448-5000; www.fortyounghotel.com; Victoria St; r US$158-276, ste US$364; ❇@🔊⛱) The old cannons that decorate this full-service 71-room hotel are a testament to its origin as a fort built in 1770 by Sir William Young, Dominica's first British governor. It's Roseau's ritziest option to hang your hat, especially if you score an oceanfront room with a balcony. The rooftop spa is great for post-sightseeing relaxation.

🍴 Eating

⭐Pearl's Cuisine   CARIBBEAN $
(✆767-448-8707; 25 Old St; mains EC$25-50; ⊙9am-5pm Mon-Sat) Although in new digs at the Sutton Hotel, this 25-year-old Roseau institution is still the go-to place for local old-school staples such as bullfoot soup, chicken callaloo or stewed agouti (a rodent). It gets busiest on Saturdays when all dishes cost just EC$20. Leave room for the soursop ice cream.

Cocorico Café   CREOLE $
(✆767-449-8686; www.cocoricocafe.com; cnr Dame Eugenia Charles Blvd & Kennedy Ave; mains EC$15-40; ⊙8:30am-4pm Mon-Fri, to 2pm Sat & Sun on cruise-ship days; 🔊) Local art and good-mood-inducing colors form the backdrop of this upstairs lair that's always buzzing with tousled tourists, gabby girlfriends and bronzed expats enjoying its tasty crepes, crisp salads and hot Creole lunches, such as jerk chicken or *sancoche* (codfish in coconut sauce).

J Astaphan & Co   SUPERMARKET $
(✆767-448-3221; 65 King George V St; ⊙8am-6pm Mon-Thu, to 7pm Fri, to 5pm Sat) This well-stocked supermarket is a good place to pick

up trail food, dinner fixings or rum at local prices. Department store upstairs.

★ **Old Stone Grill & Bar** CARIBBEAN $$
(☑ 767-440-7549; Castle St; mains EC$32-55; ⊙ 5-9pm Mon-Sat; 🐾) Leonard Lewis' locally adored bistro in, yes, an old stone building doubles as an art gallery and has tables inside and out. The extensive menu truly shines when it comes to the fresh fish paired with a choice of sides: order the croquettes or the 'spinach delight' and you won't regret it. The bartenders shake things up with skill and confidence.

🍷 Drinking & Nightlife

Central Roseau has a bunch of dive bars (and we're not talking about the sport here) that are busy with tourists in the daytime and hard-scrabble locals at night, especially on Friday and Saturday. There's a score of simple places to go for a drink along the narrow beach south of town.

Ruins Rock Cafe PUB
(☑ 767-440-5483; www.facebook.com/The-Ruins-Rock-Café-516331095159351; cnr King George V & Hanover Sts; ⊙ 9am-6pm Mon-Sat; 🐾) As busy as a beehive on cruise-ship days, this rustic, colorful beer hall–sized pub in an actual ruin lures punters with cold Carib and cocktails and the *muy macho* with bizarre bush rums (infused with snake, centipedes or grasshoppers!). There's a short menu of burgers and local dishes (lunch mains EC$30 to EC$62) to restore balance to the brain.

Warner's Bar BAR
(☑ 767-448-5000; www.fortyounghotel.com; Fort Young Hotel, Victoria St; ⊙ 11am-11pm) This genteel bar at the Fort Young Hotel is a popular spot to ring in the weekend during Friday's 'cocktails and conversations' event with live music. It has sweeping views over the water and is at its most atmospheric at sunset. Locals also invade for Monday night's 'Manager's Rum Punch' party and Wednesday's 'Unwine' wine evening.

Garage Bar & Grill BAR
(☑ 767-448-5433; 15 Hanover St; ⊙ 11am-late Mon-Sat) The name and the bar stools with tires as their base recall this joint's former incarnation. The bar tender pours strong drinks with abandon, which is much welcomed by the mostly local crowd. There's bar food including ribs and wings for sustenance. On weekends, it's often among the last places to shut down in Roseau.

🛍 Shopping

★ **New Market** MARKET
(River Bank; ⊙ 8am-4pm Mon-Sat) As much a place for locals to gather and chat with friends as a source of fresh produce, this bustling riverfront market is busiest on Saturday mornings. It's a great spot to pick up the local vibe, try a bowl of goat water (stew) or put together a picnic.

ℹ Information

INTERNET ACCESS

Cyberland Internet Café (☑ 767-440-2605; cyberland@cwdom.dm; cnr Cork & Great George Sts; per 30min EC$3; ⊙ 8:30am-6pm Mon-Fri, 10am-5pm Sat)

MEDICAL SERVICES

Princess Margaret Hospital (p387) Main hospital on the island.
New Charles Pharmacy (☑ 767-448-3198; 20 Cork St; ⊙ 8am-4:30pm Mon-Fri, to 1:30pm Sat)

MONEY

First Caribbean International Bank (☑ 767-255-7900; Old St, opposite Hodges Lane; ⊙ 8am-2pm Mon-Thu, to 5pm Fri)
Royal Bank of Canada (☑ 767-448-2771; cnr Dame Eugenia Charles Blvd & King George V St)

POST

Main Post Office (☑ 767-266-5209; Dame Eugenia Charles Blvd; ⊙ 8am-5pm Mon, to 4pm Tue-Fri) Check out the mural detailing the history of Dominica's postal service. Set up in 1856 by Anthony Trollope, by 1906 mail arrived by steam ship and policemen were the first mail carriers.

TOURIST INFORMATION

Tourist Office (☑ 767-448-2045; www.dominica.dm; cnr Dame Eugenia Charles Blvd & King George V St; ⊙ 8am-5pm Mon, to 4pm Tue-Fri)

ℹ Getting There & Away

BOAT

L'Express des Îles (p389) Regular scheduled ferry service between Roseau, Guadeloupe, Martinique and St Lucia leaves from the ferry terminal on Dame Eugene Charles Blvd (Bayfront Rd).

BUS

All bus routes originate in Roseau, but there is no central bus station. Instead, stops serving different destinations are scattered around the downtown grid. Buses run from Monday to Saturday between 6am and 7pm and come in the form of minivans with license plates starting with 'H' or 'HA.' The main bus stops:

New Market bus stop (River Rd) Buses to west-coast villages and Portsmouth, to Calibishie and Vielle Case, and to Kalinago Territory and east-coast villages.

Old Market bus stop (Old St) Buses south as far as Soufriere and Scotts Head.

King George V St (King George V & Independence Sts) & **Valley Rd bus stops** (Valley Rd) Buses east to Trafalgar, Wotten Waven, Morne Prosper and Laudat.

West Bridge bus stop (River Bank & Great George St) Buses to Canefield, Massacre, Mahaut and St Joseph.

ⓘ Getting Around

The narrow maze of the downtown area is best explored on foot. Destinations further afield can be reached by bus or taxi.

Flag down a taxi on the street, pick one up at a taxi rank or call **Dominica Taxi Association** (☑767-235-8648).

Roseau Valley

East of Roseau, the Roseau Valley is a ribbon of rural villages giving access to some of Dominica's most dramatic terrain and top wilderness sites. The village of Trafalgar is famous for its twin waterfalls, while Wotten Waven's hot sulfur springs are said to have medicinal benefits. In the north, Laudat is the gateway to the Unesco-protected Morne Trois Pitons National Park, a stunning pastiche of lakes, fumaroles, volcanoes, hot springs and dense forest.

Trafalgar Falls

Your camera will have a lovely affair with these spectacular twin waterfalls about a mile east of the village of Trafalgar. Their easy access puts them on the must-see list of just about every Dominica visitor, so expect crowds unless you're visiting in the low season or early or late in the day.

As a testament to the power of nature, the look of the falls changed when Tropical Storm Erika came through in 2015, causing boulders to shift at the base of the taller fall, unveiling hot sulfur springs that had been buried by a rockslide two decades ago.

⊙ Sights

★**Trafalgar Falls** WATERFALL
(http://tourism.gov.dm/news-and-media/bro chures/81-trafalgar-falls; Pailotte Rd, Trafalgar village; site pass US$5; ℗) An easy 0.4-mile trail runs from the visitor center near Papillote Wilderness Retreat to a platform with full-on views of the two side-by-side falls: the 125ft 'Father' fall and 75ft 'Mother' fall. Following the narrow, rocky trail beyond the platform means negotiating slippery boulders, so wear sturdy shoes and watch your step. You can cool off in the swimming hole below Mother fall. If you want to hike to the hot springs below Father fall, a guide is recommended.

🛏 Sleeping & Eating

Cocoa Cottage INN $$
(☑767-448-0412; www.cocoacottages.com; Papillotte Rd, Roseau Valley; d US$125, breakfast/dinner US$15/35; 🛜) 🍃 Connect with your soul at this serene charmer with five cottages dotted around fecund grounds. Made from local wood, lava stone, bamboo and other natural materials, each reflects the artistic vision and gentle spirit of Iris, the elfin-like owner. Days end with guests gathered around a communal table in the outdoor kitchen for delicious organic dinner prepared from local produce.

Papillote Wilderness Retreat HOTEL $$
(☑767-448-2287; www.papillote.dm; Pailotte Rd, Trafalgar village; s/d US$121/139, ste US$157/174, breakfast US$18, breakfast & dinner US$62.50; ℗@🛜) Jungly gardens with nearly 100 types of tropical flowers and trees (tours US$10), a location within walking distance of Trafalgar Falls and three volcanic mineral pools are among the assets of this popular inn. Rooms are rustic but comfortable, but avoid those next to the hydroelectric plant.

River Rock Cafe & Bar CARIBBEAN $
(☑767-225-0815; www.facebook.com/River-Rock-Cafe-bar-106457806144816/; Paillotte Rd; sandwiches EC$15, mains EC$25-50; ⊙10am-sunset, dinner at 7pm by reservation) This airy cafe is a popular pit stop for Trafalgar Falls pilgrims. It serves sandwiches as well as big platters of filling Creole fare featuring chicken, goat, beef or fish alongside a pile of provisions. Order a cold Kubuli and relax at a veranda table with a river-valley view.

ⓘ Getting There & Away

Buses leaving from Roseau's King George V St and Valley Rd bus stops make the trip to Trafalgar Falls village in about 30 minutes. The falls themselves are about 1 mile further north – you might be able to persuade the driver to take you straight there by offering a little extra money.

Wotten Waven

The tiny, steep village of Wotten Waven is well known for its natural hot sulfur springs that are said to have medicinal qualities and help cure everything from rheumatism to foot fungus. After a hard day on the trail, even skeptics will likely be happy to take off those boots and soothe sore muscles in the naturally muddy water. Enterprising villagers have created a trio of spas where relaxation-seekers can wallow in open-air pools surrounded by lovely gardens. All stay open after sunset, allowing you to chill under the stars, Kubuli in hand and serenaded by tree frogs.

Note that swimwear must be worn at all times. The water looks 'dirty' but is actually naturally orange. Clean water is piped into the pools so that there's circulation. Rinse your suit after you're done bathing.

🏃 Activities

'Taking the waters' in Wotten Waven's spas is the thing to do. The Waitukubuli Trail also passes through the village.

⭐**Screw's Sulfur Spa**   SPA
(☑767-440-4478; www.screwsspa.com; Wotten Waven; US$20; ◷10am-10pm; 🛜) 🏊 Screw's is a never-ending project masterminded by a charismatic local Rasta. He's spent years fine-tuning his natural sulfur spas, adding stonewalled pools, landscaping, bridges, twinkle lights and, of late, slides. This watery warren welcomes cruise-ship guests during the day but exudes a magical stillness when visited at night.

Ti Kwen Glo Cho   SPA
(☑767-295-4432; https://tikwenglocho.com; Wotten Waven; adult/child US$10/5; ◷8:30am-11pm) *Ti kwen glo cho* is Creole for 'little corner of water,' a fitting name for this charming spa surrounded by tropical gardens at the top of the village. Hot sulfurous water bubbles up from below and is cooled down with fresh water from a waterfall before gushing into two communal stone pools from bamboo pipes.

Tia's Bamboo Cottages & Sulphur Spa   SPA
(☑767-448-1998; tiacottages@hotmail.com; Wotten Waven; US$10; ◷9am-11pm) Right in the village and set amid beautiful tropical gardens, Tia's has three open-air pools and two private ones inside bamboo huts.

🛏 Sleeping

Le Petit Paradis   GUESTHOUSE $
(☑767-448-5946; www.lepetitparadisdominica.com; Wotten Waven; r US$28-45; P🛜) Popular with Waitukubuli Trail hikers, this rambling inn is presided over by the big-hearted Joan and surrounded by flowery gardens. There are private rooms with valley views, simple ones in apartments with shared facilities and a small camping area in back. With advance notice, Joan will cook delicious meals (US$7 to US$20) served in the open dining room.

❶ Getting There & Away

Buses to Wotten Waven in the Roseau Valley make the trip from the King George V St and Valley Rd bus stops in Roseau in about 20 minutes.

Morne Trois Pitons National Park

The village of Laudat is a main gateway to the Unesco-protected Morne Trois Pitons National Park, an evocative pastiche of lakes, fumaroles, volcanoes, waterfalls, hot springs and dense forest. It comprises five vegetation zones, mainly secondary rainforest but reaching up to cloud forest at the highest elevations.

Established in 1975, it stretches across 17,000 acres surrounding the eponymous 4672ft-high three-peaked dormant volcano. Other volcanoes within the park are Morne Micotrin, Morne Watt and Morne Anglais.

The park has been a Unesco World Heritage site since 1997.

🏃 Activities

Ti Tou Gorge   SWIMMING
(near Laudat) The short swim from a swimming hole through a narrow gorge to a rather powerful waterfall is charmingly spooky, as it's dark down there with steep vine-clad lava walls no more than 5ft or 7ft apart. It's an ethereal and unusual place, but since it's also a cruise-ship darling, come early or late in the day for relative serenity.

⭐**Boiling Lake**   HIKING
(site pass US$5) Dominica's pre-eminent trek, and one of the hardest, travels 4 miles to a 207ft-wide boiling lake, which is actually a

flooded fumarole – a crack in the earth that allows hot gases to vent from the molten lava below. Take the trailhead at Ti Tou Gorge and budget no less than six hours for the round-trip.

It's the world's second-largest such lake (the largest is in New Zealand). Inexperienced hikers should consider hiking with a guide (about US$40 per person, more with car transfer).

Middleham Falls HIKING

(site pass US$5) The trail to one of Dominica's highest waterfalls (200ft) traverses thick rainforest with towering trees and ferns. Although well built and not terribly long, the trail gets slippery and requires rock clambering and fording several creeks. Bring a swimsuit to cool off in the pool, where the heavy spray will literally take your breath away. Allow about two to three hours round-trip. The main trailhead is just off the Laudat Rd.

Boeri Lake Trail HIKING

(near Laudat; site pass US$5) At 2800ft, moody Boeri Lake is Dominica's highest lake and fills a volcanic crater wedged between Morne Trois Pitons and Morne Macaque. For the trailhead, take the road to Freshwater Lake just before Laudat and turn left at the T-junction. The 1.25-mile-long rocky and sometimes slippery trail to the lake goes past streams and hot and cold springs.

En route, you'll enjoy sweeping views of the mountains, Freshwater Lake and the Atlantic Ocean from the ridge – weather permitting. The water is cold, so a dip will be quite refreshing indeed. Also keep an eye out for scurrying zandoli (tree lizards), hummingbirds and butterflies.

Freshwater Lake HIKING

(near Laudat; site pass US$5) Shimmering shades of blue and green, Freshwater is the largest of Dominica's four lakes and the source of the Roseau River. It is easily reached via a paved road that veers uphill just before Laudat and delivers sweeping views of the valley, Morne Anglais and the sea.

At the T-junction, turn right for the lake parking lot and pick up the easy 2.5-mile trail around the lake to the right of the visitor center, past a hydroelectric station. The montane forest vegetation at this elevation (2500ft) is very different from the rainforest; trees are short and thin, and shrubs, ferns and herbs blanket the forest floor. Birders

should keep an eye out for the mountain whistler, hummingbirds and egrets. Bring a sweater or light jacket; it gets chilly up here.

Emerald Pool Trail HIKING

(http://tourism.gov.dm/news-and-media/brochures/76-emerald-pool; Imperial Rd, near Point Cassé; US$5) This flat 0.7-mile loop trail leads to a swimming hole fed by a 40ft waterfall and hemmed in by sumptuous foliage that gives it its distinctive green tinge. It's deep enough for a dip but the water can be on the cool side.

The path winds through dense rainforest and past two viewpoints, one looking out over the rainforest canopy to Morne Laurent and another treating you to panoramic views of the Atlantic coast. It's generally a serene place, except on cruise-ship days when one packed minivan after the other pulls up to the parking lot. Show up past 3pm and you'll have the place more or less to yourself. The well-marked turnoff to Emerald Pool is on the cross-island road linking Canefield and Castle Bruce. There's a visitor center with toilets and a snack bar.

Morne Trois Pitons Trail HIKING

(Imperial Rd, Pont Cassé; site pass US$5) At 4672ft, this dormant volcano is the highest elevation within the eponymous national park. The hike to the top is challenging, as it cuts through patches of razor grass and requires scrambling over steep rocks. You'll need not only good lungs and thighs but also a solid sense of balance. Budget about six hours and consider hiring a guide. The trailhead is off Imperial Rd at Pont Cassé.

👉 Tours

Extreme Dominica ADVENTURE SPORTS

(📞767-295-7272, 767-295-6828; www.extreme dominica.com; Paillotte Rd; canyoning tour US$160) This pro outfit runs exhilarating half-day expeditions that have you rappelling down waterfalls, jumping from pool to pool and floating in crystal-clear swimming holes at the bottom of deep canyon walls. It also offers guided hikes to Boiling Lake, and a turtle-watching tour (April to July only). Rates include pick-up, all gear and a training session.

🛏 Sleeping

Symes Zee Villa GUESTHOUSE $

(📞767-448-2494; www.symeszeevilla.com; Valley Rd, Laudat; s US$55, d US$66-77; ❄ 🛜) This abode is set amid tropical gardens and promises crisp mountain air and cool mountain views from its lofty perch above Laudat. Rooms are smallish and low-frills but handy for hikers. With advance notice, food can be delivered from the owner's Roseau restaurant.

Roxy's Mountain Lodge INN $$
(📞767-448-4845; www.roxymountainlodge.com; Laudat; s US$75, d US$100-150; P@) This traditional mountain lodge has appealing Swiss-chalet looks and is naturally popular with hikers. Some rooms have porches with lovely forest views.

❶ Getting There & Away
Buses to Laudat (40 minutes) leave from the King George V St and Valley Rd bus stops in Roseau. A taxi from Roseau to Laudat costs EC$80.

Soufriere & Southwest Coast

The coastal road south of Roseau takes you through a handful of seaside villages past ethereal Champagne Beach via the Mediterranean-style hillside village of Soufriere with its hot sulfur springs, to land's end in scruffy Scotts Head. The entire drive takes about 30 minutes.

Soufriere Bay, which is the rim of a sunken volcanic crater, is prime snorkeling and diving territory protected as the Soufriere-Scotts Head Marine Reserve. Segment 1 of the Waitukubuli Trail starts at Scotts Head promontory.

East of here and reached by turning inland at Loubiere, is sweeping Grand Bay and, just beyond, the villages that were most affected by Tropical Storm Erika in 2015: Dubique and Petite Savanne. Many residents were relocated to Grand Bay. The coastal road to Delices remained closed at the time of research.

◉ Sights

Soufriere Sulfur Springs HOT SPRINGS
(Soufriere; site pass US$5; ⊘24hr) Soufriere's undisputed 'hot spot' are the naturally heated mineralized waters draining from two streams into four stone pools in the hills above Soufriere. Changing rooms and a large pool are on your left as you walk past the information center, while a snack shack and picnic tables await on your right. Three more – smaller and nicer – pools are

tucked into the forest, a short walk away on segment 2 of the Waitukubuli Trail, which begins here.

Scotts Head Point HISTORIC SITE
(Land's end, Scotts Head; US$2) A narrow isthmus separating the fierce Atlantic and the calm Caribbean leads to the eponymous 'Scotts Head,' the rocky headland named for an 18th-century British lieutenant governor. A short hike leads up to a smattering of ruins that remain of the fort he erected in defense of Soufriere Bay. There's great snorkeling off the pebbly beach, and a bar that rents gear and serves cold drinks.

Grand Bay BAY
(Grand Bay) This sweeping bay is on Dominica's south coast. Turn inland at Loubiere onto a wide and largely pothole-free curving road skirting the base of Morne Anglais and crossing a few rivers before reaching the coast.

🏃 Activities

★ Bubble Beach Spa & Bar HOT SPRINGS
(Soufriere; by donation) A hot bath in the Caribbean Sea? That's what you get on Bubble Beach where warm sulfurous water percolates right up from below the ocean floor. Enterprising local Dale Mitchell has created a lovely little retreat with a stone-walled hot pool for soaking, a sandy beach with loungers (US$5), and a small bar with cold beers and homemade bush rum.

Diving & Snorkeling

★ Champagne Beach & Reef SNORKELING
(Victoria St, near Point Michel; marine reserve fee US$2; 🚻) One of Dominica's most popular underwater playgrounds has you snorkeling amid volcanic bubbles emerging from vents beneath the sea floor and rising up as drops of liquid crystal, making it feel like you're swimming in a giant glass of champagne. Best of all, you can snorkel right off the (rocky) beach. Technicolor fish and coral abound.

Soufriere-Scotts Head Marine Reserve DIVING
(📞767-616-0404; Soufriere & Scotts Head; fee EC$5) The sweeping bay stretching from Soufriere to Scotts Head is a vast volcanic crater of unknown depth and a haven for divers and snorkelers with nearly 30 different sites. With its dramatic drop-offs, walls, pinnacles, coral reefs and underwater

fumaroles, it delivers Caribbean diving at its finest and most pristine. The Kalinago associate many legends with these mysterious waters.

Nature Island Dive DIVING
(☑ 767-449-8181; www.natureislanddive.com; Gallion Rd, Soufriere; 1-/2-tank dive incl all gear US$80/112) Within a 10-minute boat ride of spectacular dive sites, this operator specializes in small groups ranging from two to eight divers.

Champagne Reef Dive & Snorkel DIVING
(☑ 767-440-5085; www.champagnereef.com; 2-tank dive US$89) Right at the famous Champagne Beach, this outfit rents snorkeling gear for US$19, including the US$2 marine reserve fee, and also organizes boat dives, dive courses and rainforest tours. If your underwater explorations have left you hungry or thirsty, there's cold beer and upscale local fare to restore energies.

🛏 Sleeping & Eating

Zandoli Inn INN $$
(☑ 767-616-5999; www.zandoli.com; Roche Cassée, Stowe; s/d US$135/145, breakfast & dinner per person US$45; P@☎) Despite being battered by Tropical Storm Erika, this artistic clifftop retreat run by a Canadian mother-and-daughter team once again induces a state of Zen, Caribbean-style. The five sun-

---

WAITUKUBULI NATIONAL TRAIL

Completed in 2011, the **Waitukubuli National Trail** (WNT; www.waitukubulitrail.com) is the Caribbean's first long-distance hiking trail. It links Scotts Head in the far southwest with Cabrits National Park in the northwest, hitting all the key beauty spots along the way, including Boiling Lake and Emerald Pool. Its 115 miles are divided into 14 segments of various lengths and difficulty but each one is designed to be completed in one day. Accommodations are available close to the trailheads. The website has maps, addresses, guide referrals and other details.

Segments

➡ Segment 1: Scotts Head to Soufriere Estate

➡ Segment 2: Soufriere Estate to Bellevue Chopin

➡ Segment 3: Bellevue Chopin to Wotten Waven

➡ Segment 4: Wotten Waven to Pont Casse

➡ Segment 5: Pont Casse to Castle Bruce

➡ Segment 6:Castle Bruce to Hatten Garden (Pagua Bay)

➡ Segment 7: Hatten Garden (Pagua Bay) to First Camp Heights

➡ Segment 8: First Camp Heights to Petite Macoucherie Heights

➡ Segment 9: Petite Macoucherie Heights to Colihaut Heights

➡ Segment 10: Colihaut Heights to Syndicate

➡ Segment 11: Syndicate to Borne

➡ Segment 12: Borne to Penville

➡ Segment 13: Penville to Capuchin

➡ Segment 14: Capuchin to Cabrits

Passes & Fees

A day pass for one segment is US$12, a 15-day pass to hike all 14 segments costs US$40. Passes are sold at or near the trailheads, including Rubis Filling Station in Portsmouth, the Sea Breeze Inn in Castle Bruce, Kalinago Barana Aute, the Waitukubuli National Trail Management Unit in Pont Casse, Ken's Hinterland Adventure Tours in Roseau and Rodney's Wellness Retreat in Soufriere. Passes are also sold at Courtesy Car Rental at Douglas Charles Airport and at the Forever Young Classic Souvenir Shop on Dame Mary Eugenia Charles Blvd in Roseau.

drenched rooms have private balconies, dreamy views of scalloped Grand Bay, beautiful artwork and solar hot-water showers.

Oceanview Apartments APARTMENT $$

(☎767-449-8266; http://oceanviewapartments.weebly.com; Bay front, Scotts Head village; s/d US$60/70, extra person US$15; P 📶) The three handsome hilltop apartments (sleeping three to five) face a garden where guests can help themselves to cherries, limes and coconuts and watch the sun drop into the ocean. Simple apartments are kitted out with TV, kitchenette and fans. The beach and the bus stop are a short walk away.

Melvina's Champagne Bar & Restaurant SEAFOOD $$

(☎767-440-5480; Victoria St, Pointe Michel; mains EC$20-40; ⏰10am-9pm, Fri til late) Despite the lofty name, Melvina's is actually a salty oceanfront bar and seafood restaurant between Roseau and Champagne Beach. On Friday nights it's a scene and a half when locals swing by for steamed fish, barbecued chicken and rum punches.

Getting There & Away

Buses down the main highway as far as Scotts Head depart from the Old Market bus stop in Roseau.

Mero & Salisbury

About halfway up the coast, the long and grayish-black beach at Mero is the west coast's most popular sandy strand. It's accessed via a narrow one-way road off the main highway. A few bars serve drinks and meals and rent beach chairs. Salisbury sits above the Batoui River valley and affords some nice coastal views.

There are some beautiful dive sites just a 10-minute boat ride offshore, including Coral Gardens, Rena's Reef and Whale Shark Reef. East Carib Dive (p377) runs trips and snorkeling tours.

Tropical Storm Erika destroyed three bridges along the west-coast highway, but sturdy Bailey bridges ensure that traffic flow is not affected until they can be properly rebuilt (with Chinese funding).

Activities

Macoucherie Distillery DISTILLERY

(☎767-449-6409; Shillingford Estate, Mero; ⏰tours by appointment) FREE Shillingford Estate near Mero has been distilling premium rum from pure sugarcane juice for more than half a century. During tours of the compound you'll learn that the company grows its own sugar and still uses a traditional water-powered mill to crush the cane, a process as authentic and old school as it gets.

East Carib Dive DIVING

(☎767-449-6575; www.dominicadiving.com; Salisbury; 1-/2-tank dives US$50/80) This outfit has run boat dives, night dives and snorkeling trips for more than 20 years. There's diving at Doudou Reef right in front of the dive center and half a dozen more fecund sites just a 10-minute boat ride away.

Sleeping & Eating

Tamarind Tree Hotel HOTEL $$

(☎767-449-7395; www.tamarindtreedominica.com; Salisbury; s US$104-134, d US$134-164; ⏰closed Sep; ❄@📶≋) 🍃 Run by a Swiss-German couple, a relaxing vibe hangs over this 15-room property on a seaside cliff amid nicely landscaped grounds. All rooms have a fridge, fans and solar-heated water; the upper units feature air-con, while three new two-bedroom cottages come with kitchen. The restaurant (mains EC$40 to EC$65) serves Kubuli on tap.

★**Romance Cafe** CARIBBEAN $$

(☎767-449-7922; www.facebook.com/RomanceDominica; Mero Beach, Mero; mains EC$20-50; ⏰10am-9pm) Run by the affable Frederique from France, this locally adored nosh spot on the beach serves up three squares a day created from bounty from the land and sea, plus all the beer, juice and coffee you could wish for. Also has a small shop with quality souvenirs.

Getting There & Away

Mero Beach sits about halfway between Portsmouth and Roseau. Driving takes about 30 to 40 minutes from either. If coming by bus, ask the driver to drop you at the turnoff to Mero Beach and walk five minutes into the village.

About 1.5 miles north of Mero, a sign points the way up to the village of Salisbury.

Portsmouth

Snuggled against sweeping Prince Rupert Bay, Dominica's second-largest town still feels rough around the edges, but that should change once a couple of long-planned five-star hotels finally get off the ground. For now, development is focused on the southern township of Picard, home to the Ross University School of Medicine that's a cornerstone of the local economy. There's a good crop of lively restaurants and bars near the slick modern campus.

North of downtown, in an area called Lagoon, the road parallels a wide yellow-sand beach whose funky restaurant-bars get busy on weekends. Ahead awaits the colonial-era Fort Shirley at Cabrits National Park.

Prince Rupert Bay, by the way, was the site of the Battle of the Saints, one of the major battles in Caribbean history, that saw the British navy give the French fleet a drubbing in 1792.

◎ Sights & Activities

★ Cabrits National Park NATIONAL PARK
(Bay St; site pass US$5; ⊙ 8am-6pm; P 🛜) The star attraction of this national park on a forested headland a mile north of downtown is Fort Shirley, an impressively restored 18th-century British garrison, just a five-minute uphill walk from the park entrance. Views over Prince Rupert Bay are especially lovely in the late afternoon. Three longer trails also crisscross the park, leading past the officers' quarters, the soldiers' barracks, the powder magazine and other vestiges from the past.

Indian River Boat Ride BOATING
(site fee US$5, boat ride US$15) The 1½-hour boat ride along this shady mangrove-lined river has you gliding past buttressed bwa mang trees with a chance to spot egrets, crabs, iguanas, hummingbirds and other creatures. Trips include a stop at 'Cobra's Bush Bar' for juice, snacks and 'The Dynamite,' the signature rum drink. Rowers wait by the bridge at the mouth of the river.

JC Ocean Adventures DIVING
(☑ 767-449-6957, cell 767-295-0757; www. jcoceanadventures.com; Cabrits National Park Rd; 2-tank boat dive US$85) JC are Jorge and Cindy, the owners of this dive center within Cabrits National Park, just past the entrance booth. Their operation includes boat, shore and night dives, as well as PADI certification courses. Equipment rental available.

🛏 Sleeping

There's a cluster of good, budget-friendly lodging options near the university in Picard and an off-grid eco-lodge in the mountains north of Portsmouth.

Sisters Sea Lodge APARTMENT $
(☑ 767-235-5454; www.sistersealodge.com; Lizard Trail, Picard; apt US$70-90; P) Walk past mango, guava and frangipani trees while strolling to your functionally furnished studio apartment with kitchen. Each of the six units sleeps up to four people and sits within a coconut toss from a narrow black-sand beach. There's wi-fi and excellent drinks and food in the seafront restaurant.

Hotel The Champ HOTEL $$
(☑ 767-445-4452; www.thechampsdm.com; Picard; r incl breakfast US$119-149; ❄ 🛜) This family-run hotel clings to a steep hill above the university suburb Picard, meaning superb views are guaranteed. There are two rooms at garden level and three upstairs, all with fridge, TV and a porch with lounge chairs. The restaurant with outdoor bar serves pizza, dinner and cold drinks. Check the website for special deals.

★ Manicou River Resort BOUTIQUE HOTEL $$$
(☑ 767-616-8903; www.manicouriverresort.com; Everton Hall Estate, Tanetane; cottage from US$195, 3-night minimum; P 🛜) 🍃 This dreamy back-to-nature retreat sits about 400ft above the Caribbean and affords picture-perfect views of Douglas Bay and the Cabrits. The octagonal, open-plan cottages have elegantly rustic wooden furniture and latticed walls that let in the rainforest sounds. If you're not staying, swing by for a sunset drink, but note that you need a 4WD to get up here.

Picard Beach Cottages RESORT $$$
(☑ 767-445-5131; www.picardbeachcottages.dm; Picard; cottage US$170-240; P ❄ 🛜) In a garden setting on an old coconut plantation right by a narrow black-sand beach, this cluster of 18 wooden cottages offers atmospheric digs but has seen better days. Each unit has a kitchenette big enough to prepare a small meal to enjoy on your private porch.

🍴 Eating

Shacks STREET FOOD $
(Michael Douglas Blvd, Picard; dishes EC$10-20; ⊙ approximately 8am-10pm) This row of food stalls caters primarily to the local student population but anyone is welcome to fill up on the cheap with pizza, burgers, barbecued meats, nachos, crepes and other comfort foods. Not all stalls are open all the time.

MORNE DIABLOTIN NATIONAL PARK

Established to protect the habitat of the national bird, the Sisserou parrot, and its pretty red-necked cousin, the Jaco parrot, this national park covers some 8242 acres. It's named for Dominica's tallest peak.

There is no public bus service to the park. You will need your own wheels or hire a driver.

Bring water and a picnic.

Morne Diablotin Trail (near Dublanc; US$5) The trek up to 4747ft-high Morne Diablotin, Dominica's highest mountain, takes you from the rainforest to the cloud forest. It may only be 1.25 miles long, but it's all steeply uphill and involves clambering over rocks, roots and trees. Budget at least two to 2½ hours each way, including stops to look for endemic Sisserou and Jaco parrots.

Prepare to get muddy and bring a jacket as it gets chilly at the top. The trailhead is on the road to the Syndicate Nature Trail, which veers off the village of Dublance. Look for the sign.

Syndicate Nature Trail (US$5) This easy 1-mile loop trail through the rainforest on the western slopes of Morne Diablotin is beloved by birders for the good chance of spotting Sisserou and Jaco parrots. The best spotting time is in the early morning and late afternoon. Also watch for hummingbirds and several dozen other feathered species.

To get to the reserve, turn onto the signposted road just north of the village of Dublanc and continue to Syndicate Estate, about 4.5 miles inland.

★**Sisters Beach Bar & Restaurant**   CARIBBEAN **$$**
(☑767-445-5211; www.facebook.com/Sisters BeachBarRestaurantandLodge; Lizard Trail, Picard; mains EC$35-85; ⊙11am-9:30pm Mon-Sat; P �((·))) Grab a seat in this feel-good beachfront dining room with mix-and-match furniture, nurse a Patricia Colada (named after the owner) and wait for Chef Francis' delicious concoctions to appear. The menu changes biweekly, but by popular demand the mussels and shrimp in white-wine sauce and the lionfish with curry-coconut sauce always make appearances. Lovely at night.

★**Blue Bay Grill & Bar**   FRENCH **$$**
(☑767-612-1144; www.facebook.com/Blue.Bay. Restaurant; Lagoon; mains EC$33-70; ⊙1-10pm; �((·))) It looks just like any other funky beach restaurant, but Blue Bay's eclectic mix of French, Creole and Swiss cuisine is a step up from the run-of-the-mill fare served elsewhere in town. The seafood platters never fail to impress, but the goat and pork dishes are also respectable. Reservations required.

Purple Turtle Beach Club Bar & Restaurant   CARIBBEAN **$$**
(☑767-445-5296; Bay St, Lagoon; mains EC$30-50; �((·))) This Portsmouth institution sits on the main beach right in the yellow sand and is a favorite end-of-day drinking spot for locals and boaters alike. Also a reliable lunch

spot to or from touring Cabrits National Park, with a menu featuring all the expected Caribbean favorites, from Creole chicken to barbecued ribs.

Tomato Cafe   INTERNATIONAL **$$**
(☑767-445-3334; Banana Trail, Picard; dishes EC$22-65; ⊙9am-9pm Mon-Sat; P �((·))) Essentially an off-campus student cafeteria, Canadian-owned Tomato feeds homesick tummies with soul food from back home, be it hummus, nachos, baked brie, pastrami, bratwurst or pizza. For dessert try the chocolate cake named in honor of Orlando Bloom who apparently became a fan during the filming of *Pirates of the Caribbean*.

❶ Information

Computer Resource Center (☑767-445-3370; Bay Rd; internet per 30min EC$5; ⊙9am-10pm Mon-Sat)

National Bank of Dominica (☑767-255-2300; Michael Douglas Blvd)

Police (Bay St)

❶ Getting There & Away

Buses to Roseau's New Market bus stop leave from the south end of Bay St on the waterfront. For Calibishie and the Douglas Charles Airport, board on Granby St on the south side of Benjamin's Park.

Northeastern Coast

The narrow road cutting to the east coast from Portsmouth across Dominica's remote and sparsely populated north is a stunning drive past massive ferns, towering palms, wild helliconias and thick banana groves. Budget about two hours for the extremely curvy drive. Numerous scenes from *Pirates of the Caribbean* were filmed in this area.

Calibishie

Calibishie is the main village on the scenic north coast with its dramatic mosaic of steep cliffs, red rocks and rivers gushing down from the mountains. The coast cradles some fine beaches, and although they can't compete with your usual white-sand wonders, they certainly have a mystique all of their own. No wonder many scenes from *Pirates of Caribbean* were filmed around here.

Although still sleepy and slow-paced, Calibishie has seen its tourism infrastructure grow in recent years and there are now some excellent places to stay and eat along the highway and in the hills. Even if you're not spending the night, it's a worthwhile stop for a meal and/or a swim en route to nearby Douglas Charles Airport.

◉ Sights

If you plan to snorkel, it's best to have your own gear, because the closest rental is JC Ocean Adventure (p378) in Portsmouth.

★ Batibou Beach   BEACH
(admission US$5) This coconut palm-fringed crescent has good swimming and snorkeling

---

HOLLYWOOD'S TREASURE ISLAND

With its wild coast, thick jungle and hidden coves, Dominica has always been a popular haunt of pirates between pillages, so it was only natural that Hollywood came calling when location scouting for the *Pirates of the Caribbean* films. In 2005, hundreds of cast and crew, led by Johnny, Orlando and Keira, invaded the island to shoot scenes of films two and three in locations such as Batibou Beach, Ti Tou Gorge, Soufriere and the Indian River.

---

with a coral reef just offshore, and there's a cafe as well. It sits at the end of a 0.6-mile bumpy dirt road that's usually only accessible by 4WD. Since it goes through private land, there may be someone asking for a US$5 toll.

Number One Beach   BEACH
(Hampstead Beach) This moody 550yd-long black-sand beach is fringed by coconut palms, sea grape and white mangrove. The currents are too strong for swimming but it's a nice spot for a picnic or a stroll. It's about a 15-minute to walk from the road – look for the sign.

Point Baptiste Beach   BEACH
Accessed via the Red Rock Haven hotel, this beautiful and quiet strand at the foot of a massive rock face has reddish sand, shallow waters and lots of shady coconut palms. You can snorkel right off the beach.

🛏 Sleeping

A number of properties flank the main highway, although the nicest overlook the rugged shore or are tucked into the hills above town. All are small and privately run, often by jovial (and sometimes eccentric) expats.

★ Jacoway Inn   B&B $$
(☎767-445-8872, 767-265-8882; www.jacowayinn.com; John Baptist Ridge Rd; apt US$75-85, cottage US$65; P 🖥) Thumbs up, way up for this darling B&B run by the irrepressible Carol Ann, gourmet cook, bon vivant, dog adopter and hostess with the mostest. All three units, including a 'new' salvaged 110-year-old wooden cottage, reflect her knack for color and design and come with kitchen. Home-cooked breakfast are memorable and served in the tropical garden gazebo.

Veranda View B&B   B&B $$
(☎767-445-8900, 767-613-9493; www.lodging-dominica.com; Main Rd, Calibishie; apt US$75-95; 🖥) This brightly decorated inn with three studio apartments sits right above the sand and has great beachfront vistas. Owner Hermien is a consummate host and excellent cook who will happily whip up a tasty lunch or dinner for you upon request. Optional breakfast is an extra US$10.

★ Cloud 9 Dominica   APARTMENT $$$
(☎767-295-0890; www.cloud9dominica.com; Calibishie; apt US$159-249, 3-night minimum; P ❄ 🖥) This new arrival with to-die-for views of ocean, beach and river kicks accommoda-

tions on Dominica up a notch. Naturally cooled by the sea breezes, all four apartments pack plenty of contemporary design cachet, the latest hi-tech gadgets and full kitchens into an ample frame. Nice touch: the porch hammocks. Great for adventurers craving end-of-day comforts and a cold drink at the rooftop bar.

The charming on-site hosts Tom and Sharie know Dominica's secret nooks and crannies and are expert in customizing adventures and experiences that forge a deep connection with the land and locals.

Pointe Baptiste Guesthouse   VILLA $$$

(✆767-445-7368; www.pointbaptiste.com; villa US$270-350) Mick Jagger spent the night and Princess Margaret had tea on the porch of this rambling wooden villa on the ancestral estate of the Napier family, who came from England in the 1930s. The charmingly musty place oozes history from every nook and cranny, and sleeps up to eight people. The garden grounds give access to two sandy beaches. Proprietor Alan Napier operates a small chocolate factory on the estate grounds.

Calibishie Gardens   CABIN

(✆767-612-5176; cabin incl breakfast US$125; P🐾📶🏊) 🐾 At this feel-good place handbuilt by congenial Canadian expat Troy (aka 'Poz'), you'll sleep like a log in wooden cabins perched atop stone pillars – it's like an eco-conscious Smurf house. The interior is rustic in style but first-rate in terms of comfort and amenities (cable TV, fridge, mosquito net). Enjoy jungle views from your private porch. The on-site restaurant is one of the best in the area.

✕ Eating & Drinking

Not much of a party place, Calibishie. One of the liveliest hangouts is Poz Restaurant & Bar, especially on Friday nights and during the Sunday-afternoon pool party.

A&A Low Price Center   SUPERMARKET $

(✆767-445-7655; Main Rd, Calibishie; ⊙6am-9pm Mon-Sat, 6-9am & 4-9pm Sun) Small but well-stocked supermarket to help with all your self-catering needs. Also has an ATM.

★Poz Restaurant & Bar   INTERNATIONAL $$

(✆767-612-5176; off Main Rd, Calibishie; mains EC$40-60; ⊙4-10pm Mon-Sat, 1-10pm Sun) 'Poz' is really Troy from Toronto, a dreamer and a doer whose magical wonderland in the

jungle quickly evolved into a community hangout for expats, visitors and villagers. From pizza to oxtail stew and lionfish fillet, the tastes are superb, and the poolside outdoor dining area built entirely from local woods is a funky delight. Ask about his 'very special rum'...

★Rainbow Beach Bar & Restaurant   CARIBBEAN $$

(✆767-245-9995; www.facebook.com/rainbow beachbarrestaurant; Main Rd, Calibishie; mains EC$40-100; ⊙8am-10pm Mon-Sat; 🐾) Chef Karine and her reggae musician husband Michael preside over one of the best restaurants on the north. Sit on the deck above the waves and tuck into French Creole culinary magic starring locally foraged ingredients whenever possible. Killer: the curried-chicken pineapple, served in an actual fruit. Goes well with the sorrel rum punch.

ℹ Information

ATM (A&A Low Price Centre grocery store, Calibishie)

Tourist Office (✆767-445-8344; www.calibishiecoast.com; ⊙ usually 9am-4pm Mon-Fri)

ℹ Getting There & Away

Buses linking Douglas Charles Airport and Portsmouth leave from the main highway. In Portsmouth you can change to a service all the way down to Roseau.

Marigot & Pagua Bay

Marigot encompasses Douglas Charles Airport and several neighborhoods strung along the highway. Aside from the gas station (the only one for miles), there's little to make you want to stop. Instead, push on to gorgeous Pagua Bay, which has a rocky beach suitable for bodysurfing and some outstanding places to hang your hat.

🛏 Sleeping & Eating

Hibiscus Valley Inn   GUESTHOUSE $$

(✆767-445-8195; www.hibiscusvalley.com; Dr Nicholas Liverpool Hwy, Marigot; r US$49-135; P📶) This convivial rainforest lodge 15 minutes from Douglas Charles Airport has both 'nature bungalows' down by the Pagua River with shared facilities and a veranda for lounging in a hammock, as well as hotel-standard rooms with air-con, TV and fridge. Meals and an extensive tour program are also available.

★**Pagua Bay House** BOUTIQUE HOTEL $$$
(☑767-445-8888; www.paguabayhouse.com; Dr Nicholas Liverpool Hwy, Pagua Bay; r US$230-400, 3-night minimum; P❋🛜) Some 6 miles south of Douglas Charles Airport, this sophisticated boutique hotel could easily grace the pages of *Architectural Digest*. The six luxe cabanas and suites mix industrial and wooden accents and come with walnut platform beds, Frette linens and walk-in showers. The equally stylish open-air restaurant has views across to the pounding surf.

★**Pagua Bar & Grill** MODERN AMERICAN $$
(☑767-445-8888; www.paguabayhouse.com; Dr Nicholas Liverpool Hwy, Pagua Bay; mains lunch US$9-14, dinner EC$60-130; ☺noon-4pm; 🛜) Part of the Pagua Bay House, this open-air restaurant comes with breathtaking views of the pounding surf, an urban hip look and delicious modern American food with Caribbean accents. It's a popular lunch spot and famous for its ceviche and fish tacos. The bar is a classy stop en route to the airport.

❶ Getting There & Away

There is bus service to Roseau via Portsmouth.

Kalinago Territory

Dominica is the only island in the Eastern Caribbean that's still home to pre-Columbian indigenous people, the Kalinago. Their ancestors are believed to have migrated north from South America around 1200 AD.

About 3000 of them live in the 3700-acre Kalinago Territory, an 8-mile-long coastal stretch south of Bataka on the east coast. Formed by the British in 1903, the communally owned territory is a remote and mountainous area where bananas, breadfruit trees and wild heliconia grow along the roadside. Some private homes are traditional wooden structures on log stilts, others are simple cement structures and, in the poorer areas, shanties made of corrugated tin and tar paper.

The Kalinago are a proud people who cherish their heritage and maintain their customs, traditions and crafts including basket weaving, cassava bread making and canoe carving.

◉ Sights

★**Kalinago Barana Autê** CULTURAL CENTER
(☑767-445-7979; www.kalinagobaranaaute.com; Old Coast Rd, Salybia; site pass & tour US$10; ☺10am-5pm Tue-Sun mid-Oct--mid-Apr, Tue & Fri-Sun mid-Apr--mid-Oct) ✎ This recreated traditional village on the Crayfish River near the Isukulati Falls is a good spot to get an overview of Kalinago history and culture. The 30- to 45-minute tour leads to various huts where locals demonstrate the crafts of basket weaving, canoe making and cassava baking. An architectural highlight is the huge Karbet (men's house) where dances and cultural presentations take place. En route you get to enjoy awesome views of the falls and the crashing waves.

Touna Kalinago Heritage Village CULTURAL CENTER
(☑767-285-1830; www.kalinagoterritory.com/attractions/touna-kalinago-heritage-village; Concord; ☺tours by arrangement; P🚻) Created by former Kalinago chief Irvince Auguiste, this living village on the Pagua River was created to introduce visitors to the way of life of Dominica's indigenous people. On guided 90-minute tours, you visit the actual private homes of basket weavers and craftsmen, and a traditional herbalist. Visits include a stop at Auguiste's own home. The project encourages active exchange between visitors and locals to break down cultural barriers. With advance notice, it's also possible to stay overnight in the village.

🛏 Sleeping

Kalinago Territory Home Stay Programme ACCOMMODATION SERVICES $
(www.kalinagoterritory.com; per person US$30-50) The manager of the Kalinago Barana Autê heritage village can organize homestays with local Kalinago families so you can get a deeper understanding of the traditional ways and contemporary issues of Dominica's indigenous people. Stay either in modern homes or traditional thatched or wooden huts. Meals can be provided as well (breakfast/lunch/dinner US$10/15/10). Booking is via the website.

Sea Breeze Inn HOTEL $
(☑767-446-0269; www.seabreezedominica.com; beachfront, Castle Bruce; r incl breakfast US$80; P🛜) Watch the sun rise over the sea from your room on this beachfront inn, a labor of love created by local couple Joan and Joey

in the heart of Castle Bruce. The restaurant serves home-cooked local food from morning to night.

Domcan's Guest House   APARTMENT **$**

(☑767-445-7794; www.domcansguesthouse.com; Castle Bruce; apt US$40; 🅿🛜) A great pit stop for Waitukubuli hikers (it's on segment 5), this guesthouse has you sleeping in basic but comfortable apartments with kitchenette, sitting area and balcony. The restaurant serves international and local fare.

⭐ **Aywasi Kalinago Retreat**   COTTAGE **$$$**

(☑767-235-4455; info@aywasiretreat.com; Aywasi St, Salybia; d US$150, 2-night minimum stay; 🅿🛜) Feel in harmony with nature when staying in one of these five A-frame wooden bungalows in a peaceful forest setting on a coastal bluff. The elegantly rustic units with handcrafted furniture consist of a downstairs sitting area with porch and a sleeping loft. Waitukubuli hikers should ask about pitching a tent or sleeping in a hammock in a traditional *ajoupa* (open hut). The restaurant serves Kalinago-inspired Creole cuisine.

Beau Rive Hotel   HOTEL **$$$**

(☑767-445-8992; www.beaurive.com; Coastal Rd, north of Castle Bruce; s/d incl breakfast US$165/200, 2-night minimum; ⊘closed Aug & Sep; 🅿@🏊) 🏊 Set in tropical gardens with a pool overlooking Wakaman Point, this hushed and remote retreat welcomes guests to 10 oversized rooms with polished wooden floors and balconies with views of the waves. Days start with breakfast on the terrace and conclude with an optional three-course dinner (US$38, guests only) at the elegant restaurant. No children aged under 16.

✖ **Eating**

Islet View Restaurant & Bar   CARIBBEAN **$**

(☑767-446-0370; New Rd, Castle Bruce; mains EC$20-40; ⊘8am-9pm) Looking just like any other humble roadside feeding and drinking station, this convivial joint actually delivers local color galore along with breathtaking views of Castle Bruce beach and bay. Sip your drink from a coconut on the breezy porch or peruse its famous bush-rum selection while salivating in anticipation of the delicious home-cooked local fare.

Daniel's Cassava Bakery   BAKERY **$**

(☑767-617-5058; Main Hwy, Salybia; ⊘8am-4pm Mon-Fri) A staple of the Kalinago diet, cassava bread is traditionally made just from ground manioc, but local baker Daniel Frederick

likes to add a bit of coconut for sweetness. Stop over at his little bakery for this cake-like bread hot from the oven (EC$5) as you explore the Kalinago Territory or visit on your way to the airport.

ℹ **Getting There & Away**

Buses to Castle Bruce and other points in the Kalinago Territory leave from the New Market bus stop in Roseau.

UNDERSTAND DOMINICA

History

Thanks to its abundance of water, Dominica has long been popular with settlers. After its discovery by Columbus in 1493, it was for centuries engaged in a tug of war between British and French colonizers and the indigenous Kalinago. Dominica achieved independence from Britain in 1978 and is a member of the Commonwealth.

Colonization

Dominica was the last of the Caribbean islands to be colonized by Europeans due chiefly to the fierce resistance of the Kalinago, the indigenous people whose ancestors are believed to have migrated here from South America around 1200 AD. They called the island Waitukubuli, which means 'Tall is her body.' Christopher Columbus, with less poetic flair, named the island after the day of the week on which he spotted it – a Sunday ('Domenica' in Italian) – on November 3, 1493.

Daunted by the Kalinago and discouraged by the absence of gold, the Spanish took little interest in Dominica. France laid claim to the island in 1635 and wrestled with the British over it through the 18th century.

In 1805 the French burned much of Roseau to the ground and from then on the island remained firmly in the possession of the British, who established sugar plantations on Dominica's more accessible slopes.

Independence

In 1967 Dominica gained autonomy in internal affairs as a West Indies Associated State and became an independent republic within the Commonwealth on

JEAN RHYS

Dominica's most celebrated author, Jean Rhys, was born in Roseau in 1890. Although she moved to England at age 16 and made only one brief return visit to Dominica, much of her work draws upon her childhood experiences in the West Indies. Rhys touches lightly upon her life in Dominica in *Voyage in the Dark* (1934) and in her autobiography, *Smile Please* (1979). Her most famous work, *Wide Sargasso Sea* (1966), a novel set mostly in Jamaica and an unmentioned Dominica, was made into a film in 1993.

November 3, 1978 (the 485th anniversary of Columbus' discovery).

The initial year of independence was a turbulent one. In June 1979 the island's first prime minister, Patrick John, was forced to resign after a series of corrupt schemes surfaced, including one clandestine land deal to transfer 15% of the island to US developers. In August 1979 Hurricane David, packing winds of 150mph, struck the island with devastating force. Forty-two people were killed and 75% of the islanders' homes were destroyed or severely damaged.

In July 1980 Dame Mary Eugenia Charles was elected prime minister, the first woman in the Caribbean to hold the office. She survived two unsuccessful coups right after her inauguration and subsequently managed to stay in office for 15 years.

Dominica in the 21st Century

Dominica's more recent political history has also been somewhat of a roller-coaster ride. After the sudden death of popular prime minister Roosevelt Douglas ('Rosie') in 2000, after only eight months in office, his successor Pierre Charles also died on the job, four years later. In 2004 31-year-old Roosevelt Skerrit stepped into the breach. A popular choice with young people, Skerrit comes from a Rastafarian farming family in the north of the island; he was re-elected in 2009 and 2014.

Skerrit moved quickly to sever long-standing diplomatic relations with Taiwan in favor of ties with mainland China in exchange for US$100 million in aid. The filming of the second and third *Pirates of the Caribbean* movies in 2005 was another boost to the island's economy.

In January 2008 Dominica joined the Bolivarian Alternative for the Americas (ALBA) – a trade group that includes Venezuela, Cuba, Bolivia and Nicaragua, designed to counterbalance American trade power. Following a special ALBA meeting in February 2009, Skerrit announced that he had secured at least part of a US$49 million fund to boost food security in the Caribbean.

In 2013 the first long-distance hiking trail in the Caribbean, the 115-mile-long Waitukubuli Trail, was officially inaugurated.

Dominica has been repeatedly devastated by hurricanes and tropical storms, most recently in August 2015 by Tropical Storm Erika. Heavy rains and winds caused floods and mudslides, and destroyed buildings, roads, bridges and the entire village of Petite Savanne on the southeast coast. At least 20 people were killed, and at the time of research the island is still recovering from the devastation.

Culture

Dominica draws on a mix of cultures: French place names feature as often as English; African language, foods and customs mingle with European traditions as part of the island's Creole culture; and the indigenous Kalinago (formerly known as Caribs) still carve dugouts (canoes), build houses on stilts and weave distinctive basketwork. Rastafarian influences are strong here.

About a third of Dominica's 74,870 people live in and around Roseau. Some 87% are of African descent and about 3000 are Kalinago.

With a 61.5% Roman Catholic population and religious observance commonplace, conservative values are strong and family holds an important place in Dominican society.

Much ado has been made of the fact that Dominica has three times the number of centenarians than more developed nations. The most famous was Ma Pampo who died in 2003 at 128 years of age. There are currently more than 30 centenarians. Dominica's government contributes to their care with free cooking gas and a monthly cash stipend.

Landscape & Wildlife

Dominica is an island of dramatic mountains that drop straight down to the sea, and what few beaches there are have been very lightly developed. For the most part, the nature here is untouched, save for the rusted cars that dot the roadsides like so many memorials to bad driving.

The Land

Dominica is 29 miles long and 16 miles wide and embraces the highest mountains in the Eastern Caribbean; the loftiest peak, Morne Diablotin, is 4747ft high. The mountains, which act as a magnet for rain, serve as a water source for the island's purported 365 rivers. En route to the coast, many of the rivers cascade over steep cliffs, giving the island an abundance of waterfalls. Three hydroelectric plants on the Roseau River produce 27.4% of the electricity supply.

The most abundant tree on the island is the gommier, a huge gum tree used by the Kalinago to make dugouts

Wildlife

Whales and dolphins patrol the deep waters off Dominica's sheltered west coast. Sperm whales, which grow to a length of 70ft, breed in the waters around here and are the most commonly sighted cetacean, although chances of seeing pilot and humpback whales as well as bottlenose dophins are also pretty good. The main season is November to March.

For near-shore divers, the marine life tends to be of the smaller variety – sea horses included – but there are spotted eagle rays, barracuda and sea turtles as well.

More than 160 bird species have been sighted on Dom&inica, giving it some of the most diverse birdlife in the Eastern Caribbean. Of these, 59 species nest on the island, including two endemic and endangered parrot species: Dominica's national bird, the Sisserou parrot, and the smaller Jaco parrot.

The island has small tree frogs, many lizards, 13 bat species, 55 butterfly species, boa constrictors that grow nearly 10ft in length and four other types of snake (none poisonous).

Dominica also used to have an abundance of large frogs known as 'mountain chicken,' which live only here and on Montserrat. It is now critically endangered because of a virulent fungus.

Environmental Issues

In 2015 Dominica was again named among the top 10 Developing World's Best Ethical Destinations by *Ethical Traveler,* a San Francisco–based all-volunteer, nonprofit organization affiliated with the Earth Island Institute.The decision was based on the country's record of environmental protection, social welfare and human rights. Contributing to the distinction was that, since 2008, Dominica no longer allows the Japanese to engage in commercial whaling in its waters. It was also lauded for its pilot project to reduce energy consumption in business sectors.

Nevertheless, environmentalists are worried about the impact of the growing number of cruise ships that dock here to refill water supplies and dump waste, as well as about the physical impact caused by 300,000 passengers.

SURVIVAL GUIDE

ℹ Directory A–Z

ACCOMMODATIONS

Dominica has no big resorts, but it does have cottages tucked into the jungle, boutique inns and remote hideaways. In most cases, listed room rates do not include the 10% value-added tax (VAT).

ACTIVITIES

Trail maps published by Dominica's Forestry Division are available for a small fee at the forestry office in Roseau's Botanic Gardens. The division can also refer you to guides who are expert in the flora and fauna of the island. Certified guides are also recommended for some of the hikes, most notably the one to Boiling

---

SLEEPING PRICE RANGES

The following price ranges refer to a double with bathroom during high season (December to April). Unless otherwise stated, breakfast is not included.

$ less than US$50

$$ US$50–US$150

$$$ more than US$150

ℹ ECOTOURISM SITES PASSES

Dominica's ecotourism sites are its biggest attraction. In order to help maintain them, a fee of US$5 per site is levied on all foreign visitors for the following dozen sites:

Boeri Lake, Boiling Lake, Indian River, Morne Trois Pitons, Middleham Falls, Freshwater Lake, Morne Diablotin Trail, Cabrits National Park, Emerald Pool, Trafalgar Falls, Soufriere Sulphur Springs and the Syndicate Forest.

A weekly pass for unlimited entry to all 12 costs US$12.

Passes are available at site entrances, from nearby vendors or from the national parks office inside the Botanic Gardens in Roseau.

In addition, there is a US$2 user fee per entry to the Soufriere-Scotts Head Marine Reserve, which includes Champagne Beach & Reef.

For more information, contact the Forestry, Wildlife and Parks Division at ☏767-266-3817 or forestry@cwdom.dm.

Lake. The **tourist office** (p371) can also make referrals.

CHILDREN

If you don't pack too much into the day and calibrate your nature adventures to your children's interests and abilities, Dominica can be a great destination for family travel. Some of the trails may be too long or challenging for younger kids, but even easy ones such as Emerald Pool and the Syndicate Nature Trail have their rewards. Riding a boat on the Indian River, swimming on the west-coast beaches, splashing around sulfur springs and snorkeling at Champagne Reef are all kid-suited, water-based activities.

EATING PRICE RANGES

The following price ranges refer to a main course. Listed menu prices may or may not include 15% VAT and a service charge of 10% or 15% – check ahead to avoid any surprises.

$ less than US$10

$$ US$10–20

$$$ more than US$20

Nappies (diapers) and baby foods are available in the larger supermarkets in Roseau and Portsmouth.

ELECTRICITY

220/240V, 50/60 cycles; North American two-pin sockets. Some accommodations have dual 220/110 voltage.

EMBASSIES & CONSULATES

The nearest US embassy is in Bridgetown, Barbados.

UK Honorary Consulate (☏767-275-7800)

EMERGENCY NUMBERS

Fire, Police & Ambulance	☏999

FOOD

With very few exceptions, dining out in Dominica is a very casual affair. Most meals revolve around some sort of fish or meat served with a selection of 'provisions,' which refers to any kind of root vegetable – from dasheen and breadfruit to sweet potato. Lunch is the main meal of the day and many restaurants close around 3pm.

Essential Food & Drink

Callaloo A creamy thick soup or stew blending a variety of vegetables (eg dasheen, spinach, kale, onions, carrots, eggplant, garlic, okra) with coconut milk and sometimes crab or ham.

Fresh fruit Dominica grows all sorts of fruit, including bananas, coconuts, papayas, guavas and pineapples, and mangoes so plentiful they litter the roadside in places.

Sea moss Nonalcoholic beverage made from seaweed mixed with sugar and spices and sometimes with evaporated milk. It's sold in supermarkets and at snackettes.

Kubuli Dominica uses the island's natural spring water for its home-grown beer label; you'll see red-and-white signs all over the island with Kubuli's slogan – 'The Beer We Drink.'

Macoucherie Rum connoisseurs crave this local concoction. Don't be fooled by the plastic bottles or cheap-looking label; it's an undiscovered gem.

GLBT TRAVELERS

Consensual same-sex sexual activity is still on the books as being illegal for both men and women and punishable by up to 10 years in prison. Even though the law is not enforced, it's worth remembering that Dominica is a socially conservative and deeply religious country. To avoid offense or confrontation, discretion is advised – stay clear of public displays of affection.

HEALTH

The standard of the medical care and equipment on Dominica are likely not as high, modern or comprehensive as you may be used to. Sophisticated diagnostic tests such as CT and MRI scans, anything but minor surgeries and other treatments must be performed outside Dominica. Make sure your insurance policy covers medical transport and emergency repatriation.

Princess Margaret Hospital (☎767-448-2231; Federation Dr) Located in Roseau, Dominica's main facility has a hyperbaric chamber and a small intensive-care unit.

LEGAL MATTERS

Dominica's legal system is based on English common law. If you find yourself in trouble, you have the right to legal representation and are eligible for public legal aid if you can't afford to pay for private services. Foreign nationals should receive the same legal protections as nationals.

MONEY

ATMs dispense EC dollars but are scarce outside of Roseau and Portsmouth. There is no ATM at the airport. Few business accept credit cards.

Cash

Unless prices rates are posted in US dollars, as is usual with accommodations, it usually works out better to use EC dollars. If you pay in US dollars you will likely get change in EC dollars.

Exchange Rates

AUSTRALIA	A$1	EC$1.93
CANADA	C$1	EC$1.98
EURO ZONE	€1	EC$2.81
JAPAN	¥100	EC$2.30
NEW ZEALAND	NZ$1	EC$1.86
UK	UK£	EC$3.29
US	US$	EC$2.68

Tipping

Hotels US$0.50 to US$1 per bag is standard; gratuity for cleaning staff is at your discretion.

Restaurants If the service charge is not automatically included in the bill, tip 10% to 15%; if it is, it's up to you to leave a small additional tip.

Taxi Tip 10% to 15% of the fare.

PUBLIC HOLIDAYS

New Year's Day January 1

Carnival Monday & Tuesday Two days preceding Ash Wednesday (the beginning of Lent, 46 days before Easter)

Good Friday/Easter Monday March/April

Labour Day First Monday in May

Pentecost/Whit Monday 40 days after Easter

① DEPARTURE TAX

Departure tax for non-nationals is EC$59 (US$22) payable in cash at the airport or port.

Emancipation Day (August Monday) First Monday in August

Independence Day November 3

Community Service Day November 4

Christmas/Boxing Day December 25/26

TAXES & REFUNDS

Value-added tax (VAT) of 15% is levied on most goods and services. It drops to 10% on hotel rooms. Visitors are not eligible to reclaim VAT paid during their trip to Dominica.

TELEPHONE

➡ Dominica's country code is ☎767.

➡ To call from North America, dial ☎1-767 + the seven-digit local number. From elsewhere, dial your country's international access code, + 767 + the local number.

➡ To call abroad from Dominica, dial ☎011 + country code + area code + local number.

➡ For directory information dial ☎118.

TIME

Clocks in Dominica are set to Eastern Caribbean Time (Atlantic Time), which is four hours behind GMT. The island does not observe daylight savings time.

TOURIST INFORMATION

Dominica (www.dominica.dm) Official tourist office website

TRAVELERS WITH DISABILITIES

Dominica is harder than most countries for disabled travelers to navigate. Uneven, broken or nonexistent sidewalks and high curbs make wheelchair-travel nearly impossible. Some of the bigger hotels in Roseau, Castle Comfort and Portsmouth may be able to accommodate disabled travelers.

Download Lonely Planet's free Accessible Travel guide from http://lptravel.to/Accessible Travel.

VOLUNTEERING

Look for Dominica-based listings on the volunteer work exchange platforms HelpX (www.helpx.net) or Workaway (www.workaway.info). A popular option is to help locals run off-grid lodges, which may involve building, gardening, cooking, web work and other chores. There are also community-based programs focused on improving the lives of local children through arts projects.

Founded by former Peace Corps volunteers, Ready, Willing, Enable! (www.rwenable.org) needs volunteers to provide training and resources to children with disabilities, as well as their communities and families.

Getting There & Away

GETTING TO NEIGHBORING ISLANDS

There are regular ferries from Dominica to Guadeloupe, Martinique and St Lucia, as well as regular scheduled flights to Antigua, Barbados, Guadeloupe, St-Martin/Sint Maarten, Martinique and Puerto Rico.

AIR

Douglas Charles Airport (DOM; ☎ 767-445-7109; Marigot) Most flights arrive at this small airport, previously known as Melville Hall Airport. It's near Marigot on the northeast side of the island and about a 90-minute drive from Roseau. **LIAT** (☎ toll-free within Caribbean Region 888-844-5428; www.liat.com), Winair, Hummingbird Air, Air Sunshine, Air Antilles and Seabourne Airlines provide service within the region.

Canefield Airport (DCF; Edward Olivier LeBlanc Hwy) This tiny airport is on the west coast near Massacre about 15 minutes north of Roseau. Winair flies to St-Martin/Sint Maarten from here but other flights are mostly private planes.

There are no flights to or from North America and Europe. You need to connect in Antigua, Barbados, St-Martin/Sint Maarten, Puerto Rico, Guadeloupe or Martinique.

SEA
Cruise Ship

Cruise ships dock in central **Roseau** (Dame Eugenia Charles Blvd), at Woodbridge Bay north of Roseau, and at Cabrits, north of Portsmouth. Downtown Roseau and popular places such as Champagne Reef and Trafalgar Falls get very busy when those giant vessels are in port. Independent travelers wishing to avoid the crowds might want to check the cruise-ship schedule (eg at www.cruisetimetables.com/cruises-to-roseau-dominica.html) to plan their itinerary accordingly.

Getting Around

BUS

Government-licensed private minivans with number plates starting with 'H' serve communities on an erratic schedule along the main roads. All routes originate at various stop in downtown Roseau.

Buses can be flagged down anywhere along the route – just stick out your arm. Unless they're full, they will stop. Service runs from 6am to 7pm Monday to Saturday.

Fares are set by the government and cost EC$1.75 to EC$11.

CAR & MOTORCYCLE

Driving is the most convenient way to explore Dominica, although it can be quite stressful because of the terrain, poor road conditions and local driving practices.

Drivers need a local license issued by a car-rental agency. It costs US$12 or EC$30 and is valid for one month. Officially, you must be aged between 25 and 65 and have at least two years of driving experience, although this varies from company to company.

Car Rental

Several international agencies plus a few reputable local ones have offices in a separate building right outside the airport terminal. Because of poor road conditions, it's well worth investing in a high-clearance vehicle, preferably a (small) 4WD, especially if you're going to be exploring the mountains. Some agencies have offices in Roseau.

Before signing anything, carefully check the car for damage and take photographs of anything you find in addition to having the agent record it on the rental agreement. Make sure that the tires are in good condition.

Daily rates start at US$22 per day for sedans and US$50 for 4WD, plus 15% VAT; many of the local agencies give discounts for rentals longer than two days. All companies offer free pickups and drop-offs, unlimited mileage and cell-phone rentals.

FERRY

The ferry service **L'Express des Îles** (☏ +590 (0) 590 91 95 20; www.express-des-iles.com; Roseau ferry terminal, Dame Eugenia Charles Blvd; one way adult/child under 2yr €69/39) connects Roseau several times weekly on 300-seater catamarans with the following nearby islands. Flexible tickets cost €10 more each way; children under two years pay a flat €39.

DESTINATION	PRICE ONE WAY/ RETURN (€)	DEPARTURES	DURATION (HR)
Pointe-à-Pitre (Guadeloupe)	69/100	Wed-Fri & Sun	2½
Saint Pierre (Martinique)	69/100	Wed-Fri & Sun	1½
Castries (St Lucia)	69/100	Mon, Wed, Fri & Sun	4½

Courtesy Car Rental (☏767-445-7677; www.dominicacarrentals.com; Douglas Charles Airport; ⊙ per day from US$49)

Island Car Rentals (☏767-255-6844; www.islandcar.dm; Douglas Charles Airport; per day from US$22; ⊙7am-7pm)

Road Runner Car Rental (☏767-275-5337; www.roadrunnercarrental.com; Canefield Hwy; per day from US$49; ⊙ office 8am-5pm Mon-Fri)

Valley Car Rental (☏767-275-1310; www.valleyrentacar.com; Douglas Charles Airport; per day from US$39)

Road Conditions

Tropical Storm Erika did a lot of damage to the roads but conditions are improving slowly. Still, driving in Dominica is not for the faint of heart. Roads are narrow and curving, have no dividing lines and are often hemmed in by deep, axle-killing rain gutters: 3in too far to the left and your wheels will enter a yawning concrete ditch; 3in too far to the right and you risk swapping rear-view mirrors with oncoming cars. Or worse.

Other dangers: potholes big enough to swallow small goats, blindingly blind curves, visitors not accustomed to driving on the left and locals getting impatient with them.

As a result, actual driving times are much greater than distances would suggest, especially when driving between the coasts through the vertiginous center. The smoothest driving is on the coastal road between Portsmouth and Roseau. The road from Portsmouth to the airport has been improved but is still narrow and winding, so the going is slow. Road conditions are worst in the Kalinago Territory and in the storm-battered southeast.

Road Rules

Driving is on the left. Honk the horn often around the blind curves. Always keep an eye out for potholes and drive around them. Avoid driving at night because roads are not lit and you'll need to use your high beam to navigate. Of course, other drivers do the same but many don't bother dimming their lights for oncoming traffic, causing you to be temporarily blinded.

To local drivers, speed limits seem to be more of a suggestion than a rule. If you're driving slowly and causing a backup, pull over to the side of the road whenever it's safe to let traffic pass.

Outside of Roseau, gas stations are few and far between. You'll find some in larger towns, including Canefield, Portsmouth and Marigot. Some take credit cards, many do not.

HITCHING

Hitching is never entirely safe, and we don't recommend it. Travelers who hitch should understand that they are taking a small but potentially serious risk.

However, locals of either sex and of all ages hitchhike here, and picking up hitchhikers, especially if there is only one of them and two or more of you, is a great way to meet locals and pick up good insider tips. Solo women travelers, though, should be extra careful.

TAXI

Taxis on Dominica have number plates beginning with 'H' or 'HA'. There are no meters and no standard fares, so use your negotiating skills and make sure you understand if the quoted fare is in US dollars or EC dollars. To order a cab, call ☏767-440-0944, ☏767-440-8126 or ☏767-276-2228.

Airport transfers from Douglas Charles Airport are regulated by the government. The following quoted fares are per person in a shared taxi:

Roseau or Portsmouth	US$30
Calibishie or Kalinago Territory	US$17
Scotts Head	US$32
Castle Comfort	US$28

Dominican Republic

POP 10,649,000 / ☏

Best Places to Eat

➡ Las Palmas (p411)

➡ El Monte Azul (p413)

➡ Passion by Martín
Berasategui (p407)

➡ Ñam Ñam (p407)

➡ Pat'e Palo (p398)

Best Places to Sleep

➡ Hostal Nicolás de Ovando
(p397)

➡ Natura Cabañas (p419)

➡ Casa El Paraíso (p413)

➡ Eco del Mar (p402)

➡ Zoetry Agua (p406)

Why Go?

The Dominican Republic is defined by its hundreds of miles of coastline – some with picturesque white-sand beaches shaded by rows of palm trees, other parts lined dramatically with rocky cliffs. The sea is the common denominator across remote fishing villages, sun-soaked and indulgent tourist playgrounds, charming small towns and the capital Santo Domingo – the Caribbean's largest and the site of so many New World firsts.

Beyond the capital, much of the DR is distinctly rural. Further inland are vistas reminiscent of the European Alps: four of the Caribbean's five highest peaks rise above the fertile lowlands surrounding Santiago. Remote deserts extend through the southwest, giving the DR a complexity not found on other islands. The country's past is writ large in the diversity of its people, and in the beautifully restored monasteries and cobblestone streets where conquistadors once roamed.

When to Go

Dec–Feb Peak tourist season, with higher prices and crowded beaches.

Feb Great weather, and you can enjoy Carnival and the whales in Samaná.

Nov You'll miss the whales, but catch baseball season.

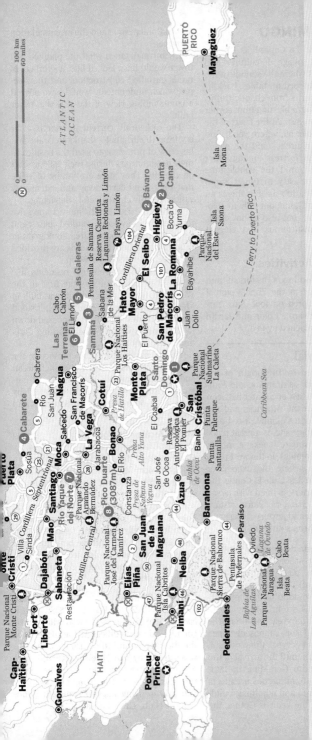

ATLANTIC OCEAN

PUERTO RICO

Mayagüez

Isla Mona

Ferry to Puerto Rico

100 km
60 miles

Dominican Republic Highlights

1 Zona Colonial (p392)
Taking a walk through history in Santo Domingo.

2 Bávaro and Punta Cana (p403) Basking on idyllic beaches of soft, white sand and aquamarine waters.

3 Península de Samaná (p409) Watching 30-ton humpbacks breaching on a whale-watching trip.

4 Cabarete (p416)
Kitesurfing the year-round offshore breezes in Cabarete.

5 Las Galeras (p412)
Relaxing into a sleepy fishing village in this remote paradise.

6 Las Terrenas (p413)
Mellowing in this cosmopolitan beachfront town.

7 Jarabacoa (p422) Rafting the turbulent Río Yaque del Norte.

8 Pico Duarte (p423)
Scaling the country's highest mountain and taking in views of both the Atlantic and the Caribbean.

SANTO DOMINGO

Santo Domingo, or 'La Capital' as it's typically called, is a collage of cultures and neighborhoods. It's where the sounds of life – domino pieces slapped on tables, backfiring mufflers and horns from chaotic traffic, merengue and *bachata* blasting from corner stores – are most intense. At the heart of the city is the Zona Colonial, where you'll find one of the oldest churches and the oldest surviving European fortress among other New World firsts. Amid the cobblestone streets, it would be easy to forget Santo Domingo is in the Caribbean. But this is an intensely urban city, home not only to colonial-era architecture, but also to hot clubs, vibrant cultural institutions and elegant restaurants.

◉ Sights & Activities

Most of Santo Domingo's historical and interesting sites are in the Zona Colonial and are easily explored on foot. Sites further afield, like the Faro a Colón and Jardín Botánico, are best reached by taxi.

◎ Zona Colonial

For those fascinated by the origin of the so-called New World – a dramatic and complicated story of the first encounter between the native people of the Americas and the Europeans – the Zona Colonial, listed as a Unesco World Heritage site, is a great place to explore. It is 11 square blocks, a mix of cobblestone and pavement on the west bank of the Río Ozama, where the deep river meets the Caribbean Sea. Calle El Conde, the main commercial artery, is lined with *casas de cambio* (money changers); cafes; restaurants; shoe, clothing and jewelry stores; and vendors hawking cheap souvenirs.

★ **Catedral Primada de América**   CHURCH
(Nuestra Senora de la Anunciacion; ☑809-682-3848; Parque Colón; adult/child RD$60/free; ☺9am-4:30pm Mon-Sat) The first stone of this cathedral, the oldest standing in the Western hemisphere, was set in 1514 by Diego Columbus, son of the great explorer (the ashes of father and son supposedly once resided in the chapel's crypt). Construction, however, didn't begin until the arrival of the first bishop, Alejandro Geraldini, in 1521. From then until 1540, numerous architects worked on the church and adjoining buildings, which is why the vault is Gothic, the

arches Romanesque and the ornamentation baroque.

It's anyone's guess what the planned bell tower would have looked like: a shortage of funds curtailed construction, and the steeple, which undoubtedly would have offered a commanding view of the city, was never built.

The cathedral's current interior is a far cry from the original – thanks to Drake and his crew of pirates, who used the basilica as their headquarters during their 1586 assault on the city. They stole everything of value that they could carry away and extensively vandalized the church before departing.

Among the cathedral's more impressive features are its awesome vaulted ceiling and its 14 interior chapels. Bare shoulders and legs are prohibited, but shawls are provided for those who need to cover up.

Although Santo Domingo residents like to say their cathedral was the first in the Western hemisphere, in fact one was built in Mexico City between 1524 and 1532; it stood for four decades, until it was knocked down in 1573 and replaced by the imposing Catedral Metropolitano.

Tickets, purchased at the entrance in the southeastern corner of the site, include an audio guide available in a variety of languages (RD$40 without audio guide). Daily Mass is at 5pm Monday to Saturday and noon and 5pm Sundays.

Museo Alcázar de Colón   MUSEUM
(Museum Citadel of Columbus; ☑809-682-4750; Plaza España; adult/child RD$100/20; ☺9am-5pm Tue-Sat, to 4pm Sun) Designed in the Gothic-Mudéjar transitional style, this was the early-16th-century residence of Columbus' son, Diego, and his wife, Doña María de Toledo. The magnificent edifice underwent three historically authentic restorations in 1957, 1971 and 1992, and the building itself, along with the household pieces on display (said to have belonged to the Columbus family), are worth a look.

Fortaleza Ozama   HISTORIC SITE
(☑809-686-0222; Las Damas; RD$70; ☺9am-5pm Tue-Sun) This is the New World's oldest colonial military edifice. At the meeting of the Río Ozama and the Caribbean, the site was selected by Fray Nicolás de Ovando and construction began in 1502. Over the centuries, the fort served as a military garrison and prison, flying flags of Spain, England, France, Haiti, Gran Columbia, the US and

the DR. Public tours began in the 1970s. Multilingual guides at the entrance charge around US$3.50 per person for a 20-minute tour.

Museo Memorial de la Resistencia Dominicana   MUSEUM

(Arzobispo Nouel 210; adult/child under 12yr RD $150/50; ⊙9:30am-6pm Tue-Sun) For those interested in the details of one of the darkest periods of Dominican history, this austere memorial honors Dominicans who fought against the brutal regime of dictator Rafael Trujillo. 'El Chivo' (the goat) ruled with an iron fist from 1930 until 1961, often touting his own greatness and wiping out some 50,000 political dissenters. The museum features torture-center replicas and 160,000 photographs, films and other objects belonging to resistance fighters. Admission includes an audioguide (English or Spanish).

Museo de las Casas Reales   MUSEUM

(Museum of the Royal Houses; ☑809-682-4202; Las Damas; adult/child under 7yr RD$100/free; ⊙9am-5pm Tue-Sat, to 4pm Sun) Built in the Renaissance style during the 16th century, this building was the longtime seat of Spanish authority for the Caribbean region, housing the governor's office and the powerful Audiencia Real (Royal Court). It showcases colonial-period objects, including treasures recovered from sunken Spanish galleons. Rooms have been restored according to their original style, with Taíno artifacts and period furnishings displayed.

Panteón Nacional   MONUMENT

(National Pantheon; Las Damas; ⊙8am-7pm Tue-Sun, from 11am Mon) Built in 1747 as a Jesuit church, this was also a tobacco warehouse and a theater before dictator Trujillo restored it in 1958 for its current use as a mausoleum. Today many of the country's most illustrious persons are honored here, their remains sealed behind two marble walls. The building, including its neoclassical facade, was constructed with large limestone blocks.

Larimar Museum   MUSEUM

(☑809-689-6605; www.larimarmuseum.com; 2nd fl, Isabel la Católica 54; ⊙9am-6pm Mon-Sat) **FREE** Thorough exhibits on larimar – a rare, light-blue mineral found only in the remote southwestern mountains of the Dominican Republic – have signage in Spanish and English. Of course, the museum is meant to inspire you to make a purchase from the jewelry store on the 1st floor.

Amber World Museum   MUSEUM

(☑809-682-3309; www.amberworldmuseum.com; cnr Arzibispo Merino & Restauracion; RD$50; ⊙9am-6pm Mon-Sat, to 1pm Sun) This museum features an impressive collection of amber samples from around the world and excellent exhibits explaining in Spanish and English amber's prehistoric origins, its use throughout the ages, Dominican mining processes, and its present-day value to the science and art worlds. The 1st-floor shop sells jewelry made from amber, larimar and more ordinary stones.

Las Damas   HISTORIC SITE

(Ladies' Street; Calle de las Damas) Heading north and south in front of Fortaleza Ozama is the first paved street in the Americas. Laid in 1502, the street acquired its name from the wife of Diego Columbus and her lady friends, who made a habit of strolling the road every afternoon, weather permitting.

Monasterio de San Francisco   HISTORIC SITE

(Hostos) The first monastery in the New World belonged to the first order of Franciscan friars who arrived to evangelize the island. Dating from 1508, the monastery originally consisted of three connecting chapels. It was set ablaze by Drake in 1586, rebuilt, devastated by an earthquake in 1673, rebuilt, ruined by another earthquake in 1751 and rebuilt again. Later it served as a mental asylum until a hurricane shut it down; today the dramatic ruins host wild dance nights every Sunday (p396).

Plaza España   PLAZA

The large, open area in front of the Alcázar de Colón has been revamped many times, most recently during the 1990s in honor of the 500th anniversary of Christopher Columbus' New World 'discovery.' Running along its northwest side is **Calle la Atarazana**, fronted by half a dozen restaurants in buildings that served as warehouses through the 16th and 17th centuries.

This is a great place for a meal or drink at an outdoor table around sunset.

⊙ Other Neighborhoods

Faro a Colón   MONUMENT

(Columbus Lighthouse; ☑ext 251 809-592-1492; Parque Mirador del Este; RD$100; ⊙9am-5pm Tue-Sun) Resembling a cross

Zona Colonial

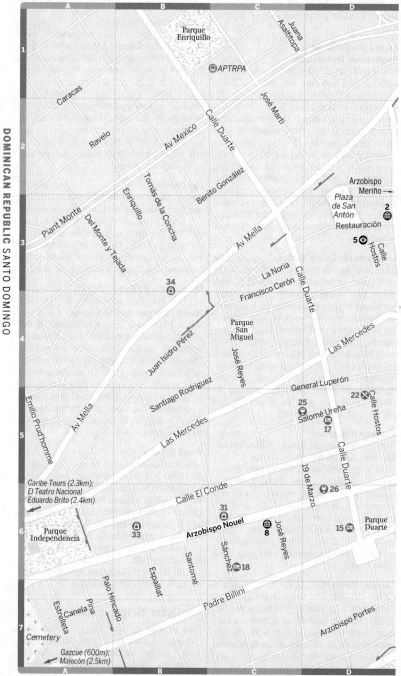

DOMINICAN REPUBLIC SANTO DOMINGO

between a Soviet-era apartment block and a Las Vegas–style ancient Mayan ruin, this massive monument is worth visiting for its controversial history. Located on the east side of the Río Ozama, the Faro's cement flanks stand 10 stories high, forming the shape of a cross. At the intersection of the cross's arms is a tomb, guarded by white-uniformed soldiers and purportedly

DON'T MISS

ZONA COLONIAL STREET LIFE

As might be expected, many of the structures in the Zona Colonial that still have their 16th-century walls have more recently altered facades and structural additions such as new floors and roofs. Keep your eyes open for the nooks and crannies and street scenes: small pedestrian alleys, men playing dominoes at an aluminum folding-table set on the street. These scenes, as much as the historical sites and buildings, make the Zona Colonial unique.

containing Columbus' remains. Spain and Italy dispute that, however, both saying *they* have the Admiral's bones.

Los Tres Ojos   CAVE
(Three Eyes; Parque Mirador del Este; RD$100; ☉8am-5pm) Consisting of three humid caverns with dark blue lagoons connected by stalactite-filled passages, this site is lovely if you show up early to beat the crowds. Upon entrance, a long stairway takes visitors down a narrow tunnel in the rock, and a cement path at the bottom leads through the caves. At the third *ojo*, a small boat can be hired for RD$20 to visit a fourth *ojo*, which is actually a gorgeous lake beneath open sky, filled with fish.

Jardín Botánico Nacional   GARDENS
(National Botanic Garden; ☎809-385-2611; Av República de Colombia; RD$200; ☉9am-5pm; ⊕) The lush grounds span 2 sq km and include vast areas devoted to aquatic plants, orchids, bromeliads, ferns, palm trees, a Japanese garden and much more. The grounds are spotless and the plants well tended, and it's easy to forget you're in the middle of a city with a metropolitan population of more than two million people. The exhibits in the on-site Ecological Museum explain the country's ecosystems, including mangroves and cloud forests, plus a display on Parque Nacional Los Haitises.

☞ Tours

Trikke   TOUR
(☎809-221-8097; www.trikke.do; Padre Billini 54; 1hr US$35; ☉9am-6pm Mon-Sat, from 10am Sun) A tour that rents motor scooters that resemble a cross between a Segway and a tricycle. City tours (US$35) and a popular

bar-hopping night tour (US$45) are also available. Group tours depart at 10am and 4:30pm each day, and all tours include a guide, water and riding lessons.

Horse-drawn Carriages   CARRIAGE TOUR
(cnr Las Damas & El Conde; with/without guide US$50/30) A leisurely option is a horse-drawn carriage tour. Look for them pulled to the side of the road near the corner of Calle Las Damas and El Conde.

Zona Colonial Walking Tours   WALKING
Interesting and informative walking tours of the Zona Colonial are offered daily by official guides – look for men dressed in khakis and light-blue dress shirts, and ask to see their state-tourism license. Many hang out in and around Parque Colón (cnr El Conde & Isabel la Católica), but you will likely encounter them near major attractions, also. Be sure to agree upon a fee before setting out.

☆☆ Festivals & Events

Monastery Sundays   MUSIC
(Hostos; ☉5-10pm Sun) FREE Every Sunday night, the 16th-century ruins of the Monasterio de San Francisco (p393) come to life for a raging dance party. Beloved band Grupo Bonye plays a mix of salsa, *bachata*, merengue and Caribbean rhythms, and hundreds of locals and tourists gather to drink and dance. The City Council has declared the event part of Santo Domingo's 'artistic patrimony.'

Carnival   CARNIVAL
Carnaval (in Spanish) is celebrated throughout the country every Sunday in February, culminating in a blowout in Santo Domingo during the last weekend of February or first weekend of March. Av George Washington (the Malecón) becomes an enormous party scene day and night. Central to the celebration are the competitions of floats, and costumes and masks representing traditional Carnival characters.

Merengue Festival   MUSIC
(☉late Jul-early Aug) The largest in the country, this two-week celebration of merengue, *bachata*, salsa, Caribbean rhythms, reggaeton and reggae is held yearly. Most of the activity is on the Malecón, but there are related events across the city.

🛏 Sleeping

The Zona Colonial is the most distinctive part of the city and therefore where most travelers stay. Sights and restaurants are within walking distance and there's an excellent choice of midrange and top-end hotels to choose from, including several European-owned boutique-style places in restored colonial-era buildings. A few new options for budget travelers have opened recently.

🛏 Zona Colonial

★ Island Life Backpacker's Hostel
HOSTEL $

(☏809-333-9374; http://islandlifebackpackershostel.com; Isabel La Católica 356; dm incl breakfast from RD$695, d from RD$1620, tr from RD$1760; ✳@🛜🏊) The expat owner of this Colonial Zone oasis traveled the world for years observing what backpackers like. Then he found a derelict colonial abode from the 1600s and transformed it into the best hostel in Santo Domingo. From the comfy dorm beds and courtyard hammocks to the super-chill bar and dipping pool, this is a true traveler's paradise.

The two-story building, which is also a Unesco World Heritage site, houses several dorms and private rooms, giving travelers options at different price points. Coffee and pancakes are provided each morning in a small kitchen in the leafy courtyard, and a full bar – along with a pool table and a dartboard – keeps the party going around the clock. The hostel also arranges all-inclusive day tours at bargain prices to attractions all over the country.

Portes 9
B&B $

(☏849-943-2039; info@portes9.com; Arzobispo Portes 9; r incl breakfast from US$55; ✳🛜) In a 400-year-old home, eight tastefully furnished rooms with wood floors and high ceilings make up this lovely, family-owned B&B fronting a quiet plaza in the neighborhood's southeast corner. It's an intimate spot where guests socialize over breakfast, and a rooftop deck features ocean views and a Jacuzzi. The location and atmosphere are superlative at this price point.

Casa Naemie
HOTEL $

(☏809-689-2215; www.casanaemie.com; Isabel la Católica 11; s/d incl breakfast RD$2000/3000; ✳🛜) This charming oasis only a few blocks from the oldest cathedral in the Americas

feels like a European pension. Surrounding a narrow central courtyard are three floors of cozy, clean rooms with large modern bathrooms. An elegant lobby with a vaulted entranceway and brick flooring does double duty in the morning when the excellent breakfast is served.

★ Hotel Villa Colonial
HOTEL $$

(☏809-221-1049; www.villacolonial.net; Sánchez 157; s/d incl breakfast US$75/95; 🛜🏊) The French owner has created an idyllic oasis, an exceptionally sophisticated combination of European elegance with a colonial-era facade and an art-deco design. The rooms lining the narrow garden and pool area all have high ceilings and four-poster beds, as well as flat-screen TVs and bathrooms with ceramic-tile floors.

★ El Beaterío Guest House
GUESTHOUSE $$

(☏809-687-8657; http://elbeaterio.fr; Duarte 8; s/d incl breakfast US$80/100; ✳🛜) Get thee to this nunnery – if you're looking for austere elegance. Each of the 11 large rooms is sparsely furnished, but the wood-beamed ceilings and stone floors are truly special; the tile-floored bathrooms are modern and well maintained. It's easy to imagine the former function of this 16th-century building, with its heavy stone facade, and dark and vaulted front room.

Hotel Palacio
HOTEL $$$

(☏809-682-4730; www.hotel-palacio.com; Duarte 106; r incl breakfast from US$117; 🅿✳🏊) Cross colonial with a touch of medieval and you have the Palacio, a maze-like hotel occupying a 17th-century mansion only a block north of El Conde. Service is exceptional and you'll need it to find your way past the charming nooks and crannies, which include reading areas, a gym, a small bar, a lush interior courtyard and stone-walled walkways.

★ Hostal Nicolás de Ovando
HISTORIC HOTEL $$$

(☏809-685-9955; Las Damas; r US$209-354, ste US$365; 🅿✳🛜🏊) Even heads of state must get a thrill when they learn they're sleeping in the former home of the first governor of the Americas. Oozing old-world charm, the Nicolás de Ovando was recently purchased by local hotel chain Hodelpa, but it remains one of the nicest stays in the city, featuring 97 rooms packed with 21st-century amenities.

🛏 Malecón

Catalonia Santo Domingo HOTEL $$$
(☎809-685-0000; www.cataloniacaribbean.com; Av George Washington 500, Malecón; r from US$166; [P][✳][@][🛜][🏊]) Among the nicest of the luxury hotels on the Malecón, Catalonia Santo Domingo is part of a huge complex including a casino and movie theater. The highest of the high-rises, it's a long elevator ride from the atrium to the 21st floor at the top. Rooms have better views than nearby competitors, and a bar and restaurant feature stunning ocean views.

🛏 Downtown

JW Marriott Santo Domingo HOTEL $$$
(☎809-807-1717; www.marriott.com/hotels/travel/sdqjw-jw-marriott-hotel-santo-domingo; Blue Mall, Av Winston Churchill 93; r RD$320; [P][✳][@][🛜][🏊]) Housed within the upper floors of downtown's chic Blue Mall, the new JW Marriott Santo Domingo is stylish and modern, with a snazzy cocktail bar, a relaxing infinity pool and a Peruvian restaurant with Asian flair. Rooms are pristine and state-of-the-art, with an option for an LED mirror TV in the bathroom. Amenities also include a 24-hour gym and cinema.

✖ Eating

Unsurprisingly, Santo Domingo is the culinary capital of the country. It offers the full range of Dominican cuisine, from *pastelitos* (pastries with meat, vegetable or seafood fillings) sold from the back of street-vendors' carts to extravagantly prepared meals in picturesque colonial-era buildings. The Zona Colonial has some of the best restaurants and is most convenient for the majority of travelers.

✖ Zona Colonial

Mesón D'Bari DOMINICAN $$
(☎809-687-4091; cnr Hostos & Salomé Ureña; mains RD$350; ⊙noon-midnight) A Zona Colonial institution popular with tourists and sophisticated *capitaleños* on weekends, Mesón D'Bari occupies a charmingly decaying colonial home covered with large, bright paintings by local artists. The menu has Dominican and international standards, and different versions of grilled meats and fish; the long attractive bar is equally appealing. Live music on some weekend nights.

★ Pat'e Palo SPANISH, MEDITERRANEAN $$$
(☎809-519-9687; La Atarazana 25; mains RD$650-1200; ⊙noon-1am) The most happening and deservedly longest surviving of Plaza España's restaurant row, Pat'e Palo is for anyone tired of the same old bland pasta and chicken. Large, both physically and in terms of its selection, the menu includes creatively designed dishes such as foie gras with dark-beer jam and risotto in squid ink and shrimp *brunoise* with lobster tail and roasted arugula.

The lobster ravioli (RD$630), one of the least expensive items on the menu, is excellent. Stick around for dessert – crème brûlée is the specialty – and an extensive wine and cigar list are for those who want to spend an extra hour or two hanging out in the candlelight.

Because of its popularity (or maybe a reason for it), there's something of a prepackaged vibe to the efficiently professional waitstaff's service; pirate-like headscarves are part of the uniform. English and French menus available.

Lulú Tasting Bar TAPAS $$$
(☎809-687-8360; www.lulu.do; cnr Arzobispo Meriño & Padre Billini; all-you-can-eat tapas RD$800, Sun brunch RD$1920; ⊙6pm-3am Mon-Sat, from 11am Sun) Class it up at Lulú, the most recent concept from the same team that brought Santo Domingo Pat'e Palo (the city's best restaurant) and Jalao (its most ostentatiously Dominican). This Colonial Zone tapas bar lures a fabulous after-work crowd looking to unwind over cigars and cocktails and nibble on small plates of *carpaccio de foie gras* and salmon satay.

✖ Malecón

Adrian Tropical DOMINICAN $
(☎809-221-1764; Av George Washington; mains RD$200; ⊙24hr; 🚼) This popular family-friendly chain occupies a spectacular location overlooking the Caribbean. Waiters scurry throughout the two floors and outdoor dining area doling out Dominican specialties including yucca or plantain *mofongo* as well as standard meat dishes. An inexpensive buffet (RD$200) is another option and the fruit drinks hit the spot. There are three other outposts in Santo Domingo.

D'Luis Parrillada DOMINICAN $$
(☎809-686-2940; Paseo Presidente Billini; dishes RD$350; ⊙8am-1am Sun-Thu, to 3am Fri & Sat)

This casual, open-air restaurant perched over the ocean only a few blocks from the Zona Colonial is one of only a few restaurants to take advantage of the Malecón's setting. The large menu includes fajitas, grilled and barbecue meats, sandwiches, seafood and little-found *pulpofongo* (*mofongo* with Creole-style cuttlefish; RD$330). Wonderful place for a drink as well.

Vesuvio Malecón   ITALIAN $$$
(☑ 809-221-1954; Av George Washington 521; mains RD$700; ⊙ noon-midnight) A Malecón institution only a few blocks from Hotel Catalonia and one of the city's better restaurants since 1954. Vesuvio is elegant without being snooty. Expect refined Neapolitan-style seafood and meat dishes; lobster and shellfish are featured in beautifully plated antipasti.

🍸 Drinking & Nightlife

⭐ **La Alpargatería**   COCKTAIL BAR
(☑ 809-221-3158; Salome Ureña 59; margaritas RD$185; ⊙ 10am-midnight Tue-Sun) At the entrance, guests step into a shoe shop where artisans craft espadrilles (light canvas shoes people started making in the Pyrenees in the 14th century). Continuing to the back, though, the store opens into a trendy cafe with comfy seating within intimate nooks and a leafy courtyard. The craft cocktails stand out here, especially the ginger-lemon margarita.

Mercado Colón   BEER GARDEN
(☑ 809-685-1103; Arzobispo Nouel 105; ⊙ noon-1am Tue-Sun) Channeling the Spanish *mercat* concept, this collection of artisanal food and alcohol vendors is housed under one Zona Colonial roof, with communal courtyard seating. Options include fresh sushi, piping-hot pizza and a variety of tapas, all assembled with local ingredients and innovative flavor combinations. It's a good place to drink craft beer and feel like part of a revolution.

Cultura Cervecera   CRAFT BEER
(www.facebook.com/ccervecerard; Rafael Augusto Sánchez 96b; draft beer from RD$210; ⊙ 4pm-midnight Mon-Thu, to 2am Fri & Sat, 3pm-midnight Sun; 🔊) A place of refuge for hopheads both Dominican and foreign, this is the country's best bet – so far – to escape the Presidente stranglehold on beer geeks. Nearly 150 craft beers by the bottle along with six taps, often dedicated to local brews from Republica Brewing and Santo Domingo Brewery, among others.

Mamma Club   CLUB
(☑ 809-868-8002; www.facebook.com/Mamma ClubRD; Av Gustavo Mejia Ricart 75; cover varies; ⊙ 9pm-3am Thu-Sat) If the thickness of the bouncers' necks is any indication of how good the bar is, consider Mamma Club the hottest place in town. In the heart of the burgeoning Piantini neighborhood, it attracts the beautiful people with its epic light and sound systems, top-notch DJs and VIP bottle service. Ladies drink free on Thursdays. Just don't start any fights.

Parada 77   BAR
(☑ 809-221-7880; Isabel la Católica 255; ⊙ 7pm-1am Sun-Thu, to 3am Fri & Sat) Thankfully, there's no dress code at this laid-back, grungy place with graffiti-covered walls. The vibe becomes decidedly high-energy on Sunday nights, when everyone heads here after the dance night at the nearby Monasterio de San Francisco (p396) winds down.

☆ Entertainment

⭐ **Colonial Gate 4D Cinema**   CINEMA
(☑ 809-682-4829; www.thecolonialgate.com; Padre Billini 52; adult/child RD$400/350; ⊙ 10am-11pm, closed Mon) Tucked away in the deep southeastern corner of the Zona Colonial, this hidden treasure is the country's first '4D' movie theater. The first three dimensions are what you'd expect, but fourth brings in the elements – mist, fog, wind, heat, smells, motion seats and bubbles. Admission includes three short films and headsets that translate them into nine languages.

The Great Wall of China and *Pirates 7D* are fantastic films for the thrills, but the most impressive (and award-winning) flick is *The Battle of Santo Domingo*, which the theater itself produced. During the film, which re-envisions the 1586 invasion of Sir Francis Drake, old Santo Domingo is brought to life as viewers feel they are flying over the city walls, getting slashed by pirate swords and dodging cannon balls.

Estadio Quisqueya   SPECTATOR SPORT
(☑ 809-616-1224; www.facebook.com/estadioquisqueya; 3456 Tiradentes Ave; tickets RD$250-1000; ⊙ games 5pm Sun, 8pm Tue, Wed, Fri & Sat) One of the best places to experience Dominican baseball is at the home field of two of the DR's six professional teams, Licey and Escogido. You can get tickets to most games

by arriving shortly before the first inning; games between the hometown rivals or Licey and Aguilas sell out more quickly.

Casa de Teatro CULTURAL CENTER
(📞809-689-3430; www.casadeteatro.com; Arzobispo Meriño 110; admission varies; ⊗9am-6pm & 8pm-3am Mon-Sat) Housed in a renovated colonial building, this fantastic arts complex features a gallery with rotating exhibits by Dominican artists, an open-air bar, and a performance space and theater that regularly host dance and stage productions.

El Teatro Nacional Eduardo Brito THEATER
(National Theater; 📞809-687-3191; Plaza de la Cultura; tickets RD$150-500) Hosts opera, ballet and musical performances, from classical to Latin pop stars. Tickets for performances at this grandly ornate 1700-seat theater can be purchased in advance at the box office from 9:30am to 12:30pm and 3:30pm to 6:30pm daily. For show dates and times, call or check the weekend editions of local newspapers.

🛍 Shopping

More than anywhere else in the country, Santo Domingo has stores that run the gamut from cheap tourist kitsch to high-end quality collectibles. The easiest – and best – neighborhood to shop in is the Zona Colonial, where you'll find rows of shops offering locally made products at decent prices.

Bolós Galería ART
(📞809-781-1654; http://galeriabolos.blogspot.com; cnr Isabel la Católica & Padre Billini; ⊗7:30am-8pm) Manuel Bolós has never seen a piece of wood he didn't like. The energetic young artist builds stylish furniture from recycled wood he collects around the Zona Coloinal

---

AMBER & LARIMAR

If you're considering buying something in amber or larimar (the DR's unique pale-blue stone), shop around since these stones, considered national treasures, are virtually ubiquitous in Santo Domingo. Typically they're presented as jewelry, but occasionally you'll find figurines, rosaries and other small objects. Quality and price vary greatly and fakes aren't uncommon. In Zona Colonial, recommended places are the **Amber World Museum** (p393) and the **Larimar Museum** (p393).

---

and beyond, and he displays it here in his gallery alongside avant-garde art he scours for across the DR and Haiti. Look for the 6ft seahorse composed entirely of recycled household goods.

Casa Quien ART
(📞809-689-0842; www.casaquien.com; cnr Arzobispo Nouel & Sánchez; ⊗11am-7pm Wed-Sun) Ensconced in an elegant, 16th-century home in the Colonial Zone, Casa Quien exhibits and sells contemporary fine art, crafts, books and other curios created by Dominican artists in limited quantity. The artist-managed space also hosts exhibitions and other events, oftentimes in support of emerging talent, and has received international praise for its mission and works.

Choco Museo CHOCOLATE
(📞809-221-8222; www.chocomuseo.com; Arzobispo Meriño 254; ⊗10am-7pm) More a shop than museum, Choco Museo nonetheless has signs in Spanish and English that explain the history of chocolate and manufacturing processes in the DR. It has a small cafe and shop, as well as workshops where you can make your own bars (organic and fair-trade bars for sale US$6).

Mapas Gaar MAPS
(📞809-688-8004; 3rd fl, cnr El Conde & Espaillat; ⊗8am-5:30pm Mon-Fri, 9am-1pm Sat) Located on the 3rd floor of an aging office building, Mapas Gaar has the best variety and the largest number of maps in the Dominican Republic. Maps are designated by city or region and include a country map, as well as several city maps on the back of each (RD$250).

Mercado Modelo MARKET
(Av Mella; ⊗8am-6pm Mon-Sat, to 1pm Sun) Bargain hard at this crowded market, which sells everything from love potions to woodcarvings, jewelry and, of course, the ubiquitous 'Haitian-style' paintings. The more you look like a tourist, the higher the asking price. The market is housed in an aging two-story building just north of the Zona Colonial in a neighborhood of fairly rundown stores and souvenir shops.

ℹ Information

EMERGENCY
For general police, ambulance and fire dial 📞911.

Cestur (☎809-222-2026; www.cestur.gob.do; cnr Jose Reyes & El Conde; ⊙8am-5pm) The Tourist Police can handle most situations.

Policia Nacional (☎809-682-2151)

INTERNET & TELEPHONE

Internet cafes are scarce, whereas wi-fi is common at cafes and restaurants.

Cyberworld (☎809-606-3831; Av Dr Delgado 102, Gazcue; per hr RD$30; ⊙8am-6pm)

Internet Express Ciber Cafe (☎809-689-9264; El Conde; per 30min RD$20; ⊙8am-9pm Mon-Fri, from 9am Sat & Sun) Inside the small plaza on Calle El Conde.

MEDICAL SERVICES

Clínica Abreu (☎809-688-4411; http://clinicaabreu.com.do; Arzobispo Portes 853; ⊙24hr) Widely regarded as the best hospital in the city.

Hospital Padre Billini (☎809-333-5656; www.hdpb.gob.do; cnr Santomé 39 & Arzobispo Nouel; ⊙24hr) The closest public hospital to the Zona Colonial, service is free but expect long waits.

POST

Both **Caribe** (p401) and **Metro** (p401) bus companies have package-delivery services based in their respective terminals; these are the best options for mailing anything within the country.

Federal Express (☎809-565-3636; www.fedex.com; cnr Av de los Próceres & Erick Leonard Ekman)

Post Office (Isabel la Católica; ⊙8am-5pm Mon-Fri, 9am-noon Sat)

TOURIST INFORMATION

Colonial Zone (www.colonialzone-dr.com) A detailed site with information and reviews on everything – historical sites, hotels, restaurants, bars – as well as discussions on Dominican history, superstitions and more.

Tourist Office (☎809-686-3858; Isabel la Católica 103; ⊙9am-7pm Mon-Sat) Located beside Parque Colón, this office has a handful of brochures and maps for Santo Domingo and elsewhere in the country, as well as a half-dozen ones with a variety of Zona Colonial walking tours. Some English and French spoken.

TRAVEL AGENCIES

Colonial Tour & Travel (☎809-688-5285; www.colonialtours.com.do; Arzobispo Meriño 209) This long-running professional outfit is good for booking flights, hotel rooms, and any and all excursions from mountain biking to rafting to whale-watching. English, Italian and French spoken.

Explora Eco Tours (☎809-567-1852; www.exploraecotour.com; Gustavo A Mejia Ricart 43, Naco) Specializes in organizing customized tours, from a single day to a week long, of national parks, nature preserves and rural communities. Website announces regularly scheduled trips open to the general public.

Giada Tours & Travel (☎809-682-4525; www.giadatours.com; Hostal Duque de Wellington, Av Independencia 304) Friendly professional outfit arranges domestic and international plane tickets, and also conducts area tours.

Tody Tours (☎809-686-0882; www.todytours.com; José Gabriel Garcia 105; per day US$250) Former Peace Corps volunteer who specializes in tropical birding tours all over the country.

❶ Getting There & Away

AIR

Santo Domingo has two airports: the main one, **Aeropuerto Internacional Las Américas** (p432), is 22km east of the city. The smaller **Aeropuerto Internacional La Isabela Dr Joaquin Balaguer** (JBQ, Higüero; ☎809-826-4003), around 20km north of the Zona Colonial, handles mostly domestic carriers and air-taxi companies.

Most international flights use Las Américas.

BOAT

The DR's only international ferry service, *Caribbean Fantasy*, run by **America Cruise Ferries** (p432) connects Santo Domingo with San Juan, Puerto Rico. The ticket office and boarding area are in the **Puerto Don Diego** (Av del Puerto, Zona Colonial), opposite Fortaleza Ozama. The ferry departs Santo Domingo at 7pm on Sunday, Tuesday and Thursday, before returning from San Juan at 7pm Monday, Wednesday and Friday. The trip from Santo Domingo takes 12 hours (eight hours in the other direction; difference is because of prevailing currents) and costs around US$200 round-trip.

The other major terminal that handles cruise ships is the **Puerto Sans Souci** (www.sansouci.com.do/en/port/sansouci-port-of-santo-domingo) on the eastern bank of the Rio Ozama, directly across from the Zona Colonial.

BUS

The country's two main bus companies – **Caribe Tours** (☎809-221-4422; www.caribetours.com.do; cnr Avs 27 de Febrero & Leopoldo Navarro) and **Metro** (☎809-544-4580; www.metroserviciosturisticos.com; Francisco Prats Ramírez) – have individual depots west of the Zona Colonial. Caribe Tours has the most departures, and covers more of the smaller towns than Metro does. In any case, all but a few destinations are less than four hours from Santo Domingo. Caribe Tours has a much larger terminal with a

WORTH A TRIP

BAHÍA DE LAS ÁGUILAS

Bahía de Las Águilas is the kind of beach that fantasies are made of. This pristine utopia is located in the extremely remote southwestern corner of the DR, but those who make it here are rewarded with 10km of nearly deserted shore, forming a gentle arc between two prominent capes. It's reachable mainly by boat from Playa Las Cuevas – the ride weaves in and out of rocky outcrops and past gorgeous cliffs with cacti clinging to their craggy edges and sea-diving pelicans nearby. Paradise found.

To get to the beach, take the paved (and signposted) road to Cabo Rojo, about 12km east of Pedernales. You'll reach the port of Cabo Rojo after 6km.

Eco del Mar (☑ 829-576-7740, 809-906-8170; www.ecodelmar.com.do; Playa Las Cuevas; camping per person incl breakfast RD$900-1500) Fancy glamping in paradise? Professional-style camping tents, strewn about the sands of Playa Las Cuevas, come in two sizes and are equipped with hotel-equivalent mattresses. There's an excellent restaurant (mains RD$350 to RD$1150), but the real coup here is the stylish beach bar in the round, offering the kind of seaside drinking of which tropical dreams are made.

Boat trips to Bahía de Las Águilas run at RD$2500 and massages on the sands cost RD$800.

Rancho Tipico (☑ 809-753-8058; cuevasdelasaguilas@hotmail.com; Playa Las Cuevas; mains RD$250-750; ⊗ 8am-7pm) A longstanding cradle for sustenance at Playa Las Cuevas, the closest point to Bahía de Las Águilas with infrastructure, Rancho Tipico does fresh seafood and some of the best *mofongos* (mashed plantains with meat or seafood; RD$400 to RD$750) you will ever eat (try the *pulpo*). The stunning location is one of the most storied settings in the DR.

gift shop, though both have ATMs and a limited food selection.

It's a good idea to call ahead to confirm the schedule and always arrive at least 30 minutes before the stated departure time. Both bus lines publish brochures (available at all terminals) with up-to-date schedules and fares, plus the address and telephone number of their terminals throughout the country.

Expreso Bávaro Punta Cana (☑ 809-682-9670; Juan Sánchez Ramirez 31) has a direct service between the Gazcue neighborhood (just off Av Máximo Gómez) in the capital and Bávaro. Departure times in both directions are 7am, 9am, 11am, 1pm, 3pm and 4pm (RD$400, three hours). Drivers are flexible and let passengers off at other stops in the city.

Another option is **APTRPA** (☑ 809-686-0637; www.aptpra.com.do; Ravelo), located amid the chaos of Parque Enriquillo, which services Higuey (RD$250), Bávaro and Punta Cana; there are six daily departures (on the hour) from 7am to 4pm for the latter two (RD$400).

CAR

Numerous international and domestic car-rental companies have more than one office in Santo Domingo proper and at Las Américas International Airport, including **Avis** (☑ 809-535-7191; Av George Washington 517; ⊗ 7am-6pm), **Dollar** (☑ 809-479-9806; Av Independencia 366; ⊗ 7am-6pm), **Europcar** (☑ 809-688-2121; Av Independencia 354; ⊗ 7am-6pm) and **Hertz**

(☑ 809-221-5333; Av José Ma Heredia 1; ⊗ 7am-6pm). All are open daily roughly from 7am to 6pm in Santo Domingo (sometimes later) and from 7am to 11:30pm at the airport.

ⓘ Getting Around

TO/FROM THE AIRPORT

There are no buses that connect directly to either of Santo Domingo's airports.

Aeropuerto Internacional Las Américas A taxi into the city costs US$40; an Uber is around US$30.

Aeropuerto Internacional La Isabela Dr Joaquín Balaguer The fare from La Isabela is more reasonable at US$15.

BUS

The cost of a bus ride from one end of the city to the other is around RD$25 (6:30am to 9:30pm). Most stops are marked with a sign and the word *parada* (stop). The routes tend to follow major thoroughfares – in the Zona Colonial, Parque Independencia is where Av Bolívar (the main westbound avenue) begins and Av Independencia (the main eastbound avenue) ends. If you're trying to get across town, just look at a map and note the major intersections along the way and plan your transfers accordingly.

CAR

Driving in Santo Domingo can challenge the nerves and test the skills of the most battle-hardened driver. Heavy traffic, aggressive drivers, especially taxis and buses, and little attention to, or enforcement of, rules means it's a free-for-all. Many of the city's major avenues are gridlocked during rush hour and you're better off walking.

Finding parking is not typically a problem, though if you are leaving your car overnight, ask around for a parking lot. Many midrange and top-end hotels have parking with 24-hour guards. In any case, be sure not to leave any valuables inside your car.

METRO
Caribbean islands and underground metros usually don't appear to go together, but in January 2009 Santo Domingo joined San Juan, Puerto Rico, as the second city in the region to have a commuter train system. Line 1 from La Feria (Centro de los Héroes) near the Malecón to the far northern suburb of Villa Mella is a 14.5km route with 16 stations running primarily north–south above and below ground along Av Máximo Gómez. In April 2013, Line 2 which runs east–west for 10.3km (entirely underground) along Av John F Kennedy, Expreso V Centenario and Av Padre Castellanos began operating. The master plan calls for six lines.

It's worth a trip for travelers to get a sense of Santo Domingo's size and sprawl, and on Line 1 for the rather stunning views over the rooftops, and scattered palm trees and mountains in the distance. The entrances, stations and subway cars are modern and clean, certainly a world away from New York City subways. The fact that stations are named after well-known Dominicans (and foreigners including John F Kennedy and Abraham Lincoln) rather than streets may be inconvenient, but it may also lead some to brush up on their history.

Each ride costs RD$20 or a 24-hour pass costs RD$80; however, it's best to purchase a card at one of the ticket booths for RD$60, which can then be refilled when needed. Place the card on top of the turnstile to enter the station (6:30am to 10:30pm).

PÚBLICO
Even more numerous than buses are the *públicos* – mostly beaten-up minivans and private cars that follow the same main routes but stop wherever someone flags them down. They are supposed to have *público* on their license plates, but drivers will beep and wave at you long before you can make out the writing. Any sort of hand waving will get the driver to stop, though the preferred gesture is to hold out your arm and point down at the curb in front of you. The fare is RD$25 – pay when you get in. Be prepared for a tight squeeze.

TAXI
Taxis in Santo Domingo don't have meters, so you should always agree on the price before climbing in. The standard fare is around RD$250 from one side of the city to another; rates tend to be higher in the evening. Within the Zona Colonial it should be even cheaper. Taxi drivers don't typically cruise the streets looking for rides; they park at various major points and wait for customers to come to them. In the Zona Colonial, Parque Colón and Parque Duarte are the best spots.

You can also call for a taxi or ask the receptionist at your hotel to do so. Service is usually quick, the fare should be the same, and you don't have to lug your bags anywhere. Many of the top hotels have taxis waiting at the ready outside, but expect to pay significantly more for those. Reputable taxi agencies with 24-hour dispatches include **Apolo Taxi** (✆ 809-537-0000) and **Aero Taxi** (✆ 809-686-1212, 829-613-0713).

PUNTA CANA & THE SOUTHEAST

A Caribbean workhorse of sun and sand, the southeast is synonymous with go-big-or-go-home tourism and carries the weight of the Dominican Republic's most dramatic beaches and turquoise seas on its deeply tanned shoulders. Sprawling resort developments, some like city-states unto themselves, line much of the beachfront from Punta Cana to Bávaro, offering families, couples and the young and restless alike a hassle-free Caribbean holiday in some of the most idyllic environs in the region.

Bávaro & Punta Cana
It wouldn't be out of line to equate the eastern coast of the Dominican Republic as a sort of sea and sun Disneyland – after all, it is here where the all-inclusive resorts snatch up broad swaths of cinematic beaches faster than the real estate agents can get the sun-soaked sands on the market. The beaches along the coastline from Punta Cana to El Macao rival those anywhere else in the Caribbean, both in terms of their soft, white texture and their warm aquamarine waters. Despite a lack of restraint on development in the area, the resorts and beaches here still manage to offer an idyllic Caribbean seascape for a seemingly endless crowd of sunseekers.

Bávaro & Punta Cana

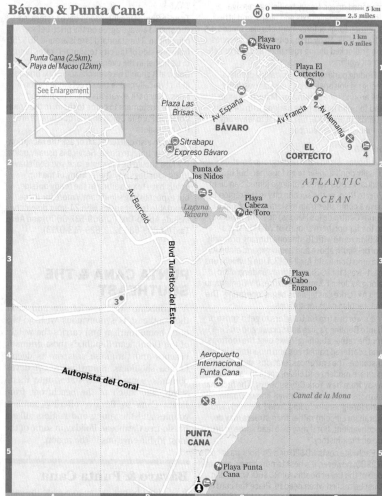

0 — 5 km
0 — 2.5 miles

0 — 1 km
0 — 0.5 miles

Punta Cana (2.5km);
Playa del Macao (12km)

See Enlargement

Av Barceló

Blvd Turístico del Este

Autopista del Coral

Plaza Las Brisas

Av España

BÁVARO

Playa Bávaro
6

Av Francia

Playa El Cortecito

2 Av Alemania

EL CORTECITO

9

4

Sitrabapu
Expreso Bávaro

Punta de los Nidos

5

Laguna Bávaro

Playa Cabeza de Toro

ATLANTIC

OCEAN

Playa Cabo Engano

3

Aeropuerto Internacional Punta Cana

8

Canal de la Mona

PUNTA CANA

Playa Punta Cana

1 7

🏖 Beaches

Ten or so beaches fall under the Punta Cana umbrella, stretching across more than 50km of coastline. Public access is protected by the law, so you can stroll from less-exclusive parts such as **Playa El Cortecito/Los Corales**, the former of which tends to be crowded with vendors, to nicer spots in front of resorts – but without the proper color wrist bracelet you won't be able to get a towel or chair.

North of El Cortecito is **Playa Arena Gorda**, lined with all-inclusive resorts and their guests on banana boats, parasailing or just soaking in the sun. A further 9km north of here is the best accessible surf beach, **Playa del Macao**, a gorgeous stretch of sand best reached by car. It's also a stop-off for a slew of 4WD tours that tear up and down the beach every day – there's less noise at the far northern end of the beach. The golden sands of **Playa Uvero Alto**, the area's northernmost beach, are 10km further north.

In the other direction, south of Bávaro and El Cortecito, is **Playa Cabo Engaño**, an isolated beach that you'll need a vehicle, preferably a 4WD, to reach. And then there's the furthest southern beach, the gorgeous,

Bávaro & Punta Cana

snaking stunner **Playa Juanillo**, whose sands are cleaned daily by Cap Cana staff – just maybe the fairest of them all!

🏃 Activities

Ojos Indígenas Ecological Park & Reserve
NATURE RESERVE

(☑829-470-1368; www.puntacana.org; adult/child US$25/10, with guided tour US$50/30; ⊙8:30am-5pm) 🕊 Though development may eventually cover every inch of the Dominican coastline, for now there are still large areas of pristine coastal plains and mangrove forests. About 500m south of (and part of) the **Puntacana Resort & Club** (☑809-959-2714; www.puntacana.com; Punta Cana; P🅿❄@🛜🏊) 🕊, this ecological park covers more than 6 sq km of protected coastal and inland habitat and is home to some 100 bird species (27 of which are indigenous species native only to the DR), 160 insect species and 500 plant species.

Visitors can take very worthwhile three-hour **guided tours** in English, French or Spanish through a lush 30-hectare portion of the reserve, with 12 freshwater lagoons (three of which you can take a dip in) all fed by an underground river that flows into the ocean. Additional tours also include visits to the park's botanical and fruit gardens, iguana farm (part of a conservation program) and a farm-animal petting zoo.

The visitor center has a great collection of insects that was compiled by entomology students from Harvard, and interesting

maps and photos of the area. The park is operated by the Puntacana Ecological Foundation, a nonprofit organization created in 1994 that works to protect the area's ecosystems – including 8km of coral reef along the reserve's shoreline – and to promote sustainable tourism and hotel practices. Nearly 4 hectares of the reserve are dedicated to the Center for Sustainability, a joint project with Cornell and other American universities to survey and study native plants, birds and insects. Guests of Puntacana Resort & Club get in free and can do self-guided tours; otherwise transportation from local hotels is included in the guided-tour prices.

Cap Cana
GOLF

(☑809-469-7767; www.capcana.com; Punta Cana) Cap Cana has one Jack Nicklaus Signature golf course, Punta Espada Golf Club, open for play since 2006 (nonguest greens fees from May to October are US$295, from November to May they're US$395), and two more on the way at the time of research. Punta Espada is considered one of the top courses in the Caribbean and in the world's top 100.

Hispaniola Aquatic Adventures
BOATING, SNORKELING

(☑800-282-5784; www.catamarantourpuntacana.com; from US$99) Runs highly popular party-boat catamaran tours for up to 25 people (or privately), taking in snorkeling at Cabeza del Toro as well as a seafood lunch and lesser-known beaches and swimming holes. Prices include transportation and alcohol. They don't allow middleman sales and a portion of the price goes to a homeless children and dogs charity in the DR.

🗺 Tours

Runners Adventures
TOURS

(☑809-455-1135; www.runnersadventures.com; Av Barcelo; ⊙7am-7pm) A well-established outfitter offering a range of adventure and cultural tours, including their most popular, Bávaro Runners, which takes in a sugarcane plantation, cigar museum, beach and horseback riding. Also offers city tours to Santo Domingo, a squirrel-monkey reserve and the longest zipline in the Caribbean.

RH Tours & Excursions
TOURS

(☑809-552-1425; www.rhtours.com; El Cortecito; ⊙9am-2pm Mon-Sat) If you're looking to explore the region, this tour operator offers a number of decent day trips for tourists.

PLAYA LIMÓN

North of Bávaro is Playa Limón, a 3km-long, isolated Atlantic beach lined with coconut trees leaning into the ocean – coveted property that you're likely to have to yourself for much of the time. Horseback-riding tours from Rancho La Cueva sometimes descend upon it for a few hours a day, generally from late morning to early afternoon, but it's otherwise all yours.

The rugged area surrounding Playa Limón has two important wetland areas, including **Laguna Limón**, a serene body of freshwater surrounded by grassy wetlands and coastal mangroves. The lagoon feeds into the ocean on the eastern end of Playa Limón and is known for birdwatching; tours are organized by Rancho La Cueva. The other lagoon – **Laguna Redonda** – is just 5km away, but is more commonly visited from Punta El Rey.

Rancho La Cueva (☎ 809-519-5271; www.rancholacueva.com; Playa Limón; s/d/tr with fan US$30/40/45; P ☎) is the only sleeping option in Playa Limón.

Popular excursions include exploring Parque Nacional Los Haitises (US$138), boat trips to Isla Saona (US$99 to US$115) and tours of Santo Domingo's Zona Colonial (US$89). All full-day trips include lunch and drinks. English, German and Spanish are spoken.

🛏 Sleeping

There is finally a blossoming hostel scene in Bávaro, a refreshing alternative for independent travelers, and it's here where you will find the biggest bulk of independent restaurants and services in one place. El Cortecito is a scruffier beach enclave nearby.

🛏 Bávaro

⭐ **Macao Beach Hostel**   HOSTEL $
(☎ 829-913-6267; www.facebook.com/macao beachhostelpuntacana; El Macao; camping s/d without tent US$10/15, with tent US$15/20, dm US$14, r without bathroom US$35, all incl breakfast; P ☎) Friendly Colombian musician Andrés has cultivated a rural Dominican village experience at this new hostel spread among several colorful traditional Caribbean clapboard shacks. Despite being a mere 10 minutes' walk from Macao Beach, it feels worlds away, with cows and horses grazing in pastures across the road, and chickens, cats, dogs and a community donkey roaming freely.

There are four rustic private rooms with mosquito nets and a five-bed dorm along with simple, bamboo-walled bathrooms and a guest kitchen. Village kids hang around and a community chef whips up Dominican meals with advance notice (RD$150). Guests can take surf lessons or horseback rides or kick back in hammocks during the day, and sit around the fire at night with Andrés and fellow musicians providing the soundtrack.

**NaturaPark Beach
Ecoresort & Spa**   HOTEL $$$
(☎ 809-221-2626; www.blau-hotels.com; Cabeza de Toro; d from US$270; P ✳ @ ☎ ☎) 🏊 NaturaPark has a narrow beach outside the village of Cabeza de Toro, halfway between Bávaro and Punta Cana. From the Lincoln Logs–style recycled coconut-wood lobby furniture to the beautiful free-growing mangroves on the property, it's all got a sustainable edge and the 524-room resort has won awards for reducing its environmental impact.

It's extra popular with those who care more about reducing their carbon footprint than hopping in and out of bars and clubs at night. The pool is a bit small, but the beach is quite nice. Free-range swans, geese and flamingos and the Laguna Bávaro on its doorstep mean nature is never too far away here.

⭐ **Paradisus Punta Cana**   RESORT $$$
(☎ 809-687-9923; www.melia.com; Playa Bávaro; all-incl d from US$400; P ✳ @ ☎ ☎) Almost jungly and discerningly quiet, this resort feels nothing like most in the area. It attracts singles and families alike and takes appreciated steps to keep them separate where desired. Newly made-over standard rooms feature soft white and beige accents, an additional sitting area with sofa bed and sexy dual showers.

🛏 Punta Cana

⭐ **Zoetry Agua**   RESORT $$$
(☎ 888-496-3879; www.zoetryresorts.com; Uvero Alto; s/d from US$426/692; P @ ☎ ☎) 🏊 The moment you walk into the intimate Zoetry, relaxation befalls you. Wooden accents and Balinese touches abound at this small prop-

erty, with 96 suites that radiate out from the dramatic, cathedral-style lobby forged from bamboo and palm leaves. Spacious rooms deport you from typical all-inclusive fare to Asian-style luxury, with hardwood floors, stone showers and sink-in bathtubs.

Several rooms have direct access to the serpentine pool that snakes throughout the property. Wellness-focused daily activities (yoga, water spinning, pilates) rule here over party activities and drinking games, but guests who want a touch of nightlife can access any of the company's more hedonistic resorts nearby. The spa is predictably inviting and all food on premises is organic. Pretty perfect. Kids are allowed but are charged as adults, a clever way to keep their numbers low.

✖ Eating

Resort buffets ensure most folks keep hunger pains at bay, but there are enough condos and villas and locals to support numerous independent eateries. Most are in shopping centers, easily reached by *moto-concho* or taxi.

Brot
CAFE **$$**

(Puntacana Village, Punta Cana; breakfast RD$255-375; ⊙7am-10pm Mon-Sat, 8am-5pm Sun; 🛜) Slammed at breakfast, this is where Punta Cana comes for its bagel fix. Fab bagelwiches (also available on baguettes) are the call, in such rarely seen flavors as Hummus Supreme and Montecristo, among others. There are also breakfast burritos, a wealth of salads and wraps, and scorching coffee. Homesickness cured!

★ Ñam Ñam
CAFE **$$**

(www.nam-nams.com; Plaza Sol Caribe, Bávaro; mains RD$119-549; ⊙11am-2:30pm & 6-11pm Tue-Sat, 7-10pm Sun; 🛜✍) Ñam Ñam means 'yummy' in Serbian: that ain't no lie. The friendly Belgradian couple behind this tiny Los Corales kitchen – they do it all themselves – know a thing or two about making your belly happy. The now-famous burgers (RD$399 to RD$549), in regular, gourmet (minced with bacon and chili) and stuffed (with ham, cheese and mushrooms) versions, are superb.

But the menu of international comfort food doesn't stop there. There are also crepes, sandwiches, a wealth of veggie options and even Serbian *chevap*, a type of minced-meat kebab from the motherland. You can't go wrong dousing anything on the menu in

the house-made pureed habanero-carrot hot sauce (serious burn), or the homespun mayo with parsley. You're welcome.

Balicana
FUSION **$$**

(www.balicana.com; Los Corales Beach Village, Los Corales; mains RD$420-550; ⊙8am-midnight Mon-Sat; 🛜) Give your taste buds a shock: this immensely pleasurable spot to eat – unbeknown to most folks who don't wander into **Los Corales Beach Village** (☑809-552-1262; www.loscoralesvillage.com; Calle Los Corales, Los Corales; r from US$126; 🅿❄🛜☒) – serves up Asian recipes normally missing in action in the DR. Thai (green curries, pad Thai), Indonesian (nasi goreng) and Malaysian (coconut curries) offerings are all devourable under a fan-cooled poolside *palapa* next to the pool.

★ Passion by Martín Berasategui
BASQUE **$$$**

(Paradisus Punta Cana, Bávaro; 7-course prix-fixe guest/non-guest US$55/60; ⊙6:30-10pm; 🛜) Chef Martín Berasategui hails from San Sebastián in Spanish Basque country – not a bad place to eat for those who might not know – and he packed a few recipes in his gastro-luggage on his way to overseeing what is considered the best fine-dining experience in the Dominican Republic, at the Paradisus Punta Cana (p406).

The seven-course tasting menu is the way to go, where you might encounter dishes a wonderful truffled ravioli; a fabulous crust-perfected salmon with fennel beads and fresh watercress, exploding chocolate olives and basil; a slow-cooked pressed veal cheek with romesco sauce; and a decadent little petit-four plate that's as pretty as it is sweet. You do need to temper your expectations a tad – despite seven Michelin stars amid various restaurants to Berasategui's name, he isn't over the stove here – but it's priced in your favor and the chef and line cooks have all worked under Berasategui's watch in Spain.

❶ Information

EMERGENCY

The main **Cestur** (Cuerpo Especializado de Seguridad Turística; ☑809-754-3082; www.cestur.gob.do; Av Estados Unidos, Bávaro; ⊙24hr) station is in Friusa, next to the bus terminal in Bávaro, with additional stations at the Punta Cana airport, Cabeza de Toro and and Uvero Alto.

MEDICAL SERVICES

All-inclusive hotels have small on-site clinics and medical staff, who can provide first aid and basic care. Head to one of several good private hospitals in the area for more serious issues.

Centro Médico Punta Cana (☎ 809-552-1506; www.centromedicopuntacana.com; Av España 1, Bávaro) Name notwithstanding, this is the main private hospital in Bávaro, with multilingual staff, 24-hour emergency room and in-house pharmacy.

Hospitén Bávaro (☎ 809-455-1121; www. hospiten.es; Carretera Higüey-Punta Cana) Best private hospital in Punta Cana, with English-, French- and German-speaking doctors and a 24-hour emergency room. The hospital is located on the old Hwy 106 to Punta Cana, 500m from Cruce de Verón.

MONEY

There is always an ATM around until you need one, in which case they are always far away, despite nearly every Dominican bank having a branch in Punta Cana! Many resorts have their own, of course. Otherwise, the closest ATMs to the hostel scene around Los Corales are **Ban-Reserves/Banco Popular ATMs** (Av Alemania, Palma Real Shopping Village) 2.2km southwest.

ⓘ Getting There & Away

AIR

Several massive thatched-roof huts make up the three terminals – Terminal A (Departures), Terminal A (Arrivals) and the new Terminal B – of the **Aeropuerto Internacional Punta Cana** (p432), located on the road to Punta Cana about 9km east of the turnoff to Bávaro. The arrival process, including immigration, purchase of a tourist card (US$10), baggage claim and customs, moves briskly.

Commercial airlines serving the Punta Cana airport year-round include the following: from Terminal A: Aerolineas Argentinas, Aeromexico, Air Canada, Frontier, JetBlue, LATAM, Southwest, Spirit, Sunwing and United; from Terminal B: Air Berlin, Air France, American Airlines, Avianca, British Airways, Copa, Delta Airlines, Edelweiss/Swiss and GOL. There are additional airlines and flights (including many charters), especially in high season.

There are Banco Popular ATMs located in the departure areas of Terminal A and B.

Rental-car agencies at Terminal A (Arrivals), which generally open from 9am to 10pm, include:

AmeriRent (☎ 809-687-0505; www.amerirent. net)

Avis (☎ 809-688-1354; www.avis.com.do)

Budget (☎ 809-466-2028; www.budget.com)

Europcar (☎ 809-688-2121; www.europcar. com)

Hertz (☎ 809-959-0365; www.hertz.com)

InterRent (☎ 809-480-8188; www.interrent. com)

National/Alamo (☎ 809-959-0434; www. nationalcar.com)

Payless (☎ 809-959-0287; www.paylesscar. com)

Sixt (☎ 829-576-4700; www.sixt.com)

Thrifty (☎ 809-959-0597; www.thrifty.com)

Resort minivans transport the majority of tourists to nearby resorts, but taxis are plentiful – look for the Siutratural guys in pink shirts. Fares between the airport and area resorts and hotels range between US$30 and US$80 depending on the destination.

BUS

The 70km toll-road, Autopista del Coral, from La Romana to Punta Cana, opened in 2012 to great fanfare, cutting the drive time from Santo Domingo to Punta Cana by two hours.

The bus terminal is located on Av Estados Unidos in Friusa, near the main intersection in Bávaro, almost 2km inland from El Cortecito.

Expreso Bávaro (☎ 809-552-1678; www. expresobavaro.com; Cruce de Friusa) has direct 1st-class services between Bávaro and the capital (RD$400, four hours), with a stop in La Romana. Departure times in both directions are 7am, 9am, 11am, 1pm, 3pm and 4pm.

From the same terminal, **Sitrabapu** (☎ 809-552-0771; Av Estados Unidos), more or less the same company, has departures to La Romana at 6am, 8:20am, 10:50am, 1:20pm, 3:50pm and 6:20pm (RD$225, 1¼ hours); and to Higüey (RD$120 to RD$130, one hour, every 20 minutes, 3am to 10:30pm). To all other destinations, head for Higüey and transfer there. You can also get to/from Santo Domingo this way, but it's much slower than the direct bus.

For Sabana de la Mar (where you can catch the ferry to Península de Samaná), Miches-based Sitrahimi passes by the Sitrabapu station on its way to Miches (RD$250, 1¾ hours, 10:30am, 12:30pm and 5:30pm), from where you can switch for Sabana de la Mar; or you can transit via Higüey and Hato Mayor. A taxi from Punta Cana direct to Sabana de la Mar costs US$200.

ⓘ Getting Around

Local buses start at the main bus terminal, passing all the outdoor malls on the way to El Cortecito, then turn down the coastal road past the large hotels to Cruce de Cocoloco, where they turn around and return the same way. Buses have the local drivers' union acronyms – Sitrabapu or Traumapabu – printed in front and cost around RD$40, depending on distance.

They generally pass every 30 minutes between 5am and 8pm, but can sometimes take up to an hour.

Daytime traffic is sometimes gridlocked between the resorts clustered just north of Bávaro and El Cortecito. Despite the stop-and-go pace of driving, renting a car for a day or two is recommended if you prefer to see the surrounding area independently. Agencies outside the airport that are handy for Baváro include **5 Star Rentals & Excursions** (☑829-917-7212; roberto.5starpuntacana@gmail.com; ☺9am-7pm Mon-Sat, noon-7pm Sun) in Los Corales, **Europcar** (☑809-686-2864; www.europcar.com.do; Av España, Bávaro; ☺8am-5pm) near Plaza Brisas de Bávaro and **Avis** (p408), **Budget** (p408), **Payless** (p408) and **National/Alamo** (p408) all near Cruce de Cocoloco.

There are numerous taxis in the area – look for stands at El Cortecito, Plaza Bávaro and at the entrance of most all-inclusive places. You can also call a cab – try Siutratural in **Bávaro** (☑809-552-0617; www.taxibavaropuntacana.com) and El **Cortecito** (☑809-552-0617; El Cortecito) or **Taxi Turístico Beron** (☑809-466-1133; www.taxituristicoberon.com).

PENÍNSULA DE SAMANÁ

This sliver of land is the antithesis of the Dominican-Caribbean dream in the southeast, where resorts rule and patches of sand come at a first-class premium. Far more laid-back and, in certain senses, more cosmopolitan, Samaná offers a European vibe as strong as espresso; it's where escape is the operative word, and where French and Italian are at least as useful as Spanish. The majority of visitors come to gasp at the North Atlantic humpback whales doing their migratory song and dance from mid-January to mid-March, but the peninsula is no one-trick pony. Sophisticated Las Terrenas is the place for those who crave a lively social scene, and sleepy Las Galeras boasts several of the best and most secluded beaches in the Dominican Republic.

Samaná

The first expedition to see North Atlantic humpback whales passing through the waters off Samaná was in 1985, and every year since then, from mid-January to mid-March, the otherwise somnolent town springs to life as an influx of tourists comes to catch glimpses of these magnificent aquatic mammals. Because North Atlantic humpbacks find the bay water particularly suitable for their annual version of speed dating, the commercialization of this natural spectacle has single-handedly catapulted the town's tourism status – for a few months each year, at least – to world-renowned.

◉ Sights & Activities

Cayo Levantado   ISLAND
A gorgeous public beach lies on the western third of this lush island, 7km from Samaná. It's the only section that's open to the public – a five-star hotel occupies the rest. Boatmen at Samaná's pier can get you there for RD$250 per person round-trip; groups of up to 15 people can negotiate a private full-day boat for RD$3000 round-trip.

★ Whale Samaná   WHALE-WATCHING
(☑809-538-2494; www.whalesamana.com; cnr Mella & Av la Marina; adult/5-10yr/under 5yr US$59/30/free; ☺office 8am-1pm & 3-6pm Jan-Mar, 9am-1pm Mon-Fri Apr-Dec) ◙ Samaná's most recommended whale-watching outfit is owned and operated by Canadian marine-mammal specialist Kim Beddall, the first person to recognize the scientific and economic importance of Samaná's whales way back in 1985. The company uses a large two-deck boat with capacity for 60 people.

Tour Samaná with Terry   ADVENTURE SPORTS
(☑809-538-3179; www.toursamanawithterry.com) This outfit offers recommended day trips to El Limón (p414), whale-watching (working alongside Whale Samaná, adding transport and credit-card facilities to its services) and more adventurous horseback-riding and ziplining or quad-biking and ziplining combos starting from US$60. It also does a recommended four-beach trip to Las Galeras (p412) that includes a lobster lunch.

⊨ Sleeping

Aire y Mar   GUESTHOUSE **$**
(☑809-538-2913; aparthotel-aireymar@hotmail.com; Calle 27 de Febrero 4; r with air-con from RD$1300-2000; ☎) A gold budget star goes to this six-room hilltop guesthouse. Rooms are bare bones (but clean!) and there's a nice communal kitchen, but the real highlight – and the reward for climbing the street from the *malecón* (waterfront path) and then a steep staircase – is the view from the hammock-strewn patio. The good-soul owner, Noelia, looks after guests with motherly care.

★**Dominican Tree
House Village** TREEHOUSE $$$

(☑800-820-1357; www.dominicantreehousevillage.
com; El Valle; r without bathroom incl breakfast &
dinner from US$235, VIP r with bathroom US$345;
🔲) 🌿 Tucked away discreetly in El Valle,
this lush sustainable-ecotourism project is
the spot to live out your dream of sleeping in
a stilted cabin in the jungle. The 19 standard
tree houses here are open on three sides and
feature queen beds and hammock chairs, all
with a dose of privacy and dramatic tropical-
forest views.

**Gran Bahía Principe Cayo
Levantado** HOTEL $$$

(☑809-538-3232; www.bahia-principe.com; Cayo
Levantado; all incl s/d from RD$19,520/24,400;
🔲@🛜🔲) This romantic five-star place has
a lot going for it, including its 'private' beach
on Cayo Levantado's idyllic sands. The 268-
room hotel sits on extra-lush grounds and
offers classic luxury á la the Ritz-Carlton
(ie slightly stuffy). However, the excellent
rooms, with hardwood floors, and some
with patio ocean views and vaulted ceilings,
suffer from stuffiness less than the lobby.

✖ Eating & Drinking

The majority of restaurants are located
along Av Malecón, while cheaper eats can be
found in converted wooden kiosks along the
waterfront and along Av Francisco de Rosario Sánchez.

★**L'Hacienda Restaurant** STEAK, SEAFOOD $$

(Santa Barbara; mains RD$480-640; ⊙7pm-mid-
night Thu-Tue; 🛜) José, the friendly French
chef-owner with a Spanish name – who
comes from a family of nine, five of whom
are chefs – has been running this intimate
French-Caribbean spot since 1987. It's a
small and simple nightly chalkboard menu
of meat and seafood grills, served up in a
soothing, baby-blue atmosphere fit for the
Caribbean. Easily Samaná's best.

Cafe de Paris BAR

(Av Malecón 6; cocktails RD$100-350; ⊙8am-mid-
night daily Jan-Mar, 10am-10pm Wed-Mon Apr-
Dec; 🛜) Samaná's one welcoming bar, this
French-owned mainstay offers more beers
than most, a good selection of rum (includ-
ing Nicaragua's excellent Flor de Cana) and
standard cocktails in a makeshift, loungy
environment. There's also an extensive
menu of bar food, from salads and sand-

wiches to crepes and pizza (mains RD$80
to RD$590).

ℹ Information

Cestur (Cuerpo Especializado de Seguridad
Turística; ☑809-200-3500; www.cestur.gob.
do; Av Francisco de Rosario Sánchez; ⊙24hr)
Tourist police; located behind Av Malecón on a
small parallel street near the third traffic circle
coming from the sea.

Scotiabank (Av Francisco de Rosario Sánchez;
⊙8:30am-4:30pm Mon-Fri, 9am-1pm Sat)
Closest ATM to the guagua (local bus) terminal
and the municipal market.

Ministerio de Turismo (Ministry of Tourism;
☑809-538-2332; www.godominicanrepublic.
com; Puerto Principe, Av Francisco de Rosario
Sánchez 5; ⊙8am-3pm Mon-Fri) Small national
tourism office. Helpful for maps and other info,
though not as well stocked with brochures as
it should be.

Centro Médico de Especialidades Samaná
(☑809 538-3999; www.cmes.com.do; Coronel
Andrés Diaz 6; ⊙24hr) Samaná's best hospital,
run by Cuban doctors.

ℹ Getting There & Away

AIR

Aeropuerto Internacional El Catey (p431),
40km west of Samaná, receives international
flights. The closest airstrip to Samaná, Aer-
opuerto Internacional Arroyo Barril, mostly
receives domestic charter flights.

BOAT

Various operators run a ferry service – pas-
sengers only, no vehicles – across the Bahía de
Samaná to Sabana de la Mar (RD$200, one hour
plus, 7am, 9am, 11am and 3pm daily). Buy tick-
ets on board. From there, it's possible to catch
guaguas to several destinations in the southeast
and then on to Santo Domingo.

BUS

Caribe Tours (☑809-538-2229; www.caribe
tours.com.do; Puerto Principe, Av Francisco
de Rosario Sánchez) offers services to Santo
Domingo at 7am, 8am, 9am, 10am, 1pm, 2pm,
3pm and 4pm (RD$340, 4½ hours, daily),
alternating between the faster highway route
or the route via San Pedro de Macorís. Stops
include Sánchez (RD$70, 30 minutes), Nagua
(RD$100, one hour) and San Francisco de
Macorís (RD$140, 1½ hours), but double-check
the stops for your particular bus.

For direct services to Puerto Plata, 210km to
the west, there are now three options. **Gingo**
(☑829-376-8346) leaves from in front of the
little park next to Banco Popular on Av Malecón
at 8am. **Santo Canario** (☑829-944-3041)

BEST OF THE REST

Bayahibe, 22km east of La Romana, was originally founded by fishermen from Puerto Rico in the 19th century. Today, it's a tranquil beach village caught in a schizophrenic power play. In the morning it's the proverbial tourist gateway, when busloads of tourists from resorts further east hop into boats bound for Isla Saona. Once this morning rush hour is over it turns back into a sleepy village. There's another buzz of activity when the resort tourists return, and then after sunset another transformation. What sets Bayahibe apart is that it manages to maintain its character despite the continued encroachment of big tourism (and the arrival of paved roads, which now canvas the entire village).

Las Palmas (☎829-850-2665, 809-972-5735; Playa Dominicus; prix-fixe from US$40; ⊙7:30-11pm Mon-Fri) This made-to-order fresh-lobster madhouse offers a meal to remember for crustacean lovers. Call ahead and make a reservation so they know to send a fisherman out to catch the right number of lobsters, which will then be quickly thrown on the grill right in the middle of diners! The prix-fixe menu includes fresh fish, drinks and desserts.

Parque Nacional Los Haitises (caves RD$100; ⊙7am-8pm) – 'land of the mountains' – is a 1375-sq-km park at the southwestern end of the Bahía de Samaná, 9km west of Sabana de la Mar. It does indeed contain scores of lush hills, jutting some 30m to 50m from the water and coastal wetlands. The knolls were formed one to two million years ago, when tectonic drift buckled the thick limestone shelf that had formed underwater.

The area receives a tremendous amount of rainfall, creating perfect conditions for subtropical humid forest plants such as bamboo, ferns and bromeliads. In fact, Los Haitises contains more than 700 species of flora, including four types of mangrove, making it one of the most highly biodiverse regions in the Caribbean. There are also 110 species of birds, 13 of which are endemic to the island.

Casa de Campo (☎800-877-3643; www.casadecampo.com.do; Av Libertad; r from US$275, villas from US$1530, all-incl supplement per adult/child US$275/152; P❄@🛜🏊) is known as much for its celebrity guests (LeBron James, Beyoncé, Jay Z, Michael Jordan) and villa owners (Marc Anthony, Sammy Sosa, Pitbull) as for its facilities. It is an all-inclusive, super-sized place that remains discerning despite its enormity. The 185 or so hotel rooms have masculine hardwood furnishings, wonderful local art, 42-inch LCD TVs, Nespresso machines and a golf cart for all.

The enormous, 28-sq-km complex is home to 16 restaurants, an equestrian center, polo fields, an exclusive beach, a shooting range – the list goes on and on. It truly resembles a city-state, albeit one with G8 summit security and a disproportionate number of 'beautiful people' per capita.

leaves at 11am beside Banco Popular on the park's western side. **Papagallo** (☎ask for Salvador 809-749-6415) offers a service at 1:45pm from under the mango tree on the eastern side of the park. If you miss him there, he waits at the municipal market until 2pm. All charge RD$300 and the trip takes about 3½ to four hours. Call ahead to double-check the day's departure. Arrive 30 to 45 minutes early to reserve a seat.

For service to towns on the peninsula, *guaguas* congregate haphazardly near the *mercado municipal*, 450m west of the Cestur station, near Calle Angel Mesina. From here, minivans head to Las Galeras (RD$100, one hour, every 10 minutes from 6:30am to 6pm), El Limón (RD$70, 50 minutes, every 15 minutes, 6:30am to 6pm) and Las Terrenas (RD$100, 1¼ hours, every 90 minutes, 6:30am to 4:45pm). Destinations fur-

ther afield also leave from the same block at the more organized **Asotrapusa Terminal** (☎829-222-0368; Av Francisco de Rosario Sánchez). Destinations include Santo Domingo (RD$325, 2½ hours, every 45 minutes, 4:30am to 4:45pm) and Santiago (RD$325, three hours, every 45 minutes, 4:45am to 2:30pm). The Puerto Plata services also make a stop here on their way out of town, but seats may be full by then.

TAXI

The **Sitratusa** (☎809-538-3131 ext 1246) taxi stand is operated by and sits just outside the entrance to Gran Bahía Principe Cayacoa resort. Fares are expensive. Samples include Las Galeras (US$45), Las Terrenas (US$55), Aeroporto El Catey (US$70), Caberete (US$170), Puerto Plata (US$190), Santo Domingo (US$190), Santiago (US$200) and Punta Cana (US$380).

ℹ Getting Around

Samaná is walkable, but if you're carrying luggage, catch a *motoconcho* (motorcycle taxi) – they're everywhere. 4WD vehicles are your only option in terms of car rental – roads on the peninsula are bad enough to warrant the extra expense. Rates average around US$50 per day (tax and insurance included) and discounts are typically given for rentals of a week or longer. Try **Xamaná Rent A Motor** (☑ 809-538-2833; fabianking1812@hotmail.com; Av Malecón; ☉ 8am-6pm Mon-Sat, to noon Sun).

Las Galeras

The road to this small fishing community 28km northeast of Samaná ends at a shack on the beach. So does everything else, metaphorically speaking. One of the great pleasures of a stay here is losing all perspective on the world beyond – even the beautiful and isolated outlying beaches seem far away. By all means succumb to the temptation to do nothing more than lie around your bungalow or while the day away at a restaurant. But – if you summon the will to resist – Las Galeras offers a variety of land- and water-based activities.

🏖 Beaches

Playa Rincón
BEACH

Pitch-perfect Playa Rincón, with soft, nearly white sand and multihued water good for swimming, stretches an uninterrupted 3km – enough for every day-tripper to claim their own piece of real estate. There's a small stream at the far western end, which is great for a quick freshwater dip at the end of your visit, and a backdrop of thick palm forest. Several restaurants serve seafood dishes and rent beach chairs, making this a great place to spend the entire day.

Playa Frontón
BEACH

Playa Frontón boasts some of the area's best snorkeling. Apparently it's also popular with drug smugglers, Dominicans braving the Mona Passage on their way to Puerto Rico, and reality-show contestants – in 2002 *Expedición Robinson*, Colombia's version of *Survivor*, was filmed here. Trails lead to the beach, but it's easy to get lost, so hire a local guide (contact Karin at **La Hacienda** (☑ 829-939-8285; http://lahaciendahostel.com) or, preferably, come by boat: **Asoldega** (Asociación de Lancheros de Las Galeras) charges about RD$3000 to Playa Frontón (RD$1000 per person with four or more).

Playa Madama
BEACH

Playa Madama is a small beach framed by high bluffs at the edge of the country; keep in mind there's not much sunlight here in the afternoon. Asoldega (p412) charges around RD$2500 to Playa Madama (RD$800 per person with four or more people).

🏃 Activities

Cabo Cabrón
DIVING

(Bastard Point) For experienced divers, Bastard Point is one of the north coast's best sites. After an easy boat ride from Las Galeras, you're dropped into a churning channel with a giant coral formation that you can swim around; you may see dolphins here.

Las Galeras Divers
DIVING

(☑ 809-538-0220; www.las-galeras-divers.com; Plaza Lusitania; ☉ 8am-6pm) Las Galeras Divers is a well-respected, French-run dive shop at the main intersection. One-/two-tank dives including all equipment cost US$55/85 (US$10 less if you have your own gear). Discounted dive packages are offered. Various PADI-certification courses can also be arranged.

🛏 Sleeping

⭐ Todo Blanco
BOUTIQUE HOTEL $$

(☑ 809-729-2333; www.hoteltodoblanco.com; r with/without air-con US$100/90; P ❄ 🗢) Living up to its 'All White' name, this whitewashed, well-established inn sits atop a small hillock a short walk from the end of the main drag. Rooms are large and airy, with high ceilings, private terraces overlooking the sea, pastel headboards and new AC, while the multi-level grounds are nicely appointed with gardens and a gazebo.

Casa Por Qué No?
B&B $$

(☑ 809-712-5631; casaporqueno@live.com; s/d incl breakfast US$50/65; ☉ closed May-Oct; P ❄ 🗢) Pierre and Monick, the charming French-Canadian owners of this B&B, are consummate hosts and have been renting two rooms on either side of their cozy home for nearly 30 years – each room has a separate entrance and hammock. It's only 25m or so north of the main intersection on your right as you're walking toward the beach.

Casa Dorado
B&B $$

(☑ 829-577-6777; www.casadoradodr.com; s/d from US$60/70; P 🗢) This beautiful house, 1km from both the main intersection and

Playita beach, features Mexican-influenced interiors styled by the American owner. Four rooms are available; the largest and most expensive comes with a Jacuzzi.

★ Casa El Paraíso
B&B $$$

(☑809-975-1641; www.facebook.com/CasaElParai soRD; La Guázuma; r incl breakfast US$150-190; ❄☒) ✎ Santo Domingo veterinarians Nora and José, a gourmet Italian chef named Mirko and a gaggle of Italian greyhounds are your hosts at this extraordinary six-room B&B in La Guázuma that practically tumbles out of the jungle into the whale-packed sea below. Room 5 (nicknamed 'Africa') is completely open on two sides, framing jungle, mountain and sea as you've never seen.

✗ Eating

End of the Road
FAST FOOD $

(Principal; mains RD$150-190; ⊗8am-9pm; ☎) Right at the town intersection, this small traveler's hub serves gourmet Angus-beef burgers and massive burritos (including an awesome breakfast version) cooked by locals trained by the French chef of what was the town's chicest eatery.

★ El Monte Azul
SEAFOOD, THAI $$

(☑849-249-3640; www.restaurantsamana-monte azul.com; mains RD$450-790; ⊗11am-2:30pm & 5-11pm Wed-Mon; ☎) Clinging spectacularly to the edge of the DR, this rustic, postcard-perfect restaurant with amazing views offers some of the island's most dramatic dining. Go at sunset, when a kaleidoscopic flurry of hues melts into the sea as you nurse a signature passion-fruit libation and watch families of whales from a few small tables lining the cliff edge.

Restaurante Isabel
DOMINICAN, SEAFOOD $$

(La Playita; ⊗RD$300-800) The simplest – and best – of the three restaurants at Playita beach sits right on the sand. Owner-chef Isabel has done little more than throw a steel grate over a clay oven to cook you whatever's fresh that day. Expect grilled fish, lobster or chicken and heaps of side dishes. Isabel's French-Canadian daughter-in-law whips up good cocktails as well.

Rincon del Marisco
DOMINICAN, SEAFOOD $$

(☑809-380-7295; Principal; mains RD$350-700; ⊗10am-10pm Wed-Mon) Local chef Rubi's gastronomic feats were previously the main event at a wonderful Playa Rincón beach restaurant. While she's traded in that dramatic setting for a simple open-air place

in town, the food continues to shine: fresh fish, *langosta* (lobster), grilled chicken etc. Order anything in the wonderful coco sauce and douse your coconut rice in the excellent vinaigrette.

❶ Information

Cestur (Cuerpo Especializado de Seguridad Turística; ☑849-452-5536; Principal; ⊗24hr) Tourist police.

BanReservas (www.banreservas.com; Principal) ATM one block north of the Malecón and another at Grand Paradise Samaná resort.

Clinica Bahia Azul (☑809-538-0042; Principal; ⊗24hr) A small, well-run clinic in town.

❶ Getting There & Away

The paved road coming from Samaná winds along the coast and through lovely, often forested countryside before reaching the outskirts of Las Galeras.

Guaguas head to Samaná (RD$100, one hour, every 10 minutes from 6:30am to 6pm) from the beach end of Calle Principal, and they also pick up passengers as they cruise slowly out of town. There are three daily buses to Santo Domingo (RD$375, three hours, 5:30am, 1pm and 3pm).

Taxis (☑809-481-8526) are available at a stand just in front of the main town beach (as well as a more expensive stand near the beach at Grand Paradise Samaná resort). Sample one-way fares are RD$3000 to Aeropuerto Catey, RD$2500 to Las Terrenas, RD$1000 to Samaná and RD$7000 to Santo Domingo. You may be able to negotiate cheaper fares, especially to Samaná.

Renting a car is an excellent way to explore the peninsula on your own. Prices are generally around RD$2700 per day with insurance; **RP Rent-a-Car** (☑809-538-0249; jreyes.jdrv@ gmail.com; Principal; ⊗8am-5pm Mon-Fri, to 3pm Sat) is one option.

Las Terrenas

Once a rustic fishing village, Las Terrenas is now a cosmopolitan town and seems as much French (approaching a colony) and Italian as Dominican. Fashionable-looking European women in designer sunglasses ride their personal ATVs with a bag of baguettes in tow, battling on roads with way too many *motos*. The balancing act between locals and expats has produced a lively mix of styles and a social scene more vibrant than that anywhere else on the peninsula. Walking in either direction along the beach road leads to a beachfront scattered with

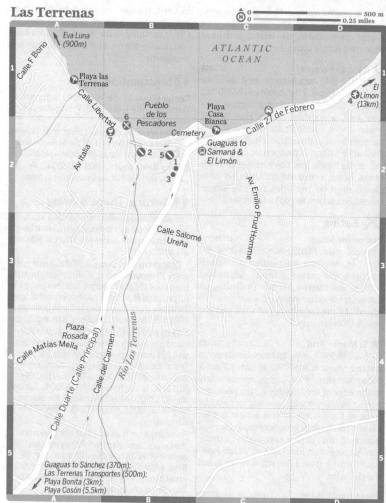

Las Terrenas

ATLANTIC OCEAN

Eva Luna (900m)

Calle F Bono

Playa las Terrenas

Calle Libertad

Pueblo de los Pescadores

Playa Casa Bianca

Calle 27 de Febrero

El Limón (13km)

Cemetery

Guaguas to Samaná & El Limón

Av Italia

Av Emilio Prud'Homme

Calle Salomé Ureña

Plaza Rosada

Calle Matías Mella

Calle Duarte (Calle Principal)

Calle del Carmen

Río Las Terrenas

Guaguas to Sánchez (370m); Las Terrenas Transportes (500m); Playa Bonita (3km); Playa Cosón (5.5km)

hotels, tall palm trees and calm, aquamarine waters.

Las Terrenas is well suited to independent travelers and a good place to hook up with fellow nomads.

☉ Sights

Cascada El Limón
WATERFALL

Tucked away in surprisingly rough landscape, surrounded by peaks covered in lush greenery, is the 52m-high El Limón waterfall. A beautiful swimming hole at the bottom can be a perfect spot to wash off the sweat and mud from the trip here, though it's often too deep and cold for a dip. The departure point is the small town of El Limón, only half an hour from Las Terrenas.

🏃 Activities

Las Terrenas has reasonably good diving and snorkeling and at least three shops in town to take you out.

LT'Kite
WATER SPORTS

(☎809-801-5671; www.lasterrenas-kitesurf. com; Calle 27 de Febrero; ☉10am-6pm) Recommended kitesurfing school run by a friendly Frenchman who speaks Spanish and English

Las Terrenas

as well. It rents surfboards (per day US$30) and kitesurfing equipment (per day US$70) and provides lessons and IKO certifications for the latter. Six hours of kitesurfing lessons (really the minimum needed to have a sporting chance of making it work) cost US$300.

Turtle Dive Center DIVING
(☑829-903-0659; www.turtledivecenter.com; El Paseo shopping center, Paseo de la Costanera; ☉10am-12:30pm & 4-7pm) A highly recommended SSI-affiliated shop, run by a safety-first Frenchman. Also runs snorkeling trips to Playa Jackson (full-day US$90) if booked in advance with five or more people, and daily trips to Isla Las Ballenas (snorkeling/two-tank dive US$35/100).

Dive Academy DIVING
(☑829-577-5548; www.diveacademy.co; 2nd fl, Beach Garden Plaza, Libertad; ☉8am-9pm) This English-run NAUI outfitter, a Las Galeras transplant, offers a 10% discount for online bookings.

👉 Tours

Flora Tours ECOTOUR
(☑829-923-2792; www.flora-tours.net; Principal 278; ☉8:30am-12:30pm & 3:30-6:30pm Mon-Sat) 🖋 This French-run agency takes top honors in town for eco-sensitive tours to Parque Nacional Los Haitises and hard-to-access beaches, as well as more tranquil catamaran trips, culturally sensitive quad-bike tours to remote villages, mountain-bike excursions of varying levels and kayak tours through the mangroves at Playa Cosón.

Casa de las Terrenas ADVENTURE
(☑809-666-0306; www.lasterrenas-excursions.com; Principal 280; ☉8:30am-noon & 3:30-6:30pm Mon-Sat) Small, friendly, French-run operation based in a little kiosk in front of Plaza Taína.

🛏 Sleeping

★ Hotel Atlantis HOTEL $$
(☑809-240-6111; www.atlantis-hotel.com.do; F Peña Gomez, Playa Bonita; s/d/q from $90/120/170; 🅿✳🛜) This rambling and charming hotel is straight out of a fairy tale – all twisting staircases, covered walkways and odd-shaped rooms. The furnishings are comfortable, not luxurious, and each of the 18 rooms is different – some have balconies and fine ocean views.

★ Peninsula House GUESTHOUSE $$$
(☑809-962-7447; www.thepeninsulahouse.com; Playa Cosón; r US$650-800; 🅿@🛜🏊) One of the Caribbean's most exquisite hotels, this Victorian B&B perched high on a hill overlooking Playa Cosón was previously the DR's hands-down top choice for utmost exclusivity and service. But plans by new owners were in the works in 2017 to construct a massive, 36-room expansion over the original six rooms, leaving to chance whether the place's soul can be salvaged.

★ Eva Luna VILLA $$$
(☑809-978-5611; www.villa-evaluna.com; Marico, Playa Las Ballenas; villas for 2/4 incl breakfast US$120/240; 🅿✳@🏊) A paragon of understated luxury, these five Mexican-style villas come with fully equipped kitchens, gorgeously painted living rooms, and terraces where a delicious gourmet breakfast is served. The bedrooms are a bit cramped, but the serenity and exquisite decor more than make up for it.

🍴 Eating & Drinking

★ Restaurante Luis SEAFOOD $$
(☑809-601-8772; Playa Cosón; mains RD$300-400, lobster per lb RD$650; ☉10am-5pm) Practically a legend at this point, this ramshackle sea shack on Playa Cosón serves up some of Samaná's best seafood. Dig your toes into the sand, shoot the breeze with the server over the daily catch (there's no menu), and sit back and wait for simplicity at its finest. French expats flock here at weekends for lobsters the size of Fiats.

★ La Terrasse FRENCH $$
(Pueblo de los Pescadores; mains RD$380-730; ☉11:30am-2:30pm & 6:30-11pm; 🛜) The Dominican chef at this sophisticated French bistro deserves a few Michelin stars for his steak *au poivre* (RD$550), one of the most perfect meals in the entire DR – you'll be

genuflecting at his kitchen's door after it graces your lips.

★ **El Mosquito** COCKTAIL BAR
(Pueblo de los Pescadores; cocktails RD$250-400; ☺5pm-2am Mon-Thu, to 4am Fri & Sat, 6:30pm-2am Sun; 🛜) The hottest bar in Las Terrenas by a landslide, this newly re-opened, open-air lounge that was destroyed in the 2012 Pueblo de los Pescadores fire is a good-time juxtaposition of rustic lounge furniture, fairy light–lit trees, exposed brick and local art that caters to a who's who of expats and tourists.

❶ Information

BanReservas (www.banreservas.com; Duarte 254; ☺8am-5pm Mon-Fri, 9am-1pm Sat)

Cestur (Cuerpo Especializado de Seguridad Turística; ☏809-754-5042; Libertad; ☺24hr) The tourist police are located inside the Centro de Atención al Ciudadano at the Las Terrenas police station.

Clínica Especializada Internacional (☏809-240-6701; www.ceiterrenas.com; Villa de Las Flores, Fabio Abreu; ☺24hr) An excellent private hospital run by Cuban doctors.

Colonial Tours (☏809-240-6822; www.colonialtours.com.do; Plaza Rosada; ☺9am-1pm & 3-7pm Mon-Fri, to noon Sat) The town's main full-service travel agency; helpful for bus info as well.

❶ Getting There & Away

AIR

International flights arrive at **Aeropuerto Internacional El Catey** (p431), located 8km west of Sánchez and a 35-minute taxi ride (US$70) to Las Terrenas. Air Canada, Westjet and Air Transat, among others, serve Canadian destinations; XL Airways goes to Paris. There's also a handful of charter flights.

BUS

For Santo Domingo, **Las Terrenas Transportes** (☏809-240-5302) operates direct coaches via the main highway (RD$375, 2½ hours, 5am, 7am, 9am, 2pm and 3:30pm), Puerto Plata (RD$325, three hours, 6:30am), Santiago (RD$320, three hours, 6:30am, 8:30am and 12:40pm) and Nagua (RD$150, 1¼ hours, 7am and 2pm). Buses leave from the Esso gas station on the outskirts of town, 2.5km south of the sea.

Guaguas to Samaná leave in front of Casa Linda at the corner of Calle Principal and the coastal road eight times daily (RD$100, 1¼ hours, 7:15am to 5pm). For those going to El Limón, 14km away, *guaguas* leave from the same stop (RD$50, 35 minutes, every 15 minutes from 7:15am to 7pm).

For Sánchez, **guaguas** (Uchotesa; ☏809-237-9550) leave from the Uchotesa depot on the outskirts of town (RD$70, every 20 minutes, 7am to 6pm).

CAR

Las Terrenas is easily accessible by road if you're motoring on your own. A portion of the US$150-million Blvd Turístico del Atlántico connects Las Terrenas with Aeropuerto Internacional El Catey, 24km to the west, avoiding the former need to transit through Sánchez. The toll charges, relative to kilometers, are high (RD$528), and it hasn't exactly been embraced by locals, but it's a beautiful drive all the same.

TAXI

The local **taxi consortium** (☏809-240-6339) offers rides for one to six passengers to just about anywhere. Some sample one-way fares are Playa Cosón (US$25), El Limón (US$25), Samaná (US$70), Las Galeras (US$100), Santo Domingo (US$150) and Punta Cana (US$400).

NORTH COAST

From east to west on the Dominican Republic's north coast, you'll find world-class beaches, water sports galore and out-of-the-way locales evocative of timeless rural life. There are waterfalls to climb, sleepy little Dominican towns with laundry ubiquitously drying on clotheslines and mile after mile of sandy beaches. Independent travelers will find accommodations of all stripes and several good places to base themselves for explorations further afield, especially Cabarete, where you can kitesurf, surf or just plain bodysurf.

Cabarete

This one-time fishing and farming hamlet is now the adventure-sports capital of the country, booming with condos and new development. Cabarete is an ideal spot to base yourself for exploring the area – you're within two hours' drive of the best that the coast has to offer, and if you want to go surfing, or windsurfing, or kitesurfing, heck, you don't even need to leave town.

🏄 Beaches

Cabarete's beaches are its main attractions, and not just for sun and sand. They're each home to a different water sport, and

DRIVING TOUR: RUTA PANORAMICA

Start Montellano

End La Cumbre

Length 30km; two hours

Tim Hall, Canadian consul and owner of **Tubagua Plantation Eco-Village** (☎809-696-6932; www.tubagua.com; El Descanso; r incl breakfast from US$30; ℗ ☎) 🍴, has been central in helping to develop the 30km Ruta Panoramica (www.rutapanoramica.com) sightseeing route, which runs between Montellano in the north (12km east of Puerto Plata) and La Cumbre in the south.

The 'highway', rough in patches, winds up and over the **Cordillera Septentrional**, climbing to 670m at La Cumbre – a nearby monument marks the spot where the bodies of political dissidents the Mirabal sisters were left by dictator Rafael Trujillo's assassins. The mountain slopes in the area are pockmarked with **amber mines** (blue amber, the most valuable variety, is found here), which are essentially small shovel- and pickax-dug holes with plastic tarps strung up as makeshift shelters. Amber mining is a fairly desperate and unpredictable undertaking. Carmen, a miner's wife, will prepare lunch and coffee in her modest home, and she and her sons will answer questions about the life of an amber miner.

A small coffee-growing region is also nearby, around the pretty little town of **Pedro Garcia**, about 10km north of La Cumbre. In Pedro Garcia itself, you can buy coffee (RD$300 for a 1lb bag) and locally produced trinkets at **Artesania La Factoria** (Calle JP Duarte 125), a shop attached to the area's sole coffee-processing plant (there were once six). After an epidemic of berry-borer beetles wiped out most of the beans in 2000, the mountainsides were cleared and converted into cattle ranches. The impact has been felt economically and environmentally, and there has been an exodus of villagers – the population is a quarter of what it was in 1970. There's a fledgling effort to obtain a reforestation grant, develop organic single-origin-coffee production and promote ecotourism. In the meantime, you can ask staff at Tubagua Eco-Village to arrange a roasting and tasting demonstration in a small hilltop shelter with beautiful views of the countryside.

are great places to watch beginner and advanced athletes alike.

Kite Beach
BEACH

Two kilometers west of town. A sight to behold on windy days, when scores of kiters of all skill levels negotiate huge sails and 30m lines amid the waves and traffic. On those days there's no swimming here, as you're liable to get run over.

Playa Encuentro
BEACH

Four kilometers west of town. The place to go for surfing, though top windsurfers and kitesurfers sometimes come to take advantage of the larger waves. The beach itself is a long, narrow stretch of sand backed by lush tropical vegetation; strong tides and rocky shallows make swimming here difficult. To find the beach, look for the fading yellow archway and sign that says 'Coconut Palms Resort.' Definitely not safe to walk around here at night.

Playa Cabarete
BEACH

Main beach in front of town. Ideal for watching windsurfing, though the very best windsurfers are well offshore at the reef line. Look for them performing huge high-speed jumps and even end-over-end flips.

🏃 Activities

Kite Club
KITESURFING

(☎809-571-9748; www.kiteclubcabarete.com; Kite Beach) This well-run club is at the top of Kite Beach, and has a fantastic atmosphere for hanging out and relaxing between sessions. The tiny kitchen delivers delicious fresh ahi tuna salads and sandwiches.

Kitexcite
KITESURFING

(☎829-962-4556; www.kitexcite.com; Kite Beach) This school was one of the first in Cabarete. Several of its instructors are Dominican, and the school uses radio helmets, video-based learning and optional offshore sessions to maximize instruction.

KITESURFING IN BUEN HOMBRE

Remember how in *The Beach* Leonardo DiCaprio hears about a super-secret island in Thailand and then goes on a crazy adventure to get there? This is what is now happening on the north coast of the Dominican Republic, with Buen Hombre.

Rumors of wind-whipped shallows in this new, off-the-grid kitesurfing paradise are circulating in the bars of Cabarete, luring away some of its most intrepid adrenaline junkies. If half of what they hear of Buen Hombre is true, they want to see it for themselves, and so they zip out into the DR's northwestern desert past gnarled cacti and herb-eating goats in search of a new thrill. At the end of the road they find a tiny fishing village, eight beachfront bungalows, a simple restaurant and a hut full of kiteboarding equipment. Oh, and a former pro tennis player and Estonian-Swedish filmmaker who speaks eight languages and built the place.

That's Riin Urbanik. She came to the area first as a traveler, and when she beheld Buen Hombre's arid, undulating landscape and felt the wind's strength, she dropped everything and started a **kiteboarding school** (☏ 829-521-2367; www.kitebuenhombre. net; Buen Hombre; s/d bungalow US$30/35, weeklong kitesurfing course US$900). She soon came to know the community of Buen Hombre, which means 'good man' and comes from kind villagers who risked their lives attempting to save passengers from ships that were wrecked in the area centuries ago. The good men of Buen Hombre also helped Riin build her dream, and one of its good women was hired as the chef.

Today people come from around the world to stay at Buen Hombre, where they take up kitesurfing or perfect their skills, bond with a group of like-minded travelers (often including diplomats, tech nerds and NGO types) and go on excursions to nearby mangrove islands and sandbars. In the evenings, when there's a full moon, they kitesurf in its glow and throw parties. On darker nights, they sit around a bonfire telling stories, drinking rum and preparing for another day in the wind.

Unlike *The Beach*, Buen Hombre is accessible via a recently paved road. Many visitors rent cars or catch a ride out with Riin, traveling west on Autopista Duarte until they reach Botoncillo, and then hanging a right and winding out over the mountains, toward the coast. The drive itself is worthwhile, and even non-kitesurfers have been known to show up in Buen Hombre for the night, just to see it for themselves.

Carib Wind Center BOATING
(☏ 809-571-0560; www.caribwindcabarete.com; Principal) With more than 20 years' experience, the Israeli-owned Carib Wind Center is for those who prefer an actual boat attached to your sail. It also rents Lasers and catamarans and provides instruction.

Vela Windsurf Center WINDSURFING
(☏ 809-571-0805; www.velacabarete.com) Vela Windsurf Center, on the main beach, uses excellent gear and works in conjunction with kitesurfing school Dare2Fly. It also rents sea kayaks (per hour US$10).

Pau Hana Surf Camp SURFING
(☏ 809-884-2828; www.pauhanasurfcamp.com; Playa Encuentro) One of the first schools on the beach, Pau Hana has a good reputation and primarily employs local kids.

Kele Surf School SURFING
(☏ 829-846-6930; www.kelesurf.com; group lesson per hr US$40, board rental per day $US25;

⊙7am-4pm) Owned by an inspiring young woman who grew up in Encuentro and works as a fashion model, Kele Surf School is hands down the best choice for aspiring female surfers. Unlike some of the smarmy instructors known to populate Encuentro, Kele's won't try any 'hanky panky.' Also her equipment is top quality and her prices are competitive.

Cabarete Surf Camp SURFING
(☏ 829-548-6655; www.cabaretesurfcamp.com) One of the most popular camps in Cabarete, with fantastic accommodations and instructors. Also offers kitesurfing lessons.

Northern Coast Diving DIVING
(☏ 809-571-1028; www.northerncoastdiving.com) Well-respected Sosúa-based dive shop with a representative in Iguana Mama. Organizes excursions from Laguna Dudu in the east to Monte Cristi in the west.

☞ Tours

★ Iguana Mama
OUTDOORS

(☏ 809-654-2325, 809-571-0908; www.iguana mama.com; Principal) This professional and family-run adventure-sports tour operator is in a class of its own. Its specialties are mountain biking (from easy to insanely difficult, from US$50) and canyoning. Trips to Damajagua (US$89) go to the 27th waterfall, and Iguana Mama pioneered a canyoning tour to Ciguapa Falls, which only this operator offers. The highest jump is more than 10m.

⚜ Festivals & Events

Dominican Jazz Festival
MUSIC

(www.drjazzfestival.com; ⊙ Nov) Held in Puerto Plata and Santiago, this long-running festival attracts top musical talent from around the country and abroad. Most of the visiting musicians run workshops for kids; one year Bernie Williams, former Yankee turned guitarist, taught both baseball and jazz.

Master of the Ocean
SPORTS

(www.masteroftheocean.com; ⊙ last week Feb) A triathlon of water sports – surfing, windsurfing and kitesurfing. From the beach you can watch some spectacular performances.

🛏 Sleeping

★ Surf Break Cabarete
B&B $

(☏ 829-921-4080; www.surfbreakcabarete. com; Playa Encuentro; s/d incl breakfast from US$35/42; P❄🛜🏊) The best value stay in Playa Encuentro offers both surf and yoga packages, along with a range of darling, *palapa*-topped accommodations in two lush complexes. The pool area and yoga studio are superbly tranquil, and the owner is friendly and helpful. This is the hotel of choice for women traveling alone (and anybody else, really).

★ Cabarete Surf Camp
HOSTEL $

(☏ 829-548-6655; www.cabaretesurfcamp.com; s incl breakfast & dinner US$25-44, d US$33-66, apt US$75-120; P❄🛜🏊) On the edge of a lagoon a five-minute walk inland, this lushly landscaped property has small, colorful and rustic backpacker-style cabins; larger, modern rooms with kitchenettes in a two-story, Victorian-style building; and, best of all, two colonial-style, all-wood rooms with louvered windows in a 'tower' above the kitchen and dining area.

Extreme Hotel
HOTEL $$

(☏ 809-571-0330; www.extremehotels.com; Kite Beach; r US$60; P🛜🏊) 〽 Trapeze, kickboxing, physical therapy camp, a half-pipe for skateboarders, certainly not your standard hotel offerings. Then again, this ecologically minded, solar-powered and self-described 'upscale hostel' is meant for those seeking an unconventional beach holiday. No TVs and no air-con in the spacious and simply furnished fan-cooled rooms.

Agualina Kite Resort
HOTEL $$

(☏ 809-571-0787; www.agualina.com; Kite Beach; r US$107; P❄🛜🏊) Opened in 2004, this is the most comfortable lodging on Kite Beach. Studios and apartments have stylish, well-equipped kitchens – stainless-steel refrigerators are an especially nice touch – and large modern bathrooms with glass showers and gleaming fixtures. There's free wi-fi throughout the building.

★ Natura Cabañas
RESORT $$$

(☏ 809-571-1507; www.naturacabana.com; r incl breakfast US$236; P@🏊) Owned and designed by an expat husband-wife team, this collection of marvelously designed thatched-roof bungalows about halfway between Cabarete and Sosúa is the epitome of rustic chic. Everything is constructed from natural materials – mahogany, bamboo and stone – and a gravel path leads to a secluded beach. Two open-air restaurants serve exquisitely created dishes (US$15 to US$30).

Velero Beach Resort
HOTEL $$$

(☏ 809-571-9727; www.velerobeach.com; La Punta 1; r from US$175; P❄@🏊) Distinguished by boutique-style rooms and its location down a small lane at the relatively low-traffic eastern end of town, Velero is an excellent choice. True to its four-star rating in service, professionalism and property maintenance, the Velero has recently opened a new restaurant, and the pool and lounge area are also top notch.

🍴 Eating

Dining out on Cabarete's beach is the quintessential Caribbean experience – paper lanterns hanging from palm trees, a gentle ocean breeze and excellent food (even if it does cost the same as you'd pay back home). Many of the bars on the beach serve good food as well, but note that many close for part of October.

TWENTY-SEVEN WATERFALLS

Travelers routinely describe the tour of the **waterfalls** (☑829-639-2492; www.27charcos. com; Damajagua; highest waterfall RD$500, organized tour US$80-100) at Damajagua as 'the coolest thing I did in the DR.' We agree. Guides lead you up, swimming and climbing through the waterfalls. To get down you jump – as much as 8m – into the sparkling pools below. At the time of research, extreme flooding had taken out a suspension bridge that visitors once used to cross a river and arrive at the attraction. In the meantime, guests were fording the river, but tour operators insisted that the bridge would be replaced promptly.

It's mandatory to go with a guide, but there's no minimum group size, so you can go solo if you wish. You can go up to the seventh, 12th or 27th waterfall, though most 'jeep safari' package tours only go to the seventh. You should be in good shape and over the age of 12. Foreigners pay RD$500 to the highest waterfall and less to reach the lower ones (US$1 of every entrance fee goes to a community development fund). Tour companies in Puerto Plata, Sosúa and Cabarete organize trips here. The falls are open from 8:30am to 3pm, but go early before the crowds arrive. A visitors center and restaurant are near the entrance.

To get to the falls, go south from Imbert on the highway for 3.3km (and cross two bridges) until you see a sign on your left with pictures of a waterfall. From there it's about 1km down to the visitors center. Alternatively, take a **Javilla Tours** (☑809-970-2412; cnr Camino Real & Av Colón; ⊙ buses every 15min 5am-7:30pm) *guagua* (bus) from Puerto Plata and ask to get off at the entrance. The big Texaco station at Imbert serves as a crossroads for the entire area. There is a frequent *guagua* service to Santiago (RD$80, one hour) and Puerto Plata (RD$40, 30 minutes).

★**Mojito Bar**　　　SALADS, SANDWICHES $
(mains RD$170; ⊙11am-2am, closed Tue; ☂🍴)
One of the few reasonably priced beachfront places, Mojitos has an excellent selection of natural juices, healthy salads, Dominican food and sandwiches (some vegan and vegetarian). It's a sliver of a space near the middle of the beach. Happy hour is from 4pm to 8pm (two mojitos RD$200).

Wilson's at La Boca　　　BARBECUE $
(☑809-667-1968; mains RD$200) This is a little barbecue shack on the Yasica River in Islabon, around 8km southeast of town on the way to Sabaneta de Yasica. The eponymous Wilson, who speaks perfect English, serves up wood-fired fish, chicken and lobster.

★**Eze Bar & Restaurant**　　　ITALIAN $$$
(☑809-571-0586; www.ezerestaurant.com; Plaza Carib Wind; mains US$15-25; ⊙8am-11pm) Eze Bar is not visible from the main drag, and unless you approach it from the beach, to get there you must walk through a windsurfing shop. The place is small but chic, with a fairly unoriginal Miami Beach vibe, so it's a bit of a shock when the Italian food arrives and blows your mind.

**Restaurante Chez
Arsenio**　　　DOMINICAN, SEAFOOD $$$
(☑809-571-9948; restaurantechezarsenio@hot mail.com; Hideaway Beach Resort; mains RD$500; ⊙11am-10pm Mon-Fri, from 9am Sat & Sun) Occupying a spectacular stretch of the western end of Playa Encuentro, the restaurant at Hideaway Beach Resort (primarily condo rentals) serves up a wide variety of Dominican, Italian and especially recommended seafood dishes. Choose either the open-air, poolside dining room or a table on the perfectly manicured lawn under a towering palm tree.

🍷 Drinking & Nightlife

Kahuna　　　BAR
(☑809-571-0064; Cabarete Beach; ⊙9pm-3am)
An excellent sports bar with NFL, NHL, NBA and games from many other league acronyms on the big screen, along with regular food and drink specials. Late nights here are especially fun, with lots of dancing and two beer-pong tables.

Voy Voy　　　BAR
(⊙6pm-late) Vela Windsurf Center by day, bar by night, this small, hip cafe also serves sandwiches and snacks. Monday karaoke is

a mandatory part of Cabarete beach life, as are the regular open-mic and dance nights.

ℹ Information

Banco Popular (Principal; ⊙9am-4:30pm Mon-Fri, to 1pm Sat)

Cestur (Tourist Police; ☑ 809-571-0713, 809-754-3036; Principal) At the eastern entrance to town.

Fujifilm Digital (☑ 809-571-9536; Principal; per hr RD$30) Fast internet connection and headphones.

Servi-Med (☑ 809-571-0964; Principal; ⊙24hr) English, German and Spanish are spoken, and travel medical insurance and credit cards accepted.

ℹ Getting There & Around

BUS

None of the main bus companies offer service to Cabarete – the closest depots are in Sosúa. They zip through town without stopping on their way to Nagua before turning south to Santo Domingo.

A large, white bus with air-con on its way from Puerto Plata to Samaná stops at the gas station just east of town every day at 1:30pm. From Cabarete, the three-hour trip costs RD$250.

CAR & MOTORCYCLE

If you want to rent a car, you can do so at the airport or in town. One fantastic option is **Easy Rider** (☑ 849-863-9560; www.facebook.com/easyridercabarete; ⊙8am-7pm), where prices are reasonable and full insurance coverage is provided (you will not be held responsible for damaged windows, tires or anything else). If you're in town and prefer to rent at the airport, you can take a *guagua* (30 minutes) to the airport road (just past Sosúa), walk 500m to the terminal and shop around at the numerous car-rental agencies there.

GUAGUA

Heaps of *guaguas* ply this coastal road, including east to Sabaneta (RD$25) and Río San Juan (RD$80, one hour) and west to Sosúa (RD$25, 20 minutes) and Puerto Plata (RD$50, 45 minutes). Hail them anywhere along Cabarete's main drag.

MOTOCONCHO

Transportation in town is dominated by *motoconchos*, who will attempt to charge you two to three times the price you'd pay for a similar ride in Puerto Plata. Don't be surprised if you can't haggle them down. A ride out to Kite Beach should cost RD$50 and Playa Encuentro RD$100.

SCOOTER

A popular option is to rent a scooter or a motorcycle. Expect to pay around US$20 per day, less if you rent for a week or more. There are lots of rental shops along the main drag, and some hotels rent two-wheeled transportation too. Be aware that helmets aren't always available, so if that's important to you consider bringing your own.

TAXI

The motorcycle-shy can call a **taxi** (☑ 809-571-0767; www.taxisosuacabarete.com), which will cost RD$500 to Encuentro, US$45 to Aeropuerto Internacional Gregorío Luperón 18km west, and US$35 to Puerto Plata. For the Santiago airport it's around US$100, and for Santo Domingo its US$200. There's also a taxi stand in the middle of town.

CENTRAL HIGHLANDS

Even die-hard beach fanatics will eventually overdose on sun and sand. When you do, the cool, mountainous playground of the Central Highlands is the place to come; where else can you sit at dusk, huddled in a sweater, and watch the mist descend into the valley as the sun sets behind the mountains? Popular retreats, roaring rivers, soaring peaks and the only white-water rafting in the Caribbean beckon. Down below in the plains of the Valle del Cibao is where merengue spontaneously erupted onto the

DON'T MISS

CARNIVAL IN LA VEGA

La Vega hosts the DR's largest and most organized Carnival celebrations in February. Townspeople belong to one of numerous Carnival groups, which range from 10 to 200 members and have unique names and costumes. The costumes (which can cost up to US$1000) are the best part of Carnival here, featuring colorful baggy outfits, capes and diabolical masks with bulging eyes and pointed teeth.

Groups march on a long loop through town, and spectators watch from bleachers set up alongside or march with them. The latter do so at their own risk – the costumes include a small whip with an inflated rubber bladder at the end, which is used to whack passersby on the backside.

musical landscape, and where you'll find some of the best Carnival celebrations in the country. Economic life in the Central Highlands revolves around Santiago, the DR's second-largest city and the capital of a vast tobacco- and sugarcane-growing region. So of course a visit here requires sipping rum and puffing a local cigar.

Jarabacoa

Nestled in the low foothills of the Cordillera Central, Jarabacoa maintains an under-the-radar allure as the antithesis of the clichéd Caribbean vacation. Nighttime temperatures call for light sweaters, a roiling river winds past forested slopes that climb into the clouds, and local adventurers share stories of their exploits over a beer in the handful of bars near the town's Parque Central. The fact that thousands of well-to-do Dominicans from Santo Domingo and Santiago have built summer homes here is a testament to Jarabacoa's laid-back charm as the 'City of Eternal Spring.'

🏃 Activities & Tours

Jarabacoa is an adventure capital, with popular excursions for canyoning, hiking and white-water rafting.

Rancho Baiguate   TOURS
(☑ 809-574-6890; www.ranchobaiguate.com; Carretera a Constanza) Rancho Baiguate is recommended for safety and reliability. Its main clientele are Dominican groups from the capital and foreign guests from the all-inclusive resorts near Puerto Plata, but independent travelers can join any of the trips, usually by calling a day or two ahead (except for Pico Duarte trips, which should be arranged weeks in advance).

Activities (prices include breakfast and lunch) range from rafting (US$50) to canyoning at **Salto de Baiguate** (US$50 including all gear) to mountain biking (US$25 to US$40); there are also waterfall tours (from US$9 without lunch). Pico Duarte trips range in price depending on the number of people and side trips; a three-day trip for four people with no side trips costs US$365 per person.

Flying Tony   ADVENTURE SPORTS
(☑ 809-854-5880, 809-848-3479; www.flyindr.com; tandem flights US$60, course US$800) Antonio Rosario Aquino is the proprietor of this long-standing paragliding operation and

one of the most experienced pilots on the island. The outfit offers tandem flights and courses to prepare the bold for solo flights. After take-off, paragliding only requires an ability to sit in a comfortable contraption (and endure a 360-degree whirl or two). Remember to bring your camera.

🛏 Sleeping

⭐ **Jarabacoa Mountain Hostel**   HOSTEL $
(☑ 809-574-6117; www.jarabacoahostel.com; s/d/tr/q from US$25/32/42/48; P ✳ 🖻) About 15 minutes' walk from town, this 'hostel' is actually a modern, two-story home, with a state-of-the-art, fully equipped kitchen and a variety of plush rooms, the best of which offer a balcony and a Jacuzzi (including bath salts!). The friendly, knowledgeable owners provide complimentary coffee, laundry machines and bicycles.

Sonido del Yaque   CABIN $
(Cabanas Cazuelas de Dona Esperanza; ☑ 809-727-7413; sonidodelyaque@gmail.com; Los Calabazos; all-incl per person RD$1000) This community-tourism project consists of wood and concrete cabins, each with bunks and a porch, set amid lush jungle above the roaring Río Yaque del Norte. There's electricity, hot showers and mosquito nets. Meals are available with notice. It's not signposted, so, coming from Jarabacoa, look for a tiny shop at the right-hand side of the road.

⭐ **Rancho Baiguate**   RESORT $$
(☑ 809-574-6890; www.ranchobaiguate.com; Carretera a Constanza; all-inclusive s US$65-72, d US$103-135, tr US$158, q US$198; P 🖻 🌊) 🛶 A wonderful base for exploring the mountains, Baiguate is a rustic resort set in an enormous 72-sq-km compound. Ask for a room in the building beside the river that runs through the complex – its large, comfortable, tile-floored rooms have patios with wicker chairs. For fun, there's a pool, beach volleyball, ping pong, zip lining, miniature horses and a trout pond.

Hotel Gran Jimenoa   HOTEL $$
(☑ 809-574-6304; www.granjimenoahotel.com; Av La Confluencia; s/d/tr incl breakfast from RD$2475/3110/3790; P ✳ @ 🖻 🌊) Set several kilometers north of town right by the roaring Río Jimenoa, this is the Cordillera Central's most upscale hotel. It's neither on the beach nor an all-inclusive hotel, but you could easily spend a week here without leaving the extensive grounds, which include a footbridge to a bar on the far riverbank.

CLIMBING PICO DUARTE

Pico Duarte was first climbed in 1944, as part of a celebration commemorating the 100th anniversary of Dominican independence. During the late 1980s, the government began cutting trails in the parks and erecting cabins, hoping to increase tourism to the country by increasing the accessibility of its peaks.

Up to around 2000m the mountain is covered in rainforest, with foliage thick with ferns and some good bird life. Above this elevation it's mostly *pino caribeño* – a mono culture plantation that looks suspiciously like Monterey pine (the stuff loggers like because of its spindly, knot-free branches). Forest fires have left the landscape a bit barren in some spots, and the wildlife consists mostly of bands of crows and a wild boar or two. There's the occasional colorful epiphyte amid the bleakness.

Routes to the Top

There are two popular routes up Pico Duarte. The shortest and easiest (and by far the most used) is from La Ciénaga. It's 23km in each direction and involves 2275m of vertical ascent en route to the peak. It's strongly recommended to do this route in three days: one long slog of a day to arrive at the La Compartición campground (2450m), one easy day to hike up and enjoy the views (and, if you're an early riser, the sunrise), and one long day back out again. The trip can be done in two days by getting up at 4am for a dawn summit, but afterward it's a grueling, hot slog down the mountain. Consider adding a fourth day to do a side trip to the Valle del Tétero, a beautiful valley at the base of the mountain.

The second most popular route is from Mata Grande. It's 45km to the summit and involves approximately 3800m of vertical ascent, including going over Pico La Pelona, a peak only slightly lower than Pico Duarte itself. You'll spend the first night at the Río La Guácara campground and the second at the Valle de Bao campground. You can walk this route in five days (return), but it's far more interesting to walk out via the Valle del Tétero and La Ciénaga (also five days). **Camping Tours** offers the hike from Mata Grande, which tends to begin from the town of San José de las Matas.

It's also possible to reach the peak from Sabaneta, Las Lagunas and Constanza. These routes are little traveled, significantly more difficult, and not offered by any tour companies – you'll need to organize a guide and mules yourself.

Tours & Guides

The easiest way to get to the summit is to take an organized tour. Prices vary widely and depend on how many people are going and for how long. Expect to pay roughly US$100 to US$200 per person per day. It's best to book as far in advance as possible.

➡ **Rancho Baiguate** (p422) is the best overall choice for non-Spanish speakers, as it's based in Jarabacoa and also offers a detour through Valle del Tétero. Its three-day, two-night 'Pico Express' trip is around US$380 per person.

➡ **Iguana Mama** (p419) in Cabarete is good if you want transportation to and from the north coast. It has only four officially listed dates a year but can likely arrange customized group trips, which cost around US$450 per person.

➡ **Camping Tours** (☎ 809-583-3121; www.campingtours.net; Villa Olga, Calle Two 2) in Santiago is the cheapest choice, as it caters primarily to Dominicans, but the guides speak only Spanish. This is your only option if you want to walk Mata Grande to Pico Duarte and exit at La Ciénaga.

Sleeping

There are approximately 14 campgrounds in the parks, each with a first-come, first-served cabin that hikers can use for free. Each cabin can hold at least 20 people and consists of wooden floors, walls and ceiling, but no beds, cots, mats or lockers of any kind, and latrines are outside. If you have a tent, consider bringing it along.

✖ Eating

La Baita ITALIAN $$

(☑ 829-451-0379, 809-365-8778; marco.brand@hotmail.it; Av La Confluencia 74; mains RD$390-650; ☺ 11am-11pm) A newcomer to Jarabacoa's restaurant scene, this little Italian place north of town nails it with homemade pastas, wood-fired pizzas and imported meats and cheeses. The affable owner-chef helps guests select the perfect glass of Italian wine to go with any main dish, be it the mouthwatering linguine with *langostinos* (little lobsters) or a tender slab of Argentine beef.

De Parrillada INTERNATIONAL $$

(☑ 809-574-7656; Dambury Conn 3; steak RD$695; ☺ noon-10pm Mon-Fri, to midnight Sat & Sun) Set back from town on a quiet side street, this rustic and charming establishment is candlelit by evening, and serves up adventurous dishes combining imported meats with local produce and flavors – for example, rosemary pork stuffed with mozzarella and drizzled with homemade passion-fruit sauce. The friendly owner-chef often emerges to socialize with guests.

★ Aroma de la Montana INTERNATIONAL $$$

(☑ 829-452-6879; http://aromadelamontana.com; mains RD$600-1500; ☺ noon-10pm Mon, 10am-10pm Tue-Thu, 9am-11pm Fri-Sun, top fl 1-11pm Sat, 12:30-6pm Sun; ✼ 🛜) Sweeping, practically aerial views of the entirety of the Jarabacoa countryside are available from the balcony seating at this sophisticated mountaintop restaurant. Lunchtime has a family atmosphere, but there's a distinctly romantic candlelit vibe on weekend nights, particularly on the top floor, which rotates 360 degrees at weekends. The menu includes rib-eye steak, chicken, salmon, and a *parrilla* for two.

ℹ Information

Banco Popular (☑ 809-544-5555; Av La Confluencia; ☺ 9am-5pm Mon-Fri, to 1pm Sat) In Plaza La Confluencia.

Cestur (Tourist Police; ☑ 809-754-3072, 809-754-3068; Miguel Castillo) Behind the Caribe Tours terminal.

Clínica Dr Terrero (☑ 829-460-1691; Av Independencia 2A)

ℹ Getting There & Away

BUS

Constanza Públicos (RD$150, 40 minutes, about 9am, 11:30am and 1:30pm) leave from diagonally opposite the Shell petrol station (at the corner of Duverge and Calle El Carmen).

La Ciénaga Públicos (RD$100, 1½ hours, about every two hours) leave from Calle Odulio Jiménez near Calle 16 de Agosto. The road is 42km long, of which the first 33km is mostly paved. (Returning can be a challenge, especially if you're coming back from an afternoon hike. Hail any truck heading towards Jarabacoa; chances are the driver will let you hop aboard.)

La Vega A **guagua terminal** (cnr Av Independencia & José Duran) provides frequent service to La Vega (RD$85, 30 minutes, every 10 to 30 minutes 6am to 6pm).

Santo Domingo The only 1st-class bus service to/from Jarabacoa is offered by **Caribe Tours** (☑ 809-574-4796; Leopoldo Jiménez). It has four daily departures to Santo Domingo (RD$270, 2½ hours, 7am, 10am, 1:30pm and 4:30pm), which stop in La Vega (RD$75, 45 minutes).

CAR

The asphalt road to Constanza has made this scenic drive a breeze as far as your car's shock absorbers are concerned; dozens of switchbacks, however, will test your driving skills. Once you hit El Río, the remaining 19km passes through a lush valley.

TAXI

A cab to La Vega costs around RD$800.

UNDERSTAND THE DOMINICAN REPUBLIC

History

First Arrivals

Before Christopher Columbus arrived, the indigenous Taínos (meaning 'Friendly People') lived on the island now known as Hispaniola. Taínos gave the world sweet potatoes, peanuts, guava, pineapple and tobacco – even the word 'tobacco' is Taíno in origin. Yet the Taínos themselves were wiped out by Spanish diseases and slavery. Of the 400,000 Taínos who lived on Hispaniola at the time of European arrival, fewer than 1000 were still alive 30 years later. None exist today.

Independence & Occupation

Two colonies grew on Hispaniola, one Spanish and the other French. Both brought thousands of African slaves to work the land. In 1804, after a 70-year struggle, the French colony gained independence. Haiti, the Taíno name for the island, was the first majority-black republic in the New World. In 1821 colonists in Santo Domingo declared their independence from Spain. Haiti, which had long aspired to unify the island, promptly invaded its neighbor and occupied it for more than two decades. But Dominicans never accepted Haitian rule and on February 27, 1844, Juan Pablo Duarte – considered the father of the country – led a bloodless coup and reclaimed Dominican autonomy. The country resubmitted to Spanish rule shortly thereafter but became independent for good in 1864. The young country endured one disreputable *caudillo* (military leader) after the other. In 1916 US President Woodrow Wilson sent the marines to the Dominican Republic, ostensibly to quell a coup attempt, but they ended up occupying the country for eight years. Though imperialistic, this occupation succeeded in stabilizing the DR.

The Rise of Caudillo

Rafael Leonidas Trujillo, the then chief of the Dominican national police, maneuvered his way into the presidency in February 1930 and dominated the country until his assassination in 1961. He implemented a brutal system of repression, killing and imprisoning political opponents. Trujillo was also known to be deeply racist and xenophobic. In October 1937, after hearing reports that Haitian peasants were crossing into the DR, perhaps to steal cattle, he ordered the execution of all Haitians along the border and in a matter of days some 20,000 were killed. Trujillo never openly admitted a massacre had taken place, but in 1938, under international pressure, he and Haitian president Sténio Vicente agreed the DR would pay US$750,000 (US$50 per person) as reparation. During these years Trujillo and his wife established monopolies and by 1934 he was the richest man on the island. Many Dominicans remember Trujillo's rule with a certain amount of fondness and nostalgia, in part because he did develop the economy. Factories were opened, a number of grandiose infrastructure and public-works projects were carried out, bridges and highways were built and peasants were given state land to cultivate.

Caudillo Redux

Joaquín Balaguer was president at the time of Trujillo's assassination. Civil unrest and another US occupation followed Trujillo's death, but Balaguer eventually regained the presidency, to which he clung fiercely for the next 12 years. And like his mentor, Balaguer remained a major political force long after he gave up official control. In 1986 he became president again, despite frail health and blindness. Repressive economic policies sent the peso tumbling. Dominicans whose savings had evaporated protested and were met with violence from the national police. Many fled to the US. By the end of 1990, 12% of the Dominican population – 900,000 people – had moved to New York.

After the 1990 and 1994 elections, widely accepted as being rigged by Balaguer, the military had grown weary of Balaguer's rule. He agreed to cut his last term short, hold elections and, most importantly, not run as a candidate. But it wouldn't be his last campaign – he would run once more at the age of 92, winning 23% of the vote in the 2000 presidential election. Thousands would mourn his death two years later, even though he had prolonged the Trujillo-style dictatorship for decades. His most lasting legacy may be the Faro a Colón, an enormously expensive monument to the discovery of the Americas that drained Santo Domingo of electricity whenever the lighthouse was turned on.

Breaking with the Past

The Dominican people signaled their desire for change in electing Leonel Fernández, a 42-year-old lawyer who grew up in New York City, as president in 1996; he edged out three-time candidate José Francisco Peña Gómez in a runoff. Still, the speed of his initial moves shocked the nation. Fernández forcibly retired two dozen generals, encouraged his defense minister to submit to questioning by the civilian attorney general and fired the defense minister for insubordination – all in a single week. In the four years of his first presidential term, he presided over strong economic growth and privatization, and lowered inflation and high rates of unemployment and illiteracy – accusations of endemic corruption, however, remained pervasive.

Hipólito Mejía, a former tobacco farmer, succeeded Fernández in 2000 and immediately cut spending and increased fuel prices, not exactly the platform he ran on. The faltering US economy and September 11 attacks ate into Dominican exports, as well as cash remittances and foreign tourism. Corruption scandals involving the civil service, unchecked spending, electricity shortages and several bank failures, which cost the government in the form of huge bailouts for depositors, all spelled doom for Mejía's re-election chances.

More of the Same

Familiar faces reappear again and again in Dominican politics and Fernández returned to the national stage by handily defeating Mejía in the 2004 presidential elections. In May 2008, with the US and world economies faltering and continued conflict with Haiti, Fernández was re-elected to yet another presidential term. He avoided a run-off despite mounting questions about the logic of spending US$700 million on Santo Domingo's subway system, rising gas prices, the fact that the DR still had one of the highest rates of income inequality in Latin America and the government's less-than-stellar response to the devastation wrought by Tropical Storm Noel in late October 2007.

Though considered competent and by some even forward-thinking, Fernández was also a typical politician beholden to special interests. The more cynical observers long claimed that the Fernández administration was allied with corrupt business and government officials, and they were proven correct long after Fernández left office, when the Odebrecht scandal unraveled in 2016. During Fernandez's term, a Brazilian construction company caught bribing DR officials with US$92 million – which in turn allowed the company to collect US$163 million in profit, according to US Justice Department documents – had nine projects going on in the country.

Dominican Republic Today

The Dominican Republic has enjoyed an economic heyday of late, with tourism booming and free-trade zones flourishing, but stubborn problems have lingered, namely corrupt politicians and trouble with Haiti. Add to that some pretty bad weather and you can bet that average Dominicans, who are no strangers to hardship, approach the present with a healthy dose of skepticism.

In 2015, GDP was growing at 7%, the fastest rate of any country in Latin America, thanks to healthy tourism, construction and mining industries. Inflation was relatively low, and around US$1 billion was coming in via remittances from more than a million Dominicans living abroad. Although sugar, coffee and tobacco had for decades been the country's largest employers, the service sector overtook agriculture both in the number of jobs it provided and the revenue it brought in. In 2016, more than six million tourists are predicted to have visited the DR, which generated more than US$6.5 billion in revenue.

Unfortunately, corruption has remained a problem in the Dominican Republic, at all levels of government and within the private sector. The most recent example of this is the Odebrecht scandal.

Trouble with Haiti also persists, and in September 2013, the Dominican Constitutional Court ruled that 'people born in the Dominican Republic to undocumented parents' weren't automatically afforded citizenship themselves. The decision, which applied to anyone born after 1929, was condemned by many as a racist ruling that targets Dominicans of Haitian descent. In response to this, the government created a 'regularization process' in 2015 that allowed people to apply for residency.

In late 2016, just after Hurricane Matthew swung through and decimated southern Haiti, heavy rains fell for more than two weeks on the DR's north coast, causing widespread damage to the country's agriculture and infrastructure and forcing the president to declare a national emergency.

Culture

History is alive and well in the DR. With a past filled with strong-arm dictators and corrupt politicians, the average Dominican approaches the present with an ironic smile – why should things change now? What is extraordinary to the traveler is that despite this there's a general equanimity, or at the very least an ability to look on the bright side of things. It's not a cliché to say that Dominicans are willing to hope for the best and expect the worst – with a fortitude and patience that isn't common.

In general, it's an accepting and welcoming culture, though Dominicans' negative attitudes toward Haitian immigration has not subsided. 'If the country could just solve the "Haiti problem" things would work out' is not an unusual sentiment to hear. Almost a quarter of Dominicans live in Santo Domingo, which is without question the country's political, economic and social center. But a large percentage of Dominicans still live by agriculture (or by fishing, along the coast).

Dominican families are large and very close-knit. Children are expected to stay close to home and help care for their parents as they grow older. That so many young Dominicans go to the United States creates a unique stress in their families – it's no surprise that Dominicans living abroad send so much money home. The DR is a Catholic country, though not to the degree practiced in other Latin American countries – the churches are well maintained but often empty – and Dominicans have a liberal attitude toward premarital and recreational sex. This does not extend to homosexuality, though, which is still fairly taboo.

Baseball

Not just the USA's game, *beísbol* is an integral part of the Dominican social and cultural landscape. Dominican ballplayers who have made the major league are the most revered figures in the country, and more than 400 have done so, including stars David Ortiz, Albert Pujols, Robinson Canó and Sammy Sosa. In 2015, 83 players on the opening day rosters came from the DR, and pitchers Juan Marichal and Pedro Martinez have both been inducted into the Hall of Fame.

The Dominican professional baseball league's season runs from October to January, and is known as the Liga de Invierno (Winter League; the winner of the DR league competes in the Caribbean World Series against other Latin American countries). The country has six professional teams. Because the US and Dominican seasons don't overlap, many Dominican players in the US major leagues and quite a few non-Dominicans play in the winter league in the DR as well.

Needless to say, the quality of play is high (the DR went undefeated in winning the World Baseball Classic in 2013), but even if you're not a fan of the sport, it's worth checking out a game or two. It's always a fun afternoon or evening. Fans are decked out in their respective team's colors waving pennants and flags, as rabidly partisan as the Yankees–Red Sox rivalry, and dancers in hot pants perform to loud merengue beats on top of the dugouts between innings. Games usually don't start on time and the stands aren't filled until several innings have passed. The best place to take in a game is Estadio Quisqueya (p399) in Santo Domingo. For tickets, head to the stadium with time to spare before the start of play (as early as possible for big games).

From June to August there is also a Liga del Verano (Summer League) if you're in the DR outside of regular season. Various major-league franchises – the San Francisco Giants, the Toronto Blue Jays, the Arizona Diamondbacks and the New York Yankees, to name a few – maintain farm teams in the DR, and summer-league play is a semiformal tournament between these teams. Games are held at smaller stadiums around town.

Music & Dance

Life in the Dominican Republic seems to move to a constant, infectious rhythm, and music has always been an important part of the country's heritage. Despite, or perhaps in part because of, the country's tumultuous history of bitter divisions, revolutions and dictatorial rule, the DR has made significant contributions to the musical world, giving rise to some of Latin music's most popular and influential styles.

Merengue is the national dance music of the Dominican Republic. From the minute you arrive until the minute you leave, merengue will be coming at you full volume: in restaurants, public buses, taxis, at the beach or simply walking down the street. Rhythmically driven and heavy on the downbeat, merengue follows a common 2-4 or 4-4 beat pattern and Domnicans dance to it with passion and flair. But what sets merengue apart from other musical forms is the presence of traditional signature instruments and how they work within the two- or four-beat structure. Merengue is typically played with a two-headed drum called a tambora, a guitar, an accordion-like instrument known as a melodeon, and a güira – a metal instrument that looks a little like a cheese grater and is scraped using a metal or plastic rod.

Whereas merengue might be viewed as an urban sound, *bachata* is definitely the nation's 'country' music, of love and broken hearts in the hinterlands. Born in the poorest of Dominican neighborhoods, *bachata* emerged in the mid-20th century, after Trujillo's death, as a slow, romantic style played on the Spanish guitar. The term initially referred to informal, sometimes rowdy backyard parties in rural areas, finally emerging in Santo Domingo shanties.

The term '*bachata*' was meant as a slight by the urban elite, a reference to the music's supposed lack of sophistication. Often called 'songs of bitterness', *bachata* tunes were no different from most romantic ballad forms, such as the Cuban bolero, but were perceived as low class, and didn't have the same political or social support as merengue. In fact, *bachata* was not even regarded as a style per se until the 1960s – and even then it was not widely known outside the Dominican Republic.

Salsa, like *bachata*, is heard throughout the Caribbean, and is very popular in the DR. Before they called it salsa, many musicians in New York City had already explored the possibilities of blending Cuban rhythms with jazz. In the 1950s, the Latin big-band era found favor with dancers and listeners alike, and in the mid-1960s, Dominican flutist, composer and producer Johnny Pacheco founded the Fania label, which was exclusively dedicated to recording 'tropical Latin' music.

With Cuba cut off from the United States politically as well as culturally, it was no longer appropriate to use the term 'Afro-Cuban'. The word 'salsa' (literally 'sauce') emerged as a clever marketing tool, reflecting not only the music but the entire atmosphere, and was the perfect appellation for a genre of music resulting from a mixture of styles: Cuban-based rhythms played by Puerto Ricans, Dominicans, Africans and African Americans.

Landscape & Wildlife

If wealth were measured by landscape, the DR would be among the richest countries in the Americas. Sharing the island of Hispaniola, the second-largest island in the Caribbean (after Cuba), it's a dynamic country of high mountains, fertile valleys and watered plains, and an amazing diversity of ecosystems.

The island's geography owes more to the Central American mainland than its mostly flat neighboring islands. The one thing that Hispaniola has in spades is an

abundance of mountains. Primary among mountain ranges is the Cordillera Central that runs from Santo Domingo into Haiti, where it becomes the Massif du Nord, fully encompassing a third of the island's landmass. The Cordillera Central is home to Pico Duarte, the Caribbean's highest mountain (at 3087m), which is so big it causes a rain shadow that makes much of southwest DR very arid. Other ranges include the Cordillera Septentrional, rising dramatically from the coast near Cabarete, and the Cordillera Orientale, along the southern shoreline of Bahía de Samaná.

Between the ranges lies a series of lush and fertile valleys. Coffee, rice, bananas and tobacco all thrive here, as well as in the plains around Santo Domingo. In comparison, sections of southwest DR are semi-desert and studded with cacti. The rich landscape is matched by an equally rich biodiversity with more than 5600 species of plants and close to 500 vertebrate species on the island, many of these endemic.

More than 300 species of bird have been recorded in the DR, including more than two dozen found nowhere else in the world. Abundant, colorful species include the white-tailed tropicbird, magnificent frigatebird, roseate spoonbill and greater flamingo, plus unique endemic species such as the Hispaniolan lizard-cuckoo, ashy-faced owl and Hispaniolan emerald hummingbird.

Environmental Issues

The DR has a rapidly growing population and millions of tourists a year, all of whom put severe pressure on the land. Water use, damage to marine ecosystems and, most of all, deforestation present acute environmental challenges. Despite the government's continual efforts in setting aside pristine land, and at times banning commercial logging, parks and reserves remain chronically underfunded, and illegal logging and agricultural encroachment remain a problem, especially in the central highlands. It's estimated that the DR has lost 60% of its forests in the last 80 years.

One of the more puzzling issues concerns the rising and receding waters of Lago Enriquillo. In 2004 the waters began rising, and by 2014, tens of thousands of acres previously occupied by yuca, banana and cattle farms had become eerily submerged, with the government attempting to move an entire town threatened by flooding. The Ministry of the

Environment, to the outrage of many residents and environmentalists, began clearing the Loma Charco Azul Biological Reserve (part of the Jaragua-Barahuco-Enrquillo Biosphere) in 2013 in order to replace lost agricultural acreage. But later that year, the lake began to recede, and it has continued to do so, apparently due to drought. Scientists don't fully understand what's happening with lake, but Isla Cabritos, an island and national park surrounded by the lake, has closed indefinitely to visitors.

Coastal resorts and villages continue to have a tremendous impact on the very seas that provide their livelihood. Pollution, runoff and other consequences of massive developments have destroyed many of the island's foremost reefs. Overfishing and the inadvertent destruction caused by careless humans transform reefs into gray shadows of their former selves.

Vertebrate species particularly endangered on Hispaniola include the West Indian manatee, American crocodile, rhinoceros iguana, Hispaniolan ground iguana and dozens of frog, turtle and bird species.

SURVIVAL GUIDE

ℹ Directory A–Z

BUSINESS HOURS

Opening hours vary throughout the year. We've provided high-season opening hours; hours generally decrease in the shoulder and low seasons.

Banks 9am to 4:30pm Monday to Friday, to 1pm Saturday

Bars 8pm to late, to 2am in Santo Domingo

Government Offices 7:30am to 4pm Monday to Friday, officially; in practice more like 9am to 2:30pm

Restaurants 8am to 10pm Monday to Saturday (some closed between lunch and dinner); to 11pm or later in large cities and tourist areas

Supermarkets 8am to 10pm Monday to Saturday

Shops 9am to 7:30pm Monday to Saturday; some open half-day Sunday

DANGERS & ANNOYANCES

The Dominican Republic is not a particularly dangerous place to visit, but tourists should be aware of the following:

➧ Street crime is rare, but locals advise tourists to avoid talking on or looking at cell phones in public (thieves are known to snatch them).

➧ Don't walk on beaches at night, and consider taking a cab when returning home late from bars.

➧ Car theft is not unheard of, so don't leave valuables inside your car.

➧ Tensions along the Haitian border flare up occasionally: check the situation before crossing.

➧ To prevent cholera, use purified water for drinking, brushing teeth and hand washing.

EMBASSIES & CONSULATES

All of the following are located in Santo Domingo.

Canadian Embassy (☑ 809-262-3100, Av Winston Churchill 1099)

Cuban Embassy (☑ 809-537-2113 Calle Francisco Prats Ramírez 808)

Dutch Embassy (☑ 809-262-0320, Nuñez de Cáceres 11)

French Consulate (☑ 809-695-4300, Calle Las Damas 42)

German Embassy (☑ 809-542-8950, Av Gustavo Mejia Ricart 1986)

Haitian Embassy (☑ 809-686-7115, Calle Juan Sánchez Ramírez 33)

Israeli Embassy (☑ 809-920-1500, Calle Pedro Henriquez Ureña 80)

Italian Consulate (☑ 809-732-6971, Av Lope de Vega)

Japanese Embassy (☑ 809-567-3365, Torre Citigroup Bldg, 21st fl, Av Winston Churchill 1099)

Spanish Embassy (☑ 09-535-6500, Av Independencia 1205)

UK Embassy (☑ 809-472-7111, Av 27 de Febrero 233)

US Embassy (☑ 809-567-7775, Av República de Colombia 57)

FOOD

Some visitors to the Dominican Republic never experience a meal outside of their all-inclusive resort, which can seem like a bargain. For travelers hoping to eat out on their own, food can be surprisingly expensive. Of course, prices tend to be much higher in heavily touristed areas, such as the Zona Colonial in Santo Domingo (comparable to US and European prices), and cheaper in small towns and isolated areas. However, outside of informal food stands and cafeteria-style eateries, a meal without drinks at most restaurants will cost a minimum of RD$325 or US$7 (after the 16% ITBIS tax and 10% service charge have been added on).

Essential Food & Drink

Beer Local brews include Quisqueya, Bohemia, Soberante and the ubiquitous Presidente. The most popular way to enjoy a beer is to share a grande (large) with a friend or two.

EATING PRICE RANGES

The following price ranges refer to the average cost of a main course including tax.

$ Less than RD$230 (US$5)

$$ RD$230–700 (US$5–15)

$$$ More than RD$700 (US$15)

Chivo Goat meat is popular and presented in many ways. Two of the best are pierna de chivo asada con ron y cilantro (roast leg of goat with rum and cilantro) and chivo guisado en salsa de tomate (goat stewed in tomato sauce). It's a specialty of the northwest: the highway between Santiago and Monte Cristi is lined with restaurants serving chivo.

Coco Coconut juice from a cocotero (a street vendor who hacks out an opening with a machete), is available everywhere.

Guineos (bananas) A staple of Dominican cuisine and served in a variety of ways, including boiled, stewed and candied, but most commonly boiled and mashed, like mashed potatoes. Prepared the same way, but with plantains, the dish is called mangú; with pork rinds mixed in it is called mofongo.

Jugo de caña (sugarcane juice) A drink sold from vendors, usually on tricycles with a grinder that mashes the cane to liquid; equally popular are the sticky pieces inside that people chew on.

La Bandera The most typical Dominican meal consists of white rice, habichuela (red beans), stewed meat, salad and fried green plantains. It's good, cheap, easy to prepare and nutritionally balanced. Red beans are sometimes swapped for small moros (black beans), gandules (small green beans) or lentejas (lentils).

Locrio Also known as arroz con pollo (chicken with rice), the dish features caramelized chicken and vegetables atop fluffy flavored rice sometimes colored with achiote.

Ron (Rum) Dominican rum is of a quality that's tough to beat. Dozens of local brands are available, but the big three are Brugal, Barceló and Bermudez. Within these brands, there are many varieties, including blanco (clear), dorado (golden) and añejo (aged), which contains caramel and is aged in special wooden casks to mellow the taste. Bermudez, established in 1852, is the oldest of the distilleries.

Seafood Most commonly a fish fillet, usually mero (grouper) or chillo (red snapper), served in one of four ways: al ajillo (with garlic), al coco (in coconut sauce), al criolla (with a mild tomato sauce) or a la diabla (with a spicy tomato sauce). Other seafood such as cangrejo (crab), calamar (squid), camarones (shrimp), pulp (octopus), langosta (lobster) and lambí (conch) are similarly prepared or al vinagre (in vinegar sauce), a variation on ceviche.

HEALTH

From a medical standpoint, the DR is generally safe as long as you're reasonably careful about what you eat and drink. As always, though, you should purchase travel or health insurance that covers you abroad. Typhoid and hepatitis A and B vaccinations should be considered, along with a prescription for a malaria prophylaxis such as Atovaquone-proguanil, chloroquine, doxycycline or mefloquine.

INTERNET ACCESS

The Dominican Republic has a surprisingly limited number of internet cafes; most charge RD$35 to RD$70 per hour. Many of these cafes also operate as call centers.

Wi-fi access is widespread in cafes and restaurants, as well as at midrange and top-end hotels and resorts throughout the country. Travelers with laptops won't have far to go before finding some place with a signal. However, the majority of the all-inclusives, as opposed to most midrange and even budget hotels, charge daily fees (around US$15 and up) for access. Many hotels that advertise the service free for guests only have a signal in public spaces like the lobby and limited or poor access in guest rooms.

MONEY

The Dominican monetary unit is the peso, indicated by the symbol RD$ (or sometimes just R$). Though the peso is technically divided into 100 centavos (cents), prices are usually rounded to the nearest peso. There are one- and five-peso coins, while paper money comes in denominations of 10, 20, 50, 100, 500, 1000 and 2000 pesos. Many tourist-related businesses, including most midrange and top-end hotels, list prices in US dollars, but also accept pesos at the going exchange rate.

ATMs & Credit Cards

ATMs can be found throughout the DR. Credit and debit cards are widely accepted in cities and tourism-related businesses.

Money changers

Money changers will approach you in a number of tourist centers. They are unlikely to be aggressive. You will get equally favorable rates, however, and a much securer transaction, at an ATM, a bank or an exchange office (cambio).

Tipping

A shock to many first-timers, most restaurants add a whopping 28% (ITBIS of 18% and an automatic 10% service charge) to every bill. Menus don't always indicate whether prices include the tax and tip.

Restaurants Tipping generally not expected since 10% automatically added to total. If especially impressed, you can add whatever else you feel is deserved.

Taxis Typically, you can round up or give a little extra change.

Hotels A 10% service charge is often automatically included; however, a US$1 to US$2 per night gratuity left for cleaning staff is worth considering.

Tours You should also tip tour guides, some of whom earn no other salary.

PUBLIC HOLIDAYS

New Years Day January 1

Epiphany January 6

Lady of Altagracia January 21

Juan Pablo Duarte Day January 26

Independence Day February 27

Good Friday Friday before Easter

Easter Sunday March/April

Labor Day May 1

Corpus Christi June 15

Restoration Day August 16

Our Lady of Mercedes Day September 24

Constitution Day November 6

Christmas Day December 25

TELEPHONE

Remember that you must dial ☑ 1 + 809, 829 or 849 for all calls within the DR, even local ones. Toll-free numbers have ☑ 200 or ☑ 809 for their prefix (not the area code).

The easiest way to make a phone call in the DR is to pay per minute (average rates per minute: to the US US$0.20; to Europe US$0.50; to Haiti US$0.50) at a Codetel Centro de Comunicaciones (Codetel) call center or an internet cafe that operates as a dual call center.

Calling from a hotel is always the most expensive option.

VISAS

The vast majority of tourists entering the Dominican Republic arrive by air. Independent travelers typically arrive at the main international airport outside of Santo Domingo, Aeropuerto Internacional Las Américas. Passing through immigration is a relatively simple process. Once disembarked, you are guided to the immigration area where you must buy a tourist card (US$10). You're expected to pay in US dollars (euros and GBP are accepted, but you lose out substantially on the rate); then join the queue in front of one of the immigration officers. You're allowed up to 30 days on a tourist card. The procedure is the same if you arrive at one of the other airports such as Puerto Plata or Punta Cana; the latter is

ACCOMMODATIONS

Compared to other destinations in the Caribbean, lodging in the Dominican Republic is relatively affordable. That said, there is a limited number of options for independent travelers wishing to make decisions on the fly and for whom cost is a concern.

The following price ranges refer to a double room with bathroom in high season (December to March and July to August). We've listed prices in the currency they are most commonly quoted on the ground – either RD$ or US$. Unless otherwise indicated the room tax of 23% is included in the price. We indicate when breakfast is included, which is often.

$ Less than RD$2335 (US$50)

$$ RD$2335 to RD$4670 (US$50 to US$100)

$$$ More than RD$4670 (US$100)

easily the busiest airport in the country in terms of tourist arrivals.

ℹ️ Getting There & Away

There are a variety of ways to get to and from the Dominican Republic, including flights into international airports, overland crossings, international cruise ships and ferries. Flights, cars and tours can be booked online at lonelyplanet.com/bookings.

AIR

There are nine so-called international airports, though at least three are used only for domestic flights. For information on most, check out www.aerodom.com. Perhaps the cheapest route between North America and the DR is Spirit Airlines' Fort Lauderdale to Santiago (around US$195 round-trip).

Aeropuerto Internacional Arroyo Barril (DAB; ☑ 809-248-2718) West of Samaná, a small airstrip used mostly during whale-watching season (January to March).

Aeropuerto Internacionál del Cibao (☑ 809-233-8000; www.aeropuertocibao.com.do) Santiago's airport is the third-largest in the country, and offers frequent international air service to major destinations. There's a good selection of car-rental agencies at the airport, too.

Aeropuerto Internacional Samaná El Catey (Presidente Juan Bosch) (AZS; Presidente Juan Bosch; ☑ 809-338-0150) Located around

40km west of Samaná; Península de Samaná's main air gateway.

Aeropuerto Internacional de Puerto Plata (Gregorio Luperón) (POP; ☏ 809-291-0000; www.puerto-plata-airport.com) Most convenient airport for north-coast destinations including the beach resorts around Puerto Plata, Sosúa and Cabarete.

Aeropuerto Internacional La Isabela Dr Joaquín Balaguer (p401) This airport is just north of Santo Domingo proper. It handles mostly domestic flights.

Aeropuerto Internacional La Romana (☏ 809-813-9000; www.romanaairport.com; Casa de Campo) Near La Romana and Casa de Campo; handles primarily charter flights from the US, Canada, Italy and Germany; some flights from Miami, NYC and San Juan, Puerto Rico.

Aeropuerto Internacional Las Américas (José Francisco Peña Gómez) (SDQ; José Francisco Peña Gómez; ☏ 809-947-2220) The country's main international airport is located 20km east of Santo Domingo.

Aeropuerto Internacional María Montez (BRX; ☏ 809-524-4144) Located 5km from Barahona in the southwest; charters only.

Aeropuerto Internacional Punta Cana (☏ 809-959-2473; www.puntacanainternationalairport.com; Carretera Higüey-Punta Cana Km 45) Serves Bávaro and Punta Cana, and is the busiest airport in the country.

LAND

These are the four points where you can cross between Haiti and the DR. Note that in recent years, tensions at the borders have sometimes been high due to new policies in the DR that have led to an increase in deportations of Haitians and even Dominicans of Haitian descent.

Jimaní–Malpasse This, the busiest and most organized crossing, is in the south on the road that links Santo Domingo and Port-au-Prince. Disputes here have created strong tension according to a local news source.

Dajabón–Ouanaminthe Busy northern crossing on the road between Santiago and Cap-Haïtien (a six-hour drive); try to avoid crossing on market days (Monday and Friday) because of the enormous crush of people and the risk of theft.

Pedernales–Ainse-a-Pietres In the far south; there's a small bridge for foot and motorcycle traffic; cars have to drive over a paved road through a generally shallow river. Migrant camps are set up on the Haitian side of this border for those who have been deported and have nowhere else to go.

Comendador (aka Elías Piña)–Belladère Certainly the dodgiest crossing, but also the least busy. On the Haiti side, the immigration building is several hundred meters from the actual border. Transportation further into Haiti is difficult to access.

SEA

International cruise ships on Caribbean tours commonly stop in Santo Domingo, Cayo Levantado in the Península de Samaná and at the new Amber Cove port near Puerto Plata.

Caribbean Fantasy, run by **America Cruise Ferries** (☏ San Juan, Puerto Rico 787-622-4800, Santiago 809-583-4440, Santo Domingo 809-688-4400; www.acferries.com), offers a passenger and car ferry service between Santo Domingo and Puerto Rico (San Juan). The trip takes about 12 hours and departs three times weekly.

❶ Getting Around

The DR is a fairly small country, so in theory at least it's easy to drive or take public transportation from one side of the country to the other. In practice, however, the inadequate road network will behoove some with limited time and a sufficient budget to consider flying.

Car Most convenient option if seeking freedom of movement, especially if interested in exploring rural and mountain regions.

Bus Two major companies, Caribe Tours and Metro, provide comfortable, frequent service between a network of major cities and towns.

Guaguas Basically small buses or minivans, ubiquitous, least expensive and least comfortable, however, often the only available public transport.

Air Useful if short on time, though the most expensive option and sometimes unreliable depending on time of year.

Grenada

POP 111,219 / ✆ 473

Best Places to Eat

➡ BB's Crabback (p436)

➡ Coconut Beach (p439)

➡ Andy's Soup House (p438)

➡ Bogles Round House (p449)

Best Places to Sleep

➡ Calabash Hotel (p442)

➡ Almost Paradise (p445)

➡ La Sagesse Manor House (p443)

➡ Mermaid Hotel (p447)

Why Go?

The most southerly islands in the Windward chain, Grenada and Carriacou (plus little Petit Martinique) are best known for their gorgeous beaches: from palm-backed white sand and translucent water to gray-black dunes and rolling breakers. But Grenada's corrugated coastline rises up to mist-swathed rainforest laced with hiking trails and swimmable waterfalls; while St George's, with its market, forts and postcard-perfect Carenage harbor, makes for a picturesque and friendly capital, and is the departure point for ferries to the laid-back sister isles of Carriacou and Petit Martinique. And though cruise ships inject a regular flow of short-stay visitors to Grenada, you'll find all three islands refreshingly quiet and uncrowded.

They're not called the Spice Islands for nothing – you really can smell the nutmeg in the air on Grenada. And it could be called the Fruit Island for the luscious bounty growing in the green hills. Then again, it could be called the Beach Island for the plethora of idyllic sandy strands. We could go on...

When to Go

The steamy tropical climate is tempered by northeast trade winds, and in January the average daily high temperature is 84°F (29°C) and the average low is 75°F (24°C), rising to a high of 86°F (30°C) and a low of 77°F (25°C) in July.

Jun–Nov Rainy season, an average 22 days of rainfall per month in St George's.

Jan–Apr The driest months, this is the best time to visit if you like to party, the raucous August Carnival is also a brilliant time to be in Grenada.

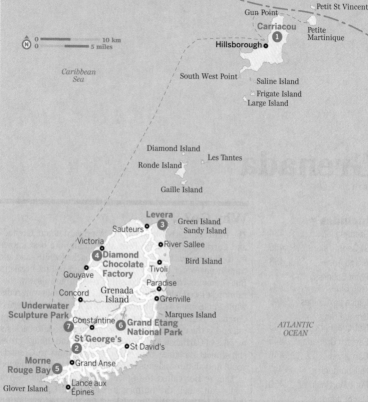

Grenada Highlights

① **Carriacou** (p446)
Enjoying peace, quiet and beautiful beaches on this friendly island.

② **St George's** (p435)
Exploring one of the Caribbean's prettiest capitals and taking in the panoramic views from its imposing forts.

③ **Levera** (p446)
Reveling in the isolation of the ultimate deserted beach with only sea turtles for company.

④ **Diamond Chocolate Factory** (p444) Following the chocolate process from bean to bar at this locally owned cooperative.

⑤ **Morne Rouge Bay** (p440) Sinking your toes into the soft white sand and super-blue water.

⑥ **Grand Etang National Park** (p443) Hiking the trails and checking out the volcanic lake surrounded by rainforest.

⑦ **Underwater Sculpture Park** (p435) Swimming among unforgettably surreal coral-encrusted sculptures in shallow waters a short boat ride from the capital.

GRENADA ISLAND

The island of Grenada is an almond-shaped, beach-rimmed gem of a place with 75 miles of coastline surrounding a lush interior, which is filled with tropical rainforest.

ⓘ Getting There & Away

The island of Grenada is the main entrance point to the country, with the vast majority of visitors arriving through the international airport at Point Salines. International cruise ships also dock on the island at a purpose-built facility right in the St George's city center.

Local boat services connect St George's with Carriacou and Petit Martinique.

St George's

St George's is one of the most picturesque towns in the Caribbean. It's a fabulous place to explore on foot, from handsome old buildings to the Carenage harbor. Interesting shops and cafes dot the narrow and busy streets.

⊙ Sights

★**Underwater Sculpture Park**　DIVE SITE
(Molinière Bay) An underwater gallery beneath the surface of the sea, just north of St George's in Molinière Bay. The project was founded by British artist Jason de Caires Taylor and there are now around 80 works in varying condition all slowly becoming encrusted with coral growth. The life-size sculptures include a circle of women clasping hands and a man at a desk. Fish and sponges have also colonized the area, making the site a fascinating mix of culture with nature.

The park is accessible to both snorkelers and divers, and all the dive shops on the island organize visits.

Fort George　FORT
(Church St; EC$5; ☉7am-5pm) Grenada's oldest fort was established by the French in 1705 and it's the centerpiece of the St George's skyline. You can climb to the top to see the cannons and bird's-eye views. Just outside the main fort area is a series of dark defensive tunnels to explore.

A plaque in the parade ground marks the spot where revolutionary leader Maurice Bishop was executed, which set in motion events that led to the US invasion in 1983.

Grenada National Museum　MUSEUM
(☑440-3725; cnr Young & Monckton Sts; adult/child EC$5/2.50; ☉9am-4:30pm Mon-Fri, 10am-1:30pm Sat) Staffed by enthusiastic members, this museum has displays that are a little haphazard. It is mostly dedicated to the original indigenous inhabitants of the island, the colonial period and slavery – there's precious little about Maurice Bishop's revolution. That said, with a history as colorful as that of Grenada, there's plenty here and it can easily absorb an hour. On some Friday evenings there are drumming performances and folk dancing.

St George's Anglican Church　CHURCH
(Church St) Erected in 1825, St George's is topped by a squat four-sided clock tower that serves as the town's timepiece, and which didn't cease to work when the building was heavily damaged in the 2004 hurricane. Repairs to the structure are almost complete, with the church boasting a wonderfully crafted new wooden ceiling and gallery.

St George's Market Square　MARKET
(Halifax St; ☉8am-3pm Mon-Sat) Busiest on Friday and Saturday mornings, this is the largest market in Grenada, with stalls heaped with fresh island produce. It's a colorful sight that is worth checking out even if you're not buying.

Cathedral of the Immaculate Conception　CHURCH
(Church St) Sitting pretty at the top of the capital's hill, St George's Roman Catholic cathedral provides a great vantage point over the town. Though Hurricane Ivan all but gutted the structure in 2004, it's since been painstakingly restored.

Carenage　HARBOR
A scenic inlet, the Carenage is a great place for a stroll along the water's edge, taking in the colorful fishing boats and the bustle of supplies being loaded for other islands. At the north end, some of the sturdy Georgian buildings overlooking the water have been restored.

★**Fort Frederick**　FORT
(Richmond Heights; EC$5; ☉8am-5pm) Constructed by the French in 1779, Fort Frederick was soon used – paradoxically – by the British in defense against the French, although it never fired a cannon in anger. It's the island's best-preserved fort, and offers striking panoramic views. If you're lucky, the gate to the tunnels will be open – bring a torch as there is no lighting down there. The fort is atop Richmond Hill, 1¼ miles east of St George's on the road to St Paul's.

🏃 Activities

★**Savvy Sailing**　SNORKELING, SAILING
(Port Louis Marina; tours US$45-100) Offers snorkeling trips on a traditional wooden sailboat made on Petit Martinique – a tranquil and atmospheric way to see Grenada's offshore wonders. Also has sunset cruises and two-day sailing trips to the Grenadines.

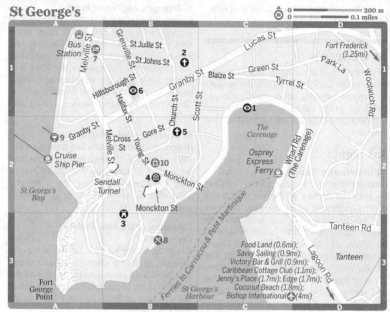

St George's

Sleeping

Deyna's City Inn
GUESTHOUSE $$

(☏ 435-7007; cityinn@spiceisle.com; Melville St; s/d US$84/90; ❄ @) Right in the town center, this brilliant little place has a range of well-equipped rooms (some a little small) with cable TV and bright, modern decor. Friendly staff, great local food from the restaurant downstairs, and a very convenient location for city sightseeing and transport around the island complete the offer. There are lots of stairs, however, and no lifts.

Eating & Drinking

During the day you'll find plenty of good cheap eats in the downtown area. For a nice sit-down meal, check out the restaurants at the Carenage.

Deyna's Tasty Foods
CARIBBEAN $

(Melville St; mains from EC$18; ⊙ 8am-9pm) The perfect place to sample Grenadian food, with daily breakfasts of salt fish and bakes or local-style porridge. Lunchtime sees scrummy rotis and the likes of curried *lambi* (conch), Creole fish or baked chicken served with callaloo, macaroni pie, salad and rice.

House of Chocolate
CAFE $

(☏ 440-2310; www.houseofchocolategnd.com; Young St; items EC$3-10, drinks EC$8-16; ⊙ 10am-6pm Mon-Sat, to 2pm Sun) Part cafe, part museum, part gift shop, this welcoming place is dedicated to all things cocoa. You can sample chocolate in both its liquid and solid forms, and buy bars from different local producers to take home. There are also delicious cakes and brownies.

Foodland
SUPERMARKET $

(Lagoon Rd; ⊙ 7:30am-8pm Mon-Thu, to 10pm Fri & Sat) A well-stocked and well-maintained grocery store; has an ample selection of local favorites and imported goodies.

★ BB's Crabback
CARIBBEAN $$

(☏ 435-7058; www.bbscrabback.co.uk; The Carenage; mains EC$58-79; ⊙ 9am-10pm Mon-Sat) The namesake waterfront restaurant of celebrity chef and local bon vivant Brian Benjamin is on the water at the end of the Carenage. Local faves like callaloo soup (a rich stew) and fresh seafood are popular, as is the signature goat curry. Fussier appetites can order pancakes and everyone loves the chocolate dessert.

St George's

Victory Bar & Grill   INTERNATIONAL $$
(☑435-7263; Port Louis Marina; mains EC$36-97, light meals EC$29-39; ☺7am-11pm; 🖭) Located in the upmarket Port Louis marina, with tables overlooking boats and the occasional megayacht. It's busy with happy yachties eating fresh salads, burgers and seafood brochettes. The atmosphere is fun, and the food is great.

Native Food and Fruits   SMOOTHIES
(Granby Street; juices EC$9-11.50; ☺9am-6pm Mon-Sat) On one side of the market plaza, this great local smoothie bar knocks out refreshing fruit-based beverages, as well as more filling shakes, that are full of flavor. Try the sea moss or order the oats, peanut and Guinness version and you'll happily skip a meal.

🔒 Shopping

One of the best reasons to wander the atmospheric streets is to discover little shops selling artful goods, unlike those near the cruise-ship docks.

Art Fabrik   ARTS & CRAFTS
(☑440-0568; Young St; ☺9am-5pm Mon-Fri, to 1pm Sat) A small shop filled with beautiful batik creations made right on Grenada. Ask to see the dyeing process. Also has a small gallery out back featuring paintings by a number of local artists.

Craft market   GIFTS & SOUVENIRS
(☺8am-6pm) Next to the market square, this craft market sells a broad collection of souvenirs including, of course, everything connected to spices.

ℹ️ Information

There are free wireless hot spots in the center of the Esplanade mall.

Astral Travel (☑440-5127; The Carenage; ☺8am-5pm Mon-Fri, to noon Sat) Astral's a switched-on travel agency with info on and affiliation to all the relevant airlines and travel services.

Grenada Tourist Board (☑440-2279; www. grenadagrenadines.com; ☺8am-4pm Mon-Fri) At the southern end of the Carenage.

Main Post Office (☑440-2526; Lagoon Rd; ☺8am-4pm Mon-Fri)

Republic Bank (Melville St; ☺8am-2pm Mon-Thu, to 4pm Fri) Reliable ATM

Scotiabank (☑440-3274; cnr Halifax & Granby Sts; ☺8am-3pm Mon-Thu, to 5pm Fri) Has a 24-hour ATM.

ℹ️ Getting There & Around

St George's is best explored on foot – lose the rental ASAP as streets in the center are narrow and congested and driving is a huge headache.

Buses depart from St George's **central terminal** (Melville St) to destinations all over the island.

A taxi to Grand Anse costs about EC$45.

BOAT

Osprey Express Ferry (☑440-8126; www. ospreylines.com) Boats to Carriacou depart from the Carenage in front of the tourism office. You can buy tickets on board, but when it's busy consider buying in advance from the office across the water in the Huggins building.

CAR & MOTORCYCLE

Grenada Island has numerous car-rental agencies. Most offer jeeps/SUVs (from around US$65/US$80 per day), and some have regular cars (from US$55).

Archie Auto Rentals (☑444-2535; www. archierentalsgrenada.com) Local rental company based in Lance aux Épines.

Indigo Car Rentals (☑439-3300; www.indigo carsgrenada.com)

Nedd's Rentals (☑440-5599; www.neddsrent. net) A small laid-back rental company offering good deals.

Sanvics 4x4 (☑444-4753; www.sanvics.com) Large rental company with a good range of vehicles.

Grand Anse

Running alongside the famous beach of the same name, Grand Anse is more a collection of hotels, restaurants and services than a real town. The beach here is one of the island's best and is justifiably popular.

To escape crowds, look for the small access road that spurs off the Grand Anse Rd toward the southern reaches of the bay; it leads to a small parking area and uncrowded sands.

◉ Sights & Activities

Grand Anse   BEACH
Grenada's main resort area is a lovely long sweep of white sand fronted by turquoise water and backed by hills. It has the highest concentration of big hotels, bars, eateries and water sports on the island but its essence has not been totally lost to development. Unlike some beaches in the Caribbean, it gets a good mix of visitors and locals, who come here to swim, exercise and play sports. It remains the essential Grenadian experience for many.

Camerhogne Park   PARK
(Grand Anse) A meticulously maintained green space running from the Spiceland Mall down to the white sands of Grand Anse. If you're visiting for the day, it's a good place to base yourself – here you'll find change rooms (EC$1), loungers for rent, plenty of shade, snack bars and even free public wi-fi.

Dive Grenada   DIVING
(⌨ 444-1092; www.divegrenada.com; Mount Cinnamon Resort; 1/2 tank dives incl rental US$85/155; ⊘ 8am-4pm) A highly rated and professionally run dive shop based in the Grand Anse area.

Aquanauts Grenada   DIVING
(⌨ 444-1126; www.aquanautsgrenada.com; Grand Anse; 1/2 tank dives incl rental US$90/150; ⊘ 8am-5pm) Runs diving and snorkeling trips around the island. Check out the scheduled dives on their website. Free nitrox for certified divers.

⊨ Sleeping

With the highest concentration of accommodations on the island, Grand Anse has everything from big resorts right on the sand to budget cottages up on the hillside.

Caribbean Cottage Club   HOTEL $
(Greystone Rd; cottages from US$60; ✲) Located on a breezy hillside just off the road between Grand Anse and the marina, this chilled little place has a handful of comfortable wooden cottages with small kitchens and panoramic sea views. There's air-con in the bedrooms and the staff is extremely helpful.

Jenny's Place   GUESTHOUSE $$
(⌨ 439-5186; www.jennysplacegrenada.com; ste US$95-165; ✲ 🛜) Set in gardens just off the beach, Jenny's Place has just four suites and two apartments. All are brightly decorated and comfortable, and the suites are very spacious, with full kitchen or kitchenette and patio. The staff is friendly, there's a good restaurant and it's a great alternative to the more anonymous large hotels.

Coyaba Beach Resort   RESORT $$$
(⌨ 444-4129; www.coyaba.com; Grand Anse Beach; r US$420; ✲ @ 🛜 ✲) Set upon a great stretch of beach, the 80 rooms here exude relaxed luxury. The beachfront grounds are beautifully landscaped and there's also a spa.

Radisson Grenada Beach Resort   HOTEL $$$
(⌨ 444-4371; www.radisson.com; r US$318-471; ✲ @ ✲) 🌿 Don't let the big exterior put you off; this enormous complex has a fairly intimate feel. The rooms are nothing special, but the facilities are impressive – the river-like pool is a hit with little ones. The staff is friendly and there seems to be every amenity you'd need on-site.

✕ Eating

★ **Andy's Soup House**   CARIBBEAN $
(⌨ 406-1600; Grand Anse Valley Rd, Woodlands; soups EC$12-15; ⊘ 7am-10pm) This humble roadside diner is our favorite place on the whole island for fantastic local eats. They serve a variety of traditional dishes and snacks including great rotis, but the main reason to come here is for the 'waters' (soups). There are usually at least five different varieties on offer; pick any, they're all delicious.

If you're feeling adventurous go for the 'mannish water,' a goat soup that is said to be a powerful aphrodisiac. They also prepare vegetarian dishes and great juices made from local fruits.

Jam Down   JAMAICAN $
(Grand Anse Valley Rd, Mount Tout; chicken EC$10-15; ⊘ 5-9pm Mon-Sat) It's worth making the trip slightly off the beaten path to this

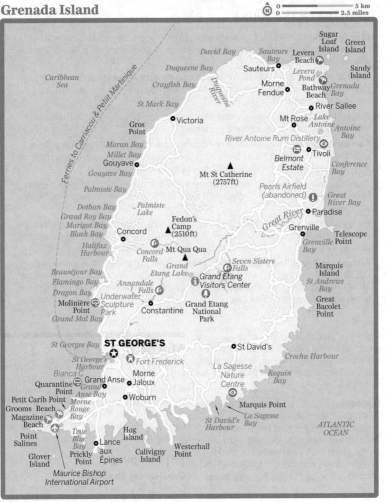

0   5 km
0   2.5 miles

Sugar Loaf Island
Green Island
Sandy Island
Grenada Bay
David Bay
Sauteurs Bay
Levera Beach
Sauteurs
Levera Pond
Duquesne Bay
Morne Fendue
Bathway Beach
Crayfish Bay
River Sallee
St Mark Bay
Mt Rose
Lake Antoine
Victoria
Antoine Bay
Gros Point
River Antoine Rum Distillery
Tivoli
Maran Bay
Millet Bay
Gouyave
Belmont Estate
Conference Bay
Gouyave Bay
Mt St Catherine (2757ft)
Palmiste Bay
Pearls Airfield (abandoned)
Great River Bay
Palmiste Lake
Dothan Bay
Grand Roy Bay
Marigot Bay
Black Bay
Fedon's Camp (2510ft)
Paradise
Concord
Grenville
Telescope Point
Halifax Harbour
Concord Falls
Mt Qua Qua
Grenville Bay
Beauséjour Bay
Flamingo Bay
Dragon Bay
Grand Etang Lake
Seven Sisters Falls
Marquis Island
Annandale Falls
Grand Etang Visitors Center
St Andrews Bay
Molinière Point
Underwater Sculpture Park
Constantine
Grand Etang National Park
Great Bacolet Point
Grand Mal Bay
St Georges Bay
ST GEORGE'S
St David's
Crochu Harbour
St George's Harbour
Fort Frederick
Bianca C
Grand Anse
Morne Jaloux
La Sagesse Nature Centre
Requin Bay
Quarantine Point
Grand Anse Bay
Woburn
Petit Carib Point
Grooms Beach
Morne Rouge Bay
Marquis Point
La Sagesse Bay
Magazine Beach
St David's Harbour
ATLANTIC OCEAN
Point Salines
True Blue Bay
Hog Island
Glover Island
Lance aux Épines
Prickly Point
Calivigny Island
Westerhall Point
Maurice Bishop International Airport

Caribbean Sea

Ferries to Carriacou & Petit Martinique

Duquesne River

Great River

humble roadside wooden shack. It sells just one thing – outrageously tasty jerk chicken cooked the original Jamaican way. Come early, as they sell out fast. It's about half a mile up the hill from the intersection. You'll know you're getting close when you see the smoke and smell jerk seasonings thick in the air.

Real Value   SUPERMARKET **$**
(Spiceland Mall; ⊙8am-9pm Mon-Thu, 8am-10pm Fri & Sat, 10am-7pm Sun) The biggest grocery store on the island; has everything you'd ever need to self-cater.

★**Coconut Beach**   SEAFOOD **$$**
(🖉444-4644; Grand Anse Beach; mains EC$48-95; ⊙noon-10pm Wed-Mon) French- and Creole-accented seafood is served up inside this old beachfront house, or at tables right on the sand. Famous for its lobster, this family-run restaurant puts just the right amount of nutmeg in the rum punch. Try outstanding *lambi* in a subtle creamy ginger sauce.

Carib Sushi   JAPANESE **$$**
(🖉439-5640; Le Marquis Centre; mains EC$38-82; ⊙11:30am-2pm Mon-Sat, 6-9pm daily) Local seafood is rolled into the mix at this casual

GRENADA ISLAND TOURS

Mandoo Tours (☑ 440-1428; www.grenadatours.com) Offers full- and half-day tours of the island, which can be tailored for historical or photographic interests. Quality vehicles with air-conditioning.

Grenada Seafaris (☑ 405-7800; www.grenadaseafaris.com) Powerboat coastal tours, with stops for snorkeling – including the Underwater Sculpture Park – and informed commentary on local fauna and flora.

Sunsation (☑ 444-1594; www.grenadasunsation.com) One of the larger companies, with well-organized island tours, hiking and sailing.

Conservation Kayak (☑ 449-5248; www.conservationkayak.com; Whisper Marina; tours US$70-145) Offers guided nature tours by kayak through bays and coves on the south side of the island. Beginners are welcome – instruction is included.

Tropical Adventures (www.tagrenada.com) A new tour company specializing in nature hikes and birdwatching in the interior of the island. It's already very popular – book in advance.

Henry's Safari Tours (☑ 444-5313; www.henrysafari.com) Various treks into the interior are offered by this company, which specializes in hiking tours. Lunch and drinks are included. Try the five-hour tour that includes a hike to the Seven Sisters Falls (p443).

Adventure Tours Grenada (☑ 444-5337; www.adventuregrenada.com; rental per day US$20, tours per hour US$15) A reputable operator that runs jeep tours around the island as well as river-tubing adventures. Also rents out mountain bikes (delivered to your hotel) and offers guided bike tours.

sushi bar. Mix and mingle on the outdoor picnic tables (or cool off inside) before diving into top-quality tempura, sushi, sashimi and noodles. Or cool off with their green-tea ice cream.

Umbrellas   AMERICAN $$
(☑ 439-9149; Grand Anse Beach; mains EC$25-75; ☺ 11am-10pm; ⛵) A stylish two-floor wooden building just back from the sand, with tables on the upper deck and inside. It's good for a frosty cocktail, cold beer or tasty meal. Salads counterbalance the long burger menu.

Edge   CARIBBEAN $$
(☑ 535-3343; Jenny's Place; lunch EC$22-28, dinner mains EC$40-85; ☺ 8am-10pm Tue-Sat, 11am-6pm Sun) Located on the northern reaches of Grand Anse, this welcoming waterside restaurant serves up good Caribbean plates as well as burgers, lasagna and salads. It's also a nice spot for breakfast.

❶ Getting There & Away

Bus The St George's–Grand Anse corridor is the busiest on the island with buses passing every couple of minutes.

Taxi Easy to find anywhere on the Grand Anse main road.

Morne Rouge Bay

Though just down the way from Grand Anse Beach, development on this excellent stretch of beach has been modest so it's uncrowded. It's a brilliant example of the snow-white sand and crystal-clear blue water that the Caribbean is known for. It has shade but limited services.

🛏 Sleeping

Gem Holiday Beach Resort   HOTEL $$
(☑ 444-4224; www.gembeachreort.com; s/d from US$103/126, s/d with sea view US$144/155; ❂❄@❅) Just up from the beach, this place is a real gem. The rooms are nothing too fancy, and perhaps a bit dated, but have all the basics you'd need including a small kitchen. Tidy, friendly and a great budget option on one of the best beaches on the island.

Kalinago   HOTEL $$
(☑ 444-5254; www.kalinagobeachresort.com; s/d US$175/182; ❂❄❅❊) This cheerful resort has spacious rooms with nice wooden furnishings overlooking the water (and just above the beach). There's also a pleasant oceanside pool with a swim-up bar and a restaurant on-site.

★ La Luna
HOTEL $$$

(☎ 439-0001; www.laluna.com; cottages US$545-825; @ 🛜 ☀) One of the Caribbean's best resorts. There's a simple elegance to these 16 Balinese-inspired cottages, with private plunge pools and open-air bathrooms. It's at a secluded end of spectacular Morne Rouge Bay beach.

✕ Eating

Sangria
MEDITERRANEAN $$

(☎ 439-7491; mains EC$50-70; ⊙ noon-midnight) Perched high up at the north end of the bay, this open-air restaurant has superlative views from its large deck and an interesting menu of Mediterranean-influenced dishes. Even if you don't eat here, it's worth coming for an evening drink.

❶ Getting There & Away

To reach Morne Rouge, head to the western end of Grand Anse and follow the road up and over the hill.

Point Salines & True Blue

The filigreed coastline around Point Salines is dominated by Maurice Bishop International Airport. It's notable for the string of lovely beaches to the north of the runway, just off the airport road.

South of the airport, True Blue is a relaxed corner of the island with some nice top-end hotels, good eateries and multiple yacht marinas.

Crowning the peninsula enclosing True Blue Bay, St George's Medical School (SGU) is a sprawling campus inhabited almost exclusively by young Americans seeking offshore medical degrees (notoriously, President Ronald Reagan said he was defending these students when he ordered the American invasion in 1983).

◉ Sights

★ Grooms Beach
BEACH

(Parc a Beouf) A lovely secluded bay with a swath of powdery white sand and warm blue waters that are good for snorkeling. It's close to the popular Beach House restaurant, north of the airport.

Magazine Beach
BEACH

The final port of call for travelers getting a last-minute dose of sea and sand before hopping on a plane, Magazine Beach has been nicknamed by locals 'the Caribbean's prettiest departure lounge.' Its white sands and invigorating waters are bordered by a picturesque tumble of boulders at its southern end. It boasts fine snorkeling right from the shore.

🏃 Activities

Aquanauts Grenada
DIVING

(☎ 444-1126; www.aquanautsgrenada.com; True Blue Bay Resort) The dive-shop juggernaut on the island. It has it all, from the boats to the gear to an army of staff. Expect to pay around US$90 for a one-tank dive including gear rental and US$150 for two tanks. Open-water courses cost US$550. There's also a branch (p438) at the Spice Island Resort on Grand Anse.

Mocha Spoke
CYCLING

(☎ 533-2470; www.mochaspoke.com; True Blue Dr; tours EC$150) A hip cafe just outside the university that rents out bicycles and runs guided cycling tours around the island.

🛏 Sleeping

★ Maca Bana
HOTEL $$$

(☎ 439-5355; www.macabana.com; Point Salines; villas US$660-1020; ❄ @ 🛜 ☀) 🖉 Maca Bana has gorgeous villas spreading down a hillside, with fabulous views down the coast to St George's and every possible detail attended to, from smartphone docks and flat-screen TVs to espresso machines and spacious wooden decks with private hot tubs. Solar panels provide all the power and everything is done with sustainability in mind.

True Blue Bay Resort & Marina
HOTEL $$$

(☎ 443-8783; www.truebluebay.com; True Blue; r US$330-443; ❄ @ 🛜 ☀) Built at the edge of a yacht-filled bay, this family-owned resort is an island favorite, with multicolored huts that pop off the green grass like a carpet of children's jellybeans lining the hill. All accommodations are elegantly furnished and feature touches of art throughout. Apartments have full kitchens; the luxurious tower rooms have great 360-degree views.

✕ Eating & Drinking

The area just outside the SGU campus gates is awash with food vans serving up comfort food to homesick Americans – think wings, gyros and tacos. You can also get good gringo-style coffees here.

Dodgy Dock
INTERNATIONAL $$

(☑443-8783; True Blue Bay Resort; mains EC$26-45; ☉7am-10pm) An inviting waterside bar/restaurant on an open-air deck, this place is good for a bite to eat or drink at any time and gets lively in the evenings. The menu has a bit of everything but it's dominated by Caribbean and Mexican flavors. There's live music on Tuesday, Friday and Saturday.

★Beach House
FUSION $$$

(☑444-4455; www.beachhousegrenada.com; Portici Bay; mains EC$68-140; ☉11am-2pm & 6-10pm Mon-Sat) Beautifully set right on the beach, just north of the airport, this casually elegant bistro serves a changing menu of salads, sandwiches and complex dinner mains that reflects the island's bounty. Book in advance and ask about the shuttle service. During low season, it's only open for dinner.

Aquarium
RESTAURANT $$$

(☑444-1410; www.aquarium-grenada.com; Point Salines; lunch EC$39-105, dinner EC$55-118; ☉10am-10pm Tue-Sun; 🅿🍴) Built right on the sands of Magazine Beach beneath some massive boulders, this ever-popular place has burgers and salads among the many options for lunch, plus some more sophisticated choices at dinner, with plenty of seafood and a wealth of choices for meat lovers. The Sunday barbecue with live music is always oversubscribed – book ahead.

❶ Getting There & Away

Bus The St George's–Grand Anse bus runs to Calliste, near the airport, which is a 10- to 15-minute walk from the attractions of Point Saline to the north and True Blue to the south.

Taxi From Grand Anse to Point Salines or True Blue cost around EC$40.

Lance aux Épines

Lance aux Épines (*lance*-a-peen) is a peninsula that forms the southernmost point of Grenada. It's home to a pretty beach and a marina.

If you're arriving on your own boat, head for the customs and immigration office (p456) at the Prickly Bay marina.

Lance aux Épines is a 10-minute taxi ride from Grand Anse.

🏃 Activities

ScubaTech
DIVING

(☑439-4346; www.scubatech-grenada.com; Calabash Hotel; 1/2 tank dives US$110/150) A small and well-run outfit offering the full gamut of snorkeling and diving trips.

🛏 Sleeping

Coral Cove Cottages
HOTEL $$

(☑444-4422; www.coralcovecottages.com; 1-/2-bedroom cottages US$150/230; ❄@🛜❄) On a breezy hillside that rolls down to coral-filled waters at the end of the Lance aux Épines peninsula, these excellent-value cottages offer privacy, tranquility and nature. The cottages themselves are nothing fancy but are clean, functional and offer fantastic views.

★Calabash Hotel
HOTEL $$$

(☑444-4334; www.calabashhotel.com; r incl breakfast US$850-1650; ❄@🛜❄) Easily the area's nicest place to bed down for the night. The beautifully manicured grounds sit hand in hand with a standard of service that is second to none. Lovely touches include having breakfast delivered to your room, and the sweeping lawns and swaying palms on the beach make the setting ripe for relaxation.

Rates include breakfast and afternoon tea, kayaking, snorkeling and sailing.

Lance aux Épines Cottages
HOTEL $$$

(☑444-4565; www.laecottages.com; r US$205-300; ❄@🛜) Beautiful beach views are enjoyed here by 11 attractive rooms, which come complete with kitchens and large living areas. It's a peaceful and friendly place that is well set up for families. Extras abound including free kayaks.

🍴 Eating & Drinking

Prickly Bay Marina Pizzeria
PIZZA $$

(☑439-5265; pizzas EC$35-45; ☉noon-11pm) Pizzas that are renowned as the best in Grenada are baked, sliced and munched dockside. Picnic tables, a pool table and a cozy seaside bar all add up to a very chilled mix of food and fun. There's live music on Fridays – a steel-pan ensemble followed by the house band or a DJ – and a daily happy hour (5pm to 6pm).

West Indies Beer Company
CRAFT BEER

(☑232-2337; www.westindiesbeer.com; Lance aux Épines Main Rd; ☉1pm-1am Mon-Thu, to 2am Fri-Sat, 4pm-1am Sun) At last! Good craft beer has finally arrived in the Windward Islands.

This neat local brewery started out as the house brewery at the True Blue Bay Resort and has now expanded into smart new premises. It produces a good variety of real ales and ciders.

La Sagesse Bay

La Sagesse Bay is a lovely palm-lined crescent with protected swimming, backed by a wall of jungle hiding saltwater ponds that are home to egrets and herons. It has a secluded vibe and feels a world away from the more developed coves on the west of the island.

◉ Sights

La Sagesse Nature Centre　　NATURE RESERVE
(☑ 444-6458; packages incl lunch & transport US$55; ⊙ 8am-5pm) The former estate of the late Lord Brownlow, cousin to Queen Elizabeth II, this nature center occupies the entire length of La Sagesse Bay. Unfortunately, the trails through the property are in poor condition and hikes are no longer available. Packages are available including transfers to and from your hotel, a meal and access to the beach facilities.

The on-site restaurant (mains EC$40 to EC$62) serves good Caribbean meals in a lovely waterside setting.

◉ Sleeping

La Sagesse Manor House　　INN $$$
(☑ 444-6458; www.lasagesse.com; r US$185-210; ☏) At La Sagesse Nature Centre, Lord Brownlow's beachside former manor house, built in 1968, has been turned into a small inn. The stylish rooms in the new block are simple and alluring, with screened windows, while those in the old manor house and the more secluded cottage have ocean views and verandas.

❶ Getting There & Away

La Sagesse is about a 25-minute drive from St George's on the Eastern Main Rd. The entrance is opposite an old abandoned rum distillery. Buses bound for the province of St David can also drop you here (EC$5).

Grand Etang National Park

Two and a half miles northeast of Constantine, after the road winds steeply up to an

GRAND ETANG ROAD

Overhung with rainforest and snaking uphill in a series of switchback turns, the Grand Etang Rd shoots right up the island's spine. The mountainous center of the island is often awash with misty clouds, and looks like a lost primordial world, its tangle of rainforest brimming with life – including monkeys that often get a bit too friendly.

Grenada's verdant splendor is on full display here; look for cassava, nutmeg, star fruit, cinnamon, clove, hibiscus, passion fruit, pineapple, avocado, mango, banana, coconut and much more.

Annandale Falls (EC$5; ⊙ 8am-4pm) is an idyllic waterfall with a 30ft drop, Annandale Falls is surrounded by a grotto of lush vegetation and has a large pool where you can take a refreshing swim. It's a two-minute walk from the visitor center. It gets crowded when cruise ships are in port.

elevation of 1900ft, you enter Grand Etang National Park, a natural wonderland centered around a lovely lake. At the visitor center you can pay your admission, learn a little about the park and get a refreshment.

Within the park you'll find four of Grenada's tallest peaks, the highest of which, bizarrely enough, is the only one without a name.

St George's–Grenville buses will drop you at the park entrance.

🏃 Activities

There are many hiking trails within the park, varying in duration and difficulty. Some are well maintained while others are overgrown and require the use of a guide. Most trails begin at or close to the visitor center (p444) and the helpful staff can arrange guides.

Hiking trails in the park include:

➡ **Concord Falls** For serious adventurers only, this hike involves branching off towards the end of the Mt Qua Qua trek and continuing on to the Concord Falls. It is a five-hour trip one way and the trail is overgrown and even nonexistent in some parts – check on conditions before heading out. It's imperative to take a guide. From the falls it's another 1.5 miles on to the

WORTH A TRIP

DIAMOND CHOCOLATE FACTORY

This **chocolate factory** (☑ 437-1839; www.jouvaychocolate.com; Diamond Estates, Victoria, St Marks; ☺ 8am-4pm Mon-Fri, 9am-5pm Sat & Sun) housed in a former distillery built by French monks, produces the Jouvay brand of chocolate that you'll see on sale around the country. The company is owned as a cooperative by local cocoa growers. Call ahead to book a tour around the buildings and chocolate-making machinery followed by a chance to taste the various products.

There's a cafe on-site serving all things chocolate as well as a gift shop.

village of Concord, from where you can pick up bus transport.

➜ **Grand Etang Shoreline** This 1½-hour loop walk around Grand Etang Lake is gentle but it's very muddy. Bring adequate footwear.

➜ **Morne La Baye** This easy 15-minute walk starts behind the visitor center and takes in native vegetation.

➜ **Mt Qua Qua** This is a moderately difficult three-hour round-trip hike that leads to the top of a ridge, offering some of the best views of the rainforest.

➜ **Seven Sisters Falls** This two-hour hike passes seven waterfalls in the rainforest. It is a challenging trek but is considered one of the best hikes in Grenada. It starts 1.25 miles north of the visitor center. You will be asked to pay EC$5 admission to the private property at the trailhead.

❶ Information

There's a cafe next to the visitor center and a couple of other options, including a restaurant, outside around the car park.

There are no accommodations within the park boundaries; the park is best accessed from those in St George's.

Grand Etang Visitor Center (☑ 440-6160; admission EC$5; ☺ 8am-4pm)

Gouyave

Gouyave, roughly halfway up the west coast from St George's, is an attractive fishing vil-

lage. It is well worth spending a couple of hours just walking around, having a drink and taking in the ambience.

◉ Sights

★ **Nutmeg Processing Cooperative** FACTORY

(☑ 444-8337; EC$2.70; ☺ 8am-3:30pm Mon-Fri) On Gouyave's main road, you can literally smell one of the most important aspects of Grenada's heritage: nutmeg. This large nutmeg processing station is a vast, drafty old facility where workers sort the fragrant and tasty pods. Tours leave constantly and are a bargain.

Concord Falls WATERFALL

There are a couple of scenic waterfalls along the Concord River. The lowest, a picturesque 100ft cascade, can be viewed by driving to the end of Concord Mountain Rd, a side road leading 1.5 miles inland from the village of Concord. These falls are on private property and the owner charges a small fee to visit them.

The half-mile trail to the upper falls begins at the end of the road. There have been some muggings in this area, although security has improved. Even so it is recommended that you don't hike alone, and leave valuables at your hotel.

✖ Eating

Gouyave Fish Fry CARIBBEAN $

(meals EC$20; ☺ 7-10pm Fri) Gouyave is Grenada's fishing capital, a fact that is celebrated in style with the festive Friday Fish Fry. Local vendors grill and fry fresh fish right off the boat, and serve it up with local sides. It's as much a party as a dining experience, with most locals sticking around for a few drinks well after their meal is done.

❶ Getting There & Away

Buses running between St George's and Victoria along the Western Main Rd stop in Gouyave in both directions.

Sauteurs

On the northern tip of the island, the town of Sauteurs (whose French name translates as 'Jumpers') is best known for its grim history. In 1651, local Carib families elected to throw themselves off the 130ft-high cliffs that line the coast rather than surrender to the advancing French army.

Modern Sauteurs is a pretty little town with colorful houses and a magnificent Anglican church. Just to the northwest of town there is an inviting long beach backed by coconut palms that offers views over to the Grenadine islands. It's got a village vibe, especially in the late afternoon when locals come down to relax.

◉ Sights

Leaper's Hill MONUMENT
(EC$5; ⊙10am-5pm) It is from this cliff face that indigenous Carib families are said to have leapt in order to avoid advancing French forces. The small museum is no longer in operation but you can still visit the lookout point and imagine the macabre events. To get here, either walk through the Catholic cemetery behind the church or take the slightly rougher path down the right-hand side beside the school.

🛏 Sleeping & Eating

The best accommodations are outside town to the west, on the jungle-backed hillsides that slope down to the water.

Sauteurs has a couple of unpretentious diners serving up good local plates; most close early.

★ Almost Paradise HOTEL $$
(☑442-0608; www.almost-paradise-grenada.com; r/cottages US$99/129; @☀) The cottages at this popular little guesthouse are simple and bright with netted beds, kitchenette, and hammocks on the balcony. But what really seals the deal are the fantastic views over to the Grenadine islands. The restaurant serves a range of excellent Mediterranean-influenced food and delicious cocktails.

Petite Anse HOTEL $$$
(☑442-5252; www.petiteanse.com; s/d from US$268/283; P☀☎☀) By far the most upmarket of the two places to stay in this stretch, Petite Anse also has more in the way of facilities, including a slip of beach. Rooms are beautifully decorated, with four-poster beds and private decks or patios. The restaurant has everything from salads and pasta to seafood.

❶ Getting There & Away

Grenville There are two bus routes from Sauteurs to Grenville. One passes by Rose Hill close to Lake Antoine and the other goes through Hermitage near Belmont Estate.

St George's Buses link Sauteurs with the capital via the Western Main Rd.

Eastern Grenada

Sparsely populated Eastern Grenada is often overlooked by visitors but is well worth shuffling your itinerary for, especially if you want to get close to some rugged nature. As you drive form village to village you'll encounter working cocoa plantations, traditional rum distilleries, remote beaches and hidden lagoons teeming with birdlife.

Be advised that apart from Bathway, the beaches in this area are mostly dangerous and not suitable for swimming.

Halfway up the east coast, bustling Grenville is the area's agricultural hub and its busy streets offer a good insight into typical life, amid a smattering of old stone buildings.

◉ Sights

Pearl Airfield MONUMENT
Once the island's main airport, this airfield just north of Grenville was taken over by marines during the US invasion, leaving two Cuban planes stranded beside the runway. Now it's a peculiarly peaceful scene with goats nibbling away at green pastures beneath the mangled wings. You can climb inside the Russian-built Antonov jet, but bring sturdy footwear as there are loose bits of metal with sharp edges.

★ Belmont Estate FARM
(☑442-9524; www.belmontestate.net; Belmont; tours adult/child EC$13/5; ⊙8am-4pm, closed Sat) Cocoa is Grenada's main crop and it's celebrated at this 300-year-old working organic plantation. Among the other crops here: cinnamon, cloves, bay leaf, ginger and nutmeg. Guided tours explain cocoa production, and you can walk the landscaped gardens and have a tasty lunch (EC$60). The estate is about 2 miles northwest of Tivoli.

River Antoine Rum Distillery DISTILLERY
(☑442-7109; Tivoli; tours EC$5; ⊙8am-4pm Mon-Fri) River Antoine has produced rum since 1785. Tours here cover all aspects of the smoky, pungent production process, from the crushing of cane to fermentation and distillation. Of course there are tastings and you can buy bottles to go.

Bathway Beach BEACH

From River Sallee, a road leads to Bathway Beach, a lovely long stretch of coral sands. A rock shelf parallels the shoreline, creating a very long sheltered pool that's great for swimming. There are usually lifeguards here from 9am to 6pm, and there are a couple of stands and small cafes selling drinks and meals.

★ Levera Beach BEACH

Backed by low, eroding sea cliffs, Levera Beach is a wild, beautiful sweep of sand that gets few visitors. Just offshore is the high, pointed Sugar Loaf Island, while the Grenadine islands dot the horizon to the north.

The road north from Bathway to Levera is unpaved, but it's fairly solid and shouldn't pose a problem to most vehicles. Walking it will take about 30 minutes. It's a very remote place; there's security during the day but avoid coming up here after dark.

The beach, the mangrove swamp and the nearby pond have been incorporated into Grenada's national-park system, and are an important waterfowl habitat and sea-turtle nesting site.

✖ Eating

Outside of Grenville and Bathway Beach there are not many restaurants on this side of the island. Consider packing a picnic to enjoy on some isolated windswept shore.

My Place CARIBBEAN $

(doubles EC$2.50, rotis EC$10-12; ⊙ 9am-5pm) A hole-in-the-wall takeout joint on the main drag selling great Trinidadian food. Pick up some doubles (curried chickpeas wrapped in roti skins) and rotis to enjoy by the water somewhere.

Melting Pot CARIBBEAN $

(mains from EC$12; ⊙ 10am-8pm Mon-Sat) Grenadian classics are served up from the buffet at this popular upstairs bar and cafe. It's great food for an even better price, but the best thing is the rear dining room – from here, you can gaze out at the sea.

🔒 Shopping

Grenada Chocolate Company CHOCOLATE

(☑ 442-0050; Belmont Estate; ⊙ 7am-4pm Mon-Fri) You can buy this company's great organic chocolate bars all over the island but it's worth visiting this little showroom on the Belmont Estate (p445) to taste all the different varieties as well as tuck into brownies, cakes and individual gourmet chocolates.

ℹ Getting There & Away

While local buses will get you to most villages on this side of the island, many attractions are off the main road. It's best to hire a vehicle or negotiate with a taxi to fully explore the area.

Local buses from Grenville to Sauteurs run on two routes: 9A goes through River Sallee passing Lake Antoine and the turnoff to Bathway, while 9B goes inland via Belmont Estate.

CARRIACOU

The fact that most people don't realize that there are in fact *three* islands in the nation of Grenada is a fitting introduction to Carriacou (*carry*-a-cou). You won't find cruise ships, big resorts or souvenir shops – this is Caribbean life the way it was 50 years ago: quiet, friendly and relaxed.

★ Festivals & Events

Carriacou Carnival CULTURAL

(⊙ Feb/Mar) A vibrant event featuring fun street parades, live bands and the quirky 'Shakespeare Mas' – like a rap battle but with men dressed in bright garb reciting verses from the Bard of Avon. Get ready to be covered in paint and party. It takes place over two weeks after the beginning of Lent.

Carriacou Regatta SAILING

(⊙ Aug) Being a proud boat-building island, Carriacou takes its regatta very seriously. The four-day festival takes place in the first week of August and attracts participants from all over the Caribbean and beyond.

Carriacou Maroon & String Band Festival MUSIC

(www.carriacoumaroon.com; ⊙ May) Bands from a number of islands come to Carriacou for this traditional music festival that takes place over three days at the end of May. A delicious sideshow is the preparation of traditional smoked foods.

ℹ Getting There & Away

To check on flights between Grenada Island and Carriacou, contact **SVG Air** (☑ 444-3549; www. svgair.com).

Osprey Lines (www.ospreylines.com; Patterson St; ⊙ 8am-5pm) runs a fast boat service from Grenada Island to Carriacou at

9am, returning from Hillsborough at 3:30pm, although they often depart a little late.

ℹ️ Getting Around

BUS

Minivans serve as local buses and depart from the **terminal** behind **Ade's Dream hotel**, stopping to pick up passengers pretty much anywhere along their set route. The number 10 bus heads south while the number 11 heads up north. It costs EC$3.50 per ride.

Buses run during the day only, and on Sunday there's no service.

CAR & MOTORCYCLE

Carriacou is small and you can get most places on public transportation. However, if you want wheels, there are a few places to rent vehicles, with rates typically around US$50 to US$60 per day. **Wayne's Jeep Rental** (p448), in Hillsborough just up from Ade's Dream hotel, has good prices. There is a gas station on Patterson St in Hillsborough.

Hillsborough

Carriacou's gentle pace is reflected in the sedate nature of its largest town, Hillsborough. There are a couple of streets lined with a mixture of modern blocks and classic Caribbean wooden structures. Go for a wander, appreciating glimpses of the turquoise waters at breaks in the buildings.

⊙ Sights

Beauséjour Bay   BEACH
(Silver Bay) Hillsborough's beach isn't the island's best, but it's decent nonetheless. Fishing boats pull in along the Esplanade, where there are a couple of shady gazebos, and there's some nice shell collecting beyond this toward the northern headland. South of Hillsborough, it's a wilder affair, with crashing waves and pelicans roosting on the spines of long-gone piers.

Sandy Island   ISLAND
Sandy Island, off the west side of Hillsborough Bay, is a favorite daytime destination for snorkelers and sailors. It's a tiny postcard-perfect reef island of glistening sands surrounded by turquoise waters. Water taxis (US$25) run from Hillsborough (15 minutes). Be clear about when you want to be picked up – as the island takes only a couple of minutes to walk around, and has little shade, a whole afternoon can tick by very slowly.

Snorkelers take to the shallow waters fronting Sandy Island, while the deeper waters on the far side are popular for diving.

🏃 Activities & Tours

Deefer Diving   DIVING
(☑ 443-7882; www.deeferdiving.com; Main St; 2-tank dives from US$105; ⊙ 8am-5pm Mon-Sat) A top local dive shop that runs trips to 33 dive sites around Carriacou. PADI open-water courses are available for US$550. Also runs snorkeling trips.

Isle of Reefs Tours   OUTDOORS
(☑ 404-0415; www.carriacoutours.com) Runs hiking tours on the island as well as turtle-watching tours and boating trips in the surrounding waters, including to the Tobago Cays (US$150 per visitor).

Simply Carriacou   BOATING
(☑ 449-2029; www.simplycarriacou.com) Organizes tours to the Tobago Cays (US$150 per visitor) including lunch on one of the islands and visits to Mayreau and Palm Island.

🛏️ Sleeping

Hillsborough is a convenient base from which to explore the island – restaurants and transport are at your doorstep and nothing is far away.

Ade's Dream   GUESTHOUSE $
(☑ 443-7317; www.adesdream.com; Main St; r US$32-60; ❄️🛜) Popular with interisland travelers, those on a budget and people wanting to be right among the action, Ade's is in the dead center of town, above a bustling grocery/hardware/liquor/everything-else store. There are basic rooms with shared facilities and self-contained units with kitchens, and it's often booked to the hilt when the rest of the island is a ghost town.

Mermaid Hotel   HOTEL $$
(☑ 443-8286; www.mermaidhotelcarriacou.com; Main St; r US$107-165; ❄️🛜) This modern two-story hotel right by the water is the most comfortable place to crash in town. Bright and spacious rooms with modern bathrooms surround an internal courtyard. Go for one of the two front rooms with sea views. Walk-ins can often get a good discount when things are slow.

Green Roof Inn   HOTEL $$
(☑ 443-6399; www.greenroofinn.com; s/d from US$75/95; 🛜❄️) Half a mile up the road from Hillsborough, this is a quiet and beautiful

place to stay. The simple rooms have mosquito-netted beds, and some have fab sea views. Rates include a fine buffet breakfast at the attached restaurant.

🍴 Eating & Drinking

Laurena II
CARIBBEAN $

(mains from EC$18; ⊘8am-9pm; 🐾) Overlooking the Esplanade, this is often the liveliest spot in town. The Jamaican chef cooks up piles of jerk, fried or barbecued chicken, curried *lambi* or oxtail served up with rice and peas and salad to queues of hungry locals. The bar is also a nice option for a rum, beer or local juice.

Patty's Deli
MARKET $

(☑443-6258; Main St; sandwiches EC$15-19; ⊘9am-4:30pm Mon-Fri, to noon Sat) Upmarket groceries, from deli meats and cheeses to fresh quiches and cakes, plus wines and excellent sandwiches.

Callaloo
CARIBBEAN $$

(Mermaid Restaurant; ☑443-8286; Main St; lunch EC$14-35, mains EC$40-45; ⊘noon-9pm) Pull up a chair and enjoy quality Caribbean plates on the spacious wooden deck right over the sands at this popular place attached to the Mermaid Hotel. The menu is not extensive but the flavors tend to be spot on, and it's often open when not much else is on offer around town. Just make sure to bring repellent in the evenings or the mosquitoes may just spoil your meal.

ℹ GETTING TO ST VINCENT

It's possible to travel from Carriacou to Union Island in St Vincent; from here, boats depart for other islands in the Grenadines and up to Kingstown. A water taxi from Hillsborough to Union Island will cost US$75.

For a more economical trip, ask around town for Troy of the **Lady JJ** (☑in St Vincent 1-784-432-5728; gellizeautroy@gmail.com; adult/child EC$50/25), a working boat which runs a couple of times a week across to Union Island.

Every first Wednesday a cheap slow boat leaves directly from Carriacou for Kingstown, stopping at most of the Grenadine islands on the way with the exception of Bequia.

★ Green Roof Inn
FUSION $$$

(☑443-6399; www.greenroofinn.com; mains from EC$69; ⊘5-9pm Tue-Sun; 🐾) The most sophisticated option in the Hillsborough area, with tables on a veranda overlooking the sea and fine meals to match the view. The menu changes according to what's fresh and available: it may feature fresh fish, steak or lobster if you're lucky, but it's all beautifully presented. Be sure to reserve a spot as the tiny dining area fills fast.

Though the cooking is refined, it's a laid-back place; the owners have children and are happy to accommodate kids.

La Playa
BAR

(Beausejour Bay; ⊘10am-6pm) Right at the north end of Beausejour Bay, this great little beach bar serves up cocktails and light meals, including burgers and panini, in a cute little wooden house right on the water.

ℹ Information

Ade's Dream Internet (☑443-7317; Main St; per hour EC$10; ⊘6am-10pm) Reasonably fast internet connection, friendly folks and a nice spot.

Hillsborough Immigration and Customs (☑443-8399; ⊘8am-4pm Mon-Fri) Get your stamps here when leaving by boat for Union Island or elsewhere in St Vincent and the Grenadines.

Hillsborough Tourist Office (☑443-7948; Main St; ⊘8am-noon & 1-4pm Mon-Fri) Helpful; located across from the pier.

Post Office (☑443-6014; Main St; ⊘8am-3pm Mon-Fri) Located at the pier.

Princess Royal Hospital (p455) In Belair, outside of Hillsborough.

Republic Bank (☑443-7289; Main St; ⊘8am-2pm Mon-Thu, to 4pm Fri) Has a 24-hour ATM.

ℹ Getting There & Away

The *Osprey* ferry from St George's docks right in the heart of town, as do boats from Union Island in St Vincent and the Grenadines.

Water taxis will take you from Hillsborough to anywhere on Carriacou and beyond including Sandy Island (US$25), Anse la Roche (US$35), White Island (US$45), Petit Martinique (US$60) and Petit St Vincent (US$60).

Wayne's Jeep Rental (☑443-6120; Main Rd; vehicles EC$120-160) Rates are around EC$120 for a two-door vehicle and $160 for a regular four-door model.

North of Hillsborough

The northern part of Carriacou is a delightful place to explore, with good scenery and tiny villages.

The first is cute little **Bogles**. Continuing on, the road traverses the crest of **Belvedere Hill**, providing sweeping views of the tiny islands of Petit St Vincent and Petit Martinique. Nearby are the remains of a couple of old sugar mills – one is close to the road.

From here, the route northeast (called the High Rd) leads down to **Windward**, a charming small village where, if you're lucky, some of the friendly locals will be out building a traditional Carriacou sloop.

Just north of Windward is a wetland that is a good spot for birdwatching.

◎ Sights

Anse La Roche   BEACH

Getting here is a bit of a mission, but Anse la Roche is an idyllic stretch of soft sand backed by bush and flanked by headlands. Protected by cliffs, this secluded beauty – an important nesting spot for sea turtles – is a private paradise. You'll usually have it to yourself, although you may emerge from the jungle to find some yachties hanging around.

From Bogles, take a left at the (white) sign for the High North Park. Follow that road, which quickly turns to dirt, for 25 minutes on foot, veering right where the power lines end, until you see a small wooden sign nailed to a tree pointing to the narrow path. Follow that path down through the forest

for 15 minutes. It's steep and a bit hard to follow at times but just keep heading down and towards the sound of the waves.

Alternatively you can just drop in with a water taxi from Hillsborough (US$35 per visitor round trip).

🛏 Sleeping & Eating

Bayaleau Point   HOTEL **$$**

(📞 443-7984; www.carriacoucottages.com; Windward; US$110-185; 📶) A great choice if you're after some peace and quiet, these wooden cottages are basic but neat and have everything you need including balconies, hammocks, kitchenettes and mosquito-netted beds. There's also a nice wooden deck area with views over to Petit Martinique and Petit San Vincent.

★**Bogles Round House**   CAFE **$$**

(📞 443-7841; Bogles; mains from EC$50-85; ⊙ noon-2:30pm & 6-9pm Mon-Sat) It is a round house and it's run by award-winning chef Roxanne Russell. The food – European dishes infused with Caribbean flavors – is inventive and up there with the best on the island. Three recently renovated cottages (US$100 incl breakfast) are scattered around the grounds and there's a small private beach.

ℹ Getting There & Away

The northern part of the island is walkable if you're energetic and not in a hurry. It's worth taking the number of a local taxi to pick you up just in case.

The number 11 bus runs up past Bogles and through the center of the island to Windward.

HIKING: BOGLES TO WINDWARD

A good hike will take you from Bogles to Windward or vice versa via the High North Park, with possible detours to see **Anse La Roche** and the wetlands at Petit Carenage. It is partially shaded for most of the way and in some points affords good views of neighboring islands.

Heading out from Bogles, take the left road at the sign to the High North Park. This will quickly turn into a dirt road – it's a vehicle track but traffic is rare and you probably won't see any at all. Veer right where the power lines end; the road then continues along the hillside passing through bushland. After about a 30-minute hike, you'll reach the turnoff to Anse La Roche. Keep an eye out for iguanas and manicous (a local opossum) along the way.

The road then continues on through more bush and down an incline to the small collection of houses that marks the beginning of Petit Carenage, from where it's paved down to Windward. Turn down towards the water just after Petit Carenage to access the lagoon, a good spot for birdwatching.

From Bogles to Windward without detours will take around an hour and a half depending on your pace. Be sure to bring water and a hat, as there are no shops along the way.

South of Hillsborough

The biggest reason to venture to this part of the island is the aptly named **Paradise Beach**, a superb stretch of sand bordered by palms and sea-grape trees. Further on, **Tyrrel Bay** is a deep, protected bay. It's a popular anchorage for visiting yachts and there are a couple of cafes.

◉ Sights & Activities

White Island   ISLAND
White Island makes for a nice day trip, with a good, sandy beach and a pristine reef for snorkeling. It's about a mile off the southern tip of Carriacou. Water taxis run from Tyrrel Bay (about US$45 round trip, 30 minutes).

Lumbadive   DIVING
(☑ 443-8566; www.lumbadive.com; Tyrrel Bay; ◷ 8:30am-5pm Mon-Sat) A great little dive shop in Tyrrel Bay with friendly and professional staff that offers two-tank dives for US$110 including equipment and six-dive packages for US$315. Also arranges accommodations in local apartments (US$55 to US$85).

🛏 Sleeping

There are a couple of accommodations options on Paradise Beach. Around Tyrrel Bay there are often houses to rent; ask in the dive shops or restaurants.

Sunset Beach Paradise Inn   HOTEL $
(☑ 443-8409; sunset.beach.paradise@gmail.com; Paradise Beach; r US$57-125; 🕸) Charming sand-side living, right on Paradise Beach. Eight rooms open onto a brightly painted porch overlooking a grassy courtyard and are only steps from the sea; larger ones have kitchenettes. There's a great little restaurant and bar (mains EC$25), tucked under a tree even closer to the waves, that serves up a good meal.

🍴 Eating

Beachside bars on Paradise Beach serve tasty local meals, and Tyrrel Bay has a couple of great casual restaurants.

Hard Wood Bar & Snacket   CARIBBEAN $
(Paradise Beach; mains EC$20-25; ◷ 9am-10pm) Near the center of Paradise Beach, this green, yellow and red shack dishes out cold beers and meals of fresh fish, oozing with local flavor. It's a serene, quintessentially Caribbean setting: locals, lifers, expats and the odd traveler pony up to the bar and settle in for a cold one on a hot day.

Slipway   BURGERS $$
(☑ 443-6500; Tyrrel Bay; mains lunch EC$25-36, dinner EC$50-86; ◷ 11:30am-2pm & 6-9pm) A chilled little open-air place, right by the water at the end of the bay, famed for its top-quality burgers and fish tacos. As an added bonus it serves West Indies Beer Company ales, too.

Lazy Turtle   ITALIAN $$
(☑ 443-8322; Tyrrel Bay; pizzas EC$30-50, mains from EC$43; ◷ 11am-11pm; 🕸) Makes excellent thin-crust pizzas and authentic Italian pasta. It's well worth the drive from Hillsborough.

🔒 Shopping

Fidel Productions   GIFTS & SOUVENIRS
(☑ 404-8866; Paradise Beach; ◷ 9am-4:30pm Mon-Sat) This charming little shop, built into an old shipping container, is a creative cave of niceties featuring locally made T-shirts, original artworks, jewelry, ceramics and some great photographs. Everything is well made and reasonably priced.

ℹ Getting There & Away

The local number 10 bus will drop you right at Paradise Beach. If you're heading to Tyrrel Bay it will drop you at the turnoff, from where it's a 10-minute walk down to the dive shops and restaurants.

PETIT MARTINIQUE

They don't call it Petit for nothing – this little island is a scant 1 mile in diameter. It's an ideal spot to get away from everything.

With a steep volcanic core rising a stout 740ft at its center, there is little room on the island for much else. The solitary road runs up the west coast, but it is rarely used – locals prefer to walk. Nothing is very far and what's the hurry? The population subsists on the fruits of the sea, either as fishers or boat-taxi operators.

With barely a thousand inhabitants, most of whom are related to each other, this is a place to find peace, quiet – and precious little else.

🛏 Sleeping & Eating

Melodies   GUESTHOUSE $
(☑ 443-9052; r US$31-44; 🕸) Melodies has neat and simple rooms, some with balconies

facing the impossibly blue ocean; it is worth the couple of extra dollars for an ocean-view room. The downstairs restaurant and bar serves good local food and stiff cocktails – sometimes followed by a round of drunken karaoke. Guests have access to a shared kitchen upstairs.

Millenium   GUESTHOUSE $
(📞444-9243; Back St; s/d US$45/55, without bathroom US$35/45; ❄) If you want air-conditioning, this is pretty much your only option on the island. It's a friendly place with decent rooms, but the downside is it's on the back road away from the water.

Palm Beach   CARIBBEAN $
(📞443-9103; www.petitemartinique.com/palm beachguesthouse; lunch EC$25-35, dinner EC$33-55; ⊙8am-10pm) Boasting the biggest menu on the island, Palm Beach serves up plates of conch, fish and lobster alongside burgers and chicken in a waterside setting. Vegetarian dishes are available on request. They also run a basic guesthouse with two simple rooms overlooking the bay (US$52 to US$67), which include a kitchenette.

❶ Getting There & Away

The *Osprey* catamaran (p457) ferries passengers between Hillsborough, on Carriacou, and Petit Martinique daily, except on weekends when there is no service. It leaves Carriacou around noon and comes back from Petit Martinique around 2pm. Another service leaves Carriacou at 3pm and returns at 7:15am the next morning.

A cheaper way to get over is to take the mail boat from the small town of Windward, directly across from Petit Martinique on Carriacou. It takes school children from Petit Martinique over early in the morning and pretty much turns right back around at around 8am. It makes the round trip again in the afternoon.

A water taxi from Hillsborough to Petit Martinique costs US$60 per visitor. From Windward you should be able to negotiate a much cheaper price with local boat owners.

UNDERSTAND GRENADA

History

Colonial Competition

In 1498 Christopher Columbus became the first European to sight the island of Grenada, during his third voyage to the New World.

It wasn't until 1609, however, that English tobacco planters attempted to settle; within a year, most were killed by Caribs, who had first established communities on Grenada in around 1100, having displaced the more peaceful Arawaks, the island's first inhabitants. Some 40 years later, the French 'purchased' the island from the Caribs for a few hatchets, some glass beads and two bottles of brandy. But not all Caribs were pleased with the land deal and skirmishes continued until French troops chased the last of them to Sauteurs Bay at the northern end of the island. Rather than submitting to the colonists, the remaining Caribs – men, women and children – jumped to their deaths from the cliffs.

French planters established crops that provided indigo, tobacco, coffee, cocoa and sugar, and imported thousands of African slaves to tend to the fields. Grenada remained under French control until 1762, when Britain first recaptured the island. Over the next two decades, colonial control of the land shifted back and forth between Britain and France – until 1783, when the French ceded Grenada to the British under the Treaty of Paris.

Animosity between the new British colonists and the remaining French settlers persisted after the Treaty of Paris. In 1795 a group of French Catholics, encouraged by the French Revolution and supported by comrades in Martinique, armed themselves for rebellion. Led by Julien Fedon, an African-French planter from Grenada's central mountains, they attacked the British at Grenville, capturing and executing the British governor and other hostages. Fedon's guerrillas controlled much of the island for more than a year, but were finally overcome by the British navy. Fedon was never captured. It's likely he escaped to Martinique, or drowned attempting to get there, though it's sometimes said that he lived out his days hiding in Grenada's mountainous jungles.

In 1877 Grenada became a Crown colony, and in 1967 it converted to an associated state within the British Commonwealth. Grenada, Carriacou and Petit Martinique adopted a constitution in 1973 and gained collective independence on February 7, 1974.

Independence

One-time trade unionist Eric Gairy rose to prominence after organizing a successful labor strike in 1950, and was a leading voice in Grenada's independence and labor movements. He established ties with the British government and monarchy, and was groomed to become the island's first prime minister when Britain relinquished some of its Caribbean colonies. After independence, Gairy's Grenada United Labour Party (GULP) swept to power.

Gairy made early political missteps, such as using his first opportunity to speak in front of the UN to plead for more research into UFOs and the Bermuda Triangle. There were rumors of corruption, of ties with General Augusto Pinochet of Chile and of the use of a group called the Mongoose Gang to intimidate and eliminate adversaries. Power went to Gairy's head and this former labor leader was soon referring to his political opposition as 'sweaty men in the streets.'

Revolutions, Coups & Invasions

Before dawn on March 13, 1979, while Gairy was overseas, a band of armed rebels supported by the opposition New Jewel Movement (NJM) party led a bloodless coup. Maurice Bishop, a young, charismatic, London-trained lawyer and head of the NJM, became prime minister of the new People's Revolutionary Government (PRG) regime.

As the head of a communist movement in the backyard of the US, Bishop tried to walk a very fine line. He had ties with Cuba and the USSR, but attempted to preserve private enterprise in Grenada. A schism developed between Bishop and hard-liners in the government who felt that he was incompetent and was stonewalling the advance of

true communism. The ministers voted that Bishop should share power with the hard-line mastermind (and Bishop's childhood friend) Bernard Coard. Bishop refused and was placed under house arrest. While Coard had the support of the majority of the government and the military, Bishop had support of the vast majority of the public.

On October 19, 1983, thousands of supporters spontaneously freed Bishop from house arrest and marched with him and other sympathetic government ministers to Fort George. The army was unmoved by the display and Bishop, his pregnant girlfriend (Minister of Education Jacqueline Creft) and several of his followers were taken prisoner and executed by a firing squad in the courtyard. To this day, it is unclear if the order came directly from Coard – although most believe that it did.

Meanwhile, America became ever more nervous of another potentially destabilizing communist nation in the Caribbean, and six days later 12,000 US marines (along with soldiers from half a dozen Caribbean countries) were on Grenadian shores. US President Ronald Reagan cited the risk to the safety of students at the US-run St George's University as a justification for the invasion; 70 Cubans, 42 Americans and 170 Grenadians were killed in the fighting that ensued. Most of the US forces withdrew in December 1983, although a joint Caribbean force and 300 US support troops remained on the island for two more years. The US sunk millions of dollars into establishing a new court system to try Coard and 16 of his closest collaborators.

A PHOENIX RISES

On September 7, 2004, Hurricane Ivan made landfall on Grenada. The first major storm to hit the island in 50 years, Ivan struck with huge force, leaving a wave of destruction that saw 90% of buildings damaged or destroyed, towns decimated and staple crops like nutmeg obliterated.

The following months and years were a dark chapter for this small Caribbean nation, whose economy was left in ruins. Nonetheless, new crops were sown (with fast-growing cocoa replacing nutmeg as the nation's main agricultural export), and homes, shops and offices rebuilt, with Caribbean neighbors lending support to help repair the damage. But within this period of rebirth, instead of simply rebuilding what was once there, opportunity was found.

Hotels, schools, churches and restaurants have been rebuilt bigger and better, incorporating sustainable practices and larger floor plans. Structures that were long overdue to be upgraded were leveled and the new buildings are a massive improvement to what was once there. Today, the only real evidence of Ivan's path is the odd roofless building – and a certain wariness among locals come hurricane season.

Fourteen people, including Coard, were sentenced to death for the murder of Bishop. His death sentence was repealed in 2007 by Britain's Privy Council, and he was released from prison in September 2009.

The New Era

After the US invasion, elections were reinstituted in December 1985, and Herbert Blaize, with his New National Party, won handily. Many PRG members reinvented themselves politically and found jobs in the new administration. From 1989 to 1995 different political parties jockeyed for control and a few short-term leaders came and went, but all within the democratic process.

In 1995 Dr Keith Mitchell became prime minister, and remained in power for 13 years. Though he had some success building the tourism economy, his government was plagued by accusations of corruption and financial misdealing, and was sharply criticized for a weak initial response to the devastation of 2004's Hurricane Ivan. The 2008 election saw the center-left National Democratic Congress (NDC) take over the reins under Tillman Thomas.

People & Culture

Grenadian culture is an eclectic mix of British, French, African and East and West Indian influences. A growing number of expats from the UK, Canada and, to a lesser extent, the United States are making Grenada home, bringing with them new attitudes and ways of life, while wider Caribbean influences also hold sway: as well as local calypso and soca, you'll hear Jamaican dancehall music blaring from speeding buses and nightclub dance floors.

Almost 60% of all Grenadians are Roman Catholic. There are also Anglicans, Seventh Day Adventists, Methodists, Christian Scientists, Presbyterians, Baptists, Baha'is and an increasing number of Jehovah's Witnesses. Because of the pervasive influence of Christian ideals, Sunday is a pretty quiet day around the islands, when many shops and services close.

The largely religious population makes for a fairly conservative culture, though once you scratch beneath the squeaky-clean veneer, you can see a population that enjoys having a few drinks and kicking up its heels, especially during the annual Carnival.

Education is on the rise and the population is quite learned. Political awareness is high, thanks in part to Grenada's brush with international infamy in the '80s. The shake-up of Hurricane Ivan in 2004 forced a deep cultural reexamination, something that many feel has led to a more mature and forward-thinking nation.

Grenadians themselves are friendly and welcoming. They are proud of their tiny nation and take care of it – there is less rubbish in the ditches and a sense of civic responsibility is palpable.

Though football is making inroads, cricket is followed with near fanaticism here, and remains the unofficial national sport.

Landscape & Wildlife

The Land

Grenada Island, Carriacou and Petit Martinique comprise a total land area of 133 sq miles. Grenada Island, at 121 sq miles, measures 12 miles wide by 21 miles long. The island is volcanic, though part of the northern end is coral limestone. Grenada's rainy interior is rugged, thickly forested and dissected by valleys and streams. The island rises to 2757ft at Mt St Catherine in the northern interior. Grenada's indented southern coastline has jutting peninsulas, deep bays and small nearshore islands.

Carriacou, at just under 5 sq miles, is the largest of the Grenadine islands that lie between Grenada and St Vincent. Most of the others are uninhabited pinnacles or sandbars in the ocean.

Wildlife

Grenada has a wide range of distinct ecosystems. The lush rainforests that cover the hilly interior are home to armadillo, opossum and mongoose, while Mona monkeys were introduced from Africa a century ago.

The islands also support a rich array of birdlife, both migratory and resident. The interior of the islands is home to tiny hummingbirds; osprey and endangered hook-billed kites cruise the thermals; and pelicans, brown boobies and frigate birds patrol the coasts.

In the ocean, sea turtles cruise the grassy shoals and come ashore to nest and lay their eggs. Despite protected status, they are still sometimes slaughtered for their meat and shells; be sure to avoid buying anything made from turtle shell, or eating turtle meat.

Many different types of reef fish populate the surrounding waters. Snorkelers and divers have the pleasure of swimming among barracuda, butterfly fish and the odd nurse shark, as well as browsing forests of brightly colored hard and soft corals.

SURVIVAL GUIDE

ⓘ Directory A–Z

ACCOMMODATIONS

Most of Grenada's accommodations are in the Grand Anse area, from big beach hotels to smaller guesthouses.

Though not on the beach, St George's makes a lively base for exploring by public transportation and has excellent places to eat and drink.

Along the beaches close to the airport and in True Blue are top-class hotels alongside good places to eat and drink.

Lance aux Épines is quieter, with an exclusive and secluded feel.

Carriacou has a string of accommodations in the capital and on Paradise Beach, often the liveliest places to be on this super-quiet island. There are great options further afield, though they can feel a bit isolated.

Petit Martinique is so small that you'll be sure to mix with the locals – they'll be your neighbors.

ACTIVITIES

Grenada has some first-class diving both on reefs and among the many wrecks that can be found in its waters. Many dive sites are found around the southwest of the island offshore from St George's, Grand Anse and Point Salines.

The Grenada Marine Protected Area covers a large area just north of St George's that includes many of the best reefs on the island.

Among the top dive sites:

MV Bianca C Referred to by locals as the *Titanic* of the Caribbean, this enormous cruiser is an awesome high-adrenaline swim through for advanced divers.

SLEEPING PRICE RANGES

The following price ranges refer to a double room with bathroom.

$ less than US$85

$$ US$85–200

$$$ more than US$200

Underwater Sculpture Park (p435) Located in the Grenada Marine Reserve, this underwater gallery is popular with fish as well as divers and snorkelers.

MV Shakem A sunken cement freighter remains for the most part intact – intriguing underwater industrial scenery.

Veronica L An easy shallow wreck dive right by the entrance to St George's – makes a good night dive.

Flamingo Bay In the northern part of the marine reserve, this all-level reef has an amazing variety of coral, sponges and fish. Also a top snorkeling spot.

Dragon Bay Sand channels between volcanic rocks provide a fantastic backdrop at this reef, which has many beautiful sponges, angelfish, morays and octopuses.

CHILDREN

Grenada has many calm, gently shelving beaches perfectly suited to children, such as La Sagesse (p443), Lance aux Épines (p442) and Morne Rouge (p440); in Carriacou, Paradise Beach (p450) is a good bet.

Keep your eye on small children around the roads in St George's as the traffic can be on the wild side; and bear in mind that some of the forts are without sufficient railings or barriers.

If you're taking water taxis, sit towards the rear where the boat moves less.

ELECTRICITY

The electrical current is 220V, 50 cycles. British-style three-pin plugs are most common, but you'll sometimes see US-style two-pin plugs.

EMBASSIES & CONSULATES

US Embassy (✆ 444-1173; usemb_gd@carib surf.com; Lance aux Épines)

EMERGENCY NUMBERS

Country Code	✆ 473
Emergency Line	✆ 911

FOOD

You'll find a full range of restaurants on the island of Grenada, from roadside shacks selling fantastic local dishes to formal waterside dining around St George's and Grand Anse.

On Carriacou things are a bit more low key, but there are still plenty of places to dine and the influence of travelers and yachties is evident in the presence of many international flavors. Petit Martinique has just a handful of simple restaurants.

Essential Food & Drink

Roti A tasty flat bread wrapped around curried meat and vegetables.

Oil down Beef and salt pork stewed with coconut milk.

Salt fish and bake Seasoned salt fish with onion and veg, and a side of baked or fried bread.

Lambi The local name for conch.

Carib beer Brewed in Grenada and always served ice cold.

Jack Iron rum Ice sinks in this lethal local belly wash.

GLBT TRAVELERS

Attitudes to same-sex couples in Grenada (and the Caribbean generally) are not modern or tolerant. Gay and lesbian couples should be discreet in public to avoid hassles.

HEALTH

There is a hospital (☑ 440-2051; Fort George Point) in **St George's** and another on the hill above **Hillsborough** (☑ 443-7400) on Carriacou.

For an emergency ambulance dial ☑ 911.

Private clinics can be found around St George's and the Grand Anse area.

MONEY

The official currency is the Eastern Caribbean dollar (EC$). There are 24-hour ATMs dispensing EC$ all over Grenada and in Hillsborough, Carriacou.

Major credit cards are accepted by most hotels, top-end restaurants, dive shops and car-rental agencies.

Currency

➡ Most hotels, shops and restaurants accept US dollars, but you'll get a better exchange rate by changing to Eastern Caribbean dollars at a bank and using local currency.

➡ Accommodation is usually priced in US dollars, as are tours and meals in more upmarket hotels; otherwise, EC$ is used.

➡ Be clear about whether prices are being quoted in Eastern Caribbean or US dollars, particularly with taxi drivers.

Exchange Rates

The Eastern Caribbean dollar is pegged to the US dollar at a rate of 2.70 to 1. For current exchange rates, see www.xe.com.

AUSTRALIA	A$	EC$1.99
BARBADOS	B$1	EC$1.35
CANADA	C$1	EC$2
EUROPE	€1	EC$2.85
JAPAN	¥100	EC$2.40
NEW ZEALAND	NZ$1	EC$1.89
UK	UK£1	EC$3.35
US	US$1	EC$2.70

EATING PRICE RANGES

The following price ranges relate to the cost of a main meal:

$ less than EC$35

$$ EC$35–70

$$$ more than EC$70

Tipping

A 10% tax and 10% service charge is added to many hotel and restaurant bills. If no service charge is added at restaurants, a 10% tip is generally expected. Prices quoted here do not include the tax and charge.

PUBLIC HOLIDAYS

In addition to those observed throughout the region, Grenada has the following public holidays:

Independence Day February 7

Labor Day May 1

Corpus Christi Ninth Thursday after Easter

Emancipation Days First Monday & Tuesday in August

Thanksgiving Day October 25

TAXES & REFUNDS

A 15% VAT is included on most purchases in Grenada.

TELEPHONE

Grenada's country code is ☑ 473. When calling from within Grenada, you only need to dial the seven-digit local phone number.

TIME

Grenada, along with the rest of the Windward Islands, is on Atlantic Time (GMT/UTC minus four hours).

CITY	TIME DIFFERENCE
Auckland	+17
Cape Town	+6
London	+4
Los Angeles	-4
Miami	-1
New Delhi	+9.5
Sydney	+15
Tokyo	+13

TOURIST INFORMATION

➡ The Grenada Board of Tourism has offices on **Grenada** (p437) and **Carriacou** (p448).

➡ There's also an information booth at **Maurice Bishop International Airport** (p456), just before immigration, where you can pick up maps and brochures; staff can also help you book a room.

TRAVELERS WITH DISABILITIES

➡ Grenada is a difficult place to get around for travelers with disabilities and many hotels have yet to prioritize accessibility.

➡ Getting around poses particular problems. Minivan buses are crowded and hard to access as a result of seats being crammed in, and many taxis are vans that are high off the ground.

➡ There are many places with no sidewalks and those that do exist are often damaged or uneven.

➡ While there are few dedicated resources for travelers with disabilities, Grenadians are helpful and will usually be willing to lend a hand in any situation.

➡ Download Lonely Planet's free Accessible Travel guide from http://lptravel.to/Accessible Travel.

VOLUNTEERING

Volunteer tourism has yet to really pick up in Grenada and there are limited opportunities on the ground. There are occasionally conservation programs that look for volunteers.

Ocean Spirits (www.oceanspirits.org) works to protect leatherback turtles in northern Grenada.

🛈 Getting There & Away

AIR

Grenada has direct air links to the US and UK as well as Barbados, St Vincent and Trinidad and Tobago.

Airports

Maurice Bishop International Airport (GND; ☑ 444-4555; www.mbiagrenada.com) is large and has full services. It has flights from North America and the UK as well as regional Caribbean destinations. **SVG Air** flies from here to Union Island in St Vincent and the Grenadines.

Lauriston airport in Carriacou is a very modest affair with just one international flight – the short hop over to Union Island in St Vincent.

Airlines

American Airlines (www.aa.com; Maurice Bishop International Airport) Regular flights between Grenada and Miami.

Caribbean Airlines (www.caribbean-airlines.com; Maurice Bishop International Airport) Direct flights linking Grenada with Port of Spain.

LIAT (www.liatairline.com; Maurice Bishop International Airport) Links Grenada with many other regional destinations. Even if you book

a direct flight, you may be sent through other islands.

SEA
Boat

There is a small mail boat that runs between Carriacou and Union Island (EC$20, one hour) in St Vincent and the Grenadines a couple of times a week.

The commercial ships that haul goods back and forth between Grenada, Carriacou, Petit Martinique and Union Island sometimes accept foot passengers.

Cruise Ship

Grenada is a port of call for numerous cruise ships. They dock at the purpose-built pier just north of the harbor in St George's, Grenada Island. If more than two ships are in port, the old dock on the Carenage is also sometimes used; it's a short walk from the center of town.

Water Taxi

Water taxis between Union Island and Carriacou cost around US$100; it's a bumpy (and often wet) 40-minute ride. Boats can be chartered in Hillsborough or Windward in Carriacou, and Clifton in Union Island.

Yacht

Immigration (open 8am to 3:45pm Monday to Friday) can be cleared on Grenada Island at the following places:

Prickly Bay Marina (☑ 444-4509; ⊗ 8am-4pm Mon-Fri, 9am-2pm Sat & Sun) Prickly Bay

Grenada Yacht Club (☑ 440-3270; Port Louis Marina) St George's

La Phare Bleu Marina (☑ 444-2400; ⊗ 8am-4pm Mon-Fri, 9am-2pm Sat & Sun) Calivigny

Grenada Marine (☑ 443-1065; ⊗ 8am-noon Tue & Thu) St David

On Carriacou, clearance can be made in **Hillsborough** .

The most frequented anchorages are Prickly Bay, Mt Hartman Bay, Hog Island and True Blue Bay along the southwest side of Grenada; and Hillsborough and Tyrrel Bay in Carriacou.

🛈 Getting Around

AIR

SVG Air (☑ 444-3549; www.grenada-flights.com) has a couple of flights a day between Grenada and Carriacou.

BICYCLE

➡ Cycling is not big in Grenada, and good equipment is hard to come by, but it is slowly gaining popularity. Many roads are poorly lit and drivers are not used to encountering cyclists, so extra care is needed when getting around.

→ It's possible to ride a full 62 mile circuit around the island, although the road is steep and winding in parts so endurance is necessary.

→ The road between Grande Anse and the airport is wide and flat and has little traffic, making it a popular place for local cyclists and a good place to meet riding partners.

→ **Mocha Spoke** (p441) in True Blue rents out cycles and also offers guided tours.

BOAT

The **Osprey** (☑ 440-8126; www.ospreylines.com) is a large, fast boat connecting Grenada, Carriacou and Petit Martinique in less than two hours (per person one way Grenada to Carriacou EC$80, Carriacou to Petit Martinique EC$20). The boats run one to two times daily.

Reservations are rarely required, except on holidays. Tickets from Grenada are purchased on board, and from Carriacou at the office on Patterson St, Hillsborough. The Osprey arrives and departs at the east side of the Carenage in Grenada, and from the Hillsborough pier in Carriacou.

Cargo Boats

Island hopping on the cargo boats that sail between Grenada, Carriacou and Petit Martinique is an adventurous and inexpensive way to travel. Departure times and dates are unscheduled and the best way to find out what's available is to ask around at the docks. On Grenada, head for the large boats that moor on the north side of the Carenage in St George's; on Carriacou, they dock at Tyrrel Bay or Hillsborough pier.

Yacht

Horizon Yacht Charters (☑ 439-1000; www.horizonyachtcharters.com; True Blue Bay Marina) is one of Grenada's largest yacht charter operators. You can arrange to have a crewed yacht, where all you have to do is sit back and enjoy the ride; or, if you have sailing experience and are traveling with suitable crew, you can get a 'bareboat' charter where you get sole charge of the vessel.

BUS

→ Buses are a great way to get around Grenada and Carriacou. These privately operated minivans run a series of set, numbered routes crisscrossing the islands, and are inexpensive and fun – though they often reach madcap speeds, with drivers maniacally tooting their horn at friends and potential passengers as they go.

→ Although main destinations are posted on the front of the bus, alongside the route number, you may need to ask the conductor or driver which bus is best to get to smaller places outside St George's and Hillsborough.

PRACTICALITIES

Magazines *Lime & Dine* is a glossy magazine with general information on the island and listings of restaurants and entertainment.

Radio & TV Grenada has three local TV stations and four radio stations.

Smoking Not particularly common in Grenada. You'll still find some bars that permit smoking but almost all hotels and resort rooms and most restaurants are now smoke free.

Weights & Measures Grenada uses the imperial system for the most part.

→ There are stops along all the major routes, and you can also flag down a bus pretty much anywhere. When you're ready to get off, tap on the roof; if that doesn't work, shout 'bus stop please driver.'

CAR & MOTORCYCLE

Main roads on Grenada are fairly good. Some major firms have agencies here but most rental companies are locally based. You can arrange for pickup at the airport and ferry dock.

Grenada's larger towns, including Grenville, Gouyave and Victoria, have gas stations. On Carriacou there's just one gas station, in Hillsborough.

Driver's License

To drive a vehicle you need to purchase a Grenadian driver's license (EC$60), which all car-rental companies can issue.

Road Rules

→ Driving is technically on the left-hand side of the road, but you can expect buses in particular to be going full bore wherever the hell they want to, with full-beam lights on permanently after dark.

→ The roads are very narrow and curvy, and local drivers attack them with great speed. For safety, slow down when approaching blind curves and use your horn liberally.

→ There are few road signs in Grenada, so a road map and a measure of caution are useful when driving.

TAXI

→ You'll find plenty of taxis on Grenada and Carriacou.

→ Fares to most destinations are preset.

→ Taxis don't tend to circulate but rather wait at dedicated ranks.

→ It's worth picking up a couple of cards with numbers for pickups.

Guadeloupe

POP 405,700 / ☎ 590

Best Places to Eat

➡ La Touna (p473)

➡ Le Mabouya dans La Bouteille (p467)

➡ Iguane Café (p467)

➡ La Playa (p481)

➡ Couleurs du Monde (p478)

Best Places to Sleep

➡ Tendacayou Ecolodge & Spa (p470)

➡ La Toubana Hôtel & Spa (p465)

➡ Auberge Les Petits Saints (p476)

➡ Hostellerie des Châteaux (p466)

➡ E.Gwada Hostel (p463)

Why Go?

Guadeloupe is an archipelago of over a dozen islands that combine to offer travelers a wealth of attractions from deserted beaches to soaring mountains. Guadeloupe's two main islands look like the wings of a butterfly and are joined together by just a couple of bridges and a mangrove swamp. Grande-Terre, the eastern of the two islands, has a string of beach towns that offer visitors marvelous stretches of sand to laze on and plenty of activities. Mountainous Basse-Terre, the western island, is home to the wonderful Parc National de la Guadeloupe, which is crowned by the spectacular La Soufrière volcano.

As well as the 'mainland' of Guadeloupe, there are a number of small offshore islands including Les Saintes, Marie-Galante and La Désirade, each of which gives visitors its own taste of Guadeloupe's yesteryear. These are some of the most evocative and untouched destinations in the French Antilles, and shouldn't be missed.

When to Go

Dec–May Guadeloupe's busiest time; the weather is warm and dry, and the average humidity is around 77%.

Jul–Nov The wettest period, when rain falls about 14 days a month and the average humidity reaches 85%. Try to avoid Christmas, the French February holidays and July and August, as prices are sky-high and rooms scarce at this time.

Jan–May The drier months are the best time for diving and snorkeling.

Map labels:

Pointe de la Grande Vigie
Caribbean Sea
Anse Bertrand
Porte d'Enfer
Pointe des Gros-Caps
Pointe d'Antigues
Beauport Le Pays de La Canne
Gros-Cap
ATLANTIC OCEAN
Plage de Clugny
Port-Louis
Les Mangles
Anse Maurice
Îlet à Kahouanne
Pointe Allègre
Îlet à Fajou
Anse du Canal
Petit-Canal
Le Moule
Grande Anse
Duzer
Îlet Caret
Vieux-Bourg
Rosette
7 La Désirade
Plage de Léroux
Deshaies **2**
Ste-Rose
Grand Cul-de-Sac Marin
Morne-à-l'Eau
Château-Gaillard
Anse à la Gourde
Anse Tarare
Pointe Ferry
Pointe-Noire
Lamentin
Baie-Mahault
Les Abymes
Guadeloupe-Le Raizet Airport
Grande-Terre
Douville
St-François
Pointe des Châteaux
Anse Caraïbe
Mahaut
Les Mamelles (768m)
Jarry
Pointe-à-Pitre
Gosier
Ste-Anne
Pigeon Island **3**
Vernou
Petit-Bourg
Saint Félix
Îlet du Gosier
Pigeon
Cascade aux Écrevisses
Bouillante
Goyave
Parc National de la Guadeloupe
Ste-Marie
Basse-Terre
La Soufrière **1**
Capesterre-Belle-Eau
Vieux-Habitants
St-Claude
Chutes du Carbet **5**
Grosse Pointe
Anse du Vieux Fort
Anse du Coq
Anse Chapelle
Baillif
St-Sauveur
Anse Canot
Bananier
Basse-Terre **1**
Gourbeyre
Trois-Rivières
Baie de Saint-Louis
St-Louis
Anse Piton
Anse Turlet
Vieux-Fort
Marie-Galante **6**
Pointe du Vieux Fort
Terre-de-Haut
Anse Ballet
Grand-Bourg
Capesterre
Les Saintes **4**
Bourg des Saintes
Airport
ATLANTIC OCEAN

0 – 20 km
0 – 10 miles

Guadeloupe Highlights

1 La Soufrière (p471) Hiking through the rainforest to the misty summit of this brooding, active volcano.

2 Deshaies (p470) Nourishing your inner gourmet and encountering boaties from around the world in this charming fishing village.

3 Pigeon Island (p472) Touching the underwater

Jacques Cousteau statue at the reserve that bears his name.

4 Terre-de-Haut (p475) Discovering the gorgeous beaches of this mountainous island full of low-key sophistication and Caribbean history.

5 Chutes du Carbet (p471) Hiking through the rainforest on well-marked

trails to see these wonderful double waterfalls.

6 Marie-Galante (p479) Finding your own slice of beach heaven on the unspoilt sands of this much-overlooked island.

7 La Désirade (p482) Escaping the mainland's crowds for the day on the beaches of this little slice of paradise.

GRANDE-TERRE

Grande-Terre – which despite its name is far smaller than Basse-Terre – is the most visited island of Guadeloupe. Its southern coast, with its reef-protected waters and golden-sand beaches, is Guadeloupe's main

resort area, with a particular concentration in and around the town of Gosier.

By comparison the eastern side of the island is barely touched by tourism: it's largely open to the Atlantic's waves, and instead of beaches has crashing surf off much of its rocky coastline. It is popular with surfers, however, who converge on the town of Le Moule.

Northern Grande-Terre is one of the most scenically impressive parts of Guadeloupe, but its tourism industry is very undeveloped. It's a wonderful place to spend a day driving around – towering sea cliffs on one side and excellent beaches on the other make it a great choice for those wanting to avoid the crowds elsewhere.

ⓘ Getting There & Away

Most people arrive in Grande-Terre at **Guadeloupe Pôle Caraïbes Airport** (p486), from where it's easy to connect by rental car, bus or taxi to anywhere in the island.

It's also possible to arrive on Grande-Terre by boat from outlying islands in Guadeloupe, as well as from neighboring Caribbean islands including Dominica, Martinique and St Lucia. Most boats arrive at Pointe-à-Pitre's **Gare Maritime de Bergevin** (Blvd de l'Amitié des Peuples de la Caraïbe), although there are also ferry services from La Désirade, Marie-Galante and Les Saintes to the town of St-François.

Pointe-à-Pitre

Pointe-à-Pitre is a fairly uninviting place – a concrete jungle of brutalist architecture, decaying traditional houses and terrible traffic – but it's the main town on Grande-Terre and due to its central location between Guadeloupe's two biggest islands, it serves as the de facto capital. It's well worth getting off the beach for half a day to visit, if only to see the superb Mémorial ACTe, a brand-new museum dedicated to slavery and colonialism. The first of its kind in the world, Mémorial ACTe has quickly become the closest Guadeloupe has to a national museum and it's an absolute must-see for anyone interested in the history and culture of these islands.

Despite its unlovely appearance, Pointe-à-Pitre is working hard to improve itself. Its central square, Place de la Victoire, is looking superb following a full renovation, and the port has been tidied up and is also looking better than it has done for years.

◎ Sights

Marché de la Darse   MARKET
(Inner Harbor; ⊘6am-2pm Mon-Sat) This popular market on the seafront in front of Place de la Victoire is Pointe-à-Pitre's main

fruit-and-vegetable market. It's full of characters and you will nearly always be offered some free samples.

Musée St-John Perse   MUSEUM
(☑0590-90-01-92; 9 Rue de Nozières; adult/child €2.50/1.50; ⊘9am-noon & 1-5pm Mon-Fri, 8:30am-12:30pm Sat) This three-level municipal museum occupies an outstanding example of 19th-century colonial architecture and is dedicated to the renowned poet and Nobel laureate Alexis Leger (1887–1975), better known by his nom de plume Saint-John Perse, who spent his childhood in Guadeloupe. The house offers a glimpse of a period Creole home and displays on Perse's life and work.

★ **Mémorial ACTe**   MUSEUM
(MACTe; ☑0590-25-16-00; www.memorial-acte.fr; Rue Raspail, Carénage; adult/student €15/10; ⊘9am-7pm Tue-Thu, 9am-8pm Fri-Sat, 10am-6pm Sun) Opening in 2015, this massively important museum of the slave trade and slavery is quite simply a must-see for any visitor to Guadeloupe. Housed in a spectacular silver-latticework structure on the site of the former Darboussier sugar factory on Pointe-à-Pitre's long-neglected waterfront, MACTe tackles its heartbreaking subject head-on, documenting the subjugation of the peoples of the Caribbean, the mass importation of African slaves, their brutal existence under their European masters and the long and painful struggle for freedom.

⚡ Activities

Antilles Sail   BOATING
(☑0590-90-16-81; www.antilles-sail.com; 1 Résidence les Boutiques du Moulin, Marina de Bas du Fort) This long-established company rents out catamarans and provides all services for anyone wanting to undertake a boat trip around Guadeloupe.

Dream Yacht Charter   BOATING
(www.dreamyachtcharter.com) Worldwide yacht charter company, providing crews and all other services to boaters.

★ Festivals & Events

Carnival   CARNIVAL
Starts warming up in January with roving groups of steel-band musicians and dancers, but officially runs between the traditional weeklong Mardi Gras period and Ash Wednesday (46 days before Easter).

Pointe-à-Pitre

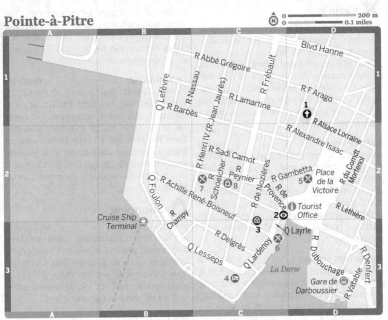

Fête des Cuisinières FESTIVAL
(Festival of Women Cooks) A colorful event held in early August. Women in Creole dress, carrying baskets of traditional foods, parade through the streets to the cathedral (Rue de l'Eglise), where they are blessed by the bishop.

🛏 Sleeping

Avoid spending the night in Pointe-à-Pitre if possible, as its hotels are very lackluster. Indeed, normally the only reason to stay here is if you're catching a flight or ferry early the next morning.

Hôtel Saint-John Perse HOTEL **$$**
(☑0590-82-51-57; www.saint-john-perse.com; Quai Lesseps; s/d €77/96; ✴🅰) This midrange option is totally unexciting, but it's perfectly located between the harbor and the Gare Maritime and extremely convenient if you're catching an early-morning boat. It has 44 fairly cramped rooms with shared balconies. There is also free luggage storage for guests who want to travel light to the outlying islands.

★La Case En Mer B&B **$$$**
(☑0590-26-45-13; www.im-caraibes.com/les-ilets; Îlet Boissard; d incl breakfast €150; ✴🅰) In

Pointe-à-Pitre

◎ Sights
1 Cathédrale de St-Pierre et St-Paul D1
2 Marché de la Darse C2
3 Musée St-John Perse C3

🛏 Sleeping
4 Hôtel Saint-John Perse C3

✗ Eating
5 Café de France D2
6 Le Yacht Club C3
7 Restaurant Fairouz C2

🛍 Shopping
8 Marché Couvert C2

search of an escape? This lovely B&B on a quiet islet, a free two-minute boat ride from the shore of Pointe-à-Pitre, offers guests the chance to unplug in two cocoonlike rooms set amid beautifully landscaped gardens, with the added bonus of a Jacuzzi. Dinner costs €25, and the affable owners speak good English. There's a three-night minimum.

Transfers to and from Pointe-à-Pitre can be arranged at any time and are free of charge.

✗ Eating

Pointe-à-Pitre's middle class seems to spontaneously vanish from the city at dusk – thereafter they're all usually to be found at the Marina de Bas du Fort (www.marina guadeloupe.com), 3km to the west of town. Here a number of decent restaurants surround a harbor full of yachts, while in the center there are just a few places to choose from in the evening.

Café de France   BAKERY $
(Place de la Victoire; pastries from €1, sandwiches €5; ⊘6am-3pm Mon-Sat; 🕾) This friendly bakery has a street terrace from where to absorb the colorful goings on of Place de la Victoire. It's a great breakfast spot, serving decent coffee, croissants and other freshly made pastries. It also does good made-to-order sandwiches.

Restaurant Fairouz   LEBANESE $
(17 Rue Jean Jaurès; mains €5-8; ⊘noon-3pm & 6-10pm Mon-Sat; ▨🖉) Housed in a charming old colonial house painted in white and red, this restaurant brings a dash of welcome Levantine relief to the ubiquitous Creole menus elsewhere in town. The excellent meze plate for two is the obvious choice for any first-time guest here, and orders for collection are also possible.

Chez Dolmare   SEAFOOD $$
(☑0590-91-21-32; Port de Pêche de Lauricisque; mains €11-15; ⊘noon-3pm Mon-Sat) You'll find the best seafood in town here, and it's no wonder – this unpretentious locale is located at the small fishing harbor of Lauricisque,

northwest of Pointe-à-Pitre's center. The menu is limited to a couple of daily specials, but they're well prepared and sizzling-hot value. Service can be both indifferent and slow, however, so plan accordingly.

Le Yacht Club   FRENCH $$$
(☑0690-74-57-11; Quai Lardenoy; mains €20-25; ⊘noon-3pm daily, 7pm-10pm Thu-Sat; 🕾) The smartest place to eat in the center of town, Le Yacht Club has a waterside location. Here, it serves up high-class French cooking from a changing daily menu in a pleasant semi-open-air dining room with fashionable decor. There's a popular barbecue at Sunday lunchtime.

🔒 Shopping

Marché Couvert   ARTS & CRAFTS
(cnr Rues Peynier & Schoelcher; ⊘6am-4pm Mon-Sat) A good place to buy island handicrafts, including straw dolls, straw hats and primitive African-style woodcarvings. It's also a good spot to pick up locally grown coffee and a wide array of fragrant spices.

ℹ Information

Drug abuse is a problem in Pointe-à-Pitre and you should take care after dark in the town's empty streets. The Place de la Victoire area has enough people until late at night to feel safe, but other parts of the city are downright spooky.

Change Caraïbes (www.changecaraibles.com; 21 Rue Frebault; ⊘8am-4:45pm Mon-Fri) A money exchange.

Post Office (Rue Wachter; ⊘8am-6pm Mon-Fri, to noon Sat)

Tourist Office (☑0590-82-09-30; www.lesilesdeguadeloupe.com; Place de la Victoire; ⊘8am-5pm Mon-Fri, to noon Sat)

ℹ Getting There & Away

BOAT
Pointe-à-Pitre has ferries that connect internationally to Dominica, Martinique and St Lucia. The following companies operate ferries to Les Saintes (Bourg des Saintes) and Marie-Galante (Grand-Bourg), departing from the **Gare Maritime de Bergevin** (p460), an easy walk from the city center.

Val'Ferry (p487)

Jeans for Freedom (p486)

BUS
There are two bus stations in Pointe-à-Pitre, one serving Grande-Terre, another serving Basse-Terre. Buses to most destinations leave at least

---

WHAT'S IN A NAME?

At first glance, the names given to the twin islands that make up Guadeloupe proper are perplexing. The eastern island, which is smaller and flatter, is named Grande-Terre, which means 'big land,' while the larger, more mountainous western island is named Basse-Terre, meaning 'flat land.'

The names were not meant to describe the terrain, however, but the winds that blow over them. The trade winds, which come from the northeast, blow *grande* (big) over the flat plains of Grande-Terre but are stopped by the mountains to the west, ending up *basse* (flat) on Basse-Terre.

hourly, though they stop after dark and only a few services run on Sunday.

Buses to Grande-Terre leave from the **Gare de Darboussier** (Rue Dubouchage) on the eastern side of the harbor in Pointe-à-Pitre.

DESTINATION	FARE (€)	DURATION, MIN
Anse Bertrand	3.50	50
Gosier	1.80	15
Le Moule	2.50	40
St-François	4	55
Ste-Anne	2.50	30

Buses to places in Basse-Terre leave from the **Gare Routière de Bergevin** (p470), right next to the **ferry terminal**.

DESTINATION	FARE,(€)	DURATION, MIN
Bouillante	3.50	55
Deshaies	2	40
Plage de Malendure	3.50	50
Ste-Rose	2	30
Trois-Rivières	4	60

ⓘ Getting Around

It's perfectly feasible to get around Pointe-à-Pitre on foot, as it's a small town with a compact center.

The bus from Pointe-à-Pitre to Gosier runs every 15 minutes, costs €1.80 (pay the driver) and takes about 15 minutes. If you're going to the Bas du Fort marina, take this bus and get off just past the university (€1, 10 minutes)

You can call for a taxi by dialing **Radio Taxis** (☏ 0590-82-00-00) or **Taxi Leader** (☏ 0590-82-26-26) in the Pointe-à-Pitre area.

Gosier

Gosier is really two towns: a cluster of high-rise hotels full of families enjoying the enviable sandy beaches on one side, and a friendly (if rather built-up) Caribbean town next door. There's little interaction between the two, however, and your experience will be strongly colored by which side of town you find yourself in.

Just 8km from Pointe-à-Pitre, Gosier is the biggest tourist spot in Guadeloupe. The hotels are packed close together and share a series of scalloped soft-sand coves, which make it an obvious spot for a family beach holiday.

The town center, about 1km away from hotel central, feels a little run-down and lacks the fine beaches found in the main hotel area, but it is more local in character. It also has a small but attractive beach and a good view across the water to Îlet du Gosier.

🛏 Sleeping

Gosier has the highest concentration of hotels in Guadeloupe, and it's precisely for this reason that most travelers will prefer to stay elsewhere on the island in search of some tranquility and privacy. That said, if you've been sold a package to Guadeloupe then this is very likely where you'll end up. Hotels are generally rather smart in Gosier, though competition is fierce and there are often bargains to be had.

★ **E.Gwada Hostel** HOSTEL **$**
(☏ 0690-11-89-74, 0590-55-67-86; www.egwada hostel.com; 2 Plateau Marcimain, Mare Gaillard; campsite s/d €15/26, dm from €18, s/d without bathroom €35/50; P @ 🛜 ⛱) Guadeloupe's only hostel is a superb, friendly and great-value breath of fresh air. Run by the informative and well-traveled Jean, the hostel has several rooms, and multiple dorms of varying sizes. Meals are available. It's in a residential area in Mare Gaillard, half-way between Gosier and Ste-Anne, which actually makes it a superb base for beach exploration.

Hôtel Les Bananiers HOTEL **$$**
(☏ 0590-84-10-91; www.les-bananiers.com; Rue des Phares et Basils, Perinet; d/studio incl breakfast €77/87; P ❄ 🛜 ⛱) It's a 1km walk to the town beach from this pretty little complex, but if you don't fancy that there's a small pool around which the four rooms and four studios with kitchenettes are arranged, surrounded by a charming garden. The welcome is very warm here and breakfast on the terrace is lovely. A good find, but book ahead.

🍴 Eating

★ **Casa Datcha** INTERNATIONAL **$**
(☏ 0690-92-56-54; www.casadatcha.com; ⏰ 11am-8pm) It's great to see a bit of panache on Gosier's neglected town beach, and Datcha provides just that. It has a fabulous location on the sand, an inventive menu that takes in everything from gorgeous salads to superb club sandwiches, and surely the best juice bar on the island, where you can design your own fresh drink to cool off with.

Le Pirate Caribéen BRASSERIE, BAR **$$**

(☑ 0590-90-73-00; Marina de Bas du Fort; mains €15-25, menus €18-30; ☺ 8am-1am; 🖥) This marina institution is housed in an atmospheric all-wood building that's slightly set back from the waterfront. It has served up endless plates of *ouassous* (freshwater crayfish), salads, steak, pasta and fresh fish for almost two decades. It's also a good place to hang out and just enjoy the fashionable buzz with a fresh beer in hand.

Le Bord de Mer CREOLE, FRENCH **$$**

(☑ 0590-84-25-23; Blvd Amédée Clara, Chemin de la Plage; mains €12-20; ☺ 9am-11pm Mon-Sat, 9:30am-5:30pm Sun) This friendly Creole place opens directly onto the sea, and so almost any table has a cracking view toward Îlet du Gosier. Familiar French and Creole fare leans heavily on fish and seafood as you'd expect, but there's also a selection of grilled meats and fresh salads.

Restaurant de l'Auberge FRENCH, CREOLE **$$$**

(☑ 0590-84-23-23; Montauban; mains €20-28; ☺ noon-3pm & 6-11pm; 🖥) The restaurant inside Auberge de la Vieille Tour serves traditional French and Creole cuisine in a very smart setting, and is certainly one of the best fine-dining experiences on the island. It's a good idea to reserve a table if you're not staying at the hotel.

🛍 Shopping

Créole Village SHOPPING CENTER

(Route des Hotels; ☺ 8am-midnight) This popular dining and shopping complex next to Gosier's marina is full of restaurants, cafes and bars to choose from.

ℹ Getting There & Away

There are regular buses between Gosier and Pointe-à-Pitre (€1.80, 15 minutes). Simply pick up any bus heading west along Gosier's Blvd Charles de Gaulle.

Services to the rest of Grande-Terre are much less frequent, and the main island bus operator, Karu'lis, doesn't go beyond Gosier. Pick up other buses heading towards Ste-Anne (€2.80, 20 minutes) or St-François (€2.80, 40 minutes) from Blvd Amédée Clara.

Despite having a marina, there is no port in Gosier and there are no scheduled ferry services to elsewhere in Guadeloupe from here – instead head to Pointe-à-Pitre for island ferries, or book an excursion at any hotel.

Marina de Bas du Fort (☑ 0590-93-66-20; www.marinaguadeloupe.com) Between Pointe-à-Pitre and Gosier. There's a large number of restaurants, bars, cafes and excellent facilities here.

Ste-Anne

The busy town of Ste-Anne sees a lot of tourists but retains plenty of village character. While the main road between Pointe-à-Pitre and St-François runs through the middle of town, bringing a constant flow of traffic, Ste-Anne has an attractive seaside promenade, a lively market and a fine white-sand beach stretching along the east side. The beach, which offers good swimming and is shaded by sea-grape trees, is particularly popular with islanders, who come here to surf, kayak and paddleboard.

⊙ Sights & Activities

Plage de la Caravelle BEACH

White-sand Plage de la Caravelle stretches along the east side of the Caravelle Peninsula, about 2km west of Ste-Anne's center, and is one of Guadeloupe's very finest. Its main tenant is Club Med, but the entire beach is public: anyone is free to walk right in, despite the guarded gate.

Excursion Guadeloupe CRUISE

(☑ 0590-74-80-57; www.excursionguadeloupe. com; Club Med) Tarzan and his crew's excellent day trips to Petite-Terre and boat tours of southern Grande-Terre, local mangrove ecosystems and snorkeling trips to various different reefs are all highly recommendable. The team also offers tours of Grande-Terre's interior by jeep and quad bike. Tarzan's 'office' is on Plage de la Caravelle, in front of Club Med, where you'll find him every morning.

🛌 Sleeping

Casa Boubou COTTAGE **$$**

(☑ 0590-85-10-13; www.casaboubou.fr; Durivage; d from €75; P ✻ 🖥 ⛱) A good deal for chill-seekers. The 10 cottages here are comfortable, practical (most have kitchens) and clean. They're closely packed but buffered by lush gardens. Guests enjoy free use of snorkeling equipment, and there's a tiny pool. One downside: the nearest beach, Plage de la Caravelle, is a 1km walk. Minimum stay of three nights.

Le Relais du Moulin HOTEL **$$**

(☑ 0590-88-48-48; www.relaisdumoulin.com; Le Helleux; ☺ r/ste €169/229; P ✻ @ ⛱) This impressive place, topped by its namesake windmill dating from 1843, is looking superb following a full renovation in 2016. It's a large place, with 70 bungalows spread out among the attractive tropical gardens, divided up into standards and suites. There's a fantastic pool area, tennis courts, a spa and an on-site Italian restaurant. It's a 500m walk to the nearest beach.

★**La Toubana Hôtel & Spa** LUXURY HOTEL **$$$**
(☑0590-88-25-78; www.toubana.com; Fonds Thézan; d incl breakfast from €280; ❊ 🛜 ➿) About 2km west of central Ste-Anne, La Toubana is magical. Poised on a quiet coastal cliff, it proffers cardiac-arresting views of the sea, Marie-Galante and Les Saintes. The 32 bungalows and the recently added 12 suites are all stylishly decorated and there's a small private cove down the hill, an excellent on-site restaurant and a superb infinity pool to chill beside.

✖ Eating

Le Kontiki CREOLE, FRENCH **$**
(☑0590-23-55-42; Rue de la Plage; mains €8-20; ☾noon-3pm) We give a big thumbs up to this popular restaurant, which boasts a fantastic location at the western end of Ste-Anne beach and a satisfying menu that includes fish and meat grills, salads, omelets, pancakes and sandwiches. There's a quieter section in the garden at the back. Last orders before 4pm.

Kouleur Kreol SEAFOOD **$$**
(☑0590-91-45-76; Rue de la Plage; mains €9-20; ☾noon-3pm Tue-Sun, 7-10pm Tue-Sat) A colorful spot that serves big, tasty seafood grills and a variety of fresh salads accompanied by lovely sea views. There's also a live band on Friday evenings.

Le Grand Bleu FUSION **$$$**
(☑0590-88-25-57; www.toubana.com; Fonds Thézan, La Toubana Hôtel & Spa; mains €22-35; ☾1:30-2:30pm & 7:30-10pm; 🛜) The sublime poolside dining at hotel La Toubana is a real treat. Expect an elegant lineup of dishes and fabulous desserts – it's pricey, but worth it for a romantic and memorable evening. Pick out a table on the breezy veranda and savor the swoony views onto the ocean. Wednesday nights feature a lavish Creole buffet.

Koté Sud CREOLE, FRENCH **$$$**
(☑0590-88-17-31; Rte de Rotabas; mains €20-25, menus €32-42; ☾7-11pm Mon-Sat; ❊) This sophisticated and long-established restaurant is outside Ste-Anne itself, on the road to Plage de la Caravelle. This is where to come for the most impressive local cuisine, which combines Creole favorites (such as conch) with traditional European dishes (such as duck breast in mascarpone sauce).

🛍 Shopping

Géograines ARTS & CRAFTS
(☑0590-88-38-74; Durivage; ☾9am-noon & 2-6pm Mon-Sat) This quirky place specializes in making things out of seeds – and it all looks good. It has seed wall hangings and even a coffee table where black and white seeds are arranged to make a chess board set under glass. The shop only shows the work of Guadeloupean artisans, made from local materials. It's clearly signposted off the main road through Ste-Anne.

Village Artisanal GIFTS & SOUVENIRS
(☾9am-7pm) A bit west of the town beach at the end of Ste-Anne's promenade, it may look tacky at first glance but it's a good place to go for the bigger souvenirs (hammocks, sculptures) that are hard to find at the souvenir market in Ste-Anne.

ℹ Information

Office de Tourisme (☑0596-76-73-45; Ave Frantz Fanon; ☾8:30am-1:30pm Mon-Fri)

ℹ Getting There & Away

Ste-Anne is easy to reach by bus, as it's on the main road between Gosier (€2, 30 minutes) and St-François (€2, 30 minutes). Pick up buses at any of the bus stops along the main road through town.

St-François

St-François represents the smarter side of tourism in Guadeloupe. Its hotels are distinctly higher end, its restaurants are outstanding and its marina is the playground of the rich and French. You'll even find Guadeloupe's only golf course here, not to mention an airfield from where incredible (but pricey) Cessna tours depart.

All this doesn't disbar the less financially fluid from visiting, but if the resorts of Gosier aren't your thing then St-François is a good alternative. There's a wide range of water sports on offer, from surfing and diving to kitesurfing and kayaking. St-François is also a major jumping-off point for trips to Guadeloupe's smaller islands, and there are services to all of them from here.

Just beyond St-François is windswept Pointe des Châteaux. This gorgeous peninsula boasts limestone cliffs pounded by crashing waves, some wonderful beaches and views of La Désirade. All in all, St-François should not be missed.

◎ Sights

Pointe des Châteaux   VIEWPOINT
This long peninsula right at the eastern tip of Grande-Terre is a gorgeous stretch of landscape. With some good beaches on both sides, it's popular with locals who head here to escape the crowds in St-François. It's also enormously popular with cyclists who love the scenic flat road. The culmination of the peninsula is a cliff, topped with a giant cross, that looks towards La Désirade and offers spectacularly scenic views.

Plage des Raisins Clairs   BEACH
On the western outskirts of St-François, Plage des Raisins Clairs is a popular sand beach where it's safe to swim. There's a gradual slope, no drop-off, a long stretch of relatively shallow water and plenty of shade.

🏃 Activities & Tours

Golf Municipal de St-François   GOLF
(☏0590-88-41-87; http://golf-saintfrancois.fr/; Ave de l'Europe) St-François has Guadeloupe's only golf course, this 18-hole, par-71 course designed by Robert Trent Jones. It's opposite the marina.

Surf Action   SURFING
(☏0690-31-88-28; www.surfantilles.com; Base Nautique de St-François) The place to come for surfing, windsurfing or stand-up paddleboarding. Surf Action has been one of the best-known surfing outfits in Guadeloupe for years.

Paradoxe Croisières   BOATING
(☏0590-88-41-73; www.paradoxe-croisieres. com; Marina de St-François) Runs day trips on the *Paradoxe II* catamaran to the island of Petite Terre for a spot of iguana-watching, beach-lounging, lunch and snorkeling. Boats leave at 8am and return to St-François at 5:30pm and cost €85/65 adult/child under 12. Other catamaran day trips include Marie-Galante (Thursdays only, €90/70 adult/child under 12), including a bus tour and lunch.

🛏 Sleeping

★Hostellerie des Châteaux   HOTEL $$
(☏0590-85-54-08; www.hostellerie-des-chateaux.com; Pointe des Châteaux; d incl breakfast €110-130; 🅿❄🛜🏊) Set on a spacious lawn inland from the road to Pointe des Châteaux, this is a wonderful place for escape – there are just four rooms and four bungalows on the grounds, giving total privacy in sublime surroundings. The on-site restaurant is open to the public and has great views, while some superb beaches are just a short walk away.

Sunset Surf Camp   GUESTHOUSE $$
(☏0590-21-51-10, 0690-41-66-69; www.sunset surfcamp.com; Rte Touristique; s €40-70, d €75; 🅿@🛜🏊) One of the few budget-friendly places to stay in St-François, this friendly place within easy distance of the fantastic Raisins Clairs beach has comfortable rooms (though no air-con), a festive atmosphere, a thick tropical garden *and* charming owners. As well as surfing courses, the owners arrange kitesurfing, paddleboarding, diving and hiking. Free bikes are also provided to all guests.

La Métisse   HOTEL $$
(☏0690-26-16-32, 0590-88-70-00; www. hotel-lametisse.com; 66 Les Hauts de Saint François; d €150; ❄🛜🏊) Tucked away in a complex of hotels above St-François, this pretty place sports a pool in the abstracted shape of Guadeloupe and seven beautifully refitted rooms that combine Creole notes with minimalism. This is a sublime place to escape to and you'll feel miles away from the town, which is in fact just 1km from here.

★La Maison Calebasse   B&B $$$
(☏0690-34-07-77; www.lamaisoncalebasse.com; Sainte-Madeleine; d incl breakfast €135-260; 🅿❄🛜🏊) This gleaming and stylish villa is nestled amid sugarcane fields about 2.5km north of St-François. Brigitte, your affable host, has applied all her flair to the decor; choose from the gîtes (small cottages; rented by the week) and an exceptionally bright room with a handsomely designed bathroom. One of Guadeloupe's very best hideaways.

Hôtel Amaudo   HOTEL $$$
(☏0590-88-87-00; www.amaudo.fr; Anse à la Barque; d €150-180; ❄🛜🏊) This special little place is in the hamlet of Anse à la Barque,

a short distance to the west of St-François itself. It's a beautiful spot, with all of the communal areas attractively done in a colonial style and all 10 rooms having fantastic sea views and private outdoor areas. There's no beach, but there is a fabulous infinity pool.

✖ Eating

Giving a culinary punch way above its weight, St-François has some of Guadeloupe's best restaurants. During the busy months be sure to reserve a table at any of the destination dining spots, and, in fact, at almost anywhere worth going to.

Le Métis Café   SEAFOOD $$
(☑0690-53-81-50; Salines Est; mains €15-30; ⊙6-11pm Tue-Sun; ☎) Hugely popular (reservations are always a good idea), this warm and convivial painted-timber restaurant serves up great food and drinks and enjoys a buzz you'll find in few other places in Guadeloupe. Their brochettes are just as giant as advertised – come hungry! There's live music on Thursdays and Fridays.

Le Zagaya   CARIBBEAN $$
(☑0590-88-67-21; 21 Rue de la République; ⊙noon-3pm & 6pm-midnight Mon-Sat.) This friendly and very popular restaurant specializes in seafood and enjoys a cool breeze coming off the sea. Choose a lobster from the tank or just enjoy the superb tuna tartare. Reserve ahead to get a table with a view and be aware that lunch is not served on Mondays or Wednesdays.

Le Restaurant du Lagon   CREOLE $$
(☑0590-23-47-52; Rte du Lagon; mains €12-20; ⊙noon-3pm) At this jetty restaurant, south of the marina that shelters a big lagoon, the setting is ideal for a plate of freshly caught fish, and there's a gently buzzing ambience. It's also a great place to grab a ti-punch or juice and drink in the view.

**★ Le Mabouya dans La
Bouteille**   FUSION $$$
(☑0590-21-31-14; www.lemabouya.fr; 17 Salines Est; mains €23-40; ⊙7-11pm Wed-Mon; ☎) This outstanding restaurant in the heart of St-François boasts a notably more sophisticated menu than its nearby competitors, with standouts such as duck breast with tamarind and ginger, yam mousse and sweet pumpkin. The improvised space itself is gorgeous, with bottle openers used

as wall decorations, a fabulous wine cellar, mood lighting and jazz in the background.

★ Iguane Café   GASTRONOMY $$$
(☑0590-88-61-37; www.iguane-cafe.fr; Chemin Rural La Coulée; mains €25-30, menus €70-80; ⊙noon-3pm & 7-10:30pm Sun, 7-10:30pm Wed-Mon; ✸☎) For a true culinary experience, the Iguana is hard to beat. On the road out of St-François toward Pointe des Châteaux, you'll find what is probably Guadeloupe's finest restaurant. Sample dishes include lobster ravioli in an oyster-cream sauce with Chinese cabbage and black mushrooms. The degustation menus and wine lists are both superb.

ℹ Information

Office de Tourisme (☑0590-68-66-81; www. destination-stfrancois.com; Ave de l'Europe; ⊙8am-5pm Mon-Fri, Sat & Sun 9am-3pm)

Post Office (Rue Ste-Aude Ferly; ⊙8am-1pm Mon-Sat)

ℹ Getting There & Away

BUS

St-François is well connected by buses to towns along the south coast of Grande-Terre, including Pointe-à-Pitre (€4, 55 minutes), Gosier (€2.50, 45 minutes) and Ste-Anne (€2, 30 minutes). Buses run at least hourly during the day from the town's **Gare Routière**.

BOAT

St-François also has a Gare Maritime from where it has multiple weekly services to La Désirade (€27 return, 45 minutes), St-Louis (Marie-Galante, €20, 40 minutes) and Bourg des Saintes (Les Saintes, €25, one hour). Timetables and prices vary throughout the year, so enquire at the Gare Maritime.

Comatrile (☑0590-22-26-31; www.comatrile. com; Gare Maritime de St-François; ⊙7am-7pm) Runs the *Iguana Beach*, which connects St-François to Les Saintes each morning, stopping at St-Louis (Marie-Galante) on the way. It returns from Les Saintes via Marie-Galante to St-François each afternoon. Check the website for exact timings and prices, as these vary enormously.

Achipel'1 (☑0690-49-49-33; Gare Maritime de St-François) Connects St-François to La Désirade twice a day in both directions (€27 return, 45 minutes).

Marina de St-François (☑0590-88-47-28) In the center of St-François, Guadeloupe's biggest marina is the playground of the Caribbean yachting classes.

Le Moule

The town of Le Moule may have served as an early French capital of Guadeloupe, but it was an important Native American settlement in precolonial times too, with some two millennia of history to its name (which, by the way, is supposedly from the Creole word for a pier, and has nothing to do with mussels). That said, unless you're a surfer or a pre-Columbian history nut, Le Moule is unlikely to be on your itinerary.

Those passing through will enjoy the wide town square with a few historic buildings, including the prettily painted town hall and a neoclassical Catholic church. Along the river are some discernible waterfront ruins from an old customs building and a fortress dating back to the original French settlement. Parc Oüatibi-tibi, on the seafront, is an important Native American archaeological site, but the results of excavations here are now nearly all in the town's museum.

☉ Sights

Edgar Clerc Archaeological Museum
MUSEUM

(Rte de la Rosette; ☉9am-5pm Mon-Fri) `FREE` Following a full renovation, this small but excellent museum is open again, and has a fascinating display of Carib pottery, jewelry and tools made of shells and stone. There is now good lighting, panels in English, and displays about Carib culture and traditions including a large model of a traditional pre-Columbian village. Don't miss the chilling sections on slavery (including irons once used on slaves).

The museum is about 1km north on La Rosette road (D123), on the western outskirts of Le Moule.

⌆ Sleeping

The tourist office can provide a list of vacation rentals, including gîtes and apartments in the area. Apart from that there are almost no accommodation options in Le Moule and most visitors prefer to stay on Grande-Terre's southern coast.

✖ Eating

Le Moule is a busy place with a large population and there are restaurants and small cafes throughout it, mainly concentrated on the seafront and the main road through the center of town.

Le Spot
CAFE $$$

(☏0590-85-66-02; Blvd Maritime; mains €16-26; ☉noon-3pm & 6-10pm Tue-Sat, 6-10pm Sun; ☎) There are incredible views into the churning waters below from this gourmet open-air bar and restaurant on Le Moule's seafront. It's the perfect place to watch the surfers frolicking in the waves over a fancier-than-usual assortment of fish and seafood dishes.

❶ Information

Office de Tourisme (☏0590-23-89-03; www. officetourismelemoule.fr; Blvd Maritime; ☉8:30am-noon & 2-5pm Mon-Fri, 8:30am-noon Sat) Lots of maps and free booklets (in French) on the area. It can also provide a list of vacation rentals, including gîtes and apartments in the area.

❶ Getting There & Away

There are hourly buses between Le Moule and both Pointe-à-Pitre (€2.50, 40 minutes) and St-François (€1.50, 20 minutes). These start and end at the scrap of land in the center of town that is rather ambitiously termed the **Gare Routière** (Rue François Serdot).

Northern Grande-Terre

Northern Grande-Terre offers large chunks of semiwilderness, spectacular scenery and a smattering of delightful beaches, which makes it all the more surprising that nearly all visitors overlook this slice of Guadeloupe (mainly as there are so few well-established hotels here). Locals seem to like it that way, however, and the laid-back fishing villages and traditional Caribbean towns you'll come across have an untouched charm you rarely find elsewhere on the island.

☉ Sights

Anse Bertrand
BEACH

This beach in the small town of the same name has golden sand and is backed by palm trees. It's rarely too crowded and is one of the loveliest beaches in northern Grande-Terre.

Anse Laborde
BEACH

Make a beeline for this oft-overlooked beach that lies about 1.5km north of Anse Bertrand. Strong riptides make it dangerous for swimming but the peace you find sitting here under a tree may be as good as it gets on northern Grande-Terre. A rightly popular beach restaurant, Au Coin des Bons Amis restaurant is also here.

Pointe de la Grande Vigie VIEWPOINT
The island's northernmost point, Pointe de la Grande Vigie offers scenic views from its high sea cliffs. A rocky path – walkable in flip-flops but better in tennis shoes – makes a loop from the parking lot to the cliffs and back, and has some fantastic views. On a clear day you can see Antigua to the north and Montserrat to the northwest, each about 75km away.

Porte d'Enfer NATURAL FEATURE
'Hell's Gate' is actually a long and narrow lagoon that could be mistaken for a river. Its calm waters are a great place to picnic, swim or snorkel. The rather dramatic names comes from the water crashing at the mouth of the lagoon, best seen by taking the road up the hill, from where there's a fantastic viewpoint.

Anse du Souffleur BEACH
(Port-Louis) This long, gently arching beach on northwestern Grande-Terre has fabulous views of mountainous Basse-Terre in the distance, soft pale sand and lapis-lazuli waters. Despite being very popular at weekends, it remains very gently developed with just a couple of simple restaurants, and instead of hotels at one end there's a large cemetery!

✖ Eating

There are a few good choices in northern Grande-Terre, and you can easily stop and get a meal of freshly cooked fish or seafood at almost any beach and in most towns.

Au Coin des Bons Amis CREOLE $
(Anse Laborde; mains €8-10; ⊗11am-4pm) Right on Anse Laborde beach, this place raises the bar in beach-shack cuisine. You'll be surprised such good stuff can come from such an unprepossessing place. Excellent grilled freshwater prawns and tasty catch-of-the-day grilled fish are just some of the few specialties on offer.

★Chez Coco CREOLE $$
(☑0690-31-97-74; Porte d'Enfer; mains €12-18; ⊗noon-4pm) Dining under the trees on the beach right on the lagoon at Porte d'Enfer is the main draw at this charming place. The menu abounds in local flavor, and includes everything from grilled fish to skewered conch. Coconut sorbet for dessert is a must,

WORTH A TRIP

BEAUPORT LE PAYS DE LA CANNE

Since it ceased operations, this former sugar factory has been converted into **Beauport Le Pays de La Canne** (☑0590-22-44-70; www.beauportle paysdelacanne.com; Port-Louis; adult/child €10.50/7.50; ⊗9am-5pm), a learning center about the local region and the history of sugar growing in the Caribbean. Taking the 50-minute train ride through the old sugar plantation is great fun, and there are some excellent exhibits to see in and around the surviving buildings that make up the large complex.

and don't forget to try one of their many specialty rums or excellent cocktails.

ⓘ Getting There & Away
Hourly buses from Pointe-à-Pitre run through Petit-Canal (€2.50, 30 minutes) and Port-Louis (€3, 40 minutes) before ending at the town of Anse Bertrand (€3.50, 50 minutes). Services are rather erratic, however, and far less frequent on the weekend.

ⓘ Getting Around
Your best bet for getting around northern Grande-Terre is to have your own wheels, as a number of places, including **Pointe de la Grande Vigie** and **Porte d'Enfer**, are not reachable by bus services.

BASSE-TERRE ISLAND

Basse-Terre is Guadeloupe's trump card. Despite its name meaning 'low land,' it rather confusingly boasts soaring peaks, including the active La Soufrière volcano, and is by far the more dramatic of Guadeloupe's two main islands. Indeed the entire center of Basse-Terre is covered in thick rainforest and makes up the impressive Parc National de la Guadeloupe.

But this magnificent scenery is not at the expense of good beaches, and you'll find some wonderful stretches of sand on Basse-Terre as well as one of the best dive sites in the Caribbean around Pigeon Island. The northwestern corner of Basse-Terre is the most scenic. Starting from the west side of Route de la Traversée, most of the west coast

BASSE-TERRE TOWN

Do note that the capital of both Basse-Terre island and Guadeloupe as a whole is the very unremarkable town of Basse-Terre. There's nothing to detain visitors here, except perhaps the **Marina de Rivière-Sens** (☎ 0590-86-79-43; www.marina-rivieresens.com) on the southern outskirts which may interest seafaring travelers, so we have not covered the town here.

is rocky and many of the drives snake along the tops of towering sea cliffs, with tantalizing glimpses into the azure bays below. Whatever you do in Guadeloupe, do not miss Basse-Terre.

ⓘ Getting There & Around

Most travelers to Guadeloupe rent a car at the **airport** (p486) for their entire stay.

It is perfectly possible to reach Basse-Terre by bus, however: from Pointe-à-Pitre's **Gare Routière de Bergevin** (Blvd de l'Amitié des Peuples de la Caraïbe), there are regular buses to all towns on the island. Sample prices and travel times include Deshaies (€2, 40 minutes), Plage de Malendure (€3.50, 50 minutes) and Trois-Rivières (€4, one hour). All buses go at least hourly during daylight hours, though they stop after dark and generally don't run on Sunday.

Deshaies

The charmingly sleepy spot of Deshaies has just the right balance of traditional fishing village and good eating and drinking options to keep visitors coming here year-round. There's a sweet little beach framed by green hills all around, but as it's a working fishing port, the best beach for swimming and sunbathing is at nearby Grande Anse. Thanks to its sheltered bay, the village is a popular stop with yachties and sailors and has a cosmopolitan air despite its dinky size.

⊙ Sights

Grande Anse   BEACH

This superb golden-sand beach with no hotel development in sight is just 2km north of Deshaies. This is one of Basse-Terre's longest and prettiest stretches of sand. The entire place is no secret though, and you won't be alone, but it's easy to escape the crowds by

walking down the bay. There are a number of beachside restaurants.

Plage de Clugny   BEACH

Between Grande Anse (p470) and Ste-Rose (p474), at the northern tip of Basse-Terre, is this dazzling stretch of golden sand lapped by jade waters that just beg to be swum in. It has views toward a dramatic islet in the bay and, beyond that, to Montserrat. Bar one little terrace restaurant at the far end of the beach, Plage de Clugny is totally undeveloped. Be very careful as the water can be rough.

🛏 Sleeping

While there are no sleeping options in Deshaies itself, there's a great number of charming guesthouses and hotels in the surrounding hilly countryside, and nearly all of them come with superb views.

Ali Naïs   GUESTHOUSE $$

(☎ 0690-42-07-01; www.gite-cabane-ali-nais.com; Allée Capado, Bas Vent; d/cabaña/ste €96/126/136; @ 🖨 🖥 🏊) This adults-only guesthouse is run by the warm and welcoming Valérie, who has created three gorgeous rooms (well, a room, a *cabaña* and a suite) on the grounds of her own mountainside home, all with great views toward the sea. It's the perfect place for a romantic escape with the option of sociability during breakfast or at the pool.

Caraïb'Bay Hotel   HOTEL $$

(☎ 0690-70-38-68, 0590-28-41-71; www.hotels-guadeloupe.org; Allée du Coeur, Grande Anse; s/d/tr incl breakfast €154/184/228; P 🅿 @ 🖨 🏊) Set in gorgeous tropical gardens just a few minutes' walk from one of Guadeloupe's best beaches, this very pleasant family-friendly hotel has comfortable and brightly painted duplexes and villas scattered through its grounds. All the accommodations are clean, and while the decor can sometimes be a little uninspiring, the whole place exudes a friendly and relaxing atmosphere.

★**Tendacayou Ecolodge & Spa**   BOUTIQUE HOTEL $$$

(☎ 0590-28-42-72; www.tendacayou.com; Matouba, Hauts de Deshaies; d incl breakfast €169-360; 🖨 🖥 🏊) This incredible hideaway in the mountains above Dehaies is run with flair by a French architect and his wife, and it may well be the most memorable and unique accommodation in Guadeloupe. The 11 spacious duplexes include three full-on villas and one multilevel wooden treehouse.

All are wonderfully designed and set in fabulous tropical grounds.

No expense has been spared here, whether it be the natural materials, a decadent spa, the unusual pool with a bridge over it or the gourmet restaurant. A little slice of kooky heaven.

★ **Le Rayon Vert** HOTEL **$$$**
(☏0590-28-43-23; www.hotels-deshaies.com; La Coque Ferry; d incl breakfast €169-199; ❈❀❈) This sunset-friendly seducer is a great place to enjoy a small-scale resort complete with an amazing infinity pool that boasts incred-

ible sea views. The 22 rooms are spacious and functional while enjoying sleek design elements. It's well worth paying for the higher category rooms for the extra space. There's a minimum four-night stay during high season.

Domaine de la Pointe Batterie LUXURY HOTEL **$$$**
(☏0590-28-57-03; Chemin de la Batterie; studios/villas €175/270; ❈❀❈) At this terraced property just outside Deshaies, every luxurious room has a sea view and the villas each have a small private pool. The entire complex

---

PARC NATIONAL DE LA GUADELOUPE

Guadeloupe's only national park, **Parc National de la Guadeloupe** (☏0590-41-55-55; www.guadeloupe-parcnational.fr; Montéran; ⊙6am-6pm), is an absolute stunner, covering much of the interior of Basse-Terre and including such sights as Les Chutes du Carbet and La Soufrière, the active volcano that soars over the island. There are a large number of well-signed and well-maintained hiking paths and several useful information offices, the most helpful of which is the Maison de la Forêt, which is in the middle of the park on the Route de la Traversée.

Chutes du Carbet (adult/child €3/1.50; ⊙8am-4:30pm) Unless it's overcast, the drive up to the Chutes du Carbet lookout gives a view of two magnificent waterfalls plunging down a sheer mountain face. From the lookout you can see the two highest waterfalls from the upper parking lot, where a signboard marks the trailhead to the falls' base. The well-trodden walk to the second-highest waterfall (110m) takes 20 minutes; it's about a two-hour hike to the highest waterfall (115m).

Starting from St-Sauveur on the N1, the road runs 8.5km inland, making for a nice 15-minute drive up through a rainforest. Nearly 3km before the end of the road is a marked stop at the trailhead to Grand Etang, a placid lake circled by a loop trail. It's just a five-minute walk from the roadside parking area down to the edge of the lake, and it takes about an hour more to stroll the lake's perimeter.

La Soufrière For an adventurous 1¾-hour hike to La Soufrière's sulfurous, moonscape-like summit, a well-beaten trail starts where the road to the volcano ends with a parking lot. The trail travels along a gravel bed and continues steeply up the mountain through a cover of low shrubs and thick ferns. In addition to a close-up view of the steaming volcano, the hike offers some fine vistas of the island. Start early in the morning.

There are a couple of ways to get to La Soufrière, the active 1467m volcano that looms above the southern half of the island. The most direct route is to follow the N3 from Basse-Terre town in the direction of St-Claude. From St-Claude, signs point to La Soufrière, 6km to the northeast on the D11.

Cascade aux Ecrevisses (Rte de la Traversée) This idyllic little jungle waterfall drops from a Basse-Terre mountainside into a small pool by a river, where you can swim. It's a popular place and can be rather crowded on the weekend, mainly as it's right on main road through the Parc National de la Guadeloupe.

Information

The **Maison de la Forêt** (Rte de la Traversée; ⊙8:30am-1pm & 1:30-4:30pm Mon-Sat, 9am-1:15pm Sun), is a useful and well-run tourist information center for anyone wanting to explore the Parc National de la Guadeloupe. It includes a staffed exhibit center with French-signed displays and English-language pamphlets, plus maps of the geographical features of the park. It's located along the Route de la Traversée, the main road through the park.

is set in beautiful gardens, and the on-site spa, one of the main attractions of the hotel, means that you can spend days here being pampered: that's good news as there's a three-night minimum.

✖ Eating

Les Hibiscus
CREOLE $$

(☑ 0590-28-22-50; Grande Anse; mains €8-15, menus €12-20; ⏱11am-3pm) This joyous, welcoming open-air eatery overlooking the beach serves classic Creole fare, and it serves it done right: rich, filling and more compellingly seasoned than in its nearby competitors.

Mahina
SEAFOOD $$

(☑ 0590-88-95-38; Blvd des Poissonnières; mains €16-27; ⏱noon-2.30pm & 7-10pm Wed-Sun; 🛜) Overlooking the bay and boasting a great terrace as well as a second-floor dining room with good views, this simple-looking place churns out far more sophisticated food than you might expect. As well as the usual seafood offerings, there is a daily-changing tapas menu and in the evening excellent pizzas made in a wood-fired oven.

La Savane
FRENCH $$

(☑ 0590-91-39-58; Blvd des Poissonnières; mains €18-23; ⏱noon-3pm Sun, 7-10pm Thu-Tue) Ignore the tacky gorilla sculpture at the entrance – this restaurant wins plaudits for its high-quality cuisine and divine location right on the seafront, with a terrace from which to drink it all in. Classic French food such as veal kidneys in mustard sauce and lamb fillet with rosemary anchors the menu. Wonderful desserts round out the offerings.

Le Coin des Pêcheurs
CREOLE, SEAFOOD $$

(☑ 0590-28-47-75; Rue de la Vague Bleue; mains €14-20, menu €18; ⏱noon-3pm & 6:30-10pm Wed-Mon) This colorful one-story beach restaurant has a great position overlooking the bay. With such breathtaking surroundings, many alfrescoholics would go back to this breezy veranda by the sea for the location alone; but the well-priced Creole-eclectic fare is delightful too, especially the *brochette de poisson* (skewered fish) and the conch fricassee.

Hemingway
INTERNATIONAL $$

(☑ 0590-47-42-04; Domaine de la Pointe Batterie; mains €15-25; ⏱lunch, dinner Wed-Sat) Down the road from the Domaine de la Pointe Batterie hotel, this appealing venue has unbeatably good views of the bay and a terrace that's a treat to dine on (as long as the wind isn't too strong). The whole place exudes style and the dishes, heavy on seafood and fish, are surprisingly affordable.

★ La Table du Poisson Rouge
INTERNATIONAL $$$

(☑ 0590-28-42-72; www.tendacayou.com; Tendacayou Ecolodge & Spa, Matouba, Hauts de Deshaies; mains €20-30, dinner menu €30; ⏱noon-3pm & 6-11pm Wed-Sun; 🛜🍴) This elegant restaurant within the Tendacayou Ecolodge & Spa is an atmospheric place for destination dining. And you could lose yourself in the homemade *moelleux au chocolat* (chocolate cake) that arrives at the end of the meal. Judging by the tuna tataki in granadilla sauce, the beautifully presented mains are just as yummy, though.

L'Amer
FRENCH, CREOLE $$$

(☑ 0590-28-50-43; Blvd des Poissonnières; mains €17-28, lunch/dinner menu €18/20; ⏱8am-11pm Mon-Sat; 🛜) Unmissably orange on the outside, refined and stylish inside, this is a Deshaies institution. The interesting (and pricey) menu takes in seafood and swordfish, and combines French tradition with an eye to local flavors. Downstairs has a simple vibe during the day, when you can eat a good sandwich on the sunny terrace; upstairs in the evenings is more formal.

ℹ Information

Office de Tourisme (www.tourisme-deshaies. com; Rue de la Liberté; ⏱9am-noon & 1-5pm Mon-Fri)

ℹ Getting There & Away

There are at least hourly direct buses to Deshaies (€2, 40 minutes) from Pointe-à-Pitre's **Gare Routière de Bergevin** (p470), and connections to other towns in Basse-Terre from Deshaies. Buses arriving in Deshaies run along the coastal road or the road behind it, depending on what direction they're heading, and there are multiple bus stops along both roads where buses stop and can be flagged down.

Plage de Malendure & Pigeon Island

This long stretch of overlapping beachside towns and villages is an ideal destination for divers: they come to dive and snorkel at the superb Réserve Cousteau around little Pigeon Island, and to relax on Plage de Malendure's dark-sand beaches. The entire area is backed by steep hills and driving along this stretch of coast is pure pleasure. Plage de Malendure is not the best beach in the area, but it is one of the best in Guadeloupe for activities, and the competition keeps the prices reasonable. The main town here is Bouillante, named after the river of the same name, which flows into the sea here. The town itself has little to offer, but has a pleasant fishing port and seafront.

◉ Sights

Réserve Cousteau   NATURE RESERVE
Jacques Cousteau brought Pigeon Island to international attention by declaring it to be one of the world's top dive areas. The waters surrounding the island are now protected as an underwater park. The majority of the dive sites around Pigeon Island are very scenic, with big schools of fish and coral reefs that are shallow enough for good snorkeling. It's only a 10- to 15-minute boat ride to the dive sites.

🏃 Activities

Gwada Pagaie   KAYAKING
(☑ 0590-10-20-29, 0690-93-91-71; www.gwada pagaie.com; Plage de Malendure) Wanna see the Réserve Cousteau from a different perspective? With a kayak, you can reach Pigeon Island at your own pace. This outfit rents kayaks for €25/35 per half-/full day. A map of the marine park is provided, as well as life jackets; bring a picnic.

Canopée   HIKING
(☑ 0590-26-95-59; www.canopeeguadeloupe.com; Plage de Malendure) This is the area's best canyoning and hiking operation, offering a huge number of trips into the nearby mountains from half-day walks (€35) to more challenging canyoning outings (from €55).

PPK-Plaisir Plongée Karukera   DIVING
(☑ 0590-98-82-43; www.ppk-plongee-guadeloupe. com; Plage de Malendure) This efficiently run dive shop gets good reviews. An introductory/single dive costs €45/35. Also fits snorkeling in during its dive outings (€15).

Centre de Plongée des Îlets   DIVING
(☑ 0590-41-09-61; www.plongee-guadeloupe.fr; Plage de Malendure) Diving here starts at an incredibly good-value €38 for divers with their own equipment. An introductory dive costs €47. With two boats, this operation tends to have larger groups and offers all kinds of instruction for beginners.

Les Heures Saines   DIVING
(☑ 0590-98-86-63; www.heures-saines.gp; Le Rocher de Malendure, Bouillante) This extremely versatile operation is based under Le Rocher de Malendure restaurant. In addition to the standard dive offerings, it can organize La Soufrière hikes, canyoning and dolphin-watching trips.

Archipel Plongée   DIVING
(☑ 0590-98-93-93; www.archipel-plongee.fr; Plage de Malendure) This friendly place right on the beach offers a range of diving courses as well as regular diving in the Réserve Cousteau. Dive prices start at €45.

Centre International de Plongée   DIVING
(☑ 0590-98-81-72; www.cip-guadeloupe.com; Plage de Malendure) This diving outfit offers one-tank dives for €35, as well as competitive package prices for divers who plan to get a lot of underwater time in.

🛏 Sleeping

There are several accommodations options in and around Plage de Malendure, but most are private accommodation such as gîtes or studios, and there are currently almost no hotels here. One excellent option is Le Jardin Tropical, a perfect base if you plan to spend a few days doing various activities.

Le Jardin Tropical   HOTEL $$
(☑ 0590-98-77-23; www.guadeloupeheberge ment.fr; Rue de Poirier, Bouillante; d from €80; P ❄ 🛜 ⛱) Le Jardin Tropical stands out for its friendly owners, a pool that feels nearly private and its super location on a greenery-shrouded hillside with killer sea views. The bungalow rooms are sparkling clean, simply furnished and good value, and all have outdoor patios and kitchens. Dinner meals are available by arrangement.

🍴 Eating

⭐ La Touna   SEAFOOD $$
(☑ 0590-98-70-10; www.la-touna.com; Bouillante; mains €14-25, menus €22-28; ⊙ lunch & dinner Tue-Sat, lunch Sun; 🛜) This fantastic and riotously popular seafront restaurant with friendly staff and an enticing and innovative menu is the best place to eat along this part of the coast. The sumptuous Creole menu with a French twist specializes in fresh seafood (there's a lobster tank here where you can choose your dinner), while the terrace has great views toward Pigeon Island.

WORTH A TRIP

MAISON DU CACAO

At **Maison du Cacao** (☑ 0590-98-25-23; www.maisonducacao.fr; Rte de Grande Plaine, Pointe-Noire; adult/child €7/3; ⊙ 9:30am-5:30pm Mon-Sat year-round & Sun Dec-Feb) you'll find an interesting display on the religious and spiritual history of cacao on Guadeloupe. Afterwards you can treat yourself to a cup of hot chocolate that's closer to the Mayan's sacrament of divinity than any mere powdered drink.

Le Rocher de Malendure   INTERNATIONAL $$$
(☑ 0590-98-70-84; Bouillante; mains €18-35, menus €20-32; ⊙ lunch & dinner Thu-Tue) The best-established restaurant in Bouillante, this sprawling complex is actually built on the eponymous rock, and has incredible views on all sides. The restaurant offers everything from beef fillet to the fresh lobsters it keeps in a small pool.

❶ Getting There & Away

Hourly buses between Pointe-à-Pitre and Basse-Terre town pass through Plage de Malendure (€3.50, 50 minutes) and Bouillante (€3.50, 55 minutes), and will drop you at one of several bus stops along the main road through both towns. Similarly priced, hourly buses between Pointe-à-Pitre and Vieux Habitants also stop in both places.

Ste-Rose

Ste-Rose was once a simple little village, primarily involved with fishing and agriculture. While sugarcane is still an important crop in the area, Ste-Rose is increasingly becoming a tourist destination in its own right, not least because it's the main launching pad for boat excursions to Grand Cul-de-Sac Marin, a marine park dotted with idyllic islets ringed by sandy beaches, mangrove swamps and healthy reefs. Don't miss it.

◉ Sights

Musée du Rhum   MUSEUM
(Rum Museum; ☑ 0590-28-70-04; www.musee-du-rhum.fr; Viard; adult/child €6/4; ⊙ 9am-5pm Mon-Sat) Those who want to understand how the ambrosia called rum starts in the sugarcane fields and ends on their palates should really head to this excellent museum, which

has thorough explanations in English. It's at the site of the Reimonenq Distillery, about 500m inland from the N2 in the village of Bellevue, just southeast of Ste-Rose. Exhibits include an old distillery, cane-extraction gears and a vapor machine dating from 1707.

★ **Grand Cul-de-Sac Marin**   NATURE RESERVE
This Unesco Biosphere Reserve just off the coast of Basse-Terre makes for a superb day trip. A chain of small coral islets sitting atop a 25km-long coral wall, the reserve supports unique ecosystems including mangrove forest, rich birdlife and reefs bursting with tropical fish. There are also some gorgeous white-sand beaches, and you'll never have to worry about overcrowding. Book through an agency in Ste-Rose.

☞ Tours

BleuBlancVert   BOATING
(☑ 0690-63-82-43; www.bleublancvert.com; Ste-Rose; half-day adult/child €40/20) This well-regarded operator runs half-day lagoon and mangrove tours on a motorized raft. The guide imparts environmental and geological knowledge, and you'll have the opportunity to snorkel along the barrier reef. Operates small groups only (four people maximum). Prices include drinks.

Nico Excursions   BOATING
(☑ 0590-28-72-47, 0690-53-09-65; www.nicoexcursions.com; Ste-Rose; half-day adult/child €40/20) This reputable outfit runs very popular half-day trips to nearby islands and reefs, including îlet Blanc, with a maximum of 12 people. It includes swimming and snorkel stops.

✕ Eating

Le Poulpe   SEAFOOD $$
(☑ 0590-28-74-21; Blvd St-Charles; mains €12-25; ⊙ noon-3pm Mon-Sat) This small place is a local institution and locals tell you it is the place to go to for the best Creole take on seafood dishes. Do not miss their excellent *fricassé de chatroux* (octopus stew).

Chez Clara   CREOLE, FRENCH $$
(☑ 0590-28-72-99; Blvd St-Charles, Bord de Mer; mains €16-21, menu €18; ⊙ lunch Thu-Tue, dinner Mon, Tue & Thu-Sat) Across the road from Ste-Rose's small fishing harbor, this casually gracious place has sea views and serves up classics such as tuna tartare, veal cutlet and lamb steak. Don't come here in a hurry –

this is the classic place for a relaxed, boozy lunch.

❶ Getting There & Away

Ste-Rose is on the main road between Pointe-à-Pitre and Deshaies. Any of the half-hourly buses between Pointe-à-Pitre to Deshaies can drop you off here (€2, 40 minutes): there are various bus stops along the main road skirting the town.

Trois-Rivières

Despite its wonderful natural position – scattered across a series of steep, verdant hillsides that tumble dramatically into the Caribbean Sea with the glorious silhouettes of Les Saintes in the distance – Trois-Rivières is a place that is rarely visited for its own attractions. The reason is far more prosaic: Trois-Rivières has the shortest and most regular ferry connections to Terre-de-Haut in Les Saintes. Few stop here for long, but there are basic facilities and the town is perfectly pleasant if you need to kill a bit of time before your boat leaves.

❶ Getting There & Away

There are hourly buses to Trois-Rivières from Pointe-à-Pitre (€4, one hour). Buses wind their way along the main road through the town and end their journey at the port.

Trois-Rivières is also the main point of departure for Les Saintes, and there are regular ferries throughout the day connecting Trois-Rivières to Bourg des Saintes (on Terre-de-Haut). Prices vary enormously, but you can expect to pay around €15/25 single/return. The journey takes around 30 minutes. Services are run by the following three operators:

CTM Deher (p487)

Val'Ferry (☑ 0590-91-45-15, 0590-94-97-09; www.valferry.fr; Allée des Espadons; ⊙7am-7pm)

Vedette Beatrix (☑ 0590-25-08-06; Rue de la Dissidence; ⊙7am–7pm)

LES SAINTES

These tiny islands 10km to the south of Basse-Terre are many people's highlight of Guadeloupe, as they allow visitors to enjoy a slice of the old Caribbean, far from the development and urban sprawl that has affected the mainland. As mountainous charmers with great beaches, Les Saintes may not exactly be a secret to the many Basse-Terre day-trippers, but they are still probably Guadeloupe's least explored corner, and easily one of its most beautiful. As well as splendid beaches, there's first-class diving and some wonderful restaurants.

Terre-de-Haut is where nearly everyone means when they speak of coming here, though some also visit next-door Terre-de-Bas, the only other inhabited island in the chain. Do not miss this charming corner of Guadeloupe.

Terre-de-Haut

Lying 10km off Guadeloupe is Terre-de-Haut, the largest of the eight small islands that make up Les Saintes. Since the island was too hilly and dry for sugar plantations, slavery never took hold here. Consequently, the older islanders still trace their roots to the early seafaring Norman and Breton colonists, and many of the locals have light skin and blond or red hair.

Terre-de-Haut is unhurried and feels like a small slice of southern France transported to the Caribbean. Lots of English is spoken here thanks to a big international sailing scene, and it's definitely the most cosmopolitan of Guadeloupe's outlying islands. Divers love the waters around Terre-de-Haut for their good visibility and healthy reefs.

Home to most of the island's residents, Bourg des Saintes is a picturesque village with a decidedly Norman accent. Its narrow streets are lined with whitewashed, red-roofed houses with shuttered windows and yards of flowering hibiscus.

◉ Sights

Fort Napoléon   FORT
(adult/child €5/2.50; ⊙9am-12:30pm) Built in 1867, on the site of an earlier fort destroyed by the British in 1809, this impressive defensive installation affords a heart-stopping view of Bourg des Saintes and the surrounding islands. You can walk through on your own or join a guided tour conducted in French. The naval museum inside is only of interest to hard-core naval historians – the 1782 battle of Les Saintes is documented in exacting detail. It's a surprisingly exhausting 1.5km walk uphill from the town.

Baie du Marigot   BEACH
Baie du Marigot is a pleasant little bay with a calm protected beach about 1km north of Bourg des Saintes. It's fairly close to Fort

Napoléon so you could combine a visit to the two; after visiting the fort, turn left at the bottom of the winding fort road and bear left again a few minutes later as you near the bay.

★ Baie de Pompierre   BEACH

The horseshoe-shaped Baie de Pompierre is perhaps Terre-de-Haut's loveliest: a reef-protected beach with golden sand and a splendid setting. There are even tame goats that mosey onto the beach and lie down next to sunbathers, as well as a small island to swim out to. The beach is an easy 1.6km walk northeast of Bourg des Saintes, although the walk is steep. There are showers and bathrooms on the beach and plenty of wooden picnicking areas.

Anse Rodrigue   BEACH

South of Grande Anse and about 2km from town is Anse Rodrigue, a nice beach on a protected cove that usually has good swimming conditions.

Pain de Sucre   MOUNTAIN

(Anse à Cointe) The Pain de Sucre (Sugarloaf) is an imposing 53m-high basalt peninsula. You'll find good snorkeling and a sandy beach here.

Anse à Cointe   BEACH

Two kilometers southwest of Bourg des Saintes is Anse à Cointe, a good beach for combining swimming and snorkeling. The snorkeling is best on the north side.

Anse Crawen   BEACH

Anse Crawen is a secluded, clothing-optional beach just a couple of minutes' walk down a dirt path that starts at the southwestern end of the Terre-de-Haut coastal road.

Le Chameau   VIEWPOINT

A winding cement road leads to the summit of Le Chameau, which at 309m is Terre-de-Haut's highest point. From town it's a moderately difficult hour-long walk to the top. Note that you're not allowed to use scooters to get up here, so prepare to hike!

🏃 Activities

Pisquettes Diving   DIVING

(📞0590-99-88-80; www.pisquettes.fr; Bourg des Saintes) A professional and highly recommended dive shop that offers the full range of scuba activities. Introductory dives go for €56 while single dives cost €51. Dive packages and certification courses are also available.

La Dive Bouteille   DIVING

(📞0690-49-80-91, 0590-99-54-25; www.dive-bouteille.com; Plage de la Colline, Bourg des Saintes) A reputable outfit at the southwestern end of the bay. It charges €110 for a two-tank dive outing and €69 for an introductory dive.

🛏 Sleeping

★ Auberge Les Petits Saints   BOUTIQUE HOTEL $$

(📞0590-99-50-99; www.petitssaints.com; Rue de la Savane; d €116-185; ❄🛜⛲) This former mayor's residence is set in an opulent villa and has quite a wonderful location with unique and interestingly furnished rooms. Each room is different, but terraces with sea views and big canopy beds come as standard, and it manages to have a refined feel without being stuffy. The decked swimming pool has fabulous views over the bay.

Kanaoa   HOTEL $$

(📞0590-99-51-36; www.hotelkanaoa.com; Rue de Coquelet, Anse Mire, Bourg des Saintes; s/d incl breakfast from €100/120, bungalows from €190; ❄🛜⛲) Right at the northern end of Bourg des Saintes, this two-star hotel sits on the beach and has a private pier and restaurant. Its rooms have rather a cheesy tropical decor, so you won't be overwhelmed by its style, but a number do have gorgeous sea views. As well as the standard rooms, there are four duplex bungalows with kitchenettes.

LoBleu Hôtel   HOTEL $$

(📞0690-63-80-36, 0590-92-40-00; www.lobleu-hotel.com; Rue Benoît Cassin; r from €122; ❄🛜) LoBleu is a real heartbreaker. Slap-bang on the beach, you couldn't ask for a more enviable setting. Unfortunately, only two rooms (out of 10) have direct sea views. They're all cheerful, with mural paintings, a small balcony and plenty of natural light. Kayaks are available for rent. Good English is spoken.

🍴 Eating

For such a small place, there are some superb restaurants on Terre-de-Haut. Most are in and around Bourg des Saintes, the only real town, though there are a few casual beach places elsewhere on the island.

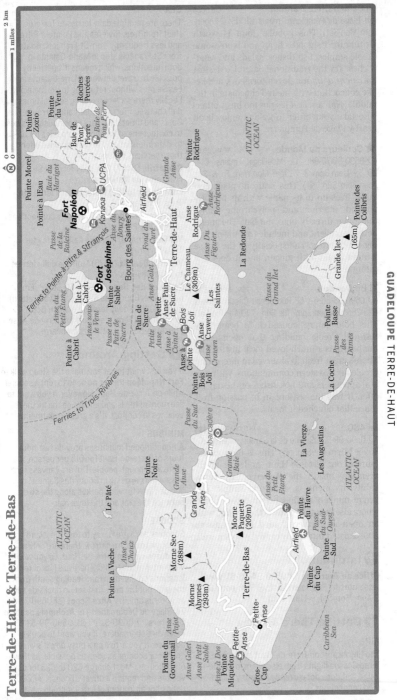

Terre-de-Haut & Terre-de-Bas

N

0   1 miles
0   2 km

Terre-de-Haut

Pointe Zozio
Pointe du Vent
Roches Percées
Pointe Morel
Baie de Pont Pierre
Baie de Pont Pierre
ATLANTIC OCEAN
Baie du Marigot
Pointe à l'Eau
UCPA
Pointe à l'Eau
Kanaoa
Fort Napoléon
Pointe du Vent
Grande Anse
Pointe Rodrigue
Pointe Rodrigue
Airfield
Anse Rodrigue
Anse du Bourg
Fond du Curé
Anse du Petit Étang
Passe de la Baleine
Ferries to Pointe-à-Pitre & St-François
Fort Joséphine
Îlet à Cabrit
Pointe à Cabrit
Anse sous le Vent
Pointe du Pain de Sucre
Passe du Pain de Sucre
Bourg des Saintes
Pointe Sable
Anse Galet
Anse Rodrigue
Anse Du Figuier
Terre-de-Haut
Le Chameau (309m)
La Redonde
Passe du Grand Îlet
Pointe des Colibris
ATLANTIC OCEAN
Grande Îlet (165m)
Grande Îlet
Pain de Sucre
Petite Anse
Petite Anse de Sucre
Bois Joli
Les Saintes
Pointe Basse
Anse à Cointe
Anse à Cointe
Anse Crawen
Anse Crawen
Pointe Bois Joli
Pointe Bois Joli
Passe des Dames
La Coche
Ferries to Trois-Rivières
Passe du Sud
Embarcadère
Pointe Noire
Grande Anse
Grande Anse
Grande Baie
La Vierge
Les Augustins
ATLANTIC OCEAN
Grande Anse
Le Pâté
Anse à Chaux
Morne Sec (288m)
Morne Abymes (293m)
Morne Paquette (209m)
Anse du Petit Étang
Pointe du Havre
Pointe du Sud-Ouest
Passe du Sud-Ouest
Airfield
Pointe du Sud
Terre-de-Bas
Pointe à Vache
Pointe du Gouvernail
Anse Pajot
Anse Galet
Anse Petit Sable
Anse à Dos
Pointe Miquelon
Gros-Cap
Petite Anse
Petite Anse
Pointe du Cap
Caribbean Sea

Le Salako Chez Z'amour CREOLE $

(off Plage de Pompierre; mains €10-15; ⊙noon-3pm Mon-Sat) This popular joint is worth visiting for its good, cheap and wholesome Creole staples, fish dishes, salads and sandwiches. Try the traditional Saintoise dessert *tourment d'amour* (love's torment), a cake-like concoction with melted chocolate in the middle. Nab a seat if it's not too busy, otherwise take your order to go and enjoy it on nearby Plage de Pompierre.

★**Couleurs du Monde** SEAFOOD $$

(☑0590-92-70-98; Le Mouillage; mains €14-20; ⊙11am-3pm & 7-10pm Mon-Wed, Fri & Sat, noon-3pm Sun; 🐾) This seafront place certainly lives up to its name with its brightly painted interior and polychrome tables that open directly onto the bay. The menu here is excellent and includes a daily-changing set of tapas. The specialty of the house is tuna tataki with ginger, and it does not disappoint.

Ti Bo Doudou FRENCH, CREOLE $$

(☑0590-98-56-67; 58 Rue Benoît Cassin; menus €23-25; ⊙noon-3pm Tue-Sun, 7-10pm Tue-Sat) This bold eatery, housed in a beautifully restored Creole building that opens onto the beach, is a much-loved local institution. There's great fresh food served in interesting Creole and Western combinations, with several appetizers and hot dishes of the day on offer. It was the sea bream in passion-fruit sauce that clinched it for us.

Le 480 INTERNATIONAL $$$

(☑0590-99-50-99; Rue de la Savane; mains €20-30; ⊙7-11pm Tue-Sun; 🐾) This is the top restaurant on Terre-de-Haut, and has lovely premises inside the Auberge Les Petits Saints. Its menu is short and simple, but you're unlikely to find better cooking anywhere else. Another draw is the setting, with an open-air terrace shaded by a massive 200-year-old intricately carved wooden wall.

ℹ Information

Office de Tourisme (☑0590-94-30-61; www.lessaintes.fr; Rue Jean Calot; ⊙9am-noon & 2-4pm Mon-Sat, 9-11am Sun)

ℹ Getting There & Away

AIR

The tiny airport on Terre-de-Haut takes chartered Cessna flights from elsewhere in Guadeloupe, but does not currently have any scheduled connections.

SEA

There are multiple daily ferries to Terre-de-Haut from Trois-Rivières and Pointe-à-Pitre, and less frequently from St-François. Boats from St-François stop in Marie-Galante in both directions, which means it's perfectly possible to travel between Marie-Galante and Les Saintes without returning to the mainland. Locally there's a ferry running several times daily between Terre-de-Haut and Terre-de-Bas. Costs and timetables vary enormously: it's best to contact one of the ferry companies for up-to-date information. Ferry companies offering these services include:

Comatrile (p467) One daily ferry to St-Françoise via Marie-Galante.

CTM Deher (p487) Multiple daily ferries to Trois-Rivières.

Jeans for Freedom (p486) Daily connections to Pointe-à-Pitre.

Val'Ferry (p475) Multiple daily ferries to Trois-Rivières.

Vedette Beatrix (p475) Multiple daily ferries to Trois-Rivières.

Le Soleil des Îles (☑0690-50-36-28; Embarcadère, Bourg des Saintes; €10.50 return) Runs multiple daily ferries between Bourg des Saintes (Terre-de-Haut) and Grande Anse (Terre-de-Bas). Buy tickets on board.

ℹ Getting Around

If you just want to eat and make the steep walk to **Fort Napoléon** there's no need to rent a scooter while on Terre-de-Haut. However, if you want to see more of the island and reach the furthest beaches in comfort, it's a great investment.

MINIBUS

Air-conditioned minibuses provide two-hour tours of Terre-de-Haut for €15 per person, if there are enough people. Drivers canvass ferry passengers arriving in Bourg des Saintes, or you can look for vans parked along the street between the pier and the town hall.

SCOOTER

Scooters are a great way to tour the island. Although roads are narrow, there are only a few dozen cars on Terre-de-Haut, so you won't encounter much traffic. There are lots of rental locations on the main road leading south from the pier, but the ones that set up dockside seem as good as any. Try **Alizé Scoot** (☑0690-72-80-74; Place du Débarcadère) or **Archipel Location Scooters** (☑0690-31-99-91, 0590-99-52-63; Place du Débarcadère) if you want to book in advance. If you arrive on a busy day, it's wise to grab your scooter as soon as possible, as they often sell out. Most charge €20 to €25 for day visitors and require a driver's license, a €200 deposit or an imprint of a major credit card.

Scooters come with gas but not damage insurance, so if you get in an accident or spill the bike, the repairs will be charged to your credit card. Driving a scooter is prohibited in the center of Bourg des Saintes and helmets are obligatory.

Terre-de-Bas

Lying just 1km to the west of Terre-de-Haut, Terre-de-Bas is the only other inhabited island in Les Saintes. It's an idyllic place that was historically home to sugar and coffee plantations. With these long gone, the island relies on fishing for its livelihood and tourism has yet to take root. Despite this, there is a regular ferry service between the islands, making it possible for visitors to poke around on a day excursion, or even stay overnight.

The main village, Petite-Anse, is on Terre-de-Bas' west coast. It has hilly streets lined with trim houses, a small fishing harbor, and a quaint church with a graveyard of tombs decorated with conch shells and plastic flowers. Grande Anse, diagonally across the island on the east coast, is a small village with a little 17th-century church and a good beach.

🛏 Sleeping & Eating

There are no hotels on Terre-de-Bas, but there are a couple of locals offering holiday homes, so it's perfectly possible to stay overnight. Most people visit from Terre-de-Haut on a day trip, though.

On Terre-de-Bas, Petite-Anse has a good bakery and pastry shop, and both Petite-Anse and Grande Anse have a couple of reasonably priced local restaurants serving up seafood.

ℹ Getting There & Away

A ferry, **Le Soleil des Îles** (€10.50 return), travels between Grand-Bourg, Terre-de-Haut and Anse des Mûriers, a pier near to Grande Anse, before continuing to Petite-Anse, the port and de facto capital of Terre-de-Bas. It makes the journey five times a day in each direction during the week, and twice a day in each direction on the weekend. The journey takes around 10 minutes to Anse des Mûriers, and 15 minutes to Petite-Anse. Buy tickets on the boat.

ℹ Getting Around

If you enjoy long country walks, it's possible to make a loop walk between Terre-de-Bas' two villages, Petite-Anse and Grande Anse. It's about 9km round-trip, going out on one road (either the cross-island or the south-coast road) and returning on the other.

Otherwise, there's sometimes a private minibus (€2, five minutes) that runs between the villages. Ask a local where it's stopping these days.

MARIE-GALANTE

Marie-Galante is a delightfully undeveloped island beloved by those who enjoy the quieter pleasures in life and particularly by beach bums who want to escape the crowds. Compared with the archipelago's other islands, Marie-Galante is relatively flat, its dual limestone plateaus rising only 150m, but even if it doesn't enjoy a dramatic landscape, it has knock-out beaches, some fascinating old buildings, and some top-notch eating and sleeping options. Plan at least two full days here to do the island justice.

There are three settlements on Marie-Galante. Grand-Bourg is the commercial and administrative center of the island, while the other two villages, Capesterre on the southeast coast and St-Louis on the northern coast, are both dreamily laid-back fishing ports with good beaches in the vicinity. However, as the island can be crossed in half an hour and nearly everyone hires a car, it makes little difference where you decide to base yourself.

◎ Sights

Rum distilleries are Marie-Galante's main sights, and you have three to choose from. Idyllic beaches include Plage de la Feuillère and Plage de Petite Anse, just west of Capesterre, as well as Plage de Vieux-Fort and Plage de l'Anse Canot, which both lie north of St-Louis.

Distillerie Poisson DISTILLERY
(☑0590-97-03-79; Habitation Edouard, Rameau, Grand-Bourg; ⊙7am-1pm Mon-Sat) FREE Midway between St-Louis and Grand-Bourg, this famous distillery bottles the island's best-known rum under the Père Labat label. There's also a good restaurant on the premises and plenty of chances to buy souvenir samples.

Distillerie Bielle DISTILLERY
(☑0590-97-93-62; www.rhumbielle.com; Section Bielle, Grand-Bourg) FREE Between Grand-Bourg and Capesterre, this historic distillery

offers free tours of its age-old operation and a fully stocked gift shop.

Domaine de Bellevue
DISTILLERY

(☑0590-97-26-50; www.habitation-bellevue. com; Section Bellevue, Capesterre; ⊙9am-1pm) 🍃 FREE This remotely located rum distillery on Marie-Galante has a historic setting and a wonderful old windmill. The distillery nowadays uses totally sustainable and nonpolluting methods to produce its rums and is a local leader in responsible rum production.

🛏 Sleeping

Marie-Galante has some superb accommodation options, although you'll find yourself with much more choice if you're spending more than a night or two – many of the best guesthouses do not accept visitors for less than two or three nights.

Au Village de Ménard
BUNGALOW $

(☑0590-97-09-45; www.villagedemenard.com; Section Vieux Fort, St-Louis; d €80-95, tr €125; ❄🛜🌊) An attractive cluster of 11 comfortable bungalows and villas, Au Village de Ménard is the perfect place to relax after a long day's adventures, with an enviable position on a cliff next to an old mill overlooking the bay, a great poolside restaurant and a nicely laid-out tropical garden. The owners rent cars at unbeatable rates. It's 2km from the nearest beach.

Village de Canada
COTTAGE $

(☑0690-50-55-50, 0590-97-86-11; www.villagede canada.com; Section Canada, Grand-Bourg; d €77-99; ❄🛜🌊) This Creole-style venture consists of eight cottages and an apartment resting in a flowery plot. The casual atmosphere and quiet location make this the kind of place where you quickly lose track of the days. The cottages are nothing special but are well kitted out. There's a good pool, too. Minimum stay of two nights.

★ Coco Beach Resort
GUESTHOUSE $$

(☑0690-49-86-66, 0590-97-10-46; www.coco beachmariegalante.com; Grand-Bourg; s/d/ste €89/99/129; ❄🛜🌊) Pint-sized, this place can hardly call itself a resort, and it will appeal to anyone who would never dream of staying at a big impersonal hotel complex. There are just eight rooms here, all facing the sea and overlooking a gorgeous little beach with views towards Dominica. The welcome is warm and the whole place feels like a shared house.

Le Touloulou
HOTEL $$

(☑0590-97-32-63, 0690-39-13-06; www.letou loulou.com; Plage de Petite Anse; d/q €75/150; ❄🛜) Le Touloulou has two major advantages: it's set right on the beach and has a wonderful restaurant. It's otherwise a fairly basic setup, but all five rooms have porches overlooking the beach, and the family rooms have little kitchens. Being on the beach for these prices is a great deal, and management is friendly.

Villa Les Bougainvilliers
B&B $$

(www.location-marie-galante.fr; 22 Les Hauts de Beaufils, Grand-Bourg; d incl breakfast €83, studio €99; 🅿❄🛜🌊) An atmosphere of dreamlike tranquility wafts over this superb property just over 2 miles east of Grand-Bourg. It features an alluring pool and an Eden-like garden with million-dollar views of the coast. There's one compact room and one larger studio. It's secluded and not on the beach, so you'll need your own wheels to stay here. There's a two-night minimum stay.

L'Oasis
GUESTHOUSE $$

(☑0590-97-59-55, 0690-50-87-38; http:// oasis-mariegalante.monsite-orange.fr; Rue Sony Rupaire, Grand-Bourg; d €80-120; ❄🛜) Each one of the three apartments here has something special to recommend it – a small tropical garden, a Jacuzzi or a terrace with views to Dominica. It's located in the center of the village, 1km from the seafront, toward the Grande-Savane area. Prices drop for stays longer than one night.

🍴 Eating

L'Ornata
BRASSERIE $

(Place Félix Eboué, Grand-Bourg; mains €8-16; ⊙8am-10pm; 🛜) A great-value option in a pleasant old Creole house right across from the ferry dock. Food-wise, it features all the Creole classics as well as moderately priced *plats du jour* (specials) and snack options, best enjoyed on the breezy terrace. Takeaway is available, and it's also a good place to come for drinks in the evening.

Sun 7 Beach
SEAFOOD $$

(☑0590-97-87-58; Grand-Bourg; mains €18-32; ⊙noon-3pm & 7-10.30pm Mon-Sat; 🛜) This charming beach restaurant with serious culinary credentials is run by a young and friendly team trying to enliven the gastronomic offerings on the island. It's just a timber shack, but it's been painted in bright colors and is an alluring and fun place for a meal, with dishes such as *magret de canard* (duck fillet) cooked with honey and cumin on offer.

Chez Henri
GRILL, BAR **$$**

(☑ 0590-97-04-57; www.chezhenri.net; 8 Ave des Caraïbes, St-Louis; mains €12-20; ⊘ noon-3pm & 7-11pm Mon-Sat; 🐾) This is an unexpected gem for such a tiny backwater: a lively jazz bar and a great beachside restaurant perfect for whiling away Caribbean evenings. Local art is on display, handmade local crafts are for sale, the live music is good and the simple Creole food is delicious (try the excellent Creole omelet).

Footy
CREOLE **$$**

(☑ 0690-39-80-17; Blvd de la Marine, Grand-Bourg; mains €12-18; ⊘ noon-3pm Mon-Sat, 7-11pm Fri & Sat) Owned by a former soccer player, this place has a great sea-view terrace and a local reputation for the best pork chops on the island. It has live music in the club area in the back most Friday and Saturday nights. Make a right from Grand-Bourg's ferry dock on the main pier and head down the main road for a few minutes.

★ La Playa
INTERNATIONAL **$$$**

(☑ 0590-93-66-10, 0690-51-84-77; Rte du Littoral, Capesterre; mains €20-35; ⊘ noon-3pm Thu-Sun, 7-10pm daily mid-Dec–mid-May, 7-10pm Wed-Sun mid-May–mid-Dec; 🐾) For a menu that strays a little off the familiar Creole path, try this well-respected restaurant in a cute house located across the road from Petite Anse beach. At lunchtime, toothsome specialties may include fish tartare and skewered beef. Dinner is a more formal affair; standouts may include lobster in mango sauce, crab in coconut sauce or paella.

❶ Information

Office du Tourisme (☑ 0590-97-56-51; www. ot-mariegalante.com; Rue du Fort, Grand-Bourg; ⊘ 9am-noon & 1-4pm Mon-Thu, Sat 8am-4pm Fri, 8am-noon Sat & Sun)

❶ Getting There & Away

AIR

Air Caraïbes (p486) has daily flights to Marie-Galante from Pointe-à-Pitre. The airport is midway between Grand-Bourg and Capesterre, 5km from either.

BOAT

There are daily ferry connections between Pointe-à-Pitre and Grand-Bourg (one hour), while St-Louis has daily connections to both St-François (45 minutes) and Les Saintes (45 minutes). Prices vary enormously and depend on deals and the current level of competition on each route. Companies running these routes:

Comatrile (p467) Runs services to Les Saintes and St-François from St-Louis.

Express des Îles (p487) Runs services to Pointe-à-Pitre from Grand-Bourg.

Val'Ferry (p487) Runs services to Pointe-à-Pitre from Grand-Bourg.

The interisland crossing to Marie-Galante can be a bit rough, so if you're not used to bouncy seas it's best to travel on a light stomach and sit in the middle of the boat. One saving grace is that the boats leaving from Pointe-à-Pitre are very big (and more stable) and quite comfortable.

St-Louis is the island's main anchorage for yachters.

❶ Getting Around

BUS

During the day, except for Sunday, infrequent minibuses make runs between Grand-Bourg, Capesterre and St-Louis (€1 flat fare, approximately 15 minutes between each village). It's not a very convenient way to get around Marie-Galante, however, and it's far easier to hire a car or scooter to explore properly. Find the bus stops on the main road through each village.

CAR

You really need your own transport to get the most out of Marie-Galante. Car and scooter hire are both cheap and readily available at both ports of entry to the island, Grand-Bourg and St-Louis. Cars generally start at €25 per day and motorbikes at €15 to €20. Be sure to inspect your vehicle closely as some of them, especially scooters, can be haggard.

Auto Moto Location (☑ 0590-97-19-42; www. automoto-location.com; Ave des Caraïbes, St-Louis)

Hertz (☑ 0590-97-59-80; www.hertzantilles. com; Rue du Fort, Grand-Bourg)

Toto Location (☑ 0690-65-64-99, 0590-97-59-16; www.toto-location.com)

MINIBUS

Minibus tour drivers are usually waiting for arriving ferry passengers at both ferry ports, Grand Bourg and St-Louis. A four-hour guided tour that makes a nearly complete circle around Marie-Galante costs between €12 and €15. Stops on the tour usually include a distillery, the Ste-Marie Hospital parking lot (best view on the island), a shop where people make manioc flour, and an abandoned sugar plantation.

The buses will sometimes leave you on the town beach in St-Louis for a few hours and pick you up in time to make whichever boat back you plan to take. Some of the tour guides don't speak much standard French, let alone English, so be sure to converse a bit beforehand to make sure they can explain sights clearly in your language.

LA DÉSIRADE

With its soaring central mountain, thick vegetation and palm-strewn beaches, tiny La Désirade is the quintessential Caribbean Island of popular fantasy. Its unusual name comes from the fact that it was the first sight of land caught by Columbus on his second voyage in 1493 – thus 'the desired' landfall that his crew were hoping for. Indeed, it's hard to imagine them being disappointed, and today La Désirade retains much of its natural charm. From from one side at least, it looks pretty much as it did in Columbus' time, albeit now with a couple of prominent wind farms.

Just 11km long and 2km wide, La Désirade makes for a wonderful day trip from Grande-Terre. Even the best beaches are nearly deserted, and there are some excellent restaurants where you can enjoy a long lunch.

🛏 Sleeping

There are three hotels on La Désirade. One we do not list as it organizes cockfights for visitors, but the other two are both decent value and well located within walking distance of the port.

★ Hôtel Oasis   HOTEL $
(☎0590-20-01-00; www.oasisladesirade.com; Rue de la Dési, Beauséjour; s/d/tr incl breakfast €48/52/57; ❄☎) Situated within easy walking distance from the ferry and Fifi Beach, this brightly painted two-level Creole-style house could not be more of a deal, with six compact but tidy rooms and studios. The interiors are rather modern and stylish, and the welcome is very warm.

Oualiri Beach Hotel   HOTEL $
(☎0590-20-20-08; www.rendezvouskarukera.com; Beauséjour; s/d €70/80; ☎) The simple and rather small rooms here would be totally unremarkable were they not directly on the beach. Yes, it's a small and rather rocky cove, and management is a little too relaxed for this place to really live up to its

potential, but if being on the beach is what you want – this is your place. There's no sign.

🍴 Eating

The name of the game here is seafood, of course, and La Désirade specializes in lobster, conch and octopus, which are on the menu in practically every restaurant. Restaurants are concentrated around Beauséjour, the main settlement, and can also be found on several of the more picturesque beaches.

Rose-Ita   SEAFOOD $$
(mains €4-35; ☉10am-4pm Fri-Wed, dinner Fri-Mon; ☎) This pink and breezy new addition to La Désirade's eating options is a real winner, with gorgeous sea views from a bluff overlooking a small fishing beach below. The menu is wider than at most other places locally, so as well as the splash-out *assiette de langouste* (lobster platter, €35), you can order a far simpler burger or *croque-monsieur* (ham-and-cheese toastie, €4).

Chez Nounoune   SEAFOOD, CREOLE $$
(☎0590-20-03-59, 0690-74-62-15; Baie-Mahault; menus €14-36; ☉9am-2pm) Overlooking pretty Petite Rivière beach, rather chaotic but very friendly Chez Nounoune is the kind of open-air joint you tell your friends about when you get home. As all dishes are prepared from scratch, they ask that you call and order their seafood dishes by 11am. It's worth it: you won't be disappointed by the generous portions or the sublime views.

La Roulotte   CREOLE $$
(☎0690-54-19-64; Plage du Souffleur; mains €18-23; ☉noon-3pm) Despite its appearance this is no mere beach shack slap-bang on gorgeous Souffleur beach, but a La Désirade institution open for over 15 years. Jean-Edouard does everything alone here – so order and enjoy a leisurely swim before lunch – and you won't find better grilled fish, conch stew, octopus curry or lobster on the island.

La Payotte   CREOLE, SEAFOOD $$
(☎0590-20-01-29; Grande Anse, Beauséjour; mains €12-20; ☉9am-3pm daily, 6.30-11pm Fri & Sat) Right on La Désirade's own Grande Anse beach, La Payotte serves a tasty variety of Creole dishes as well as a small breakfast menu on its charming beachside terrace. Don't miss the stir-fried chicken with cashew nuts and the grilled lobster.

ℹ Getting There & Away

There are two crossings per day on the **Achipel'1** (p467) between St-François and La Désirade (€27 return, 45 minutes). Buy tickets shortly before departure at the St-François Gare Maritime. From St-François, the ferry leaves at 8am; it leaves La Désirade at 3:45pm. From La Désirade there is a 7am crossing and a 5pm return. Outside of high season there are no boats on Tuesdays.

ℹ Getting Around

Scooter rentals are available at the ferry dock of La Désirade for €20 to €25 a day. Cars can be rented for €40 per day. There is a bus that theoretically runs up and down the island, but it was not working during our last visit.

UNDERSTAND GUADELOUPE

History

Caribs in Karukera

When sighted by Columbus on November 14, 1493, Guadeloupe was inhabited by Caribs, who called it Karukera (Island of Beautiful Waters). The Spanish made two attempts to settle Guadeloupe in the early 1500s but were repelled both times by fierce Carib resistance, and finally in 1604 they abandoned their claim to the island.

Three decades later, French colonists sponsored by the Compagnie des Îles d'Amérique, an association of French entrepreneurs, set sail to establish the first European settlement on Guadeloupe. On June 28, 1635, the party, led by Charles Liénard de l'Olive and Jean Duplessis d'Ossonville, landed on the southeastern shore of Basse-Terre and claimed Guadeloupe for France. They drove the Caribs off the island, planted crops and within a decade had built the first sugar mill. By the time France officially annexed the island in 1674, a slavery-based plantation system had been well established.

France vs Britain in Guadeloupe

The English invaded Guadeloupe several times and occupied it from 1759 to 1763. During this time, they developed Pointe-à-Pitre into a major harbor, opened profitable English and North American markets to Guadeloupean sugar, and allowed the planters to import cheap American lumber and food. Many French colonists actually grew wealthier under the British occupation, and the economy expanded rapidly. In 1763 British occupation ended with the signing of the Treaty of Paris, which relinquished French claims in Canada in exchange for the return of Guadeloupe.

Amid the chaos of the French Revolution, the British invaded Guadeloupe again in 1794. In response, the French sent a contingent of soldiers led by Victor Hugues, a black nationalist. Hugues freed and armed Guadeloupean slaves. On the day the British withdrew from Guadeloupe, Hugues went on a rampage and killed 300 royalists, many of them plantation owners. It marked the start of a reign of terror. In all, Hugues was responsible for the deaths of more than 1000 colonists, and as a consequence of his attacks on US ships, the USA declared war on France.

In 1802 Napoléon Bonaparte, anxious to get the situation under control, sent General Antoine Richepanse to Guadeloupe. Richepanse put down the uprising, restored the prerevolutionary government and reinstituted slavery.

Guadeloupe was the most prosperous island in the French West Indies, and the British continued to covet it, invading and occupying the island for most of the period between 1810 and 1816. The Treaty of Vienna restored the island to France, which has maintained sovereignty over it continuously since 1816.

Modern Guadeloupe

Slavery was abolished in 1848, following a campaign led by French politician Victor Schoelcher. In the years that followed, planters brought laborers from Pondicherry, a French colony in India, to work in the cane fields. Since 1871 Guadeloupe has had representation in the French parliament, and since 1946 it has been an overseas department of France.

Guadeloupe's economy is heavily dependent upon subsidies from the French government and upon its economic ties with mainland France, which absorbs the majority of Guadeloupe's exports and provides 75% of its imports. Agriculture remains a cornerstone of the economy. The leading export crop is bananas, the bulk of which grow along the southern flanks of La Soufrière.

People & Culture

Guadeloupean culture draws from a pool of French, African, East Indian and West Indian influences. The mix is visible in the architecture, which ranges from French colonial buildings to traditional Creole homes; in the food, which merges influences from all the cultures into a unique Creole cuisine; and in the widely spoken local Creole language, the local dialect that is a heavily accented and very colloquial form of French. Guadeloupe is also one place in the Caribbean where you're likely to see women wearing traditional Creole dress, especially at festivals and cultural events.

The total population of Guadeloupe is about 405,000, with a third of the population aged under 20. About three-quarters of the population is of mixed ethnicity, a combination of African, European and East Indian descent. There's also a sizable population of white islanders who trace their ancestry to the early French settlers, as well as a number of far more recently arrived French from the mainland.

The predominant religion is Roman Catholicism. There are also Methodist, Seventh Day Adventist, Jehovah's Witness and evangelical denominations, and a significant Hindu community.

The island is fertile ground for the literary imagination, apparently. Guadeloupe's most renowned native son is Saint-John Perse, the pseudonym of Alexis Leger, who was born in Guadeloupe in 1887. Perse won the Nobel Prize for literature in 1960 for the evocative imagery in his poetry. One of his many noted works is *Anabase* (1925), which was translated into English by TS Eliot.

The leading contemporary novelist in the French West Indies is Guadeloupe native Maryse Condé. Many of her best-selling novels have been translated into English. The epic *Tree of Life* (1992) centers on the life of a Guadeloupean family, their roots and the identity of Guadeloupean society itself. *Crossing the Mangrove* (1995) is a perfect beach read. Set in Rivière au Sel near the Rivière Salée, it unravels the life, and untimely death, of a controversial villager.

Landscape & Wildlife

Beaches line nearly every shore in Guadeloupe, explaining its enduring attraction to generations of French holidaymakers. Outside of the mountainous Parc National de la Guadeloupe (p471), the interior is made for the most part of gently rolling fields of sugarcane. The beaches, hiking trails and picnic areas here are almost always completely litter-free.

Underwater life includes small sea horses, lobsters, lots of parrot fish, and crabs. Divers may occasionally spot a ray or barracuda, but for the most part the waters here support large schools of smaller fish.

Birds found on Guadeloupe include various members of the heron family, pelicans, hummingbirds and the endangered Guadeloupe wren. A common sighting is the bright yellow-bellied banana quit, a small nectar-feeding bird that's a frequent visitor at open-air restaurants, where it raids unattended sugar bowls.

You'll probably see drawings of raccoons on park brochures and in Guadeloupean advertising; it is the official symbol of Parc National de la Guadeloupe and its main habitat is in the forests of Basse-Terre, but visitors are unlikely to see them in person.

Guadeloupe has mongooses aplenty, introduced long ago in a futile attempt to control rats in the sugarcane fields. Agoutis (short-haired, short-eared rabbitlike rodents that look a bit like guinea pigs) are found on La Désirade. There are iguanas on Les Saintes and La Désirade. All of these animals are fairly commonly seen by visitors.

SURVIVAL GUIDE

❶ Directory A–Z

ACCOMMODATIONS

Most hotels in Guadeloupe are midsized and midrange, and prices are reasonable by the standards of the region. You'll also find private *chambres d'hôte* (rooms for rent in private homes) or villas and *gîtes* (cottages) to rent, but they generally require booking by the week. Guadeloupe has one excellent hostel, but otherwise provides poorly for the needs of travellers on a serious budget.

CHILDREN

Because of all the French families that come here, there are a number of child-friendly hotels and activities. Many hotels have play areas and activities just for kids and a special children's menu. All restaurants will allow children to dine, and they'll often have a simple and good-value *menu enfant* (children's set meal) to offer them.

Practically all hotels will provide cots, and some hotels provide babysitting services. European brands of baby formula, foods and diapers can be bought at pharmacies.

ELECTRICITY

220V, 50 cycles; European-style, two-round-pin plugs.

FOOD

Guadeloupe has some fantastic eating opportunities, from simple beachside grills serving up the catch of the day to gastronomic multicourse blowouts to rival anywhere. Seafood lovers will be particularly happy here, with fresh lobster, conch, octopus and shrimp on most menus. That said, there is limited choice on the island if you don't want Creole or French food.

Essential Food & Drink

➡ **Acras** A universally popular hors d'oeuvre in Guadeloupe, *acras* are fried fish, seafood or vegetable fritters in tempura. *Acras de morue* (cod) and *crevettes* (shrimp) are the most common and are both delicious.

➡ **Ti-punch** Short for *petit punch,* this ubiquitous and strong cocktail is the normal *apéro* (aperitif) in Guadeloupe: a mix of rum, lime and cane syrup, but mainly rum.

➡ **Crabes farcis** Stuffed crabs are a typical local dish. Normally they're stuffed with a spicy mixture of crabmeat, garlic, shallots and parsley that is then cooked in the shell.

➡ **Blaff** This is the local term for white fish marinated in lime juice, garlic and peppers and then poached. It's a favorite dish in many of Guadeloupe's restaurants.

GLBT TRAVELERS

Guadeloupe usually earns OK marks from gay travel organizations, as gay and lesbian rights are protected under French law. However, attitudes on the ground tend to be far less tolerant and prejudice against gay people is not unusual, although it's not nearly as extreme as on some Caribbean islands. Gay couples usually do not publicly express affection or advertise their sexual orientation, although hoteliers don't seem to mind if same-sex couples share a bed. There is little or no gay scene here – most introductions happen via the internet.

HEALTH

Medical care in Guadeloupe is equivalent to mainland France: very good. The biggest hospital is the **Centre Hospitalier Universitaire** (CHU; ☑ 0590-89-10-10; www.chu-guadeloupe. fr; Rte de Chauvel; ⊙ 24hr) in Pointe-à-Pitre, though there are smaller hospitals in almost every region. There are plenty of pharmacies everywhere; look for the green cross, often flashing in neon. EU citizens can get healthcare costs refunded through their European Health

> ### SLEEPING PRICE RANGES
>
> The following price categories are based on the cost of a double room in high season (from December to April and July to August).
>
> **€** less than €80
>
> **€€** €80–150
>
> **€€€** more than €150

Cards. When paying for medical care, nationals of other countries should keep all receipts to reclaim money from their health-insurance providers.

LEGAL MATTERS

French law governs legal matters in Guadeloupe, and there is a presumption of innocence, as well as the right to a lawyer. Most travellers will have no interaction with the police at all.

MONEY

Guadeloupe, as a department of France, uses the euro. Hotels, larger restaurants and car-rental agencies accept Visa and MasterCard. ATMs are common.

Exchange Rates

AUSTRALIA	A$1	€0.69
CANADA	C$1	€0.72
JAPAN	¥100	€0.82
NEW ZEALAND	NZ$1	€0.66
SOUTH AFRICA	ZAR100	€7.24
SWITZERLAND	CHF1	€0.94
UK	UK£1	€1.19
US	US$1	€0.96

For current exchange rates, see www.xe.com.

Tipping

Tipping is not common or expected in Guadeloupe.

PUBLIC HOLIDAYS

New Year's Day January 1

Labor Day May 1

Victory Day May 8

Ascension Thursday 40th day after Easter

Slavery Abolition Day May 27

Bastille Day July 14

Schoelcher Day July 21

Assumption Day August 15

All Saints' Day November 1

Armistice Day November 11

Christmas Day December 25

EATING PRICE RANGES

The following price categories are based on the cost of a main course.

€ less than €12

€€ €12–20

€€€ more than €20

TAXES & REFUNDS

If you do not live in France, it is possible to claim back VAT on certain purchased items at the airport when leaving Guadeloupe. This isn't possible if you're flying from Guadeloupe to France.

TELEPHONE

The country code for Guadeloupe is ☑ 590. Confusingly, all local landlines also begin with ☑ 0590: these numbers are separate, however, and therefore must be dialed twice when calling from abroad. Cell-phone numbers begin with ☑ 0690.

To call Guadeloupe from abroad, dial your country's international access code, followed by the ☑ 590 country code and the local number (dropping the initial zero). When calling from within the French West Indies, simply dial the local 10-digit number.

TIME

Guadeloupe uses GMT/UTC -4 hours. Daylight saving time are not used.

TRAVELERS WITH DISABILITIES

By comparison with other Caribbean Islands, Guadeloupe makes good provision for travelers with disabilities, with many hotels having wheelchair accessible rooms, and many public places having disabled toilets.

ⓘ Getting There & Away

AIR

Guadeloupe's only international airport is **Guadeloupe Pôle Caraïbes Airport** (☑ 0590-21-14-98; www.guadeloupe.aeroport.fr; Les Abymes), which is north of Pointe-à-Pitre, 6km from the city center.

A number of airlines serve Guadeloupe:

Air Canada (☑ 0590-21-12-77; www.aircanada.com) From Montreal.

Air France (☑ 0820-82-08-20; www.airfrance.com) From Paris, Cayenne, Miami and Port-au-Prince.

Air Caraïbes (☑ 0820-83-58-35; www.aircaraibes.com; ⊘ 8am-8pm) From Paris.

American Airlines (www.aa.com) From San Juan and Miami.

Corsair (www.corsair.fr; ⊘ 8am-6pm) From Paris.

Norwegian (www.norwegian.com) From Baltimore, Boston and Miami.

There are direct regional services to Antigua, Barbados, Dominica, Fort-de-France, Port-au-Prince, St-Barthélemy, St-Martin/Sint Maarten, Santo Domingo, St Lucia and Trinidad and Tobago. Regional airlines serving Guadeloupe include **Air Caraïbes** (☑ 0820-83-58-35; www.aircaraibes.com; Guadeloupe Pôle Caraïbes Airport; ⊘ 8am-8pm), **Air Antilles Express** (☑ 0890-64-86-48; www.airantilles.com; Guadeloupe Pôle Caraïbes Airport; ⊘ 3hrs before flights), **LIAT** (☑ 0590-21-13-93; www.liat.com; Guadeloupe Pôle Caraïbes Airport; ⊘ 3hr before flights) and **Winair** (www.fly-winair.sx; Guadeloupe Pôle Caraïbes Airport; ⊘ 3hr before flights).

SEA

There are excellent connections to nearby Caribbean islands from Guadeloupe, as well as the possibility to charter your own yacht or catamaran to make the trip.

Cruise Ship

Cruise ships don't always call at Pointe-à-Pitre, as neither the port area nor the city itself is particularly attractive. However, when cruise ships do call, they normally dock right in the city at **Centre St-John Perse** (Quai Ferdinand de Lesseps), Pointe-à-Pitre's old port complex, and at the new cruise ship terminal just a short walk from the center of town.

Ferry

There are plenty of connections between Guadeloupe and neighboring islands, particularly Martinique, although if your destination is Martinique, do bear in mind that it's nearly always cheaper – and certainly faster – to fly.

L'Express des Îles (☑ 0825-35-90-00; www.express-des-iles.com; Gare Maritime de Bergevin) and **Jeans for Freedom** (☑ 0825-01-01-25; www.jeansforfreedom.com; Gare Maritime de Bergevin; ⊘ 7am-7pm) both run ferries between Guadeloupe and its neighboring islands of Dominica, Martinique and St Lucia. The two companies are always offering special deals and promotions, and competition is fierce. In general it pays to book ahead as far as possible.

There are usually crossings on Sunday, Wednesday and Friday from Pointe-à-Pitre to Roseau, Dominica (one way/round-trip €69/106, 1½ hours), continuing to Fort-de-France, Martinique (one way/round-trip €69/106, three hours), and then on some days continuing to Castries, St Lucia (one way/round-trip €72/110, 4½ hours).

In the other direction there are departures from Castries in St Lucia on Monday, Thursday and Saturday calling at Fort-de-France and Roseau before arriving in Pointe-à-Pitre.

Departure days and times for these services change frequently and, due to weather conditions, often bear no relation to the printed schedule. The only way to be sure is to call the ferry companies on the day of travel.

Yacht

Popular with yachties and sailors, Guadeloupe has three marinas:

➡ **Marina de Bas du Fort** (p464) Between Pointe-à-Pitre and Gosier.

➡ **Marina de St-François** (p467) In the center of St-François, Grande-Terre

➡ **Marina de Rivière-Sens** (p470) On the southern outskirts of the town of Basse-Terre.

Customs and immigration offices are located in Pointe-à-Pitre, Basse-Terre and Deshaies.

The yacht charter companies **Antilles Sail** (p460) and **Dream Yacht Charter** (p460) are based at Marina de Bas du Fort.

ⓘ Getting Around

For travelers visiting more than one place in Guadeloupe, a rental car is almost a necessity. The main tourist spots on the southern coast of Grande-Terre are navigable without one, but for the most part a vehicle comes in handy and rental prices are very low. Most visitors pick up a car at the airport and keep it throughout their stay, although as transporting cars to the outlying islands is expensive, most people hire scooters or cars on each island rather than taking one with them.

AIR

Air Caraïbes has almost daily flights between Pointe-à-Pitre and Marie-Galante, and these are the only scheduled domestic flights in Guadeloupe at present.

BICYCLE

The flat roads of Grande-Terre are very popular with cyclists, particularly the stretch between St-François and Pointe des Châteaux. Bicycles are an adventurous and fun way to get around the islands of Terre-de-Haut, La Désirade and Marie-Galante. Rentals start at €10 per day.

BOAT

Ferries are the principal way to get around between the various islands of Guadeloupe. Multiple ferry operators run services between Grande-Terre and Terre-de-Haut, Marie-Galante and La Désirade. There are also ferries from Trois-Rivières on Basse-Terre to Terre-de-Haut in Les Saintes. Prices tend to be similar, though

Newspaper *France-Antilles* (www.guadeloupe.franceantilles.fr) is the main daily newspaper for the French West Indies. French newspapers and magazines are commonly found everywhere; print editions in English are far rarer.

Radio & TV Tune into Réseau Outre-Mer 1ère (http://la1ere.francetvinfo.fr) or catch up on local TV on Guadeloupe 1ère (www.guadeloupe.la1ere.fr).

Smoking France has a comprehensive smoking ban that is also observed in Guadeloupe. Smoking in all enclosed public spaces is against the law.

Weights & Measures Guadeloupe uses the metric system for everything, and the 24-hour clock.

it's hard to give exact costs as most companies have promotions or other discounted fares available and seem to be in a constant price-war with each other. Shop around on the ground for the best deal, and always confirm sailing times by phone as schedules change regularly.

CTM Deher (☑ 0590-92-06-39; www.ctmdeher.com; Allée des Espadons; ⊙7am-7pm)

Jeans for Freedom (p486)

L'Express des Îles (☑ 0825-35-90-00; www.express-des-iles.com; Gare Maritime de Bergevin; ⊙7am-7pm)

Val'Ferry (☑ 0590-91-45-15; www.valferry.fr; Gare Maritime de Bergevin)

Vedette Beatrix (p475)

BUS

Guadeloupe has a good public bus system that operates from about 5:30am to 6:30pm on weekdays, with fairly frequent service on main routes. The Saturday-afternoon service is much lighter, and there are almost no buses on Sunday.

Many bus routes start and end in Pointe-à-Pitre and destinations are written on the buses. Bus stops have blue signs picturing a bus; in less-developed areas you can wave buses down along their routes. Pay the driver when you board.

CAR & MOTORCYCLE

In Guadeloupe, drive on the right. Traffic regulations and road signs are identical to those in mainland France. Exits and intersections are clearly marked, and speed limits are posted.

Rental

Multiple car-rental companies have offices at the airport and in major resort areas. Some agents will let you rent a car near your hotel and drop it off free of charge at the airport, which can save you a hefty taxi fare.

Companies generally drop their rates the longer you keep the car, with the weekly rate working out to be about 15% cheaper overall than the daily rate. Nearly all companies use an unlimited-kilometers rate.

Rates for small cars are advertised from around €35 per day, although the rates offered on a walk-in basis and availability of cars can vary greatly with the season. It's a good idea to reserve ahead from December to May.

Road Conditions

Roads are excellent by Caribbean standards and almost invariably hard-surfaced, although secondary and mountain roads are often narrow.

Around Pointe-à-Pitre there are multilane highways, with cars zipping along at 110km/h. Outside the Pointe-à-Pitre area, most highways have a single lane in each direction and an 80km/h speed limit.

HITCHHIKING

Hitchhiking is fairly common on Guadeloupe, particularly when the bus drivers decide to go on strike. The proper stance is to hold out an open palm at a slightly downward angle. All the usual safety precautions apply.

TAXI

Taxis are plentiful but expensive in Guadeloupe. There are taxi stands at the airport in Pointe-à-Pitre, and you can call one almost anywhere on Grande-Terre, Basse-Terre and Marie-Galante. Fares are 40% higher from 9pm to 7am nightly, as well as all day on Sunday and holidays.

Haiti

Best Places to Eat

➜ Papaye (p494)

➜ Lakou Lakay (p499)

➜ L'Estaminet (p494)

➜ Café 36 (p494)

Best Places to Sleep

➜ El Rancho (p493)

➜ Habitation des Lauriers (p497)

➜ Royal Decamero (p498)
n Indigo Beach Resort & Spa (p498)

➜ Abaka Bay Resort (p502)

➜ Cormier Plage Resort (p499)

Why Go?

The most common phrase in Haiti might surprise you. It's *'pa gen pwoblem,'* and it translates to 'no have problem.' Haitians use it in a dizzying array of contexts: responding to thank-yous, asserting well-being, filling awkward silences. Despite Haiti's well-documented struggles, exacerbated lately by natural disasters, proud Haitians use the phrase sincerely, conveying an uncanny ability to live in the moment and appreciate what they do have, which is quite a lot.

Tranquil beaches, tumbling waterfalls and pine-tree-capped mountains dot the varied and striking landscape, easily rivaling the natural beauty found anywhere else in the Caribbean. The world's only successful slave rebellion happened here, and the music, art and culture that came with it make Haiti entirely unique. As those who come to assist Haiti often learn, an encounter with the soul of this fascinating, beautiful country often benefits a traveler just as much.

When to Go

Nov–Mar The hottest, driest days in most of the country (with the exception of some rain in the north); these months are also ideal for travel due to attractions such as the countrywide Fet Gédé Vodou festival (November), and Carnival in Port-au-Prince and Jacmel (February).

Apr–Jun Quite a bit of rain in the south, as well as in Port-au-Prince.

Aug–Oct Hurricane season, and many days are humid with considerable rainfall. Still, travel is perfectly feasible if there are no big storms.

Haiti Highlights

1 Jacmel Carnival (p500)
Joining the country's liveliest street party, celebrating Vodou, sex and, death.

2 Citadelle Laferrière (p498) Discovering the mountain fortress and Versailles-like ruined palace, proud symbols of the world's first black republic.

3 Parc National la Visite (p496) Hiking alongside local farmers in Haiti's pine forest, with views out to the Caribbean Sea.

4 Vodou Ceremony (p499) Heading out from Gonaïves and attending a Vodou ceremony.

5 Île-à-Vache (p502) Kicking back on this white-sand sliver of paradise.

6 Port-au-Prince (p491) Exploring the soul of the country via thriving art, music and cultural scenes within the buzzing capital.

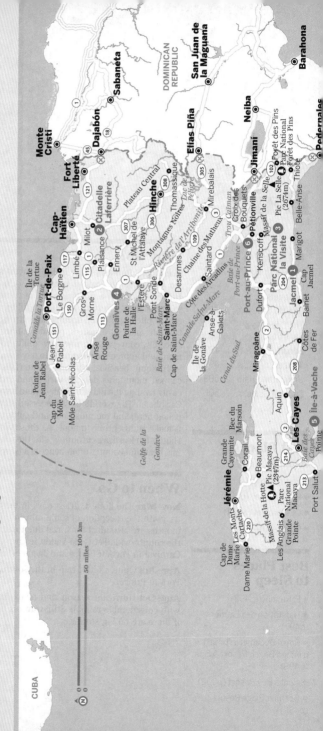

PORT-AU-PRINCE

POP 978,000

Let's admit the obvious: Port-au-Prince doesn't have the image of somewhere you'd visit for fun. A true city of the developing world, just a couple of hours by air from Miami, the city was preceded by a reputation for impoverished chaos even before the 2010 earthquake shook it to its foundations. Years later the recovery is still slow going, the gulf between rich and poor remains as wide as ever, and the streets remain cluttered with trash and rubble.

And yet the city remains one of the most vibrant and exciting in the Caribbean. Like a bottle of local *klerin* liquor, Port-au-Prince takes the raw energy of Haiti and distills it into one buzzing shot, and witnessing the self-sufficient spirit of its people might be the most life-affirming experience you have on your travels. It's a chaotic, exhilarating, compelling place, and if you're not careful, it may well capture your soul.

🛈 Dangers & Annoyances

It's unwise to walk around after dark, particularly near Champs de Mars and in Pétionville, as street crime is an issue. Avoid being ostentatious with possessions, and don't visit slum areas unless you are accompanied by a trusted local guide.

⦿ Sights

Champs de Mars   PARK

A series of parks split by wide boulevards that collectively make up the Place des Héros de l'Independence, with the former site of the demolished Palais National at its center, this broken heart of Port-au-Prince suffered greatly in the 2010 earthquake and is no longer a place to linger. A tall fence has been constructed around the parks, but intrepid travelers may ask permission from guards to enter; a guided city tour with **Voyages Lumière** (☑ 3607-1321; www.voyageslumiere.com/haiti) also takes you in.

Musée du Panthéon National   MUSEUM

(Mupanah; ☑ 3417-4435; Pl du Champs de Mars; US$5; ⊘ 8am-4pm Mon-Thu, to 5pm Fri, 10am-4pm Sat, noon-5pm Sun) This modern, mostly subterranean history museum, set below gardens, hosts a permanent exhibition chronicling Haiti's history, from the Taínos and slavery to independence and the modern era. Fascinating exhibits include exquisite Taíno pottery; the rusting anchor of Columbus' flagship, the *Santa María;* a copy of the fearsome Code Noir that governed the running of the plantations; the silver pistol with which Christophe took his own life; Emperor Faustin's ostentatious crown; and 'Papa Doc' Duvalier's trademark black hat and cane.

★**Grand Rue Artists**   ARTS CENTER

(www.atis-rezistans.com; 622 Grand Rue; ⊘ 8am-8pm) While most of Haiti's artists are represented in the rarefied air of Pétionville's galleries, a collective of sculptors and installation artists produces spectacular work in an unlikely setting, squeezed into the cinder-block houses among mechanics and body workshops on Grand Rue. In this Caribbean junkyard gone cyberpunk, the artists turn scrap and found objects into startling Vodou sculpture, exploring a heady mix of spirit, sex and politics, all grounded in the preoccupations of daily Haitian life.

⌖ Tours

The vast majority of people who visit Haiti will be better off exploring the country with a knowledgeable guide, as getting around on one's own, particularly without speaking French or Creole, is very challenging. **Voyages Lumière** and **Pale Dlololo** (☑ 4608-3366; www.paledlololoinstitute.com; 1 week US$200, private tutoring per hr US$20, online Skype classes per hr US$30) are two excellent operators.

🛏 Sleeping

🛏 Port-au-Prince

★**St Joseph's Home for Boys Guest House**   GUESTHOUSE $

(☑ 3892-6071; www.sjfamilyhaiti.org; Delmas 91, Delmas; r shared per person incl full board US$55; 🛜) Rebuilt with great fortitude after the original house collapsed in the 2010 earthquake, this home for ex-street boys offers a fantastic Haitian experience. The tall, sleek new building includes a rooftop lounge offering amazing city and mountain views, and well-kept shared rooms include bunk beds and pristine bathrooms. Delicious meals are taken communally. The guesthouse is located opposite Radio Haiti-Inter.

Hôtel Oloffson   HOTEL $$

(☑ 3810-4000; www.hoteloloffson.com; 60 Ave Christophe; r/ste from US$100/200; 🅿✳@🛜🏊) If Haiti has an iconic hotel, it's the Oloffson. Immortalized as Hotel Trianon in Graham Greene's *The Comedians,* the

Port-au-Prince

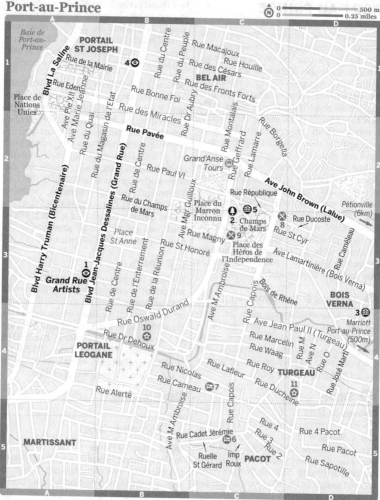

HAITI PORT-AU-PRINCE

---

elegant gingerbread building is one of the city's loveliest, further tricked out with paintings and Vodou flags. There's a sociable bar for your rum punches, and every Thursday the house band RAM plays up a storm.

⭐ **Inn at Villa Bambou**   BOUTIQUE HOTEL **$$$**
(☎3702-1151; www.villabambouhaiti.com; 1 Rue Marfranc, Pacot; r incl half board from US$250; P❄☀🛜🏊) A 1920s house rebuilt since the earthquake, this is a truly gorgeous boutique hotel. There are half a dozen rooms, each named for a herb and beautifully decorated. The quality of the food is a particular selling point, along with the leafy garden – and if there's a guesthouse offering better views of Port-au-Prince, we'd like to know about it.

Karibe Hôtel   HOTEL **$$$**
(☎2812-7000; www.karibehotel.com; Juvenat 7, Juvenat; s/d from US$174/191, ste from US$285; P❄☀@🛜🏊) One of Haiti's fanciest, this hotel-cum-conference-center is where you'll find the richest businessfolk, international consultants and even presidents (Bill Clinton and 'Baby Doc' Duvalier have been guests). Rooms and service are impeccable, and the rooftop bar gets packed on Friday nights.

Port-au-Prince

Marriott Port-au-Prince　　　　HOTEL **$$$**

(☑2814-2800; www.marriott.com; 147 Ave Jean-Paul II, Turgeau; r US$187; P✳🛜❄) When the Marriott opened near downtown Port-au-Prince in 2014, it set a new bar (and price point) for hotels in its class. The ceilings are a bit higher, the counter tops glisten whiter, and the staff is a touch more professional. When expats grow weary of daily struggles in Haiti, they make for the Marriott and its potent rum sours.

🛏 Pétionville

★**La Lorraine**　　　　BOUTIQUE HOTEL **$$$**

(☑2816-8300; www.lalorrainehaiti.com; 36 Rue Clerveaux, Pétionville; r/ste incl breakfast US$125/143; P✳🛜) This newly restored 1950s home-turned-boutique-hotel is perhaps the most relaxing stay in all of Pétionville. Apart from the high-arching door

frames, each room is uniquely arranged with contemporary furnishings and fine Haitian art, with some rooms featuring balconies and hammocks and others containing mini gardens. The owner's meticulous attention to detail is apparent at every turn; service is impeccable.

★**El Rancho**　　　　BOUTIQUE HOTEL **$$$**

(☑2815-1000, in USA 212-219-7607; www.nh-hotels. com; 5 Rue Jose Martin, Pétionville; r from US$165; P✳🛜❄) In 2013 the Spanish hotel Chain NH took the reins at this upscale Pétionville hotel and casino, revamping the snazzy, fountain-lined entryway and the 72 modern rooms surrounding an alfresco restaurant and pool. The outdoor area is stunning, and often hosts nightlife events with performers including the likes of Sweet Micky, the famous *compas* singer and former president.

Hotel Kinam　　　　HOTEL **$$$**

(☑2955-6000, 2944-6000; www.hotelkinam.com; Pl St-Pierre, Pétionville; r old/new incl breakfast US$80/169; P✳@🛜❄) This large, historic gingerbread hotel recently underwent a US$26-million expansion, adding a shiny new wing. Rooms in the new section are well sized and modern, while vintage rooms are more basic and budget-friendly. The effect is charming, particularly on evenings when the pool is lit up and guests congregate for renowned rum punches.

✗ Eating

✗ Port-au-Prince

Les Jardins du Mupanah　　　　CARIBBEAN **$$**

(☑2811-6764; lesjardinsdumupanah@gmail.com; Rue Oswald Durand, Champs de Mars; sandwiches US$8, mains US$13; ⊙11am-4pm Mon-Sat) With floor-to-ceiling windows looking out over

---

PORT-AU-PRINCE'S GINGERBREAD ARCHITECTURE

The vast majority of Haiti's unique gingerbread buildings are in Port-au-Prince, almost entirely the product of just three Parisian-trained Haitian architects: Georges Baussan, Léon Mathon and Joseph-Eugène Maximilien.

　　The key gingerbread characteristics are brick-filled timber frames adorned with lacy wooden latticework, high ceilings, and graceful balconies set over wide porches – all designed to take advantage of the prevailing winds. **Hôtel Oloffson** (p491) is Port-au-Prince's most photographed example of gingerbread style, and recently, the exquisite and refurbished gingerbread home **Maison Dufort** (☑2813-1694; studiofokal@fokal.org; Rue du Travail, Turgeau; ⊙9am-4pm) opened to the public.

　　The loveliest gingerbread in Pétionville is the **Hotel Kinam**, although this was built in the 1950s, long after the original gingerbread boom.

leafy gardens, Mupanah's cafe and restaurant offers one of the most elegant lunching experiences in the city. Artsy white imitation trees adorn the dining area, and well-dressed waitstaff provide top-notch service. The Caribbean-themed menu includes such items as Creole shrimp and a tropical chopped salad with grilled lobster and green papaya.

Café Terrasse
INTERNATIONAL $$

(☑ 3736-3132, 2944-1033; 11 Rue Capois, Port-au-Prince; sandwiches US$5, mains US$12-24; ⊙ 10am-8pm Mon-Sat; ☜) In downtown Port-au-Prince, Café Terrasse is a long-standing haunt for embassy and NGO types, serving up large, fresh salads, custom omelets and hearty French fare. The eccentric owner has tastefully adorned the cafe with antique furnishings and old-timey art, and patio seating looks over Champs de Mars. Surprisingly cheap burgers and sandwiches are also available to go.

✕ Pétionville

Pâtisserie Marie Beliard
BAKERY $

(☑ 2813-1515, 2813-1516; www.patisseriemariebeliard.com; cnr Rues Faubert & Lambert, Pétionville; pastries US$1-5; ⊙ 6am-6:30pm Mon-Sat, to 1pm Sun) Hands down the best bakery in Pétionville, this bright French cafe is the perfect stop to fuel up before a city tour or a road trip. The *pain au chocolat* is divine, as are the cupcakes, croissants, sandwiches and pizzas. The quaint kitchen-utensil wallpaper and inlaid brick give the place a homey vibe.

★ Café 36
INTERNATIONAL $$

(☑ 2233-3636; www.cafe36haiti.com; La Lorraine Hotel, 36 Rue Clerveaux, Pétionville; tapas US$8-10, mains US$12-18; ⊙ 6am-10pm; ℗☜) Attached to the boutique hotel La Lorraine, this classy but chilled-out restaurant, event space and art gallery is the kind of place where you could eat for a week. And drink. And do trivia. And see some art. And eat more. The menu offers traditional Dominican dishes such as *kibbeh* and *acra*, along with healthy, international salads and beef carpaccio.

★ L'Estaminet
BRASSERIE $$

(☑ 4873-2163, 4824-1329; 157 Rue Chavannes, Pétionville; mains US$11-22; ⊙ 7:30am-11:30pm Mon-Sat, 4pm-11:30pm Sun) Recently opened by Jean Pierre, a whimsical, serial restaurateur who rarely ceases to delight, L'Estaminet is his best offering yet. The stylish brasserie boasts an extensive wine list along with cheese plates, homemade pastas and a tender beef filet drizzled with a decadent sauce of your choosing. Art and books abound, and jazz seems to emanate from the very walls.

★ Papaye
FUSION $$$

(☑ 4656-2482; 48 Rue Métellus, Pétionville; mains US$18-28; ⊙ noon-2:30pm & 7-11pm Tue-Fri, 1-11pm Sat) 'Caribbean fusion' aren't words you expect to see written in a Haitian restaurant review, but Papaye carries off the idea with considerable aplomb, taking Creole dishes and jamming them up against Asian, European and other culinary influences. Somehow it works, producing one of Haiti's classiest restaurants.

Caribbean Supermarket
SUPERMARKET

(☑ 3113-3333; 51 Rue Métellus, Pétionville; ⊙ 8am-8pm Mon-Sat, to 2pm Sun; ℗) This enormous supermarket in Pétionville is a one-stop shop for food. The glistening aisles include imported and gourmet products and there's also an attached cafe serving some of the best coffee and sandwiches around. The caprese sandwich with prosciutto is particularly mind-blowing.

🍷 Drinking & Nightlife

This is a city that knows how to party. On any given night of the week, residents pour into their regular haunts to throw down, oftentimes until the wee hours. Mondays are trivia night at La Lorraine (p493), Tuesdays are karaoke night at **Zest** (☑ 4429-4994; 81 Rue Gregoire, Pétionville; ⊙ noon-late). Wednesdays are US$5 appetizers at **Magdoos** (☑ 4823-2665, 3821-2121; www.facebook.com/magdoosresto; Rue Ogé, Pétionville; mains US$7-15), Thursdays are rum sours at **Yanvalou** (☑ 4329-1347; yanvaloubar@gmail.com; Ave N, Pacot; ⊙ 11am-11pm), and so on.

☆ Entertainment

Hôtel Oloffson
LIVE MUSIC

(☑ 3810-4000; 60 Ave Christophe) On Thursday nights, from about 11pm, crowds gather here to dance until the small hours to the Vodou rock and roots music of RAM – the hotel band. A potent blend of African rhythms, *rara* horns, guitar and keyboards, the shows have an irresistible atmosphere. At the center of everything is band leader (and Oloffson owner) Richard A Morse.

Sylvio Cator Stadium
SPECTATOR SPORT

(cnr Rue Oswald Durand & Ave Mgr Guilloux) Hosts Port-au-Prince's two biggest soccer clubs: Racing Club Haïtien and Violette Athletic.

🛍 Shopping

Port-au-Prince is Haiti's marketplace. For the most memorable of all souvenirs, head to the Grand Rue Artists (p491), a Vodou junkyard extraordinaire. Down the street at the **Marché de Fer** (Grand Rue, Port-au-Prince; ⊘7am-5pm), you can also find everything from paintings and *artisanat* (handicrafts) to Vodou flags.

ℹ Information

Most hotels have wi-fi, but internet cafes are plentiful and cost around HTG150 per hour.

Ministry of Tourism (☑3816-3208; www.haititourisme.gouv.ht; 8 Rue Légitime, Port-au-Prince)

Police station (☑2257-2222, 2222-1117, emergency 114; Rue Légitime, Port-au-Prince; ⊘24hr)

Post Office (Rue Bonne Foi, Port-au-Prince; ⊘8am-4pm Mon-Sat)

Post Office (Pl St-Pierre; ⊘8am-4pm Mon-Sat)

MONEY

ATMs are widespread. To beat bank queues and maximize safety, head to supermarkets to change money; most have dedicated counters and security guards.

Sogebank (Rte de Delmas 30, Delmas; ⊘8:30am-3:30pm Mon-Fri)

Scotiabank (cnr Rues Geffrard & Louverture, Pétionville; ⊘9am-4:30pm Mon-Fri)

Unibank (118 Rue Capois, downtown Port-au-Prince; ⊘8am-4:30pm Mon-Fri)

MEDICAL SERVICES

Haiti Air Ambulance (☑2812-8700, 2812-8701; www.haitiairambulance.org; Sonapi industrial Park) Helicopter ambulances accessible to those who buy a membership (two weeks/one year US$25/36).

Hôpital Bernard Mevs (☑3771-8247; 2 Rue Solidarite; ⊘24hr) A reputable hospital with a trauma center, run in partnership with Project Medishare.

Hôpital du Canapé Vert (☑2245-0984, 3767-8191; 83 Rte de Canapé Vert, Canapé Vert; ⊘24hr) Excellent doctors and emergency service, recommended by expats.

Hôpital François de Sales (☑2223-2110, 2222-0232; 53 Rue Charéron, Port-au-Prince; ⊘24hr) Decent hospital for visitors and expats.

St Luke Family Hôpital (www.stlukehaiti.org; Next to Petit Freres, Tabarre; ⊘8am-5pm) A leader in internal medicine; down the street from the US Embassy.

ℹ Getting There & Away

International flights depart from **Aéroport International Toussaint Louverture** (p508) and domestic flights from **Aérogare Guy Malary** (p508); the two are adjacent on the northern outskirts of Port-au-Prince.

Airlines running domestic flights to and from Aérogare Guy Malary include **Sunrise Airways** (p508) and **Mission Aviation Fellowship** (p508).

Port-au-Prince has no central bus station; instead, there is a series of mildly anarchic departure points according to the destination. Most buses and *taptaps* (local minibuses) leave when full – exceptions are for Cap-Haïtien, Les Cayes and Jérémie, which you can buy seats for in advance.

ℹ Getting Around

Moto-taxis are good for weaving through traffic jams, but certainly not the safest form of transport. They cost around HTG50 for short trips; haggle for longer distances. Taptaps run along set routes and are a very cheap and convenient way of getting around. The usual fare is HTG10 per trip.

AROUND PORT-AU-PRINCE

The clamor of Port-au-Prince can tire even the most die-hard traveler after a while – luckily there are several worthwhile sights within striking distance of the capital.

Croix des Bouquets

Almost sucked in by Port-au-Prince's inexorable urban sprawl, Croix des Bouquets is the setting for one of Haiti's most vibrant art scenes. Its Noialles district is home to the *boss fé* (ironworkers), who hammer out incredible decorative art from flattened oil drums and vehicle bodies.

Steel drums are the most common material for the art. They're cut in half and flattened, the designs chalked and then cut out with chisels. Once free, the edges are smoothed and relief work is beaten out. The smallest pieces are the size of a book; the most gloriously elaborate can stand over 2m. Popular designs include the Tree of Life, the Vodou *lwa* La Siren (the mermaid), birds, fish, musicians and angels.

Buses from Port-au-Prince (US$1, 30 minutes) depart from the junction of Rue des

Fronts Forts and Rue du Centre. Taptaps from Port-au-Prince (HTG20, 30 minutes) leave from Carrefour Fleuriot in Tabarre, on Boulevard du 15 Octobre. Get out at the police post, where the road splits left to Hinche and right to the DR. Take the right-hand road, then turn right at Notre Dame Depot. For Noailles, turn right at the Seventh Day Adventist Church, and follow the sound of hammered metal: the artist village is signed.

Route de Kenscoff

The main road from Pétionville's Pl St-Pierre winds steeply uphill toward the cool of the mountains. After just a few kilometers you're in a rich agricultural area, with steep terraced fields clinging to the sides of the mountains, and the congestion of the city replaced by sweet cool breezes.

The crisp air of **Kenscoff** makes it a popular weekend destination for city dwellers – at 1980m above sea level, it's often referred to as the Switzerland of the Caribbean (there are even a few weird Caribbean–Alpine architectural hybrids). With sweeping views everywhere you look and the brooding cloud-capped backdrop of Massif de la Selle behind you, it's tailor-made for day walks. Coffee and vegetables are grown in great quantities here, giving Kenscoff an interesting local market.

Le Florville (☏ 3289-9911; 19 Rte de Kenscoff, Kenscoff; r incl breakfast US$65-100; P) is a lovely hotel on the Route de Kenscoff, with just five tidy rooms and a winning restaurant, and just off the Route de Kenscoff, **L'Observatoire de Boutilliers** is a romantic mountain-top restaurant with an incredible view of Port-au-Prince and beyond.

Taptaps leave Pétionville throughout the day from the corner of Rue Gregoire and Villate, departing when full (HTG20, 30 minutes) and passing through Fermathe. Change at Kenscoff for Furcy.

Furcy

In the tiny, picturesque village of Furcy, pine trees abound and the whiff of fresh cilantro is in the air. There are stellar views of the Massif de la Selle, and locals rent out horses (around US$5 per hour) to take visitors to a waterfall above the village (it's 1½ hours on foot). Whatever your plans, don't forget some warm clothes – temperatures drop once the sun starts to dip.

Furcy offers three amazing options:

O-zone the Village (☏ 4806-6929, 2811-5170; www.facebook.com/pg/ozonethevillage; Pl Furcy; dm incl breakfast from US$30, s/d incl breakfast US$40/60; P ☏) A rustic lodge constructed almost entirely with recycled materials (including a tree-house option).

HIKING IN PARC NATIONAL LA VISITE

The Massif de la Selle, a series of spectacular ridges still dotted with pine forest, divides Haiti's southeast. You can do one of Haiti's best hikes here – a day of trekking that takes you through the western section of the mountains, known as Park National la Visite, and toward the Caribbean. The route traverses four mountains and takes in some truly beautiful terrain, from wooded slopes to almost-rolling green hills, as well as offering lovely views out to sea. Once you reach Seguin you'll find the weird *kraze dan* (broken teeth) rock formations – great slabs of karst jutting up from the ground like so many discarded giant's dentures. A decent degree of fitness is required to do the trek, which usually takes six to eight hours. Take plenty of water and some food, as well as suitable clothing: the altitude ascends above 2000m in places, so there can be strong sun and wind, as well as unexpected rain and chill.

To reach the trailhead, take a taptap from Pétionville to Kenscoff, and change for Furcy. From there, you can walk to Carrefour Badyo, then bear left to follow the track to Seguin. By 4WD, it's a 15-minute drive to Badyo, and then you have to start hiking. Once at Seguin, you descend to Marigot (another couple of hours), and from here it is a taptap ride to Jacmel (US$1, one hour). At Furcy it's possible to hire horses with guides, but you'll have to pay for the return trip from Seguin.

In Seguin, about half way between Furcy and Marigot, the **Auberge de la Visite** (☏ 2246-0166, 3851-0159; www.facebook.com/auberge.lavisite; Seguin; r per person incl full board US$80) is a delightful place to rest.

Lodge (☑3458-5968; s/d/tr incl breakfast US$100/120/140; P❄@) A Canadian-style stone-and-wood cottage (including one room with its own sauna).

Sesanet (Madame Helene's; ☑3443-0443; s/d incl half board US$125/150; P) A homey guesthouse that also offers French and Middle Eastern fusion cuisine.

To arrive in Furcy, rent a car or hop a moto-taxi from Kenscoff (HTG150, 45 minutes) up the mountain. Make a left at Kenscoff Commissariat, then right after the fast-food places and continue uphill.

Ville-Bonheur & Saut d'Eau

An otherwise unprepossessing town, Ville-Bonheur and the nearby waterfall Saut d'Eau become the focus of Haiti's largest Vodou pilgrimage every July 16.

During the pilgrimage, the area around the Church of Our Lady of Mt Carmel is turned into a huge campground. The few guesthouses are inundated. One great accommodations option is the bright and clean **Auberge du Mont Carmel** (☑4844-8935; r incl breakfast US$50; P❄☞❅), just before the waterfall. Alternatively, there are accommodations in nearby Mirebalais, including the **Mirage Hotel** (☑2210-0631; 11 Rte Départementale; s/d incl breakfast US$85/105; P❄☞❅).

Buses and taptaps leave from Estasyon Mirebalais in Port-au-Prince (US$2.50, 2½ hours) between Grand Rue and the cathedral, at the junction of Rues des Fronts Forts and du Centre.

NORTHERN HAITI

If you're interested in how Haiti came to be as it is today, head north. From Columbus' first landfall on Hispaniola to the key events of the slave revolution, it all happened here.

Cap-Haïtien

POP 171,000

Haiti's second city feels a world away from the throng and hustle of Port-au-Prince. During the French colonial era it was the richest city in the Caribbean, and even if that grandeur has long since faded, the city still maintains a relaxed atmosphere. The old port architecture of high shop fronts and balconies makes it a pleasant place to wander.

🛏 Sleeping

Hotels in Cap-Haïtien have upped their game in recent years, with excellent budget accommodations alongside a number of good midrange and high-end options, including **Hostellerie du Roi Christophe** (☑3687-8915; hotroi24b@hotmail.com; cnr Rues 24 & B; s/d US$105/126; P❄☞❅) and **Hôtel Les Jardins de l'Ocean** (☑2260-1655; Rue 9, Carenage; r incl breakfast from US$90; P❄☞). Rooms fill fast on the weekend, so advance booking is advised.

★**Habitation des Lauriers** HOTEL **$$**
(☑3836-0885; www.habitationdeslauriers.com; cnr Rues 13 & Q; s/d with fan US$50/60, with air-con US$90/120; P@☞❅) The best-value option in Cap-Haïtien offers striking views of the city from its mountaintop perch on the western outskirts, along with top-notch service, delicious home-cooked meals, and charming accommodations for every budget. A diverse mix of guests socialize on the veranda of the historic main house and around the dipping pool, surrounded by lush gardens, hummingbirds and butterflies.

Budget travelers stay in more basic rooms up the hill, but the warm owners provide welcome cocktails, affordable excursions and complimentary airport pickup to all.

✗ Eating & Drinking

NGO workers living just outside Cap-Haïtien salivate when speaking of weekend forays into the city, where they can feast on a variety of international and local cuisines, either on the seafront or within upscale hotels. Top choices include **Lakay** (☑3188-6881; info@lakayhaiti.com; Blvd de Mer; mains US$8-19; ☉11:30am-3am), **Cap Deli** (☑2817-2807; www.facebook.com/pg/capdelihaiti; cnr Rues 29 & A; mains US$6-15; ☉10am-10pm Mon-Sat, 1-10pm Sun; ☞) and **Kokiyaj** (☑3227-4821; Blvd de Mer; mains US$8-15; ☉8am-midnight).

Cap-Haïtien also offers a lively nightlife scene, with most of the bar-restos, including the excellent **Boukanye** (☑4453-6344, 3354-6344; www.facebook.com/Boukanye; Blvd de Mer, btwn Rues 24 & 25; ☉7am-late Mon-Sat, 6pm-late Sun), concentrated along the Blvd de Mer and emanating *compas* music late into the night. For a more local scene, head to the Place d'Armes, where Haitians gather to watch football matches over Prestige beer and popcorn.

WORTH A TRIP

CÔTE DES ARCADINS

From Port-au-Prince, Rte National 1 stretches north along the coast before turning inland toward Gonaïves and Cap-Haïtien. The area is named for the Arcadins, a trio of sand cays surrounded by coral reefs in the channel between the mainland and Île de la Gonâve.

Beach hotels are the order of the day along the Côte des Arcadins, including the **Royal Decameron Indigo Beach Resort & Spa** (☏ 2815-0111, in USA 855-308-0375; www.decameron.com; Km 78, Rte National 1; all-incl r from US$79; P ❄ @ ☎), a bright and breezy hotel on a gorgeous white-sand beach with dazzling turquoise water, and cocktails flowing freely from four bars and three tasty restaurants. The recently renovated **Moulin sur Mer** (☏ 3701-1918, 2813-1042; www.moulinsurmer.com; Km 77, Rte National 1; r incl breakfast from US$115; P ❄ @ ☎) is a large and charming complex with a nice selection of rooms, including 'gingerbreadized' rooms near the beach and more Spanish-hacienda style ones further back. The **Musée Colonial Ogier-Fombrun** (☏ 3701-1918; Km 77, Rte National 1; US$5; ☉ 10am-6pm) is a short (complimentary) golf-buggy ride away.

Diving is a popular activity in these parts, and can be arranged by **Pegasus** (☏ 3411-4775; nicolemarcelinroy@yahoo.com; Kaliko Beach Club, Km 61, Rte National 1; ☉ 8am-5pm) or **Marina Blue Dive & Excursion Center.** (☏ 2811-4043; www.marinabluehaiti.com; Moulin sur Mer, Km 77, Rte National 1; open water certification US$275, dives US$100; ☉ 8am-5pm)

Hotels offer private transport to and from the area.

❶ Information

There's a useful cluster of banks and ATMs along Rue 10-11A.

Hôpital Justinien (☏ 2262-0512, 3356-2004; cnr Rues 17 & Q; ☉ 24hr) Cap-Haïtien's main hospital.

Rien Que Pour Vos Yeux (82 Rue 17) Well-stocked pharmacy.

Sogebank (cnr Rues 11 & A) Has an ATM open during banking hours.

Unibank (cnr Rues 11 & A)

❶ Getting There & Away

AIR

Hugo Chavez International Airport (p508) is 3.5km east of the city (US$7/1.50 by taxi/moto-taxi). **Sunrise Airways** (p508) has four daily flights to Port-au-Prince (from US$55, 30 minutes).

BUS

San-Souci Tours (☏ 4855-7071; Rte National 1) offers bus service to and from Port-au-Prince; **Caribe Tours** (cnr Rues 29 & A) goes to Santiago and Santo Domingo in the DR.

The Citadelle & Sans Souci

The awe-inspiring mountain fortress of Citadelle Laferrière is a short distance from Cap-Haïtien on the edge of the small town of **Milot**. Built to repel the French, it's a monument to the vision of Henri Christophe, who oversaw its construction. A visit here is an essential part of any trip to Haiti, and actually takes in two sites – the Unesco World Heritage–listed fortress itself and the palace of Sans Souci.

One recommended guide here is Maurice Etienne, who also runs the excellent Lakou Lakay hotel, restaurant and cultural center. A reasonable fee for a guide is US$20 to US$30, plus the hire of a horse (US$15 plus a US$5 tip for the guide).

◉ Sights

★**Citadelle Laferrière**　FORTRESS
(Citadelle Henry; Sans Souci & Citadelle US$25; ☉ 7am-4pm) Haitians call the Citadelle the eighth wonder of the world and, having slogged to the 900m summit of Pic Laferrière (or ridden horseback for US$15), you'll likely agree. This battleship-like fortress gives commanding views in every direction. Completed in 1820, it employed 20,000 people and held supplies to sustain the royal family and a garrison of 5000 troops for a year. With 4m-thick walls up to 40m high, the fortress was impenetrable, although its cannons were never fired in combat.

Sans Souci　HISTORIC SITE
(US$15; ☉ 7am-4pm) Built as a rival to Versailles in France, Henri Christophe's palace of Sans Souci has lain abandoned since it was ruined in the 1842 earthquake. The years of neglect have left an elegantly crumbling edifice, slightly alien against its tropical backdrop. Finished in 1813, Sans Souci was more than just a palace, designed to be

the administrative capital of Christophe's kingdom, housing a hospital, a school and a printing press, as well as an army barracks.

🛏 Sleeping & Eating

Lakou Lakay   CREOLE $$
(☎ 3614-2485; Milot; meals US$10-20) This cultural community center is a longstanding institution that has seen better economic times but remains delightful. Run by guide Maurice Etienne and his family, the center welcomes visitors with traditional dancing, folk songs and drumming, along with a huge Creole feast (reservations required). Rooms for visitors (US$50 per person) are very simple.

ⓘ Getting There & Away

Taptaps from Cap-Haïtien (HTG20, one hour) drop you a short walk from Sans Souci. Don't plan to return too late, as transport dries up by late afternoon.

Gonaïves

Gonaïves may not be much to look at, but travelers keen on understanding Haiti's history will appreciate a stop in this large, political city. On January 1, 1804, it was here that Dessalines signed the act of Haitian independence, creating the world's first black republic. Just outside Gonaïves, the town of Dessalines is surrounded by historic, mountain-top forts that defended the city throughout the 1800s.

Souvenance and Soukri – the two biggest Vodou festivals in the country – are two more reasons travelers might opt to base themselves in the area. The best hotel in town is **Hotel Admiral Killick** (☎ 3498-2605; 90 Av des Dattes; r incl breakfast from US$80; P ❊ 🐀 ☀) and dining options consist of mediocre bar-restos.

Souvenance begins on Good Friday, and continues for a week, to the constant sound of *rara* music. Prayers are offered to sacred tamarind trees, initiates bathe in a sacred pond and bulls are sacrificed for the Vodou spirits.

Soukri is a ritual dedicated to the Kongo *lwa*. The service is divided into two branches: 'the father of all Kongo' takes place on January 6, and the second, larger ceremony, 'the mother of all Kongo,' occurs on August 14. The rituals last two weeks each, a true test of endurance. Many of the celebrations are similar to those in Souvenance.

ⓘ Getting There & Away

Gonaïves is roughly halfway between Port-au-Prince and Cap-Haïtien, with a bus station east of the main square next to the National gas station on the main highway. There are buses to Port-au-Prince (HTG350, 3½ hours) and Cap-Haïtien (HTG250, three hours).

SOUTHERN HAITI

Haiti's south is about taking it easy. Pulling out of Port-au-Prince, the urban hustle is soon replaced by a relaxed air as you head toward the Caribbean.

Jacmel

POP 48,000
Sheltered by a beautiful 3km-wide bay, the old port of Jacmel is one of the most friendly and tranquil towns in Haiti, and host to one of its best Carnivals.

Part of Jacmel's charm lies in its old town center, full of mansions and merchants'

WORTH A TRIP

BEACHES WEST OF CAP-HAÏTIEN

A rough road leads west from Cap-Haïtien, winding along the northwest coast of the cape toward some of the loveliest coastal scenery in the country, where green hills tumble straight into the Atlantic, the two divided by sheer cliffs or stretches of delicious golden sand. Here you'll find **Cormier Plage Resort** (☎ 3702-0210; www.cormierhaiti.com; Rte de Labadie; s/d incl half board US$120/198; P ❊ @ 🐀) a pleasant resort with 34 big and airy rooms looking out to sea, meters from the gently shelving golden beach. The property also features an aviary, a spa and a tennis court, and the restaurant is great for seafood (though service can be slow). **Plage Labadie** is a walled-off peninsula rented by Royal Caribbean Lines for its cruise-ship guests, who arrive three or four times a week.

From there, *bateaux-taxis* (water taxis) ferry passengers to the uninhabited island of Île-à-Rat, one of the country's most beautiful places to spend a day sunning, snorkeling, and feasting on freshly caught seafood.

warehouses with a late-Victorian grace poking out from behind the wrought-iron balconies and peeling facades. Although some of Jacmel's historic buildings were damaged in the earthquake, the town has received a facelift in recent years, including the installation of innumerable urban mosaics.,The most impressive mosaics are displayed along the new, kilometer-long beachfront boardwalk, **Promenade du Bord de Mer** (Jacmel waterfront), which buzzes with activity day and night.

◉ Sights

★Bassin Bleu   WATERFALL
(HTG100; ⊘dawn-dusk) Tucked into the mountains 12km northwest of Jacmel, Bassin Bleu is a series of three cobalt-blue pools linked by waterfalls that make up one of the prettiest swimming holes in Haiti. Experience Jacmel will take you to a hamlet close to the pools via moto-taxi, then a local guide will escort you down an uneven path (at one point you'll rappel down a rock face) to the gorgeous pools, where kids often jump from high rocks.

Cayes Jacmel   VILLAGE
From the small fishing village of Cayes Jacmel, about 14km east of Jacmel, the beach spreads a further 3km to **Plage Ti Mouillage**, a gorgeous white-sand beach fringed with coconut palms, plus a bar for drinks and seafood. Cayes Jacmel is known for making the rocking chairs seen throughout Haiti.

☞ Tours

Experience Jacmel   ADVENTURE
(☎3322-7557, 3722-5757; www.experiencejacmel.com; Promenade du Bord de Mer; ⊘8am-1pm) The most reputable tour company in the south, Experience Jacmel offers city tours, Carnival-focused art excursions, journeys to Bassin Bleu, and even a Vodou night tour involving an encounter with a Vodou priest.

DON'T MISS

FESTIVALS & EVENTS

Jacmel's **Carnival** (⊘Feb) celebrations are famous across Haiti, and every year thousands of partygoers descend on the city to take part in this fantastic spectacle. Jacmel turns into one giant street theater for the event: it's a world away from the sequins and sparkle of Carnival in Rio de Janeiro.

Local owner Markensy is as nice and helpful as they come, and incredibly knowledgeable about the town.

☐ Sleeping

★Cyvadier Plage Hôtel   HOTEL $$
(☎3844-8264; www.hotelcyvadier.com; Rte de Cyvadier; s/d with fan US$60/73, with air-con US$80/95; P✳@☀) Off the main highway, this is the furthest of the beach hotels from the center of Jacmel, but also one of the best. Good rooms in a cluster of buildings face the terrace restaurant and out to the private cove of Cyvadier Plage (nonresidents welcome).

Cap Lamandou Hôtel   HOTEL $$
(☎3720-1892, 3920-9135; www.cap-lamandou.com; Rte de Lamandou; r US$118; P✳@☎☀) On the edge of Jacmel, but a bit of a hike off the main road, the Cap Lamandou is one of Jacmel's glitziest hotels. Rooms are immaculate, with wi-fi throughout and lovely views over the bay. The bar leads onto the central terrace and pool, which has more steps descending to the sea if you're in need of a dip.

✗ Eating & Drinking

The best restaurants in the city are housed in hotels, including Hôtel Florita, Colin's Hotel and Cyvadier Plage Hôtel. A local specialty are tiny sweet *ti malice* (bananas), and there's plenty of street food around. Between July and January, look out for women selling *pisquettes,* tiny fish sautéed in huge numbers. Nightlife in Jacmel is lively on the Promenade du Bord de Mer and Ave Baranquilla, where the music and partying go as late as the patrons feel like staying.

☐ Shopping

Jacmel is a souvenir-buyer's paradise. Its most famous output is the papier-mâché Carnival masks, but other handicrafts include hand-painted boxes, wooden flowers, and models of taptaps, jungle animals and boats. Prices are cheap, and there's no hard sell. Most of the shops and a number of galleries can be found on Rue St-Anne near the Hôtel la Jacmelienne sur Plage. **Moro** (☎3467-4518, 3166-6363; 21 Rue du Commerce; ⊘hours vary Mon-Sat) is one of the better galleries.

❶ Information

Banque Nationale de Crédit (Grand Rue; ⊘8:30am-4pm Mon-Fri)

Dola Dola (cnr Aves Baranquilla & de la Liberté; ⊘8am-4pm Mon-Sat) Moneychanger.

MÔLE SAINT-NICOLAS

The prosperous town of Môlê Saint-Nicolas is well worth a visit, not only because it is the site where Christopher Columbus first made landfall on Hispaniola in 1492, but also because it is the first town in Haiti to offer its residents 24-hour electricity, mostly generated by solar power. The grid was set up in 2016 by Sigora, a San Francisco–based technology company, and as you stroll through the town you'll see solar panels atop street lights, homes and businesses.

The surrounding areas are also brimming with historical sites, including caves with Taíno paintings, forts, a powder warehouse and a watchtower. The biggest attraction, though, is the kitesurfing camp **Boukan Guinguette** (www.boukanguinguette.com; beach camping HTG850, s/d incl breakfast US$65/80). Incredibly far-flung but more than worth the drive, this is the first and only kitesurfing school in Haiti, with well-constructed bungalows and a top-notch restaurant-bar. Reaching the area is a lengthy and difficult process. Contact Boukan Guinguette for information.

Hôpital St Michel (☏2288-2151; Rue St-Philippe; ⊙24hr) For emergencies, but not great.

Pharmacie St-Cyr (48 Ave Baranquilla; ⊙8am-8pm)

Philippe Agent de Change (Ave Baranquilla; ⊙8am-7pm Mon-Sat) Changes euros and Canadian dollars.

Post office (☏4890-0000; Place Touissaint L'Ouverture; ⊙8am-4pm Mon-Sat)

Unibank (Ave de la Liberté; ⊙8:30am-4pm Mon-Fri) Gives Visa advances.

❶ Getting There & Away

La Source (☏4300-9525; 16 Av de la Liberté, near Maré Geffard) buses (HTG200, three hours) and taptaps (HTG100, 2½ hours) to Port-au-Prince leave from the Bassin Caïman station 2km out of town.

Kabic

About 30 minutes east of Jacmel, just down the street from Cayes Jacmel, this small fishing village turned lush bohemian beach getaway graced the map just a few years ago, attracting artist types with a desire to feel closer to nature and further from the gritty capital. The town is tiny, with just a few hotels and restaurants, and a picturesque azure beach that offers decent waves for surfers. The friendly locals, referred to as Kabiquois, make guests feel welcome and are one of the main reasons so many return time and again.

🏃 Activities

During the day people relax on the beach or go surfing; the reef and rock breaks off Kabic are suitable for all levels. The area is home to Haiti's first and only surf school, **Surf Haiti**

(☏3159-9414, 4906-2119; www.surfhaiti.org; Kabic Beach; lessons US$15, board rental half-/full day US$10/20; ⊙dawn-dusk), which also runs its own guesthouse up the mountain. Kabic has increasingly attracted surfers and hosted its first international surf competition in 2016.

🛏 Sleeping & Eating

From the eccentric guesthouse **Chic Chateau** (☏4751-6703; www.facebook.com/ChicChateauHaiti; Kabic Beach; s/d incl breakfast US$50/60; P 🛜 🐾) 🐾 to the beachfront resort **Kabic Beach Club** (☏2274-1220, 3780-6850; www.kabicbeachclub.com; Kabic Beach; s/d with air-con US$120/130, r without air-con US$115, all incl breakfast; P ❄ 🛜 🐾) to a bungalow-style stay **La Colline Enchantée** (☏3703-0448; www.facebook.com/collineenchantee; Marigot; s/d incl breakfast from US$77/99; P 🛜 🐾), Kabic has a good mix of overnight options for all budgets. And just off the main drag, a small but impressive collection of open-air, beachfront restaurants serve up seafood dishes and Creole cuisine. At **Villa Nicole** (☏3389-4500, 3387-4500; www.villanicolejacmel.com; Kabic Beach; s/d incl breakfast $121/154; ❄ 🛜) and **La Reference** (Kabic Beach; mains US$5; ⊙9am-9pm), expect just-caught lobster, conch, fish and octopus, served with coconut rice and fried plantains. Wash it all down with fresh coconut water. **Sur Le Toit** (☏2209-4038; Kabic Beach; barbecue HTG175) has an ambitious menu but often only serves BBQ.

❶ Getting There & Away

Moto taxis from Jacmel to Kabic run around HTG75 in the daytime and HTG125 at night, and taptaps (HTG25) travel up and down the beachfront road from sunrise until 8pm. Jacmel's taptap station is on the corner of Ave Baranquilla and Rue des Beaux Enfants, and the ride from Jacmel to Kabic takes around 30 minutes.

The Southwest

From Port-au-Prince, Rte National 2 runs the length of Haiti's southern 'claw' to Les Cayes. After crawling through Carrefour, the road winds through a succession of medium-sized towns along the coast: Léogâne, known for its distilleries and stone sculptors; Grand-Goâve, a jumping-off point for dolphin- and whale-watching trips and visits to secluded and outrageously beautiful beaches (boating tour company **Toupamer** (☑ 3685-7505; richardboyer1@hotmail.com) can take you there); and Petit-Goâve, famous for its sweet *dous makos* (a type of Haitian fudge).

Les Cayes

You'd be hard-pressed to find a sense of urgency in Haiti's fourth-largest city. More popularly known as Aux Cayes, Les Cayes is an old rum port sheltered by a series of reefs that has sent many ships to their graves (its first recorded victim was one of Columbus' ships on his final voyage to Hispaniola). Pirates were another threat, notably from nearby Île-à-Vache. Today Les Cayes has little to offer the visitor, although it's a good stopping-off point for other destinations in the south. The best place to stay is **Cayenne Hôtel** (☑ 3105-3959; lacayenneht@yahoo.fr; Rue Capitale; s/d incl breakfast from US$60/80; P ❀ @ ☎) and the best place to eat is **Bistro Gourmand** (☑ 2270-5718; Rue Geffrard; mains HTG400; ⊙ 9am-10pm).

WORTH A TRIP

ABAKA BAY RESORT

This hotel (☑ 3721-3691; www.abakabay.com; Anse Dufour; s/d incl full board US$135/220; ❀ @) has one of the most fabulous beaches in the Caribbean, a smooth white curve of a bay, met by lush foliage and a series of pleasant bungalows and villas. The atmosphere is laid-back, but the service is still exacting. Private transport to and from the island costs an additional US$50 per boat.

Voyageur (☑ 3633-2361; voyageurbus@gmail.com; Meridien Hotel, Rte National 2) and **Transport Chic** (☑ 3630-2576; 227 Ave des Quatre Chemins) have luxury air-conditioned minibuses running daily between Les Cayes and Port-au-Prince (US$10, four hours). Buy tickets the day before, and take photo ID.

Île-à-Vache

The so-called 'Island of Cows,' Île-à-Vache lies about 15km south of Les Cayes. In the 16th century it was a base for the Welsh pirate Henry Morgan as he terrorized Santo Domingo and Colombia. Three centuries later Abraham Lincoln tried to relocate emancipated black American slaves here, but it was a short-lived and ill-provisioned experiment.

The island's dreamy hotels include Abaka Bay Resort (p502), which offers one of the most fabulous beaches in the Caribbean, and **Port Morgan** (☑ 3923-0000; www.port-morgan.com; Cayes Coq; s/d incl full board from US$115/205; P ❀ @ ☎), a collection of bright-and-breezy gingerbread chalets with lovely views out to sea.

Hotels on Île-à-Vache offer transfers from the Les Cayes wharf from US$50 to US$60 per trip (which can be split among groups). Otherwise, *bateaux-taxis* (water taxis) leave from the wharf several times daily (US$2, 30 minutes) for the island's main town, Madame Bernard.

Port Salut

A once-picturesque road leads west from Les Cayes to the spectacular beaches of Port Salut, but the view is diminished by broken trees, trashed buildings and other hurricane damage. At the time of writing, electricity had not yet been restored; all area businesses were running on generators and lacked wi-fi.

The one-street town is strung for several kilometers along the coast, and still offers wide swaths of palm-fringed white sand with barely a person on it, and the gorgeously warm Caribbean to splash around in. The largest cave in Haiti, **Grotte Marie Jeanne** (☑ 3702-3941, 3638-2292; HTG100; ⊙ 8am-4pm), is about 45 minutes up the coast in Port-à-Piment, and definitely worth a visit.

Auberge du Rayon Vert (☑ 3713-9035, 3779-1728; www.aubergedurayonvert.com; Rue Point-Sable; s/d US$77/88; P ❀ @) remains a great place to stay and eat, and **Chez Kaliko** (☑ 3878-9601; Port Salut beach; mains US$12;

⊘hours vary) is an excellent restaurant on the beach serving fresh conch and lobster.

Jérémie

Jérémie, the capital of Grand'Anse Départment, was hit hard by Hurricane Matthew, which took out many of the city's trees and blew the tin roofs off innumerable homes. Hard work on the part of locals and visiting NGO employees has gotten the city back up and running, though, making this one of the most pleasant and surprisingly tidy places to visit in all of Haiti.

Place Charmant (☑3882-0965, 3701-5874; www.placecharmant.com; 2 Calasse; r incl half board from $US77; P@✖) is hands down the best accommodations option in the city, but there are several decent places on Ave Emile Roumer, including **Auberge Inn** (☑3727-9678; info@aubergeinnhaiti.com; s/d/tr without bathroom US$75/120/150; P@).

Jérémie offers an array of cheap eateries and local spots, along with a popular new restaurant focusing on healthy fare, **Ilan-Ilan** (☑3724-6662, 4865-7564; 85 Rue Source Dommage; mains HTG300; ⊘8am-11pm).

The quickest way in and out is the Mission Aviation Fellowship (p508) flight from Port-au-Prince (US$135, 35 minutes), with scheduled flights every Tuesday and Thursday.

Grand'Anse Tours (☑3746-6777, 2811-8064; 81 Rue Geffard, Port-au-Prince) runs buses every morning for Port-au-Prince (HTG500, eight hours) from a lot on the southern outskirts.

UNDERSTAND HAITI

History

Haiti's earliest inhabitants called their island Quisqueya – 'cradle of life.' Despite its size, it has often played a key role in world history: Christopher Columbus founded the first European settlement in the Americas here, and under French slavery it became the richest colony – an iniquity that led to two firsts: the only successful slave revolution in history and the founding of the world's first black republic. Unfortunately, modern Haiti has suffered from self-serving leaders, foreign interventions and natural disasters, preventing it from living up to the promise of its revolutionary heroes.

JÉRÉMIE'S SWEET TREATS

Baked goods are a big deal in Jérémie, which is home to the famous Haitian ginger bun known in Creole as *konparet*. This translates roughly to 'when you smell it you appear at the bakery' and it's made with a mouthwatering mix of coconut, cinnamon, ginger, flour, sweet banana, butter and sugar. Other popular confections include *bonbon siwo*, a molasses and flour cookie, and *tablet wowoli*, a sesame brittle. Try them all at **Konparet Madam Senec** (☑2714-4489; Rue Stenio Vincent; konparet US$1).

The Taínos, Spanish & French

Hispaniola's earliest inhabitants arrived around 2600 BC in huge dugout canoes from what is now eastern Venezuela. They were called the Taínos, and by the time Christopher Columbus landed on the island in 1492, they numbered some 400,000. However, within 30 years of Columbus' landing, the Taínos were gone, wiped out by disease and abuse.

The Spanish neglected their colony of Santo Domingo, and through the 17th century it became a haven for pirates and, later, ambitious French colonists. In 1697 the island was formally divided, and the French colony of St-Domingue followed soon after.

The French turned St-Domingue over to sugar production on a huge scale. By the end of the 18th century it was the richest colony in the world, with 40,000 colonists lording it over half a million black slaves. Following the French Revolution in 1789, free offspring of colonists and female slaves demanded equal rights, while the slaves themselves launched a huge rebellion. Led by the inspiring slave leader Toussaint Louverture, the slaves freed themselves by arms and forced France to abolish slavery.

The World's First Black Republic

French treachery dispatched Toussaint to a prison death, but in May 1803 his general, Jean-Jacques Dessalines, took the French tricolor flag and, ripping the white out of it, declared he was ripping the white man out of the country. The red and blue were stitched together with the motto *Liberté ou la Mort* (Liberty or Death), creating Haiti's flag.

Dessalines won a decisive victory against the French at the Battle of Vertières, near Cap-Haïtien, and on January 1, 1804, at Gonaïves, Dessalines proclaimed independence for St-Domingue and restored its Taíno name, Haiti, meaning 'Mountainous Land.'

Dessalines crowned himself Emperor of Haiti and ratified a new constitution that granted him absolute power. However, his tyrannical approach to the throne inflamed large sections of society to revolt – his death in an ambush at Pont Rouge in 1806 marked the first of many violent overthrows that would plague Haiti for the next 200 years.

Dessalines' death sparked a civil war between the black north, led by Henri Christophe, and the south, led by Alexandre Pétion. Christophe crowned himself king, while Pétion became president of the southern republic. It took both their deaths (Christophe by suicide) to reunite the country, which happened in 1820 under new southern leader Jean-Pierre Boyer, who established a tenuous peace.

During his reign Boyer paid a crippling indemnity to France in return for diplomatic recognition. The debt took the rest of the century to pay off and turned Haiti into the first third-world debtor nation. Boyer also sought to unify Hispaniola by invading Santo Domingo. The whole of the island remained under Haitian control until 1849, when the eastern part proclaimed independence as the Dominican Republic.

The next half-century was characterized by continued rivalry between the ruling classes of wealthy mixed race families and blacks. Of the 22 heads of state between 1843 and 1915, only one served his full term in office; the others were assassinated or forced into exile.

US Intervention

By the beginning of the 20th century, Haiti's strategic proximity to the new Panama Canal and increased German interests in the country reignited American interest. When Haitian President Vilbrun Guillaume Sam was killed by a mob in 1915, the US sent in the marines to stabilize the country.

During its nearly 20-year occupation of the country, the US replaced the Haitian constitution and built up the country's infrastructure by instituting the hated *corvée*, labor gangs of conscripted peasants.

The occupation brought predictable resistance, with the Caco peasant rebellion led by Charlemagne Péraulte from 1918 to 1920, in which thousands of Haitians were killed before the assassination of Péraulte effectively put an end to the uprising – an episode of Haitian history still bitterly remembered in the country today. The occupation proved costly and the US pulled out in 1934.

The Duvaliers & Aristide

Haiti's string of tyrannical rulers reached its zenith in 1956 with the election of François 'Papa Doc' Duvalier, whose support came from the burgeoning black middle class and the politically isolated rural poor.

Duvalier consolidated his power by creating the notorious Tontons Macoutes (named after a Haitian folk-story character who carries off small children in a bag at night), a private militia who used force with impunity in order to extort cash and crops from a cowed population.

'Papa Doc' died on April 21, 1971, and was succeeded by his son Jean-Claude 'Baby Doc' Duvalier. Periodic bouts of repression continued until major civil unrest forced Baby Doc to flee to France in February 1986.

Control changed hands between junta leaders until finally the Supreme Court ordered elections for December 1990. A young priest named Father Jean-Bertrand Aristide, standing as a surprise last-minute candidate with the slogan 'Lavalas' (Flood), won a landslide victory.

Aristide promised radical reforms to aid the poor, but after just seven months he was pushed out of office. An alliance of rich mixed race families and army generals staged a bloody coup. Despite international condemnation, an embargo against the junta was barely enforced, and thousands of Haitians fled political repression in boats to the USA.

Many had seen Aristide as a radical socialist, so when a joint US–UN plan was finally brokered for his return, it was on the condition that he sign up to an economic restructuring plan that eviscerated his original ideas for reform.

Haiti Today

Haiti is now the poorest country in the western hemisphere, and has long been a major recipient of international aid. The 2010 earthquake and 2016 hurricane not only created new challenges, but also laid bare the fault lines in Haitian society and the body politic.

In 2016 violent protests and dubious accusations of voter fraud repeatedly delayed the presidential election, forcing an interim government and an extra round of voting in which only 21% of the country took part. The winner, a banana exporter with no previous political experience, was finally declared in 2017. But President Jovenel Moïse faces some pretty enormous obstacles: Haiti's economic growth continues to slow, inflation and unemployment are spinning out of control, and on top of it all, Hurricane Matthew caused an estimated US$2.7 billion in damage.

Even if Moïse comes up with a viable plan, he'll likely end up thwarted by Haiti's parliament, which seems configured to create political gridlock. Meanwhile, the mainly mixed-race oligarchies who speak only French and own half the country's wealth continue dominating manufacturing and import/export, and remain the powers standing behind the president's throne. Within the high walls of Pétionville are the best French restaurants and boutiques and riches unimaginable by the vast majority of Haitians.

People & Culture

Vodou

It's hard to think of a more maligned and misunderstood religion than Vodou. Even its name sparks an instantly negative word-association game of voodoo dolls, zombies and black magic – less a religion than a mass of superstitions. The truth is somewhat distant from the hype.

Vodou is a sophisticated belief system with roots in Haiti's African past and the slave rebellion that brought the country to independence in 1804. Central to Haiti's national identity, these roots have also led to the demonization of Vodou in the West. For three centuries, slaves were shipped to Haiti from the Dahomey and Kongo kingdoms in West and Central Africa. As well as their labor, the slaves brought with them their traditional religions; Vodou is a synthesis of these, mixed with residual Taíno rituals and colonial Catholic iconography.

Vodou played a large part in both the inspiration and organization of the struggle for independence. The Vodou ceremony at Bois Cayman in 1791, presided over by the slave and priest Boukman, is considered central to sparking the first fires of the Haitian slave revolution. However, Vodou's relationship to power has always been a rocky one. Both Toussaint Louverture and Jean-Jacques Dessalines outlawed Vodou during their reigns, fearing its political potential. Overseas, the 'bad example' of slaves emancipating themselves led to Vodou being castigated in the US and Europe. It wasn't until 1991 that Vodou was finally recognized as a national religion alongside Christianity.

Music

Haitian music has been used for many things: an accompaniment to Vodou ceremonies, a form of resistance in politics, and also just to dance the night away.

HAITI'S EARTHQUAKE

At 4:53pm on January 12, 2010, Haiti was shaken to its core when shock waves from a fault line 13km below the earth's surface caused a 7.0-magnitude earthquake. Haitians quickly dubbed the earthquake *Godou-Godou,* named for the sound it made as the buildings collapsed. It's thought that 230,000 people were killed, 300,000 injured and 2.3 million people displaced, while over 180,000 buildings were either damaged or destroyed. Striking at the heart of what was already the poorest country in the Americas, *Godou-Godou* is one of the largest natural disasters on record.

The earthquake prompted an enormous humanitarian response, with billions of dollars in international assistance flooding into Haiti, and tens of thousands of volunteers and soldiers arriving to assist. But much of that 'help' was misguided and even counterproductive, undermining Haiti's potential to help itself. The Interim Haiti Recovery Commission (IHRC) set up to coordinate billions of dollars in reconstruction aid and led by Bill Clinton delivered only disorganized development experiments and unfinished projects. The Red Cross raised half a billion dollars and claimed to have built 130,000 homes, but investigative reports revealed it had only built six permanent homes. Even today, not all of the rubble has been cleared, and tens of thousands of people remain in tent cities.

One of the most popular forms is *rara*. During Carnival, Port-au-Prince and Jacmel fill with rivers of people who come to hear *rara* bands moving through the streets on floats. Cuban *son* has influenced the troubadour bands that entertain in restaurants and hotels, singing and gently strumming guitars. Merengue, the Dominican big-band sound, has always been played enthusiastically on dance floors, and in the 1950s evolved into *compas direct* (or just *compas* for short), with its slightly more African beat.

Racines (roots) music grew out of the Vodou-jazz movement of the late 1970s and was propelled by Vodou rhythms overlaid with electric guitars, keyboards and vocals. The most notable *racines* bands are Boukman Eksperyans, Boukan Ginen and RAM.

Haitian popular music and politics seem destined to be intertwined: in the 2010 presidential election, musician Wyclef Jean was only disqualified from running for office on a technicality, while *compas* singer Michel 'Sweet Micky' Martelly went on to win the vote for high office.

SURVIVAL GUIDE

❶ Directory A–Z

ACCOMMODATIONS

With new, higher-end stays in the works in Cap-Haïtien and Labadie, northern Haiti is on the rise. Midrange boutique hotels and guesthouses remain plentiful, and budget travelers will be happy to learn that **Habitation des Lauriers** (p497) has plans to open the area's first dorm room. There are also camping opportunities on far-flung beaches and deserted islands.

DANGERS & ANNOYANCES

Many governments advise against nonessential travel to Haiti, and certainly caution is advised.

> ### SLEEPING PRICE RANGES
>
> ....
>
> The following price ranges refer to a double room with bathroom, breakfast usually included. Air-conditioning is often included in midrange and top-end properties.
>
> **$** less than US$70
>
> **$$** US$70–130
>
> **$$$** more than US$130

→ UN troops have helped the country deal with large-scale gang and kidnapping problems, but keep your ear to the ground for protests around election time, which can get violent and should be avoided.

→ To avoid street crime, use hotel safes for anything you're not willing to lose. Hide your money in pockets, and avoid taking out smart phones on the street.

→ Common annoyances include a poor electricity supply, snarling traffic, begging, and getting stared at or called *blanc*, which is a generic word for a foreigner.

ELECTRICITY

Haiti uses flat-pronged plugs with 110V at 60 Hz.

EMBASSIES & CONSULATES

All of the embassies and consulates are in Port-au-Prince or Pétionville. Australia, New Zealand and Ireland do not have diplomatic representation in Haiti; British citizens can seek assistance at the UK Embassy in Santo Domingo.

Brazilian Embassy (☎ 2256-0900; ppinto@mr.gov.br; 168 Rue Darguin, Pétionville)

Canadian Embassy (☎ 2812-9000; www.port-au-prince.gc.ca; Rte de Delmas btwn Delmas 71 & 75, Port-au-Prince; ☺ 7am-3:30pm Mon-Thu, to 12:30pm Fri)

Cuban Embassy (☎ 2256-3504; www.cubadiplomatica.cu/haiti; 3 Rue Marion, Pétionville; ☺ 8am-12:30pm Mon-Fri)

Dominican Embassy (☎ 2813-0887; embadomhaiti@gmail.com; 121 Ave Pan Américaine, Pétionville)

French Embassy (☎ 2999-9000; www.ambafrance-ht.org; 51 Rue Capois, Port-au-Prince)

Mexican Embassy (☎ 2229-1040; embmxhai@yahoo.com; 2 Musseau cnr Delmas 60, Port-au-Prince)

US Embassy (☎ 2229-8000; http://haiti.usembassy.gov; 41 Rte de Tabarre, Tabarre; ☺ 7am-3:30pm Mon-Fri)

Venezuelan Embassy (☎ 3443-4127; embavenezhaiti@hainet.net; 2 Blvd Harry Truman, Port-au-Prince)

FOOD

Fresh seafood abounds on Haiti's northern coast, including lobsters and giant crabs, and a traveler can't go wrong with these options. A more adventurous (if controversial) local delicacy is horse meat, which is sold in roadside stands to the east of Cap-Haïtien. Many of the popular restaurants in the cities specialize in American-style dishes such as hamburgers and hot dogs.

HEALTH

Travel in Haiti is generally safe as long as you're reasonably careful about what you eat and drink. The most common travel-related illnesses, such as dysentery and hepatitis, are acquired by consumption of contaminated food and water. There is a small but significant malaria risk in certain parts of the country, and you should check before travel as to required prophylaxis. Following the 2010 earthquake, Haiti suffered a widespread cholera outbreak.

INTERNET ACCESS

Online access isn't a problem in any decently sized Haitian town, and internet cafes open and close frequently. Broadband connections are increasingly standard, along with webcams, CD burning and USB connections for uploading digital photos. Prices cost around HTG50 (US$0.75) per hour. The more expensive the joint, the better the electricity supply is likely to be. If you're bringing a laptop, wi-fi access is increasingly widespread.

MONEY
ATMs

Automated teller machines are increasingly common in Port-au-Prince, Pétionville and Cap-Haïtien, but have yet to catch on in much of the rest of the country. Always be aware of your surroundings when using an ATM and pocketing a wad of cash – use machines in large grocery stores that staff security guards when possible.

Credit Cards

Most midrange and all top-end hotels (and many Port-au-Prince restaurants) will happily let you flash the plastic.

OPENING HOURS

Many restaurants and most businesses close on Sunday.

Banks 8:30am to 1pm Monday to Friday; some major branches also open 2pm to 5pm.

Bars & Clubs 5pm to late.

Offices 7am to 4pm Monday to Friday; many close earlier Friday; government offices close for an hour at noon.

Restaurants 7am to 9pm.

Shops 7am tp 4pm Monday to Saturday; some close earlier Friday and Saturday.

PHOTOGRAPHY

Taking photos of airports and police buildings is forbidden, and it's a good idea to obtain permission first before snapping a policeman or a UN soldier. Haitians are well aware of their country's poverty, and often dislike being photographed in work or dirty clothes. Always ask permission.

PUBLIC HOLIDAYS

Government offices and most businesses will be closed on the following days:

Independence Day January 1
Ancestors' Day January 2

Carnival February (three days before Ash Wednesday)
Good Friday March/April
Agriculture and Labor Day May 1
Flag and University Day May 18
Ascencion Day 39 days after Easter
Corpus Christi May/June
Anniversary of the death of Jean-Jacques Dessaline October 17
Anniversary of the death of Toussaint Louverture November 1
All Soul's Day November 2
Anniversary of the Battle of Vertières November 18
Christmas Day December 25

TELEPHONE

Landlines Connections can sometimes be patchy. Most businesses list several numbers on their cards and many people carry two cell phones on different networks.

Cell/Mobile Phones Haiti uses the GSM system. The main operators are Digicel and Natcom. Coverage is generally good. Providers have international roaming agreements with foreign networks, but it can be cheaper to buy a local handset on arrival in Haiti for about US$20, or a SIM card for about US$5. Take a copy of your passport to the dealer for identification.

Costs Within Haiti calls cost around US$0.10 per minute, and to call overseas around US$0.90 per minute. Top-up scratch cards are available from shops and street vendors.

Codes Haiti's country code is ☎509. There are no area codes. To make an international call, first dial ☎00.

Calling The quickest option is to find a phone 'stand' – usually a youth on the street with a cell phone that looks like a regular desk phone, who will time your call and charge accordingly.

TIPPING

Most Haitians don't tip, but in tourist areas it is usual to tip and certainly all gratuities are happily accepted. Restaurant bills generally include a 10% tax and a 5% service charge.

WORK

Paid work is in short supply in Haiti, but ReliefWeb (www.reliefweb.int) and DevNet (www.

devnetjobs.org) are good places to look for jobs in the development sector in Haiti.

ⓘ Getting There & Away

Most travelers enter Haiti by air through Port-au-Prince, with the most common flight routes being from Miami, Fort Lauderdale and New York. The international airport at Cap-Haïtien also handles a small number of incoming flights.

By land, there are several border crossings with the Dominican Republic, and direct bus services link Port-au-Prince with Santo Domingo, and Cap-Haïtien with Santiago.

Flights and tours can be booked online at www.lonelyplanet.com/bookings.

AIR

Haiti has two international airports: **Aéroport International Toussaint Louverture** (☑ 4865-6436) in Port-au-Prince and **Hugo Chávez International Airport** (☑ 4478-5057, 2262-8539) in Cap-Haïtien. Numerous international carriers offer services to Haiti, including Sunrise Airways, JetBlue Airways, American Airlines, Spirit Airlines, Air France, Air Antilles Express, Insel Air, InterCaribbean Airways, Delta, Cubana, Copa, Aeromexico and Avianca.

LAND

The Haitian–Dominican border has three official crossing points. Most useful to travelers is the Malpasse–Jimaní crossing between Port-au-Prince and Santo Domingo, followed by the northern Ouanaminthe–Dajabón crossing on the road between Cap-Haïtien and Santiago. A third, and little-used, crossing is from Belladère to Comendador (aka Elías Piña).

There are direct coach services linking the two capitals, and also Cap-Haïtien to Santiago. Included in the cost of the tickets are border fees that all travelers have to pay. Entering the DR you must pay US$10 for a tourist card. The situation with fees entering and leaving Haiti by land is fluid – officials regularly ask for US$10 to stamp you in or out.

The Haitian border can be slightly chaotic if you're traveling independently, particularly at Ouanaminthe with its sprawling local market. Onward transport is plentiful, however.

ⓘ Getting Around

AIR

Domestic flights operate from **Aérogare Guy Malary** (☑ 2250-1127), near the international terminal. The two airlines that operate there are **Sunrise Airways** (☑ 2811-2222, 2816-0616; www.sunriseairways.net; Aérogare Guy Malary) and **Mission Aviation Fellowship** (MAF; ☑ 3791-9209, 2941-9209; www.maf.org; Aérogare Guy Malary; ☺7am-4pm Mon-Sat).

Haiti's small size means that flights are short (none longer than 40 minutes), saving hours on bad roads. The planes are small, typically carrying 16 passengers or fewer. One-way tickets usually cost around US$100.

BOAT

Public boat taxis are common and relatively affordable in the north and south of Haiti for transport between locations not connected by roads. Hiring private boats is less economical.

BUS

Getting around Haiti by bus and minibus isn't always comfortable, but it's the cheapest way to travel within the country, and services run to most places. Sturdy buses have the advantage of taking you to places that you'd usually need a 4WD to reach.

CAR & MOTORCYCLE

Terrible roads, a lack of road signs, and the perils of wayward pedestrians and oncoming traffic mean that you need both nerves of steel and a sense of humor to drive in Haiti.

MOTO-TAXI

The quickest and easiest way to get around any town is by moto-taxi (motorcycle taxi), often just referred to as a 'moto'. A trip will rarely cost more than about US$0.75, although rates can climb steeply if you want to travel any serious distance. Motos in Port-au-Prince are more expensive than elsewhere.

If you want to wear a helmet, you'll need to have one with you. This is a very good idea, considering how people drive in Haiti. Moto drivers and passengers are regularly injured and even killed in accidents.

TAPTAP & CAMIONETTE

A taptap is a converted pickup, often brightly decorated, with bench seats in the back. Fares are slightly cheaper than a bus. The same rules for buses apply to taptaps, which leave from the same *estasyon*: they go when full, the comfy seats next to the driver are more pricey, and you can hail one and get off where you like.

Taptaps are better suited for short trips, and in many areas are likely to be the only feasible way to get around. Halfway between a taptap and a bus is the *camionette*, with no seats, just a few ropes dangling from the ceiling to hold on to.

TAXI

Port-au-Prince and Cap-Haïtien operate collective taxis called *publiques* for getting around town. You might find them hard to spot initially, as they look like any other battered car, but look for the red ribbon hanging from the front mirror and license plates starting with 'T' for transport.

Major towns sometimes have radio-taxi firms with meters.

Jamaica

📞 +876 / POP 2.68 MILLION

Best Places to Eat

➡ Wilkes Seafood (p524)
➡ Mi Hungry (p515)
➡ Stush in the Bush (p521)
➡ Jack Sprat (p540)
➡ Houseboat Grill (p531)

Best Places to Sleep

➡ Katamah Beachfront Resort (p539)
➡ Rockhouse (p536)
➡ Goldeneye (p522)
➡ Neita's Nest (p514)
➡ Germaican Hostel (p523)

Why Go?

Jamaica is one of those countries that everyone thinks they know before they arrive, such is the power of its cultural branding. Who hasn't listened to a Bob Marley song, or gawped at the lightning feet of Usain Bolt?

The island is more than just a parade of clichés about dreadlocked Rastas and hot-heeled athletes though. Long white beaches are twinned with steep green mountains; relaxed resorts are contrasted against adrenaline-charged ghettoes, the sophistication of the capital Kingston and the charm of fishing villages. Sweet reggae and slack dancehall vie with gospel and the sound of a country mixing up its (very visible) African roots with the opportunities of some 21st-century hustle – all in one of the most beautiful islands in the Caribbean. Jamaica has a complicated national soundtrack, but one that's impossible not to groove along to

When to Go

Dec–Mar High season. Expect sunny, warm days, especially on the coast. There is little rainfall, except in Port Antonio and the northeast. At night it can become chilly, particularly in the mountains.

Apr & May This is a good time to visit; the weather is still pretty dry (again, except in Port Antonio). Rates drop for accommodations, and there are far fewer tourists, especially in the big resorts/cruise ports.

Jun–Nov Low season. There is sporadic heavy rainfall across the island, except the south coast. Heavy storms, including hurricanes, gear up August to October. Many of Jamaica's best festivals happen in midsummer.

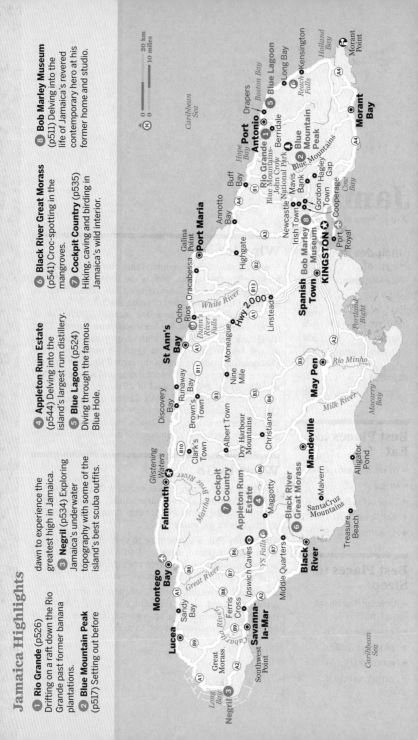

Jamaica Highlights

1 Rio Grande (p526)
Drifting on a raft down the Rio Grande past former banana plantations.

2 Blue Mountain Peak (p517) Setting out before dawn to experience the greatest high in Jamaica.

3 Negril (p534) Exploring Jamaica's underwater topography with some of the island's best scuba outfits.

4 Appleton Rum Estate (p544) Delving into the island's largest rum distillery.

5 Blue Lagoon (p524) Diving through the famous Blue Hole.

6 Black River Great Morass (p541) Croc-spotting in the mangroves.

7 Cockpit Country (p535) Hiking, caving and birding in Jamaica's wild interior.

8 Bob Marley Museum (p511) Delving into the life of Jamaica's revered contemporary hero at his former home and studio.

KINGSTON

Squeezed between the Blue Mountains and the world's seventh-largest natural harbor, Kingston simultaneously impresses you with its setting and overwhelms you with its noise and hustle. This is the island's cultural and economic heart, and a place named a Creative City of Music by Unesco in 2015. Like a plate of spicy jerk washed down with a cold Red Stripe beer, a visit to Kingston is essential to taste the rich excitement of modern Jamaica.

Kingston is a city of two halves. Downtown is home to historic buildings, the courts, banks, street markets and one of the Caribbean's greatest art museums. By contrast, Uptown holds the city's best hotels and restaurants, largely confined to New Kingston, with its cluster of tall buildings around Emancipation Park.

Uptown and Downtown seldom mix, but taken together they form a compelling and sometimes chaotic whole. Kingston is certainly never boring – we encourage you to jump right in.

◎ Sights

◉ Uptown

★**Bob Marley Museum**   MUSEUM
(☎927-9152; www.bobmarleymuseum.com; 56 Hope Rd; adult/child J$3000/1500; ⊗9:30am-4pm Mon-Sat) The large, creaky, colonial-era wooden house on Hope Rd, where Bob Marley lived and recorded from 1975 until his death in 1981, is the city's most-visited site. Today the house functions as a tourist attraction, museum and shrine, and much remains as it was in Marley's day.

The hour-long tour provides fascinating insights into the reggae superstar's life after moving uptown. His gold and platinum records are there on the walls, alongside Rastafarian religious cloaks, Marley's favorite denim stage shirt, and the Order of Merit presented by the Jamaican government. One room is entirely wallpapered with media clippings from Marley's final tour; another contains a replica of Marley's original record shop, Wail'n Soul'm. Marley's simple bedroom has been left as it was, with his favorite star-shaped guitar by the bed. At the rear of the house you'll see the spot where gunmen attempted to kill him in 1976.

The former recording studio out back is now an exhibition hall with some wonderful photos of Bob, and a theater, where the tour closes with a 20-minute film. Photography isn't allowed inside the house, but you'll almost certainly be instructed to sign 'One Love' at some point.

★**Devon House**   MUSEUM
(Map p516; ☎929-6602; www.devonhouseja maica.com; 26 Hope Rd; adult/child J$1000/500; ⊗9:30am-5pm Mon-Sat) This beautiful colonial house was built in 1881 by George Stiebel, the first black millionaire in Jamaica. Antique lovers will enjoy the visit, highlights of which include some very ornate porcelain chandeliers. Note the trompe l'oeil of palms in the entrance foyer and the roundabout chairs, designed to accommodate a man wearing a sword. Amid the grand surroundings, Stiebel even managed to discreetly tuck a gambling room away in the attic. Admission includes a mandatory guided tour.

The tree-shaded lawns of Devon House attract Kingstonians who come here to canoodle and read. The popular former carriage house and courtyard are home to several shops – tours include a scoop from **Devon House I-Scream** (Map p516; Devon House, 26 Hope Rd; scoops J$250; ⊗10am-10pm), Jamaica's best.

◉ Downtown

★**National Gallery of Jamaica**   GALLERY
(Map p512; ☎guided tours 922-1561; www.natgal ja.org.jm; 12 Ocean Blvd; admission J$400, 45min guided tours J$3000; ⊗10am-4:30pm Tue-Thu, to 4pm Fri, to 3pm Sat) The superlative collection of Jamaican art housed by the National Gallery is the finest on the island and should on no account be missed. As well as offering a distinctly Jamaican take on international artistic trends, the collection attests to the vitality of the country's artistic heritage as well as its present talent.

The collection is organized chronologically, introduced by Taíno carvings and traditional 18th-century British landscapes, whose initial beauty belies the fact that their subjects include many slave plantations. Ten galleries represent the Jamaican school, from 1922 to the present. Highlights include the boldly modernist sculptures of Edna Manley, the vibrant 'intuitive' paintings of artists including John Dunkley and David Pottinger, and revivalist bishop Mall-

Downtown Kingston

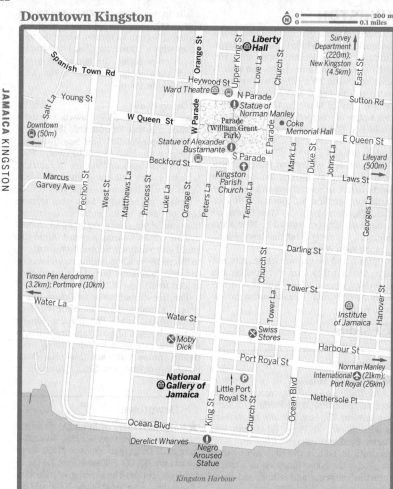

ica 'Kapo' Reynolds. Later galleries chart the course of 'Jamaican art for Jamaicans' up to the recent past, including abstract religious works by Carl Abrahams, Colin Garland's surrealist exercises, ethereal assemblages by David Boxer, and the work of realist Barrington Watson.

Temporary exhibition spaces frequently offer up the best of contemporary Jamaican art, as seen during the superb **biennial temporary exhibition** (www.natgalja. org.jm; ☉ Dec-Mar) that takes place on alternate, even-numbered years between mid-December and March.

Parade   SQUARE

(William Grant Park) William Grant Park, more commonly known as 'Parade,' is the bustling heart of Downtown, and originally hosted a fortress erected in 1694 with guns pointing toward the harbor. The fort was replaced in 1870 by Victoria Park, renamed a century later to honor Black Nationalist and labor leader Sir William Grant. The north and south entrances are watched over by cousins and political rivals **Norman Manley** (Map p512) and **Alexander Bustamante** (Map p512), respectively. A large fountain stands at its center.

At North Parade, the distinguished **Ward Theatre** (Map p512; www.wardtheatrefoundation.com; North Parade), built in 1911, once hosted the annual Boxing Day pantomime – a riotous, irreverent social satire. Sadly, the building has fallen into disrepair over the years, although there are plans to restore it to its former glory. For now, you can admire the cracked sky-blue facade with white trim.

The gleaming white edifice facing the park's southeast corner is **Kingston Parish Church** (Map p512), which replaced an older church destroyed in the 1907 earthquake. Note the tomb dating to 1699, the year the original was built. The tomb of Admiral Benbow, commander of the Royal Navy in the West Indies at the turn of the 18th century, is near the high altar, while plaques commemorate soldiers of the colonial West Indian regiments.

The crenelated redbrick building facing East Parade is the 1840 **Coke Memorial Hall** (Map p512), named after the founder of the Methodist churches in the Caribbean, Thomas Coke.

South Parade, packed with street vendor stalls and the blast of reggae, is known as 'Ben Dung Plaza' because passersby have to bend down to buy from hawkers whose goods are displayed on the ground. King St leads from here to the waterfront, and to a replica of Edna Manley's **Negro Aroused statue** (Map p512; King St), depicting a crouched black man breaking free from bondage; the original is in the National Gallery of Jamaica.

Institute of Jamaica   MUSEUM

(JCDT; Map p512; ☑922-0620; www.instituteofjamaica.org.jm; 10-16 East St; adult/child J$400/200; ☺10am-6pm Tue-Sun) The Institute of Jamaica is the nation's small-scale equivalent of the British Museum or Smithsonian, housed in three separate buildings. The institute hosts permanent and visiting exhibitions. Buy your ticket at the **Natural History Museum**, accessed by a separate entrance around the corner on Tower St. In late 2016 the institute was undergoing a multimillion-dollar refit, so expect the layout to change and improve.

★ Liberty Hall   MUSEUM

(Map p512; ☑948-8639; http://libertyhall-ioj.org.jm; 76 King St; adult/child J$400/200; ☺9am-5pm Mon-Fri) At the end of a tree-lined courtyard, decorated with cheerful mosaics and a mural depicting Marcus Garvey, stands Liberty Hall, the headquarters of Garvey's UNIA (United Negro Improvement Association) in the 1930s. The building now contains a quite excellent multimedia museum about the man and his work, which allows the visitor to appreciate Garvey's impact as a founder of pan-Africanism.

Trench Town Culture Yard   CULTURAL CENTER

(☑859-6741; 6-8 Lower First St; tours J$1000; ☺6am-6pm) Trench Town, which began life as a much-prized housing project erected by the British in the 1930s, is widely credited as the birthplace of ska, rocksteady and reggae music. It has been immortalized in numerous reggae songs, not least Bob Marley's 'No Woman No Cry,' the poignant anthem penned by Marley's mentor, Vincent 'Tata' Ford, which was written here.

The yard's museum is stocked with Wailers memorabilia, along with the rusted-out carcass of a VW bus that belonged to the Wailers in the 1960s and the small bedroom that was Bob and Rita Marley's home before superstardom. As with many things Marley-related, tours can be rather brisk, with visitors steered toward the gift shop.

Also on-site is the **Trench Town Development Association**, responsible for transforming the home into a community-based heritage site, and dedicated to promoting social justice and self-reliance.

Visits are best arranged in advance – it's safe to visit, but we don't advise wandering elsewhere around Trench Town on your own.

🏃 Activities

Tuff Gong Recording Studios   MUSIC

(☑923-9380; www.tuffgong.com; 220 Marcus Garvey Dr; tours J$1000) Tuff Gong is one of the Caribbean's largest and most influential studios. Bob Marley's favorite place to record, it's run by his son Ziggy. Visitors are welcome to take a 45-minute tour with the entire music production process explained, provided you call in advance – but if someone's recording, you may not be allowed to see all sections of the studio.

Excitingly, the studio is set to start pressing vinyl again in 2017 for the first time in years, and it's hoped that future tours will encompass this.

👉 Tours

Jamaica Cultural Enterprises   CULTURAL

(☑540-8570; www.jaculture.com; Kingston tours half-/full day US$65/90) Highly recommended

LIFEYARD

An innovative art and permaculture scheme, **Lifeyard** (Paint Jamaica; ☑809-3198, 298-4313; www.facebook.com/lifeteam360; Fleet St; donation requested), is regenerating an area of downtown Kingston once beset with gang problems. The program is centered on an urban farming project, and its Rastafari organizers have also worked with the community and visiting artists to cover the whole street with beautiful and uplifting murals. It's not just pretty pictures though – the art is backed-up by youth projects including breakfast and homework clubs, workshops, educational support and media training so the community can tell their own stories.

cultural tours in and around Kingston, including to the Blue Mountains. Excellent themed tours include history, food, music and art – there's even a boozy Kingston rum tour – either as a group or tailor-made. Every Thursday they offer a free Kingston walking tour, starting at 9am at Emancipation Park.

Sun Venture Tours TOURS
(☑924-4515; www.sunventuretours.com; 32 Russell Heights) Offers a city tour of Kingston, incorporating a walking tour of Port Royal and a visit to Devon House (US$85 per person, minimum four people, including entrance fees), as well as longer day tours including Kingston's musical heritage. Sun Venture also offers hiking tours of the Blue Mountains and Maroon country, excursions to coffee plantations and more.

🛏 Sleeping

⭐ **Reggae Hostel** HOSTEL $
(☑920-1596; www.reggaehostel.com; 8 Burlington Ave; dm/d US$25/70; P✸@🛜) Close to Half Way Tree, this excellent hostel has a relaxed, friendly vibe. Dorms are simple, with fans, while private rooms (one with its own bathroom) are spacious and have air-con. There's a communal kitchen, patio bar and helpful staff. Highly sociable – helpful if you're looking for people to hook up with to go to a dancehall street party or on a weekend beach trip.

⭐ **Neita's Nest** GUESTHOUSE $$
(☑469-3005; www.neitasnest.com; Stony Hill, Bridgemount; s/d US$90/120; 🛜) A truly delightful art-filled B&B tucked up high in Stony Hill, with great views from the terrace of Kingston and the mountains. Cozy rooms and a gracious host who welcomes you into the family make this feel like a perfect retreat away from the city. Dinner is available on request (and is highly recommended).

The excellent value is compounded by the discount offered for stays of more than two nights.

Knutsford Court Hotel HOTEL $$
(Map p516; ☑929-1000; www.knutsfordcourt.com; 16 Chelsea Ave; r/ste US$147/205; P➔✸@🛜⛱) Fine hotel with a garden setting, popular with Jamaican families and businesspeople. The rooms – some with private balconies and work desks – are modern and well appointed. Rates include continental breakfast, served in the Melting Pot restaurant, which also offers exemplary Jamaican fare and room service at other times.

⭐ **Spanish Court Hotel** BOUTIQUE HOTEL $$$
(Map p516; ☑926-0000; www.spanishcourthotel.com; 1 St Lucia Ave; r US$199-209, ste US$245-319; P✸@🛜⛱) A favorite with Jamaica's business elite, this hotel is big enough to offer everything you need but small enough to remain intimate. Thoroughly modern rooms have Jamaican-designed furniture. Relaxation options include the rooftop pool, a gym and a spa. The Gallery Café serves food throughout the day, while the restaurant has beautifully presented international and Jamaican dishes.

🍴 Eating

🍴 Downtown

Swiss Stores CAFE $
(F&B Downtown; Map p512; cnr Church & Harbour Sts; meals from J$800; ☻8am-4:30pm Mon-Fri; 🛜) Pasta, pepperpot soup, sandwiches, roti wraps and a glass of wine inside a welcome bubble of air-con – what more could you ask of a jewelry store! The setting seems incongruous, but Swiss Stores is an essential downtown lunch and meeting spot. All the items on the small menu are fresh and tasty, and the coffee and cake are delicious.

★ Moby Dick
JAMAICAN $$

(Map p512; 3 Orange St; meals J$1100-2000; ⊙9am-7pm Mon-Sat) Don't let the plastic tablecloths fool you, this unassuming hangout has been popular with besuited lawyers and judges for nearly a century. The curried goat (J$1100) is outstanding, as is the conch version (J$1700) when available, served with roti, rice and salad and washed down with one of the excellent fresh fruit juices.

✗ Uptown

★ Mi Hungry
VEGETARIAN $

(Shop 24a, Marketplace; pizza half/whole J$500/1000, salads J$500-700; ⊙8:30am-11pm Mon-Sat, noon-10pm Sun) Mi Hungry serves up 'sun cooked' I-tal food that you wouldn't believe. Their 'pleaza' comes with a base of seeds and grains, topped with sun-dried tomatoes and crunchy veg (we recommend ackee with a few chilies) and is delicious in a way that the words 'raw vegan pizza' can't convey – you'll definitely want to come back for more.

The salads are equally hearty, and there's a fabulous array of fresh juices on offer. Made with love.

★ Andy's
JERK $

(49 Mannings Hill Rd; meals J$700; ⊙8am-11pm Mon-Sat) If you're after the best authentically prepared jerk chicken and pork in Kingston, then Andy's is well worth the travel. This nondescript corner stop gets particularly busy in the evenings, when locals line up for their meats accompanied by fried breadfruit, *festival* (fried dumplings), sweet potato or plantain. There's good soup in the morning.

M10 Bar & Grill
JAMAICAN $$

(☑930-2112; www.facebook.com/M10BarAndGrill; 6 Vineyard Rd, Vineyard Town; 3-course menu J$2500; ⊙11am-midnight) Where else but in Kingston would you find a daytime truck stop transforming into a slick open-air restaurant, with crisp white tablecloths and waiters in black ties? M10 is one of the city's best-kept secrets. The menu leans toward Jamaican and international – good stews, fish ribs and the like, with divine saltfish fritters to start and sticky desserts to finish.

Red Bones Blues Café
FUSION $$$

(Map p516; ☑978-8262; www.facebook.com/RedbonesBluesCafe; 1 Argyle Rd; mains J$3000-6000; ⊙11am-11pm Mon-Fri, 6-11pm Sat) This restaurant, bar and live-music venue has long been a beehive of cultural and culinary activity. Inside, the walls are beguilingly bedecked with photographs of jazz and blues legends. The menu offers Jamaican twists on European tastes (callaloo strudel, anyone?) with good fish, pasta and salads. The 'Nyam & Scram' lunch menu (J$1200) is excellent value.

There are quality live bands throughout the week, including blues, jazz and reggae, showcasing well-chosen local and international talent, as well as regular poetry slams.

Opa
GREEK $$$

(75 Hope Rd; mains J$2000-3500; ⊙4pm-midnight) Jamaica's only Greek restaurant, this is the place to go if you're craving good lamb, sharp feta and fresh seafood. The Greek classics hold true, but other things get an inventive twist, such as the lamb burger that comes in a phyllo wrapper rather than a bun (the ackee burger is an unexpected hit too).

We could eat the grilled octopus all day and into the night, when the outside bar becomes a chilled Mediterranean-Caribbean lounge.

🍷 Drinking & Nightlife

★ Dub Club
CLUB

(www.facebook.com/officialkingstondubclub; Skyline Dr, Jack's Hill; J$500; ⊙8pm-2am Sun) Dub Club is a house party that's become a Jamaican brand. And what a house! Set high on Jack's Hill, it looks down over the lights of Kingston, twinkling in the night. The huge sound system treats you to the deepest dub and rootsiest reggae you can imagine, with the selector standing at a pair of decks under a huge mango tree.

There's a laid-back bar and I-tal food, and the doors open from 8pm, so you can treat it as a fine early drinking spot, though things don't get going until way after 10pm. Every reggae artist and DJ worth their salt rotates through the Dub Club at some time – if there's a cooler night out in Kingston, we'd like to know about it.

Tracks & Records
BAR

(☑906-3903; www.facebook.com/UBTracks; Market Pl, 67 Constant Spring Rd; ⊙11:30am-11:30pm) Music meets athletics at this doubly punning sports bar owned by Usain Bolt. The atmosphere is lively, with plenty of drinks and bar food, plus some surprisingly good karaoke, and live music on 'Behind the Screens' Tuesday.

Uptown Kingston

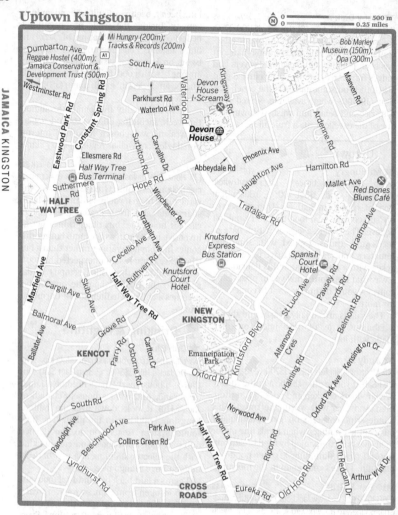

Information

Andrews Memorial Hospital (☎926-7401; www.amhosp.org; 27 Hope Rd) Well-equipped private hospital with well-stocked pharmacy.

Downtown Police Station (☎922-9321; 11 East Queen St) Downtown police headquarters.

Half Way Tree Police Station (142 Maxfield Ave, Half Way Tree)

Half Way Tree Post Office (Map p516; Half Way Tree Rd; ☺8am-5pm Mon-Thu, 9am-4pm Fri, 8am-1pm Sat)

University Hospital (☎927-1620; http://uhwi.gov.jm; University of the West Indies campus,

Mona) The best, most up-to-date public hospital, with 24-hour emergency department.

Getting There & Around

AIR

Norman Manley International Airport (KIN; ☎924-8452; www.nmia.aero) Around 11km southeast of Downtown Kingston, Manley handles international flights. There's a tourist information desk in the arrivals hall, and a money-exchange bureau before customs. As you exit there's a bank, car rental booths and a booking station for official taxis. Outside, you'll find phone shops to buy local SIM cards.

WORTH A TRIP

PORT ROYAL

A dilapidated, ramshackle sprawl of tropical lassitude, Port Royal is replete with important historical buildings collapsing into dust. Today's fishing hamlet was once the pirate capital of the Caribbean. Later it was the hub of British naval power in the West Indies, but the remains give little hint of the town's former glory. The English settled the isolated cay in 1656, called it 'Cagway' or 'the Point' and built Fort Cromwell (renamed Fort Charles after the Restoration in 1660). The town boomed, but a massive earthquake in 1692 put an end to Port Royal's ascension, and survivors crossed the harbor to settle in what would become Kingston.

Port Royal's highlight is historic **Fort Charles** (☑ 967-8438; adult/child J$1000/500; ⊘ 9am-5pm), where Nelson was once stationed. **Gloria's** (5 Queen St; fish J$1300, lobster J$1750; ⊘ 10:30am-11pm Mon-Thu & Sun, to 1am Fri & Sat) is a famous seafood restaurant, much beloved of Kingstonians.

Bus 98 operates between the international airport (arrivals hall) and Parade, Downtown (J$100, 35 minutes, every 30 minutes).

A taxi between the international airport and New Kingston costs about US$35.

BUS

Knutsford Express (☑ 971-1822; www.knutsfordexpress.com) Comfortable Knutsford Express buses run from their own **terminal** (p548) in New Kingston, serving all major destinations on the island. Coaches are air-conditioned and have wi-fi. There's a discount for buying tickets more than 24 hours in advance. Be at the bus station at least 15 minutes before departure to register your ticket.

Downtown Bus Station (Beckford St) Downtown Kingston's moderately anarchic bus and minibus station, serving destinations across the country.

CAR

Most car-rental companies offer free airport shuttles. Some reputable companies with offices at Norman Manley International Airport:

Avis (☑ 924-8293; www.avis.com.jm; Norman Manley International Airport)

Hertz (☑ 924-8028; www.hertz.com; Norman Manley International Airport)

Island Car Rentals (☑ 926-8012; www.islandcarrentals.com; 17 Antigua Ave) Local car rental firm.

PUBLIC TRANSPORTATION

Buses, minibuses and route taxis arrive and depart from **North** (Map p512) and **South Parade** (Map p512) in Downtown; **Half Way Tree bus station** (Map p516) in Uptown; **Cross Roads**, between Uptown and Downtown; and **Papine** (Main St), at the eastern edge of town off Old Hope Rd.

Jamaica Urban Transport Co Ltd (JUTC; www.jutc.com; city fares J$100) operates a fleet of yellow Mercedes-Benz and Volvo buses. Most are air-conditioned. JUTC buses stop only at official stops.

Minibuses and route taxis (look for their red license plates) ply all the popular routes (J$100), stopping on request.

BLUE MOUNTAINS

The Blue Mountains are a hiker's dream, and 30 recognized trails lace the hills. Many are overgrown due to lack of funding and ecological protection programs, but others remain the mainstay of communication for locals.

The most popular route is the steep, well-maintained trail to 'The Peak,' which in Jamaica always means **Blue Mountain Peak**.

These trails (called 'tracks' locally) are rarely marked. Get up-to-date information on trail conditions from the main ranger station at Holywell. If a trail is difficult to follow, turn back. Mountain rescue is slow and you could be lost for days. When asking for directions from locals, remember that 'jus a likkle way' may in fact be a few hours of hiking.

If you're hiking alone, normal precautions apply:

➡ Wear sturdy hiking shoes.

➡ Bring snacks, plenty of water and a flashlight (torch).

➡ Let people know where you're headed.

➡ Buy the 1:50,000 or 1:12,500 Ordnance Survey topographic map series, available from the **Survey Department** (☑ 750-5263; www.nla.gov.jm; 23½ Charles St, Kingston).

Guides can be hired at the guesthouses in Hagley Gap and Penlyne Castle, or through most local accommodations for J$5000/7000 per half-/full day, while guided hikes in the Blue Mountains are also offered:

Forres Park Guest House & Farm (p518)

Jamaica Conservation & Development Trust (☑ 960-2848; www.jcdt.org.jm; 29 Dumbarton Ave, Kingston 10) Manages trails in the national park and can recommend hiking guides.

Mount Edge B&B (☑ 351-5083, 944-8151; www.17milepost.com; r without bathroom J$3000-4000, with bathroom J$4000-6000; [P][@][🛜]) 🚲

🛏 Sleeping

Jah B's Guest House GUESTHOUSE $
(☑ 377-5206; www.jahbguesthouse.com; Abbet Green; dm/r US$20/30; [P]) This friendly place, run by a family of Bobo Rastas and particularly popular with shoestring travelers, has a basic but cozy guesthouse with bunks and simple rooms. I-tal meals are prepared amid a cloud of ganja smoke and a nonstop volley of friendly banter; the manager can help arrange transfers from Kingston.

Forres Park Guest House & Farm GUESTHOUSE $$
(☑ 927-8275; www.forrespark.com; cabins US$75, r US$90-220; [P]) This guesthouse is a top choice for birdwatchers. All rooms have balconies and the plushest sports a whirlpool tub. Excellent meals are cooked on request and available to nonguests. You can rent mountain bikes and enjoy the on-site spa treatments after tackling the steep, rewarding hiking trail. Excellent tours and guided hikes offered.

ℹ Getting There & Away

BUS

Buses 60 and 68 run hourly from Half Way Tree in Kingston up Hope Rd to Papine (J$100, 20 minutes), from where you connect to the Blue Mountains. Minibuses and route taxis depart from near the Park View Supermarket on the main square in Papine. There are two main routes: to Mavis Bank and Hagley Gap via Gordon Town (for Blue Mountain Peak), and to Newcastle and Section via Irish Town. Frequency of service depends on demand, but there's at least one morning run and one in the afternoon for the two main routes.

CAR

From Kingston, Hope Rd leads to Papine, from where Gordon Town Rd (B1) leads into the mountains. Papine is your last opportunity to fill up with gas, so make sure you have a full tank. The B1 continues across the mountains all the way to Buff Bay. A 4WD is recommended; this road is sometimes closed by landslides, so check before setting out.

THE NORTH COAST

Ocho Rios

Ocho Rios is a former fishing village on a wide bay that was developed for tourism in the mid-1980s. The frequent docking of cruise ships (sometimes three in a day) at the central pier that commands the town's focus gives 'Ochi' a slightly 'packaged' feel, spiced up by the entreaties of 'guides' and souvenir sellers. The hassle quotient is relatively minor, however, and the town has a relaxed vibe when there's no ship in dock.

Tourism has endowed the town with a great eating scene, lively nightlife, and a plethora of guiding companies offering everything from scuba diving to zip-line tours. Throw in some of Jamaica's best waterfalls on its doorstep, and Ocho Rios makes an excellent base for exploring the north coast.

◎ Sights

⭐**Irie Blue Hole** WATERFALL
(Thatch Hill; US$10) High on the White River, the heavenly Irie Blue Hole is a vision of what Dunn's River Falls was 20 years ago, and an undisputed highlight of the north coast. You make your way up a series of magical falls and blue pools surrounded by forest, with ample opportunity to swim, dive and swing off ropes into the water. Guides accompany you through the cascades on a well-marked trail (with steps and ropes where necessary for safety). The tiny cave climb under one of the falls is safe but isn't for claustrophobes. The guides are excellent, know the best places to take photos of you (and show off their diving skills), and are very attentive to both kids and more senior visitors who might be uncertain on some of the climbs. Vendors sell jelly shoes at the entrance, and life jackets are also available for those who want to enjoy the falls but aren't strong

swimmers. There are food and drink stands at the entrance to the falls. Take nothing you aren't happy to get wet.

Dunn's River Falls
WATERFALL

(☑ 974-2857; www.dunnsriverfallsja.com; adult/child US$20/12; ☺ 8:30am-4pm Sat-Tue, 7am-4pm Wed-Fri) These famous falls, 3km west of town, are Jamaica's top-grossing tourist attraction. Great throngs of people can sometimes make it seem more like a theme park than a natural wonder, but this doesn't make the climb up the falls any less exhilarating. You clamber up great tiers of limestone that step down 180m in a series of beautiful cascades and pools. The water is refreshingly cool, with everything shaded by tall rainforest. Guides can help with the climb (tip expected), but aren't strictly necessary; although the current is strong in places, the ascent is easily achieved by most able-bodied people. Swimwear is essential. There are changing rooms, and you can rent lockers (J$500) and buy jelly shoes from vendors.

The park also includes food stalls and a restaurant, a kids' playground, and a hard-selling craft market. Try to visit when the cruise ships aren't in dock, and ideally when the gates open in the morning. Route taxis (J$100) from Ocho Rios to St Ann's Bay can drop you at the entrance.

Mahogany Beach
BEACH

FREE The small and charming Mahogany Beach is particularly popular with locals; it comes to life on weekends with loud music, smells of jerk cooking and impromptu football matches. There is plenty of parking plus showers, and a small shop selling beach goods. The beach is about 1km east of the town center – it's quickest to jump in a taxi to get here.

🏃 Activities

Virtually the entire shoreline east of Ocho Rios to Galina Point is fringed by a reef, and it's great for snorkeling and scuba diving. One of the best sections is **Devil's Reef**, a pinnacle that drops more than 60m. Nurse sharks are abundant at **Caverns**, a shallow reef about 1km east of the White River estuary; it has many tunnels plus an ex-minesweeper, the *Kathryn*. Most resorts have their own scuba facilities. As well as independent operators, upscale hotels also offer water sports.

Garfield Diving Station
DIVING

(☑ 395-7023; www.garfielddiving.com; Turtle Beach) Ocho Rios' longest-running water-sports operator with more than 30 years' experience. Dive packages include one-tank dives (US$50), PADI certification courses (US$475) and wreck dives. Other activities offered include snorkeling excursions (US$35), glass-bottom boat rides (US$30) and Jet Ski rental (prices on request). Boat charter is available for deep-sea fishing (half-day for up to four people US$650).

Resort Divers
DIVING

(☑ 881-5760; www.resortdivers.com; Salem; 1-/2-tank dives US$50/95) The oldest diving operator in the region, with an excellent reputation. Besides standard dives, there are certification courses (from US$420), night dives (US$60) and snorkeling excursions (US$30).

👉 Tours

Hooves
HORSEBACK RIDING

(☑ 972-0905; www.hooves-jamaica.com; 61 Windsor Rd; half-day horseback tours incl refreshments adult/child US$70/50) Offers guided horseback tours along the beach, with a bareback ride into the sea (beginners welcome), and the 'honeymoon ride,' which includes a beach meal with fizz. Reservations required.

Chukka Cove Farm
ADVENTURE SPORTS

(☑ 619-1382; www.chukkacaribbean.com; Priory) This former polo field west of Priory is home to the Caribbean-dominating adventure group Chukka, which offers an ever-growing list of guided excursions and activities. Popular excursions include the three-hour Horseback Ride 'n Swim (US$79), which culminates in an exciting bareback trot into the sea; ATV driving (US$115); zip-line tours (US$79); and the Zion Bus to Bob Marley's Mausoleum in Nine Mile (US$104).

🛏 Sleeping

★ Reggae Hostel
GUESTHOUSE $

(☑ 974-2607; www.reggaehostel.com; 19 Main St; dm/r US$20/60; ⓟ❄🛜) An ever-popular hostel, this relaxed guesthouse is perfectly located in the center of Ocho Rios. There's a good mix of simple, air-con, private rooms, some with mini-verandas, and dorms (some with fan, others with air-con). There's a kitchen and a rooftop bar that's made for socializing. The staff have great info on backpacker-friendly excursions.

HIKING BLUE MOUNTAIN PEAK

Highest of the highlights, Blue Mountain Peak reaches 2256m above sea level, and no visit to the area should omit a predawn hike to its summit for a sunrise view. Most hikers set off from Penlyne Castle around 2am to reach Blue Mountain Peak for sunrise. Fortified with a breakfast of coffee and cereal, you set out single file in the pitch black along the 12km round-trip trail (you'll need a flashlight and a spare set of batteries, just in case). The first part of the trail – a series of steep scree-covered switchbacks named Jacob's Ladder – is the toughest. Midway, at Portland Gap (4km above Abbey Green), there's a ranger station where you pay the US$5 park fee. You should arrive at the peak around 5:30am, while it is still dark.

Don't hike without a guide at night. Numerous spur trails lead off the main trails and it is easy to get lost. Although hiking boots or tough walking shoes are best, sneakers will suffice, though your feet will likely get wet. At the top, temperatures can approach freezing before sunrise, so wear plenty of layers. Rain gear is also essential, as the weather can change rapidly.

Hibiscus Lodge HOTEL $$
(☑ 974-2676; www.hibiscusjamaica.com; 83 Main St; r US$150-192; P 🅿️ ❄️ @ 🏊) A stairway descends alongside a cliff overhang, past flowering gardens overflowing with bougainvillea, and down to a private sunning deck, perfect for a spontaneous jump in the sea. A small gallery of contemporary Jamaican art complements the main building nicely. Rooms are modestly furnished, though a refit to freshen things up was taking place when we visited.

★ **Cottage at Te Moana** COTTAGE $$
(☑ 974-2870; www.harmonyhall.com; cottages US$150-180; P ❄️) With its small clifftop garden overhanging a reef, this exquisite reclusive property with two delightful cottages offers a wonderful alternative to Ochi's resorts. Think wicker furniture and a host of art collected from across the Caribbean. Both cottages have fully equipped kitchens, separate living areas, plus verandas with hammocks. Steps lead down to a coral cove good for snorkeling.

Sea kayaks and paddleboards are also available. There's a three-night minimum stay (five nights in high season).

★ **Jamaica Inn** GUESTHOUSE $$$
(☑ 974-2514; www.jamaicainn.com; ste US$569-879, cottages US$989-2389; P 🅿️ ❄️ 🛜 🏊) Winston Churchill loved this place (and this is echoed in the colonial-era prints and furnishings), an exquisite family-run 'inn,' tucked in a private cove, that exudes patrician refinement. There's a library and a bar with a warm clubby feel, and an on-site spa. Dining requires a collared shirt and trousers for men. Water sports include scuba diving, snorkeling and fishing.

Blue House GUESTHOUSE $$$
(☑ 994-1367; www.thebluehousejamaica.com; White River Bay; r US$200-260; P ❄️ @ 🛜 🏊) This gem offers luxurious bedrooms in cool blue hues – a real home from home. The separate two-bedroom Cozy Cottage provides even greater seclusion, with its private patio and hammock hidden behind a curtain of flowers. The resident Barefoot Chef cooks up superb fusion cuisine, drawing on Chinese and Indian influences, and the lavish three-course dinners are worth every penny.

✖ Eating

★ **Live Food** VEGAN $
(19 Main St; mains from J$800; ⊙9am-10pm) This Rastafari-run joint – a cute thatched shack enlivening an otherwise boring strip of shops – is a great way to get an injection of I-tal food. The big salads are filling and delicious, and the raw take on a pizza is a definite surprise. If you're in a rush, go for the fabulous and healthy smoothies. Opening hours can be somewhat relaxed.

Ocho Rios Jerk Centre JERK $
(☑ 974-2549; 16 Da Costa Dr; meals J$550-1000; ⊙11am-midnight) The liveliest jerk joint in town serves excellent jerk pork, chicken and conch, as well as barbecue ribs. There are daily specials, the best being curry goat (J$550) and goat-head soup. Grab a Red Stripe and watch sports on the big-screen TV while you're waiting for your food. There are DJs on Friday nights.

Mongoose
Restaurant and Lounge JAMAICAN $
(Main St; mains J$900-2500; ⊙9am-1am) Lively restaurant and bar that quickly serves up big plates of hearty food. If you want Jamaican, go for the stews (particularly the oxtail); otherwise you can get really good burgers, grilled fish, pizzas and the like. It's pretty empty during the day unless there's a cruise ship in town, when it heaves.

Mom's
JAMAICAN $
(7 Evelyn St; mains around J$1000; ⊙8am-10pm Mon-Sat) This home-style restaurant has few frills but is a gem nonetheless. Eat in or takeout generous servings of oxtail stew, chicken, pork and fish, and all the Jamaican classics. If you had a Jamaican auntie, this is how she'd cook for you.

★Toscanini
ITALIAN $$$
(📞975-4785; Harmony Hall; mains US$18-45; ⊙noon-2pm & 6:30-10pm Tue-Sun; 🅿) In a gingerbread house, this is one of the finest restaurants in Jamaica. It's run by two gracious Italians who use the freshest local ingredients in the recipes – the manager greets guests and explains the use of local herbs in the cooking. The daily menu ranges widely, from prosciutto with papaya to rich rabbit ragù with tagliatelle.

🍷 Drinking & Nightlife

John Crow's Tavern
SPORTS BAR
(10 Main St; ⊙10am-1am) The big TV above the bar screens the latest football games and the outdoor terrace is perfect for a beer, a burger and a spot of people-watching on the main street. The beer is cold and there's a wide selection of rum.

Ocean's 11 Watering Hole
BAR
(Fisherman's Point; ⊙4pm-midnight) With its prime spot on the pier, it's little surprise that Ocean's 11 is popular with cruise-ship passengers, who knock back the potent cocktails and cheer each other on during Tuesday-night karaoke. The upstairs space doubles as a small art gallery and coffee shop. There's dancehall on Friday and oldies ska and reggae on Sunday.

🛍 Shopping

Olde Craft Market
ARTS & CRAFTS
(Main St; ⊙9am-5pm) This market features fair-quality ceramics and art, as well as the usual T-shirts with chirpy Jamaican slo-

DON'T MISS

STUSH IN THE BUSH

This organic farm-to-table Rasta dining experience, **Stush in the Bush** (📞562-9760; www.stushinthebush.com; Bamboo; meals US$55-75; 🅿), is home to some of the best food you'll eat in your entire trip to Jamaica. Your experience here starts with a walking tour of the farm, learning about what you'll eat, and then proceeds to a gorgeous rustic cabin with tremendous views for your meal.

There are two options, the gourmet pizza (US$55) and the full spread (US$75), of four and five courses respectively, with sides of delicious salads, crunchy plantain chips with zingy dips, rich soups and lively juices. It's vegan-friendly too – even the chocolate cake. Advance booking essential.

gans and Rasta tams with fake dreadlocks attached.

Island Village
MALL
(📞974-8353; village free, beach J$200; ⊙9am-midnight) Since its 2002 opening, this self-contained entertainment park has changed the face of Ocho Rios. The 2-hectare development claims to resemble a 'Jamaican coastal village.' It doesn't remotely, but you'll still find a peaceful beach, upscale craft shops, a **cinema** (📞675-8886; Island Village), **Jimmy Buffett's Margaritaville bar** (📞675-8800; Island Village; ⊙11am-4am), several cafes, and an amphitheater for live performances.

ℹ Information

Computer Whizz (Shop 11, Island Plaza; per 30min/1hr J$150/250; ⊙8:30am-7:30pm Mon-Sat) Has 10 computers as well as wi-fi access for those with their own laptops.

Kulkarni Medical Clinic (📞974-3357; 16 Rennie Rd) Private medical practice used by many upmarket hotels in the area.

Police Station (📞974-2533; Da Costa Dr) Near the clock tower.

Tourist Information (📞974-7705; Shop 3, Ocean Village Plaza, Main St; ⊙9am-5pm Mon-Thu, to 4pm Fri) Represents the Jamaica Tourist Board. Staff can help you suss out Ochi's transportation, lodging and attractions options. Also operates an information booth on Main St, but it's open only when cruise ships are in port.

❶ Getting There & Away

CAR

Avis (☑ 974-8047; avis.com.jm; 15 Milford Rd)

Bargain Rent-a-Car (☑ 974-8047; Shop 1a Pineapple Place Shopping Centre, Main St)

Salem Car Rental (☑ 974-0786; www.salemcarrentals.com; Shop 7, Sandcastles Resort) Reliable locally run car rental agency.

BUS

Buses, minibuses and route taxis arrive at and depart from Ocho Rios' **Transportation Center** (Evelyn St). During daylight hours there are frequent departures – fewer on Sundays – for Kingston (via the old A3 through the mountains, rather than the toll highway) and destinations along the north coast. There is no set schedule: they depart when full. Sample destinations:

Discovery Bay J$180, 30 minutes

Kingston J$350, 2½ hours

Montego Bay J$500, 90 minutes

Port Maria J$180, 50 minutes

Runaway Bay J$150, 30 minutes

St Ann's Bay J$100, 10 minutes

Knutsford Express (www.knutsfordexpress.com; Island Village) has scheduled departures on comfortable air-con coaches to Kingston and Montego Bay from its depot at Island Village. Arrive 15 minutes prior to departure to register your ticket. Sample fares include Kingston (J$1950), Montego Bay (J$1950), Negril (J$2700) and Port Antonio (J$2050).

TAXI

JUTA (☑ 974-2292) is the main taxi agency catering to tourists. A licensed taxi will cost about US$110 for Montego Bay, and about US$100 for Kingston (US$110 to the international airport at Kingston).

Minibuses and route taxis ply Main St and the coast road, costing J$100 for short hauls.

Around Ocho Rios

The seaside resorts of Ocho Rios quickly give way to isolated villas and fishing villages like Port Maria as the coastal road winds its way east along cliffs and bluffs. The sense of leaving tourist Jamaica behind is enhanced by the drop in road quality.

Drawn by its coastal beauty and unspoiled character, two of Jamaica's most famous visitors, author Noël Coward and James Bond creator Ian Fleming, made their homes in the area. While Coward settled in Firefly, with its spectacular view down on the coastline, Fleming found refuge at Goldeneye, now an exclusive resort.

★ **Firefly** HISTORIC BUILDING

(☑ 997-7201, 994-0920; J$1000; ☺ 9am-5pm Mon-Thu & Sat) Set amid wide lawns high atop a hill 5km east of Oracabessa and 5km west of Port Maria, Firefly was the home of Sir Noël Coward, the English playwright, songwriter, actor and wit, who was preceded at this site by the notorious pirate Sir Henry Morgan. When he died in 1973, Coward left the estate to his partner Graham Payn, who donated it to the nation.

Your guide will lead you to Coward's art studio, where he was schooled in oil painting by Winston Churchill. The studio displays Coward's original paintings and photographs of himself and a coterie of famous friends. The drawing room, with the table still laid, was used to entertain such guests as the Queen Mother, Sophia Loren and Audrey Hepburn. The upper lounge features a glassless window that offers one of the most stunning coastal vistas in all Jamaica. The view takes in Port Maria Bay and the coastline further west. Contrary to popular opinion, Coward didn't write his famous song 'A Room with a View' here (it was written in Hawaii in 1928).

Coward lies buried beneath a plain white marble slab on the wide lawns where he entertained many illustrious stars of stage and screen. A dance floor nearby covers his old pool – the house is now used as an exclusive venue for society weddings.

★ **Goldeneye** HOTEL $$$

(☑ 622-9007; www.goldeneye.com; beach huts US$725-980, cottages US$1220, villas US$1960-3975; P ❄ ☎ ☒) One of Jamaica's most exclusive properties, Ian Fleming's old villa has been expanded into a stylish resort, with a selection of gorgeous beach huts and villas sprinkled across expansive grounds on a quaint cove. Staff are pampering yet discreet. The restaurants serve gourmet meals, the beach bar is a chilled-out delight, and there's plenty of access to water sports.

You can even kayak gently across the lagoon to a charming wellness center. Fleming's old residence, where he wrote the Bond novels, is now a private resort-within-a-resort, with its own beach, butler and cook. Up to 10 guests can stay here for a cool US$8000 per night. We understand that Beyoncé is a fan, but if you can't run to that, console yourself with the entertainment room for Bond movies and a Goldeneye cocktail from the Bizot Bar.

Port Antonio

We're hesitant to describe anywhere as the 'real' Jamaica, but Port Antonio, with its charming mess of markets, higglers (street vendors) and Georgian architecture in various states of disrepair, its greenery and nearby beaches, does a pretty good approximation. There are definitely no Margaritavilles here; just a capillary-like tangle of backstreets, browsing goats and friendly locals. Wandering past the old houses lining the Titchfield Peninsula, it's very easy to think you've roamed into some quaint colonial ghost town.

◉ Sights

Port Antonio's heart is the Town Sq, at the corner of West St and Harbour St. It's centered on a clock tower and backed by a handsome redbrick **Georgian courthouse** from 1895; the building is surrounded by a veranda supported by Scottish iron columns and topped by a handsome cupola, and is now a branch of National Commercial Bank. About 50m down West St is the junction of William St, where the smaller Port Antonio Sq has a **cenotaph** honoring Jamaicans who gave their lives in the two world wars.

On the west side of Port Antonio Sq is **Musgrave Market** (West St; ⊙Mon-Sat), decked out in yellows and blues, a quintessential chaotic developing-world market supported by thick limestone columns. Following William St south to Harbour St, you can turn left to peek inside **Christ Church**, a redbrick Anglican building constructed in neo-Romanesque style around 1840 (much of the structure dates from 1903). Look for the brass lectern donated by banana-magnate Captain Lorenzo Dow Baker.

On the north side of the Town Sq is the marvelously baroque facade of the **Royal Mall**, a three-story complex painted a striking red, now more or less a covered shopping parade decorated and designed in a plethora of styles, including Tudor and Renaissance.

Folly RUINS
This rather appropriately named two-story, 60-room mansion on the peninsula east of East Harbour was built entirely of concrete in pseudo-Grecian style in 1903 by Olivia Tiffany Mitchell, heiress to the Tiffany fortune. It was only lived in for 35 years before being abandoned and given to the govern-

ment in lieu of unpaid taxes, after which it fell into disrepair.

Bikini Beach BEACH
(J$500; ⊙noon-10pm) A small private beach with a pretty lick of sand near the marina on the Titchfield Peninsula. Hopefully the shuttered beach restaurant will reopen soon.

🛏 Sleeping

★**Germaican Hostel** HOSTEL $
(dm US$25-27, d US$62, cottages US$80; 🛜) Superb hilltop German-run hostel outside Port Antonio, with astounding views over the coast. The dorm is spacious and the doubles are well presented, plus there's a cottage, 'hammock house' and new annex that was being built when we visited. The kitchen is well set up but the real gem is the veranda with views, and the peace of getting away from it all.

It's some distance from town, but the managers will pick you up and do a run into Port Antonio a couple of times a day (a route taxi from Port Antonio to Stony Hill will take you most of the way).

Finjam Cottage GUESTHOUSE $
(☏293-2265; www.finjamcottage.com; r US$45, with sea view & balcony US$55; 🛜) On the highest point of Titchfield Hill, Finjam is a very homely and laid-back place, with simple rooms, a pleasant veranda to chill out on, use of the kitchen and a great location close to town. The friendly hosts are Finnish-Jamaican, hence the name.

DeMontevin Lodge GUESTHOUSE $
(☏993-2604; www.demontevinlodgehotel.com; 21 Fort George St; d US$70-100, without bathroom US$45) This venerable Victorian guesthouse – built in 1881 – has a homey ambience that blends modern kitsch and antiques reminiscent of granny's parlor – the place could almost be the setting of a tropical Sherlock Holmes novel. The simple bedrooms (six with private bathrooms) are timeworn, but clean as a whistle.

Hotel Timbamboo HOTEL $$
(☏993-2049; www.hoteltimbamboo.com; 5 Everleigh Park Rd; r US$75-95; 🅿🌀🛜🏊) The Timbamboo has spacious, sunny rooms with modern furniture, carpeted floors and cable TV. Some rooms have balconies with views of the Blue Mountains, though it's set a little too far back for a proper sea breeze. The hotel's sun deck is a great place to unwind.

✗ Eating

★ The Italian Job

ITALIAN $

(29 Harbour St; pasta J$1000-2000, pizza J$740-1400, salads J$500-1000; ☺ noon-10pm Mon-Sat) This is a jolly, Italian-run, checked-tablecloth sort of a place, with great pasta dishes, pizza and salads, plus crepes for dessert. Keep an eye on the specials board too, as the chef puts a great twist on local offerings, such as lobster ravioli dressed with avocado. The wine is pretty good too.

Yosch Café

INTERNATIONAL $

(Allen Ave; sandwiches J$350-500, mains J$550-1200; ☺ 9am-9pm Sun-Thu, to 10pm Fri & Sat) This cafe on the edge of the craft village complex is all decking, driftwood and bamboo, open to the sea breeze and looking back onto Titchfield and the bay. The breakfasts and sandwiches are winners, as is the fish if you come here for dinner. Very refreshing.

★ Wilkes Seafood

SEAFOOD $$

(Allen Ave; salads J$500-1000, catch of the day J$2500; ☺ 7:30-10:30am, 11:30am-4pm & 5:30-9pm) This place looks like an unassuming beach bar from the front, but is a delightful small restaurant inside, overlooking the sea and with a semi-open kitchen that lets the cooking aromas make you hungry. Nothing you order will disappoint, though we found the coconut curried fish to be a particular winner. Dining here is a real Port Antonio highlight.

❶ Information

National Commercial Bank (☑ 993-9822; 5 West St) Bank with ATM.

Police station (☑ 993-2546, 993-2527) Port Antonio's central police station.

Port Antonio Hospital (☑ 993-2646; Nuttall Rd; ☺ 24hr) Above the town on Naylor's Hill, south of West Harbour. Has a basic emergency services department.

Scotiabank (☑ 993-2523; 3 Harbour St) Has an ATM.

❶ Getting There & Away

There's a **transportation center** (Gideon Ave) that extends along the waterfront, with minibuses leaving regularly for Kingston (to Half Way Tree bus station; J$500, two hours) via Buff Bay and Port Maria (where you change for Ocho Rios). Route taxis depart constantly for Fairy Hill (J$100, 10 minutes), Boston Bay (J$150, 20 minutes) and Manchioneal (J$250, 40 minutes).

Knutsford Express has two buses a day to Kingston (J$2200, four hours) via Ocho Rios.

Around Port Antonio

The road east of Port Antonio has some of the prettiest landscape in Jamaica – gorgeous beaches and lush green hills. Reach Falls (p527), a particularly beautiful waterfall in a country that abounds in them, is a highlight.

Port Antonio remains the main transport hub for this region, and route taxis run all day between the city and Manchioneal, stopping at all points en route. With your own vehicle, it's possible to continue along into St Thomas parish and all the way to Kingston.

Port Antonio to Fairy Hill

The A4 meanders east of Port Antonio through thick forest, jagged-tooth bays, pocket coves and the coastal villages of Drapers, Frenchman's Cove and Fairy Hill. This is where most visitors to Port Antonio, and indeed to Portland, will find accommodations and explore the nearby Rio Grande Valley and Blue Lagoon as well as the luxuriant sands of Winnifred Beach, and Frenchman's Cove.

◎ Sights

★ Blue Lagoon

LAGOON

The waters that launched Brooke Shields' movie career are by any measure one of the most beautiful spots in Jamaica. The 55m-deep 'Blue Hole' (as it is known locally) opens to the sea through a narrow funnel, but is fed by freshwater springs that come in at about a depth of 40m. As a result the water changes color through every shade of jade and emerald during the day, thanks to cold freshwater that blankets the warm mass of seawater lurking below.

You may encounter boat operators eager to take you on a short boat ride (US$20) to nearby Cocktail Beach (where parts of the Tom Cruise movie *Cocktail* were filmed) and rustic Monkey Island, a short distance away.

The lagoon is accessible from the road and is public property, but the area is under development so an entrance fee may soon be on the cards. Note that if it's been raining heavily, run-off water from the hills turns the lagoon a disappointing murky green.

★ Winnifred Beach

BEACH

FREE Perched on a cliff 13km east of Port Antonio is the little hamlet of Fairy Hill and a rugged dirt track. Follow that road steeply downhill and you'll reach Winnifred Beach, yet another totally gorgeous beach that puts a lot of the sand in more famous places to shame. It's the only truly public beach on this stretch of the coast, and has a great vibe, with food and drink stands, weekend sound systems and Jamaicans from all walks of life.

Frenchman's Cove BEACH
(J$1000; ⊘9am-5pm) This beautiful little cove just east of Drapers boasts a small but perfect white-sand beach, where the water is fed by a freshwater river that spits directly into the ocean. The area is owned by the **Frenchman's Cove resort** (☑933-7270; www.frenchmanscove.com; r/ste US$112/145, 2-/3-bedroom cottages US$260/360; P❋☎☀). There's a snack bar serving jerk chicken and fish, alfresco showers, bathrooms, a secure parking lot and the option of taking boat tours (US$20) to the Blue Lagoon.

🛏 Sleeping

Drapers San Guest House GUESTHOUSE $
(☑993-7118; www.draperssan.com; Hwy A4, Drapers; r US$65-85; ☎) Run by an Italian expat, activist and font of local knowledge, this cozy little house comprises two cottages with five doubles and one single room (two share a bathroom), all with fans, louvered windows and hot water. It's all very welcoming and family-oriented; there's a comfy lounge and communal kitchen, and (excellent) dinners can be served by arrangement.

⭐**Hotel Mocking Bird Hill** HOTEL $$$
(☑993-7267; www.hotelmockingbirdhill.com; Mocking Bird Hill Rd; r US245-295; ☎☀) 🍃 The Mocking Bird is one of the most vigorous proponents of ecotourism in Portland. The property is a lovely house at the end of a winding dirt road; all rooms are lovingly appointed with well-chosen fabrics and art, ocean views and private balconies. Meals at the **Mille Fleurs** (☑993-7267; 3-course dinners US$55; ⊘noon-2pm & 7-9pm; ♪) restaurant are sublime. Trails through the hillside gardens are fabulous for birdwatching.

🍴 Eating

⭐**Woody's** JAMAICAN $
(Hwy A4, Drapers; mains J$300-800; ⊘noon-8pm) This truly brilliant spot – with an outdoor patio and an indoor counter that doubles as a local meeting place – prepares tremendous hot dogs and burgers, grilled cheese and Jamaican dinners to order. There's a great veggie burger heaped with stewed callaloo, and sublime homemade ginger beer. Service

is anything but rushed, but the charming hosts make this a winning experience.

Boston Bay

Boston Bay is a lick of a town with a cute pocket-size beach shelving into turquoise waters. High surf rolls into the bay, making it a popular place to catch some waves.

Near the entrance to Boston Bay beach on the main road you'll see half a dozen smoky jerk pits on the roadside. Vendors vie for your custom, but they're all equally good, serving up hot and sweet jerk with *festival*, plantain and breadfruit, washed down with a cold drink. They'll also sell jars of locally made jerk sauce (J$800) to take home – a great souvenir.

⊙ Sights

Boston Bay Beach BEACH
(Boston Bay; J$200) Boston Bay's beach sits in a small pretty cove, and while its golden sand is draw enough, the shape of the bay and prevailing weather makes it a perfect surf spot. There are showers, changing rooms, a lifeguard and a small restaurant.

🏃 Activities

Boston Bay Surfing SURFING
(board hire US$20, 1hr surf lessons with board US$20) The cove at Boston Bay is a perfect place to learn to surf, or to hire a board for the day and hit the waves yourself. The instructors here will have you standing up on the board in no time – or at least enjoy the splash as you topple into the water.

🛏 Sleeping

⭐**Great Huts** RESORT $$
(☑353-3388; www.greathuts.com; Boston Beach Lane; huts per person US$55-80, tree houses US$163-255; ☎) A green 'ecovillage' meets sculpture park overlooking Boston Bay, this is a distinctive and imaginative collection of African-style huts and tree houses with open verandas, bamboo-walled bedrooms and alfresco showers. There's a private beach, a walking trail along the cliff, an Afro-centric library and a great restaurant-bar with live music on Saturday. If only all resorts in Jamaica felt this 'inclusive.'

Rio Grande Valley

Errol Flynn supposedly initiated rafting on the Rio Grande during the 1940s, and moonlight raft trips were considered the ultimate activity among the fashionable.

Today paying passengers make the 11km journey of one to three hours (depending on water level) from Grant's Level (Rafter's Village), about 2km south of Berridale, to Rafter's Rest at St Margaret's Bay. When the moon is full, unforgettable nighttime trips are offered. These are less regimented; your guide will be happy to pull over on a moon-drenched riverbank so that you can canoodle with your sweetie or just open the ice chests to release the beer.

Reserve at **Rio Grande Experience** (☑ 993-5778; per raft US$65) or at Rafter's Village at Grant's Level if you don't have reservations. This is a one-way trip, so if you're driving you need to hire a driver to bring your car from Berridale to St Margaret's Bay (Rio Grande Experience will help for US$15; the drivers are insured, but make clear to them that you expect them to drive slowly and safely).

A route taxi from Port Antonio to Grant's Level costs J$200; they depart from the corner of Bridge St and Summers Town Rd. Licensed taxis cost about US$20 roundtrip.

MONTEGO BAY & NORTHWEST COAST

Montego Bay

Montego Bay has two distinct faces: there's the smooth tourist countenance that grins contentedly from the pages of a thousand glossy Caribbean brochures; and there's MoBay proper, a pretty gritty city, second only to Kingston in terms of status and chaos. Most of the big all-inclusive resorts are located well outside the urban core in the fancy suburb of Ironshore. Stay in the city, however, and you're faced with an entirely different proposition – a riot of cacophonous car horns and bustling humanity that offers an unscripted and uncensored slice of Jamaican life, warts and all.

The Hip Strip (aka Gloucester Ave), with its midrange hotels and ubiquitous souvenir shops flogging Bob Marley T-shirts, acts as a kind of decompression chamber between MoBay's two halves. You won't find many hipsters here, but in among the hustlers and smoky jerk restaurants there's a detectable Jamaican rhythm to the action on the street.

◉ Sights

Doctor's Cave Beach   BEACH
(☑ 876-952-2566;   www.doctorscavebathingclub. com; adult/child US$6/3; ☺ 8:30am-sunset) It may sound like a rocky hole inhabited by lab-coated troglodytes, but this is actually Montego Bay's most famous beach and the one with the most facilities. A pretty arc of sugary sand fronts a deep-blue gem studded with floating dive platforms and speckled with tourists sighing happily. Er, *lots* of tourists – and a fair few Jamaicans as well. The upside is an admission charge keeps out the beach hustlers, though it doesn't ensure that the beach is kept clean.

Founded as a bathing club in 1906, Doctor's Cave earned its name when English chiropractor Sir Herbert Barker claimed the waters here had healing properties. People flocked to Montego Bay, kick-starting a tourism evolution that would culminate in the appearance of *Homo Margaritavillus* decades later. There are lots of facilities on hand including a restaurant, a grill bar, an internet cafe and water sports, and lots of things to rent (beach chairs, towels, snorkeling gear).

★ National Museum West   MUSEUM
(☑ 940-6402; http://museums-ioj.org.jm/; Sam Sharpe Sq, Montego Bay Cultural Centre; J$400; ☺ 9am-5pm Tue-Sun) This well-curated, revamped museum, peppered with period objects, takes you through the history of western Jamaica, from the Cohaba ceremonies of the indigenous Taínos and the arrival of the Spanish, followed by the English, to the trans-Atlantic slave trade, the advent of king sugar, Maroon rebellions, emancipation and the development of 20th-century Montego Bay as a tourist destination. A separate room introduces you to the rise of Rastafarianism, the alleged divinity of Haile Selassie and the back-to-Africa movement.

**Montego Bay Marine Park
& Bogue Lagoon**   NATURE RESERVE
(☑ 952-5619) The waters of Montego Bay are gorgeous to behold both above and below the surface, but they have long been compromised by the effects of fishing, water sports and pollution. With the creation in 1991 of the Montego Bay Marine Park, environmental regulations at last began to be strictly enforced to protect the area's coral reefs, flora and fauna, and shoreline mangroves.

The park extends from the eastern end of the airport westward (almost 10km) to the

REACH FALLS

Even in a country that abounds in waterfalls, **Reach Falls** (adult/child US$10/5; ⊘ 8:30am-4:30pm Wed-Sun) stands out as one of the most beautiful places in Jamaica. The white rushing cascades are surrounded by a bowl of virgin rainforest; the water tumbles over limestone tiers from one hollowed, jade-colored pool into the next. It's possible to walk, wade and swim your way up to the edge of the falls, by an unmarked jungle path some way below the main entrance.

Once you enter the falls, guides will offer their services – crucial if you want to climb to the upper pools, which we highly recommend (there's a little underground, underwater tunnel a bit up the falls; plunging through is a treat). The Mandingo Cave, the crown jewel of the falls, can be accessed at the top of the cascades, but you need to bring climbing shoes and be prepared for a long climb.

Excellent local guides **Leonard Welsh** (☑ 849-6598) and **Kenton Davy** (☑ 438-3507) can take you and point out plants and wildlife along the way if you choose to hike to the falls.

The turnoff to Reach Falls is well signed about 2km north of Manchioneal. Any Port Antonio–Manchioneal route taxi can drop you; it's a further 3km uphill to the falls.

Great River, encompassing the mangroves of Bogue Lagoon and the fishing waters around Airport Point.

You can hire canoes or set out with a guide to spot herons, egrets, pelicans and waterfowl; swimming and crawling below are barracudas, tarpon, snapper, crabs and lobsters. Request a guide two days in advance; there's no charge but donations are gladly accepted.

Indigenous Rastafarian Village COMMUNITY
(☑ 285-4750; www.rastavillage.com; Fairfield Rd; 2hr/1-day tour US$25/100; ⊘ tours by appointment) If you want to learn about the Rastafarian movement, come out to this... hmmm... 'theme park' is definitely not the right description. How about 'living interpretive exhibit?' There's not exactly a natural mystic floating in the air, but this 'village' is still a good introduction to Jamaica's most famous indigenous religion. If coming from downtown MoBay, head south on Barnett St and then drive east along Fairfield Rd for around 5km. Book your visit in advance

You'll be taken through a pretty, jungly settlement, shown medicinal plants (not what you're thinking) and given a coherent breakdown of what the Rasta faith traditionally believed in. As most travelers don't learn much about Rastafarians past the ramblings of dreadlocked hustlers, this is a pretty valuable experience, and the all-day tour includes some lovely treks into the surrounding countryside, complete with swimming in paradisiacal natural pools.

Sam Sharpe Square SQUARE
(Fort St) This bustling cobbled square is named for Samuel Sharpe (1801–32), national hero and leader of the 1831 Christmas Rebellion); it is also where he was hanged in its aftermath. At the square's northwest corner is the **National Heroes' Monument**. Nearby is the **Cage**, a tiny brick building built in 1806 as a lockup for vagrants and other miscreants.

🏃 Activities

Deep Drop Fishing Charters FISHING
(☑ 572-0010; www.fishinginjamaica.com; Montego Bay Yacht Club; 4hr trip US$480) Runs recommended deep-sea fishing trips. They take up to four people.

Montego Bay Yacht Club FISHING
(☑ 979-8038; www.mobayyachtclub.com; Montego Bay Freeport, GPS N 18.462452°, W -77.943267°; ⊘ 10am-10pm) Apart from being a major docking point for yachts, this is also from where deep-sea fishing tournaments take place.

Dreamer Catamaran Cruises BOATING
(☑ 979-0102; www.dreamercatamarans.com; cruise incl transfer US$80; ⊘ cruises 10am-1pm & 3-6pm Mon-Sat) An outfit that offers a catamaran adventure on three swift boats specially designed for partying, with an open bar and a snorkeling stop in the marine park. Cruises depart from Doctor's Cave Beach Club. A bus will pick you up at your hotel.

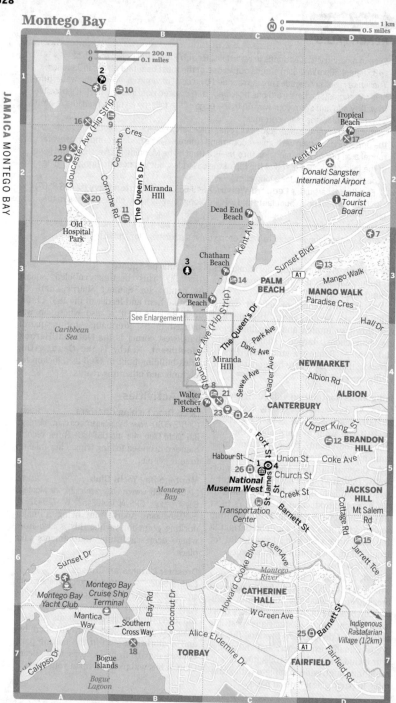

Montego Bay

0 ——— 1 km
0 ——— 0.5 miles

0 ——— 200 m
0 ——— 0.1 miles

2
7 6
10

16
9

Corniche Cres

19
22

Gloucester Ave (Hip Strip)

Corniche Rd

20

11

The Queen's Dr

Miranda Hill

Old Hospital Park

See Enlargement

Tropical Beach

17

Kent Ave

Donald Sangster International Airport

Jamaica Tourist Board

7

Dead End Beach

Sunset Blvd

13

A1

Mango Walk

MANGO WALK
Paradise Cres

Chatham Beach

14

PALM BEACH

Hall Dr

Cornwall Beach

3

Gloucester Ave (Hip Strip)

The Queen's Dr

Park Ave

Davis Ave

Miranda Hill

Sewell Ave

Leader Ave

NEWMARKET

Albion Rd

ALBION

Caribbean Sea

8

Walter Fletcher Beach

21

CANTERBURY

23
24

Upper King St

12 **BRANDON HILL**

Coke Ave

Fort St

Habour St

St James St

Union St

26
1
4
Church St

National Museum West

Creek St

JACKSON HILL

Mt Salem Rd

Cottage Rd

Transportation Center

Barnett St

15

Jarrett Tce

Montego Bay

5

Sunset Dr

Montego Bay Yacht Club

Montego Bay Cruise Ship Terminal

Mantica Way

Southern Cross Way

Bay Rd

Coconut Dr

Green Ave

Montego River

CATHERINE HALL

W Green Ave

Howard Cooke Blvd

Alice Eldemire Dr

25

Barnett St

Indigenous Rastafarian Village (1.2km)

18

TORBAY

FAIRFIELD

Fairfield Rd

A1

Bogue Islands

Bogue Lagoon

Calypso Dr

Montego Bay

JAMAICA MONTEGO BAY

Rafters Village
RAFTING

(☎940-6398; www.jamaicarafting.com; per raft 1-2 people US$60) Contact them for trips along the **Martha Brae** (☎952-0889; www.jamaicarafting.com; Martha Brae Rd; per 2-person raft US$60; ⊗8:30am-4:30pm), near Falmouth on the northwest coast, within easy day-tripping distance of Montego Bay and Ironshore.

🏃 Diving

MoBay offers a few good dive sites. For advanced divers, the Point/Basket Reef north of the airport has a good wall dive due to the fish, sharks, rays and dense coral that are fed by crystal-clear waters scoured by currents. The wall here starts at 20m and drops to at least 90m. Airport Reef, off the southwestern edge of the airport, is considered by some to be the best site on the island, with masses of coral canyons, caves and tunnels, and a DC-3 wreck that's become a multicolored mansion for masses of fish.

With all this said, don't dive here expecting top-rate macrodiving (ie lots of big fish). There are mantas, nurse sharks and the like in these waters, but most divers report seeing nothing larger than barracuda, reef fish and rock lobsters.

Most dive centers also offer snorkeling trips and provide multiple levels of PADI certification.

★ Dressel Divers
DIVING

(☎in Spain 321-392-2338; www.dresseldivers.com; Iberostar Rose Hall Resort, Rose Hall; 1-/2-tank dive US$55/90) Acclaimed international diving outfit with a scuba center in Iberostar Rose Hall Resort, 20km east of MoBay. Nonhotel guests are welcome on trips. For customized dive-package prices, use the online form on the website.

Dive Seaworld
DIVING

(☎953-2180; www.diveseaworld.com; Ironshore; 1-/2-tank dive US$65/100) Located northeast of Montego Bay. Offers night dives and PADI certification courses as well as regular dives.

☆✦ Festivals & Events

★ Red Stripe Reggae Sumfest
MUSIC

(www.reggaesumfest.com; ⊗mid-Jul) The largest reggae festival in Jamaica typically includes more than 50 world-class reggae and dancehall artists. Held in July at the Catherine Hall Entertainment Center, it starts with a beach party on Walter Fletcher Beach, followed by a week of nonstop partying. Past performers have included Luciano, Beenie Man, Gregory Isaacs, Damien 'Jr Gong' Marley and Alicia Keys.

🛏 Sleeping

Ridgeway Guest House
GUESTHOUSE **$**

(☎952-2709; www.ridgewayguesthouse.com; 34 Queens Dr; s/d US$60/70, without air-con

US$45/55; ✱ 🛜) The rooms here surround a pretty garden and are as good a deal as any you'll find in MoBay. They're comparable to midrange digs: cozy beds, tiled floors, nice furnishings, all kept quite clean and presentable. The cheapest ones are fan-cooled. Located away from the beaches near the airport, but a free shuttle gets you to the sea and sand.

View Guest House
GUESTHOUSE $

(📞952-3175; www.theviewguesthouseja.com; 56 Jarrett Tce; s/d from US$45/65; ✱ 🛜 ⊠) On the southeast edge of town on the downslope of Mt Salem Rd is this family-run, extremely friendly option. Rooms are basic but clean and come with a lot of love. Return guests are fanatic in their loyalty to this place. Home-cooked meals are served, and it has a communal kitchen and bar, plus a view overlooking the city.

Caribic House
HOTEL $

(📞876-979-6073; 69 Gloucester Ave; d with/without sea view US$74/65; ✱ 🛜) This no-frills spot across the street from Doctor's Cave Beach is a favorite for the budget-minded. The rooms are basic, with cracked floor tiles, the hot water doesn't always work and there's no real communal area, but, what the hell – you're a backpacker, right?

★Polkerris B&B
B&B $$

(📞877-7784; www.montegobayinn.com; 31 Corniche Rd; r incl breakfast US$194-202; P ✱ 🛜 ⊠) The best B&B in Montego Bay? No question. Hanging above the Hip Strip, Polkerris, run by a British expat and his Jamaican wife, is sublime in every detail. There's the trickling waterfall, the swimming pool, the view-embellished veranda, the stupendous breakfast and – most importantly – the one-of-the-family style of service that reminds you that you're in the real Jamaica.

Deja Resort
RESORT $$

(📞876-940-4173; www.dejaresort.com; 92 Gloucester Ave; s/d incl full board $176/240; P ✱ 🛜 ⊠) A recent refurb and management change has added some modern boutique touches to the hotel – the faux-grand facade wouldn't look out of place in a British seaside resort, circa 1973. Investigate closer and you'll find some welcome extras including a gym, a Jacuzzi, a swimming pool and a most elegant bar and restaurant. All meals and access to Doctor's Cave Beach included.

Richmond Hill Inn
HOTEL $$

(📞952-3859; www.richmondhillinnja.com; Union St; s/d/ste US$130/153/228; P ✱ 🛜 ⊠) Stay in a historic great house within Montego Bay's city limits. This spectacularly located gem atop a small hill once belonged to the Dewars Scotch whiskey heirs and is bedizened with fine local art, antique furniture and the ghosts of prestigious former guests. Richard Nixon and James Bond in his third incarnation (Roger Moore) both stayed here. Good bar, too.

Toby's Resort
HOTEL $$

(📞952-4370; www.tobyresorts.com; cnr Gloucester Ave & Sunset Blvd; r US$122-132; P ✱ 🛜 ⊠) Located just off the 'top' of the Hip Strip, Toby's provides an admirable local vibe with amenities geared toward international travelers. Staff make Toby's feel like a gracious guesthouse, but with the benefits of large grounds, comfy rooms, a big pool and a smaller pool, and a good bar and restaurant (p531) serving a mix of Jamaican and international dishes.

Altamont West
HOTEL $$

(📞979-9378; www.altamontwesthotel.com; 33 Gloucester Ave; r US$110-210; P ✱ 🛜 ⊠) Bright Caribbean colors lure hotel window-shoppers into one of the Hip Strip's better accommodations options. A baby grand piano furnishes the front veranda (good sign!) and there are plenty of local Jamaican motifs dotted around to remind you this is the real deal. Rooms don't quite match the salubrious common areas, particularly the characterless cheapies facing the corridor.

🍴 Eating

Evelyn's
JAMAICAN $

(📞952-3280; Kent Ave, Whitehouse; mains J$500-1000; ⊙9am-9pm Mon-Sat, 10am-6pm Sun) Fantastic choice: a true local's spot, this rustic seafood shack (near Sandals Montego Bay) is also patronized by some very in-the-know tourists. Come here for the likes of curried conch with dhal or rice, and even filled rotis.

Pork Pit
JERK $

(📞952-1046; 27 Gloucester Ave; mains J$500-800; ⊙11am-11pm; 🛜) At this glorified food shack on the Hip Strip, a half-roasted chef slaves over a blackened barbecue fashioned from pimento wood sticks laid over smoking hot coals. His meat-cooking travails send a delicious aroma wafting down Gloucester Ave and provide a perfect advert for the Pork Pit's obligatory jerk pork (and jerk chicken). Eat it under the 300-year-old cotton tree.

Nyam 'n' Jam
JAMAICAN $

(✒952-1922; 17 Harbour St; mains J$500-1000; ⊙8am-11pm) On the cusp of the craft market, you can retreat to check out this truly authentic Jamaican dining experience. Settle down for snapper with a spicy sauce; jerk or brown stew chicken; curried goat; or oxtail with rice and peas. There's a round-the-clock branch at the City Centre Mall, too.

★Houseboat Grill
JAMAICAN $$

(✒979-8845; http://thehouseboatgrill.com; Southern Cross Blvd; mains US$17-35; ⊙4-11pm Tue-Sun) Moored in Bogue Lagoon at Montego Bay Freeport, this converted houseboat is the best restaurant in the city. The changing menu offers eclectic Caribbean fusion cuisine: tiger shrimp in a fiery red curry, smoked marlin tartare, or beef medallions with goat's cheese and plantain-mashed potatoes. You can dine inside or reclusively out on the moondeck. Reservations strongly recommended.

Toby's Good Eats
JAMAICAN $$

(Tobys Resort, cnr Gloucester Ave & Sunset Blvd; mains J$600-1400; ⊙7:30am-10:30pm; 🐾) As casual eats go, Toby's is a good choice, especially if you're staying on Sunset Dr and don't feel like venturing onto the actual Hip Strip. The menu features red snapper prepared the local way (steamed in foil with Jamaican veggies and spices), vegetable dishes and pasta. Stick around for some stick (ie pool) after dinner.

Biggs BBQ Restaurant & Bar
AMERICAN $$

(✒952-9488; www.biggsbbqmobay.com; Gloucester Ave; mains US$15-29; ⊙noon-midnight; ▦) Perched on a terrace above a thin ribbon of accessible beach, this sports-bar-cum-diner lives up to its name – the portions are BIG in an unashamedly American way, and dishes range from pulled pork and ribs to steamed snapper. Choose between watching the big-screen TVs showing American football and sipping a Man Go Kill Yoself cocktail on the deck instead.

Pelican
JAMAICAN $$

(✒952-3171; Gloucester Ave; mains J$1390-3850; ⊙7am-11pm; ▦🐾) Loved by upper-crust Jamaicans and tourists both, Pelican is good for goat curry and oxtail, and the seasonal lobster dishes aren't bad either. Opened the

same year Jamaica gained independence (1962) and armed with the same chef since the early 1980s, this seminal Hip Strip restaurant has fully earned its right to be called a MoBay institution.

★Marguerite's
FUSION $$$

(✒952-4777; Gloucester Ave; mains US$32-48; ⊙6-10:30pm) This celebrated restaurant provides a lovely setting from which to watch the sunset while drinking cocktails, followed by dinner on the elegant clifftop patio. The pricey (some would say overpriced) menu edges toward nouvelle Jamaican and fresh seafood, but also includes sirloin steak and inventive pasta. The chef displays his culinary chops at a central flambé grill.

🍷 Drinking & Nightlife

Jimmy Buffett's Margaritaville
BAR

(✒979-8041; www.margaritavillecaribbean.com; Gloucester Ave; after 10pm cover US$10; ⊙11am-midnight) Of the three Margaritavilles in Jamaica, this one actually offers something like a local nightlife experience. By day, yes, it's a tourist trap. A water slide carries revelers through the plumbing and flushes them ignominiously into the ocean, where their fellow booze cruisers await on a docked catamaran. But as night falls, locals like to come here and, well, dance.

MoBay Proper
BAR

(✒940-1233; www.facebook.com/mobayproper-sportsbar/; Fort St; ⊙noon-1am) Proper is often packed with locals and expats returned to the motherland. It's a friendly, occasionally raucous spot and probably the easiest bar for tourists to access off the Hip Strip. Beneath a 'chandelier' of Heineken bottles, the pool table generates considerable heat, while dominoes are the rage with an older crowd out on the patio.

🛍 Shopping

★Gallery of West Indian Art
ART

(✒952-4547; www.galleryofwestindianart.com; 11 Fairfield Rd; ⊙10am-5pm Mon-Fri) In the suburb of Catherine Hall, this is the best quality gallery in town. It sells genuinely original arts and crafts from around the Caribbean including Cuban, Haitian and Jamaican canvases, hand-painted wooden animals, masks and handmade jewelry. Most of the work here is for sale. Call ahead.

Harbour Street Craft Market
GIFTS & SOUVENIRS

(Harbour St; ⊙7am-7pm) The largest selection of typical Jamaican souvenirs in MoBay – coconut-palm baskets, woven hats, towels and clothing in Rasta colours, wood carvings and art – is found at this market, which extends for three blocks between Barnett and Market Sts.

Fort Montego Craft Market
GIFTS & SOUVENIRS

(off Gloucester Ave; ⊙8am-7pm) This crafts market behind the fort sells a good selection of Jamaica wood carvings, vibrant paintings ripped off from Haitian art, locally made items woven from coconut palm, and mass-produced Chinese tat. We like the friendly proprietresses of stalls 121, 132 and 97.

ⓘ Information

Fairview Medical (☑940-7063, 275-1119; www.themontegobaydoctor.com; Alice Eldermire Dr; ⊙7am-7pm Mon-Fri, 9am-5pm Sat, 10am-3pm Sun) Private clinic with emergency services.

First Global Bank (☑971-5260; 53 Gloucester Ave; ⊙9am-3pm Mon-Thu, 9am-4pm Fri)

Jamaica Tourist Board (☑952-3009; www.visitjamaica.com; Donald Sangster International Airport; ⊙for flight arrivals) In the arrivals hall at Donald Sangster International Airport.

Police Station (☑952-5310, 952-4396; 29 Church St)

Scotiabank (Gloucester Ave) Handy Hip Strip ATM.

DANGERS & ANNOYANCES

The well-policed Hip Strip (Gloucester Ave) is safe from criminals, but hustling may be an issue. There are aggressive hucksters in MoBay who will size you up and either try to charm or intimidate you out of a few bucks (or more) if they think you're green. Walk with purpose wherever you go; if you look lost or confused, you'll be an easier mark.

ⓘ Getting There & Away

AIR

The majority of international visitors arrive at **Donald Sangster International Airport** (MBJ; ☑952-3124; www.mbjairport.com) , 3km north of Montego Bay. There's a Jamaica Tourist Board (JTB) information booth in the arrivals hall and a 24-hour money-exchange bureau immediately beyond immigration. There is also a transportation information counter plus desks representing tour companies, hotels and rental cars immediately as you exit customs, as well as a booth for taxis. The adjacent terminal serves domestic flights. The terminals aren't linked by walkways but there are connecting shuttles.

You'll find taxis waiting outside the arrivals lounge at the airport. There is an official taxi booth immediately outside customs. A tourist taxi to Gloucester Ave costs US$15. Alternatively, you can catch a minibus or route taxi from the gas station at the entrance to the airport (J$100).

BOAT

Cruise ships berth at the **Montego Bay Cruise Ship Terminal** (Freeport) in the Montego Freeport, about 3km south of town. Taxis to downtown MoBay cost US$15. The savvy walk out of the port gates and flag cheaper route taxis.

Montego Bay Yacht Club (☑979-8038; www.mobayyachtclub.com; Montego Freeport) has hookups, gasoline and diesel, and will handle immigration and customs procedures.

BUS & MINIBUS

Public buses other than Knutsford Express (p517), minibuses and route taxis arrive and depart from the **transportation center** (Barnett St) at the south end of St James St. Destinations are written on the bus/van/taxi and people will direct you to the correct vehicle if you ask around.

Minibuses (ie vans) and shared taxis run directly to Ocho Rios (J$500, two hours; onward transfers to Port Antonio and Kingston), Lucea (J$225, one to 1½ hours; onward transfers to Negril), Negril (J$350, 1½ hours), Kingston (J$950, five hours), some inland villages and also Ironshore and Rose Hall (J$150, 30 minutes).

Montego Bay Metro Line bus service links MoBay with the suburbs and outlying villages, such as Anchovy and Grange Hill.

You can almost always find a route taxi early in the morning or around 4pm to 5pm (ie commuting hours); there will likely be a wait at other times of the day, and long-distance taxi service slacks off after sunset. It's always easier to get a ride to towns on the coast compared to towns in the interior.

CAR

Avis (☑952-0762; www.avis.com.jm; Donald Sangster International Airport)

Hertz (☑979-0438; www.hertz.com; Donald Sangster International Airport)

Island Car Rentals (☑952-7225; www.islandcarrentals.com; Donald Sangster International Airport)

ⓘ Getting Around

Route taxis ply set routes and charge set fares for set distances and are the cheapest way to get around Montego Bay. The usual cost for a route is about J$100, perhaps double that if heading to the outer suburbs.

Rose Hall to Greenwood

East of Montego Bay is Jamaica's most famous (and allegedly haunted) mansion, Rose Hall, while Greenwood, with its own great house, is further east again. Several restaurants are clustered around Half Moon Village, en route to Rose Hall from Montego Bay.

◉ Sights

★ Rose Hall Great House   HOUSE
(☑ 953-2323; www.rosehall.com; off Hwy A1; adult/child under 12yr US$20/10; ⊘ 9am-5:15pm & 6:30-9pm) This 1770s mansion is the most famous great house in Jamaica. John Palmer, a wealthy plantation owner, and his wife, Rose (after whom the house was named), hosted some of the most elaborate social gatherings on the island. Much of the attraction is the legend of Annie Palmer, alleged to have murdered three husbands and whose ghost is said to haunt the house. Rose Hall is 3km east of Ironshore. Entry is by tour only.

Beyond the Palladian portico the house is a bastion of historical style, with a magnificent mahogany staircase and doors, and silk wall-fabric that is a reproduction of the original designed for Marie Antoinette during the reign of Louis XVI. Unfortunately, because the house was cleaned out by looters back in the 19th century, almost all of the period furnishings were brought in from elsewhere, and quite a few are from the wrong century. With that said, the exquisite imported antique furnishings are the genuine article, and many are the work of past leading English master carpenters.

Slaves destroyed the house in the Christmas Rebellion of 1831 and it was left in ruins for more than a century. In 1966 the three-story building was restored to its haughty grandeur.

Tours take in the rooms, including Annie Palmer's bedroom upstairs, which has been (re)decorated in crimson silk brocades because, y'know, red is the color of blood; the secret passage through which she was visited by her slave lover; her tomb; and the cellar with period objects and an English-style pub.

Day tours focus on the sumptuous furnishings, while evening tours are more theatrical and are not really suitable for under-12s.

★ Greenwood Great House   HOUSE
(☑ 953-1077; www.greenwoodgreathouse.com; adult/child US$20/10; ⊘ 9am-6pm) This marvelous estate, sitting high on a hill, may not have Rose Hall's fame, but offers a far more intimate and interesting experience. Unique among local plantation houses, Greenwood survived unscathed during the slave rebellion of Christmas 1831. Most of the furnishings are authentic, and some of the rare objects are truly remarkable. Greenwood is 11km east of Ironshore and around 10km west of Falmouth, off Hwy A1; turn inland and follow the pitted road uphill.

Construction of the two-story, stone-and-timber structure was begun in 1780 by the Honorable Richard Barrett, whose family arrived in Jamaica in the 1660s and amassed a fortune from its sugar plantations. (Barrett was a cousin of the famous English poet Elizabeth Barrett Browning.) In an unusual move for his times, Barrett educated his slaves.

The original library is still intact, as are oil paintings, a 1626 map of Africa and plentiful antiques, including a mantrap used for catching runaway slaves (one of the few direct references we found in any Jamaican historical home to the foundations of the plantation labor market, ie slavery). Among the highlights is the rare collection of musical instruments, including an exquisitely inlaid piano made for Edward VII by Thomas Broadwood (who made pianos for Beethoven), one of three working barrel organs in the world and two polyphones, one of which the guide is happy to bring to life. The resident ghost is decidedly low-key and you can drink in the view of the entire coast from the upstairs veranda.

A great number of minibuses and route taxis ply the A1 road, traveling to and from Donald Sangster International Airport and Montego Bay. You'll pay about J$120 to travel from MoBay to Ironshore; J$150 to Rose Hall. Private taxis cost US$35.

Falmouth

Built on riches amassed from sugar and slavery, and advanced enough by the early 19th century to have running water before even New York City, Falmouth feels like a sunken *Titanic* recently raised from the deep. Little altered architecturally since the 1840s, when slave emancipation dramatically reversed its fortunes, the town retains one of the finest ensembles of Tropical-Georgian buildings in the Caribbean.

For anyone with even a passing interest in Jamaican history and architecture, Falmouth is an essential stopover. It is a bustling, proper Jamaican town, where old ladies in their Sunday best congregate outside the limestone-bricked, English-style church and market traders ply roasted yam and sugarcane under the pretty gingerbread verandas of commerce-packed Harbour Lane. This quintessential Jamaican-ness is under threat, as there is talk of banishing the produce market from the town center and turning it into a sanitized version of Jamaican life for cruise-ship passengers.

◎ Sights

Water Square
SQUARE

The best place to orient yourself is Water Sq, at the east end of Duke St. Named for an old circular stone reservoir dating from 1798, the square (actually a triangle) has a fountain topped by an old waterwheel. Back in the day this fountain pumped fresh water (before New York City had any such luxury). In the evening, the square really comes to life, with people limin' under the coconut trees, blaring reggae and delicious smells wafting from stalls.

Many of the wooden shop fronts in this area are attractively disheveled relics.

William Knibb Memorial Church
CHURCH

(cnr King & George Sts; ⊘ hours vary) On July 31, 1838, slaves gathered outside William Knibb Memorial Church for an all-night vigil, awaiting midnight and then the dawn of full freedom (to quote Knibbs: 'The monster is dead'), when slave-shackles, a whip and an iron collar were symbolically buried in a coffin. Behind the church you can find Knibb's grave. A plaque inside the church displays the internment of these tools of slavery; to get in, ask at the Leaf of Life Hardware store on King St.

☞ Tours

★ Falmouth Heritage Walks
HISTORICAL

(☑ 407-2245; www.falmouthheritagewalks.com; ⊘ on cruise ship days and by reservation) This excellent outfit consists of a knowledgeable guide offering three ways of exploring history-rich Falmouth. The Heritage Walking Tour (adult/child US$25/15) is an inter-

esting two-hour look at Falmouth's handsome Tropical-Georgian architecture. The Food Tour (adult/child US$45/25) combines snippets of culture with tastings of street food, while the Jewish Tour (adult/child US$15/10) visits Falmouth's Jewish cemetery with gravestones etched in Hebrew.

❶ Getting There & Away

Buses, minibuses and route taxis arrive and depart on opposite sides of Water Sq for Martha Brae (J$120, 15 to 20 minutes), Montego Bay (J$200, 45 minutes), Albert Town (J$250, 1½ hours) and Ocho Rios (J$350, 80 minutes).

Glistening Waters

Glistening Waters (Luminous Lagoon; 30min boat trip per person US$25; ⊘ tours from 6:45pm) actually lives up to the hype. Located in an estuary near Rock, 1.6km east of Falmouth, the water here boasts a singular charm – it glows an eerie green when disturbed. The green glow is due to the presence of microorganisms that produce photochemical reactions when stirred; the concentrations are so thick that fish swimming by look like green torpedoes and when you swim, sparks run down your body.

Swimming through the luminous lagoon is semihallucinogenic, especially on starry nights, when it's hard to tell where the water ends and the sky begins. The experience is made all the more surreal thanks to the mixing of salt- and freshwater from the sea and the Martha Brae River; the freshwater 'floats' on the saltwater, so you not only swim through green clouds of phosphorescence, but alternating bands of cold and warm.

You have to take a boat out to reach the bioluminescent spots. Half-hour boat trips are offered from Glistening Waters Marina and two other locations next to it; the three boat companies are comparable. Any hotel from Ocho Rios to Montego Bay should be able to organize a trip out here.

NEGRIL & WEST COAST

Negril

Stuck out on the island's western tip and graced with its finest and longest natural beach, Negril was first colonized by hippies

OFF THE BEATEN TRACK

HIKING IN COCKPIT COUNTRY

Just over 30 crow-flying kilometers from the roasting sunbathers of Montego Bay glowers a foreboding wilderness that challenges popular images of Jamaica as tame, well trodden and bereft of backcountry. Cockpit Country is a broad, barely penetrable thicket of dense foliage and intricate karst topography scattered with caves, hollows and conical hills that, metaphorically speaking, resembles an upturned egg carton.

A few hunters' tracks and farmers' footpaths lead into and even across Cockpit Country. Most are faint paths, often overgrown, and hiking away from these trails can be dangerous going. The rocks are razor sharp and sinkholes are everywhere, often covered by decayed vegetation and ready to crumble underfoot. Never travel alone, as there is no one to hear you call for help should you fall into a sinkhole. Take lots of water: there is none to be had locally.

It is imperative you take a trusted guide. The one company that regularly organizes tours in the Cockpits is the **Southern Trelawny Environmental Agency** (STEA; ☑ 393-6584; www.stea.net/ccat_main.htm; Rock Spring; tours US$25-50), based in Rock Spring. STEA works with reputable local guides, simultaneously empowering local communities while giving visitors access to this little-explored corner of Jamaica. These locals are versed in ecotourism practices and know their way around these hills and caves. You'll still need to bring stout walking shoes (or water shoes if caving), rain gear and a powerful flashlight in the event of a delay past sunset. Take warm clothing if you plan on overnighting, as nights can get cold. Rates for guides vary based on hike length.

STEA's most popular hike - and a great introduction to the Cockpits – is a 20km walk along the abandoned B10 road from Kinloss to Spring Garden that passes through Barbecue Bottom. Along the way, you get a real appreciation for the beautiful scenery – the honeycombed limestone cliffs and verdant valleys. It's a long hike, but with gentle inclines, so accessible to any moderately fit hiker, and with beautiful views – something you don't get if hiking through the Cockpits' interior. Shorter hikes along that route are also possible.

---

in the early 1970s. Unsurprisingly, 40 years of development has left its mark – not all of it good: Negril is renowned for its hustlers. But it's not all hassle. A strong local business community, fueled by a desire to safeguard Negril's precious ecology, has kept the area from becoming a full-on circus. Consequently Negril remains a laid-back place of impromptu reggae concerts and psychedelic sunsets.

◉ Sights & Activities

There's plenty to keep you busy in Negril, from sunset boat cruises and glass-bottom-boat outings to getting in the water with a snorkeling mask or beneath the waves with a scuba tank. Fishing, parasailing and kayaking are other watery pursuits. Most lodgings can also arrange tours to Jamaican attractions further afield.

★**Seven Mile Beach**   BEACH
(Negril Beach, Long Beach) Seven Mile Beach was initially touted on tourism posters as 'seven miles of nothing but you and the sea.' True, sunbathers still lie half submerged in

the gentle surf, and the sweet smell of ganja smoke continues to perfume the breeze, but otherwise the beach has changed a great deal. Today it's cluttered with restaurants, bars and nightspots, and every conceivable water sport is on offer. It is still beautiful to behold, but if you're looking for solitude, look elsewhere.

It's worth noting that the Seven Mile Beach is actually only 4 miles long.

🏃 Activities

★**Negril Adventure Diver**   DIVING
(☑ 412-2502; www.negriladventurediver.com; Norman Manley Blvd, Coral Seas Beach Resort; 1-/2-tank dives US$60/100) This diving outfit gets particularly high marks for the patience and friendliness of its diving instructors. Particularly good for beginners, though they tend to get rave reviews from most customers.

★**Dream Team Divers**   DIVING
(☑ 957-0054; www.dreamteamdiversjamaica.com; One Love Dr, Sunset on the Cliffs Resort; 1-/2-tank dives US$40/70) Highly recommended, professional diving outfit. A full range of PADI

courses on offer, as well as discover scuba dives (US$80).

Negril Cruises
BOATING

(☑430-0596; www.negrilcruises.com; Hedonism II; US$40-60) Offers several variations of long, drunken party cruises; good times.

Ray's Water Sports
WATER SPORTS

(☑957-4349) Parasailing and other water sports are offered by Ray's Water Sports at the north end of Seven Mile Beach.

✵ Festivals & Events

Rastafari Rootzfest
CULTURAL

(www.rastafarirootzfest.com; ⊘Dec) Held for three days in December in Negril, this new festival celebrates the Rastafarian lifestyle, from music and art to I-tal cuisine, ganja cultivation and religious beliefs.

🛏 Sleeping

🛏 Long Bay

Negril Yoga Centre
RESORT $

(☑957-4397; www.negrilyoga.com; Norman Manley Blvd; r US$51-91; ❄🛜) A hearkening back to hippie days of yore, these rustic yet atmospheric rooms and cottages surround an open-air, wood-floored, thatched yoga center set in a garden. Options range from a two-story, Thai-style wooden cabin to an adobe farmer's cottage; all are modestly furnished. Naturally, yoga classes are offered (US$10 for guests and US$20 for visitors).

Rondel Village
RESORT $$

(☑957-4413; www.rondelvillage.com; Norman Manley Blvd; r from US$127, 2-bedroom villas US$302; ❄🛜🏊) 🏊 Rondel is a charmer. Rooms encased in beautiful white chalets are set off with sharp purple accents and are surrounded by snaking swimming pools and verdant (largely edible) natural foliage. Eschewing big-resort ambitions, it is the epitome of Negrilian calm – relaxed, hassle-free and filled with all the ingredients for a week enjoyed doing absolutely nothing. Service is exemplary.

Blue Cave Castle
HOTEL $$

(☑957-4845; www.bluecavecastle.com; West End Rd; s/d US$75/145; ❄🛜) Winner of Negril's 'quirky hotel' prize is this mock castle that sits like a crenelated fortification warding off invaders on the cliffs of the West End. Fourteen fit-for-a-king rooms and a private grassy terrace create a less swashbuckling

atmosphere inside. Repeat visitors testify to fine service and a blissful ambience. There's a swimming cave accessed via a slippery staircase.

Firefly Beach Cottages
HOTEL $$$

(☑957-4358; www.jamaicalink.com; Norman Manley Blvd; r US$166, ste & apt US$206-324; ❄🛜) Not to be mixed up with the Noël Coward estate, Firefly Negril is a more modest affair where little wooden cabins and a pretty pink house shelter simple, nonfancy rooms with an ocean breeze. Out in the communal areas you'll see hammocks slung between sea grapes, a rough-and-ready gym, and washing hung out to dry. It's rustic but real.

🛏 West End

★ Judy House Cottages & Rooms
HOSTEL $

(☑957-0671, 424-5481; www.judyhousenegril.com; Westland Mountain Rd; s/d US$25/40, cottages US$90; 🛜) This lush tropical garden on a hill above the West End guards two self-contained cottages with kitchen and five additional rooms (three singles and a couple of dorms, all with shared bathroom) aimed at backpackers. English owner Sue is a mine of candid info, the honesty bar and the friendly discourse are refreshing, and the hammocks in the garden are...zzzzzz.

The luxury here isn't in the gilded bath taps, it's in the unscripted extras.

Catcha Falling Star
HOTEL $$

(☑957-0390; www.catchajamaica.com; West End Rd; r US$135,1-/2-bedroom cottages incl breakfast US$110-350; 🅿🛜) In inimitable West End style, these pleasant fan-cooled cottages – including several with two bedrooms – sit on the cliffs. Each is named for an astrological sign and the rooms do have the genuine variety of the zodiac; some peek into gardens abloom with tropical flowers, while others lip out on to the blue-on-blue vista of ocean. Breakfast is delivered to your veranda.

★ Rockhouse
HOTEL $$$

(☑957-4373; www.rockhousehotel.com; West End Rd; r/studio/villa US$180/220/410; ❄🛜🏊) One of the West End's most beautiful and well-run hotels, with luxury thatched rondavels (African huts) built of pine and stone, plus studio apartments that dramatically cling to the cliffside above a small cove. Decor is basic yet romantic, with net-draped poster beds and strong Caribbean colors. Catwalks

ZIMBALI RETREAT

In the hills above Little London, the wonderful **Zimbali Retreat** (485-2789; www.zim-baliretreats.com; Caanan Mountain, Little London; 4-course lunch/5-course dinner US$50/60; Mon-Sat;) is an organic farm which has become the go-to destination for some of Jamaica's most sophisticated meals (including imaginative vegetarian options), served in a strikingly stylish yet rustic bar. Book ahead for a morning or evening slot; the farm tour is included. Head north from Little London for 5km, or take a tour from Negril.

Better yet, you can stay in one of the seven snug rooms on the property (US$99 per person incl full board), swing in a hammock overlooking the lush hillside, commune with the friendly resident dogs and cats and do numerous outings in the hills – hiking, swimming in the river and enjoying a cookout with a local Rasta over a wood fire. Pickups from Negril cost US$15.

lead over the rocks to an open-sided dining pavilion overhanging the ocean.

🍴 Eating

🍴 Long Bay

Cosmo's SEAFOOD $
(957-4784; Norman Manley Blvd; mains J$600-1200; 10am-11pm;) A tatty hippie outpost that sits like an island of good taste amid an ocean of insipid all-inclusive buffets. Cosmo's, in Negril-speak, is a synonym for 'fantastic seafood.' Eschew fine dining for burying your toes in the sand at a beachside picnic table – the plates of melt-in-your-mouth lobster, grilled fish and curried conch are deliciously spicy.

Lobster House ITALIAN $$
(957-4293; Sunrise Club; mains US$10-27; 7:30am-11pm) Renowned for its pink gnocchi in a Parmesan cream and its signature lobster dishes, this congenial outdoor spot has attained the status of best pizzeria in town, thanks to its brick oven. Many, however, come for a cup of what is arguably the best espresso on the island, made using Blue Mountain coffee and the proprietor's vintage 1961 Faema espresso machine.

🍴 West End

⭐ 3 Dives Jerk Centre JERK $
(957-0845; West End Rd; quarter-/half-chicken J$400/650; 3pm-midnight) This colorful shack, which looks like it'll blow away in the next category one hurricane, serves up what may be the best jerk chicken in Negril, plus other Jamaican classics. Let your nose and taste buds be the judge. Feast your eyes on those sizzling lobsters or that smoking

jerk and be prepared for a loooong, totally worthwhile, wait.

⭐ Rockhouse Restaurant & Bar FUSION $$$
(957-4373; www.rockhousehotel.com/eat; West End Rd; mains US$15-30; 7:30am-10pm;) Lamplit at night, this relaxed cliffside spot leads the pack when it comes to nouvelle Jamaican cuisine in the western parishes. Dine and gush over dishes such as vegetable tempura with lime and ginger, specialty pastas and daily specials such as watermelon spare ribs and blackened mahi-mahi with mango chutney. At the very least, stop by for a sinful bananas Foster.

🍷 Drinking & Nightlife

⭐ Rick's Cafe BAR
(www.rickscafejamaica.com; West End Rd; 3-10pm;) You'll be joining the touristy throng at this ever-popular West End institution, but why not? Just for one evening. The drinks menu features empty-your-wallet cocktails and US$7 Red Stripes (skip the food): you're paying for the ambience, pool access and the live band. While you sip your drink, local divers try to outdo each other from the 10m-tall cliffs.

Sir D's Firewater Love Nest BAR
(521-0260; West End Rd; 4-10pm) If all you want is to watch the greatest show on earth – Negril's fiery sunset – with a Red Stripe in your hand, then this friendly little place that clings to the clifftop fits the bill perfectly.

LTU Pub BAR
(957-0382; www.facebook.com/LTUPUB; West End Rd; 8am-11pm) A friendly and comfortable clifftop haunt centered on a small yet lively tiki bar, LTU is the perfect place to strike up a conversation at sunset or to enjoy

a Bloody Mary before noon. Good international food, too.

☆ Entertainment

Negril's reggae concerts are legendary, with live performances every night in peak season. Several venues offer regular weekly jams, so they all get a piece of the action. You will also find sound-system jams where the DJs play shatteringly loud music – usually dancehall – on giant speakers. Most bars start the night playing reggae oldies and bust out the dancehall later.

★ **Bourbon Beach**   LIVE MUSIC
(🖉 957-4432; www.bourbonbeachnegril.com; Norman Manley Blvd; entry fee varies; ☺ from 8pm Mon, Thu & Sat) The best spot for live reggae on Seven Mile Beach, Bourbon Beach has hosted such greats as John Holt and Gregory Isaacs; younger talent appears on Thursdays. Saturday is dancehall night. The lively bar is open daily and the jerk is excellent, too.

Jungle   CLUB
(🖉 954-4005; www.junglenegril.com; Norman Manley Blvd; US$7-10; ☺ 10pm-4am Thu-Sat) The only bona fide nightclub outside the all-inclusives, Jungle, with its tacky decor, is not the most urbane place, but the DJs *definitely* know what they're doing; during high season guest talent from Miami and New York regularly takes command of the turntables. Thursday is Ladies' Night and Saturday is great for partying until dawn.

ℹ Information

Negril Minor Emergency Clinic (Norman Manley Blvd; ☺ 9am-5pm, doctor on call 24hr) Handles minor medical emergencies.

Police Station (🖉 957-4268; Sheffield Rd)

Post Office (West End Rd; ☺ 8am-5pm Mon-Fri) Between A Fi Wi Plaza and King's Plaza.

Scotiabank (🖉 957-4236; Negril Sq; ☺ 9am-5pm Mon-Sat) Northwest of Plaza de Negril; offers currency exchange and ATMs.

DANGERS & ANNOYANCES

Hustlers stalk Negril like nowhere else in Jamaica. You can expect to be endlessly offered everything from drugs to the hustlers themselves. Usually – but not always – you can shake them off with a firm 'no,' but Negril hustlers can be pretty in your face. Do not walk between Seven Mile Beach and the West End at night. Tourists have been,

and continue to be, mugged while walking through this area.

ℹ Getting There & Away

From the **transportation center** (Sheffield Rd), dozens of minibuses and route taxis run between Negril and Montego Bay. The 1½-hour journey costs between J$350 and J$500. Minibuses and route taxis also leave for Negril from Donald Sangster International Airport in Montego Bay (the price is negotiable, but expect to pay about US$15).

The handy and comfortable **Knutsford Express** (🖉 971-1822; www.knutsfordexpress.com; Norman Manley Blvd; ☺ 6:15am-8pm) runs one daily bus at 8am to Kingston (J$3100, five hours) via Savanna-la-Mar (J$600, 40 minutes) and Mandeville (J$2250, 3¼ hours), and two daily buses to Kingston (J$3100, 5¼ hours) that stop in Montego Bay (J$1600, 1½ hours), Falmouth (J$1850, two hours) and Ocho Rios (J$2500, 3½ hours) en route. Buses depart across the street from Times Square Plaza.

ℹ Getting Around

Negril stretches along more than 16km of shoreline, and it can be a withering walk. Route taxis cruise the length of Seven Mile Beach and West End Rd all the time. You can flag them down anywhere. The fare between any two points was J$130 at research time during the day; in the evenings, it can be up to J$200 per hop.

SOUTH COAST & CENTRAL HIGHLANDS

Treasure Beach

Welcome to a unique part of Jamaica that gets all the facets of the quintessential Caribbean experience exactly right. Winding country lanes, a dearth of hustlers, a local population of poets and artists, sublime deserted beaches, no gimmicky resorts, and – above all – a proud, foresighted local community that promotes sustainability and harbors a bonhomous but mellow culture. Too good to be true? Not at all.

A bicycle is a good means of getting around quiet Treasure Beach; some lodgings rent them out for a small fee.

🏖 Beaches

Several fishing beaches beckon within easy walking distance of the major accommodations. Ask about best swimming spots, as there can be strong undertows.

Fishermen's Beach
BEACH

(Frenchman's Bay) This is the most centrally located beach running east from the Treasure Beach Hotel as far as Jack Sprat Beach. It is watched over by a landmark buttonwood tree that has long attracted the attention of poets, painters and wood-carvers who ply their wares. It's a good place for sunning and swimming, and a popular spot for watching the sunset.

Great Bay Beach
BEACH

(Great Bay) All the way at the eastern 'bottom' of Treasure Beach, this is its least developed portion, where the main business remains a Fishermen's Co-op building. There are a couple of beachside shacks serving beer and cooking up fresh seafood. Swimming is possible.

Jack Sprat Beach
BEACH

(Frenchman's Cove) At the western edge of Jake's Hotel, brightly painted wooden fishing boats are pulled up on the sand, and there is invariably a fisher or two on hand tending the nets. Good for swimming, as it's somewhat sheltered.

Calabash Bay Beach
BEACH

(Calabash Bay) The long, narrow arc of Calabash Bay Beach has a few beach shacks plying rum and – if you're lucky – some basic potluck cuisine (fish, mainly). Swimming is possible but can be choppy.

Tours

Treasure Tours
OUTDOORS

(965-0126; www.treasuretoursjamaica.com; 9:30am-5:30pm Mon-Fri) This excellent local outfit supports local communities around the south coast and arranges trips to YS Falls, Appleton Rum Estate, Black River, Negril and turtle-spotting in Treasure Beach. Airport transfers to Kingston and MoBay also arranged.

Mr Nice Guy
BOATING

(433-0252; bebesutherland@yahoo.com) Mr Nice Guy in question is Bernard 'BeBe' Sutherland, a fisherman who's active in the protection of Treasure Beach's critically endangered hawksbill turtles. This experienced boat captain runs trips to Black River and Pelican Bar, as well as fishing outings.

Festivals & Events

Calabash International Literary Festival
LITERATURE

(965-3000; www.calabashfestival.org; late May/early Jun, even-numbered years) A daring, acclaimed literary festival at Jake's Hotel, drawing literary voices both domestically and internationally.

Sleeping

Welcoming Vibes
GUESTHOUSE $

(538-8779; www.welcomingvibes.org; Church St; r US$39;) The amazing open-air terrace of this house on the hill drinks in the full expanse of Frenchman's Bay while the common area fills with the aromatic smoke of di 'erb. The four spacious, en-suite, bug-netted rooms are airy and cool and friendly owner Paul is happy to shoot the breeze. Park below and take the steep footpath up.

Ital Rest
GUESTHOUSE $

(421-8909, 473-6145; Great Bay; r US$50) In the right setting, a lack of electricity rockets a property right into the super-romantic category. Two exquisite all-wood thatched cabins is the deal here. Hang with the Rasta owners as the sun sets, then retire to a candlelit room with a loved one. All rooms have toilets and the upstairs room has a great sundeck. Kitchen facilities are shared.

Katamah Beachfront Resort
BOUTIQUE HOTEL $$

(567-9562; www.katamah.com;) There's something for everyone at this adorable beachside place – from the three sensual, Moroccan-style rooms and the Berry Suite in the main house to the two breezy little cabins with hammocks under the trees. There are even three large glamping tents and thatched beachside gazebos for chilling. Owner Ricky can hook you up with a reliable local boat captain.

Jake's Hotel
BOUTIQUE HOTEL $$$

(965-3000, in the USA 800-688-7678; www.jakeshotel.com; r US$145-480;) If you haven't been to Jake's, you haven't really been to Treasure Beach. This romance-drenched boutique hotel is the nexus of pretty much everything in the area – cooking courses, yoga classes and mosaic workshops all happen here. Individually crafted rooms spurn TVs but are big on style and atmosphere.

It's owned by Jason Henzell, son of film director Perry Henzell who conceived

Jamaica's great seminal movie *The Harder They Come* in 1972.

✕ Eating

Hold a Vibz Cafe CAFE $

(☑540-7981; off Main Rd, Calabash Bay; smoothies J$450; �9am-4pm; ☑) This friendly little cafe has won local and visiting fans with its excellent fruit smoothies, revitalizing veggie juices, and tasty sandwiches and salads. Heading up Main Rd, turn into the little lane just before the gaudy, cakelike yellow-and-green building and walk for around 100m.

Gee Whiz VEGETARIAN $

(☑573-5988; Maylen Plaza, Main Rd; meals J$600-1000; ☑11:30am-7pm Tue-Sun) Run by delightful Rasta Delroy, this simple restaurant is a great stop for vegetarian dishes, prepared to order, as well as fish dishes and freshly pressed fruit juices. I-tal, mon!

★ Strikie-T JAMAICAN $$

(☑869-8516; Billy's Bay; mains J$1200-2000; ☑noon-10pm Mon-Sat Nov-Apr) A seasonal affair run by the energetic, ever-friendly Chris 'Strikie' Bennett, who has worked as a professional chef in the US and at Jake's. This understated food shack in Billy's Bay, festooned with fairy lights, is anchored by secret recipes and a hand-built jerk smoker. The food is great: Jamaican favorites, from jerk to lobster, home-cooked and mouth-watering.

★ Jack Sprat FUSION $$

(☑965-3583; mains J$700-2400; ☑10am-11pm) Seafood and pizza aren't obvious bedfellows until you wander into Jack Sprat's, where they put fresh lobster on their thick Italian-style pies. For many it's enhanced by the dreamy location (candlelit tables under twinkle-lit trees) and bohemian interior (a mix of retro reggae and movie posters). The pizza is the best in Jamaica and the homemade crab cakes are ace.

There are open-air movie screenings some evenings.

▼ Drinking & Nightlife

★ Pelican Bar BAR

(Caribbean Sea; ☑10:30am-sunset) A thatched hut on stilts, built on a submerged sandbar 1km out to sea after owner Floyd saw it in a dream, is still Jamaica's – and perhaps the planet's – most enjoyable spot for a drink. You can carve your name into the floorboards, play a game of dominoes, or just chill with a Red Stripe while wading in the shallows.

Getting there is half the fun: hire a local boat captain in Treasure Beach (around US$40) or Parottee (around US$20), who will call ahead to arrange things if you want to eat. This is essential for those who want to take a meal out here (mains are US$10 to US$20), which is novel but frankly not necessary – you'll get better food on land. It's best to come here for a cold Red Stripe (or rum, if such is your fancy). The bar's fame has spread far and wide, and the clientele is a mix of enchanted travelers and repeat-business fishers who while away the hours exchanging pleasantries with the owner.

❶ Information

Treasure Beach Foundation (Breds; ☑965-3000; www.breds.org; Kingfisher Plaza; ☑9am-5pm) The Treasure Beach Foundation – or Breds (short for brethren) – is dedicated to fostering heritage pride, sports, health and education among the community, and represents a partnership between the Treasure Beach community, expats and stakeholders (Jamaican and foreign) in the local tourism industry. This little place also acts as the unofficial tourist office.

Work includes restoring decrepit housing, sponsorship of both a soccer team and a basketball team, the introduction of computer labs at local schools and education for the children of fishers lost at sea.

❶ Getting There & Away

There is no direct service to Treasure Beach from Montego Bay, Negril or Kingston. Route taxis run to/from Black River (J$250 to J$350); from Mandeville, you'll need to get a route taxi to Junction or Santa Cruz and another taxi to Treasure Beach (J$200). Most hotels and villas arrange transfers from Montego Bay or Kingston for US$120.

Black River

The capital of St Elizabeth, Black River is a busy little place that was the most prosperous port in Jamaica in the late 19th century. The namesake river is a slow-moving slick of moldering tannins patrolled by crocodiles and boats full of curious tourists. Most visitors opt to stay in nearby Treasure Beach.

The best way to get a feel for the Great Morass is to explore it by small watercraft or tour boat; quick excursions are easily arranged in Black River, but if you are heading on to Treasure Beach, lengthier forays up the river can be arranged there. Along the way, with the right guide, you can eat at delightful riverside shacks, discover hidden swimming holes and, of course, spot some grinning, sunning crocodiles.

J Charles Swaby's
Black River Safari BOATING
(☑965-2513, 962-0220; tour US$19; ☺tours 9am, 11am, 12:30pm, 2pm & 3:30pm) Longest-established operator of croc safari tours offering five daily from the east side of the river.

St Elizabeth River Safari BOATING
(☑965-2229, 965-2374; tour US$19; ☺tours 9am, 11am, 2pm & 3:30pm) Tours of Great Morass on large watercraft depart from behind the Hendricks Building.

Idlers' Rest Beach Hotel BOUTIQUE HOTEL $$
(☑965-9000; www.idlersrest.com; Crane Rd; r from US$110; P❄☎) A worthwhile non-Treasure Beach option a little way out of town, Idlers' Rest redefines 'Irie'. Owned by a friendly lawyer, the hotel is a tasteful boutique decorated in a comfy mix of modern chic, Caribbean color and pan-African art, with rooms cooled by gentle sea breezes. Our one quibble is maintenance: rooms could be cleaner and in better nick.

★Cloggy's on the Beach SEAFOOD $$
(☑634-2424; www.facebook.com/pages/Cloggys-on-the-Beach/139402596166094; 22 Crane Rd; mains J$700-2400; ☺noon-10pm) This beachside joint is your best culinary bet in Black River; it's an all-round pleaser with a relaxed vibe, great bar ambience and excellent seafood. Try a cup of conch soup for a revelation, and follow that up with some gorgeous curried lobster or conch on the breezy terrace. It occasionally throws well-attended beach sound-system parties, too.

Black River is a nexus for route taxis that shoot off in all directions. Taxis on High St depart for Treasure Beach (J$250). Minibuses go to Montego Bay (J$250 to J$300) from the transportation center behind the market.

YS Falls

YS Falls (☑997-6360; www.ysfalls.com; B6; adult/child US$19/10; ☺9:30am-5pm Tue-Sun, last entry 3:30pm, closed public holidays), a series of eight cascades hemmed in by limestone cliffs and surrounded by lush jungle, are among the most beautiful in Jamaica. The cascades fall 36m from top to bottom, separated by cool pools perfect for swimming. Lifeguards assist you with the rope swing above one of the pools and a stone staircase follows the cascades to the main waterfall. There are no lockers, so watch your stuff.

Get here by tour or drive the 5.5km road from Middle Quarters.

The waters of YS (why-ess) take their name from the original landowners, ranchers John Yates and Richard Scott.

The more adventurous can fly, screeching, over the falls along a canopy zip line for US$50/35 per adult/under-12. A tractor-drawn jitney takes all visitors to the cascades, where you'll find picnic grounds, changing rooms, a tree house and a shallow pool fed with river water.

Almost every tour operator in Jamaica (and many hotels) offers trips to YS Falls, but if you want to get here ahead of the crowds, drive yourself (or charter your own taxi) and arrive right when the grounds open.

The YS Falls entrance is just north of the junction of the B6 toward Maggotty. From the A2 (a much smoother road if you're driving), the turnoff is 1.5km east of Middle Quarters; from here you'll head 5.5km north to the falls. Public transport is not a reliable way of reaching the falls.

UNDERSTAND JAMAICA

History

Columbus & the Arawaks

Christopher Columbus landed on Jamaica in 1494. At the time there were perhaps 10,000 peaceful Arawaks, who had settled Jamaica around AD 700. Spanish settlers arrived from 1510 and quickly introduced two things that would profoundly shape the island's future: sugarcane production and slavery. By the end of the 16th century the Arawak population had been entirely wiped out, worn down by hard labor, ill-treatment and European diseases.

Arrival of the English

In 1654 an ill-equipped and badly organized English contingent sailed to the Caribbean. After failing to take Hispaniola, they turned to weakly defended Jamaica. Despite the ongoing efforts of Spanish loyalists and the guerilla-style campaigns of freed Spanish slaves (cimarrones – 'wild ones' – or Maroons), England took control of the island.

Slave Colony

New slaves kept on arriving; bloody insurrections kept occurring. The last and largest was the 1831 Christmas Rebellion, inspired by Sam Sharpe, an educated slave who incited passive resistance. The rebellion turned violent as up to 20,000 slaves razed plantations and murdered planters. When the slaves were tricked into laying down arms with a false promise of abolition – and 400 were hanged and hundreds more whipped – there was a wave of revulsion in England, causing the British parliament to finally abolish slavery.

The transition from a slave to wage-labor economy caused chaos, with most slaves rejecting the starvation wages offered on the estates and choosing to fend for themselves.

Road to Independence

A banana-led economic recovery was halted by the Great Depression of the 1930s, and then kick-started again by WWII, when the Caribbean islands supplied food and raw materials to Britain. Adult suffrage for all Jamaicans was introduced in 1944, and virtual autonomy from Britain was granted in 1947. Jamaica seceded from the short-lived West Indies Federation in 1962 after a referendum called for the island's full independence.

Postindependence politics have been dominated by the legacy of two cousins: Alexander Bustamante, who formed the first trade union in the Caribbean just prior to WWII and later formed the Jamaican Labor Party (JLP); and Norman Manley, whose People's National Party (PNP) was the first political party on the island when it was convened in 1938. Manley's son, Michael, led the PNP toward democratic socialism in the mid-1970s, causing capital flight at a time when Jamaica could ill afford it. Bitterly opposed factions engaged in open urban warfare preceding the 1976 election, but the PNP won the election by a wide margin and Manley continued with his socialist agenda.

Power Struggles

The US government was hostile to the path Jamaica was taking and when Manley began to develop close ties with Cuba, the CIA purportedly planned to topple the government. Businesses pulled out, the economy went into sharp decline and the country lived virtually under siege. Almost 700 people were killed in the lead-up to the 1980 elections, which were won by the JLP's Edward Seaga. Seaga restored Jamaica's economic fortunes somewhat, severed ties with Cuba and courted Ronald Reagan's USA. Seaga was ousted in 1989 and replaced by Manley, who took a short, second crack at the prime ministerial office. He retired in 1992, handing the reins to his deputy, Percival James Patterson, Jamaica's first black prime minister.

Present & Future

In 2007 Bruce Golding of the JLP was elected prime minister, ending 18 years of PNP rule. Three years later the USA called for the extradition of Christopher 'Dudus' Coke, the don of Tivoli Gardens ghetto and one of the most powerful men in Jamaica. The demand for extradition was originally refused by Golding, who claimed that the evidence against Dudus was gathered illegally, but after American pressure the police moved against Dudus in a bloody battle that left 67 dead. Dudus himself was apprehended at a roadblock, disguised as a woman and en route to the US embassy to negotiate his surrender.

Jamaica's current prime minister is Andrew Holness of the JLP. Most Jamaicans will tell you the greatest issues facing the country are crime and the brain drain to the USA, Canada and the UK. Illiteracy is also a major concern, as are threats to the environment through deforestation and overdevelopment. In the meantime the Jamaican people face the future with resolve and a measure of good humor – they've endured worse in the past.

Culture

Religion

Jamaica professes to have the greatest number of churches per square kilometer in the world. Although most foreigners associate the island with Rastafari, more than 80% of Jamaicans identify themselves as Christian and the Church remains a powerful political lobby group in the country.

Literature

The current star on Jamaica's literary scene is undoubtedly Marlon James, author of *A Brief History of Seven Killings* and *The Book of Night Women*, but other hot names to look out for include Kei Miller (*The Last Warner Woman, August Town*), Olive Senior (*Dancing Lessons*), and Garfield Ellis (*For Nothing At All*). Nicole Dennis-Benn's debut novel *Here Comes the Sun* announced the arrival of another great Jamaican writer in 2016.

The novels of Anthony Winkler are celebrated for the wry eye they cast over Jamaican life, most notably in *The Lunatic, The Duppy* and *The Family Mansion*.

Music

Modern Jamaican music starts with the acoustic folk music of mento. In the early 1960s this blended with calypso, jazz and R&B to form ska, the country's first popular music form. This evolved, via the intermediate step of rocksteady, into the bass-heavy reggae of the 1970s, the genre that ultimately swept all before it. Dancehall, a faster and more clubby sound than its predecessors, followed thereafter, and continues to dominate the contemporary music scene today. For all that these styles are distinct, they constantly blend and feed off each other – this syncretism is the true magic of Jamaican music.

REGGAE

In his song 'Trench Town,' Bob Marley asked if anything good could ever come from Jamaica's ghettoes. In doing so, he challenged the class-based assumptions of Jamaican society, with the minority elite ruling over the disenfranchised masses. Of course, the answer came in the message of pride and spiritual redemption contained in the music itself, as reggae left the yard to conquer the world, in the process turning Bob Marley into a true global icon.

Bob Marley's band, The Wailers, sprang from the ska and rocksteady era of the 1960s. Producers Lee 'Scratch' Perry, Clement 'Sir Coxsone' Dodd and King Tubby played a key role in evolving the more spacious new reggae sound, while the resurgence of Rastafarianism that followed Haile Selassie's 1966 visit to Jamaica inspired the music's soul. Through his signing of The Wailers, the Jamaican-born founder of Island Records, Chris Blackwell, helped introduce reggae to an international audience.

Reggae is more than just Marley. His original bandmates Peter Tosh and Bunny Wailer both became major stars, joining a pantheon that runs from Desmond Dekker and Dennis Brown to Burning Spear and Gregory Isaacs. While dancehall has since taken over as Jamaica's most popular domestic music, in recent years there has been something of a roots reggae revival, with artists such as Chronixx, Proteje and Jah9 bringing back some rasta consciousness to rejuvenate the genre for the new century.

RASTAFARI

Dreadlocked Rastas are as synonymous with Jamaica as reggae. Developed in the 1930s, the Rastafari creed evolved as an expression of poor, black Jamaicans seeking fulfillment, boosted by Marcus Garvey's 'back to Africa' zeal.

Central to Rastafari is the concept that the Africans are one of the displaced 12 Tribes of Israel. Jamaica is Babylon, and their lot is in exile in a land that cannot be reformed. The crowning of Ras Tafari (Haile Selassie) as emperor of Abyssinia in 1930 fulfilled the prophecy of an African king and redeemer who would lead them from exile to the promised land of Zion, the black race's spiritual home.

Ganja smoking is a sacrament for many (if not all) Rastas, allowing them to gain wisdom and inner divinity through the ability to 'reason' more clearly. The parsing of Bible verses is an essential tradition, helping to see through the corrupting influences of Babylon. The growing of dreadlocks is an allegory for the mane of the Lion of Judah.

Despite its militant consciousness, the religion preaches love and nonviolence, and adherents live by strict biblical codes advocating a way of life in harmony with Old Testament traditions. Some Rastas are teetotalers who shun tobacco and keep to a strict diet of vegetarian I-tal food, prepared without salt; others, like the 12 Tribes Rastafari, eat meat and drink beer.

WORTH A TRIP

A TASTE OF RUM

You can smell the yeasty odor of molasses wafting from the **Appleton Rum Estate** (☑963-9215; www.appletonrumtour.com; factory tour & rum tasting US$25; ⊘9am-3:30pm Mon-Sat, closed public holidays) well before you reach it, 1km northeast of Maggotty. The largest and oldest distillery in Jamaica has been blending rums since 1749. The tour explains how molasses is extracted from sugarcane, then fermented, distilled and aged to produce the Caribbean's own rocket fuel, which you can taste in the John Wray Tavern. Undergoing renovation during research time; due to reopen in November 2017.

Around 17 varieties – including the lethal Overproof – are available for sampling. Unsurprisingly, the well-stocked gift shop does brisk business with visitors whose inhibitions have understandably been lowered over the course of the tour (and by the way, you get a complimentary bottle of the stuff at the end of the tour, so don't get too soused!).

Of all of Jamaica's rum factory tours, this is the best organized and most fairly priced. Every tour company in Jamaica can get you onto one of the busloads of tourists that truck to and from the Appleton estate (the 'from' part is pretty fun after 17 varieties of rum). Otherwise, it's easiest to get here from Maggotty; the factory is 1km east, and taxis will take you there and back for around J$600.

DANCEHALL

The modern sound of Jamaica is definitely dancehall: rapid-fire chanting over bass-heavy beats. It's simplistic to just call dancehall Jamaican rap, because the formation of the beats, their structure and the nuances of the lyrics all have deep roots in Jamaica's musical past.

The new sound sprang up at the close of the 1970s with DJs such as Yellowman, Lone Ranger and Josey Wales, who grabbed the mic, and powered the high-energy rhythms through the advent of faster, more digital beats. This was a period of turmoil in Jamaica, and the music reacted by moving away from political consciousness towards a more hedonistic vibe. The scene centered on the sound systems and 'sound clashes' between DJs, dueling with custom records to win the crowd's favor and boost their reputation.

By the 1990s the success of artists such as Shabba Ranks turned dancehall global, but stars including Buju Banton, Beenie Man, Bounty Killer and Sizzla continue to be criticized for lyrics celebrating violence and homophobia. This came to a peak in 2014 with the conviction for murder of 'World Boss' Vybz Kartel, dancehall's biggest and most innovative star. Curiously, his prison sentence has barely slowed his music release schedule. Criticism of dancehall's more outlandish facets is a staple of the Jamaican press, but for all this, dancehall remains in rude health – Sean Paul and Konshens have long ascended into international stardom, while acts such as Cham and Tommy Lee ride the riddims at home.

Sports

If anyone can wrest away Bob Marley's mantle as the world's most recognizable Jamaican, it's the ultra-charismatic Usain Bolt, currently the fastest man on the planet, and 'triple-triple' Olympic gold winner, winning gold in the 100m, 200m and 400m relay at the Beijing, London and Rio games. He's part of Jamaica's astonishing home-grown crop of athletics champions, along with Shelly-Ann Fraser-Pryce and Elaine Thompson (both Olympic 100m and 200m gold medal holders).

Jamaica is cricket mad, and cricketers like fast bowler Courtney Walsh and batsman Chris Gayle are revered. Jamaica plays nationally as part of the West Indies team, who were quarter-finalists in the 2011 and 2015 World Cups, and champions in the 2012 and 2016 World Twenty20. Jamaican cricket's home is Sabina Park in Kingston, which hosts national and international test matches as well as the Caribbean Premier League (CPL) – of which the Jamaican Tallawahs are the 2016 champions.

Landscape & Wildlife

The Land

At 10,991 sq km (roughly equal to the US state of Connecticut, or half the size of Wales), Jamaica is the largest of the English-speaking Caribbean islands. It is one of the Greater Antilles, which make up the westernmost Caribbean islands, and is a near neighbor to Cuba and Haiti.

'Mainland' Jamaica is rimmed by a narrow coastal plain, except for the southern broad flatlands. Mountains form the island's spine, rising gradually from the west and culminating in the Blue Mountains in the east, which are capped by Blue Mountain Peak at 2256m. The island is cut by about 120 rivers, many of which are bone dry for much of the year but spring to life after heavy rains, causing great flooding and damage to roads. Coastal mangroves, wetland preserves and montane cloud forests form small specialized ecosystems that contain a wide variety of the island's wildlife. Offshore, small islands called cays offer further habitats for marine life.

Wildlife

The island has more than 255 bird species. Stilt-legged, snowy-white cattle egrets are ubiquitous, as are 'John crows' (turkey vultures), which are the subject of several folk songs and proverbs. Jamaica's national bird is the 'doctor bird' or red-billed streamertail – an indigenous hummingbird with shimmering emerald feathers, a velvety black crown with purple crest, a long bill and curved tail feathers.

Coral reefs lie along the north shore, where the reef is almost continuous and much of it is within a few hundred meters of shore. Over 700 species of fish zip in and out of the exquisite reefs and swarm through the coral canyons. Last but not least, three species of endangered marine turtles – the green, hawksbill and loggerhead – lay eggs on Jamaica's beaches.

SURVIVAL GUIDE

❶ Directory A–Z

ACCOMMODATIONS

If you're traveling on a shoestring, head to simple guesthouses or hostels. In the midrange category there's a wide range of choice in appealing small hotels, many with splendid gardens, sea views or both. If traveling with your family or a group, consider one of the hundreds of villas available to rent across the island. And if you've

PRACTICALITIES

Newspapers The *Jamaica Gleaner* (www.jamaica-gleaner.com) is the high-standard newspaper. Its rival is the *Jamaica Observer*, followed by the gossipy tabloid *Jamaica Star*.

Radio Of the 30 radio stations, Irie FM (105.1FM; www.iriefm.net) is the most popular.

Smoking Banned in public places (including bars and restaurants).

TV There are seven channels; most hotels have satellite TV with US channels.

Weights & measures Metric and imperial measurements are both used. Distances are measured in meters and kilometers, and gas in liters, but coffee (and ganja) is most often sold by the pound.

decided to splurge, Jamaica's luxury hotels rank among the finest in the world.

Low season (summer) is usually mid-April to early December; the high season (winter) is the remainder of the year, when hotel prices increase by 40% or more. All-inclusive packages are usually based on three-day minimum stays.

BUSINESS HOURS

The following are standard hours for Jamaica; exceptions are noted in reviews. Note that the country virtually shuts down on Sunday.

Banks 9:30am to 4pm Monday to Friday.

Bars Usually open around noon, with many staying open until the last customer stumbles out.

Businesses 8:30am to 4:30pm Monday to Friday.

Restaurants Breakfast dawn to 11am; lunch noon to 2pm; dinner 5:30pm to 11pm.

SLEEPING PRICE RANGES

Unless otherwise stated, the following price ranges refer to a double room in high season with European Plan (room only with bathroom), with the compulsory 6.25% to 15% GCT included in the price.

$ less than US$90

$$ US$90–200

$$$ more than US$200

GANJA

Ganja is an integral part of life for large sections of Jamaica's population – whether as a recreational toke or Rastafari sacrament – though it has long been illegal. In 2015, however, the Jamaican parliament decriminalized possession. Possession of up to 2oz (56g) is now treatable in the same manner as a parking offense, garnering a fine of up to US$100 but no criminal record. Full legalization is on the cards, if not immediately imminent. For now, the only way to buy ganja legally is with a permit from the Health Ministry if you have a prescription for medical marijuana.

While some travelers are keen to seek it out, even those wanting to avoid it are unlikely to get through their trip without at least a whiff of secondhand smoke. You'll undoubtedly be approached by people offering to sell you ganja, whether a 'nudge wink' hustler, or a vendor at a dancehall street party openly selling it alongside candies and rum. If you want to smoke, we still recommend doing so discreetly, at your hotel. Some local strains are particularly strong, and tourists have reported suffering harmful side effects from ganja, especially from ganja cakes and cookies.

Shops 8am or 9am to 5pm Monday to Friday, to noon or 5pm Saturday, late-night shopping to 9pm Thursday and Friday.

DANGERS & ANNOYANCES

Jamaica is probably more plagued by bad media about safety than it is by violent crime that affects tourists. Many travelers fear the worst and avoid the country; those who do make it here are far more likely to come away with positive impressions than horror stories. Petty crime is the most serious issue, although some travelers may be more concerned with the increasingly fluid legality of ganja.

EMBASSIES & CONSULATES

If your country isn't represented in this list, check 'Embassies & High Commissions' in the Yellow Pages of the Greater Kingston telephone directory.

Canadian High Commission (926-1500; www.canadainternational.gc.ca/jamaica-jamaique; 3 West Kings House Rd, Kingston)

Dutch Embassy (926-2026; Victoria Mutual Bldg, 53 Knutsford Blvd, Kingston 5)

French Embassy (946-4000; www.ambafrance-jm-bm.org; 13 Hillcrest Ave, Kingston 6)

German Embassy (631-7935; www.kingston.diplo.de; 10 Waterloo Rd, Kingston 10)

Italian Embassy (968-8464; 10 Surbiton Rd, Kingston 10)

Japanese Embassy (929-7534; www.jamaica.eab-japan.go.jp; NCB Tower 6th fl, 2 Oxford Rd, Kingston 5)

UK High Commission (936-0700; www.gov.uk; 28 Trafalgar Rd, Kingston)

US Embassy (702-6000, after hours 702-6055; http://kingston.usembassy.gov; 142 Old Hope Rd, Kingston)

ELECTRICITY

Jamaica uses 110V voltage at 50Hz. Sockets are usually two- or three-pin as per US standard.

EMERGENCY NUMBERS

Jamaica's country code is 876, which is dropped if dialing within the country.

Ambulance	110
Directory assistance	114
International operator	113
Police	119
Tourism board	929-9200

GLBT TRAVELERS

There is a gay scene in Kingston, but it is an underground affair as Jamaica is a largely homophobic society. Sexual acts between men are prohibited by law and punishable by up to 10 years in prison. Many reggae dancehall lyrics by big-name stars could be classified as antigay hate speech. Gay-bashing incidents are almost never prosecuted, with law enforcement, in most cases, looking the other way.

Nonetheless, you shouldn't be put off from visiting the island. In the more heavily touristed areas you'll find more tolerant attitudes, and hotels that welcome gay travelers, including all-inclusives. Publicly, though, discretion is important and open displays of affection should be avoided.

Useful websites:

Gay Jamaica Watch (http://gayjamaicawatch.blogspot.com)

J-FLAG (www.jflag.org)

Quality of Citizenship Jamaica (www.qcjm.org)

HEALTH

Acceptable health care is available in most major cities and larger towns throughout Jamaica, but may be hard to locate in rural areas. To find a good local doctor, your best bet is to ask the management of the hotel where you are staying or contact your embassy in Kingston or Montego Bay. Note that many doctors and hospitals expect payment on the spot, regardless of whether you have travel health insurance.

Many pharmacies are well supplied, but important medications may not be consistently available. Be sure to bring along adequate supplies of all prescription drugs.

LEGAL MATTERS

➜ Jamaica's drug and drink-driving laws are strictly enforced.

➜ Don't expect leniency just because you're a foreigner. Jamaican jails are distinctly unpleasant.

➜ Ganja has been decriminalized, and possession of up to 2oz attracts a fine, rather than arrest.

➜ If arrested, insist on your right to call your embassy in Kingston to request assistance.

MONEY

➜ The unit of currency is the Jamaican dollar, the 'jay,' which uses the same symbol as the US dollar ($). Jamaican currency is issued in bank notes of J$50, J$100, J$500, J$1000 and (rarely) J$5000. Prices for hotels and valuable items are usually quoted in US dollars, which are widely accepted.

➜ Commercial banks have branches throughout the island. Those in major towns maintain a foreign-exchange booth.

➜ Most towns have 24-hour ATMs linked to international networks such as Cirrus or Plus. In more remote areas, look for ATMs at gas stations. In tourist areas, some ATMs also dispense US dollars.

➜ Traveler's checks are little used and attract fees for cashing.

➜ Major credit cards are accepted throughout the island, although local groceries and the like will not be able to process them, even in Kingston.

PUBLIC HOLIDAYS

New Year's Day January 1

Ash Wednesday, **Good Friday** & **Easter Monday**

Labor Day May 23

Emancipation Day August 1

Independence Day First Monday in August

National Heroes Day Third Monday in October

Christmas Day December 25

Boxing Day December 26

EATING PRICE RANGES

The following price structure is based on the cost of an average meal at a Jamaican restaurant. Watch out for menus adding 16.5% government tax and a further 10% service charge to the bill.

$ less than US$15 (J$1900)

$$ US$15–25 (J$1900–3200)

$$$ more than US$25 (J$3200)

TELEPHONE

Jamaica's country code is 876. To call Jamaica from the US, dial 1-876 + the seven-digit local number. From elsewhere, dial your country's international dialing code, then 876 and the local number.

For calls within the same parish in Jamaica, just dial the local number. Between parishes, dial 1 + the local number. We have included only the seven-digit local number in Jamaica listings.

Cell phones

You can bring your own cell phone into Jamaica (GSM or CDMA). Be aware of hefty roaming charges or buy a local SIM card.

If your phone is unlocked, buy a local SIM card from one of the two local cell-phone operators, Digicel (www.digiceljamaica.com) or Flow (www.discoverflow/jamaica), or you can buy a cheap handset. You'll need to bring ID to buy either. SIM cards are free – ask for the best current offers, usually from around J$500 for calls plus data. Prepaid top-up cards are sold in denominations from J$$50 to J$1000, and you'll find them at many gas stations and grocery stores.

JAMAICAN CUISINE

Jamaican cuisine has the weight and heft of a peasant's diet, with heavy starches and the colorful flavor you associate with the crossroads of the Caribbean. The Taínos introduced callaloo, cassava, corn, sweet potatoes and tropical fruits; the Spanish tossed in escoveitch (a variation on ceviche); Africa added yams, rice, stews and smoked meat; India its curries and rotis; the Chinese added a dash of heat; and the English wrapped it all up in a meat pie.

ℹ Getting There & Away

ENTERING JAMAICA

Passports valid for at least six months from the date of entry are required for all visits to Jamaica.

Most nationals require no visa to visit Jamaica. Most of those who do can obtain one on arrival.

AIR

Jamaica has two international airports, **Norman Manley International Airport** (p516) in Kingston and **Donald Sangster International Airport** (p532) in Montego Bay.

Jamaica is well served by international carriers from cities across North America and Europe.

Useful regional airlines:

Caribbean Airlines (☑ 744-2225; www.caribbean-airlines.com)

Cayman Airways (www.caymanairways.com)

COPA Airlines (www.copaair.com)

Fly Jamaica (☑ 656-9832; www.fly-jamaica.com)

SEA

Jamaica is a popular destination on the cruise roster, mainly for passenger liners but also for private yachts.

For maps and charts of the Caribbean, contact **Bluewater Books & Charts** (☑ 800-942-2583; www.bluewaterweb.com). The **National Oceanic & Atmospheric Administration** (☑ 888-990-6622; www.nauticalcharts.noaa.gov) sells US government charts.

Many yachties make the trip to Jamaica from North America. Upon arrival in Jamaica, you *must* clear customs and immigration at Montego Bay, Kingston, Ocho Rios or Port Antonio. In addition, you'll need to clear customs at *each* port of call. The main ports for yachts:

➡ **Errol Flynn Marina** (☑ 715-6044, 993-3209; www.errolflynnmarina.com; Port Antonio, GPS N 18.168889°, W -76.450556°)

➡ **Montego Bay Yacht Club** (p527)

➡ **Royal Jamaican Yacht Club** (☑ 924-8685; www.rjyc.org.jm; Palisadoes Park, Norman Manley International Airport, Kingston, GPS N 17.940939°, W -76.764939°)

ℹ Getting Around

BICYCLE

Mountain bikes and 'beach cruisers' (bikes with fat tires, suitable for riding on sand) can be rented at most major resorts (US$10 to US$30 per day). Road conditions can be poor when off the main highways, and Jamaican drivers are not considerate of cyclists. For serious touring, bring your own mountain or multipurpose bike.

BUS

Large buses are few and far between in Jamaica due to the narrow twisting roads. Throughout the island there are bus stops at most road intersections along routes, but you can usually flag down a bus anywhere except in major cities. If the bus doesn't have a bell to indicate when you want to get off, shout out 'let down' or 'one stop' to the driver.

Knutsford Express (Map p516; ☑ 971-1822; www.knutsfordexpress.com; 18 Dominica Dr, New Kingston Shopping Center parking lot) operates big comfortable, air-conditioned coaches and covers most destinations. Sample fares/times are Kingston–Ocho Rios (J$1850, two hours), Kingston–Montego Bay (J$2950, four hours). Online booking is available, along with student, senior and child fares.

CAR

Driver's License

To drive in Jamaica, you must have a valid International Driver's License (IDL) or a current license for your home country or state, valid for at least six months, and be at least 21 years of age.

Fuel & Spare Parts

Many gas stations close at 7pm or so. In rural areas, stations are usually closed on Sunday. At the time of writing, gasoline/diesel cost about J$120/112 per liter.

Rental

Most major international car-rental companies operate in Jamaica, including **Avis** (www.avis.com.jm) and **Hertz** (www.hertz.com).

Local car-hire firms can be a lot cheaper than the international brands. Recommended firms:

Beaumont Car Rentals (☑ 926-0311; www.beaumontcarrentalja.com)

Island Car Rentals (☑ 929-5875; www.island-carrentals.com)

Road Conditions

Jamaica's roads run from modern multilane highways to barely passable tracks.

Jamaica's best road is the new highway between Kingston and Ocho Rios, which has dramatically cut transit times to the north coast. It's a toll road – cars pay around J$1000.

You can expect any road with the designation 'A' to be in fairly good condition. 'B' roads are generally much more narrow and often badly potholed, but still passable in the average rental car. Minor roads, particularly those in the Blue Mountains and Cockpit Country, can be hellish. If you plan to drive off the major routes, it's essential to have a stalwart 4WD.

Road Hazards

Laid-back Jamaica has some of the world's rudest and most dangerously aggressive drivers. Cars race through towns and play chicken with one another with daredevil folly. Use extreme caution and drive defensively, especially at night when you should be prepared to meet oncoming cars that are either without lights or blinding you with high beams. Use your horn liberally, especially when approaching blind corners, and watch for pedestrians.

Road Rules

➡ Always drive on the left.

➡ Jamaica has a compulsory seat-belt law.

➡ Speed limits range from 50km/h to 80km/h and vary from place to place across the island.

➡ Carry ID and all relevant car-rental paperwork at all times.

MINIBUS

Private minibuses, also known as 'coasters,' have traditionally been the workhorses of Jamaica's regional public transportation system. All major towns and virtually every village in the country are served.

Licensed minibuses display red license plates with the initials PPV (public passenger vehicle) or have a JUTA (Jamaica Union of Travelers Association; ☑ 974-2292) insignia. JUTA buses are exclusively for tourists. Public coasters don't run to set timetables, but depart their point of origin when they're full. They're often overflowing, and the drivers seem to have death wishes.

ROUTE TAXI

Communal route taxis are the most universal mode of public transportation, reaching every part of the country. They run on set routes, picking up as many people as they can along the way. They're very convenient and are a cheap way of getting around the island. Simply pick them up at their terminal in town (they go when full), or flag them down on the road and tell the driver where you want to get off. If you get in an empty taxi – particularly at the taxi station – be clear if you just want to pay the regular fare instead of a charter.

Most route taxis are white station wagons marked by their red license plates. They should have 'Route Taxi' marked on the front door, and they are not to be confused with similar licensed taxis, which charge more. Avoid any taxi that lacks the red license plate.

1. Dancing the salsa in Cuba 2. Steel drum 3. Cuban musician 4. Bob Marley statue by artist Alvin Marriott

DANEFROMSPAIN / GETTY IMAGES ©

Sounds of the Caribbean

From the brassy swagger of a salsa band to the lolling gait of reggae, the music of the Caribbean draws influences from both plantation fields and colonial parlors, and is as elemental to the islands as the sound of crashing surf.

Steel Pan & Calypso

Hammered from oil barrels, the ringing drums of steel-pan bands are a testament to the adaptive ingenuity of Caribbean musicians. The drums play buoyant calypso, often punched up with braggadocio lyrics or laced with social commentary.

Reggae

Born in the late '60s, reggae is the musical descendant of uniquely Jamaican genres ska and rocksteady. With a languid offbeat shuffle and an ambassador in Bob Marley, it's a cornerstone of island culture.

Cuban Music

Though every destination has its own musical language, no place speaks as fluently as Cuba, where music seems to pour out of every alleyway.

Salsa

Like trade winds circling Puerto Rico, the Dominican Republic, Cuba and Nueva York, salsa's hip-grinding groove is a prized multi-island export. The sound has roots in African rhythms and indigenous islander instruments.

Merengue

The blistering rhythms of this Dominican genre of music are inseparable from the highly stylized, passionate dance bearing the same name.

1. Wallilabou Bay (p733), St Vincent & the Grenadines **2.** El Morro (p593), San Juan, Puerto Rico **3.** Brimstone Hill Fortress (p671), St Kitts & Nevis **4.** Fort Charles, Port Royal (p517), Jamaica

PROARTWORK / GETTY IMAGES ©

Pirates, Forts & Ruins

The Caribbean has a bounty of booty for pirate fans. Old forts and other crumbling ruins recall the days when sailing-ship dramas played out on the high seas.

Port Royal, Jamaica

A dilapidated, ramshackle place of tropical lassitude, today's funky fishing hamlet was once the pirate capital of the Caribbean. Later, it was the hub of British naval power in the West Indies. There are fascinating historic sites here, including old Fort Charles.

Old San Juan, Puerto Rico

Two Unesco World Heritage forts are a commanding presence in Old San Juan. Secrets and surprises wait around every ancient corner, all in the huge shadow of 16th-century El Morro (Fuerte San Felipe del Morro) and Fuerte San Cristóbal.

Brimstone Hill Fortress, St Kitts

More than 8000 French troops fought with 1000 British troops for a month in order to seize Brimstone Hill Fortress. This amazing Unesco World Heritage fort has views north, west and south across the Caribbean.

St Vincent

You can walk the very beaches and bay where much of the first *Pirates of the Caribbean* was filmed. Although the sets are fading away like old buccaneers, the small village and bay of Wallilabou is still recognizable.

Île-à-Vache, Haiti

About 15km off the coast of Les Cayes, Île-à-Vache was the hideout in 1668 of Captain Morgan, the Welsh pirate who looted every Spanish galleon he saw. Today it's home to some good resorts.

BRENT BARNES / SHUTTERSTOCK ©

1. Diving in Little Cayman (p278) 2. Mayreau (p740), St Vincent & the Grenadines 3. Anegada (p284), British Virgin Islands 4. Male frigate bird (p115), Barbuda

Hidden Caribbean

While more than 90% of the Caribbean's 7000 islands are minute and uninhabited, these are largely inaccessible to the average traveler. But there is a small club of islands well off the tourist track that are *almost* uninhabited, offering the adventurous traveler the kind of escape many dream about.

Little Cayman

Little Cayman has a population that barely cracks three figures – and that's the iguanas. Come here for some of the world's best wall diving.

Mayreau

A double crescent of perfect beaches awaits on Mayreau, an island near the southern end of the Grenadines. The killer diving at Tobago Cays is nearby and it's possible to rent a room in a home.

Anegada

The nicknames of Anegada say it all: 'Mysterious Virgin' and 'Ghost Cay.' Hang your hammock in this magical, remote bit of sand in the British Virgin Islands.

Barbuda

Frigate birds outnumber humans on Barbuda, an island that's happy to remain in the shadow of Antigua. Some beach cottages can only be reached by boat.

Petit Martinique

Grenada itself isn't exactly on the beaten path, and its island of Petit Martinique is almost unknown. The little beach here is just 10 minutes by foot from the guesthouses serving the island.

Martinique

POP 396,000 / ☑596

Best &Places to Eat

➡ La Cave à Vins (p560)

➡ New Cap (p564)

➡ 1643 (p573)

➡ Le Guérin (p573)

➡ Cocoa Beach Cafe (p575)

Best Places to Sleep

➡ Domaine Saint Aubin (p573)

➡ L'Anse Bleue (p564)

➡ Maison Rousse (p572)

➡ Hotel Bakoua (p563)

➡ Hotel Simon (p559)

Why Go?

Volcanic in origin, Martinique is a mountainous stunner crowned by the still-smoldering Mont Pelée, the volcano that wiped out the former capital of St-Pierre in 1902. Offering a striking diversity of landscapes and atmospheres, Martinique is a cosmopolitan and sophisticated island that boasts stunning beaches, superb hiking, top-notch culinary experiences, an enormous array of activities and rich cultural life.

While it suffers from overcrowding and urban sprawl in some places, particularly in and around the busy capital, Fort-de-France, life – and travel – becomes more sedate as one heads north or south through some of the island's alluring scenery. The rainforested, mountainous northern part is the most spectacular, but the south has its fair share of natural wonders, including lovely bays and miles of gorgeous beaches. Add to this a dash of Gallic joie de vivre and you'll understand why so many people love Martinique.

When to Go

Dec–May The dry season, and the busiest time of the year, although Martinique enjoys a year-round tropical climate. Expect the island to be crowded with French holidaymakers and hotel costs to be at a premium.

Jun–Nov The rainy season with heavy showers most days. September is the rainiest month and, along with August, is most prone to hurricanes – these are the better times to avoid Martinique.

Oct–May The best months for diving, although most dive schools run trips year-round.

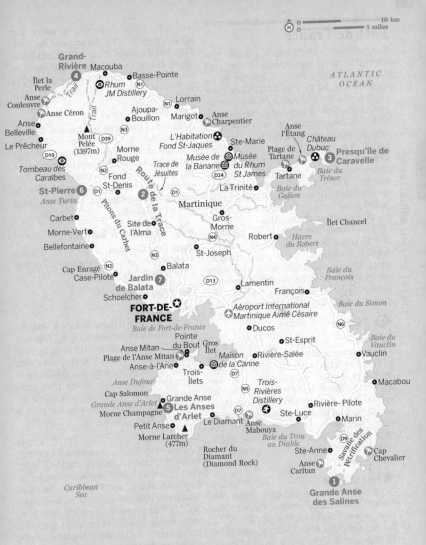

Martinique Highlights

1 Grande Anse des Salines (p568) Swimming and sunning yourself at one of the island's most beautiful beaches.

2 Route de la Trace (p571) Driving the scenic road through the center of the island, stopping for a walk in the foothills of Mont Pelée.

3 Presqu'île de Caravelle (p574) Soaking up the sun and sand by day and the gourmet flavors by night.

4 Grand-Rivière (p573) Hiking the dramatic 20km trail along Martinique's pristine and dramatic northern coast.

5 Les Anses d'Arlet (p565) Enjoying a day on the

beach at a gorgeous cove in southwestern Martinique.

6 St-Pierre (p570) Seeing the devastation of Mont Pelée first hand in the former capital, .

7 Jardin de Balata (p560) Putting your botanist's hat on and exploring this excellent botanical garden.

Fort-de-France

Fort-de-France, Martinique's capital, has undergone immense change in the past decade. Beginning the 21st century as an economically backward, dilapidated kind of place, the city has very successfully reinvented itself as a cruise-ship destination, with the construction of two impressive new terminals. More than that, Fort-de-France has rejuvenated its central park, given a coat of paint to many of its buildings and enhanced itself with several pieces of modern architecture. All this has served to breathe fresh life into the largest city in the French West Indies, and cruisers and travelers alike now flock to the place.

The obvious attraction is the fabulous Fort St-Louis, from which the city takes it name. Less obvious is the rich and engaging street life, the ubiquitous music and some excellent eating options. Even if you've come to Martinique for the beaches, you'll be very glad to spend a day in Fort-de-France.

◎ Sights

La Savane
PARK

This gorgeous rectangular park is the heart of Fort-de-France, and after a huge makeover over the last several years, it's looking better than ever. As well as a hallowed central lawn that nobody walks on, there are all sorts of spaces here to sit and relax, plus a large strip of cafes, restaurants and bars along the park's western side, which serves as the city's main evening entertainment area.

★ Fort St-Louis
NOTABLE BUILDING

(☑0596-75-41-44; adult/child €8/4; ⊙9am-4pm Tue-Sat) The hulking fortress that gave the city its name lurks on the far side of La Savane and dates from 1640, although most of what stands today is the result of subsequent additions. After years of being closed to the public, Fort St-Louis is finally open to tours, and it's easily the top sight in town. Buy tickets and join tours at the Tourist Information Kiosk (p561) on La Savane.

Bibliothèque Schoelcher
NOTABLE BUILDING

(Rue de la Liberté; ⊙1-5:30pm Mon, 8:30am-5:30pm Tue-Thu, 8:30am-5pm Fri, 8:30am-noon Sat) **FREE** Fort-de-France's most visible landmark, the Bibliothèque Schoelcher is an elaborate, colorful building with a Byzantine dome and an interesting ornate interior. The library was built in Paris and displayed at the 1889 World Exposition. It was then dismantled, shipped in pieces to Fort-de-France and reassembled in its current location.

☞ Tours

A variety of tours can be arranged through Fort-de-France's tourist office (p561). The offerings include a walk through the town's history, a tour of the area's churches, and a bus trip to nearby waterfalls and tropical gardens. The tourist office can also help to arrange English-speaking guides for hikes around the island.

✯✯ Festivals & Events

Mardi Gras Carnival
CARNIVAL

A spirited festival during the five-day period leading up to Ash Wednesday.

🛏 Sleeping

Hotel Hortensia
HOTEL $

(☑0596-60-29-59; 11 Rue de Redoute du Matouba; r with/without bathroom €48/40; ❄ 🛜) This very simple hotel is the cheapest place to lay your head in Fort-de-France. The six rooms with private facilities are only marginally more expensive than the six rooms that share bathrooms. Don't expect an overwhelmingly friendly welcome, but otherwise this place is fine for a night.

L'Impératrice
HOTEL $$

(☑0596-63-06-82; www.limperatricehotel.fr; 15 Rue de la Liberté; r €105-140, ste €160; ❄ 🛜) Central and with a sleek art-deco facade, the Impératrice is a local landmark almost as famous for its downstairs cafe as its upstairs hotel. All 23 rooms are excellent, with laminate floors, dark-wood furniture, sparkling bathrooms and all modern comforts. Ask for a room on the upper floors; if you can, go for room 53, which has the best views.

Fort Savane
BUSINESS HOTEL $$

(☑0596-80-75-75; www.fortsavane.fr; Rue de la Liberté; r/studio/ste €110/130/180; ❄ 🛜) Despite what we can only describe as a frosty welcome (you need to be buzzed into the hotel as you would an apartment building and staff seem rather unnecessarily suspicious), this place is excellent value, superbly located and rather stylish. All rooms come with espresso makers and rather minimalist furnishings, while studios have kitchens and suites have kitchens and lounges.

Fort-de-France

Fort-de-France

◉ Top Sights
1 Fort St-Louis.................................... C4

◉ Sights
2 Bibliothèque Schoelcher C2
3 La Savane C3

🛏 Sleeping
4 Fort Savane C3
5 Hotel Hortensia C2
6 Hotel Simon A3
7 L'Impératrice C3

🍴 Eating
8 Hasta la Pizza B3

La Baie .... (see 8)
9 La Cave à Vins A2
10 Le Vieux Foyal B3
11 Le Yellow B3

🍷 Drinking & Nightlife
12 Black Pearl B3

✪ Entertainment
13 Croisière Bar A3
14 Tropiques Atrium D2

🛍 Shopping
15 Cour Perrinon B2

★ **Hotel Simon**　　　　BUSINESS HOTEL $$$
(☎0596-50-22-22; www.hotel-simon.com; Ave Loulou Boilaville; r from €240; ❄ 🖥) This impressive hotel next to the cruise terminal opened its doors in 2016 and overnight raised the stakes in the Fort-de-France hotel market. The pricey rooms all boast espresso machines and flat-screen TVs, and are gorgeous, spacious and furnished with an appreciation of minimalist aesthetics. Public

JARDIN DE BALATA

Just 10km outside of Fort-de-France, **Jardin de Balata** (📞0596-64-48-73; www.jardindebalata.fr; Rte de la Trace; adult/child €13.50/7.50; ⊗9am-6pm (last admission 4:30pm); 🅿️ 🚹), a mature botanical garden in a rainforest setting, is one of Martinique's best attractions and will please anyone with even a passing interest in botany. The hour-long walk around the garden is clearly marked, and a series of tree walks will keep kids interested. An audioguide in English is available.

To get there from Fort-de-France, take a taxi (€15, 20 minutes) or a suburban bus (€1.50, 20 minutes) from Rue André Aliker.

areas are similarly impressive, making this a cool oasis away from the city.

✗ Eating

Hasta la Pizza
PIZZA $

(Rue de la Liberté; pizza €8-20; ⊗9am-10:30pm Mon-Sat, 4-11pm Sun; 🛜) This friendly pizzeria has a prime seafront location and always seems to be busy with people crowding around its roadside tables and waiting for takeout. The pizza is delicious and cooked in a wood-fired oven. This place is indispensable on Sunday evenings, when it's one of the few places open at all.

★ Le Vieux Foyal
CREOLE $$

(📞0596-77-05-49; 22 Rue Garnier Pagès; mains €14-20; ⊗10am-3pm & 7-10pm Mon-Sat; ❄️) Brimming with good cheer, this restaurant in a street running parallel to the seafront is that easy-to-miss 'secret spot' that local gourmands like to recommend. Everything is fresh and tasty – unfussy market cuisine at its best. Its plant-filled patio at the back is a haven of peace. Live dinnertime jazz on Thursday cranks the hip atmosphere up a notch.

Le Yellow
FRENCH $$

(📞0596-75-03-59; www.the-yellow.fr; 51 Rue Victor Hugo; ⊗noon- 3pm & 7-11pm Mon-Fri, 7-11pm Sat; ❄️✎) Charm, warmth and conviviality rarely seen elsewhere in Fort-de-France are the main draws to this 1st floor restaurant, where a small but delightful and regularly changing menu of French-Creole specialties

includes such dishes as sea-urchin risotto with squash and black mushrooms or conch stew with coconut milk. Reservations are normally essential.

La Baie
CREOLE, BRETON $$

(📞0596-42-20-38; Rue de la Liberté; mains €18-25; ⊗noon-2.30pm & 6-11pm Mon-Sat; 🛜) This friendly place is run by a native from Brittany and enjoys an intimate 1st-floor dining room with sea and park views. The menu, which stretches from seafood and fish to delicious galettes (savory crepes made with buckwheat flour), is enticing day or night. Book ahead for the evening.

★ La Cave à Vins
FRENCH $$$

(📞0596-70-33-02; 124 Rue Victor Hugo; mains €20-26; ⊗noon-3pm & 6-10pm Tue-Sat; 🛜) This charming little place is the smartest dinner address in Fort-de-France, serving up a small menu of elaborate main dishes (such as veal rib, lamb rack or duck breast cooked in a honey sauce), a superb wine list (for which the restaurant is rightly named), and a warm and convivial atmosphere. Book ahead.

🍷 Drinking & Nightlife

Fort-de-France is a lively place after dark. The seafront is full of bars, particularly toward the Pointe Simon part of town, and these are busiest when there's a cruise ship or two in port. Most locals head to La Savane to spend the cool evenings watching impromptu musical performances, including some incredible drumming displays. Plenty of kiosks here sell beer, wine and cocktails until around 1am.

Black Pearl
BAR

(36 Rue Ernest Deproge; ⊗8am-1am) This ever-busy seafront place has a popular restaurant, but it's mostly employed as a bar and gets quite rowdy at weekends. With tables outside on the street as well as inside, it's probably the buzziest place in Fort-de-France for some beers.

☆ Entertainment

★ Tropiques Atrium
CULTURAL CENTER

(📞0596-70-79-29; www.tropiques-atrium.fr; 6 Rue Jacques Cazotte; ⊗9am-7pm Tue-Fri, 10am-1pm Sat; 🛜) This superb cultural center runs an interesting program of indie films and documentaries, and hosts theatrical and musical shows in its state-of-the-art auditoriums. There's a pleasant cafe-bar-restaurant here, too, and it's definitely the best place in town to pick up on cultural and artistic events. Check the website for the current program.

Croisière Bar
LIVE MUSIC

(cnr Rues Ernest Deproge & Isambert; ⊘noon-11pm; 🐾) This spacious restaurant and bar has a live band on Friday and Saturday evenings, and sometimes during the week when there are cruise ships in town. It's certainly one of the best places to hear live music in Fort-de-France.

🛍 Shopping

The busy streets of downtown Fort-de-France are crammed with shops selling all manner of trinkets, clothing, jewelry and perfumes. The main boutique area is along Rue Victor Hugo, particularly from Rue de la République to Rue de la Liberté. The large **Cour Perrinon** (Rue Perrinon; ⊘8am-6pm Mon-Sat) shopping mall has some of the best shops in town, with the extra attraction of air-con.

ℹ Information

MEDICAL SERVICES

CHU de Martinique (Centre Hospitalier Universitaire de Martinique; ☑0596-55-20-00; www.chu-martinique.fr; Ave Zobda Quitman)

Pharmacie Glaudon (cnr Rues de la Liberté & Antoine Siger; ⊘7:30am-6pm Mon-Fri, 7:30am-noon Sat)

MONEY

Banks with ATMs are easy to find in the center, while money can be changed at **Change Caraïbes** (4 Rue Ernest Deproge; ⊘8am-5:30pm Mon-Fri, to 12:30pm Sat).

POLICE

Police Station (Rue Victor Sevère; ⊘24hr)

POST

Main Post Office (cnr Rues Antoine Siger & de la Liberté; ⊘7am-6pm Mon-Fri, to noon Sat)

TOURIST INFORMATION

Tourist Office (☑0596-60-27-73; www.tour-ismefdf.com; 76 Rue Lazare Carnot; ⊘8am-5pm Mon-Fri, 9am-noon Sat) Has some useful brochures in English on activities and accommodations, and can arrange English-language walking tours.

Tourist Information Kiosk (La Savanne; ⊘8am-5pm Mon-Sat) Behind tinted, possibly bulletproof glass lurks an employee of the tourist office who can give out maps and sells tickets to **Fort St-Louis**.

ℹ Getting There & Away

The **Aéroport International Martinique Aimé Césaire** (p580) is just a 15-minute drive from Fort-de-France. Taxis are readily available at the airport (about €30 to Fort-de-France).

BOAT

There are boats from Fort-de-France to Trois-Îlets, Anse Mitan, Anse à l'Ane and Pointe du Bout. The ferries dock at the quay fronting the minibus parking lot.

Vedettes Tropicales (☑0596-63-06-46; www.vedettestropicales.com; Blvd Alfassa; ⊘8am-6pm) runs multiple daily ferries between Fort-de-France's **ferry terminal** (⊘24hrs) and the resort towns of Trois-Îlets (€5), Pointe du Bout (€5), Anse Mitan (€2.50) and Anse à l'Ane (€2.50). See the website for exact schedules, as they change according to season. All trips are approximately 20 to 30 minutes long.

Cruise ships dock at either **Pointe Simon** (Rue des Caraïbes; ⊘24hr) or Quai des Tourelles.

BUS

The busy main **bus station** (Blvd Alfassa; ⊘24hrs) is on Rue de la Pointe Simon, from where *taxis collectifs* (privately run minivans) fan out to every town on the island. It's a well-organized place – each stand has the name of the town or towns it serves and normally a waiting bus that will leave when full. Most destinations are served at least hourly during daylight hours. There are very few services after 5pm and none on Sundays. Pay the driver.

Sample fares from Fort-de-France:

DESTINATION	COST (€)	DURATION (MIN)
Carbet	4.10	35
Diamant	6.20	45
Grand-Rivière	11.20	75
St-Pierre	4.80	45
Ste-Anne	8.80	60
Tartane	4.10	50
Trois-Îlets	2.90	30

For buses to Morne Rouge (€2.50, 45 mins) and the Jardin de Balata (€1.50, 20 minutes), head to Rue André Aliker south of the Parc Floral in Fort-de-France; they leave every 30 minutes during the day, Monday to Saturday.

Southern Martinique

Martinique's south has by far the best beaches and is definitely the island's center of gravity for tourism. Those looking for a straightforward beach holiday should head to Ste-Anne's beaches, probably the best on the island. Those who have their own transportation should consider basing themselves in Diamant or Ste-Luce, both of which have several good beaches within easy driving distance and some great eating options nearby.

The largest concentration of places to stay is in the greater Trois-Îlets area, which encompasses the busy resort town of Pointe du Bout. While there are some lovely stretches of beach and plenty of activities on offer here, this is also as touristy as Martinique gets. A far more charming and less heavily trafficked alternative are the gorgeous coves and tranquil villages of Les Anses d'Arlet, which remain pleasingly undeveloped and retain a calm, local feel even in high season.

Trois-Îlets

Directly across the bay from Fort-de-France is the commune of Trois-Îlets, which includes several distinct towns and villages. First of all, there's Trois-Îlets itself, a historic town that retains quite a bit of charm and is well known as the birthplace of Marie Josèphe Rose Tascher de la Pagerie, later Empress Josephine of France through her marriage to Napoléon Bonaparte. Her childhood plantation home is now an interesting museum.

Also here is Pointe du Bout, Martinique's most developed resort, home to the island's most-frequented yachting marina and to some of its largest hotels. There are some good beaches here, but you'll be sharing them with some serious crowds. Overall it's a popular place for a beach holiday, and a great base for families, though many travelers will prefer to explore other spots on the coast to find a true Caribbean vibe.

◉ Sights

Maison de la Canne   MUSEUM
(Sugarcane Museum; ☑0596-68-32-04; Rte de Trois-Îlets; adult/child €3/1; ☉8:30am-5:30pm Tue-Thu, 8:30am-5pm Fri & Sat, 9am-5pm Sun; ℗) This museum occupies the site of an old sugar refinery and rum distillery, and tells the fascinating and sad story of Martinique through the history of the slave trade, colonialism and eventual emancipation. Inside the main building are period photos and items such as the Code Noir, which outlined appropriate conduct between slaves and their owners. Displays are in French and English, though the English texts are significantly less detailed than the French ones.

Musée de la Pagerie   MUSEUM
(☑0596-68-38-34; Quartier Pagerie; adult/child €5/2; ☉9am-4:30pm Tue-Sun, 9:30am-2:30pm Sat & Sun; ℗) This former sugar estate was the birthplace of Marie Josèphe Rose Tascher de la Pagerie, the future Empress Josephine. A picturesque stone building, formerly the family kitchen, has been turned into a museum containing Josephine's childhood bed and other memorabilia. Other buildings contain such things as the Bonaparte family chart, old sugarcane equipment and love letters to Josephine from Napoléon.

🏃 Activities & Tours

Schéhérazade   BOATING
(☑0696-39-45-55; www.scheherazade.fr; Marina de la Pointe du Bout; half-day tours adult/child €50/30) This company runs boat tours to the superb Rocher du Diamant (p564), allowing you to swim on the reef, see a cave of bats and just get up close to this amazing but hard-to-reach place. It also runs dolphin-watching trips that come highly recommended. Tours include snacks and drinks.

Dauphins Martinique   DOLPHIN-WATCHING
(☑0696-02-02-22, 0596-76-89-78; www.dauphin-martinique.com; Marina de la Pointe du Bout; half-day tours adult/child €55/35) ⊘ This reputable outfit runs small-group dolphin-watching trips with environmental awareness and with minimal impact on the animals. Trips include a swimming/snorkeling stop.

TOURS DE LA MARTINIQUE

If you like your holidays with a healthy dose of competition, don't miss these island-wide racing events.

Tour des Yoles Rondes (www.yoles-rondes.net) Weeklong race of traditional sailboats in late July/early August.

Tour Cycliste de la Martinique (www.cyclismemartinique.com) Weeklong bicycle race in mid-July.

Fort-de-France Semi-Marathon A 22km half-marathon around the city is held in November.

Espace Plongée DIVING
(📞0596-66-01-79; www.epm972.fr; Marina de la Pointe du Bout) This outfit offers morning and afternoon dives every day and, if enough people want to go, night dives. It's located right beside the water in the marina and English is spoken. Introductory dives cost €60, normal ones €55.

Attitude Plongée DIVING, SNORKELING
(📞0696-72-59-28; www.attitudeplongee.com; Marina de la Pointe du Bout) Right in the heart of Pointe du Bout, this diving outfit charges €65 for an introductory dive and €50 for a single dive.

Héliblue HELICOPTER TOURS
(📞0596-66-10-80; www.heliblue.com; Domaine Château Gaillard, Trois-Îlets) This helicopter tour operator offers a range of aerial journeys around Martinique from the Domaine Château Gaillard heliport near Trois-Îlets. Prices range from €34 per person for a six-minute flight to €195 per person for a tour around Mont Pelée.

🛏 Sleeping

Most of Trois-Îlets' hotels and resorts are concentrated in and around the Pointe du Bout area and tend to be rather closely packed-together, large hotels popular with package tourists. While they are decent value and have plenty of facilities, they will be unlikely to appeal to independent travelers.

Le Panoramic Hotel HOTEL $$
(📞0596-68-78-48; www.lepanoramic.fr; Anse à l'Ane; d incl breakfast from €144; ❄🛜⛱) This hillside hotel in Anse à l'Ane, a few kilometers west from Trois-Îlets, has a stunning location with views over the bay and a gorgeous tropical-garden setting. The 36 fully equipped rooms are brightly furnished, sharing a simple but comfortable style; be sure to ask for a room with a sea view. There's a good beach nearby.

Hotel Bakoua RESORT $$$
(📞0596-66-02-02; www.hotel-bakoua.fr; Pointe du Bout; d incl breakfast from €185; ❄🛜⛱) Perched on a hillside, this resort features 132 units of varying sizes and shapes. They are comfortably furnished (the best of the lot are right on the beach), and have a minimalist, contemporary vibe. Guests have access to a small artificial beach which comes complete with water-sports

equipment, as well as an infinity pool with incredible views.

🍴 Eating & Drinking

Pointe du Bout's marina is the place to head for nightlife, with several cocktail bars, live-music venues and pubs by the waterfront. You won't find anything much more than this, save the odd party in the high season – ask around at your hotel and the marina.

Baguet Shop BAKERY $
(Rue Cha-Cha, Pointe du Bout; sandwiches €4-7; ⏰6:30am-7:30pm; 🛜) This simple places does tasty sandwiches made to order, great coffee and mouthwatering pastries that will make you think you're in Paris. It has seating available, including tables outside. A good option for breakfast or a quick lunch.

★La Mandoline FRENCH $$
(📞0596-69-48-38; www.poterie-village.fr; Le Village de la Poterie, Rte de Trois-Îlets; mains €17-26; ⏰noon-2.30pm Tue-Sat, 7.30-10pm Fri & Sat; 🛜) Inside this adorable complex of shops and restaurants, about 1km down a dirt road from the main road, is the most charming restaurant in Trois-Îlets. Choose between sitting outside surrounded by greenery, or inside the historic building's cozy dining room, before sampling the famous piña colada and then perusing the refined gourmet-style traditional French cooking on the menu.

ℹ Information

There's an **Otitour** (L'Office du Tourisme de Trois-Îlets; 📞0596-68-47-63; Rue Cha-Cha; ⏰8am-1pm & 2-5pm Mon-Fri, 9am-1pm Sat) tourism kiosk by the marina.

ℹ Getting There & Away

Trois-Îlets is served by regular ferries (€5, 20 minutes) from Fort-de-France, which makes getting to this part of Martinique a doddle. Ferries are run by **Vedettes Tropicales** (p561) and also serve Pointe du Bout (€5, 20 minutes), Anse Mitan (€2.50, 25 minutes) and Anse à l'Ane (€2.50, 30 minutes).

There are also regular bus connections between both Trois-Îlets and Pointe du Bout and Fort-de-France (€2, 40 mins). In Trois-Îlets buses stop by the town square. In Pointe du Bout they stop on Rue des Bougainvilliers, near the marina.

MARTINIQUE SOUTHERN MARTINIQUE

Le Diamant

Le Diamant, both a town and a commune, is one of the most scenic destinations in southern Martinique, although there's no real center here as things are scattered along about 2km of sandy, wave-tossed shore and in the hills immediately behind. For visitors, this seaside town is a good base to explore the western horn of the island. It's also an obvious launching pad for the superb dive sites located around Le Rocher du Diamant, while the haunting Anse Cafard Slave Memorial gives some much-needed historical perspective on Martinique's brutal colonial history.

◎ Sights

★ Rocher du Diamant   NATURAL FEATURE
This extraordinary-looking 176m-high volcanic islet that's just under a mile offshore from the village of Le Diamant is a very popular dive site, with interesting cave formations but tricky water conditions. Various companies also organize boat excursions that take in the islet – don't miss your chance to get close to this natural wonder.

Plage du Diamant   BEACH
This beautiful stretch of white sand extends for 2km to the west of Le Diamant. Swimming is not recommended as the waves can be very strong, but it's the picture-perfect place for sunbathing, beachcombing, having a picnic lunch or simply enjoying the view of nearby Rocher du Diamant.

Anse Cafard Slave Memorial   MEMORIAL
(Anse Cafard; ⊙24hr) This haunting memorial overlooking the sea and Le Rocher du Diamant in the distance depicts a mass of formless humanity in stone. It commemorates the fate of the scores of slaves who lost their lives in a shipwreck off the coast here in 1830, and more generally, the tens of thousands of enslaved Africans who were taken to Martinique as part of the trans-atlantic slave trade.

Musée des Coquillages et de la Mer   MUSEUM
(☑0596-76-41-92; Hotel l'Ecrin Bleu, Morne La Croix; adult/child €5/3; ⊙9am-6pm; ℗) Just north of Le Diamant's center, the long-running Musée des Coquillages et de la Mer shelters hard-to-find shells gathered by collectors over centuries from different beaches around the world, including specimens from Japan in the 1760s and South Africa in the 1880s. It's a must for anyone keen on the sea and its majestic creatures.

🏃 Activities

Antilles Sub Diamond Rock   DIVING
(☑0596-76-10-65, 0696-82-14-35; www.plongee-martinique.fr; Port de Pêche Départemental de la Taupinière) A small outfit capably managed by a French couple, it's known for friendly service and small groups. Has introductory dives (€60), three-dive packages (€135), certification courses and snorkeling trips.

🛏 Sleeping

There are a few independently run guesthouses in Le Diamant, which stand out far more than the many larger, far-less-enticing resorts along the coast.

★ L'Anse Bleue   BUNGALOW $$
(☑0596-76-21-91; www.hotel-anse-bleue.com; La Dizac; d €70-95; ❈ 🐾 🖥 🏊) This place is very simple, but somehow manages to get things just right – there are 25 delightful bungalows (either one room or two) spread out across spacious grounds, a decent-sized pool, a superb on-site restaurant, friendly management and a peaceful location – all adding up to make this one of our favorite hotels in Martinique. It's a short walk to the beach.

Rêve Bleu   GUESTHOUSE $$
(Ecrin Bleu; ☑0596-76-41-92; www.ecrinbleu.com; Rte des Anses d'Arlet; d from €85; ℗❈🖥) This excellent-value place on the hillside overlooking Le Diamant has spacious, clean and well-equipped rooms, each of which comes with a large terrace that includes a kitchenette, making it a great choice for families. It's a short drive into town, so it's a good idea to have your own transport.

🍴 Eating

★ New Cap   INTERNATIONAL $$
(☑0596-76-12-99; Anse Cafard; mains €15-22; ⊙noon-3pm & 7-10pm Wed-Mon; 🖥) This beachfront restaurant with divine Rocher du Diamant views quite simply wins the popular vote and is always packed on the weekend. Choose from their 'legendary salads,' tapas, burgers and daily fish and seafood specials chalked up on the blackboard. A wonderful *tarte au citron* (lemon tart) will finish you

off sweetly. It's at Anse Cafard, 3km west of Le Diamant.

La Paillotte Bleue
FRENCH $$

(☑ 0596-58-33-21; La Dizac; mains €16-23; ⊙ 7:30-10pm; 🛜) Sublime poolside dining at this superb restaurant is a real treat. Located at L'Anse Bleue (but run separately to the hotel), La Paillotte Bleue serves up classic French dishes with a dash of Caribbean influence, such as a sautéed octopus cooked with aromatic herbs, or curried chicken. There's a good wine list and service is excellent.

Chez Lucie
CREOLE $$

(☑ 0596-76-40-10; 64 Rue Justin Roc; mains €15-28; ⊙ 11am-3pm & 6:45-10pm Mon & Wed-Sat, 11am-3pm Sun) There are few places in the world where the waves crash this close to your table, and Chez Lucie earns plaudits for being possibly the best place on the coast to watch the sea, especially on rougher days. The broad menu offers all sorts of tempting goodies, starting with codfish fritters, which you might follow with catch of the day.

ℹ️ Getting There & Away

Le Diamant can be reached by hourly bus from Fort-de-France's bus station (€4, 45 minutes). There is no service after dark or on Sundays. Buses stop in the center of Le Diamant next to the main roundabout.

Multiple buses run along the south coast and connect Le Diamant to its beaches and on to Les Anses d'Arlet (€2, 20 minutes) as well as to Ste-Luce (€1, 15 minutes) in the other direction.

Les Anses d'Arlet

Les Anses d'Arlet is without a doubt the most charming corner of southern Martinique, retaining as it does an undiscovered feel, some gorgeous scenery and wonderful beaches. The commune of Les Anses d'Arlet contains a string of villages, each named descriptively after its respective *anse* (cove): Grande Anse, Anse Noire, Anse Dufour and – confusingly – Anse d'Arlet Bourg, the administrative center of Les Anses d'Arlet. The villages are connected by a steep and winding coastal road from where there are superb glimpses down to the waves below.

Anse d'Arlet Bourg itself is crowned by an 18th-century Roman Catholic church whose doors open almost directly onto the beach, and the entire scene is framed with

steep, verdant hills. The next-door village of Grande Anse is set along a beachfront road lined with brightly painted boats and a string of restaurants, while lovely Anse Dufour and Anse Noire remain almost untouched by tourism.

◎ Sights

Plage Anse d'Arlet
BEACH

This gorgeous stretch of sand in front of Anse d'Arlet Bourg is backed by the village's 18th-century church and is one of the most lovely places to swim in Martinique. Further down there are a host of beach restaurants and bars, and it's rarely difficult to find your own spot on the plentiful golden sand.

Anse Dufour
BEACH

Approximately halfway between Anse Mitan and Grande Anse, a secondary road peels off the D7 and plunges straight to Anse Dufour 2km below. You'll be smitten by the mellow tranquility of this fishing hamlet, which has a golden-sand beach and a handful of Creole restaurants, though it's well known to local day-trippers, who come here in droves on the weekend.

Anse Noire
BEACH

If you're after an intimate, secluded strip of sand, head to lovely Anse Noire, which is reached by taking the side road to Anse Dufour and continuing around the hillside. This tiny, dreamlike cove lapped by jade waters offers a small patch of black sand studded with palm trees. Swimming and snorkeling are excellent.

🏃 Activities

L'Arlésienne
BOATING

(☑ 0696-82-54-41; http://baladesdelarlesienne. free.fr; Ave Robert Deloy, Grande Anse; half-/full-day tour €30/55) This operator offers an interesting tour that takes in the bays and coves between Grande Anse and Le Diamant. It's an ideal way to gain an overview of the coast's delights. There is a stop for a swim in a lovely little cove. Trips to northern Martinique can also be arranged.

Kayak de l'Anse Noire
KAYAKING

(☑ 0696-34-86-36; Anse Noire; 1hr €6, half-day €13, full day €20) This beachfront operation rents out kayaks, a great way to explore the nearby bays a gentle pace.

Alpha Plongée DIVING, SNORKELING
(☎ 0596-48-30-34, 0696-81-93-42; www.alpha-plongee.com; 138 Ave Robert Deloy, Grande Anse) This low-key diving venture specializes in small groups and offers an intimate feel to its aquatic adventures. Single-dive trips cost €45 while introductory dives are €50. Certification courses and dive packages are available. Also offers *randonnée palmée* (guided snorkeling tours; €20) and rents snorkeling gear (€10 per day).

Plongée Passion DIVING
(☎ 0596-68-71-78; www.plongeepassion.com; 1 Allée des Raisiniers, Grande Anse) On the beach, this friendly and well-known dive outfit offers morning and afternoon outings daily. A single dive, including equipment, costs €45.

🛏 Sleeping

By some incredible stroke of luck, Les Anses d'Arlet are still rather undeveloped, but this means they have hardly any provision for people who want to base themselves here. This, of course, also accounts for their continued charm, as nearly everyone who comes here is a day-tripper. Grande Anse and Anse d'Arlet Bourg both have small guesthouses where it's possible to stay.

Résidence Madinakay HOTEL $
(☎ 0596-68-70-76; 3 Allée des Arlésiens, Anse d'Arlet Bourg; d €58; ❉ 🕸) Right in the thick of things and just across the road from Anse d'Arlet Bourg's beach, this small hotel is excellent value for money given its prime location. The eight studios are fairly functional and not particularly exciting, but they are clean and equipped with all the necessary comforts.

Oukaé GUESTHOUSE $
(www.location-oukae.com; 3 Allée des Raisiniers, Grande Anse; d per week from €640; ❉ 🕸) One of the few guesthouses in Grande Anse, here you can only rent rooms by the week. However, as it's just moments from the beach and there's a whole roster of good restaurants nearby, it's a great choice as a Martinique base. The rooms come in various styles and sizes, but are all adorable timber-fronted huts with creature comforts included.

Résidences Colombier VILLA $$
(☎ 0596-68-63-38, 0696-80-51-52; Rue General de Gaulle, Anse d'Arlet Bourg; d from €80; ❉ 🕸) The kindly host here offers a number of apartments and gîtes (cottages) in the heart of Anse d'Arlet Bourg for families and couples, normally for rental by the week. They're very comfortable, have all been renovated recently and are just moments from the beach here. All in all, a superb place to base yourself.

🍴 Eating

There are plentiful eating possibilities along the Anse d'Arlet coast, most particularly in Grande Anse, which has a seafront full of wonderful little seafood restaurants right on the beach. Seafood is – of course – the name of the game here, and you're spoiled for choice about where to get it.

Au Dessous du Volcan CREOLE, SEAFOOD $
(☎ 0596-68-69-52; 79 Rue des Pêcheurs, Petite Anse; mains €12-20; ⏱ noon-3pm & 7-10pm Fri-Wed; 🕸) This attractive place serves up a very high standard of Creole food in a beautiful tropical garden. Order in advance for the signature dish: roast lobster flambéed in rum.

Bidjoul CREOLE $
(Ave Robert Deloy, Grande Anse; mains €8-18, set meals €14-20; ⏱ 10am-10pm; 🕸) This charming wooden house on the beach has a very reasonably priced menu, and serves up all the Creole favorites, as well as pizza. Best of all, it has tables on the sand and you can easily have a dip while you're waiting for your meal.

⭐ Ti Sable INTERNATIONAL $$
(☎ 0596-68-62-44; www.tisablemartinique.com; 35 Allée des Raisiniers, Grande Anse; mains €13-23; ⏱ noon-3pm & 7-10pm; 🕸) Head to this rather fabulous complex at the northern end of Grande Anse's beach for a lovely waterside-eating experience. The food (a scrumptious assortment of fish dishes, exotic salads and barbecued meats) is of very high quality and the setting is magical. On Sundays it lays on an excellent lunch buffet (€28) and there's live music in the evening.

Le P'ti Bateau SEAFOOD $$
(☎ 0596-53-17-35; 108 Ave Robert Deloy, Grande Anse; mains €15-35; 🕸) This great little beachside place in Grande Anse has loungers its guests can use on the beach out front, while inside is a great little seafood menu that includes a great-value set menu for kids (€8.50) or a rather more extravagant lobster

menu (€48). In between these you'll find local favorites such as conch fricassee and fish tartare.

Valy et Le Pêcheur
CREOLE $$

(☑ 0696-93-60-87; Anse d'Arlet Bourg; mains €10-22, menus €16-35; ⊗ noon-3pm Wed-Mon) This beachside kiosk is run by a dynamic crew who serve excellent local specialties, among them pork ribs, conch fricassee and braised chicken. Servings are large and this is definitely the pick of the bunch of beach shacks in Anse d'Arlet Bourg.

Ti Payot
CREOLE $$

(☑ 0596-69-07-38; http://plongeepassion.com/ti-payot; 1 Allée des Raisiniers, Grande Anse; mains €13-19; ⊗ 8am-7pm; 🛜) At this beautiful spot overlooking the water you can enjoy the waves running up under its wooden terrace as you eat. It's a lovely place for lunch (especially after a couple of dives with Plongée Passion, who run the restaurant) and there are always new chef's suggestions determined by what's been landed fresh each morning.

ℹ️ Getting There & Away

Buses connect Les Anses d'Arlet with Fort-de-France (€3.20, 50 minutes, every 30 minutes), passing through Le Diamant and Petite Anse beforehand. Buses simply run along the main coastal road and stop at several points in each village – wait at any bus stop.

A local minivan runs along the coastal road between Le Diamant and Trois-Îlets (€2, 30 minutes) and connects each village, though it only runs seven times a day in each direction during the week. It runs five times a day on Saturday and three times a day on Sunday.

Ste-Luce

This busy town is, in itself, not really worth visiting, but the stretch of hotels along the coast in the suburbs of Gros Raisin and Trois-Rivières keeps visitors coming, not to mention the historic Trois-Rivières Distillery, Martinique's most famous. The hotels are far enough away from the main road for you not to feel like you're living on a freeway, but close enough to make this a great base to explore the southern half of the island, with the lovely beaches at Ste-Anne and Les Anses d'Arlet both within easy reach for enjoyable day trips.

West of St-Luce's center, along the D7 that leads to Trois-Rivières, the coastline is dotted with a string of beaches – Anse Gros Raisin, Anse Corps de Garde, Anse Mabouya, among others. They aren't the most scenic, but for those staying in the area they provide a pleasant break and are rarely crowded.

🏃 Sights & Activities

Trois-Rivières Distillery
DISTILLERY

(☑ 0596-62-51-78; www.plantationtroisrivieres. com; Quartier Trois-Rivières; guided tour €3; ⊗ 9am-5:30pm Mon-Fri, to 1pm Sat) One of Martinique's oldest rum distilleries, this interesting place offers self-guided tours, with signs in English, starting from near the parking lot. However, as with all distilleries in Martinique, many of the 'exhibits' are actually on-site souvenir and snack shops. The guided tour (six daily) ends with a tasting at the rum boutique; it sells hard-to-find aged rums, but if you're just after normal rums you'll find them cheaper at most supermarkets.

Kawan Plongée
DIVING

(☑ 0696-76-58-69; http://sainteluce.kawanplongee.com; Blvd Kennedy) Éric, Cécile and their team welcome you to this friendly dive operator in the middle of Ste-Luce. Introductory dives cost €55, while a normal dive is €45, with numerous packages and courses available.

🛏️ Sleeping

Much of the accommodation in and around Ste-Luce is made up of rather unexciting, mass-market resorts, but there are a few gems.

Hotel Le Panoramique
HOTEL $

(☑ 0596-62-31-32; www.hotel-le-panoramique. com; Trois-Rivières; d from €75; ❄️🛜🏊) Just a little north of Le Verger de Ste-Luce, some way out of the town, this place is handy for access to the beach. Five of the 15 rooms have kitchenettes, not to mention the best views, though they also suffer from having a road right below them. There's a bar and restaurant on the property, too.

⭐ Ti' Paradis
B&B $$

(☑ 0696-96-39-40, 0596-62-78-20; www. ti-paradis-martinique.com; 69 Anse Gros Raisin, Ste-Luce; d incl breakfast €130-150; ❄️🛜🏊) Somewhere between a boutique hotel and B&B, Ti' Paradis harbors seven immaculate rooms that are furnished in muted earth tones and boast sparkling bathrooms as well as superb sea views. Laze on the shady terrace, lounge by the pool or step down to Gros Raisin beach just below. Evening meals are available by arrangement, but there is a two-night minimum.

Hotel Corail Résidence
HOTEL $$

(✆0596-62-11-01; www.hotelcorail.com; Anse Mabouya; d €125; ✳🛜≋) This is definitely one of the best spots to base yourself in Ste-Luce. It's supremely laid-back, and all 25 rooms have kitchenettes and little porches with amazing views of the bay. There's a great pool area and a top-notch on-site restaurant. It's also just a short stroll to the beach at Anse Mabouya, the best in town.

Le Verger de Ste-Luce
BUNGALOW $$

(✆0596-62-20-72; www.facebook.com/Vergerde SainteLuce; d/q €85/115; ✳🛜≋) For a warm welcome, look no further than this charming place. Bungalows surround a small pool with sun chairs and there's a stand-alone Jacuzzi – and the friendly owner loves to practice her English. The simple bungalows all have their own porch with a kitchenette, while a good amount of greenery keeps the small place feeling private.

✖ Eating

★ Le Mabouya
FRENCH, CREOLE $$

(www.hotelcorail.com/le-restaurant-le-mabouya; Hôtel Corail Résidence; mains €15-28; ⊙7-10pm daily, noon-2:30pm Sat & Sun; 🛜) This superb restaurant is one worth splurging on, with a fantastic and inventive French-Creole menu that is way more sophisticated than your average Martinique beach shack. Try signature dishes such as lobster ravioli, scallops with risotto or just the life-affirming crème brûlée. Reservations are a good idea.

La Pura Vida
CREOLE, FRENCH $$

(✆0596-53-89-35; http://restaurantpuravida.fr; Gros Raisin; ⊙noon-2pm Tue-Sun, 7-10pm Tue-Sat; 🛜) Combining French traditional cookery and locally available products, La Pura Vida is a stand-out addition to Ste-Luce's dining scene. Its premises alone are a breath of fresh air: a big airy terrace with attractive wooden tables and lounging sofas – this is also a great place for a cocktail. Choose your own lobster from the tank or just order the excellent conch stew.

Case Coco
FRENCH $$

(✆0596-62-32-26; 58 Rue Schoelcher; mains €18-25; ⊙noon-3pm Wed-Sun, 6:30-10pm Tue-Sun; ✳🛜) In a beautifully restored Creole house, this atmospheric establishment provides a winning combination of innovative French fare and tropical flair, and warmth and intimacy – not to mention an enviable position along the seafront promenade. Order the rum-flambé pork fillet if it's on the menu. Not a bad place for a romantic dinner.

❶ Getting There & Away

There are hourly buses between Fort-de-France and Ste-Luce throughout the day (€3.80, 1 hour). Buses in Ste-Luce stop at Place des Cocotiers, on Rue Anatole France. From here there are also half-hourly to hourly buses to Le Diamant (€1, 20 minutes) and Ste-Anne (€1.80, 45 minutes).

Ste-Anne

The southernmost town on Martinique, Ste-Anne has an attractive seaside setting with painted wooden houses, a lovely central square with a brightly painted stone church on one side and lots of good restaurants. Despite the large number of visitors that flock to the town on weekends and during the high season, Ste-Anne remains a casual, low-key place and never feels swamped by visitors.

For some serious sunbathing, make your way to Grande Anse des Salines, at the undeveloped southern tip of the island. There's also an excellent town beach with abundant near-shore reef formations that make for good snorkeling.

A 15-minute drive – and just 6km east as the crow flies – to the northeast transports you to yet another world, along the Atlantic-battered east coast. Here, around impressive Cap Chevalier, you'll find some great isolated beaches.

◎ Sights

★ Grande Anse des Salines
BEACH

Immense, crystalline and glossy, Grande Anse des Salines doesn't disappoint the bevy of swimmers who dabble in its gorgeous depths or the sun worshippers who lie out on the ribbon of golden sand. Les Salines gets its name from Etang des Salines, the large salt pond that backs it; it's about 5km south of Ste-Anne along the D9. There are food vans and snack shops along the beach, but otherwise it's wonderfully undeveloped, a slice of fabulously raw nature.

Pointe Marin
BEACH

Ste-Anne's most popular swimming beach is the long, lovely strand that stretches along the peninsula 800m north of the town center. It's backed by restaurants and bars, and though it can be quite crowded, the beach is long enough to be able to find a quiet spot on most occasions.

Anse Michel
BEACH

The steady winds that buff this part of the coast, mixed with the reef-sheltered lagoon, are the perfect combination for kitesurfing and windsurfing. This *anse* also offers excellent sunbathing and swimming opportunities.

🏃 Activities & Tours

⭐Taxi Cap
BOATING

(☎0696-45-44-60, 0596-76-93-10; www.taxi-cap.com; Cap Chevalier; full-day excursion adult/child €38/15) The best way to discover the lagoon, the nearby islets and the mangrove ecosystems around Ste-Anne is by joining a boat excursion. Taxi Cap runs a whole raft of these, and the return crossing to the Îlet Chevalier costs as little as €4. The classic full-day excursion costs €38 and includes lunch and a whole host of activities.

Alize Fun-Lagon Evasion
WATER SPORTS

(☎0696-91-71-06; www.alizefunkitemartinique.com; Cap Chevalier, Anse Michel) To brush up on your windsurfing or kitesurfing skills, or try a first lesson (from €95), contact this small outfit right on the beach. It also rents kayaks (€16 per hour) and can arrange guided kayak tours to nearby islets.

Natiyabel
OUTDOORS

(☎0696-36-63-01; http://plongee-martinique.fr; Bourg, Ste-Anne) This well-run dive center organizes a variety of dive trips and certification. Introductory/single dives cost €50/45. Snorkeling is €15. Kayaks are available for rent (€15 per half-day).

🛏 Sleeping

Salines Studio
HOTEL $

(☎0596-76-82-81, 0596-76-90-92; salinestudios@hotmail.fr; 7 Rue J-M Tjibaou, Ste-Anne; d €70-80; ❄️🅿️) Salines Studio is dependable, low-key and quiet. It resembles a typical motel and would best suit budget travelers looking for kitchenette studios. It's in the center of the village, so has easy access to local services and transport.

⭐Airstream Paradise
CARAVAN PARK $$

(☎0696-19-86-76; www.airstreamparadise.fr; Pointe Marin; d/q from €89/119; ❄️🅿️) This park, right on Pointe Marin beach, has a collection of revamped Airstream luxury trailers, which can accommodate between two and four people. Each Airstream includes an outdoor Jacuzzi, an espresso machine, a grill and a flat-screen TV. Management is proactive and friendly, and it's great for kids. Definitely a unique approach to a caravan holiday in Martinique!

🍴 Eating

⭐Otantik
CREOLE $$

(☎0696-08-40-26; Rue Frantz Fanon; mains €12-19; ⏱noon-3pm & 6-10pm Wed-Sun; 🅿️) We love this hilltop shack with dazzling sea views, where seasonal ingredients are paired with the catch of the day and a small, great-value and wonderfully tasty menu is newly created each day. There's more than a slight hippyish air, and vegetarians are well provided for. Try the excellent mix-plates and don't miss the plantain salad, the house specialty.

⭐Les Tamariniers
CREOLE, FRENCH $$

(☎0596-76-75-62; 30 Rue Abbé Saffache; mains €14-30, menus €20-35; ⏱noon-2pm & 7-9:30pm Thu-Tue; ❄️) Definitely the best in town, this friendly place has a varied menu of Creole food and French specialties. Be sure to sample the rum flambé shrimp on a kebab, and if you're really pushing the boat out, order the full seafood grill, which at €93 for two people should keep you going for a while.

Basilic Beach
SEAFOOD $$

(☎0696-32-67-92; Pointe Marin; mains €14-23; ⏱noon-3pm Tue-Sun) This wooden shack overlooks the water between Ste-Anne and Pointe Marin beach, and also has a pleasant seating area on a grassy knoll for the perfect lunch by the sea. Food is typical of Martinique: *acras* (deep-fried balls of dough filled with fish or shrimp), tuna tartare, catch of the day and conch are all on the menu, as is a superb basil mojito.

Le Coco Neg'
CREOLE $$

(☎0596-76-94-82; 4 Rue Abbé-Hurard; mains €14-25; ⏱7pm-midnight Mon-Sat; ❄️) This traditional Caribbean spot near the church serves up wonderful home-cooked Creole cuisine in a brightly painted dining room, where eating feels rather like being a guest in someone's home. It gets lively on Friday evenings when meals are followed by Creole tunes to shake your body to.

🍷 Drinking & Nightlife

La Dunette BAR
(☑0596-76-73-90; www.ladunette.com; Rue J-M Tjibaou, Ste-Anne; ⊙noon-11pm; 🛜) In the center of town, this hotel restaurant is one of the best spots to grab a drink. The location alone – a wooden deck and a pontoon overlooking the water – guarantees memorable sunset cocktails. There's live music on Thursday, Friday and Saturday evenings.

ℹ Information

Tourist Office (☑0596-76-73-45; www.sainteanne-martinique.fr; Ave Frantz Fanon; ⊙8:30am-1.30pm Mon-Fri)

ℹ Getting There & Away

Buses run between Fort-de-France and Ste-Anne roughly every hour during daylight hours (€4, one hour 15 minutes). There are also half-hourly local buses running along the coast to Ste-Luce (€2.20, 45 minutes). Ste-Anne's **Gare Routière** (Rue Abbé Saffache) is in the center of town.

Northern Martinique

Northern Martinique is the side of the island that few travelers see. Rugged, windswept and mountainous, it contains much of the island's most impressive scenery and best hiking opportunities, including its trump card, massive Mont Pelée, the semi-active volcano that has profoundly shaped both Martinique's geology and history.

Unlike the south, this is not a region known for its beaches, though there are a few terrific ones here if you know where to look. This absence means that there are no resorts, and consequently far fewer tourists than you'll find down south. With fantastically scenic landscapes such as that of the Presqu'île de Caravelle and Grand Rivière, not to mention the historic charm of St-Pierre, it's easy to see why northern Martinique is for Caribbean connoisseurs.

St-Pierre

Packed full of Caribbean charm, St-Pierre is undoubtedly one of Martinique's loveliest towns, with a tranquil azure bay backed by steamy rainforest on the mountainside behind it. Full of colonial-era buildings, St-Pierre also boasts an attractive dark-gray sand beach and the perfect location for superb sunsets.

What's hard to believe amid all this tranquility is that St-Pierre was once Martinique's capital and at one point perhaps the most cosmopolitan city in the entire Caribbean. That all ended abruptly on May 8, 1902, when Mont Pelée erupted and wiped out the town (and some 30,000 of its inhabitants) in just 10 minutes, leaving just three survivors. Unsurprisingly St-Pierre has never recovered from the tragedy. The capital was moved to Fort-de-France and St-Pierre became the sleepy seaside village you see today. Whether you come for its dark history or its laid-back, rather agreeable present, St-Pierre is a treat.

◉ Sights

Ruins RUINS
(Rue Bouillé) St-Pierre's most impressive ruins are those of the old 18th-century theater. While most of the theater was destroyed, enough remains to give a sense of the former grandeur of this building, which once seated 800 and hosted theater troupes from mainland France. On the northeast side of the theater you can enter the tiny, thick-walled jail cell that housed Louis-Auguste Cyparis, one of the town's three survivors. Another area rich in ruins is the Quartier du Figuier, also along Rue Bouillé.

Musée Volcanologique et Historique MUSEUM
(Musée Frank A Perret; ☑0596-78-15-16; Rue Victor Hugo; adult/child €5/2; ⊙9am-5pm Mon-Sat; P) This small but very interesting museum, founded in 1932 by American adventurer and volcanologist Frank Perret, gives a glimpse of the devastating 1902 eruption of Mont Pelée. On display are items plucked from the rubble and historic photos of the town before and immediately after the eruption.

Zoo de Martinique ZOO
(Habitation Latouche; ☑0596-52-76-08; www.zoodemartinique.com; Anse Latouche; adult/child €15.50/9; ⊙9am-6pm; 🐾) This former botanical garden on the southern outskirts of St-Pierre has undergone an impressive transformation and is now an excellent privately run zoo. Set within the ruins of

ROUTE DE LA TRACE

The Route de la Trace (known more prosaically on maps as the N3) winds up into the mountains north from Fort-de-France. It's a beautiful drive through a lush rainforest of tall tree ferns, anthurium-covered hillsides and thick clumps of roadside bamboo. The road passes along the eastern flanks of the volcanic mountain peaks of the Pitons du Carbet. Several well-marked hiking trails lead from the Route de la Trace into the rainforest and up to the peaks.

The road follows a route cut by the Jesuits in the 17th century: the Trace de Jésuites. Islanders like to say that the Jesuits' fondness for rum accounts for the twisting nature of the road.

Less than a 10-minute drive north of Fort-de-France, in the village of Balata, is **Sacré-Coeur de Balata,** a scaled-down replica of the Sacré-Coeur Basilica in Paris. This domed church, in the Roman-Byzantine style, has a stunning hilltop setting – the Pitons du Carbet rise up as a backdrop, and there's a view across Fort-de-France to Pointe du Bout below.

On the west side of the N3, 10 minutes' drive north of the Balata church, is the **Jardin de Balata** (p560), a mature botanical garden in a rainforest setting. After the garden, the N3 winds up into the mountains and reaches an elevation of 600m before dropping down to Site de l'Alma, where a river runs through a lush gorge. There are riverside picnic tables, trinket sellers and a couple of short trails into the rainforest.

Beyond Site de l'Alma, Route de la Trace passes banana plantations and flower nurseries before reaching a T-junction at **Morne Rouge,** which was partially destroyed by an eruption from Mont Pelée in August 1902, several months after the eruption that wiped out St-Pierre. At 450m it has the highest elevation of any town on Martinique, and it enjoys some impressive mountain scenery.

About 2km north of the T-junction, a road (D39) signposted to Aileron leads 3km up the slopes of **Mont Pelée,** from where there's a rugged trail (four hours round-trip) up the volcano's south face to the summit.

a sugar mill dating from the 18th century, the wonderful grounds are as full of tropical plants and trees as ever, but have now had animal enclosures added to them, which include habitat for a leopard, a boa constrictor, an enormous anteater, iguanas, parrots and various monkeys.

Centre de Découverte des Sciences de la Terre   MUSEUM

(☑0596-52-82-42; www.cdst.e-monsite.com; Rte du Prêcheur; adult/child €5/3; ☺9am-5pm Tue-Sun Sep-Jun, 10am-6pm Tue-Sun Jul & Aug; ℗) Just 1.5km north of town, the earth-science museum looks like a big white box set on top of some columns. It hosts a permanent exhibit on Mont Pelée, in French. Documentaries are screened all day long, but the one to watch is *Volcans des Antilles,* which recounts Pelée's eruption and the dire consequences. It's subtitled in English and shown at 9:30am, 11:30am, 2pm and 4pm.

Distillerie Depaz   DISTILLERY

(☑0596-78-13-14; www.depaz.fr; Plantation de la Montagne Pelée; ☺10am-5pm Mon-Fri, 9am-4pm

Sat; ℗) FREE Learn how rum is made at this operation perched on a hillside amid sugarcane fields on the northern outskirts of St-Pierre. This interesting place offers self-guided tours, with signs in English. In the tasting room you can sample different rums, including *rhum vieux* (vintage rum), the Mercedes of Martinique rums, which truly rivals cognac. There's an on-site restaurant.

Domaine de l'Émeraude   NATURE RESERVE

(☑0596-52-33-49; www.pnr-martinique.com/visiter/domaine-demeraude; adult/child €6/3; ☺9am-4pm; 🐾) This wonderful natural reserve has been curated with exhibits and labeling to allow visitors to get the most out of its many trails, making it a slice of wild nature with great learning possibilities. Give yourself plenty of time to do the three different walks through the forest, ranging from 1km to 5km, where you'll see all manner of indigenous plants, flowers and trees.

🏃 Activities

Hiking

Mont Pelée is the island's most famous natural attraction and a must-do for walkers. There are strenuous trails leading up both the northern and southern flanks. The shortest and steepest is up the southern flank, beginning at Réfuge de L'Aileron in Morne Rouge (it's signposted), and takes about four hours round-trip. Ask at the tourist office (p573) for a map. Early morning is the best time to climb the volcano, as you stand a better chance of clear views.

Diving

Diving is St-Pierre's trump card, with a fantastic collection of wrecks lying just offshore – a number of ships sank in the 1902 eruption. The catch? They lie deep, and most of them are accessible to experienced divers only. For beginners, there are some excellent canyon dives. Further north, Îlet La Perle is an exposed seamount that consistently sizzles with fish action, in less than 25m of water.

Centre de Plongée à Papa D'Lo DIVING
(☑0696-50-13-68; www.apapadlo.net; Rue Bouillé) This excellent dive outfit specializes in wreck diving and has good premises right on the seafront, as well as modern equipment. Individual dives start at €36 and introductory ones at €60.

Tropicasub DIVING
(☑0696-24-24-30; www.tropicasub.com; Anse Latouche; ⊙Tue-Sun) One of the most experienced dive operators in the area is Tropicasub, on the southern outskirts of St-Pierre. Introductory dives go for €55 while single dives cost €50. Certification courses and dive packages are also available.

🎊 Festivals & Events

Mai de St-Pierre MUSIC, EXHIBITIONS
The island commemorates the May 8, 1902, eruption of Mont Pelée with live jazz performances and a candlelight procession through the former capital of St-Pierre from the cathedral along the seafront.

🛏 Sleeping

St-Pierre itself has just one hotel, a sign of just how little this lovely destination is on the traveler radar, but there are several other hotels and guesthouses in the vicinity. In nearly all cases, you'll need a car if you plan to stay anywhere but the town center.

Le Fromager CHALET $
(☑0596-78-19-07; Quartier St-James; d €39; ℗) This popular hilltop restaurant also has four superb-value timber studios, each with its own balcony and mind-blowing sea views. At these prices it's no wonder they're usually booked up – do reserve ahead.

Hôtel de l'Anse HOTEL $
(☑0596-78-30-82, 0696-38-91-70; Anse Latouche; s/d from €43/45, bungalow €60-80; ℗ ❄ 🛜) On a charming cove between Carbet and St-Pierre, this well-priced abode is in an atmospheric converted chapel that offers nine impeccably simple and airy rooms. The upstairs rooms are a tad smaller than those downstairs and supremely basic, though they're a good deal. Behind the main hotel there are also three cozy bungalows in a beautiful tropical garden.

★ La Maison Rousse GUESTHOUSE $$
(☑0596-55-85-49; www.maisonrousse.com; Quartier Fonds Mascret, Fonds St-Denis; r €110-130, ste €210; ❄ 🛜) This gorgeous retreat in the middle of the thick jungle in the heights of Fonds St-Denis is one of Martinique's most exquisite escapes. Rooms sleep up to four people and are simple, brightly painted and surround a small pool with dizzying views down to the river below. The best rooms are the gorgeous and spacious suites with their own private terraces.

Hôtel Villa Saint-Pierre HOTEL $$
(☑0596-78-68-45; www.hotel-villastpierre.fr; Rue Bouillé; d €137-147, tr €182; ℗ ❄ 🛜) The best place in town is right on the waterfront and has a small beach just meters from the front door. The nine modern and comfortable rooms, complete with locally made wood furniture, have an almost boutique feel to them, and the welcome is friendly. Rooms with a sea view are inundated with natural light – well worth the extra €10.

🍽 Eating

There are some excellent restaurants in and around St-Pierre, though outside high season it can be an effort to locate one that's open. Evenings are particularly tough, with only a few perennials staying open year-round. Wonderful seafood is available, and Le Guérin (p573) on the seafront at lunchtime is the best place to eat it.

★ **Le Guérin** CREOLE $
(☑0596-78-18-07; Rue Bouillé; menu €12; ⊗lunch Mon-Sat) There's no contest about the most popular lunch spot in town, upstairs within the old market – there can be a wait during the lunch rush, but with some of the best *acras* and *boudin créole* (blood sausage) on Martinique, the wait is worth it.

Chez Marie-Claire CREOLE $
(☑0596-69-48-21; Rue Bouillé; mains €10-15, menus €12-15; ⊗noon-2:30pm Mon-Sat) Upstairs on a metallic mezzanine overlooking the covered market, Chez Marie-Claire is about as unfussy and informal as dining gets on this French island, but that doesn't make its Creole dishes such as stewed beef, freshwater crayfish and conch any less delicious. The various *menus* (set meals) are a steal.

★ **Le Fromager** CREOLE $$
(☑0596-78-19-07; Quartier Saint-James; mains €10-15; ⊗lunch Tue-Sun; ℗) What's not to love at this superb-value lunchtime-only place, with its incredible sea views from the mountainside overlooking St-Pierre? The welcome is warm and the Creole cooking in the kitchen is both wonderful and authentic. Sunday lunchtime is a popular buffet (€25 per person) with Creole dancing – it's massively popular and a local cultural highlight, and so reservations are essential.

Beach Grill SEAFOOD $$
(Carbet; mains €16-29; ⊗11:30am-2pm Tue-Sun, 7-10pm Thu-Sat; 🕿) This hugely popular sand-floor place on Carbet's beach (about 4km south of St-Pierre) is very professionally run, with attentive staff and an excellent menu of fresh seafood and meat dishes. The salads are huge – if somewhat unwieldy in their boatlike presentation jugs – and the fish is fresh and delicious.

Le Tamaya FRENCH, CREOLE $$
(☑0596-78-29-09; 85 Rue Gabriel Péri; mains €14-18, lunch menu €15; ⊗lunch daily, dinner Thu-Tue; ❋) This great little number near the imposing Maison de la Bourse on the seafront road is a reliable choice. It prepares delectable French-inspired dishes with a tropical twist. The fricasseed octopus will certainly

DOMAINE SAINT AUBIN

The **Domaine Saint Aubin** (☑0596-69-34-77; www.ledomainesaintaubin.com; Petite Rivière Salée; d/tr from €179/210; ❋🕿❋) is an atmospheric boutique hotel housed in an absolutely gorgeous former plantation house, surrounded by acres of forested land. Rooms are decorated with antique furniture, but are comfortable and well maintained. The owners, whose family have lived in Martinique since 1715, take very good care of their guests. There's an on-site restaurant and a sumptuous breakfast.

win your heart. The lunchtime *menu* is brilliant value.

★ **1643** FRENCH $$$
(☑0596-78-17-81; www.restaurant1643.com; Anse Latouche; mains €23-30; ⊗noon-2pm & 7-9pm Tue-Sat, noon-2:30pm Sun; 🕿) This delightful restaurant is in the same historic property as the Hotel de l'Anse, even though it's separately run. The name refers to the year in which the Habitation Anse Latouche was founded, and 1643 is the best place in St-Pierre for an extravagant gastronomic experience. The house specialty is *magret de canard* (duck fillet) with foie gras. Need we say more?

❶ Information

Tourist Office (☑0596-78-10-39; ⊗8am-4pm Mon-Fri, 9am-noon Sat) Offers guided tours of St-Pierre in French (though some guides speak some English) at 9:30am and 2:30pm Monday to Friday.

❶ Getting There & Away

There are regular buses between St-Pierre and Fort-de-France (€4.80, 45 minutes) throughout the day, though these end around 4pm and don't run on Sundays. Buses leave from the seafront on Rue Bouillé near to the Hôtel Villa Saint-Pierre but pick up passengers at any bus stop along the main road.

Grand-Rivière

Nestled away at Martinique's most northern point, Grand-Rivière is an isolated and unspoiled fishing village full of 19th-century buildings with a gorgeous position beneath coastal cliffs covered in jungle. Mont Pelée forms a rugged backdrop to the south, while there's a fine view of neighboring Dominica to the north and black-sand beaches on either side. This is Martinique at its wildest and most remote.

The main road dead-ends at the sea, where there's a fish market and rows of brightly colored fishing boats in the small harbor. There's little to do here and the town has certainly seen better days, but it's the starting place for the immensely scenic hike along the northwest side of Mont Pelée all the way to Le Prêcheur, and it's also a very worthwhile day trip for a good lunch and some dramatic scenery.

🏃 Activities

Au Fil des Anses   BOATING

(☑ 0696-38-90-68, 0696-44-50-66; Grand-Rivière; full day adult/child €60/35) Run by the friendly Omer, this well-organized operation runs good-value boat excursions that take you to various scenic spots along the wild coast between Grand-Rivière and Le Prêcheur for swimming, snorkeling and trying your hand at fishing. The itinerary is flexible.

🛏 Sleeping & Eating

Tante Arlette   GUESTHOUSE $$

(☑ 0596-55-75-75; www.tantearlette.com; 3 Rue Lucy de Fossarieu; r from €105; ✳🔊) The only option in Grand-Rivière if you want to stay overnight, Tante Arlette (who despite her smiling avatar isn't always quite as warm and welcoming as she sounds) has a very smart set of 10 rooms upstairs from her popular restaurant. The superior rooms at the back are a big step up from the poky standards at the front.

Tante Arlette   CREOLE, SEAFOOD $$$

(☑ 0596-55-75-75; www.tantearlette.com; 3 Rue Lucy de Fossarieu; mains €20-43; ⊙ lunch 12:30-3pm Tue-Sun, dinner for hotel guests only; 🔊) This longstanding favorite is the best place in northern Martinique to try out authentic Creole food. The house specialty is the seafood grill (€45), which includes half a lobster, conch and shrimp, or – for the same price – a stew of the same creatures.

ℹ Getting There & Away

There is a bus from Fort-de-France (€11.20, one hour 20 minutes), which leaves a few times a day. It's often quicker to take a bus to the town of Basse-Pointe (€10.50, one hour) and try to get on a minibus (€1.50, 20 minutes) heading to Grand Rivière from there. Be prepared to wait in Basse-Pointe, however, and make the journey in the morning if you want to avoid spending the night in Grand-Rivière. Buses arriving in Grand-Rivière stop at several stops along the main road through the town.

Presqu'île de Caravelle

The wonderful Presqu'île de Caravelle is a little-visited peninsula with some gorgeous stretches of beach and a wild, untamed feel. A gently twisting road with spectacular views runs through sugarcane fields to the charming main village of Tartane, and then on to Baie du Galion. On the north side of the peninsula are a couple of protected beaches, including some spots favored by surfers. With several superb restaurants and hotels, a very atmospheric colonial ruin and some excellent walking, it's surprising that there's so little tourism here. This is, of course, all the more reason not to miss it.

⊙ Sights

Anse de Tartane   BEACH

Fronting the village of Tartane, this long strand of soft beige sand has lots of fishing shacks, a fish market and colorful *gommier* (gum tree) boats. It can get crowded on weekends, but is a lovely place to swim, with calm waters and an island the intrepid can swim out to.

Plage de La Brèche   BEACH

On the eastern outskirts of Tartane, this crescent of sand edged by manchineel trees is a stunning beach to sun yourself on. The sand here is brown-gray and there are picnic tables and a beach restaurant.

Anse l'Etang   BEACH

This gently shelving, palm-fringed beach is one of Martinique's most appealing. It's not suitable for swimming, though, because the waters are rough, with lots of wave action. It's popular with surfers.

Plage des Surfeurs   BEACH

(Anse Dufour) This is where most surfers in Martinique are heading, a fantastic beach with great waves crashing onto golden sand. There's nothing on the beach other than lots of other surfers, but several surf schools are located in the houses directly behind the beach, and some instructors even hang out on the beach looking for customers.

Château Dubuc   RUINS

(☑0596-58-09-00; Presqu'île de Caravelle; adult/child €5/2.50; ☉9am-4:30pm) The ruins of this 17th-century estate are set almost at the end of the peninsula and are a haunting and atmospheric sight. The master of the estate apparently gained notoriety by using a lantern to lure ships into wrecking off the coast, and then gathering the loot. Now it's a superbly run attraction, and your entry fee gets you an excellent audio-tour that really brings the place to life. Give yourself plenty of time here, as it's an enormous site.

Several hiking trails start from here too, including a 3km walk to the site of a historic lighthouse from where there are great views.

To get here from Tartane, you'll need to have your own wheels (the road is unpaved, but you don't need a 4WD).

🏃 Activities

Surf Up   SURFING

(☑0696-77-73-60; www.martinique-surf.com; 19 Rue de Surf) Offering surfing and paddleboarding courses, this enthusiastically run place just by Plage des Surfeurs is good value. English is spoken.

Ecole de Surf Bliss   SURFING

(☑0696-70-23-60, 0596-58-00-96; www.surf martinique.com; Rue de Surf, Anse Bonneville; private lessons per hr €40) Offers group or private surf lessons for people of all ages and experience levels on the nearby beach; also rents surfboards and bodyboards. English is spoken.

🛌 Sleeping

Hôtel Résidence Océane   HOTEL $$

(☑0596-58-73-73; www.residenceoceane.com; Rte du Château Dubuc, Anse l'Etang; d €99-125; ❀🞲🏊) The Océane ticks all the right boxes. It's small enough to be low-key and relaxed, but big enough to have a bit of buzz with the surfer crowd that likes to stay here. Best of all, it's blessed with stunning ocean views, and the nearest beach – Plage des Surfeurs – is within easy walking distance. Some rooms have terraces with kitchenettes.

Hotel Le Manguier   HOTEL $$

(☑0596-58-48-95; www.hotel-martinique-le-man guier.com; Tartane; d garden view/sea view €82/94; ❀🞲🏊) A great-value port of call. This charming collection of whitewashed units

is perched high above the center of Tartane. The simple yet rather sleek rooms have small outdoor hot-plate kitchens, redone bathrooms and great balconies, many of which face the Atlantic Ocean. There's a small pool, and breakfast is served with a sea view.

Hotel Restaurant Caravelle   HOTEL $$

(☑0596-58-07-32; www.hotel-la-caravelle-mar tinique.com; Rte du Château Dubuc; s/d from €76/83; 🞲🏊) This small, friendly, family-run hotel is a great choice. There is a hibiscus-covered terrace with glorious views of the Atlantic, and the public areas are all beautifully furnished and well looked after. Rooms are very pleasant and come in several different sizes, including studios that have well-equipped kitchenettes on a spacious front porch with great views. There's an excellent on-site restaurant.

🍴 Eating

Le Kalicoucou   PIZZA $

(☑0596-58-02-38; Rte du Château Dubuc; pizza €8-20; ☉11am-3pm Wed-Fri, 7-10pm Tue-Sun) On the eastern end of the main strip in Tartane, this is the place for excellent pizza and ice-cold beer – or, if you needed a reminder of the French influence, crepes and wine. While delivery and takeout are available, it's actually a charming place to come in the evening, with a friendly local crowd dining in the cool breeze.

Ti Carbet   CREOLE $

(☑0696-27-17-01; Tartane; mains €10-15; ☉lunch) We love this little local treasure overlooking the attractive Plage de la Brèche, on the eastern outskirts of Tartane. It concocts good, fresh food at competitive prices given the enviable location. You won't get much variety but tasty staples usually include grilled fish, octopus stew and curried chicken.

★Cocoa Beach Cafe   INTERNATIONAL $$

(☑0696-80-66-07; Anse l'Etang; mains €14-18; ☉noon-6pm Tue-Sun; 🞲) This fantastic addition to the eating options in Tartane has a wonderfully eclectic menu that draws together cuisines from around the world, all right on the gorgeous beach at Anse l'Etang. Dishes include Balinese-style chicken, Tahitian-style raw fish, *bò bun* of beef and a superb *mi cuit de thon teriyaki* (semicooked tuna teriyaki). Service is friendly and efficient.

Le Ratelot
FRENCH, SEAFOOD $$

(☑0596-63-26-11; Anse l'Etang; mains €16-24, lunch menu €25; ☺noon-3pm Fri-Wed, 7-10pm Fri, Sat, Mon & Tue; 🐾) Right on the most attractive beach in Tartane, this excellent restaurant turns out superb dishes that include beefsteak, tuna with morel mushrooms or marlin with gorgonzola cheese. There's dining on the terrace and, from virtually all points, a superb view of the beach.

Le Phare
FRENCH $$

(☑0596-58-08-48; Anse Bonneville; mains €15-25, menus €16-20; ☺noon-2:45pm Tue-Sun, 7-9:45pm Tue-Sat; 🐾) In a terrific hilltop setting next to the end of the road that leads to Château Dubuc, the Phare is famous for the incredible views of Anse Bonneville and the sea from its open-air deck; you may never have a tuna tartare or a kangaroo fillet with a view to rival this one.

L'Escapade
CREOLE $$

(☑0596-58-43-08; Tartane; mains €15-20; ☺10am-3pm & 7-10pm Mon, Tue, Thu & Fri) It doesn't get much simpler than this but that's why we like it. On the western end of the main strip in Tartane, this family-run eatery serves up simple yet well-executed Creole dishes such as conch stew or spicy goat stew, and packs them in at lunchtime. A real slice of local life.

Restaurant La Tartanaise
CREOLE $$

(Rte du Château Dubuc; mains €9-15, set menu €16; ☺8am-10pm) This ramshackle place in the middle of the seafront serves up popular fish, seafood and grilled meat dishes, including excellent *acras*. This is where many of the locals go for a ti-punch at day's end.

★ La Table de Mamy Nounou
FRENCH, CREOLE $$$

(☑0596-58-07-32; Hôtel Restaurant Caravelle, Rte du Château Dubuc; mains €15-30, menu €28; ☺noon-2pm & 7-9pm Wed-Mon; 🐾) This much-lauded restaurant at the Hôtel Restaurant Caravelle is a winner, thanks to its breezy veranda with lovely sea views, sophisticated mains and wonderful homemade desserts. Stand-out dishes might include *grenadin de porcelet* (larded fillet of suckling pig) and lamb with aromatic herbs. The flambéed-banana dessert is a treat, but do be mindful of the restrictive opening hours.

❶ Information

There's a small but helpful **Office de Tourisme** (☑0596-38-07-01; Tartane; ☺9am-noon & 1pm-5pm Mon-Fri) on Tartane's seafront.

❶ Getting There & Away

The gateway to Presqu'île de Caravelle is the town of La Trinité, which has direct hourly buses to and from Fort-de-France (€4.10, 45 minutes), which stop at its small bus station in the town center. Here you'll need to transfer to the local *navette* (shuttle bus) to Tartane (€1.10, 15 minutes, every 30 minutes). Buses run into the center of Tartane and stop along the seafront.

UNDERSTAND MARTINIQUE

History

When Christopher Columbus first sighted Martinique it was inhabited by Caribs, who called the island Madinina, meaning 'island of flowers.' In 1635 the first party of French settlers, led by Pierre Belain d'Esnambuc, landed on the northwest side of the island. There they built a small fort and established a settlement that would become the capital city, St-Pierre. The next year, on October 31, 1636, King Louis XIII signed a decree authorizing the use of African slaves in the French West Indies.

The settlers quickly went about colonizing the land with the help of slave labor; by 1640 they had extended their grip south to Fort-de-France, where they constructed a fort on the rise above the harbor. As forests were cleared to make room for sugar plantations, conflicts with the native Caribs escalated into warfare, and in 1660 those Caribs who had survived the fighting were finally forced off the island.

The British also took a keen interest in Martinique, invading and holding the island for most of the period from 1794 to 1815. The island prospered under British occupation; the planters simply sold their sugar in British markets rather than French ones. Perhaps more importantly, the occupation allowed Martinique to avoid the turmoil of the French Revolution. By the time the British returned the island to France in 1815, the Napoleonic Wars had ended and the

French empire was again entering a period of stability.

Not long after the French administration was re-established on Martinique the golden era of sugarcane began to wane, as glutted markets and the introduction of sugar beets on mainland France eroded prices. With their wealth diminished, the aristocratic plantation owners lost much of their political influence, and the abolitionist movement, led by Victor Schoelcher, gained momentum.

It was Schoelcher, the French cabinet minister responsible for overseas possessions, who convinced the provisional government to sign the 1848 Emancipation Proclamation, which brought an end to slavery in the French West Indies. Widely reviled by the white aristocracy of the time, Schoelcher is now regarded as one of Martinique's heroes.

In 1946 Martinique went from being a colony to an overseas *département* of France, with a status similar to those of metropolitan *départements*. In 1974 it was further assimilated into the political fold as a Department of France.

People & Culture

The earliest settlers on Martinique were from Normandy, Brittany, Paris and other parts of France; shortly afterward, African slaves were brought to the island. Later, smaller numbers of immigrants came from India, Syria and Lebanon. These days, Martinique is home to thousands of immigrants, some of them here illegally, from poorer Caribbean islands such as Dominica, St Lucia and Haiti. Martinique's population today hovers around 400,000 – more than a quarter of whom live in the Fort-de-France area.

The majority of residents are of mixed ethnic origin. The Black Pride movement known as *négritude* emerged as a philosophical and literary movement in the 1930s, largely through the writings of Martinique native Aimé Césaire, a *négritude* poet who was eventually elected mayor of Fort-de-France. The movement advanced black social and cultural values and re-established bonds with African traditions, which had been suppressed by French colonialism.

The beguine, an Afro-French style of dance music with a bolero rhythm, originated in Martinique in the 1930s. Zouk is a more contemporary French West Indies creation, drawing on the beguine and other French-Caribbean folk forms. Retaining the electronic influences of its '80s origins with its Carnival-like rhythm and hot dance beat, zouk has become as popular in Europe as it is in the French Caribbean.

Landscape & Wildlife

At 1080 sq km, Martinique is the second-largest island in the French West Indies. Roughly 65km long and 20km wide, it has

THE ERUPTION OF MONT PELÉE

At the end of the 19th century, St-Pierre – then the capital of Martinique – was a flourishing port city. Mont Pelée, the island's highest mountain at 1397m, was just a scenic backdrop to the city.

In the spring of 1902, sulfurous steam vents on Mont Pelée began emitting gases, and a crater lake started to fill with boiling water. Authorities dismissed it all as the normal cycle of the volcano, which had experienced harmless periods of activity in the past.

But at 8am on Sunday May 8, 1902, Mont Pelée exploded into a glowing burst of superheated gas and burning ash, with a force 40 times stronger than the later nuclear blast over Hiroshima. Between the suffocating gases and the fiery inferno, St-Pierre was laid to waste within minutes.

Of the city's 30,000 inhabitants, there were just three survivors. One of them, a prisoner named Louis-Auguste Cyparis, escaped with only minor burns – ironically, he owed his life to having been locked in a tomblike solitary-confinement cell at the local jail. He went on to tour the world with the Barnum & Bailey's Circus as part of their 'Greatest Show on Earth.'

Pelée continued to smolder for months, but by 1904 people began to resettle the town, building among the crumbled ruins.

a terrain punctuated by hills, plateaus and mountains.

The highest point is the 1397m-high Mont Pelée, an active volcano at the northern end of the island. The island's center is dominated by the Pitons du Carbet, a scenic mountain range reaching 1207m. Martinique's irregular coastline is cut by deep bays and coves, while the mountainous rainforest in the interior feeds numerous rivers.

The Land

The Carib name for Martinique was Madinina, meaning 'island of flowers,' and it's not difficult to see why. Martinique has lots of colorful flowering plants, with the vegetation varying with altitude and rainfall. Rainforests cover the slopes of the mountains in the northern interior, luxuriant with tree ferns, bamboo groves, climbing vines and hardwood trees like mahogany, rosewood, locust and *gommier* (gum tree).

The drier southern part of the island has brushy savanna vegetation such as cacti, frangipani trees, balsam, logwood and acacia shrubs. Common landscape plantings include splashy bougainvillea, the ubiquitous red hibiscus and yellow-flowered allamanda trees. To truly appreciate the range and magnificence of the island's varied flora, head to the unbeatable Jardin de Balata (p560) on the mountainous Route de la Trace (p571) and see the many flowers that gave Martinique its name.

Wildlife

Martinique is home to anole lizards, manicous (opossums), mongooses and venomous fer-de-lance snakes. The mongoose, which was introduced from India in the late 19th century, preys on eggs and has been responsible for the demise of many bird species. Some native birds, such as parrots, are no longer found on the island at all, while others have significantly declined in numbers. Endangered birds include the Martinique trembler, white-breasted trembler and white-breasted thrasher.

The underwater life tends to be of the smaller variety; lots of schools of tiny fish that swim by in a cloud of silver or red. There are a decent amount of lobsters hiding under rocks, and occasionally a ray will glide by.

SURVIVAL GUIDE

ⓘ Directory A–Z

ACCOMMODATIONS

Hotel accommodations in Martinique aren't particularly charming or cheap, and in the case of many guesthouses, are often run in a semiprofessional manner, meaning owners frequently have other jobs. You can expect receptions to be unstaffed, so arranging your accommodations ahead of time is always a good idea. On the plus side, hotels here are generally small by Caribbean standards and large resorts are rare.

CHILDREN

Children will be welcome on vacation in Martinique. Many hotels are family oriented and the island is a very safe place overall. Practically all hotels will provide cots, and some hotels provide babysitting services.

All restaurants will allow children to dine, and they'll often have a simple and good-value *menu enfant* (children's set meal) to offer them. European brands of baby formula, foods and diapers can be bought at pharmacies.

ELECTRICITY

Martinique runs on 220V, 50 cycles; plugs have two round prongs; a plug adaptor will come in handy.

EMERGENCY NUMBERS

Ambulance	☑ 15
Police	☑ 17
Fire	☑ 18
Martinique country code	☑ 596
International access code	☑ 00

FOOD

Martinique will thrill anyone who loves good food. Not only is there the French influence on the island – which has placed food and drink at the center of life and led to the preponderance of competitive and inventive restaurants – but there's also the superb quality of the local fish and seafood, which make it almost impossible to cook badly here. Almost every town has an outstanding restaurant, while it's also hard to go wrong at any simple beach shack.

Essential Food & Drink

➡ **Acras** A universally popular hors d'oeuvre in Martinique, *acras* are fish, seafood or vegetable tempura. *Acras de morue* (cod) and *crevettes* (shrimp) are the most common and are both delicious.

➡ **Ti-punch** Short for *petit punch*, this ubiquitous and strong cocktail is the normal *apéro* (aperitif) in Martinique. It's a mix of rum, lime and cane syrup – but mainly rum.

➡ **Crabes farcis** Stuffed crabs are a common local dish. Normally they're stuffed with a spicy mixture of crabmeat, garlic, shallots and parsley, and cooked in their shells.

➡ **Blaff** This is the local term for white fish marinated in lime juice, garlic and peppers, then poached. While it's popular across the Caribbean, its true home is Martinique.

GLBT TRAVELERS

Gay rights are legally protected in Martinique, as a part of France. However, overall homophobia is still very prevalent and there is little or no gay scene on the island. Gay and lesbian travelers have nothing to worry about though – in general, those working in the hotel industry are perfectly used to gay travelers and same-sex couples booking a double room will cause no problems.

LEGAL MATTERS

French law governs legal matters in Martinique, and there is a presumption of innocence, as well as the right to a lawyer. Most travelers will have no interaction with the police at all.

MONEY

Martinique uses the euro. Hotels, restaurants and car rental agencies accept most credit and debit cards. ATMs are common across the island and it's no problem accessing money with international cards.

Exchange Rates

AUSTRALIA	A$1	€0.69
CANADA	C$1	€0.72
JAPAN	¥100	€0.82
NEW ZEALAND	NZ$1	€0.66
SWITZERLAND	CHF1	€0.94
UK	UK£1	€1.19
US	US$1	€0.96

For current exchange rates, see www.xe.com.

Tipping

Tipping is not normally expected in Martinique, though it's polite to round up your bill to the nearest euro, and to give a tip for any exceptional service.

PUBLIC HOLIDAYS

New Year's Day January 1
Easter Sunday Late March/early April
Ascension Thursday Fortieth day after Easter
Pentecost Monday Eighth Monday after Easter
Labor Day May 1
Victory Day May 8

Slavery Abolition Day May 22
Bastille Day July 14
Schoelcher Day July 21
Assumption Day August 15
All Saints' Day November 1
Armistice Day November 11
Christmas Day December 25th

TAXES & REFUNDS

If you do not live in France, it is possible to claim back VAT on certain purchased items at the airport when leaving Martinique. This isn't possible if you're flying from Martinique to France.

TELEPHONE

The country code for Martinique is ☎ 596. Confusingly, all local numbers begin with ☎ 0596 as well. These numbers are separate, however, and therefore must be dialed twice when calling from abroad. Local mobile numbers begin with ☎ 0696.

When calling from within the French Antilles, simply dial the local 10-digit number. From elsewhere, dial your country's international access code, followed by the ☎ 596 country code and the local number (omit the first zero).

TIME

Martinique uses GMT/UTC -4 hours. Daylight saving time is not used.

TOURIST INFORMATION

The **Martinique Promotion Bureau** (www.martinique.org) is a good source of information on the island – in English and several other languages. Many towns have at least one small tourism office where the staff will speak English and can usually give you free maps and some useful local advice. Pamphlets, mainly in

PRACTICALITIES

Newspapers *France-Antilles* (www.martinique.franceantilles.fr) is the main daily newspaper for the French West Indies.

Radio & TV Tune into Réseau Outre-Mer 1ère (www.la1ere.fr) or catch up on local TV on networks RFO 1 and RFO 2.

Smoking Smoking in all enclosed public spaces is against the law.

Weights & Measures Martinique uses the metric system for everything, and the 24-hour clock.

French but with enough pictures and maps to get the gist, are available at airports and many hotels.

TRAVELERS WITH DISABILITIES

By comparison with other Caribbean Islands, Martinique makes good provision for travelers with disabilities, with many hotels having wheelchair-accessible rooms, and many public places having disabled toilets.

ℹ️ Getting There & Away

AIR

The island's only airport is **Aéroport International Martinique Aimé Césaire** (FDF; ☎ 0596-42-18-77; www.martinique.aeroport.fr; Lamentin), near the town of Lamentin in the southeast of Martinique, a short distance from Fort-de-France.

A number of airlines serve Martinique:

Air Canada (☎ 590-0590-21-12-77; www.aircanada.com; Martinique Aimé Césaire International Airport; ⊙ 7am-7pm) From Montreal.

Air France (☎ 0596-48-55-93; www.airfrance.com; Aéroport International Martinique Aimé Césaire; ⊙ 8am-8pm) From Paris.

American Airlines (www.aa.com; Aéroport International Martinique Aimé Césaire; ⊙ 9am-5pm) From San Juan and Miami.

Corsair (☎ 0890-64-86-48; www.corsair.com; Aéroport International Martinique Aimé Césaire; ⊙ 8am-6pm) From Paris.

There are direct regional services to Dominica, Guadeloupe, Port-au-Prince (Haiti), Havana (Cuba), San Juan (Puerto Rico), St-Barthélemy, St Lucia, St-Martin/Sint Maarten and Santo Domingo (Dominican Republic).

Regional airlines serving Martinique include **Air Caraïbes** (☎ 0820-83-58-35; www.aircaraibes.com; Aéroport International Martinique

Aimé Césaire; ⊙ 7am-7pm), **Air Antilles Express** (☎ 0596-42-16-71; www.airantilles.com; Aéroport International Martinique Aimé Césaire; ⊙ 8am-8pm) and **LIAT** (www.liatairline.com; Aéroport International Martinique Aimé Césaire; ⊙ 8am-8pm).

SEA
Ferry

L'Express des Îles (☎ 0825-35-90-00; www.express-des-iles.com; Ferry Terminal, Rue Bouillé, Fort-de-France; ⊙ 7am-6pm) operates large, modern catamarans between Fort-de-France and Pointe-à-Pitre in Guadeloupe (one way/round-trip €79/119, three hours), with a stop at Roseau in Dominica (one way/round-trip €79/119, 1½ hours). In the other direction there are departures from Fort-de-France to Castries in St Lucia (one way/round-trip €79/119, 80 minutes). There are three to five weekly crossings in both directions.

Jeans for Freedom (☎ 0825-01-01-25; www.jeansforfreedom.com; Ferry Terminal, Rue Bouillé, Fort-de-France; ⊙ 8am-5pm) operates services between St-Pierre and Pointe-à-Pitre (one way, €79). There are one to three weekly services depending on season.

There are discounts of 50% for children aged under two, 10% for students and passengers under 12 years old, and 5% for passengers younger than 26 or older than 60. Departure days and times for these services change frequently and, due to weather conditions, often bear no relation to the printed schedule. The only way to be sure is to call the ferry company or check with a local travel agent.

Yacht

The main port of entry is in Fort-de-France, but yachts may also clear at St-Pierre or Marin, both of which have marinas.

Yachting and sailing are very popular in Martinique and numerous charter companies operate on the island, including **Sparkling Charter** (☎ 0596-74-81-68; www.sparkling-charter.com; Porte de Plaisance, Marin), which is based at the **Marina du Marin** (☎ 0596-74-83-83; www.marina-martinique.fr), and **Star Voyage** (www.starvoyage.com; Port de Plaisance, Marin), based at the **Marina de la Pointe du Bout** (Marina des Trois-Îlets; ☎ 0596-66-07-74; www.marina3ilets.com).

ℹ️ Getting Around

Getting around Martinique is generally a doddle. Most visitors hire a car for their time here, as car hire rates are low and the road network is good, though traffic jams around Fort-de-France can slow things down considerably.

Boat

A regular *vedette* (ferry) between Martinique's main resort areas and Fort-de-France provides a nice alternative to dealing with heavy bus and car traffic; it also allows you to avoid the hassles of city parking and is quicker.

Bus

Although there are some larger public buses serving the urban area around Fort-de-France, most buses elsewhere in Martinique are minivans marked 'TC' (for *taxis collectifs*) on top. Destinations are marked on the vans, sometimes on the side doors, and sometimes on a small sign stuck in the front window. Traveling by bus is best for shorter distances – and for visitors with a lot of extra time in their itinerary.

Bus stops are marked *'arrêt de bus'* or have signs showing a picture of a bus.

Car & Motorcycle

Renting a car is the most reliable form of transportation in Martinique. Car rental is a breeze, rates are low and the road network is excellent.

Rental

There are numerous car-rental agencies at Martinique's airport. You'll find the best rates on their websites, and local firms are generally cheaper than international agencies. You must be at least 21 years of age to rent a car, and some companies add a surcharge for drivers under the age of 25.

All major international rental companies can be found at the airport, as well as the following local outfits:

Carib Rentacar (☑ 0596-42-16-15; www.rentacar-caraibes.com; Aéroport International Martinique Aimé Césaire; ☺ 8am–6pm)

Pop's Car (☑ 0596-42-16-84; www.popscar.com; Aéroport International Martinique Aimé Césaire; ☺ 8am–6pm)

Road Conditions

Roads in Martinique are excellent by Caribbean standards, and there are multilane freeways (along with rush-hour traffic) in the Fort-de-France area.

Road Rules

In Martinique, drive on the right side of the road. Traffic regulations and road signs are the same as those in Europe, speed limits are posted, and exits and intersections are clearly marked.

Montserrat

POP 5300 / ☎ 664

Best Places to Eat

➡ Pont's Beach View (p586)

➡ People's Place (p586)

➡ Olveston House Restaurant (p586)

Best Places to Sleep

➡ Gingerbread Hill (p585)

➡ Olveston House (p586)

Why Go?

Before its lower two thirds became devastated by cataclysmic eruptions of the Soufrière Hills Volcano in 1995, Montserrat was a carefree little island paradise famous as the birthplace of the late Alphonsus Cassell, creator of the soca hit 'Hot, Hot, Hot,' and as the home of Air Montserrat, the famous recording studio founded by Beatles producer Sir George Martin. Sting and Eric Clapton were among the stars who recorded here.

Two decades later, this modern-day Pompeii is slowly recovering. The population is growing, and sand mining and geothermal energy provide new sources of income.

Tourists are returning too, a trickle to be sure, mostly for volcano-related day trips. Those who stay longer are drawn by the slow rhythm, the friendly locals, the fabulous hiking and birdwatching, and the blessedly tranquil ambience. The volcano is always a wild card, but by and large Montserrat is a safe place to visit.

When to Go

Mar Help locals paint the island even greener during St Patrick's Week (March 10 to 17), which celebrates Montserrat's Irish heritage.

Jul–Nov Hurricane season, although storms can disrupt transport to and from the island at any time. Runners can sweat it out during the Volcano Half Marathon in November.

Dec The Montserrat Festival, the local version of Carnival, runs from Christmas to New Year.

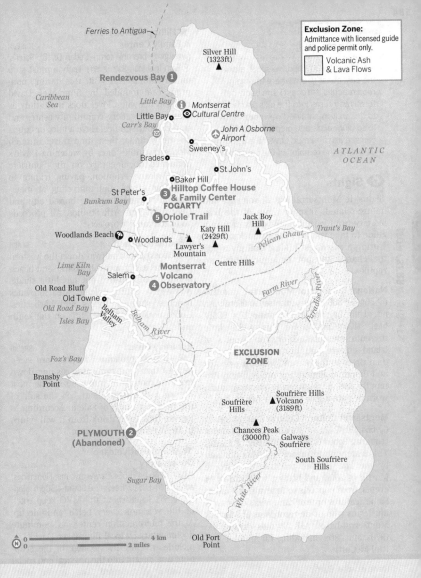

Ferries to Antigua

Silver Hill
(1323ft) ▲

Rendezvous Bay 1

Caribbean
Sea

Little Bay
Little Bay ○

Carr's Bay

1 Montserrat
Cultural Centre

John A Osborne
Airport

Sweeney's ○

Brades ○

St John's ○

Baker Hill ○

3 Hilltop Coffee House
& Family Center
FOGARTY

St Peter's ○

Bunkum Bay

5 Oriole Trail

Jack Boy
Hill ▲

Pelican Ghaut

Trant's Bay

ATLANTIC
OCEAN

Woodlands Beach ○

Woodlands ○

Katy Hill
(2429ft) ▲

Lawyer's
Mountain

Lime Kiln
Bay

Salem ○

Old Road Bluff
Old Towne ○

Old Road Bay

Isles Bay

Belham
Valley

Belham River

Montserrat
Volcano
Observatory 4

Centre Hills

Farm River

Paradise River

EXCLUSION
ZONE

Fox's Bay

Bransby
Point

PLYMOUTH 2
(Abandoned)

Soufrière
Hills

Soufrière Hills
Volcano
(3189ft) ▲

Chances Peak
(3000ft) ▲

Galways
Soufrière

South Soufrière
Hills

Sugar Bay

White River

N
0   4 km
0   2 miles

Old Fort
Point

Exclusion Zone:
Admittance with licensed guide
and police permit only.

Volcanic Ash
& Lava Flows

Montserrat Highlights

1 Rendezvous Bay
(p584) Swimming and
snorkeling on Montserrat's
only white-sand beach.

2 Exclusion Zone Tour
(p585) Getting close-ups of
the destruction wreaked on
Plymouth and the way nature
is reclaiming the area.

**3 Hilltop Coffee House
& Family Center** (p584)
Stopping by this nonprofit for
unique art and memorabilia, a
volcano video and fresh juices.

**4 Montserrat Volcano
Observatory** (p584)
Enjoying panoramic views
of the Exclusion Zone and

unraveling the mysteries of
the volcano.

5 Oriole Trail (p585)
Plunging on through the
rainforest on this moderate
hike perfect for birders and
nature lovers.

JACK BOY HILL

After about a 3-mile drive south along the east coast (from where the main road reaches the coast), the badly battered road turns into the hills and leads to this well-maintained viewpoint with fixed binoculars and picnic tables. You can see ash and mud flows to the south as well as the remains of the old airport.

⊙ Sights

'Sights' in Montserrat are all volcano- and nature-related. Take in views of the buried city from various viewpoints or hire a guide to take you into the Exclusion Zone. Hitting a rainforest hiking trail gives you the chance to spot endemic birds and reptiles.

National Museum of Montserrat   MUSEUM

(☑ 664-491-3086; www.montserratnationaltrust.ms; Little Bay; adult/child under 12yr EC$5/free; ⊙ 10am-2pm Mon-Fri) This modest little museum presents exhibits on aspects of island culture and history from Amerindian times to the present, including photos and dioramas illustrating pre-eruption Plymouth and a flamboyant stage costume worn by native soca superstar Arrow.

Montserrat Cultural Centre   CULTURAL CENTER

(☑ 664-491-4242; www.themontserratculturalcentre.ms; Robert Griffith Dr, Little Bay; P) FREE
This stately performance hall was donated by the late Beatles producer Sir George Martin in 2006 and hosts a wide variety of events, from concerts to funerals. A 'Wall of Fame' features bronze handprints of famous musicians who made recordings at Martin's Montserrat-based AIR Studios during the 1970s and '80s, including Elton John and Paul McCartney.

Rendezvous Bay   BEACH

Montserrat's only white sandy beach is a lovely (though facility-free) crescent perfect for swimming, snorkeling and diving. It can only be accessed via a steep 0.7-mile trail from Little Bay. Alternatively, get there by kayak. Rentals are available in Little Bay.

If you're hiking, budget about 20 minutes, including a stop at the top of the trail, to enjoy great views.

★ Hilltop Coffee House & Family Center   MUSEUM

(www.gingerbreadhill.com; Cedar Dr, St Peter's; ⊙ 8am-1pm Mon-Sat; P 🛜) Truly a must stop on any Montserrat visit, this darling nonprofit cafe founded by filmmaker David Lea and his wife Clover does multi-duty as museum, art gallery, community center and de facto tourist office. Have a juice or cuppa on the veranda, then time travel through Montserrat milestones by watching David's acclaimed documentary on the Soufrière Hills Volcano eruption, paying tribute to soca star Arrow, and marveling at memorabilia rescued from the buried city and George Martin's AIR Studios. All proceeds go to community projects.

Woodlands Beach   BEACH

(Woodlands) About halfway down the western coast, this easily accessible dark-sand beach is often footprint-free but has little shade. A covered clifftop picnic area provides benches, showers, toilets and barbecues. Good snorkeling by the cliffs on the south end.

Runaway Ghaut   SPRING

🖉 Ghauts (pronounced 'guts') are steep ravines that send rainwater rushing down from the mountains into the sea. The most famous is Runaway Ghaut, on the side of the road just north of Salem. According to legend, those who drink from it will return to Montserrat time and again.

★ Montserrat Volcano Observatory   MUSEUM

(MVO; ☑ 664-491-5647; www.mvo.ms; Flemmings; adult/child EC$10/free; ⊙ 8:30am-4:30pm Mon-Fri; P 🛜) Scientists at the MVO keep track of the volcano's every belch and hiccup. At the interpretation center, an 18-minute documentary by local filmmaker David Lea includes riveting live footage of the eruptions and insight into the physical and social upheaval they caused. The terrace offers sweeping views of the volcano, Belham Valley and Plymouth.

Get there by driving up a steep hill at the intersection where the Storm Bar is located. Turn right at the top, then left onto a paved road.

Isles Bay   BEACH

(Garibaldi Hill) This small beach at the mouth of the Belham River is great for swimming and is home to a popular beach bar called Hank's. Gets busy with locals on weekends.

🏃 Activities

Scriber's Adventures & Tours HIKING
(📞664-492-2943; www.scribersadventures.com)
For close encounters with Montserrat's
unique flora and fauna, sign up for a hiking
tour with James 'Scriber' Daly, who seems
to know every bird, bat, turtle or lizard
by name and has a knack for spotting the
national bird, the elusive Montserrat Oriole. Outings run from 90 minutes to three
hours and can be tailored to your fitness
level.

Oriole Trail HIKING
(St Peter's) This moderate 1.3-mile trail cuts
through the rainforest to the top of Lawyer's
Mountain, from where you'll have bird's-eye
views of the island. It can easily be done
without a guide, although having someone who can explain the flora and fauna
along the way can deepen your experience.
The trailhead is up from the Hilltop Coffee
House (ask for directions here).

Scuba Montserrat DIVING
(📞664-496-7807; www.scubamontserrat.com;
Main Island Rd, St Peter's; 2-tank dive US$88; ⊙of-
fice 8am-5pm) Aside from underwater adventures, this dive shop also runs snorkeling
trips to Rendezvous Bay, and the Volcano
Boat Tour to the shores off the buried city of
Plymouth. Snorkeling gear and kayak rentals are also available.

👉 Tours

★ Aqua Montserrat TOURS
(📞664-496-9255; www.aquamontserrat.com; Little Bay; tours US$30-150; ⊙Tue & Sat) Founded
by Veta Wade, a young and energetic Mont-
serratian returnee from England, this

outfit takes visitors on customized adventure tours that show off the island's secret
nooks and crannies above and below the
water. Tours must be booked at least 72
hours in advance. Aqua also rents kayaks
and snorkeling equipment, and runs a fun
shopping tour where you meet community
artists and artisans.

Veta is also the creator of Fish N Fins, a
year-round program teaching local kids how
to swim and snorkel.

★ Montserrat Island Tours TOURS
(📞664-491-2124, 606-658-0077; www.montser-
ratislandtours.com; half-/full-day tours per person
US$45-65; ⊙office 8am-5pm Mon-Fri) These
small private-island tours are run with passion, dedication and first-hand know-how
by charismatic local Sun Lea and provide
an in-depth experience of Montserrat's
unique features. Tours can even include
a foray into the buried city of Plymouth
(dependent on seismic and weather conditions and subject to a permit fee of US$100
per group).

🛏 Sleeping

★ Gingerbread Hill GUESTHOUSE $$
(📞664-491-5812; www.gingerbreadhill.com; St
Peter's; d US$45-125; 🅿 ❄ 🛜) Created by David
and Clover, American hippie transplants and
devoted Montserrat champions, this charismatic refuge consists of four cheerfully hued
and artistically decorated self-catering units
with spacious verandas, ultra-comfy beds
and sublime ocean views. The crown jewel
is the Heavenly Suite with a rooftop terrace
for counting the stars. The 'Sweet & Simple'
room downstairs is the best budget pick on
the island.

VOLCANIC APOCALYPSE

Montserrat has seen more than its fair share of nature's destructiveness but never
more so than in July 1995 when the Soufrière Hills Volcano (now 3180ft) ended its 400
years of dormancy. A series of ash falls, pyroclastic flows and mud flows destroyed the
capital, Plymouth, smaller settlements, farmland and forests. Around 11,000 residents
were evacuated and resettled in the north or emigrated to Britain. Eruptions continued until the last major one in 2010, but since then Soufrière has, by and large, been
peaceful.

Two-thirds of the island is still an Exclusion Zone, with life now focused in Brades
and Little Bay in the north. But nature is slowly reclaiming the destroyed areas. You
can take in the spectacle from safe viewing points that include the Montserrat Volcano
Observatory, on boat trips and helicopter flyovers. With a guide and police permit,
it's even possible to visit Plymouth for a firsthand look at the destruction wrought by
nature.

Essence Guesthouse
GUESTHOUSE $$

(☑664-491-5411; www.essencemontserrat.com; Old Towne Bluff Dr, Old Towne; r US$70-115; P🛜❄) Run with a personal touch by Belgian couple Annie and Eric, this charismatic place has views out over Belham Valley and the volcano from roomy apartments with full kitchen and private patio or balcony. For more privacy rent the new Pool House with a private pool and deck.

Erindell Villa
GUESTHOUSE $$

(☑664-491-3655; www.erindellvilla.com; Gros Michael Dr, Woodlands; r incl breakfast US$85; P@❄) This friendly guesthouse near the rainforest offers plenty of freebies, including snorkeling gear and cell phones, as well as a personal experience thanks to hosts Shirley and Lou. Both are great storytellers who like to share the dinner table with their guests (extra charge).

★Olveston House
GUESTHOUSE $$$

(☑664-491-5210; www.olvestonhouse.com; Loblolly Lane, Salem; r US$110-119; P❄🛜❄) The former winter home of the late Sir George Martin is now an utterly delightful inn run by the affable trio of Margaret, Sarah and Carol. There are six charming rooms (three with air-con, three with access to the wraparound porch), and lots of memorabilia and photographs of famous musicians. Wi-fi works in the lobby and bar only.

✖ Eating & Drinking

People's Place
CARIBBEAN $

(☑664-752-8491; Main Island Rd, St Peter's; meals EC$10-25; ⊙9am-7pm Mon-Thu, to midnight Fri & Sat) John's blue hilltop shack enjoys a cult following among islanders, especially on Friday and Saturday nights when every gathers for beer and a gab. The Caribbean fare is simple, ample and

delicious, and served with a big smile. You can't go wrong with the roti, but if it's Friday, try goat water, a stew and the national dish.

Nostalgia
CARIBBEAN $

(☑664-496-9925; Main island Rd; dishes EC$5-30; ⊙8am-4pm Mon-Fri, to 7pm Sat; P) This canary-yellow food truck parked by the side of the road just before Carr's Bay is a local favorite for bulging sandwiches but also does burgers and fried or grilled chicken or fish. Service tends to be slow as molasses, though, so the clued-in call ahead for their order and avoid the lunchtime rush.

★Pont's Beach View
CARIBBEAN $$

(☑664-496-7788; johnponteen@gmail.com; Little Bay; mains EC$25-45; ⊙10am-4pm Tue-Sun, dinner 6-9pm by reservation; 🛜) John Ponteen is a man with a big heart who serves big platters of top Caribbean food – from catch of the day to succulent baby back ribs and spicy Creole chicken. Sit at handcrafted mahogany tables in an enchanted garden pergola festooned with detritus washed up by the sea, or grab a table on the breezy octagonal deck overlooking Little Bay.

Time Out Bar & Restaurant
CARIBBEAN $$

(☑664-491-9046; Look Out Circle, Little Bay; mains EC$15-55; ⊙noon-11pm Mon-Sat) Right next to the beach, this contemporary grill feeds hungry tummies with big burgers, barbecued ribs, and wings and pasta dishes. Thanks to a full bar, this is also one of the few places on the island where you can get a drink at night.

Olveston House Restaurant
BRITISH $$

(☑664-491-5210; www.olvestonhouse.com; Loblolly Lane, Salem; mains EC$25-55; ⊙7:30am-9pm; P🛜) At this all-day restaurant in the winter home of the late Sir George Martin you get to tuck into Caribbean-infused English cuisine with a view of the tropical garden. Friday pub nights are great for eavesdropping on gossiping islanders, as are the barbecue feasts that draw capacity crowds every other Wednesday.

Hank's Beach Bar
CARIBBEAN $$

(Isles Bay Beach; dishes EC$30-90; ⊙11am-sunset Wed-Sun) This beach-bum hangout sits right on Isle's Bay Beach at the mouth of the Belham River and gets busy with locals on Sundays. Aside from burgers, chicken and salads, it also has good pizza (sometimes) and a killer lemon-blueberry cheesecake.

Soca Cabana CARIBBEAN **$$**
(✆664-493-1820; www.socacabana.com; beachfront, Little Bay; mains EC$30-40; ⊗8am-4pm Sun-Thu & dinner by reservation, 8am-late Fri & Sat; ⊛) Dance in the sand at this chilled beach bar, which gets packed for Saturday-night karaoke. The wooden bar was rescued from Sir George Martin's AIR recording studio.

🛍 Shopping

Montserrat's few shops do a brisk trade in volcano-related souvenirs, such as bottled ash and volcano rum. For handmade local crafts try the Arts & Craft Association in Brades and the National Trust's gift shop. The store at the airport also has a decent selection. For a comprehensive chronicle of the island's volcanic legacy, pick up David Lea's DVD series *The Price of Paradise* or his book *Through My Lens*.

Arts & Crafts Association GIFTS & SOUVENIRS
(✆664-496-1398; Main Island Rd, Brades; ⊗9am-2pm Mon-Fri) Pick up locally made crafts such as the island cotton and ceramics, as well as volcano-related souvenirs.

ℹ Information

Montserrat Post Office (✆664-491-2457; Brades Rd; ⊗8:15am-3:55pm Mon-Fri) In Brades.

Montserrat Tourist Office (✆664-491-4700; www.visitmontserrat.com; EK Osbourne Bldg, Little Bay; ⊗8:30am-4:30pm Mon-Fri)

UNDERSTAND MONTSERRAT

Culture

The small population of Montserrat is tightly knit. More than 90% is of African descent with a strong influence of Irish blood. The flag bears Montserrat's coat of arms, which depicts a white woman clutching a harp and hugging a cross.

An increasing number of the displaced are returning to the island as new houses are built. Many say that they never felt at home in Britain and miss their lives on the island. Still, the population remains at less than half its total pre-eruption and the economy is still trying to recover.

Quite predictably, cricket is huge and when the national team practices on the pitch near Little Bay, few cars pass without pausing for a critical look. More surprising, perhaps, is the passion for the national soccer (football) team, which plays in a beautiful, brand-new stadium.

Landscape & Wildlife

Volcanic eruptions destroyed about 60% of Montserrat's forest ecosystem, leaving the Centre Hills as the main refuge for flora and wildlife. Laced with hiking trails, they harbor numerous species, including the endemic Montserrat Oriole, the practically extinct 'mountain chicken' (actually a huge frog) and a shy lizard called Montserrat Galliwasp. The island is also home to three species of sea turtle. The Montserrat National Trust arranges turtle-watching treks during nesting time in August and September.

SURVIVAL GUIDE

ℹ Directory A-Z

ACCOMMODATIONS

Montserrat does not have any resorts or large hotels. If you're spending just a night or two, it's best to stay in a small guesthouse run by affable locals who will be happy to help you maximize your time on the island. If you're staying longer, consider renting a self-catering apartment or villa. Rates overall are low and the quality high. The hotel tax is either 7% or 10%.

Booking Services

Montserrat Enterprises (✆664-491-2431; www.montserratenterprises.com/rentals; villas

---

SLEEPING PRICE RANGES

The following price ranges refer to a double with bathroom during peak season (December to April). Unless otherwise stated, breakfast is not included.

$ less than US$60

$$ US$60–100

$$$ more than US$100

EATING PRICE RANGES

The following price ranges refer to a main course. Most places add a 10% service charge.

$ less than EC$20

$$ EC$20– 50

$$$ more than EC$50

per week US$600-2000) Rents villas with pool and views around the island, and arranges for car pick-up from the airport or ferry. Minimum rental is one week.

CHILDREN

Montserrat is very laid-back and part of its charm is that there just isn't that much to do. Consider taking the older ones to the Montserrat Volcano Observatory and on hikes, take a boat ride out to Plymouth or rent a kayak. The four beaches are small but offer good swimming and snorkeling (bring equipment).

DANGERS & ANNOYANCES

The Soufrière Hills Volcano has been active since 1995, but there's been no major volcanic activity since February 2010. Still, about two-thirds of Montserrat are still vulnerable. The former capital of Plymouth and the entire south belong to the so-called 'Exclusion Zone.' Visits here are subject to current threat levels and only possible with a licensed tour guide, who needs to obtain prior authorization from police. Note that there's a US$100 fee per entry in addition to any tour charges.

On occasion, southern winds blow ash and volcanic gases across the entire island, which can lead to flight cancellations. The situation is constantly monitored by Montserrat Volcano Observatory staff. Sirens warning of impending volcanic activity are tested at noon daily. If they go off at other times, immediately turn your radio to 88.3 FM or 95.5 FM and follow instructions.

ELECTRICITY

Most places have dual 220/110 voltage; North American two-pin sockets are prevalent but three-pins are around too, so bring an adapter.

EMERGENCY NUMBERS

| Fire | ☏911 |
| Police | ☏999 |

FOOD

From simple food trucks to (the one) hotel dining room, there's some excellent eating

on Montserrat. The fare is classic Caribbean and value for money is high. Self-caterers can pick up supplies at a handful of small supermarkets.

Essential Food & Drink

➜ **Goat water** Montserrat's national dish is far more loved than its dubious-sounding name would suggest. 'Got some?' is a frequent conversation starter and refers to the spicy clove-scented broth accented with floating chunks of goat meat. It's eaten hot with a crusty bread roll.

➜ **Fruit juices** Exotic fruits grow in abundance on Montserrat and make delicious fresh juices. Depending on the season, you'll find mango, guava and papaya as well as the more unusual West Indian cherry and soursop, which tastes a little like a creamy strawberry with hints of pineapple and coconut.

GLBT TRAVELLERS

Homosexuality is legal under Montserrat law, but most people are quite conservative and don't approve of public displays of affection between same-sex couples. There's no problem for same-sex couples sharing a room.

HEALTH

Only basic medical care is available on Montserrat, the best option is **St John's Hospital** (☏ 664-491-5218). The nearest full-service hospital is in Antigua, the nearest hyperbaric chamber in Guadeloupe.

LEGAL MATTERS

Montserrat's legal system is based on British common law. In case of legal difficulties, you have the right to legal representation and are eligible for legal aid if you can't afford to pay for private services. If you are arrested, local police must notify your nearest embassy or consulate of your predicament.

MONEY

There are ATMs at Royal Bank of Canada and Bank of Montserrat in Brades; both dispense EC dollars 24/7. Few shops, hotels and restaurants accept credit cards.

Exchange Rates

AUSTRALIA	A$1	EC$1.93
CANADA	C$1	EC$1.98
EURO ZONE	€1	EC$2.81
JAPAN	¥100	EC$2.30
NEW ZEALAND	NZ$1	EC$1.86
UK	UK£1	EC$3.29
US	US$1	EC$2.68

For current exchange rates, see www.xe.com.

Tipping

Restaurants If the service charge is not automatically included in the bill, tip 10% to 15%; if it is, it's up to you to leave a small additional tip.

Taxi Tip 10% to 15% of the fare.

PUBLIC HOLIDAYS

In addition to holidays observed throughout the region, Montserrat celebrates the following public holidays:

New Year's Day January 1

St Patrick's Day March 17

Good Friday/Easter Monday March or April

Labor Day May 1

Pentecost/Whit Monday 40 days after Easter

Queen's Birthday First, second or third weekend in June

Emancipation Day First Monday in August

Christmas/Boxing Day December 25/26

TAXES & REFUNDS

Hotels add 10% accommodation tax (7% at guesthouses) to the final bill. There is no sales tax or value-added tax (VAT).

Visitors are not eligible to reclaim VAT paid during their trip.

TELEPHONE

➡ Montserrat's country code is ☑664.

➡ To call from North America, dial 011 + 1 + 664 + local number. From elsewhere, dial your country's international access code + 1 + 664 + local number.

➡ To call abroad from Montserrat, dial 011 + country code + area code + local number.

TIME

Clocks in Montserrat are set to Eastern Caribbean Time (Atlantic Time), which is four hours behind GMT. The island does not observe daylight saving time, but since other countries do, the following times are indicative only:

CITY	NOON IN MONTSERRAT
Auckland	5am + 1 day
Frankfurt/Milan	5pm
London	4pm
Los Angeles	8am
New York	11am
Sydney	3am + 1 day

TRAVELERS WITH DISABILITIES

Not much is done on Montserrat to aid mobility-impaired and other disabled persons. Access to buildings and transportation is very difficult, sidewalks (where they exist) are uneven, curbs high and ramps rare.

Download Lonely Planet's free Accessible Travel Guide from http://lptravel.to/AccessibleTravel.

VOLUNTEERING

Coral Cay Conservation (www.coralcay.org) This UK-based nongovernmental environmental organization needs volunteers for its scientific surveys to collect data from tropical forest and coral reefs and to run community education programs about conservation skills and sustainability.

Turtle Conservation Montserrat (http://ccoleby2001.wixsite.com/turtlesmontserrat) Volunteers working with local turtle conservationist John Jeffers help monitor the annual arrival of leatherback, loggerhead, hawksbill and green turtles who come to nest in Montserrat, and assist with the release of hatchlings at the beach.

🛈 Getting There & Away

AIR

Tiny **John A Osborne Airport** (MNI; near Gerald's village) is served several times daily by seven- or eight-passenger aircraft from Antigua by **Fly Montserrat** (www.flymontserrat.com) and **SVG Air/ABM Air** (☑ in Antigua 268-562-7183, in Montserrat 664-491-4200; www.montserrat-flights.com). High winds, heavy rain or volcanic ash may delay service for hours or days.

SEA

Jaden Sun Ferry (☑ in Antigua 268-778-9786, in Montserrat 664-496-9912; round-trip adult/child 2-12yr EC$300/150) On-and-off ferry service from St John's in Antigua to Little Bay on Montserrat in 90 minutes for EC$300 round-trip (children two to 12 years EC$150). Call or check www.visitmontserrat.com for the latest schedule. Bad weather will suspend service.

🛈 Getting Around

If you're staying on Montserrat, your host will arrange for a pick-up from the airport or the ferry dock. If you're just here for the day, it's best to prearrange for a guided tour. See the tourist office website (www.visitmontserrat.com) for details.

BUS

Minibuses ply the main road from Monday to Saturday between 7am and 5pm. There is no schedule and no official stops, so just hail one as it passes. The fare is EC$3 to EC$5. For an additional fee, buses will travel off route to where you need to go.

ⓘ DEPARTURE TAX

The combined departure and security tax for stays longer than 24 hours is EC$55 or US$21 – cash only.

CAR

Hiring a car on Montserrat requires obtaining a local driver's license (EC$50) at the airport, ferry port or the police station in Brades. Arrange a car through your accommodation or contact any of the agencies listed on www.visit-montserrat.com/get-around.

Driving is on the left. The speed limit is 20mph because of the curvy roads and steep terrain. Use your horn at hairpin curves. There are no traffic lights.

HITCHING

Naturally, there are some inherent risks in accepting a ride from strangers but on Montserrat this is actually a common way to get around the island. It's customary to waggle your forefinger rather than stick out your thumb.

Hitching is never entirely safe, and we don't recommend it. Travelers who hitch should understand that they are taking a small but potentially serious risk.

TAXI

Taxis wait at the ferry terminal and the airport and may also be arranged by phone. Ask at your accommodation or contact a driver directly (see www.visitmontserrat.com/get-around for a list). Cars are not metered, so agree on the fare in local currency before setting off.

All drivers double as guides and charge about US$25 per hour for all passengers.

Puerto Rico

POP 3.5 MILLION / 🖉 787

Why Go?

Golden sand, swashbuckling history and wildly diverse terrain make the sun-washed backyard of the United States a place fittingly hyped as the 'Island of Enchantment.' It's the Caribbean's only island where you can catch a wave before breakfast, hike a rainforest after lunch and race to the beat of a high-gloss, cosmopolitan city after dark. Between blinking casinos and chirping frogs, Puerto Rico is also a land of dynamic contrasts, where the breezy gate of the Caribbean is bedeviled by the hustle of contemporary American culture.

A quick visit for Puerto Rico's beaches, historic forts and nightclubs will quicken a visitor's pulse, but the island's singular essence reveals itself to those who go deeper, exploring the misty crags of its mountains and pastel facades of the island's remote corners.

Best Places to Eat

➡ José Enrique (p601)
➡ Luquillo Beach Kiosks (p606)
➡ El Quenepo (p612)
➡ El Vejigante (p615)

Best Places to Sleep

➡ The Dream Catcher (p599)
➡ Condado Vanderbilt Hotel (p599)
➡ Hacienda Tamarindo (p611)
➡ Tres Sirenas (p617)

When to Go

Mid-Dec–mid-Apr & Jul Crowds escaping the frosty US mainland in winter see hotel rates go up and seasonal attractions come to life. In July, local families create a second high season, filling beach towns.

Sep–Nov & mid-Apr–May Puerto Rico's tourist infrastructure takes a breather to regroup during shoulder season, though there isn't a significant fluctuation in prices or services.

Jun–Nov Apart from July, things get pretty lethargic during hurricane season; some resorts offer discounted packages, but prices at small hotels don't drop precipitously.

Puerto Rico Highlights

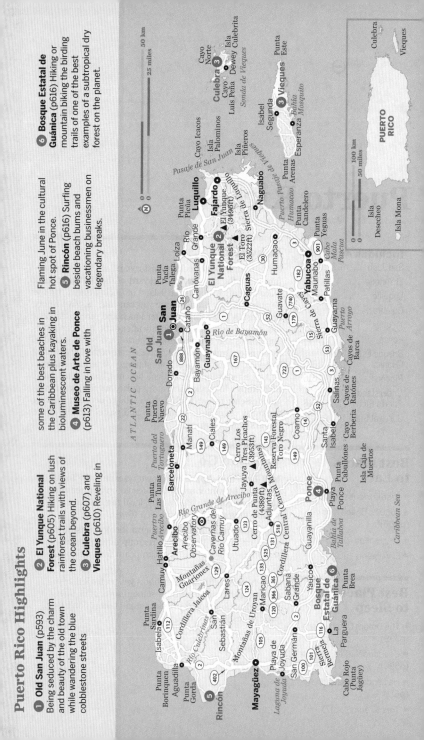

❶ Old San Juan (p593) Being seduced by the charm and beauty of the old town while wandering the blue cobblestone streets

❷ El Yunque National Forest (p605) Hiking on lush rainforest trails with views of the ocean beyond.

❸ Culebra (p607) and **Vieques** (p610) Reveling in some of the best beaches in the Caribbean plus kayaking in bioluminescent waters.

❹ Museo de Arte de Ponce (p613) Falling in love with Flaming June in the cultural hot spot of Ponce.

❺ Rincón (p616) Surfing beside beach bums and vacationing businessmen on legendary breaks.

❻ Bosque Estatal de Guánica (p616) Hiking or mountain biking the birding trails of one of the best examples of a subtropical dry forest on the planet.

SAN JUAN

Established in 1521, San Juan is the second-oldest European-founded settlement in the Americas and the oldest under US jurisdiction. Shoehorned onto a tiny islet that guards the entrance to San Juan harbor, the old town was inaugurated almost a century before the *Mayflower* laid anchor in present-day Massachusetts, and it is now a historic wonderland that juxtaposes historical authenticity with pulsating modern energy.

Beyond its timeworn 15ft-thick walls, San Juan is far more than a collection of well-polished colonial-era artifacts – it's also a mosaic of ever-evolving neighborhoods such as Santurce, which has a raw vitality fueled by street art, superb restaurants and a bar scene that takes over the streets at night.

And then there's the beaches. Silky ribbons of sand line San Juan's northern edge from swanky Condado to resort-filled Isla Verde. You can land at the airport and be splashing in the azure waters an hour later.

◉ Sights

Most of San Juan's major attractions, including museums and art galleries, are in Old San Juan. Beaches dominate the appeal of Condado, Ocean Park and Isla Verde (as they should), while Santurce offers buzzy, gritty delights. Be aware that most museums are closed on Mondays.

◉ Old San Juan

★ El Morro
FORT

(Fuerte San Felipe del Morro; Map p594; ☑787-729-7423; www.nps.gov/saju; 501 Norzagaray, Old San Juan; adult/child US$5/free; ⊙9am-6pm; 🚌Fort) The star of Old San Juan, El Morro juts aggressively over bold headlands, glowering across the Atlantic at would-be conquerors. The 140ft walls (some up to 15ft thick) date back to 1539 and El Morro is said to be the oldest Spanish fort in the New World. Displays document the construction of the fort, which took almost 200 years, as well as El Morro's role in rebuffing attacks on the island by the British, the Dutch and, later, the US military. A short film providing a historical overview of the fort is screened every 15 minutes.

ℹ TUNNEL TOURS

Hour-long free guided tours roam the tunnels at **Fuerte San Cristóbal** every Saturday (English) and Sunday (Spanish) at 10:30am and 12:30pm. Come at least half an hour beforehand (or earlier) and add your name to the sign-up list. Guides walk you through three of the fort's tunnels, including one that's otherwise closed to the public.

★ Fuerte San Cristóbal
FORT

(San Cristóbal Fort; Map p594; ☑787-729-6777; www.nps.gov/saju; 501 Norzagaray, Old San Juan; adult/child $5/free; ⊙9am-6pm; 🚌Fort) San Juan's second major fort is Fuerte San Cristóbal, one of the largest military installations the Spanish built in the Americas. In its prime, San Cristóbal covered 27 acres with a maze of six interconnected forts protecting a central core with 150ft walls, moats, booby-trapped bridges and tunnels. The fort has a fascinating museum, a store, military archives, a reproduction of military barracks, and stunning Atlantic and city views.

★ Museo de las Américas
MUSEUM

(Museum of the Americas; Map p594; ☑787-724-5052; www.museolasamericas.org; cnr Cuartel de Ballajá, Norzagaray & Calle del Morro, Old San Juan; adult/child $6/4; ⊙9am-noon & 1-4pm Tue-Fri, 10am-5pm Sat, noon-5pm Sun; 🚌Fort) This museum presents an impressive overview of cultural development in the Americas, including indigenous, African and European influences. Four permanent exhibits integrate art, history and sociology in thoughtful and provocative ways; the coverage of slavery is particularly moving, including a recreation of travel on a slave ship. Audiovisual highlights and knowledgeable guides enrich visits.

Paseo de la Princesa
WATERFRONT

(Walkway of the Princess; Map p594; Old San Juan) Evoking a distinctly European feeling, the Paseo de la Princesa is a 19th-century esplanade just outside the city walls. Lined with antique streetlamps, trees, statues, benches, food vendors' carts and street entertainers, this romantic walkway ends at the magnificent **Raíces Fountain** (Roots Fountain; Map p594), a stunning sculpture

PUERTO RICO SAN JUAN

Old San Juan

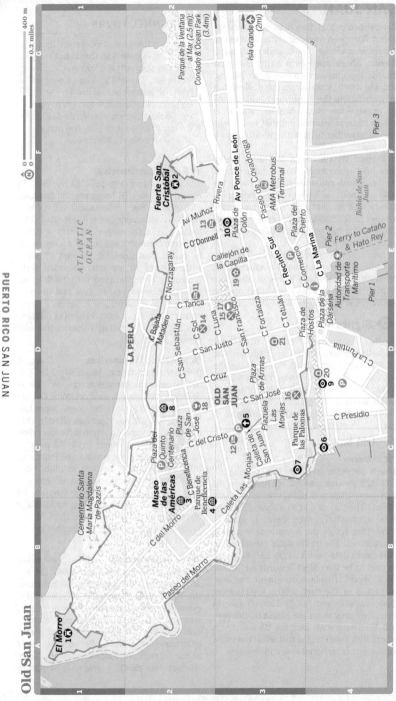

Old San Juan

and water feature that depicts the island's eclectic Taíno, African and Spanish heritage. Festivals and fairs are often held here, including the weekend **artisans fair** (Map p594; ⊙ noon-8pm Fri-Sun).

Plaza de Colón   SQUARE
(Columbus Plaza; Map p594; cnr San Francisco & Tetuán, Old San Juan) Tracing its roots back more than a century to the 400-year anniversary of Columbus' first expedition, the Plaza de Colón is dominated by its towering statue of Columbus atop a pillar. Ringed with tall trees and outdoor cafes, the plaza sees a lot of action. At this end of Old San Juan, the city wall was torn down in 1897 and the plaza stands on the site of one of the city's original gated entries, Puerta Santiago.

La Fortaleza   HISTORIC SITE
(El Palacio de Santa Catalina; Map p594; 🖉 ext 2211 787-721-7000; www.fortaleza.gobierno.pr; Calle Recinto, Old San Juan; suggested donation $3; ⊙ tours 9am-3:30pm Mon-Fri) Guarded iron gates mark La Fortaleza. This imposing building, dating from 1533, is the oldest executive mansion in continuous use in the western hemisphere. The original fortress for the young colony, La Fortaleza eventually yielded its military preeminence to the city's newer and larger forts and was remodeled and expanded to domicile island governors for more than three centuries. You can take a 30-minute guided tour that includes the mansion's Moorish gardens, the dungeon and the chapel.

Casa Blanca   HISTORIC BUILDING
(White House; Map p594; 🖉 787-725-1454; Calle San Sebastián, Old San Juan; entrance $3; ⊙ 8am-noon & 1-4pm Wed-Sun) First constructed in 1521 as a residence for Puerto Rico's pioneering governor, Juan Ponce de León (who died before he could move in), Casa Blanca is the oldest continuously occupied house in the western hemisphere. Today it's a historic monument containing a sparse museum and an Alhambra-style garden with a series of fountains. The interior rooms are furnished with antiques and paintings from the 16th and 17th centuries; the views of the bay from the 2nd floor are among the best in Old San Juan.

Museo de San Juan   MUSEUM
(Map p594; 🖉 787-480-3547; museodesanjuan@sanjuanciudadpatria.com; 150 Norzagaray, Old San Juan; by donation; ⊙ 9am-noon & 1-4pm Tue-Sat, 11am-5pm Sun; 🚌 Fort) Located in what was once the city marketplace, the Museo de San Juan offers the definitive take on the city's 500-year history. A permanent exhibit showcases well-laid-out pictorial and photographic testimonies from the Caparra ruins to modern-day neighborhoods. There's also a half-hour video about the history of San Juan and a temporary exhibition space that often features work from emerging artists. Every Saturday morning a small **farmers market** (Map p594; www.mercadoagricola natural.com; snacks from $2; ⊙ 8am-1pm Sat; 🚌; 🚌 Fort, El Morro) 🖉 is held in the pretty inner courtyard.

PUERTO RICO SAN JUAN

DON'T MISS

SANTURCE ART SCENE

For eye-popping examples of Puerto Rico's vivid visual art, head to San Juan's Santurce district. Museums, galleries, outdoor art and impromptu graffiti combine for a visual riot as vibrant as the best salsa.

Catedral de San Juan CHURCH
(Map p594; ☑787-722-0861; 153 Calle del Cristo, Old San Juan; ⊙8am-4pm) FREE Although noticeably smaller and more austere than other Spanish churches, the Catedral de San Juan nonetheless retains a simple earthy elegance. Founded originally in 1521, the first church on this site was destroyed in a hurricane in 1529. A replacement was constructed in 1540 and, over a period of centuries, it slowly evolved into the neoclassical-inspired monument seen today.

⊙ Santurce

★Museo de Arte de Puerto Rico MUSEUM
(MAPR; Map p598; ☑787-977-6277; www.mapr. org; 299 Av de Diego, Santurce; adult/concession $6/3, Wed after 2pm free; ⊙10am-8pm Wed, to 5pm Thu-Sat, 11am-6pm Sun; ☑T5, T21) San Juan boasts one of the largest and most celebrated art museums in the Caribbean. Housed in a splendid neoclassical building that was once the city's Municipal Hospital, MAPR boasts 18 exhibition halls spread over an area of 130,000 sq feet. The artistic collection includes paintings, sculptures, posters and carvings from the 17th to the 21st century, chronicling such renowned Puerto Rican artists as José Campeche, Francisco Oller, Nick Quijano and Rafael Ferrer.

⊙ Carolina

Museo del Niño de Carolina MUSEUM
(☑787-257-0261; www.museodelninocarolina.com; Av Campo Rico, Carolina; adult/child $10/6, mini-zoo extra $2/1, go-carts $5; ⊙9am-5pm Wed-Fri, 10am-6pm Sat & Sun; ☑☑) Kids go to town at this sprawling hands-on museum in suburban San Juan. Inside, interactive and fun displays get kids thinking about things like volcanoes, electricity and music. Dress-up areas, a mini-city and construction sites let them play at being grown up. Outside, an MD-82 American Airlines plane is perfect for exploring. A small petting zoo and go-carts also are big hits. Worth the short trip to Carolina, especially on a rainy day.

🏖 Beaches

★Balneario Escambrón BEACH
(off Av Muñoz Rivera, Puerta de Tierra; parking $5; ⊙8:30am-6pm; ☑D53, T3, T5, T21) A sheltered arc of raked sand, decent surf breaks, plenty of local action and a 17th-century Spanish fort shimmering in the distance are the hallmarks of this fine beach only a stone's throw from Old San Juan and the busy tourist strip of Condado. Best of all, it's often uncrowded.

★Playa Ocean Park BEACH
(Map p598; off McLeary, Ocean Park) Ocean Park's lesser fame is its hidden blessing. Fronted by leafy residential streets and embellished by B&Bs, its wide sweep of fine, diamond-dust sand is protected by offshore reefs and caressed by cooling seasonal trade winds. The neighborhood's namesake beach is perfectly tranquil, yet open to all: just pick a road through the low-rise gated community and follow it toward the water.

★Playa Isla Verde BEACH
(off Av Isla Verde, Isla Verde) With its legions of tanned bodies and dexterous beach bums flexing their triceps around the volleyball net, Playa Isla Verde basks in its reputation as the Copacabana of Puerto Rico. Serenity seekers may prefer to head west to Ocean Park and dodge the extended families and colonizing spring-break hedonists that stake space here. Whatever your view, this broad, mile-long wedge of sand that lies between Punta Las Marías and Piñones is an undeniable beauty.

Playa Condado BEACH
(Map p598; off Av Ashford, Condado) Hemmed in by hotel towers and punctuated by rocky outcrops, Condado's narrow beaches are busier than Ocean Park's, but less exclusive than Isla Verde's. Expect boisterous games of volleyball and plenty of crashing Atlantic surf. Families congregate around the big hotels, while gay men like the beach at the end of Calle Vendig. **Parque de la Ventana al Mar** (Window to the Sea Park; Map p598; Av Ashford, Condado) has lovely waterfront views.

🏃 Activities

The glittering azure waters are an obvious draw for outdoor fun in San Juan. Beaches that open to the Atlantic are great for kite-surfing and surfing, while the reefs draw snorkelers and divers. The city's glassy lagoons and waterways are perfect for kayaking and paddleboarding. On land you can get out and about in the nearby green hills and mangrove forests.

Velauno WATER SPORTS
(Map p598; ☑787-470-9099; www.velauno.com; 860 Av Ashford, Condado; 1hr paddleboard & kayak rental from $25, tours from $55; ⊙9am-5pm) Velauno offers stand-up paddleboarding classes and rentals. It also has single and double kayak rentals and tours.

Pine Grove Surf Club WATER SPORTS
(☑787-361-5531; www.pinegrovesurfclub.com; tours/lessons from $35/45; ⊙7am-6pm) Owned and operated by the friendly Nogales brothers, this operation offers fun surf lessons on Pine Grove beach, paddleboarding tours in the lagoons of Piñones and snorkeling excursions off gorgeous Balneario Escambrón.

15 Knots KITESURFING
(☑787-215-5667; www.15knots.com; Beach House Hotel, 4851 Av Isla Verde, Isla Verde; rental per hour from $50, lessons from $295; ⊙10am-6pm) The often-gusty conditions off San Juan's beaches make the waters prime kitesurfing territory. This recommended outfit offers rentals and lessons.

Scuba Dogs DIVING, SNORKELING
(☑787-783-6377; www.scubadogs.net; Parque del Tercer Milenio, Puerta de Tierra; dives from $75; ⊙9am-7pm Mon-Sat) This large, long-running outfit has been a tireless supporter of the offshore coral wonderland that is **Escambrón Marine Park** (off Av Muñoz Rivera, Puerta de Tierra; ▣D53, T3, T5, T21). The Dogs offer gear rental, an array of shore and boat dive trips, plus training. Its shop is in Parque del Tercer Milenio.

⌲ Tours

Excursiones Eco TOURS
(☑787-565-0089; www.excursioneseco.com; walking/boat tours from $15/45) This community-oriented tour company offers various guided trips to lesser visited areas of San Juan, including boat tours through the city's lagoons and excursions into squatter communities and other economically underserved neighborhoods. Tours include historical background, flora and fauna details, and information about the current struggles faced in the city. Approximately

85% of all proceeds go directly to the guides themselves.

Flavors of San Juan FOOD & DRINK
(☑787-964-2447; www.sanjuanfoodtours.com; adult/child $80/70) If eating your way around the old town is your style, Flavors of San Juan conducts three-hour walking tours that give you a tasty dose of the local cuisine. Rum tastings and a primer on prepping the popular dish *mofongo* folded in too.

✺✺ Festivals & Events

★**Fiestas de la Calle San Sebastián** CULTURAL
(Calle San Sebastián, Old San Juan; ⊙mid-Jan) For a full week around the third weekend of January, Old San Juan's Calle San Sebastián hums with processions, music, food stalls and larger-than-ever crowds. During the day, it's folk art and crafts; at night, it's raucous revelry.

★**Festival Casals** MUSIC
(☑787-723-5005; http://corporacionartesmusicales.pr; El Centro de Bellas Artes Luis A Ferré, 22 Av Ponce de León, Santurce; tickets $15-75; ⊙late Feb-early Mar) Since 1956 renowned soloists and orchestras have come from all over the world to join the Puerto Rico Symphony Orchestra in performing virtuoso concerts night after night, primarily at El Centro de Bellas Artes Luis A Ferré (p602). The performances usually stretch over about three weeks from late February into March.

Culinary Festival FOOD & DRINK
(www.facebook.com/sofoculinaryfest; ⊙Aug & Dec) SoFo's alfresco culinary festival is a moveable feast that in recent years has

---

A WEEKEND IN SAN JUAN

Stay in Old San Juan. Start your first day with an exquisite cup of Puerto Rican coffee at **Finca Cialitos** (Map p594; ☑939-207-9998; www.fincacialitos.com; 267 San Francisco, Old San Juan; snacks from $3; ⊙7:30am-4:30pm Tue-Fri, 8am-5pm Sat & Sun). Explore the historical sights of the **colonial quarter** and catch the sunset from an old wall. Wander till you find the perfect eatery before heading to **Nuyorican Café** (p602) for salsa music. Hit **Isla Verde** (p596) on day two for some beach time and then consider **Ocean Park** for dinner.

Condado & Ocean Park

tended to happen twice a year, in August and December. During the three-night event, a two-block wedge of Fortaleza is closed to traffic and commandeered by local restaurateurs who set up their tables in the street and rustle up their best dishes. Live bands drop by, belly dancers entertain diners and the food is sizzlingly good.

🛏 Sleeping

🛏 Old San Juan

Posada San Francisco HOSTEL, GUESTHOUSE $
(Map p594; ☎787-996-0324; www.posada-colonial-puertorico.com; Plaza de Colón, 405 San Francisco, Old San Juan; dm $22, d with shared bathroom $60, all incl breakfast; ❄🛜; 🚇El Morro, Fort) This family-run posada makes up for lackluster service by being spacious and clean. Double- and twin-bedded rooms have high ceilings, fridges and classic tile floors. Exquisite 5th-floor-patio views, plenty of bathrooms (no waiting in line for the showers) and a guest kitchen top it off. Continental breakfast included. The elevator can be cranky – take the stairs if you don't want to chance it.

★Casa Sol B&B $$
(Map p594; ☎787-980-9700, 787-399-0105; www.casasolbnb.com; 316 Sol, Old San Juan; r $170-230; ❄🛜) This charming B&B is located in a beautifully restored 18th-century building in the heart of the old town. Rooms are spacious and nicely decorated, each with unique furnishings, folk art and touches like fresh flowers. The cheery central courtyard doubles as a dining area where a homemade breakfast is served each morning; fittingly for its name and address, it's done up in a radiant yellow. The affable owners live on-site and are generous with their local knowledge.

★Hotel El Convento HISTORIC HOTEL $$$
(Map p594; ☎787-723-9020; www.elconvento. com; 100 Calle del Cristo, Old San Juan; r $270-400, ste $660-1440; 🅿❄@🛜❄) Historic monument, tapas restaurant, meeting place, coffee bar and evocative colonial-era building – El Convento is Puerto Rico's most complete atmospheric and multifaceted hotel. Built in 1651 as the New World's first Carmelite convent, the 67 rooms and five suites (2nd-floor rooms have the highest ceilings) are gorgeously decorated with Andalusian tiles, mahogany and thick rugs. Service is impeccable from reception to the bar.

🛏 Condado

★Coral Princess Hotel HOTEL $$
(Map p598; ☎787-977-7700; www.coralpr.com; 1159 Magdalena, Condado; r incl breakfast $100-175; ❄🛜❄) The Coral Princess is a 25-room boutique hotel that punches way above its weight. Sitting in Condado's midrange bracket, it offers all the luxuries of the fancy resorts – spacious rooms, flat-screen TVs, marble floors and original art – but with enough intimacy and Latin flavor to remind you that you're still in Puerto Rico. A rooftop Jacuzzi and well-maintained pool make it that much better.

Condado & Ocean Park

◎ Top Sights
1 Museo de Arte de Puerto Rico E2
2 Playa Ocean Park......................................F1

◎ Sights
3 Parque la Ventana al Mar......................C1
4 Playa Condado D1

◎ Activities, Courses & Tours
5 Velauno B1

⌂ Sleeping
6 Condado Vanderbilt Hotel......................C1
7 Coral Princess Hotel................................D1
8 Dream Inn G1

9 The Dream Catcher...................................G1

◎ Eating
10 Cocobana G1
11 José Enrique..D2
12 Kabanas Food Truck C1
13 Kasalta G1
14 Perla D1
15 Santurce Food Trucks C2

◎ Drinking & Nightlife
16 La Placita de Santurce............................D2

◎ Shopping
17 Santurce POP C2

★Condado Vanderbilt
Hotel   LUXURY HOTEL $$$
(Map p598; ☑787-721-5500; www.condadovan-
derbilt.com; 1055 Av Ashford, Condado; r/ste from
$350/445; P❋@🛜⊠) One of the most
opulent hotels when it opened in 1919, the
Condado Vanderbilt Hotel reopened in 2014
after a lavish restoration and expansion. Its
323 rooms, including 90 rooms in the orig-
inal building, are spacious and exude mod-
ern elegance; many have breathtaking city
or ocean views. Service is tops, with conci-
erges stationed on every floor and doormen
who greet you by name.

Ocean Park

★Dream Catcher   B&B $$
(Map p598; ☑787-455-8259; www.dreamcatch-
erpr.com; 2009 España, Ocean Park; r $125-190, ste
$230-290; ❋🛜) The Dream Catcher wows

with its whimsical elegance: fine art and
knick-knacks, luxurious linens and quirky
wallpaper, designer furnishings and lazy
hammocks, plants and sunlight everywhere,
the outdoors brought in. It's high-end boho
living at its best. Guests enjoy outdoor
showers, quiet nooks for relaxing, common
kitchens for socializing and a vegetarian
restaurant serving some of the best breakfasts in town. Service is impeccable. And the
beach is just two blocks away.

★Dream Inn   HOTEL $$
(Map p598; ☑787-200-6340; www.dreaminnpr.
com; 2009 McLeary, Ocean Park; r incl breakfast
$140-175; P❋🛜⊠) A hipster with a big
heart, that's how Dream Inn feels. It's an
urban architectural beauty – cement rules
– with ecofriendly features like cross-breeze
walls, solar panels and rainwater-collection
bins. Units are bright and spotless with art

by local artists; many enjoy private balconies. A rooftop terrace and a lap pool are perfect places to relax. Breakfast at nearby Kasalta (p601) is included.

Isla Verde

La Playita   INN $$
(Hotel La Playa; ☑787-791-1115; 6 Amapola, Isla Verde; r $110-120; ❀☎) ❀ Yes, you can stay oceanfront in Isla Verde without breaking the bank. And be green about it – La Playita has solar hot-water heaters, low-power air-con units and a 2000-gallon water-catchment system. A small garden leads to modern rooms with tasteful beachy decor. The breezy restaurant opens directly onto the water – a million-dollar view (perfect for breakfast!).

Ritz-Carlton   RESORT $$$
(☑787-253-1700; www.ritzcarlton.com; 6961 Av Los Gobernadores, Isla Verde; r/ste from $500/700; ❀❀@☎❀) Decked out in expensive marble and embellished with Alhambra-esque lions that line the path to the swimming pool, this is San Juan at its swankiest and is a favorite hangout of visiting celebrities. Rooms are plush, service is heavy on the 'yes sirs' and 'yes madams', and the communal areas shimmer like winning entries in an international design competition.

✕ Eating

✕ Old San Juan

★ La Bombonera   PUERTO RICAN $
(Map p594; ☑787-705-3370; 259 San Francisco, Old San Juan; $5-17; ❀7:30am-5pm Tue-Sun; ❀❀; ❀City Hall, El Morro) This historic diner shines with a recent renovation including Tiffany stained-glass windows, marble-top tables and a gleaming bronze coffee machine. Even the wait staff is gussied up in bow ties and bolero jackets. *Mallorcas* (a type of sweet bread), pastries and steaming cups of coffee are the favorites here but tasty breakfasts and daily specials make it easy to come for more.

El Jibarito   PUERTO RICAN $$
(Map p594; ☑787-725-8375; www.eljibar-ito1977.com; 280 Sol, Old San Juan; mains $10-27; ❀10:30am-9pm; ❀❀) Welcome to the neighborhood, *hermano*. El Jibarito is the kind of mom-and-pop place you just know will serve a good and garlicky *mofongo* (mashed

plantains) or *arroz con habichuelas* (rice and beans). Which it does. A favorite of local families and visitors, the meals are simple but hearty.

★ Verde Mesa   CARIBBEAN $$$
(Map p594; ☑787-390-4662; www.verdemesa.com; 107 Tetuán, Old San Juan; mains $15-25; ❀6-10pm Tue-Sat; ❀❀) Hidden in plain sight on a bustling Old San Juan street, this little gem of a restaurant is lauded for its vegetarian and seafood fare. Take a break from *mofongo* and enjoy Verde Mesa's fresh and flavorful food. Many of the ingredients are sourced from local organic farms. Pressed-tin ceilings, antiques and mood lighting give meals a romantic patina. Don't miss the crème brûlée.

✕ Condado

Kabanas Food Truck   BURGERS, MEXICAN $
(Map p598; ☑787-969-2180; www.facebook.com/kabanas413; 1014 Av Ashford, Condado; meals $7-12; ❀8am-10pm Mon-Thu, to 1am Fri-Sun) Condado on the cheap – it can be done, and done well. This food truck serves mouthwatering burgers with homemade *tostones* (fried banana chips), hefty tacos with parmesan-encrusted tortillas and breakfast options like waffles, eggs Benedict and açaí bowls. It can get busy, but the wait staff is friendly and efficient. Almost best of all – the ocean views while you eat!

Perla   STEAK, SEAFOOD $$$
(Map p598; ☑787-977-7886; www.perlarestaurant.com; La Concha, 1077 Av Ashford, Condado; mains $25-55; ❀6-10pm Sun-Thu, to 11pm Fri & Sat; ❀) Dine inside an architectural oyster – literally – at romantic Perla, where hand-blown glass lamps cast a flattering glow and pearlescent walls undulate and echo into the nighttime sea. Aquatic options feature on the menu along with steaks, and a voluminous wine list (many by the glass) highlights French and Californian selections. Book ahead for the coveted window seats.

✕ Ocean Park

★ Cocobana   VEGETARIAN $
(Map p598; ☑787-268-7758; 2000 Loíza, Ocean Park; ❀11am-5pm Mon-Sat; ❀☎❀) A mural of a cow with a toothy smile and a flower behind its ear will be the first sign that you've arrived at one of the best vegetarian restaurants in town. Cocobana has an exten-

sive menu of innovative sandwiches, wraps, salads and smoothies – oh so many smoothies. Ingredients are fresh and local, prepared in an open kitchen, the bustling chef in full sight.

Be sure to look beyond the menu though. The daily specials, served cafeteria-style, entice many meat eaters to the veggie side. The special includes a *criollo* main, rice and beans, salad, soup and a drink. All for 10 bucks. Swap in a smoothie for some extra change.

★**Kasalta** CAFE **$$**
(Map p598; ☑787-727-7340; www.kasalta.com; 1966 McLeary, Ocean Park; mains $5-25; ⏱6am-10pm; P✺) Oh the garbanzo (chickpea) soup! Tucked into Ocean Park's residential enclave, Kasalta is the sort of authentic Puerto Rican bakery and diner that you'll find yourself crossing town to visit daily. The coffee here is as legendary as the sweets that fill a long glass display case and include everything from Danish pastries to iced buns.

✕ Isla Verde

Playa Papaya BISTRO **$$**
(☑787/399-1007; Ocean Tower, 5757 Av Isla Verde, Isla Verde; meals $8-15; ⏱8am-3pm Mon-Thu, to 5pm Fri-Sun; ✺✐) This Tiki-inspired bistro serves up a mean breakfast – from coconut pancakes and Oreo waffles to steak and eggs with sweet papaya sauce. Looking for lighter fare? Check out the half dozen açaí bowls with ingredients like chia, bee pollen, hemp and agave. Or opt for a fresh fruit smoothie made to order. Service is hit or miss.

Metropol PUERTO RICAN, CUBAN **$$**
(☑787-791-5585; http://metropolrestaurant.com; Av Isla Verde, Annexo Club Gallistico, Isla Verde; dishes $11-22; ⏱11:30am-10pm; P✺🍴) Find this neighborhood favorite right next to the cockfighting arena. It's well known for the plentiful portions and simple (but not plain) local and Cuban fare. The stuffed Cornish hen is popular. There are several other locations around the island, though it's a family-run endeavor.

✕ Santurce

★**Santurce Food Trucks** STREET FOOD **$**
(Map p598; cnr Av Ponce de León & Cerra, Santurce; meals $4-8; ⏱11am-11pm Wed-Sun) A set of upscale food trucks set up shop most days in an enclosed parking lot on Santurce's main drag. Meatballs. Dumplings. Tacos. Bagels. Gelato. It's a veritable international marketplace. Picnic tables are set up streetside for diners to eat side by side. Evenings bring twinkling lights, adding to the festive feel.

★**José Enrique** BISTRO **$$$**
(Map p598; ☑787-725-3518; www.joseenriquepr.com; 176 Duffaut, Santurce; mains from $18; ⏱11:30am-10pm Tue-Fri, 6:30-10pm Sat; ✺) Though hidden in a pink house without a sign, you'll have no problems finding one of the western hemisphere's best restaurants – just follow the excited hordes in the know. Reservations aren't possible, so be prepared to wait on the sidewalk; your meal is definitely worth the minor inconvenience. The namesake chef is a multiple-award winner and he combines local ingredients brilliantly.

SAN JUAN FOR CHILDREN

Puerto Rico is a family-friendly destination and children are very much a part of daily life across San Juan. You'll see children at all manner of restaurants and events, and no doubt running around plazas late into the evening. Sidewalks are typically in decent condition and wide enough for strollers (though baby-changing facilities are few and far between).

Most resorts have children's clubs or programs; only a few boutique properties have age restrictions. Large swaths of the beaches are reef-protected so waves are gentle. **Playa Ocean Park** (p596) and **Playa Isla Verde** (p596) are particular favorites for families.

In and around San Juan there are several attractions that children really enjoy. The **Museo del Niño de Carolina** (p596) is always a big hit, as are the must-visit sights **El Morro** (p593) and **San Cristóbal** (p593) in Old San Juan. What could be better than huge fortresses complete with tales of gold, plunder and pirates? Kids can explore the walls and tunnels for hours.

Drinking & Nightlife

★ **La Placita de Santurce** STREET PARTY
(Map p598; Calle Dos Hermanos, Santurce; ☺5pm-late Thu-Sat; ☐T3, T5) Santurce's famous market – La Placita – is known as the hub of San Juan's hottest nightlife scenes. Especially good on Thursday and Friday nights, the historic market plaza and its surrounding streets host what becomes a veritable street party: people meeting up, drinking, eating and, as soon as the salsa band warms up, dancing until the wee hours.

★ **La Factoría** BAR
(Map p594; ☏787-412-4251; www.facebook.com/lafactoriapr; 148 San Sebastián, Old San Juan; ☺6pm-4am) You've gotta wedge your way in on weekend nights for DJs, acoustic guitars or sing-along sets. And that's just the start. The so-named *Hijos de Borinquen* (or 'Sons of Puerto Rico') has three speakeasies hidden inside – one a wine bar, another a salsa dance club, the last a snazzy lounge. Great craft cocktails throughout plus tapas for filler.

Club Brava CLUB
(☏787-791-2781; www.bravapr.com; El San Juan Hotel, 6063 Av Isla Verde, Isla Verde; cover $20; ☺10pm-late Thu-Sat) This club inside El San Juan Hotel, gets packed with 'beautiful people' and garners rave reviews from all-night clubbers. A mix of house, reggaeton and salsa fills the small, two-level club, and the atmosphere is electric. Dress up, bring your credit card and get ready to get down to what's touted as the best sound system in the Caribbean.

☆ Entertainment

San Juan has an eclectic entertainment scene. From salsa performances in backstreet bars to the symphony at Bellas Artes. Resort hotels also have live entertainment most nights, and Santurce's galleries and artsy cafes offer up indie films, performance art and live music.

★ **Nuyorican Café** LIVE MUSIC
(Map p594; ☏787-977-1276; www.nuyorican-cafepr.com; 312 San Francisco, Old San Juan; cover $5; ☺8pm-late) If you came to Puerto Rico in search of sizzling salsa music, you'll find it at the Nuyorican Café. San Juan's hottest nightspot – stuffed into an alley off Fortaleza, opposite a nameless drinking hole –

is a congenial hub of live Latino sounds and hip-gyrating locals. Six-piece salsa bands usually get hopping around 11pm.

El Centro de Bellas Artes
Luis A Ferré THEATER
(Bellas Artes; ☏787-724-4747; www.cba.gobierno.pr; 22½ Av Ponce de León, Santurce; ☺box office 10am-6pm Mon-Sat, to 4pm Sun; ☐T3, T5) Built in 1981, this center has more than 1900 seats in the festival hall, about 750 in the drama hall and 200 in the experimental theater. The Puerto Rican Symphony Orchestra holds its weekly winter performances at the complex's newer 1300-seat Pablo Casals Symphony Hall. International stars perform here and it's the major host of the annual Festival Casals (p597).

🛍 Shopping

★ **Puerto Rican Art & Crafts** ARTS & CRAFTS
(Map p594; ☏787-725-5596; www.puertorican-craft-crafts.com; 204 Fortaleza, Old San Juan; ☺10am-6pm Mon-Sat, noon-5pm Sun; ☐City Hall) A large shop specializing in Puerto Rican folk art, paintings and jewelry. Items come from artist workshops found throughout the island. The prices are on the high end, but so is the quality.

★ **Santurce POP** SHOPPING CENTER
(Map p598; www.santurcepop.com; 1116 Av Ponce de León, Santurce; ☺10am-6pm Tue-Sat; ☐T3, T5) In the heart of Santurce, this boho design mart has several booths of handcrafted and locally sourced goods. You'll find everything from hipster T-shirts and unique jewelry to fine leather goods and smoking accessories. Oftentimes the designers themselves are on hand to answer questions. The vegetarian and vegan eatery here is a perfect fit.

ℹ Information

EMERGENCY
In any kind of emergency, call 911.

INTERNET ACCESS
Almost all lodgings have wi-fi, though many in common areas only. A number of plazas in Old San Juan have free hot spots.

MEDICAL SERVICES
Ashford Presbyterian Community Hospital
(☏787-721-2160; www.presbypr.com; 1451 Av Ashford, Condado; ☺24hr; ☐T21) El Presby is the best-equipped and most convenient hospital for most travelers.

MONEY

Banco Popular (www.popular.com; 206 Tetuán, Old San Juan; ⊙8am-4pm Mon-Fri) Banco Popular is the most, well, popular bank in town. Full-service locations and ATMs are found in most neighborhoods, including Condado, Santurce, Ocean Park and Isla Verde.

POST

Old San Juan Post Office (Map p594; ☑787-724-2098; www.usps.com; 100 Paseo de Colón, Old San Juan; ⊙8am-4pm Mon-Fri, to noon Sat; 🚌 city hall)

TOURIST INFORMATION

Puerto Rico Tourism Company (PRTC; Map p594; ☑800-866-7827, 787-722-1709; www.seepuertorico.com; Edificio Ochoa, 500 Tanca, Old San Juan; ⊙8am-4pm Mon-Fri, 9am-5pm Sat; 🚌 City Hall, Fort, El Morro)

ℹ Getting There & Away

AIR

Luis Muñoz Marín International Airport (SJU, LMM Airport; ☑787-253-2329; www.aeropuertosju.com; off Hwy 26, Isla Verde; ⊙24hr) San Juan's busy international airport is only 8 miles from Old San Juan. Plenty of ATMs are located around the entrances and there's a tourist information center (PRTC; ☑787-791-1014, 800-866-7827; www.seepuertorico.com; Terminal C, ⊙9am-8pm) near the baggage claim area in Terminal C. There also are a handful of eateries, coffee stands and gift shops in each terminal. It's barely 10 minutes by cab from Isla Verde.

Isla Grande Airport (SIG, Fernando Luis Ribas Dominicci Airport; ☑787/729-8790; www.prpa.gobierno.pr; Calle Lindbergh, Isla Grande, Miramar) Private aircraft, charter services and some flights serving the islands of Culebra and Vieques use San Juan's Isla Grande Airport, on the Bahía de San Juan in the city's Miramar district.

BOAT

Almost 20 cruise lines call on San Juan, with many cruisers starting and ending their voyages here. It's the second-largest port for cruise ships in the western hemisphere, serving nearly two million passengers each year. Most ships dock at the piers along Calle La Marina near the Customs House, just a short walk from the cobblestoned streets of Old San Juan; others dock at the Pan American Pier on nearby Isla Grande. Popular cruise lines serving San Juan include Royal Caribbean and Viking Ocean Cruises.

PÚBLICO

While there's no island-wide bus system, *públicos* (public vans) offer an alternative option, providing an inexpensive though often time-consuming link between San Juan and other major towns like Fajardo, Ponce or Mayagüez.

In San Juan, *público* centers include LMM international airport and the **Terminal de Carros Públicos** (Terminal de Carros Públicos de Río Piedras; ☑787-294-2412; cnr Arzuaga & Vallejo, Río Piedras) in Río Piedras. Vans leave once they're full and make frequent stops, dropping off and picking up passengers along the way. Service runs Monday through Saturday. Cash only.

ℹ Getting Around

TO/FROM THE AIRPORT

From Luis Muñoz Marín International Airport, fixed-price taxis cost per carload (with up to five passengers) $10 to Isla Verde, $15 to Condado and Ocean Park, and $19 to Old San Juan. Add $1 for each piece of luggage, and $1 between 10pm to 6am. Taxis line up outside of baggage claim areas, where taxi touts hustle passengers into cabs in a remarkably efficient way. Rates are visibly posted. If you find others going your way, consider splitting the cost – just agree on a final destination (ie only one stop per cab).

The bus is the cheapest option into town at $0.75 a ride. Look for the 'Parada' sign outside the arrivals concourse. The D53 and T5 buses serve Old San Juan. The D53 via Isla Verde, Ocean Park and Condado; the latter via Isla Verde and Santurce.

PUBLIC TRANSPORTATION

AMA Metrobus (Autoridad Metropolitana de Autobuses, Metropolitan Bus Authority; ☑787-294-0500; http://ati.pr; fare $0.75, coins only; ⊙most routes 5am-8pm Mon-Sat) AMA Metrobus operates San Juan's public buses. The buses are clean and air-conditioned; however the system itself is not easy for visitors. Route maps and information are hard to find and few bus stops have any indication of what buses stop there. Service can also be erratic, with wait times between 30 and 60 minutes.

Routes taken most often by visitors (bus numbers are followed by associated route descriptions):

➡ **T3** Old San Juan, Puerta de Tierra, Av Ponce de León (Miramar/Santurce), Sagrado Corazón (Tren Urbano station)

➡ **T5** Old San Juan, Puerta de Tierra, Av Ponce de León (Miramar/Santurce), Isla Verde (via Loíza), Luis Muñoz Marín International Airport

➡ **T9** Old San Juan, Puerta de Tierra, Convention Center, Av Fernández Juncos (Miramar/Santurce), Sagrado Corazón (Tren Urbano station), Río Piedras

➡ **T21** Old San Juan, Puerta de Tierra, Av Ashford (Condado), Av Ponce de León (Santurce), Sagrado Corazón (Tren Urbano station)

➤ **C35** Convention Center, Av Ponce de León (Miramar/Santurce), Sagrado Corazón (Tren Urbano station), Av Fernández Juncos (Miramar/Santurce)

➤ **D45** Sagrado Corazón (Tren Urbano station), Isla Verde, Piñones, Loíza

➤ **D53** Old San Juan, Puerta de Tierra, Condado, Ocean Park (via McLeary), Isla Verde, Luis Muñoz Marín International Airport

Tren Urbano (Urban Train; ☑787-294-0500; http://ati.pr; fare $1.50; ◉5:30am-11:30pm) Connects Bayamón with downtown San Juan as far as Sagrado Corazón on the southern side of Santurce. Modern trains run every eight to 16 minutes, serving 16 stations.

TAXI

Taxi fares are set in the main tourism zones. From Old San Juan, trips to Condado, Ocean Park or Isla Grande Airport cost $12, and $19 to Isla Verde and Luis Muñoz Marín International Airport. Journeys within Old San Juan cost $7. You'll also pay a $2 gas surcharge per trip plus $1 for each piece of luggage; add a $1 surcharge between 10pm and 6am.

Taxis line up at the eastern end of Calle Fortaleza in Old San Juan; in other places you will likely need to call one. Try **Metro Taxi** (☑787-725-2870; ◉24hr) or **Rochdale Radio Taxi** (☑787-721-1900; www.taxiprrochdale.com; ◉24hr).

A growing alternative is to use drive share services like Uber (www.uber.com), a private car service offered by freelance drivers. Fares are cheaper than taxis and the service is reliable; all fares are paid by credit card, using an app.

AROUND SAN JUAN

You can be three-quarters of the way across the island and still be within an hour or two's drive of San Juan (traffic permitting). Day trips from the capital can thus take you almost anywhere in the commonwealth. If you're keen to probe deeper, it's worthwhile traveling slower and making an overnight stop.

◉ Sights

★ **Birth of the New World Statue** STATUE
(Estatua de Cristóbal Colón; www.terravistaparkland.com; Km 9.5, Hwy 681) Undeniably Puerto Rico's biggest, most bizarre new attraction, the 362ft likeness of Christopher Columbus (Cristóbal Colón) navigating toward the New World is the work of Russian sculptor Zurab Tsereteli and is the linchpin of the north coast's flashy new tourist development.

The statue, the tallest in North America and Puerto Rico's highest structure, stands astride a green rise overlooking an alluring expanse of beaches and mangroves: a wild area poised to become the TerraVista Park, a future adventure complex in which the statue will take center stage. By 2020 there should be new hotels, restaurants, helicopter rides and 'mangrove adventure' activities such as kayaking and ziplining in this spot.

Officially opened in 2017, the statue is the first (and currently only) part of this megaproject. You can ascend to a viewing gallery about halfway up and imagine the crowds-to-be descending on this peaceful place.

The irony surrounding the statue is as much a talking point as the structure itself. First, that it should be raised within sight of an important ceremonial site for the Taíno, whose culture was decimated following the explorer's arrival on these shores; and second, that it should be raised at all with construction costs of millions of dollars to a heavily debt-saddled island. Many are also concerned about the statue's environmental impact in an ecologically sensitive area.

Love it or hate it, the statue exhibits some splendid workmanship and has launched a revival of this entire stretch of coast.

★ **Observatorio de Arecibo** NOTABLE BUILDING
(☑787-878-2612; www.naic.edu; Hwy 625; adult/child $12/8; ◉9am-4pm mid-Dec–mid-Jan, Jun & Jul, Wed-Sun rest of the year) Puerto Ricans reverently refer to it as 'El Radar', to everyone else it is simply the largest radio telescope in the world. Resembling an extraterrestrial spaceship grounded in the middle of karst country, the Arecibo Observatory looks like something out of a James Bond movie – probably because it is (007 aficionados will recognize the saucer-shaped dish and craning antennae from the 1995 film *Goldeneye*).

The 20-acre dish, operated in conjunction with SRI International, is set in a sinkhole among clusters of haystack-shaped *mogotes*, like earth's ear into outer space. Supported by 50-story cables weighing more than 600 tons, the telescope is involved in the SETI (Search for Extraterrestrial Intelligence) program and used by on-site scientists to prove the existence of pulsars and quasars, the so-called 'music of the stars.' Past work has included the observation of the planet Mercury, the first asteroid image and the discovery of the first extra-solar planets.

Top scientists from around the world perform ongoing research at Arecibo, but an informative visitors center with interpretative displays and an explanatory film provide the public with a fascinating glimpse of how the facility works. There's also a well-positioned viewing platform offering you the archetypal 007 vista.

To get to the observatory, follow Hwys 635 and 625 off Hwy 129. It's only 9 miles south of the town of Arecibo as the crow flies, but the roller-coaster ride through karst country will make it seem more like 90.

EL YUNQUE & EASTERN PUERTO RICO

The east coast is Puerto Rico shrink-wrapped; a tantalizing taste of almost everything the island has to offer squeezed into an area you can drive across in a couple of hours.

Sodden rainforest teems with noisy wildlife and jungle waterfalls at El Yunque National Forest, the commonwealth's tropical gem. Down at sea level, beach lovers bask on the icing-sugar sand of Playa Luquillo. And just east is one of Puerto Rico's stunning bioluminescent bays in the pristine ecological reserve of Las Cabezas de San Juan Reserva Natural.

Separated from mainland Puerto Rico by an 8-mile stretch of blue water, the two bejeweled Caribbean havens of Culebra and Vieques have an irresistible charm thanks to mellow locals, laid-back expats and itinerant sailors. Their beaches and unblemished countryside glimmer invitingly with nary a golf course, casino or huge resort.

El Yunque

◉ Sights

El Yunque National Forest FOREST
(☏787-888-1880; www.fs.usda.gov/elyunque; Northern Entrance, Km 4, Hwy 191; adult/child $4/free; ☺7:30am-6pm; P🚻) is one of Puerto Rico's crown jewels. It boasts nearly 29,000 acres of lush mountainous terrain, with waterfalls dotting the landscape, rushing rivers and gurgling brooks, bromeliads clinging to towering trees, and bamboo groves opening to spectacular ocean views.

The only rainforest in the US National Forest System, El Yunque (named after the Taíno god, Yúcahu) has 23 miles of trails, some short and paved, others long, steep and barely there. Almost all gain some elevation; one of the toughest is to El Yunque's peak, El Toro, almost 3609ft above sea level. Both casual and experienced hikers are sure to find rewarding trails.

El Portal Visitors Center (p606), near Luquillo, is a good place to get your bearings before setting out to explore. The park has two entrances. The northern side, 23 miles east of San Juan, receives the majority of visitors and has lots of well-marked trails. The southern side, near Naguabo, is wilder and less developed, making for beautiful off-the-beaten track experiences. Several guesthouses here have private trails leading into El Yunque, making it easy to hike an entire day and not see a soul.

🛏 Sleeping

★El Hotelito INN $$
(☏787-980-7402; www.yunquehotelito.com; off Hwy 976; r incl breakfast $160; P🖙❄) Set on a 25-acre tropical flower farm, this seven-en-room inn offers serenity and beauty. Once a private home, there's art, family heirlooms and loads of books in the welcoming common areas. A pool overlooks the rainforest. Rooms are upscale and artsy, all with private balconies with mountain or ocean views. Three miles of private trails lead directly to El Yunque.

★Casa Flamboyant B&B $$$
(☏787-559-9800; www.casaflamboyantpr.com; Km 22.2, Hwy 191; r incl breakfast $230-295; P🖙❄) Tucked way up in the mountains with panoramic views of El Yunque, Casa Flamboyant makes the most of its breathtaking location. Three well-appointed rooms (two with private terraces), a cozy living room and an infinity pool are as elegant as Puerto Rico's rainforest gets. Private trails lead to gorgeous waterfalls and swimming holes, which guests often have to themselves. Adults only.

🍴 Eating

Palmer, the colorful strip where Hwy 191 heads south from Hwy 3 toward El Yunque, has some attractive eating options. Inside the park, there are several cheerful roadside stands and the visitors center has a good cafe.

★ **Mi Vida Café & Burger** CAFE, BURGERS **$**

(☑ 787-888-7356; 5 Principal, Palmer; burgers $3-12; ⊙ 10am-6pm; 🖊) This mom-and-pop cafe serves up some of the best burgers on the coast – some stuffed with chorizo – with purple yam fries on the side. Swap out the bun for huge plantain or *mofongo* patties. Freshly made and well-stuffed *pastelillos* (turnovers) and all manner of wraps are great to-go options. Vegetarian choices abound.

★ **Lluvia** CAFE **$**

(☑ 787-657-5186; www.lluviapr.com; 52 Principal, Palmer; mains $5-12; ⊙ 7am-3pm Wed-Sun; 🛜🖊♿) With a setting seemingly straight out of an IKEA catalogue, this contemporary cafe dishes up a range of creative meals, from excellent breakfasts to thick sandwiches, salads, flatbread pizza and more at lunch. The orange juice is freshly squeezed and the coffee made from premium Puerto Rican beans.

ℹ Information

El Portal Visitors Center (☑ 787-888-1880; www.fs.usda.gov/elyunque; Northern Entrance, Km 4, Hwy 19; adult/child $4/free; ⊙ 9am-5pm) Make this sprawling visitors center your first stop. There are interactive exhibits, a short overview film (in Spanish and English), a walkway through the forest canopy and a gift shop. Vending machines serve up drinks and snacks, plus there is a good small cafe. Pick up free basic maps and information, then admire some stunning tree ferns.

ℹ Getting There & Away

Since there's no public transportation to El Yunque, you will need to get here with private vehicle, taxi (from $85) or on a guided tour. Driving from San Juan, there will be signs directing you from Hwy 3 to Hwy 191. Turn south at Palmer and follow the signs to El Yunque National Forest.

Luquillo

In many ways Luquillo is a typical Puerto Rican town: a coastal strip of magnificent beaches backed by a mishmash of condo towers, strip malls and urban sprawl. But here, in the island's busy northeastern corner, beauty easily outweighs the beast. Playa Luquillo, the mile-long crescent of surf and sand to the west of the town, is regularly touted as being the commonwealth's finest *balneario* (public beach) and the proverbial home of Puerto Rican soul food. Because

of Luquillo's popularity with sanjuaneros (people from San Juan), your best time to visit is on a weekday.

⊙ Sights

★ **Playa Luquillo** BEACH

(Balneario La Monserrate; off Frontage Rd, Luquillo; parking $5; 🅿) Luquillo is synonymous with the fabulous Playa Luquillo. Set on a calm bay facing northwest and protected from the easterly trade winds, the public part of this beach makes a mile-long arc to a point of sand shaded by evocative coconut palms. The beach itself is a plane of broad, gently sloping sand that continues its gradual slope below the water.

With crowds converging here at weekends and during holidays, Luquillo has always been more about atmosphere than solitude. Many come just for the famous long strip of food kiosks (p606) at its western end. Umbrellas ($10) and beach loungers ($5) can be rented near the **balneario** (☑ 787-889-5871; Playa Luquillo, Luquillo; tent/powered sites $10/17, parking $4; 🅿).

🛏 Sleeping & Eating

Luquillo Sunrise Beach Inn HOTEL **$$**

(☑ 787-889-1713; www.luquillosunrise.com; Herminio Díaz Navarro, Luquillo; r incl breakfast $150-190; 🅿❄🛜) The Luquillo Sunrise is caressed by cooling breezes in its 17 ocean-facing rooms. Each is very '80s tropical in decor – think *Golden Girls* – but comfortable nonetheless. There's a communal patio and all upper-floor rooms have large balconies overlooking Playa Azul. Luquillo plaza is two blocks away and the famous balneario (p606) is a 30-minute stroll along the beach.

★ **Luquillo Beach Kiosks** PUERTO RICAN **$**

(Playa Luquillo, off Hwy 3, Luquillo; dishes $3-20; ⊙ hours vary, generally noon-10pm; 🅿♿) Luquillo's famous line of 60 or so beachfront *friquitines* (also known as *quioscos, kioskos* or just plain food stalls) along the western edge of Hwy 3 serve often-excellent food at very popular prices. It's a fine way to sample local food and snack culture, including scrumptious *surullitos* (fried cornmeal and cheese sticks).

ℹ Getting There & Around

Hwy 3 leads directly to Rte 193 (aka Calle Fernandez Garcia), which is the main artery of Luquillo.

Públicos run from the **Río Piedras terminal** (p603) in San Juan to Luquillo's central plaza ($5) from Monday to Saturday. Trips take from 2½ to 3½ hours, depending on the traffic. If you're going to the beach, make sure you disembark next to the food kiosks, a mile or so before Luquillo *pueblo*. Taxis cost $72 from San Juan each way.

CULEBRA & VIEQUES

Culebra

Long feted for its diamond-dust beaches and world-class diving reefs, sleepy Culebra is probably more famous for what it hasn't got than for what it actually possesses. There are no big hotels here, no golf courses, no casinos, no fast-food chains, no rush-hour traffic and, best of all, no stress. Situated 16.5 miles off mainland Puerto Rico, it's home to a range of gorgeous natural areas, bays, snorkeling sites, hiking trails and all manner of fine beaches. Come, join the local vibe and explore one of Puerto Rico's most gorgeous destinations.

◉ Sights

★ Culebra National Wildlife Refuge
WILDLIFE RESERVE

(☎787-742-0115; www.fws.gov/caribbean/refuges/culebra) More than 20% of Culebra is part of a spectacular national wildlife refuge, which US President Theodore Roosevelt signed into law more than 100 years ago. Most of this land lies along Culebra's coastline and includes more than 20 cays. Containing three different ecosystems, the refuge serves as a habitat for endangered sea turtles and is also the largest seabird nesting grounds in the Caribbean. For visitors, it is a place for hiking, birdwatching and enjoying secluded beaches.

★ Playa Flamenco
BEACH

(end of Hwy 251) Stretching for a mile around a sheltered, horseshoe-shaped bay, Playa Flamenco is not only one of Culebra's best beaches, it's also generally regarded as the finest in the Caribbean. Backed by low scrub and trees rather than craning palms, Flamenco gets very crowded on weekends, especially with day-trippers from San Juan. Alone among Culebra's beaches, it has a range of amenities. Weekdays are good for a visit, when crowds are few.

★ Playa Carlos Rosario
BEACH

(off Hwy 251) Remote Playa Carlos Rosario is a thin, white-sand beach with one of the best snorkeling areas in Puerto Rico. This is mostly due to a barrier reef that almost encloses the beach's waters; you can snorkel on either side of it by swimming through the boat channel – look for the floating white marker – at the right-hand side of the beach. But be very careful: water taxis and local powerboats cruise this channel, and swimmers have been hit.

★ Playa Zoni
BEACH

(off Hwy 250) Head to the eastern end of the island and you'll eventually run out of road at Playa Zoni. Many locals think this is a better beach than Flamenco and it's hard to argue. Zoni isn't quite as big and curving, but it certainly is stunning in its own right with soft sand, turquoise waters and idyllic views of Cayo Norte, Isla Culebrita and even Charlotte Amelie on the horizon. Do like the locals do and bring a cooler for a picnic.

★ Isla Culebrita
ISLAND

If you need a reason to hire a water taxi, Isla Culebrita is it. This small island, just east of Playa Zoni, is part of the national wildlife refuge. With its six beaches, tide pools, reefs and nesting areas for seabirds, Isla Culebrita has changed little in the past 500 years. The north beaches, especially the long crescent of Playa Tortuga, are popular nesting grounds for green sea turtles – you might even see them swimming near the reefs just offshore.

🏃 Activities

★ Culebra Snorkeling & Dive Center
DIVING, SNORKELING

(☎787-435-3662; www.culebrasnorkelingcenter. com; Pedro Márquez, Dewey; ⊙8:30am-5pm Mon-Thu, to 1:30pm Sun) This friendly shop offers excellent snorkeling excursions around the island where you're sure to see turtles, stingrays and all sorts of tropical fish. If DIY is more your thing, staffers will share snorkeling maps and tips, and point you in the right direction. High-end snorkel gear, kayaks, underwater cameras, even rash guards are available for rent too.

Kayaking Puerto Rico
KAYAKING, SNORKELING

(☎787-742-0523; www.kayakingpuertorico.com; Hwy 251; 3hr tours $55-60) These tours, cheerfully called 'aquafaris', combine kayaking and snorkeling the rich waters of the Luis

Peña Channel Natural Reserve, ending with some time on Playa Flamenco. You can also start at Fajardo at the ferry port (p622) at 8am ($75, includes transfers). This outfit also rents gear (snorkel equipment, paddleboards and kayaks) at reasonable prices.

🛏 Sleeping & Eating

Most of Culebra's restaurants are in the tiny town of Dewey. Beyond town, look for food trucks, which offer cheap, tasty eats. Shoestringers will save by renting a place with a kitchen and cooking for themselves.

Culebra International Hostel   HOSTEL $
(📞 732-547-8831; www.culebrahostel.com; Calle Fulladoza, Dewey; dm/r $33/$90; ❄ 🛜) Once an auto-parts shop, this rambling hostel offers two spacious dorms (including one female-only) with good bunk beds and air-con. There's a simple kitchen and lots of outdoor seating, mostly in a wild garden of potted plants (over 350 at last count). Expat manager Tommy often cooks dinner for guests, served family style.

★ Villa Fulladoza   APARTMENT $$
(📞 787-742-3576; www.villafulladoza.wix.com/culebra; 350 Fulladoza, Dewey; apt $80-95; 🛜) Super-cute and vividly turquoise and salmon, unfussy Villa Fulladoza offers seven bright fan-cooled studio apartments with ocean breezes and plenty of room. The shared patio is shaded by a swaying mango tree, while many of the units have large

---

HIKING CULEBRA'S COUNTRYSIDE

Rejoice! The island is your oyster. The 2.5 mile (4.5km) hike from Dewey to Playa Flamenco is along a paved road with some inclines, but the destination is idyllic. You can veer off to **Playa Tamarindo** from a junction just before the lagoon. Playa Carlos Rosario is reached via a trail that starts at the western end of Playa Flamenco. The hike to **Playa Brava** begins at the end of a back road that cuts north from Rte 250 just past the island's graveyard. The trail rises to a ridge and then drops to the beach through thick scrub. The toughest hike on the island is the rough trail to **Playa Resaca** that traverses the eponymous mountain; the trailhead is just under 2 miles (about 3km) from Dewey.

---

terraces (get one upstairs for great views). If you are lucky enough to enjoy your own private water transportation, there's a boat dock.

★ Villa Flamenco Beach   APARTMENT $$
(📞 787-742-0023, 787-383-0985; www.villaflamencobeach.com; off Hwy 251; studio $135-145, 1-bedroom apt $155-180; 🅿 ❄ 🛜) Gentle waves lulling you to sleep, a night sky replete with twinkling stars and one of the best beaches on the planet just outside your window: this six-unit place is an absolute winner. Enjoy the getaway with self-catering kitchen facilities, inviting hammocks and little more than palms, sand and turquoise waters for atmosphere. Closed October and November.

★ El Panino   FOOD TRUCK, SANDWICHES $
(📞 787-501-1441; Calle Escudero, Dewey; $8-12; 🕐 8am-4pm; 🚸) Sitting in a gravel lot with a handful of other food trucks, El Panino is far and away the heavy hitter here. Gourmet sandwiches, served hot and gooey (like the breakfast melt made with chorizo, egg and cheese) or cool and flavorful (try the roasted veggie sandwich with pesto and goat cheese), are mouthwatering good.

★ Zaco's Tacos   MEXICAN $
(📞 787-742-0243; www.zacostacos.com; 21 Pedro Márquez, Dewey; mains $6-9; 🕐 noon-9pm Mon-Fri, 9:30am-2:30pm Sun; 🚸) This hip open-air restaurant dishes up ultra-fresh Mexican fare plus a smattering of tasty salads. If you're hungry, order a monster-sized burrito with all the fixings. Enjoy your meal in the clapboard dining room or on the shady back patio. Daily specials are worth a look.

ℹ Information

EMERGENCY
Police Station (📞 787-742-3501; Fulladoza, Dewey; 🕐 24hr) Located on the road headed out of Dewey, toward Punta Soldado.

INTERNET ACCESS
Most accommodations have wi-fi, as does the **tourist information center** (p609), whose internet extends to the little park outside.

MEDICAL SERVICES
Hospital de Culebra (📞 787-742-3511; Calle Font, Dewey; 🕐 24hr) Adjoining the Culebra Health Clinic (📞 787-742-3521; Calle Font, Dewey; 🕐 8am-5pm Mon-Sat), Culebra's hospital has a 24-hour emergency room. The island also keeps a plane on emergency standby at

the airport for medical transport to the main island.

MONEY

Banco Popular (☑787-742-3572; www.popular. com; 9 Pedro Márquez, Dewey; ☺8am-3:30pm Mon-Fri) The only full-service bank in Culebra it has a 24-hourr ATM.

POST

Post Office (☑742-3862; www.usps.com; 26 Pedro Márquez, Dewey; ☺9am-4pm Mon-Fri, to noon Sat) Super-efficient, well cooled and right in the center of town.

TOURIST INFORMATION

Tourist Information Office (☑787-742-1033; Calle Pedro Márquez, Dewey; ☺8am-noon & 1-4:30pm Mon-Fri; 🛜) Islandwide information can be found at this tourist information counter, a block from the ferry terminal. Wi-fi is free and extends to the shady plaza right outside its doors.

US Fish & Wildlife Service (☑787-742-0115; www.fws.gov/caribbean/refuges/culebra; off Km 4.2, Hwy 250; ☺7am-4pm Mon-Fri) This government agency is responsible for managing the Culebra National Wildlife Refuge. Stop by the office on the eastern side of Ensenada Honda for maps, information about the refuge, its flora, fauna and hikes, and permission to visit other sections of the refuge.

ⓘ Getting There & Away

AIR

Culebra's **Benjamín Rivera Noriega Airport** (CPX; ☑787-742-0022; Hwy 251) is a tiny affair with a snack bar, a couple of car-rental booths and check-in counters. There's frequent service from San Juan, Ceiba and, handily for island-hoppers, Vieques. Airlines serving the airport include **Air Flamenco** (☑877-535-2636, 787-742-1040; www.airflamenco.net), **Vieques Air Link** (☑787-742-0254, 888-901-9247; www. viequesairlink.com) and **Cape Air** (☑800-227-3247; www.capeair.com). Charter flights can be arranged through **M&N Aviation** (☑787-791-7090, 877-622-5566; www.mnaviation.com).

The approach to Culebra's airport over Playa Flamenco and then between two peaks is one of the world's most spectacular.

BOAT

The most popular – and cheapest – way to Culebra from the mainland is on the **Autoridad de Transporte Marítimo** (ATM, Maritime Transportation Authority; ☑787-494-0934; https:// ati.pr/rutas-y-mapas; Calle Pedro Márquez, Dewey; one way adult/child $2.25/1; ☺office open before sailings) ferry service from Fajardo on either passenger or cargo boats. The service

is reliable, though past problems gave it a bad rep it's still trying to shake.

Be sure to get to the ferry terminal at least an hour early to buy your ticket (advance sales or reservations are not accepted). Schedules vary by day, but there are usually at least three round-trips. Trip times run between one to two hours, depending on the boat (passenger boats are fastest). Check times locally or on tourist information websites.

On busy weekends, especially during the summer, travelers may get bumped by island residents.

ⓘ Getting Around

Arriving by ferry, you can easily walk to any point in Dewey proper, while another 45 minutes will take you to Playa Flamenco. Elsewhere you'll want your own transport (a bike or golf cart will do).

BOAT

Water taxis provide round-trip service to Culebra's nearby cays, including Isla Culebrita, Cayo Norte and Cayo Luis Peña. Fares range from $35 to $50 per person, depending on the destination. Try **Cayo Norte Water Taxi** (☑787-435-6546; per person $35-50) or **Water Taxi** (☑787-685-5815; amarog1281@hotmail.com; per person $35-50).

CAR & GOLF CART

Mainland rental companies forbid you to bring cars to Culebra on the ferry. Locally, rental agencies push 4WDs hard but there's no reason for these on Culebra's well-maintained paved roads. Golf carts are good alternatives.

Avis (☑787-742-0726; www.avis.com; 98 Escudero, Dewey; rental from $68; ☺9am-5pm) The only international car-rental agency on the island.

Carlos Jeep Rental (☑787-742-3514; www. carlosjeeprental.com; Hwy 250; golf cart rental from $28, 4WDs from $45; ☺5am-9:30pm)

Jerry's Jeep Rental (☑787-742-0587; www. jerrysjeeprental.com; Hwy 251; golf carts from $30, 4WD rental from $45; ☺8am-6pm Sat-Thu, 7am-7pm Fri)

PÚBLICO

Públicos have one route on the island, from the ferry terminal to Playa Flamenco (per person $3). As long as there's room, passengers can flag them down anywhere along the route. The fare remains the same, regardless where you get on.

TAXI

There's taxi service on the island, mostly *público* drivers supplementing their income. (You'll likely be picked up in a van.) Fares run from $5 to $20, depending on where you're headed on the island.

Raul Transportation (☑787-358-4816, 787-955-9238)

Willy's Transportation (☑787-449-0580, 787-449-0598)

Xavier Transportation Services (☑787-463-0475; cortes_xh@yahoo.com)

Vieques

Measuring 21 miles long by 5 miles wide, Vieques is substantially bigger than Culebra and distinctly different in ambience. Though still a million metaphorical miles from the bright lights of the Puerto Rican mainland, the larger population here has meant more choice of accommodations, swankier restaurants and generally more buzz. It's renowned for its gorgeous beaches, semi-wild horses and unforgettable bioluminescent bay.

◉ Sights & Activities

★**Bahía Mosquito**   NATURE RESERVE
(Bioluminescent Bay; off Hwy 997) Locals claim that this magnificent bay, a designated wildlife preserve about 2 miles east of Esperanza, has the highest concentration of phosphorescent dinoflagellates not only in Puerto Rico, but in the world. A trip through the lagoon – take a tour – is nothing short of psychedelic, with hundreds of fish whipping up fluorescent-blue sparkles below the surface as your kayak or electric boat passes by (no gas-powered boats are permitted – the engine pollution kills the organisms that create the phosphorescence).

Abe's Snorkeling & Bio-Bay Tours   KAYAKING, SNORKELING
(☑787-741-2134; www.abessnorkeling.com; 136 Flamboyán, Esperanza; tours from adult/child

$40/20; ⊙9am-6pm) Abe's offers guided kayaking and snorkeling trips to the wildlife refuge, Cayo Afuera, Bahía Mosquito and other locations around the island. Its tours are particularly geared toward beginners and children; it even has kayaks that can accommodate families of three or four.

★**Vieques Adventure Company**   ADVENTURE
(☑787-414-4101; www.viequesadventures.com; tours from $50; ⊙hours vary) This outfit runs well-organized tours of the island, including hiking and historical tours, beach-hopping and snorkeling excursions, and mountain-bike trips. Groups are small. Gear rentals available too.

🏖 Beaches

Vieques' beaches are as legendary as Culebra's – and there are a lot more of them. The beaches in the national wildlife refuge are among the best on the island. Elsewhere you'll find numerous strips of sand, including a gorgeous public one in the south, where days can easily pass into weeks.

Vieques National Wildlife Refuge   NATURE RESERVE
(☑787-741-2138; www.fws.gov/caribbean/refuges/vieques; Km 3.2, Hwy 997; ⊙6am-6:30pm Oct-Mar, to 7:30pm Apr-Sep; P♿) Lying within these protected confines are the best reasons to visit Vieques. This 18,000-acre refuge occupies the land formerly used by the US military. The 3100-acre western segment was used mainly as a storage area during the military occupation and is very quiet. The 14,700-acre eastern segment, which includes a former live firing range (still off-limits), has the island's best beaches along its southern shore. Both sections have beaches that are considered among the most beautiful in Puerto Rico.

VIEQUES BY BIKE

Free from the mainland's traffic jams and unforgiving drivers, Vieques has become a little-heralded biking center. The island's main bike outlets organize guided rides, though going it alone is a good option too. A couple of suggestions:

➡ Some of the best bicycling is along Hwys 995, 996 and 201, which wind through the countryside north and west of Esperanza and are light on traffic.

➡ The ultimate Vieques loop involves heading west out of Isabel Segunda on Hwy 200 all the way to Punta Arenas (the last section is unpaved). After some shore snorkeling and an idyllic picnic lunch, swing south through the old military bunkers to Playa Grande before linking up with Hwy 996 to Esperanza.

★ Playa Caracas
BEACH

(Red Beach; Vieques National Wildlife Refuge, off Km 3.2, Hwy 997, Southern Shore) Calm and clear Playa Caracas is reached on a paved road and has gazebos with picnic tables to shade bathers from the sun; there's excellent snorkeling – lots of healthy sea fans and underwater life – off the eastern side of the beach. Walking west, Playuela is a lesser-known cove with less shade, meaning you'll find few people here and you can enjoy the view back to lovely Playa Caracas.

★ Sun Bay
BEACH

(Balneario Sun Bay; ☑787-741-8198; off Hwy 997, Parque Nacional Sun Bay; admission Wed-Sun only $4; ⊙8:30am-5pm Mon-Thu, to 6pm Fri-Sun; P♠) Part of Puerto Rico's national park system, Sun Bay is a long half-moon-shaped bay, less than a half-mile east of Esperanza. It's the island's *balneario* (public beach), with all the amenities you could hope for, including lifeguards and a cafe (11am to 5pm daily) serving up *criollo* treats. Measuring a mile in length, Sun Bay rarely seems busy – even with 100 people sunning and playing on it, it will still appear almost deserted. The surf is gentle.

★ Playa La Plata
BEACH

(Silver Beach; Vieques National Wildlife Refuge, off Km 3.2, Hwy 997, Southern Shore; ⊙6am-6:30pm Oct-Mar, to 7:30pm Apr-Sep) Playa La Plata is as far east as you can go at present. This gorgeously secluded beach is on a mushroom-shaped bay and has sand like icing sugar and a calm sea that seems to shimmer in a thousand different shades of turquoise, cobalt and blue. The snorkeling is good toward the western side of the beach. The road here is very rough; only a 4WD will get you close without walking.

Playa La Chiva
BEACH

(Blue Beach; Vieques National Wildlife Refuge, off Km 3.2, Hwy 997, Southern Shore; ⊙6am-6:30pm Oct-Mar, to 7:30pm Apr-Sep) FREE Gorgeous Playa La Chiva, at the eastern end of the main road, is long and open with occasionally rough surf. It's easy to find your own large patch of sand and you can find shade in the shrubs. There's good snorkeling toward the eastern side of the beach, just off a small island; park at spot No 5 through 10 for the best access.

🛏 Sleeping

★ Lazy Hostel
HOSTEL $

(☑787-741-5555; www.lazyhostel.com; 61a Orquideas, Esperanza; dm/r $30/75, all incl breakfast; ❉ ?) Created from shipping containers, the two dorms (one female-only) at this hostel are surprisingly comfortable. Both have four bunks, each bed with privacy curtain, power strip and night-light. Private rooms are simple and equally inviting. All have aircon and share spick-and-span bathrooms. An outdoor kitchen makes cooking (and saving a bit of dough) easy. Guest age limit is 'about' 50.

★ Casa de Amistad
GUESTHOUSE $$

(☑787-741-3758; www.casadeamistad.com; 27 Benitez Castaño, Isabel Segunda; r $105-125; P❉?☰) Casa de Amistad is everything a great holiday guesthouse should be: welcoming, comfortable, well located, stylish and well priced. It fits the bill (and more) with eight mid-century-meets-Caribbean-chic rooms, all with air-con, modern bathrooms and flat-screen TVs. Some have balconies to enjoy the balmy air. The ferry is a five-minute walk and there are great restaurants close by.

★ Malecón House
INN $$$

(☑787-741-0663; www.maleconhouse.com; 105 Flamboyán, Esperanza; r $180-300, ste $325, all incl breakfast; P❉?☰) With its travertine floors, beautiful fabrics and light-wood furniture, this spacious 13-room upmarket inn is a gracious choice. Looking out over the water from a quiet section of the main street, two rooms have private seaside balconies, one has a four-poster mahogany bed and all have a clean and uncluttered feel.

★ Hacienda Tamarindo
GUESTHOUSE $$$

(☑787-741-8525; www.haciendatamarindo.com; Km 4.5, Hwy 997; r $200-265, ste $250-315, 2-bedroom villa $375; P❉?☰) Perched on a hill looking out to a fine Caribbean vista, this 17-room guesthouse has lashings of style leavened by a relaxed island vibe. Rooms have a decidedly Caribbean *luxe motif* – tropical wood furnishings, elegant doors, wrought-iron balconies, colorful textiles and fine art – while the manicured grounds enjoy bursts of bougainvillea and hammocks strung here and there.

✖ Eating

✖ Esperanza

Rancho Choli
PUERTO RICAN $

(☎787-698-4464; Calle Almendro, Esperanza; $6-11; ⊙10am-10pm; 🖤) Down-home cooking is what you'll find at this casual restaurant. The menu changes daily but prepare to be delighted by mouthwatering plates of stuffed *mofongo*, *lechón asado* (roast pork) and freshly caught whole lobster. Order a side of *tostones* and wash it all down with a glass of tamarind juice. Just a block from the main drag.

★ El Quenepo
SEAFOOD $$$

(☎787-741-1215; www.elquenepovieques.com; 148 Flamboyán, Esperanza; mains $26-34; ⊙5:30-10pm Mon-Sat) Upscale El Quenepo has a lovely interior and an equally delectable menu. The food is catch-of-the-day fresh – a family of seven brothers supplies the seafood – and the decor is contemporary. Specialties include whole Caribbean lobsters, *mofongo* made with breadfruit grown in the backyard, and delicately pan-seared scallops with coconut crème fraiche and caviar. Be sure to book ahead.

✖ Isabella Segunda

★ Panadería La Viequense
BAKERY $

(☎787-741-8213; 352 Antonio G Mellado, Isabel Segunda; mains $3-11; ⊙6am-4pm) If it's breakfast you're after, this is the place for early eggs or hangover-obscuring coffee. If you miss the 11am cutoff, you can feast instead on decent baked goods and sandwiches. Service is no-nonsense and fast, the decor clean and modern, and the clientele local with a smattering of in-the-know tourists. Don't miss its photo gallery of early-20th-century Vieques.

★ Coqui Fire Cafe
MEXICAN $$

(☎787-741-0401; 421 Quiñones, Isabel Segunda; $12-25; ⊙5-9pm Mon-Fri) Sitting on a quiet corner in Isabel Segunda, Coqui Fire lights up the foodie scene with delicious Mexican dishes served with flair. Try the *carnitas* (pork shoulder braised in chilies and papaya juice) or go big with the blackened shrimp served with coconut *mole*. The signature margarita is a hit, prepared with a dash of homemade heat. Reservations recommended.

ⓘ Information

EMERGENCY
Dial 911 for emergencies.

INTERNET ACCESS
Wi-Fi is available at most inns and guesthouses. There's also a free hot spot in Isabel Segunda's central plaza, right in front of city hall.

MEDICAL SERVICES
Hospital Susan Centeno (☎787-741-2151; Km 0.4, Hwy 997; ⊙clinic 7am-4pm Mon-Fri, emergency 24hr) Located just south of Isabel Segunda on Hwy 997.

MONEY
Banco Popular (☎787-741-2071; www.bancopopular.com; 115 Muñoz Rivera, Isabel Segunda; ⊙8am-3:30pm Mon-Fri) Fully operating bank with ATM.

POST
Post Office (☎787-741-3891; www.usps.com; 97 Muñoz Rivera, Isabel Segunda; ⊙8am-4:30pm Mon-Fri, to noon Sat) The island's only post office.

TOURIST INFORMATION
US Fish & Wildlife Service (☎787-741-2138; www.fws.gov/southeast/maps/vi.html; Km 3.2, Hwy 997; ⊙8am-noon & 1-3pm Mon-Fri) Manages several refuges, including those at Cabo Rojo, Culebra and Vieques. The emphasis is on preserving places where wildlife breed, migrate or simply live. On Vieques, the US Fish & Wildlife Service maintains a **visitors center** in the **Wildlife Refuge** (p610)'s eastern side, which is manned by knowledgeable staff.

Puerto Rico Tourism Company (PRTC; ☎787-741-0800; www.seepuertorico.com; Central Plaza, Calle Carlos Lebron, Isabel Segunda; ⊙9am-4pm Mon-Fri) Friendly, helpful and bilingual staff on hand to give out information, brochures and Vieques maps. Located inside the *alcaldía* (city hall).

ⓘ Getting There & Away

AIR
Vieques' tiny **Antonio Rivera Rodríguez Airport** (VQS; ☎787-729-8715; Hwy 200, Km 2.6; 🖤) has frequent service from San Juan, Ceiba and, handily for island-hoppers, Culebra. Airline options include **Air Flamenco** (p609), **Air Sunshine** (☎787-741-7900, 800-327-8900; www.airsunshine.com), **Cape Air** (p609) and **Vieques Air Link** (p609). Charter flights can be arranged through **M&N Aviation** (☎787-791-7090, 877-622-5566; www.mnaviation.com).

Check bag size and weight limits before flying. Typically, medium-sized suitcases meet the requirements but airlines limit baggage weight, including carry-ons, to 30lb. Any amount over that is charged by the pound.

Públicos greet most flights and will take you anywhere you want to go on the island.

BOAT

By far the cheapest way to and from Vieques and the mainland (Fajardo) is by ferry (adult/child $2/1, 75 minutes). Though the service suffers from a bad reputation, it's relatively reliable. For the best outcome, arrive at the **ferry terminal** (ATM, Maritime Transportation Authority; ☑787-565-2717; https://ati.pr/rutas-y-mapas; German Rieckehoff, Isabel Segunda; ◐office open before sailings) at least an hour early and buy your ticket; advance sales and reservations are not accepted. Sometimes there are delays but rarely longer than an hour. Note that on summer weekends, the ferry from Fajardo can sell out, in which case residents are given priority.

Schedules vary by day but there are usually three round-trips. Check times locally or at tourist info websites.

❶ Getting Around

CAR & SCOOTER

Cars are highly useful for exploring Vieques, as the island is large and most of the best beaches are off the main routes. Expect to pay about $55 to $85 a day for a small car or 4WD. The latter are useful if you want to get to the outer beaches in the wildlife refuge. There's no need for a large SUV unless you're traveling in a group. Reliable rental agencies include **Fun Brothers** (☑787-435-9372; www.funbrothers-vieques. com; Malecón, Esperanza; scooters per day $55; ◐8:30am-5:30pm) and **Maritza's Car Rental.** (☑787-741-0078; www.maritzascar-rental.com; Km 2, Hwy 201; per day $55-110; ◐8am-6pm)

PÚBLICO

Públicos typically greet both ferries and airplanes – they read '*Vieques y Sus Barrios*' (Vieques and Its Neighborhoods) on the windshields. These vans cover the entire island, but don't be in a hurry to get where you're going. The trip between Isabel Segunda and Esperanza costs $3, with *públicos* running regularly from 7am to 11pm. Sometimes there's an additional $0.50 charge per bag.

TAXI

A fare of $10 to $20 should get you anywhere on the island. Try **Coqui Ayala** (☑787-374-6820), **Edna Robles** (☑787-630-4673), **Nate** (☑787-364-5911) or **741 Taxi** (☑787-741-8294; www.741taxi.com; ◐24hr).

SOUTHERN & WESTERN PUERTO RICO

Ponce

Ponce es ponce (Ponce is Ponce), runs a simple yet telling Puerto Rican saying: the explanation given as to why the nation's haughty second city does things, well, uniquely – and in defiance of the capital. Native son and author Abelardo Díaz Alfaro went further, calling Ponce a *baluarte irreductible de puertorriqueñidad* – a bastion of the irreducible essence of Puerto Rico.

Strolling around the sparkling fountains and narrow, architecturally ornamented streets of the historic center certainly evokes Puerto Rico's stately past. Unfortunately, the neighborhoods that surround the central square exhibit woeful characteristics of Puerto Rico's present: irreducible snarls of congested traffic, economic stagnation and cookie-cutter urban sprawl.

◉ Sights

★ Museo de Arte de Ponce   GALLERY

(MAP; ☑787-848-0505; www.museoarteponce. org; 2325 Av Las Américas; adult/concession $6/3; ◐10am-5pm Wed-Sat & Mon, noon-5pm Sun) *Brush Strokes in Flight,* a bold primary-colored totem by American pop artist Roy Lichtenstein, announces the smartly remodeled MAP, where an expertly presented collection ranks among the best in the Caribbean. It is itself worth the trip from San Juan. A $30-million renovation celebrated the museum's 50th anniversary and the smart curation – some 850 paintings, 800 sculptures and 500 prints presented in provocative historical and thematic juxtapositions – represents five centuries of Western art.

Plaza Las Delicias   SQUARE

Within this elegant square you'll discover Ponce's heart as well as two of the city's landmark buildings, Parque de Bombas (p614) and Catedral Nuestra Señora de Guadalupe (p614). The Fuente de los Leones, a photogenic fountain rescued from the 1939 World's Fair in New York, is the square's most captivating attraction. The smell of *panaderías* (bakeries) follows churchgoers across the square each morning, children squeal around the majestic fountain under the midday heat, and lovers stroll under its lights at night.

Ponce

Ponce

◎ Top Sights
1 Museo de Arte de Ponce.....................B4

◎ Sights
2 Catedral Nuestra Señora de
   Guadalupe......................................C2
3 Fuente de los Leones C2
4 Parque de Bombas................................C2
5 Plaza Las Delicias................................C2
6 Teatro La Perla......................................C1

⌂ Sleeping
7 Hotel Bélgica B2
8 Ponce Plaza Hotel & Casino................B1

✕ Eating
9 El Vejigante C1
10 Sabor y Rumba C1

Parque de Bombas NOTABLE BUILDING
(☎787-840-1045; ⊙9am-5pm) FREE *Ponceños*
(people from Ponce) claim that the eye-

popping Parque de Bombas is Puerto Rico's
most frequently photographed building,
which is not too hard to believe as you
stroll around the black-and-red-striped,
Arabian-style edifice and make countless
unwitting cameos in family photo albums.
Since 1990 the landmark has been a tourist
information center (p615), where pleasant,
bilingual staff will sell you tickets for a trolley and direct you to local attractions.

**Catedral Nuestra Señora de
Guadalupe** CATHEDRAL
(Our Lady of Guadalupe Cathedral; Plaza Las Delicias; ⊙7am-7pm) The twin bell towers of
this striking cathedral cast an impression
of noble piety over Ponce's Plaza Las Delicias. It was built in 1931, in the place where
colonists erected their first chapel in the
1660s, which (along with subsequent structures) succumbed to earthquakes and fires.
Its stained-glass windows and interior are
picturesque. There are several services daily.

Centro Ceremonial Indígena de Tibes
ARCHAEOLOGICAL SITE

(Tibes Indian Ceremonial Center; ☑787-840-5685; http://ponce.inter.edu/tibes/tibes.html; Km 2.2, Hwy 503; adult/child $3/2; ⊙9am-3:30pm Tue-Sun, closed major holidays) The ancient ceremonial center of Tibes is one of the Caribbean's most important archaeological sites, due largely to evidence found here of pre-Taíno civilizations, such as the Igneris. Though Tibes lacks the dramatic scale of sites such as Mexico's Uxmal, it is a quiet spot, ideal for imagining the people who once dwelt here (brought alive by enthusiastic staff and an excellent interpretation center), and is a highly recommended way to spend an afternoon.

🛏 Sleeping & Eating

⭐ Hotel Bélgica
HOTEL $

(☑787-844-3255; www.hotelbelgica.com; 122 Villa; r $75-100; ❄🛜) Just off the southwest corner of Plaza Las Delicias, this traveler-favorite has a creaking colonial-era ambience, with 15ft ceilings and wrought-iron balconies. The hallways are a bit of a maze and dimly lit, but the place is charming, with delightful old furniture in many of the 20 rooms.

Rooms near the front allow you to stare out over the plaza from private balconies, but be prepared for noise on weekend nights. The wi-fi is spotty.

Ponce Plaza Hotel & Casino
HOTEL $$

(☑787-813-5050; www.ponceplazahotel casino.com; cnr Reina Isabel & Unión; d from $110; 🅿❄🛜♨) Standing grandly over a corner of the plaza, this building's lemon-yellow colonial-era facade has emerged from the scaffolding after years of preservationist dispute. The historic building, location and clutch of amenities, and mix of classic colonial and modern rooms, keep it among the top options in the city center.

⭐ El Vejigante
CARIBBEAN $

(www.facebook.com/elveji; cnr Cristina & Mayor Canera; mains $8-15; ⊙midday-1am) A diminutive, cool, cozy little joint perfect for pre- or post-theater dinner and drinks since Teatro La Perla (Pearl Theater; ☑787-843-4322; cnr Mayor & Cristina; ⊙lobby 8am-4:30pm Mon-Fri) FREE is just around the corner. El Vejigante is far-reaching in its wine list, innovative in its food (Caribbean and Latin American fusion) and impeccable in its service. The walls are decorated with *vejigantes* (masks) and creations from the Ponce carnival.

Sabor y Rumba
CARIBBEAN $

(Reina Isabel 66; mains $10; ⊙11am-11pm) An otherwise run-down courtyard has been spruced up to provide one of Ponce's best-value restaurants. There are outside tables and generous portions of *mofongo* or *cerdo relleno* (stuffed pork). Read the electric scoreboard to find out what's cooking. There are also music classes, regular live music, an espresso machine and graffiti. Simple – and yet an engine of inspiration.

ℹ Information

INTERNET ACCESS
The **Plaza Las Delicias** (p613) has free wi-fi, and all accommodation options and even some restaurants have wi-fi too.

MEDICAL SERVICES
Hospital Manuel Comunitario Dr Pila (☑787-848-5600; 2445 Av Las Américas) A hospital with a 24-hour emergency room.

MONEY
Banks line the perimeter of Plaza Las Delicias so finding a cash machine is no problem. Most of the banks are open from 9am to 4pm weekdays, plus Saturday mornings.

POST
Post Office (93 Atocha; ⊙8:30am-3:30pm Mon-Fri, to noon Sat) Four blocks north of Plaza Las Delicias, this is the most central of the city's four post offices.

TOURIST INFORMATION
Puerto Rico Tourism Company (PRTC; ☑787-284-4141, 787-840-1045; Plaza Las Delicias; ⊙9am-5:30pm) You can't miss the big red-and-black structure in the middle of Parque de Bombas, where friendly, English-speaking members of the tourist office are ready with brochures, answers and suggestions.

ℹ Getting There & Around

AIR
Aeropuerto Mercedita (Hwy 1) Four miles (seven km) east of the town center off Hwy 1, Ponce's airport looks dressed for a party, but is still waiting for the guests to arrive. JetBlue (☑787-651-0787, 800-538-2853; www.jetblue.com; Aeropuerto Mercedita), the only airline currently serving the airport, has services to New York and Orlando, but no domestic flights. There is car rental available here. A taxi to the center costs $15.

CAR

Swooshing down to Ponce from San Juan is easy on the smoothly paved Hwy 52, a partially toll-controlled highway called the Autopista Luis A Ferré.

PÚBLICO

There's a nice, new **público terminal** (cnr Victoria & Unión) three blocks north of the plaza, with connections to most major towns, including San Juan. Pack unlimited patience for the indefinite wait.

TAXI

Hailing a cab at the Plaza Las Delicias is much quicker than calling for one, but if you do need to call try **Ponce Taxi** (☏787-840-0088; Plaza Las Delicias). It's $1 to drop the flag and roughly $1 per kilometer, but meters are used infrequently, so ask about the price before you get an unpleasant surprise.

Bosque Estatal de Guánica

The immense 10,000-acre expanse of the Guánica Biosphere Reserve is one of the island's great natural treasures. Located in two wonderfully untrammeled sections just east and west of Guánica, this remote desert forest is among the world's best examples of subtropical dry forest vegetation, containing extraordinary flora and fauna as a result. In the larger, more tourist-friendly eastern portion, numerous trails intersect this astonishing ecosystem, lending themselves well to mountain biking, birdwatching and hiking.

Scientists estimate that only 1% of the earth's original spread of dry forests of this kind remain, and the fact that there is such a vast acreage here renders this a rare sanctuary.

Over 700 varieties of plants, many near extinction, thrive in the reserve. Some of the unusual species here include the squat melon cactus with its brilliant pink flowers that attract hummingbirds. Another plant, with the unseemly name of the Spanish dildo cactus, grows into huge treelike shapes near the coast and attracts bullfinches and bats. Of the fauna, nine of Puerto Rico's 14 endemic bird species can be found here, including the Puerto Rican woodpecker, the Puerto Rican emerald hummingbird and – the ultimate prize for birdwatchers – the exceedingly rare 'prehistoric' Puerto Rican nightjar, of which there are estimated to be as few as 1500.

When out hiking or biking, the 30-odd miles of trails hammer you with contrasts at every turn, alternating between arid, rocky, scrub-covered highlands and almost 12.5 miles of remote, wholly untouched coast.

🛏 Sleeping

★**Mary Lee's by the Sea** APARTMENT $$
(☏787-821-3600; www.maryleesbythesea.com; 25 San Jacinto; studios $130-300; P ❋) This charismatic guesthouse run by Mary Lee Alverez is one of the island's most isolated, idiosyncratic stays. It's set on a steep hillside overlooking the mangrove cays and the Caribbean, so guests have little choice but to unplug (limited wi-fi, no TVs) and relax. Each apartment is appointed with bright marine-themed furnishings and many have private decks, hammocks and barbecue facilities. One room even has a bathroom that opens out to a private garden shower.

ℹ Information

Ranger Station (☏787-821-5706; ⊘7am-4pm) A solitary ranger is usually in evidence at this small center next to the main parking area at the end of Hwy 334 in the eastern portion of the Bosque Estatal de Guánica.

ℹ Getting There & Around

The Bosque Estatal de Guánica can be reached from Guánica via two main routes. To get to the eastern section of the reserve and the Ranger Station, follow Hwy 116 northeast from Guánica toward Hwy 2 and then turn right onto the narrow Hwy 334 to wind up to the reserve entrance. The southern extent of the eastern section of the forest – including the ferry to Gilligan's Island and Guánica's plushest accommodations possibilities – is also accessible by Hwy 333, to the southeast of Guánica.

Rincón

You'll know you've arrived in Rincón – 'the corner' – when you pass the sun-grizzled gringos cruising west in their rusty 1972 Volkswagen Beetle with surfboards piled on the roof. Shoehorned in the island's most remote corner, Rincón is Puerto Rico at its most unguarded, a place where the sunsets shimmer scarlet and you're more likely to be called 'dude' than 'sir.' This is the island's surfing capital, and one of the premier places to catch a wave in the northern hemisphere.

Not surprisingly, Rincón's waves are often close to perfect. Breaking anywhere from 2ft to 25ft, the names are chillingly evocative: Domes, Indicator, Spanish Wall and Dogman's. The crème de la crème is Tres Palmas, a white-tipped monster that is often dubbed the 'temple' of big-wave surfing in the Caribbean.

Rincón's town center has been revitalized recently and now boasts great bars and restaurants.

🏃 Activities

Surf 787
SURFING

(☎787-448-0968; http://surf787.com; Km 8.3 Hwy 115, Behind Spyce Bar Restaurant; group surf lessons from $70) The coolest kid on the block, Surf 787 has a suite of packages, all-inclusive surf vacations, adult getaways and a kids surf camp. The instructors here, who are all CPR- and water-safety certified, also offer lessons for couples and small groups as well as private tuition.

★ Puerto Rico Technical Divers
DIVING

(☎787-477-3368; www.facebook.com/Prtekdiving center; Km 12 Hwy 115; ⊙8am-5pm) This is one of the island's best-equipped dive facilities, specializing in shore diving around Rincón, Aguadilla and Isabela. They have a comprehensive range of gear to buy and to rent, too. It's a bit hard to spot from the road: look for the Vacas Gauchas *parrilleria* (grillhouse) and you'll know you're close.

🛏 Sleeping & Eating

Rincón Surf Hostel
HOSTEL $

(☎678-744-8556; www.rinconsurfhostel.com; Km 0.5 Hwy 413; dorm/s/d $25/70/80) This hostel is a particularly tempting option for surfers and beachgoers, one block back from the beach on the northwestern side of Rincón. Clean dorms and small private rooms, a communal kitchen and a little takeaway coffee shack out front make this a good stopover for those on a budget.

Que Chévere
INN $$

(☎787-823-6452; http://quecheverepr.com; 17 Muñoz Rivera; r $75-125) 'Que Chévere!' is how most Latin Americans say 'how cool' and when you see what you get for your money at this clean, tasteful new inn on Rincón's Plaza de Recreo, you might want to utter the same words. This is a new concept for the town: its first bang-in-the-center accommodation and its first backpacker hotel.

★ Tres Sirenas
B&B $$$

(☎787-823-0558; www.tressirenas.com; 26 Sea Beach Drive; d inc breakfast $190-295; ❄ 🛜 🛗)

This is Rincón's best guesthouse and probably one of the Caribbean's finest. A stone's throw from two of the bigger, more luxurious hotels, true indulgence beckons at this tranquil end-of-street detached house, from the freshly brewed coffee in your room to the lovingly prepared breakfasts served to all guests at their private terraces (with views out to the glimmering ocean).

La Cambija
PUERTO RICAN $

(Cambija 17; $4.50-12; ⊙noon-10pm Wed-Mon) In a town where so many successful restaurants are expat-owned, it's nice to see Puerto Rican–helmed La Cambija doing well. Locals and tourists mix around the bar, or at the informal, open-air tables, feasting on *pinchos* (marinated pork and plantain kebabs, mmm) or a fillet of mahimahi. It's packed in the evenings, with a bubbly Puerto Rican feel.

★ La Copa Llena
INTERNATIONAL $$

(☎787-823-0896; http://attheblackeagle.com; Black Eagle Marina; mains $20-40; ⊙3-9:30pm Wed-Sat, 11am-9:30pm Sun; Ⓟ) Is your glass half empty or half full? It's hard not to look on the bright side of life at La Copa Llena (the full cup). Down by the Black Eagle Marina, this is one of the best restaurants in Rincón, for the elegantly understated interior and huge sea-fronting patio but mostly for the innovative food.

🍷 Drinking & Nightlife

Rincón's nightlife is varied, but there are few 'bars' per se: many restaurants rather become animated places come night time. Some focus more on drinking, some on eating, but it's invariably undertaken under the same roof.

However, Rincón has its own central dedicated cocktail bar, **Roots** (cnr Progreso & Comercio; ⊙5pm-midnight Sun-Thu, until 2am Fri & Sat). Locals currently favor a couple of open-air joints just south of the Plaza de Recreo (p618) on the intersection of Muñoz Rivera and Cambija, such as **Barca** (cnr Muñoz Rivera & Calle B; ⊙3-10pm Mon-Thu, noon-midnight Fri & Sat, noon-10pm Sun).

ⓘ Information

EMERGENCY

Police Station (☎787-823-2020; cnr Nueva & Nueva Final) The local cops are based in the southeast corner of central Rincón, off Nueva.

INTERNET ACCESS

Almost every place to stay and many restaurants have free wi-fi.

MEDICAL SERVICES

Rincón Centro de Salud (☑787-823-5555, 787-823-5500; www.costasalud.com; 28 Muñoz Rivera, cnr Calle A; ☺clinic 8am-4pm Mon-Fri, emergencies 7am-11pm Mon-Fri) In Rincón town, this health center is a block south of Plaza de Recreo.

MONEY

There are ATMs in the lobby of almost every hotel and in many bars, so finding cash won't be a problem. The nearest ATM to Plaza de Recreo is **Cooperativa de Ahorro y Credito** (cnr Calle B & Muñoz Rivera; ☺8:15am-4pm Mon-Fri, 8am-11:30am Sat).

POST

Post Office (Hwy 115; ☺7:30am-4:30pm Mon-Fri, 8:30am-noon Sat) North of the **Plaza de Recreo** (p618) on Hwy 115.

TOURIST INFORMATION

Tourist Information Center (☑787-823-5024; Sunset Bldg, Cambija s/n; ☺8am-4:30pm Mon-Fri) Rincón's tourist office is in the Sunset Building adjacent to Rincón public beach.

❶ Getting There & Away

The easiest way to approach the town is via Hwy 115, which intersects Hwy 2 both at the northern end of the Rincón peninsula near Aguadilla and the southern end, not far north of the Mayagüez airport, Aeropuerto Eugenio Maria de Hostos. As Hwy 115 sweeps into town, it becomes Calle Muñoz Rivera.

❶ Getting Around

Rincón – despite its mantle as an 'alternative' beach haven – has little provision for nonmotorized transport. The spread-out community with minimal public transport has few sidewalks and almost no facilities for bicycles.

The only reliable way to get around the area is by rented car, taxi, irregular *públicos* or – if you're energetic and careful – walking. Car rentals can be found at **Angelos** (☑787-823-3438; Hwy 115 Km 12) in central Rincón. The **público stand** (cnr Muñoz Rivera & Comercio, Plaza de Recreo) is just off Plaza de Recreo on Nueva. However, you're here in Rincón for the wild coastal scenery and it must be emphasized this is a pretty miserable way of getting about.

You will pay around $40 for a taxi from either the Aguadilla or Mayagüez airports. Car rentals can be found at both of these destinations, as well as in Rincón itself.

UNDERSTAND PUERTO RICO

History

Taino Roots

Indigenous peoples are thought to have arrived – via a raft from Florida – around the 1st century AD, quickly followed by groups from the Lesser Antilles. The Taínos created a sophisticated trading system on the island they named Borinquen and became the reigning culture, although they were constantly fighting off Carib invaders.

Colonization of the Taino

All that changed forever in 1508, when Juan Ponce de León came back to the island he had glimpsed from one of Christopher Columbus' ships. Driven by a desire for gold, Spanish conquistadores enslaved, murdered, starved and raped natives with impunity. Virtually wiped out by war, smallpox and whooping cough, a few remaining Taínos took to the mountains. Soon Dutch and French traders became frequent visitors, dropping off human cargo from West Africa. By 1530 West African slaves – including members of the Mandingo and Yoruba tribes – numbered about half the population of 3000 in Puerto Rico.

And so it went for several generations. The Spanish-American War of 1898 finally pried Puerto Rico out from under the yoke of the Spanish empire, but it established the small island as a commonwealth of the United States – Borinquen was liberated from Spain, but not quite free.

From Spanish Colony to American Commonwealth

Operation Bootstrap poured money into the island and set up highways, post offices, supermarkets and a few military posts. Puerto Ricans have accepted the US economic and military presence on their island, with varying degrees of anger, indifference and satisfaction, for more than 100 years now – and the strong independentista movement that wanted to cut all ties with the US in the 1950s has mostly receded into the background. The biggest question for Puerto Ricans – a passionately political people who muster at least a 90% voter turnout on election days – is whether to keep the status quo or become, officially, the United States' 51st state.

Political Turmoil

In May 2006 a stalemate between Governor Aníbal Acevedo and the Puerto Rican legislature led to a massive budgetary crisis that forced the government to literally shut down after it ran out of funds to pay over 100,000 public-sector employees. The crisis lasted two weeks before a grudging compromise was reached, but it drew intense criticism from business leaders, Puerto Rican celebrities and the general public. The grand jury investigation that charged Acevedo with corruption eventually found him not guilty.

People & Culture

Most Puerto Ricans live a lifestyle that weaves together two primary elements: the commercial and material values of the United States and the social and traditional values of their 'enchanted' island. Because of the strong connection to the mainland United States, Puerto Ricans have espoused many of the same social values as their cousins in New York. Even so, the Puerto Rican flags that fly from the fire escapes of NYC leave no doubt that many Puerto Ricans will never fully lose themselves to mainstream American culture.

Modern practicalities of the island's political and cultural position have meant that, for three or four generations now, many Puerto Ricans have grown up bouncing between mainland US cities and their native soil. Even those who stay put assimilate by proxy: young people in a wealthy San Juan suburb may wander the mall past American chain stores and chat about Hollywood blockbusters; obversely, their counterparts living in the uniformly Puerto Rican neighborhoods of New York or Chicago may have a day-to-day existence that more closely resembles Latin America. This makes the full scope of their bilingual and multicultural existence difficult to comprehend for outsiders. Many Puerto Ricans are just as comfortable striding down New York's Fifth Ave for a little shopping during the week as they are visiting the friquitines (roadside kiosks) with their families at Playa Luquillo on the weekend.

Arts

Abundant creative energy hangs in the air over Puerto Rico (maybe it has something to do with the Bermuda Triangle) and its effects can be seen in the island's tremendous output of artistic achievement. Puerto Rico has produced renowned poets, novelists, playwrights, orators, historians, journalists, painters, composers and sculptors. The island's two most influential artists are considered to be rococo painter José Campeche and impressionist Francisco Oller. As well as being a groundbreaking politician, Puerto Rican Governor Luís Moñez Marín was also an eloquent poet. In the world of entertainment Rita Morena is the only Puerto Rican to have won an Oscar, a Grammy, a Tony and an Emmy, while the island's hottest film talent is actor Benicio del Toro, star of Steven Soderbergh's recent two-part biopic of Che Guevara. While it's known for world-class art in many mediums, music and dance are especially synonymous with the island.

Landscape & Wildlife

The Land

It is the astonishing beaches that captivate most minds planning a first visit to Puerto Rico. But as seasoned aficionados know, the sand and surf intimate only a part of the full, rich picture of the topography. Shores also yield internationally crucial swathes of mangrove reserve, and behind the beachside hotels the mythical, densely forested contours of the Central Mountains cascade invitingly upwards. The island rears a number of crops: bananas, coffee, yams and citrons are of great importance.

Wildlife

Seeking out the wildlife of Puerto Rico can be very rewarding. The island's jungle-clad mountains and surreal variety of terrain – including some of the wettest and driest forests in the subtropical climate – have a bit of everything (albeit no huge beasts or flocks of colorful birds). The island's most famous creature is the humble common coquí. The nocturnal serenade of this small endemic frog is the poignant soundtrack of the island, an ever-present reminder of Puerto Rico's precious natural environment.

SURVIVAL GUIDE

ℹ Directory A–Z

ACCOMMODATIONS

Puerto Rico has a wide range of accommodations. Book ahead in high season.

Hotels Available islandwide in price ranges from $60 to $400+ nightly, with a good selection under $200.

B&Bs A relatively new mid-range accommodation option; owners always live on or near the premises and breakfast is included.

Guesthouses These range from family-run places with a few rooms to larger motel-like stays; many can also be apartments under another name.

Resorts World-class properties line San Juan's beachfront and other coastal areas. There are, however, few all-inclusive resorts.

Camping Possible on Culebra and in a handful of nature parks.

ACTIVITIES

The possibilities are endless here, as the island is adept at packaging up particular elements of its hugely varying landscape into exactly the thrill you fancy. Where there are rambunctious waves, there are surf schools; where there is tropical jungle, there are operators waiting to whisk you into the thick of it.

ELECTRICITY

Puerto Rico has the 110V AC system used in the USA.

EMBASSIES & CONSULATES

Most nations' principal diplomatic representation is in Washington, DC, which means many countries do not maintain consulates in Puerto Rico. Consulates in Puerto Rico tend to be the honorary kind that have very limited services – if any – for travelers. The following consulates may be of use:

French Consulate (☑787-767-2428; www. consulfrance-miami.org; 270 Av Muñoz Rivera, Suite 301, Hato Rey; ☺ phone inquiries 9am-noon Mon, Wed & Fri, in-person by appointment only; Ⓜ Roosevelt)

Spanish Consulate (☑787-758-6090; www. exteriores.gob.es; Mercantil Plaza, 2 Av Ponce de León; ☺8:30am-1:30pm Mon-Fri)

Netherlands Consulate (☑787-399-0830; www.the-netherlands.org; Mercantil Plaza, 2 Av Ponce de León; ☺by appointment only)

Dominican Republic Consulate (☑787-725-9550; www.domrep.org; 1607 Av Ponce de León, Suite 101, Santurce; ☺9am-2pm Mon-Fri)

EMERGENCY & IMPORTANT NUMBERS

Fire, Police & Ambulance	☑911

FOOD

Puerto Rico's traditional cuisine hauls in influences from North America, its Caribbean neighbors, Africa and Spain, and is spliced together by the succulent dominance of *lechón* (pork) in as many forms as you could shake some barbecue tongs at. A network of experimental chefs is striving islandwide to spice up the food scene with their own bold influences, which run from European to Middle Eastern.

GLBT TRAVELERS

Puerto Rico is probably the most gay-friendly island in the Caribbean. San Juan has a well-developed gay scene, especially in the Condado district and Santurce. Vieques and Culebra are popular destinations for an mix of gay and lesbian expatriates and travelers. Rincón and Ponce, whilst some way behind in specifically gay venues, are gay-friendly destinations.

HEALTH

If you have a medical emergency or a need for healthcare in Puerto Rico, the array of pharmacies and hospitals is good compared to most other places in the Caribbean.

➡ For medical emergencies, dial 911.

➡ Tap water does not taste great but is safe to drink.

INTERNET ACCESS

Wi-fi is common in places to stay, cafes and many public places and squares. In this book, the wi-fi symbol means that wi-fi is available throughout the property unless otherwise noted, while the internet symbol means there are public internet terminals available.

MONEY

ATMs

ATMs dispensing US currency are easily found. Credit and debit cards are widely accepted. Watch for mandatory fees at upscale hotels and resorts.

Exchanging Money

Major bank offices in San Juan and Ponce will exchange foreign currencies. There are also

---

SLEEPING PRICE RANGES

The following price ranges refer to a double room with bathroom in high season. Unless otherwise stated a tax of 9% to 15% is included in the price.

$ less than US$90

$$ US$90–200

$$$ more than US$200

exchange desks at San Juan's Luis Muñoz Marín International Airport and major resorts (which offer terrible rates).

Tipping

Generally, you tip in Puerto Rico as you would on the US mainland.

Bars $1 per drink.

Luggage attendants $1 to $2 per bag for anyone who helps with your luggage.

Restaurants 15% of the bill.

Taxis 15% of the fare.

Check for service charges included in your bill at touristy restaurants, even for groups smaller than six.

If possible, tip servers with cash even when paying by credit card; this precludes management taking a cut.

OPENING HOURS

Hours can vary from those posted and they change sporadically, so check before setting off.

Banks 8am-4pm Monday to Friday, 9:30am-noon Saturday

Bars 2pm-2am, often later in San Juan

Government offices 8:30am-4:30pm Monday to Friday

Museums 9:30am-5pm, often closed Monday and Tuesday

Post offices 8am-4pm Monday to Friday, 8am-1pm Saturday

Restaurants 11am-10pm, later in San Juan

Shops 9am-6pm Monday to Saturday, 11am-5pm Sunday, later in malls

PUBLIC HOLIDAYS

In addition to holidays observed in the region, Puerto Rico also celebrates the following public holidays:

Three Kings Day (Feast of the Epiphany) January 6

Eugenio María de Hostos' Birthday January 10

Martin Luther King Jr Day Third Monday in January

Emancipation Day March 22

Palm Sunday Sunday before Easter

Easter A Sunday in late March/April

José de Diego Day April 18

Memorial Day Last Monday in May

Luis Muñoz Rivera's Birthday July 18

José Celso Barbosa's Birthday July 27

Labor Day First Monday in September

Columbus Day Second Monday in October

Thanksgiving Fourth Thursday in November

TIME

Puerto Rico is on Atlantic Standard Time (GMT-4). Clocks in this time zone read an hour later

EATING PRICE RANGES

The following price ranges refer to a standard one- or two-course meal. Tipping is extra.

$ less than US$18

$$ US$18–30

$$$ more than US$30

than the Eastern Standard Time zone, which encompasses such US cities as New York and Miami. There is no Daylight Saving Time observed on the island.

TELEPHONE

Puerto Rico's country code is 1 and the area code is +787. To call locally, just dial the local seven-digit telephone number. To call the island from the US, dial 1 + 787 + the seven-digit number. From elsewhere, dial your country's international access code followed by 787 + the seven-digit number.

All major US cell-phone carriers provide service in Puerto Rico without any extra charges.

TOURIST INFORMATION

Puerto Rico Tourism Company is the commonwealth's official tourist bureau. It has a fair range of general interest materials and a decent website, **See Puerto Rico** (www.seepuertorico.com). Privately produced tourist magazines and brochures are abundant.

Check out Eye Tour Puerto Rico (http://places.eyetour.com) for short videos posted on the website that give good insights into Puerto Rico.

Welcome to Puerto Rico (http://welcome.topuertorico.org/) is part encyclopedia, part travel guide, and an excellent online resource on the island of Puerto Rico.

TRAVELERS WITH DISABILITIES

Travel to and around Puerto Rico is becoming easier for people with disabilities as the country is subject to the Americans with Disabilities Act (ADA). Public buildings are now required to be wheelchair-accessible and to have appropriate restroom facilities. Similarly, public transportation services must be made accessible to all, and telephone companies are required to provide relay operators for the hearing impaired.

VISAS

You only need a visa to enter Puerto Rico if you need a visa to enter the US, since the commonwealth follows the United States' immigration laws. Residents of many countries must still apply for an Esta (Electronic System for Transport authorization, https://esta.cbp.dhs.gov/esta).

PRACTICALITIES

Useful Websites El Nuevo Dia (www.elnuevodia.com/english) provides the latest news online from Puerto Rico's main news publication. Puerto Rico Day Trips (www.puertoricodaytrips.com) has good sightseeing tips across the commonwealth.

TV & Radio American TV is broadcast across the island. Radio is mostly in Spanish.

Weights & Measures Puerto Rico follows the imperial system with two exceptions: all distances on road signs are in kilometers and gas (petrol) is pumped in liters.

Smoking Banned in most public places, including hotel rooms and restaurants

Getting There & Away

ENTERING PUERTO RICO

US nationals need proof of citizenship (such as a driver's license with photo ID or birth certificate) to enter Puerto Rico, but be aware that if traveling to another country in the Caribbean (other than the US Virgin Islands, which, like Puerto Rico, is a US territory), you require a valid passport in order to reenter the US. Visitors from other countries must have a valid passport to enter Puerto Rico.

AIR

There are a few airports on Puerto Rico that service international flights:

Luis Muñoz Marín International Airport (San Juan Airport; www.aeropuertosju.com) This is San Juan's main airport, and where almost all flights arrive or depart.

Rafael Hernández Airport (Aguadilla Airport; http://aguadilla.airport-authority.com) Aguadilla's airport receives a few international flights, mostly from the United States, Santo Domingo, St Lucia and Aruba.

Small planes fly to the British Virgin Islands from **Isla Grande Airport** (San Juan's secondary airport), **Benjamín Rivera Noriega Airport** (Culebra Airport) and **Antonio Rivera Rodríguez Airport** (Vieques Airport).

International airlines serving Puerto Rico include American Airlines, United, Delta, Spirit, LATAM, Air Canada, Emirates, Air France, KLM and British Airways.

SEA

San Juan is the second-largest port for cruise ships in the western hemisphere (after Miami).

Over one million cruise-ship passengers pass through the ports in Old San Juan annually, and all the major cruise-ship lines operate cruises from here.

Following substantial investment, Ponce's **Port of the Americas** (Muelle de Ponce) also now has cruises calling.

Getting Around

AIR

Because Puerto Rico is such a small island, its domestic air transportation system is basic. **Cape Air** (1-800-227-3247; www.capeair.com) and **JetBlue** (1-800-538-2583; www.jetblue.com; Luis Muñoz Marín INternational Airport) connect San Juan with Mayagüez on the mainland several times daily; airlines serving the offfshore islands of Culebra and Vieques from San Juan include **Vieques Air Link** (San Juan (Isla Grande) 787-722-3736; www.viequesairlink.com) and **Air Flamenco** (787-724-6464; www.airflamenco.net).

BOAT

The **Autoridad de Transporte Marítimo** (ATM, Maritime Transportation Authority; ext 2736 787-494-0934; https://ati.pr/rutas-y-mapas; Calle Playa; adult/child to Culebra $2.25/1, to Vieques $2/1) offers daily service to Vieques and Culebra on *lanchas* (passenger boats) and *ferries* (cargo boats). Service runs three to four times daily.

CAR

Despite the occasional hazards of operating a car in Puerto Rico, driving is currently the most convenient way to see the island; public transport is about as poor as it gets, and cycling is deemed too dangerous.

Puerto Rico has the same basic rules of the road as the US: traffic proceeds along the right side of the road and moves counterclockwise around traffic circles.

Car rental rates run $30 to $60 per day. A valid driver's license issued from your country of residence is all that's needed to rent. Major international car-rental companies as well as local firms operate on the island. Most prohibit taking rentals from the mainland to Culebra and Vieques.

PÚBLICO

Públicos are essentially public minibuses that run prescribed routes during daylight hours, typically Monday to Saturday. Traveling via *público* offers an inexpensive local experience, but requires a lot of patience and time. Some *públicos* make relatively long hauls between places such as San Juan and Ponce or Mayagüez, but most make much shorter trips, providing a link within and between communities.

Saba

POP 1991 / ☎ 599

Best Places to Eat

➡ Island Flavor (p630)

➡ Chez Bubba (p627)

➡ Brigadoon (p627)

Best Places to Sleep

➡ Queen's Garden Resort (p630)

➡ Cottage Club (p626)

➡ Selera Dunia (p626)

Why Go?

Rising like an otherworldly peak from the Caribbean, this cloud-shrouded volcanic island – a 'special municipality' of the Netherlands – is as vertiginous as its motherland is flat.

Dense vegetation draping Saba's dramatic crags and valleys made it the ideal silhouette of Skull Island in the original 1933 *King Kong* movie, with some of its scenes set deep in the jungle also filmed here. Amid the foliage, its tiny main villages – commercial center, Windwardside, and capital, the Bottom – harbor enchanting traditional red-roofed, white-timber houses with forest-green shutters and gingerbread trim.

Below the waterline lies a colorful kingdom of coral teeming with sharks, turtles and luminous tropical fish. Scuba diving is renowned here, but there are also opportunities for free diving, snorkeling or swimming at one of Saba's two ocean coves.

Saba is an easy day trip from neighboring islands, but its unique rugged landscape and astonishing aquatic ecosystems reward longer exploration.

When to Go

Jul–Sep Due to its elevation, Saba's weather is refreshingly temperate compared to neighboring islands.

Oct Each October, the two-week Sea & Learn festival hosts a range of ecological activities.

Nov–early Dec Bask in the pre-season rush after the hurricanes clear out.

Windwardside

Filled with traditional gingerbread-trimmed Saban cottages, the quaint hamlet of Windwardside is Saba's commercial heart, with amenities including a dive shop, tourist office (p629) and the Trail Shop (p629), which has a wealth of advice on hiking. From the center, the 'suburb' of Booby Hill is an exceptionally steep 600m trek southeast.

Though light on sights, Windwardside has a couple of small, intriguing museums and a clutch of art galleries and craft shops. Up at Booby Hill, you can take jewelry-making classes at Jobean Glass Art Studi.

◉ Sights

Dutch Museum MUSEUM
(☑416-5856; www.museum-saba.com; by donation; ⊘1-5pm) Inside a classic Saban gingerbread cottage, this little museum's displays include Dutch tiles, lacework, porcelain, crystal, copper engravings, paintings, mirrors and furniture ranging from 150 to 400 years old. A free hour-long film about the Dutch West India Company's operations between 1600 and 1800 screens every Tuesday at 5pm (reservations recommended).

Harry L Johnson Museum MUSEUM
(www.museum-saba.com; US$2; ⊘10am-3pm Tue-Sat) Surrounded by wildflowers, this pint-sized museum occupies a quaint 1840-built sea-captain's cottage and is crammed with an eclectic collection. Highlights include vintage photographs of Dutch royalty, Saba's first telephone, the Steinway piano hoisted up the Ladder (p626) by eight strong Saban lads, and an old rock oven (the cottage's original kitchen remains intact). A museum guide brings the stories behind the objects to life. Outside, look for the large cistern used to gather water and, above it, the family cemetery.

★ Mt Scenery MOUNTAIN
A dormant volcano that last erupted in 1640, Mt Scenery (887m) is the pinnacle of pyramid-shaped Saba, and officially the highest point in the Kingdom of the Netherlands. It's covered by elfin forest (cloud forest) with 200-year-old mountain mahogany trees smothered in orchids, bromeliads and other epiphytes. The **Mt Scenery Stairway** starts behind the Trail Shop (p629) in Windwardside and climbs 1064 stairs. Check the weather forecast before setting out as the steps can become extremely slippery in rain.

The best time to get started is about 9am or 10am, so you can reach the summit around noon, the least cloudy part of the day.

Established in 2017, a second trail, the **Elfin Forest Trail**, branches off from the Sandy Cruz Trail close to Hell's Gate, and also leads to the summit.

🏃 Activities & Tours

Cabbies double as island guides with tours costing US$50 for up to four people. Hotels will call a guide for you or order one from George on ☑416-3367 or Wayne on ☑416-7170. There are usually taxis waiting at the port and airport.

To hike with a guide such as the legendary Crocodile James, contact the Trail Shop (p629).

Sea Saba DIVING
(☑416-2246; www.seasaba.com; Lambee's Place; 1-/2-tank dives from US$65/131, night dives US$85; ⊘by appointment) Passionate about marine education and keeping Saba a pristine place to visit, PADI-affiliated Sea Saba runs a range of dive trips and various courses including introductory courses from US$120 and open-water courses from US$330. Night dives take place on Tuesday, Thursday and Sunday. It also runs four-hour snorkeling trips (US$39 including gear) and rents snorkeling gear (per day US$15).

🍴 Courses

★ Jobean Glass Art Studio ART
(☑416-2490; http://jobean.glass.com; Booby Hill; half-/full-day glass workshop US$95/150; ⊘10am-5pm Mon-Sat, to 3pm Sun, classes by appointment) Local artist Jobean works out of her colorful studio up on Booby Hill. During a half-day glass workshop, you're set up with a torch and an unlimited supply of thin glass shafts that you melt down into swirling balls or cylinders, before making beads of all shapes and sizes while incorporating gold foil and quirky objects.

Your creations are yours to keep; otherwise just drop by and browse the shop. Some of Jobean's more unusual designs include plates made from Heineken bottles and wine bottles and a huge array of animals large and small.

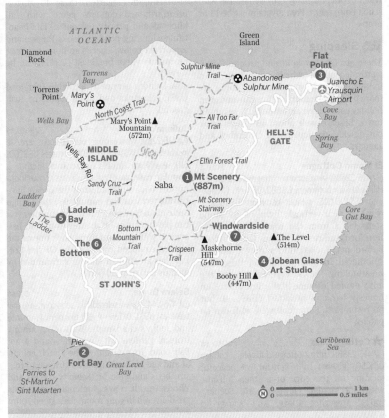

Saba Highlights

❶ Mt Scenery (p624) Hiking to the summit of Saba's soaring volcano while taking in dizzying views of the sea far below.

❷ Diving (p633) Scuba diving among submerged pinnacles teeming with nurse sharks and large colorful fish on a trip from Fort Bay.

❸ Juancho E Yrausquin Airport (p635) Landing on the world's smallest commercial runway alongside sheer, steep cliffs at Flat Point.

❹ Jobean Glass Art Studio (p624) Crafting jewelry on a course with glass artist Jobean in Booby Hill.

❺ Ladder Bay (p626) Tackling the hundreds of steps hewn into the rock where supplies and even visiting royalty were hauled up.

❻ Island Flavor (p630) Dining on fruit, veggies and herbs from the owners' gardens at this tree-shaded restaurant in the Bottom.

❼ Harry L Johnson Museum (p624) Learning about the island's pioneering history in a traditional Windwardside gingerbread-trimmed cottage.

Saba Freediving School   WATER SPORTS
(☎416-9213; www.sabafreediving.com; half-/2-/3-day course US$150/220/345; ☺by appointment) Saba's clear waters are a superb place to try the increasingly popular sport of free diving.

Affiliated with both PADI and AIDA (the International Association for the Development of Apnea), instructor Luis Fonseca teaches techniques for holding your breath and the mental and physical disciplines needed to reach depths normally only achievable with scuba equipment. Free divers must be 18 or over.

🛏 Sleeping

There are five hotels in and around Windwardside, all of which have their own unique flavor. If you're looking for a bit more privacy, the tourist office can advise on holiday cottage rentals scattered throughout town. Reserve well ahead as places book out quickly, particularly in December and January.

El Momo Cottages
HOTEL $

(☏416-2265; www.elmomocottages.com; Booby Hill; s/d with bathroom US$80/95, with kitchenette US$100/115, without bathroom US$60/75; 🛜🏊) A near-vertical flight of 69 stone steps leads from the road to the reception for these rustic cottages with outdoor bathrooms. Tucked into a rugged hillside smothered in tropical foliage, they have breathtaking views, especially from the aptly named 'Cottage in the Sky.' There's an honesty bar and breakfast (US$8.50) but no restaurant. Some cottages' wi-fi can be patchy.

⭐ Cottage Club
COTTAGE $$

(☏416-2386; http://cottage-club.com; cottage US$150; P🛜🏊) In a central yet peaceful location on the edge of a steep hillside, with spectacular views of Mt Scenery (p624) towering above, and across to St-Martin/Sint Maarten, these 10 gingerbread-trimmed cottages come with full kitchens and private balconies. The beautiful swimming pool overlooks the sea and airport far below. There's an honesty bar in reception, where breakfast (US$15) can be served.

A laundry service is available (per load US$15). Iguanas and goats roam the lush grounds.

Juliana's
HOTEL $$

(☏416-2269; www.julianashotelsaba.com; s/d/ste incl breakfast US$140/165/200, cottages US$200-310; P❄🛜🏊) Juliana's amenities include a popular cafe-bar, Tropics (p628), overlooking the pool. Rooms facing the ocean have private terraces and hammocks; the Mango Suite has a four-poster bed – in summer you can pick mangoes off the tree from your balcony. If you're self-catering, book one of the kitchen-equipped cottages; the Orchid Cottage has an outdoor shower surrounded by orchids and tropical plants.

Selera Dunia
B&B $$

(☏416-5443; www.seleradunia-saba.com; s/d incl breakfast US$120/135; P🛜) Owners Hemmie and Jenny's charismatic B&B is set among tropical gardens with waterfalls and a koi fish pond. Its two suites, the Dutch colonial and the Malaysian, have extra-long king-size beds and epic Mt Scenery (p624) and Windwardside views. Homemade breakfasts are delivered to your room. It's a steep 700m walk or US$8 taxi ride from town.

WHERE TO SWIM & SNORKEL IN SABA

Wells Bay Backed by sheer cliffs, this rocky little bay has a small, coarse sandy beach that comes and goes depending on the northerly swell – ask locally to find out when's best to visit while you're here. There's great snorkeling (including a marked underwater trail); rent gear from **Sea Saba** (p624) in Windwardside. It's a steep 2.5km walk back up to the Bottom, so it's best to prebook a taxi for the return trip (one way US$15.50).

Cove Bay Behind a breakwater constructed from boulders to keep currents at bay, this little cove is one of the island's two ocean swimming spots, with excellent snorkeling in calm weather. It's sunniest in the morning; there's a small strip of coarse sand but no amenities. From the airport, it's a 150m walk downhill. Order a taxi at the airport for the return trip or hike the precipitous 4km **Spring Bay Trail** to Windwardside.

Ladder Bay Until the mid-20th century, before Fort Bay was enlarged as a port, everything – from supplies to the Queen – was hauled up to the Bottom via the Ladder, a series of more than 800 steps hewn into the rock on the island's west coast. Panoramic views aside, these days there's not much here other than an abandoned customs house halfway along the 800m-long route. Snorkeling is possible in the bay when the weather's calm.

Scout's Place   HOTEL $$
(☑416-2740; www.scoutsplace.com; d incl breakfast US$129-252, cottage US$319; ❋❄⊠) Adjoining Windwardside's busiest pub (p628), Scout's has standard and deluxe rooms (with shared walkway balconies) and 'cottage rooms' with ocean-view balconies (C2 has the largest, sunniest deck). All have fridges and tea- and coffee-making facilities. The detached two-bedroom Pirate Cottage has a kitchen, lounge area and terrace. Rates include basic continental breakfast but be quick as the kitchen often shuts early.

✗ Eating

Windwardside is home to most of the island's dining options, from cheap snack bars to a couple of fine-dining establishments. Book ahead for dinner as many restaurants only cook enough food for guests with reservations and/or have a limited number of tables.

If you're self-catering, you can stock up at supermarkets including Saba's largest (albeit still small), Big Rock Market (p627).

Bizzy B Bakery   BAKERY $
(dishes US$3-9.50; ☺7am-4pm Mon-Fri, to 3pm Sat; ☎) Bizzy B bakes most of the island's bread fresh daily (including baguettes and delicious corn-rich maize loaves), along with pastries, cakes and cookies. It also sells filled sandwiches and a soup of the day to take away or eat at picnic tables in the courtyard out front.

Big Rock Market   SUPERMARKET $
(☺8am-7pm Mon-Sat) Windwardside's largest grocery store stocks frozen meat, fresh veggies and local Saba Spice rum as well as some pharmacy items.

Saba Snack   FAST FOOD $
(dishes US$8.50-11.50, mains US$12-25; ☺8am-7:30pm Wed-Mon) This little fast-food shack opens to a covered terrace and serves cheap Mexican and international fare – burritos, quesadillas, chicken fajitas, burgers, Creole-spiced grouper, coconut shrimp, garlic snapper – to eat on-site or take away. Sides include rice, red beans and chips. Food can be hit-and-miss.

★Brigadoon   INTERNATIONAL $$
(☑416-2380; mains US$20-36; ☺dinner 6-11pm, takeaway 4-6pm) Housed in a romantic cottage, Brigadoon is one of Saba's best restaurants. Frequently changing dishes might

include a sublime Saba lobster bisque, rack of lamb with truffle sauce, lion fish with lobster and shrimp sauce, and silky crème brûlée. There's a live-seafood tank and two vegetarian mains nightly. Regular events include lobster night and prime rib night.

Movie nights also occasionally take place.

Swingin' Doors   BARBECUE $$
(☑416-2506; chicken&ribs/steak US$15.80/20.80; ☺6-8pm Tue, Fri & Sun) Bookings are a must for this wildly popular, smoke-filled barbecue venue when the saloon-style wooden doors swing open for finger-lickin' chicken and ribs (Tuesday and Friday) or steak (Sunday), as only enough food is ordered to cater for reservations. Sides include salads, roast potatoes, rice and beans; the well-stocked bar has US and South American wines and Caribbean beers.

Long Haul Grill & Bar   INTERNATIONAL $$
(☑416-2013; mains US$12-29; ☺10am-10pm Tue-Sun) Long Haul's pizzas are named for Saban locales, including Hell's Gate (sausage, peppers and mushrooms), Ladder Bay (anchovies, shrimp and smoked ham) and Mt Scenery (chicken, bacon and goat's cheese). Fantastic sandwiches include a Cubano (pulled pork, dill pickles, Swiss cheese and honey mustard) and Freedom Fighter (chargrilled veggies, black beans and horseradish mayo). There's a covered terrace out front.

It's as much a good-time bar as a restaurant, with beer, cocktails and a small wine selection, sports screenings and live music on Fridays.

★Chez Bubba   FRENCH $$$
(☑416-2539; www.chezbubbabistro.com; mains US$24.50-34.50, tapas US$12.50-18.50; ☺5:30-10pm Wed-Sat & Mon, noon-10pm Sun) Tucked up a flight of stairs, this little bistro seats just 16 people on its terrace and in its tiny dining room, so reservations are essential. Steak tartare, baked brie, snails, filet mignon with foie gras, grilled Saban lobster tail with herb butter, and duck à l'orange star on the menu; everything including the bread is prepared from scratch.

Save room for spectacular desserts such as molten chocolate lava cake with homemade rum-and-raisin ice cream or piña colada pudding. A changing array of tapas dishes (garlic-sautéed frogs' legs, beef carpaccio) is served from noon to 5pm on Sundays.

Windwardside & Around

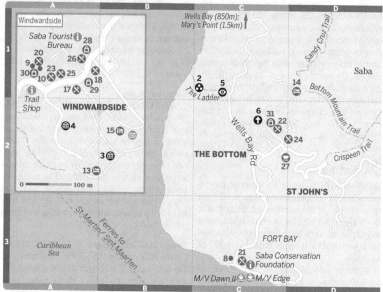

🍷 Drinking & Nightlife

Windwardside has the island's only real drinking scene, with several bars (some of which double as restaurants and vice versa). Scout's Place (p628) hosts karaoke on Friday nights, while Long Haul Grill & Bar (p627) has live music the same night. Tropics Cafe (p628) has various special events.

Tropics Cafe
BAR

(www.sabatropics.com; ⊙11am-11pm Tue-Sun; 🛜) Edging the swimming pool of Juliana's (p626) hotel, relaxed hangout Tropics hosts loads of events such as film screenings of island hikes on Wednesdays at 6:30pm. Happy hour is 4pm to 6pm; Friday's happy hour rings in the weekend with free wine and Jell-O shots. Decent food (mains US$25 to US$36) includes whole snapper and Caribbean jerk chicken.

Scout's Place
PUB

(http://scoutsplace.com; ⊙7:30am-11pm; 🛜) Village-center pub Scout's is hopping during happy hour (4pm to 6pm), when locals and visitors congregate for half-price beers on its two open-sided covered terraces overlooking the surrounding hills, valley and ocean. Karaoke kicks off at 8pm on Fridays. It's

adjacent to the hotel (p627) of the same name. Skip the food.

🛍 Shopping

⭐ Five Square Art Gallery
ARTS & CRAFTS

(www.fivesquareart.com; ⊙9am-6pm Mon-Sat, noon-3pm Sun) Paintings, sketches, drawings, prints, silk screening, cards, carvings, sculptures and other unique works by artists from Saba and around the Caribbean are all for sale at this gallery in Windwardside's village center. Look out for watercolors by Dutch-born local artist Heleen Cornet, who painted the stunning mural inside the Sacred Heart Church (p630) in the Bottom.

Kakona
ARTS & CRAFTS

(www.kakonasaba.com; ⊙9am-5pm) 🌿 Seven Saban artists and craftspeople working on the island sell their wares here, many of which are made from indigenous plants and natural products (such as Saba Spice shampoo and conditioner, sea salt, soaps, herbal teas and natural insect repellent). There's also jewelry and artworks crafted from recycled materials (Heineken bottles included). Look out for locally made knives too.

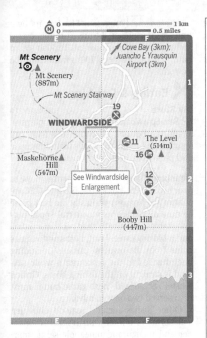

Jewel Cottage JEWELRY
(www.thejewelcottage.com; ⊙9:30am-6pm mid-Dec–Apr, closed Sun May–mid-Dec) Drop by the adorable gingerbread-trimmed traditional cottage of jeweler Mark Johnson to browse unique pieces including necklaces, bracelets and earrings for men and women. Designs inspired by Saba's extraordinary flora and fauna incorporate dazzling gems set in gold and silver.

⊕ Information

Post Office (⊙8am-noon & 1-5pm Mon-Fri, 8am-noon Sat)

RBC Bank (⊙8:30am-3:30pm Mon-Fri) Has a 24-hour ATM.

Saba Tourist Bureau (☑416-2231; www.sabatourism.com; ⊙8am-5pm Mon-Thu, 8am-4:30pm Fri) Has maps and brochures, and can help arrange island tours and diving trips.

Trail Shop (☑416-2630; www.sabapark.org; ⊙noon-4pm Mon, 10am-4pm Tue-Fri, 10am-2pm Sat & Sun) If you plan on hitting the trails, make this your first stop for maps, nature books and the latest on trail conditions. Guides including ranger James Johnson aka Crocodile James lead two-hour guided hiking treks (US$20 including transport) that will open your eyes to Saba's extraordinary eco-diversity.

⊕ Getting There & Away

From Windwardside, a taxi to the airport costs US$12.50; to the Bottom it's US$10 and to Fort Bay it's US$15.

Morgan Car Rental (p635) rents cars from US$65 per day.

The Bottom

Although home to Saba's administrative and government buildings, the island's tiny capital is at no risk of being staid on account

SABA THE BOTTOM

of the approximately 500 students studying at the Saba University School of Medicine, which is located in the village. There isn't a lot on offer for tourists, but it's a pretty spot for a quick wander and a number of hiking trails start or end here.

◉ Sights

Sacred Heart Church CHURCH
(☉sunrise-sunset) Locals refer to this charming 1935-built stone church as 'Saba's Sistine Chapel' thanks to Dutch-born local artist Heleen Cornet's colorful and stunningly detailed altar mural, which infuses biblical scenes with a Saban rainforest twist.

You can browse and buy Cornet's works at the Five Square Art Gallery (p628) in Windwardside.

🛏 Sleeping

★ Queen's Garden Resort BOUTIQUE HOTEL $$$
(☎416-3494; http://queensaba.com; Troy Hill Dr; ste incl breakfast from US$284; P ✳ 🛜 🐾) With regal views over the Bottom, rainforest and ocean, the hillside 'Queen' has indeed welcomed Dutch royalty. The 12 spacious suites each occupy an entire floor and are filled with elegant Caribbean furnishings; most have a private Jacuzzi. For the ultimate evening meal, request the private 'Bird's Nest' platform high up in a mango tree (restaurant mains US$24 to US$39).

The on-site Frangipani Spa has its own line of Caribbean beauty products and includes a Finnish sauna and Turkish steam bath. It's a super-steep 700m walk from the Bottom.

🍴 Eating & Drinking

My Store SUPERMARKET $
(☉8am-6pm Mon-Sat) The largest supermarket in the Bottom, My Store sells fruit and veggies, and imported goods including wine and plenty of frozen ready meals.

★ Island Flavor INTERNATIONAL $$
(mains US$11-25, lobster US$39.50; ☉7:30am-5:30pm Wed-Mon; 🛜) 🍽 Easily the best place to dine on Saba, this wonderful spot's outdoor tables sit beneath shady coconut palms and a Moringa tree. Fruit, herbs and veggies come from the owners' gardens (including one attached to the restaurant), while seafood is straight off the fishing boats. Grilled lobster served with herb garlic butter must be reserved two days in advance.

Other dishes include seafood chowder, a fisherman's burger with blackened snapper and mango and pineapple salsa, spicy chicken skewers with Thai green curry sauce, slow-braised pastrami on rye with sauerkraut and Swiss cheese, and herb-crusted beef tenderloin with amaretto and mushroom sauce. Freshly pressed juices, smoothies, herbal teas and Illy coffee are served alongside beer, wine and cocktails.

SABA FESTIVALS & EVENTS

Saba Triathlon (☉late Jan) An 800m open-water swim from Fort Bay, 7km road cycle (with a 600m elevation gain) and a 7km run on mountain trails (with a 350m elevation gain) ending in Windwardside make up Saba's arduous triathlon, held on the last Saturday in January. Registration costs per individual/team are US$60/110; alternatively you can cheer the athletes on along the route.

Saba Summer Festival (☉late Jul) The island's Carnival takes place over the last week of July and includes a Carnival queen contest, a calypso king competition, a costumed parade around the Bottom and a grand-finale fireworks display.

Sea & Learn (www.seaandlearn.org; ☉Oct) For around two weeks in October (dates change annually), the entire island becomes a learning center for naturalists, scientists and enthusiasts, who discover the richness of Saban flora and fauna in a range of activities, from helping out on a shark research project to learning how to use tropical plants to make medicinal teas.

Saba Lobster Fest (☉early Nov) Over the first weekend in November, from Friday to Sunday, several of the island's restaurants offer discounted specials at lunch and dinner incorporating the local delicacy, Saba Bank spiny lobster, caught on the Saba Bank offshore.

Saba Days (☉early Dec) Held in the first week in December, this island-wide festival features sporting events, steel bands, dance competitions, donkey races and barbecues.

Bottom Bean Cafe COFFEE
(☑ 416-3385; http://bottombeancafe.com; ⏲ 7am-5pm Mon-Fri, 10am-3pm Sat) Maple and bacon, caramel pecan, chocolate mint and chocolate cookie are among the bean flavors at this coffee bar, along with traditional varieties, which are ground and brewed in styles including espresso, cappuccino, latte and macchiato. Fresh juices, smoothies, milkshakes, beer, wine and cocktails are also available. On Mondays and Fridays it serves gourmet burgers (US$8 to US$14) from 3pm.

🛍 Shopping

⭐ **Saba Artisan Foundation** ARTS & CRAFTS
(☑ 416-3260; ⏲ 8:30am-4pm Mon-Fri) A small guild of locals produces an eclectic assortment of Saba-specific arts, crafts and souvenirs, including intricate Saba lace as well as hats, T-shirts, bags and hand-screened linens (tablecloths, tea towels and curtains), sewn on-site. Homemade jams and potent liqueurs including Saba Spice rum, guava rum, guavaberry rum and ginger rum (free tastings available) are also on the shelves.

ℹ Information

WIB (⏲ 24hr) The bank branch here closed in 2016, but WIB still has a 24-hour ATM.

ℹ Getting There & Away

A taxi between the Bottom and Windwardside costs US$10; to Fort Bay it's US$7.50, and to the airport it's US$20.

Fort Bay

Saba's working port, Fort Bay, serves ferries and yachts as well as fishing vessels and dive boats.

🏃 Activities

⭐ **Saba Divers** DIVING
(☑ 416-2526; www.sabadivers.com; single-tank shore/boat dive US$45/58, night dive US$60/73; ⏲ by appointment) PADI-affiliated Saba Divers heads out to 30 different locations such as Third Encounter and Twilight Zone at the Pinnacles, which rise from the ocean floor up to 30m with black-tip reef sharks, turtles and Nassau groupers; and Hot Springs, where you can experience underwater volcanic activity. Gear is super-new and groups are small and well organized. Prices include free nitrox.

OFF THE BEATEN TRACK

MARY'S POINT

The far-flung village of **Mary's Point** was once a 45-minute walk from even the next village. In 1934 the Dutch government decided to move every single villager and house to an area behind Windwardside known as the 'Promised Land,' thus lessening the isolation of being so far from any other signs of civilization. You can see the ruins of Mary's Point while hiking on the North Coast Trail (guide required).

🍴 Eating

Deep End Bar & Grill SEAFOOD, INTERNATIONAL **$$**
(☑ 416-3438; mains US$16-28; ⏲ 8:30am-3:30pm Tue-Sun) Panoramic glass windows look out over Fort Bay's port from Deep End's light-filled dining room. Fresh-as-it-gets seafood comes straight off the boats docking out front; the restaurant also cooks hearty breakfasts along with burgers, sandwiches, salads and pastas.

ℹ Information

Saba Conservation Foundation (☑ 416-3295; www.sabapark.org; ⏲ 8am-4pm Mon-Fri) Established in 1987, nonprofit management organization Saba Conservation Foundation is in charge of keeping Saba in pristine condition, both on land and in the surrounding ocean, and has information about hiking trails and the Saba Marine Park.

ℹ Getting There & Away

Saba's two ferries, the **M/V Dawn II** (p635) and **M/V Edge** (p635) serve St-Martin/Sint Maarten. Taxis meet arriving ferries; a fare to Windwardside costs US$15.

UNDERSTAND SABA

History

Saba was intermittently inhabited by the Arawaks and Caribs before Columbus sailed past the island in 1493 on his second voyage to the New World. Although English pirates and French adventurers briefly inhabited the island, it wasn't until 1640 that the Dutch set up a permanent settlement, the remains of which are still scattered around the island.

Saba changed hands a dozen times or so over the next 200 years, resulting in mostly Irish and English settlers, but Dutch ownership. Life on Saba was difficult at best. Many of the men made their living from the sea, as fishermen or as pirates such as Hiram Beakes (who coined the phrase 'dead men tell no tales'), leaving so many women on the island that it became known as 'The Island of Women.'

Because the steep topography of the island precluded large-scale plantations, colonial-era slavery was quite limited on Saba. Those colonists who did own slaves generally had only a few and often worked side by side with them in the fields, resulting in a more integrated society than on larger Dutch islands.

The close-knit community beat seemingly impossible conditions and thrived in this little outpost. Tourism found Saba when an airport was built in 1959, but it wasn't until 1970 that Saba got uninterrupted electricity.

Saba was a part of the Netherlands Antilles until 2005, when the five islands (Saba, Curaçao, Bonaire, Sint Eustatius and Dutch Sint Maarten) met on the Jesurun Referendum to decide the fate of the Netherlands Antilles. Saba, along with Bonaire, voted overwhelmingly to become administered directly by the Netherlands. In October 2010, after many round-table discussions during the previous two years, the Netherlands Antilles was officially dissolved. Saba, along with Sint Eustatius and Bonaire became 'special municipalities' of the Netherlands, which effectively strengthened the bond between these islands and the mainland. As 'overseas countries and territories' they now share similar rights to those living in the Netherlands and have a more closely linked government system. On January 1, 2011, Saba adopted the US dollar as its currency.

People & Culture

Most locals are descendants of British, Irish, Scottish, Dutch and Scandinavian settlers, along with those from other Caribbean islands and the descendants of African slaves.

The island is tolerant of differences, an attitude that came about hundreds of years ago when slave and master had to work side by side to allow the island to thrive. Today Saba's small population continues to be a village-like, close-knit community that's welcoming to newcomers and visitors.

Artists and artisans have long been inspired by the island's natural beauty and Saba has a small but vibrant handicraft scene. Saba's most famous craft is lace making, a skill that was brought to the island in the 1870s by a woman who'd been sent to live in a Venezuelan convent. Older women in the community still weave the lace in their spare time.

Landscape & Wildlife

Saba has an extraordinary bounty of orchids, bromeliads, mountain fuchsia, mahogany, elephant and sea grape trees, wild plantains, massive ferns and other flora. Across the island, you'll see Saba's national flower, the yellow-petaled, dark-centered black-eyed Susan; petals can also be white or orange.

You'll also encounter a multitude of birds such as the red-billed tropic and Audubon's shearwater along with endemic critters such as Saba green iguanas (also known as black dragons), the anoles lizard and the (harmless) red-bellied racer snake, which is only found on Saba and Sint Eustatius.

Mosquitoes are far less prevalent here than on neighboring islands, but they do still exist so it's worth using repellent to guard against them.

SURVIVAL GUIDE

ℹ Directory A–Z

ACCOMMODATIONS

Most accommodations are midrange and reasonably priced considering there are very few options on the island (advance reservations are strongly recommended).

Private vacation rentals are listed at www.sabatourism.com/stay.html. Most cottages are located in Windwardside or Hell's Gate.

Hotels add a 5% government room tax; a 10% to 15% service charge is usually at the discretion of the visitor. Each guest must also pay a US$1 per day conservation fee.

ACTIVITIES
Diving & Snorkeling

Saba's otherworldly beauty extends to 29 diverse dive sites, including sheer wall dives and submerged pinnacles. Evidence of the island's volcanic activity can be felt at sites such as **Hot Springs** and nearby **Ladder Labyrinth**, with yellow-tinged sand that's hot to the touch even at depths of 16m. Dazzling multicolored corals, sponges and marine life from barracudas to turtles, sea horses and black-tipped reef sharks abound.

Since 1987, the area has been protected as the Saba Marine Park by the nonprofit **Saba Conservation Foundation** (p631). All divers must go through a dive operator and pay a US$3 fee per dive. Saba has two diving outfits, **Sea Saba** (p624) in Windwardside, and **Saba Divers** (p631) by the port in Fort Bay. Both are PADI five-star centers and offer several boat dives daily and the gamut of courses and certifications.

For snorkelers, **Wells Bay** (p626) and adjacent **Torrens Point** are ideal spots, with a marked underwater trail. **Ladder Bay** (p626) is also good, but it's a 30-minute hike down to the shore from the road and double that back up. **Cove Bay** (p626), near the airport, is an idyllic snorkeling spot when conditions are calm. Sea Saba rents snorkeling gear.

Hiking

Saba is a hiker's paradise with many of the century-old trails once used by the earliest settlers to get from village to village. Before setting out, drop by the **Trail Shop** (p629) for maps, nature books and the latest on trail conditions. When you're hiking, dress in layers, wear sturdy walking shoes and bring water. Some hikers might appreciate a walking stick (available for free at the Trail Shop) to navigate steep and slippery sections.

New routes are being created all the time. Currently, some 15 marked trails cut across seven ecosystems, including coastal meadows, rainforests and elfin forests (cloud forests).

After **Mt Scenery** (p624), the most popular hikes are the moderately strenuous **Sulphur Mine Trail** (40 minutes one way), which offers views of the airport landing strip (exploring the mine is possible but flashlights/torches are essential; enter at your own risk); the **Spring Bay Trail**, from the airport to Windwardside (three hours one way); the **Bottom Mountain Trail** (90 minutes one way), from Windwardside to the Bottom; and the long but easy **Sandy Cruz Trail** (three hours one way) from Hell's Gate to the Bottom.

Established in 2017, the new 800m **Elfin Forest Trail** branches off from the Sandy Cruz Trail close to Hell's Gate, and provides an alternative route to the summit of Mt Scenery.

The only trail you shouldn't attempt without a guide is the **North Coast Trail** (three hours one way), from Hell's Gate to Wells Bay, which leads past the deserted old village ruins of **Mary's Point** (p631) en route. All of the others are accessible to reasonably fit hikers, although they're much more fun in the company of a ranger such as Crocodile James.

CHILDREN

Saba's steep hills and streets are difficult for parents to navigate with prams/buggies. Activities for children are also extremely limited, although older kids may enjoy hiking.

Cribs (cots) and high chairs are rare. Supermarkets sell baby-care items such as diapers (nappies).

ELECTRICITY

Saba's electric current is 110V, 60 cycles. North American–style plugs are used.

EMERGENCY NUMBERS

COUNTRY CODE	☑ 599
INTERNATIONAL ACCESS CODE	☑ 011
EMERGENCY	☑ 911

SLEEPING PRICE RANGES

The following price ranges refer to a double room with private bathroom in the high season (mid-December to mid-April).

$ less than US$100

$$ US$100–200

$$$ more than US$200

EATING PRICE RANGES

The following prices are for a main course.

$ less than US$15

$$ US$15–30

$$$ more than US$30

FOOD

Except for a smattering of gems, Saba's few eating options are not good. Most restaurants are concentrated in Windwardside, with fewer in the Bottom and one at Fort Bay along with a bar.

Even self-caterers may struggle as the supply ship only comes in once a week (on Wednesday mornings); there are small supermarkets in **Windwardside** (p627) and the **Bottom** (p630).

The **Saba Lobster Fest** (p630) takes place in early November.

GLBT TRAVELERS

There's no gay and lesbian nightlife scene. Sabans tend to be very tolerant so public displays of affection or booking into a double room shouldn't pose any problems. Same-sex marriage was legalized in 2012.

HEALTH

Thanks to the Saba University School of Medicine, located in the Bottom, healthcare on the island is excellent.

AM Edwards Medical Center (☑ 416-3288; www.sabahealthcare.org; Paris Hill Rd) In the Bottom.

Saba Dispensary (☑ 416-3400; www.sabadispensary.com; ◷ 9am-5pm Mon-Fri, 10am-noon Sat) The island's only pharmacy is located in the Bottom.

Saba Marine Park Hyperbaric Chamber (☑ 416-3295; ◷ 24hr) Opposite the pier at Fort Bay.

LEGAL MATTERS

Drugs of all kinds are prohibited; being caught with any in your possession will result in prosecution.

Saba is very environmentally conscious and importation and exportation of wildlife such as lizards is illegal.

MONEY

Saba uses the US dollar. There are ATMs in Windwardside and the Bottom. Credit cards (including foreign cards) are accepted at larger establishments.

> **ⓘ TAP WATER**
>
> Sabans are extremely environmentally aware. The island's water supply mostly comes from rain gathered on rooftop cisterns, or a small desalination plant, so it's best to drink bottled water.
>
> Visitors should be mindful about not taking long showers and not running the water longer than absolutely necessary.

ATMs

RBC Bank (p629) In Windwardside; has a 24-hour ATM.

WIB (p631) In the Bottom; there's a 24-hour ATM but no other banking facilities.

Exchange Rates

AUSTRALIA	A$1	US$0.72
CANADA	C$1	US$0.74
FRANCE	€1	US$1.05
JAPAN	¥100	US$0.85
NEW ZEALAND	NZ$1	US$0.69
SWITZERLAND	Sfr1	US$0.98
UK	UK£1	US$1.23

For current exchange rates, see www.xe.com.

Tipping

Service charges are included on restaurant bills, so no further tipping is necessary. At hotels, a 10% to 15% service charge is generally at the discretion of the guest. Tipping taxi drivers and guides is at visitors' discretion.

PUBLIC HOLIDAYS

New Year's Day January 1
Good Friday March/April
Easter Sunday March/April
Easter Monday March/April
King's Day (Koningsdag) April 27
Labor Day May 1
Ascension Thursday 40th day after Easter
Pentecost Seventh Sunday after Easter
Carnival Monday July 31
Saba Day December 1
Christmas Day December 25
Boxing Day December 26

TELEPHONE

➡ Saba's country code is ☑ 599.
➡ Local numbers are seven digits.
➡ There are no area codes on Saba.
➡ If you are calling locally, just dial the seven-digit number.
➡ To call the island from overseas, dial your country's international access code + 599 + the local number.

TIME

Saba is on Atlantic Time (GMT/UTC minus four hours). Daylight saving time is not observed.

TOURIST INFORMATION

Saba Tourist Bureau (p629) In Windwardside; has maps and brochures, and can help arrange island tours and diving trips.

Trail Shop (p629) If you plan on hitting the trails, make Windwardside's Trail Shop your first stop for maps, nature books and the latest on trail conditions. It can also arrange hiking guides.

TRAVELERS WITH DISABILITIES

Wheelchair users and travelers with limited mobility may have a problematic time on Saba, as the island is extremely steep and riddled with thousands upon thousands of stairs.

Accommodations and restaurant bathrooms invariably aren't wheelchair-friendly.

VOLUNTEERING

Volunteering opportunities such as maintaining hiking trails, monitoring reefs and marine life, and assisting staff at the **Trail Shop** (p629) are available through the **Saba Conservation Foundation** (p631). Projects run for a maximum of two to three months.

ⓘ Getting There & Away

AIR

Flying into Saba is a hair-raising experience: its airport is home to the world's shortest commercial runway (400m), with flights coming in breathtakingly close to the sheer cliffs (fear not: Saba pilots must pass regular tests).

Saba's **Juancho E Yrausquin Airport** (SAB; ☑ 416-2255; Flat Point) is served by **Winair** (☑ 416-2255; www.fly-winair.com), with daily flights to St-Martin/Sint Maarten's **Princess Juliana International Airport** (p723) and weekly flights to St-Barthélemy. There's no ATM; taxis meet flights.

Avoid booking the last flight of the day, as flights are not allowed to land at St-Martin/Sint Maarten's airport after sunset.

The airport has a small bar named the Flight Deck.

SEA

Two ferries run visitors between St-Martin/Sint Maarten and Saba. No cruise ships serve Saba.

Ferry

M/V Dawn II (☑ 416-2299; www.sabactransport.com; adult/child one way US$58/35, return US$100/55, same-day return US$78/45) The smoother of Saba's two ferries if you're prone to motion sickness, with comfy seats, air-conditioning and free Heineken. It departs from Fort Bay at 7am Tuesday, Thursday and Saturday for Bobby's Marina, Philipsburg, St-Martin/Sint Maarten; journey time is 90 minutes. Check in at least 45 minutes prior to departure. There's a US$10 departure tax.

M/V Edge (☑ in Sint Maarten 545-2640; www.stmaarten-activities.com; one way adult/child US$55/27.50, return US$110/55, day trip US$80/40) This high-speed catamaran departs Fort Bay at 3:30pm Wednesday, Friday and

Sunday for the often-rough 90-minute trip to Pelican Marina, Simpson Bay, St-Martin/Sint Maarten. Arrive 45 minutes before departure. Departure tax is US$10.

Yacht

Contact the harbor master between 6am and 6pm on VHF channel 16 to arrange docking and customs and immigration clearance.

ⓘ Getting Around

There is no bus service on Saba. Most travelers use taxis, walk or hitchhike. Cab fares are fixed and drivers meet arriving flights and ferries; otherwise, locals can call you a taxi. Renting a vehicle is not recommended for short stays.

CAR & MOTORCYCLE

Saba's only roads are narrow, exceptionally steep and winding, with tight corners, and driving conditions are difficult. The island's sole **gas station** (☑ 416-3272; ⊙ 9am-5pm Mon-Sat) is located in Fort Bay.

If you decide to drive, a driver's license from your home country will suffice. Driving is on the right-hand side of the road. Drivers tend to drive slowly as there are many sharp turns and two-way streets that only fit one car at a time. **Morgan Car Rental** (☑ 416-2881; www.icssaba. com; Island Communication Services; car-rental per day from US$65; ⊙ 9am-6pm Mon-Fri, 10am-3pm Sat) in Windwardside rents cars from US$65 per day.

HITCHHIKING

Hitching is never entirely safe, and we don't recommend it. Travelers who hitch should understand that they are taking a small but potentially serious risk. However, hitching on Saba is common and often necessary, and the island is one of the safest destinations in the region.

TAXI

➡ There is no central taxi dispatch number on Saba, but prices are fixed to prevent overcharging.

➡ A taxi between the airport and Windwardside costs US$12.50; between Fort Bay and Windwardside it's US$15. Between the Bottom and Windwardside, a taxi costs US$10.

➡ There is an additional US$1 for transporting luggage.

➡ Fares increase by 25% between 9pm and 6am.

➡ Your hotel or restaurant can arrange a cab; try Peddy (416-7062) or Garvis (416-6114).

Sint Eustatius

POP 3200 / ✒ 599

Best Places to Eat

➡ Franky's (p641)

➡ Old Gin House Restaurant (p642)

➡ Cool Corner (p642)

➡ Para Mira (p641)

Best Places to Sleep

➡ Old Gin House (p641)

➡ Harbor View Apartments (p641)

➡ Statia Lodge (p643)

Why Go?

'The Caribbean's Hidden Treasure' – the tourism slogan of tiny Sint Eustatius (more commonly known as Statia) is especially apt. The jewels of this castaway-style outpost lie under the sea: dazzling reefs, teeming marine life, rusting wrecks and vestiges of the Lower Town – part of the capital (and only town), Oranjestad – which is now largely submerged.

Incredibly, Statia was the world's busiest seaport for cargo transported between Europe and the American colonies in the 18th century, when the island became a tax-free haven under the Dutch. By the 1790s, over 3000 ships landed in 'Golden Rock' each year and the population exceeded 30,000. In 1796 the French took over Statia and instituted heavy taxes, driving merchants away. Later part of the since-dissolved Netherlands Antilles, Statia became a 'special municipality' of the Netherlands in 2010.

Today, Statia's few visitors are intrepid scuba divers, and hikers exploring its rugged, volcanic terrain.

When to Go

Dec–Jan While neighboring islands swell with visitors, Statia stays remarkably calm.

Apr–May Savor the last of the dry season before the thundershowers plow through.

Jul Celebrate Carnival with locals amid live music and seafood feasts.

Oranjestad

The only town on Sint Eustatius, tiny Oranjestad evokes a bygone era with its colorfully painted wooden cottages, historic ruins (including its centerpiece Fort Oranje (p637)) and dusty, virtually traffic-free streets.

Oranjestad is split into the waterfront Lower Town (most of which now lies ruined underwater following hurricanes, with only four 17th-century buildings remaining), and the Upper Town, where most services are located, including the government headquarters.

◉ Sights

★ Lower Town Beach   BEACH

This narrow strip of oyster-gray sand is an extraordinary place to snorkel in pristine waters among the ruins of 18th-century warehouses, now caked in coral and teeming with multicolored fish. The ruins comprise most of the former Lower Town, which had been built on sand behind a sea wall and over time sank into the water as hurricanes wreaked destruction.

Government Guesthouse   NOTABLE BUILDING

(Emmaweg, Upper Town) This handsome 18th-century stone-and-wood building was thoroughly renovated in 1992 with funding from the EU. It's now the government headquarters, with the offices of the lieutenant governor and commissioners on the ground floor and the courtroom on the upper floor. The building, which once served as the Dutch naval commander's quarters, came by its name in the 1920s, when it was used as a guesthouse. Its interior is closed to the public.

★ Fort Oranje   FORT

(Fort Oranje Straat, Upper Town; ⊗ 24hr) FREE
Soak up history and sweeping views from this extensively restored fort, a mighty citadel complete with cannons, triple bastions and cobblestone parade grounds. The current stone structure was built by the British in 1703, replacing the original wooden fort the French erected in 1629. It's the best preserved of the 16 remaining defensive forts on the island and is where the first salute was fired in recognition of US independence on November 16, 1776, now commemorated as Statia Day.

SALUTE TO AMERICA

A plaque in the courtyard of **Fort Oranje**, commissioned by US President Franklin D Roosevelt, commemorates Statia's most famous moment in history. On November 16, 1776, the American war vessel *Andrew Doria* sailed into the harbor and fired a 13-gun salute (one for each of the rebellious colonies). Statia's governor Johannes de Graaff gave orders to fire Fort Oranje's cannons in a counter-salute, thereby becoming the first foreign nation to recognize the sovereignty of the new United States of America.

Dutch Reformed Church   RUINS

(Kerkweg) The thick 60cm stone walls of the old Dutch Reformed Church, built in 1755, remain perfectly intact, but the roof collapsed during a 1792 hurricane and the building has been open to the heavens ever since. The grounds are the resting place of many of the island's most prominent citizens of the past.

Sint Eustatius Museum   MUSEUM

(☑ 318-2288; http://ssecar.org; cnr Van Peereweg & De Graaffweg, Upper Town; adult/child US$5/3; ⊗ 9am-5pm Mon-Thu, to 3pm Fri, to noon Sat) Set inside an 18th-century house built by wealthy merchant Simon Doncker, this eclectic collection showcases pre-Columbian artifacts and exhibits on slavery, Statia's Jewish community, nautical history, and colonial relics including ceramics and mahogany furniture. There are also period rooms in the style of an upper-class colonial-era villa.

Synagogue Ruins   RUINS

(Mansionweg, Upper Town) These ruins are the roofless and slowly decaying yellow-brick walls of the Honen Dalim ('She Who is Kind to the Poor'), an abandoned synagogue dating from 1739, which makes it the second-oldest synagogue in the western hemisphere. The synagogue's *mikvah* (a cleansing bath for women) has been left intact. The ruins are 30m down the alleyway with art nouveau lampposts, opposite the south side of the library.

Jewish Cemetery   CEMETERY

(Mansionweg, Upper Town) About 50m south of the Honen Dalim synagogue ruins is a

Map of Sint Eustatius showing Boven Bay, Boven (294m), Venus Bay, Gilboa Hill, Jenkins Bay, Little Mtn (200m), ZEELANDIA, Zeelandia Bay, Zeelandia, Concordia Bay, ATLANTIC OCEAN, Tumble Down Dick Bay, Signal Hill (234m), Franklin Delano Roosevelt Airport, Great Bay, CONCORDIA, Compagnie Bay, GOLDEN ROCK, Oranjestad, Interlopers Point, Corre Corre Bay, Lower Town Beach, Sint Eustatius Museum, Fort Oranje, Caribbean Sea, ORANJESTAD, Gallows Bay, The Quill, Mazinga (601m), Miriam Schmidt Botanical Gardens, Hangover Reef, White Cliffs, Charles L Brown Wreck, Kay Bay, Fort de Windt, Buccaneers Bay, Statia Lodge, Back-off Bay

Sint Eustatius Highlights

1 Diving (p645)
Cavorting with reef sharks and sea turtles at one of Statia's shipwrecks-turned-artificial-reefs.

2 The Quill (p643)
Ascending Statia's dormant volcano before winding your way down to the bottom of the crater.

3 Volunteering (p647)
Uncovering the island's rich history or getting closer to Statia's flora and fauna as a volunteer with a local project.

4 Fort Oranje (p637)
Visiting the fort dominating the island's sole town, Oranjestad, with views radiating out to sea.

5 Lower Town Beach (p637) Snorkeling between sunken ruins to spot hidden blue beads and spawning fish.

6 Sint Eustatius Museum (p637) Checking out the fascinating museum to find a collection of annotated artifacts, including a 2000-year-old skeleton.

Jewish cemetery, with gravestones dating from 1742 to 1843. It was here that some Jews tried to avoid British plundering. Troops noticed an extremely large number of funerals for such a small community and, upon opening a casket, found valuables instead of bodies.

🏃 Activities

Scubaqua Dive Center   DIVING
(☎318-5450; www.scubaqua.com; Oranjebaai, Lower Town; per day/night dive incl air, nitrox & marine park fees US$52/67, gear per day US$30; ⊗closed Sep) Owned and operated by an international team of scuba pros, Scubaqua organizes superb day and night dives. UV torches to illuminate the nighttime waters

cost US$10 per dive. Snorkeling equipment costs US$7 per day.

Golden Rock Dive Center   DIVING
(☑318-2964; www.goldenrockdive.com; Oranjebaai, Gallows Bay; 1-/2-tank dives incl gear US$60/110 plus marine park fee per dive US$6; ☺closed Sep) Michele and Glenn run this friendly, professional diving outfitter with two dive boats and loads of high-quality equipment, including Glenn's own invention, the buoyancy glider – a nonmotorized submersible that allows you to get up close to fish without deterring them. Golden Rock also offers four-hour coastal or offshore deep-sea fishing charters (per two people including rods, reels and bait US$350).

Secar   VOLUNTEERING
(Sint Eustatius Center for Archaeological Research; ☑524-6770; http://secar.org; Lampeweg, Upper Town) Secar is the island's sanctioned organization dedicated to unearthing and restoring relics from the past. Volunteers have the opportunity to work at one of the island's 600 documented archaeological sites.

⭐ Festivals & Events

King's Day   CULTURAL
(Koningsdag; ☺Apr 27) King's Day (Koningsdag) celebrates the birthday of the Netherlands' King Willem-Alexander on April 27 (April 26 if the 27th is a Sunday). There's singing, dancing, sporting competitions including cricket matches, and *oranjekoorts* (orange fever), where everyone dresses outlandishly in orange.

Statia Carnival   CULTURAL
(☺Jul) Music, beauty and calypso competitions, parades with themed floats, and sizzling local food all feature at Statia's biggest festival, with events all over Oranjestad. Founded in 1964, it's held over 10 days in the second half of July, culminating on a Monday with the burning of a King Momo effigy (the symbolic spirit of festivals in many Latin American countries).

Statia Day   CULTURAL
(☺Nov 16) Fort Oranje (p637) is the site of ceremonies held on Statia Day, November 16, which commemorates the date in 1776 when Statia became the first foreign land to salute the US flag and recognize the country's independence. On this date in 2004, Statia adopted a new flag. Parties, barbecues and celebrations kick off all over the island from the preceding week.

Golden Rock Regatta   SAILING
(☺mid-Nov) This colorful sailing race is held between Statia and the nearby islands of St-Martin/Sint Maarten and St-Barthélemy over four days. It commemorates Statia's importance during the American Revolution and the 11-gun salute that was fired from the island on November 16, 1776.

STATIA DIVE SITES

Blair Lobsters, sea horses and schooling fish call this underwater coral reef home.

Blue Bead Hole One of the most photogenic sites, due to the friendly and prolific schools of colorful fish, Blue Bead is also one of the best spots for finding a coveted cobalt-colored bead.

Charles L Brown Cable-laying ship the *Charles L Brown*, measuring 100m long, was sunk in 2003 as an artificial reef for divers. Most of its superstructure is intact and is now inhabited by schools of barracuda. Divers can explore the interior.

Chien Tong A 52m Taiwanese fishing vessel, the *Chien Tong* is home to multicolored fish and reef sharks and is best at night, when you'll see green and hawksbill turtles.

Gibraltar So named for the 14m-high, 16m-wide rock here, Gibraltar is covered in deep-water sea fans, and frequented by schools of sennet fish. Nurse sharks rest nearby.

Grand Canyon Like its US namesake, this awesome site is dwarfed by steep sides, which are covered in black coral. Eagle rays, sharks and jackknife fish are among the marine life here.

Lost Anchor Barracuda and rabbitfish live around two huge anchors on this offshore reef, along with queen angelfish.

Oranjestad

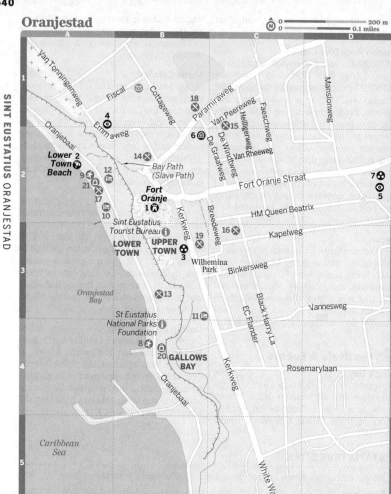

🛏 Sleeping

The best place to base yourself is along the waterfront, with cooling sea breezes and stunning sunsets.

Country Inn Guesthouse   GUESTHOUSE $
(📞 318-2484; www.countryinn-statia.com; 3 Passionfruit Rd; s/d US$60/70; ❄️🌐) Near the airport, 1.8km from Fort Oranje, Iris Pompier's little inn offers excellent value in half a dozen simple but tidy and clean rooms in a whitewashed building surrounded by nicely landscaped grounds. All have fridges, queen-size beds and cable TV, and ceiling fans as well as air-con. Breakfast is available by prior request for US$10. Cash only.

Golden Era Hotel   HOTEL $$
(📞 318-2345; http://goldenerahotel.com; Oranjebaai, Lower Town; s/d incl breakfast from US$120/150; ❄️🌐🏊) Set over two stories, the 20-room Golden Era has certainly seen better days, although there are some aspects to recommend it, including the Lower Town location and large waterfront swimming pool. Rooms, however, are little better than hostel standard, with worn furnishings, but all have balconies. Singles come with

Oranjestad

fridges only, but doubles have kitchenettes and overlook the water.

★ **Old Gin House**   HOTEL **$$$**
(☑ 318-2319; www.oldginhouse.com; Oranjebaai, Lower Town; d/ste incl breakfast from US$195/355; ✳🛜❄) Restored to its 17th-century glory, this stately cotton-seed ginning station makes a romantic spot to unwind. Most of the traditionally furnished rooms are in a yellow two-story complex behind the historic structure and come with comfy mahogany sleigh beds, along with tea- and coffee-making facilities and fridges. Across the street, two oceanfront suites open onto terraces overlooking the water.

Harbor View Apartments   APARTMENT **$$$**
(☑ 586-0923; www.statiaharborviewapartments. com; Kerkweg 8, Upper Town; apt US$250, per week US$1400; 🅿✳🛜) Self-sufficient travelers will find it hard to beat this contemporary block of four light, bright one-bedroom apartments sleeping up to four people (living rooms have convertible sofa beds). Set behind a security gate with a shared garden and terrace with barbecue facilities, apartments come with full kitchens, washing machines and balconies with sweeping ocean views. Minimum stay is two nights.

✖ **Eating**

Even in Statia's town, dining options are limited: there are a few spots serving local recipes and seafood, along with a handful of casual cafes and Chinese restaurants.

The island's only supermarkets, including its largest, **Duggins** (De Windtweg, Upper Town;

8am-8pm Mon-Sat, to 6pm Sun), are located here.

Sandbox Tree Bakery   BAKERY **$**
(☑318-2404; Kerkweg 3, Upper Town; dishes US$2-12.50; ⏱5:30am-2:30pm Mon-Sat) What looks like an unassuming residential house, trimmed in sky-blue, is in fact the island's best bakery.Try Dutch specialty breads such as *krentenbollen* with raisins, cookies like spiced *speculaas,* sweet pastries including *zeeuwse bolus* (brown sugar, lemon zest and cinnamon) and *vlaaien* (fruit pie), and savory options like *worstenbroodje* (sausage rolls). It also makes ready-to-eat sandwiches, salads and burgers.

Para Mira   CAFE **$**
(Paramiraweg, Upper Town; dishes US$2-6.50; ⏱10am-2pm Tue-Sat) An adorable cream-painted, turquoise-trimmed wooden cottage houses this traditional Dutch lunchroom. Croquettes, sandwiches such as ham and Gouda, tomato and onion, or curried egg, doughnuts, cinnamon rolls, coffee and tea can be enjoyed on the porch or garden terrace shaded by blue umbrellas.

★ **Franky's**   BARBECUE, CARIBBEAN **$$**
(☑318-0166; Black Harry Lane; mains US$12-28; ⏱11am-11pm Wed-Sun) If at all possible, plan to be at Franky's between noon and 6pm on a Saturday, when half the island turns out for Statia's most popular barbecue. Lobster, ribs, chicken and freshly caught fish take center stage on the smoky grill and are dished up in huge portions, accompanied by

OFF THE BEATEN TRACK

STATIA FORTS

Besides the imposing Fort Oranje (p637), there are 18 forts scattered throughout the island, all built in the 18th century. Most of these have been consumed by island foliage, and others lie in various states of disrepair, but a few are worth a glimpse if only for the magnificent views out to sea. Apart from Fort de Windt , all face the gentler Caribbean side of the island.

deep-fried johnnycakes and mountainous salads such as coleslaw.

Cool Corner   CHINESE $$
(☑318-3386; Emmaweg 3, Upper Town; mains US$12-22; ⊙11am-11pm, hours can vary; 🛜🚬) Painted in lavender and fuchsia-pink, with a honey-colored pine interior, Cool Corner is an island favorite. *Char siu* (barbecued pork), *kung pao* (hot garlic chicken), fish hot pot and salt-and-pepper shrimp complement veggie options such as spicy tofu with sesame and garlic sauce, scallion pancakes and *chow mien* (noodles with local vegetables). Dishes change regularly; portions are enormous (takeaway available).

Blue Bead Bar
& Restaurant   INTERNATIONAL $$
(☑318-2873; Oranjebaai, Gallows Bay; mains US$12.75-30; ⊙noon-2pm & 6-9pm; 🛜🚼) A sprawling bright-blue deck makes an idyllic perch for dining on specialties including its nine varieties of pizza, from the Farmer (bacon and eggs) to Blue Bead (sweet peppers and olives). There's a good kids' menu; on Saturday nights, the place is a popular hangout for local families. The deck comes into its own during sunset drinks. Cash only.

Old Gin House Restaurant   INTERNATIONAL $$$
(☑318-2319; www.oldginhouse.com; Oranjebaai, Lower Town; mains lunch US$14-29, dinner US$24-42, bar snacks US$8-16; ⊙7-11am, noon-2pm & 6-9pm; 🛜) Statia's best hotel is also home to its most refined restaurant. Dinner is a classy affair with options ranging from pork tenderloin and goat's cheese salad to rib-eye steak with potato gratin and grilled lobster with garlic-and-herb butter. Key lime cream-filled crêpes with mango coulis are the house-specialty dessert. Don't miss a predinner drink with front-row sunset views.

🛍 Shopping

Mazinga on the Bay   GIFTS & SOUVENIRS
(www.mazingaonthebay.com; Oranjebaai, Lower Town; ⊙1-6pm Thu-Sun; 🛜) Inside one of the four remaining 17th-century Lower Town buildings, Mazinga is named for Statia's highest peak, the Quill (Mazinga is the highest point on the extinct volcano's rim). It stocks locally made crafts and jewelry, books, Statia-themed T-shirts, sun hats, beach bags, beachwear and towels. It carries a good selection of Dutch snacks (cheeses, cookies and more) too.

Little House on the Bay   ARTS & CRAFTS
(☑318-2288; http://secar.org; Oranjebaai, Gallows Bay; ⊙9am-noon Wed, Fri & Sat or by appointment) Run by the Sint Eustatius Historical Foundation, this gift shop sells local art and crafts such as jewelry, ceramics, paintings, photographs and driftwood carvings as well as secondhand books. Proceeds support the Sint Eustatius Museum (p637) and historical research on Statia. Hours can vary.

ℹ Information

First Caribbean Bank (www.cibcscib.com; cnr Fort Oranje Straat & Emmaweg, Upper Town; ⊙8:30am-3:30pm Mon-Fri) Has an ATM (which frequently runs out of cash).

Post Office (Fiscal, Upper Town; ⊙7:30am-4pm Mon-Fri)

Sint Eustatius Tourist Bureau (☑318-2433; www.statia-tourism.com; Fort Oranje, Upper Town; ⊙8am-noon & 1-5pm Mon-Thu, to 4:30pm Fri) Has maps, brochures and helpful staff. The airport **tourist information desk** (p646) is staffed for arriving flights.

St Eustatius National Parks Foundation (Stenapa; ☑318-2884; www.statiapark.org; Oranjebaai, Gallows Bay; ⊙7am-5pm Mon-Fri) This nonprofit organization was started in 1998 to protect Statia's ample natural resources. It manages the Statia National Marine Park, Quill National Park and **Miriam Schmidt Botanical Gardens**. Stop by the office to pick up free maps and brochures, and for advice about exploring Statia above and below the waterline. Stenapa also has opportunities for volunteering (p647) around the island.

ℹ Getting There & Away

Statia has no public transport. A taxi between the airport and Oranjestad costs US$8.50.

Car-rental companies can meet you at the airport.

Quill National Park & Around

⊙ Sights & Activities

★ The Quill
HIKING

(per hiker US$10) Statia's looming dormant volcano, the Quill (derived from the Dutch word *kuil,* meaning pit or hole) soars 601m high. Designated a national park in 1998, it's the island's most popular hiking destination. From the trailhead at the end of Rosemarylaan in Oranjestad, it takes about 45 minutes to ascend the moderately steep but densely canopied trail to the crater rim.

Pay hiker fees in advance at the tourist office or St Eustatius National Parks Foundation (Stenapa).

The volcano last erupted in AD 400. There's a viewpoint down into the junglelike crater, which lies 273m above sea level, but for close-ups you need to continue down a sheer, slippery 500m-long trail to the bottom; ropes and ladders help you make the descent. En route you'll pass through four vegetation zones, including a small elfin forest. Look out for rare fauna including the Antillean iguana, the (harmless) red-bellied racer snake, found only on Statia and Saba, and the bridled quail dove. Make sure you bring plenty of water. A cab ride to the trailhead from the airport is US$10, from town US$8. Altogether there's a network of 10 trails but some are very rough and steep and should not be attempted without a guide; you can arrange one with Stenapa.

Fort de Windt
RUINS

(White Wall) Sweeping views of St Kitts to the south and the Quill and White Cliffs to the northeast extend from this historic fort at the island's southern tip, 3.3km southeast of Oranjestad's Fort Oranje. Between January and April, keep an eye out for whales offshore. The stone structure was completed in 1756 and used to monitor shipping routes before it was abandoned in 1815. It retains a pair of forest-green-painted cannons atop a cliffside wall.

Miriam Schmidt Botanical Gardens
GARDENS

(📞 318-2884; www.statiapark.org; Upper Company, the Quill; suggested donation US$5; ⊙ dawn-dusk) Started in 1988 on a former sugar plantation, these semiwild botanical gardens grow across the southeastern slopes of the island's dormant volcano, the Quill, 5km east of Oranjestad. It's a fragrant introduction to the island's rich flora, with a Sensory Garden, Palm Garden and Kitchen Garden, Bird Observation Trail and Lookout Garden (with telescope) overlooking St Kitts. Check road conditions before setting out as the road's often impassable, even by 4WD. Otherwise be prepared to hike (taxis don't run here).

🛏 Sleeping

Statia Lodge
APARTMENT $$

(📞 318-1900; www.statialodge.com; White Wall; 1-bedroom bungalow s/d US$145/165, 2-bedroom bungalow tr/q US$260; ⊙ closed Sep; ❄️🛜🏊) Statia Lodge's cluster of 10 timber- and terracotta-furnished, kitchen-equipped wooden bungalows sits on a windswept bluff 2.3km southeast of Fort Oranje. Knock back a cold beer on your terrace or at the bar by the L-shaped waterfront pool. Small bungalows sleeping one to two people include a complimentary scooter; the large ones, sleeping three to four, come with a car.

BLUE-BEAD FEVER

When Peter Minuit purchased the island of Manhattan (the heart of present-day New York City) from its local inhabitants, he paid for the land with 60 Dutch guilders' worth of trinkets, including several alluring blue beads.

These glassy pentagonal balls were produced in Amsterdam and traded throughout all of the Dutch holdings around the world. According to legend, several hundred years ago a large wooden vessel that sank off the coast of Statia was carrying these precious beads by the barrelful. And even today a lonely little bead will, once in a while, wash ashore.

Although the price of the blue beads hasn't risen in value quite like the real estate of New York, these shimmering talismans are considered to be quite a find. They are the only historical artifacts that are allowed to leave the island and, after years of avid plundering, the chance of finding one is slim. However, as the local saying goes, 'you don't find the beads; the beads find you.'

UNDERSTAND SINT EUSTATIUS

History

Statia has a rich and fascinating history that lives on in the island's extraordinary collection of ruins.

By the time Columbus came across the island in 1493, Caribs had already left. Consequently, when the French arrived there was no indigenous population to be devastated by disease or enslavement. The Dutch established the first permanent settlement in 1636. Statia changed hands 22 times among the Dutch, French and British over the next couple of centuries.

Statia was a primary link between Europe and the Atlantic world for much of the later 18th century. As the English and French levied duty after duty on their islands, the Dutch made Statia duty free in 1756. Subsequently, thousands of ships used Oranjestad as their main stopping point between Europe and the American colonies. In its heyday, Statia was home to no fewer than 10,000 full-time residents, both European colonists and African slaves. The population rose to around 30,000 when taking into account the sailors who were in port for months at a time.

Britain was none too pleased, though, contrary to popular belief, it wasn't the British navy's attack on Statia in 1781 that started the island's downward spiral. It was taxes imposed by the French in 1795 that eventually drove merchants away to nearby islands.

From 1954 Statia was part of the Netherlands Antilles, together with Aruba, Bonaire, Curaçao, Saba and Sint Maarten. On Statia Day, November 16, 2004, the island adopted a new flag, but in 2005 it voted to remain part of the Netherlands Antilles. However, other members voted to disband the island nation group, effectually leaving Statia the sole member. In October 2010, the Netherlands Antilles was officially dissolved and Statia – along with Saba and Bonaire (Aruba had seceded in 1986) – became a 'special municipality' of the Netherlands. Statians now share similar rights to those living in the Netherlands. On January 1, 2011, Statia adopted the US dollar as its currency.

Culture

Most islanders are descendants of African slaves brought over to work in the warehouses in Lower Town and on the long-vanished plantations. The culture is a mix of African and Dutch heritages along with other expats. The population expanded in the mid-1990s, with a surge in immigrants from the Dominican Republic and Aruba in particular. Following the dissolution of the Netherlands Antilles, it declined by 13% between 2011 and 2016 due to a lack of employment opportunities.

Landscape & Wildlife

The Land

The Quill looms above the southern half of the island. This extinct volcano, which reaches 601m at Mazinga, the highest point on the rim, is responsible for the high, conical appearance Statia has when viewed from neighboring islands. Volcanologists maintain the Quill is one of the most perfectly shaped volcanoes in the world.

Cliffs drop straight to the sea along much of the shoreline, resulting in precious few beaches. At the north side of Statia there are a few low mountains, while the island's central plain contains the airport and the town of Oranjestad.

The Dutch Caribbean Nature Alliance (www.dcnanature.org) has a wealth of information about the island's flora and fauna.

Flora & Fauna

Most of the northern end of the island is dry with scrubby vegetation, although oleander, bougainvillea, hibiscus and flamboyant flowers add a splash of color here and there. The greatest variety of flora is inside

---

PRACTICALITIES

Smoking Banned inside hotel rooms and enclosed spaces such as restaurants. Outdoor areas, including dining areas, however, are generally not smoke-free.

Weights & Measures The metric system is used in Statia.

the Quill, which collects enough cloud cover for its central crater to harbor an evergreen seasonal forest (which is closely related to a rainforest), with ferns, elephant ears, bromeliads, bananas, and tall kapok and silk cottonwood trees that are many centuries old. The island also has over two dozen varieties of orchid; new species are still being found today.

At certain locations across the island, including the Miriam Schmidt Botanical Gardens (p643), look out for the fuchsia-pink flowers of the *Ipomoea sphenophylla urban* (Statia morning glory), which is unique to the island. Once thought to be extinct, it's now the most rare and endangered species in the Kingdom of the Netherlands.

Statia has 75 resident and migratory species of bird, including white-tailed tropic and purple-throated carib birds that nest on the cliffs along the beach north of Lower Town, in Oranjestad. There are also harmless red-bellied racer snakes, which are only found on Statia and Saba, as well as iguanas, lizards, tree frogs, fruit-eating bats, land crabs and hawksbill and green turtles, which nest on Statia's beaches. Invertebrates such as monarch butterflies also call Statia home, along with the *glyphyalus quillensis* land snail, discovered in 2015 and named for the Quill , where it lives. Most other terrestrial animal life is limited to goats, chickens, cows and donkeys.

For divers and snorkelers, marine life offers additional diversity, with hundreds of fish species, extensive coral reefs, schools of cuttlefish and large families of Caribbean spiny lobster.

SURVIVAL GUIDE

ℹ️ Directory A–Z

ACCOMMODATIONS

Accommodations options on Statia are severely limited; there's only a handful of properties on the entire island, so be sure to book ahead. Away from the waterfront in particular, accommodations can be very hit-and-miss – choose carefully.

There are a couple of homestay options; check www.statia-tourism.com/stay/homestay-program.

Unlike other Caribbean islands, prices tend to remain static throughout the year.

ACTIVITIES

The nongovernment organization **Stenapa** (p642) was established in 1998 to protect Statia's ample natural resources. It manages the Statia Marine Park, the above-ground national park and the **Miriam Schmidt Botanical Gardens** (p643). The office, situated in a traditional timber building, has detailed information about diving and hiking, as well as everything you need to know about Statian flora and fauna.

Diving & Snorkeling

Among aficionados, Statia's diving is regarded as some of the best in the Caribbean. Protected as the Statia Marine Park since 1996, the waters are blessed with coral reefs, drop-offs, canyons and wrecks inhabited by a host of underwater creatures from ethereal sea horses to giant octopuses, plus stingrays, barracudas, coral, lobster and tropical fish. Also submerged in the clear waters is plenty of colonial detritus, including anchors and cannons. Whales come through between January and April. The submerged 18th-century ruins off the beach in Lower Town offer fascinating snorkeling.

Diving is only allowed through the two local dive shops, **Scubaqua Dive Center** (p638) and the **Golden Rock Dive Center** (p639), both in Lower Town. Each operates all manner of day and night dives as well as PADI certification courses. Divers must purchase a dive tag for US$6 per dive or US$30 per year to help maintain the pristine conditions. There's a recompression chamber at the **Queen Beatrix Medical Centre**.

Hiking

After diving, exploring the island's pristine nature on foot is the second-most popular pastime on Statia. A hiker's fee of US$10 is payable at the **St Eustatius National Parks Foundation** (Stenapa), which also has free maps and brochures with trail descriptions as well as the latest on trail conditions, and can organize guided tours.

EATING PRICE RANGES

The following price ranges are for a main course.

$ less than US$15

$$ US$15–35

$$$ more than US$35

CHILDREN, TRAVEL WITH

Children are warmly welcomed on Statia. However, facilities catering specifically to them, such as high chairs or baby-changing areas, are minimal, so parents need to be self-sufficient. Footpaths are narrow or nonexistent, so they're not ideal for prams/buggies. Baby-care products such as nappies/diapers are sold in the island's small supermarkets.

ELECTRICITY

Statia's electric current is 110V, 60 cycles; North American–style sockets are common.

EMERGENCY NUMBERS

Police	☎ 911
Fire department	☎ 912
Ambulance	☎ 913

FOOD

Oranjestad is home to almost all of Statia's limited dining options. Locally caught seafood, especially lobster, is a delicacy.

There's a handful of small supermarkets for self-caterers.

GLBT TRAVELERS

Statia is not overly tolerant, so public displays of affection are not advised. Since 2012, same-sex marriage has been legal on the island but it's strongly opposed by many locals.

HEALTH

Oranjestad's **Queen Beatrix Medical Centre** (☎ 318-2211, emergency 912; http://sehcf.org; HM Queen Beatrix, Upper Town; ⊙7am-3pm Mon-Fri) has quite a good reputation considering the island's remoteness and minuscule population. There are always two doctors on call 24 hours a day.

ⓘ DRINKING WATER

Statia's water comes from a variety of sources including rainfall collection and runoff; it's best to drink bottled water.

MONEY

ATMs are located in Oranjestad and at the airport, but can be unreliable; it's best to bring cash, which is preferred by many establishments.

ATMs

ATMs often run out of cash and won't work for all foreign cards.

First Caribbean Bank (p642) Near Fort Oranje; has an ATM.

Exchange Rates

AUSTRALIA	A$1	US$0.72
CANADA	C$1	US$0.74
EUROPE	€1	US$1.05
JAPAN	¥100	US$0.85
NEW ZEALAND	NZ$1	US$0.69
SWITZERLAND	Sfr1	US$0.98
UK	UK£1	US$1.23

For current exchange rates, see www.xe.com.

Tipping

Tipping is not necessary or expected.

PUBLIC HOLIDAYS

New Year's Day January 1

Good Friday March/April

Easter Sunday March/April

Easter Monday March/April

King's Day (Koningsdag) April 27

Labor Day May 1

Ascension Thursday 40th day after Easter

Emancipation Day July 1

Statia Day November 16

Kingdom Day December 15

Christmas Day December 25

Boxing Day December 26

TAXES & REFUNDS

Statia is duty-free.

TELEPHONE

Statia's country code is ☎ 599. To call the island from overseas, dial your country's international access code + 599 + the local number.

TIME

Statia is on Atlantic Time (GMT/UTC minus four hours). Daylight saving time is not observed.

TOURIST INFORMATION

At Fort Oranje, the **Sint Eustatius Tourist Bureau** (p642) has free island maps that show the roads and hiking trails. The airport's tiny **tourist information desk** (www.statia-tourism.com; Franklin Delano Roosevelt Airport, Max T

Pandt Blvd; ⊙ hours vary) opens when flights are landing.

TRAVELERS WITH DISABILITIES

Statia's rugged terrain and poor infrastructure are problematic for travelers with disabilities and limited mobility.

VOLUNTEERING

Statia is a good stop for educational volunteering trips. **Stenapa** (p642) connects long- and short-term volunteers with opportunities like tagging sea turtles on Zeelandia beach, maintaining the **Miriam Schmidt Botanical Gardens** (p643), staffing the office and cataloguing Statian flora.

Secar (p639) is the island's sanctioned organization dedicated to unearthing and restoring relics from the past. Volunteers have the opportunity to work at one of the island's 600 documented archaeological sites.

ⓘ Getting There & Away

AIR

Franklin Delano Roosevelt Airport (EUX; ☑ 316-2887; Max T Pandt Blvd) is Statia's only airport. It's tiny and currently only accommodates **Winair** (☑ 318-2303; www.fly-winair.com) puddle jumpers from St-Martin/Sint Maarten, from where you can connect to other islands and intercontinental flights.

Facilities are minimal; there's an ATM outside, but no car-hire desks. A small tourist information desk is staffed for arriving flights.

SEA

No cruise ships alight here. Ferries to/from St-Martin/Sint Maarten and to/from St Kitts have long been mooted but there are no services at present; check with Statia's **tourist office** (p642) for updates.

Yachts need to radio the **Marine Park** (p642), part of the St Eustatius National Parks Foundation (Stenapa), at VHF channel 16 or 17 as there are many protected spots around the island and there is only anchorage for 12 yachts at a time. There's a US$20 harbor fee, plus Marine Park fees per day/week of US$10/30.

ⓘ Getting Around

CAR & MOTORCYCLE

Driving is on the right side of the road. Road conditions are spotty outside of Oranjestad and the road to the Miriam Schmidt Botanical Gardens is often impassable. Watch out for roaming goats, cows and chickens all over the island, even in town. Also keep an eye out for surprise one-way streets – they tend to appear out of nowhere and

> ### ⓘ DEPARTURE TAX
>
> Departure tax is US$15, payable only in cash.

the locals can get very upset if you're heading the wrong way.

Car Rental

Little Statia has a ridiculous number of car-rental agencies. Expect to pay around US$40 to US$55 per day for a car or 4WD. Just remember, you get what you pay for. Cash is preferred but credit cards are sometimes accepted.

Rental companies don't have offices open to the public or desks at the airport, but meet customers at the airport for pick-up and drop-off. If you haven't prebooked, the airport tourist information desk can usually arrange a rental at short notice.

Operators:

ARC Car & Jeep Rental (☑ 318-2595) Rents 2WDs and 4WDs.

Brown's Car Rental (☑ 318-2266) Has a good range of 4WDs.

Rainbow Car Rental (☑ 318-2811) Offers a small range of 2WDs.

Reddy Car Rental (☑ 318-2880; reddyrentals@yahoo.com) Rents a small selection of 2WDs; booking via email is possible in addition to phone reservations.

Rivers Car Rental (☑ 318-2566) Hires out a limited number of 2WDs and 4WDs.

HITCHHIKING

Hitching is never entirely safe, and we don't recommend it. Travelers who hitch should understand that they are taking a small but potentially serious risk. While the usual safety precautions apply, hitching on Statia is generally safer than many other destinations in the region.

TAXI

The island's handful of taxis are independently run. The airport tourist information desk will call you one. Elsewhere ask a local, hotel or restaurant to phone for you. Prices average US$8 to US$15 per person per trip, plus an extra US$1 if you're carrying luggage, and an additional US$2 after sunset.

St-Barthélemy

POP 9035 / ☎ 590

Best Places to Eat

➡ Le Petit Deauville (p651)

➡ Le Grain de Sel (p658)

➡ On the Rocks (p654)

➡ Taïno (p657)

➡ La Boulangerie Choisy (p655)

➡ LT (p655)

Best Places to Sleep

➡ Tom Beach Hotel (p654)

➡ Eden Rock (p654)

➡ Hôtel Le Toiny (p655)

Why Go?

In the treasure-packed Caribbean, St-Barthélemy (or, as it's locally known, St-Barth) is a multifaceted jewel. This exquisite island blends French urban flair with a lush tropical landscape of soaring mountains, isolated stretches of sunsoaked, powder-soft sand, windswept cliffs, scrubby green hills, flowering gardens filled with bougainvillea, hibiscus and fragrant frangipanis, and turquoise bays dotted with myriad sailboats.

With such a dreamlike setting, St-Barth is, unsurprisingly, a destination of choice for the rich, famous and beautiful for its laid-back tempo, luxurious small-scale hotels, designer-label boutiques and outstanding restaurants. But although St-Barth is undeniably an expensive destination, all beaches are accessible, public and free, and activities from surfing, windsurfing and kitesurfing, to sailing, diving and snorkeling are all possible here. If you visit outside of high season, you can score fantastic accommodation deals.

When to Go

Dec–Jan Share the island with Academy Award winners and tycoons.

Feb–Apr Low-season prices start to kick in by April, late in the *carème* (dry season).

Jul–Aug *L'hivernage* (hurricane season) officially runs from June 1 to November 30; grab bargains before the rains hit.

St-Barthélemy Highlights

1 Kitesurfing (p656)
Soaring above the translucent waters of Grand Cul-de-Sac.

2 Anse de Gouverneur (p656) Rolling out your towel on a perfect stretch of sand.

3 Le Petit Deauville (p651) Cooling off with a sublime sorbet while eyeing Gustavia's super-yachts and chic boutiques.

4 On the Rocks (p654)

Dining on groundbreaking gastronomy high up on a rocky promontory.

5 Anse de Colombier (p652) Following scenic walking trails down to St-Barth's most secluded beach.

6 St Bartholomew's Anglican Church (p650)
Hearing renowned local choir La Chorale de Bons Choeurs

at this Gustavia church built in 1855.

7 Le Ti St Barth Catching a cabaret amid sumptuous surrounds at this Pointe Milou club.

Gustavia

Back in the 1950s, St-Barthélemy's capital was a windswept fishing village. Change came in the 1960s, when wealthy visitors including the Rockefeller and Rothschild families jetted in, followed by super-yachts carrying Hollywood stars and influential Europeans in the 1970s. Today this port town is nothing short of majestic. Although relatively small when compared to other capitals in the Caribbean, Gustavia has a string of high-end boutiques, upmarket restaurants and a handful of historical sights.

◉ Sights

St Bartholomew's
Anglican Church   CHURCH
(www.stbartholomewsanglicanchurch.com; Rue Samuel Fahlberg; ⊙8:30am-6pm) Built in 1855 from French bricks and limestone, local stone and Sint Eustatius volcanic black rock, white-painted St Bartholomew's has an open-sided design with louvered shutters that let in celestial rays of light and original pine pews. Services are held in French and English; it also hosts concerts in April and November by renowned local choir La Chorale de Bons Choeurs, which regularly rehearses here. Look for the enormous anchor across the road.

Shell Beach   BEACH
(Rue des Normands) A short stroll from the harbor, Shell Beach is an ideal Caribbean strand. As its name suggests, the beach is awash with seashells, and although the water gets deep quickly, it's generally calm, making it ideal for swimmers and snorkelers (bring your own gear). It's a favorite with kids from the nearby school, and is at its most peaceful late afternoon as the sky deepens to orange.

⚗ Activities & Tours

Jicky Marine Service   BOATING, TOURS
(☑0590-27-70-34; www.jickymarine.com; Rue Jeanne d'Arc; boat hire per half-/full day from €390/490) Just northwest of the Yacht Club, this full-service center offers boat charters and runs various trips including 90-minute sunset Champagne cruises (€85), half-day catamaran cruises (from €99), one-hour Jet Ski tours (€99) and customized fishing charters. Other activities include fly-boarding (per ride €150), using the propulsion of a Jet Ski to shoot you high into the air, dolphin-style.

Yellow Submarine Tours   BOATING
(☑0690-71-83-01; Rue de la République; adult/child €40/25; ⊙11am & 2pm mid-Oct–late Apr) If you're keen to explore underwater without getting wet, a one-hour tour aboard this semi-submersible canary-yellow vessel allows you to peer out below the waterline through the glass panels (there's also seating up on deck). Tours take you to a local reef, fishing trawler wreck and a sandy area where sea turtles congregate. Buy tickets from Great Bay Express (p661).

Saint-Barth Plongée   DIVING, SNORKELING
(☑0690-41-96-66; www.st-barth-plongee.com; Quai de la Collectivité; 1-/2-tank dive €80/140; ⊙8am-8pm, closed Sep & Oct) Reputable outfit Saint-Barth Plongée offers dive trips to some 22 sites including wrecks, canyons, caves and reefs (some just a few minutes from the harbor) that feel personalized due to a 10-person maximum. Introductory dives and night dives both cost €90; snorkeling trips lasting two to four hours start from €60. Its qualified instructors have decades of experience in St-Barth's waters.

✦ Festivals & Events

Carnival   CARNIVAL
(⊙late Feb/early March) Held for five days before Lent, St-Barth's carnival celebrations include a pageant, costumes and street dancing, and end with the burning of a King Carnival figure at Shell Beach.

Festival of St-Barth   CULTURAL
(⊙24 Aug) August 24, the feast day of the island's patron saint and namesake, Saint Barthélemy, is celebrated with fireworks, a public ball, boat races and other competitions. Most events take place in Gustavia.

🛏 Sleeping

Sunset Hotel   HOTEL $
(☑0590-27-77-21; www.st-barths.com/sunset-hotel; Rue de la République; s/d/tr from €130/150/200; ❄🛜) If you're looking to save and stay close to the action, Sunset is a bonanza. Its 10 rooms come with fridges; pricier ones have a stunning harbor and sunset views but also some street noise. Breakfast (€8) is served on the panoramic terrace. Two caveats: it's on the 3rd floor, with no lift/elevator, and wi-fi is in public areas only.

✕ Eating

⭐ Le Petit Deauville   ICE CREAM $

(✆ 0590-52-37-67; 15 Rue de la République; ice cream per 1/2/3 scoops €3/5/7; ⊙ 11am-12.30pm & 3.30-7pm Mon-Sat; ⚑) The sublime, all-natural, fruit-based sorbets (such as pineapple, mango, guava and passionfruit) and rich, creamy ice creams (including roast chestnut, pistachio, chocolate and crème brûlée) handmade at this tiny shop by *maître glacier* (master ice-cream maker) Yan Colin star on the menus of some of St-Barth's finest restaurants. There are no tables; head to the marina directly opposite.

Thai to Go   THAI $

(✆ 0590-52-92-32; www.blackgingersbh.com; Rue Samuel Fahlberg; dishes per 100g €4-10; ⊙ 11.30am-2.30pm & 5-8.30pm) Adjacent to refined Thai restaurant Black Ginger, this hole-in-the-wall's delicious Thai dishes can be heated up on-site for a portside picnic or bought cold for reheating in your apartment or villa kitchen. Choices include rice vermicelli with vegetables, red curry with squid, chicken with Thai basil and mahi-mahi massaman curry.

Eddy's   FUSION $$

(✆ 0590-27-54-17; Rue du Samuel Fahlberg; mains €21-32; ⊙ 7-9:30pm Mon-Sat, bar to midnight, closed late Aug-Oct) Tucked behind a timber gate (look for the iguana motif on the stone pavement out front), this hideaway filled with tropical plants and wooden furniture is a perennial favorite among locals. The menu blends French, Caribbean and Asian influences in dishes such as lime and basil calamari, blackened lamb cutlets, and shrimp in coconut milk. Don't miss Eddy's homemade rum.

Black Ginger   THAI $$

(✆ 0590-29-21-03; www.blackgingersbh.com; Rue Samuel Fahlberg; mains €26-33; ⊙ 6:30-10pm Wed-Mon) Filled with glossy timber furniture and lush plants and lit by oversized lamps, this split-level space is a seductive spot for spicy Thai flavors; try the *pla pik* (mahi-mahi with black pepper), *seua rong hai* (grilled beef with papaya and mango salad) and *pla neung see eiw keeng nai bai tong* (sea bass steamed in a banana leaf with fresh ginger).

L'Isoletta   ITALIAN $$

(✆ 0590-52-02-02; Rue du Roi Oscar II; mains €14-18, pizzas half-meter/meter from €25/46; ⊙ noon-11pm Tue-Sat, 6-11pm Sun) The casual sibling of fine-dining establishment L'Isola (✆ 0590-51-00-05; Rue du Roi Oscar II; mains €36-58; ⊙ 6-11pm Nov-Apr, 6.30-11pm Tue-Sun May-Aug, closed Sep & Oct) has a chic terrace with outsized wooden furniture strewn with cushions. Pizzas (by the half-meter or meter, served on wooden planks) are the mainstay, along with toasted panini sandwiches, homemade focaccia, parmigiana and lasagne. All are made with imported Italian ingredients, with meals accompanied by Italian wines.

Pipiri Palace   CREOLE $$

(✆ 0590-27-53-20; Rue du Général de Gaulle; mains €18-34; ⊙ noon-2:30pm & 7-10pm Mon-Sat) Inside a large Creole cottage amid a miniature tropical forest, longstanding institution Pipiri cooks up casual lunches (Creole crab cakes, mahi-mahi tartare, grilled rock lobsters) and intricate evening mains (pan-fried foie gras with papaya ginger jam, local fish curry in a banana leaf, breaded rack of lamb with mango sauce). Its chateaubriand steak (€86 for two) is renowned island-wide.

Le Repaire   BRASSERIE $$

(✆ 0590-27-72-48; Rue de la République; mains €18-28; ⊙ 11am-11pm) In a prime spot on Gustavia's waterfront opposite the ferry terminal, this locally loved, reasonably priced brasserie serves well-prepared French mains (steak tartare with raw egg, duck breast with honey and spices, bavette steak with Béarnaise sauce...) along with pub staples. There's a 30-strong cocktail list and Gustavia's only pool table. Breakfast, from 7am, is the earliest option in town.

L'Entracte   INTERNATIONAL $$

(✆ 0590-27-70-11; Rue du Bord de Mer; mains €16-28; ⊙ noon-3pm & 7-11pm Mon-Fri, 7-11pm Sat, closed Sep & Oct) Inside a converted warehouse, this Gustavia harborside classic is best known for its steaming thin-crust pizzas, which many consider to be the best on the island. Other dishes include pan-fried calamari, chicken cordon bleu, black Angus steaks and whole red snapper, along with freshly baked bread.

Maya's   INTERNATIONAL $$$

(✆ 0590-27-75-73; www.mayas-stbarth.com; Public Beach, Public; mains €37-58; ⊙ 7-11pm Mon-Sat) Prices here have the potential to flag a credit-card red alert, but Maya's is a quintessential St-Barth experience. A celebrity magnet,

ST-BARTHÉLEMY GUSTAVIA

WORTH A TRIP

ANSE DE COLOMBIER

The tropical paradise you've been daydreaming about is **Anse de Colombier**: a dazzling secluded white-sand beach that's fronted by turquoise waters and backed by undulating hills. One scenic walking trail here begins at the end of the road in La Petite Anse, just beyond Flamands (750m; around 20 minutes); another leads downhill from the viewpoint at the end of the road at Colombier (600m; about 15 minutes downhill). The sandy bay is ideal for swimming; there's excellent snorkeling on the north side.

this shabby-chic waterfront venture has a daily changing, market-inspired menu that might include ginger-marinated shrimp, filet mignon with béarnaise sauce, blackened dorade with a micro-herb salad, langoustine gratin and Maya's world-famous coconut tart. Book well in advance.

Drinking & Entertainment

★ **Tom's Juice Bar**   JUICE BAR
(www.tomsjuicebar.com; Passage de la Crémaillère, Rue du Général de Gaulle; ⊙8am-7pm Mon-Sat; 🕾) Hidden up a flight of steps above Gustavia's town center, Tom's is a diamond find for freshly squeezed juices with names such as 'sweet green' (spinach, cucumber, apple and lime), smoothies called 'purple rain' (acai, banana and coconut water) and bottled varieties including an invigorating ginger drink (fresh ginger, lemon filtered water and honey), which is also available at the island's supermarkets.

At breakfast, it serves acai bowls including 'mylky' (acai, cashew milk, dates, granola, goji berries, shredded coconut and honey), followed by raw salad bowls at lunch.

Le Select   BAR
(📞0590-27-86-87; cnr Rue de la France & Rue du Général de Gaulle; ⊙noon-1:30am Mon-Sat) Although it was actually a meal in the British Virgin Islands that inspired Jimmy Buffett's famous song *Cheeseburger in Paradise*, it hasn't stopped Le Select from making it its anthem. Plastered in beer coasters, the space completely lacks glamor, but has plenty of charm to spare. Live bands regularly play in the beer garden, and branded T-shirts are sold at the next-door shack.

Bar Baz   LIVE MUSIC
(www.bazbar.com; Rue Samuel Fahlberg; ⊙4pm-1am Mon-Sat) Live bands (reggae, rock, funk and blues) and international DJs play every night from 9pm at this wood-shingled harborside venue. It's strewn with red, yellow and apricot-cushioned timber chairs; posters signed by musicians who've performed here adorn the bar. Its on-site restaurant specializes in sushi.

🛍 Shopping

Les Petits Carreaux   ARTS & CRAFTS
(Passage de la Crémaillère, Rue du Roir Oscar II; ⊙10am-7pm Mon-Sat) Artist Véronique Vandernoot's iconic hand-painted ceramic tiles appear at the entrance to every beach on the island, with bright Caribbean colors vividly evoking each location. You can watch Véronique paint and buy her tiles here at her studio-shop, along with other items incorporating her iconic designs, such as coffee mugs, coasters, place mats, jewelry, postcards, bags, books and clothing.

ℹ Information

Banque Nationale de Paris (Rue du Bord de Mer; ⊙8am-noon & 2-3:30pm Mon-Fri) Has an ATM.

Police (📞24hr 0590-27-66-66; www.comst-barth.fr; Rue du Roi Oscar II; ⊙8am-noon & 2-5pm Mon, Tue, Thu & Fri, 8am-noon Wed)

Post Office (Rue Samuel Fahlberg; ⊙8am-3pm Mon, Tue, Thu & Fri, to noon Wed & Sat)

Tourist Office (Comité Territorial du Tourisme; 📞0590-27-87-27; www.saint-barth-tourisme.com; Quai Général de Gaulle; ⊙8:30am-12:30pm & 2-5:30 Mon-Thu, 8:30am-12:20pm & 2-5pm Fri) St-Barth's tourist office can help with accommodation bookings, restaurant recommendations, island tours and activities.

Flamands

Set below steep cliffs, this small settlement stretches to St-Barth's longest beach, Anse des Flamands.

⊙ Sights

Anse des Flamands   BEACH
Anse des Flamands' clear waters are very popular with beachgoers and surfers when the swell's up. Although there's no shade, upmarket hotels at the eastern end have bars, sun loungers and umbrellas for paying

customers. There's easy beach access with streetside parking at the low-key westernmost end, which is a relaxed spot to spread out your towel. You also may find parking on the main road, from where several laneways also lead down to the beach.

🛌 Sleeping

Auberge de Terre-Neuve   COTTAGE $
(📞0590-27-75-32; www.aubergedeterreneuve. com; Rte de Flamands, Flamands; cottages s €90, d €170-180; ❄️🛜) On the way down into Flamands, this cluster of cottages is a great affordable option if you don't mind not being right on the beach (it's a 650m walk down a *steep* hill). The apricot-colored cabins have basic but comfy furniture, sparkling white tiles, kitchenettes and terraces with Weber barbecues. From April to November, car rental is included in the lodging price.

Auberge de la Petite Anse   BUNGALOW $$
(📞0590-27-64-89; www.auberge-petite-anse. com; Anse des Flamands; cottages s/d/tr €150/200/220; ❄️🛜) As the snaking stone road starts to peter out at the far end of Flamands, little Auberge de la Petite Anse emerges. Its 16 semidetached bungalows have terraces overlooking the cerulean waters. If you fancy a dip, the beach is a 200m walk east. It's brilliant value, especially from April to November, when car rental is included.

Cheval Blanc   RESORT $$$
(📞0590-27-61-81; www.chevalblanc.com; Anse des Flamands; d/ste/villa from €820/1220/2960; ⊙closed Sep–mid-Oct; 🅿️❄️🛜🏊) If you're searching for a cocoon-like sanctum where daily stresses melt away, the White Horse is it. Opening onto the white sand of St-Barth's longest beach, this refined resort has 40 white-on-white-painted rooms, suites and villas, ranging from hillside garden suites amid tropical plants to beachside suites with private Jacuzzis and villas with private pools. Its spa is St-Barth's best.

🍴 Eating

Most restaurants are along the beachfront.

Chez Rolande   CARIBBEAN $
(📞0590-27-51-42; Flamands; sandwiches €3.50-14, mains €19-24; ⊙noon-3pm & 7-10pm Tue-Sat, noon-3pm Sun, closed Sep & Oct; 🛜) Hummingbirds flutter through the palm-filled garden of this cute-as-a-button golden-yellow shack with turquoise trim and a red roof. A local favorite, it's a great stop for sandwiches such as saltfish and salad or lobster and garlic butter; regional specialties including goat curry in Creole sauce, traditional black sausage with coleslaw and chicken with ginger and coconut; and potent rum punch.

La Langouste   SEAFOOD $$
(📞0590-27-63-61; www.flamandsbeachhotel.com; Hôtel Baie des Anges, Flamands; mains €20-44; ⊙noon-2:30pm & 7-9:30pm, closed Sep) A Flamands icon, La Langouste is famous for its live tank filled with crustaceans, which are grilled and served with a trio of sauces – a feast best enjoyed at a white tablecloth–covered table on the veranda overlooking the pool. Other menu highlights include Pastis-flambéed sea bass with zucchini gratin, and an outstanding lobster bisque. There's an excellent wine list.

St-Jean

After Gustavia, spread-out St-Jean is St-Barth's second-busiest settlement. Its beach curves on either side of the landmark Eden Rock, St-Barth's first hotel, which sits up on a bluff. The western end of beach is situated at the end of St-Barth airport's runway, and is a great spot to watch the hair-raising takeoffs and landings.

🏃 Activities

Hookipa Surf Shop   WATER SPORTS
(📞0590-27-71-31; snorkeling gear/bodyboard/ surfboard/longboard rental per day €7/9/24/40; ⊙9am-7pm Mon-Sat, 10am-12:30pm Sun) A one-stop shop for renting water-sports equipment, Hookipa can also let you in on the island's surfing hot spots, including where conditions are best on the day, and also put you in touch with local instructors. It also sells boards, wax, sunscreen, clothing, footwear and water-sports accessories.

Carib Waterplay   WATER SPORTS
(📞0690-61-80-81; www.caribwaterplay.com; Baie de St-Jean) This small outfit on the beach rents out kayaks (single/double per hour €20/25), SUPs (per hour €25), bodyboards (per hour €10), longboards (per hour €20) and snorkeling gear (per hour €10). You can also set sail on catamarans (per two hours €80) and windsurf (per hour €30). One-hour windsurfing lessons cost €90.

🛏 Sleeping

⭐ Tom Beach Hotel

BOUTIQUE HOTEL **$$**

(✆0590-52-81-20; www.tombeach.com; Baie de St-Jean; incl breakfast d from €320, beachfront d from €500; 🅿❄🛜🏊) Amid tropical gardens right on the beach, this exquisite property has just 12 rooms and a contemporary, breezy, beach house–style design. Midrange rooms look out over the gardens or the beach, while heading up the price scale gives you direct access onto the sand. All rooms have private terraces, king-size four-poster beds and high-tech facilities including bluetooth sound systems.

Rates include sumptuous breakfasts, airport or marina transfers and free use of beach sun loungers; water-sports equipment is available.

Le Village

HOTEL **$$**

(✆0590-27-61-39; www.levillagestbarth.com; Colline de St-Jean; d incl breakfast €275-710, family cottage €890, villas €3900-6930; ❄🛜🏊) Comfort, charm and atmosphere: this place has the lot. Accommodations vary from standard hotel rooms to traditional cottages with mahogany furniture, kitchenettes and wraparound patios; its two villas are a haven of luxury. A real hit is the dazzling infinity pool, with stunning ocean views. It's a 250m walk uphill from the beach. The spa offers nine different massage treatments.

⭐ Eden Rock

LUXURY HOTEL **$$$**

(✆0590-29-79-99; www.edenrockhotel.com; Baie de St-Jean; cottage/ste from €1150/1850; ❄🛜) Dating from 1950, St-Barth's first hotel stretches over a rocky promontory down to St-Jean's powdery white beach. Some of the luxuriously appointed cottages can be connected to form family apartments; eight suites open directly onto the beach. Exceptional amenities include two restaurants – the beachfront Sand Bar and the swooningly romantic On the Rocks – as well as a panoramic bar.

There's no communal swimming pool, but some accommodations come with private pools including the pièce de résistance 'villa rockstar', which also has a recording studio complete with the 1970s mixing console John Lennon used when recording 'Imagine'. Service exceeds even the highest expectations.

Eco-focused initiatives include solar power, rainfall collection and electric vehicles.

🍴 Eating

Maya's to Go

DELI **$**

(✆0590-29-83-70; www.mayastogo.com; Les Galeries du Commerce; dishes €6.50-19; ⊙7am-7pm Tue-Sun; 🛜) Run by Maya's famous restaurant (p651) in Public, this small *traiteur* (delicatessen) across the road from the airport is the ultimate place to pick up gourmet beach-picnic supplies: quiches, *tartines* (open-faced sandwiches), salads and pastries, as well as treats including crisps, chocolates and organic marshmallows. There's also a good range of French wines.

Kiki-é Mo

DELI **$$**

(✆0590-27-90-65; www.kikiemo.com; St-Jean; breakfast €9-15, sandwiches €7-16, mains €17-26; ⊙7am-9pm; 🛜) 🖉 In the heart of St-Jean, this laid-back deli uses organic ingredients in its French and American breakfasts, outstanding sandwiches (on baguettes, ciabatta or panini) and vitamin-packed salads. Roast scallops in black-truffle foam, and local lobster with orange hollandaise, are among the more substantial mains. It's an equally great spot for a smoothie, a freshly squeezed juice, or a cocktail. Takeaway available.

⭐ On the Rocks

GASTRONOMY **$$$**

(✆0590-29-79-99; www.edenrockhotel.com; Eden Rock, Baie de St-Jean; mains €58-72; ⊙7-10pm) Celebrated chefs Jean-Georges Vongerichten and Eric Desbordes helm the kitchen at this flagship restaurant of iconic hotel Eden Rock, set high on the rock with glittering million-dollar views. Inspired creations include artichoke and black-truffle ravioli, sake-caramelized black cod, veal filet with smoked chili glaze and banana soufflé with banana and passionfruit sorbet. Spectacular cocktails are served from 6pm.

Sand Bar

INTERNATIONAL **$$$**

(✆0590-29-79-99; www.edenrockhotel.com; Eden Rock, Baie de St-Jean; mains €30-69, pizzas €26-45, tapas €18-33; ⊙7:30-9:30am, noon-3pm & 7-10pm) The elegant beach bar at the celebrity-filled Eden Rock hotel serves a daily breakfast buffet (€55), early-evening tapas, and classy mains at both lunch and dinner, from a black Angus cheeseburger to wood oven–roasted lobster. The wood-fire oven also turns out pizzas such as black truffle and fontina cheese. It hosts a 'jungle barbecue' on Tuesday nights (per person €85).

ANSE DE TOINY

....

Hôtel Le Toiny (☑0590-27-88-88, in USA 800-680-0832; www.letoiny.com; Anse de Toiny; ste/1-bedroom villa from €1095/1215; ⓟ✳❡⚊) Stretching across 42 acres in one of the most remote corners of the island, these 14 all-suite villas are fresh from head-to-toe renovations by switched-on new owners. Suites have private swimming pools and terraces with gorgeous views over the bay. A shuttle service runs 400m to the beach (watch out for strong currents). Its restaurant, LT, is superb.

LT (☑0590-29-77-47; www.letoiny.com; Hôtel Le Toiny, Anse de Toiny; mains lunch €21-28, dinner €36-55; ⊘noon-3:30pm & 7-10pm) An out-of-the-way location at the far-flung Hôtel Le Toiny makes LT one of St-Barth's culinary secrets. Japanese-style yellowfin-tuna *tataki* (tartare), Tahitian mahi-mahi *poisson cru* (lime and coconut-marinated raw fish) and Caribbean gulf shrimp with squid-ink risotto are among the menu highlights. The open-sided dining room overlooks the infinity pool, and the bay beyond. Reservations are essential.

🍷 Drinking & Nightlife

Le Papillon Ivre   WINE BAR
(☑0590-52-02-15; Centre Commercial Les Amandiers; ⊘4pm-1am Mon-Sat; ☎) St-Barth's first traditional wine bar looks like it was plucked from a hip Parisian back street and set down here. A timber bookcase-style cabinet of bottles lines an entire wall; wines by the glass start at €6, while bottles start from €32. Soak up your tipple with tapas dishes (€12 to €24) or charcuterie and/or cheese platters (€32 to €39).

Modjo   CLUB
(Centre Vaval; ⊘11pm-4am Mon-Fri, to 5am Sat) A resident DJ and international guests spin until the early hours of the morning at St-Barth's most sizzling club, set beneath vaulted dark timber-beamed ceilings, with outdoor lounge-strewn areas to cool down in. Live bands play occasionally; check its Facebook page for the current schedule. Dress to impress to get past the door.

ℹ Information

American Express (☑0590-52-97-06; La Savane Commercial Center; ⊘8am-noon & 2-3:30pm Mon-Fri) St-Barth's ATMs don't accept Amex cards but its American Express office in St-Jean fills the gap with services for members including emergency cashing of checks in euros or US dollars.

Lorient

The site of St-Barth's first French settlement, in 1648, Lorient fans out from its lovely white-sand surf beach. Charming historic stone structures here include a small Caribbean-style convent and one of the island's three Catholic churches.

👁 Sights

Plage de Lorient   BEACH
With calm waters at its eastern end and gentle surf at the western end, this gorgeous curve of golden sand is one of St-Barth's most family-friendly beaches. The reef is ideal for snorkeling amid friendly barracuda, sea turtles and rays. The nearest place to rent surfboards and snorkeling gear is Hookipa (p653) in St-Jean.

🍴 Eating

⭐**La Boulangerie Choisy**   BAKERY $
(☑0590-27-96-96; Centre Commercial de Oasis; dishes €1.20-6.40, breakfast €6.90; ⊘5:30am-1pm) Glass display cases at Choisy tantalize with exquisite pastries and cakes. Sweet varieties include éclairs, shell-shaped Madeleines, multilayered *mille-feuilles* and *clafoutis* (cherry flan); quiches (Lorraine, zucchini and eggplant, goats cheese) are among the savory options, along with freshly baked breads. The indoor and outdoor space flows to a courtyard dining area for brilliant-value breakfasts (coffee, pastry or baguette, cooked-to-order eggs and juice).

JoJo Burger   BURGERS $
(☑0590-27-50-33; burgers €10-29, sandwiches €6-12; ⊘10am-10:30pm) Huge burgers at this open-sided shack range from the 'old school' (beef, bacon, cheddar and mustard) to the vegetarian 'hippie' (chickpea patty, carrot, alfalfa and tomato, cooked on a separate grill), the 'Tex-Mex' (beef, guacamole, beans and cheese) to the 'mahi mahi' (fish,

mayo, red pepper and red onion). Choose from regular beef or premium black Angus patties.

Grand Cul-de-Sac & Pointe Milou

Arcing across a large horseshoe-shaped bay, Grand Cul-de-Sac's sandy beach is one of the island's top spots for water sports including windsurfing and kitesurfing. The protected lagoon-like waters are ideal for beginners; those who are more advance can catch some great wave action beyond the reef.

To its northwest is the steep, predominantly residential settlement of Pointe Milou.

🏃 Activities

⭐ 7ème Ciel Kitesurf
KITESURFING

(☑0690-69-26-90; www.saintbarthkite.com; Grand Cul-de-Sac; 1/1½hr lesson for 1 person €145/210, 2hr lesson for 2 people €290; ⊙dawn-dusk) The shallow, reef-protected waters at Grand Cul-de-Sac average 27°C year-round, making it an ideal spot to learn to kitesurf. Champion kitesurfer Enguerrand Espinassou offers lessons for up to two people at a time; if you're already experienced, you can rent equipment here (prices on request). One-on-one SUP instruction is also available (per half-hour €40, SUP rental €10).

Ouanalao Dive
DIVING

(☑0590-63-74-34; www.ouanalaodive.com; Grand Cul-de-Sac; 2-tank/introductory dive €150/95, instruction from €230; ⊙8am-6pm, closed early Sep) This professional outfit runs three dives daily (9am, 11am and 2:30pm) as well as night dives on request. There are special rates for multiday diving. It also rents out snorkeling gear (€20), SUPs, glass-bottomed canoes and pedal boats (per hour €25). Two-hour snorkel

---

WORTH A TRIP

ANSE DE GOUVERNEUR

Bookended by high cliffs, **Anse de Gouverneur** is a gorgeous, broad, secluded sandy beach fringing a U-shaped bay. It's splendid for sunbathing, and for picnics. The lack of visitors – even in high season – means beachgoers often sunbathe *au naturel*.

---

trips to one of several nearby islands cost €65 including gear.

🛏 Sleeping

Hôtel Christopher
HOTEL $$$

(☑0590-27-63-63; www.hotelchristopher.com; Pointe Milou; d incl breakfast from €460; P❄🛜🏊) One of the swankiest options on the island, the Christopher has 42 streamlined rooms and suites, a small spa and two restaurants: the casual Mango, and ultra-gourmet Taïno. There's no beach, but the sprawling pool area – surrounded by sand and with a timber-decked poolside bar – is a fair trade. Minimum stay is three nights.

Hotel Guanahani & Spa
LUXURY HOTEL $$$

(☑0590-52-90-00; https://leguanahani.com; Grand Cul-de-Sac; d/ste from €700/950; P❄🛜🏊) With 67 renovated rooms and suites, this retreat is the island's largest – a hidden village of tropical-toned bungalows spread over 18 acres of hibiscus-, frangipani- and palm-filled grounds with two swimming pools, a state-of-the-art spa, three restaurants, tennis courts, a kids club and a water-sports center. Its position on the headland provides access to two beaches, each with different orientations.

Le Sereno
LUXURY HOTEL $$$

(☑0590-29-83-00; www.lesereno.com; Grand Cul-de-Sac; d/villa incl breakfast from €630/1155; P❄🛜🏊) Pass through the entryway of this classy boutique property to uncover a mesmerizing decked pool ringed by sun loungers and coconut palms, and a cache of top-notch amenities including two restaurants (one Italian, the other casual) and a serene indoor-outdoor spa. The grounds adjoin a lovely stretch of beach but be aware that not all rooms have sea views.

🍴 Eating & Drinking

O'Corail
CAFE $

(☑0590-29-33-27; Grand Cul-de-Sac; breakfast €3.50-10, small dishes €12-17, lunch mains €19-33; ⊙9am-6pm Tue-Sun; 🛜) Taste the salt of the sea in the breeze blowing through this laid-back beachfront terrace dining area and in the fresh fish dishes served here. The menu also features burgers, grilled meats and daily specials, as well as freshly squeezed juices and smoothies. The service is quite slow when it's crowded, but you'll be too busy watching the kitesurfers out front to care.

★ **Taïno** GASTRONOMY $$$

(☎0590-27-63-63; www.hotelchristopher.com; Hôtel Christopher, Pointe Milou; mains €31-46; ⊙7-10pm) Fine dining reaches celestial heights at the culinary star of the swish Hôtel Christopher (p656). A meal might start with goat's-cheese panna cotta and olive-oil sorbet before you move onto a main such as suckling pig with spiced sweet potato, or smoked lobster ceviche with pan-fried grouper and lemongrass jus, and finish with mango tarte Tatin with passionfruit and rum mousse.

Le Ti St Barth CLUB

(☎0590-27-97-71; www.letistbarth.com; Pointe Milou; ⊙9:30pm-5am Tue-Sat) Like an evening in Baz Luhrmann's *Moulin Rouge*, Le Ti St Barth is a sumptuous jumble of wrought-iron chandeliers and velvet drapes. From 9.30pm it hosts a small cabaret; by 11pm it morphs into a full-blown DJ-fueled nightclub that's frequented by a roll call of international superstars. Between 7:30pm and 9:30pm it serves upmarket barbecue fare (mains €36 to €64).

MONTBARS 'THE EXTERMINATOR'

Monsieur the Exterminator (Daniel Montbars) was a French-born pirate – and a fearsome one at that. He was present when his uncle was killed in a battle with Spanish conquistadors, and he spent the rest of his life exacting revenge (and borrowing a bit of plunder). Legend has it that Montbars buried treasure somewhere between Anse de Gouverneur and Anse de Grande Saline, but it has never been found...

Trézor (Grand Fond; ⊙9am-8pm) Notorious pirate Montbars the Exterminator (Daniel Montbars) reputedly hid his still-undiscovered treasure hereabouts, but if you don't have time to search for it, stop into this overflowing boutique instead. Guarded by a life-sized pirate statue out front, its pirate-themed gifts include jewelry, figurines, T-shirts, skull-adorned belts and walking canes, and fancy-dress costumes such as hooks, eye patches and beards.

Anse de Grande Saline

Behind its beautiful beach, this remote, rugged area spreads out around St-Barth's largest salt pond and towering mountains. Amid the cacti and scrub, look out for wildlife including iguanas and land tortoises.

◉ Sights

★ **Anse de Grande Saline** BEACH

Secluded Anse de Grande Saline is the most photogenic of all St-Barth's beaches. This sweep of golden sand is ideal for working on your tan and frolicking in the crashing surf, but be aware that there's no shade. From the car park, it's a 500m walk through the scrub and over the dunes. Like many of St-Barth's more remote beaches, it's a favorite spot with nudists.

🛏 Sleeping

The few places to stay here are around the salt pond and the hills above; there are no beachfront properties.

Fleur de Lune B&B $

(☎0590-27-70-57, mobile phone 0690-56-59-59; www.saintbarthgitefleurdelune.com; Grande Saline; d incl breakfast €150-450; ❄🛜🏊) Situated 900m from Anse de Grande Saline, this B&B is a refined, minimalist cocoon. Free apéritifs at 6:30pm are a great way to meet other guests; low-season rates include use of a car. There's a two-night minimum stay mid-April to mid-December, a minimum four-night stay from early January to mid-April, and a minimum 10-night stay from mid-December to early January.

Salines Garden Cottages COTTAGE $$

(☎0690-41-94-29; www.salinesgarden.com; Grande Saline; d incl breakfast €200-250; 🅿❄🛜🏊) Inland on the Grande Saline's parched terrain, five semidetached cottages – each styled after one of owner Jean-Phillipe's favorite surf spots around the world: Essaouira, Pavones, Padang Padang, Cap Ferret and Waikiki – huddle around a small plunge pool shaded by pandanus trees. Minimum three nights (14 over the Christmas and New Year period). Rates include transfers to/from the airport or marina.

🍴 Eating

The northeastern side of the salt pond is home to the handful of restaurants.

★ **Le Grain de Sel** CREOLE, FRENCH **$$**
(📞0590-52-46-05; Anse de Grande Saline; mains €13-27; ⊘noon-3pm & 7-10:30pm, closed Sep; 🍴) Built into the side of the hill behind desert shrubs, this timber-decked spot is an oasis for French-accented Creole cuisine. Menu highlights include conch fricassée, white rum–flambéed lobster, vanilla- and ginger-marinated duck, Caribbean-spiced steak, octopus and shrimp skewers, and paprika- and garlic-marinated whole red snapper. There's a great two-course kids menu (€15) and an astute wine list.

UNDERSTAND ST-BARTHÉLEMY

History

Due to its inhospitable landscape and lack of fresh water, St-Barth never had a big Arawak or Carib presence. When Christopher Columbus sighted the island on his second voyage in 1493, he named it after his older brother Bartolomeo. The first Europeans who attempted to settle the island, in 1648, were French colonists. They were soon killed by Caribs. Norman Huguenots gave it another try in 1659 and prospered, not due to farming (which was near impossible) or fishing, but by setting up a way station for French pirates plundering Spanish galleons.

In 1784, the French king Louis XVI gave St-Barth to the Swedish king Gustaf III in exchange for trading rights in Göteborg. There are still many reminders of Swedish rule on the island – such as the name Gustavia, St-Barth's continuing duty-free status,

and several buildings and forts. However, Sweden sold St-Barth back to France in 1878 after declining trade, increasing disease and a destructive fire affected the island.

Throughout the 19th and early 20th centuries, St-Barth wasn't much more than a quaint French backwater, and life was tough for residents. Without the lush vegetation typical of the Caribbean, farming was difficult. Many former slaves emigrated to surrounding islands to find work, leaving St-Barth one of the only islands in the region without a substantial African population.

In 1946, St-Barth, as a member of Guadeloupe, was part of an overseas *région* and *département*. By the 1950s tourists slowly started arriving at the tiny airport on small planes and private jets. The rugged island suddenly found new natural resources: beaches, sunsets, quiet. Quick-thinking islanders created laws limiting mass tourism to guard their hard-earned lifestyle; as a result, you won't see casinos, high-rise hotels or fast-food chains, but you will pay for the unspoiled atmosphere.

An overwhelming 90% of St-Barth's population voted in a referendum for more fiscal and political independence from France and Guadeloupe in 2003, which was achieved in 2007. After separation, the island became an 'overseas collectivity', which meant that the island gained a municipal council rather than having a single island-wide mayor. Despite the separation, the island has remained part of the EU, but retains its duty-free port status.

People & Culture

Most residents of St-Barth fall into one of three categories: descendants of the pioneers from Normandy who have called St-Barth home for more than 300 years; mainland French setting up expensive shops and restaurants; or foreigners looking for a more relaxed lifestyle. As tourism blossomed, the first group of residents largely traded in their fishing careers for tourism-related jobs, so virtually everyone is working in hospitality of some sort.

Despite the island's location, the general atmosphere is much more that of a quiet seaside province in France than a jammin' Caribbean colony.

For hundreds of years, St-Barth's residents were too busy toiling in near-impos-

---

CULTURAL FESTIVALS

St-Barth Film Festival (www.stbarthff. org; ⊘late Apr) Going strong strong since 1996, the five-day St-Barth Film Festival showcases Caribbean talent in film and documentary. Screenings take place at venues around the island, including beaches.

St-Barth Music Festival (www. stbartsmusicfestival.org; ⊘mid-late Jan) Beaches are among the venues for January's St-Barth Music Festival festival, which features two weeks of jazz, chamber music, opera and ballet performances.

sible conditions to create much art, thus the traditional handicrafts were largely utilitarian, such as hats and baskets woven from the leaves of latanier palms.

Today there's a smattering of art galleries and workshops around the island devoted to exhibiting the work of local artisits. For more information about visiting artists' studios, stop by the tourist office (p652).

Landscape & Wildlife

St-Barth's total land area is a mere 24 sq km, although its elongated shape and hilly terrain make it seem larger. The island lies 25km southeast of St-Martin/Sint Maarten.

St-Barth has numerous dry and rocky offshore islets. The largest, Île Fourchue, is a half-sunken volcanic crater whose large bay is a popular yacht anchorage and a destination for divers and snorkelers.

St-Barth's arid climate sustains dryland flora, such as cacti and bougainvillea. Local fauna includes the red-footed land tortoise, the Lesser Antillean iguana, the Anguilla Bank Anole lizard, and the endangered Anguilla Bank racer snake (all snakes on St-Barth are harmless, though they can bite). From April to August, sea turtles lay eggs along the beaches on the northwest side of the island. The islets off St-Barth support seabird colonies, including those of frigate birds.

Considering the island's minuscule size, St-Barth has an impressive 16 beaches. Those looking for 'in-town' beaches will find that St-Jean, Flamands, Lorient and Shell Beach all have beautiful sandy strands. The most famous secluded beaches – Colombier, Grande Saline and Gouverneur – are as close to the picture-perfect Caribbean beach as possible, with long, powdery expanses of sand and gently lapping warm waves.

In recent years St-Barth has taken environmental concerns very seriously, and has committed to sustainable methods of energy production. The island utilizes a color-coded recycling system; be sure to toss glass in green containers and plastic in blue containers.

In 2001 St-Barth pioneered the first eco friendly trash incinerator of its kind in the Caribbean. The incinerator is able to simultaneously burn trash, create energy and produce drinkable water, all with less pollution than older incinerators. It comes with a higher price tag, but it's worth it.

PRACTICALITIES

Smoking Under French law, smoking is banned in all enclosed public spaces including hotel rooms, restaurants, cafes and bars.

Weights & Measurements The metric system and 24-hour clock are used.

SURVIVAL GUIDE

ⓘ Directory A–Z

ACCOMMODATION

St-Barth's largest hotel has a mere 67 rooms and the island's second biggest has barely half that number. The others are small, typically with fewer than a dozen rooms. Private villas are also located across the island. During high season, everything books up fast. There's no easy way to do St-Barth on the cheap, but rates drop significantly in low season.

ACTIVITIES

Although St-Barth is celebrated for its leisurely pursuits, swimming, snorkeling, surfing, windsurfing, kitesurfing, scuba diving, fishing, kayaking, hiking and horseback-riding are all possible here, with operators located across the island.

To dive on your own, you must pay a fee and register with the **St-Barth Natural Marine Reserve** (☑ 0590-27-88-18; www.reservenaturellestbarth.com; Quai de la République, Gustavia; ☺ 8:30am-12:30pm Mon-Sat).

ELECTRICITY

The current used is 220V (50/60 cycles); wall plugs are Western European style. Many hotels offer American-style shaver adapters.

EMERGENCY NUMBERS

Fire/ambulance	☑ 18
Police (Gustavia)	☑ 0590-27-66-66

SLEEPING PRICE RANGES

The following price ranges refer to a double room with bathroom per night in high season (mid-December to mid-April):

€ less than €200

€€ €200–€400

€€€ more than €400

EATING PRICE RANGES

The following price ranges refer to a main dish.

€ less than €20

€€ €20–€40

€€€ more than €40

FOOD

St-Barth has a sophisticated dining scene, with *boulangeries* (bakeries) turning out fabulous breads and exquisite pastries, casual beachside restaurants offering great-value prix-fixe menus, and fine-dining restaurants run by celebrated chefs.

For self-caterers, French supermarkets including **Marché U** (www.magasins-u.com; St-Jean; ⊘ 8am-8pm Mon-Sat, 9am-1pm Sun), opposite the airport, and **Oasis** (Centre Commercial de Oasis; ⊘ 9am-9pm), in Lorient, stock quality products.

GLBT TRAVELERS

In 2013 France (and thus St-Barth) became the 13th country in the world to allow same-sex marriage. Even beforehand, it's long been said that St-Barth is the most gay-popular spot on Earth without a gay bar, which pretty much sums up the nature of the island's gay tourism today. Locals and other travelers are very laid-back and it's not uncommon to see gay couples holding hands at the beach or having a romantic dinner, although there's no major nightlife scene.

HEALTH

Medical facilities in Gustavia include the small hospital, **Hôpital De Bruyn** (☑ 0590-27-60-35, emergency 0590-51-19-00; Rue du Père Irenée de Bruyn; ⊘ 24hr), and eight local doctors. There are two pharmacies on the island: one in **Gustavia** (☑ 0590-27-61-82; Rue de la République; ⊘ 8am-7:30pm Mon-Fri, 8am-1pm & 3:30-7pm Sat & public holidays) and one in **St-Jean** (☑ 0590-29-02-12; La Savane Commercial Center; ⊘ 8am-7:30pm Mon-Fri, 8am-1pm & 3:30-7pm Sat & public holidays).

MONEY

The currency used in St-Barth is the euro. ATMs are easy to find in Gustavia and in St-Jean, but they don't always accept foreign cards.

Exchange Rates

AUSTRALIA	A$1	€0.69
CANADA	C$1	€0.72
JAPAN	¥100	€0.81
NEW ZEALAND	NZ$1	€0.66
SWITZERLAND	Sfr1	€0.93
UK	UK£1	€1.16
US	US$	€0.95

For current exchange rates, see www.xe.com.

Tipping

Service fees are included in prices so tipping is not necessary or expected, but people commonly round up restaurant bills and taxi fares to the nearest euro.

PUBLIC HOLIDAYS

New Year's Day January 1

Easter Sunday Late March/early April

Labor Day May 1

Victory Day May 8

Ascension Thursday 40th day after Easter

Pentecost Monday Seventh Monday after Easter

Bastille Day July 14

Assumption Day August 15

Slavery Abolition Day Oct 9

All Saints' Day (Toussaints) November 1

All Souls Day November 2

Armistice Day November 11

Christmas Day December 25

TELEPHONE

➡ St-Barth's country code is +590.

➡ Be aware that the island's landline numbers then begin with 0590 (mobile phones start with 0690).

➡ If you're calling from abroad, dial your country's international access code, then St-Barth's country code, then drop the initial '0' of the local 10-digit number. For example, calling from North America, dial 011 + 590 + 590-12-34-56.

➡ To call from within the French phone system, dial the full 10-digit local number including the initial '0'.

TIME

St-Barth is on Atlantic time (GMT/UTC minus four hours). Daylight saving time is not observed.

❶ Getting There & Away

AIR

St-Barth's only airport, **Gustaf III** (Aéroport de St-Barthélemy; SBH; ☑ 0590-27-65-41), has the second-shortest runway in the world (the shortest is on Saba). Only teeny-tiny puddle jumpers can land on the island, and only during daylight hours. The majority of flights are to/from St-Martin/Sint Maarten's two airports but there are also less frequent and seasonal flights to/from regional destinations including Anguilla, Antigua, Guadeloupe, Puerto Rico, Saba and St Thomas. Airlines serving St-Barthélemy include **Air Antilles Express** (☑0590-29-62-79; www.airantilles.com), **Air Caraïbes** (☑0590-87-14-80; www.aircaraibes.com), **St-Barth Commuter** (☑0590-27-54-54; www.stbarthcommuter.com), **Tradewind Aviation** (www.flytradewind.com) and **Winair** (☑0590-27-61-01; www.flywinair.sx).

SEA
Cruise Ship

No cruise ships dock at St-Barth, but a few anchor offshore and launch tenders to Gustavia's ferry terminal.

Ferry

The ferry service between St-Barthélemy and St-Martin/Sint Maarten often hits choppy water so it's a good idea to take motion-sickness medication beforehand. The €20 departure tax is included in most ferry ticket prices.

Voyager (☑0590-87-10-68; www.voy12.com; ☺ferry one way €71) has two high-speed boats to St-Martin/Sint Maarten. One goes from Gustavia to Oyster Pond, St-Martin (30 minutes, 10:15am daily plus 8am and 5:45pm Tuesday, Wednesday and Thursday and 8:15am and 5:45pm Sun); the other travels to Marigot (one hour, 7:25am and 5:15pm Monday, Friday and Saturday). Day-trip tickets cost €87 round-trip; returning on a different day costs €104 return.

High-speed catamaran **M/V Edge** (☑Sint Maarten 721-544-2640; www.stmaartenactivities.com) makes the 45-minute trip from Gustavia to Pelican Marina on Simpson Bay, Sint Maarten, at 4pm on Tuesday, Thursday and Saturday; it returns at 9am the following day. You need to check in at least 15 minutes in advance.

Great Bay Express (www.greatbayferry.com; Gustavia Ferry Terminal; one way adult/child €70/45, return €105/55) runs six daily services from Monday to Saturday, three on Sunday from St-Barth's marina to Philipsburg, St-Martin/Sint Maarten (Dutch side). Same-day return tickets per adult/child cost €75/45.

Yacht

If you're arriving by yacht, you must contact the **port office** (☑0590-27-66-97; www.portdegustavia.fr; Rue du Bord de Mer, Gustavia) on VHF channel 12 two hours prior to arrival. Upon arrival, proceed to the port office with all passenger and crew passports and your vessel's registration details.

ⓘ Getting Around

There is no bus system on St-Barth. Taxis are pricey, so strongly consider renting a car.

CAR & MOTORCYCLE

Driving is on the right-hand side, and the speed limit is 45km/h, unless otherwise posted. Land tortoises have right of way on roads.

Fuel

There are only two gas stations on the island, one in St-Jean (7:30am to noon and 2pm to 7pm Monday to Saturday) and one in Lorient (7:30am to 5pm Sunday to Wednesday and Friday; 7:30am to 2pm Thursday to Saturday).

Rental

All major car-rental companies have desks at the airport. Prices between December and April start at around €70 per day for a compact car, while low-season prices start at around €40.

Car-rental companies include the following:

Budget (☑0590-27-66-30; www.budget.com; car rental per day from €46; ☺8am-6.30pm)

Chez Beranger (☑0590-27-89-00; www.beranger-rental.com; Rue du Général de Gaulle; scooter/quad bike rental per day from €45/56; ☺8.30am-6pm)

Europcar (☑0590-29-41-86; www.europcar.com; car rental per day from €38; ☺8am-6pm)

Gumbs Rental (☑0590-27-75-32; www.gumbs-car-rental.com; car rental per day from €30; ☺by appointment)

Soleil Caraibes (☑0590-27-67-18; www.soleilcaraibes.com; car rental per day from €35; ☺8am-6pm)

Scooter rental outlets include **Barth'Loc** (☑0590-27-52-81; http://barthloc.com; Rue de la France; scooter/car/quad bike rental per day from €45/70/90; ☺7:30am-6:30pm Mon-Sat, 7:30am-12:30pm & 4-6pm Sun), which also has ATV quad bikes, and **Meca Moto** (☑0590-29-72-28; Marigot; motorbikes/scooters/quad bikes per day €95/30/75; ☺8am-noon & 2-6pm Mon-Wed, 8am-noon Sat), which also rents Harley-Davidson motorbikes.

TAXI

Taxi fares range from pricey to outrageous, even for short distances. There are no set fares, so prices are all over the board. At minimum, it costs between €15 and €45 from Gustavia to the airport, and between €30 and €60 from Gustavia to Petit Cul-de-Sac. All prices then increase by about 50% between 8pm and 6am and all day on Sunday.

To book a taxi in Gustavia, call 0590-27-66-31; at the airport, call 0590-27-75-81. There are taxi stands in Gustavia. You can also contact drivers directly – a list of drivers and their phone numbers is available at the tourist office.

St Kitts & Nevis

POP 56,900 / ☎ 869

Best Places to Eat

➜ Bananas Restaurant (p678)

➜ Gin Trap Bar & Restaurant (p676)

➜ Golden Rock Inn (p677)

➜ Sprat Net Bar & Grill (p673)

Best Places to Sleep

➜ Ottley's Plantation Inn (p672)

➜ Golden Rock Inn (p677)

➜ Belle Mont Farm (p672)

➜ Hermitage Plantation Inn (p678)

Why Go?

Near-perfect packages – that's how you might think of St Kitts and Nevis. The two-island nation combines beaches with beauteous mountains, activities to engage your body and rich history to engage your mind. The local culture is mellow, friendly and infused with a pulsing soca beat.

But if the pair offer much that's similar, they differ in the details. St Kitts is larger and feels that way, from bustling Basseterre and mighty Brimstone Hill Fortress to the party strip and resorts of Frigate Bay. New roads and tourist development have generated additional verve and excitement.

Across the Narrows, tranquil Nevis is a neater package, anchored by a single volcanic mountain buttressed by a handful of beaches and a tiny colonial capital, Charlestown. Nature walks take you to verdant upper reaches of the peak. History here centers on the big names of British admiral Horatio Nelson and US founding father Alexander Hamilton.

When to Go

Late Nov–early Dec The best time to visit, price- and weatherwise, when hurricane season should have stopped. The hurricane (and rainy) season is from July to November.

Mid-Dec–mid-Apr High-season rates start.

Feb–Jun The driest months are February to June, and Winter days average a temperature of 81°F (27°C), while summers shoot up to 86°F (30°C).

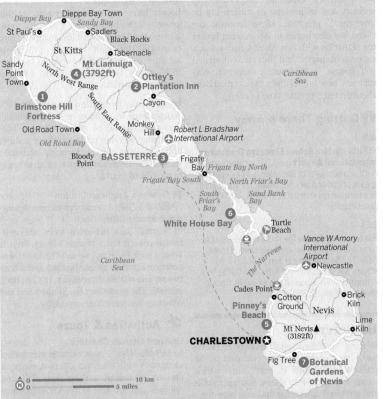

St Kitts & Nevis Highlights

1 Brimstone Hill Fortress (p671) Marveling at British colonial might at this superbly preserved hilltop citadel with dreamy views out to sea.

2 Ottley's Plantation Inn (p672) Taking a break from island explorations with a lazy lunch at this grand old estate.

3 Basseterre (p664) Soaking up the verve and history of St Kitts' vibrant capital.

4 Mt Liamuiga (p672) Staring into the crater of a volcano after a thigh-burning trek.

5 Pinney's Beach (p675) Giving in to slothdom during a long day at this wide and long beach on Nevis' west coast.

6 White House Bay (p669) Enjoying a swim and a snorkel followed by sunset drinks at urban-stylish Salt Plage beach bar.

7 Botanical Gardens of Nevis (p677) Calming down amid a symphony of flowers, trees, exotic statues and water-lily ponds.

ST KITTS

St Kitts definitely has a beat, and it's not just the one blasting from the many minibuses hauling folks hither and yon. Its capital, Basseterre, is a bustling place to explore, while the Unesco-recognized Brimstone Hill Fortress National Park ranks among the Caribbean's prime historic sights. Hedonistic pleasures, meanwhile, rule the island's glorious beaches, whose funky to chic bars invite rum-fueled tanning sessions.

Sugar drove the local economy for centuries but since the last plant closed in 2005, St Kitts has put most of its eggs into the tourist basket, especially the cruise-ship industry and by pushing its 'citizenship by investment' program. More recently, the island has also begun to tap into the luxury travel market with new resorts, ritzy villas, a superyacht marina and Tom Fazio–designed golf course. Infrastructure improvements such as a new tunnel and a bypass road have also injected a healthy dose of energy.

ℹ️ Getting There & Away

AIR

St Kitts' modern **Robert Llewellyn Bradshaw International Airport** (p682) is located on the northern outskirts of Basseterre. The departure area is bright and airy but amenities are limited to a bare-bones snack bar. There is an ATM before security.

SEA

Passenger ferries ply the route between Basseterre and Charlestown on Nevis several times daily. The **Seabridge car ferry** (p682) links Majors Bay in southern St Kitts with Cades Bay in northwestern Nevis. Water taxis link Cockleshell Beach and Oualie Beach.

Basseterre

St Kitts' bustling capital, Basseterre (basstear), has a compact downtown next to the cruise-ship terminal in Port Zante, which teems with duty-free shops, souvenir stalls and outdoor bars. If that and cold beer don't do it for you, bone up on island history at the National Museum, then plunge into the charmingly ramshackle maze of narrow streets radiating out from the Circus, a roundabout anchored by a Victorian-style clock tower. On your wanderings, keep an eye out for the occasional architectural gem (Princes St is especially rewarding), then wrap up by joining locals in 'liming' on grassy Independence Sq.

⊙ Sights

National Museum   MUSEUM
(☑ 869-466-2744; www.stkittsheritage.com; Bay Rd; adult/under 12yr EC$8/free; ⊙ 9:15am-5pm Mon-Fri, to 1pm Sat) This modest museum is a good place to start your explorations of St Kitts. Displays deal with colonial and sugar history, the road to independence, and local lifestyle and traditions. It's housed in the 1894 Old Treasury Building, a stately pile built from hand-cut volcanic limestone.

Independence Square   SQUARE
Locals 'lime' and exchange gossip on this grassy patch anchored by a circular fountain crowned by three topless nymphs. Once called Pall Mall Sq, it was used in the 1790s for slave auctions and is bordered by a few 18th-century Georgian buildings and the dignified cathedral.

Immaculate Conception Cathedral CHURCH
(Independence Sq; ⊙ hours vary) This hulking gray-stone house of worship has a barrel-vaulted wooden ceiling evoking a ship's hull. Sunlight filters through elaborate stained-glass windows above an altar made of multihued marble.

St George's Anglican Church   CHURCH
(☑ 869-465-2167; www.facebook.com/stgeorge withstbarnabasstkitts; Cayon St; ⊙ hours vary) In a small park behind a fence, this red-roofed church has a stormy history. French Jesuits built the first one in 1670, but it was destroyed by fire, an earthquake and a hurricane, and rebuilt three times, the last time in 1869. The tower can be climbed and the cemetery has some fancy epitaphs.

🏃 Activities & Tours

Leeward Islands Charters   BOATING
(☑ 869-465-7474; www.leewardislandscharters stkitts.com) This class act offers a range of options, including a three-hour Sail and Snorkel trip for US$45 (Nevis departures US$62); a full day of sailing, snorkeling, drinks and beach barbecue for US$87; and two-hour sunset cruises for US$50. Boats leave from Port Zante Marina on St Kitts or the Four Seasons pier on Nevis.

Blue Water Safaris   BOATING
(☑ 869-466-4933; www.bluewatersafaris.com; Port Zante Marina, Basseterre; full-day cruise US$95) This well-respected company runs a variety of catamaran cruises, including a popular all-day trip to Nevis with a snorkeling stop, lunch and an hour on Pinney's Beach. Departures are tied to the cruise-ship schedule but private charters are also available.

Pro Divers St Kitts   DIVING
(☑ 869-660-3483; www.prodiversstkitts.com; Fisherman's Wharf, Fort Thomas Rd; 2-tank dive incl gear US$115; ⊙ closed 3 weeks Aug) Owner Austin and his team have explored every nook and cranny of the Kittitian underwater world, and offer the gamut of underwater experiences for novice to veteran divers as well

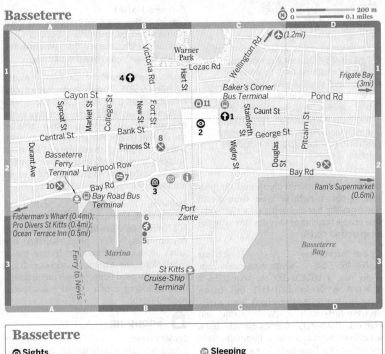

Basseterre

◉ Sights
- **1** Immaculate Conception
  Cathedral C1
- **2** Independence Square C2
- **3** National Museum B2
- **4** St George's Anglican Church B1

◈ Activities, Courses & Tours
- **5** Blue Water Safaris B3
- **6** Leeward Islands Charters B3

◉ Sleeping
- **7** Seaview Inn B2

◈ Eating
- **8** Ballahoo B2
- **9** El Fredo's D2
- **10** Farmers' Market A2

◉ Shopping
- **11** Gallery Cafe C1

as all levels of certification courses. Rates include all gear and transportation.

✨ Festivals & Events

Carnival   CARNIVAL
(www.stkittsneviscarnival.com; Basseterre; ⊘ Dec 26-Jan 2) FREE Also known as Sugar Mas, Carnival is the biggest yearly event on St Kitts. It starts in mid-November but kicks into high gear for two weeks on 26 December with dance and music competitions, beauty pageants, costumed parades and steel-pan music enlivening streets and venues throughout town.

St Kitts Music Festival   MUSIC
(www.stkittsmusicfestival.com; Warner Park, Basseterre; ⊘ late Jun) This three-day festival brings top-name Caribbean performers from all musical genres – calypso to soca, reggae to salsa, jazz to gospel – to Basseterre's Warner Park. Recent line-ups have included Damian Marley (Bob's son) and 50 Cent.

🛏 Sleeping

There are a few simple guesthouses in downtown Basseterre, but unless you're catching an early ferry there's really no reason to stay here, since the town all but shuts down after dark.

Seaview Inn   GUESTHOUSE **$**
(☑ 869-663-6554; www.seaviewinnstkitts.net; Bay Rd; r US$88; ❅ 🖥) The 10 dark, tiny but newly revamped rooms of this walk-up near the bus/ferry terminal don't invite lingering

ST KITTS & NEVIS BASSETERRE

GREG'S SAFARIS

Greg Pereira heads up **Greg's Safaris** (☑869-465-4121; www.gregsafaris.com), offering a half-day 4WD tour into the forest with stops at a viewpoint and a beach as well as a lunch of local fruit and pastries. Considerably more challenging is the rugged all-day tour up to the Mt Liamuiga volcano crater rim for US$110 (children US$80), including lunch.

but they are certainly cheap and the only lodging option right in town. Grab a cold one from the bar and settle down for some fine people watching (*sans* sea views) on the wraparound porch.

Ocean Terrace Inn HOTEL $$$
(☑869-465-2754; www.oceanterraceinn.com; Wigley Ave; r US$220-290, ste from US$325; P✴@☎☒) Nicknamed OTI, this Basseterre institution has emerged from a rigorous refurb with renewed sparkle and comfort. The hotel's 69 units cascade down a bayfront hillside about a 15-minute walk west of central Basseterre. The staff is superfriendly, rooms with private patios are classily furnished and three smallish pools compensate for the lack of beach.

✖ Eating

Central Basseterre brims with small local eateries that get flooded at lunchtime and often sell out by 2pm. Food trucks and street-food stalls set up at and around Port Zante, especially on cruise-ship days.

El Fredo's CARIBBEAN $
(☑869-466-8871; www.facebook.com/ElFredos RestaurantandBar; cnr Bay & Sanddown Rds; mains EC$20-35; ☺11am-4pm Mon-Sat) Every day, there are some Kittitian faves cooking in the kitchen of this local lunchtime hot spot, be it creole snapper and garlic shrimp or more challenging pigtail soup and goat stew, all paired with a potpourri of provisions (starchy sides). The setting is classic Caribbean cool but the homemade sauce is hot!

Ram's Supermarket SUPERMARKET $
(☑869-466-7777; Bay Rd; ☺8:30am-7pm Mon-Thu, 8:30-8pm Fri & Sat, 9am-1pm Sun; P☎) This large branch of Ram's has a great selection of local and imported food to stock the refrigerator in your rental unit.

Farmers' Market MARKET $
(Bay Rd; ☺Mon, Wed & Sat mornings) Bag great pictures and bargain-priced fresh produce and fish at Basseterre's tin-roofed market, which is busiest on Saturday morning.

Fisherman's Wharf SEAFOOD $$
(☑869-466-5535; www.fishermanswharfstkitts. com; Fort Thomas Rd; mains EC$40-115; ☺6:30-9:30pm Mon-Sat; P☎) Enjoy sweeping views of sparkling Basseterre from your table on the deck of this breezy alfresco dining spot, where an open charcoal fire tickles fresh snapper, lobster and other piscine delights to juicy perfection. All produce and seafood are sourced locally.

Ballahoo CARIBBEAN $$
(☑869-465-4197; www.ballahoo.net; Circus; mains EC$29-65; ☺8am-3pm Mon-Wed, to 9pm Thu-Sat; ☎) From its 1st-floor perch, Ballahoo has great people watching from terrace tables overlooking the Circus roundabout. It's a dependably good hangout with menu standouts including conch chowder and oven-roasted lamb.

🔒 Shopping

Gallery Cafe GALLERY
(☑869-765-5994; www.facebook.com/TheGallery-CafeOnTheSquare; 10 N Independence Sq; ☺9am-4pm Mon-Sat) This gallery in an attractive 18th-century colonial cottage showcases paintings, pottery, jewelry and other crafts by local artists.

ℹ Information

Banks with ATMs orbit the Circus in downtown Basseterre.

Post Office (☑869-465-2521; Pelican Mall, Bay Rd; ☺8am-3:30pm Mon-Fri)

St Kitts Tourism Authority (☑869-465-4040; www.stkittstourism.kn; upstairs Pelican Mall, Bay Rd, Basseterre; ☺7:30am-4:30pm Mon-Fri)

ℹ Getting There & Away

Buses heading up the west coast as far as St Paul's leave from the **Bay Road bus terminal** (p683) next to the ferry terminal, while buses heading east as far Saddlers leave from **Baker's Corner bus terminal** (p683).

Frigate Bay

Frigate Bay, some 3 miles southeast of Basseterre, is an isthmus dividing the calm Caribbean side and the surf-lashed Atlantic side, which is dominated by the hulking Marriott Resort. The road leading to the resort – Zenway Blvd – is restaurant row, but the area's key draw is 'the Strip,' a row of funky beach bars along Frigate Bay South. Swimming is good on both sides, although the Caribbean waters are calmer, of course.

◉ Sights & Activities

Frigate Bay South   BEACH
In season, the party never stops along the Strip, a bar-backed golden sweep of sand with mellow, kid-friendly waves.

Royal St Kitts Golf Club   GOLF
(☑ 869-466-2700, ext 7604; www.royalstkittsgolfclub.com; 858 Zenway Blvd, Frigate Bay; greens fee 9/18 holes US$95/165; ☺ tee times 7am-5pm; ☎) Around since the 1970s, this central 18-hole, par 71 course got a makeover by Tom McBroom in 2003 to 2004, with the final four holes being played within earshot of the Atlantic waves.

🛏 Sleeping

Frigate Bay has the greatest concentration of lodging options on St Kitts, ranging from B&Bs to full-service beach resorts like the Marriott.

Timothy Beach Resort   HOTEL $$
(☑ 869-465-8597; www.timothybeach.com; South Frigate Bay; r US$170-245,1-/2-bedroom ste US$270/410; ☎❄🐾🏊) This low-key pad is right on a fine beach and snorkeling reef, and within stumbling distance of the row of raucous bars called the Strip. Rooms are distributed across several two-story buildings and, though not of the latest vintage, they're large and comfortable enough. Ask for an ocean-facing one on the upper floor.

Rock Haven B&B   B&B $$
(☑ 869-465-5503; www.rock-haven.com; Scenic Dr, Frigate Bay; ste incl breakfast US$200-210; ☎❄☎) This lovely Caribbean home is a great find for those not in need of buckets of privacy. It has just two suites with handpicked furniture and floral bedspreads. The larger one (called Sanctuary) even has a full kitchen and a flower-filled patio. The warm host, Judith, makes memorable breakfasts and can happily help you plan your stay.

St Kitts Marriott Resort   RESORT $$$
(☑ 869-466-1200; www.marriott.com; Frigate Bay Rd; r from US$270; ☎❄@☎🏊) This hulking resort on a wide sandy beach and within strolling distance of Frigate Bay's 'restaurant row' is like a small village unto itself with multiple pools, restaurants and bars, a gym, a spa, a nightclub, duty-free shops and even a casino. It's the perfect choice for those who need all the comforts of home in a blue-sky locale.

✕ Eating

Patsy's Beach Bar & Grill   CARIBBEAN $
(☑ 869-664-3185; www.facebook.com/Patsys-Beach-Bar-and-Grill-739843656041604; the Strip, South Frigate Bay; burgers EC$10-20, mains EC$25-80; ☺ 11am-10pm or later; ☎☎) Beach gourmets flock to Patsy's for her fingerlickin' barbecued ribs and mouthwatering shrimp pasta served in her cheerfully painted outpost toward the northern end of the Strip.

Ram's Express   SUPERMARKET $
(Zenway Blvd; ☺ 9am-7pm Mon-Sat, 10am-5pm Sun; ☎) This small but well-stocked supermarket is handy for picking up supplies for a day on the beach.

Rock Lobster   MEDITERRANEAN $$
(☑ 869-466-1092; www.rocklobsterstkitts.com; Zenway Blvd; mains EC$58-120, tapas selections EC$45-135; ☺ 5-10pm Thu-Tue; ☎☎) Like clam shells, you'll be clapping for the meat and seafood at this relaxed open-sided patio and bar. Aside from the locally caught namesake crustacean, top choices include the mixed seafood pasta and the blackened mahimahi. The tapas platters are great for sharers.

Mr X's Shiggidy Shack
Bar & Grill   CARIBBEAN $$
(☑ 869-762-3983; the Strip, South Frigate Bay; mains EC$40-120; ☺ 4pm-midnight Mon-Fri, 8am-midnight Sat & Sun; ☎☎) Lanterns on battered picnic tables on the sand put you in instant party mood at this high-energy joint popular with expats and tourists. On bonfire night (Thursday), bands hook up to the generator and jam, while on Saturdays, karaoke drives many to drink (more). Burgers and fresh fish help keep brains balanced.

Marshall's   INTERNATIONAL $$$
(☑ 869-466-8245; www.marshallsdining.com; Fort Tyson; mains US$20-40; ☺ 6-10pm; ☎) Hypnotic views compete with the expertly crafted continental fare at this romantic and elegant hilltop villa with seating placed around a swimming pool. The menu ranges from tried-and-true favorites like grilled veal chops to lobster, and local dishes like ackee and saltfish. Reservations recommended.

ST KITTS & NEVIS FRIGATE BAY

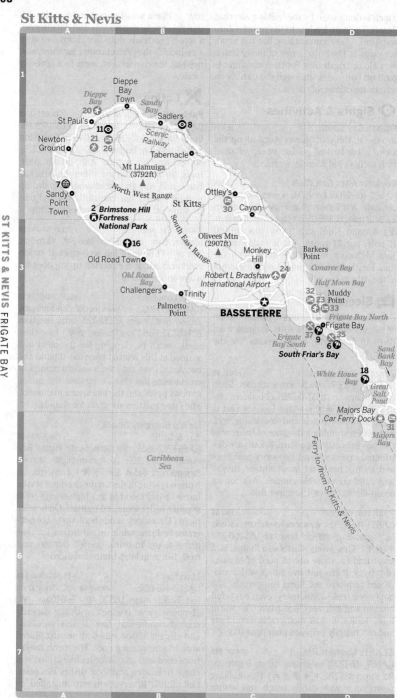

Dieppe
Bay
20

Dieppe
Bay
Town

Sandy
Bay

Sadlers
8

St Paul's

11

Scenic
Railway

Newton
Ground

21
26

Tabernacle

Mt Liamuiga
(3792ft)

7

Sandy
Point
Town

North West Range

Ottley's

30

Cayon

St Kitts

2 Brimstone Hill
Fortress
National Park

South East Range

Olivees Mtn
(2907ft)

Monkey
Hill

Barkers
Point

16

Conaree Bay

Old Road Town

Old Road
Bay

Robert L Bradshaw
International Airport

24

Half Moon Bay

Challengers

Trinity

32
23

Muddy
Point

Palmetto
Point

BASSETERRE

33

Frigate Bay North

Frigate
Bay South

37
9

Frigate Bay

35

6

South Friar's Bay

18

Sand
Bank
Bay

Caribbean
Sea

White House
Bay

Great
Salt
Pond

Majors Bay
Car Ferry Dock

31

Ferry to/from St Kitts & Nevis

Majors
Bay

🍷 Drinking & Nightlife

⭐ Mill St Kitts
CAFE

(www.facebook.com/millstkitts; Zenway Blvd; ⏱6:30am-6:30pm) At this industrial-chic cafe inside a converted container ensemble, sip excellent cuppas surrounded by corrugated walls plastered in sheets from the *Pravda* newspaper from the owner's native Russia. Stop en route to the beach to pick up baked goods, fresh and inventive salads and sandwiches (EC$22 to EC$50). A new bar was being added to take the place from day to night.

Southeast Peninsula

St Kitts' south is a scrubby, wild and hilly peninsula ringed by sublime sandy beaches. There are no villages down here and, until recently, no residential development to speak of. That all changed with the development of Christophe Harbour, which centers on a superyacht marina and includes luxurious villas, a members-only beach club and a Tom Fazio–designed golf course. The long-awaited opening of the Park Hyatt is also bringing more traffic down here.

Heading south on the main road, which runs for 8 miles from Frigate Bay, you cross over steep St Timothy's Hill before shooting downhill via a new tunnel that opened in 2016. Hold onto the steering wheel, for your breath will likely be taken away by the view that unfolds as you exit the tunnel. The road itself – called Kennedy A Simmons Hwy after the islands' first prime minister – has been completely resurfaced.

◉ Sights

⭐ South Friar's Bay
BEACH

(🅿 🛜) There are excellent tanning and snorkeling possibilities along this lovely beach backed by palm trees and sea grapes, and bookended by two restaurants: the snazzy Carambola Beach Club and the funky Shipwreck Bar & Grill. Both get busy on cruise-ship days when crowd-evaders should stroll over to one of the locally owned bars set up in between the two.

White House Bay
BEACH

The beach itself ain't much, but there's some pretty good snorkeling here thanks to offshore reefs and a couple of sunken wrecks. These days, though, the reason most people visit is for sublime sunset drinks at the chic Salt Plage beach bar.

St Kitts & Nevis

★ **Cockleshell Beach**   BEACH

Enjoy great views of Nevis across the Narrows on this pretty but often busy crescent of white powdery sand with calm and shallow waters and several bars, restaurants and water-sports concessionaires.

🛏 Sleeping

Aside from the new Park Hyatt in Banana Bay, the only places to stay in the south are private villas or luxury apartments.

★ **Park Hyatt**   RESORT $$$

(☎ 869-468-1234; https://stkitts.park.hyatt.com/en/hotel/home.html; Banana Bay; d from US$450; P 🐾 🛜 🏊) The Caribbean's first Park Hyatt snuggles into crescent-shaped Banana Bay and has 126 units designed to feel like a contemporary beach retreat. The social hub is the 'Great House' with restaurants, 24-hour fitness facilities and shops. The family-friendly lagoon pool and kids' club keep little ones entertained, while grown-ups

seeking peace and quiet can spread their towel by the infinity pool.

🍴 Eating & Drinking

All the Caribbean-side beaches have at least one restaurant-bar where you can fuel up in the daytime. With the opening of the Park Hyatt, staying for dinner is an option as well.

Reggae Beach Bar   CARIBBEAN $$

(☎ 869-762-5050; www.reggaebeachbar.com; Cockleshell Beach; mains EC$27-85; ⊗ 9am-sunset Sat-Thu, to 11pm Fri; P 🛜) A rough-and-ready crowd fuels up on Caribs and coladas at this castaway bar on picturesque Cockleshell Beach. Sleep it off on an umbrella-shaded beach chair (US$10), get a massage or snorkel with tropical fish hiding out in the protected reef. Best night: Fridays for the lobster fest (reservations recommended).

The place used to be home to Wilbur, a legendary pot-bellied pig that died in 2012. Look for the memorial under the trees.

Sadly, today a bunch of caged monkeys is kept as an 'attraction.'

Spice Mill Restaurant CARIBBEAN $$$

(☑869-765-6706; www.spicemillrestaurant.com; Cockleshell Beach; mains lunch US$13-22, dinner US$30-45; ⊙beach bar 10am-sunset, restaurant noon-4pm daily, 5:30-9:30pm Fri-Wed; P🐾) With its shingle roof, crayfish-trap lamps and dugout canoe bar, Spice Mill gives the rustic beach shack a hipster makeover. The menu is just as zeitgeist-compatible, with local produce and fresh fish and seafood getting a flavorful workout with international spices and homemade rubs and hot sauces.

Carambola Beach Club INTERNATIONAL $$$

(☑869-465-9090; www.carambolabeachclub.com; South Friar's Bay; mains lunch US$11-22, dinner US$27-46; ⊙6-9pm Tue-Sat, 9am-9pm on cruise-ship days; P🐾) If you like your beach bars sophisticated instead of funky, saunter up to this snazzy hangout on one of St Kitts' dreamiest sandy patches. The stylish restaurant features pastas, salads and sushi for lunch, and more elaborate fish and meat dishes for dinner. It gets packed on cruise-ship days. Beach chairs and umbrellas rent US$10 each.

★Salt Plage BAR

(☑869-466-7221; www.facebook.com/SaltPlage; Whitehouse Bay; ⊙4-10pm; 🐾) Urban industrial meets Caribbean lounge chic at this sophisticated imbibing spot right on sweeping Whitehouse Bay. Follow up a swim or shipwreck snorkel with craft beer or cocktails and reflect on the day's adventures while watching the sun dip into the ocean. Tapas and fresh fish beckon if you get the munchies.

Northern St Kitts

A drive around the windswept, rural northern half of the island is a must. The entire circuit is about 35 miles and can easily fill half a day, especially with an extended stop at the landmark Brimstone Hill Fortress. Beyond here the road narrows, sheep graze on fields of grass and old sugarcane fields run up the hills to Mt Liamuiga, the 3792ft dormant volcano that dominates the interior.

Civilization thins out here, with only a handful of villages clinging to the breezy windward side, punctuated by pretty parish churches and homes tinged with tangerine, turquoise and mint-green facades. Without stopping, the drive should take about an hour and a half.

Alternatively, cover the route aboard the historic St Kitts Scenic Railway.

⊙ Sights

Romney Manor HISTORIC BUILDING

(☑869-465-6253; www.caribellebatikstkitts.com; Old Road Town; adult/child under 11yr EC$5/free; ⊙8:30am-4pm Mon-Fri, also 9am-1pm Sat Nov-Apr; P) A favorite pit stop on island tours, the former residence of the owners of the Wingfield Estate sugar plantation has since 1964 been the home of the Caribelle Batik workshop and store. Horticulturists will feel in floral heaven in the surrounding gardens (note the 350-year-old saman tree) that also hide an old bell tower used to regulate the working-day routine of slaves. Stand in the viewing gallery, from where plantation owners kept an eye on the sugar works.

Wingfield Estate St Kitts HISTORIC SITE

(Old Road Town; ⊙24hr; P) FREE Wingfield is one of the island's oldest sugar estates, founded in 1625 and in operation until all cane processing was centralized in Basseterre in the 1920s. As you wander among the salt-and-pepper stones of the partly restored mill, smoke stack, aqueduct, lime kiln and other structures, picture the slaves who once toiled to produce sugar, molasses and rum on these grounds. There's decent signage to explain what you're looking at.

St Thomas Anglican Church CHURCH

(Middle Island) The oldest Anglican church in the Caribbean was built in 1625, shortly after the arrival of British sea captain and colony founder Thomas Warner. He is buried beside his friend Samuel Jefferson, believed to be the great-great-great-grandfather of US President Thomas Jefferson. The current stone building dates to 1860.

★Brimstone Hill Fortress National Park FORT

(☑869-465-2609; www.brimstonehillfortress.org; adult/child US$10/5, audio guide US$5; ⊙9:30am-5:30pm) Even if you're not a fan of military anything, this massive hilltop compound with its citadels, bastions, barracks and ramparts will likely leave a lasting impression. The British began construction of what was then a state-of-the-art fortress in 1690 and, using slave labor, kept refining it for about a century. In 1999 it became a Unesco World Heritage site.

Start your visit by watching the 10-minute video on the history of the island and the construction of the fortress, then wander up to polygonal Fort George to stand on the gun deck, take in the views and imagine the cannons firing all the way out to sea. One floor below are exhibits on the construction of the fortress, life at the fort, slavery, punishment and other topics, along with a recreated barrack room where six soldiers slept side by side in hammocks. For a more in-depth experience, pick up an audio guide at the ticket gate.

The fortress sits at the end of a steep 0.75-mile-long road.

Amazing Grace Experience   MUSEUM

(☑ 869-465-1122; www.amazinggraceexperience. com; Main Island Rd, Sandy Point Town; US$5; ⊙ 9am-4pm Mon-Fri, to 1pm Sat; 🅿️) This small, private museum tells the spiritual journey of John Newton, from British slave trader to abolitionist and writer of 'Amazing Grace', through exhibits and a 12-minute video that is as saccharine as the hymn. Call ahead to confirm opening times.

Kate Spencer Art Studio   ARTS CENTRE

(☑ 869-465-7740; www.katespencerfineart.com; ⊙ by appointment) **FREE** British-born Kate Spencer has lived on St Kitts since 1989 and is one of the island's top artists. Aside from her boldly pigmented acrylic paintings, she has of late focused her creativity on wispy silk scarves. Her work also decorates walls at the Belle Mont Farm resort near her studio in northern St Kitts. Call ahead for an appointment if you'd like to visit the studio.

Black Rocks   LANDMARK

(near Sadlers village; 🅿️) **FREE** Wind and water have chiseled black lava belched up eons ago by Mt Liamuiga into fanciful coastal rock formations. There are lovely views of the waves crashing onto the rocks from the parking lot where, on some days, souvenir and drinks vendors set up shop.

Coming from the north, turn off the main road about 220yd past an old stone church in a field.

🏃 Activities & Tours

Mt Liamuiga Volcano Hike   HIKING

Getting to the crater rim of Mt Liamuiga, at 3792ft the country's highest volcanic peak, involves a lung-busting, thigh-burning 2.5-mile trek. The deep crater with its active fumaroles and seasonal lake would make a great *Star Wars* movie set. The entire trip takes about 4½ to five hours and is tough, tough, tough. Since the trail is not well marked and partly overgrown, it's easy to get disoriented, which is why a guide is recommended.

Irie Fields Golf Course   GOLF

(☑ 869-466-1712; www.kittitianhill.com/experience/golf; Kittitian Hill, St Paul's; 🕸️) 🏌️ The newest kid on the golfing block is this sustainable par 71 golf course where you tee off amid organic crops and fruit trees. Designed by Ian Woosnam, it's the potentially fierce breezes that present an additional challenge.

St Kitts Scenic Railway   RAIL

(☑ 869-465-7263; www.stkittsscenicrailway. com; Needsmust train station; adult/child from US$89/44.50; ⊙ Dec-Apr) This cheerfully painted historic train previously transported sugarcane from the plantations to the factory in Basseterre. Today, it takes tourists along 18 miles of the original tracks, followed by a 12-mile bus ride. The upper deck is great for sightseeing and the lower deck has air-con. The entire trip takes three hours, but trains only run if a cruise ship is in port.

🛏️ Sleeping

⭐ Belle Mont Farm   RESORT $$$

(☑ 869-465-7388; www.bellemontfarm.com; Kittitian Hill, St Paul's; villa from US$400; 🅿️🕸️🏊) 🏌️ Hugging the foothills of Mt Liamuiga, this luxe boutique resort has you checking into sublime West Indian–style villas set within an organic, sustainable farm. Expect lots of unusual treats like outdoor bathrooms with claw-foot tubs, private plunge pools, porches with views out to Saba and Sint Eustatius, and a restaurant that turns produce foraged on-site into culinary miracles.

⭐ Ottley's Plantation Inn   HOTEL $$$

(☑ 869-465-7234, in the US 800-772-3039; www. ottleys.com; Ottley's village; d US$285-479, cottages US$779; 🅿️❄️@🕸️🏊) At this immaculately restored vestige of colonial times, the great house gives way to a manicured lawn and cottages with antique- and chintz-filled rooms and, in some cases, private plunge pools. The wonderful jungle trail and the alfresco restaurant (both open to nonguests) are great for soaking up the supreme serenity of the place.

✗ Eating

Sprat Net Bar & Grill
CARIBBEAN $$

(☏ 869-465-7535; www.facebook.com/Sprat-Net-Bar-Grill-122539311164912/; Old Rd, Middle Island; mains EC$30-115; ⏰ 6-11pm Wed-Sun; P ☎) Join local families at this fuss-free waterfront institution for humongous platters of grilled fish and lobster, served family-style on plastic plates amid nautical decor and cheap beers. Everything's caught by the owners that day and cooked up in the open kitchen. Best night: Wednesdays when a band whips everyone into a shimmying frenzy.

If you're self-catering, buy the catch of the day next door starting around 4pm.

★ Kitchen
CARIBBEAN $$$

(☏ 869-465-7388; www.bellemontfarm.com/food/the-kitchen; Belle Mont Farm, Kittitian Hill, St Paul's; lunch small plates US$12-20, dinner mains from US$75; ⏰ 7am-9pm; P ❋ ☎) 🍴 The main restaurant at sustainable Belle Mont Farm resort flaunts decor that pays tribute to the island's sugary past while capturing the zeitgeist with a literal farm-to-table concept that sees its French chef, Christophe Letard, sourcing 90% of its ingredients from its own land or local suppliers. The menu is constantly in flux, although the *dasheen* (taro root) risotto is a perennial palate pleaser.

★ Royal Palm Restaurant
INTERNATIONAL $$$

(☏ 869-465-7234; www.ottleys.com; Ottley's Plantation Inn, Ottley's village; mains lunch US$14-32, dinner US$30-55; ⏰ 7:30am-9pm; P ☎) The historic stone walls of the old sugar boiling house hem the fine-dining restaurant at Ottley's Plantation Inn, which is a popular stop on island tours. The menu is mostly international infused with island flair and best consumed on the covered terrace with lavish garden views. Try the coconut-crusted chicken and the soursop ice cream.

🛍 Shopping

Caribelle Batik
ARTS & CRAFTS

(☏ 869-465-6253; www.caribellebatikstkitts.com; Romney Manor, Old Road Town; adult/child under 11yr EC$5/free; ⏰ 8:30am-4pm Mon-Fri, also 9am-1pm Sat Nov-Apr) Set in a former plantation great house tinged in shades of citrus, mint and tangerine, Caribelle Batik has churned out gorgeous batik products since 1974. Local ladies demonstrate and explain the process of creating the often-intricate designs that you can buy in the attached store. Combine a visit here with a spin around the surrounding gardens with their 350-year-old saman tree.

NEVIS

Coin-shaped Nevis (nay-vis) is sprinkled with rustic charm and infused with a keen historical awareness and appreciation. Many visitors come here just for the day but those in the know stay much longer.

There's nothing brash about this sweet and unhurried island, whose blissfully uncrowded beaches fringe a forested interior that rises to majestic, often cloud-shrouded, Mt Nevis (3182ft). The coastal lowlands support bougainvillea, hibiscus and other flowering bushes that attract numerous hummingbirds. It's this lush landscape that makes Nevis so popular with bikers, hikers, birders and other nature and outdoor fans. History buffs, meanwhile, can snoop around the legacy of Horatio Nelson and Alexander Hamilton.

❶ Getting There Away

Vance W Amory International Airport (p682), in Newcastle, is a small operation with an ATM. It gets regional flights only. Some air services are seasonal and only weekly.

Passenger ferries ply the Charlestown–Basseterre route several times daily. The **Seabridge car ferry** (p682) links Cades Bay on Nevis with Majors Bay on St Kitts.

Charlestown

The ferry from St Kitts docks right in charismatic Charlestown, Nevis' toy-town-sized capital whose narrow streets are steeped in colonial history and lined with both brightly painted gingerbread Victorians and Georgian stone buildings. It's well worth strolling up and down the main street with its banks, businesses, tourist office, bars and restaurants. At night the town all but shuts down. The closest beach, lovely Pinney's, is about 1.5 miles north of Charlestown.

👁 Sights & Activities

Museum of Nevis History
MUSEUM

(Hamilton House; ☏ 869-469-5786; www.nevis heritage.org; Main St; adult/child US$5/2; ⏰ 8:30am-4pm Mon-Fri, 9am-noon Sat) American statesman Alexander Hamilton (1757–1804) was many things in his short life: soldier, lawyer, author of the *Federalist Papers*,

LIMING WITH THE LOCALS

Nevis is a tight-knit community. Just how tight is in evidence every Friday and Saturday night, when roadside cookouts draw locals into the streets for barbecued chicken and ribs, gossip and music. Locals even have a name for this activity: liming, ie chilling or hanging out. The biggest event is hosted by the Water Department on Pump St, near Charlestown, on Friday from about 5pm.

US founding father, the country's first Secretary of the Treasury and, finally, the victim of a fatal duel with his political nemesis Aaron Burr. He was born – scandalously out of wedlock – in or near the restored 1840 building that today contains a modest museum chronicling his rags-to-riches career.

Horatio Nelson Museum　　　　MUSEUM
(☑ 869-469-0408; www.nevisheritage.org; Building Hill Rd; adult/child US$5/2; ☺ 9am-4pm Mon-Fri, to noon Sat) This small museum trains its focus on Horatio Nelson, the British naval commander who married a local widow, Fanny Nisbet, in 1787 and met his demise at the Battle of Trafalgar in 1805. An endearing collection of maps, paintings, documents, busts, vases and other memorabilia help tell his story.

Bath Hot Spring　　　　HOT SPRINGS
Right on the banks of the Bath Stream, you can join locals taking the 107°F hot mineral waters of a natural spring bubbling forth through layers of crushed stones through the bottom of five pools. It's said to have therapeutic qualities and to even cure arthritis and gout.

★☆ Festivals & Events

Culturama　　　　CULTURAL
(www.culturamanevis.com; ☺ late Jul-early Aug) FREE Since 1974, Nevisians have celebrated their heritage with a joyous program of street jams, calypso tents, fashion shows, boat rides, parades, parties, dance and various pageants – from Mr Cool to Ms Culture Swimsuit.

🛏 Sleeping

Aside from a few locally run and inexpensive guesthouses, Charlestown does not have any lodging options.

JP's Guest House　　　　GUESTHOUSE $
(☑ 869-469-0319; www.nevisisland.com/guest-houses/jps-guest-house; Lower Prince William St; r US$72; ❇🛜) Two minutes' walk from the ferry dock, this tidy upstairs place in a modern building has 10 rooms that are a tad twee but spotless, and outfitted with air-con, cable TV and fridge. Self-caterers may make use of the communal kettle and microwave.

🍴 Eating & Drinking

★ **Wilma's Diner**　　　　CARIBBEAN $
(☑ 869-663-8010; www.facebook.com/Wilmas-diner; Main St; mains lunch EC$47, dinner US$40; ☺ 11am-3pm Mon-Sat) The gracious Wilma is a wizard in the kitchen and dishes out a daily-changing menu of hearty local fare like barbecue pork ribs or stewed chicken in her quaint and green-trimmed cottage next to the police station. A more fanciful three-course dinner is available by reservation only. Call at least one day ahead.

Cafe des Arts　　　　CAFE $
(☑ 869-667-8768; www.facebook.com/thecafede-sarts; Bayfront, Samuel Hunkins Blvd; sandwiches EC$20-40; ☺ 8:15am-2pm or later Mon-Sat Nov-May; P🛜) Infused with charming boho flair and set in a little banana tree–shaded park by the sea, this colorful outdoor cafe does brisk business with its cooked breakfasts and freshly made sandwiches, salads and quiches. Locals and clued-in visitors roll in on Tuesdays after 6pm for the ritual burger bonanza.

Charlestown Public Market　　　　MARKET $
(Market St; ☺ 7am-4:30pm Mon-Sat) A few stalls set up by the ferry pier sell local fruit and vegetables. It's busiest on Saturday morning. Bargaining recommended.

Chinese Supermarket　　　　SUPERMARKET $
(Memorial Sq; ☺ 8am-11pm) A little overpriced but stocked with basic supplies, this market is open when everything else is not.

Octagon Bar　　　　CARIBBEAN
(☑ 869-469-0673; Samuel Hunkins Blvd; dishes EC$8-18; ☺ 11am-8pm; 🛜) For a big dose of local color, belly up to this outdoor bar on the waterfront or order one of its cheap, simple lunches (salt fish, johnnycakes, chicken stew etc) and chow down amid trippy mermaid and dolphin murals on the shaded patio.

ℹ Information

Plenty of banks with ATMs line up on Main St.

Post Office (nevispostoffice@nia.gov.kn; Main St; ◷8am-3:30pm Mon-Fri)

Public Library (☑869-469-0421; www.face book.com/nepublib/; Main St)

ℹ Getting There & Away

The ferry from St Kitts drops anchor at the pier right in the heart of Charlestown. If you're arriving via the Seabridge car ferry, you need to arrange for a taxi to pick you up. A taxi ride from the airport costs US$20.

Northern Nevis

Nevis' west and north coast are ringed with superb beaches, from long and lovely Pinney's and busy Oualie to romantic Lovers and white-sand Nisbet and Herbert's. The island's only five-star resort, the Four Seasons, is a major presence on Pinney's Beach, which is also home to a cluster of jumpin' beach bars and restaurants. Further north, Cades Bay is the launchpad for the Seabridge car ferry to St Kitts. Some of Nevis' best dive sites are a short boat ride off the west coast.

◉ Sights

St Thomas' Lowland Church CHURCH
(Main Island Rd, Cotton Ground; P) About 3 miles north of Charlestown, Nevis' oldest church (1643) stares serenely out to sea from its hilltop perch. Goats keep the cemetery grounds trimmed. Take a walk around the moody cemetery where the oldest graves belong to some of the original settlers. The oldest is from 1649.

★ Pinney's Beach BEACH
(Main Island Rd; P 🛜) This 3-mile-long stretch of tan sand along the west coast has decent snorkeling right offshore. The northern end is punctuated by the Four Seasons Resort and several beach bars, but quiet patches abound. Sundays are busiest.

Oualie Beach BEACH
(Main Island Rd; P 🛜) In the northwest, family-friendly Oualie has grayish sand, shallow water and sunset views of St Kitts. The eponymous resort provides drinks and eats, beach chairs and water-based activities.

Lovers Beach BEACH
(Main Island Rd) Curtained off by sea grapes, mile-long Lovers Beach charms with white sands and an untamed beauty. Its lack of facilities keeps it nearly deserted, but currents and a steep drop make the water less suitable for kids or inexperienced swimmers.

Park by the side of the road next to the sign saying 'Sea Haven Beach' and walk 500ft through the trees to the sea. Between April and November, the beach is a turtle-nesting ground.

Nisbet Beach BEACH
(Main Island Rd; P 🛜) This Atlantic-facing beach near the airport is a divine palm-lined strip of soft white sand, but windy conditions can make the sea quite choppy. An upscale beach bar belonging to Nisbet Plantation Beach Club provides sustenance and facilities.

★ Herbert's Beach BEACH
(just south of Nisbet Plantation Beach Club) A quarter-mile dirt track spills out into this practically deserted Atlantic-side beach with white sand buttressed by clumps of sea grapes. Several reefs close to shore make it a popular spot with snorkelers provided the sea isn't too choppy. No facilities, little shade.

⚡ Activities & Tours

Four Seasons Golf Course GOLF
(☑869-469-1111; www.fourseasons.com/nevis/services_and_amenities/golf/course; Main Island Rd, Pinney's Beach; 9/18 holes US$165/230; 🛜) Get into the tropical swing at this acclaimed 18-hole, par 71 course designed by Robert Trent Jones II and spread across a dramatic mix of steep slopes, rainforest ravines and beachfront.

Nevis Equestrian Centre HORSEBACK RIDING
(☑869-662-9118; www.nevishorseback.com; Clifton Estate, Main Island Rd, Cotton Ground; rides US$75; ◷rides 9am, 2pm, sunset) Saddle up and explore the verdant and sandy scenery on a variety of rides, including the popular 90-minute Beach & Trail Ride (US$75), which also takes in a secluded beach, a lagoon and historic villages. Lessons are US$30 per hour.

Mt Nevis HIKING
Nevis' highest peak (3182ft) is seemingly perpetually cloaked in clouds, a phenomenon that gave the island its name: *nieve* is

Spanish for snow. Since the climb to the top is steep and strenuous, and the trail is not always marked, it should only be attempted by experienced hikers or with a guide.

Scuba Safaris
DIVING

(☑ 869-469-9518; www.divenevis.com; Oualie Beach Resort, Main Island Rd; 2-tank dive US$110) This five-star PADI outfit at the Oualie Beach Resort runs boat dives to coral reefs and wrecks around Nevis and St Kitts, and also offers certification courses and snorkel safaris.

Wheel World Cycle Shop
CYCLING

(☑ 869-469-9682; www.bikenevis.com; Oualie Beach Resort, Main Island Rd; bike rentals per day from US$25; ☺ 8am-4pm Mon-Sat) From his base at the Oualie Beach Resort, Winston Crooke gets visitors in the saddle on guided tours. The most popular is the Island Discovery Tour (US$65), an easy two-hour spin along historic sugarcane trails with stops in small villages and at plantations. Hike-and-bike combination tours (US$85) are also available, as are bike rentals.

🛏 Sleeping

Oualie Beach Resort
RESORT $$

(☑ 869-469-9735; www.oualiebeach.com; Oualie Beach; r US$150-280; P ✳ 🛜) Tailor-made for families and sporty types, character-ful Oualie has 32 breezy white rooms with four-poster beds and floral touches in gingerbread cottages on a calm, coconut palm–studded beach. The restaurant serves island cuisine, while the bar gets hopping nightly with a mix of locals and guests. A top-rated dive shop and bike-tour outfit are on-site.

Four Seasons Resort Nevis
LUXURY HOTEL $$$

(☑ 869-469-1111; www.fourseasons.com/nevis; Pinney's Beach; r from US$900; P ✳ @ 🛜 ☒) This full-service luxury resort on the manicured grounds of a former sugar and coconut plantation has 196 rooms discreetly set in low-rise garden cottages along Pinney's Beach. The oversized rooms face either Mt Nevis or the ocean, are dressed in soothing natural tones and outfitted with all expected luxe amenities.

Nisbet Plantation Beach Club
RESORT $$$

(☑ 869-469-9325, in the US 800-724-2088; www.nisbetplantation.com; Nisbet Beach, Newcastle; d incl breakfast, afternoon tea & dinner US$739-996; P ✳ 🛜 ☒) This former plantation is where Nelson met and fell in love with Fanny Nisbet. It attracts traditionalists keen on

afternoon tea and the 'no shorts after 6pm' policy. The 36 sun-yellow cottages exude casual glam and are less luxurious than the price tag might suggest. They're set around the 'Avenue of Palms,' a long sweep of lawn flanked by soaring palms.

🍴 Eating

★ Gin Trap Bar & Restaurant
CARIBBEAN $$

(☑ 869-469-8230; www.thegintrapnevis.com; Main Island Rd, Jones Bay; mains US$18-35; ☺ noon-2:30pm & 6-9pm Tue-Sun) Sunset views out to St Kitts are positively dreamy at this worldly farm-to-table outpost whose kitchen is helmed by Mary Parks, Cordon Bleu grad and former figure skater. Kick things off in the stylish bar with a jalapeño-laced Gin Trap cocktail before feasting on inspired international fare in the louvered dining room. Ceviche and the homemade ravioli are recommended.

★ Sunshine's Beach Bar & Grill
CARIBBEAN $$

(☑ 869-469-5817; www.sunshinesnevis.com; Pinney's Beach; mains lunch US$8-15, dinner US$15-30; ☺ 11am-late; P 🛜) This legendary rum-and-reggae joint has been getting people in a party mood for decades. A cold Carib goes well with its 'secret sauce'–marinated grilled ribs and chicken, but the signature 'Killer Bee' rum punch demands your respect: its 'sting' has been documented by hundreds of photos decorating the walls.

Chrishi Beach Club
INTERNATIONAL $$$

(☑ 869-469-5959; www.chrishibeachclub.com; Main Island Rd, Cades Bay; mains US$18-24; ☺ noon-10pm Tue-Sat, 11am-5pm Sun; P 🛜) A contemporary Caribbean vibe hangs over this Norwegian-owned white beachfront pavilion on a quiet stretch of sand close to the Seabridge car ferry. It's mostly a daytime venue but now also serves dinners in season. Sunday brunch gets busy. The burgers are great but we also like the Deep French Kiss (prosciutto and brie baguette).

❶ Getting There & Away

Northern Nevis is served by bus and by taxi.

South Nevis

The circular island road traverses the lush southern part of Nevis between cloud-shrouded Mt Nevis and Saddle Hill, skirting crumbling sugar mills and plantation estates–turned-hotels. In the east, the population thins out and the sloping green flatlands – once sugarcane plantations – run down to the turbulent Atlantic. It's a desolate and dramatic landscape.

⊙ Sights

★ Botanical Gardens of Nevis   GARDENS
(☎869-469-3509; www.botanicalgardennevis.com; St John Figtree; adult/child 6-12yr EC$35/21.50; ⊙9am-4pm Mon-Sat) It's easy to spend a couple of hours wandering around this enchanting symphony of orchids, palms, water-lily ponds, bamboo groves and other global flora interspersed with sculpture, pools, ponds and fountains. In the Rainforest Conservatory parrots patrol the huge tropical plants, waterfalls and Mayan-style sculpture. A Thai restaurant serves lunch and refreshments. Note that the gardens may close on occasion between mid-August to mid-October – call ahead. Benches, swings and shaded pergolas invite relaxing surrounded by beauty and tranquility.

Nevisian Heritage Village   MUSEUM
(☎869-469-5521; Fothergills Estate, Gingerland; adult/child EC$8/2.50; ⊙9am-3:30pm Mon-Sat) This open-air museum illustrates Nevisian social history, from Carib times to the present, through a collection of recreated traditional buildings furnished with period relics. Exhibits include a Carib chief's thatched hut, slave houses and a blacksmith's shop.

🏃 Activities & Tours

Golden Rock Nature Trail   HIKING
(Gingerland) The Golden Rock Inn is the departure point for this easy-to-moderate rainforest hike along a ridgeline and down a gentle ravine past giant ferns and trees. Keep an eye out for troops of vervet monkeys. A free map is available at the inn's reception desk.

Upper Round Road Trail   HIKING
Built in the late 1600s, this trail once linked the sugar estates, cane fields and villages surrounding Mt Nevis. Today, it travels 9 miles from Golden Rock Inn in the east to Nisbet Plantation Beach Club in the north, past farms, orchards, gardens and rainforest.

Sunrise Tours   HIKING
(☎869-669-1227; www.nevisnaturetours.com; per person US$25-40; ⊙by request) For a delightful and informative nature experience, hit the trail in the company of Nevis native and environmentalist Lynell Liburd, whose hiking menu ranges from a gentle village walk to the strenuous trek up Mt Nevis.

LOCAL KNOWLEDGE

NEVIS HERITAGE TRAIL

As you drive the island ring road, look for the blue road markers pointing out locations on the **Nevis Heritage Trail**, including churches, sugar estates, military installations and natural sites. For orientation, pick up a leaflet at the tourist office or the museums.

🛏 Sleeping & Eating

Three plantation estates – one arty, another traditional, the third contemporary – offer wonderful stays that beautifully connect you with Nevis' history and its sweet and unhurried character.

★ Golden Rock Inn   INN $$$
(☎869-469-3346; www.goldenrocknevis.com; Gingerland; d from US$250, 2-night minimum; ⊙closed mid-Aug–mid-Oct; P❖🐾❄) Fall asleep to a symphony of tree frogs and crickets at this intimate retreat that's perfect for unplugging from the daily grunt in comfort while fully cocooned by nature. The 11 funkily classy cottages are tucked into a riotous tropical garden where vervet monkeys chase butterflies. Up above, a good-sized pool beckons.

The restaurant (lunch US$11 to US$19, dinner US$22 to US$32) down below is famous for its lobster sandwiches.

Several hiking trails leave right from the grounds (maps available at reception).

Montpelier Plantation Inn & Beach   LUXURY HOTEL $$$
(☎869-469-3462; www.montpeliernevis.com; St John Figtree; r incl breakfast US$405-445, ste US$885; ⊙closed mid-Aug–early Oct; P🐾❄) This blissful hideaway on the estate where Nelson wed Fanny consists of a great house with a lavish art-, flower- and antique-filled parlor and garden grounds dotted with modern-colonial-chic bungalows. Despite vestiges from the past, such as the old sugar mill, the overall ambience is classy and contemporary. A private beach is a free 20-minute shuttle-bus ride away.

Hermitage Plantation Inn INN $$$

(☑ 869-469-3477; www.hermitagenevis.com; Hermitage Rd, St John Figtree; r incl breakfast US$255-425, cottage US$555-850; P 🛜 🕿) Country comfort and Caribbean flair combine effortlessly at this cluster of candy-colored gingerbread stone cottages set amid beautiful gardens on a former plantation. Even if you're not staying, swing by to soak up the charmingly old-school ambience along with a nutmeg-dusted rum punch during its famous West Indian Pig Roast on Wednesdays.

★ Bananas Restaurant INTERNATIONAL $$

(☑ 869-469-1891; www.bananasrestaurantnevis.com; Upper Hamilton Estate, Morning Star village; mains lunch US$15-25, dinner US$22-35; ⊙ 11am-11pm; P 🛜) A torchlit walkway leads to this enchanting hideaway hand-built by British transplant and former dancer Gillian Smith. Enjoy the tranquil vibe ensconced on the veranda, slurping tropical drinks and tucking into food inspired by her travels around the world. Local flavors such as conch gratin, salt fish and goat water round out the menu. Reservations advised.

☆ Entertainment

Indian Castle Race Track HORSE RACING

(☑ 869-663-2208; www.facebook.com/ntajc/; Indian Castle Estate, Hanley's Rd; hours vary; ⊙ several times per year) Aside from cricket, there are few things that get the locals more excited than a 'day at the races.' Several times a year, usually around major holidays, the Nevis Turf and Jockey Club sponsors horse races starring mostly local equines. Live music, barbecue chicken and rum punches keep the party going well into the evening.

UNDERSTAND ST KITTS & NEVIS

History

First sighted by Christopher Columbus in 1493 on his second voyage to the New World, St Kitts and Nevis became the oldest British colonies in the Caribbean in 1623 and 1628, respectively. Like many islands in the region, their growth was fueled by sugar and the African slaves that worked on the plantations. Even after St Kitts and Nevis became independent of Britain in 1983, sugar continued to drive the economy until 2005.

European Discovery

The island known today as St Kitts was called Liamuiga (Fertile Island) by the Caribs, who arrived about AD 1300 and chased out the peaceable agrarian bands who'd been in the area for hundreds of years. When Columbus sighted the island on his second voyage to the New World, in 1493, he named it St Christopher after his patron saint, later shortened to 'St Kitts.'

Columbus used the Spanish word for 'snow,' *nieve*, to name Nevis, presumably because the clouds shrouding its mountain reminded him of a snowcapped peak. Caribs knew the island as Oualie (Land of Beautiful Waters).

Colonial Times

St Kitts was colonized under Sir Thomas Warner in 1623, only to be joined soon after by the French, a move the British only tolerated long enough to massacre the Caribs. In one day, 2000 of them were slaughtered, causing blood to run for days at the site now known as Bloody Point.

A century and a half of Franco-British battles culminated locally in 1782, when a force of 8000 French troops laid siege to the important British stronghold at Brimstone Hill on St Kitts. Although they won this battle, they lost the war and the 1783 Treaty of Paris brought the island firmly under British control.

Nevis had a colonial history similar to St Kitts. In 1628 Warner sent a party of about 100 colonists to establish a British settlement on the west coast of the island. Although the original settlement, near Cotton Ground, fell to an earthquake in 1680, Nevis eventually developed one of the most affluent sugar plantation societies in the Eastern Caribbean. As on St Kitts, most of the island's wealth was built upon the labor of African slaves who toiled in the island's sugarcane fields. Sugar continued to play a role in the local economies until the last plantation closed in 2005.

By the late 18th century, Nevis, buoyed by the attraction of its thermal baths, had become a major retreat for Britain's rich and famous.

Road to Independence

In 1816 the British linked St Kitts and Nevis with Anguilla and the Virgin Islands as a single colony. In 1958 these islands became part of the West Indies Federation, a grand but ultimately unsuccessful attempt to combine all of Britain's Caribbean colonies as a united political entity. When the federation dissolved in 1962, the British opted to lump St Kitts, Nevis and Anguilla together as a new state. Anguilla, fearful of domination by larger St Kitts, revolted against the occupying Royal St Kitts Police Force in 1967 and returned to Britain as an overseas territory.

In 1983 St Kitts and Nevis became a single nation within the British Commonwealth, with the stipulation that Nevis could secede at any time. In the 1990s, a period of corruption on St Kitts and pro-independence on Nevis almost brought an end to the federation. A referendum held on Nevis in 1998, however, failed to produce a two-third majority needed to break away.

Looking Ahead

St Kitts' future is quite literally under construction as parts of the unpopulated southern part of the island are being developed into Christophe Harbour, a high-end residential area with villas, a private-member beach club, a superyacht marina and a Tom Fazio–designed golf course. The area is also home to a new Park Hyatt resort, the brand's first in the Caribbean. A new tunnel and resurfaced road have also been completed. In the north, the big news is the opening of the Belle Mont Farm, a visionary sustainable resort set on its own 400-acre farm at the foot of Mt Liamuiga.

Nevis, on the other hand, is looking to the past as its greatest asset. The expanded Nevis Heritage Trail goes a long way toward education and heritage preservation.

People & Culture

Although the population of St Kitts and Nevis is predominantly (90%) of African descent, culturally the islands draw upon a mix of European, African and West Indian traditions.

Rather than selling their soul and identity to mass tourism, both islands still exude unhurried Caribbean flair. Walk through a residential area on St Kitts on any given night and locals will be out in the streets, listening to reggae or calypso blaring out of homes and chatting with friends. On weekends, villagers on Nevis organize communal barbecues.

Kittitians are obsessed with cricket. Both international matches as well as those featuring the national Caribbean Premier League team, the St Kitts and Nevis Patriots, are played at Warner Stadium in Basseterre.

Landscape & Wildlife

Both islands have grassy coastal areas, a consequence of deforestation for sugar production. Forests tend to be vestiges of the large rainforests that once covered much of the islands, or they are second-growth.

Away from developed areas, the climate allows a huge array of beautiful plants to thrive, especially on Nevis. Flowers such as plumeria, hibiscus and chains-of-love are common along roadsides and in garden landscaping.

ST KITTS & NEVIS PEOPLE & CULTURE

WILD VERVET MONKEYS

You'll see them on the beach, the trail and the golf course – packs of wild vervet monkeys brought from Africa to St Kitts and Nevis by French settlers in the 17th century. Since then, they have flourished so well that they outnumber humans two to one. They may look cute and are even used in promoting the islands to tourists, but to local farmers they're a nightmare because of their ravenous appetite for fruit and vegetable crops.

In order to get the problem under control, a nonprofit company called Arnova Sustainable Future has partnered with the Department of Agriculture to set up feeding stations on the upper slopes to curb the incentive to come down from the mountain to forage for food at lower-lying farms. Other planned measures include a spay and neuter program as well as taste, smell and hearing aversions.

Meanwhile, according to the Animal Rights Foundation of Florida, another way to decimate the Kittitian monkey population is by trapping and selling the animals to medical research and testing laboratories worldwide. Two such facilities on St Kitts also use local monkeys in their research.

Nevis is fairly circular and the entire island benefits from runoff from Mt Nevis. St Kitts' shape resembles a tadpole. The main body is irrigated by water from the mountain ranges. However, this is of little value to the geographically isolated, arid southeast peninsula, which is covered with sparse, desert like cacti and yucca.

Aside from the vervet monkey, another ubiquitous creature is the mongoose, imported from Jamaica by plantation owners to rid their sugarcane fields of snakes. Both islands provide plenty of avian life for bird watchers.

Reefs around the two islands face the same threats as elsewhere in the region. On St Kitts, some of the best reefs ring the southeast peninsula.

SURVIVAL GUIDE

ℹ️ Directory A–Z

ACCOMMODATIONS

There are large resorts on both islands, but most accommodations are still small- to medium-sized hotels, plantation inns, guesthouses and apartment rentals. The government-mandated hotel tax (10%) and a 10% service fee are not always included in quoted rates. Always check what's included when making a reservation.

CHILDREN

Children receive a warm welcome on St Kitts and Nevis. Many restaurants have kids' menus or are happy to cook up simple dishes. Larger resorts provide organized children's activities, kids' clubs and day-care or babysitting.

Most beaches are safe for children to play on and many of the southern and western beaches are calm enough for younger swimmers. Older kids enjoy water sports, zip-lining, historic fortresses, guided hikes and bike trips.

SLEEPING PRICE RANGES

The following prices ranges refer to a double room with bathroom. Unless otherwise stated, breakfast is not included in the price.

$ less than US$100

$$ US$100–200

$$$ more than US$200

ELECTRICITY

220V, 60 cycles; North American–style two-pin sockets.

EMERGENCY NUMBERS

To call a phone number in St Kitts and Nevis, dial your international access code, the country code (☎ 869) and then the local number.

Ambulance	☎ 911
Fire	☎ 333
Police	☎ 911

FOOD

Eating in St Kitts and Nevis is more often than not a farm-to-table and sea-to-table experience, and a palate-rewarding endeavor at all budget levels. Even at roadside stands and humble snackettes you can often fill up for little. On Nevis, some of the best food is served at the restaurants of the plantation inns.

Essential Food & Drink

➜ **Stewed salt fish** Official national dish; served with spicy plantains, coconut dumplings and seasoned breadfruit.

➜ **Pelau** Also known as 'cook-up,' this dish is the Kittitian version of paella: a tasty but messy blend of rice, meat, saltfish, vegetables and pigeon peas.

➜ **Conch** Served curried, marinated or soused (boiled).

➜ **Cane Spirit Rothschild** More commonly known as CSR, this locally distilled libation is made from pure fermented cane juice and best enjoyed on the rocks mixed with grapefruit-flavored Ting soda.

➜ **Brinley Gold Rum** Locally blended rum comes in such flavors as vanilla, coffee, mango, coconut and lime. The shop in Port Zante does tastings.

➜ **Carib** Locally brewed lager.

GLBT TRAVELERS

There is no real gay and lesbian scene on St Kitts and Nevis and, though rare, discrimination does occur. So better be safe and don't engage in public displays of affection, especially outside the resorts and in villages. Officially, homosexual 'acts' between men (though not women) are on the books as being punishable with up to 10 years' imprisonment. However, the law is not enforced.

HEALTH

For minor illnesses, nearly all hotels will have a doctor on call or will be able to help you find assistance. The CDA Technical Institute of the West Indies on Bay Rd in Basseterre operates two hyperbaric chambers.

Joseph N France General Hospital (JNF Hospital; ☑ 869-465-2551; Cayon St, Brumaire; ☺ 24hr) Main hospital on St Kitts with emergency room and trauma department.

Alexandra Hospital (☑ 869-469-5473; Government Rd)

LEGAL MATTERS

St Kitts and Nevis' legal system is based on British common law. In case of legal difficulties, you have the right to legal representation and are eligible for legal aid if you can't afford to pay for private services. Foreign nationals should receive the same legal protections as local citizens.

Note that you can get fined for using foul language in public, but drinking alcohol while driving is legal (of course, this doesn't mean you can drive drunk!). Wearing camouflage clothing is illegal.

MONEY

ATMs at the airports and in Basseterre and Charlestown. Credit cards widely accepted.

Cash

St Kitts and Nevis use the East Caribbean dollar (EC$), but US dollars are widely accepted. However, unless rates are posted in US dollars, as is the norm with accommodations, some restaurants and dive shops, it usually works out better to use EC dollars. If you pay in US dollars, you will likely get change in EC dollars.

Exchange Rates

AUSTRALIA	A$1	EC$1.93
CANADA	C$1	EC$1.98
EUROPE	€1	EC$2.81
JAPAN	¥100	EC$2.30
NEW ZEALAND	NZ$1	EC$1.86
UK	UK£	EC$3.29
US	US$	EC$2.68

Tipping

→ **Hotels** US$0.50 to US$1 per bag is standard; gratuity for cleaning staff is at your discretion.

→ **Restaurants** If the service charge is not automatically added to the bill, tip 10% to 15%; if it is, it's up to you to leave a little extra.

→ **Taxi** Tip 10% to 15% of the fare.

PUBLIC HOLIDAYS

New Year's Day January 1

Good Friday/Easter Monday March/April

Labor Day First Monday in May

Pentecost/Whit Monday Forty days after Easter

Emancipation Day First Monday in August

Culturama Day August 8

EATING PRICE RANGES

The following price ranges refer to a main course.

$ less than US$10

$$ US$10–25

$$$ more than US$25

National Hero's Day September 16

Independence Day September 19

Christmas/Boxing Day December 25/26

TAXES & REFUNDS

Hotels and restaurants charge 12% value-added tax (VAT) and a 10% service fee, although this is not always included in quoted rates.

VAT on goods and services is 17% but food, medicine and funeral expenses are exempt.

Visitors are not eligible to reclaim VAT paid during their trip.

TELEPHONE

→ The country code for St Kitts and Nevis is ☑ 869.

→ To call from North America, dial ☑ 011 + 869 + local number.

→ From elsewhere, dial your country's international access code + 869 + local number.

→ To call abroad from St Kitts and Nevis, dial ☑ 011 + country code + area code + local number.

→ If making a call within or between the islands, you only need to dial the seven-digit local number.

→ For directory assistance, dial ☑ 411.

→ In hotels, local calls are often free but international calls are charged at exorbitant rates.

TIME

Clocks in St Kitts and Nevis are set to Atlantic Time, which is four hours behind GMT. The islands do not observe daylight-saving time, but since other countries do, the following times are indicative only:

CITY	NOON IN ST KITTS AND NEVIS
Auckland	5am + 1 day
Frankfurt/Milan	5pm
London	4pm
Los Angeles	8am
New York	11am
Sydney	3am +1 day

TRAVELERS WITH DISABILITIES

International resorts generally have good accommodations for people with disabilities. Otherwise, both of the islands are something of a challenge. Fortunately, almost everything of interest can be reached directly by car. The must-see Brimstone Hill Fortress has both accessible and inaccessible areas.

VOLUNTEERING

Care Nevis Animal Society (www.carenevis. org) Needs volunteers to walk the sheltered dogs and socialize the pups and traumatized canines.

Nevis Turtle Group (www.nevisturtlegroup. org) Needs volunteers to collect information about turtles nesting on beaches from June to October.

ⓘ Getting There & Away

AIR

Robert L Bradshaw International Airport (SKB; ☑ 869-465-8121; Basseterre) is on the northeastern outskirts of Basseterre. It is served seasonally by Air Canada (Toronto), **American Airlines** (www.aa.com) (Miami, New York City, Charlotte), British Airways (London-Gatwick), **Delta** (www.delta.com) (Atlanta) and United Airlines (New York-Newark).

Regional carrier **LIAT** (www.liat.com) provides year-round services to Antigua, Tortola, US Virgin Islands, St-Martin/Sint Maarten, St Croix and San Juan. Winair has direct flights to and from St-Martin/Sint Maarten. Trans Anguilla Airways flies to Anguilla.

Nevis' diminutive **Vance W Armory International Airport** (NEV; ☑ 869-469-9040; www. nevisports.com; Newcastle; ☎) is in Newcastle, on the island's northeastern edge, and is only served by such regional airlines as **Winair** (www.

fly-winair.com) (St-Martin/Sint Maarten), Air Sunshine (Anguilla, St Thomas, Virgin Gorda, Tortola, Dominica), Seaborne Airlines (San Juan) and Tradewind Aviation (St Barths, San Juan).

SEA
Cruise Ship

Scores of cruise ships on Eastern Caribbean itineraries visit St Kitts. Sometimes two or three of these behemoths are docked at Basseterre's deep-water-harbor **cruise-ship terminal** (Port Zante, Basseterre). On those days, the beaches in the south or the St Kitts Scenic Railway get very busy. Independent travelers might want to check the cruise-ship schedule (eg at www. cruisetimetables.com/cruises-to-basseterre-st-kitts.html) to plan their itinerary accordingly.

Nevis lacks a dock that can handle the enormous boats so visits are limited to passengers brought ashore by tender from small ships (usually under 300 passengers) anchored offshore, or those on day excursions from St Kitts.

Yacht

St Kitts and Nevis are right on the Eastern Caribbean yachting circuit, although their lack of natural harbors like those on Antigua keep the numbers of people mooring for any period of length low.

The two ports of entry are Basseterre and Charlestown. There's a customs office at Zante Marina in Basseterre, while the immigration office is at the adjacent cruise-ship terminal. Open since 2015, the ultraluxe Christophe Harbour marina is tailor-made for superyachts and has its own customs house.

Vessels headed for Nevis must contact the port authority in order to be assigned a mooring within 24 hours of arrival. Customs and immigration are near the ferry dock in Charlestown.

If moving between St Kitts and Nevis, no special clearance is required.

ⓘ Getting Around

BOAT

St Kitts and Nevis are linked by passenger ferry between Basseterre and Charlestown, by car ferry between Majors Bay and Cades Bay, and by on-demand water taxis between Cockleshell Beach and Oualie Beach.

Car Ferry

The **Seabridge car ferry** (☑ 869-662-7002, 869-662-9565; car & driver EC$150, passengers EC$20; ⊙7am-7pm) service links Majors Bay in the south of St Kitts with Cades Bay on Nevis' northwest coast in about 20 minutes.

There are six scheduled departures in either direction from Monday to Saturday and three on Sunday. The first ferry leaves **Cades Bay** at 7am and **Majors Bay** (Majors Bay, St Kitts) at

---

8am; the last at 6pm and 7pm, respectively. The schedule often runs late and services may get cancelled because of bad weather. If demand is high, the captain sometimes runs an additional trip.

If you have a rental car, check with your rental company if you're allowed to take it across to the other island. Cars must be backed onto the ferry and parked with just a few inches between them. Ask one of the deckhands to help you, if necessary.

Passenger Ferry

Six passenger ferries shuttle between **Basseterre** (Bay Rd, Basseterre) and Charlestown. The trip takes about 45 minutes and is both a pleasant and scenic way to travel. The main companies are **MV Mark Twain/Sea Hustler** (☑ 869-469-0403; adult/child EC25/10) and **MV Caribe Breeze/Caribe Surf** (☑ 869-466-6734; mmtscaribe@hotmail.com; fare EC16-21).

Fares are set at adult/child EC$25/15 one way. The actual schedule varies day by day. For the latest, ask at your hotel, call 869-466-4636, check www.sknvibes.com/travel/ferry.cfm or text 'Ferry' to 7568 to get the schedule on your cell phone.

Tickets are sold from about 30 minutes before sailings. It's a good idea to arrive early as some boats sell out.

Water Taxi

Using a water-taxi service between the islands can be a good way to go if you want to be independent. Boats run between Reggae Beach Bar on Cockleshell Beach, St Kitts, and Oualie Beach on Nevis. The cost for the 10-minute trip costs US$20 to US$30 per person, usually with a two-person minimum. Rides must be scheduled in advance.

Local operators include the following:

Seabrat (☑ 869-662-9166)
Perfect Life (☑ 869-663-3595)
Black Fin (☑ 869-663-3301)

BUS

Government-licensed private minivans serve communities on an erratic schedule along the main roads. All have green license plates starting with 'H' or 'HA' and many are hilariously painted and festooned with names like 'De Punisher' or 'Love Bug.'

Buses can be boarded at designated stops in Basseterre and Charlestown or flagged down anywhere along the route. Service is more frequent in the morning and in the afternoon, and all but stops around 7pm or 8pm. Sunday service is less frequent.

Fares cost EC$2.50 to EC$5 and are payable to the driver. Sometimes it's possible to pay a

> ### ⓘ DRINKING WATER
>
> Many people drink tap water without incident but the US-based Center for Disease Control (CDC) recommends bottled water, which is cheap and widely available.

little extra to be dropped off at places off the main route.

St Kitts

There is no bus service south to Frigate Bay and beyond and in the far north between St Paul's and Ottley's.

Basseterre has two bus terminals:

Bay Road bus terminal (Bay Rd) Buses heading up the west coast as far as St Paul's.
Baker's Corner bus terminal (Cayon St) Buses heading east as far as Sadlers.

Nevis

From Charlestown, buses travel both clockwise and counterclockwise along the Main Island Rd. Buses leave when full.

Memorial Square bus stop Destinations north of Charlestown.
DR Walwyn Plaza bus stop Destinations south of Charlestown.

CAR

A local driving permit, available from car-rental agencies, is required for driving on St Kitts and Nevis. It costs US$24 or EC$62.50 and is valid on both islands for three months.

Drive on the left side of the road, often around goats, cows and pedestrians. The steering wheel is usually on the right.

The speed limit is posted in miles per hour and is generally 20mph in built-up areas and 40mph on highways.

There are no traffic lights on either island but traffic circles are common.

If you have an accident, call the police and don't move the vehicle.

Car Rental

Rental companies will usually meet you at the airport, ferry port or your hotel. Daily rates start at about US$45. You really won't need a 4WD for going anywhere – unless it's rainy season. Most of the major international firms have local affiliates.

St Kitts

Local companies include the following:

Avis (☑ 869-465-6507; www.avis.com; Bay Rd, Basseterre; ⊙8am-5pm Mon-Fri, to noon Sat, 9-11am Sun)

Caines Rent a Car (☎ 869-465-2366; Princes St, Basseterre)

Sunny Blue Scooter Rentals (☎ 869-664-8755; www.sunnybluerental.com; Pond Rd, Basseterre)

TDC/Thrifty Car Rental (☎ 869-465-2991; www.thrifty.com; Central St, Basseterre)

Nevis

Local rental companies include the following:

1st Choice Car Rental (☎ 869-469-1131; www.neviscarrental.com; Shaws Rd, Newcastle)

Nevis Car Rentals (☎ 869-469-9837; www.neviscarrentals.com; Shaws Rd, Newcastle; per day from US$45; ⏰7am-7pm)

TAXI

Taxis on St Kitts and Nevis are usually minibuses with yellow license plates beginning with 'T' or 'TA.' Fares are regulated by the government, with one tariff applying to up to four passengers. However, it's best to confirm the price (and which currency is quoted) before riding away. Service between 10pm and 6am adds 50% extra.

Taxis meet scheduled flights on both islands. Taxi island tours on both islands cost around US$80. Those short on time can take a three-hour half-island tour for US$60.

St Lucia

POP 165,595 / ☏ 758

Best Places to Eat

➡ Rainforest Hideaway (p695)

➡ La Terrasse (p691)

➡ Spice of India (p691)

➡ Orlando's (p699)

➡ Reef Cafe (p701)

➡ Boucan (p699)

Best Places to Sleep

➡ East Winds Inn (p690)

➡ Boucan (p698)

➡ Cap Maison (p693)

➡ Fond Doux Holiday Plantation (p698)

➡ Balenbouche Estate (p700)

➡ Bay Guesthouse (p690)

Why Go?

Blessed by nature, St Lucia has geographic and cultural riches enough to embarrass far bigger nations. Notwithstanding, it remains a down-to-earth place that wears its breathtaking beauty with nonchalance.

Noted for its oodles of small and luxurious resorts that drip color and flair, it is really two islands in one. Rodney Bay in the north offers lazy days and modern comforts amid a beautiful bay. In the south, Soufrière is at the heart of a gorgeous region of old plantations, hidden beaches and the geologic wonder of the impossibly photogenic Pitons.

When to Go

Dec-Mar As with most Caribbean destinations the winter season is the most popular time to visit St Lucia. The very unwintry weather brings the crowds and jacks up the prices, especially during the driest period from December to March. Winter weather is sublime with average temperatures around 81°F (27°C).

July Summer is quiet and hot, with the July temperatures averaging 85°F (29°C).

Jun-Oct Hurricane season – expect more rain this time of year and maybe the odd storm.

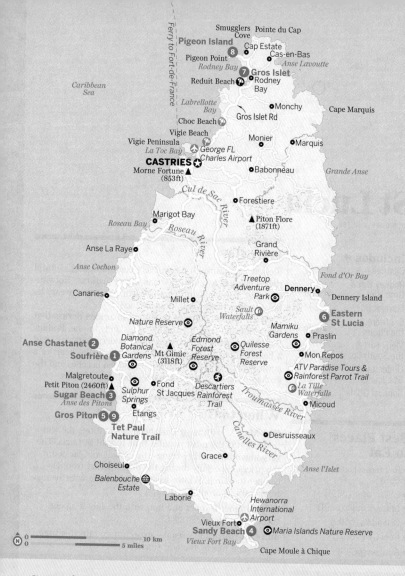

St Lucia Highlights

1 **Soufrière** (p695) Hunting heritage among the colonial buildings of grand estates.

2 **Anse Chastanet** (p696) Snorkeling or diving in the fish-filled waters.

3 **Sugar Beach** (p696) Sipping a cocktail on one of the Caribbean's most dramatic stretches of sand.

4 **Sandy Beach** (p700) Gliding across the brilliant blue waters after kiteboarding.

5 **Gros Piton** (p697) Huffing and puffing up the steep trail for astounding views.

6 **Eastern St Lucia** (p693) Taking a drive through the fishing villages to hidden waterfalls and lush gardens.

7 **Gros Islet** (p689) Dancing the night away in the middle of the street at Gros Islet's famous Friday-night bash.

8 **Pigeon Island** (p692) Unpacking a picnic lunch on the beach beneath wonderful ruins.

9 **Tet Paul Nature Trail** (p697) Enjoying a gentle hike through gorgeous landscapes.

Castries

The main city of St Lucia is worth a stop, with its best feature being the soaring Morne Fortune (2795ft), which serves as Castries' scenic backdrop. Most of the city's historic buildings were destroyed by major fires between 1785 and 1948, but it still makes for an interesting stroll. The markets are mostly given over to selling tat to cruise-ship passengers but you can find interest back in the recesses.

◎ Sights

Cathedral of the Immaculate Conception   CATHEDRAL
(Laborie St; ⊘8am-5pm) The city's Catholic cathedral, built in 1897, looks like a fairly typical grand stone church from the outside, but step inside and check out the splendidly painted interior of trompe l'oeil columns and colorfully detailed biblical scenes. The island's patron saint, St Lucia, is portrayed directly above the altar. When children's choirs are practicing, it's magical.

Fort Charlotte   FORT
(Morne Fortune) Sitting atop the 2795ft Morne Fortune, about 3 miles south of Castries center, is Fort Charlotte, whose construction began under the French and was continued by the British. Because of its strategic hilltop vantage point overlooking Castries, the fort was the location of fierce fighting between the French and British in colonial times. The fort buildings have been renovated and given a new life as the Sir Arthur Lewis Community College, but there's still some interesting places to see.

🏃 Activities

Hackshaw's   BOATING
(☑453-0553; www.hackshaws.com; Vigie) Hackshaw's runs whale- and dolphin-watching outings (from US$60) as well as deep-sea fishing trips (from US$100).

Carnival Sailing   BOATING
(☑452-5586; www.carnivalsailing.com; Pointe Seraphine) Runs popular party-yacht cruises down to Soufrière, including side trips to the sulfur springs and a waterfall. Also organizes sunset cruises.

🎊 Festivals & Events

St Lucia Jazz Festival   MUSIC
(www.stluciajazz.org; ⊘May) Concerts and jam sessions featuring big names from the international jazz scene.

Carnival   CARNIVAL
(www.luciancarnival.com; ⊘Jul) The biggest show on the island's calendar. Castries' streets buzz with music, a costume parade and calypso.

Creole Heritage Month   CULTURAL
(⊘Oct) A nationwide festival celebrating all things Creole with cultural activities in several host communities. It culminates in a big food fair.

🛏 Sleeping

Eudovic's Guesthouse   GUESTHOUSE $
(☑452-2747; www.eudovicart.com; Morne Fortune; r US$60-65; ❋ 🛜 ☀) Everything is simple and ultra-laid-back at this low-key guesthouse run by master artisan Eudovic. There are eight rooms, four with air-conditioning, which are clean and utilitarian. Fan-cooled rooms 1 and 2 open onto a jungle-like garden and get more light than some of the air-con options. Downtown Castries is a five-minute bus ride away.

Auberge Seraphine   INN $$
(☑453-2073; www.aubergeseraphine.com; Pointe Seraphine; s/d from US$125/140; ❋ 🛜 ☀) This inn has a heavy focus on regional business-people, so it's not exactly a vacation environment, though it is convenient to downtown Castries and the airport. All the rooms are functional and clean. Be sure to ask for one with a marina view – rooms 301 to 304 are the best. There's also an on-site restaurant.

🍴 Eating

For good rotis and local dishes, try the stalls on the north side of **Castries Central Market** (Jeremie St; ⊘6am-5pm Mon-Sat).

Gobble   CAFE $
(Jeremie St; mains EC$16.50-22; ⊘7am-5pm Mon-Fri, 9am-3pm Sat) An air-conditioned oasis in downtown Castries, this modern cafe serves classic St Lucian dishes as well as burgers, salads and sandwiches. There's also a selection of scrumptious desserts and good coffee, natural juices and milkshakes. Hands down the best place to eat in the center.

★ **Pink Plantation House**   CREOLE **$$**

(☑ 452-5422; Chef Harry Dr, Morne Fortune; mains EC$40-75; ⏱ 11:30am-3pm Mon-Fri, 6:30-9pm Fri, 9am-noon Sun) This art gallery housed in a splendid colonial mansion sitting on a lush property doubles as a fantastic restaurant. The views from the veranda are to die for. The Sunday brunch buffet, at EC$65, is unmissable. Wonderful cocktails, too.

Coal Pot   CARIBBEAN **$$**

(☑ 452-5566; Vigie Cove; mains EC$47-81; ⏱ noon-3pm & 6:30-9pm Mon-Sat, 6:30-10pm Sun) Follow the road around the harbor to find this little hidden gem. It's right on the water and far enough from town that the tranquility of the sea lulls you into a diner's dream. The cooking is modern French-Creole, with fresh produce and local spices combining in dishes bursting with flavor.

🔒 Shopping

★ **Eudovic's Art Studio**   ART

(☑ 452-2747; www.eudovicart.com; Morne Fortune; ⏱ 8am-4:30pm Mon-Fri, to 2pm Sat & Sun) Vincent Joseph Eudovic is a renowned master carver, and his studio at Morne Fortune is a magnificent art gallery. The craftsman is now in his seventies and doesn't work as much anymore but his son Jallim has followed in his father's footsteps and is very active. You can watch the carvers in action in the workshop.

Caribelle Batik   ARTS & CRAFTS

(☑ 452-3785; Old Victoria House, Morne Fortune; ⏱ 8am-5pm Mon-Sat) Housed in an enticing Victorian Caribbean mansion nestled amid lush tropical gardens, this working batik studio is a feast for the eyes. All the batik items incorporate tropical motifs and are handmade downstairs. There is also a variety of items (purses, bags, jewelry) made by other artisans around the island. Make sure to visit the rear balcony for amazing views over town.

Pink Plantation House   ART

(☑ 452-5422; Chef Harry Dr, Morne Fortune; ⏱ 11:30am-3pm Mon-Sat, 9am-3pm Sun) Michelle Elliot's eye-goggling paintings and hand-painted ceramics are sure to enliven your bedroom. This place is also famous for its good-value restaurant (p688) and wrap-around views of Castries.

ℹ Information

Most banks have branches with ATMs in the center.

Tourist Office (☑ 452-4094; www.stlucia.org; La Place Carenage, Jeremie St; ⏱ 8am-4:30pm Mon-Fri)

Castries

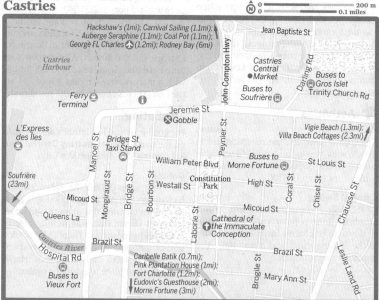

ⓘ Getting There & Away

BUS

Frustratingly, bus services in Castries don't depart from one central location but rather from dedicated stops spread around the city.

Buses for Gros Islet and Rodney Bay depart from the northern side of town, a block away from the market, while those to Vieux Fort and the south depart from the other side on Lower Hospital Rd.

Soufrière buses leave from the south side of the market, while Morne Fortune services are found in the center of town.

TAXI

There are many taxi ranks within central Castries. The one on Bridge St is generally manned by friendly older gentlemen who charge fair prices right off the bat.

You always ask hotels and restaurants to call a cab on your behalf.

Around Castries

Going north past George FL Charles Airport along Gros Islet Rd from Vigie Peninsula, the oceanside highway snakes its way to Rodney Bay. This stretch is far busier and more built-up than any other area in St Lucia.

Heading south from Castries the old highway quickly begins to wind up into the hills, passing scenic La Toc.

⊙ Sights

Vigie Beach   BEACH
This 2-mile beach runs parallel to the George FL Charles Airport runway. Vigie Beach is where you can find locals taking a quick dip on hot days. The color of the sand? Brown-gray.

Choc Beach   BEACH
A promontory separates Vigie and Choc Bays. The southern section of this long swath of honey-colored sand is flanked by the highway (noise!) but if you walk to the north it gets much quieter.

La Toc Beach   BEACH
South of Castries, this splendid golden-sand beach remains largely off the tourist radar, not least because it's a bit hard to find. Go in the direction of Morne Fortune, then head to the lower gate of the Sandals Regency Golf Resort & Spa, where the guards will show you the path that leads down to the beach.

WORTH A TRIP

BABONNEAU PARK

Enjoy the rainforest from a Tarzan perspective? Just 30 minutes east of Rodney Bay, **Rainforest Adventures** (☑ 458-5151; www.rainforestadventure.com; Chassin; tours from US$50; ⊙ 9am-3pm Mon-Fri & Sun) offers zip lines through the trees in the lush, protected Babonneau park (US$80). For the less adventurous, it offers a 1½-hour aerial 'tram' ride (US$80) over the canopy, and birdwatching tours (US$60) and hikes (US$50).

⏹ Sleeping

Villa Beach Cottages   HOTEL $$$
(☑ 450-2884; www.villabeachcottages.com; Choc Bay; 1-bedroom villas US$265-330) Offering around a dozen spacious and elegantly furnished villas, this polished place on Choc Beach is more personal than some of the bigger resorts and offers outstanding value. All rooms have full kitchens, comfy living spaces and private balconies overlooking the sea. The only downside: it's fairly close to the main road.

ⓘ Getting There & Away

With Castries being the transport hub of the island, local buses pass through all areas surrounding the capital. Most attractions around Castries can also be reached by taxi for around EC$30 to EC$40.

Rodney Bay & Gros Islet

About 6 miles (10km) north of Castries, the vast horseshoe of Rodney Bay boasts the island's most diverse tourist facilities. Within the bay is a large, artificial lagoon and marina, flanked by Rodney Bay Village, a somewhat bland assemblage of bars, restaurants, shops and more.

Far more interesting is the fishing village of Gros Islet to the north. Here the historic streets are lined with rum shops and fishing shacks draped with drying nets.

⊙ Sights

Reduit Beach   BEACH
This long stretch of white sand is the most popular beach on the island. The sea ranges from turquoise to azure, the waves are benign and there are plenty of beach

activities and cafes at hand. The central part of the beach gets mobbed, so head to the south end on the far side of the vast Rex Resorts. It's less crowded and has more shade.

🏃 Activities

Boating

Seeing St Lucia from the sea is a real treat. Several companies organize day sails and motorboat trips (from US$100) along the west coast from Rodney Bay. Sunset cruises are also hugely popular.

Sea Spray Cruises *BOATING*
(www.seaspraycruises.com; Rodney Bay Marina; cruises US$66-121) Offers a variety of cruises including day trips to Soufrière and pirate-themed party cruises aboard the *Black Magic*, a replica Spanish galleon.

Endless Summer Cruises *CRUISE*
(☑ 450-8651; www.stluciaboattours.com; Rodney Bay Marina; cruises US$83-120) A popular operator with full-day sailing trips down to Soufrière as well as sunset cruises. Also offers charter trips.

Diving & Snorkeling

There are several dive sites and snorkeling spots of note off the northwestern coast. You'll find dive operators in many of the larger resorts.

Scuba Steve's Diving *DIVING*
(☑ 450-9433; www.scubastevesdiving.com; Flamboyant Dr, Rodney Bay; 2-tank dives from US$85; 🖐) Offers dives across the island and snorkel trips (US$60 to US$75). It's located inside the Harmony Suites hotel.

🛏 Sleeping

★ Bay Guesthouse *GUESTHOUSE $*
(☑ 450-8956; www.bay-guesthouse.com; Bay St, Gros Islet; s/d from US$40/45, apt US$100; ❄ 🛜) Within easy walking distance of Gros Islet, this simple waterfront guesthouse is excellent value. It's run by a charming couple who have a great insight into the needs of travelers. Rooms range from compact to spacious; some offer kitchens and stunning views. The grounds have hammocks.

Harmony Suites *HOTEL $$*
(☑ 452-8756; www.harmonysuites.com; Flamboyant Dr, Rodney Bay; r with/without kitchen US$155/120, luxury ste US$240; 🅿❄🛜🏊) Located a convenient short walk away from both the beach and the Rodney Bay shops,

Harmony Suites offers spacious suites with and without kitchens, some with views of the lagoon. It's not luxurious but the rooms are bright, there's powerful air-con, the grounds are well kept and the staff are friendly. Hard to beat for the price around here.

La Terrasse *GUESTHOUSE $$*
(☑ 572-0389, 721-0389; www.laterrassestlucia. com; Seagrape Ave, Rodney Bay Village; d from US$100; ❄🛜) This delightful guesthouse run by a French couple feels remarkably homey. It has a tropical courtyard and dining deck, and there are four handsomely decorated rooms with modern fixtures. It's in a quiet street off the main avenue and a five-minute walk from the beach.

★ East Winds Inn *RESORT $$$*
(☑ 452-8212; www.eastwinds.com; Labrellotte Bay, Gros Islet; s/d all-inclusive per night from US$685/985; ❄🛜🏊) Understated yet beautiful, relaxed yet luxurious, this all-inclusive inn is one of St Lucia's most appealing beachside resorts. It has a mere 30 rooms spread over a garden- and bird-filled site. Service is superb, as is the food.

Ginger Lily Hotel *HOTEL $$$*
(☑ 458-0300; www.thegingerlilyhotel.com; Reduit Beach Ave; r US$175-230; ❄🛜🏊) An excellent alternative to the bigger resorts nearby, Ginger Lily Hotel is functional, intimate and blissfully quiet. Set in a peaceful garden, the 11 well-designed rooms have balconies and terraces with hammocks but no sea views. They are delightfully cool inside. Reduit Beach is just across the road.

Coco Palm *HOTEL $$$*
(☑ 456-2800; www.coco-resorts.com; Reduit Beach Ave, Rodney Bay Village; d US$230-370; ❄🛜🏊) A harmonious blend of modern lines and Creole styling. Although the Coco Palm isn't on the beach, it has an inviting setting on a grassy terrace overlooking Rodney Bay Village. With varied accommodations, it's appropriate for singles, couples and families alike. Some rooms have private steps into the enormous pool, which is sure to be a hit with younger travelers.

Bay Gardens Beach Resort & Spa *RESORT $$$*
(☑ 457-8500; www.baygardensresports.com; Reduit Beach Ave; d/ste US$365/560; ❄🛜🏊) An excellent choice if you prefer a full-service

resort, the BGBR has an idyllic beachfront location. Rooms are in three-story buildings designed with a neoclassical flair; many overlook the large cloverleaf pool or the beach. The suites have functional kitchens, making them a great choice for families.

✕ Eating

Gros Islet Fish Fry
SEAFOOD $

(Bay St, Gros Islet; meals EC$20-25; ⊙5-10pm Wed, Fri & Sat) A couple of open-air joints across from the water serve up excellent seafood grills a few nights a week at the Gros Islet Fish Fry. They are ultracasual: wait for a plate of barbecued fresh fish, get a few sides, then find a spot in the dark at a picnic table.

Elena's
ICE CREAM, PIZZA $

(☑572-2900; Rodney Bay Marina; ice cream EC$5-13, pizzas EC$22-55; ⊙7am-11pm Mon-Sat, 8am-11pm Sun) Elena's whips up a scrumptious assortment of real gelati to cool you down after a day in the sun. Also serves up great pizza from the waterside oven, plus snacks and pasta. There's another branch (ice cream only) in the Baywalk Mall.

Cafe Ole
CAFETERIA $

(Rodney Bay Marina; mains EC$16-40; ⊙7am-10pm Mon-Sat, 8am-10pm Sun) This sprightly eatery sitting on a covered wooden deck overlooking the marina is the perfect venue for enjoying a drink, snack or a meal – and to people-watch. It serves some of the best coffee on the island (EC$5 to EC$11).

★ Spice of India
INDIAN $$

(☑458-4253; www.spiceofindiastlucia.com; Baywalk Mall, Rodney Bay; mains EC$51-72; ⊙noon-4pm & 6-11pm Tue-Sun) You'd never guess it from the outside but this restaurant next to the mall complex at the beginning of the Rodney Bay strip consistently serves some of the best Indian food in the Caribbean. Everything is carefully prepared by veteran Indian chefs; the delectable curries are perfectly spiced and the lamb biryani is phenomenal. Book in advance.

Blue Olive
MEDITERRANEAN $$

(☑458-2433; Seagrape Ave, Rodney Bay; mains EC$55-75; ⊙11:30am-10pm Mon-Sat, 6:30-10pm Sun) A welcoming restaurant right by the water serving up high-quality French and other Mediterranean classics alongside great local seafood dishes.

Flavours of the Grill
CARIBBEAN $$

(☑450-9722; Mare Therese St, Gros Islet; mains EC$28-55; ⊙12 noon-10pm Mon-Sat) An intimate eatery in a colorful, quirky Creole home in the center of Gros Islet, offering refined versions of Caribbean classics. The seafood is locally caught. There is a buffet at lunch while dinner is from the menu.

★ La Terrasse
FRENCH $$$

(☑572-0389; www.laterrassestlucia.com; Seagrape Ave, Rodney Bay Village; mains EC$74-125; ⊙6:30-10pm Wed-Mon) Frogs' legs and *escargot* in St Lucia? Yes, it's possible at this wonderfully intimate little French restaurant on the backstreet, which uses fresh, local ingredients to prepare some of the best meals on the island. Reserve in advance.

Big Chef
STEAK $$$

(☑450-0210; www.bigchefsteakhouse.com; Reduit Beach Ave, Rodney Bay Village; mains EC$79-219; ⊙6-11pm Mon-Sun) If you fancy splashing out on something other than lobster, step into the classy air-conditioned dining room and tuck into quality imported cuts at St Lucia's favorite steakhouse. You'll have to change out of the shorts and sandals but it's worth it for a top-quality meal.

🍸 Drinking & Nightlife

Rodney Bay is the most 'happening' area in St Lucia. Most restaurants feature a bar section. You can also check out the bars in the large hotels.

On Friday nights in Gros Islet the weekly **jump-up** gets going. Stalls sell fresh fish, grilled chicken and other delights. The music plays at full volume and there's dancing in the streets. Popular with locals and visitors alike, it's St Lucia's best party.

Felly Belly
JUICE BAR

(Rodney Bay Mall, Rodney Bay; smoothies EC$14-20; ⊙7:30am-8pm Mon-Sat) Pop into this tiny place in the Rodney Bay mall for great juices and smoothies. Take your pick from the two boards full of different mixes or make your own from scratch.

Delirius
BAR

(Reduit Beach Ave, Rodney Bay Village; ⊙11am-late Fri-Wed) Come for rollicking times on the terrace and good cocktails. Also serves good meals including a full range of items from their very own smokehouse. Get there before 11pm if you want to eat.

ST LUCIA RODNEY BAY & GROS ISLET

🛍 Shopping

Island Mix Art Emporium ARTS & CRAFTS
(Seagrape Ave, Rodney Bay Village; ⊙10am-6pm
Fri-Wed, to 8pm Thu) A bright waterside gallery
featuring works by artists and craftspeople
from across the island. There is a good cafe
on-site serving lunch, and Thursday evenings from 6pm to 8pm they prepare fish
and chips.

❶ Getting There & Away

Minibus Both Rodney Bay and Gros Islet can
be reached from Castries via the same regular
public minivan service.

Taxi There are usually taxi drivers hanging out
in front of the malls in Rodney Bay, and there is
a taxi booth at the Rodney Bay Marina.

Water Taxi From the Reduit Beach area it's
quicker and more fun to travel to Gros Islet via
water taxi (☑518-8236; Reduit Beach). Boats
also serve Rodney Bay Marina and Pigeon
Island. Expect to pay around EC$25 one way
and EC$40 return per passenger.

Pigeon Island

This former island was joined to the mainland in the 1970s when a sandy causeway
was constructed; it's one of Rodney Bay's
best sights.

Pigeon Island has a fascinating range of
historic sites scattered across the bucolic
former 'island'. Its spicy history dates back
to the 1550s, when St Lucia's first French
settler, Jambe de Bois (Wooden Leg), used
the island as a base for raiding passing
Spanish ships. Two centuries later, British
admiral George Rodney fortified Pigeon Island, using it to monitor the French fleet on
Martinique.

Most of the coastline around Pigeon Island is rocky, but you'll find two small sandy
beaches pricked with palm trees within the
reserve. The water is safe for swimming and
snorkeling. Loungers are available for rent
for EC$8.

There is a much larger beach just outside the grounds but it's often overrun with
visitors.

◎ Sights

Pigeon Island
National Landmark HISTORIC SITE
(☑452-5005; www.slunatrust.org; adult/child
EC$19/5; ⊙ticket booth 9am-5pm) Pigeon Is-
land is a fun place to explore, with paths
winding around the remains of barracks,

batteries and garrisons; the partially intact
stone buildings create a ghost-town effect.
The grounds are well endowed with lofty
trees, manicured lawns and fine coastal
views. Bring a picnic and make a day of it.
Guided tours of the site can be arranged at
the ticket office for EC$59 for groups of one
to seven visitors.

🍴 Eating

★ **Jambe De Bois** CARIBBEAN $
(☑450-8166; Pigeon Island National Landmark;
mains EC$32.50-37.50; ⊙9am-10pm Tue-Sun,
to 5pm Mon) Locals, yachties and frequent
visitors know they'll get a delicious meal
and a wonderful view of the bay here. The
menu is fairly small but varied, with local
specialties lining up with Mediterranean
plates.

Pick out a table on the breezy veranda for
a romantic meal. On weekends there is great
live music.

❶ Getting There & Away

Public buses do not run all the way to Pigeon
Island but it's a short taxi ride from Rodney Bay
or Gros Islet.

It's possible to walk all the way up the beach
from Gros Islet to Pigeon Island. When you get to
the channel at the luxurious Landings Hotel, ring
the bell and a small boat will carry you across.
Then make your way through the sea of sun
loungers in front of Sandals – it's a public beach,
don't mind the security guards.

The easiest way to get to Pigeon Island from
Rodney Bay is via a water taxi from Reduit
Beach, which costs around EC$25 per passen-
ger.

The Northern Tip

Once you've left bustling Rodney Bay, life
becomes more sedate as you head toward
the island's northernmost reaches. On Cap
Estate the hilly terrain is dotted with chichi
villas, large estates and the island's only public golf course. From there it's an easy drive
downhill to secluded Cas En Bas beach. This
is the wilder side of the island – the winds
and surf here can be lively.

◎ Sights

Smugglers Cove BEACH
Close your eyes and imagine a hidden cove,
framed on three sides by steep sheltering
cliffs. You've just pictured Smugglers Cove,
a secluded crescent of brown sugary sand.

Cas En Bas
BEACH

Apart from kitesurfers who come here for the excellent winds, few visit this wide curve of gray sand because it's a bit off the beaten track. It's a stunning beach to sun yourself on.

🏃 Activities

Horseback Riding

There are a number of stables in the area offering trail rides as well as beach canters along Cas En Bas beach (p693). Expect to pay US$65 for two hours. Free pickup services can be arranged from most hotels in the Rodney Bay area. Children are welcome.

Holiday Riding Stables HORSEBACK RIDING
(holidayridingstables@gmail.com; Cas En Bas; US$60) A flexible stables offering different riding trips along remote Cas En Bas beach, including time in the water with the horses.

Kitesurfing

Cas En Bas always has a stiff breeze, which makes it an excellent kitesurfing spot. There are a couple of kite places located here but they're not always open so reserve in advance.

Aquaholics KITESURFING
(☑726-0600; www.aquaholicsstlucia.com; Cas En Bas; lessons per hour US$90) A recommended kitesurf school run by charismatic instructor Simon. He runs right alongside beginners on a jet ski to offer instant tips and training. Introductory classes are US$60 per hour and can be shared with a friend.

Kitesurfing St Lucia KITESURFING
(☑714-9589; www.kitesurfingstlucia.com; Cas En Bas Beach; lessons 1/2hr US$90/150, rental per hour from US$35; ⊙hours vary) Offers lessons with an instructor on a jet ski as well as two-hour discover kitesurfing introductions (US$120). Also rents out gear to experienced kiters.

🍴 Sleeping & Eating

★**Cap Maison** BOUTIQUE HOTEL $$$
(☑457-8679; www.capmaison.com; Cap Estate; d incl breakfast from US$435; ❊🛜🏊) Privacy, luxury and service are hallmarks of this sanctuary built on a seaside bluff. The elegant Moroccan-Caribbean architecture features suites that are elegantly furnished and decorated. Another draw is the superb Cliff at Cap restaurant (open to nonguests).

DENNERY FISH FRY

The big culinary event on this side of the island is the Dennery fish fry, which takes place every Saturday from around 4pm onward. While similar fish festivals in Gros Islet and Anse La Raye are major parties, the Dennery edition is more focused on the food, with a wider variety of seafood on offer. It takes place at the collection of colorful wooden huts right by the waterside near the town fish market.

Downside: the nearest beach requires hiking down (and back up) 92 steps.

Marjorie's Beach Bar & Restaurant CARIBBEAN $$
(☑520-0001; Cas En Bas Beach; mains EC$40-65; ⊙8am-6pm) Feel the sand between your toes at this funky cafe on the sand. Enjoy tasty Creole dishes and wicked rum punch. The management also organizes guides for a two-hour nature hike (US$30 per visitor) in the area that visits Donkey Beach, Secret Beach and Cactus Valley.

ℹ️ Getting There & Away

There's no public transport in this corner of the island but there are unmarked pirate buses that run irregularly from Gros Islet up to Cap Estate. Wait at the bus stop on the highway on the north side of the entrance road to Gros Islet. They're usually beaten-up old white vans.

Eastern St Lucia

A 30-minute drive from Castries transports you to yet another world, along the Atlantic-battered east coast, where you can experience a St Lucia that's very Creole, laid-back and little visited.

While this coast lacks the beaches of the west, it makes up for it with lovely bays backed by spectacular cliffs, a rocky shoreline pounded by thundering surf, and a handful of picturesque fishing towns, including Dennery and Micoud.

👁 Sights

La Tille Waterfalls WATERFALL
(☑489-6271; EC$21; ⊙9am-6pm) Off the beaten track and rarely visited, La Tille is one of the better waterfalls on the island, with

BIRDING IN ST LUCIA

Twitchers are sure to get a buzz in St Lucia – there are a number of desirable new ticks for their list, including five endemic species: the St Lucia parrot, the St Lucia warbler, the St Lucia oriole, the St Lucia peewee and the St Lucia black finch. The St Lucia parrot (*Amazona versicolor*), locally called the Jacquot, is the national bird and appears on everything from T-shirts to St Lucian passports.

Good birdwatching spots include Millet Bird Sanctuary and the Des Cartiers Rainforest Trail.

a high-volume cascade falling into a large pool surrounded by greenery. But a visit here is about more than just the falls; the Rasta guardians of the site constantly work on the flower-filled grounds and a relaxed, natural vibe abounds. There is a nature trail and rope swing, and vegetarian meals are offered.

Mamiku Gardens GARDENS
(☎455-3729; www.mamikugardens.com; EC$20; ☼9am-5pm) A relaxing focal point for any eastern day trip, the Mamiku botanical gardens are located on the grounds of a former plantation and boast an extensive collection of tropical flora including some wonderful orchids. Upon arrival you'll be given a booklet to assist in identifying the 247 named species in the gardens. But it's not just about the plants, there are also historical ruins to explore, hiking trails and birdwatching tours.

🏃 Activities

Between March and August the long stretch of Grande Anse on the northeast coast is a favorite nesting ground for hundreds of leatherback turtles. Visitors are allowed to check out the turtle rookeries at night and observe eggs being laid or hatching – a fantastic spectacle. A licensed guide must accompany all visitors. Note that Grande Anse beach is only accessible by 4WD.

Des Cartiers Rainforest Trail HIKING
(☎715-0350; Desruisseaux; EC$27; ☼8am-3pm Mon-Fri) A 1-mile (2km) loop through stunning, rarely visited rainforest. If you're lucky

you might spot the St Lucia parrot, but even if you don't it's a breathtaking hike. Admission includes the services of a guide. The trailhead is around 6 miles inland from the Dennery highway. It's possible to link this trail with the Edmund Rainforest Trail (p697) above Soufrière.

🛏 Sleeping

Zamaca B&B $$
(☎454-1309; za_ma_ca@hotmail.com; Fond Bay Dr, Escap, Micoud; r US$114) Set in a large modern house overlooking wild Fond Bay, this welcoming B&B features five spacious and comfortable rooms. It's about a 15-minute walk down to the rugged beach, which, like most on this side of the island, is not suitable for swimming. It's an isolated location so you may want to rent a vehicle.

ℹ Getting There & Away

The Castries–Vieux Fort Hwy runs through the heart of the region, and buses running between those cities will drop you anywhere along the route.

The northern reaches of the east side of the island are rugged and isolated. To reach many of the beaches here you'll need a good 4WD or be prepared to hike in.

Marigot Bay

Deep, sheltered Marigot Bay is an exquisite example of natural architecture. Sheltered by towering palms and the surrounding hills, the narrow inlet is said to have once hidden the entire British fleet from French pursuers. Yachts play the same trick these days – the bay is a popular place to drop anchor and hide away for a few nights while enjoying nearby beaches.

◉ Sights & Activities

Millet Bird Sanctuary NATURE RESERVE
(☎519-0787; Millet; walking EC$27, birdwatching EC$81; ☼8:30am-3pm Mon-Fri) This nature reserve lies about 6 miles (10km) inland from the west-coast highway, in Millet. Here's your chance to spot endemic species, including the St Lucia parrot and the St Lucia warbler. Book in advance and a knowledgeable forest ranger will take you on a tour. There's also a scenic 2-mile loop hiking trail that alternates between thick forests and wide-open hilltops.

Dive Fair Helen
WATER SPORTS

(☑451-7716; www.divefairhelen.com; ☺8:30am-4:30pm Mon-Fri, to 12:30pm Sat) Based at Marigot Beach Club, Dive Fair Helen charges US$126 for a two-tank dive, including equipment, and US$78 for a snorkeling excursion (US$56 for kids). It also offers kayaking tours along the coast and up a river (US$66) or further afield to Anse Cochon for lunch and snorkeling, returning by boat (US$132).

🛏 Sleeping

Marigot Bay has an excellent range of accommodations, both down by the waterside and up in the surrounding hills. Most are toward the upper end of the budget spectrum.

Nature's Paradise
B&B $$

(☑458-3550; www.stluciaparadise.com; r incl breakfast US$155-225; 🛜🗶) Nature's Paradise is magical, if you don't mind the rough dirt road between the bay and the B&B. Poised on a greenery-shrouded promontory, it offers cracking views of sea and bay. The two rooms in the main building are a tad small, while the two cottages nestled in a Garden of Eden are roomy and fully equipped.

★ Inn on the Bay
B&B $$$

(☑451-4260; www.saint-lucia.com; r from US$265; 🛜🗶) Outstandingly positioned atop a secluded hill (views!), this peach of a place, run by a Canadian couple, features bright and spacious rooms that open onto a pool and a sunset-friendly deck. A free shuttle takes you to the bay. Alternatively you can take the 300-odd steps down to a secluded cove with good snorkeling.

Capella
HOTEL $$$

(☑458-5300; www.capellahotels.com; r from US$740; ❄🛜🗶) Occupying a nicely landscaped plot on the southern shores of the bay, this upmarket resort is the most comfortable place to stay in the area. The smartly finished rooms boast dark-wood features, clean lines, ample space and heaps of amenities. Service is courteous and professional.

🍴 Eating & Drinking

There are several great places to eat right on the bay. For very cheap eats hike back up the hill into Marigot Village where you'll find a bakery and, in the evenings, a local pizza place.

Masala Bay
INDIAN $$

(☑451-4500; mains EC$32-71; ☺noon-10pm) On a high 2nd-floor balcony at the marina, this Indian place serves up fine curries with great views.

Chateau Mygo
CREOLE $$

(☑451-4722; mains EC$35-90; ☺8am-11pm) This unfussy little eatery could hardly be better situated: the dining deck is right on the waterfront. The menu concentrates on simply prepared seafood and meat dishes served in generous portions.

★ Rainforest Hideaway
FUSION $$$

(☑451-4485; www.rainforesthideawaystlucia.com; menus EC$125-150; ☺5-10pm) This stylish restaurant is perfect for a tête-à-tête. Subdued lighting, elegant furnishings and a breezy deck overlooking the bay will rekindle the faintest romantic flame. The emphasis is on local dishes with a contemporary twist and there's live jazz most nights. It's accessible by a small ferry from the docks.

ℹ Getting There & Away

There's no public transport all the way down to the bay, but Castries–Jacmel buses will drop you at Marigot Village, from where it's a 10-minute walk down the hill.

You'll find a taxi stand right outside the marina. A taxi to or from Castries costs around EC$60.

Soufrière & the Pitons

If one town were to be the heart and soul of St Lucia, it would have to be Soufrière. Its attractions include a slew of colonial-era edifices scattered amid brightly painted wooden storefronts and a bustling seafront.

The surrounding landscape is little short of breathtaking: the skyscraping towers of rock known as the Pitons stand guard over the town. Jutting from the sea, covered in vegetation and ending in a summit that looks otherworldly, these are St Lucia's iconic landmarks.

The area boasts beauty above and below the water as well as historic and natural sights aplenty.

Many visit only as a day trip from the north – don't join them! There are far too many attractions to pack into a couple of hours. Spend a couple of nights down here soaking up the ambience accompanied by the hum of the rainforest.

⊙ Sights

Anse Chastanet   BEACH
Stretched out in front of the resort of the same name, Anse Chastanet is a fine curving beach. The sheltered bay is protected by high cliffs. The snorkeling just offshore is some of the best on the island; hassle-free access is through the resort, which also offers day passes if you want to use the sun loungers and water-sports facilities.

It's a moderate 1-mile walk from Soufrière – just watch out for vehicles along the sheer mountain road. It's also possible to take a water taxi (EC$100 round-trip) from the main dock in town.

★ Anse Mamin   BEACH
Backed by lush rainforest, this dreamy secluded enclave of sand edges a gently curved cove that's about a 10-minute walk north of Anse Chastanet, or about 30 minutes from town. The resort also has sun loungers and a grill restaurant here but they are tastefully done and don't take away from the absolute tranquility.

★ Sugar Beach   BEACH
The most famous beach on the island, gorgeous Sugar Beach is spectacularly situated between the two Pitons, ensuring phenomenal views both from the sand and in the water. Like most in the area, it was originally a gray-sand beach – the soft white sands are imported from abroad. There are free basic public loungers at the far northern end; alternatively, when occupancy is low, you can rent one of the resort's more luxurious models.

Public access is through the Viceroy resort – if you plan on dining at the beachside restaurant or **renting water-sports gear** (☑456-8000; 1/2 tank dives US$85/110) they'll send a shuttle for you. Otherwise it's a long walk from the entrance gate; it feels even longer on the way back up.

Fond Doux Holiday Plantation   PLANTATION
(☑459-7548; www.fonddouxestate.com; tours with snack/lunch US$25/33; ⊙11am-4pm) 🐾 At this bijou hideaway you can catch an informative one-hour walking tour that allows you to take in the plantation, a cocoa-processing plant and a lookout with fine views of the Pitons.

Malgretoute Beach   BEACH
This lovely rugged gray-sand and pebble beach, just north of looming Petit Piton, has some good snorkeling just offshore. There is an interesting petroglyph covered in moss on a large rock about 200m north of the entrance. It faces the jungle so you have to walk around the back to spot it. Or ask local guide Kaya to show you the way – he's usually hanging around the entrance.

Malgretoute is south of Soufrière. Head along the Vieux Fort Rd then take the small road toward Sugar Beach and keep a lookout for the beach access road down the hill. The entire area around Malgretoute has been bought for yet another mega resort, so access may become limited.

Pitons Waterfall   WATERFALL
(☑487-9564; EC$7.50; ⊙6am-5:45pm) In the mood for a dip in tepid waters? Make a beeline for this picturesque cascade surrounded by lush forest that is fed by a mix of natural streams and underground thermal sulfur springs from Soufrière volcano. There are two small concrete pools fed by the main waterfall and another at the end of a side channel. You can shower under the flow but watch out for the slippery rocks.

It's on the road to Jalousie Plantation.

Diamond Falls Botanical Gardens
& Mineral Baths   GARDENS
(☑459-7565; www.diamondstlucia.com; adult/child EC$17.50/8.75, baths from EC$15; ⊙10am-5pm Mon-Sat, to 3pm Sun) Wander amid tropical flowers and trees at this old estate. Mineral baths date from 1784, when they were built atop hot springs so that the troops of France's King Louis XVI could take advantage of their therapeutic effects. You can take a dip in small public pools among the nature or in the less appealing enclosed private bathhouse. The gardens are 1 mile east of Soufrière town center.

There is a lovely trail that ends at a waterfall running down the rock face – but it's for viewing only, visitors are not permitted to bathe under it. Guides congregate outside the entrance and will talk you through the flora as you stroll. They are not permitted to charge a fee but a reasonable gratuity is expected.

Sulphur Springs   LANDMARK
(☑459-7686; admission EC$24, with thermal baths EC$38; ⊙9am-5pm) Looking like something off the surface of the moon, the Sulphur Springs are saddled with the unfortunate tagline of being the world's only drive-in volcano. The reality is far from

CLIMBING THE PITONS

If you have time for only one trek during your stay, choose the Gros Piton (2617ft) climb. Starting from the hamlet of Fond Gens Libres, you walk mostly through a thick jungle. The final section is very steep, but the reward is a tremendous view of southern St Lucia and the densely forested mountains of the interior. Allow roughly four hours there and back. A guide is mandatory; contact **Gros Piton Nature Trail Guides** (p697).

While climbing Petit Piton is discouraged by local authorities – some sections involve clambering on near-vertical slabs of rock – many experienced hikers and climbers do journey to the summit. Expect to take around three to four hours round-trip. The smaller peak affords better views of the island's Caribbean beaches than Gros Piton does.

You can find guides (US$60) at the **Pitons Waterfall** (p696), which is just across from the entrance to the trail, or keep an eye out for the wooden signs advertising guide services on the road on the way in. It's best to begin early as it gets hot on the climb.

the garish description. There isn't a classic crater, or a cauldron of magma, to check out – but it's still an awe-inspiring place. Stinky pools of boiling mud are observed from platforms surrounded by vents releasing clouds of sulfur gas. Younger travelers will love it.

There is a thermally heated river that has been dammed to form a pool where visitors can relax in the mineral-rich waters and apply mud facials. You can even purchase a ball of dried volcano mud to take home and apply in the comfort of your own bathroom.

The springs are a couple of miles south of Soufrière, off the Vieux Fort Rd.

Gateway to Soufrière VIEWPOINT
Around a mile and a half up the road to Castries this lookout at the side of the road affords fantastic views across the Soufrière valley to the Pitons.

🏃 Activities

Diving & Snorkeling
The waters off Soufrière, which have been designated a marine park, are a magnet for divers of all levels. There's a good balance of reef dives, drop-offs and easy dives, as well as a couple of wrecks.

For snorkeling, Anse Chastanet, Anse Mamin and Jalousie Beach offer optimal conditions.

Scuba St Lucia DIVING
(☑459-7000; www.scubastlucia.com; Anse Chastanet Resort; 1/2 tank dives incl equipment US$90/140) Well-organized Scuba St Lucia is right on the beach at Anse Chastanet and has a fleet of good boats.

Action Adventure Divers DIVING
(☑459-5599, 485-1317; Hummingbird Beach Resort) A recommended outfit that offers a wide range of trips and usually keeps groups small.

Hiking
⭐**Tet Paul Nature Trail** HIKING
(☑457-1122; tetpaul2016@gmail.com; off Vieux Fort Rd; tours adult/child EC$27/13.50; ⊗9am-5pm) 🏆 Don't miss this community-run nature trail. During the 45-minute tour, a guide will show you an organic farm and take you to a lookout; the view of the Pitons jabbing the skyline is stunning, but even better are the insights into traditional local life. It's signposted, 3.1 miles south of Soufrière.

Gros Piton Nature Trail Guides CLIMBING
(☑459-3965, 285-7431; www.soufrierefoundation.org; per visitor EC$88) Official guides for climbs up Gros Piton work on a turn-based system out of this office at the trailhead. Turn up before 1pm to ensure a trip.

Edmund Rainforest Trail HIKING
(☑457-1427; EC$27; ⊗8am-3pm Mon-Fri) High in the mountains above Soufrière you'll find the trailhead for this challenging hike into the heart of the St Lucian rainforest. At the entrance there is a van from the Ministry of Agriculture where you'll need to pay the admission fee.

The main route passes up to the island divide to offer views down to the east side. A spur route off the main trail, the Enbas Saut trail, leads to waterfalls deep in the jungle.

If you choose the full route, it's possible to join up with the Des Cartiers trail which finishes at a trailhead above Micoud;

the trail exit is in a remote area so you should organize transport to pick you up in advance.

The trails here are not well signed and guides are highly recommended. The Agriculture Department in Castries can point you in the right direction.

🜄 Tours

★ Jungle Biking
CYCLING

(☑ 457-1400; www.bikestlucia.com; Anse Mamin; 2½hr trips US$65; ⊙ 8am-3:30pm Mon-Sat) This outfit, which is part of the Anse Chastanet Resort (nonguests are welcome), offers mountain-biking tours along trails that meander through the remnants of an old plantation, just next to Anse Mamin beach. It's suitable for all fitness levels. Various stops are organized along the way, where the guide will give you the lowdown on flora, fauna and local history.

Mystic Man Tours
BOATING

(☑ 459-7783; www.mysticmantours.com; Bridge St, Soufrière; ⊙ 8am-4pm Mon-Sat) Runs quality boat excursions in the area, from whale-watching and snorkeling trips to sunset cruises and deep-sea fishing outings.

Real St Lucia Tours
TOURS

(☑ 486-1561; www.realstluciatours.com) A quality operation based out of Soufrière, run by a group of enthusiastic young locals. They offer tailor-made tours across the island.

Rabot Estate
TOURS

(☑ 572-9600; Vieux Fort Rd; tours US$28-61; ⊙ 9-11:30am Mon, Tue & Thu, 1-3:30pm Wed & Fri) The team at the Boucan hotel (p698) offer two interesting chocolate-themed tours on their plantation. The Tree to Bean Tour (US$28) explains everything about cocoa growing and processing while the Bean to Bar Experience (US$61) lets visitors make their own chocolate using beans from the estate. Call to make reservations.

🛏 Sleeping

Most places to stay are fairly isolated, so a rental car is advised. Some hotels provide shuttle services to nearby beaches.

Downtown Hotel
HOTEL $

(☑ 459-7185; www.thedowntownhotel.net; Bridge St; r US$76-92; ❋ 🛜) The Downtown doesn't exactly scream vacation (it's within a small shopping mall), but it's very central,

convenient, well maintained and affordable. Aim for a room at the back for sea views and to avoid the road noise.

Hummingbird Beach Resort
RESORT $$

(☑ 459-7232; www.istlucia.co.uk; Soufrière; r US$100-350; ❋ 🛜 🌊) Friendly, low-key and peaceful, this modest resort is a short walk from both town and Anse Chastanet. The best rooms are the cute cottages with private balconies offering ocean vistas and Piton-centered panoramas. Some of the air-con rooms are a little drab. It's right on the edge of town, making for easy exploration.

★ Fond Doux Resort & Plantation
RESORT $$$

(☑ 459-7545; www.fonddouxestate.com; off Vieux Fort Rd; cottages US$360-510; 🛜 🌊) 🍴 Hidden in the hills to the south of Soufrière, this 250-year-old working cocoa plantation (p696) is a great place to unwind. Fifteen tastefully refurbished cottages with private balconies are surrounded by tropical gardens. Some boast private plunge pools. There is also a fine split-level communal pool with great views, and guests are offered a free plantation tour.

Boucan
RESORT $$$

(Hotel Chocolat; ☑ 572-9600; www.thehotel-chocolat.com; Rabot Estate; r incl breakfast from US$525-775; 🛜 🌊) 🍴 What sets this place apart is the design scheme; cocoa is the dominant theme, and it's no wonder – the resort is set in a cocoa plantation where they make their own chocolate. And all of it is every bit as decadent as fine chocolate – especially the wonderful Piton-view infinity pool. The hotel also prides itself on its engaged ethics.

Viceroy Sugar Beach
RESORT $$$

(☑ 456-8000; www.viceroyhotelsandresorts.com; Anse des Pitons; d incl breakfast US$850; ❋ 🛜 🌊) Boasting the best location on the island, nestled in a coconut grove smack between the Pitons, this luxurious resort opens onto a perfect white-sand beach (p696) – the sand was imported from abroad. Rooms have private plunge pools, hardwood floors and all the amenities you'd expect.

Jade Mountain
RESORT $$$

(☑ 459-4000; www.jademountainstlucia.com; Anse Chastanet; ste US$1185-2835; 🛜 🌊) Sitting castle-like atop a hill, this exclusive resort offers stadium-sized suites (called 'sanctuaries'), many with their own private infinity pools.

Each unit has an open fourth wall with a heavenly view of the Pitons. Rooms also come with 24-hour butler service.

Crystals BOUTIQUE HOTEL $$$
(📞 285-1984; www.stluciacrystals.com; Soufrière; villas from US$250; ❈ 🛜 ☒) Indian and Caribbean touches, wood-carved furnishings and a tree-house bar are just some of the features at this wonderful off-beat retreat. No two cottages are alike, but they all have air-conditioning, private barbecue areas and plunge pools. The views of the Pitons and the valley of Soufrière are mesmerizing.

Stonefield Estate Villa Resort RESORT $$$
(📞 459-5648; www.stonefieldvillas.com; off Vieux Fort Rd; 1-bedroom villas US$400-650; ❈ 🛜 ☒) 🍃 This historic lime plantation estate sports a cache of well-proportioned gingerbread-style cottages with private plunge pools scattered amid a lush property, and glorious views over Petit Piton. Perks include an on-site restaurant, a spa and a pool. The property also has a superb petroglyph inscribed on a big basaltic boulder. It's on the southern outskirts of Soufrière.

Anse Chastanet Resort RESORT $$$
(📞 459-7000; www.ansechastanet.com; Anse Chastanet; r from US$575; ❈ 🛜) The hillside-beachside location is supremely enjoyable. Whether you want to dive, snorkel, cycle, get pampered, experience fine dining or simply do nothing, this resort on its dreamy namesake beach has it all. Rooms down by the beach have air-con while those on the hill get the views.

Ladera RESORT $$$
(📞 459-7323; www.ladera.com; off Vieux Fort Rd; ste incl breakfast US$995-1480; 🛜 ☒) The location is one of the best in St Lucia: an 1100ft-high ridge with full-frame views of the Pitons and the ocean. The spacious rooms have a rich, naturalistic design and their own plunge pools; there's also a spa. It's 2.5 miles south of town.

✖ Eating

Fedo's CARIBBEAN $
(Soufrière; mains EC$12-50; ⊘9am-5pm Mon-Sat) Hidden away on the eastern edges of town several blocks back from the waterfront, this no-nonsense diner serves up quality Creole dishes at reasonable prices. It's difficult to find; ask any local for directions.

Martha's Tables CARIBBEAN $$
(📞 459-2770; off Vieux Fort Rd, Malgretoute; meals from EC$40; ⊘11:30am-2pm Mon-Fri) Just up the hill from Malgretoute Beach, this home-style restaurant is in Martha's actual home. Each day she prepares a spread of excellent comfort food using local flavors. Grab a plastic chair and enjoy.

Hummingbird Beach Resort CARIBBEAN $$
(📞 459-7232; Soufrière; mains EC$58-95; ⊘7am-11pm) Mouth-watering local dishes are intermixed with old favorites to form a perfect culinary balance. The fish is prepared with style and flavor and served up with a great view.

Bamboo CARIBBEAN $$
(Jardin Cacao; 📞 459-7545; www.fonddouxestate.com; Fond Doux Holiday Plantation; mains lunch EC$38-46, dinner EC$43-78; ⊘10am-10pm) 🍃 The emphasis here is on local cuisine, using vegetables that are organically grown on the estate (p696). Some desserts are prepared with cocoa.

★ Orlando's CARIBBEAN $$$
(📞 459-5955; www.orlandosrestaurantstl.com; Cemetery Rd; 3-course meals US$50; ⊘6-9pm Wed-Sun) Chef Orlando Sachell made a name for himself basically inventing the concept of farm-to-table cuisine at some of St Lucia's best resorts. Now he has his own fine restaurant right in Soufrière. The menu changes constantly but the high level of service doesn't. Book in advance.

★ Boucan Restaurant & Bar FUSION $$$
(📞 457-1624; www.hotelchocolat.com/uk/boucan; Rabot Estate; mains EC$57-116; ⊘7am-10am, noon-2:30pm & 6-9:30pm) Succulent cocoa-inspired cuisine in relaxed, contemporary surrounds. You'll find cocoa from the plantation in many plates over all three courses. The dessert menu alone is reason enough to come here – don't miss the crème brûlée, flavored with cocoa. Reserve ahead, as this is one of the island's high-profile spots.

Dasheene CARIBBEAN $$$
(📞 459-7323; Ladera; mains EC$81-130; ⊘7am-9:30pm Mon-Sun) This open-air place in the Ladera resort (p699) serves Caribbean and European fare in magical surrounds, headlined by incomparable Pitons views. Reservations are mandatory.

Shopping

Zaka Masks ARTS & CRAFTS
(☑ 457-1504; www.zaka-art.com; Waterfront; ☺ 9am-5pm Mon-Sat, to 1pm Sun) Walk into this quirky studio on the waterfront in Soufrière and you'll be welcomed by friendly Zaka, who creates lovely wooden masks that are painted in vivid colors. His works embellish a number of hotels on the island. They are irresistible and highly collectible, so bring plenty of cash (or a credit card) if you're thinking of buying.

ⓘ Information

First Caribbean Bank (Church St; ☺ 9am-2pm Mon-Thu, to 4pm Fri) Reliable ATM in town.
Tourism Office (☑ 453-1121; ☺ 9am-5pm Mon-Fri)

ⓘ Getting There & Away

➤ Regular buses connect Soufrière to Castries and the north of the island by a scenic winding mountain road (EC$8, 45 minutes). Take care if driving, as local vehicles often fly around the corners.

➤ There's also a regular bus service connecting the town to Vieux Fort (EC$6, 30 minutes).

Vieux Fort & the South Coast

St Lucia's expansive south coast is stunning, yet most travelers just see it from the window of a taxi after landing at the Hewanorra International Airport.

St Lucia's second-largest town lies on a vast plain at the southern tip of the island, where the azure waters of the Caribbean Sea blend with those of the rough Atlantic Ocean. Vieux Fort won't leap to the top of your list of preferred destinations in St Lucia but the coastal area is scenic. The town fronts a lovely bay that is recognized as a prime destination for kitesurfing and windsurfing; it's also a lovely place for a walk.

◉ Sights & Activities

The combination of constant strong breezes, protected areas with calm water, and a lack of obstacles make the bay of Anse de Sables a world-class destination for kitesurfers and windsurfers.

Sandy Beach BEACH
At the southern tip of the island, Sandy Beach is a beautiful strand of white sand that always has a stiff breeze, which makes it a hot spot for kitesurfers. It's also suitable for swimming – on a calm day. It's never crowded.

★ **Atlantic Shores Stables** HORSEBACK RIDING
(☑ 285-1090; atlanticshores758@gmail.com; adult/child from US$65/55) Professionally run stables offering a range of great rides along beaches and through the lush countryside in the south of the island. The horses are in great condition and the landscapes here are wild and inspiring.

Reef Kite & Surf KITESURFING
(☑ 454-3418; www.slucia.com/kitesurf; Sandy Beach, Anse des Sables, Vieux Fort; rentals per half-day from US$70) A two-hour 'taster session' is US$100; a three-hour course costs US$220. It also rents kayaks (US$12 per hour) that can be paddled over to the Maria Islands.

🛏 Sleeping

Accommodations in Vieux Fort are very limited. There are a couple of simple hotels in town but they mainly cater to regional business travelers and don't have much island atmosphere.

Reef Beach Huts GUESTHOUSE $
(☑ 454-3418; www.kitesurfstlucia.com; Sandy Beach, Anse de Sables, Vieux Fort; r incl breakfast US$65) There are four simple rooms in a wooden lodge out the back of the Reef Cafe (p701). They don't have any views, get quite hot during the day and suffer from road noise from the highway – but the location is a hit: you're just steps from the water.

Charlery's Inn HOTEL $
(☑ 454-6448; www.charlerysinnslu.com; r from US$65) Located in a building that looks like an office block right beside the bus stops, the rooms here are nothing special, but they're clean and will do the trick if you just need a place to crash close to the center. If there's no one in reception ask in the gas station across the road.

★ **Balenbouche Estate** HERITAGE HOTEL $$
(☑ 455-1244; www.balenbouche.com; Balenbouche; r US$120-180; ☎) Between Choiseul and Laborie you'll find this tranquil 18th-century estate home with an eco-bent, comprising four simple yet delightful all-wood garden cottages. You really feel that you've stepped back in time here; complete

the experience with a stroll round the grounds and the truly atmospheric jungle-covered mill ruins. There is no pool, but there are two dark-colored sandy beaches nearby.

✕ Eating

★ Reef Cafe
INTERNATIONAL $

(☎ 454-3418; Anse de Sables; mains EC$24-32, light meals EC$10-20; ⊙ 8am-10pm Tue-Sun, to 6pm Mon) Sit under the trees at tables with sea views and tuck into some of the best cuisine on the south of the island at this casual cafe. The Creole seafood dishes are delectable and there's also great lasagna and salads. Excellent value.

Island Breeze
CARIBBEAN $$

(☎ 454-6754; Anse de Sables; mains EC$35-60; ⊙ 9am-10pm) Pull up a table at this attractive wooden restaurant right on the sand and enjoy quality Caribbean specialties with a view. The seafood plates are great, and the ribs and jerk dishes are also winners. It's also a fresh spot to get out of the sun and enjoy a drink.

❶ Getting There & Away
➡ Public minivans for Soufrière (EC$6, 50 minutes) leave when full from the intersection near the Sol gas station.

➡ Buses for Castries (EC$8, one hour) depart from near the roundabout on the eastern edge of town and take the eastern road via Dennery.

UNDERSTAND ST LUCIA

History
Archaeological finds on the island indicate that St Lucia was settled by Arawaks between 1000 BC and 500 BC. Around AD 800 migrating Caribs conquered the Arawaks and established permanent settlements.

St Lucia was outside the routes taken by Columbus during his four visits to the New World and was probably first sighted by Spanish explorers during the early 1500s. Caribs successfully fended off two British attempts at colonization in the 1600s, only to be faced with French claims to the island a century down the road, when they established the island's first lasting European settlement, Soufrière, in 1746 and went about developing plantations. St Lucia's colonial history was marred by warfare, however, as the British still maintained their claim to the island.

In 1778 the British successfully invaded St Lucia and established naval bases at Gros Islet and Pigeon Island, which they used as staging grounds for attacks on the French islands to the north. For the next few decades possession of St Lucia seesawed between the British and the French. In 1814 the Treaty of Paris finally ceded the island to the British, ending 150 years of conflict during which St Lucia changed flags 14 times.

Culturally the British were slow in replacing French customs, and it wasn't until 1842 that English nudged out French as St Lucia's official language. Other customs linger, and to this day many speak a French-based patois among themselves, attend Catholic services and live in villages with French names.

St Lucia gained internal autonomy in 1967 and then achieved full independence, as a member of the Commonwealth, on February 22, 1979. Politics has stabilized in recent times, with election results usually coming in the form of landslide victories for the opposing party. The downturn in the banana industry has meant that a diversification of industry is vital for economic prosperity. Tourism is now the main source of revenue.

In late 2010 the island was severely hit by a hurricane, which caused much damage in the Soufrière area.

People & Culture
St Lucians are generally laid-back, friendly people influenced by a mix of their English, French, African and Caribbean origins. For instance, if you walk into the Catholic cathedral in Castries, you'll find a building of French design, an interior richly painted in bright African-inspired colors, portraits of a Black Madonna and child, and church services delivered in English. About 85% of St Lucians are Roman Catholics.

The population is about 170,000, one-third of whom live in Castries. Approximately 85% are of pure African ancestry. Another 10% are a mixture of African, British, French and Indian ancestry, while about 4% are of pure Indian or European descent.

The predominantly African heritage can be seen in the strong family ties that St Lucians hold and the survival of many traditional customs and superstitions. Obeah (Vodou) is still held in equal measures of respect and fear in places like Anse La Raye.

The local snakeman is visited by islanders for his medicinal powers. One such muscular remedy he uses involves massaging the thick fat of the boa constrictor on aching limbs.

There is an eclectic mix of cultural ideologies within St Lucia. But with the arrival of globalization, economic disparity has had a negative effect on the cultural identity of some young people. Violent crime, mostly drug-related, is on the rise.

Landscape & Wildlife

The Land

The striking landmass of St Lucia is one of its defining features. At only 27 miles long, the teardrop-shaped island packs a variety of topography into its 238 sq miles. Standing nearly as tall as they are long, the rolling hills and towering peaks of the interior make this green island an apparition of altitude rising from the sea.

Banana plantations dominate every flat section of land, and some not so flat. The Caribbean cash crop is a staple industry for St Lucia. Lush tropical jungle forms a rat's nest of gnarled rainforest, filling the interior of the island with thick bush.

In the north the island flattens out a little and the beaches get a bit wider – allowing infrastructure to get a foothold. In the south the land rises sharply and continues in folds of green hills that stretch right to the shoreline. It's in this portion of the island, near Soufrière, that St Lucia's iconic

landmarks are found. The twin peaks of the Pitons, which are extinct volcano cones, rise 2600ft from the sea and dominate the horizon.

Wildlife

St Lucia's vegetation ranges from dry and scrubby areas of cacti and hibiscus to lush, jungly valleys with wild orchids, bromeliads, heliconias and lianas.

Under the British colonial administration much of St Lucia's rainforest was targeted for timber harvesting. In many ways the independent St Lucian government has proved a far more effective environmental force, and while only about 10% of the island remains covered in rainforest, most of that has now been set aside as nature reserve. The largest indigenous trees in the rainforest are the gommier, a towering gum tree, and the chatagnier, a huge buttress-trunked tree.

Fauna includes endemic birds, bats, lizards, iguanas, tree frogs, introduced mongooses, rabbitlike agoutis and several snake species, including the fer-de-lance and the boa constrictor.

SURVIVAL GUIDE

ℹ Directory A–Z

ACCOMMODATIONS

St Lucia has a pretty wide range of accommodations options. In addition to swish hotels and all-inclusive resorts, which form the core of the market, it offers a range of more intimate ventures, including boutique inns and self-catering villas.

Most accommodations are concentrated in the area from the northeast down to Marigot Bay. If you prefer a quiet retreat, opt for the Soufrière area. Many hotels have an on-site restaurant.

CHILDREN

Although purpose-made kids' attractions are scarce, St Lucia is an eminently suitable destination for those traveling with children. With its abundance of beaches and opportunities for outdoor activities, including horseback riding, snorkeling, zip-lining and diving, there's plenty to do in a generally safe environment. Whale- and dolphin-watching excursions are also popular with families.

SLEEPING PRICE RANGES

Taxes, which include a 10% service charge and a 10% government tax, are included in our listed prices. Watch out, though, because most places will quote before-tax prices.

$ less than US$85

$$ US$85 to US$200

$$$ more than US$200

There are some hotels that won't take children under a certain age, but a number of all-inclusive resorts cater specifically to families and have an impressive range of amenities for children. Most hotels also offer reduced rates for children staying in their parents' room.

ELECTRICITY
220V (50 cycles); three-pronged, UK-style plugs.

EMBASSIES & CONSULATES
UK High Commission (📞 452-2485, 452-2484; Francis Compton Bldg, 2nd fl, PO Box 227, Castries)

EMERGENCY NUMBERS

Country Code	📞 758
Emergency Line	📞 999

FOOD
Dining options on St Lucia are fantastically varied, with local French-Creole– inspired dishes jostling for space on menus alongside pan-Caribbean classics and quality international cuisine.

All over the island you'll find 'fish fry' events where local seafood is grilled outside on massive barbecues and eaten at communal picnic tables.

Rodney Bay Village and the nearby marina on the north side of the island are lined with modern, high-end international eateries.

Essential Food & Drink
Seafood Dorado (also known as mahimahi), kingfish, marlin, snapper, lobster, crab and shellfish feature high on the menu.
Meat dishes Chicken and pork dishes are commonly found.
Local specialties Try callaloo soup, *lambi* (conch) and salt fish with green fig (seasoned salt cod and boiled green banana).
Piton The beer of St Lucia; crisp and sweet, it's perfectly light and refreshing.
St Lucian rum The island's sole distillery produces white rums, gold rums and flavored rums.

GLBT TRAVELERS
As with most destinations in the region, St Lucia isn't all that friendly to those identifying as LGBT. While problems aren't as serious as in some larger Caribbean nations, gay men should be especially aware that homosexuality is generally not accepted in St Lucian society.

HEALTH
You'll find major public medical facilities in Castries and Vieux Fort, as well as smaller clinics

---

EATING PRICE RANGES

Eating places can be categorized according to the following price brackets, based on the cost of the cheapest main meal, inclusive of taxes.

$ less than EC$35

$$ EC$35 to EC$70

$$$ more than EC$70

---

around the island; however, the public system is for the most part slow and inefficient. There are good private clinics in the north of the island, the best of which is the **Tapion Hospital** (📞 459-2000; www.tapion-hospital.com; Tapion Rd, La Toc) just south of Castries.

MONEY
The Eastern Caribbean dollar (EC$) is the island's currency.

Visa, American Express and MasterCard are widely accepted at hotels, car-rental agencies, shops and restaurants.

Currency
Prices for many tourist services, including accommodations, activities, excursions and car hire, are often quoted in US dollars and can be paid in US dollars. But you can also pay the equivalent in EC dollars or with a major credit card.

Exchange Rates
The Eastern Caribbean dollar is pegged to the US dollar at a rate of 2.70 to 1.

AUSTRALIA	A$1	EC$1.99
BARBADOS	B$1	EC$1.35
CANADA	C$1	EC$2
EUROPE	€1	EC$2.85
JAPAN	¥100	EC$2.40
NEW ZEALAND	NZ$1	EC$1.89
UK	UK£1	EC$3.35
US	US$1	EC$2.70

For current exchange rates, see www.xe.com.

Tipping
A 10% tax and 10% service charge are added to the bill at all but the cheapest hotels and restaurants; there's no need for additional tipping.

PRACTICALITIES

Newspapers *The Voice* (www.thevoic-eslu.com) is the island's main, triweekly newspaper.

Radio Tune into music, news and patois programs on Radio Caribbean International (101.1FM).

Smoking St Lucia does not yet have blanket regulations on smoking. In general smoking is not permitted in enclosed spaces. Most restaurants and bars no longer permit smoking.

Weights & Measures St Lucia uses the imperial system.

PUBLIC HOLIDAYS

In addition to holidays observed throughout the region, St Lucia has the following public holidays:

New Year's Holiday January 2
Independence Day February 22
Labor Day May 1
Corpus Christi Ninth Thursday after Easter
Emancipation Day August 3
Thanksgiving Day October 5
National Day December 13

TAXES & REFUNDS

St Lucia has a 15% VAT on most retail products. There is no mechanism in place for visitors to reclaim taxes upon leaving the country.

TELEPHONE

St Lucia's area code is ☎ 758. To call from abroad, dial your country's international access code plus 758 and the seven-digit local number.

TIME

St Lucia is on GMT/UTC-4; the same as its Windward Island neighbors.

CITY TIME	DIFFERENCE
Auckland	+17
Cape Town	+6
London	+4
Los Angeles	-4
Miami	-1
New Delhi	+9.5
New York	-1
Sydney	+15
Tokyo	+13

TRAVELERS WITH DISABILITIES

➟ Most resorts have some facilities for travelers with disabilities, but it is best to inquire before heading out.

➟ The area around Rodney Bay Village has good wide sidewalks and some ramps but the rest of the country is difficult for travelers with limited mobility.

➟ Public transport is not designed for travelers with disabilities, and getting in and out of minivans is likely to pose some difficulty.

ⓘ Getting There & Away

AIR

St Lucia receives direct long-haul flights from the US, UK and Europe. It also has regional connections to Antigua, Martinique, Trinidad and Tobago, Barbados and St Vincent.

St Lucia has two airports:

Hewanorra International Airport (UVF; www.slaspa.com) in Vieux Fort is at the remote southern tip of the island. It handles flights from North America, the UK and Europe plus a few regional flights.

George FL Charles Airport (SLU; www.slaspa.com) is conveniently located in Castries but due to the short runway is only served by regional flights on prop planes from Liat (www.liat.com), Air Caraibes (www.aircaraibes.com) and Caribbean Airlines (www.caribbeanairlines.com).

SEA
Cruise Ship

Cruise ships dock in Castries, either at Pointe Seraphine or right in town at La Place Carenage. Smaller vessels sometimes call at Soufrière; they anchor offshore and bring passengers ashore via tenders.

Ferry

The fast-ferry service **L'Express des Îles** (☎ 456-5022; www.express-des-iles.com) operates a daily 80-minute express catamaran between the **ferry terminal** in Castries and Fort-de-France on Martinique. It also has continuing service to Dominica (four hours) and Guadeloupe (seven hours). Departure days and times change frequently; check in advance.

Yacht

Customs and immigration can be cleared at Rodney Bay, Castries, Marigot Bay, Soufrière or Vieux Fort. Most yachties pull in at Rodney Bay, where there is a full-service marina and a couple of marked customs slips opposite the customs office.

It's easy to clear customs and immigration at Marigot Bay, where you can anchor in the inner harbor and dinghy over to the customs office.

Castries is a more congested scene, and yachts entering the harbor are required to go directly to the customs dock. If there's no room you should head for the anchorage spot east of the customs buoy. In Soufrière the customs office is right on the waterfront. At Vieux Fort you can anchor off the big ship dock, where customs is located.

Popular anchorages include Reduit Beach, the area southeast of Pigeon Island, Rodney Bay Marina, Marigot Bay, Anse Chastanet, Anse Cochon and Soufrière Bay.

Yacht charters are available in Marigot Bay and Rodney Bay.

Bateau Mygo (☑721-7007; www.bateaumygo. com)

Caribbean Yachting (☑522-4861; www.caribbeanyachtingbj.com; Rodney Bay Marina)

DSL Yachting (☑452-8531; www.dsl-yachting. com; Rodney Bay Marina)

Moorings (☑451-4357; www.moorings.com)

❶ Getting Around

AIR

There is a domestic helicopter link (per passenger US$165, 10 minutes) between George FL Charles Airport, near Castries, and Hewanorra International Airport, near Vieux Fort, which is convenient if you're staying in the north and have a long-haul flight.

BOAT

Water taxis can be hired to travel to virtually anywhere on the west side of the island, with the most popular routes running between Rodney Bay in the north and Marigot Bay or Soufrière in the south.

BUS

Bus service is via privately owned minivans. They're a cheap way to get around. St Lucia's main road forms a big loop around the island, and buses stop at all towns along the way. They're frequent between main towns and generally run until around 7pm, except on the busy Castries–Gros Islet corridor where they run until after 10pm. With the exception of services in the north, very few run on Sunday.

In urban areas buses are only permitted to stop at designated bus stops. In rural areas, if there's no bus stop nearby, you can wave buses down anywhere on the route as long as there's space for the bus to pull over. When you want to get off, announce your intention by calling out 'stopping driver' well in advance of your stop.

Sample fares from Castries to Gros Islet or Marigot Bay are EC$2.50, and to Soufrière, EC$8. Route numbers and destinations are displayed on the buses.

CAR & MOTORCYCLE

Drivers are required to purchase a local driving permit (US$22), which is sold by the car-rental companies, although authorities are now accepting international driver's licenses.

➡ Drive on the left-hand side.

➡ Speed limits are generally 15mph (24km/h) in towns and 30mph (48km/h) on bigger roads.

Rental

➡ You can rent a car when you arrive in St Lucia, be it at the airport or in town.

➡ Most companies require the driver to be at least 25 years old and to have had a driver's license for at least three years.

➡ Some major rental firms have franchises here but you'll often find better prices with local outfits.

➡ The cheapest cars rent for about US$60 a day.

➡ Nearly all car-rental agencies offer unlimited mileage.

➡ If you're planning an extensive tour of the island, it's advisable to hire a 4WD, as many of the roads are steep and smaller ones can become little more than potholed mudslides after a bout of rain.

Avis (www.avisstlucia.com; George FL Charles Airport)

Courtesy Car Rentals (☑452-8140; www. courtesycarrentals.com)

H&B Car Rental (☑452-0872; Reduit Beach Ave, Rodney Bay Village; ⊗8am-6pm)

National (☑450-8721; www.stlucia-car-rental. com)

Sixt (www.sixt.com)

West Coast Jeeps (☑459-5457; www.westcoastjeeps.com)

Road Conditions

Main roads are generally good, while conditions on secondary roads vary greatly with some sections being newly surfaced and others peppered with abyssal potholes. Make sure you have a workable jack and spare tire available. Many of the interior and southern roads are also very winding and narrow.

Gas stations are distributed around the island.

TAXI

Taxis are available at the airports, the harbor, in front of major hotels and at taxi ranks in towns. They aren't metered but more or less adhere to standard fares, especially on short trips. On longer journeys prices are somewhat negotiable. Confirm the fare before getting in.

Poly's Tours (☑452-8525) Offers transport and tours all over the island at affordable rates.

St-Martin/Sint Maarten

POP ST-MARTIN 36,824; SINT MAARTEN 40,917 / ☏ ST-MARTIN 590; SINT MAARTEN 1-721

Best Places to Eat

➡ Le Pressoir (p716)

➡ Le Shambala Restaurant (p716)

➡ Côté Plages (p718)

➡ Canoa (p719)

➡ L'Escargot (p709)

Best Places to Sleep

➡ Le Temps des Cerises (p715)

➡ L'Esplanade (p715)

➡ Les Balcons d'Oyster Pond (p719)

➡ Marquis Boutique Hotel (p718)

Why Go?

The world's smallest area of land divided into two nations, this half-French, half-Dutch island's fascinating cultural mix incorporates a rich African heritage and 120 different nationalities speaking 80-plus languages, giving rise to some of the finest cuisine in the Caribbean.

A major cruise-ship port and air hub, St-Martin/Sint Maarten's number-one focus is tourism. Spread out around the island are 37 white-sand, palm-fringed beaches, from busy stretches lined with pumping bars to tranquil hidden bays and coves. Water sports from snorkeling and diving to Jet Skiing abound, along with land-based adventures like hiking and treetop ziplining.

It's a remarkable recovery for an island that has been ravaged by hurricanes. In the last two or so decades alone, it's experienced eight ferocious storms including 1995's Luis, which decimated large swathes of the island and left thousands of residents homeless, and 2014's Gonzalo. Today, you'll see signs of ongoing reconstruction as rebuilding continues.

When to Go

Feb–Mar The party's in full swing during the Heineken Regatta and Carnival festivities.

May–Jun Capitalize on reduced prices and quieter beachscapes before hurricane season roars up.

Nov–early Dec Stop by just before the massive crowds roll in for the holiday season.

St-Martin & Sint Maarten Highlights

1 **Loterie Farm** (p714)
Flying through the treetops on a zipline or lounging in a cabana by this oasis-like plantation's spring-fed pool.

2 **Topper's Rhum** (p710)
Bottling your own rum as part of a behind-the-scenes tour of Topper's distillery in Simpson Bay.

3 **Îlet Pinel** (p710)
Hopping on a boat for a day of snorkeling and sunbathing on this tiny islet off St-Martin's northeast coast.

4 **Corail Helicopters** (p714) Swooping over the dazzling turquoise waters aboard a helicopter departing

from the Aéroport de Saint-Martin Grand Case.

5 **Flavors of St Martin** (p708) Setting off from Philipsburg's Amsterdam Cheese & Liquor Store on an island-wide food tour with plenty of tastings en route.

SINT MAARTEN

Sint Maarten, the Dutch side of the island, is completely different from the French side. With its tourist-friendly nightlife, slew of shopping centers including duty-free shops in capital Philipsburg, tacky casinos, numerous condo units and sprawling resorts, it can sometimes feel overdeveloped and artificial, but you'll also find a few peaceful, picturesque beaches around Simpson Bay and Little Bay.

Philipsburg

Philipsburg, the capital of St-Martin/Sint Maarten's Dutch side, sprawls out along a wide arcing bay that mostly functions as an outdoor shopping mall (and red-light district) for cruise-goers. There are some older buildings that survived the hurricanes mixed among the new, but overall the town is far more commercial than quaint. Most of the duty-free shops are along Front St, while one block south, the Boardwalk is jammed with boisterous beach bars.

◉ Sights

Sint Maarten Museum MUSEUM
(☑542-4917; www.museumsintmaarten.org; 7 Front St; by donation; ⊙10am-4pm Mon-Fri) Arawak pottery shards, plantation-era artifacts, period photos and a few items from HMS *Proselyte*, the frigate that sank off Fort Amsterdam in 1801, are among the displays at this island history museum, along with exhibits covering 1995's devastating Hurricane Luis, the salt industry and slavery. The little shop downstairs sells an assortment of Caribbean arts and crafts.

★ That Yoda Guy Museum MUSEUM
(☑542-4009; http://netdwellers.com/mo/ygme/index.html; 19 Front St; US$12; ⊙10:30am-4pm Mon & Sat, 9:15am-5pm Tue-Fri, plus 10:30am-4pm Sun when cruise ships in port) Run by Nick Malley, who helped create Yoda of *Star Wars* fame, this 1st-floor museum starts with a short film about the creator and his work on *Star Wars*. It then winds though an exhibit of movie memorabilia including photos, Han Solo frozen in carbonite, a functioning robotic Yoda puppet, scripts, posters, storyboards, and items from other films Malley has worked on including *Men In Black*, *Alien*, *Terminator* and *Hellraiser*. Malley is often here in person and can autograph gift-shop purchases.

🏃 Activities

Sea Trek Diving WATER SPORTS
(☑520-2346; www.seatrekstmaarten.com; Bobby's Marina; sea trek per person US$109; ⊙by reservation) Experience dazzling marine life without scuba diving on a 'sea trek': a 30-minute guided walk along the sea floor at a depth of around 6m wearing a full-head helmet hooked up to an air hose so you can breath normally. A water taxi whisks you to Little Bay, where there are natural and artificial reefs including a sunken helicopter.

Octopus Diving DIVING
(☑in St-Martin 0590-29-11-27; http://octopusdiving.com; Bobby's Marina; 2-tank dive US$99, snorkeling excursion US$55, snorkeling-gear rental per day US$10; ⊙7am-5pm) Based in Grand Case, PADI-affiliated Octopus (p714) also has this handy second location in Philipsburg.

Trisport OUTDOORS
(☑588-6009; www.trisportsxm.com; Bobby's Marina; ⊙10am-5pm Mon-Sat) This versatile outfit has a range of bike, kayak and snorkeling tours (from US$49) and an 'Amazing Race' (styled after the TV show; US$75). It also offers rentals of bikes (per day US$25), stand-up paddleboards (per hour US$25), surf-ski kayaks (per hour US$25) and kayaks (per hour US$15).

☞ Tours

★ Flavors of St Martin FOOD & DRINK
(☑in Puerto Rico +787-964-2447; http://stmartinfoodtours.com; adult/child US$120/90) A 4½-hour tour by air-conditioned bus is a fantastic way to discover the French, Dutch and Caribbean flavors of this multicultural island. Tours meet at the Amsterdam Cheese & Liquor Store (p709), starting with a cheese tasting, before heading off to sample sizzling barbecue fare, local rum, seafood and Sint Maarten–made gelato, learning about the island's history en route. Arrive hungry.

🛏 Sleeping

Philipsburg is largely the domain of cruise-ship passengers, so it's not the best place if you're looking for a secluded paradise. There is a handful of sleeping options but be aware that some properties here are rented on an hourly basis. If you're keen to stay on the Dutch side, Maho and Simpson Bay are more appealing options.

Pasanggrahan Royal Guest House
HOTEL $$

(542-3588; www.pasanhotel.net; 19 Front St; d/ste/penthouse from US$185/289/1500; ❋ 🛜) The restaurant and lobby of this historical property occupy a former plantation-style governor's residence, which has a prime spot on both the beach and Front St. Some of its spacious, dark-timber-furnished rooms have kitchenettes. Suites have four-poster beds; the penthouse sleeps up to six people.

Holland House Beach Hotel
HOTEL $$

(542-2572; www.hhbh.com; 43 Front St; d/top-floor ste incl breakfast from US$255/600; ❋ 🛜) Opening directly onto the beach, Holland House has spacious rooms facing either the ocean or the street; oceanfront ones have balconies overlooking the cruise ships when they're in port. Some have kitchenettes; the penthouse suite has a patio, outdoor Jacuzzi and unrivaled views. Its Ocean Lounge Restaurant & Bar (p709) is always buzzing.

🍴 Eating & Drinking

Beach bars crowd the Boardwalk. Be sure to sample the island's specialty Guavaberry liqueur at the Guavaberry Emporium (p709).

⭐ L'Escargot
FRENCH $$$

(542-2483; www.lescargotrestaurant.com; 96 Front St; snail menus US$10.50-14.50, mains US$24.50-44.50; 11:30am-3pm & 6-10:30pm) An enchanting traditional Creole cottage painted a rainbow of vivid colors, this charmer is even more inviting inside with sepia lighting, embroidered tablecloths and Édith Piaf recordings playing in the background. House-specialty escargots (snails) are served in the shell with garlic and parsley butter or baked in mushroom caps. Other French classics include sole meunière or cognac-flambéed duck breast.

Ocean Lounge Restaurant & Bar
SEAFOOD, INTERNATIONAL $$$

(542-2572; www.hhbh.com; Holland House Beach Hotel, Boardwalk; mains US$16-38, whole lobster US$65, seafood platter for 2 US$115; kitchen 7am-10pm, bar to midnight) With a breezy terrace opening onto the seafront, the restaurant and bar at the Holland House Beach Hotel (p709) is a popular place for a sunset beverage or all-out meal of fish, gourmet burgers (including a lobster surf-and-turf option) or grilled whole lobster. Seafood

CARNIVAL TWO WAYS

On the French side of the island, Carnival celebrations (www.sxm-carnival.com) are held during the traditional five-day Mardi Gras period that ends on Ash Wednesday. On the Dutch side, which has the larger Carnival, activities usually begin the second week after Easter and last for two weeks. Events are centered at Carnival Village on the north side of Philipsburg.

platters come with grilled lobster, sashimi tuna, king crab, fresh oysters and shrimp.

🛍 Shopping

Amsterdam Cheese & Liquor Store
FOOD & DRINKS

(581-5408; 26 Juancho Yrausquin Blvd; 8:30am-5:30pm Mon-Sat, 11am-4pm Sun) Free samples of Dutch cheeses including Gouda, Old Amsterdam, Edam and Maaslander are on offer at this emporium, which sells cheeses in varying sizes (vacuum packed on request) alongside *jenever* (Dutch gin), spicy *speculaas* cookies, tulips, delftware and Texel wine. Get your car-park ticket stamped upon purchase for free parking.

Guavaberry Emporium
DRINKS

(http://guavaberry.com; 8 Front St; 9:30am-5:30pm) Located inside an original Dutch West Indies town house built in the late 1700s, this emporium produces the official liqueur of St-Martin/Sint Maarten. It's made from rum, cane sugar and wild guavaberries from the island's interior, and has a bittersweet spiced flavor. There are free tastings and bottles for sale.

ℹ Information

Post office (2 N Debrot St; 7:30am-5pm Mon-Thu, to 4:30pm Fri, 8-11:30am Sat)
Sint Maarten Tourist Bureau (542-2337; www.visitstmaarten.com; Vineyard Office Park, 33 WG Buncamper Rd; 9am-5pm Mon-Fri) Limited tourist information.

GETTING THERE & AWAY

Philipsburg is home to the **Port St Maarten** (p724) cruise-ship terminal, where you'll find taxis and car-rental companies, as well as marinas with services to St-Barthélemy and Saba. Buses are infrequent, so a taxi or your own wheels are best.

Simpson Bay

Although close to the runway at Princess Juliana International Airport (p723), beautiful Simpson Bay has some of the most captivating crystal tidewater out of all the beaches on the island. Swimming and sunbathing aside, other pursuits here include boating, horseback riding and heading behind the scenes of a rum distillery (p710).

🏃 Activities

Seaside Nature Park
HORSEBACK RIDING

(☑544-5255; www.seasidenaturepark.com; 64 Cay Bay Rd; 2hr ride from US$65, 2hr sunset ride US$90; ⏱1-5pm Wed, Sat & Sun) Canter through the headland's dry scrub and cacti to the beach for a horseback ride along the sand (or in the shallow water). Sunset rides finish with a beachside bonfire and champagne. Lessons lasting 45 minutes cost US$45. The property also has a small farm where you can see and pet miniature horses, rabbits, turtles, peacocks, geese and ducks.

Random Wind
BOATING

(☑587-5742; www.randomwind.com; Skip Jack's Marina, Welfare Rd; day trip adult/child US$109/55) The 54ft yacht *Random Wind* has circumnavigated the globe twice and now runs day trips for up to 20 passengers out to some of the quieter bays around the island. Trips include snorkeling gear, lunch and an open bar.

Aqua Mania Adventures
BOATING

(☑544-2640; www.stmaarten-activities.com; Pelican Marina, Simpson Bay Resort) Aqua Mania has a host of tours, including half-day snorkeling trips (from US$45), sunset lagoon cruises (from US$40), and day trips (from US$75) such as round-island trips and excursions to Îlet Pinel and Tintamarre island, as well as Anguilla's Prickly Pear Cays. It also operates the M/V Edge (p724) ferry to/from St-Barthélemy, and can arrange transfers to/from Princess Juliana International Airport .

☞ Tours

★ Topper's Rhum
DISTILLERY

(☑520-4903; www.toppersrhumtours.com; Bay 3, 9 Well Rd; tour US$20; ⏱tours by reservation) Tours lasting 1½ hours take you behind the scenes of this distillery, where you learn the history of rum-making in the Caribbean and view the creation, blending and bottling processes, followed by a tasting session. Infusions include coconut; spice; banana, vanilla and cinnamon; mocha; and white chocolate and raspberry. You can bottle your own rum to take home.

✨ Festivals & Events

Heineken Regatta
SAILING

(http://heinekenregatta.com; ⏱early Mar) This hugely popular, long-running annual event bills itself as 'serious fun' and features competitions for racing yachts, large sailboats and small multihulls around the island.

🛏 Sleeping

The southern end of Simpson Bay is home to several resorts and hotels (of varying quality). Just south of the airport you'll find a handful of hotels opening onto the beach.

Mary's Boon
HOTEL $$

(☑545-7000; http://visitmarysboon. com; 117 Simpson Bay Rd; studio/1-bedroom/2-bedroom apt from US$135/225/275; ❖❢❅) A stone's throw from the airport runway, this plantation-style inn with bright Caribbean colors is bang on the beach. Options span plain, partially underground rooms with no view to pricier options opening onto the sand. It's undergoing rolling renovations, so check on their progress before you book. All rooms have kitchenettes; its restaurant also serves breakfast, lunch, dinner and 60-plus wines.

🍴 Eating & Drinking

Beach bars south of the airport serve barbecue fare and international dishes such as burgers. A string of restaurants also overlook Simpson Bay Lagoon.

Self-caterers should head to the well-stocked **Carrefour** (Union Rd, Cole Bay; ⏱8am-8pm Mon-Sat, 9am-6pm Sun) supermarket.

Top Carrot
VEGETARIAN, CAFE $

(☑544-3381; 68 Welfare Rd; dishes US$8-16; ⏱7:30am-6pm; ❢❢) 🌿 Boho hangout Top Carrot serves up scrumptious, mostly veggie options in a chilled-out cushion-clad dining room adjoining a New Age shop selling crystals, candles et al. It makes its own Bulgarian yogurt, pastries such as quiches and cinnamon scrolls, and market-fresh salads, using primarily locally grown ingredients. There's also a wide range of freshly squeezed juices, smoothies and herbal teas.

Carousel   GELATO **$**
(http://carouselstmaarten.com; 60a Welfare Rd; gelato or ice cream per 1/2/3 scoops US$4/6/9; ⏰2-10:30pm Mon-Thu, to 11pm Fri-Sun; 🛜) After you've deliberated over 30-plus ice cream and gelato flavors, and peeked through the glass windows to watch them being made, head out the back to ride this gelateria's beautiful old-fashioned carousel (aka merry-go-round; per ride US$2), which was imported piece by piece from Italy. Mouthwatering gelato flavors include soursop, grapefruit and mint, tamarind, guavaberry, raspberry, passionfruit and pineapple.

★ Karakter   INTERNATIONAL **$$**
(☎523-9983; http://karakterstmaarten.com; Simpson Bay; mains US$10-32; ⏰kitchen 9am-10pm, bar to 11pm Mon-Fri, to midnight Sat & Sun) Footsteps from the turquoise water, just behind the airport runway, this fabulous dilapidated bus-turned-beach bar serves breakfast (including fresh OJ and strong coffee), and gourmet salads, sandwiches and burgers at lunch. Dinner mains include barbecued lobster, crab, snapper, triggerfish and tuna, grilled rack of lamb, chicken cordon bleu, and veggie options such as ratatouille. Live music plays most weekend evenings.

★ Kokomo   BAR
(☎553-7815; www.kokomo-sxm.com; Little Bay; ⏰11am-7pm, kitchen to 5pm, closed Sep & Oct) Way down in Kokomo, reached by a steep, bumpy 400m drive off AJC Brouwer Rd, cabanas spread out beneath palm trees on the powdery sand and a beach bar made from raw timbers provide an idyllic spot for a drink between dips in the turquoise sea. Fabulous tropical cocktails include Caraïbes Sunrise (spiced rum, passionfruit liqueur, fresh mango and strawberries).

ⓘ Getting There & Away

Simpson Bay is home to Princess Juliana International Airport, from where **ferries** (p724) also depart for Anguilla. All the major car-rental companies have desks here.

Ferries leave for Saba from the southern end of Simpson Bay. Taxis are prevalent.

DON'T MISS

SUNSET BAR & GRILL
....

At the end of the runway, **Sunset Bar & Grill** (☎545-2084; http://sunsetsxm.com; 2 Beacon Hill Rd; ⏰7:30am-4am; 🛜) is a rite of passage for aviation buffs: where else can you sip an ice-cold beer while snapping photos of huge intercontinental jets soaring overhead? It's rocking during the two-for-one happy 'hour' between 4pm and 7pm. Afterwards, it changes name to its evening alter ego, the Refuge Restaurant & Lounge.

Buses run to Philipsburg and Marigot but schedules are unpredictable.

ST-MARTIN

Quieter than its Dutch counterpart, the French half of the island is a charming mix of white-sand beaches, cluttered town centers and stretches of bucolic mountainside. Several areas, including the capital, Marigot, still bear the scars of hurricanes that have torn through the island.

Marigot

The capital of French St-Martin, port town Marigot is a town dominated by a stone fort high up on the hill. A distinctive European flavor is palpable here, with a produce market and a handful of *boulangeries* (bakeries).

Marigot was virtually leveled by Hurricane Luis in 1995, and hard-hit by subsequent hurricanes including Lenny in 1999 and Gonzalo in 2014, but a few historic buildings with wrought-iron balconies and belle epoque lampposts remain.

Although Marigot is generally safe during the day, it's a no-go zone after dark.

⊙ Sights

Fort Louis   RUINS
(Rue du Fort Louis; ⏰24hr) **FREE** In 1767 three gun batteries were placed up on top of this hill. In 1789 Fort Louis was constructed by St-Martin's then-governor Jean Sebastian de Durat to protect Marigot's harbor warehouses storing rum, salt, coffee and sugarcane from marauding British and Dutch pirates. It's been abandoned for centuries

WORTH A TRIP

BAIE NETTLÉ

Sandy Ground is the long, narrow, curving strip of land that extends west from Marigot between the coast and Simpson Bay Lagoon. Sandy Ground's settlement is not particularly appealing (and a no-go area after dark), but the beach at **Baie Nettlé** (Nettle Bay), with views of Marigot and across to Anguilla, is a beautiful white-sand flat stretch of beach with a handful of bars and restaurants. Watch out for currents and submerged rocks if you're swimming.

and contains only remnants from bygone eras, but English and French interpretive panels detail its history and the view alone rewards the 50m climb from the road up to the ruins.

Musée de Saint Martin Antilles   MUSEUM
(St-Martin Archaeological Museum; http://musee-saintmartin.e-monsite.com; 7 Rue Fichot; ⊙9am-1pm & 3-5pm Mon-Fri) **FREE** Clay figurines from 550 BC (the oldest discovered in the Antilles), Arawak-sculpted gemstones and shells and period photography are among the historical displays that bring the island's history to life at this small but absorbing museum, which spans the Arawak period (from 3250 BC) to European colonization and island fashion in the 1930s. Interpretative panels are in English and French.

Produce Market   MARKET
(Blvd de France; ⊙food 7am-3pm Wed & Sat, bric-a-brac & clothing 7am-3pm Mon, Tue, Thu & Fri) The twice-weekly produce market on Marigot's waterfront has tropical fruit such as passionfruit and bananas, root vegetables, goat's meat and chicken, and freshly caught fish from the surrounding waters. Local rums include Mauby (bark-infused rum) and Shrub (crushed-orange-peel-infused rum). There are also plenty of souvenir stalls.

🛏 Sleeping

The few hotels in the center of Marigot cater to island folk who live on smaller islands and need a place to crash while they do their bulk grocery shopping on St-Martin. These spots are some of the cheapest places on the island, but as Marigot is not a safe place to walk around after dark,

you may want to consider staying in Grand Case, 6km to the northeast, instead.

🍴 Eating

Enoch's Place   CARIBBEAN $
(Front de Mer; mains €10-14; ⊙11am-2pm & 5:30-9pm Mon-Sat) For a down-to-earth local experience, head to this bustling eatery handily positioned on a corner of Marigot's open-air market (p712). Dishes are made fresh daily and might include spicy Creole shrimp, smoky grilled ribs, barbecued red snapper fillets, tangy goat curry, oxtail stew, conch salad and St-Martin's best johnnycakes. There's no seafood on Mondays when the fishing boats don't run.

Ô Plongeoir   INTERNATIONAL $$
(☎0590-87-94-71; Front de Mer; mains lunch €12-18, dinner €16-28, tapas €7-15; ⊙noon-9:30pm Mon-Sat; 🐾) Opposite the yacht club, this open-air eatery is a great place to gaze at Anguilla in the distance (and, often, visiting iguanas from the hillside above). Salmon gravlax, tempura tiger prawns, grilled calamari, blackened red snapper fillets, bavette steak with béarnaise sauce, honey-spiced roast duck and oven-baked Camembert are among the menu highlights. Tapas is served between 5pm and 6pm.

Le Tropicana   CARIBBEAN $$
(☎0590-87-79-07; Pont la Royale; mains €14-31.50; ⊙noon-9:30pm Mon-Sat) Right on the dock of the marina, this colorful spot's chairs and tablecloths are a mélange of sunny yellows and oranges. Poached salmon with raspberry-butter sauce, lobster-stuffed chicken breast with Jamaican pepper jus and sole meunière give it a strong local following, but the biggest winners are lush desserts like Grand Marnier soufflé and chocolate fondue.

ℹ Information

Post Office (www.laposte.fr; 25 Rue de la Liberté; ⊙7am-5:30pm Mon-Fri, 7:30am-noon Sat)
Tourist Office (☎0590-87-57-21; www.stmartinisland.org; Route de Sandy Ground; ⊙8:30am-1pm & 2:30-5:30pm Mon-Fri, 8am-noon Sat)

ℹ Getting There & Away

Public ferries (p724) to Anguilla depart from Marigot's ferry terminal at Fort Louis' marina, as do **Voyager** (p724) ferries to St-Barthélemy.

Buses serve Marigot but schedules are highly unpredictable so you're better off taking a taxi or traveling with your own wheels.

Terres Basses

Terres Basses (pronounced 'tair boss'), also known as the French Lowlands, is a verdant stretch of lush, low-lying land connected to the larger part of the island by two thin strips of land. This peaceful area has a string of beautiful sandy beaches with safe swimming and snorkeling.

◉ Sights

Baie Rouge   BEACH

Named for the red-tinged color of the sand, Baie Rouge is a long, beautiful strand with good swimming. Although it's just 150m from the main road, it retains an inviting natural setting. For the best snorkeling, swim to the eastern end of the beach toward the rocky outcrop. From the French-Dutch border at Cupecoy Bay, it's 3km northeast.

Baie aux Prunes   BEACH

(Plum Bay) A gently curving bay with polished shell-like grains of golden sand, Baie aux Prunes is popular for swimming and snorkeling when it's calm, and for surfing when the swell's up. From the French-Dutch border at Cupecoy Bay, it's 3km northwest.

Baie Longue   BEACH

(Long Bay) Baie Longue embraces two splendid miles of seemingly endless white sand and rocky outcrops, making it a great place for long strolls and enjoying quiet sunsets. The impossibly clear turquoise waters are exceptionally calm. It's 1.6km northwest of the French/Dutch border at Cupecoy; look for the entrance to the car park opposite the Grand Étang salt pond.

⛏ Sleeping & Eating

La Samanna   RESORT $$$

(☑0590-87-64-00; www.belmond.com/la-samanna-st-martin; Baie Longue; d/ste/villas from US$945/1545/2245; P✳⬆☎⬇) La Samanna is one of the most lavish – and expensive – places to stay on the island. Fronting a magnificent stretch of beach, this tropical hideaway has a state-of-the-art spa, two pools, high-quality restaurants, and rooms, suites and villas with luxurious fittings such as mahogany and teak furniture, Italian marble, private plunge pools, rooftop

sundecks and floor-to-ceiling windows with mesmerizing views.

Le Sand   INTERNATIONAL $$

(☑0690-73-14-38; Rte des Terres Basses, Baie Nettlé; mains €11-25; ⊙kitchen noon-10:30pm, bar 9am-midnight) On a pristine stretch of brilliant-white beach, Le Sand serves classy fare like saltfish fritters, lemon lobster risotto, crab ravioli with pineapple sauce, and *côte de bœuf* (beef steak) for two. Drop by on Fridays for grilled seafood specials; Saturdays for paella. Happy hour is 5pm to 7pm. Live reggae, soul and blues on Sundays from 3pm to 6pm.

Friar's Bay

Friar's Bay is a postcard-worthy cove with a broad sandy beach. This popular local swimming spot is just beyond the residential neighborhood of St Louis; the road leading in is signposted.

◉ Sights

Happy Bay   BEACH

Head to the northernmost point of Friar's Bay's beach and you'll discover a dirt path that twists for 450m over a bumpy headland to the perfectly deserted Happy Bay. Equidistant from bustling Marigot and Grand Case, this surprisingly serene strip of powdery sand is completely bare (as are those who like to hang out here).

✗ Eating & Drinking

Friar's Bay Beach Café   FRENCH, SEAFOOD $$

(☑0590-49-16-87; Rue de Friar's Bay; mains €16-36; ⊙breakfast 9-11am, lunch noon-5pm, bar 9am-sunset) Fringed by palm trees, this breezy beach cafe occupies a privileged spot with sheltered cabanas strewn on the sand. Choose from large leafy salads, club sandwiches, burgers, quiches, beef carpaccio and fish ceviche from the menu chalked daily on the huge blackboard, followed by a free shot of locally brewed rum. Live music from 6pm to 9pm on Sundays.

Kali's Beach Bar   BAR

(Rue de Friar's Bay; ⊙10am-sunset, hours can vary) Painted in Rastafarian reds, greens and yellows, Kali's has hammocks strung between shady coconut palms. Renowned across the island for its potent rum punches (some using the house-made bush rum), it also serves icy-cold beers. Full-moon reggae parties with a bonfire run from sunset to midnight. It also rents snorkeling equipment (per day €10) and kayaks (per hour €25).

Grand Case

The small beachside settlement of Grand Case has not been dubbed the 'Gourmet Capital of the Caribbean' for nothing. Each evening, a ritual of sorts takes place on Grand Case's beachfront road, Blvd de Grand Case, with restaurants placing their menus and chalkboard specials out front, and would-be diners strolling along the strip until they find somewhere that takes their fancy.

While dining is the premier attraction, there's also a decent beach for swimming and snorkeling, while other pursuits include diving (p714), boating (p714), skydiving (p714) and even perfume making (p715).

🏃 Activities

Corail Helicopters　　　SCENIC FLIGHTS
(☑0590-69-81-81; http://corailhelico-sxm. com; Aéroport de Saint-Martin Grand Case, Rte de l'Espérance; helicopter flight per person from €150; ⊙tours by arrangement) For dazzling views of the islands and turquoise waters, swoop over sights such as Anse Marcel, Pic Paradis, Oyster Pond and Anguilla's West End and Tintamarre aboard a helicopter. Rides last between 12 minutes and 25 min-

utes. You can also arrange custom tours, airport transfers and private charters.

Octopus Diving　　　DIVING, SNORKELING
(☑0590-29-11-27; http://octopusdiving.com; 3 Rue de la Petite Plage; 2-tank dive €99, snorkeling excursion €55, snorkeling-gear rental per day €10; ⊙7:30am-5pm) Run by locals Sally and Chris, this well-established PADI-affiliated operator offers dive trips and four-hour snorkeling excursions to various sites around the island, including Creole Rock, Turtle Reef, Chio, Tugboat and Old Timers' Reef. There's a second Octopus (p708) outlet in Philipsburg on the Dutch side.

SXM Parachute　　　SKYDIVING
(☑0690-77-15-41; www.sxmparachute.com; Aéroport de Saint-Martin Grand Case, Rte de l'Espérance; tandem jump €280; ⊙9am-7pm early Nov-late Apr) For the most exhilarating aerial views of the island, head up into the skies aboard a Cessna 206G then hurl yourself out to free fall 3000m on a tandem skydive with an instructor. A video costs €95; photos are €45. Takeoff is from the Aéroport de Saint-Martin Grand Case (p724).

Scoobidoo　　　BOATING
(☑0590-52-02-53; www.scoobidoo.com; Grand Case Marina; day trip to Prickly Pear Cays or Anguilla €110, to St-Barthélemy €140) Scoobidoo offers excellent catamaran trips that go to Prickly Pear Cays, Anguilla and St-Barthélemy (be sure to bring your pass-

DON'T MISS

PIC PARADIS

The 424m Pic Paradis, the highest point on the island, offers fine vistas and good hiking opportunities. The peak is topped with a communications tower and is accessible by a rough maintenance road that doubles as a hiking trail. You can drive as far as the last house and then walk the final 1km to the top.

A must for hikers and foodies, oasis-like **Loterie Farm** (☑0590-87-86-16; www.loterie farm.com; 103 Rte de Pic Paradis; self-guided/guided hikes €5/25, adult high-ropes course €40-60, children low-ropes course €25, swimming pool €25, cabanas from €200; ⊙9am-5pm Tue-Sun) on the way up to the peak is an excellent place to spend the afternoon. The quiet plantation features ziplining, a couple of hikes, a gorgeous spring-fed swimming pool and an outstanding restaurant, **Hidden Forest** (☑0590-87-86-16; www.loteriefarm.com; 103 Rte de Pic Paradis; tapas €8-15, mains €16-29; ⊙noon-3pm & 6:30-9:30pm Tue-Sat, noon-4pm Sun).

The road to Pic Paradis is 500m north of the 'L' in the road between Friar's Bay and Grand Case that splinters off to the inland community of Colombier. Take the road inland for 2km, turn left at the fork (signposted 'Sentier des Crêtes NE, Pic Paradis') and continue 500m further to the last house, where there's space to pull over and park (do not leave anything in your car).

port). Day trips include snorkeling equipment, a buffet lunch and an open bar. Boats also leave from Anse Marcel (p718). Whale-watching trips are planned during the migration season (December to April).

🎓 Courses

Tijon   PERFUME MAKING
(📞0590-22-74-70; http://tijon.com; 1 Rte de l'Espérance; ⊙9:30am-5pm Mon-Fri, by appointment Sat & Sun) As well as shopping for perfumes at this heady boutique, you can learn how to create your own fragrances from a selection of oils during a one-hour Mix-and-Match course (€89). The two- to three-hour Perfume Class 101 (€139) teaches you about the history of perfume and offers more advanced mixing. Both include a gift bag worth up to €45.

🛏 Sleeping

Grand Case has some of the most charming boutique places to stay on the island as well as a couple of budget options.

Hotel Hevea   GUESTHOUSE $
(📞0690-29-36-71; http://hotelhevea.com; 163 Blvd de Grand Case; d €85-130, tr/q 140/150; 🅿❄🕸) Freshly painted in fuchsia pink and oyster gray, this sweet establishment has nine colorful, well-equipped rooms named after local plants such as Hibiscus, Jasmin and Laurier (magnolia), an inviting patio and friendly owners. Best of all, it's ideally positioned on Grand Case's beachfront road with rare private parking (there's only a handful of spaces, so arrive early).

Grand Case Beach Club   RESORT $$
(📞0590-87-51-87; www.grandcasebeachclub.com; 21 Rue de la Petite Plage; d/q incl breakfast from €230/415; 🅿❄🕸) On the quiet northeast end of the beach, this gently sprawling resort's low-rise red-roofed buildings have airy renovated rooms facing the sea. Its sparkling pool sits out on a promontory; there's also a water-sports center and superb snorkeling a few fin-strokes away, along with an on-site tennis court. Kids under 12 stay for free in their parents' room.

⭐ Le Temps des Cerises   BOUTIQUE HOTEL $$$
(📞0590-51-36-27; www.letempsdescerisehotel. com; 158 Blvd de Grand Case; d €280-380; ❄🕸) Opening onto the beach with dazzling views, this chic laid-back property opened in late 2015 and shelters three doubles and six superior doubles decked out in airy neutral

tones with natural materials including polished hardwood floors and vintage timber furniture. All have balconies and minibars. Stand-up paddleboards, snorkeling equipment, sun loungers and beach umbrellas are included in the rate.

⭐ L'Esplanade   BOUTIQUE HOTEL $$$
(📞0590-87-06-55; www.lesplanade.com; Route de l'Espérance; studios/lofts/ste from €415/475/515; @🕸❄) A 500m stroll east of the beach, this romantic, impeccably run hillside hotel is a haven from the hustle of Grand Case, with a beautiful pool and swim-up bar. Its 24 sumptuous studios, lofts and suites have fully equipped kitchens and private oceanview terraces, along with French linens, mahogany staircases and vaulted ceilings, and handcrafted Brazilian and Balinese furniture.

Cooked-to-order breakfasts (€15) can be arranged the previous evening, and there's a luxurious on-site spa. A complimentary shuttle runs to its equally charming sister property, Le Petit Hotel (p715), where nonmotorized water-sports equipment is free.

Le Shambala   BOUTIQUE HOTEL $$$
(📞0590-29-17-09; www.leshambala.com; 28 Blvd de Grand Case; ste from €280; 🅿❄🕸❄) There are just five suites at this ultraexclusive hideaway behind a security gate with direct beach access. Each is named after a Caribbean island, and comes with a private pool, garden area and covered terrace, and beautiful interiors with raised beamed ceilings. There's also a gorgeous communal pool by the beach, a beach bar and an exceptional restaurant (p716).

Le Petit Hotel   BOUTIQUE HOTEL $$$
(📞0590-29-09-65; www.lepetithotel.com; 248 Blvd de Grande Case; studio/ste from €455/615; ❄🕸) Each of the 10 rooms at this boutique jewel – the sister property of L'Esplanade (p715) – come with sea-facing balconies, Balinese furniture, Brazilian hardwood ceilings and free nonmotorized water-sports equipment. Suites accommodating up to four people have separate living rooms with pull-out couches, along with full kitchens and dining areas. Top-floor balconies have full sun; lower ones are shaded.

🍴 Eating

The island's best restaurants line up along Blvd de Grand Case, along with smoky *lolos* (barbecue shacks) and casual cafes.

★ **Lolos** BARBECUE $

(52 Blvd de Grand Case; mains €8-14; ⊘10:30am-10:30pm) Smoke billows from these Creole *lolos*, which cluster around wooden picnic tables. Of the six individual establishments sizzling up succulent ribs, cod fritters, grilled fish, chicken and stuffed crabs cooked in the shell, favorites include **Talk of the Town**. Sides such as coleslaw, potato salad, rice or beans are usually included in the price, along with crispy johnnycakes.

Aglio e Olio PIZZA $

(⬆0690-82-11-36; 2 Rue Franklin; pizza €8-15, pasta €12; ⊘6-10pm Wed-Mon) Neapolitan pizzas are fired at 900°C (1652°F) for 60 seconds in the wood-fired oven of this authentic little pizzeria. If you can't decide, go for the house-specialty Dino (named for the owner/chef) with Italian sausage, mozzarella, onion, spinach and Parmesan. There are also two baked pasta dishes. The terrace sits on a busy road; takeout prices are €2 cheaper.

Ocean 82 SEAFOOD, FRENCH $$

(⬆0590-52-98-12; www.ocean-82.com; 82 Blvd de Grand Case; mains €22-30, lobster per kg €65; ⊘noon-10:30pm) One of the few upmarket restaurants along foodie strip Blvd de Grand Case to serve food all day, this elegant white-tableclothed spot has spectacular views of the ocean from its covered terrace. Its live tank takes pride of place in the window; dishes include homemade lobster and mushroom ravioli with truffle oil, shrimp-stuffed chicken breast, conch pie and lobster thermidor.

Sunset Café CAFE, FRENCH $$

(⬆0590-87-51-87; www.grandcasebeachclub.com; Grand Case Beach Club, 21 Rue de la Petite Plage; mains breakfast €8.50-16, lunch €9-19, dinner €17-33; ⊘8am-9:30pm) In an area that abounds with ocean views, this Grand Case Beach Club (p715) eatery, with a breezy terrace that juts out over the glittering water, takes first prize. Throughout the day it morphs from a laid-back cafe serving sandwiches, burgers and salads to a refined restaurant of an evening, when dishes might include *moules-frites* (mussels and fries), delectable steaks and grilled seafood.

Le Tastevin FRENCH, FUSION $$

(⬆0590-87-55-45; http://letastevin-restaurant.com; 86 Blvd de Grand Case; mains €22-35; ⊘noon-2:30pm & 5:30-10:30pm mid-Dec–Apr, 5:30-10:30pm May–mid-Dec) Overlooking the beach, this much-lauded restaurant is all about romance, from the candlelit tables to the white tablecloths that gently flutter under your plate as the breezy ocean air swooshes through. Around six daily blackboard specials complement standards such as scallop carpaccio with grapefruit and hazelnut oil, lobster bouillabaisse, and roast duck breast with sherry demi-glace and caramelized sweet potato.

★ **Le Shambala Restaurant** GASTRONOMY $$$

(⬆0590-29-17-09; www.leshambala.com; 28 Blvd de Grand Case; mains €21-38, 2-course lunch menu €28, 3-course dinner menu €38; ⊘noon-2:30pm & 6-9:30pm) In an enchanting setting overlooking the water right on the beach, the restaurant of Le Shambala (p715) hotel has one of the area's – and the island's – best menus. Be wowed by black-tiger-prawn carpaccio with olive-oil ice cream, thyme-crusted rack of lamb with cardamom jus, black-olive-crusted monkfish with caramelized red-pepper sauce and toffee *panna cotta* (literally 'cooked cream') with flambéed pineapple.

★ **Le Pressoir** FRENCH $$$

(⬆0590-87-76-62; www.lepressoirsxm.com; 32 Blvd de Grand Case; mains €20-34, 2-course lobster menu €51; ⊘6-11pm Dec-Apr, 6-11pm Mon-Sat May–mid-Sep & mid-Oct–Nov, closed mid-Sep–mid-Oct; ⛲) A beautiful 1871-built bright-yellow house with charming red clapboard shutters, cornflower-blue posts and romantic boudoir-style interior – one of the last remaining traditional Creole houses – sets the stage for the culinary art of feted chef Franck Mear: rum-marinated foie gras, veal sweetbreads in lobster broth, duck breast with black grape jus, roast scallops with truffled chestnut puree and wild sole meunière.

Le Cottage FRENCH $$$

(⬆0590-29-03-30; www.lecottagesxm.com; 97 Blvd de Grand Case; mains €22-37, 3-course menu with wine €75, 4-course lobster menu €59; ⊘5:30-10pm; ⛲) Classical French cuisine pairs with an outstanding wine list at this stylish restaurant. Start off with homemade foie gras or crème Chantilly lobster soup capped with a puff-pastry lid before moving onto mains like Noilly Prat–flambéed sea bass, thyme-crusted rack of lamb with garlic potato mash, or beef tenderloin with Roquefort sauce. A two-course kids' menu costs €14.

🍷 Drinking & Nightlife

★ Hidden Garden
COCKTAIL BAR

(☑ 0690-14-51-55; 49 Blvd de Grand Case; ⊘ 5:30pm-1am Sun & Tue-Fri, to 3am Sat) Tucked at the end of a narrow boardwalk, Hidden Garden is a magical spot with flickering candles, timber benches strewn with cushions, and sensational cocktails such as Basilic Bloody Maria (basil-infused tequila, tomato juice and pepper), Aquarium (rum, blue curaçao, dry vermouth, cane-sugar syrup and bitters) and Clover Club (gin, raspberry liqueur, raspberry puree, lemon juice and egg white).

La Cave de Charly
WINE BAR

(☑ 0590-29-04-15; http://lacavedecharly.com; 49 Blvd de Grand Case; ⊘ 5pm-2am) Over 1000 French wines from 150 different labels (including around 30 by-the-glass options at any one time) are available at this airy space with hardwood floors and lofty white-painted beams, with upturned barrels out front. Pair them with superb cheese and charcuterie boards or classic bistro dishes such as beef tartare. There's often live jazz and blues.

Calmos Café
CAFE

(☑ 0590-29-01-85; www.lecalmoscafe.com; 40 Blvd de Grand Case; ⊘ 11am-late; 🛜) Bury your feet in the sand (or splash them in the water if the tide's in) at this vibrantly painted local fave. Tropical rum-laced cocktails include its house-specialty Calmos with mango and peach juice (happy hour is from 4pm to 6pm). It's famed for the quality of its live music sessions featuring salsa (Thursdays) and reggae (Sundays).

ℹ️ Getting There & Away

The smaller of St-Martin/Sint Maarten's two airports, **Aéroport de Saint-Martin Grand Case** (p724), is located here. There are taxi ranks and car-rental desks for companies including Banana Location. Buses stop by but schedules are erratic at best. A taxi or your own wheels are the way to go.

Anse Marcel

Anse Marcel's hidden bay is first glimpsed from high up in the mountains as you gently descend to the coast. The hills above this quiet port are the stomping ground of wealthier vacationers, with some of St-

ÎLET PINEL

This little islet just 1km from French Cul-de-Sac is a great spot to spend a sun-soaked afternoon. Totally undeveloped (it's part of the Sint Maarten Marine Park), Pinel is the domain of day-trippers, who arrive at the island's calm west-facing beach, where there's good swimming, snorkeling and two restaurants/bars as well as a small gift shop. Rent snorkeling gear from **Caribbean Paddling** (http://caribbeanpaddling.com; Rue de Cul-de-Sac, French Cul-de-Sac; snorkeling-gear rental per day €15; ⊘ 9:30am-5pm) at French Cul-de-Sac.

If you want to make your own way over, Caribbean Paddling also rents kayaks and stand-up paddleboards. Otherwise, you can catch a small boat from the dock at the road's end in French Cul-de-Sac, departing roughly every 30 minutes from 10am to 5pm. The five-minute ride costs €12 round-trip (cash only).

Martin/Sint Maarten's fancier properties located here.

Boat tours leave from the marina; watersports-equipment rental is available on the beach.

The area is one of several places on the island still recovering from hurricane damage.

◉ Sights

Anse Marcel
BEACH

Protected by two large headlands, this gorgeous white-sand beach with clear opal-colored waters is especially popular with families. Snorkeling is particularly good (and safe) here, especially around the headlands. Caraïbes Watersports (p718) rents gear.

Petites Cayes
BEACH

One of the island's top hidden beaches, Petites Cayes is accessible via a small, 2.5km-long trail that begins just south of the marina off Rue de l'Anse Marcel; follow it along the rugged headland past flowering Pope's Head cacti (keep an eye out for iguanas). It's a bit of a walk (around 30 minutes), but definitely worth it. Surfers flock here when the swell's up.

🏃 Activities

Caraïbes Watersports   WATER SPORTS
(📞 0690-88-81-02; www.caraibeswatersports.com; ⏱ 9am-5pm) Beachside shack Caraïbes Watersports rents out kayaks and stand-up paddleboards (per hour each €20), snorkeling gear (per hour €10), flyboards (per 30 minutes €120) and Jet Skis (per 30 minutes €60); if you don't want to go it alone, you can take a two-hour Jet Ski tour (per person €180) or 90-minute snorkeling tour (€45).

Scoobidoo   BOATING
(📞 0590-52-02-53; www.scoobidoo.com; day trip to Prickly Pear Cays or Anguilla €110, to St-Barthélemy €140) Catamaran trips to Anguilla, Prickly Pear Cays and St-Barthélemy (passport required) include snorkeling equipment, a buffet lunch and an open bar. Trips also pick up from Grand Case (p714). Ask about upcoming whale-watching trips during the migration season (December to April).

🛏 Sleeping

⭐ **Marquis Boutique Hotel**   BOUTIQUE HOTEL $$$
(📞 0590-29-42-30; www.hotel-marquis.com; Pigeon Pea Hill; d from €310; 🅿 ❄ @ 🛜 ❄) The reward for the supersteep drive up here is a spectacular panorama over the bay below. Perched on a greenery-cloaked hillside, this cluster of brightly colored, light-drenched villas shelters 17 rooms with marble bathrooms, high ceilings, minibars and paintings by renowned local artist Francis Eck. You're not near the water, but there's a free guest shuttle to the beach.

Orient Beach

Although this sandy strand has become a busy resort area filled with beach bars, its southern end is quieter and a favorite spot for nudists. Snorkel-friendly reefs protect 5.5km of inviting white-sand beach. Restaurants, bars, water-sports operators and resorts all call Baie Orientale (Orient Bay) home.

⊙ Sights & Activities

Butterfly Farm   MUSEUM
(📞 0590-87-31-21; www.thebutterflyfarm.com; Rte du Galion; adult/child €15/7; ⏱ 9am-3:30pm) Wear bright colors to attract the butterflies fluttering around giant plants and a forested canopy at this mesh-encased farm. As practical as it is magical, here you can learn about chrysalis stages and how cocoons form; tickets include a 20-minute guided tour in French. Come early to see the butterflies at their most active. Admission is valid for the duration of your stay on the island. It's signposted 1.5km south of Orient Beach.

Wind Adventures   WATER SPORTS
(📞 0590-29-41-57; www.wind-adventures.com; ⏱ 8am-6pm) Situated right on the sand, this water-sports center rents equipment for a wide range of activities, including windsurfing (per hour €25), kitesurfing (per hour €50), stand-up paddleboarding (per hour €20), kayaking (per hour €15) and sailing (catamaran rental per hour €45). It also offers lessons and a range of half-day tours, and can deliver equipment anywhere on the island (€30).

🛏 Sleeping

About 700m inland from Orient Beach you'll find a handful of high-end resort hotels and timeshares. There are no budget options.

🍴 Eating & Drinking

⭐ **Côté Plages**   FRENCH $$
(📞 0590-52-47-37; www.coteplages.com; Baie Orientale; tapas €7-16, mains €14-28, 2-/3-course menus €26/33; ⏱ 6-9:30pm; 🔧) Drop by between 6pm and 7pm for tapas (roast marrow bone, frogs' legs in garlic and parsley, Burgundy snails) before feasting on Caribbean-influenced French fare: truffled lobster bisque, sautéed veal kidneys, puff-pastry-baked red snapper, duck breast in fig sauce, and sea scallop and saffron risotto, accompanied by outstanding wines. Its three-course kids' menu costs €10.

Rancho del Sol   STEAK, TEX-MEX $$
(📞 0590-51-12-12; www.elranchodelsol.com; Baie Orientale; mains €15-27.50; ⏱ 10am-10pm; 🔧) On a hill high above the fray of Orient Beach, this wagon-wheel-flanked, Texan-style steakhouse has sweeping views from its vast open terrace. Succulent steaks aside, it serves barbecued ribs, chicken burritos, beef fajitas, deep-fried chimichangas and a wide range of pizzas (with names like Desperado and Geronimo). Happy hour takes place between 5pm and 7pm.

Bikini Beach   BAR
(📞 0590-87-43-25; www.bikinibeachsxm.com; Baie Orientale; ⏱ 9am-8pm) Shaded by coconut palms, this classic beach bar has a large wooden deck and sun loungers on the

sand. Banana-and-strawberry coladas, rum punches and house-made rum infusions (passionfruit, ginger, guavaberry) are among its tropical concoctions. You could easily laze the day away here, but if you're keen to get active, it also offers Jet Ski rentals, parasailing and banana boating.

Kontiki BAR

(☑0590-87-43-27; www.kontiki-sxm.com; Baie Orientale; ☉9am-8pm) A maze of driftwood, booths and cushioned sun loungers on the sand, this good-time venue's best seats are the suspended swings, which dangle next to the bar. Local and European beers are served ice cold; there's also a small but stellar wine selection, freshly pressed juices and an extensive cocktail list. DJs spin at beach parties every Sunday.

Oyster Pond

The Dutch–French border slices straight across Oyster Pond, which actually isn't a pond at all but a stunning sunken bay nestled between two jagged hills. Yachts fill its three marinas.

🛏 Sleeping

⭐ **Les Balcons d'Oyster Pond** BUNGALOW $$

(☑0590-29-43-39; www.lesbalcons.com; 15 Ave du Lagon; bungalows €120-230; P ❄ 🛜 ≋) This charming collection of bungalows spreads across a scrubby hill, with sweeping views of the bay and quiet marina below. Each bungalow has completely different decor but all have private terraces with gas grills. Two bungalows have additional sofa beds; one has a full kitchen, laundry and private outdoor Jacuzzi.

🍴 Eating & Drinking

Stardocks CAFE $

(Emerald Merit Rd; dishes US$6-14, 2-course lunch menus US$12-14; ☉7am-3pm) Fresh smoothies, juices, homemade lemonade with ginger, good coffee and herbal teas are all reasons to stop by this welcoming little waterside cafe on the Dutch side of the border, but it's also a top spot for breakfast (French, American or Caribbean), bagels, panini, salmon and avocado wraps, quiche of the day and cakes like banana with cinnamon and nutmeg.

⭐ **Canoa** CARIBBEAN $$

(☑in Sint Maarten 543-6442; www.canoasxm. com; Emerald Merit Rd; mains US$24-40; ☉5:30-

10:30pm) Opening onto two waterside terraces overlooking the bobbing yachts on the Dutch side of the border (but invariably overflowing with residents from the French side), this traditional orange, turquoise and sky-blue timber shack turns out feisty island dishes: conch chowder, Creole stuffed crab backs, rum-marinated shrimp, *buljawou* (pickled saltfish and cinnamon-dusted fried plantains) and Jamaican jerk-spiced pork chops. Bookings advised.

Quai Ouest FRENCH $$

(☑0690-73-76-01; www.captainolivershotel.com; Captain Oliver's, Ave du Lagon; pizza €12-16, mains €20-25; ☉5-9pm Mon, noon-2pm & 5-9pm Tue-Sat) With a prime spot on the Oyster Pond waterfront within the Captain Oliver's hotel complex, this eatery is known for its lunchtime pizzas and quality French evening fare including roasted Camembert, meat both grilled and tartare, duck breast in mushroom sauce, and chocolate mousse to finish. Come early for a good table at sunset.

Mr Busby's INTERNATIONAL $$

(☑Sint Maarten 543-6088; 6 Emerald Merit Rd; mains US$16.75-36.75; ☉7:30am-6pm) On the Dutch side of the border at Oyster Pond, laid-back Mr Busby's opens directly onto Dawn Beach's sands, with sun loungers beneath the palm trees. Lobsters swim in the live tank; the extensive menu also spans homemade beef lasagna or linguini with clams, scallops with fennel and Vermouth cream sauce, filet mignon, and grilled burgers, wings, ribs and chicken.

BZH INTERNATIONAL $$

(☑0590-87-38-41; https://bzhsxm.com; Ave du Lagon; breakfast €15, crêpes €6-9, pizzas €11-15, mains €13-28; ☉8am-10pm Mon-Sat) Locally renowned for its pizzas, such as La Segain (goat's cheese, fresh tomato and pesto) or La Calabraise (bacon, egg and olives), Breton-turned-global BZH also serves breakfast; sweet crêpes such as apples flambéed with Calvados or salted caramel; and mains including beef tartare and duck breast with honey jus. Pizzas can be delivered around Oyster Pond for orders over €20.

⭐ **Dinghy Dock Bar** BAR

(Rue de l'Escale; ☉11am-midnight Mon-Fri, 9am-midnight Sat & Sun) The big draw at this self-styled Caribbean dive bar on the marina's edge is happy hour (5pm to 7pm), when customers get to mix their own drinks. Cocktails include a Tropical Iced Tea, a Fire & Ice

Bloody Mary and a chili and passionfruit caipirinha. There's live music every Sunday night and often other nights throughout the week.

❶ Getting There & Away

Voyager ferries serve St-Barthélemy.

Infrequent buses pass through en route between Marigot and Philipsburg, but you're better off arranging a taxi or traveling with your own wheels.

UNDERSTAND ST-MARTIN/SINT MAARTEN

History

For a thousand years, St-Martin/Sint Maarten was sparsely populated by the Arawaks and later the fiercer Caribs. They named the island Soualiga after the brackish salt ponds that made it difficult to settle.

Columbus sailed past on November 11, 1493, which happened to be the feast day of Saint Martin of Tours, after whom he named the island Isla de San Martin. But it was the Dutch who were the first to take advantage of the land, a nice stopping-off point between the Netherlands and their colonies in Brazil and New Amsterdam (New York City). After a few abortive attempts by the Spanish to regain the island, now found to be brimming with lucrative salt deposits, the French and Dutch ended up fighting for control of it.

As legend has it, the Dutch and the French decided to partition St-Martin/Sint Maarten from a march originating in Oyster Pond. The French walked northward, the Dutch south. While the French quenched their thirst with wine, the Dutch brought along *jenever* (Dutch gin). Halfway through, the Dutchmen stopped to sleep off the ill effects, effectively giving the French a greater piece of the pie.

St-Martin became a plantation island much like many of its neighbors. The end of slavery (1848 on the French side; 1863 on the Dutch side) brought an end to the plantation boom and by 1930 the population stood at just 2000 hardy souls. The island became duty-free in 1939. In 1943, during WWII, the US Navy built large runways on the island to use as a base in the Caribbean. The French capitalized by using the runways to fly in tourists; by the 1950s this had brought the population of St-Martin/Sint Maarten up to about 70,000 and made tourism the number-one industry on both sides of the island.

In the 1980s Aruba's secession from the Netherlands Antilles sparked movements on St-Martin/Sint Maarten toward greater independence from their parent entities. The Dutch were first in 2000, when they received a 'status aparte' with the Netherlands. The French side followed in 2003, voting to secede from Guadeloupe to form their own separate overseas collectivity (Collectivité de Saint-Martin). In 2010 the Netherlands Antilles dissolved, propelling Sint Maarten toward independence when it officially became recognized as a 'constituent country' of the Kingdom of the Netherlands.

Since the mid-1990s, St-Martin/Sint Maarten has been hit by no fewer than eight major hurricanes. Among the worst were the catastrophic Hurricane Luis in 1995, the strongest to hit in the 20th century. It killed 14 people and left thousands of residents homeless after it wreaked extensive damage, decimating large swathes of the island including Grand Case, Marigot, Simpson Bay and Philipsburg and beaching, sinking or destroying 1300 boats. Hurricane Bertha in 1996 severely damaged Grand Case's fragile post-Luis reconstruction, while Hurricane Lenny in 1999 killed 13 people and caused large-scale destruction to south-facing areas including Simpson Bay. Hurricane Gonzalo in 2014 killed one person and destroyed numerous properties and watercraft. Today, many areas are still recovering and rebuilding.

Culture

St-Martin/Sint Maarten is a melting pot of ethnicities like no other place in the Caribbean. The island culture has its roots largely in African, French and Dutch influences, though scores of more recent immigrants – including many from the Dominican Republic, Haiti and China – have added their own elements to this multicultural society. Today, the island claims 120 different nationalities speaking over 80 different languages, although French dominates St-Martin and English dominates Sint Maarten.

St-Martin/Sint Maarten has adapted to tourism better than any other island nearby. You'll rarely meet someone who was actually born on the island. As the smallest area of land in the world divided into two nations, each side functions symbiotically while attracting tourists in very different ways. The French side embraces its European roots and seeks to recreate a certain amount of 'Old World' atmosphere. Home to the cruise-ship port, the Dutch side is much more built up with solid hurricane-resistant concrete high-rises, and a constant hum of low-lying debauchery that accompanies the dozens of gentlemen's clubs, casinos and beach bars, although it also offers a huge range of water-sports activities along its coast.

Landscape & Wildlife

The west side of the island is more water than land, dominated by the expansive Simpson Bay Lagoon, which is one of the largest landlocked bodies of water in the Caribbean and has moorings for a large array of boats. The island's interior is hilly, with the highest point, Pic Paradis (p714), rising 424m from the center of French St-Martin.

Birdwatching is excellent here, with over 100 different species of bird recorded. Of them, some 60 migratory species include herons, egrets, stilts, pelicans and laughing gulls, which frequent the island's salt ponds. Frigatebirds can be spotted along the coast, and hummingbirds and yellow-breasted banana quits in gardens. Dragonflies and butterflies are prevalent all over the island.

The only native mammals are bats, of which there are eight species. There are also mongooses, racoons, iguanas, geckos, tortoises, sea turtles and several species of tree frog.

The waters on the entire Dutch side, from Cupecoy Bay to Oyster Pond, are protected by Sint Maarten Marine Park. Much of the French side is part of the protected nature reserve Réserve Naturelle de St-Martin.

SURVIVAL GUIDE

ℹ️ Directory A-Z

ACCOMMODATIONS

It's best to book in advance, especially during high season (mid-December to mid-April) and over the Christmas and New Year period in particular, when prices soar.

> ### SLEEPING PRICE RANGES
>
> The following price ranges refer to a double room with bathroom in the high season (mid-December to mid-April).
>
> **$** less than US$150
>
> **$$** US$150–US$300
>
> **$$$** more than US$300

Large resorts dominate the areas of Anse Marcel and Orient Beach on the French side, and Maho and Mullet Bay and Simpson Bay on the Dutch side. Grand Case has some charming boutique properties.

ACTIVITIES

St-Martin/Sint Maarten is a great destination for families and anyone up for an adventure. Water sports are most popular, but there are plenty of outdoor pursuits on land too, including horseback riding, hiking, ziplining, cycling and skydiving.

Cultural activities range from food tours to rum-distillery tours and perfume-making workshops.

Diving

The most popular dive spot is at **Proselyte Reef**, south of Philipsburg, where, in 1802, the 42m, 32-gun British frigate HMS *Proselyte* sank in 15m of water.

Other prime dive sites include the **Maze**, where you can go cave diving and spot turtles, angelfish, sponges and corals; **Turtle Reef**, a deep dive of up to 18m with octopuses, eels, lobster and namesake turtles; and **One Step Beyond**, which has large schools of fish along with barracudas, morays, lobster and sharks.

See www.vacationstmaarten.com for a list of dive shops around the island. Serious divers should consider a day trip to the neighboring islands of Sint Eustatius or Saba.

DANGERS & ANNOYANCES

➡ The disparity between wealthy tourists and islanders can give rise to opportunistic crime such as pickpocketing and muggings.

➡ No-go areas at night include Marigot, Sandy Ground (2km southwest of Marigot), Quartier d'Orléans (3km south of Orient Beach) and Lower Prince's Quarter (the area immediately north of Philipsburg). During the day, Marigot is generally safe to walk around, but the other places are still best avoided.

➡ Be aware that all leased cars on the Dutch side of the island have an 'R' ('Rental') marking

ST-MARTIN/SINT MAARTEN LANDSCAPE & WILDLIFE

on the license plate, making them easy targets for petty thieves and carjackers.

Rental Car Safety

Muggers have been known to follow cars home, and when the victim is driving through a quiet area, the assailants will purposefully bump the car. After you pull over to check for damages, the thief will mug you (and may take off in your car). Petty criminals have also followed victims all the way back to the victim's hotel and robbed them as they walked from the car to their lodging. Be mindful of who is behind and in front of you. If you feel like you are being followed, simply pull into a very public place, or continue driving past where you are staying until the driver goes in another direction. If you are bumped by another car, just continue driving.

ELECTRICITY

French side: 220V, 60 cycles, European-style sockets; Dutch side: 1100V, 60 cycles, North American–style sockets.

EMERGENCY NUMBERS

Ambulance (St-Martin)	☑15
Police (St-Martin)	☑17
Ambulance (Sint Maarten)	☑912
General emergency (Sint Maarten)	☑911
Police (Sint Maarten)	☑111

FOOD

Grand Case, on the French side, is the island's gourmet epicenter. There are also some great hidden beach-bar restaurants and *lolos* (barbecues) scattered around the coastline. Many resorts have top restaurants. Cruise-ship port Philipsburg is home to mainly fast-food and casual eateries (of varying quality), although there are a couple of notable standouts.

The two best-stocked supermarkets are **Marché U** (www.magasins-u.com; Howell Center, Rue de Hollande; ☺8am-8pm Mon-Sat, to 12:45pm Sun) on the French side and **Carrefour** (p710) on the Dutch side.

EATING PRICE RANGES

The following price ranges refer to a main course.

$ less than US$15

$$ US$15–US$30

$$$ more than US$30

GLBT TRAVELERS

While same-sex marriage is legally recognized on both sides of the island – and although the French side is generally more tolerant – some homophobia does exist, so it's best to avoid public displays of affection.

Larger and/or more upmarket resorts tend to be open minded, so booking a double room shouldn't pose any problems.

HEALTH

The island has two small but well-equipped hospitals.

St Maarten Medical Center (SMMC; ☑543-1111; http://smmc.sx; 30 Welgelegen Rd, Cay Hill) East of Philipsburg in the Cay Hill area on the Dutch side; has a 24-hour emergency room.

Centre Hospitalier LC Fleming de Saint Martin (☑0590-52-25-25, emergency ☑0590-52-25-52; www.chsaintmartin.org; Spring Concordia) In Marigot on the French side; has a 24-hour emergency room.

MONEY

The French side uses euros; on the Dutch side items are posted in US dollars. ATMs blanket the island but not all accept foreign cards.

Cash

If you're paying with cash, establishments on both sides invariably accept one-for-one dollars to euros and vice versa, though depending on the current exchange rate, this may work against you.

As not all ATMs accept foreign cards, it's worth keeping cash on hand.

Exchange Rates

AUSTRALIA	A$1	US$0.72
CANADA	C$1	US$0.74
EURO ZONE	€1	US$1.05
JAPAN	¥100	US$0.85
NEW ZEALAND	NZ$1	US$0.69
SWITZERLAND	Sfr1	US$0.98
UK	UK£1	US$1.23

For current exchange rates, see www.xe.com.

Tipping

Hotels Many (but not all) hotels and restaurants include a 15% service charge, in which case no further tipping is necessary (otherwise, add 15% to the bill).

Restaurants Diners commonly leave a small amount for exceptional service.

Taxis It's customary to round up taxi fares.

PUBLIC HOLIDAYS

New Year's Day January 1 (both sides)

Good Friday March/April (Dutch side)

Easter Sunday March/April (Dutch side)

Easter Monday March/April (both sides)

King's Day (Koningsdag) April 27 (Dutch side)

Labor Day May 1 (both sides)

Victory Day May 8 (French side)

Carnival Monday Monday before Ash Wednesday (both sides; unofficial)

Carnival Tuesday Tuesday before Ash Wednesday (both sides; unofficial)

Ash Wednesday February/March (both sides; unofficial)

Ascension Thursday Fortieth day after Easter (both sides)

Abolition Day May 27 (French side)

Whit Sunday Seventh Sunday after Easter (Dutch side)

Pentecost Monday Eighth Monday after Easter (French side)

Emancipation Day July 1 (Dutch side)

Bastille Day July 14 (French side)

Assumption Day August 15 (French side)

Constitution Day October 9 (Dutch side)

All Saints' Day (Toussaints) November 1 (French side)

Sint Maarten Day/Armistice Day November 11 (both sides)

Christmas Day December 25 (both sides)

Boxing Day December 26 (Dutch side)

TELEPHONE

➨ St-Martin's country code is ☏590; Sint Maarten's is ☏1-721.

➨ Be aware that St-Martin's 10-digit landline numbers then begin with ☏0590 (10-digit mobile-phone numbers begin with ☏0690); drop the initial '0' when calling internationally.

➨ Sint Maarten's local numbers are seven digits; landline numbers begin with ☏54, while mobile numbers begin with ☏55.

➨ Calls between the two sides are treated as international calls.

➨ The exit code for both sides of the island is ☏00.

➨ To call the Dutch side from the French side, dial ☏00-1-721, then the seven-digit number.

➨ To dial the French side from the Dutch side, dial ☏00-590, then drop the '0' and dial the remaining nine digits.

TIME

St-Martin/Sint Maarten is on Atlantic Time (GMT/UTC minus four hours). Daylight saving is not observed.

🛈 DRINKING WATER

Tap water on both sides of the island comes from desalination plants. It is generally safe to drink, though doesn't taste very appealing so many locals prefer to drink bottled water.

TRAVELERS WITH DISABILITIES

Although St-Martin is rugged and quite mountainous, the massive amount of tourist development has made it relatively hassle-free for travelers with disabilities to experience the island.

Many resorts have wheelchair-friendly rooms and bathrooms with rails and barrier-free showers. Not all restaurant bathrooms are equipped for wheelchair users, however – confirm when you book.

Download Lonely Planet's free Accessible Travel guide from http://lptravel.to/Accessible Travel.

VOLUNTEERING

Opportunities for volunteering are limited on both sides of the island.

➨ Check first with the French and/or Dutch representation in your home country to see whether volunteering affects your visa status.

➨ One popular volunteering option for both locals and visitors is the annual **Heineken Regatta** (p710).

➨ You could also try contacting the Nature Foundation St Maarten (www.naturefoundationsxm.org) to inquire about monitoring wildlife such as sea turtles as well as various island rehabilitation projects.

🛈 Getting There & Away

AIR

Princess Juliana International Airport (SXM; ☏546-7542; www.sxmairport.com; Airport Rd), on the Dutch side, is where all intercontinental flights arrive and depart. Major airlines fly to the island from North America, including Air Canada, American, Delta, JetBlue and US Airways. Air France connects the island with Paris and KLM has flights from Amsterdam. It is also a major hub for the region, with services to destinations including Anguilla, Antigua, Curaçao, Guadeloupe, Haiti, Jamaica, Montserrat, Saba, San Juan (Puerto Rico), Sint Eustatius, St-Barthélemy, St Kitts & Nevis, St Thomas, Tortola and Trinidad. Regional airlines serving Sint Maarten include Air Sunshine (www.airsunshine.com), LIAT (www.liat.com), Winair (www.fly-winair.com), Air Antilles Express (www.airantilles.com), Insel Air (www.fly-inselair.com) and St Barth Commuter (www.stbarthcommuter.com).

Aéroport de Saint-Martin Grand Case (L'Espérance; SFG; www.saintmartin-airport.com; Rte de l'Espérance), on the French side, has prop planes serving Anguilla, St-Barthélemy, Guadeloupe and Martinique. It's served by Air Caraïbes (www.aircaraibes.com), Air Antilles Express and St Barth Commuter.

SEA
Cruise Ship

No fewer than 18 major companies land in Philipsburg's **Port St Maarten** (www.port stmaarten.com; Juancho Yrausquin Blvd), where passengers disembark directly onto land. Sometimes up to seven ships a day are in port.

Ferry

Ferries depart from Marigot (French side) and Simpson Bay (Dutch side) for Anguilla; Marigot, Philipsburg (Dutch side) and Oyster Pond (on the border, just over the French side) for St-Barthélemy; and from Philipsburg and Simpson Bay for Saba.

M/V Dawn II (☑ in Saba 416-2299; www.sabac transport.com; Bobby's Marina; per adult/child 1 way US$58/35, return US$100/55, same-day return US$78/45) Ferries depart from Sint Maarten at 4.30pm Tuesday, Thursday and Saturday for Saba. Seats are comfortable (it's the better of the two Saba boat services if you're prone to motion sickness); free Heineken is served onboard. There's a US$10 departure tax payable in cash.

M/V Edge (☑ 544-2640; www.stmaarten-activities.com) Catamaran *M/V Edge* leaves Simpson Bay's Pelican Marina at 9am on Tuesday, Thursday and Saturday for the 45-minute trip to St-Barthélemy (one way adult/child US$65/38, day trip US$100/60). It leaves Pelican Marina at 9am on Wednesday, Friday and Sunday for the bumpy 90-minute trip to Saba (one way adult/child US$55/27.50, return US$110/55, day trip US$80/40). Arrive 45 minutes before departure. Departure tax is US$10.

Voyager (☑ 0590-87-10-68; www.voy12.com; 1 way/return €64/84) Regular services sail to/

from Marigot's ferry terminal at Fort Louis' marina (one hour) and Oyster Pond (30 minutes) in St-Martin to St-Barthélemy.

Great Bay Express (☑ 542-0032; www.greatbayferry.com; Bobby's Marina; one way adult/child US$70/45, return US$105/55) Runs five daily services Monday to Saturday (three on Sunday) from Bobby's Marina to St-Barthélemy's ferry terminal. Journey time is 45 minutes. Same-day return day-trip tickets cost US$75/45 per adult/child.

Public Ferries (Fort Louis marina) From Marigot's ferry terminal at Fort Louis' marina, public ferries serve Anguilla every 45 minutes between 8.15am and 7pm, with an additional departure at 10pm. Journey time is 25 minutes. Tickets cost €20 one way, plus a €3 security fee; there's a €20 departure tax (€5 departure tax for day trips).

GB Ferries (http://anguillaferryandcharter. com; Princess Juliana International Airport; one way day/night US$65/80) A reliable operator linking Princess Juliana International Airport in Simpson Bay with Anguilla. Journey time is 20 to 30 minutes. It departs St-Martin/ Sint Maarten between 10am and 6.30pm. In addition, it runs a high-season evening ferry between 10pm and 1am to connect with Princess Juliana International Airport's late-night flights. There's a US$20 departure tax (US$5 for day trips).

Yacht

There are marinas on the Dutch side at Great Bay (Philipsburg) and Simpson Bay Lagoon, on the border at Oyster Pond, and on the French side at Anse Marcel along with two in Marigot (Fort Louis and Port La Royale).

Those arriving by yacht must contact the **immigration office** (☑ 543-0355; www.sint maartengov.org; Clem Labega Sq, Philipsburg) on VHF channel 12 to arrange clearing immigration before docking at the island's marinas.

Two bridges rise to allow boats to enter the coves at Simpson Bay and Sandy Ground. Simpson Bay's bridge opens at 9am, 9.30am, 11am, 11.30am, 4.30pm and 5.30pm December to April (no openings from May to November). Sandy Ground's bridge opens at 8.15am and 2.30pm Monday to Saturday, and 8.15am and 5.30pm Sunday year-round. Visit www.stmartin island.org for updated timetables.

ℹ Getting Around

Although the island is divided into two separate land claims, there are no official border crossings (besides billboards welcoming drivers to each side of the island). Traffic moves freely across both sides of the island as if it were one entity.

PRACTICALITIES

Smoking On both sides of the island, smoking is banned in all enclosed public spaces including hotel rooms, restaurants, cafes and bars. It's permitted in outdoor areas, however, such as terraces, so you may still encounter smoke.

Weights & Measures Both sides of the island use the metric system and 24-hour clock.

BICYCLE

To tackle the island's hilly terrain, **Wind Adventures** (p718) in Orient Beach, on the French side, has mountain bikes for €25 per day, while **Trisport** (p708) in Philipsburg, on the Dutch side, rents bikes for US$25 per day. Take care riding on the roads, as traffic is heavy and not considerate of cyclists.

BUS

➡ Buses are by far the cheapest method of transportation, but they do not have any set schedule.

➡ Buses have their final destination posted on the front shield; most are bound for either Philipsburg or Marigot.

CAR & MOTORCYCLE

All the major car-rental companies, as well as some independents, have desks at **Princess Juliana International Airport** (p723).

In high season prices for a small car start at US$45/€45 per day. During low season they can start as low as US$28/€28.

Make sure you take a good look at your vehicle before leaving the lot, and take photos to avoid being charged for pre-existing damage. Comprehensive insurance is strongly recommended.

Rental companies include the following:

Avis (☑ Sint Maarten 545-2847; www.avis-sxm.com) At both airports.

Banana Location (☑ 0690-71-91-05; www.bananalocation.com; Rte de l'Espérance; ☺ 8am-6pm) At Aéroport de Saint-Martin Grand Case on the French side. Cars can be delivered to other arrival points or your hotel.

Budget (☑ 545-2316; www.budget.com) At Princess Juliana International Airport.

Coastal Car Rental (☑ 543-0244, toll-free 978-8361; www.coastal.sx; Juancho Yrausquin Blvd; cars per day from US$30) At the cruise-ship terminal Port St Maarten; pickup/drop-off at Princess Juliana International Airport can be arranged.

Hertz (☑ in Sint Maarten 545-4541; http://hertz.sxmrentacar.com) Has 10 locations around the island including both airports and the Port St Maarten cruise-ship terminal.

Johnny's Scooter Rental (☑ 587-0272; www.johnnysscooterrental.com; Juancho Yrausquin Blvd; scooter/ATV rental per day US$65/99; ☺ 8am-5:30pm), in Philipsburg, rents scooters and ATV quad bikes (per day US$65/99).

ⓘ DEPARTURE TAX

Departure tax is included in the ticket price for intercontinental flights. A departure tax of US$10/€10 is payable in cash for regional flights; this may be included in the ticket price.

A varying rate of departure tax is payable in cash for ferries, from US$5/€5 plus a security tax of US$3/€3 up to US$20/€20; it's sometimes included in the cost of tickets.

Paradise Island (☑ 546-7709; http://paradisecarrentalsxm.com) At Princess Juliana International Airport.

Sunshine (☑ 546-7711; www.sunshine-car-rental.com) At Princess Juliana International Airport.

Be sure to rent a vehicle on the French side, or a vehicle with French license plates on the Dutch side, as Dutch rental plates are marked with a letter 'R' ('Rental'), making them an easy target for thieves and carjackers.

HITCHHIKING

You'll often see locals hitching, but tourists shouldn't follow suit. Petty theft and violent crime are common on the island and hitchhikers are easy targets.

TAXI

➡ To book a taxi, call 9247 (Sint Maarten) or 0590-87-56-54 (St-Martin).

➡ On the Dutch side, never get in a car that doesn't have a license plate reading 'TXI' indicating that it's a registered taxi.

➡ From Juliana airport it's US$7 to Maho, US$25 to Philipsburg, US$25 to Marigot, US$35 to Grand Case, US$45 to Orient Beach and US$55 to Anse Marcel. Make sure you have change, as drivers aren't always willing or able to take larger notes.

➡ Rates increase by 25% from 10pm to midnight and by 50% between midnight and 6am; there's an additional US$4 charge per passenger for three or more people.

➡ Day or night, agree on a fare before hopping in a cab.

St Vincent & the Grenadines

POP 109,991 / ☏ 784

Best Places to Eat

➡ L'Auberge des Grenadines (p736)

➡ Sugar Reef Cafe (p738)

➡ Fig Tree (p736)

➡ Basil's Bar & Restaurant (p731)

➡ Barracuda (p743)

Best Places to Sleep

➡ Cotton House (p738)

➡ Petit St Vincent Resort (p745)

➡ Tamarind Beach Hotel & Yacht Club (p740)

➡ Palm Island Resort (p744)

➡ Bequia Plantation Hotel (p736)

Why Go?

Just the name St Vincent and the Grenadines (SVG) evokes visions of exotic, idyllic island life. Imagine an island chain in the heart of the Caribbean Sea, uncluttered by tourist exploitation, with white-sand beaches on deserted islands, sky-blue water gently lapping the shores and barely a soul around.

While it may sound like a playground for the rich and famous, you don't need your own yacht to enjoy SVG. In fact cheap ferries make exploring this archipelago nation independently a breeze and with so many islands to choose from, there's sure to be one that perfectly meets your needs.

And while it's famed for its islands and beaches, the country offers more than just a relax in a hammock. There are volcanoes to climb, refreshing waterfalls to explore and great hiking throughout.

When to Go

Jan–May The dry season is the best time to island hop through the Grenadines and laze on spectacular beaches along the way.

Jun–Aug Heavy rains scare away the crowds, but Vincy's party season gets into full swing, led by the raucous Vincy Mas Carnival.

Oct–Nov The shoulder season brings thinner crowds and lower prices and, as long as a storm isn't passing through, usually a decent amount of fine weather.

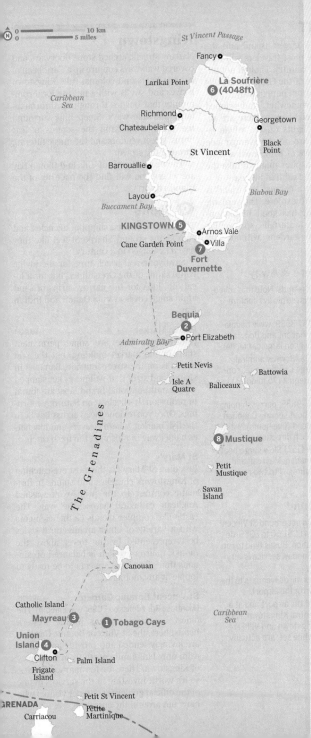

St Vincent Passage

0 — 10 km
0 — 5 miles

Caribbean Sea

Fancy

Larikai Point

La Soufrière (4048ft) **6**

Richmond

Chateaubelair

Georgetown

Black Point

St Vincent

Barrouallie

Layou

Biabou Bay

Buccament Bay

KINGSTOWN 5

Arnos Vale

Cane Garden Point

Villa

7

Fort Duvernette

Bequia **2**

Admiralty Bay

Port Elizabeth

Petit Nevis

Isle A Quatre

Battowia

Baliceaux

The Grenadines

8 Mustique

Petit Mustique

Savan Island

Canouan

Catholic Island

Mayreau 3

1 Tobago Cays

Caribbean Sea

Union Island 4

Clifton

Palm Island

Frigate Island

Petit St Vincent

GRENADA

Petite Martinique

Carriacou

St Vincent & the Grenadines Highlights

1 **Tobago Cays** (p741) Visiting these five picture-perfect islands that are the essential SVG snorkeling experience.

2 **Bequia** (p734) Tossing away your return ticket upon settling into one of the region's best small islands.

3 **Mayreau** (p740) Chilling out on postcard-perfect Saltwhistle Bay before partying the night away with new friends.

4 **Union Island** (p742) Hopping between the many bars and restaurants on this remote island outpost.

5 **Kingstown** (p728) Keeping it real on the cobblestone streets of SVG's biggest city and capital, a vibrant and decidedly nonupscale mélange.

6 **La Soufrière** (p735) Hiking to the top of this immense sulfur-spitting volcano.

7 **Fort Duvernette** (p729) Climbing the spiral staircase to the top of this rock fortress jutting out of the sea.

8 **Mustique** (p738) Kicking up your heels with rock stars at this impossibly beautiful and expensive island.

ST VINCENT

St Vincent is SVG's largest island and the hub through which most travelers will pass on their visit to the country. Though not un-inspiring, the allure of the Grenadines pulls most visitors away from here quickly.

The island is somewhat undeveloped compared to its neighbors – there are no functioning traffic lights on the whole island. The beaches are on the average side and the frenetic pace of Kingstown and its unpolished edges inspires many to take the first boat down to the calm of Bequia.

But if you give it a chance, the island is a fascinating place to explore. The verdant, rainforested interior has good hiking op-tions and there are waterfalls, spectacular old forts and lush gardens without any crowds at all.

ⓘ Getting There & Away

Several ferries link the islands. Note that sched-ules can change by whim so always confirm timings.

Bequia Express (☑457-3539; www.bequia-express.net) Links St Vincent and Bequia (one hour) several times daily on large car ferries.

MV Admiral (☑458-3348; www.admiral-tytransport.com) A large car ferry that con-nects St Vincent and Bequia (75 minutes) two to three times daily.

MV Barracuda (☑455-9835; perrysshipping@vincysurf.com) Cargo boat serving Canouan, Mayreau and Union Island (five hours), with three trips a week in each direction

MV Gem Star (☑457-4157) Slow cargo boat from St Vincent to Canouan, Mayreau and Union Island (seven hours), with two round-trips each week.

ⓘ Getting Around

Buses are a good way to get around St Vincent, with fares ranging from EC$1.50 to EC$6, de-pending on the destination. Buses tend to run from 6am to 8pm; on Sunday, service is very limited.

Car-rental companies will deliver cars to the ferry dock in Kingstown or the airport.

Taxis are available at the airport and at a couple of stands in central Kingstown. Fares from the airport to Kingstown and Villa are EC$30. Other fares, while set, are actually negotiable.

Kingstown

Narrow streets, arched stone doorways and covered walkways conjure up a Caribbean of banana boats and colonial rule. Kingstown heaves and swells with a pulsing local com-munity that bustles through its throrough-fares and alleyways. Steep hills surround the town, amplifying the sounds of car horns, street vendors and the music filtering through the crowd.

The nearby towns of Villa and Indian Bay are where you will find the majority of the island's resorts.

⊙ Sights

The narrow streets, shipping agencies and rum shops around Sharpe St feel like they haven't changed in a century.

Save your real beach time for the idyllic white sands of the Grenadines, but for a lo-cal dip, look for the narrow strips of sand amid small coves at **Villa Beach** and **Indian Bay**.

Public Market   MARKET
(☉6am-3pm) There are some permanent stalls in the market building, but the real action is on the streets outside. Bananas in shapes and sizes that will never get slapped with a multi-national-brand label are found in profusion. It's liveliest on Saturday morn-ings. Once you're done, head across Bay St to the fish market, where cleavers and machet-es bang away in unison at the fresh catch.

St Mary's   CHURCH
Brooding St Mary's is the most eye-catching of Kingstown's churches and stands in dra-matic contrast to the prim, whitewashed Anglican cathedral across the way. The castle-like complex blends Gothic elements with a variety of other architectural styles best represented by the tower above the monks' quarters, which is balanced on sin-uous thin pillars and appears to be ready to topple at any moment.

St Vincent Botanic Gardens   GARDENS
(Montrose Rd; admission EC$5; ☉6am-6pm) The oldest botanical gardens in the western hemisphere, the St Vincent Botanic Gardens are lovingly tended and provide an oasis of calm only half a mile north from the frenzy of Kingstown. There are few marked species, so it's worth investing in the services of one of the official guides (EC$10 per visitor) who hang out around the entrance.

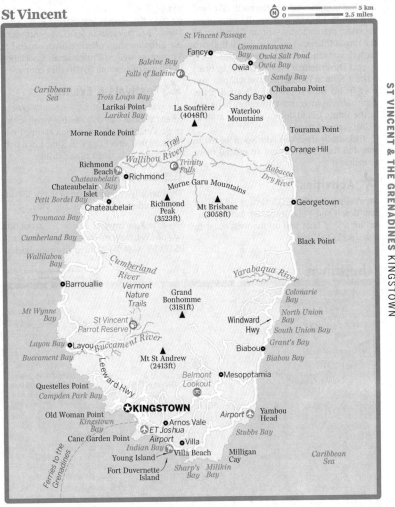

Fort Charlotte FORT

(⏱6am-6pm) **FREE** Just north of the city and standing proudly atop a 660ft-high ridge, Fort Charlotte (1806) offers commanding views of both town and the Grenadines to the south. It was once a fearsome military post with dozens of cannons, a few of which remain. There are usually a couple of local guides hanging around who will show you around for EC$10 each. It's well worth contracting their services.

It's a stiff 40-minute walk uphill from town. Walk to the west end of Tyrrel St and keep following the road as it curves uphill.

Like most roads in Vincy there's no footpath, so watch out for speeding vans. Alternatively, you can take a bus from the Leeward Bus Station to Edinboro and then walk the last 10 minutes to the fort.

★ Fort Duvernette FORT

(Rock Fort; ☎451-2921; svgntrust@gmail.com; admission EC$5; ⏱8am-6pm) Perched atop a large volcanic rock offshore from Villa, this eerie fort was constructed to defend the town of Calliaqua and affords fantastic 360-degree views of the southern shoreline. There are 225 steps in the spiral staircase that has been carved into the rock; take care as it can be slippery, with small stones often covering the walkway – bring footwear. At the top, 200ft above sea level, you'll find two batteries of cannons and a picnic area.

Fort Duvernette is only accessible by boat. Ask for Nato in Indian Bay who will take you over in his little rowboat for a good price. Alternatively, motorboat operators hang out at the Young Island dock and charge around EC$100 round-trip.

Technically there's an admission fee to the fort, but there's not always an official there to collect it.

🏃 Activities

Snorkeling can be OK a little way off Indian Bay Beach and Villa Beach. For better snorkeling take a boat trip up the west coast to some secluded bays.

Indigo Dive DIVING
(☎ 493-9494; www.indigodive.com; Blue Lagoon Marina; 1-/2-tank dives US$60/120; ⊙ 8am-6pm) An intimate shop offering dives around St Vincent as well as Professional Association of Diving Instructors (PADI) dive courses.

🎊 Festivals & Events

Vincy Mas CARNIVAL
(⊙ end of Jun or early Jul) *The* big yearly event in St Vincent. This enormous carnival culminates in a street party in Kingstown with steel-pan bands, dancers and drinks.

🛏 Sleeping

The majority of options are in the beachside communities of Indian Bay and Villa.

Skyblue Apartments APARTMENT $
(☎ 457-4394; skyblue@vincysurf.com; Indian Bay; r US$78-85; ❄@🛜) Nestled in the suburban

Kingstown

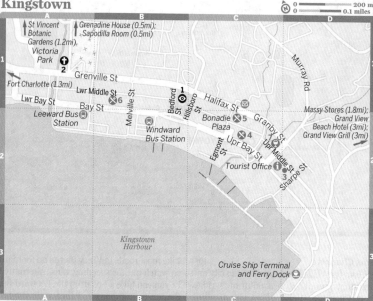

neighborhood of Indian Bay, this well-managed place is neat, tidy and just steps from the water. The tranquil rooms are comfortable, but are not liable to win design awards; all come equipped with kitchens.

★**Grenadine House**   BOUTIQUE HOTEL **$$**
(🖉458-1800; www.grenadinehouse.com; r US$150-230; 🌢@🖭) Perched in the hills overlooking Kingstown like a fortress of whitewashed luxury, Grenadine House is away from the beach and near the genteel district of the botanical gardens. The property offers fantastic views of town and the Grenadines. White linen with thread counts to brag about, wicker headboards and fresh flowers complement the bedrooms. The food and drink options are excellent.

The French governor-general, the original resident in the 1760s, would still approve.

★**Beachcombers Hotel**   RESORT **$$**
(🖉458-4283; www.beachcombershotel.com; s/d from US$96/124; @🛜🖭) This is a real find on Villa's west side. Multicolored buildings dot the landscape in true Caribbean style. The entry-level rooms are fairly basic, but the midrange options have fine furnishings and are fantastic value. The best rooms have large verandas overlooking the harbor and islands. An elegant restaurant (mains EC$45 to EC$90) and sea-view pool seal the deal.

Blue Lagoon Marina   HOTEL **$$**
(🖉458-4308; www.bluelagoonsvg.com; Ratho Mill; r with/without kitchenette US$219/199) Catering to yachties and landfarers alike, this recently renovated marina on the southern reaches of the island has comfortable modern rooms with colorful paint jobs that afford views of the bay and the bobbing yachts moored in front. Some have kitchenettes although it's not essential as there's a cafe, restaurant and a bar on-site.

Grand View Beach Hotel   RESORT **$$**
(🖉458-4811; www.grandviewhotel.com; Villa Point; s/d from US$104/125; 🌢@🛜🖭) Sweeping views of the island-dotted waters and curvaceous shore at Villa Point are reason enough to stay at this modest hillside resort with a truthful name. The 19 rooms are split between cozy but charismatic ones in an old plantation house and larger ones in a modern Spanish-style wing. The grounds are lovely and the beach is a short stroll away.

ISLAND TOURS

Bamboo Adventures (🖉430-4281; www.booksvgnow.com; Georgetown) A new operator with good customer service and quality guides, offering all the usual tours and tailor-made options.

Sailor's Wilderness Tours (🖉457-1274; www.sailorswildernesstours.com; full-day tours US$95) A popular local tour company offering a range of trips, including volcano tours and visits to waterfalls.

Young Island Resort   RESORT **$$$**
(🖉458-4826; www.youngisland.com; Young Island; s/d incl 2 meals from US$506/646; 🌢@🖭) It's only 200yd offshore from Villa, but the private, vaguely heart-shaped Young Island is a whole world away. The 29 units here include sexy villas, some with plunge pools, killer views and everything you need to forget about the little hotel ferry back to St Vincent.

Go for a room right by the water or up on the hill, and avoid those stuck in the middle. Not all rooms have air-con, but there is no difference in price so make sure to request it when booking.

The resort also offers a day package for visitors (US$120) that includes a room, lunch for two and use of all facilities.

✗ Eating

Chilli'n   CARIBBEAN **$**
(🖉456-1776; www.chillinsvg.com; Egmont St; mains EC$15-20, wraps & burgers EC$10-13; ☺7am-8pm Mon-Thu, to 11pm Fri & Sat) An unpretentious restaurant with a social vibe that's a good place to get an affordable bite to eat or just hang out for some drinks. There's a daily local-meal special as well as pizzas and sandwiches. At night the music gets turned up and it morphs into a fun bar popular with locals and expats alike.

Massy Stores   SUPERMARKET **$**
(Casson Hill Rd; ☺7am-8pm Mon-Sat, to 1pm Sun) Best supermarket on the island.

Basil's Bar & Restaurant   INTERNATIONAL **$$**
(🖉457-2713; Cobblestone Inn, Upper Bay St; mains from EC$34-69; ☺8am-late) If the food wasn't so good, you might think you'd entered a pirate's dungeon, given the moody lighting and stone walls. Food spans American

and Caribbean favorites; the lunch buffet (EC$37.50) is great. It has Kingstown's classiest bar.

Grand View Grill
CARIBBEAN $$

(☑ 458-4811; Indian Bay; mains EC$45-80; ⊗ 3-10pm Tue-Sun) Right by the sands of Indian Bay, this casual restaurant attached to the Grand View Beach Hotel is a winner, with grilled mains served with two tasty sides as well as pizzas, pasta and burgers. Look out for the regular jerk nights.

Veejays
CARIBBEAN $$

(buffet items EC$12-20, rotis EC$11-30, mains EC$30-50; ⊗10am-9pm Mon-Thu & Sat, to midnight Fri) On the northern edge of Kingstown, buzzing Veejays has a popular lunch buffet featuring traditional Vincentian dishes. Eat inside the air-conditioned dining area downstairs, or on the open-air terrace at the top. There's also an extensive menu of other dishes; locals rate Veejays' rotis as the best on the island and they're even available in meat-free soy versions.

Sapodilla Room
CARIBBEAN $$

(☑ 458-1800; www.grenadinehouse.com; Grenadine House; mains EC$43-65; ⊗ 7-10pm, terrace 7-10am & noon-3pm) The classic dining room of the Grenadine House hotel offers a small menu featuring locally sourced produce in dishes that combine Creole, Caribbean and American flavors. Start your night in the elegant Mayfair-style British pub. For casual fare outside with great views, try the terrace.

Young Island Resort
FUSION $$$

(☑ 458-4826; www.youngisland.com; lunch EC$32-47, dinner EC$168; ⊗ noon-2pm & 7-10pm) There are few places that can boast that their specialty is bread, but here at Young Island the proof is in the pumpernickel. Every meal comes with a barge full of fresh bread to accompany the equally fresh seafood and other dishes prepared with some of St Vincent's best bounty. Tables are set in beautiful gardens by the beach.

Nonguests are welcome; reserve in advance. The little hotel boat takes five minutes to reach the resort.

French Veranda
FRENCH $$$

(☑ 453-1111; www.marinershotel.com; Mariners Hotel, Villa; mains EC$65-90; ⊗ noon-10pm) It's not all French – there's also curry, satay sauce and pizza on the menu – but there is escargot and it's all served on a lovely veranda

with sweeping views in a mood of casual elegance. Portions can be a bit on the small side for the price.

🍷 Drinking & Nightlife

Impromptu bars rule the streets in the center of town as the Saturday market wanes in the afternoon. The area around Heritage Sq is Kingstown's number-one 'liming' spot.

Flow Wine Bar
WINE BAR

(☑ 457-0809; James St; ⊗ 11am-10pm Mon-Thu, to midnight Fri, 6pm-midnight Sat) Fabulously chic for grubby downtown Kingstown, Flow is a dimly lit top-floor bar with sofas to spare, a chilled soundtrack and an extensive selection of wine by the glass and bottle. The food here is inventive and excellent value – try the jalapeño wontons. A place to put your Caribbean escape on hold just for a moment.

ⓘ Information

General Post Office (☑ 456-1111; Halifax St; ⊗ 8:30am-3pm Mon-Fri, to 11:30am Sat)
Tourist Office (p748)

ⓘ Getting There & Away

BUS

There are two bus stations in Kingstown, both of which are located on Bay St near the center of town.
Leeward Bus Station For buses to the western side of the island.
Windward Bus Station Buses to the east and south of the island.

FERRY

Services to the Grenadines depart from the ferry dock on the southern side of Kingstown Bay.
MV Gem Star (p728) Slow cargo boat from St Vincent to Canouan, Mayreau and Union Island, with two trips each way each week.
MV Barracuda (p728) Slow cargo boat serving Canouan, Mayreau and Union Island, with three trips each way each week.

Leeward Highway

The Leeward Hwy runs north of Kingstown along St Vincent's west coast for 25 very slow miles, ending at Richmond Beach. Offering some lovely scenery, the road climbs into the mountains as it leaves Kingstown, then winds through hillsides and back down to deeply cut coastal valleys that open to coconut plantations, fishing villages and bays lined with black-sand beaches.

◎ Sights

Layou Petroglyph Park   ARCHAEOLOGICAL SITE

(Layou; EC$5) Around half a mile off the main road, this lovely park is centered around a large rock perched on the side of a rushing stream that was carved by St Vincent's original indigenous inhabitants. The petroglyph itself, while interesting to look at, will not hold your attention for long, but the park is a lovely place to relax. Bring a picnic lunch to enjoy in one of the gazebos.

Wallilabou Falls   WATERFALL

(☑ 531-1310; EC$5; ◷ 9am-6pm) An inviting waterfall that splits into two streams over three large boulders before filling a large swimming hole surrounded by trees and birdlife. Downstream, the river passes beneath a colonial-era dam that has been reclaimed by nature, with trees growing out from gaps in the stones.

Cumberland Bay   BEACH

A lovely secluded bay framed by jungle-covered bluffs, Cumberland is a popular anchorage for more adventurous yachties. It's also a fine place for a swim. There's a distinctly local bar-restaurant overlooking the black sands. If you're looking for even more seclusion, head to the next bay, Troumaca Bottom, which is equally beautiful and rarely visited.

Dark View Falls   WATERFALL

Set among striking mountains covered with lush foliage, this double waterfall is the most beautiful on the island that you don't need a boat to get to. The turnoff is almost at the northern end of the Leeward Hwy, between Chateaubelair and Richmond; look for the small sign on the right after passing the hydroelectric plant. From the turn, it's about a 10-minute drive on a shocking 'road'.

☆ Activities

Richmond Vale Diving & Hiking   HIKING, DIVING

(☑ 458-2255; www.richmondvalehiking.com; Richmond Vale, Chateaubelair; volcano hike US$75-85) Run out of the Richmond Vale Academy (an international school focused on environmental and social issues), this adventure shop is the only one of its kind in the island's north. It organizes treks to the summit of La Soufrière volcano, as well as along other

A PIRATE'S LIFE

Just a few years ago, remote Wallilabou Bay was one of the most recognizable places in all of SVG. The little anchorage was transformed into the pirate haven of 'Port Royal' and various parts of the first *Pirates of the Caribbean* movie were filmed here in 2002 (in addition to a couple of scenes from one of the sequels). It's easy to see why the producers selected the spot – it's a beautiful natural setting with calm waters flanked by forest that feels far from civilization. Today the last vestiges of most of the sets are long gone, but one of the building facades has been maintained for fans alongside a few props from the movie.

With a bit of imagination you can still relax in true buccaneer style at the waterside bar and restaurant.

Buses running between Kingstown and Chateaubelair will drop you at Wallilabou. Just let the driver know if you want the bay or the waterfalls. Both are right by the main road.

nature trails. The attached dive shop offers both shore and boat dives.

The academy also rents out simple rooms (single/double US$35/50) at its hilltop base, which grows organic produce and has fantastic views of the surrounding area.

Vermont Nature Trails   HIKING

(EC$5; ◷ 9am-5pm) About 5 miles north of Kingstown along the Leeward Hwy, a sign points east to the Vermont Nature Trails, 3.5 miles inland, where you'll find the Parrot Lookout Trail. The 1.75-mile loop (two hours) passes through the southwestern tip of the St Vincent Parrot Reserve, a thick rainforest where, if you're lucky, you might spot the namesake bird in its natural habitat.

ⓘ Getting There & Away

Buses run from Kingstown's Leeward Bus Station up to Chateaubelair, a short distance short of Richmond at the end of the highway. Many attractions are well off the main road, so to fully explore the area it's best to hire a vehicle.

Windward Highway

The windward (east) coast of St Vincent is a mix of wave-lashed shoreline, quiet bays and small undeveloped towns. The black-sand beaches meld into the banana plantations and the lush vegetation grows up into the hilly interior.

As you head north, you really start to get off the beaten track. The jungle gets a bit thicker, the road a bit narrower and towering La Soufrière volcano (4048ft) begins to dominate the skyline.

Continuing on you will hit Sandy Bay, a sizable village that has the island's largest concentration of Black Caribs. North is Owia Bay and the village of Owia, where you'll find the Salt Pond, a group of tidal pools protected from the crashing Atlantic by a massive stone shield. This is a popular swimming hole with crystal-clear waters and a view of St Lucia to the north.

BEQUIA

Bequia (beck-way) is the most perfect island in the whole Grenadines. Stunning beaches dotting the shoreline, accommodations to fit most budgets and a slow pace of life all help to create an environment that is unforgettable. There are fine restaurants, shops that retain their local integrity and enough golden sand and blue water to keep everybody blissful.

✦✦ Festivals & Events

Easter Regatta SAILING
Around Easter, this is SVG's main sailing event.

ℹ Information

Bequia Customs & Immigration Office
(☑ 457-3044; ⊘ 8:30am-6pm Mon-Fri, 8:30am-noon & 3-6pm Sat, 9am-noon & 3-6pm Sun)

ℹ Getting There & Away

Ferry services link Bequia with St Vincent and the southern Grenadine islands. All services arrive at and depart from the main dock in Port Elizabeth.

Bequia Express (☑ 458-3472; www.bequia-express.net) Car ferry running to St Vincent (one way/return EC$25/45, one hour) several times daily.

MV Admiral (☑ 458-3348; www.admiral-ty-transport.com) Car ferry to St Vincent (one way/return EC$20/35, one hour), running several times daily. It's an older boat and spends quite a bit of time in dry dock – call to check if it's running.

Bequia's airport doesn't see many regular flights. **SVG Air** (p749) has one flight a day between Bequia and St Vincent, although by the time you mess around at both airports it's quicker to take the boat. It also runs a direct international flight between Bequia and Barbados. Schedules change frequently so check the website before making plans.

WORTH A TRIP

MESOPOTAMIA

Montreal Gardens (EC$13; ⊘9am-4pm Mon-Fri) Tucked away at the end of a rough road at the top of the valley above Mesopotamia – the SVG version – St Vincent's other botanical gardens are in many ways superior to their more famous Kingstown counterparts. Surrounded by craggy mountains and rolling hills, the setting is spectacular and the gardens themselves are a deliciously lush and colorful affair awash with birdsong.

Belmont Lookout On the road to Mesopotamia there is an excellent lookout where you peer down into the impossibly green valley, known as the breadbasket of San Vincent. It's a lush landscape dotted with small farms and palm trees. On the other side of the road the view is equally impressive across to Bequia, Mustique and Garifuna Rock, which was the first prison of the Black Caribs before they were expelled to Honduras.

There's a small information booth next to the car park. For a spectacular loop, you can continue on the narrow, twisting roads from Belmont through the verdant valley to the southern coast road and back to Kingstown.

LA SOUFRIÈRE VOLCANO

St Vincent's La Soufrière volcano dominates the northern part of the island and a hike to its summit is a highlight for adventurous travelers.

The crater is an otherworldly environment with shag-carpet-like moss growing on the ground and mounds of black rocks all around. There are also some active sulfur outlets.

There are two routes to the top. The easiest route, and the one that is officially promoted to visitors, begins from the windward side of the island, where a proper trail leads up from the car park to the summit. It's a moderate 2½-hour hike.

But if you're looking for real adventure, consider the leeward trail that begins near Chateaubelair at the end of the Leeward Hwy. It's a longer, more challenging hike, but you'll be rewarded with views of both the volcano and the sea all the way up, and there's more bush along the trail. It takes around four hours from the trailhead and a local guide is essential as the path is not clearly marked.

ⓘ Getting Around

Bikes are easily rented; cars cost about US$60 per day.

Local minibuses run on a set route from the dock to Paget Farm, near the airport, and cost EC$2 to EC$5. If you pay extra they will detour to Lower Bay or down to the water at Friendship Bay.

Private taxis (EC$15 to EC$40) can be minivans, SUVs or open-top pickups. Prices are fixed and can be obtained at the **Bequia Tourism Association** (☑ 458-3286; www.bequiatourism. com; ☺ 9:30am-5:30pm).

Port Elizabeth

⊙ Sights

Hang around the ferry dock and make some new friends as you sit under the copious coverage of the iconic **almond tree**.

★**Princess Margaret Beach**   BEACH
Simply divine. Located just around the corner from Port Elizabeth, this is one of the loveliest stretches of sand on the island. It is backed by a wall of lush vegetation and the deep, calm waters are perfect for swimming.

To get here on foot from Port Elizabeth, follow the Belmont walkway right to the end of Admiralty Bay and look for the steps leading to a dirt path up the bluff. At the top a set of wooden stairs leads down to a short concrete path constructed out in the water that loops around the rocks to the beginning of the bay. A small section of the concrete path was washed out by Hurricane Matthew, but it's still possible to skirt around the edge. From town it's a short journey, but not ideal for those who fear heights.

Alternatively, follow the vehicular access route, traveling on the main road south and turning down the signed narrow access road to the beach (about a five-minute, EC$25 taxi trip). Or arrive in style by getting a ride on one of the water taxis idling in the harbor.

🏃 Activities

★**Friendship Rose**   BOATING
(☑ 457-3888; www.friendshiprose.com; day trips adult/child from US$140/70) This 80ft vintage schooner is a beautiful example of classic boatbuilding and once served as a mail boat. Now it runs day trips to various Grenadines islands, including Mustique and the Tobago Cays. Prices include breakfast, lunch and refreshments.

★**Ramblers Hiking Tours**   HIKING
(☑ 430-0555; www.hiking-bequia.com; hikes per person from US$25) Explore the green hills and flower-scented trails of Bequia with informative local guide Donnaka.

Dive Bequia   DIVING
(☑ 458-3504; www.divebequia.com; Walkway; 1-/2-tank dives US$78/140; ☺ 8am-4:30pm) A highly rated dive shop with plenty of local experience. Also runs snorkeling trips.

Bequia Dive Adventures   DIVING
(☑ 458-3826; www.bequiadiveadventures.com; Belmont Walkway; 1-/2-tank dive US$70/120) Dives throughout the Grenadines.

🛏 Sleeping

Port Elizabeth has the biggest range of accommodations on the island. You'll find several hotels lining the Belmont Walkway, as well as some cheaper options up in the hills right behind town.

Rambler's Rest
GUESTHOUSE $

(📞 430-0555; www.rentalsbequia.com; r/apt US$66/149; 🛜) This haven, just above the docks, is owned by the irrepressible Donna-ka, a splendid host and gentleman. He has two simple rooms (there's a shared kitchen and terrace with great views) and a larger two-bedroom apartment. He's not always on the island, but when he's around he delights in taking guests on walks and he runs Ram-blers Hiking Tours (p735).

Gingerbread Hotel
HOTEL $$

(📞 458-3800; ginger@vincysurf.com; Belmont Walkway; r US$160-270) Like a set piece from a production of *Hansel and Gretel*, Ginger-bread looks exactly as you'd expect, with ornate eaves nailed to a steep roof. The spotless rooms are spread over the lovely grounds just beside the restaurant in the main house and some offer private balconies overlooking the bay.

Bequia Plantation Hotel
HOTEL $$$

(📞 534-9444; www.bequiaplantationhotel.com; r US$250-300, cottages US$450; 🏊) Set on spa-cious grounds at the end of Admiralty Bay, this recently renovated hotel feels removed from the downtown hustle but is just an effortless stroll from the action. There are six comfortable rooms upstairs in the main building, the best of which are the two with sea-view balconies, and more private stand-alone cottages spread among the coconut palms.

🍴 Eating

Green Boley
CARIBBEAN $

(Belmont Walkway; rotis EC$10-18) Adding a bit of local character to the Belmont Walkway, this simple green wooden bar sells cheap and delicious rotis; take your pick of chick-en, conch or beef. There's also a full selection of drinks, including the famous Green Bolet rum punch. Inside has all the atmosphere, but the picnic tables outside have the first-class views.

Doris Fresh Food
SUPERMARKET $

(Back St; 🕐 8am-4:30pm Mon-Sat, to noon Sun) It looks just like a house from the street, but out the back you'll find Bequia's best selec-tion of imported products and wines. There's everything from rice noodles to artichokes and a variety of fresh fruit and vegetables.

Bequia Market
MARKET $

(🕐 7am-6pm) It's hard to miss the local fruit-and-vegetable market, just off the wa-ter, near the center of town. Vendors are famed for their aggressive sales techniques, despite the large notice on the wall that makes it clear that stuffing samples into visitors' mouths is against the rules. You've been warned.

⭐ Fig Tree
CARIBBEAN $$

(📞 457-3008; www.figtreebequia.com; Belmont Walkway; mains EC$30-60; 🕐 8am-10pm, closed Tue) A 300m stroll along the waterfront west of the docks, this open-air restaurant has views to match both the great food and hos-pitality of the owner, Cheryl Johnson. Creole touches abound; book ahead for the Friday night fish fry.

It runs a reading room for local children – book donations are appreciated.

Mac's Pizzeria
PIZZA $$

(📞 458-3474; Belmont Walkway; pizzas EC$45-70; 🕐 11am-10pm) Mac's packs in the crowds for its top-quality pizzas and snacks. A few steps from the beach, it has an elevated deck over-flowing with happy diners swapping slices and telling stories. Make sure to leave some room for the Bequia lime pie.

⭐ L'Auberge des Grenadines
CREOLE $$$

(📞 457-3555; www.caribrestaurant.com; mains EC$30-100; 🕐 noon-2pm & 6-10pm) At the north end of Port Elizabeth, this simple two-story house has a wide patio and veranda with ideal harbor views. Classic top-end island preparations combine Creole spice with French flair. Few diners seem to resist the fresh lobster. There's jazzy music several nights a week.

🛍 Shopping

Mauvin's Model Boat Shop
GIFTS & SOUVENIRS

(Front St; 🕐 9am-5pm Mon-Sat) Carefully crafted model boats are made here under a breadfruit tree and sold in a tidy little gallery.

Bequia Bookshop
BOOKS

(Front St; 🕐 8:30am-4:30pm Mon-Fri, 9am-1pm Sat) The best bookstore in the region stocks everything from charts and survey maps to yachting books and flora and fauna guides. Browse West Indian, North American and European literature, and you'll even find some long-out-of-print tomes just waiting a buyer.

ℹ Information

Bequia Tourism Association (p735) An excellent resource, located in the small building on the ferry dock and staffed by helpful locals.

Bank of San Vincent & Grenadines (☎ 458-3700; ⊗ 8am-2pm Mon-Thu, to 4pm Fri) Bank with 24-hour ATM.

Maria's Cafe (per hr EC$10; 🛜) Just down the road from the main marina, and upstairs. Sit on the balcony, grab a drink and check your email.

Post Office (⊗ 9am-noon & 1-3pm Mon-Fri, 9-11:30am Sat) Opposite the ferry dock on Front St.

ℹ Getting There & Away

James F Mitchell Airport is near Paget Farm, at the southwest end of the island. The frequent ferries from Kingstown dock right in Port Elizabeth.

Many places are accessible on foot from Port Elizabeth.

Lower Bay

The tiny beachside community of Lower Bay has the best beach on the island: the stunningly clear waters of Admiralty Bay spread out in front like a turquoise fan from a base of golden sand. It's never crowded. Vendors rent out beach chairs and there are a couple of cute beachfront cafes.

⊙ Sights

Lower Bay   BEACH
Not quite as famous as the island's star Princess Margaret Beach, this is an equally splendid stretch of sand that has a couple of places to get meals and a drink. Note: beware of manchineel trees here as they can cause a bad rash.

🛏 Sleeping & Eating

De Reef Apartments   APARTMENT $$
(☎ 458-3484; dereef@vincysurf.com; per night from US$100; ❄) Offering some of the best value on the island, these homely apartments are decked out with everything you'll need, including air-con in the bedrooms, and are set in a garden full of fruit trees just across the road from inviting Lower Bay. They all boast spacious terraces and are a great choice for peace and quiet.

De Reef   CAFE $$
(☎ 458-3484; dereef@vincysurf.com; meals EC$25-60; ⊗ 8am-late) Right on the sand (in fact, you can squish it between your toes),

this cafe serves up fresh seafood and comfort food throughout the day. The bar is skilled with rum punch and you can have yours on a lounger in the sand. Take a dip in the perfect surf and have another. Hugely popular on Sundays.

ℹ Getting There & Away

The Paget Farm bus from Port Elizabeth will drop you at the Lower Bay junction, from where its a 10-minute walk down the hill to the village. If you pay a little extra, the bus will take you all the way down.

Friendship Bay

Located over the hill on the southeast coast of the island, the gentle curve of Friendship Bay is about 1.5 miles from Port Elizabeth.

A rarely crowded crescent of sand, the beach here is a top reason to make the strenuous yet short walk over the spine of the island (or wimp out on a short taxi or bus ride). A dense thicket of palms provides shade and that nicely clichéd tropical look.

🛏 Sleeping

Sugar Apple Inn   HOTEL $$
(☎ 475-3148; www.sugarappleinn.com; r US$132-200; ❄🛜⊠) Offering outstanding value, these bright and spacious apartments have separate kitchens with walls of windows that open out to reveal phenomenal sea views. Spotless, spacious and with all the amenities, it's just a short walk from Friendship Bay. There are also a couple of cottages right down on the sand. Service is warm and public transportation runs right past the door.

★ Bequia Beach Hotel   RESORT $$$
(☎ 458-1600; www.bequiabeach.com; Friendship Bay; r US$368-580; ❄@🛜⊠) A sprawling low-rise resort with a privileged location right on Friendship Bay that manages to balance style and elegance with an unpretentious atmosphere. Accommodations range from garden-view cottages to suites overlooking the water and villas with private pools. All are finished with top-quality furnishings.

ℹ Getting There & Away

Friendship Bay is close enough to walk from Port Elizabeth, although you have to climb up and over a steep hill. Alternatively, the Paget Farm bus will drop you at the top of the hill overlooking the bay; if you pay a bit extra it will take you all the way down.

Spring Bay

On a quiet island, this is the quiet end. It's a brief hop over the central spine from Port Elizabeth. Sugar plantations still operate here, and there are good views of the oft-ten-turbulent waters to the east.

◉ Sights

Old Hegg Turtle Sanctuary   WILDLIFE RESERVE
(EC$15; ⊙9am-5pm) At this 'sanctuary,' a well-known institution on Bequia, turtle eggs are hatched and transferred to small concrete pools, ostensibly to give them a better chance in the wild. While there's no reason to doubt the ecological intentions of the owner, it's unclear whether the hand-reared turtles have the skills necessary to survive on their own or find it back to their birthplace to breed.

🛏 Sleeping & Eating

Most of the accommodations are high-end boutique hotels.

All the hotels here have their own dining areas or restaurants.

Sugar Reef   BOUTIQUE HOTEL $$
(⊡458-3400; www.sugarreefbequia.com; Spring Bay; r US$150-300; 🖥) An impeccable hotel with beautiful rooms spread over 65 acres; half are on the hillside in an imposing stone mansion and the others down by the cafe fronting a palm-shaded beach. The seaside rooms are superb with whitewashed stone walls and double doors right onto the sands. There's no air-con but you won't need it with the constant sea breeze.

★ Firefly   BOUTIQUE HOTEL $$$
(⊡458-3414; www.fireflybequia.com; r from US$215; ❋🖥⊛) Just a 10-minute drive from Port Elizabeth and you're transported to tranquil luxury. The 10 rooms are tastefully decorated with minimalist flare, accented with views worthy of royalty. It's set in a working tropical-fruit plantation that dates from the 1700s; informative walking tours (EC$10) are available.

Spring House Hotel   BOUTIQUE HOTEL $$$
(⊡457-3707; www.springhousebequia.com; r US$233-299; ❋🖥⊛) Right at the top of the hill overlooking Spring Bay, this intimate hotel feels like your private retreat on a secluded island. The rooms are elegant with hardwood floors, massive bathrooms and classic furnishings and the only sound you'll hear is the birdsong from surrounding bush. A number of terraces, including one with a jacuzzi, offer fantastic sea views.

★ Sugar Reef Cafe   CAFE $$
(⊡458-3400; mains EC$39-70; ⊙noon-9pm) Sit under fantastic driftwood chandeliers in the seaside dining room and tuck into superb gourmet delights at this wonderful cafe inside the Sugar Reef hotel. Fresh fish features prominently on the small menu, but there are always a couple of veg options, too. It's also a great place for a drink, either at the bar or out by the water.

❶ Getting There & Away

There's no public bus to Spring Bay and it's quite a long hike. A taxi will cost EC$30 to EC$40.

MUSTIQUE

What can you say about Mustique other than 'Wow!'? First, take an island that offers stunning beaches and everything else you expect to find in paradise, then add to the mix accommodations that defy description or affordability. With prices that exclude all but the superrich, film stars and burnt-out musicians, this island is the exclusive playground of the uberaffluent.

The documentary *The Man Who Bought Mustique* (2000) tells the unlikely story of Lord Glenconner, the man who turned the island into a playground for the rich. Most visitors not staying in a fabulous retreat come on widely marketed day trips from Bequia. They join the local swells for drinks and more at Basil's (p739), one of the Caribbean's great waterfront bars.

🛏 Sleeping

★ Cotton House   BOUTIQUE HOTEL $$$
(⊡456-4777; www.cottonhouse.net; r from US$865; ❋🖥⊛) Centered around a beautifully renovated colonial-era cotton warehouse, the luxurious Cotton House is set on 13 acres of beautiful grounds. Accommodations are in a range of villas and cottages, including seafront rooms with their own plunge pools. It strikes a fine balance between relaxed atmosphere and great service and facilities.

Mustique Company
VILLA $$$

(☑ 448-8000; www.mustique-island.com; villas per week US$8000-85,000) Nothing is short of perfection at these properties, and every need is catered for by your villa staff. Most of the villas were built by the rich and famous according to their personal tastes, so there's a wide variety to choose from. Log onto the website to browse.

Why buy a Ferrari when you can rent a really nice house in the Caribbean for a week?

Firefly Mustique
BOUTIQUE HOTEL $$$

(☑ 488-8414; www.fireflymustique.com; r incl breakfast US$695; ❄@🛜🏊) Set on a steep cliff overlooking Britannia Bay, each of the four supremely well-appointed rooms here has an ocean view and unique styling. Firefly's bar is a popular hangout in the evenings for the locals (read: billionaires). We dare you to emerge from your room and tell them to keep the noise down.

🍷 Drinking & Nightlife

★ Basil's
BAR

(☑ 488-8350; www.basilsbar.com; ⊙9am-late; 🛜) Famous Basil's is a delightful open-air thatch-and-bamboo restaurant that extends out into Britannia Bay, and is the place to eat, drink and meet up with others in Mustique. It's a must-stop for every day-tripper and seemingly every passing sailboat. Who could imagine that a menu that combines tasty banana pancakes *and* lobster could be such a hit?

🛈 Getting There & Away

AIR

Mustique's airport receives regular scheduled flights from Barbados. There's also private service from St Vincent and anywhere else you fancy, really. Your accommodations should be able to sort out tickets.

BOAT

A smattering of day trips run to Mustique from St Vincent and Bequia. From the latter, the *Friendship Rose* sailing boat offers the classiest mode of transport. Otherwise you can charter a small boat for the day from Port Elizabeth on Bequia for around US$80 per passenger (minimum of US$300).

CANOUAN

Canouan (cahn-oo-ahn) is literally a divided island. A beautiful hook-shaped isle, it has

TWIN BAY

Part of coming to St Vincent and the Grenadines is finding that perfect beach where you really feel like you've been stranded in paradise. On Canouan, if you're willing to take a bit of a hike, you can get to deserted **Twin Bay**, on the east side of the island, just south of the resort zone and east of E Coast Rd. Ask a local for directions, pack a lunch and get lost in paradise for the day.

some of the most brilliant beaches in the entire Grenadines chain, but unfortunately for independent travelers more than half of the island is taken up by a massive resort. Another large marina project under construction in the south of the island threatens to further diminish the slow island vibe.

Unless you have a yacht to sleep on, or manage to get a room at the one fine hotel right on the sand by town, Canouan is not the best choice as a base to explore the region. The tiny main town of Charleston lacks the sense of community that you'll find in other neighboring islands. Despite this, the island remains worth a visit for its landscapes and marine environment; you'll find lovely beaches with good snorkeling not too far from the ferry dock.

👁 Sights

If you're staying in Charlestown you have fine beaches facing both west and east just a very short walk away. Pick your favorite! If you're staying at the resort, you have your choice of some of the best and most secluded beaches in the Grenadines.

🛏 Sleeping

Canouan has very slim pickings for budget and midrange travelers. A couple of places around town rent out apartments, but these often fill up with visiting workers from the main island. Make sure to reserve something before you arrive.

Scooby's Apartment
APARTMENT $$

(☑ 532-5935; apt US$89; 🛜) Located on a hillside overlooking Charleston, this single, fully equipped apartment has fantastic views and is the best choice for budget travelers on pricey Canouan. The owner is particularly helpful.

Tamarind Beach Hotel & Yacht Club
RESORT $$$

(☎458-8044; www.tamarindbeachhotel.com; Charleston; s/d/tr incl breakfast US$250/310/480; ❋@🌐➤) Giant thatched-roof buildings stand guard over the beach and invite you in for pure relaxation. Elegant rooms, accented with white walls and chocolate-colored hardwood, entice the visitor and make it hard to return to the daily grind. The beach is right out front of every room and suite and, as is typical for Canouan, it's a fine strip of sand.

Pink Sands Club
RESORT $$$

(Canouan Resort; ☎458-8000; www.pinksandsclub.com; ste from US$1400; ❋@🌐➤) Canouan's ultraluxurious megaresort has recently been refurbished and relaunched as the Pink Sands Club. It has 26 suites and six villas, all with sea views. Services abound, including an infinity pool, tanning deck, tennis court, golf course and spa with over-the-water *palapas* with glass floors. There are five restaurants spread around the grounds.

ⓘ Information

Bank of St Vincent & the Grenadines (◷8am-2pm Mon-Thu, to 4pm Fri) The only ATM on the island. From the dock, walk up to the main road and turn left.

ⓘ Getting There & Away

AIR

Grenadine Airways (☎456-6793) flies between St Vincent and Canouan (one way/return US$51/99, 20 minutes), leaving the main island at 10:20am and returning at 5:15pm.

Canouan's airport also receives regular scheduled flights from Barbados and St Lucia with **SVG Air** (p749).

SEA

Canouan has ferry links to St Vincent and Bequia as well as neighboring islands in the southern Grenadines.

MV Barracuda (☎455-9835; perrysshipping@vincysurf.com) Slow cargo boat; serves St Vincent (EC$50), Mayreau (EC$30) and Union Island (EC$30), with three runs each way each week.

MV Gem Star (☎457-4157) Slow cargo boat; serves St Vincent (EC$50), Mayreau (EC$30) and Union Island (EC$30), with two runs each way each week.

MAYREAU

Blessed with breathtaking beauty yet very little development, the compact palm-covered island of Mayreau is the authentic Grenadines dream. With only a handful of vehicles, no airport and just a smattering of residents, it often feels like the fabled dessert isle.

Mayreau is a fantastic destination for independent travelers wanting to enjoy some of the Grenadines' best beaches and get a good dose of culture at the same time. There are no resorts and while yachts and bigger ships do dock here, once the sun goes down you'll have the place to yourself.

The island is so small you can't help get to know the friendly locals who are famed throughout the Grenadines for their hard-partying ways. With around a dozen bars for its 400-odd residents it's fairly clear it's not just a myth. It's said that tiny Mayreau's weekly beer order is more than twice that of Union Island, its far bigger neighbor.

⊙ Sights

Mayreau's main beach near the dock is a lovely thick golden stretch of sand abutted by cliffs with clear waters that are great for snorkeling. It has nice views across to Union Island's impressive peaks. When there's no wind, though, the sand flies can be vicious.

There are a number of hidden little coves around the island that rarely see visitors.

Mayreau Catholic Church
CHURCH

This cute stone church sits atop the hill in the center of the island. Make sure to head around the back for fantastic views of the Tobago Cays.

★ Saltwhistle Bay
BEACH

On the northern, uninhabited side of Mayreau you'll find Saltwhistle Bay, a double crescent of beautiful beaches split by a narrow palm-tree-fringed isthmus that seems to come right out of central casting for tropical ideals. The turquoise water laps both sides of the sandy strip, in some places only a few feet away.

Yachts drop anchor in the bay and occasional day-trippers come ashore for a bit of lunch and a sandy frolic. A few rickety huts along the shore sell cold drinks and simple snacks as well as souvenirs to passing yachties. It's a very low-key scene.

It's a 20-minute walk from the ferry dock over the steep hill.

🏃 Tours

Mayreau is the closest island to the Tobago Cays and, if you don't have your own yacht, the cheapest place from which to organize a day trip. Prices begin from around EC$120 per person for a full day trip; add a little more if you want a fresh barbecue seafood lunch thrown in – and you really do.

🛏 Sleeping

There are only two functioning hotels on the island, but it is also possible to rent a room or a house, sometimes for a good nightly rate. Ask at Robert Righteous & De Youths (p741) restaurant.

On the east side of the island, at Salt-whistle Bay, there is a small resort that features a handful of stone apartments that blend rather well into the environment. The accommodations have been closed for a while and need an overhaul, but the bar-restaurant usually opens when there's a crowd and is a fine place for a meal.

Waterloo Guesthouse GUESTHOUSE **$$**
(☑ 458-8561; apt US$100; ❄) Brand new air-conditioned apartments decked out with full-sized kitchens and everything you need. Go for the upstairs one for better views.

Dennis' Hideaway HOTEL **$$**
(☑ 458-8594; www.dennis-hideaway.com; dm/r from US$20/93; ❄🌐🖥) The eponymous Dennis seems to be related to half the island's residents, many of whom work here. Rooms are on a hill with views west to Union Island and beyond. There's also a very basic hostel-style room for those on a tight budget. The restaurant (mains EC$25 to EC$60) serves basic fare and fresh seafood – Dennis cooks a mean conch.

🍴 Eating

Simon's SANDWICHES **$**
(sandwiches EC$5-10; ⊙7am-9pm) Had enough of lobster and just hankering for a good cheese-and-salad roll? You're in luck. Head up the hill to this tiny grocery store to order a half or full fresh-baked baguette packed with cheddar and greens. Best-value feed in the Grenadines. There's no sign, but everyone knows it.

Robert Righteous & De Youths SEAFOOD **$$**
(☑ 458-8203; mains EC$55-70; ⊙6am-10pm) This place is overflowing with Rasta flavor and enough Bob photos to make you think you're in a college dorm room. With pork chops and strong drinks on the menu, it's hard to tell how authentic the Rastafarianism is – but no matter, the food is tasty and the vibe is, as you'd expect, chilled out. Go for the lobster.

ℹ Getting There & Away

MV Gem Star (☑ 457-4157) Slow cargo boat; serves St Vincent, Canouan and Union Island, with two trips each way each week.

MV Barracuda (☑ 455-9835; perrysshipping@vincysurf.com) Slow cargo boat; serves St Vincent, Canouan and Union Island, with three trips each way each week.

TOBAGO CAYS

With five small islands ringed with coral reefs, the fabled Tobago Cays offer some of the Caribbean's best diving and snorkeling.

The islands sit firmly in a national park and are only accessible by boat on a day trip from one of the Grenadines. And what a day trip it can be! The snorkeling is world class and the white-sand beaches look like strips of blinding snow. Underwater, sea turtles and parrot fish are just the start of myriad species you'll see. The coral is gorgeous.

◎ Sights

The **Tobago Cays Marine Park** (adult/child US$10/5) encompasses the five uninhabited islands of Tobago Cays – Petit Bateau, Petit Rameau, Jamesby, Baradal and Petit Tabac – as well as the populated island of Mayreau, and Catholic Island, Jondall and Mayreau Baleine to the north.

The five Tobago Cays sit above a large sand-bottomed lagoon protected by 4km-long Horseshoe Reef. The lagoon is an important habitat for sea turtles. Other dive and snorkel spots include Egg Reef and World's End Reef on the eastern side of the cays and Mayreau Gardens to the west.

Also within the boundaries of the reserve is the wreck of the *Purina*, a British gunboat, which lies just west of Mayreau.

Catholic Island is a designated sea-bird reserve, while there's a small mangrove forest on Petit Rameau.

🏃 Activities

There is a marked sea-turtle observation area for snorkelers around the beach of Baradal Cay where boating activity is prohibited.

All scuba-diving activity must be accompanied by a registered local guide. Kitesurfing is only permitted in the designated area to the north of Petit Rameau.

ⓘ Getting There & Away

You can get a day trip to the cays from any place in the Grenadines. Some good operators are found on Bequia and Union Island, while the cheapest place to visit from is Mayreau. Expect to pay from US$90 to US$200 for a full day out, depending where you set out from.

If you've got your own sails you can only anchor in the sand-bottomed areas around Baradal and the small strip in front of Petit Tabac.

UNION ISLAND

Union Island feels like an outpost at the bottom of a country – and that's just what it is. Before the introduction of fast boats, its remote location enabled it to become a base for contraband (which historically propped up the economy here) from all over the Caribbean.

The small port town of **Clifton** has an unpretentious charm and a more local feel than some of the towns on the more-visited Grenadine islands. You can easily spend a day wandering its short main street and the surrounding hills. It's an important anchorage for yachts and a transport hub – there are boats to Carriacou in Grenada. It also has decent accommodations, services and just enough nightlife.

⊙ Sights

Union Island's first-class beaches are never crowded.

Big Sand
BEACH

One of the best beaches on the island, Big Sand on Richmond Bay is around 1km north of Clifton. It has plenty of white sand and brilliant blue waters, with forest-covered mountains as a backdrop. It's an easy walk from town.

Chatham Bay
BEACH

A favorite hangout among Union Island locals and a popular anchorage for yachties in the know, Chatham Bay is a lovely thin crescent of white sand backed by steep, forest-covered hills on the western side of the island. The calm turquoise waters are perfect for snorkeling. On the edge you'll find a couple of simple bars and a restaurant.

You'll need a good 4WD vehicle to get here, or you can hike down (20 minutes) from the main road. A water taxi can drop you right on the sand.

🏃 Activities

Hike up into the hills behind Clifton, including **Fort Hill**, about 150m up, for magnificent views of the surrounding islands.

The quiet fishing village of **Ashton**, some 3km away, makes a good walk.

Excursions to **Tobago Cays** are popular. They usually include a stop in Mayreau, lunch and refreshments and cost around US$90 to US$100 per person.

Scaramouche
BOATING

(tours from US$95) Union Island's very own movie star, the wooden sailboat *Scaramouche* was built on neighboring Carriacou and featured in the original *Pirates of the Caribbean* movie. Now visitors can sail to the Tobago Cays or cruise around the Grenadines on her deck. Tours include meals and drinks.

Yannis Sails
BOATING

(☑ 458-8513; www.anchorage-union.com/Nyannis. htm; Yacht Club, Clifton; tours from US$100) Catamarans sail on day trips to Mayreau (Saltwhistle Bay), Tobago Cays and Palm Island. Rates include lunch, rum punch and lots of snorkeling. Schedules are flexible. Boats are based on Palm Island, but will pick you up at the Anchorage dock.

Grenadines Dive
DIVING

(☑ 458-8138; www.grenadinesdive.com; Clifton; 1-/2-tank dive US$80/140) Organizes custom excursions to Tobago Cays and elsewhere in the Grenadines. It also arranges pickups from other islands, including Mayreau and Canouan. Mayreau Gardens is a popular drift dive on one of the longest reefs in the region.

JT Pro Center
KITESURFING

(☑ 527-8363; www.kitesurfgrenadines.com; private/group lessons US$195/245, 3-day course US$700) Runs kitesurfing classes out on the 'Kite Beach' behind the airport. You can get information at the Snack Shack (p743) in the middle of Clifton. Also rents gear.

🛏 Sleeping

TJ Plaza Guesthouse
GUESTHOUSE $

(☑ 458-8930; http://tjplaza.weebly.com; Clifton; r US$33-61) The best bet for budget travelers, this family-run guesthouse has a variety of options, including budget rooms with fans on the 2nd floor and air-conditioned options with hot water downstairs. If there's no one around, ask at the two-story pink wooden building on Front St directly behind the guesthouse.

Bougainvilla Hotel HOTEL $$

(☑458-8678; www.grenadines-bougainvilla.com; Clifton; r incl breakfast US$132-165; ❄ 🙲) Not far from the main yacht dock, this French-accented hotel has 10 lovely rooms: six standard options and four apartments with kitchenettes and living space. Each has a nice warm palette of colors – there's plenty of marigold yellow, touches of art and classic furnishings. Service is good.

Islanders Inn HOTEL $$

(☑527-0944; www.theislandersinn.com; Belmont Bay, Zion; r US$90-130; ❄ 🙲) A fine choice if you want a bit of tranquility, this bright, small hotel has good sea views and is just a short walk from some of the best stretches of sand on the island. Rooms are simple but spacious enough and have private balconies overlooking the water. It's around a 20-minute walk from town, but feels very remote.

Kings Landing Hotel HOTEL $$

(☑485-8823; www.kingslandinghotel.com; Clifton; s/d from US$85/100; ❄ 🙲 ⛱) A very tidy two-story hotel at the south end of Clifton, set around a pool with a waterfront view. The 17 rooms are basic but clean and the hotel is well managed. A good spot for families wanting a bit of peace; kids like the pool.

Anchorage Yacht Club Hotel HOTEL $$

(☑458-8221; http://www.aycunionisland.com/hotel.html; Clifton; r US$165-250; ❄ 🙲) Right at the yacht docks and popular with visiting sailors and holidaymakers. The rooms have a simple nautical vibe and feature views of the harbor. The vast terrace bar is popular with people transacting business of all kinds and yacht passengers desperate for dry land.

David's BOUTIQUE HOTEL $$$

(www.davidsbeachhotel.com; Big Sand, Richmond Bay; r US$1100; ❄ 🙲) By far the classiest place to stay on the island, David's is an intimate all-inclusive hotel ideal for those who don't want to be stuck on a private resort island. Rooms are neat, spacious and modern and are split between a bedroom with big French windows overlooking the water and a lounge area at the back.

🍴 Eating

The Snack Shack CAFE $

(Front St, Clifton; breakfast EC$12-20, light meals EC$20-22; ⊙8am-midnight) Pull up a chair at one of the hand-crafted tables outside this popular little cafe right in the center of town and watch the gentle pace of Clifton life as you enjoy great crepes and panini. Throw in good tunes, a decent cocktail list and a fun atmosphere and you'll see why it's so busy.

Yummy Stuff Bakery BAKERY $

(Front St, Clifton; items EC$2-10; ⊙6:30am-6pm) Out the back of the mall on the main street, this inviting little bakery is a great place for a cheap bite to eat. Sit on old shipping pallets and enjoy filling chicken rotis, banana bread, brownies and more.

Captain Gourmet DELI $

(Front St, Clifton; breakfast EC$16-25, light meals EC$15-30; ⊙8am-5pm Mon-Fri, to 2pm Sat; 🙲) Enjoy an espresso and fine baked goods at a sidewalk table at this cafe-deli. A distinctive French flavor permeates, and you'll find quality quiches, sandwiches and salads.

Barracuda ITALIAN $$

(☑458-8571; Clifton; pizzas EC$20-48, mains EC$35-68; ⊙10am-10pm) Perfect for those traveling with small fussy eaters, this unpretentious place right across from the water in Clifton manages to excel with both Italian dishes and local specialties. There's good pastas, pizzas and steaks alongside tasty fish dishes and filling rotis. It might not be the most stylish, but it offers outstanding value.

Big Citi Grill CARIBBEAN $$

(☑458-8960; Front St, Clifton; burgers EC$28-30, mains EC$40-55; ⊙8am-9pm) Enjoy great burgers and wraps as well as more filling Caribbean plates at this friendly 2nd-floor restaurant overlooking Clifton's main road. Has a small, good-value lunch buffet.

Sparrows Beach Club EUROPEAN $$$

(☑458-8195; sparrowsbeachclub@gmail.com; Big Sand, Richmond Bay; mains EC$62-110) Located right on the sands of the best beach on the island, Sparrows is as much a destination as a restaurant. You can order meals right to your lounger, or sit on the deck in the brightly painted restaurant. The food is a mixed bag; the high-end dishes are excellent, but the cheaper ones are banged out without much love.

ST VINCENT & THE GRENADINES UNION ISLAND

🍷 Drinking & Nightlife

Many people begin their sundowner expedition on the near-endless terrace at the Anchorage Yacht Club.

Happy Island   BAR
(Happy Island; ⊘24hr) Located right in front of Clifton, in the bay, you'll find this one-bar island. There didn't used to be any land in this part of the bay, but local fishermen would throw conch shells in the shallows and eventually an island began to form. And what do you do with some free land? You put a bar on it!

ℹ️ Information

Erika's Marine (☑485-8335; www.erikamarine.com; Clifton) A one-stop solution to your travel needs, it offers cash advances on credit cards when the ATM is out of service. Other services include internet access, a travel agency and laundry. It also manages some rental properties around the island.

INTERNET ACCESS

Internet Cafe (Front St; per 30min session EC$5; ⊘8am-4:30pm) The cleverly named Internet Cafe is the place you can get online in town if you don't have your own device.

MONEY

Bank of St Vincent & Grenadines (☑458-8347; ⊘8am-2pm Mon-Thu, to 4pm Fri) Towards the airport, with the island's only ATMs (24 hours).

TOURIST INFORMATION

Union Island Tourist Bureau (☑458-8494; Front St, Clifton; ⊘9am-noon & 1-4pm Mon-Fri) On the main road, near the customs office. Has good info on Tobago Cays.

Tobago Cays Marine Park Office (☑485-8191; www.tobagocays.org; Clifton; admission adult/child US$10/5; ⊘8am-4pm Mon-Fri) Details on visiting the cays and a small interpretation center.

ℹ️ Getting There & Away

AIR

Clifton's airport is an easy walk from any place in town. In addition to services to St Vincent, it receives regular scheduled flights from Barbados and occasionally St Lucia.

SEA

There are three regular boats heading north into the Grenadines and St Vincent.

MV Barracuda (☑455-9835; perrysshipping@vincysurf.com) A cargo boat that runs three times a week to Mayreau, Canouan and on to Kingstown.

MV Gem Star (☑457-4157) Slow cargo boat making two trips a week to Mayreau, Canouan and Kingstown.

There is a daily school boat to Mayreau (EC$20 one way) leaving from the Grenadines Dive dock in Clifton at 6:30am and again around 3:30pm when school is in session.

The commercial ships that haul goods back and forth between Grenada, Carriacou, Petit Martinique and Union Island sometimes accept foot passengers.

PALM ISLAND

Once called Prune Island, the now more attractively titled Palm Island is just a 10-minute boat ride southeast of Union Island. It's a private island, but visitors can still come ashore at **Casuarina Beach**, which is a stopover on many day tours between Union Island and the Tobago Cays.

🛏️ Sleeping & Eating

Palm Island Resort   RESORT $$$
(☑458-8824; www.palmislandresortgrenadines.com; s/d from US$745/845; 🌢@🛜🌊) The plush Palm Island Resort is a delightful place to hole up for a week. The manicured tropical grounds are spotted with palms (obviously) and dotted with villas. The rooms are well fitted out, with an emphasis on luxury living and sea views. The large pool is a nice place for mixing with your fellow guests.

ℹ️ Getting There & Away

A water taxi to Palm Island from Union Island costs around US$20.

PETIT ST VINCENT

It's not called *petit* for nothing – this island is the smallest and southernmost in the Grenadines chain. Sequestered and exclusive, PSV has a formidable reputation as one of the best private islands in the world. That reputation isn't unwarranted – the beaches are just as spectacular as those on its neighboring islands, and having the place (almost) to yourself makes the price seem a bit more affordable.

Nonguests are able to visit a dedicated area of beach as well as the beach bar on day trips.

🛏 Sleeping

Petit St Vincent Resort   RESORT $$$
(✆ in the US +1-954-963-7401; www.psvresort.com; cottages/villas US$1470/1995; @ 🛜) A luxurious escape featuring 22 cottages and villas that are designed with comfort and privacy in mind. There are spacious sundecks only feet from the ocean, and living spaces that bristle with fine stonework and whitewashed luxury.

There are two staff members per bungalow, ensuring that your every wish is fulfilled. When you want to call on your staff, simply raise the yellow flag and they'll be right there. Prices are all-inclusive.

ℹ Getting There & Away

Cargo ships from Kingstown sometimes continue on to PSV after docking at Union Island. A water taxi from Union costs US$60.

UNDERSTAND ST VINCENT & THE GRENADINES

History

Siboneys, Arawaks & Caribs

St Vincent and the Grenadines is not as remote as it appears; it has been inhabited for some 7000 years. Originally it was sparsely populated by the hunter-gatherer Siboneys. Around 2000 years ago they were replaced by the Arawaks, who moved up from present-day Venezuela. The raiding Caribs eventually took over from the Arawaks, but held some of the islands for as little as 100 years before the arrival of the heavily armed Spanish. Fierce Carib resistance kept the Europeans out of St Vincent long after most other Caribbean islands had fallen to the colonists. This was in part because many Caribs from other islands fled to St Vincent (Hairoun, as they called it) after their home islands were conquered – it was the Caribs' last stand. On the island, Caribs intermarried with Africans who had escaped from slavery, and the new mixed generation split along ethnic lines as Black Caribs and Yellow Caribs.

We're British, Mate

In 1783, after a century of competing claims between the British and French, the Treaty of Paris placed St Vincent under British control. Indigenous rebellions followed and British troops rounded up the insurgents, forcibly repatriating around 5000 Black Caribs to Roatán island, Honduras. With the native opposition gone, the planters capitalized on the fertile volcanic soil. However, prosperity didn't last long: two eruptions of La Soufrière, the abolition of slavery in 1834 and a few powerful hurricanes stood in the way of their colonial dreams. For the remainder of British rule the economy stagnated – plantations were eventually broken up and land was redistributed to small-scale farmers.

Modern St Vincent & the Grenadines

In 1969, in association with the British, St Vincent became a self-governing state. On October 27, 1979, it was cobbled together with the Grenadines as an independent member of the Commonwealth.

The nation remains poor. It is still dependent on banana exports, though crops have been badly hit by black sigatoka disease, which has severely depleted exports. Tourism, while important, still has a long ways to go in terms of bringing in needed wealth. Crown lands continue to be sold off to foreign investors to generate funds and stimulate economic development, but the accompanying jobs boom has failed to materialize and many Vincentians have slipped well below the poverty line.

The long-serving prime minister, Ralph Gonsalves, was reelected for the fourth time in 2015 in a result that was controversial among some Vincentians. In the last decade he has been busy forming alliances with Bolivia, Venezuela, Cuba and pretty much anyone else willing to send aid to SVG, such as Canada, Japan and China. He made headlines in early 2016 by calling on the Caribbean to investigate marijuana as a possible substitute for banana crops throughout the region.

Meanwhile his critics point to delays in the long-overdue and vital new airport as evidence of the lack of progress under his government. The opposition claims that all the government's resources are being poured into the controversial project without developing the infrastructure required to receive the new visitors the facility is supposed to bring in.

Culture

Pigeonholing Vincy culture is a tough task. With 32 islands in the chain, the cultural variance is as vast as the sea in which they sit. Locals tend to be conservative, quiet and a tough nut to crack for outsiders, but then again, wash ashore on some of the tiny islands and everybody has something to say to you.

To a certain degree there is a feeling of detachment from the outside world. But the isolation of the islands is fading fast, with easy access to pop culture and mass media.

Most locals find work in traditional industries such as fishing, agriculture or laboring. Tourism is also becoming important, but is still quite modest compared to neighboring islands such as Barbados or even Grenada.

Landscape & Wildlife

The Land

St Vincent is a high volcanic island, forming the northernmost point of the volcanic ridge that runs from Grenada in the south

up through the Grenadine islands. It is markedly hilly and its rich volcanic soil is very productive – St Vincent is often called the 'garden of the Grenadines.' It has a rugged interior of tropical rainforest, and lowlands thick with coconut trees and banana estates. The valley region around Mesopotamia, east of Kingstown, has some of the best farmland and most luxuriant landscapes.

The island of St Vincent gobbles up 133 sq miles of the nation's 150 sq miles. The other 17 sq miles are spread across 31 islands and cays, fewer than a dozen of which are populated. The largest of the islands are Bequia, Mustique, Canouan, Mayreau and Union Island. The larger Grenadine islands are hilly but relatively low-lying, and most have no source of freshwater other than rainfall. All are dotted with stunning white-sand beaches and abundant sea life.

Wildlife

The crystal-clear waters surrounding St Vincent and the Grenadines are abundant with sea life. Plentiful reefs are a flurry of fish activity, with turtles, moray eels, angelfish, barracuda, octopus, nurse sharks and countless other species calling the region home. Dolphins also frequent the area and are often seen surfing the bow waves of oceangoing vessels.

On land, the fauna becomes decidedly more sparse. The sun-drenched islands are home to a few interesting species, such as the St Vincent parrot, an endangered and strikingly beautiful bird that has multicolored plumage and is seen in the jungle interior of St Vincent. This rainforest also provides the home for manicou (opossum) and agouti (a rabbitlike rodent). Agouti roam freely on Young Island, where they are easy to spot.

Environmental Issues

The concepts of climate change and environmental responsibility are slowly creeping into the collective mindsets of Vincentians. The government has started a program to try to curb damage done to the sea by overfishing and irresponsible boating practices. It's a great start, but getting locals to comply could be an uphill battle. Broken glass and ever-present fast-food wrappings are major features in gutters, ditches and roadways in Kingstown, especially.

Freshwater is also a major concern, with a combination of runoff, wells and desalination plants supplying the hydration for the islands. Demand outstrips supply when cruise ships roll up and refill their tanks and this continues to be a divisive issue for locals, depending on which side of the economic equation they sit.

SURVIVAL GUIDE

ⓘ Directory A–Z

ACCOMMODATIONS

There's a wide range of accommodations options throughout SVG, with beds to suit most budgets. On most of the main islands you can find places that are decidedly casual. At other places, however (read: Mustique), you'll have to remortgage the house to spend the week, and you're expected to dress accordingly.

Hotels are generally quite personal, with only a few rooms for the relaxed staff to look after.

ACTIVITIES

The warm, clear waters of SVG draw divers from around the globe. They come to swim with a stunning array of sea life, from reef-hopping angelfish and grass-munching sea turtles to ocean predators such as nurse sharks. The reefs are pristine, with forests of soft and hard coral colored every hue of the rainbow. Wrecks, rays and the odd whale just add to the appeal. Spearfishing is prohibited.

Visibility is often unlimited and the warm water makes for comfortable diving. Great sites can be found at the very recreational depth of 60ft to 80ft and currents are minimal.

You can find good dive operators on all the main islands. The going rates for a one-tank dive start at around US$70. Great for novices looking to get their feet literally wet are 'resort courses,' which include a couple of hours of instruction and a shallow dive geared to first-timers; they average US$85.

Most dive shops run snorkeling trips parallel to their dive excursions. The obvious destination here is beautiful Tobago Cays.

ELECTRICITY

The electric current is 220V to 240V (50 cycles). British-style three-pin plugs are used. Some resorts also have US-style outlets with 110V power.

EMERGENCY NUMBERS

Area Code	☎ 784

SLEEPING PRICE RANGES

Prices listed are for the busy high season (winter, December to April/May) and usually drop when things are quieter.

Rates listed here do not include 10% VAT that is added to all hotel rooms, or the 10% service charge that is frequently tacked on to bills – be sure to clarify exactly what price you are being quoted. Prices are in either EC$ or US$, depending on the hotel.

The following price ranges refer to a double room with bathroom.

$ less than US$85

$$ US$85–200

$$$ more than US$200

Emergency	☎ 999

FOOD

Meals in SVG are almost always enjoyed with a fantastic sea view. In the popular tourist areas on the main island and in the Grenadines, you'll find restaurants serving all kinds of international cuisine, but almost all also have at least a couple of traditional dishes on the menu and they're well worth trying out.

Essential Food & Drink

As far as West Indian food goes, SVG is one of the better destinations for enjoying its unique flavors.

Fresh produce St Vincent produces top-quality and delicious fruit and vegetables.

Seafood Lobster, shrimp, conch and fish are all popular and readily available.

Callaloo A spinach-like vegetable used in soups and stews. Many vitamins!

Savory pumpkin soup More squash-like than the American Thanksgiving staple; often like a rich stew.

Saltfish Dried fish that has been cured; delicious when made into fish cakes.

Rotis Curried vegetables, potatoes and meat wrapped in a flour tortilla are a national passion.

Hairoun (high-rone) The light and tasty local lager.

GLBT TRAVELERS

As with elsewhere in the Caribbean, the view about gays and lesbians is outdated, to say the least. You won't find any gay-friendly events, resorts or cruises here. Gay and lesbian travel-

EATING PRICE RANGES

The following price ranges are based on the cost of a main course.

$ less than EC$30

$$ EC$30–70

$$$ more than EC$70

ers should be cautious with public affection, but should otherwise be fine.

HEALTH

Milton Cato Memorial Hospital (Kingstown General Hospital; ☏ 456-1185; ⊙24hr) On the Leeward Hwy. For serious illness or decompression sickness you will be sent to Barbados.

Bequia District Hospital (☏ 458-3294) Recently refurbished hospital serving the Grenadines. Also has a walk-in clinic for minor health issues.

MONEY

The Eastern Caribbean dollar (EC$) is the local currency. Major credit cards are accepted at most hotels, car-rental agencies, dive shops and some of the larger restaurants. All of the major islands, except for Mayreau, have a bank and one or more 24-hour ATMs. But the network can go down, so carry backup cash. People will always accept US$.

There is 15% VAT that is added onto most retail items; this will already be included in the price. Most hotel rates have 10% VAT and 10% service charge added on top of them.

Exchange Rates

The Eastern Caribbean dollar is pegged to the US dollar at a rate of 2.70 to 1.

AUSTRALIA	A$	EC$1.99
BARBADOS	B$	EC$1.35
CANADA	C$1	EC$2.83
EUROPE	€1	EC$2.29
JAPAN	¥100	EC$1.91
NEW ZEALAND	NZ$1	EC$3.38
UK	UK£1	EC$2.70
US	US$1	EC$2.02

Tipping

In restaurants a tip of 10% to 15% is the norm, though it's often added to the bill; 10% is usually added to hotel bills. A 10% tip is customary in taxis.

PUBLIC HOLIDAYS

In addition to those observed throughout the region, SVG has the following public holidays.

St Vincent & the Grenadines Day January 22

Labour Day First Monday in May

Caricom Day Second Monday in July

Carnival Tuesday Usually second Tuesday in July

Emancipation Day First Monday in August

Independence Day October 27

TAXES & REFUNDS

A 15% VAT is included on most purchases in St Vincent. There is no mechanism for visitors to claim back VAT upon departure.

TELEPHONE

The country code is 1; the area code is 784. To call any other country with a country code of 1 (most of North America and the Caribbean), just dial 1 and the 10-digit number. For other countries, dial the international access code 011+country code+number.

TIME

St Vincent, along with the rest of the Windward Islands, is on UTC minus four hours.

TOURIST INFORMATION

The **Department of Tourism St Vincent & the Grenadines** (☏ 456-6222; www.discoversvg. com; NIS Building, Bay St; ⊙8am-noon & 1-4pm Mon-Fri) has an office on St Vincent. Bequia has an excellent tourist office as does Union Island. Several free publications are also highly useful, including *Ins & Outs St Vincent & the Grenadines*.

TRAVELERS WITH DISABILITIES

Travelers with disabilities, especially those in wheelchairs, will have difficulty traveling throughout SVG. There are rarely sidewalks, pathways are often sand and ferries and other seagoing transportation are not designed with special needs in mind.

❶ Getting There & Away

AIR

St Vincent is the main air hub for SVG, though tiny ET Joshua Airport in Kingstown can only handle small planes, so service is limited to nearby islands such as Barbados and Grenada. The main islands in the Grenadines also have service to Barbados.

A new airport, Argyle International Airport, is under construction on the east side of St Vincent, near Yambou Head, but is years behind schedule and may not open until 2017 or later. It will be able to handle jets and flights from North America and beyond.

SEA

There is a twice-weekly small mail boat that runs between Union Island and Carriacou in Grenada. Commercial ships that haul goods between Grenada, Carriacou, Petit Martinique and Union Island sometimes accept foot passengers.

You can charter a small open boat to take you from Clifton on Union Island to Carriacou in Grenada.

❶ Getting Around

AIR

Flights within SVG are a quick and inexpensive way to shuttle around the country. There are airports on all the main Grenadine islands except Mayreau. There are a number of airlines running regular services between the islands.

Grenadine Air Alliance (www.grenadine-air. com)

Mustique Airlines (www.mustique.com)

SVG Air (☑ 457-5124; www.svgair.com)

BOAT
Ferry

The main islands of SVG are well linked by boats. It's very important to confirm schedule details in advance as they change frequently.

Water Taxi

You can usually find someone who will get you between islands in the Grenadines. Usually this will be on a small, open fishing boat with room for, at best, four people with minimal luggage. The rides can be quite exciting and should not undertaken in rough seas. Places to stay on the islands always have reliable contacts.

Costs are negotiable – for an example, you should be able to get from Mayreau to Union Island for under EC$150.

Yacht

You just never know if you'll be able to hitch a ride somewhere. The Grenadines get a lot of traffic so there are opportunities. Hang out dockside in Union Island, or at bars popular with sailors on Bequia, and see what you can arrange.

---

❶ DEPARTURE TAX

Departure tax is now included in all tickets for travel to and from St Vincent and the Grenadines – there is no longer a fee payable at the airport.

BUS

Buses are a good way to get around St Vincent. It is possible to catch one on Bequia and Union Island, but these islands are so small that you'll rarely use them.

The buses themselves are usually minivans that are often jammed full. You can expect to get to know at least 20 fellow commuters as you are squeezed into every available space in the bus. There's usually a conductor on board who handles the cash and assigns the seats. When you get to your stop, either tap on the roof or try to get the attention of the conductor over the thumping music, and the bus will stop for you just about anywhere.

Fares vary by distance, ranging from EC$1.50 to EC$5, depending on the destination.

CAR & MOTORCYCLE

St Vincent is really the only island where you may wish to drive. It has enough roads to make exploration interesting and worthwhile. However, expect to drive slowly over its very narrow and winding roads – think 20mph as a good average.

Rental

Rentals typically cost from US$60 a day for a car and from US$70 for a 4WD.

There are car-rental agencies on St Vincent and Bequia, but most of the Grenadine islands have no car rentals at all. On some islands there are no roads.

Road Rules

Driving is on the left-hand side. To drive within SVG you must have a visitor license (EC$100), which can be obtained at the central police station on Bay St in Kingstown, or at the airport.

Trinidad & Tobago

POP 1.3 MILLION / ☎ 868

Best Places to Eat

➜ Veni Mangé (p759)

➜ Chaud Café (p759)

➜ Breakfast Shed (p757)

➜ Kariwak Village (p776)

Best Places to Sleep

➜ Kariwak Village Holistic Haven (p776)

➜ Mt Plaisir Estate (p768)

➜ Castara Retreats (p781)

➜ Miller's Guesthouse (p778)

Why Go?

Trinidad and Tobago are an exercise in beautiful contradiction. In Trinidad, pristine mangrove swamps and rainforested hills sit side by side with smoke-belching oil refineries and ugly industrial estates. Tobago has everything you'd expect from a Caribbean island, with palm trees and white sand aplenty, yet it's relatively unchanged by the tourist industry. Combined, this twin-island republic offers unparalleled birdwatching; first-class diving; luxuriant rainforests perfect for hiking, waterfall swimming and cycling; and electric nightlife, with the fabulous Carnival easily the biggest and best of the region's annual blowouts.

But don't expect anyone to hold your hand. The oil and gas industry leaves tourism low on the priority list, so it's up to you to take a deep breath, jump in and enjoy the mix.

When to Go

Feb–Mar High season sees hordes of visitors arrive for Carnival, while summer (July and August), Easter and the Christmas period are also busy.

Oct–mid-Dec & Apr–Jun Shoulder seasons mean fewer crowds and cheaper accommodations, but a good chance of some rain.

Trinidad and Tobago's southerly location keeps temperatures consistent year-round, with a daily average of 27°C (80°F). The rainy season (June to November) and the dry season (December to May) are the major weather variations. As the islands sit outside the hurricane belt, severe storms are very uncommon.

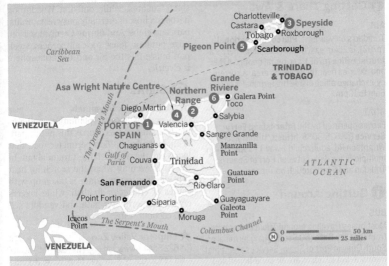

Trinidad & Tobago Highlights

1 **Port of Spain** (p752) Partying at the Caribbean's best Carnival, and sampling the live-music scene, from steel-band music to soca extravaganzas and calypso beats.

2 **Northern Range** (p766) Scouting the waterfalls, wildlife and ruggedly gorgeous Trinidad coastline.

3 **Diving** (p784) Submerging yourself among the underwater canyons and shallow coral gardens in Tobago, particularly around Speyside.

4 **Asa Wright Nature Centre** (p767) Grabbing your binoculars to spy on Trinidad's prolific birdlife.

5 **Pigeon Point** (p775) Dipping your toes into whiter-than-white sand and turquoise waters at Tobago's most popular beach.

6 **Grande Riviere** (p768) Peeking at leatherback turtles laying eggs on the beach (March to June) and holding your breath as the hatchlings make a bid for the sea (May to September).

7 **Boat Ride** (p772) Following Tobago's Caribbean coastline to snorkel at hidden coves and eat fresh fish at a beach barbecue.

TRINIDAD

Tours

Island Experiences   TOURS
(☑ 756-9677, 625-2410; www.islandexperiencestt. com; tours US$55-155, beach shuttle US$30-40) Gunda Harewood and her multilingual guides offer islandwide tours covering all the main sights, plus 'eco-cultural' trips, which reveal lesser-known places and impart local knowledge and lore. Island Experiences also offers trips out to the Bocas islands and Tobago options. There's a useful shuttle service to and from Maracas and Las Cuevas beaches, too.

Paria Springs   ADVENTURE
(☑ 620-8240; www.pariasprings.com; US$105-$150; 🚴) Run by a local mountain biker and wildlife expert, tours include kayaking/ stand-up paddling through Caroni and Nariva swamps, hiking and waterfall climbing in Chaguaramas, waterfall rappelling/canyoning in the Northern Range, visiting Gasparee Cave and Lopinot, hiking or swimming in Guanapo Gorge, and various mountain-biking options island-wide.

Caribbean Discovery Tours   TOURS
(☑ 624-7281, 620-1989; www.caribbeandiscovery-tours.com; US$100-150) Tours are conducted in a rugged Land Rover 4WD. Options range from sunrise birdwatching at Aripo Savannah to farming/culinary trips in hilly Paramin, a bean-to-bar chocolate tour in Brasso Seco and a foodie experience. Nariva Swamp hiking and kayaking, too.

ⓘ Getting There & Away

AIR

Trinidad's only airport, **Piarco International** (p792), is 25km east of Port of Spain. There's a **tourist office** (p762), car-rental booths, ATMs and eateries near the ticketing area. A currency-exchange office inside the terminal is open 6am to 10pm.

BOAT

Ferries operated by the **Inter-Island Ferry Service** (☑ 625-3055; https://ttitferry.com/; Wrightson Rd; adult/child 1-way TT$50/25) run multiple times daily between Port of Spain on Trinidad and Scarborough on Tobago.

ⓘ Getting Around

BUS

Most buses traveling around Trinidad originate from the **City Gate** (60 South Quay) terminal on South Quay in Port of Spain. Services aren't that frequent, but all buses are air-conditioned and make a cheap way to get around if you're not in a rush. Check online (www.ptsc.co.tt) or at the **information/ticket booth** (☑ 623-2341; City Gate, 60 South Quay; ⊕ 6am-8pm Mon-Fri) at City Gate for schedules.

CAR

A number of small, reliable car-rental companies operate on Trinidad. Prices average about TT$300 a day, including insurance and unlimited mileage. Discounts are usually offered for weekly rentals. **Econo-Car** (☑ 622-8072; www.econocarrentalstt.com; 191-193 Western Main Rd) and **Kalloo's** (☑ 622-9073; www.kalloos.com; 31 French St) have offices in Port of Spain, as well as booths at Piarco International Airport (p763).

Port of Spain

Spreading back from the Gulf of Paria and cradled by the Northern Range foothills, Port of Spain is a mishmash of the pretty and the gritty, with the green expanse of the central Queen's Park Savannah and a host of gorgeous fretworked buildings alongside a frenetic, gridlocked downtown area, its waterfront mostly hidden behind grimy industrial sprawl. But the city's explosive development has created a savvy, metropolitan verve that sets it apart from the average Caribbean capital. This isn't a place that kowtows to the tourist dollar, and it's all the richer for it. There may not be many designated 'sights', but there's plenty of atmosphere downtown, with its market stalls and shady squares, while outlying Woodbrook harbors a host of eternally busy restaurants, bars and clubs. And during Carnival season, huge outdoor 'fetes' rock all corners, steel-pan music fills the air and the atmosphere is electric.

⊙ Sights

★ Queen's Park Savannah   PARK

Once part of a sugar plantation, and formerly home to a racecourse, this public park is encircled by a 3.7km perimeter road that locals call the world's largest roundabout. In the early evening when the scorching heat subsides, the grassy center is taken up with games of cricket or football, while joggers crowd the perimeter path and vendors sell cold coconut water.

★ Emperor Valley Zoo   ZOO

(☑ 622-5344; www.zstt.org; Circular Rd; adult/child TT$30/15; ⊕ 8am-6pm Mon-Fri; ℗ 🛝) Just north of Queen's Park Savannah, the 2.5-hectare Emperor Valley Zoo may be small, but has some interesting residents, including indigenous red howler monkeys, ocelots and various birds and snakes native to Trinidad and Tobago. A newly landscaped section holds sea otters, flamingos and a butterfly park, while giraffes, warthogs and Bengal tigers are the newest residents.

★ Botanical Gardens   GARDENS

(☑ 622-1221; Circular Rd; ⊕ 6am-6:30pm; ℗ 🛝) **FREE** Resplendent with exotic trees and plants, and networked by gentle paths, the Botanical Gardens date from 1818. A graceful mansion built in 1875, the adjacent **President's House**, which is closed to the public, is slated for major repairs, its west wing having collapsed in early 2010.

★ National Museum
& Art Gallery   MUSEUM

(☑ 623-5941; www.nmag.gov.tt; cnr Frederick & Keate Sts; ⊕ 10am-6pm Tue-Sat, 2-6pm Sun) **FREE** Housed in a classic colonial building, the dusty historical exhibits range from Amerindian settlers to African slaves and indentured Indians. There are also geological and natural-history displays – check out the tarantulas and fearsome-looking giant centipede. The rotating collection of artwork on the top floor is the highlight, and gives an excellent introduction to the Trinbago art scene.

Woodford Square   PARK

(Frederick St) This grassy square with its fountain and ornate bandstand is the symbolic center of downtown Port of Spain. Dr Eric Williams, Trinidad and Tobago's first prime minister, gave stirring speeches here, which eventually led to independence from Britain; the 1970s Black Power demonstrations also took place here. Known as the 'University of Woodford Sq', it remains a 'speakers corner' where people can express opinions via soapbox discussions. Surrounding Woodford Sq are some interesting edifices, including the **Red House** (St Vincent St) parliament buildings.

Waterfront Park   PARK

(Wrightson Rd) Off Wrightson Rd opposite Independence Sq, the paved Waterfront Park is overlooked by high-rise offices of the International Waterfront Centre and the Hyatt Regency. Though a bit sterile, with its could-be-anywhere waterfalls and manicured landscaping, the waterside promenade does allow you to get close to the gulf, and is a popular liming spot come evening.

Independence Square   AREA

The hustle and bustle of downtown culminates along Independence Sq, two parallel streets that flank a central promenade. The commanding 1836 **Roman Catholic Cathedral** (📞 623-5232) caps the promenade's eastern end; at its western end, past the high-rise blocks of the Nicholas and Central Bank towers, and a statue of cricket hero Brian Lara, the square feeds onto Wrightson Rd, the coastal highway.

🛏 Sleeping

Port of Spain holds the bulk of Trinidad's accommodations, and as most of the country's better-known attractions are within an hour's drive, it's quite feasible to stay here and explore the whole island.

During Carnival season, most places offer packages for a set number of days, and raise rates to twice the regular room price.

Inna Citi Place   GUESTHOUSE $

(📞 622-0415; www.inna-citi-place.com; 15 Gaston Johnson St, Woodbrook; s/d incl breakfast US$40/$65; ❄@🛜) Excellent little budget choice on a quiet residential street, offering cheerful, spotlessly clean rooms with aircon, TV, wi-fi, a communal kitchen (though the cooked breakfast is pretty ample) and laundry facilities. It's well placed for Carni-

---

THE MAGNIFICENT SEVEN

Along the west side of the Queen's Park Savannah on Maraval Rd are the Magnificent Seven, a line of eccentric and ornate colonial buildings constructed in the early 20th century, and now in various states of repair; two of the most dilapidated, Mille Fleurs and White Hall, are covered by a protective roof and are mostly hidden from the road by fencing, pending restoration. From south to north, they are **Queen's Royal College**; **Hayes Court**; **Mille Fleurs**; **Roomor**; the **Catholic Archbishop's Residence**; **White Hall**; and **Stollmeyer's Castle**, this last recently refurbished.

---

val and the Ariapita Ave scene, and is a good place to meet fellow travelers.

Pearl's   GUESTHOUSE $

(📞 625-2158; peterhenry64@yahoo.co.uk; 3-4 Victoria Sq; s/d US$22/44; 🛜) Bare bones, cheap and with bags of character, Pearl's is set in a faded old gingerbread house overlooking grassy Victoria Sq. It's perfect for Carnival (just steps from one of the band-judging points) and great for linking up with other travelers. Basic fan-only rooms without bathroom, plus a shared kitchen and a communal wraparound veranda.

Johnson's   GUESTHOUSE $

(📞 628-7553; johnsonsbandb@hotmail.com; 16 Buller St; s incl breakfast US$40-50, d US$55-65; ❄🛜) Perfectly located midway between Ariapita Ave and downtown, this friendly guesthouse is an excellent budget option. There's a range of clean, basic rooms downstairs, with fan only and without bathroom, while the smarter rooms upstairs have aircon and an en suite bathroom. Often filled with visiting workers.

⭐**Culture Crossroads Inn**   GUESTHOUSE $$

(📞 622-3387; www.culturecrossroadstt.com; cnr Bengal & Delhi Sts, St James; s/d US$100/$125; P❄❄@🛜) Sparkling clean place, very professionally run and with easy access to malls, transport and the St James/Woodbrook bars and restaurants. The charming owner is a former soca performer and an effusive source of information on all things Trinidad, and the smart, modern rooms (named after

Port of Spain

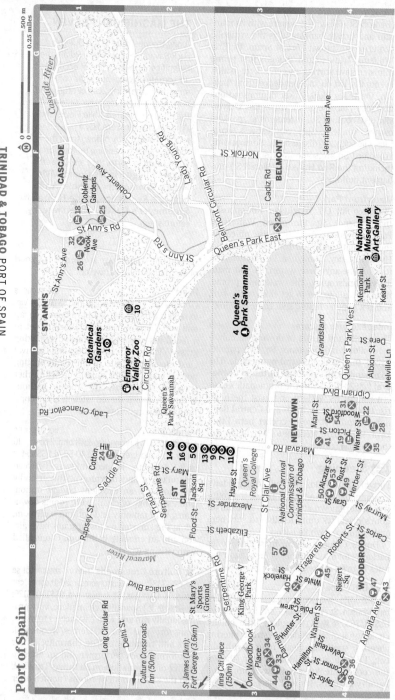

N
0   500 m
0   0.25 miles

Cascade River

CASCADE

Norfolk St

Jerningham Ave

BELMONT

Cadiz Rd

Coblentz Gardens

18
25

St Ann's Rd

Coblentz Ave

Lady Young Rd

Belmont Circular Rd

Queen's Park East

29

32
Nook Ave

26

St Ann's Ave

National Museum & Art Gallery
3

Memorial Park

Keate St

ST ANN'S

Botanical Gardens
1

10

Circular Rd

Emperor Valley Zoo
2

Queen's Park Savannah
4

Queen's Park West

Grandstand

Dere St

Albion St

Melville Ln

Lady Chancellor Rd

Queen's Park Savannah

Cipriani Blvd

NEWTOWN

Marli St

31
54
22
28

Picton St

Cotton Hill
24

Saddle Rd

Serpentine Rd

Prada St

Mary St

14
16
5
13
9
7
11

Jackson Sq

ST CLAIR

Flood St

Alexander St

Hayes St

Queen's Royal College

St Clair Ave

Woodford St

Warner St

19
41
35

Maraval Rd

National Carnival Commission of Trinidad & Tobago

50
Gray St

Alcazar St
53

Rust St
49

Herbert St

Rapsey St

Maraval River

Jamaica Blvd

St Mary's Sports Ground

Serpentine Rd

King George V Park

Elizabeth St

57

Tragarete Rd

Roberts St

Carlos St

Murray St

WOODBROOK

45

White St

Havelock St

Siegert Sq

47

43

Ariapita Ave

Delhi St

Long Circular Rd

Culture Crossroads Inn (50m)

St James (1km);
Fort George (3.6km)

Inna Citi Place (150m)

One Woodbrook Place

44
33
34
56

Damien St

Pole Carew St

Warren St

Hamilton St

Devenish St

Taylor St

Connor St

40

Hunter St

38
36

30

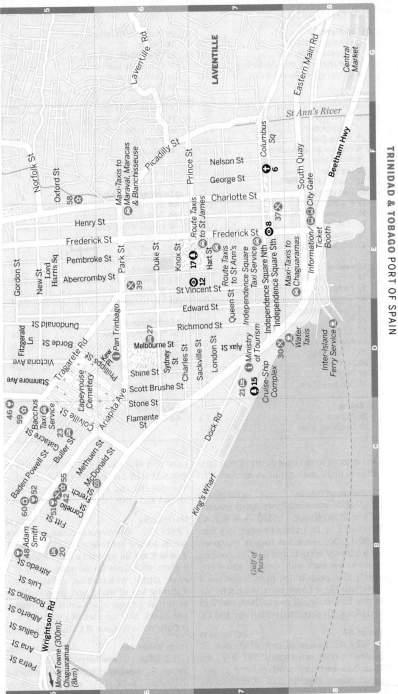

LAVENTILLE

Laventille Rd

St Ann's River

Columbus Sq

Norfolk St

Oxford St

58

Maxi-Taxis to Maraval, Maracas & Blanchisseuse

Picadilly St

Prince St

Nelson St

George St

Charlotte St

6

South Quay

Eastern Main Rd

Central Market

Beetham Hwy

Henry St

Frederick St

Pembroke St

Abercromby St

Gordon St

New St

Lord Harris Sq

Park St

Duke St

Knox St

Route Taxis to St James

Frederick St

Hart St

8

37

Information/ City Gate

Inter-Island Ferry Service

Ticket Booth

17

12

St Vincent St

39

Edward St

Richmond St

Queen St

Independence Square Nth

Independence Square Sth

Independence Square Taxi Service

Route Taxis to St Ann's

Maxi-Taxis to Chaguaramas

Dundonald St

Fitzgerald Ln

Borde St

Victoria Ave

Stanmore Ave

Tragarete Rd

Phillipps St

Lapeyrouse Cemetery

Colville St

Ariapita Ave

Pan Trinbago

Kew Pl

27

Melbourne St

Sydney St

Shine St

Charles St

Scott Brushe St

Stone St

Flamente St

Sackville St

London St

Ajax St

Ministry of Tourism

15

21

Cruise-Ship Complex

30

Water Taxis

Dock Rd

King's Wharf

Gulf of Paria

Baden Powell St

Gatacre St

Buller St

Methuen St

McDonald St

St French

Cornelio

Fitt St

Adam Smith Sq

Alfredo St

Luis St

Rosalino St

Alberto St

Gallus St

Ana St

Petra St

Wrightson Rd

MovieTowne (300m); Chaguaramas (8km)

Bacchus Taxi Service

46

59

23

60

52

55

42

51

48

20

Port of Spain

local cultural icons) have plenty of neat little extras to make your stay more comfortable.

Gingerbread House GUESTHOUSE **$$**
(☎ 627-8170; www.trinidadgingerbreadhouse.com; 8 Carlos St, Woodbrook; r US$70; ❂❈@☎❋) Renovated by its architect owner, this fretworked 1920s house has bags of character, with a breezy veranda and a stylish outdoor space at the back with sundeck and a creatively tiled pool. In the main house you'll feel much like a house guest, staying in one of two high-ceilinged rooms, both spacious and pleasantly decorated with fridge and TV.

Inn at 87 GUESTHOUSE **$$**
(☎ 622-4343; www.innat87.com; 87 Woodford St, Newtown; r incl breakfast from US$90; ❈☎) Set in a cute and airy peach-painted gingerbread house, close to lots of restaurants,

bars and the Queen's Park Oval cricket ground. Staff are excellent and attentive. The cheerful and comfy rooms come with air-con and cable TV.

Normandie HOTEL **$$**
(☎ 624-1181; www.normandiett.com; 10 Nook Ave, St Ann's; r incl breakfast US$144, ste $159; P❈@☎❋) Tucked into a quiet backstreet a short walk from the Savannah, this is a lovely retreat, with inviting, spotless rooms featuring lots of wood, and good facilities, as well as a range of self-contained studios and suites, plus a restaurant and shops. A popular concert venue at Carnival time, too.

Forty Winks Inn GUESTHOUSE **$$**
(☎ 622-0484; www.fortywinkstt.com; 24 Warner St, Newtown; s/d/tr/q incl breakfast US$90/105/136/145.50; ❈@☎) Nicely

located in Newtown and very efficiently run, this vibrantly decorated house has five cheerful rooms and a friendly, intimate atmosphere. Enjoy the sunset from the patio on top, which is lush with plants. Popular with business travelers.

L'Orchidée GUESTHOUSE $$

(✆621-0618; www.trinidadhosthomes.com; 3 Coblentz Gardens, St Ann's; s/d $110/120; P✳@🛜) Smart 12-bedroom inn, popular with business travelers, with bright, well-appointed rooms in vibrant colors and a super-professional staff. Breakfast is included in the rates, and it's walking distance from the Savannah.

Airport Inn GUESTHOUSE $$

(✆669-8207; www.airportinntrinidad.com; 60 Factory Rd, Golden Grove; s/d/tr/q US$75/100/130/150; P✳🛜) Just off the approach road to Piarco International Airport, this is a good option for a stopover before you fly, with a free shuttle to the terminal. Set in a family home, the rooms are neat and clean and the owner-operator friendly and welcoming.

Alicia's House GUESTHOUSE $$

(✆623-2802; www.aliciaspalace.com; 7 Coblentz Gardens, St Ann's; r incl breakfast US$65-100; P✳@🛜🏊) Bustling place with a comfortingly kitsch 1970s ambience. Just north of Queen's Park Savannah, it has comfortable rooms with fridges, air-con, cable TV and wi-fi, plus nice communal areas, including sundeck and pool/hot tub. Meals are served in its restaurant.

Sundeck Suites HOTEL $$

(✆622-9560; www.sundecktrinidad.com; 42-44 Picton St, Newtown; s/d/tr apt US$60/80/90; P✳🛜) A block away from Par-May-La's Inn, and owned by the same management, Sundeck offers no-frills apartments, each with a fully equipped kitchen and a small deck. Guests can enjoy mountain views from atop its broad 130-sq-meter rooftop deck.

Hyatt Regency HOTEL $$$

(✆623-2222; www.trinidad.hyatt.com; 1 Wrightson Rd; r from US$179; P♿✳@🛜🏊) Taking up a fat piece of oceanside real estate next to the ferry terminal, this is the most luxurious choice in Port of Spain. Its army of staff presides over a huge array of amenities, from stunning rooftop pool and spa to multiple restaurants and bars. Rates reduce at weekends when business guests depart.

Kapok HOTEL $$$

(✆622-5765; www.kapokhotel.com; 16-18 Cotton Hill; r US$149-185, ste US$199-214; P♿✳@🛜🏊) Not just a business hotel, the smart Kapok boasts an authentic Caribbean vibe. It's located toward the south end of Saddle Rd, within throwing distance from Queen's Park Savannah, and perfect for Carnival. Rooms and suites are decked out with pretty rattan furnishings and it has a self-service launderette and two excellent restaurants.

Holiday Inn Express HOTEL $$$

(✆669-6209; www.hiexpress.com; 1 Exposition Drive, Trincity; r from US$157; P♿✳🛜🏊) Functional airport hotel just off the highway and adjacent to a golf course. It's a little soulless but does the job if you need to be close to the airport, with comfortable beds, a decent pool and a gym. There's a free shuttle to Trinity Mall as well as to the airport.

🍴 Eating

⭐Dopson's Roti Shop INDIAN $

(✆628-6141; 25 Maraval Rd, Newtown; rotis from TT$25; ⏰6:45am-5pm Mon-Fri, 8am-5pm Sat) This renowned little place is a favorite locals' spot – many Trinis claim they make the best rotis in Port of Spain here. The fillings are fresh, succulent and generous (try the curried duck), and Dopson's also cooks up a mean traditional breakfast of eggplant and tomato choka, saltfish and smoked herring.

Breakfast Shed CARIBBEAN $

(Wrightson Rd; mains from TT$50; ⏰6:30am-4pm) Under an awning right on the water, this is the place to go for Trini tastes, with stalls ranged around the perimeter of an open-air, picnic-benched eating area. The

STREET FOOD

Street food is a big deal in Port of Spain. Trini treats are available from dusk until late into the night along Western Main Rd in St James; Ariapita Ave in Woodbrook, where you'll find a string of stands selling gyro wraps; and – on Thursday, Friday and Saturday evenings – the southeastern corner of the Queen's Park Savannah, where stalls set up offering everything from corn soup and fried chicken to bake and fish or juices made from exotic tropical fruits.

CARNIVAL

With roots in both West Africa and Europe, Carnival is the ultimate indulgence before the sober disciplines of Lent – and everyone's welcome to participate in this big daddy of Caribbean festivals.

Background information is available from the **National Carnival Commission** (☑622-1670; www.ncctt.org; 11 St Clair Ave, Port of Spain) and the **National Carnival Bands Association** (☑628-8650; www.ncbatt.com; 1 Picton St, Newtown), while Trinidad Carnival Diary (www.trinidadcarnivaldiary.com) provides mas band listings and reviews, and topical articles on all things Carnival: check out the Masquerader Corner section of the site.

Mas Camps

Mas camps are workshops where carnival bands ('mas bands') create their costumes and display them to prospective revelers. Costumes cost anything from TT$3000 for a basic outfit to TT$10,000 or more for a 'frontline' extravaganza; buying a costume allows you to parade along the Carnival route with the band on the main Monday and Tuesday festivities, and usually covers food and drinks as well. Costumes can be bought directly from mas camps or online, and they go very quickly. Latecomers can try their luck finding a costume from websites such as Carnival Junction (www.carnivaljunction.com) or Fineahban (www.fineahban.com). First-choice bands include **Tribe** (☑625-6800; www.carnivaltribe.com; 20 Rosalino St, Woodbrook), **Trini Revellers** (☑625-1881; www.trinirevellersmas.com; 35 Gallus St, Woodbrook), **Legacy** (☑622-7466; www.legacycarnival.com; 88 Roberts St, Woodbrook) and **Showtime** (☑681-6117; www.showtimecarnival.com; 51 French St, Woodbrook). For full band listings see the National Carnival Bands Association website.

Pre-Carnival Highlights

➡ Lavish pre-Carnival fetes start on January 1 and continue until Carnival.

➡ The Panorama semis and finals see steel-pan bands battle it out on the last two Sundays before Carnival weekend.

➡ There are fabulously cute Kiddie Mas parades on the final two Saturdays preceding Carnival.

➡ Watch mesmerizingly huge costumes dance across the stage at the final of the King and Queen of the Bands competition, held on the Friday before Carnival at the Queen's Park Savannah in Port of Spain.

➡ Dimanche Gras, on the Sunday before Carnival at Queen's Park Savannah, sees the crowning of the Calypso Monarch.

J'ouvert

Trinidad's Carnival opens with J'ouvert, a no-holds-barred predawn street party where revelers indulge in their most hedonistic inclinations, as they welcome in the festivities by playing 'dirty mas'. From 4am, partygoers fill the streets, slather themselves and others in mud, paint, oil and even liquid chocolate, and go mad while following trucks blasting soca. It's an anarchic scene, so you're best off signing up with an established band like **3Canal** (☑622-1001; www.3canal.com; 33 Murray St, Woodbrook), **Red Ants** (☑625-6800; 20 Rosalino St, Woodbrook) or **Chocolate City** (☑623-4627; 42 Baden Powell St, Woodbrook), which employ security and lay on drinks and music trucks as well as mud, paint and a basic costume for about TT$500. Web presence for J'ouvert bands is patchy, so check Facebook for info.

Playing Mas

On Carnival Monday and Tuesday, tens of thousands parade and dance in the streets with their mas bands, accompanied by soca trucks with DJs; steel bands also parade and attract a loyal local following. Carnival is all about participation, but if you don't join a band, you can take in the action streetside – though stewards rope off the areas for each band, and won't allow nonmasqueraders in. You can also watch from the judging points at Adam Smith Sq, South Quay and, the big daddy of them all, the main stage at the Queen's Park Savannah. Another good spot is the 'Socadrome,' an alternative stage in the Jean Pierre Complex on Wrightson Rd.

large servings of local fare include fish or chicken with macaroni pie, callaloo, stewed beans, plantain and rice. Breakfasts include saltfish buljol or smoked herring with fresh coconut bread.

Mother Nature's   VEGETARIAN $
(☑ 623-3300; cnr Park & St Vincent Sts; mains TT$25-50; ⊙ 5am-4pm Mon-Sat; ▣) Whole-wheat roti? Yes, it exists here, as do dairy-free desserts (including a showcase of ice creams) and deliciously healthy vegetarian dishes from the local repertoire. The fresh-pressed or squeezed natural juices, from barbadine to sugar cane, are delectable.

Patraj   CARIBBEAN $
(☑ 622-6219; 161 Tragarete Rd; rotis from TT$25; ⊙ 8am-5pm Mon-Sat) Opposite the Queen's Park Oval cricket ground, Patraj serves some of the most mouth-watering roti in the city, with a huge array of fillings from shrimp to beef and plenty of veggies. There's a small space in which to eat. Service can be a bit dour.

Hosein's Roti Shop   INDIAN $
(☑ 335-2259; www.hoseinsrotishop.com; cnr Independence Sq South & Henry St; rotis from TT$25; ⊙ 10am-10pm Mon-Sat; ▣) On the south side of town, this is a hugely popular carryout, with hungry workers queuing up for the tasty and generously sized rotis.

★Coloz   CARIBBEAN $$
(☑ 726-3030; Unit 14, One Woodbrook Place, Damian St, Woodbrook; lunch TT$125-150; ⊙ 11:30am-2:30pm Tue-Sun; P▣) Discerning locals have long known about this oasis of Trini delectability. The mom-and-pop team cook up a daily buffet of local delights, from seasoned kingfish to lamb chops or steak with mushrooms and peppers, backed up with an array of sides – calalloo, bhaji (spinach), lentils – and a fresh salad bar. Go early or you'll find there's little left.

★Veni Mangé   CARIBBEAN $$
(☑ 624-4597; 67a Ariapita Ave; mains from TT$105; ⊙ 11:30am-3pm Mon-Fri, plus 7-10:30pm Wed & Fri; ▣▣) West Indian flavor, art, foliage and enthusiasm infuse this vibrant restaurant. Serving Caribbean cuisine with classic French influences, it's one of the best spots for lunch in Port of Spain. Try the beef dumplings, the grilled fresh fish with tamarind sauce or the excellent veggie options.

Chaud Café   FUSION $$
(☑ 628-9845; www.chaudcafe.com; One Woodbrook Place, Damian St, Woodbrook; brunch dishes from TT$50, small plates from TT$75, mains from TT$90; ⊙ 11am-11pm Mon-Thu, to midnight Fri & Sat; ▣) Part wine bar, part upscale bistro, and operated by local chef extraordinaire Khalid Mohammed, this is a lovely spot for lunch, perhaps honey-mustard glazed mahi mahi with or seven-vegetable tagine. The pasta (including gluten-free) is always delicious. It's great for evening drinks, too, with good cocktails and wine, and tasty small plates of tapas-like bites. Great Saturday brunch offerings, too.

Ciao at the Normandie   FUSION $$
(☑ 624-1181; 10 Nook Ave, St Ann's; brunch TT$185, mains TT$75-185; ⊙ 11:30am-3pm & 6-10:30pm Mon-Sat, 8:30am-1pm Sun; P▣) For a quiet romantic dinner, take a table on the pretty terrace and enjoy excellent service and great Italian food with a Caribbean twist. Some excellent fish and seafood, plus fresh and yummy desserts. It's also worth checking out the lavish Sunday-brunch spread – one child (under eight years) goes free with each adult – and the Friday-night fish fry.

Sweet Lime   CARIBBEAN $$
(☑ 624-9983; www.sweetlime.co.tt; cnr Ariapita Ave & French St, Woodbrook; lunch TT$25-35, dinner TT$95-380; ⊙ 11:30am-midnight; ▣▣▣) This restaurant-bar has an open-air kitchen, plant-laden outdoor seating and free wi-fi. At lunch you can get a simple local meal such as fried fish, baked chicken or stewed shrimp with rice, beans and salad. The extensive and more expensive dinner menu includes salads, burgers, grilled meats and fish or seafood – all with a tasty Trini flavour.

Often puts on live music around Christmas or Carnival.

More Vino More Sushi   SUSHI $$
(☑ 622-8466; www.morevino.com; 23 O'Connor St, cnr Ariapita Ave, Woodbrook; sushi TT$28-108, mains from TT$78; ⊙ 11am-midnight Mon-Wed, to 1am Thu-Sat) This popular wine bar serves up excellent sushi, with all the familiar rolls, plus local flavors such as the spicy Maracas – all made right in front of your eyes. Japanese and Thai mains are also on offer, the wine list is excellent and it's a great spot for a cocktail. The hookah pipes are also very popular.

NIGHTLIFE TOURS

If you'd like someone to guide you through the best of Port of Spain's nightlife scene, contact **Island Experiences** (p751) for an evening entertainment tour, which usually includes visits to a couple of panyards, a calypso show and guidance in choosing the best street snacks. Tours focused on clubbing or hitting the city's bars are also available. About two hours of fun, including transportation, starts at US$60 per person.

Hakka
FUSION $$

(☑ 221-0800; www.hakkarestaurant.com; 4 Taylor St, Woodbrook; mains from TT$61; ◷ 11am-11pm Mon-Thu, 11am-midnight Fri & Sat, noon-10pm Sun) Buzzing place offering delectable Chinese cuisine with an Indian/Asian flavor, from Thai green curries to Szechuan chilli fish. Eating in can build up the bill, but inexpensive takeout is also on offer, and the terrace out front fills up with drinkers on the weekends.

★ Buzo Osteria Italiana
ITALIAN $$$

(☑ 223-2896; 6 Warner St, Newtown; pizzas TT$89-127, pastas TT$79-109, mains TT$109-290; ◷ 11:30am-11pm Mon-Sat; ☑ ⛄) Set in a gorgeous old stone building, with a courtyard that's ideal for evening cocktails, this is one of Trinidad's best restaurants. The Italian chef cooks up authentic antipasti and pasta (from beef carpaccio to pumpkin tortelli with buffalo mozzarella), plus delectable mains such as squid-ink gnocchi with lobster and shrimp or prosciutto-wrapped pork loin. Pizzas are equally sublime. Booking advisable.

Chaud
INTERNATIONAL $$$

(☑ 621-2002; www.chaudkm.com; 6 Nook Ave, St Ann's; prixe fixe 3-course lunch TT$295, mains TT$175-$350, tasting menus TT$600-800; ◷ 11am-3pm & 6-10:30pm Mon-Sat; ☑) Set in secluded St Ann's, this is Trini fine-dining at its best. The gourmet creations of local superchef Khalid Mohammed might include slow-cooked lamb shank with cassava risotto and gremolata, or geera-crusted kingfish with tomato choka, *aloo gobi* and dhal. The five-or 10-course tasting menu is unforgettable, but you can also come for the reasonably priced three-course set lunch.

Apsara
INDIAN $$$

(☑ 623-7659; www.apsaratt.com; 13 Queen's Park East; lunch set menu TT$150, mains TT$125-280; ◷ 11am-3pm daily, 6-11pm Mon-Sat; ☑) Named after the dancers of the court of Indra, who could move freely between heaven and earth, Apsara is a stalwart among Port of Spain's restaurants. Specializing in North Indian cuisine, its curries and tandoori meats and fish will melt in your mouth. Vegetarians have many options. The lunch special is good value.

🍷 Drinking & Nightlife

Port of Spain's drinking scene is concentrated along Woodbrook's Ariapita Ave, with a string of bars and clubs (and places that are somewhere between the two, with DJs and a dance floor). The nightlife scene is especially happening Thursday through Saturday, and places change quite quickly. If you're hitting the Ariapita Ave, the best plan is to start at Shakers (p761) and work your way west.

Frankie's
BAR

(☑ 622-6609; 68a Ariapita Ave, cnr Alberto St, Woodbrook; ◷ 11am-late) First opened as an inexpensive lunch spot, Frankie's has morphed into one of Ariapita Ave's best-loved liming locations. You can still get local lunches, but it's best after dark, when the friendly crowd spills out onto the pavement and the drinks flow.

Paprika
CLUB

(☑ 789-8917; https://paprikatt.wordpress.com; 15 Rust St, St Clair; ◷ 6pm-3am Thu, to 4am Fri & Sat) **FREE** Often the busiest nightspot on buzzing Rust St, this is a bohemian bazaar of Middle Eastern baroque, where an upscale crowd grooves to soca, dancehall and club anthems amid the dry ice inside, or take in the breeze on the outside deck.

Stumblin' on the Avenue
CLUB

(☑ 223-5017; 42 Ariapita Ave, Woodbrook; ◷ 3pm-4am Tue-Sat) **FREE** Laid-back bar/club, with dancing at the weekends in the air-con interior as well as the terrace out front. The playlist of soca and dancehall draws a relaxed but party-hard Trini crowd, and the drinks are inexpensive, with regular promotions on offer.

La Habana
BAR

(☑ 622-6609; 61 Ariapita Ave, Woodbrook; ◷ 4am-late Mon-Sat) An ever-busy bar that's popular with the Venezuelan community. Drinkers crowd onto the pavement outside come the weekend, and DJs spin Latin tunes as the crowd salsas the night away on the dance floor inside.

RuStreet
BAR

(☑622-2233; 20 Rust St, St Clair; ⊙11am-5pm Mon & Tue, to 2am Wed, Thu & Sat, to 3am Fri) **FREE** Though open for lunch and dinner, this is primarily a place to go for a few drinks, with excellent cocktails and regular special deals. Music from DJs at the weekends, and tables set out on an open-air terrace.

Vas Lounge
CLUB

(☑235-3224; 16 Rust St, St Clair; ⊙6pm-4am Wed-Sat, 8pm-2am Sun) **FREE** Buzzing bar-club with an air-con dance floor inside, which spills out onto a raised terrace under the stars. Expect a buzzing Trini crowd, a queue for the bar and a loud playlist of dancehall, soca and pop.

Shakers on the Avenue
BAR

(☑624-6612; cnr Ariapita Ave & Cornelio St, Woodbrook; ⊙11:30am-2am Tue-Thu, to 3am Fri & Sat) **FREE** This great little bar, with an icy indoor section and a convivial garden, is an excellent liming spot, with good cocktails, a friendly mixed-age crowd and bar snacks. Look out for the regular live-music performances, usually on Wednesday, as well as drinks promotions; DJs play at weekends.

Fifty One Degrees
CLUB

(☑627-0051; www.51degrees.biz; 51 Cipriani Blvd; weekend cover charge from TT$120; ⊙7pm-late Thu-Sat) This stalwart of the Port of Spain nightlife scene continues its reign as one of the best places to party the night away, with things heating up from 11pm onwards. Dress to impress, and don't turn up wearing sneakers, flip-flops or a hat.

Drink Lounge and Bistro
BAR

(☑223-7243; 63 Rosalino St, cnr Roberts & Warren Sts, Woodbrook; ⊙4pm-midnight Tue-Thu, to 2am Fri & Sat) **FREE** A block back from Ariapita Ave, this cool little wine bar is a popular hangout for arty types, with a host of cultural happenings, great food and, of course, an excellent selection of wine and cocktails.

Buzz Bar
BAR

(☑221-8873; One Woodbrook Place, Damian St, Woodbrook; ⊙4pm-1am Tue-Fri, 5pm-1am Sat) Set high above the street on the terrace of swish One Woodbrook Place, this is a chilled alternative to the bars of Ariapita Ave and Rust St, with twinkling fairy lights, tables under the stars and the city lights spread out below. A mixed, older crowd enjoys good cocktails and regular drinks promotions.

☆ Entertainment

Kaiso Blues Café
LIVE MUSIC

(☑477-2262; 85 Woodford St, Newtown; ⊙11am-11pm) Offering live music throughout the year – from calypso to blues, jazz, reggae and R&B – along with a little spoken word and karaoke too. Tables outside and in, bar snacks available and a friendly crowd make this a relaxing place to take in some local tunes.

PANYARDS

For much of the year, panyards are little more than vacant lots where steel bands store their instruments. Come Carnival season, they become lively rehearsal spaces, pulsating with energy and magnificent sound, with pan-lovers crowding in to buy drinks from the bar and take in the music. It's a window into one of the most important and sacred parts of Trinidad's urban landscape, with aficionados discussing every note and tempo change, and excitement building as the Panorama competition gets closer.

Steel bands start gearing up for Carnival as early as late September, and some rehearse and perform throughout the year. The best way to find out about practice and performance schedules is by asking around. You can also contact the steel-pan governing body, **Pan Trinbago** (☑623-4486; www.pantrinbago.co.tt; Victoria Suites, 14-17 Park St, Port of Spain).

Some popular panyards that welcome visitors:

Phase II Pan Groove (☑627-0909; Hamilton St)

Renegades (☑624-3348; 138 Charlotte St)

Silver Stars (☑633-4733; 56 Tragarete Rd)

Nu Pub   LIVE MUSIC

(Mas Camp Pub; ☑ 627-4042; cnr French St & Ariapita Ave) A taste of old-school Port of Spain,
with live calypso several times a week (cover
charge varies), often featuring the nation's
most celebrated calypsonians. Other nights
see anything from karaoke to Latin dance,
and there are pool tables out back, too. It's
been renamed the Nu Pub, but it's universally referred to by its original name, the
Mas Camp Pub.

🔒 Shopping

The central area of Port of Spain, especially
around Independence Sq, Charlotte St and
Frederick St, is filled with malls and arcades
selling everything from spices to fabric by
the yard. International shops cluster at the
enormous **Falls at West Mall** (Western Main
Rd), just west of town.

★**Cocobel**   CHOCOLATE

(☑ 622-1196; www.cocobelchocolate.com; 37 Fitt
St, Woodbrook; gift boxes TT$60-375; ☉ 10am-
5pm Mon-Fri) Made from the finest Trinitario
beans, Cocobel chocolates are available only
in Trinidad and Tobago, but can stand up
as some of the finest you'll taste anywhere
in the world. Each of the individual bon-
bons are works of art, hand-decorated and
incorporating local flavors such as Maracas
sea salt, sorrel, chadon beni and guava.
Beautifully packaged and a unique taste of
Trinidad.

★**Green Market**   MARKET

(☑ 221-9116; www.greenmarketsantacruz.com;
Upper Saddle Rd, Santa Cruz; ☉ 6am-1pm Sat &
Sun; ♿) Set in the verdant Santa Cruz Valley,
this fabulous market has organic produce
stalls as well as local craft. But it's best as
a place to kick back on a bench under the
trees and enjoy wonderful Sunday-brunch
offerings, from Venezuelan arepas to Creole treats, hot cocoa tea (hot chocolate) and
pure fresh juices. Children's activities, too.

ℹ Information

DANGERS & ANNOYANCES

Port of Spain has a bad reputation for crime,
with robberies and shootings (invariably
drug-related) besetting low-income areas such
as Laventille, which most travelers never venture into. Busy areas – downtown, Woodbrook,
St Clair, Newtown and the Savannah – are safe
during the day.

➤ Avoid walking solo at night around downtown
Port of Spain and across the Savannah.

➤ Take a taxi back to your hotel at night rather
than walk.

➤ Beware of parking restrictions, which are
not clearly signed. Police often tow cars, which
have to be expensively bailed out at the police
station on South Quay, so use a public parking
lot (around TT$35 per day).

INTERNET ACCESS

All hotels and guesthouses have wi-fi, as do
many cafes, bars and restaurants. The **Rituals**
(cnr Marli St & Maraval Rd; sandwiches TT$22-
45; ☉ 6:30am-7pm; ❄ 🛜 ♿) coffee shops are
always a good option when you're on the move.

MONEY

The major banks – RBTT, Republic Bank, Royal
Bank and First Citizens – all have branches on
Park St east of Frederick St, and on Independ-
ence Sq. There are also banks in West Mall,
Long Circular Mall and on Ariapita Ave. All have
24-hour ATMs.

POST

Main Post Office (☑ 625-4784; www.ttpost.
net; Wrightson Rd; ☉ 8am-4pm Mon-Fri) TT
Post has outlets all over town.

TOURIST INFORMATION

The **Tourism Development Company** (TDC;
☑ 675-7034; www.gotrinidadandtobago.com;
Maritime Centre, 19 10th Ave, Barataria; ☉ 8am-
4:30pm Mon-Fri), outreach arm of the **Ministry
of Tourism** (☑ 624-1403; www.tourism.gov.
tt; Level 8-9, Tower C, Waterfront Complex,
Wrightson Rd; ☉ 8am-4:30pm Mon-Fri), has an
office at **Piarco** (☑ 669-5196; www.gotrinida-
dandtobago.com; Piarco International Airport;
☉ 8am-11pm) airport offering basic advice on
accommodations and attractions etc, but no
outlet in Port of Spain.

The **National Carnival Commission** (p758)
can provide background information on Carnival.

ℹ Getting There & Away

Ferries from Tobago run by the **Inter-Island
Ferry Service** (p752) dock at the terminal on
Wrightson Rd. **Water Taxis** (☑ 624-5137; http://
nidco.co.tt; Wrightson Rd; 1-way TT$15; ☉ run
regularly Mon-Sat) to San Fernando also depart
regularly from Monday to Saturday. A taxi from
Piarco International Airport (p792) will cost
US$30 to Port of Spain, US$35 to Woodbrook.

ℹ Getting Around

Port of Spain is a relatively small city; you could
explore all of the downtown area on foot, though
the heat might make you want to jump in a taxi
to travel between downtown and Woodbrook, St
Clair or Newtown.

From downtown, you can take shared route taxis to **St Ann's** (Hart St) or **St James** (Hart St). Take maxi-taxis to **Chaguaramas** (cnr South Quay & St Vincent Sts), via Ariapita Ave in Woodbrook, and the north-coast towns of **Maraval, Maracas and Blanchisseuse** (cnr Charlotte & Park Sts). There are also maxis to destinations east along the highway. Private taxis wait at the large hotels; there's also a taxi stand at **Independence Sq** (🖉 625-3032). For a private taxi, call **Bacchus Taxi Service** (🖉 622-5588; Tragarete Rd).

Reliable local car-rental agencies include **Econo-Car** (p752) and **Kalloo's** (p752). Both **Econo-Car** (🖉 669-1119; www.econocarrentalstt.com; Piarco International Airport) and **Kalloo's** (🖉 669-5672; www.kalloos.com; Piarco International Airport) have branches at the airport.

Chaguaramas

Occupying Trinidad's northwest tip, the Chaguaramas (sha-gah-*ra*-mus) Peninsula was the site of a major US military installation during WWII, and was fully handed back to Trinidad only in the 1970s. Today the string of oceanside marinas draws in yachties taking advantage of dry-docking facilities or waiting out the weather – Trinidad lies safely south of the hurricane belt.

The area is a popular recreation spot, with a couple of beaches, a golf course and lovely hiking in verdant Tucker Valley; a giant waterpark is under construction along the waterfront. It's also the launching point for tours to a chain of offshore islands, the **Bocas**. Popular options are **Gasparee Island**, where you can visit caves that drip with stalactites, or the most distant, 360-hectare **Chacachacare**, a former leper colony. Boat tours, hiking, swimming and historical excursions, can be arranged with Island Experiences (p751) or the **Chaguaramas Development Authority** (🖉 634-4227; www.chaguaramas.com; tours TT$40-140), which manages the peninsula.

◉ Sights

Chaguaramas Military History & Aerospace Museum MUSEUM
(🖉 634-4391; Western Main Rd; adult/child TT$50/30; ☺9am-5pm Tue-Sun; 🅿🚼) This fascinating museum celebrates the role of Caribbean soldiers in overseas warfare by way of battle re-creations, photographs and military hardware – plus a decommissioned passenger jet slowly rusting in the ocean breeze.

WORTH A TRIP

MOUNT ST BENEDICT MONASTERY

A Benedictine monastery sits on 240 hectares on a hillside north of Tunapuna, 13km east of Port of Spain. Though not a major sight in itself, **Mount St Benedict** attracts people who want to stay or eat at its secluded guesthouse, birdwatch or walk in the surrounding forest. Unless you have a car, however, it's inconvenient to get to. The thickly wooded hills behind the monastery provide hiking opportunities and possible glimpses of hawks, owls and numerous colorful forest birds, and maybe a monkey, and the road up offers panoramic views of Trinidad's central plains.

Under the monastery, peaceful **Pax Guest House** (🖉 662-4084; www.paxguesthouse.com; Mt St Benedict, Tunapuna; s incl breakfast US$65-90, d $95-120; 🅿❄) is delightful place to come for lunch or afternoon tea (TT$15; daily 2pm to 6pm), with scones, pastries or Trinidadian sweet bread served on a veranda that makes a great spot for birdwatching. Book visits in advance. A favorite hike from here is the 30-minute trail to the fire tower, which offers eye-popping views and birding.

Tucker Valley AREA
(🖉 225-4232; www.chaguaramas.com) Just inland of Chaguaramas town, the 6000-hectare Tucker Valley is a popular recreation spot, with picnic grounds, hiking trails and a golf course.

Macqueripe Beach BEACH
(Tucker Valley, off Western Main Rd; parking TT$20; 🅿) The main road through Tucker Valley ends at Macqueripe, formerly the swimming spot of American troops and now a pretty place to dive into cool green waters, with views over to the misty Venezuelan coastline and lovely landscaped gardens around the steep path down to the sand.

🏃 Activities & Tours

Kayak Centre KAYAKING
(🖉 325-2627; trinikayak@gmail.com; Williams Bay; per hr kayaks single from TT$30, tandem TT$50, stand-up paddleboard TT$30; ☺6am-6pm) Right on the waterfront as you enter Chaguaramas from Port of Spain, this cool little

operation offers kayaking and SUP explorations of calm Williams Bay. Life jackets are available.

Zip-Itt Adventure
ADVENTURE

(☎303-7755; www.chaguaramas.com; Macqueripe Bay, Tucker Valley; zip line TT$140, kids activity park TT$85, 1hr bike rental TT$50; ☺10am-4pm Tue-Fri, to 4:30pm Sat & Sun; ⊕) Seven zip lines of varying lengths, one of which swoops right over Macqueripe Bay, plus five canopy walks/net bridges. Tickets sold at the beach entry kiosk; wear covered shoes. It also has a children's activity park, with rope walkways, and bike rental.

🛏 Sleeping

Bight
GUESTHOUSE $$

(☎634-4420; www.peakeyachts.com; Peake's Marina, 5 Western Main Rd; r US$85; P☀🛜) Simple, tidy rooms right on the water make this the nicest midrange option in the area – sit on the porch and enjoy the views of pelicans diving and yachts bobbing.

CrewsInn
HOTEL $$$

(☎607-4000; www.crewsinn.com; Point Gourde; r incl breakfast US$238-275; P☀@🛜🏊) The highest-end option in Chaguaramas, with a pool and resort-like trappings, CrewsInn has luxurious, overpriced modern rooms, all with patios and complete amenities. The hotel is within a marina complex with two restaurants.

🍴 Eating

Wheel House Pub
CARIBBEAN $$

(☎634-2339; Tropical Marine; lunch TT$45, dinner mains TT$60-150; ☺11am-11pm Mon-Sat) Great little bar-restaurant with tables on a covered waterfront terrace and an air-con interior. Inexpensive fish, pork or chicken with local sides is a bargain at lunchtime, and dinner offerings widen to shrimp, burgers, ribs and lamb or pork chops.

Lighthouse Restaurant
INTERNATIONAL $$

(☎634-4384; www.crewsinn.com; CrewsInn Marina, Western Main Rd; mains from TT$89-345, lunch special TT$99-150; ☺11am-3pm & 6-10pm; 🛜⊕) Open-air restaurant on a deck overlooking the bobbing masts of the CrewsInn Marina. The food is decent (if lacking a bit of passion), but the setting is gorgeous and it's also good for sunset drinks. Daily set-price lunch special (one to three courses) too.

Sails
INTERNATIONAL $$

(☎634-1712; www.sailsrestpub.com; Power Boats Marina; burgers from TT$56, mains TT$95-335; ☺11am-midnight; ⊕) This popular hangout has seating on the water, pool tables inside and a BBQ on Sundays. You can get bar snacks and grilled food here, as well as kebabs and local dishes such as callaloo soup and fresh fish or seafood with plentiful sides.

❶ Getting There & Away

Yellow band **maxi-taxis** (p763) run from Port of Spain into Chaguaramas, but you'll need a car or a private taxi at night.

Maracas Bay

Maracas Bay is Trinidad's most popular beach. The wide, white-sand shore, dotted with palm trees contrasting against the backdrop of verdant mountains, remains an irresistible lure for both locals and travelers. Despite the curving headland, the sand is often pounded by waves that serve up good bodysurfing. On weekends the beach can get pretty crowded, but during the week it can feel almost deserted.

However, the scene is somewhat marred by ongoing construction of new vendor huts and visitor facilities on the sand, but once beyond these, the beach itself remains glorious.

◉ Sights

Maracas Beach
BEACH

(North Coast Rd; changing rooms TT$1, car park TT$10; ☺lifeguards 10am-6pm) A white-sand shore sprinkled with palm trees and backgrounded by the verdant Northern Range. The wave-battered beach is often good for bodysurfing. During the week, the crowds thin out and it can feel almost deserted. Beach chairs, loungers and umbrellas are available to rent

🍴 Eating & Drinking

An array of huts on and opposite the beach sell bake and shark: seasoned shark steaks, served in a fried bake bread, slathered with dressings (try the tamarind, chadon beni and hot pepper) and topped with salad. Shark numbers are threatened in Trinidad, however, so a more sustainable choice is bake and kingfish. You can also get fries, burgers, hot dogs and other snacks.

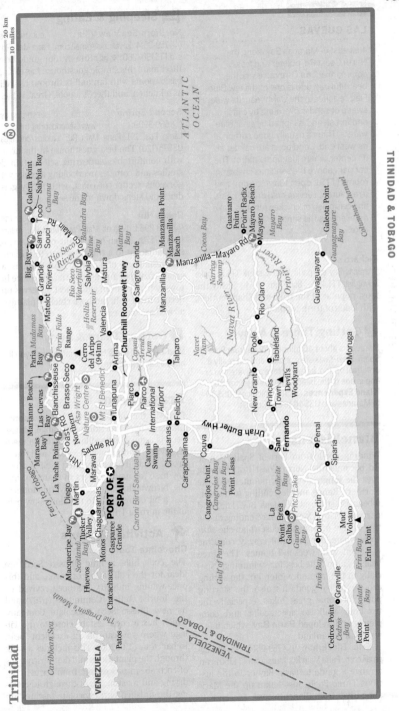

LAS CUEVAS

Just east of Maracas Bay along the North Coast Rd, quieter and less commercial **Las Cuevas** is another beautiful bay, and is one of the few Blue Flag beaches in the Caribbean. Its wide sweep of sand is overhung by cliffs and forest, and is lapped by clear blue waters. There's usually good surfing at its west end. Conditions are calmer at its center, where lifeguards patrol. The car park above the sand has changing rooms (TT$1; open 10am to 6pm) and a restaurant serving cold drinks, beers and basic fish or chicken lunches. Take repellent, as the sandflies can be bad here.

Richard's
CARIBBEAN $

(Maracas Bay car park; bake & shark TT$35, bake & kingfish TT$45; ☺8am-7pm; P 🚻) Easily the most popular of the bake-and-shark outlets, with loads of fresh toppings.

❶ Getting There & Away

Maracas is about 40 minutes' drive from Port of Spain. Maxi-taxis are irregular and not really a practical option; better to take a private taxi or hop in one of the beach shuttles organized by **Island Experiences** (p751), which cost US$30 to Maracas and US$40 to Las Cuevas.

Blanchisseuse

Winding north from Port of Spain, Saddle Rd becomes the North Coast Rd, climbing over the jungle-slathered mountains of the Northern Range and descending to the Caribbean coastline at Maracas Bay. The road narrows east of Maracas Bay, ending at the tiny village of Blanchisseuse (blan-she-*shu-hze*), where the beautiful craggy coastline is dotted with weekend homes. The three beaches aren't the best for swimming, especially in the fall and winter, but the surfing can be pretty good. It's also the starting point for some great hikes, especially the two-hour walk to spectacular and completely undeveloped **Paria Bay**, which has a waterfall just inland.

Eric Blackman (☑759-9514; kayakeric@gmail.com; Paria Main Rd; tours from TT$150) can arrange a guide to Paria Bay or to the luscious Three Pools, just 1.5km up the Marianne River from Blanchisseuse.

🛏 Sleeping & Eating

Northern Sea View Villa
GUESTHOUSE $

(☑759-9514; kayakeric@gmail.com; Paria Main Rd; s/d TT$130/260; 🛜 🌊) Run by tour guide Eric Blackman, this simple guesthouse has clean, basic rooms with fan and bathroom as well as a kitchen, and there's a pool. Great value.

Second Spring
GUESTHOUSE $$

(☑669-3909; www.secondspringtnt.com; Lamp Post 191, Paria Main Rd; studios/cottages US$75/120) The best guesthouse in the area, with comfortable, endearing self-contained studios and cottages overlooking a rocky yet gorgeous section of coast, with lovely gardens and steps down to the sea.

Cocos Hut
CARIBBEAN $$

(☑669-2963; Laguna Mar, Paria Main Rd; mains from TT$70; ☺7am-7pm) Right on the roadside, adjacent to a track down to the beach, the restaurant of Laguna Mar hotel is a small, cozy spot and usually the only place in town where you can get a meal. It serves up decent fresh fish, lamb or chicken platters, as well as cold beers.

❶ Getting There & Away

Maxi-taxis and route taxis are infrequent; you'll need a car to get here.

Brasso Seco

Plum in the middle of the lush rainforest that smothers the Northern Range, Brasso Seco is a quiet little village that once made its living from growing cocoa and other crops. Today, it has reinvented itself as a low-key base for nature lovers in search of hiking, birdwatching, cocoa-cultivation tours or just a bit of insight into the slow, slow pace of life in rural Trinidad.

🏃 Activities & Tours

Chocolate Tours

The cool hills around Brasso Seco are ideal for the cultivation of cocoa, and this once-waning industry has been revived by the Tourist Action Committee (p767) and its new Brasso Seco Chocolate Company, which has a cocoa estate close to the village where you can do an excellent 'bean to bar' tour (TT$200). This includes a walk through the plantations and demonstrations of cocoa-bean processing, from fermenting, drying and roasting, right through to creating the finished bar; chocolate tastings are included, and you can also combine the trip with a local lunch.

Hiking

There are some spectacular day hikes of varying lengths from Brasso Seco to waterfalls: Double River Waterfalls, Madamas Falls and Sobo Falls. The 13km trek to Paria Bay from Brasso Seco is one of the most gorgeous in Trinidad, passing the famous Paria Falls. You can make this hike into a fine coastal backpacking trip with camping on beautiful bays by continuing all the way to Matelot to the east. If you're a very hardy hiker, you might want to attempt the scramble up Cerro del Aripo, the tallest mountain in Trinidad (941m).

Guides, such as **Carl Fitzjames** (☑669-6054, 486-6059; carlfitzjames@hotmail.com; hikes US$20-100), can be arranged through the Tourist Action Committee (p767).

🛏 Sleeping & Eating

Brasso is a rural, residential community, so there are no restaurants, but in advance you can arrange a lovely meal at Pachenco's (p767). There are a couple of bars in the village selling drinks and snacks.

Pachenco's   GUESTHOUSE $$
(☑669-6139; s/d incl breakfast & dinner TT$350/700) You'll get a friendly welcome at the Pachenco's. This neat and tidy house, with three bedrooms and a sitting area, is by the church. It's basic and does the trick, and Mrs P's homemade meals and cocoa tea (hot chocolate) are delicious.

Petit Tacarib Campsite   CAMPGROUND $$$
(☑620-1989; www.caribbeandiscoverytours.com; per person incl meals US$130) This remote bay is accessible only via a walk along the North Coast bench trail or by boat from Blanchisseuse. Accommodations are basic, but the experience is utterly magical.

ℹ Information

Tourist Action Committee (☑718-8605, 493-4358; www.brassosecoparia.com; Madamas Rd; half-/full-day hikes TT$360/540)

ℹ Getting There & Away

Public transport isn't an option here; you'll need a car. Alternatively, visit with **Caribbean Discovery Tours** (p751), which can also arrange hard-to-reach accommodations and local food options.

Grande Riviere

The closest the northeast gets to a resort town, Grande Riviere is still a far cry from most Caribbean holiday spots. It's a quiet and peaceful place, rich in natural attractions, from a stunning beach where turtles lay eggs to the surrounding rainforest, studded with waterfalls and hiking trails and offering plenty of good birdwatching. A few small-scale hotels have sprung up to cater to lovers of the outdoors, and the village is a fantastic place to get away from it all, but the big draw are the legions of leatherback turtles that lay their eggs on the beach here between March and August. Grand

---

WORTH A TRIP

ASA WRIGHT NATURE CENTRE

A former cocoa and coffee plantation transformed into an 80-hectare nature reserve, the **Asa Wright Nature Centre** (☑667-4655; www.asawright.org; Arima-Blanchisseuse Rd; adult/child US$10/6; ☉9am-5pm, guided walks 10:30am & 1:30pm; 🅿 👶) blows the minds of birdwatchers. Even if you can't tell a parrot from a parakeet, it's still a worthwhile trip, as you can see a great number of colorful specimens from the veranda viewing gallery, as well as lizards and agouti. Located amid the rainforest of the Northern Range, the center has a **lodge** (☑667-4655; www.asawright.org; Arima-Blanchisseuse Rd; d per person inc all meals US$170; 🅿 👶 📶) catering to birding tour groups, a research station for biologists and a series of hiking trails, open to day visitors via guided tours.

Bird species commonly seen here include blue-crowned motmots, chestnut woodpeckers, channel-billed toucans, blue-headed parrots, 14 species of hummingbird and numerous raptors. The sanctuary is also home to a natural swimming pool and to the elusive nocturnal *guacharo* (oilbird). To protect the oilbirds, tours are limited.

Tour companies such as **Island Experiences** (p751) can ferry you to Asa Wright as part of a half- or full-day tour.

Riviere is one of the world's major nesting beaches, with hundreds of turtles laying here in peak season; local guides lead turtle-watching trips.

⊙ Sights

Grande Riviere Beach   BEACH
(Paria Main Rd) This long, wide beach is capped at each end by exuberantly forested headlands, with the ever-shifting lagoon of the eponymous river at its east end providing calm freshwater swimming. Scattered year-round with the broken shells of leatherback-turtle eggs, the coarse dirty-yellow sand shelves steeply down to turbulent waters, best tackled by strong swimmers.

⌲ Tours

The mainstay of the community-run Grand Riviere Nature Tour Guide Association are early-hours excursions to watch turtles lay eggs on the village beach. Each year, between March and August (and sometimes into September), mature leatherbacks and other species such as hawksbill drag themselves up from the shoreline, dig a deep hole with their powerful flippers and deposit a clutch of eggs into the sand. Hatchlings emerge about eight weeks later and make a mad dash for the sea, guided by the moonlight; few survive, however, though locals do gather up any that unearth themselves by day and release them after dark. Watching the laying process is a memorable experience and shouldn't be missed if you visit at the right time. Don't try to do this independently; turtles have protected status in Trinidad and Tobago, and you need a permit to enter the beach at night during the season.

★ Grande Riviere Nature Tour Guide Association   ECOTOUR
(☑469-1288; grntga@gmail.com; Hosang St; turtle-watching incl permit US$16, hiking from TT$200) As well as leading excellent turtle-watching excursions, where expert guides provide background information on the turtles and the laying process, this community-run outfit offers year-round birdwatching excursions and hiking tours to waterfalls, swimming holes and seldom-visited natural wonders in the area. Its base is just off the road to the beach, adjacent to Mt Plaisir Estate.

⊨ Sleeping

Grand Rivere's cluster of hotels offers relaxed beachside accommodations; ask around for less expensive homestay options in the village.

Le Grande Almandier   HOTEL $$
(☑670-1013; www.legrandealmandier.com; 2 Hosang St; s/d incl breakfast US$115/167; P❉@) Next door to Mt Plaisir Estate, the compact but decent rooms at Le Grande Almandier have quaint balconies overlooking the sea, and are a budget-friendly option. It also has a laid-back restaurant and bar.

Acajou   BOUTIQUE HOTEL $$
(☑670-3771; www.acajoutrinidad.com; 209 Paria Main Rd; bungalows incl breakfast TT$1250; P⊜🛜) Set in riverside gardens, Acajou has five bungalows replete with rich wood and bright-white linens and cushions. French doors open to hammocked patios that look toward the ocean, and there's a path down past the river to the sea. No air-conditioning, TV or phones make this a fantastic retreat. There's a restaurant on-site.

★ Mt Plaisir Estate   BOUTIQUE HOTEL $$$
(☑670-1868; www.mtplaisir.com; Hosang St; r incl breakfast US$150-225; P❉🛜) The beachside Mt Plaisir Estate was the first hotel in the area, and is still the best. Local art, murals and handcrafted furnishings adorn the quirky but comfortable rooms, which sleep two to six people, some right on the beach and others on an upper story.

Mt Plaisir Restaurant   INTERNATIONAL $$
(Hosang St; mains TT$80-220; ◷8-10:30am, 12:30-2:30pm & 6:30-8:30pm) The restaurant at Mt Plaisir Estate is the top choice in town, cooking up divine seafood, pasta and meat dishes featuring organic fruits and vegetables. It's great for breakfast, too, with homemade yogurt and fruit, eggs and bacon and local buljol or eggplant/tomato choka with coconut bake.

❶ Getting There & Away

Maxi-taxis are infrequent, so you'll need to hire a car or get a taxi; the fare from Port of Spain is about US$130. All the hotels can arrange transport.

Northeast Coast

'When you out, you out. When you in, you in,' is what they say about the remote northeast. Despite the ruggedly beautiful coastline, waterfalls, hiking trails and swimmable rivers – and the leatherback turtles that lay eggs on the beaches – tourism remains very low-key here. Inaccessible from Blanchisseuse, where the North Coast Rd ends, this quiet region is bounded by Matelot in the north and Matura in the southeast.

👁 Sights

Sans Souci
BEACH

(Toco Main Rd) A short drive west of Toco, the small village of Sans Souci has several good beaches, though as they're all lashed by pounding waves, most people come here to surf rather than swim. It's a quiet and truly scenic spot, with the waves beating against the sand and the palm trees leaning drunkenly in the constant sea breeze. The best (and the largest) beach is Big Bay, a wide sweep of smooth yellow sand that's usually all but deserted.

Galera Point
LIGHTHOUSE

(Galera Rd, Toco) Beyond Toco's Salybia Beach, Galera Rd meanders through the countryside to Trinidad's extreme northeastern tip, capped by Galera Point lighthouse. Peek through the coastal trees at the edges of the grounds to see the waves crashing onto rocks below, and the distinct line where the blue Caribbean sea meets the green Atlantic. Picnic tables dot the grounds.

Saline Beach
BEACH

(Toco Main Rd, Salybia; ⊘ lifeguards 10am-6pm; 🅿 👤) Salybia is dominated by two incongruous-looking resorts, popular with Trinidadians seeking a rural break, but the big draw here is just before the bridge spanning the Rio Seco, where a track leads down to Saline Beach, a popular locals' liming spot. The fine yellow sand meets relatively calm waters, protected by a barrier reef, and there's freshwater swimming in the river, which meets the sea here. There are lifeguards, a bathroom and kiosks selling drinks and snacks.

★ Rio Seco Waterfall
WATERFALL

(off Toco Main Rd, Salybia; 👤) Just past the bridge over the Rio Seco, a signposted trail leads inland to the Rio Seco Waterfall in Matura National Park. This stunning swimming hole and waterfall, with deep clear waters and a gorgeous canopy of rainforest overhead, is a 45-minute hike from the trailhead, and the path is signposted, well maintained and easy to follow without a guide, though it's best to go in a group.

Matura Beach
BEACH

(Toco Main Rd, Matura) This wild, undeveloped beach with its coarse gray sand offers perfect conditions for leatherback turtles to lay their eggs, but it's far too rugged and windblown to throw down a towel for some beach time. This is one of the busier laying sites in the March–August season, when you need a permit to enter after dark. Turtle-watching trips are arranged through Nature Seekers.

👉 Tours

Nature Seekers
ECOTOUR

(📞 668-7337; www.natureseekers.org; Toco Main Rd, Matura; turtle-watching US$20) Matura is home to Nature Seekers, a nonprofit community organization that runs educational programs and evening turtle tours, where you can watch leatherbacks laying eggs close up – a magical experience. It also offers hikes in the surrounding area and kayak trips.

🛏 Sleeping

Suzan's Palace
GUESTHOUSE $

(📞 398-3038; Toco Main Rd, Matura; r TT$400) Basic and very local-style rooms right in Matura, all clean and well maintained. Rooms sleep up to four. Meals are available.

Leatherback Lodge
B&B $$

(📞 691-1188; www.leatherbacklodge.com; 70 Upper Rio Grande Trace, Matura; r incl breakfast US$90-140; 🅿) Gorgeous B&B in a plant-filled location, with friendly owners who offer tours all over Trinidad. The bright rooms have ceiling fans and open out onto patios hung with feeders to attract hummingbirds. Great local meals available.

ℹ Getting There & Away

The northeast is accessed via the busy little village of Valencia, a short way beyond the end of the Churchill Roosevelt Hwy, from where the Valencia Main Rd makes a T-junction with the Toco Main Rd, which hugs the northeast coast. Getting here is easiest by far in a taxi (around US$100 from Port of Spain) or with your own vehicle, as maxi-taxis are thin on the ground.

East Coast

Trinidad's east coast is wild and rural. The mix of lonely beaches with rough Atlantic waters, mangrove swamps and seaside coconut plantations creates dramatic scenery. It's deserted most of the year, except for holidays and weekends, when people flood in to Manzanilla and Mayaro for beachside relaxation, packing coolers with food and splashing about in the gently shelving waters. Most visitors come here on a day trip bound for Nariva Swamp, with its protected wetlands and forest.

Running parallel to the sea, the Manzanilla–Mayaro Rd makes for a beautiful drive. It passes through the Cocal, a thick forest of coconut palms whose nuts are shipped all around the island, and which harbor some interesting birds, including red-chested macaws.

Mayaro has a smattering of accommodation options on the beach, but the beach isn't that appealing for swimming and it's best to visit just for the day.

◎ Sights

★ **Nariva Swamp**   WILDLIFE RESERVE
(Manzanilla-Mayaro Rd) Inland of the Cocal, the Ramsar-protected Nariva Swamp covers some 60 sq km of freshwater wetland inhabited by anacondas and a small population of elusive manatees. To fully appreciate the area's beauty, book a spot on a kayak tour with Paria Springs (p751) or Caribbean Discovery Tours (p751); trips include a walk into Bush Bush Island to see howler and white capuchin monkeys. Take insect repellent.

Mayaro Beach   BEACH
(Manzanilla-Mayaro Rd; ☺lifeguards 9am-5pm) Around the headland to the south of Manzanilla Beach, expansive Mayaro offers calmer waters than its neighbor, and the beach scene is more genial. Locals play cricket on the flat sands at low tide. One of the busier spots is adjacent to Church Rd, south of Mayaro village.

✖ Eating

★ **Ranch**
                              CARIBBEAN $$
(☏223-6798; Mayaro-Guayaguayare Rd, Mayaro; snacks TT$35-80, mains TT$45-125; ☺10am-11:30pm Wed-Sun; P✳ⓗ) Great little place past Mayaro village, with tables in an air-con indoor dining room and in a patio garden. Local food runs from chicken with Trini sides to shrimp and lobster, but the highlight is a whole grilled Mayaro snapper, seasoned to perfection. The snack fare, from crab backs to pepper squid, is equally lip-smacking. Great for a drink, too.

❶ Getting There & Away

To drive to Manzanilla, Mayaro and Nariva, you have to go through bustling Sangre Grande (sandy grandy), from where signposted minor roads head down to the Manzanilla–Mayaro Rd. Most visitors arrive in a rented car or as part of an organized tour to Nariva.

West Coast

Trinidad's west coast allows you to dig deep into Indo-Trinidadian culture. The Carapichaima area is the heartland of Trinidad's Indian population, whose forebears mostly came to Trinidad between 1845 and 1917 as indentured workers to fill the labor gap when slavery was abolished. Today, there are endless restaurants and street stalls selling delicious rotis, doubles and Indian snacks, and Hindu temples adding a splash of color to the landscape. The west also offers great birdwatching at Caroni Bird Sanctuary and the Pointe-a-Pierre Wildfowl Trust.

◎ Sights

Caroni Bird Sanctuary   BIRD SANCTUARY
(www.caronibirdsanctuary.com; Uriah Butler Hwy, Caroni; Pⓗ) Caroni Bird Sanctuary is the roosting site for thousands of scarlet ibis, the national bird of Trinidad and Tobago. In the late afternoon the birds fly in to roost in the swamp's mangroves, giving the trees the appearance of being abloom with brilliant scarlet blossoms. Even if you're not an avid birdwatcher, the sight of the ibis flying over the swamp, glowing almost fluorescent red in the final rays of the evening sun, is not to be missed.

The sanctuary is off the Uriah Butler Hwy, 14km south of Port of Spain; the turnoff is marked. Many guesthouses and hotels in Port of Spain also arrange trips, as do tour companies such as Island Experiences (p751). A round-trip in a taxi will cost around TT$400, including waiting time.

Waterloo Temple   HINDU TEMPLE
(☏681-4435; Waterloo Rd, Carapichaima; donation suggested; ☺6am-6pm; Pⓗ) Beautifully situated at the end of a causeway off the

central west coast, Waterloo Temple was constructed almost entirely by indentured laborer Sewdass Sadhu, after his previous structure (built on state land) was demolished. It was a true labor of love, with Sadhu carrying each foundation stone on his bicycle to the water's edge. It's a beautiful place, surrounded by the shallow waters of the Paria Gulf at high tide and with prayer flags fluttering in the air.

Indian Caribbean Museum MUSEUM
(☑ 673-7007; www.icmtt.org; Waterloo Rd, Carapichaima; ◷ 10am-5pm Wed-Sun) FREE Just inland from Waterloo Temple, this absorbing museum is dedicated to the Indian history and experience in Trinidad. Some gorgeous antique sitars and drums are displayed, as are photographs and informational displays about early Indian settlers. Other highlights include local art, traditional Hindi clothing, a display of a traditional Indian Trini kitchen (replete with a *chulha,* the earthen stove where roti is made) and crazy pictures of Brits with their Indian indentured servants.

Hanuman Murti and Sri Dattatreya Ashram HINDU TEMPLE
(☑ 673-5328; Orange Field Rd, Carapichaima; donations appreciated; ◷ ashram 9am-noon & 5-7pm; P ♿) Towering 26m over the Sri Dattatreya Ashram, the brightly painted Hanuman Murti is a potent icon of Trinidad's Hindu community. Devotees from all over the country come here to pray and walk devotional circles around the statue. Constructed by craftsmen from Tami Nadu in India, the ashram is equally ornate, its rich exterior covered in statuary – an incredible sight to behold in the middle of a small Trinidadian town. Other smaller statues dot the grounds.

Pointe-a-Pierre Wildfowl Trust WILDLIFE RESERVE
(☑ 658-4200, ext 2512; www.papwildfowltrust.org; Petrotrin Refinery, Southern Main Rd, Point-a-Pierre; TT$20; ◷ 9am-5pm Mon-Fri, 10am-5pm Sat & Sun, tours daily 9:30am & 1pm; P ♿) Despite being amid the island's sprawling oil refinery, this wetland sanctuary has an abundance of birdlife in a highly concentrated 26 hectares. There are about 90 bird species, both wild and in cages, including endangered waterfowl, colorful songbirds, scarlet ibis, herons and other wading birds. Guided tours help you identify all the various species.

CHAGUANAS & FELICITY

Easily accessed from the north by the Uriah Butler Hwy and the Southern Main Rd, **Chaguanas** (sha-gwaan-us) is a sprawling town known for its excellent shopping, with plenty of Indian clothing and jewelry on sale along the main street and a great produce **market** (Chaguanas Main Rd, Chaguanas; ◷ 6am-4pm Mon-Sat). South of town, at **Felicity**, the Chaguanas **potteries** (☑ 789-4079; 183 Edinburgh Village, Southern Main Rd, Felicity; pottery tour TT$20; ◷ 10am-5pm Mon-Sat) use traditional methods to make beautiful ceramic items including *deyas,* tiny earthenware lamps that are lit during the annual Hindu Divali festival each October, when crowds of people from around the country descend on Felicity to see the beautiful glowing displays. Fairy lights are strung up along the Southern Main Rd and along the area's residential streets, and the locals transform their front yards by creating wire structures in fantastical shapes, from birds to stars, hung with burning *deyas.*

☞ Tours

★**Winston Nanan Caroni Tours** BIRDWATCHING
(☑ 645-1303; www.nananecotours.com; 2½hr boat tours US$10; ♿) Long, flat-bottomed motorboats, some holding up to 30 passengers, pass slowly through Caroni Swamp's channels, with guides pointing out the snakes and anteaters often seen in the surrounding trees. Tours of the swamp leave daily at 4pm. Go to the Caroni Bird Sanctuary, where staff members will direct you. It's best to arrive 15 minutes or so early.

ⓘ Getting There & Away

From the Churchill Roosevelt Hwy, the well-signposted Uriah Butler Hwy swings south parallel to the west coast. You can also take the much slower Southern Main Rd from Curepe, which crosses over to the west side of the highway north of Chaguanas. A car is by far the best way to explore.

San Fernando

Trinidad's second-largest city, San Fernando is also the center of the island's gas and oil industries. Anyone looking for real cultural immersion will enjoy San Fernando, as few tourists come through the town. Most of the action happens at shops and stands around Harris Promenade and the main Coffee St, or you can find great views from San Fernando Hill (p772). The spectacle of Pitch Lake (p772) is just a short drive to the south.

◉ Sights

Pitch Lake　　　　　　　　GEOLOGICAL SITE
(☑ 651-1232; Southern Main Rd, La Brea; tours TT$50; ⊙9am-5pm) About 25km southwest of San Fernando, and just south of the small town of La Brea, this slowly bubbling black 'lake' is perhaps Trinidad's greatest oddity. Once thought of by the Amerindians as a punishment of the gods, the 40-hectare expanse of asphalt is around 75m deep at its center, where hot bitumen is continuously replenished from a subterranean fault. One of only three asphalt lakes in the world, it has the single-largest supply of natural bitumen.

The lake's surface looks like a clay tennis court covered with wrinkled, elephant-like skin; tour guides sagely take you across via the solid parts. Flat shoes are recommended. During the rainy season, people sit in its warm sulfurous pools, said to have healing qualities. A visitor center gives some background on the history of the lake (though it's often locked up).

San Fernando Hill　　　　　　　　HILL
(Circular Courts Rd, San Fernando; ⊙9am-6pm; [P]) FREE Looming over San Fernando, this was once a sacred Amerindian site, but today its landscaped grounds are a great place to kick back and relax, dotted with picnic tables and offering sweeping views over the central plains. It has a cafe and a children's playground. You'll need a car to get here, as the access road is some way from the center.

❶ Getting There & Away

The **water taxi** (☑ San Fernando 652-9980; http://nidco.co.tt; King's Wharf, Lady Hales Ave; 1-way TT$15; ⊙run regularly Mon-Sat) between Port of Spain and San Fernando docks at Kings Wharf. The city is on the Uriah Butler Hwy, about 1½ hours' drive from Port of Spain. PTSC (www.ptsc.co.tt) runs express buses between Port of Spain and San Fernando, dropping off at the waterfront near the water-taxi terminal, which is also where maxi-taxis arrive and depart.

TOBAGO

While Trinidad booms with industry and parties all night, tiny Tobago (just 42km across) slouches in a deck chair with a beer in hand watching its crystalline waters shimmer in the sun. Though Tobago is proud of its rainforests, fantastic dive sites, stunning aquamarine bays and nature reserves, it's OK with not being mentioned in a Beach Boys' song. It accepts its tourists without vigor, but rather with languor, and allows them to choose between plush oceanside hotels or tiny guesthouses in villages where you walk straight to the open-air bar with sandy bare feet, and laugh with the locals drinking rum.

☞ Tours

★ Island Girl Charters　　　　　　　BOATING
(☑ 620-7245; www.sailtobago.com; full day incl lunch US$90) This bright-yellow catamaran offers lovely sailing tours of Tobago, a great alternative to smaller tour boats for families, with a shaded indoor space and tanning nets stretched across the water between the hulls. Day trips include a delicious lunch. Discounts are available for children (five to 16 years); under fives go free.

★ Frankie Tours and Rentals　　　　TOURS
(☑ 631-0369; www.frankietours.com; Mt Irvine Beach; per person US$20-110) Offers turtle-watching, birdwatching and rainforest tours as well as 24-hour taxi service and car rentals. One of the best options is a full-day boat trip along the Caribbean coast, visiting some of the best snorkeling sites and stopping off for a beach-barbecue lunch.

NG Nature Tours　　　　　　　BIRDWATCHING
(☑ 660-5463; www.newtongeorge.com; half/full-day tours US$50-65/$95-125) Newton George is one of Tobago's best birdwatching guides, with many years of experience under his belt. Tours cover all the island's birding hot spots, from wetlands to Little Tobago and the Forest Reserve, and can be tailored to your requirements.

Peter Cox Nature Tours
WILDLIFE

(☑ 751-5822, 294-3086; www.petercoxnature
tours.com; per person US$50-120) A good choice
for serious birdwatchers, with avian-ori-
ented trips island-wide, plus hiking, waterfalls, turtle-watching and general island
tours.

Mountain Biking Tobago
CYCLING

(☑ 681-5695; www.mountainbikingtobago.com; per
person from US$50) Owner Sean de Freitas is
a straight-shooting guide who provides solid
rentals and cycling equipment. His Highland Falls ride is particularly awesome, ending at a splendid swimming hole and waterfall. He also guides road rides.

ⓘ Getting There & Away

AIR
Most people get to Tobago by taking the
20-minute flight from Trinidad, or fly in direct
from Europe. The **ANR Robinson International
Airport** (p792), like Tobago, is small, relaxed
and rarely rushed.

BOAT
A catamaran ferry, run by the **Inter-Island Ferry
Service** (p752), shuttles between Port of
Spain on Trinidad, and Scarborough on Tobago.

ⓘ Getting Around

Getting around any of Tobago's small towns is
easy on foot. For wider exploration, rent a car
or hire a driver for the day. Buses are slow and
infrequent but cover the whole island.

BICYCLE
Tobago has less traffic than Trinidad, especially
on the remote eastern part of the island. There
are some nice roads, usually hilly, that bring you
through amazing landscapes: Roxborough–Parlatuvier Rd, which passes straight through the
Tobago Forest Reserve; Arnos Vale Rd to Mason
Hall; Buccoo to Charlotteville along the northern
coast. If cycle touring is your thing, it's possible
to circumnavigate the island, though you'll need
strong legs – and a steely temperament to cope
with local drivers.

For mountain biking, **Mountain Biking Tobago**
(p773) is recommended.

Basic bikes can also be rented around the
Crown Point area.

BUS
The Scarborough bus terminal is a short walk
from the ferry terminal, off Milford Rd on Sangster Hill Rd, and has services to most points on
the island. Buses to/from Crown Point (TT$2)
run hourly from 5am to 8pm. For more information on services, call 639-2293.

CAR
If you want to explore the island, it's well worth
renting a car for a day or two. Gas stations are
fairly widespread in the southwest, less so elsewhere, so it's wise to fill up when you can.

Econo Car (p778)
KCNN (p778)
Sheppy's (p778)
Thrifty Car Rental (p778)

TAXI
Taxis from ANR Robinson International Airport
charge about TT$35 to hotels around Crown
Point, TT$50 to Pigeon Point, TT$80 to Scarborough, TT$70 to Mt Irvine or Buccoo and TT$380
to Charlotteville. Islandwide prices are displayed
on a board just before the exit of the arrivals
area; drivers await arriving flights. To call an
authorized taxi, dial 683-7900.

Route taxis can be a good and cheap option
for zipping between the bays here; just stick
out your hand at the roadside – official drivers
should have 'H' plates or, at least, other passengers in the car.

Crown Point

Spread over Tobago's southwest tip, Crown
Point is the island's tourist epicenter, offering a relatively wide range of accommodations, restaurants and some nightlife. The
attractive beaches and extensive services
make many tourists stay put, but anyone
wanting a deeper appreciation of Tobago's
charms should plan to push eastward to
explore other parts of the island.

⊙ Sights

Buccoo Reef
REEF

Stretching offshore between Pigeon Point
and Buccoo Bay, the extensive Buccoo Reef
was designated as a marine park in 1973
and a Ramsar site in 2006. The fringing
reef boasts five reef flats separated by deep
channels. The sheer array of flora and fauna
– dazzling sponges, hard corals and tropical fish – makes marine biologists giddy.
However, despite the efforts of conservation groups, some sections of Buccoo Reef
have been battered by too much use and not
enough protection.

Glass-bottom-boat reef tours are an
accessible way to explore the reef. Tours
leave from Store Bay and Pigeon Point.
Most operators charge TT$120 per person
for a two-hour trip. The boats pass over the
reef (much of which is just a meter or two
beneath the surface), stop for snorkeling

Tobago

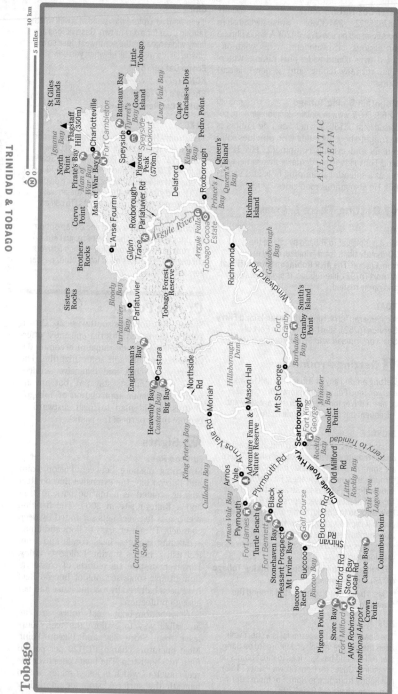

10 km
5 miles

St Giles Islands

Little Tobago

Iguana Bay
Flagstaff Hill (350m)
Charlotteville
Fort Cambleton
Batteaux Bay
Turrel's Bay
Goat Island

North Point
Pirate's Bay
Man of War Bay
Speyside
Pigeon Peak (576m)
Speyside Lookout

Lucy Vale Bay

Cape Gracias-a-Dios
Pedro Point

Corvo Point
Man of War Bay
L'Anse Fourmi
Roxborough–Parlatuvier Rd

King's Bay
Delaford
Roxborough
Prince's Bay
Queen's Island
Queen's Bay

ATLANTIC OCEAN

Brothers Rocks
Gilpin Trace
Argyle River
Tobago Cocoa Estate
Argyle Falls

Richmond Island

Sisters Rocks
Parlatuvier
Tobago Forest Reserve
Richmond

Bloody Bay
Parlatuvier Bay

Goldsborough Bay

Windward Rd

Englishman's Bay
Castara
Castara Bay
Big Bay
Northside Rd
Moriah

Hillsborough Dam

Fort Granby
Smith's Island
Granby Point

Heavenly Bay

King Peter's Bay

Adventure Farm & Nature Reserve
Mason Hall

Mt St George

Barbados Bay

Arnos Vale Rd
Plymouth Rd

Culloden Bay

Arnos Vale
Plymouth
Turtle Beach
Black Rock
Golf Course
Fort James
Fort Bennett
Stonehaven Bay
Pleasant Prospect
Mt Irvine Bay
Buccoo

Scarborough
Fort King George
Rockly Bay
Bacolet Point
Minister Bay

Claude Noel Hwy

Ferry to Trinidad

Old Milford Rd
Little Rockly Bay

Caribbean Sea

Buccoo Bay
Buccoo Reef
Shirvan Rd

Petit Trou Lagoon

Pigeon Point
Store Bay
Fort Milford
ANR Robinson International Airport
Crown Point
Milford Rd
Store Bay Local Rd
Canoe Bay
Columbus Point

and end with a swim in the **Nylon Pool**, a calm, shallow area with a sandy bottom and clear turquoise waters. All the operators are pretty similar, often playing loud soca and selling drinks on board; you'll be repeatedly approached by touts when on Store Bay and Pigeon Point beaches.

Store Bay
BEACH

(Milford Rd) You'll find white sands and good year-round swimming at Store Bay, a five-minute walk from the airport. It's also the main departure point for glass-bottom-boat trips to the Buccoo Reef, with hawkers offering these and rides on Jet Skis or banana boats, and renting umbrellas and sun loungers. Facilities include showers/bathrooms (TT$5), and food outlets selling delicious local lunches.

Pigeon Point
BEACH

(🛈 639-0601; www.pigeonpoint.tt; adult/child TT$20/$10; ⊙9am-5pm; 🅿️ 🚼) You have to pay to get access to Pigeon Point, the fine dining of Tobago's beaches, with landscaped grounds, bars, restaurants, toilets and showers spread along plenty of beachfront. The postcard-perfect, palm-fringed beach has powdery white sands and milky aqua water; around the headland, the choppy waters are perfect for windsurfing and kitesurfing with Radical Watersports (p775).

🏃 Activities & Tours

⭐ Stand-Up Paddle Tobago
KAYAKING

(🛈 681-4741; www.standuppaddletobago.com; Radical Watersports, Pigeon Point Beach; lessons US$60, snorkeling US$80, bioluminescence tour US60; 🚼) The big deal here are fantastic night-time kayak or SUP tours through the bioluminescent waters of Bon Accord Lagoon; by day you can explore the Pigeon Point surrounds by SUP or take an adventurous full-day trip. There's also a fantastic three-hour snorkeling excursion to little-visited spots. Gear is top quality and the staff knowledgeable, professional and super enthusiastic.

⭐ Radical Watersports
WATER SPORTS

(🛈 631-5150; www.radicalsportstobago.com; Pigeon Point Beach; kiteboarding US$95-135, windsurf boards per hour US$45, lessons US$75, kayak/SUP US$22, sailing lessons US$65; ⊙9am-5pm) Radical Watersports, at the northernmost end of Pigeon Point Beach, is the center for wind sports, providing quality rental and lessons. It also rents kayaks and stand-up

paddleboards that are perfect for exploring the mangrovey 'No Man's Land' and deserted beaches to the east.

Friendship Riding Stables
HORSEBACK RIDING

(🛈 620-9788; www.friendshipridingstables.com; rides from TT$350) Near Canoe Bay, aptly named Friendship Riding Stables will take you on equestrian adventures through local woodland and down to the sea.

🛌 Sleeping

Crown Point has everything from inexpensive guesthouses to luxury resorts, and is a great base if you want to be close to the area's busy beaches as well as its restaurants and nightlife.

⭐ Dimples Apartments
APARTMENT $

(🛈 660-8156, 786-8134; www.dimples-apartments.com; Store Bay Branch Rd; apt TT$300; 🅿️ 🏵️ 🛜) Fantastic value, these appealing apartments come with dining room/kitchen and air-con bedroom, and are beautifully maintained by the Tobagonian/English owners, who are constructing a second complex with a pool nearby.

Hummingbird Hotel
BOUTIQUE HOTEL $

(🛈 635-0241; www.hummingbirdtobago.com; 128 Store Bay Local Rd; r US$60-75; 🅿️ 🏵️ 🛜) Friendly and efficiently run little hotel, with inviting rooms ranged around a central pool. All are immaculate, and meals are available.

Sandy's Guesthouse
GUESTHOUSE $

(🛈 639-9221; Store Bay Local Rd; r TT$300; 🏵️) Stay with Valerie and Hugh Sandy and you're a guest in a welcoming Tobagonian home. The rooms and shared kitchen facilities are scrupulously clean, and rates are some of the lowest in the area.

⭐ Summerland Suites
HOTEL $$

(🛈 631-5053; www.summerlandsuites.info; Roberts St, Bon Accord; 1-/2-bed apt US$80/90; 🅿️ 🏵️ @ 🛜 🏊) Set in a quiet Bon Accord neighborhood, this is a peaceful and pretty option, with apartments laid out along a pool and shaded by huge samaan trees. Apartments are very well maintained with updated, tasteful furnishings and good kitchen equipment. The only drawback is the distance from the beaches.

Store Bay Holiday Resort
HOTEL $$

(🛈 639-8810; www.storebayholidays.com; Store Bay Local Rd; studios TT$540, apt TT$690-850; 🏵️ 🛜 🏊) Right at the end of Store Bay

Local Rd, and just a five-minute walk from the beach, this pleasant resort has very well-kept studios and apartments, all with cable TV and cooking facilities, as well as a small pool.

Native Abode
GUESTHOUSE $$

(☑631-1285; www.nativeabode.com; 13 Fourth St, Bon Accord; r incl breakfast US$140; P❂❋🛜) On a tree-filled side street reached via Store Bay Local Rd then Gaskin Bay Rd, this is a lovely little place. Rooms are decorated to a very high standard; they're clean, modern and appealing, and have a kitchenette. The owners' garden is a great chill-out spot, filled with fruit trees.

Sun Spree Resort
HOTEL $$

(☑631-5195; www.sunspreeresortltd.com; 40 Store Bay Local Rd; r TT$450; P❋@🏊) Long, slim property with a pool, pretty grounds and smart, well-maintained rooms with modern decor. The hotel is about 10 minutes' walk from Store Bay Beach, and there's a restaurant and bar.

★Kariwak Village Holistic Haven
HOTEL $$$

(☑639-8442; www.kariwak.com; Store Bay Local Rd; r incl breakfast from US$220; P❂@🛜🏊) Just a two-minute walk from Store Bay Beach, Kariwak feels incredibly peaceful despite its central location. The modern cabanas line paths that wind through flower-filled tropical gardens, past tinkling streams and a thatch-roofed yoga *ajoupa* (open hut). It's both rustic and refreshing. It has an organic herb garden, two pools (one with waterfall-fueled hot tub), yoga and tai chi classes, and a really excellent restaurant.

🍴 Eating

One of the best places to eat lunch is the row of food huts opposite Store Bay Beach, where local women serve delicious dishes like roti, crab and dumplin' and simple plate lunches (from TT$50). You'll also find a cluster of fast-food places at the junction of Milford Rd and Pigeon Point Rd, and opposite in D Coliseum mall.

Skewers
MIDDLE EASTERN $

(☑631-8964; cnr Milford & Pigeon Point Rds; mains TT$35-90; ⊙10am-10pm) The first of several Middle Eastern restaurants in Crown, and still the most popular, with grilled (halal) meats and all the traditional sides: *fattoush*, hummus, Arabic rice, spiced potatoes. There's also a gyro station outside, which serves food until the wee hours at weekends.

Pasta Gallery
ITALIAN $

(☑727-8200; Pigeon Point Rd; mains TT$75-95; ⊙6:30-10pm, closed Wed & Sun; 🖋🍴) Cute little pasta place with tables inside and a deck out front. There's everything from spaghetti with seafood to lasagne, plus filling salads. Check out the local art on the walls, too! Gluten-free pasta is available.

★Kariwak Village
CARIBBEAN $$

(☑639-8442; Kariwak Village Hotel, Store Bay Local Rd; breakfast TT$70-90, lunch TT$100-145, dinner TT$210-230; ⊙7:30-10am, 12:30-2:15pm & 7-9:30pm; 🖋🍴) Beneath the thatched roof and coral-stone walls of this open-air restaurant, enjoy masterpieces of Caribbean cuisine made with fresh organic herbs and vegetables from the garden. Breakfast includes local specials such as flying fish,

---

DIVING TOBAGO

Diving is excellent in Tobago. Nutrient-rich waters fed by the outflow from South American rivers attract a rich variety of marine life, from shoals of tropical fish to rays, and there is some exciting drift-diving around the island's northeast as well as many more mellow dive sites in the southwest. Although serious divers tend to stay near Speyside and Charlotteville, dive operators in Crown Point run trips all over the island. Visit www.tobagoscubadiving.com for lists of operators aligned with the Association of Tobago Dive Operators. There a recompression chamber in the east-coast village of Roxborough.

R&Sea Divers (☑639-8120; www.rseadivers.com; Shepherd's Inn, Store Bay Local Rd; dives from US$45) R&Sea Divers is safe, professional and friendly: this is a Professional Association of Diving Instructors (PADI) facility that's been around for a long time. Staff will pick up divers at any hotel.

Undersea Tobago (☑631-2626; www.underseatobago.com; Coco Reef Hotel, Milford Rd; dive US$50) Based at the Coco Reef hotel, this is a reliable dive outfit that places great emphasis on safety and uses top-notch equipment.

plus homemade yogurt and granola. The lunch and dinner set menus feature grilled fish, meat and seafood (plus a vegetarian option), and are cooked with plenty of love.

★ **La Cantina** PIZZA $$
(639-8242; www.lacantinapizzeria.com; RBTT Compound, Milford Rd; pizzas TT$90-155; noon-9:45pm Mon & Thu-Sat, noon-2:45pm & 6-9:45pm Tue & Wed, 6-9:45pm Sun;) Tucked into a bank compound off Milford Rd, this buzzing joint cooks up a huge range of authentically Italian pizzas in its wood-fired oven – you can watch the chef spinning dough and adding toppings. Good salads and fast service. Takeout available.

Mesoreen Café Bistro CARIBBEAN $$
(639-8726; Store Bay Local Rd; burgers TT$55-70, mains TT$110-180; 11am-11pm Tue-Sun;) Great new addition to the Crown Point scene, with smiling service and tables laid out around a pretty open-sided dining area. The menu is short but sweet, running from burgers to fresh fish, steak, geera pork, barbecued chicken, curried shrimp and pasta dishes, and there are a couple of veggie options too.

Dillon's Backyard Cafe CARIBBEAN $$
(639-7264; Milford Rd; mains TT$130-240; 6:30-10:30pm Mon-Sat) Under new management, this Tobago-owned cafe excels in fish and fresh seafood, from catch of the day to shrimp (curried or in rum or garlic sauce) to seafood platters and pasta dishes, and grilled whole lobster. All are served with a smile in an open-sided courtyard set back from the road.

Café Coco CARIBBEAN $$
(Off Pigeon Point Rd; mains TT$125-$300; 5:30-10pm) The wistful ambience, complemented by friendly staff, is the best thing about this handsome restaurant, which is candlelit and breezy and has waterfalls and greenery. The cocktails are decent, and the menu runs from seafood pasta to baby-back ribs and chargrilled lamb. Attached to Coco Reef Resort.

Marcia's CARIBBEAN $$
(639-0359; Store Bay Local Rd; mains from TT$70; 11am-2pm & 7-10pm;) A great place to have a sit-down meal of Tobagonian classics, from fresh fish to curried conch or baked chicken with callaloo, macaroni pie and salad. Friendly and good value. Takeout available too.

Drinking & Nightlife

★ **Shade** CLUB
(329-0082; www.theshadetobago.com; 15 Mt Pleasant Blvd, Bon Accord; 6pm-late Wed-Sat) Locals, foreigners and tourists all flock to the open-air Shade for a proper party lime. It's probably the hippest place on the island to dance the night away, though it can be a bit of a pickup joint. Small cover charge Friday and Saturday.

Jenny's BAR
(Milford Rd; 5pm-late) Bedecked with fairy lights, this streetside bar, with tables on a deck, is often the busiest liming spot in Crown Point on the weekends.

Renmars BAR
(www.renmarstobago.com; Pigeon Point Beach; cocktails from TT$50) Right on the sands of Pigeon Point Beach, this is a lovely spot to have a cocktail, and is great for sunset-watching.

Bago's Beach Bar BAR
(Pigeon Point Rd; 10am-late) Right on the sand where Pigeon Point Rd forks right, this cool little beach bar serves them cold and mixes a mean rum punch. Great for sunset.

Shopping

Pennysaver's (Milford Rd; 8am-8:30pm Mon-Sat, 8am-1pm Sun) There are several minimarts on Store Bay Local Rd, but for big grocery shops head east of Crown Point to Pennysaver's, near Canaan.

Information

In Crown Point, there are banks at the airport and along Milford Rd close to Store Bay, all of which have 24-hour ATMs.

Tourist Office (639-0509; www.visit tobago.gov.tt; ANR Robinson International Airport; 8am-10pm) The staff provide basic information and can help you book a room or find hiking and birdwatching tour guides.

Getting There & Around

International and domestic flights land at **ANR Robinson airport** (p792), where taxi drivers line up to meet arriving passengers; there's a board listing fares island-wide just before you leave the arrivals area. Taxis are easy to find throughout Crown Point: you can expect drivers to slow down and ask if you need a ride whenever you're walking around the area. Route taxis run along Milford Rd and are a good option for short hops.

CAR RENTAL

Econo Car (622-8074; www.econocar rentalstt.com; ANR Robinson Airport, Crown Point)

KCNN (682-2888; www.tobagocarhire.com; Bon Accord)

Sheppy's (639-1543; www.tobagocarrental. com; Store Bay Local Rd, Crown Point)

Thrifty Car Rental (639-8507; www.thrifty. com; ANR Robinson Airport)

Buccoo

Though its narrow strip of white sand is monopolized by fishing boats at the village end, Buccoo's sweeping palm-backed bay is pretty spectacular. Even so, it's more a place to hang out or take a horse ride than throw down your towel. This may soon change, however, as a huge Sandals resort hotel is proposed for construction on the Buccoo headland. For now the tiny village offers a taste of true local flavor: friendly folks who define easygoing, breathtaking sunsets over the bay and the infamous Sunday School party every week, staged in and around the incongruously grand new beach facility. It's also the place to come for a fabulous laid-back horseback ride along the beach.

Tours

★ **Being with Horses** HORSEBACK RIDING
(639-0953; www.being-with-horses.com; 14 Galla Trace, Buccoo; rides from US$95;) This small-scale stable, home to an ever-growing herd of rescued horses, offers rides along Buccoo Point and beach, including a swim in the sea. Great for kids, with an intuitive, holistic approach to things equestrian, it also offers therapeutic riding for children with disabilities.

Festivals & Events

Goat Races SPORTS
(www.buccoo.net; Buccoo Integrated Facility, Buccoo Main Rd; Easter) Easter weekend is a huge deal in Tobago, when everyone flocks to Buccoo for a series of open-air parties and – the highlight of it all – goat races. Taken very seriously, goat racing draws more bets than a Las Vegas casino. The competing goats get pampered like beauty contestants and the eventual champion is forever revered. The partying stretches throughout the weekend and the big races happen on Tuesday.

Sleeping

★ **Miller's Guesthouse** GUESTHOUSE $
(660-8371; www.millersguesthouse.com; 14 Miller St; s/d/tr US$35/60/70, apt US$80-110;) In a pretty location overlooking Buccoo Bay, the basic singles and doubles here are great for budget travelers. Rooms are kept sparkling fresh and clean, and there's a shared kitchen. A great place for meeting people, and next to a restaurant too.

Fish Tobago GUESTHOUSE $
(309-0062; www.fishtobago.com; 26a Buccoo Point; dm/s US$25/35, d US$40-100;) Tucked away off the main road into the village, this is a great spot for travelers. It's efficiently run and has a range of rooms from dorms to apartments, some complete with hand-painted beach scenes on the walls. A communal kitchen, and great snorkeling and fishing trips available.

Seaside Garden Guesthouse GUESTHOUSE $$
(639-0682; www.tobago-guesthouse.com; Buccoo Bay Rd; r US$42-58, apt US$100;) Friendly little guesthouse just stumbling distance from where Sunday School street party is held. Its rooms and apartments are meticulously cared for. A tastefully decorated sitting room with a bay window enhances the serenity of the place, while the communal kitchen is well equipped, and there's a washing machine for guests' use.

Eating

La Tartaruga ITALIAN $$
(639-0940; www.latartarugatobago.com; Buccoo Bay Rd; mains TT$65-345; 6:30-10pm Mon-Sat;) It's surprising to find this authentic Italian restaurant with scrumptious homemade pastas and delectable wine (it has the second-largest Italian wine cellar in the Caribbean) tucked away in tiny Buccoo. But it's a treat, indeed. The ambience melds lively Caribbean colors and art with a candlelit patio fit for a romantic Italian cafe.

Luvinia's CARIBBEAN $$$
(631-1349; Miller's St; salads and burgers TT$50-75, dinner mains TT155-250; 8am-10pm Mon;) With tables on a terrace taking in the sweep of Buccoo Bay, this is a great place to sip a drink while watching fishers land their catch. The food is excellent too, with a local dish of the day, plus pasta, pizza, sandwiches, burgers and wraps for lunch, Dinner mains range from mahi-mahi in coconut sauce to grilled lamb and a seafood platter.

Makara   FUSION $$$

(☑340-9547; Buccoo Integrated Facility, Buccoo Bay Rd; mains TT$160-325; ⊙11:30am-10pm; ☑) On a balcony high above Buccoo Bay, this fine-dining restaurant offers an upscale take on Caribbean cuisine: feast on guava-barbecue mahi-mahi, braised pork belly with roasted shrimp or curried goat. Great for a romantic dinner.

☆ Entertainment

★ Sunday School   LIVE MUSIC
(Bucco Integrated Facility, Buccoo Bay Rd; ⊙8pm-3am Sun) FREE Lacking any religious affiliation, Sunday School is the sly title for a street party held in Buccoo every Sunday night. Until around 10pm, partygoers are mostly tourists enjoying rum drinks, overpriced barbecue dinners and live steel pan. Later in the night, folks from all over the island come to 'take a wine' or just hang out, with DJs spinning reggae, soca and dance hits.

ⓘ Getting There & Away

A taxi to Buccoo from Crown Point will cost about TT$70. Route taxis run up and down the main coastal strip passing the Buccoo turnoff.

Leeward Coast

The stretch of coastline from Mt Irvine Bay to Arnos Vale has several lovely beaches, a few sizable hotels and a slew of fancy villas hugging the greens of the golf course. Like a sloppy adolescent propping its feet on the table in a fancy living room, Black Rock's tiny Pleasant Prospect is right in the middle. It's a teeny surfer haunt: a cluster of cheap unofficial accommodations, eateries and a few good places to lime.

◉ Sights

★ Mt Irvine Beach   BEACH
(Grafton Rd; P♿) This pretty public beach, 200m north of Mt Irvine Bay Hotel, has sheltered picnic tables and changing rooms, plus a beachside restaurant and bar, roti shacks and plenty of shade trees. Surfers migrate here from December to March to ride the renowned waves. You can rent sun loungers, kayaks and surfboards on the beach.

Kimme's Sculpture Museum   MUSEUM
(☑639-0257; www.luisekimme.com; Bethel; TT$20; ⊙10am-2pm Sun or by appointment) At the golf course, turn right off the main road onto Orange Hill Rd and you'll see signs leading you to the blinged-out former home of Luise Kimme, a German sculptor who died in 2013 but who had lived in Tobago for many years. Some of her fantastic, 2m to 3m wood-and-metal Caribbean-themed sculptures are displayed inside as are those of her artistic successor, Cuban sculptor Dunieski, who now lives and works here.

Stonehaven Bay   BEACH
(Grafton Rd) Northeast of Mt Irvine, this fabulous sweep of coarse yellow sand, also known as Grafton Bay, offers some good swimming and bodyboarding. A couple of large-scale hotels overlook the sand, one of which has a beach bar selling lunch and drinks; the eastern end has calmer waters.

Grafton Caledonia Wildlife Sanctuary   NATURE RESERVE
(Grafton Rd; P♿) After Hurricane Flora in 1963, Brit Eleanor Alefounder converted her 36 hectares into a bird sanctuary. It has some short hiking trails and excellent birdwatching. Visitors can come to the reserve any time, but the best time to come is around the 4pm feeding time. To get there, follow signs inland opposite the Grafton Beach Resort.

Adventure Farm and Nature Reserve   BIRDWATCHING
(☑639-2839; www.adventure-ecovillas.com; Arnos Vale Rd; US$10; ⊙9am-6pm; P♿) Adventure Farm and Nature Reserve is a 5-hectare working organic estate that has retained about 1 hectare of wild area. This is home to a wealth of bird species, which flutter in en masse when a bell is rung to signify feeding time. The center is especially revered for its huge numbers of hummingbirds, which cluster around feeders at the main house; watching them up close is a wonderful spectacle. You can also take short hikes around the estate along marked trails.

🛏 Sleeping

★ Top O'Tobago   BOUTIQUE HOTEL $$
(☑687-0121; www.topotobago.com; Arnos Vale Rd; cabanas US$150; P❄🛜🏊) A fantastic hilltop location with views over the rounded eggbox-like crags and out to the sea, this flower-bedecked place is made special by its colorful, simple style and superlative service from friendly staff. The bright, breezy self-contained cabanas are beautifully decorated, and hammocks swing in the breeze. There's a trail down to Arnos Vale Beach.

★**Cuffie River Nature Retreat** RESORT **$$**
(☑ 660-0505; www.cuffieriver.com; Runnemede; r from US$155; P ✳ 🐾 🛰) Follow signs off the Northside Rd to this charming, secluded retreat at the edge of the rainforest. Designed for birdwatching fanatics, it has an excellent birding guide on hand to lead hikes around the area. The spacious, comfortable rooms, equipped with balconies, are flooded with natural light. It also has an ecofriendly swimming pool and there are several freshwater springs nearby.

★**Adventure Eco-Villas** GUESTHOUSE **$$**
(☑ 639-2839; www.adventure-ecovillas.com; Arnos Vale Rd; apt/cottages US$85/140; P ✳ 🐾) Two self-contained one-bedroom wooden cottages within the Adventure Farm (p779) nature reserve, with kitchens, hardwood floors, tons of windows that open into the forest and a spacious deck. You feel a part of the environment as if you were camping, but you're actually in a styled-out little apartment. There's also a smaller apartment in the main house.

Seahorse Inn INN **$$**
(☑ 639-0686; www.seahorseinntobago.com; Stonehaven Bay; r incl breakfast US$88; ✳ 🐾) A nice contrast to the big resorts, this lovely spot on a ridge immediately above the sands of Stonehaven Bay is a low-key and peaceful place to stay. Its four spacious rooms have teak floors and broad balconies facing the ocean; crashing waves will lull you to sleep.

★**Mount Irvine Bay Resort** RESORT **$$$**
(☑ 639-8871; www.mtirvine.com; Grafton Rd; r US$128-288; P ✳ @ 🐾 🛰) The grand old lady of Tobago resorts, with sweeping grounds and an enviable position over Mt Irvine Bay, as well as its very own golf course. It's in the midst of a stylish refurb, with updated rooms and public areas. The pool is huge and the service excellent; and there's a path right down to the beach.

★**Plantation Beach Villas** RESORT **$$$**
(☑ 639-9377; www.plantationbeachvillas.com; Stonehaven Bay; villas for 2 people US$280; P ✳ 🐾 🛰) Right on Stonehaven Beach, this is the nicest of the villa resorts in the area, with tastefully appointed three-bedroom villas, a communal beachside pool and a cute little restaurant and bar. All villas come with a housekeeper who cleans daily and will cook for guests.

✗ Eating

Waves CAFE **$$**
(Stonehaven Bay; lunch TT$45-90, dinner TT$170-220; ⊙10am-10pm; 👪) Overhanging Stonehaven Bay, this is a casual place offering up burgers, tacos and sandwiches for lunch, plus pasta and more ambitious meat and fish dinners. There's a kids' menu, too.

★**Fish Pot** SEAFOOD **$$$**
(☑ 635-1728; Pleasant Prospect; lunch mains from TT$60, dinner TT$160-185; ⊙11am-3pm & 7-10pm Mon-Sat; 👪) This laid-back restaurant specializes in superfresh, simply prepared seafood (with some chicken and steak dishes), and is equipped with an open-air patio. Excellent homemade bread, and great starters from fish chowder to crab cakes. Don't miss it.

Seahorse Inn Restaurant & Bar CARIBBEAN **$$$**
(☑ 639-0686; www.seahorseinntobago.com; Seahorse Inn, Stonehaven Bay; mains TT$145-350; ⊙noon-3:30pm & 6-10pm) Sitting alfresco amid a tropical setting overlooking the water, with the sound of waves crashing below, this upmarket restaurant specializes in gourmet Creole cuisine.

🍷 Drinking & Nightlife

Leggers BAR
(Grafton Rd, Pleasant Prospect; ⊙6am-late) Leggers is an unpretentious bar nooked into a cliff overlooking the ocean. It catches lovely breezes and is a great spot to snag a beer after a day of sand and surf. It offers local breakfasts (to 10am) and barbecue Fridays as well.

ℹ Getting There & Away

From the airport, taxis to Mt Irvine are TT$70, TT$75 to Stonehaven Bay/Pleasant Prospect, TT$100 to Arnos Vale.

Castara

About a 45-minute drive from Plymouth, Castara is a working fishing village on the north coast that's popular with tourists not wanting the inundated Crown Point scene. People love the wide, sandy beach, relaxed atmosphere and picturesque setting. There's also a nice sense of tourism coexisting with village life, with visitors queuing up to buy bread and cakes from the clay oven just back from the main beach (order early on a Wednesday morning), or helping the fishers to pull in the seine nets. Castara is also a good base for a variety of tours and activities.

🏃 Activities & Tours

Snorkeling is good in the calm Heavenly Bay to the east of the main beach, and you can also take a freshwater swim in a small waterfall just behind the park on the west side of the village by Cheno's restaurant; just cross the playing field and follow the river.

Wild Turtle Scuba DIVING
(☑ 639-7836; www.divingintobago.com; Depot Rd, Castara; dive US$50) Wild Turtle is certified by the Professional Association of Diving Instructors (PADI) and is recommended by divers. It offers Open Water dive certification (US$450) as well as refresher, advanced and Divemaster classes.

Fitzroy Quamina Tours HIKING
(☑ 660-7836, 344-1895; hikes TT$160-300) Based in Bloody Bay, experienced guide Fitzroy Quamina leads nature walks through the Tobago Forest Reserve, as well as to local waterfalls and hidden beaches. You'll need your own transport to get to the trailheads.

Alibaba TOURS
(☑ 686-7957; www.alibaba-tours.com; Depot Rd; per person US$75-125; ⚙) Professional outfit offering boat trips and land tours throughout the island.

🛏 Sleeping

★ Castara Cottage APARTMENT $
(☑ 757-1044; www.castaracottage.com; Second Bay Rd; apt US$70-110; 🖥) Decked out in rich tropical colors, these three appealing apartments are in a great location, perched on a hillside between Big and Heavenly Bays. Each is equipped with all you need to self-cater, and has pleasant outdoor areas for liming and lounging.

Castara Bliss GUESTHOUSE $
(☑ 352-5727; www.castarablissapartments.com; Northside Rd; r US$65; ❄🖥) Set on a hillside with and with distant sea views, these cool little self-contained studios are great for budget travelers, with netted beds, cable TV and lots of local info from the helpful owner. One has bunk beds and can sleep four.

★ Castara Retreats RESORT $$
(☑ 766-1010; www.castararetreats.com; Northside Rd; 1-bed apt US$107-223; 🅿❄🖥) Beautifully

designed self-contained wooden villas on a lushly landscaped hillside that offers lovely views of the beach. Each is thoughtfully kitted out and quietly luxurious, and there are even sea views from some of the beds. It offers friendly, helpful staff and plenty of privacy, plus a fantastic restaurant and bar. It has a scenic yoga deck, and massages are available.

Alibaba's Sea Breeze GUESTHOUSE $$
(☑ 635-1017; www.alibaba-tours.com; Depot Rd; s/d US$80/90; 🅿🖥) This well-run bunch of apartments has magnificent beach-facing balconies, full kitchens and comfortable rooms with bamboo and seashell details, plus four-posters draped with mosquito nets. All are beautifully maintained and very inviting.

🍴 Eating

★ Caribbean Kitchen CARIBBEAN $$
(☑ 766-1010; www.castararetreats.com; Castara Retreats, Northside Rd; mains TT$110-160; ⊙11am-10pm; ⚙🍴) In a beautiful setting on a balcony lit with fairy lights high above the bay, this is a lovely lunch or dinner choice, with homemade pasta, bean burgers and eggplant *involtini* (rolls) as well as local-style curried lamb and excellent freshly caught seafood. The chocolate mousse, made with Tobago cocoa, is to die for. Great for fresh local juices and sunset cocktails, too.

★ Cascreole CARIBBEAN $$
(☑ 721-5700; Big Bay; mains from TT$75, Thu set menu TT$100; ⊙noon-3pm & 6:30-9:30pm; 🅿🍴) On a wooden deck built over the Big Bay sands, this is all you'd want from a beach bar: ice-cold beers and fresh and delicious fish, chicken and shrimp, served with tasty sides. Plenty of sea breezes and a Thursday-night beach bonfire and feast.

D'Almond Tree CARIBBEAN $$
(☑ 683-3593; Big Bay; mains from TT$75; ⊙6-9:30pm) Right on the sands of Big Bay, with local offerings ranging from grilled fish to curry goat. No alcohol, but you can bring your own.

Boat House CARIBBEAN $$
(☑ 483-0964; Depot Rd; lunch mains TT$70-90, dinner TT$120-135, pizzas TT$90-130; ⊙9:30am-10pm Mon & Fri, to 5pm Tue & Thu, to midnight Wed, 10am-5pm Sun; 🅿🖥🍴) Offering colorful decor, bamboo detailing and beachside ambience, this friendly bar and restaurant serves up sandwiches and burgers, as well

ENGLISHMAN'S BAY

North of Castara, the road winds past a stretch of coast that's punctuated by pretty beaches and villages, unhurried places with cows grazing at the roadside. The best place to stop is **Englishman's Bay**. This superb undeveloped beach, shaded by stands of bamboo and coconut palms, draws snorkelers to its gentle waters, where a coral reef lies 20m offshore. Eula's restaurant has local fare and rustic toilets.

as fish, chicken, beef and shrimp mains with local sides. There are good pizzas on Sundays. It's the busiest spot in town each Wednesday, with African drumming, limbo and moko jumbie dancers.

Cheno's　　　　　　CARIBBEAN **$$**
(📞704-7819; breakfast from TT$50, dinner TT$65-70; ⊗8am-1pm, dinner by reservation; 🔊) The best breakfast in town, from saltfish buljol and coconut bake to bacon and eggs. Local lunch and dinner (fish, chicken or curry goat, local-style) is also available.

🍷 Drinking & Nightlife

Glasgow's Bar　　　　　　BAR
(Northside Rd, Parlatuvier; mains from TT$40; ⊗10am-10pm) Perched at the cliffside above Parlatuvier Bay, this friendly Tobago rum shop is a great place to kick back and enjoy the views. The adjoined cookshop sells local meals and fish-and-chips, too.

❶ Getting There & Away

A taxi from Crown Point will cost TT$280, and cars are available to rent locally from **Taylor's** (📞354-5743; www.taylorstobagoautorental.com; Depot Rd, Heavenly Bay).

Scarborough

Located 15 minutes' drive east of Crown Point, Scarborough is Tobago's capital, a crowded port with bustling one-way streets and congested traffic. Tobagonians come here to bank, pay bills or go shopping, and though there are some good places to grab a bite and a neat public market, most visitors will want to push onward.

◉ Sights

Botanical Gardens　　　　　　GARDENS
(Gardenside St; ⊗dawn-dusk) **FREE** A pretty place to duck out of the heat, with a variety of flowering trees and shrubs, including flamboyants, African tulips and orchids (in an orchid house) laid out over 3 hectares of a former sugar estate. The most convenient of several entrances is just back from Carrington St on Gardenside St.

★ Fort King George　　　　　　FORT
(Fort St; 🅿 ♿) **FREE** Atop a hill at the end of Fort St, this sizable fort was built by the British between 1777 and 1779, and is worth a visit to see its restored colonial-era buildings – one of which holds the Tobago Museum – and magnificent views. Benches under enormous samaan trees allow you to gaze out over Rockly Bay, while cannons line the fort's stone walls, pointing out to sea over palm-covered flatlands below.

Tobago Museum　　　　　　MUSEUM
(📞639-3970; Fort King George, Fort St; TT$10; ⊗9am-4:30pm Mon-Fri; ♿) The Fort King George officers' quarters now contain this small but worthy museum, which displays a healthy collection of Amerindian artifacts, maps from the 1600s, military relics, paintings, a small geology exhibit and a neat collection of domestic artifacts from Tobago's more recent history.

🛏 Sleeping

Hope Cottage　　　　　　GUESTHOUSE **$**
(📞639-2179; hcghtobago@hotmail.com; Calder Hall Rd; s/d TT$110/275; 🔊) A solid, super-friendly budget option near Fort King George, a half-hour walk uphill from the dock. Within this former home of 19th-century governor James Henry Keens (acting governor from 1856 to 1857 and buried in the backyard), guests have access to a big kitchen, TV room, dining room, backyard and front porch; the more expensive rooms have private bathroom and cable TV.

Sandy's Bed & Breakfast　　　　　　GUESTHOUSE **$$**
(📞639-2737; www.tobagobluecrab.com; cnr Main & Robinson Sts; r incl breakfast US$80; ❄🔊) Behind the Blue Crab Restaurant, the three rooms are pleasantly simple with pine floors, nice furniture and views overlooking Rockly Bay.

Blue Haven Hotel   HOTEL $$$
(☑ 660-7400; www.bluehavenhotel.com; Bacolet Bay; r incl breakfast US$296-331; P✳@🛜🏊) Robinson Crusoe supposedly was stranded at the beach below this romantic, tastefully done resort hotel with a hint of faded glamour. Amenities here include a beachside pool, tennis courts and kayaks, and each room has an oceanfront balcony. A restaurant and bar are on-site.

✖ Eating

★ Ciao Café and Pizzeria   ITALIAN $
(Burnett St; pizzas TT$50-98, ice creams from TT$30; ⊘11:45am-2:45pm & 6-10pm Mon & Wed-Sat, 6-10pm Sun) Both locals and foreigners come to lime at this adorable cafe, which cooks up authentic Italian pizza in a brick oven, plus great panini, coffee and the best Italian gelato in Trinidad and Tobago.

★ Shore Things   CAFE $$
(Old Milford Rd, Lambeau; mains TT$60-115; ⊘11am-6pm Mon-Fri; ☑🍴) A couple of kilometers west of Scarborough, this is one of the most pleasant oceanside cafes on the island, serving quiche, pizza, filled crepes, salads, sandwiches and fresh juices, plus more substantial fish and meat dishes. The setting, overlooking the ocean, is lovely and breezy. Great for teatime cakes, and there's a kids' menu, too.

★ Salsa Kitchen   MEDITERRANEAN $$$
(☑ 639-1552; 8 Pump Mill Rd; tapas from TT$85, mains from TT$150; ⊘6-11pm Tue-Sun) A tiny place on a hillside veranda off Wilson Rd, and run by a wonderfully welcoming husband-and-wife team, Salsa Kitchen cooks up delicious tapas bites from lobster dumplings to eggplant mozzarella, and more substantial fare such as saddle of lamb and even pizza. Book ahead, as there are only five tables and it often gets busy.

ℹ Information

There are branches of Republic Bank and Scotiabank just east of the docks, both equipped with ATMs. There's another ATM right outside the ferry terminal.

Post Office (Post Office St; ⊘7:30am-6pm Mon-Fri, 9am-1pm Sat) There's a TT Post outlet in the ferry terminal.

Tobago House of Assembly Tourism Branch (☑ 635-0934; www.visittobago.gov.tt; 12 Sangsters Hill Rd; ⊘8am-4pm Mon-Fri) The main office is just west of the esplanade and ferry terminal; there's also an office at the cruise-ship terminal (adjacent to the ferry terminal).

ℹ Getting There & Away

Tobago's main bus terminal is just behind the waterfront at Sangster's Hill Rd; buses and maxi taxis to all points depart from here. The dock for ferries between Trinidad and Tobago, run by the **Inter-Island Ferry Service** (☑ 639-2417; https://ttitferry.com; Carrington St; adult/child 1-way TT$50/25), is on Carrington St, right in the heart of town. Taxis line up to meet foot passengers just outside.

In lower Scarborough, there are route-taxi stands: cars to Plymouth, Castara and Parlatuvier depart from opposite the market, and taxis to Crown Point leave from in front of the ferry terminal. In upper Scarborough, taxis to Speyside and Charlotteville leave from Republic Bank by James Park. Fares are TT$5 to TT$12.

Windward Road

East of Scarborough, Tobago's Windward Coast is the more rural part of the island, less appealing to tourists thanks to its rough dark-sand beaches and pounding Atlantic waves. The Windward Rd, which connects Scarborough with Speyside and Charlotteville, winds past scattered villages, jungly valleys and white-capped ocean dotted with tiny offshore islands. The further east you go, the more ruggedly beautiful the scenery becomes.

Although much of the Windward Rd is narrow and curvy, with a handful of blind corners, it's easily drivable in a standard vehicle. Journey time from Scarborough to Speyside is 1½ hours.

◉ Sights

Argyle Falls   WATERFALL
(Windward Rd; adult/child TT$60/30; ⊘7am-5:30pm) This 54m waterfall on the Argyle River is Tobago's highest, cascading down three distinct levels, each with its own pool of spring water, which you can swim in. From the parking lot, it's a 20-minute hike up. In addition to the entry fee, you can pay an authorized guide US$10 to lead the way and point out things of interest. The path is easy to follow independently, though it can get slippery after rain (which also turns the pools a muddy brown).

Tobago Cocoa Estate
TOUR

(☑788-3971; www.tobagococoa.com; Cameron Canal Rd; adult/child TT$90/45; ⊙tours 11am; 🅿🚻) In the hills above Argyle Falls, and accessed via the same approach road, Tobago Cocoa Estate offers hour-long plantation tours that give the lowdown on local chocolate production. The tours end with tastings of the estate's delectable award-winning chocolate. You must reserve in advance, and there's a 10-person minimum group size, so you may have to fall in with other travelers.

Speyside

The small fishing village of Speyside fronts Tyrrel's Bay, and attracts divers and birders. It's the jumping-off point for excursions to uninhabited Little Tobago island, a bird sanctuary 2km offshore. Protected waters, high visibility, abundant coral and diverse marine life make for choice diving, and Speyside is home to some of the best scuba sites in the Caribbean. Several dive shops operate in the village and most visitors stay in diver-oriented hotels. Nondivers can take glass-bottom-boat/snorkel tours to Little Tobago.

Speyside has a quiet, end-of-the-road feel. Above town, the off-road lookout has panoramic views out over the islands and reef-studded waters.

◉ Sights

Little Tobago
ISLAND

Also known as Bird of Paradise Island (though it isn't home to any of the eponymous birds), Little Tobago was home to a cotton plantation during the late 1800s, and is now an important seabird sanctuary that offers rich pickings for birdwatchers. Red-billed tropic birds, magnificent frigate birds, brown boobies, Audubon's shearwaters, laughing gulls and sooty terns are some of the species found here. The hilly, arid island, which averages just 1.5km in width, has a couple of short hiking trails with captivating views.

Frank's (p784) and Top Ranking Tours (p784) run glass-bottom-boat tours to Little Tobago. The trip includes guided birdwatching on the island and snorkeling at the lovely Angel Reef.

🏃 Activities

Blue Waters Dive'n
DIVING

(☑660-5445; www.bluewatersinn.com; Blue Waters Inn; single dive US$66, PADI Open Water US$495) Well-run dive shop offering certification, refresher courses and recreational dives in and around Speyside.

Extra Divers
DIVING

(☑660-4852; www.extradivers-worldwide.com; Speyside Inn, Windward Rd) Bilingual dive outfit popular with German travelers, attached to the Speyside Inn.

☞ Tours

Frank's
BOATING

(☑660-5438; Batteaux Bay; Little Tobago trip US$30; ⊙10am & 2pm) Based at Blue Waters Inn, Frank's conducts glass-bottom-boat tours to Little Tobago. The trip includes birdwatching, with guides pointing out the various species as well as plants and animals of interest along the way, and snorkeling at the lovely Angel Reef, home to one of the largest brain corals in the world. Masks and fins are provided.

Top Ranking Tours
BOATING

(☑660-4904; Little Tobago trip US$30; ⊙10am & 1pm) Top Ranking Tours, departing from the beach near Jemma's restaurant, operates tours of Little Tobago aboard its glass-bottom boats. Masks and fins are provided so you can snorkel at Angel Reef.

🛏 Sleeping

Speyside Inn
HOTEL $$

(☑660-4852; www.extradivers-worldwide. com; 189-193 Windward Rd; s/d incl breakfast US$100/144; 🅿❄@🛜🏊) Quite lovely, this butter-yellow hotel houses bright balcony rooms looking over the ocean, and cottages nestled out back in the jungly landscaping. It's very much geared toward scuba business, with the Extra Divers shop on-site. There's a restaurant and a bar, and it's often the most animated spot in town (though that's not saying much in quiet Speyside).

★ Blue Waters Inn
HOTEL $$$

(☑660-2583; www.bluewatersinn.com; Batteaux Bay; r incl breakfast from US$296; 🅿❄@🛜🏊) Speyside's most upscale accommodations, geared to divers and birdwatchers, Blue Waters sits on aquamarine Batteaux Bay, the best beach in the area. The rooms all have patios and great views. Guests get use of tennis courts, beach chairs and kayaks. It has a restaurant, bar and a full-service PADI dive center. Located 1km from the main road.

✖ Eating

Jemma's CARIBBEAN **$$**
(Windward Rd; mains TT$80-150; ⊗8am-8pm Mon-Thu & Sun, to 4pm Fri; 🍴) Nestled in a treehouse setting and blessed by sea breezes, Jemma's is a standard stop for tour groups, and service can be slow. It boasts excellent atmosphere and fresh local food, including fish, chicken and shrimp dishes, and delicious sides such as breadfruit pie or tania fritters, as well as sandwiches and burgers. No booze, but you can bring your own.

Birdwatchers Restaurant & Bar CARIBBEAN **$$**
(📞660-5438; Windward Rd; mains TT$70-200; ⊗11:30am-9pm) Kick back on the candlelit deck and enjoy fresh seafood and cold beers at this friendly place. The menu changes with the catch of the day, and also includes shrimp, chicken and lobster.

❶ Getting There & Away

You can drive to Speyside from Scarborough, along the winding Windward Rd, in about 1½ hours. Taxis from Crown Point cost TT$380, a little less from Scarborough.

Charlotteville

A delightful fishing village, Charlotteville nestles in aquamarine Man of War Bay, a short walk from glorious Pirate's Bay Beach. This secluded town accepts its trickle of off-the-beaten-track tourists with mostly jovial spirits and occasionally apathy. It's more lively than nearby Speyside, and tourist services include a sprinkling of places to stay and eat and an ATM. This may all change, though, with the construction of a large new beach facility smack in the middle of the village, which locals have been opposing to little effect.

◉ Sights

Man of War Bay BEACH
(Bay St) The large, horseshoe-shaped Man of War Bay is fringed by a palm-studded brown-sand beach with good swimming. Roughly in the middle of the beach, you'll find changing facilities (TT$1) and the Suckhole (p786) beach bar, adjacent to a swimming area watched over by lifeguards. The

pier toward the eastern end is a nice spot for fishing or sunset-watching.

★Pirate's Bay BEACH
(Pirate's Bay Rd) Past Charlotteville's pier, a dirt track winds up and around the cliff to concrete steps that descend to Pirate's Bay, which offers excellent snorkeling and fantastic beach liming, with locals and visitors making a day of it with coolers and games of beach football. There are no facilities, so bring your own drinks and food. If you don't fancy the 10-minute walk, ask one of the Man of War Bay fishers to transport you there and back.

Flagstaff Hill HILL
(Windward Rd) Reached via a signposted turnoff from the main road between Speyside and Charlotteville, Flagstaff Hill is a popular spot to picnic and watch the birds circling St Giles Island. The coastal views are stupendous.

🏃 Activities

★ERIC DIVING
(📞788-3550; www.eric-tobago.org; Northside Rd; single dive US$65) The acronym stands for Environmental Research Institute Charlotteville, and though this outfit is part dive shop, offering PADI training and recreational diving, it's also a research facility dedicated to monitoring the health of the island's reefs and ecosystems.

🛏 Sleeping

Man-O-War Bay Cottages CABIN **$**
(📞660-4327; www.man-o-warbaycottages. com; Campbleton Rd; 1-/3-bedroom cottages US$65/120; 🅿@) 🌿 Plotted in a little botanical garden, with lots of tropical trees, ferns and flowering plants, these 10 simple cottages with kitchens and generous outdoor decks are basic but have a fantastic location, open to the breeze and sounds of the surf. You'll find them beachside, about five minutes' walk south of the village.

Top River Pearl GUESTHOUSE **$$**
(📞660-6011; www.topriver.de; 32-34 Spring St; r from US$80; @🛜) Although it's not on the beach, this European-run guesthouse, just 180m up from the waterfront, is a treat with its hammocks and expansive bay views. With furnishings built from local teak, mahogany trimmings and red-tiled floors, each of the four neat but plain rooms has a balcony with ocean views, plus minikitchen.

MUSIC IN TRINIDAD & TOBAGO

Stop for a moment on the streets of Trinidad and Tobago and listen. You'll likely hear the fast beat of soca playing on a maxi-taxi radio, or the sound of steel drums drifting out from a panyard. Often festive, sometimes political or melancholy, music digs deep into the emotion of island life.

Although Carnival happens in February, there's always plenty of great live music happening, especially in the months leading up to Carnival.

Calypso

A medium for political and social satire, calypso hearkens back to the days when African slaves – unable to talk when working – would sing in patois, sharing gossip and news while mocking their colonial masters. Today, risqué lyrics, pointed social commentary and verbal wordplay are still the order of the day. Mighty Sparrow, long acknowledged the king of calypso, has voiced popular concerns and social consciousness since the 1950s, as did his contemporary, the late, great 'Grandmaster,' Lord Kitchener. Another famous calypsonian, David Rudder, helped revive the musical form in the mid-1980s by adding experimental rhythms, unearthing both the cultural importance and flexibility of calypso. Others to look out for include the distinctive voice of Shadow, and the inimitable Calypso Rose, whose recent collaboration LP with Manu Chao has brought worldwide success.

Chutney

This up-tempo, rhythmic music of Indian Trinis is accompanied by the *dholak* (Northern Indian folk drum) and the *dhantal* (a metal rod played with a metal striker). Chutney songs celebrate social situations – everything from women witnessing a birth to men partying at a bar. It's a fusion of classical Hindu music with more contemporary soca, and can't fail to get you wiggling your hips. Notable stars include Rikki Jai, Drupatee and Ravi B.

Soca

The energetic offspring of calypso, soca was born in the 1970s, and uses the same basic beat but speeds things up, creating danceable rhythms that perfectly accompany the Carnival season. Though soca is yet to break out internationally in the way of Jamaican dancehall, its biggest stars have collaborated with many international names, from Diplo to Pitbull, and many recent hits bring in elements of reggae and electronic dance music (EDM) beats. Machel Montano is the reigning king of soca; other big names include speedy lyricist Bunji Garlin, Fay-Ann Lyons, Destra and Benjai.

Steel Pan

Rhythm and percussion are the beating heart behind Carnival. Traditionally percussionists banged together bamboo cut in various lengths, or simply drummed on whatever they could – the road, sides of buildings, their knees. When African drums were banned during WWII, drummers turned to biscuit tins and then oil drums discarded by US troops, which were shaped and tuned to produce a brand new instrument. Today, steel pans come in a variety of sizes, each producing a unique note. Heard together, they become a cascading waterfall of sound. During Carnival, some bands are transported on flatbed trucks along the parade route. All bands aim to win Panorama, the national competition that runs throughout Carnival season.

Charlotte Villas GUESTHOUSE **$$**
(www.charlottevilla.com; d US$80; P🐾) In the south part of town, these three fully equipped, high-ceiling apartments are spacious, simple and relaxing, with verandas and tons of natural light flooding in.

🍴 Eating

⭐ **Suckhole** CARIBBEAN **$$**
(📞288-5820; Man of War Bay Beach, off Bay St; mains TT$45-150; ⏱10am-6pm Tue-Sun, lunch 12:30-2:30pm) Right on the beach, with tables overlooking Man of War Bay, this enigmat-

ically named place is a great lunch option, serving up burgers and huge portions of fish, ribs, chicken and shrimp. Great service and a delicious rum punch, too.

Gail's   CARIBBEAN $$

(☑688-5492; Bay St; mains from TT$70; ☺7pm-late Mon-Sat) Located at the northern end of the waterfront, Gail's serves up freshly caught fish with fantastic local side dishes, and adds in a local soup to start the meal. The welcome is always friendly, and it's a great spot for an intimate dinner.

G's   CARIBBEAN $$

(Bay St; mains from TT$50; ☺11am-9pm) This hole-in-the-wall eatery has a breezy seaside patio for enjoying simple, inexpensive meals of fish or chicken and chips, and more elaborate plates with all the local trimmings. Blaring music at weekends from the adjoining bar. Opening hours can be erratic.

ⓘ Getting There & Away

Most visitors get to Charlotteville in a rental car, as maxi-taxis and buses are sporadic. A taxi from Crown Point costs TT$380.

UNDERSTAND

History

Early History

Caribs and Arawaks were Trinidad's sole inhabitants until 1498, when Columbus arrived and christened the island La Isla de la Trinidad, for the Holy Trinity.

Initially, gold-hungry Spain gave only scant attention to Trinidad, which lacked precious minerals, but in 1592 a Spanish capital was finally established at San José, just east of present-day Port of Spain, and enslavement of the Amerindian population began in earnest. French planters descended en masse to assist the Spanish with development of the island, and West African slaves were brought in to supplement the labor forces toiling on tobacco and cocoa plantations.

British forces took the island from the Spanish in 1797. With the abolishment of slavery in 1834, slaves abandoned plantations; this prompted the British to import thousands of indentured workers, mostly from India, to labor in the cane fields and service the colony. The indentured-labor system remained in place for over 100 years.

Tobago's early history is a separate story. Also sighted by Columbus and claimed by Spain, it wasn't colonized until 1628, when Charles I of England decided to charter the island to the Earl of Pembroke. In response, a handful of nations took an immediate interest in colonizing Tobago.

During the 17th century Tobago changed hands numerous times as the English, French, Dutch and even Courlanders (present-day Latvians) wrestled for control. In 1704 it was declared a neutral territory, which left room for pirates to use the island as a base for raiding ships in the Caribbean. The British established a colonial administration in 1763, and within two decades slave labor established the island's sugar, cotton and indigo plantations.

Tobago's plantation economy wilted after the abolition of slavery, but sugar and rum production continued until 1884, when the London firm that controlled finances for the island's plantations went bankrupt. Plantation owners quickly sold or abandoned their land, leaving the economy in a shambles.

Free Colony

In 1889 Tobago joined Trinidad as a British Crown Colony. Even though Trinidad and Tobago's demand for greater autonomy grew and anticolonial sentiment ripened, the British didn't pay attention until 1956, when the People's National Movement (PNM), led by Oxford-educated Dr Eric Williams,

LOCAL KNOWLEDGE

AMERINDIAN LEGACY

Arima is home to a small Amerindian community who still follow some traditional customs. Just west of town, the small and rather dusty **Amerindian Museum** (☑645-1203; Eastern Main Rd; ☺8am-6pm; 🅿🚻) **FREE** at Cleaver Woods displays some artifacts. Local shaman **Cristo Adonis** (☑488-8539) can show you around or take you on an educational hike to learn about the medicinal plants and spirituality of the Amerindians.

took measures to institute self-government. Independence was granted in 1962, and the country became a republic of the Commonwealth in 1976.

Frustration with the leftover colonial structure led to the Black Power movement, which created a political crisis and an army mutiny, but ultimately strengthened national identity. Bankrupt and without prospects, the country's luck changed in 1970 with the discovery of oil, which brought instant wealth and prosperity. During the 1980s, when oil prices plummeted, a recession hit and political unrest ensued. Accusations of corruption and complaints from an underrepresented Indian community led to the PNM's defeat in 1986 by the National Alliance for Reconstruction (NAR).

Corruption blossomed in a judicial system congested with drugs-related trials (the country is a stopover for the South American drug trade). In July 1990 members of a minority Muslim group attempted a coup, stormed parliament and took 45 hostages, including Prime Minister ANR Robinson. Though the coup failed, it undermined the government, and the PNM returned to power.

Trinidad & Tobago Today

Vast petroleum and natural gas reserves discovered in the late 1990s helped stabilize the economy. In 1995 Basdeo Panday of the United National Congress (UNC) beat the PNM's Patrick Manning in a controversial election, seating the first prime minister of Indian descent. A stalemated political process saw Manning win the 2002 and 2007 elections. With his popularity failing amid a slew of corruption scandals, Manning called an early election in 2010 and was trounced by the People's Partnership (PP), a coalition of the UNC and COP parties led by Kamla Persad-Bissessar, who became the republic's first female prime minister. Trinidad and Tobago's party politics had long been divided along ethnic lines, with the PNM being the predominant party of Afro-Trinidadians and the UNC representing the Indian community, and for many, the PP government was seen to represent a new start by many. Nonetheless, the PP were no more successful than the PNM in dealing with the key issues of high crime and deep-seated corruption, and the 2015 general election saw the PNM return to power under PM Keith Rowley.

People & Culture

Of the country's 1.3 million inhabitants, some 60,000 live on Tobago. Trinidad has one of the most ethnically diverse populations in the Caribbean, a legacy of its checkered colonial history. The majority is of Indian (40.3%) and African (39.5%) descent. The remaining 20% are of mixed ancestry, but there are also notable European, Chinese, Syrian and Lebanese communities, while a few hundred native Caribs live in the Arima area.

Roughly one-third of all islanders are Roman Catholic. Another 25% are Hindu, 11% are Anglican, 13% are other Protestant denominations and 6% are Muslim. With its roots in African faith traditions, the Orisha religion also remains strong in some areas, as does Rastafarianism.

Cricket

Introduced by the British in the 19th century, cricket isn't just a sport in Trinidad and Tobago, it's a cultural obsession. International cricket legend Brian Lara – the 'Prince of Port of Spain' – hails from Trinidad and his popularity ranks up there with Jesus. And despite their failing fortunes, the arrival of the West Indies team for a test match still sees everything grinding to a halt as people stick to their TVs to capture the action.

The main venue is the **Queen's Park Oval** (622-4325; www.qpcc.com; 94 Tragarete Rd;), home to the Queen's Park Cricket Club, a few blocks west of the Queen's Park Savannah in Port of Spain. Originally built in 1896, with the northern hills as a spectacular backdrop, it's the site of both regional and international matches and holds 25,000 spectators who pack out the stands and create a party atmosphere at matches. It also has a small museum dedicated to cricket heritage; call to arrange a visit.

Landscape & Wildlife

Formerly part of the South American mainland, Trinidad and Tobago have a rich natural environment that's quite different to the rest of the Caribbean. Lush rainforests harbor a huge variety of plants and animals, as well as spectacular birds, while the coral reefs around Tobago, fed by nutrient-rich currents from the Orinoco River, are some of the Caribbean's best.

The Land

Boot-shaped Trinidad was once part of the South American mainland. Over time a channel developed, separating Trinidad from present-day Venezuela. The connection to South America is noticeable in Trinidad's Northern Range, a continuation of the Andes, and in its abundant oil and gas reserves, concentrated in southwestern Trinidad.

The Northern Range spreads east to west, forming a scenic backdrop to Port of Spain. The rest of the island is given to plains, undulating hills and mangrove swamps. Trinidad's numerous rivers include the 50km Ortoire River, and the 40km Caroni River dumping into the Caroni Swamp.

Tobago, 19km northeast of Trinidad, has a central mountain range that reaches almost 610m at its highest point. Deep, fertile valleys run from the ridge down toward the coast, which is fringed with bays and beaches.

Wildlife

Because of its proximity to the South American continent, Trinidad and Tobago has the widest variety of plant and animal life in the Caribbean: some 460 species of birds, 600 species of butterfly, 70 kinds of reptiles and 100 types of mammals, including red howler monkeys, anteaters, ocelots, agouti and armadillos.

Plant life is equally diverse, with more than 700 orchid species and 1600 other types of flowering plants. Both islands have luxuriant rainforests, and Trinidad also features elfin forests, savannas and both freshwater and brackish mangrove swamps.

Environmental Issues

Water pollution is a huge environmental concern on Trinidad and Tobago. Agricultural chemicals, industrial waste and raw sewage seep into groundwater and eventually the ocean. Reef damage is due mostly to pollution, as well as overuse.

Quarrying (both legal and illegal) and unsustainable development are rampant in this ecodestination. Deforestation and soil erosion are direct results. Sand erosion is a special concern on the northeast coast of Trinidad, where leatherback turtles lay eggs.

So-called 'wild meat' such as agouti, deer, wild hog, armadillo and iguana is a hugely popular delicacy in Trinidad and Tobago, and the local animal population is also threatened by rampant and unregulated hunting.

The Environmental Management Authority (www.ema.co.tt) is charged with monitoring environmental issues, but as in other developing countries, the pressure of 'progress' trumps preservation. Environment Tobago (www.environmenttobago.net) is an informative resource about issues facing Tobago.

BIRDWATCHING

Trinidad and Tobago are excluded from many Caribbean birding books because of the sheer magnitude of additional species here – about 460 in total. Torn from Venezuela, these islands share the diversity of the South American mainland in their swamps, rainforests, ocean islets, lowland forests and savannas, and the birdwatching is some of the best in the Caribbean.

For references, try *A Guide to the Birds of Trinidad and Tobago* by Richard Ffrench, which has good descriptions but limited plates; or *Field Guide to the Birds of Trinidad and Tobago* by Martyn Kenefyk, Robin Restall and Floyd Hayesm, which has a few more.

The best birding spots in Trinidad are **Asa Wright Nature Centre** (p767), **Caroni Bird Sanctuary** (p770), **Nariva Swamp** (p770) and Mt St Benedict (p763). In Tobago: **Little Tobago** (p784) and **Tobago Forest Reserve**.

SURVIVAL GUIDE

ℹ Directory A–Z

ACCOMMODATIONS

Both islands have good-value guesthouses and hotels. These are concentrated in Port of Spain in Trinidad and Crown Point in Tobago, which has other clusters around Buccoo/Mt Irvine, Castara, Speyside, Charlotteville and Scarborough. Aside from Carnival season in Port of Spain, when rates rise astronomically, Trinidad & Tobago is less expensive than elsewhere in the Caribbean, with budget options from US$40 a night;

SLEEPING PRICE RANGES

The following prices refer to a double room with bathroom during high season (December to April). A 10% service charge and a 15% value-added tax (VAT) can add 35% more to your bill. Most advertised accommodations rates include the tax and service charge, but not always.

$ less than US$75

$$ US$75–200

$$$ more than US$200

rates are often negotiable in the low or shoulder seasons (roughly April to early December).

ACTIVITIES

In Trinidad, Port of Spain is the best base for seeing most of the island's sights, as you can easily get there and back in a day. However, if you plan on exploring the northeast coast – Toco, Grande Riviere and beyond – it makes sense to overnight in Grande Riviere, as the drive in and out is long and demanding. Some of Trinidad's best birdwatching areas, such as Aripo Savannah and Caroni Arena Dam, are ecologically sensitive and all visitors need a permit to enter. These can be obtained independently, but it's time-consuming and difficult. Far better to let a recommended tour operator handle it for you.

During turtle-nesting season (March to August) you must have a permit to enter key nesting sites such as the beaches at Matura and Grande Riviere after dark. These are available from **Nature Seekers** (p769) in Matura and the **Grande Riviere Nature Tour Guide Association** (p768), and are provided when you sign up for a turtle-watching trip.

You can drive right around Tobago in a day, so it's possible to see the sights from wherever you base yourself. As in Trinidad, unless you're on a tour with a local company, you'll need your own vehicle to explore, as public transport isn't a convenient or reliable option for most places of interest.

CHILDREN

Kids of all ages flock with their parents to Tobago's beaches, and most facilities are family-oriented. In Trinidad, the tourism is less family-oriented, but higher-end hotels usually accommodate children. During Carnival, Kiddie Mas is a sight not to miss, whatever your age.

➥ Diapers (nappies), wipes, formula and baby food are available in all large supermarkets.

➥ Pharmacies stock accessories such as bottles.

➥ High chairs are available in some tourist-oriented restaurants.

➥ Nappy-changing facilities are nonexistent.

➥ Most hotels and many guesthouses can provide infant cots.

➥ Car-hire companies can provide child seats for a fee.

➥ Breastfeeding in public isn't common among local women, but if you use a cover-up, you shouldn't encounter any problems.

DANGERS & ANNOYANCES

Tobagonians warn of rampant lawlessness in Trinidad, and Trinidadians say crime is increasing in Tobago. While such claims reflect a real crime increase, they tend to exaggerate the dangers of travel on the islands.

➥ Avoid walking alone at night, especially around dark, desolate areas and particularly in Port of Spain.

➥ Theft can be a problem, especially in touristy parts of Tobago, so keep an eye on your valuables and don't bring them to the beach.

➥ Some travelers find the aggressive tactics of souvenir hawkers or boat-ride sellers annoying. Just be firm but polite and you'll usually be left alone.

➥ Women may also feel frustrated by the overt attention of men, but – again – be firm but polite. While flirting will invite more hassle, a friendly, formal 'good morning/afternoon/evening' can be disarming.

➥ If you've traveled around other Caribbean islands you may have encountered a lax attitude toward drugs. Beware – smoking weed in Trinidad and Tobago is a serious offense and getting caught can quickly ruin your holiday.

➥ Take good, strong bug spray to ward off no-see-ums (sandflies) and mosquitoes; dengue fever is present on both islands, and there have been recent outbreaks of Zika and chikungunya.

➥ Take care to avoid the manchineel tree, which grows along the coastline of both islands. Its shiny rounded leaves and apple-like fruits are extremely poisonous if ingested, and the runoff from the trees after rain can cause skin blisters. Most manchineel trees are labeled on popular beaches in Tobago.

➥ Trinidad (though not Tobago) has four species of venomous snake, including corals and pit vipers. Chance encounters are unlikely, but you should watch where you tread when walking in the forests.

ELECTRICITY

Electrical current 115/230V, 60Hz; US-style two-pin plug.

EMBASSIES & CONSULATES

Embassies and consulates/high commissions in Port of Spain include the following:

Australia (☑ 822-5450; www.trinidadand tobago.embassy.gov.au; 18 Herbert St, St Clair; ☺8am-4:30pm Mon-Fri)

Canada (☑ 622-6232; www.trinidadandtobago. gc.ca; Maple Bldg, 3-3a Sweet Briar Rd, St Clair; ☺8-11:30am Mon-Thu)

France (☑ 628-1931; www.ambafrance-tt.org; 7 Mary St, St Clair; ☺9am-1pm & 2:30-4:30pm Mon-Thu, 9am-1:30pm Fri)

Germany (☑ 628-1630; www.port-of-spain. diplo.de; 19 St Clair Ave, St Clair; ☺8-11:30am Mon-Fri)

Netherlands (☑ 625-1210; http://trinidad andtobago.nlembassy.org; Life of Barbados Bldg, 69-71 Edward St; ☺8am-5pm Mon-Thu, to 2pm Fri)

UK (☑ 350-0444; http://ukintt.fco.gov.uk; 19 St Clair Ave, St Clair; ☺9am-4pm Mon-Thu, to 1pm Fri)

US (☑ 622-6371; https://tt.usembassy.gov; 15 Queen's Park West)

Venezuela (☑ 627-9821; embve.ttpsp@mmp pre.gob.ve; 16 Victoria Ave)

EMERGENCY & IMPORTANT NUMBERS

Trinidad & Tobago area code	☑868
International access code	☑011
Police	☑999
Fire	☑990
Ambulance	☑811

FOOD

The cuisine of Trinidad and Tobago is one of its undoubted highlights, an intoxicating blend of Indian and Creole flavors. Curried crab with dumplings is a Tobago specialty, while goat, duck, chicken, shrimp and veggies are also cooked up in a curry sauce to fill the ubiquitous rotis. Fish and seafood are excellent, with king-fish, mahi-mahi, barracuda, carite and redfish such as snapper offered grilled, steamed or fried, but always delightfully seasoned.

Essential Food & Drink

Bake and shark Seasoned shark steaks, topped with salad and local sauces and served in a light fried bread. Better to go for kingfish than nonsustainable shark.

Callaloo The leaves of the dasheen tuber, cooked up with pumpkin, okra, coconut and plenty of seasoning.

Carib and Stag The national beers; always served 'beastly' cold.

Doubles Curried channa (chickpeas) in a soft fried bara bread.

Peas The local terms for beans: usually pigeon, kidney, black-eye and green lentils, stewed with spices and coconut.

Pelau Chicken and pigeon peas cooked up with rice, pumpkin and coconut.

Roti A split-pea-infused flat bread wrapped around curried meat and vegetables.

GLBT TRAVELERS

Though more progressive than some other Caribbean islands, Trinidad and Tobago remain pretty closed to the idea of same-sex relation-ships, backed up by the fact that the local laws criminalize buggery. There is a sizable LGBT community, but it's not at all visible; being out and expressing affection is not the norm, and on beaches and in rural areas you may get negative repercussions.

HEALTH

There are large general hospitals in **Port of Spain** (☑ 623-2951; 56-57 Charlotte St), San Fernando and **Scarborough** (☑ 660-4744; Signal Hill; ☺24hr), but conditions can be antiquated and waits long. Many visitors opt for private hospitals such as **St Clair Medical Centre** (☑ 628-1451; www.medcorpltd.com; 18 Elizabeth St, St Clair) in Port of Spain.

LEGAL MATTERS

If you are arrested in Trinidad and Tobago, you have the right to be told what you have been detained for, and do not have to give an oral or written statement unless you choose to. You have the right to speak to and to retain a lawyer to defend you. The police should inform the rel-evant embassy or consulate (where one exists) when a foreign national is arrested, who can in turn help with finding representation. If contact is not made on your behalf, you have the right to do this yourself.

ⓘ DRINKING WATER

Tap water is heavily chlorinated in Trin-idad & Tobago, and tastes better boiled than fresh from the tap. It can still cause upsets for those unused to it, though, so it's best to stick to bottled water.

Note that possession of drugs, including cannabis, is dealt with harshly here.

MONEY

The official currency is the Trinidad and Tobago dollar (TT$), but many goods or services are priced in US$. We quote rates as they are given, be it TT$ or US$.

Exchange Rates

AUSTRALIA	AS$1	TT$5.08
CANADA	C$1	TT$5.16
EUROPE	€1	TT$7.20
JAPAN	¥100	TT$5.95
NEW ZEALAND	NZ$1	TT$4.83
UK	UK£1	TT$8.24
US	US$1	TT$6.73

For current exchange rates, see www.xe.com.

Tipping

Tipping has not traditionally been part of Trinidad and Tobago culture, though it is increasingly common.

➨ **Restaurants** Many restaurants add a 10% service charge to bills; if not, a tip of 10% to 15% is customary.

➨ **Bars** High-end or tourist-oriented bars may have a tip box on the bar; it's up to you if you want to contribute.

➨ **Chambermaids** It's usual to leave TT$100 or so at the end of a stay.

➨ **Grocery stores** If packers bag up your shopping, wheel your trolley to your car and pack it into the vehicle for you, give a tip of TT$5 to TT$10.

➨ **Taxis** Don't tip maxi-taxi or route-taxi drivers. Tipping private taxis is not expected but will be appreciated.

PUBLIC HOLIDAYS

Carnival Monday and Tuesday are unofficial holidays, with banks and most businesses closed.

Spiritual Baptist/Shouter Liberation Day March 30

Good Friday March/April

Easter Monday March/April

Indian Arrival Day May 30

Corpus Christi Ninth Thursday after Easter

Labour Day June 19

Emancipation Day August 1

Independence Day August 31

Republic Day September 24

Divali October, dates vary

Eid ul Fitr (Muslim New Year) Dates vary

Christmas Day December 25

Boxing Day December 26

New Year's Day January 1

TAXES & REFUNDS

VAT of 12.5% is included in the prices of goods sold in shops. Hotels often don't include a 10% room tax and a 10% service charge in quoted rates; always check in advance.

TELEPHONE

The country's area code is ☑ 868. When calling from North America, dial 1-868 plus the local number. From elsewhere dial your country's international access code plus 868 plus the local number. Within the country, just dial the seven-digit local number.

To make an international call, dial the ☑ 011 international access code, followed by the country code for the place you're calling, and then the number, omitting the initial zero if there is one.

Public phones are numerous but often don't work. Your best bet is to get a local SIM card and use a cell phone.

TIME

Trinidad and Tobago is on Atlantic Standard Time (AST): four hours behind GMT/UTC in winter, five hours behind GMT/UTC in summer.

TRAVELERS WITH DISABILITIES

With tourist infrastructure already wobbly here, Trinidad and Tobago doesn't have extensive facilities for travelers with disabilities. However, the higher-end hotels and resorts are equipped to accommodate.

Towns and cities can be challenging if you use a wheelchair; dropped kerbs are rare and pavements are often nonexistent.

Download Lonely Planet's free Accessible Travel Guide from http://lptravel.to/Accessible Travel

❶ Getting There & Away

AIR

Piarco International Airport (www.tntairports. co/piarco; Golden Grove, Trinidad) in Trinidad handles the bulk of international flights; the rest fly into the much smaller **ANR Robinson International Airport** (www.tobagoairport. com; Crown Point, Tobago) in Tobago.

A number of international airlines fly to Trinidad and Tobago. Caribbean Airlines (the national carrier) and LIAT are particularly useful for flights from other Caribbean countries.

Caribbean Airlines (☑ 625-7200; www. caribbean-airlines.com) flies from Trinidad to Antigua, Barbados, Grenada, Kingston and Montego Bay in Jamaica, Nassau, St Lucia and Sint Maarten.

LIAT (☑ 1-888-895-5428; www.liat.com) flies from Trinidad to Antigua, Barbados, Curaçao, Grenada, Guyana, St Lucia and St Vincent.

SEA
Cruise Ship

In Trinidad ships dock at the King's Wharf, on ugly Wrightson Rd in Port of Spain, from where you can walk onto Independence Sq and the downtown area. In Tobago, the cruise-ship terminal is adjacent to the ferry terminal in downtown Scarborough.

Yacht

Out of the hurricane path, Trinidad and Tobago is a safe haven for yachties. Chaguaramas in Trinidad has the primary mooring and marina facilities as well as an immigration and customs office for yachties. Tobago is an upwind jaunt, but sometimes yachts moor at Charlottesville or Scarborough. For more information, contact the **Yacht Services Association of Trinidad and Tobago** (✆ 634-4938; CrewsInn Hotel & Yachting Centre, Western Main Rd, Chaguaramas).

ⓘ Getting Around

AIR

Caribbean Airlines (p792) operates the 20-minute flight between Trinidad and Tobago (one way TT$150). The checked baggage weight allowance is one piece at up to 20kg. While it's wise to book in advance, it is often possible to buy tickets at the airport on the day of departure. Note that flights are often subject to delays and cancellations.

BOAT

Fast catamaran ferries make the 2½-hour trip between Queen's Wharf in Port of Spain, Trinidad, and the main ferry dock in Scarborough, Tobago. It's a cheap, comfortable way to travel (unless you're prone to seasickness), with the added bonus of not having to get all the way to Piarco airport. The ferries have a bar, cafeteria and deck, and movies are played in the air-conditioned interior.

There are two to four departures daily from both islands, in the morning and afternoon. Tickets can be purchased from the **Inter-Island Ferry Service** (p752); do so in advance around Christmas, Easter and in Carnival season.

BUS

Buses offer travelers an inexpensive way to get around, especially on longer cross-island trips, but can be infrequent and unreliable. For shorter distances, travelers are better off taking maxi-taxis or route taxis. Check online (www.ptsc.co.tt) for schedules. For bus information, call 623-2262 in Trinidad or 639-2293 in Tobago.

CAR & MOTORCYCLE

Cars drive on the left, and the car's steering wheel is on the right (as in the UK). Your home driver's license is valid for stays of up to three months.

Twisting, narrow roads and fast, horn-happy drivers can make driving on the islands an adventure; in Port of Spain, traffic, complicated roads and poor signage can be challenging. Your best bet is to study a map before you get in the car, take a deep breath and practice Zen-like patience. You will get the hang of it, and you'll find driving much easier if you simply relax a little and follow the flow. Be aware that fellow road users (especially maxi-taxis and route taxis) will stop suddenly to drop off a friend, say 'hi' to a neighbor or pick up a cold beer. Sometimes they'll simply stop, while other times they'll wave an arm up and down to signal they are about to do something.

The ignored speed limit on highways is 80km/h, and 50km/h to 55km/h on city streets. Gas (petrol) is about TT$3.11 a liter for regular.

TAXI

Regular taxis are readily available at the airports, cruise-ship and ferry terminals and at hotels. All are unmetered but follow rates established by the government; hotel desks and airport tourist offices have a list of fares. Make sure to establish the rate before riding off, and note that fares increase after 10pm.

Maxi-Taxi

Maxi-taxis are 12- to 25-passenger minibuses that travel along a fixed route within a specific zone. They're color-coded by route, run 24 hours, are very cheap and are heavily used by locals. Rides cost TT$3 to TT$12, depending on how far you go. You can flag a maxi at any point along its route, or hop on at the appropriate taxi stand. Keep in mind that, due to their frequent stops, maxi-taxis can take a long time to get

---

PRACTICALITIES

Newspapers & Magazines There are three daily newspapers: *Trinidad Express*, *Newsday* and *Trinidad Guardian*.

TV & Radio There are three local TV stations: TV6 (channel 5), CVM (channel 6) and Gayelle (channel 7), the latter broadcasting only local programming.

Smoking It's illegal to smoke in enclosed public spaces.

Weights & Measures Trinidad and Tobago uses the metric system. Highway signs and car odometers are in kilometers, but some road markers still measure miles.

from A to B, though in Trinidad maxis that take the Priority Bus Route can be pretty speedy

On Trinidad, many maxi-taxis operate out of the maxi-taxi terminal adjacent to City Gate. On Tobago, all maxis have a blue band.

For information about maxi-taxi routes, contact **Trinidad & Tobago Unified Maxi Taxi Association** (☑ 624-3505)

Route Taxi

Route taxis are shared cars that travel along a prescribed route and can drop you anywhere along the way. They look like regular cars, except that their license plates usually start with an 'H' (for 'hire'). They run shorter set routes than maxis, mostly within towns and cities; fares start at TT$5.

Turks & Caicos

POP 51,430 / 649

Best Places to Eat

➡ Coyaba (p803)

➡ Grace's Cottage (p804)

➡ Coco Bistro (p804)

➡ Osprey (p810)

Best Places to Sleep

➡ Blue Horizon Resort (p807)

➡ Parrot Cay (p805)

➡ Island House (p810)

➡ Sibonné Beach Hotel (p801)

Why Go?

The Turks & Caicos Islands (TCI), hiding at the southern tip of the Bahamian Archipelago, elude most travelers' radars. Yet this sparsely populated string of low sand cays boasts some of the world's most spectacular coral reefs, and has built itself into a true luxury-tourism destination. The pace of life is easygoing, the local welcome genuine and the diving truly out of this world.

Providenciales is the bustling epicenter of all this, but beyond its endless beaches and world-class resorts, you'll find local festivals, jungle-wrapped ruins, perfect seaside bars and even traces of Europe's first discovery of the New World.

Venture to the less populated islands, and you'll be enchanted by colorful postcards of fading colonial glories, gobsmacked by the annual migration of thousands of humpback whales, spoiled with your pick of deserted beaches and all but forced to abandon the pace of modern life.

When to Go

Dec–Apr High season in TCI, with warm, dry and settled weather coinciding with the annual humpback migration. Accommodations are at their most expensive, especially over the winter holidays.

Mar–early Apr Major US holidays, such as spring break for college students, are generally the busiest times in the islands.

Jun–Nov Hurricane season with the severest storms typically threatening from August to October. Some tourist businesses may close for a number of weeks during this period, although those that remain open offer significantly cheaper accommodations.

Turks & Caicos Highlights

1 **Grace Bay Beach**
(p797) Counting the luxury resorts fronting this legendary stretch of icing-sugar sand.

2 **Grand Turk** (p808)
Meandering through the salt-gritted streets of the islands' colonial heyday.

3 **Iguana Island** (p805)
Getting up close to the largest thriving population of the Turks and Caicos rock iguana, on Little Water Cay.

4 **Whale watching** (p815)
Gasping at one of the world's great cetacean extravaganzas from the comfort of a beachfront bar.

5 **Mudjin Harbor** (p807)
Feeling the might of the Atlantic batter the reef wall, just offshore from this stunning Middle Caicos beach.

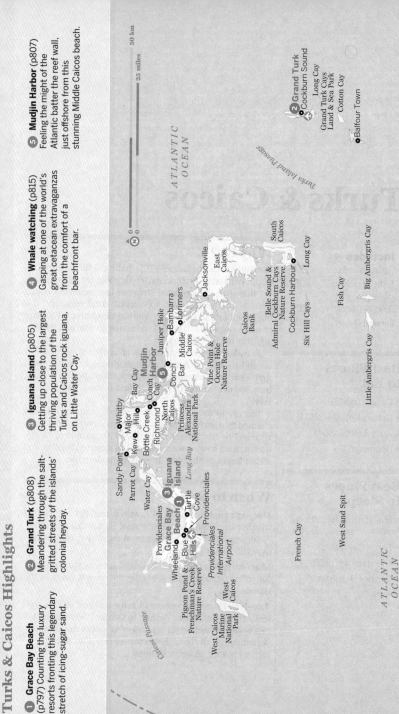

CAICOS ISLANDS

The fan of islands that forms the main landmass of this nation are the Caicos Islands, which range from the nearly uninhabited East Caicos to the condo-sprouting Providenciales.

ℹ Getting There & Away

Providenciales International Airport (☑946-4420; www.provoairport.com) The main point of entry for the Caicos Islands and the entire country. For those arriving by boat, six of TCI's seven ports of entry are in the Caicos Islands: five on Provo, and one on South Caicos.

ℹ Getting Around

From Provo there are daily connecting flights to **South Caicos Airport** (☑946-4255), but no regular, scheduled flights to North and Middle Caicos. You're now reliant on the ferry, a tour or private charter to reach these islands, although once on North Caicos you can drive to Middle Caicos across a 1-mile causeway, built in 2007, almost immediately damaged by Hurricane Hanna, then repaired in 2014 and 2015.

The passenger-only **TCI Ferry** (☑946-5406; http://tciferry.tciferry.com) runs between **Walkin Marina** (☑946-4411; Heaving Down Rock, off Leeward Hwy), Heaving Down Rock, on the leeward (west) side of Providenciales to **Sandy Point Marina** on North Caicos. There are five services a day, Monday to Saturday, and three on Sundays and public holidays; the 30-minute journey costs US$50 return for adults, and US$30 for children. The TCI Ferry to South Caicos runs to the government dock two to three times a week. It takes 90 minutes and costs US$99/70 return for adults/children.

Providenciales

Providenciales, or Provo as it's known locally, is the commercial and touristic capital of Turks and Caicos. By far the busiest and most populated of the islands, it's home to the country's major international airport and some fairly rampant development, from stunning all-inclusive resorts to the concrete shells of ill-considered ventures that never got off the ground. Its greatest attractions are miles of beautiful white-sand beaches, and the halo of reef that blooms in every direction.

Everything is modern and commercial because it's mostly new. There's no old town – just a few decades ago, this was all salt flats.

◉ Sights

Grace Bay Beach　　　　　　　　BEACH
Several miles long (the frequently boasted '12 miles' only applies if you measure the entire northern coast of Provo, which is, admittedly, one unbroken beach), this world-famous stretch of coast is powdered with white sand and close enough to the reef wall to see the Atlantic breakers. Though it's studded with hotels and resorts, its sheer size means that finding your own square of paradise is a snap.

Caicos Conch Farm　　　　　　　FARM
(☑946-5330; www.caicosconchfarm.net; off Leeward Hwy; adult/child US$12/8; ⊙9am-4pm Mon-Fri, to 2:30pm Sat; P🚻) The Caribbean Queen Conch, on menus throughout not only TCI but the whole Bahamian Archipelago, is cultivated here, purportedly the world's only commercial conch farm. An interesting 30-minute tour takes you from the egg and larval stages through to maturity and harvest. It's located at the northeast extremity of Provo.

Long Bay Beach　　　　　　　　BEACH
This windy, less frequented beach on Provo's southern shore is ideal for kitesurfing.

Cheshire Hall　　　　　　　PLANTATION
(☑941-5710; Leeward Hwy; entry & tour US$10; ⊙8:30am-4:30pm Mon-Fri; 🚻) Built in the late 1700s by a British Loyalist planter displaced by the American Revolution, Cheshire Hall was once the most important site on Provo, the hub of a 5000-acre cotton plantation. Now run by the National Trust, the remaining 15 or so buildings (including the Great House and kitchen) aren't in the best state of repair. Admission includes a 30-minute tour (8:30am to 11:30am and 2:30pm to 4pm) and there's a reproduction slave hut to poke around in.

Chalk Sound National Park　　NATIONAL PARK
Chalk Sound sums up Provo: a startlingly turquoise 5km lagoon studded with tiny cays sheltering Turks and Caicos rock iguanas, but marred by less-than-scenic development. It can be a delightful place to kayak (no powered craft are allowed) in the company of bonefish, barracuda, rays and lemon sharks, but isn't easy to access, as there are no launching places.

Sapodilla Hill　　　　　　　HISTORIC SITE
TCI's long maritime history is etched into the limestone on Sapodilla Hill, where mariners have commemorated landfall by carving names, dates and pictures into the rock

TURKS & CAICOS PROVIDENCIALES

Providenciales

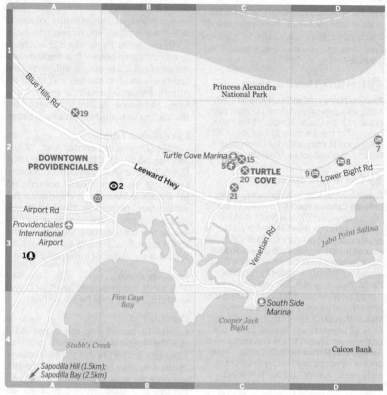

since the 1650s. Molds of the inscriptions can be seen at Provo Airport, if you don't fancy the short (but steep and usually hot) climb to see the originals.

🏃 Activities

Potcake Place VOLUNTEERING
(☑231-1010; www.potcakeplace.com; Salt Mills Plaza, off Grace Bay Rd; ⊙10am-1pm & 2-4pm Mon-Sat; 🐾) This unique charity cares for Provo's many ownerless dogs (named 'potcakes' for the practice of feeding them with the crust at the bottom of the rice pot). Visitors can help out, donate, take puppies for socialization walks on the beach (10am Monday to Saturday), and even adopt dogs they take a particular shine to.

Caicos Cyclery CYCLING
(☑941-7544, 431-6890; www.caicoscyclery.com; Salt Mills Plaza, Grace Bay Rd; ⊙10am-6pm Oct-Aug, vary Sep) The place to go if you want to

pedal around Grace Bay on something better than a clunky cruiser. Caicos Cyclery has high-quality road bikes, mountain bikes and hybrids, ideal if you want to take a bike over to North and Middle Caicos for some traffic-free touring. Cruisers/road bikes are US$20/60 per day, with discounts for three or more days. Bikes can be returned to the adjoining Big Al's Island Grill (p803) if the shop is closed.

Sky Pilot Parasail ADVENTURE SPORTS
(☑333-3000; http://skypilotparasailing.com; ⊙9am-5pm) For US$85 per person (or US$65 for direct bookings, from 9am to 10am and 4pm to 5pm) this outfit will pick you up from your Provo hotel, strap you into a tandem parasail and drag you into the skies above Grace Bay at high speed. Fun.

Diving & Snorkeling

All the dive operators offer a range of dive and snorkel options, from introductory

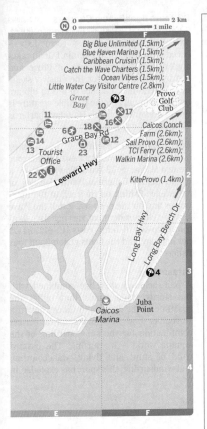

Providenciales

'discovery' or 'resort' courses to Professional Association of Diving Instructors (PADI) certification (US$300 to US$800).

Most offer free hotel pickup and drop-offs. Dive sites include **Grace Bay**, **Pine Cay** and the famous, precipitous drop-off at **Northwest Point**. The reefs of North, Middle and West Caicos are also within striking distance, although you'll need a private charter to reach the stunning sites around South Caicos.

★ **Big Blue Unlimited** WATER SPORTS
(☑946-5034; http://bigblueunlimited.com; Leeward Marina; ☺7:30am-5:30pm; ♠) Living by a sincere, ecofriendly ethos that's refreshing to see in TCI, Big Blue does it all: stand-up paddleboarding, kayaking, diving (two tanks US$195), snorkeling, kiteboarding (lessons US$150 per hour), cultural and historic tours to North and Middle Caicos, and whale-watching in season. The staff is excellent, their equipment and knowledge

top-notch and, overall, you couldn't be in better hands.

Dive Provo DIVING
(☑946-5040; www.diveprovo.com; Ports of Call Plaza, Grace Bay Rd) Has two-tank/night dives (US$156/95) at sites around the island, plus GoPro and camera rental.

Provo Turtle Divers
DIVING

(946-4232; www.provoturtledivers.com; Turtle Cove Landing; 2-tank dive US$143; 8am-5pm Mon-Sat) Going strong since the 1980s, this respected outfit offers two-tank and night dives, plus PADI courses from US$450.

Fishing

The waters around Provo are noted game-fishing territory, with the 2000m deep just 15 minutes from shore promising tuna, wahoo, dorado and even sailfish and marlin. Bonefishing among the mangroves is another popular pastime for anglers in TCI. Boat charters and trips can be arranged from Leeward and Turtle Cove Marinas.

Grand Slam Charters
FISHING

(231-4420; http://gsfishing.com; Lower Bight Rd, Turtle Cove) Offers the biggest charter boat in Turks and Caicos for some serious deep-sea fishing, and can arrange accommodations in a lovely penthouse on Grace Bay Beach.

Bite Me Sportfishing
FISHING

(231-0366; www.turks-caicos-fishing.com; Turtle Cove Marina) Operating an 11m boat with top-notch equipment and room for 10 passengers, Bite Me can take you to where the big ones (wahoo, mahi-mahi, tuna, dorado, marlin and more) lurk.

DB Tours Bonefishing Charters
FISHING

(242-4327; www.turksandcaicosbonefishing. com; departures 7:30am & noon) Experienced local fisherman Captain Darrin takes anglers into the mangroves of Provo and nearby cays to hunt for the elusive, skeletally blessed fish. Catches of 4lb to 8lb are not uncommon, and the inedible creature is released after its ordeal. Half-day charter is US$560, full-day US$952.

Catch the Wave Charters
FISHING

(941-3047; www.catchthewavecharter.com; Leeward Marina; 7:30am-5:30pm) Run by a North Caicos fisherman with decades of experience fishing on the reef, in the mangroves and on the deep sea, Catch the Wave has five charter boats of varying sizes. Bottom/deep-sea fishing costs US$1275/1475 per half-day, and the boats generally fit four fishers.

Kitesurfing

A reef-sheltered shoreline combined with the steady trade winds that buffet the coastline of the Turks and Caicos between November and May make for a perfect combination for the snowboarding of the aquatic world – kitesurfing. The bastard child of stunt kite flying, wakeboarding and windsurfing, this sport has exploded in

---

OFF THE BEATEN TRACK

THE OTHER SIDE OF PROVO

Grace Bay Beach (p797) is world famous, but by no means the only sparkling stretch of sand on Provo. Long Bay Beach (p797) is as extensive (5km) and the island's premier spot for kiteboarding. Malcolm Roads, at the northwestern extremity of the island, is delightfully quiet: from the settlement of Wheeland a rough dirt road leads to this top-notch sandy spot. The south-facing Sapodilla Beach is calm, clear and a favorite yacht anchorage, while Leeward Beach, east of Grace Bay, adds limestone escarpments to the ubiquitous icing-sugar sand.

If you feel inclined to tear yourself away from the beach and see some other sights, there are a few worth taking in. A rental car that can handle a bit of dirt road is a must to check out the lighthouse at Northwest Point, 13km from Providenciales. Caution is the word as the road has been known to swallow cars whole. The same goes for the road to Chalk Sound National Park (p797).

Protecting reefs off of Provo's west shore, Northwest Point Marine National Park also encompasses several saline lakes that attract breeding and migrant waterfowl. The largest is Pigeon Pond, inland. This part of the park is the Pigeon Pond & Frenchman's Creek Nature Reserve. Other ponds – notably Northwest Point Pond and Frenchman's Creek – encompass tidal flats and mangrove swamps along the west coast, attracting fish and fowl in large numbers. You'll have to hike here, and come equipped with food and water.

The Caicos Banks on Provo's south side are the best place to see the luminous-green marine glowworms that light up the waters just after sunset, for several days after each full moon.

recent years. Imagine flying the biggest kite you've ever seen, strapping yourself onto a wakeboard and holding on for dear life: depending on how much sugar you like in your tea, you'll be either enchanted or terrified. The warm TCI waters, especially those of Long Bay on Provo's southern shore, are firmly on the radar of the sport's elite – but don't be put off, it's also a great place to learn. KiteProvo (p801) is the natural place to start.

KiteProvo
WATER SPORTS

(☑242-2927; http://kiteprovo.com; Long Bay Beach, Shore Club beach access; ☺8am-7pm) Operating on Long Bay Beach, one of the acknowledged epicenters of the sport, KiteProvo is just the outfit to teach you kitesurfing. Multilingual instructors come from all over the world to teach, and lessons are US$175 per hour, with a two-hour minimum.

Sailing & Boat Tours

In many ways a sailor's paradise, the waters around Provo can nonetheless be treacherous, with shallow channels, sand banks and coral heads to negotiate. Boats can be chartered from the Blue Haven (p817) and Turtle Cove (p817) marinas, and most will be professionally captained to ensure you don't come unstuck.

Caribbean Cruisin'
BOATING

(☑231-4191; http://caribbeancruisin.tc; Blue Haven Marina, Leeward Going Through) One of the more prominent of the many outfits doing boat excursions from Provo, Cruisin' can take you to the nearby cays or snorkeling on Emerald Reef (US$50 per person) and even arranges seaside scavenger hunts for kids (adults/kids US$115/75). Private charters, Jet Skis and tours of North and Middle Caicos are just some of its other lines.

Sail Provo
BOATING

(☑946-4783; www.sailprovo.com; Walkin Marina, Leeward Going Through; ⊞) There are many outfits and individual vessels keen to take you sailing around the island; Sail Provo is one of the better ones. Its sleek catamaran, *Arielle II*, plies the waters between Leeward Going Through, Iguana Island (and other cays) and the reef. Half-day excursions with snorkeling and lunch start at US$81 per person, and private charters at US$875.

JOJO: A NATIONAL TREASURE

Since the mid '80s, a 7ft bottle-nosed male dolphin called JoJo has cruised the waters off of Provo and North Caicos. When he first appeared, he was shy and limited his human contact to following or playing in the bow waves of boats. He soon turned gregarious, however, and has become an active participant whenever people are in the water.

JoJo is now so popular that he has been named a national treasure by the Ministry of Natural Resources. This treasure is protected through the **JoJo Dolphins Project** (☑941-5617; www.marinewildlife.org; PO Box 153).

Like any wild dolphin, JoJo interprets attempts to touch him as an aggressive act and will react to defend himself, so please bear this in mind if you're lucky enough to experience his playfulness and companionship.

Ocean Vibes
BOATING

(☑242-4444; www.oceanvibes.com; Leeward Marina) This locally owned and run operation specializes in catamaran cruises and snorkeling adventures. Chartering a 14.5m catamaran to take up to 12 people on a skippered half-day adventure costs US$1512.

Undersea Explorer
BOATING

(☑432-0006; www.caicostours.com; Turtle Cove Marina; adult/child US$70/60; ☺hourly from low tide 10am/11am to 5pm Mon-Sat; ⊞) This moving underwater observatory, a big hit with kids and those with a phobia of getting wet, is a cool way to see three different sections of the reef. Pickup/drop-off at any hotel in Grace Bay. It also does Mermaid Adventure (with a real mermaid!) for kids.

🛏 Sleeping

Most of Provo's places to stay are right on Grace Bay Beach. Your main decision is whether you want condo-style, a resort or something else.

★ Sibonné Beach Hotel
HOTEL $

(☑946-5547; www.sibonne.com; Grace Bay; r/apt from US$185/260; ❄ @ ☎ ☀) Deservedly popular and occupying a divine stretch of sand on Grace Bay, Sibonné is a real antiresort; the vibe defines mellow. The two cheapest rooms are small but the rest of the choices are roomy and comfy.

Ports of Call Resort
RESORT $$

(☑ 946-8888; www.portsofcallresort.com; Grace Bay Rd, Grace Bay; r from US$379; ✷ ⚆ ⚌) If you're searching for an affordable resort and are willing to accept that it isn't beachfront, this is a great option. Clean and spacious rooms stack in three stories above the pool and chilled poolside bar. Nothing too special, but if you're here to dive, lie on the beach or not liquidate your finances, this is the place to stay.

Turtle Cove Inn
INN $$

(☑ 946-4203; www.turtlecoveinn.com; Turtle Cove Marina; r from US$219; ✷ ⚆ ⚌) This older property in the heart of the Turtle Cove Marina is the perfect budget choice on an island where the concept is pretty much unknown. Rooms are good sized and some have nice views of the boats. The grounds are a bit ragged.

★ Gansevoort Turks & Caicos
RESORT $$$

(☑ 941-7555; www.gansevoorthotelgroup.com; Lower Bight Rd, Grace Bay Beach; r from US$910; P ✷ ⚆ ⚌) One of the newest, slickest resorts along Grace Bay Beach, the Gansevoort brings the clean lines and minimalist chic of a big-city boutique to Provo. Its centerpiece is a vast palm-fringed infinity pool, while the rooms boast top-quality beds, 400-thread-count bedding and all the conveniences of life. The on-site restaurant, Stelle, is one of the best on the island.

Point Grace
BOUTIQUE HOTEL $$$

(☑ 941-7743; http://pointgrace.com; off Grace Bay Rd, Point Grace; ste from US$720; P ✷ ⚆ ⚌) The 28 suites and penthouses at this tasteful beachfront hotel are sophisticated and luxurious, creating a retro fantasy of the colonial-era British estate (with far better plumbing). Units come in all sizes, amenities include a pool and thalassotherapy spa, and the sweet on-site restaurant, Grace's Cottage (p804), is a wonderful place to wine and dine.

Beaches
RESORT $$$

(☑ 1-888-242-2437; www.beaches.com; Lower Bight Rd; d from US$1900; P ⚆ ⚌) This all-inclusive behemoth is a world unto itself, with four distinct 'villages' (the Caribbean, France, Italy and Key West), eight pools, a water park, 15 bars and 19 restaurants. Every conceivable diversion is available – diving, lawn chess, kids camp, even a DJ academy – making it ideal for a self-contained family vacation.

Day passes are available to those who'd like to sample Beaches' myriad luxuries. A 10am to 6pm pass costs US$520 for adults and US$180 for children.

Coral Gardens
RESORT $$$

(☑ 941-3713; www.coralgardens.com; Penns Rd, off Leeward Hwy; r from US$349; ✷ ⚆ ⚌) In the quieter environs of the Bight Settlement, on a sweep of Grace Bay protected by Princess Alexandra National Park, you'll find one of Provo's more understated and less costly resorts. It doesn't offer the range of activities that the biggest places do, but does offer diving, gym, cycling, fitness, free massages, clean-lined design and comfortable rooms.

Ocean Club West
RESORT $$$

(☑ 946-5880; www.oceanclubresorts.com; 54 Bonaventure Cres, Grace Bay Beach; r from US$500; P ✷ ⚆ ⚌) With a great location in the heart of Grace Bay, the OCW is a safe bet. The wonderful pool is complete with an arch-bridge-appointed 'river' and the requisite swim-up bar. Rooms are a bit cramped, compared to some of the palatial digs on Grace Bay, but the kitchenettes and balconies more than make up for it.

The Sands at Grace Bay
RESORT $$$

(☑ 946-5199; www.thesandstc.com; Grace Bay Rd; r from US$330; ✷ ⚆ ⚌) This mammoth place is a great family option with a kiddy pool, and kitchenettes in every room. The 118 suites cluster around the superb pool area or face onto the beach where there are tiki huts and the excellent Hemingway's Bar and Grill.

✕ Eating

Greenbean Cafe
CAFE $

(cnr Bridge & Lower Bight Rds, Turtle Cove; mains US$11-16; ⊙ 7am-6pm Sun-Wed, to 10pm Thu-Sat; ⚆ ⚋) ✐ This excellent initiative pairs healthy eating with environmental awareness and is leading where hopefully others will follow, using organic produce, compostable packaging and, where possible, locally sourced ingredients. Try its excellent salads and food bowls, get a fresh smoothie or panini to go, or just chill out with a range of tea and coffee.

★ Da Conch Shack
BAHAMIAN $$

(☑ 946-8877; www.daconchshack.com; Blue Hills Rd; mains US$16-20; ⊙ 11am-9pm; ⚆) The quintessential Provo beach bar, Da Conch Shack is a cluster of clapboard huts and sturdier concrete buildings spreading out over the sand at Blue Hills, northwest of downtown. The cracked conch is the best we've tasted, ditto the rum punch, and there's a beach party with live music (reggae, rake'n'scrape) from 7pm on Wednesdays and 1pm on Sundays.

Mr Grouper's   SEAFOOD $$

(☑242-6780; Lower Bight Rd, Diamond Stubbs Plaza; mains US$17-24; ⊙11am-10pm) Aside from American standbys such as breaded shrimp and seafood chowder, Mr Grouper's is all about the local *fruits de mer*: lobster (in season), blackened mahi-mahi, conch in every conceivable way, and the restaurant's namesake fish, either grilled whole or its meaty fillets fried to crispy perfection. Painted a suitable aquamarine, it's popular enough to have birthed a second outlet, near the airport.

Somewhere   TEX-MEX $$

(☑941-8260; http://somewherecafeandlounge. com; Leeward Hwy, Coral Gardens Resort; mains US$20-24; ⊙8am-10pm, from noon late Sep–late Nov; 🐾🏧) This laid-back beach bar and restaurant is the ideal reward for a walk on Grace Bay's endless sands. Two stylish levels are wide open to the water, with cooling breezes and live music on tap. The Tex-Mex-centric menu encompasses breakfasts such as huevos rancheros and chorizo tacos, and all-day fare such as the day's catch in tangy Veracruzano style.

Le Bouchon du Village   FRENCH $$

(☑946-5234; Regent Village Plaza, Grace Bay Rd; mains US$28-32; 🐾) It's a long way from Lyon, but this excellent little French bistro is in a village of sorts – the Regent Village retail plaza. The tropical weather may dissuade you from trying otherwise-delicious renditions of country favorites such as duck confit, but the chef's also a dab hand with the local seafood: tuna, scallops, grouper and lobster (in season).

Fresh Catch Local Bites   BAHAMIAN $$

(☑243-3167; Salt Mills Plaza, Grace Bay Rd; mains US$22-26; ⊙8am-10pm Mon-Sat; 🍴🏧) Fresh Catch has a few facets that distinguish it from Provo's many other TCI/Bahamian joints: it has a separate vegetarian menu, offers all-you-can-eat seafood (including lobster, in season) on Wednesdays, and serves 'native' breakfasts such as chicken souse

with johnnycake (stewed chicken with bay, allspice, lime and chili and served with pan-baked bread).

Yoshi's   JAPANESE $$

(☑941-3374; http://yoshissushi.net; Saltmills Plaza, Grace Bay Rd; mains US$20-36; ⊙noon-3pm & 6-10pm Mon-Sat) A favorite with Provo locals, Yoshi's sushi and grill can be a welcome respite from rice and peas. Local ingredients such as conch and lobster are put to good use (maybe as citrus-martini ceviche, or grilled and served with tangy 'Yoshi sauce') and the steaming bowls of ramen can be just the ticket after a day on the reef.

Baci Ristorante   ITALIAN $$

(☑941-3044; Harbour Towne Plaza, Turtle Cove; mains US$23-29; ⊙noon-2pm Mon-Fri, 6-10pm Mon-Sat) Wrought-iron gating encloses a breezy tiled patio at this favorite trattoria in Turtle Cove. The brick-oven pizzas are a mix-and-match affair in which you build your own from the list of imported ingredients, while the dinner menu expands to include Italian classics such as *vitello al limone* (veal in lemon sauce) and *insalata caprese* (tomato and mozzarella salad).

Big Al's Island Grill   DINER $$

(☑941-3797; http://bigalsislandgrill.com; Grace Bay Rd, Salt Mills Plaza; mains US$14-26; ⊙7am-10pm; 🐾🏧) This relaxed diner serves up American favorites such as hamburgers, plus pasta and a short vegan/veggie menu.

Tiki Hut   INTERNATIONAL $$

(☑941-5341; http://tikihut.tc; Turtle Cove Marina, Lower Bight Rd; mains US$20-22; ⊙11am-10pm Mon-Fri, 9am-10pm Sat & Sun; 🐾🏧) Back at its original home, the Turtle Cove Inn, this is a popular spot where you can sit on the broad deck under hissing palms, nursing a cold beer and watching the boats come in. You can also grab a cheap burgers (US$15) or something more substantial – perhaps grilled catch of the day or jerk chicken.

★Coyaba   FUSION $$$

(☑946-5186; www.coyabarestaurant.com; Caribbean Paradise Inn, off Grace Bay Rd; mains US$40-46; ⊙6-10pm Wed-Mon Nov-Aug) Coyaba ('heavenly' in Arawak) is a happy marriage of European technique and Caribbean flavors and ingredients. Alongside a diverse array of weekly specials (perhaps based around lobster in season) you'll find menu staples such as braised 'osso buccolettes' with jerk jus and apple and cinnamon relish, and wahoo, chargrilled with ackee, callaloo and shrimp.

★ **Grace's Cottage** INTERNATIONAL **$$$**
(☑946-5096; http://pointgrace.com; Point Grace Resort, off Grace Bay Rd; mains US$38-42; ☺6-10:30pm Fri-Wed; ☑) Tucked out of the way from the main road, this 'gingerbread' cottage has tables spread out under trees and in romantic hidden enclaves. Crisp white-linen tablecloths and smart service complement a globe-trotting menu featuring inventive seafood dishes, pasta and good vegetarian options such as *gado gado* and quinoa salad. There's also a superb wine list. Reservations are usually essential.

Coco Bistro INTERNATIONAL **$$$**
(☑946-5369; www.cocobistro.tc; Grace Bay Rd; mains US$39-43; ☺5:30-10pm Tue-Sun; P☎) Spreading out beneath the coconut palms surrounding an aggressively orange two-story house is this fine diner, one of Provo's best. A veritable army of waiters flutters from table to table, ferrying ravioli stuffed with conch and roast peppers, local lobster grilled with garlic butter and a much-lauded coconut pie to tables of well-heeled vacationers.

Magnolia Restaurant & Wine Bar INTERNATIONAL **$$$**
(☑941-5108; www.magnoliaprovo.com; 76 Sunburst Rd, Turtle Cove; mains US$27-34; ☺5:30-8:30pm Tue-Sun; ☎) Sitting on the hill overlooking Turtle Cove, Magnolia is a great place for a romantic meal, with superb cooking and an equally lovely view over the lights of the cove. The fairy-light-rimmed balcony is the perfect setting for the signature dish, a cracked-pepper and sesame-crusted rare-seared tuna, which is so tender it melts in your mouth.

Crackpot Kitchen BAHAMIAN **$$$**
(☑245-0005; www.crackpotkitchen.com; Ports of Call Plaza; mains US$30-36; ☺5-11pm Fri-Wed Nov-Aug) Run by perhaps TCI's only celebrity chef (Nikita O'Neil, who fronts the *Crackpot Kitchen Cooking Show*), this is one of the best places to try traditional island food. Conch fritters, curry goat and blackened mahi-mahi don't get much better than this, and European-inflected dishes such as Cornish game hen in beer jerk sauce are excellent too.

Mango Reef INTERNATIONAL **$$$**
(☑946-8200; http://mangoreef.com; Turtle Cove Marina, Lower Bight Rd; mains US$32-38; ☺9am-11pm Mon-Fri, to 9pm Sat & Sun; ☎) A relocation from Grace Bay to the ever-developing Turtle Cay Marina means you can tie up your boat right under the tiki lights and palm-decked terrace of this streamlined modern eatery. Once ashore, enjoy snapper grilled with garlic, basil and lemon, chargrilled T-bone with peppercorn sauce, or a kaffir-lime-spiked lobster curry.

🍷 Drinking & Nightlife

Danny Buoy's PUB
(☑946-5921; next to Salt Mills Plaza, Grace Bay Rd; ☺11am-2am; ☎) A sprawling roadside terrace, tables thronged with happy imbibers, invites the thirsty into this rambunctious island institution. There's a menu littered with delicious, calorific bar food (eg battered shrimp with popcorn and smoked jalapeño mayo) and raucous entertainment Tuesday through Saturday nights (karaoke Thursdays get particularly hyped once the crowd from the Fish Fry pours in).

🔒 Shopping

Graceway Gourmet FOOD & DRINKS
(☑941-5000; www.gracewaysupermarkets.com; Allegro Rd, Grace Bay; ☺7am-9pm) The fanciest supermarket in Provo, Graceway may be eye-wateringly expensive, but its selection of fresh fruit and vegetables can't be beaten anywhere else in the country. A good option is to put together your own fresh salad (US$20 per pound) and eat it at the cafe tables out front.

FOTTAC FOOD & DRINKS
(Flavors of the Turks and Caicos; ☑946-4081; Regent Village Plaza, Grace Bay Rd; ☺10am-6pm Mon-Sat) Alongside the salts, spices and sauces on display at this high-end local grocer, you'll find noncomestibles such as soaps and locally made clothing, jewellery and handicrafts. Perhaps the most prominent line is Bambarra rum: you can taste different versions, or buy rumcake made from the locally distilled spirit.

Mama's Gift Shop GIFTS & SOUVENIRS
(☑946-5538; Ports of Call Plaza, Grace Bay Rd; ☺10am-6pm Mon-Sat, 11am-3pm Sun) The longest-standing gift shop in the Ports of Call Plaza, and perhaps on Provo, Mama's has been run by Eleana Patrick since 1995.

It's packed with souvenirs and beachwear, much of it locally made.

❶ Information

Police Station (☎ 941-5891, emergency 911; Salt Mills Plaza, Grace Bay Rd)

Post Office (☎ 946-4676; Town Centre Mall, Old Airport Rd; ⊙ 8am-4pm Mon-Thu, to 3:30pm Fri)

Turks & Caicos Tourism (☎ 946-4970; www. turksandcaicostourism.com; Stubbs Diamond Plaza; ⊙ 9am-5pm Mon-Fri)

❶ Getting There & Around

There is no bus service from **Providenciales International Airport** (p797). A taxi from the airport to Grace Bay costs US$25 for two people. Some resorts arrange transfers.

BICYCLE

Both **Scooter Bob's** (☎ 946-4684; www. scooterbobstci.com; Turtle Cove Marina Plaza; ⊙ 8am-5pm Mon-Sat, to noon Sun) and **Caicos Cyclery** (p798) rent out bikes from US$15 per day.

CAR & MOTORCYCLE

There are a number of rental agencies on the island, with **Hertz** (☎ 654-3131; www.hertztci. com; Providenciales International Airport; ⊙ 8am-5pm) and **Budget** (☎ 946-4079; www. budget.com; Providenciales International Airport; ⊙ 10am-11pm) both represented at the airport. If you'd prefer a local company, try

Rent-a-Buggy (☎ 946-4158; www.rentabuggy. tc; 1081 Leeward Hwy; ⊙ 8am-5pm Mon-Sat, 9am-3pm Sun), **Paradise Scooters** (☎ 333-3333; http://paradisescooters.tc; Grace Bay Plaza, Grace Bay Rd; ⊙ 9am-5pm) or **Scooter Bob's** (p805).

TAXI

Taxis are a popular way of getting around the island. Most are vans; although unmetered, the pricing is consistent. It's best not to be in a hurry as they often take forever to come pick you up. Your hotel can arrange a taxi for you and they meet all flights at the airport. **Nell's** (☎ 941-3228) and **Provo Taxi & Bus Group** (☎ 946-5481) are reliable.

Unlicensed taxis called jitneys roam the island looking for fares. Usually old cars driven by Haitians, they tout for business with short beeps of the horn: acknowledge them when they toot, and agree a fare up front (US$10 should be the most you'll pay to reach any part of the island).

North Caicos

Despite its proximity to the wealth and flashy resorts of Provo, North Caicos feels a decade or two behind its neighbor, and is definitely more relaxing. Tiny settlements dot the northern and eastern parts of the island, while the south fractures into a maze of mangroves and shallow waterways. Inland lie historic plantation ruins,

---

THE CAYS

The smaller islands around Providenciales are known simply as the Cays, and most of them boast superb beaches and total isolation. They are only accessible by private boat charter.

Fort George Cay is home to the remnants of an 18th-century British-built fort. Now the only invaders are divers and snorkelers there to inspect the gun emplacements slowly becoming one with the sea bottom.

Little Water Cay is famous for its population of Turks and Caicos rock iguanas, which used to be common on the islands, but now thrive only here, thanks to conservation initiatives. Admission to the nature reserve on 'Iguana Island' is charged at the **visitor centre** (☎ 941-5710; Half Moon Bay US$5, guided tour US$10, trail access US$15). Visitors must stay on the boardwalks and refrain from touching or feeding the iguanas.

French Cay, south of Providenciales, is an old pirate hideaway now frequented by migrating birds. Just offshore the waters are teeming with stingrays. Nurse sharks gather here in summer.

Parrot Cay is home to one of the Caribbean's most luxurious and exclusive resorts, the eponymous **Parrot Cay** (☎ 946-7788; www.parrotcay.com; Parrot Cay; r/ste from US$885/2318; ❄ ☎ ☒).

There are no scheduled public services to the cays. You can only visit as part of a tour or in a privately chartered boat.

flamingo-filled waterways and small slash-and-burn farms growing corn, okra, peppers and other local staples.

◉ Sights

★ Wade's Green Plantation
PLANTATION

(☎243-6877, 232-6284; http://tcnationaltrust.org/Wades-Green-Plantation; US$10; ⊙9:30-11:30am & 2:30-4pm Mon-Fri) Granted to Loyalist Wade Stubbs by King George III in 1789 as compensation for the loss of his Florida estate, this cotton and sisal plantation struggled on until 1814, when hurricanes, boll weevils and the harsh climate led Stubbs to abandon both the estate and his slaves. Quickly claimed by dry tropical forest, it's wonderfully atmospheric and the best-preserved plantation anywhere in the Caribbean. Out-of-hours visits can be arranged (including Saturdays, but not Sundays) and tours are included. Bring insect repellent: the forest is home to clouds of small-yet-utterly-ferocious mosquitoes.

Pumpkin Bluff
BEACH

Much of North Caicos' shore is mudflats, but this beautiful spot on the northern coast has lovely fine sand, and is excellent for snorkeling. A foundered cargo ship adds to the allure.

Cottage Pond
LAKE

This tropical blue hole (43m deep), formed by karst subsidence, is fed by the tides and connects to a much larger underground chamber. While it's not visually spectacular, it's interesting and a good place to spot West Indian whistling ducks, grebes, waders and other waterbirds. Look for the unobtrusive turnoff on Sandy Point Road, about 1.2km from the T-junction with Kew Hwy.

Three Mary Cays
NATURE RESERVE

While North Caicos doesn't offer the country's best diving and snorkeling, these three protected ironshore islets are surrounded by healthy coral, and can be reached from the shore.

East Bay Islands Reserve
NATURE RESERVE

The beautiful, protected cays off North Caicos' northeast coast are a refuge for iguanas, birds and sea creatures. With sandy beaches and coral to the north, and mangroves to the south, they're delightful to explore in a kayak or boat.

🛏 Sleeping

Pelican Beach Hotel
HOTEL $$

(☎946-7112; www.pelicanbeach.tc; Whitby; d with half board US$238; ❄🤶) For those looking for a relaxed, back-to-basics place to stay, this is an excellent option. There is nothing fancy here; plain rooms without TVs sit in a row only a few feet from the beach. Take the half-board option as Chef Susie's food is excellent. Pelican Car Rentals (p807) is based here, and there are free bicycles for guests.

Hollywood Beach Suites
HOTEL $$$

(☎231-1020; www.hollywoodbeachsuites.com; Hollywood Beach Dr, Whitby; ste from US$457; P❄🤶) Four suites get prime position on an 11km beach that you'll often have to yourself. The suites have everything you need to unwind, and there are complimentary kayaks and bikes for guests. The swimming, snorkeling, diving and fishing are all fantastic too. Four-night minimum stay.

🍴 Eating

★ Silver Palm Restaurant & Bar
CARIBBEAN $$

(☎244-4186; Drake Ct, Whitby; mains US$20-25; ⊙8am-9pm Wed-Mon Nov-Jun) Lobster and conch are the specialties here – all, of course, sourced locally, and sometimes caught to order (by prior arrangement). Informal and friendly, small and intimate, it's located in an old tropical Victorian house. The homemade coconut ice cream is mandatory.

Miss B's
BAHAMIAN $$

(☎241-3939; Airport Rd, Major Hill; mains US$20-22; ⊙8am-11pm; 🤶) One of North Caicos' best, Miss B's is a restaurant with character and charm. Forego the pizza for Bahamian favorites such as conch, souse and lobster, and drop in on Saturday night if you fancy some karaoke.

ℹ Information

There's a post office in Kew.

Bottle Creek Police (☎946-7116, emergency 911; Bottle Creek)
Kew Police (☎946-7261; Kew)

ℹ Getting There & Around

TCI Ferry (p797) connects **Sandy Point Marina** (p797) on North Caicos with the Leeward Marina on Provo up to five times daily. Round-trip is US$50 for adults and US$30 for kids. Once on North Caicos you can rent a car for around US$80 per day. Try **Al's Rent-a-Car** (241-1355; www.alsrentacar.com; Major Hill Rd, Bottle Creek) or **Pelican Car Rentals** (946-7112; www.pelicanbeach.tc; Whitby).

M&M Taxi & Tours (231-6285) Can meet you at the Sandy Point marina.

Middle Caicos

If you're really looking to get away from it all, treat yourself by checking out Middle Caicos. A causeway connects North and Middle, with stunning Atlantic coastline opening up to the north of the road, and vast mangroves stretching away to the south. There are only a few tiny settlements dotted along the island; Conch Bar and Bambarra are the largest, but there isn't much to them. However, Conch Bar Caves (p807) and Bambarra Beach (p807), two of the island's more worthwhile attractions, are nearby.

There are few services to speak of on the island, save the odd seemingly abandoned gas pump (which may or may not have gas) and a few phone booths that have seen better days. The proximity to North Caicos dictates that traveling over to the neighboring island is the way to go if you want to buy groceries or head out for a meal.

⊙ Sights & Activities

Bambarra Beach   BEACH

(🖼) Bring a picnic to enjoy at the tables provided on this broad, fine-sand beach. The water is shallow a long way out, and usually calm, so it's a good choice for families. The beach is reached by a 1km track from the town of Bambarra.

Conch Bar Caves   CAVE

(247-3157; ⊙9am-3pm Mon-Fri) The largest cave system on dry land found anywhere in the Bahamian Archipelago, Conch Bar is accessible with National Trust guides charging a very steep US$20. Call for access outside normal hours.

Middle Caicos Ocean Hole   DIVE SITE

Thought to be the largest yet discovered, this 76m-deep, 600m-wide blue hole is a paradise for hammerhead sharks. Divers wishing to meet them will need to charter a flat-bottomed boat, as it's bang in the middle

DON'T MISS

MUDJIN HARBOR

One of TCI's most beautiful spots is **Mudjin Harbor**. Near Conch Bar the rocky shore rears up to form a shrub-covered escarpment above the rolling Atlantic. Walking along the clifftop you'll be surprised to see a staircase appear out of nowhere, leading into the earth. Take it down through the cave and emerge on a secluded cliff-lined beach. Looking seaward you'll be entertained by the waves crashing into the offshore rocks in spectacular fashion. If you want to explore beyond Mudjin, walk the lovely **Crossing Place Trail**.

of the shallows off Middle Caicos' southern shore.

Crossing Place Trail   HIKING

Following the historic route connecting Middle Caicos with North, this coastal trail is a fantastic way to see beautiful Mudjin Harbour, the island's dramatic Atlantic coast and the resident birdlife. Join the trail at Conch Bar or Mudjin Harbor, following the signs.

🛏 Sleeping & Eating

★**Blue Horizon Resort**   RESORT $$

(946-6141; www.bhresort.com; Mudjin Harbor; cabins from US$290; ⊙Oct-Aug; ❋🛜) This beautiful property at Mudjin Harbor boasts its own 2200ft stretch of private beach and a wonderful setting among the foliage. Bleached beach colors predominate inside five units, all equipped with basic kitchens: ask for 'Sunrise' or 'Sunset', which make the most of sensational views toward the rolling Atlantic. You'll need to self-cater to some extent, stocking up in Provo.

Dreamscape Villa   VILLA $$$

(946-7112; www.middlecaicos.com; Bambarra; per night/week from US$336/2240; ❋) This fully self-contained villa is magnificently located on a pristine section of Bambarra Beach, just a few yards from the sea. With three bedrooms, filtered water, full kitchen and everything else you'll need, all that remains is to stock up, get here and unwind. The isolation, snorkeling, fishing, birdwatching and swimming make this a wonderful family-holiday option.

Mudjin Bar and Grill   BAHAMIAN **$$**
(📞946-6141; http://bhresort.com/mudjin-bar-grill; Blue Haven Resort, Mudjin Harbour; mains US$20-22; ⏰11am-4pm Mon-Sat Oct-Aug; 📶) With peerless views over the limestone 'Dragon' to the reef wall and deep blue Atlantic beyond, the in-house restaurant for the Blue Haven Resort could rest on its laurels. However, the food – conch fritters, lobster, grilled fish, burgers and more – matches the view. Mudjin will also make you dinner by prior arrangement – perfect pretext for a sundowner on the deck.

❶ Getting There & Away

There are no direct flights or ferries to Middle Caicos, so you'll generally arrive by road from North Caicos.

Arthur's Taxi Service (📞241-0730; Conch Bar)

TURKS ISLANDS

The Turks group comprises Grand Turk and its smaller southern neighbor, Salt Cay, in addition to several tiny cays. The islands lie east of the Caicos Islands, separated by the 35km-wide Turks Island Passage.

❶ Getting There & Away

Grand Turk International Airport (📞946-2233) Has multiple daily flights to and from Providenciales.

A government ferry runs three times a week from Grand Turk to Salt Cay (round-trip US$15). Arrangements can also be made with any of the Grand Turk dive companies to take you over to Salt Cay; costs vary depending on numbers.

❶ Getting Around

BICYCLE

A few hotels on Grand Turk provide bikes for their guests as they are the perfect way to get around the tiny island. On Salt Cay, **Tradewinds Guest Suites** (p811) will get you pedaling for US$20 per day.

CAR

Car hire is very simple to arrange on both Grand Turk and Salt Cay. Expect to pay around US$70 per day. All hotels can either arrange car rental or point you in the direction of local companies.

TAXI

Taxis are an inexpensive and reliable way to get around Grand Turk. A taxi from the airport to Cockburn Town will cost you about US$10, though prices vary according to distance; the entire island can be reached from the airport for up to US$25. Be sure to settle on a price before you head out as the cabs are unmetered. Your hotel can easily sort you a cab, or call **Carl's** (📞241-8793).

Grand Turk

Happily lacking the modern development that has enveloped Provo, Grand Turk is a step back in time. At just 10.5km long, this dot amid the sea is a sparsely populated, brush-covered paradise. Cockburn Town, the main settlement, has narrow streets frequented by wild donkeys and horses. Grand Turk is the port of call for most cruises coming to the Turks and Caicos Islands, thanks to a huge facility at the island's south end. On a busy day, two ships will be in port – off-loading nearly 7000 people.

Beaches rim the land and calm blue water invites you in for a refreshing swim.

Cockburn Town

You'd be hard pressed to guess that sleepy Cockburn is the capital city of the Turks and Caicos. But what it lacks in polish and sophistication it more than makes up for in rustic charm. That charm can be seriously challenged, however, when thousands of cruise-ship passengers disembark for the day, even if most never leave the gleaming cruise-ship center in the island's south.

◉ Sights

The legacy of Grand Turk's salt-raking past survives in the salt-rotted Bermudan and Victorian architecture along Front and Duke Sts. Some are derelict (and reputedly haunted), some have been lovingly restored, several survive as inns, and some have been replaced by ugly, unfinished concrete shells, but the overall impression is of collapsing colonial charm, fringed with tropical foliage. Highlights include the **General Post Office** (📞946-1334; Front St; ⏰8am-4pm Mon-Thu, to 3:30pm Fri) and Guinep House, housing the **Turks & Caicos National Museum** (📞946-2160; www.tcmuseum.org; Front St; US$7; ⏰9am-1pm Mon-Wed, 1-5pm Thu, also open for cruise ships). To the south lies the grand 1815 home Waterloo, residence of TCI's governors.

TURKS & CAICOS GRAND TURK

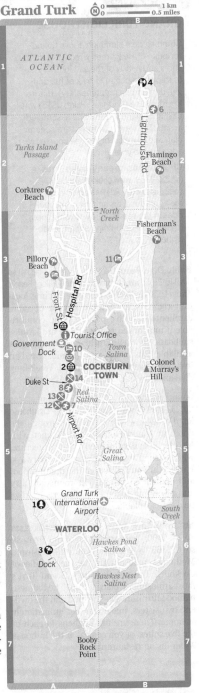

Grand Turk

🏃 Activities

⭐ Oasis Divers
WATER SPORTS

(☑946-1128; www.oasisdivers.com; Duke St; ⊙8am-4pm) Runs a huge range of diving and snorkeling tours (two tanks for US$115, night dives for US$80). Oasis also runs eco-tours to swim with the stingrays on Gibbs Cay, spot humpback whales in February and March, and other memorable activities, and has dive-and-stay-package arrangements with local hotels.

⭐ Grand Turk Diving Co
DIVING

(☑946-1559; www.gtdiving.com; Duke St; ⊙8am-4pm) Local legend Smitty runs this excellent outfit. There are two-tank dives for US$115, singles for US$80 and night dives for US$85. Full PADI courses are offered for US$450. You can also hire a bike for US$20 per day.

Screaming Reels
FISHING

(☑231-2087; www.screamingreelstours.com) Will take you out and help land the big one. Charters are based on a per-boat basis and the cost can be shared between up to eight people.

🛏 Sleeping

There are several sleeping options in both downtown Cockburn and elsewhere on the island. Everything is close enough that staying on one end of the island doesn't preclude you from enjoying the other.

TURKS & CAICOS GRAND TURK

GRAND TURK LIGHTHOUSE

Standing on a bluff high above the notorious northeast reef, wrecker of many ships and nearly of the salt industry (cargo ships began to balk at the danger, demanding greater safety), this iron **Lighthouse** (Northeast Point; US$3) was cast in England in 1852 and assembled in situ. The views out to sea are spectacular, and there's a high-rope course to add spice to your visit.

Chukka Caribbean Adventures (☑232-1339; www.chukkacaribbean. com; Lighthouse Rd) has an office near the lighthouse, organizing horseback rides in the sea, stingray-feeding trips to Gibbs Cay, zip-lining and other activities.

Bohio Dive Resort & Spa   RESORT $$
(☑946-2135; www.bohioresort.com; Pillory Beach; r from US$275; ❈☏⌘) Boasts a prime location right on a stunning stretch of sand, excellent-value dive packages and comfortable if unadorned rooms. There are kayaks, sailboats, snorkeling gear and other extras available, plus night flights, live music and an in-house restaurant, Guanahani. Week-long dive-and-stay packages start at US$2043.

Island House   GUESTHOUSE $$
(☑232-1439; www.islandhouse.tc; Lighthouse Rd; d US$244; ❈☏⌘) Walking through the doors at Island House you'll be met with Mediterranean-influenced architecture, whitewashed walls and arched doorways. Further in you'll discover the inviting pool and opulent courtyard. The rooms are airy and nicely put together, and there are dive packages available.

★Grand Turk Inn   GUESTHOUSE $$$
(☑331-9400; www.grandturkinn.com; Front St; ste US$366; ❈☏) This beautifully restored Methodist manse right in the middle of Cockburn Town is definitely Grand Turk's most atmospheric place to stay. The Balinese bamboo furniture sets the tone and the owners, two sisters, make you feel immediately at home. There are full kitchens in each of the five suites, or you can eat at the in-house Asian-fusion restaurant.

✗ Eating

Front and Duke streets boast the best and most atmospheric places to eat.

Sand Bar   PUB FOOD $
(☑243-2666; www.grandturk-mantahouse.com; Duke St; mains US$13-18; ⊙11am-1am; ☏) With a convivial open-air bar and decking stretching out over the water, the Sand Bar is justifiably the most famous and popular spot in town for an evening rum punch. The food's good too, and the whale-watching, when the humpbacks pass by close to shore in February and March, can be amazing.

★Turk's Head Inne   INTERNATIONAL $$
(☑946-1830; www.turksheadinne.com; Duke St; mains US$26-28; ⊙6-9pm Wed-Sat) The inhouse restaurant at this boutique hotel, housed in a lovely timber home dating to around 1830, is one of the best places to eat in Cockburn Town. Expect dishes such as seared tuna with ginger and soy, and lobster with heart-of-palm salad.

★Osprey   INTERNATIONAL $$
(☑946-2666; www.ospreybeachhotel.com; Duke St; mains US$18-25; ⊙7am-9pm; ☏) This terraced poolside restaurant is one of the most pleasant places to eat in Cockburn Town. There's a legendary BBQ on Wednesday and Sunday nights: amazing seafood, poultry and beef are grilled before your eyes, paired with salads and served up to a happy throng. There are great ocean views and the house band keeps the energy levels up.

🛍 Shopping

The best shopping to be found on the island is in the street stalls that open up on Duke St when the cruise ships are in port. There is a good variety of locally made goods, Haitian artwork and hand-drawn maps.

ℹ Information

Businesses and government offices close at 3pm on Friday. Some businesses open from 9am to 1pm on Saturday.

General Post Office (☑946-1334; Front St; ⊙8am-4pm Mon-Thu, to 3:30pm Fri)

Police Station (☑946-2299, emergency 911; Hospital Rd)

Tourist Office (☑946-2321; www.turksand-caicostourism.com; Front St; ⊙8am-4:30pm Mon-Fri)

ℹ️ Getting There & Away

The town center is a few kilometers north of the **Grand Turk International Airport** (p808); a taxi ride from the airport into town costs about US$10. For car rentals, try **Tony's** (☑231-1806; www.tonyscarrental.com) or **Nathan's** (☑231-4856). Ferries to Salt Cay leave from Cockburn Town's **Government Dock** (p817).

Salt Cay

If you can't quite envision what the Turks would have been like in the 19th century, take a trip to Salt Cay. It's the sort of hideaway that you search your whole life to discover. But while the land is quiet, the sea surrounding the island is awash with life: turtles, eagle rays and the majestic humpback whale all frequent the waters. Hard to get to and even harder to leave, this place is a true haven for scuba divers and for those seeking an escape from the modern world.

🏃 Activities

Thousands of North Atlantic humpback whales pass through the Columbus Passage (aka the Turks Islands Passage) every year between January and March. En route to breeding grounds in Silver and Mouchoir Banks to the south of TCI, the giants swim close enough to Salt Cay (and Grand Turk) to be spotted from the shore. Alternatively, small local boats rigged for fishing and diving will take visitors up close, to see and even swim with the whales.

Salt Cay Divers   DIVING
(☑241-1009; www.saltcaydivers.tc) Salt Cay Divers is a one-stop dive shop, offering not only diving (US$65 per tank), but accommodations and hearty meals too. The annual humpback-whale migration (February to March) is a big draw, and this operation takes pride in showing off the whales but not disturbing them (US$112 for divers, US$140 for nondivers).

🛏️ Sleeping

Tradewinds Guest Suites   RESORT $
(☑946-6906; www.tradewinds.tc; Victoria St; r from US$190; ❄️🛜) Tradewinds is a great spot to base yourself for an extended stay: there are weekly rates and the location is ideal – it's right on the beach, just a few steps from town. There are complimentary bikes and dive packages available too. The rooms are tidy, ocean-facing and good value.

COLUMBUS LANDFALL NATIONAL PARK

A scrubby patch of shorefront, most popular with mosquitoes, **Columbus Landfall National Park** commemorates Columbus' putative landing on the island in 1492. The park extends out into the water to encompass its true treasure: the reef below.

Backed by the pines and low scrub of Columbus Landfall National Park and adorned by the picturesque iron hulk of a beached ship, **Governor's Beach** is a lovely place for a quiet dip. It's also a scene of celebration, during events like October's Lobster Festival.

Pirate's Hideaway Guesthouse   GUESTHOUSE $
(☑244-1407; www.saltcayaccommodations.com; Victoria St; r from US$220; ❄️🛜♿) You can see the whales from the upstairs rooms as they pass by, or just hang out in the tropical gardens with the parrots – it is a pirate's place after all.

Castaway   VILLA
(☑946-6977; www.castawayonsaltcay.com; ste per night $349, three-night minimum; 🛜) The folks behind Porter's Island Thyme (p811), Salt Cay's most agreeable restaurant, are responsible for these four ultrarelaxing suites just inland from the island's northern shore. Each has a comfy, raised king-sized bed, a small wet area and access to communal kitchen, lounge room and terrace. They can even throw in two single beds, should you wish to bring the kids along.

🍴 Eating

Green Flash Cafe   GRILL $
(☑242-0325; Deane's Dock; mains US$15-17; ⊙7am-9pm Tue-Sun) Right off the main dock and the perfect vantage point to watch out for its namesake. Nothing pretentious here, just simple food enjoyed on picnic tables in a beautiful setting. Great burgers, conch and cold beer – what more could you want?

⭐ Porter's Island Thyme   INTERNATIONAL $$
(☑946-6977; www.islandthyme.tc; Balfour Town; mains US$28-31; ⊙8am-3pm & 6:30-10pm Mon-Sat; 🅿️♿) Comfortably the best place to eat on Salt Cay, Island Thyme exudes a sense of fun that doesn't detract from attention

to detail in the kitchen. Alongside the inevitable conch (cracked or curried), you'll find steak, pasta, lobster, tuna, snapper and more. It gets extra marks for the short, simple vegetarian menu and the open-air dining rooms overlooking the *salina* (salt-drying pan).

❶ Getting There & Away

The three little twin-propeller planes operated by **Caicos Express** (☑ 941-5730; http://caicosexpress.com) are the only ones flying regularly to Salt Cay. There are three scheduled flights per week to and from Providenciales, for US$93 per leg. There's also the thrice-weekly government ferry from Grand Turk (return US$15), but it can often be thwarted by high seas.

UNDERSTAND TURKS & CAICOS

History

Taíno History

Recent discoveries of Taíno artifacts on Grand Turk and Middle Caicos have shown that the islands originally had much the same indigenous culture as their northern neighbors. Known as the Lucayans, this branch of the Taíno people probably began arriving here around AD 750, permanently settling most islands by around 1300. Sadly, this young society soon came into contact with European rapacity. While the local claim that Columbus made his first New World landfall at Grand Turk in 1492 is unproven, what is certain is that within 30 years of that date the Lucayan civilization in these islands was gone, decimated by slavery and disease.

Salt & Cotton

The island group remained virtually uninhabited for most of the 16th and 17th centuries, passing between the nominal control of Britain, France and Spain. Permanent populations only developed from the 1670s, when Bermudian salt rakers settled the Turks Islands and used natural *salinas* (salt-drying pans, still prominent features of Grand Turk and Salt Cay) to produce sea salt. Captured by the French and Spanish in 1706, the islands were retaken by the

Bermudans soon afterwards. It was also around this time that piracy in the islands enjoyed its heyday, with famous outlaws such as Mary Read, Anne Bonny, Calico Jack Rackham, Captain Kidd and Blackbeard preying on wrecked and gold-laden shipping from the many hiding places the islands offered.

The French again took the Turks and Caicos Islands in 1783, successfully resisting the attempts of one Horatio Nelson to reclaim them for the British Crown (the Treaty of Paris, signed the same year, accomplished what he could not). British Loyalists dispossessed after American Independence were settled here, many attempting to make a go of cotton farming, until hurricanes, weevils and geopolitics wrecked their ambitions in the early 19th century.

Bermuda and the Bahamas, both British colonies, had spent much of the 18th century disputing control of the islands; in 1799 the Crown resolved the question in favor of the Bahamians. TCI enjoyed a brief period of independence from 1848 to 1873, when control passed to Jamaica, which administered the islands until 1962.

From Crown Colony to Island Paradise

Fast forward to the mid-20th century: the US military built airstrips and a submarine base in the 1950s, and astronaut John Glenn splashed down just off Grand Turk in 1962, putting the islands very briefly in the international spotlight.

Administered through Jamaica and the Bahamas in the past, Turks and Caicos became a separate Crown colony of Great Britain in 1962, then an Overseas Territory in 1981. In 1984 Club Med opened its doors on Providenciales (Provo), and the Turks and Caicos started to boom. In the blink of an eye, the islands, which had previously lacked electricity, acquired satellite TV.

The Turks and Caicos relied upon the exportation of salt, which remained the backbone of the British colony until 1964. Today finance, tourism and fishing generate most of the income, but the islands could not survive without British aid. The tax-free offshore finance industry is a mere minnow compared with that of the Bahamas, and many would be astonished to discover that Grand Turk, the much-hyped financial

THE TROUVADORE

One of the most fascinating vignettes from TCI's history is the story of the slave-ship *Trouvadore*. The slave trade had been abolished in Britain and its territories in 1807, with slavery itself fully outlawed in 1833. The *Trouvadore*, however, was Spanish. In 1841 it was carrying a cargo of up to 300 souls from the Portuguese African colony of São Tomé to the slave markets of Cuba when it ran onto the reef north of East Caicos. The crew of 20 and 192 slaves survived the wreck, and were carried to Grand Turk, where all were accommodated in the local prison.

Once a one-year 'apprenticeship' had been served in the salt works (ostensibly to pay for the cost of the rescue mission), 168 former slaves were resettled in TCI, primarily on Middle Caicos. Such an influx, equivalent to 7% of the islands' former population, represented a considerable alteration to their demographic makeup. The *Trouvadore* survivors went on to establish themselves in the islands, and many of today's Belongers can trace their ancestry to this seminal event. It's thought that the place-name Bambarra, in Middle Caicos, indicates that at least some of the settlers were of the Bambara people of modern-day Mali, Guinea, Burkina Faso and Senegal.

The 1993 discovery of letters relating to the *Trouvadore* and its settlers revived interest in the story, and a search for the wreck itself. In 2003, archaeologists found a tell-tale ballast mound off the coast of East Caicos, becoming confident with further study that they had indeed found the ill-fated slave-ship. Excavation and research continue, and can be read about at http://slaveshiptrouvadore.org.

center, is really just a dusty backwater in the sun.

British Direct Rule

Relations between islanders and British-appointed governors have been strained since 1996, when the incumbent governor's comments suggesting that government and police corruption had turned the islands into a haven for drug trafficking appeared in the *Offshore Finance Annual*, and opponents accused him of harming investment. Growing opposition threatened to spill over into civil unrest.

Things were made far worse in 2009, when the governor of the Turks and Caicos imposed direct rule on the country following a series of corruption scandals that rocked the islands in 2008. The scandals concerned huge alleged corruption on the part of the Turks and Caicos government, including the selling off of its property for personal profit, and the misuse of public funds.

The imposition of direct rule from London was attacked by members of the suspended Turks and Caicos government, who accused the UK of 'recolonizing' the country, but the general reaction across the country was a positive one, as faith in the local political system had been extremely low in the years leading up to the suspension.

In 2012 a new constitution and general elections saw the return of the Progressive National Party (PNP) to power, despite the corruption scandals of three years prior. In 2016, however, the opposition People's Democratic Movement (PDM) took power, installing the country's first female head of government.

People & Culture

The culture of the Turks and Caicos is that of a ship that is steadied by a strong religious keel. There is a very strong religious core to these islands, and the populace is friendly and welcoming, yet a bit reserved. Native Turks and Caicos islanders, or 'Belongers' as they are locally known, are descended from the early Bermudian settlers, Loyalist settlers, slave settlers and salt rakers.

There are a few expats lurking about calling the Turks home: Americans because of the proximity; Canadians because of the weather; and Brits because of the colonial heritage. Some have come to make their fortunes, some to bury their treasure like the pirates of old, and others to escape the fast-paced life that permeates much of the developed world.

PRACTICALITIES

Television Aside from cable services from neighbors (particularly the USA), TCI is served by 4NEWS and Channel 8 from Provo, and Turks and Caicos Television from Grand Turk.

Newspapers Weekly, digital and regional publications include *Turks & Caicos Weekly News* (http://tcweeklynews.com), *Caribbean News Now* (www.caribbeannewsnow.com) and TCI Enews (www.enews.tc).

Radio There are over 20 AM and FM radio stations throughout the islands, including 107.7 Radio Turks & Caicos FM, 99.9 Kiss FM and 93.9 Island FM.

Magazines Key publications covering dining, accommodations and culture are *Where When How* (www.wherewhenhow.com) and *Times of the Islands* (www.timespub.tc).

Smoking Smoking is banned in public places in Turks and Caicos, including beaches and national parks. Bars, restaurants, casinos and other liquor-licensed premises can still provide non-covered smoking areas.

Weights & Measures Imperial and metric systems are both in use.

More recently hundreds of Haitians have fled their impoverished island and landed on the Turks and Caicos Islands; for some this is only a port of call on their way to America, while others are happy to stay. Some Belongers are wary of these new immigrant communities, while some locals are sympathetic or even indifferent.

Nightlife in the Turks and Caicos is of the mellow variety for the most part. There are a few night spots in Provo, and some beachside bars on the outer islands. Those seeking a roaring party of a holiday should look elsewhere – having said that, the local rake'n'scrape music can really get the crowd going. For those not in the know, rake'n'scrape or ripsaw (as it is locally known) is a band fronted by someone playing a carpenter's saw by rhythmically scraping its teeth with the shaft of a screwdriver; sometimes other household objects are used as percussion.

The art scene in the Turks and Caicos is slowly evolving. Traditional music, folklore and sisal weaving that evolved during colonial days have been maintained to this day. Paintings depicting the scenery are popular and the quality appears to be improving. The Haitian community has had a strong influence on the Turks and Caicos art scene.

There are a few shops in Provo that have a good selection of locally produced art; unfortunately, except for a few choice locations, most of the art that's available outside Provo is tourist paraphernalia, made in China and slapped with a T&C sticker.

Landscape & Wildlife

Much of the Turks and Caicos can be described as flat, dry and barren. The salt industry of the last century saw fit to remove much of the vegetation from Salt Cay, Grand Turk and South Caicos; low-lying vegetation now covers the uninhabited sections of these islands. The larger islands are in a much more pristine state, with vegetation and a higher degree of rainfall prominent on North, Middle and East Caicos. Small creeks, inland lakes – often home to flamingos – and wetlands make up the interior of these larger land masses.

A flourishing population of bottle-nosed dolphins lives in these waters. And some 7000 North Atlantic humpback whales use the Turks Island Passage and the Mouchoir Banks, south of Grand Turk, as their winter breeding grounds between February and March. Manta rays are commonly seen during the spring plankton blooms off of Grand Turk and West Caicos.

The wetlands and inland salt waterways of TCI make it fertile ground for birdwatching, especially on the uninhabited islands. The more remote islands will naturally require effort and expense to reach, but those who do may be rewarded with sightings of ospreys, flamingos, Cuban whistling ducks and other species. The *Birding in Paradise* booklet series, covering Provo, North, Middle and South Caicos, Grand Turk and Salt Cay, is a comprehensive guide to birdwatching in the major islands.

SURVIVAL GUIDE

ℹ Directory A-Z

ACCOMMODATIONS

Accommodations in TCI are unavoidably expensive, reaching stratospheric heights at the plusher resorts. Aside from resorts, you can choose from hotels and self-contained villas/apartments. Provo in particular is ringed with resorts; we've included just those we like the best.

ACTIVITIES

TCI is an outdoorsy sort of place, and diving, snorkeling, sailing and fishing are the most popular pursuits. There's much more on offer though: kitesurfing, paddleboarding, hiking and other diversions are easy to organize.

Diving & Snorkeling

Diving highlights include Salt Cay, where you can dive with humpback whales during their annual migration; Grand Turk, with its pristine reefs and spectacular wall-diving; and even built-up Provo, where you might get the chance to share the sea with JoJo the dolphin.

In the Caicos Islands a two-tank dive typically costs around US$150 to US$200 and a half-day snorkeling trip is around US$125. Fishing can cost US$400 to US$800 per half-/full day, while windsurfing averages US$30 to US$40 per hour.

A two-tank morning dive in the Turks Islands typically costs around US$115 to US$150 and snorkeling around US$65 per half-day. Fishing is around US$300 to US$400 per half-/full day.

Fishing

Fishing is the big deal in TCI. With the islands' fringing reefs dropping away spectacularly, from around 30 to 7000 feet, the habitat of wahoo, tuna, mahi-mahi, dorado, sailfish and marlin is within easy striking distance of many of the islands. The hunt for the elusive silver bonefish among the saltwater channels of the Caicos Islands' mangroves is a local specialty. All anglers must hold a current fishing license (per day/month/year US$10/30/60), available from the marina office at **Turtle Cove** (p817).

Whale Watching

The annual migration of 2500 to 7000 Atlantic humpback whales through the Columbus Passage, the deep-water channel separating the Caicos and Turks islands, is one of the Caribbean's great sights. Moving through the channel (also known as Turks Islands Passage) between January and March, with the most reliable sightings in February and March, the mighty creatures are on their way to their breeding grounds in Silver Bank in the

Dominican Republic, and Mouchoir Bank in TCI's southern waters. Scores of local boats take visitors close to the action, and it's even possible to dive or snorkel with the whales. If you prefer terra firma, perhaps with a drink in hand, you can also watch from the shores of Grand Turk and Salt Cay, as they are close to the passage.

CHILDREN

TCI is a fantastic place to take kids. Although you may struggle to find specific programs and activities for youngsters outside major resorts, that's not such a problem when you consider the beaches, reefs, water sports and general freedom they'll enjoy. And all-inclusive megaresorts such as **Beaches** (p802) have so many diversions and activities for kids that the trick will be getting them to leave.

Kids not yet old enough to dive will be able to snorkel at reduced rates with outfits such as **Big Blue** (p799); those too young (or too timid) even for that can still come face-to-face with reef life, riding the **Undersea Explorer** (p801).

One difficulty for those with infants in strollers is the scarcity of sidewalks. Beyond Grace Bay, Turtle Cove and similarly tourist-rich areas of Provo, sidewalks don't exist, and you can be forced to walk on the shoulder of the road. The saving grace here is that, Provo excepted, traffic is negligible throughout the islands.

Dedicated changing facilities won't be found outside modern resorts and one or two restaurants and transport hubs. Prepare to improvise.

Overall, any difficulties you meet will be outweighed by the pleasures of taking kids to a warm, relaxed, beach-bedizened place where children are welcome everywhere (except perhaps the swankiest 'adult' restaurants).

ELECTRICITY

Electrical current 120V, 60Hz. Sockets are two- or three-prong US standard.

EATING PRICE RANGES

The following price indicators are based on the cost of a main dish.

$ less than US$20

$$ US$20–30

$$$ more than US$30

EMBASSIES & CONSULATES

Only Jamaica, Germany, Haiti and the US have consular representation in TCI; the UK is represented by the office of the governor, on Grand Turk. Other countries are generally represented in Nassau (the Bahamas) or Kingston (Jamaica).

EMERGENCY NUMBERS

Country Code ☑ 649

Emergency ☑ 911

FOOD

The locals might disagree, but between Bahamian and TCI food, there's precious little difference. Nearly everything bar local seafood is imported, meaning price and quality part ways (in the wrong direction) and that the catch of the day is almost always the best choice. Conch is the staple protein, and lobster (not available between April and July) the star ingredient.

GLBT TRAVELERS

As in most Caribbean destinations, the attitude toward gay and lesbian travelers in the Turks and Caicos is not progressive. While totally legal, gay sex remains a taboo subject here, particularly with reference to gay men. As more visitors arrive, and brave locals normalize identities and behaviors beyond the hetero-norm, some degree of acceptance has been forthcoming. However, there is still no openly gay scene to speak of, and GLBT travelers may decide to fly under the radar.

HEALTH

There are small hospitals on Provo and on Grand Turk, and clinics on the smaller islands. Clinics generally operate 9am to 5pm Monday to Friday, and post a number for out-of-hours emergencies.

Associated Medical Practices Clinic (☑ 946-4242; Leeward Hwy, Providenciales; ⏰ 24hr emergency) Has several private doctors. The clinic has a recompression chamber.

National Hospital (☑ 941-2900; Hospital Rd, Grand Turk)

Provo Discount Pharmacy (☑ 946-4844; Central Sq Plaza, Leeward Hwy, Providenciales; ⏰ 8am-10pm)

LEGAL MATTERS

TCI law derives largely from UK common law, with the limitations on powers of arrest and recognition of habeas corpus that entails. If you are arrested, you must be informed of the charge, can have your consular representative notified and are entitled to legal representation (at your own expense).

Recreational drugs are illegal to buy, sell or consume: any of these activities can result in fines and/or jail time. The blood-alcohol limit for drivers is 0.08, but there is little enforcement of this (consequently drunk drivers can be a real issue, especially in Provo, and especially on weekend nights).

MONEY

ATMs are found in Providenciales and Grand Turk, but are less common elsewhere. Always carry some cash – the US dollar is the official currency. Turks and Caicos crowns and quarters are issued for small change.

Exchange Rates

AUSTRALIA	A$1	$0.74
CANADA	C$1	$0.76
EUROPE	€1	$1.07
JAPAN	¥100	$0.88
NEW ZEALAND	NZ$1	$0.72
SWITZERLAND	Sfr1	$0.99
UK	UK£1	$1.26

For current exchange rates, see www.xe.com.

Tipping

Tip 15% in restaurants and for taxi drivers. However, check your bill, as many restaurants add a service charge automatically.

PUBLIC HOLIDAYS

New Year's Day January 1

Commonwealth Day Second Monday in March

Good Friday March/April

Easter Monday March/April

National Heroes' Day Last Monday in May

Her Majesty the Queen's Official Birthday June 13 (or nearest weekday)

Emancipation Day August 1

National Youth Day Last Friday in September

National Heritage Day Second Monday in October

National Day of Thanksgiving Fourth Friday in November

Christmas Day December 25 (or nearest weekday)

Boxing Day December 26 (or nearest weekday)

TAXES & REFUNDS
All services incur a nonrefundable 12% tax.

TELEPHONE
The country code ☑ 649 isn't required for inter-island calls within TCI.

TIME
TCI is on permanent Eastern Daylight Time (GMT/UTC−4).

TRAVELERS WITH DISABILITIES
Little is done in TCI to make public spaces more accessible to those with disabilities, and there are no support or advocacy organizations. Individual hotels and resorts, especially the larger and pricier ones, should have accessibility provisions, but it's important to inquire before booking.

ℹ Getting There & Away

AIR
While there are two other nominally international airports in TCI, you will certainly come through Providenciales International Airport (PLS). From there you can fly to the UK, US, Canada, the Bahamas, Antigua, Cuba, Jamaica, the Dominican Republic, Haiti and Puerto Rico. To get to elsewhere in the region, you'll have to transit, most probably through Miami or possibly Fort Lauderdale.

SEA
While there are no international ferry services between TCI and neighboring islands, it is possible to arrive by private or chartered boat, and on the cruise ships that call regularly at Grand Turk.

Private boaters must clear customs and immigration within 24 hours of arrival, and should arrange this by contacting their chosen port of entry before arrival. Ports of entry to TCI are the **Blue Haven** (☑ 946-9910; www.bluehaventci.com; Leeward Marina) (leeward), **Turtle Cove** (☑ 941-3781; www.tcmarina.com), **South Side** (☑ 231-4747; http://southsidemarina-tci.com) and **Caicos** (☑ 946-5600; www.caicosmarina.com; 1 Long Bay Hwy, Long Bay) marinas, plus **Sapodilla Bay** (all on Providenciales) and the government docks on **South Caicos** (p797) and **Grand Turk**.

If arranging clearance yourself, contact TCI Customs and Immigration (☑ 338-5493 in Provo; ☑ 946-1176 in Grand Turk; ☑ 946-3214

in South Caicos) and a customs officer will visit, between 8am and 4pm from Monday to Friday (extra charges apply on weekends and public holidays). Until pratique is granted, vessels must fly the yellow Q flag and only the captain may come ashore.

Clearance costs US$50 and a cruising permit (US$300, valid for 90 days) is required for stays of more than seven days.

ℹ Getting Around

AIR
Air is the quickest and most convenient way to get from Provo to Grand Turk and all islands further than North and Middle Caicos. TCI's main carrier is **interCaribbean** (☑ 946-4999; http://intercaribbean.com).

BOAT
TCI Ferry Service (p797), which has supplanted the regular short-trip planes to North and Middle Caicos, has two routes:
➜ **Providenciales to North Caicos** Several times daily (adult/child return US$50/30, 30 minutes)
➜ **Providenciales to South Caicos** Three times weekly (adult/child US$99/70, 90 minutes)

CAR & MOTORCYCLE
Driving is on the left-hand side. The lack of public transport means car and motorcycle hire is a common option for visitors. Provo (and to a lesser extent, North Caicos and Grand Turk) has offices for many international car-rental chains, and smaller operations are easy to engage at airports and other major ports of entry. Grand Turk and Salt Cay can be comfortably explored on ubiquitous golf carts, which rent for around US$50 per day

To rent a car, you need to be 25 or above, and hold a currently valid license. An International Driver Permit (IDP) is only required if your license is in a language other than English. The age limit is only 18 for scooters.

TAXI
Taxis are available on all the inhabited islands. Cabs are unmetered and pricing is set (but not cheap); confirm the price before setting out. Prices from the airport to the major resorts on Providenciales are advertised on the wall outside the airport taxi rank (a little beyond the international-departures door); if you don't care to check, it should be somewhere around US$25−40.

US Virgin Islands

POP 106,400 / 📞 340

Best Places to Eat

➡ Balter (p838)

➡ Daylight Bakery & Diamond Barrel (p823)

➡ Harvey's (p838)

➡ Pie Whole (p824)

Best Places to Sleep

➡ Northside Valley (p844)

➡ Concordia Eco-Resort (p834)

➡ St John Inn (p830)

➡ Arawak Bay Inn at Salt River (p842)

➡ Green Iguana (p823)

Why Go?

Hmm, which of the US Virgin Islands (USVI) to choose for hammock-strewn beaches, conch fritters and preposterously blue water? Easy: any one, though each differs in personality. St Thomas has more resorts and water sports than you can shake a beach towel at. It's the most developed island, with dizzying cruise-ship traffic. St John cloaks two-thirds of its area in parkland and sublime shores, ripe for hiking and snorkeling. It leads the way in environmental preservation. The largest Virgin, St Croix, pleases divers and drinkers with extraordinary scuba sites and rum factories. It's the furthest island and offers the greatest immersion in local life. Wherever you go, get ready for reggae rhythms, curried meats and mango-sweetened microbrews. These are US territories, but they feel a world away, mon.

When to Go

Mid-Dec–Apr The dry and sunny high season, when everything is open and activities are going full tilt.

Mid-Apr–early May The islands' biggest bash is the whopping, party-hearty St Thomas Carnival.

May & Jun The water is at its calmest and prices are a bit lower.

Mid-Dec–early Jan St Croix throws the cheery Cruzan Christmas Fiesta.

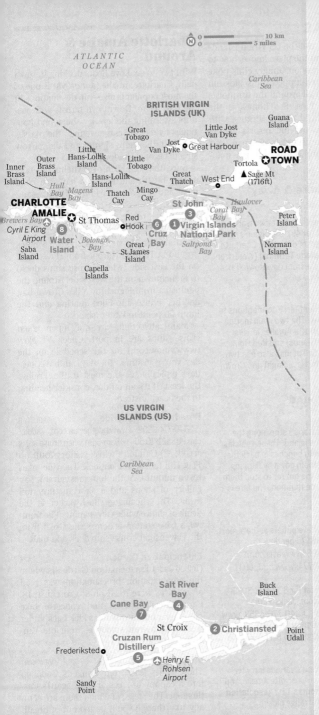

US Virgin Islands Highlights

1 **Virgin Islands National Park** (p829) Hiking to sugar-mill ruins, petroglyphs and isolated beaches rich with marine life.

2 **Christiansted** (p835) Sipping microbrews, exploring the cannon-covered fort and chowing traditional West Indian food.

3 **St John's North Shore** (p832) Choosing your favorite strand of sand, from Cinnamon Bay's water sports to Maho Bay's turtle-spotting to Leinster Bay's snorkeling with sharks.

4 **Salt River Bay** (p841) Seeing where Columbus landed by day, then kayaking the bioluminescent water by night.

5 **Cruzan Rum Distillery** (p844) Drinking the Virgin Islands' favorite attitude adjuster at its source.

6 **Cruz Bay** (p829) Raising a glass to happy-hour St John's fun-loving main town.

7 **Cane Bay** (p841) Diving the wall and peering down into the deep.

8 **Water Island** (p821) Slowing down on a jaunt to the wee 'fourth Virgin.'

ST THOMAS

Most visitors arrive at the US Virgin Islands via St Thomas, and the place knows how to strike a first impression. Jungly cliffs poke high in the sky, red-hipped roofs blossom over the hills, and all around the turquoise, yacht-dotted sea laps. St Thomas is the most commercialized of the Virgins, with cruise-ship traffic and big resorts galore, but it's also a fine island to sharpen your knife and fork, and kayak through mangrove lagoons.

ⓘ Getting There & Away

AIR

The island has two facilities for air arrivals: **Cyril E King Airport** (p849), the region's main hub, a short drive west of downtown Charlotte Amalie; and the **Seaplane Terminal** (Waterfront Hwy), right on the waterfront downtown. Taxis are easy to get at both.

BOAT

St Thomas has excellent ferry connections to the rest of the Virgins. The two main marine terminals are at Charlotte Amalie (ferries to the British Virgin Islands) and Red Hook (ferries to St John). St Thomas also has two cruise-ship terminals: Havensight and Crown Bay.

ⓘ Getting Around

BUS

'Dollar' buses (aka 'safaris') stop along the main roads around the island. These vehicles are open-air trucks with benches in back that hold 20 people. Flag them down by flapping your hand, and press the buzzer to stop them when you reach your destination. The fare is US$2.

CAR

Most rental agencies have outlets at the airport. Prices start around US$70 per day.
Avis (☑ 800-230-4898; www.avis.com)
Budget (☑ 340-776-5774; www.budgetstt.com)
Dependable Car Rental (☑ 800-522-3076; www.dependablecar.com; Jackson Dr)
Discount Car Rental (☑ 340-776-4858; www.discountcar.vi; 3308 Contant)
Hertz (☑ 340-774-1879; www.hertz.com)

TAXI

Taxis cluster at the island's various ferry terminals and in downtown Charlotte Amalie. You can also call the **St Thomas Taxi Association** (☑ 340-774-0394) to arrange pickup.

Charlotte Amalie & Around

With two to six Love Boats docking in town daily, Charlotte Amalie (a-*mall*-ya) is one of the most popular cruise-ship destinations in the Caribbean. Downtown buzzes with visitors swarming the jewelry shops and boutiques by day. By early evening, the masses clear out, the shops shutter and the narrow streets become shadowy.

Sure, the scene can overwhelm, but take a deep breath and focus on having a good meal and on your proximity to white-sand beaches.

⊙ Sights

Charlotte Amalie stretches about 2.5 miles around St Thomas Harbor from Havensight on the east side (where cruise ships dock) to Frenchtown on the west side. Around the peninsula from Frenchtown lies Crown Bay, another cruise-ship-filled marina and the jump-off point to Water Island.

Many attractions are only open when cruise ships are in port. Check VI Now (www.vinow.com) for the schedule on the day you're visiting. Tuesdays and Wednesdays typically see the most traffic, Fridays the least. If it's an off day, consider heading to the beach instead.

Paradise Point Skyride   CABLE CAR
(☑ 340-774-9809; www.ridetheview.com; adult/child US$21/10.50; ⊙9am-5pm when cruise ships in port; ☻) Gondolas whisk visitors 700ft up Flag Hill to a scenic outlook. The ride takes seven minutes. At the top a restaurant, bar, gallery of shops and a short nature trail await. The chocolatey Bushwacker is the drink of choice while view-gaping. The tramway's base station is across the street from the Havensight cruise-ship dock and mall.

Emancipation Garden   PARK
(Tolbod Gade) Emancipation Garden is where the emancipation proclamation was read after slaves were freed on St Croix in 1848. Carnival celebrations and concerts take place here, but mostly folks kick back under trees with a fruit smoothie from the Vendors' Plaza next door.

99 Steps   VIEWPOINT
These stairs lead from Kongens Gade up into a canopy of trees at Blackbeard's Castle's foot. The steps, of which there are actually 103 (though you'll be too out of breath

WORTH A TRIP

WATER ISLAND

Water Island – sometimes called the 'Fourth Virgin' – floats spitting distance from Charlotte Amalie's trafficky bustle. But with only about 100 residents and very few cars or shops, it feels far more remote. At 2.5 miles tip to tip, it doesn't take long to walk the whole thing. Most locals travel by bike or golf cart.

Honeymoon Beach is the palm-lined main attraction. It offers fine swimming and snorkeling in calm, shallow water. A couple of beach bars sell drinks, sandwiches and fish tacos, and one rents snorkel gear and kayaks. Expect peace and quiet – unless a cruise ship is in port, and then you'll have plenty of company. Honeymoon is a 10-minute walk from the ferry dock. Follow the road uphill from the landing; when the road forks, go right and down the hill to the sand.

Virgin Islands Campground (☑ 340-776-5488; www.virginislandscampground.com; cottages US$195; @ 🖥️) 🏊 is the only option if you want to spend the night, but it's an ecowinner. Each wood-frame-and-canvas cottage has beds, linens, electrical outlets and a table and chairs inside. Guests share the communal bathhouse, cooking facilities and hot tub. Captured rainwater runs through the sinks and showers; solar energy heats it. The cottages nestle into the surrounding trees, so it's a bit like sleeping in a breezy tree house. A four-night minimum stay is required.

The **Water Island Ferry** (☑ 340-690-4159; 1-way US$5) departs roughly every hour from outside Tickle's Dockside Pub at Crown Bay Marina. The journey takes 10 minutes. Taxis from downtown to the marina cost US$4 to US$5 per person.

---

to count), were constructed using ship-ballast brick in the mid-18th century. The view at the top impresses. Explore in the cool of the morning, before the cruise-ship crowds arrive.

Blackbeard's Castle HISTORIC SITE
(www.blackbeardscastle.com; US$12; ⊙ 9am-2pm by request) Set atop Government Hill, this five-story masonry watchtower was said to be the lookout post of pirate Edward Teach, alias Blackbeard, in the 18th century. Actually, historians don't lend much credence to the tale. What's known for certain is that colonial Danes built the tower as a military installation in 1678. You can climb up for good harbor views. It's only open on days cruise-ship groups request it.

St Thomas Synagogue HISTORIC BUILDING
(www.synagogue.vi; 16a & b Crystal Gade; ⊙ 9am-4pm Mon-Thu, to 3pm Fri) The second-oldest Hebrew temple in the western hemisphere (the oldest is on the island of Curaçao), peaceful St Thomas Synagogue is a National Historic Landmark. The current building dates from 1833, but Jews have worshiped here since 1796, from Sephardic Jews from Denmark to today's 110-family Reform congregation. The temple floor is made of sand to symbolize the flight of the Israelites out of Egypt and across the desert. There's a tiny museum in the back room.

Frenchtown AREA
The island's 'Frenchies,' aka Huguenots who came to St Thomas from St-Barthélemy during the mid-19th century, populated this community of brightly painted frame houses on the harbor's western side. Nowadays the fishers' neighborhood has several good restaurants that overlook the water.

Brewers Bay BEACH
This beach, located behind the University of the Virgin Islands, is beloved of students, local families and shell-spotters alike. There are no facilities other than snack vans serving *pates* (meat-filled dough pockets) and cold Heineken beers. It gets deserted fast come nighttime. Brewers is by the airport and accessible by taxis and public buses.

Magens Bay BEACH
(www.magensbayauthority.com; adult/child US$5/2; ⊙ 8am-5pm; 👪) The sugary mile that fringes heart-shaped Magens Bay, 3 miles north of Charlotte Amalie, makes almost every travel publication's list of beautiful beaches. The seas here are calm, the bay broad and the surrounding green hills dramatic, and tourists mob the place to soak it all up. The beach has lifeguards, picnic tables, changing facilities, a taxi stand, food vendors and water-sports operators renting kayaks, paddleboards and paddleboats (US$20 to US$30 per hour).

Charlotte Amalie

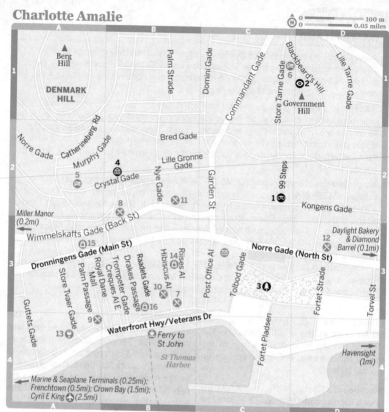

Charlotte Amalie

⊙ Sights

1 99 Steps.. C2
2 Blackbeard's Castle........................... D1
3 Emancipation Garden........................ C3
4 St Thomas Synagogue....................... B2

🛌 Sleeping

5 Crystal Palace.................................... A2
6 Green Iguana...................................... C1

😋 Eating

7 Bumpa's.. B3
8 Cuzzin's Caribbean Restaurant & Bar. B2

9 Gladys' Cafe....................................... A4
10 Greengo's Cantina............................. B3
11 MBW Cafe & Bakery........................... B2
12 Nile Valley... D3

🍸 Drinking & Nightlife

13 Greenhouse.. A4

🛍 Shopping

14 AH Riise... B3
15 Camille Pissarro Gallery..................... A3
16 Made in the Virgin Islands................. B3

Hull Bay

BEACH

On the north coast and just west of Magens Bay, Hull Bay is usually a gem of solitude when Magens is overrun. The shady strand lies at the base of a steep valley and has a fun restaurant-bar but no other facilities. It's a locals' beach: fishers anchor their small boats here and dogs lope around. Hull Bay is also the island's surfing beach; the restaurant rents a couple of surfboards (per day US$35).

It's off the beaten path, so you'll need a car to get here.

🏃 Activities & Tours

Virgin Islands Ecotours
KAYAKING

(☑340-779-2155; www.viecotours.com; French-town; 3hr tour US$89) The Frenchtown outpost of the local adventure company offers guided tours where you kayak across the harbor to uninhabited Hassel Island, hike around a 200-year-old fort and then snorkel on a coral reef.

St Thomas Scuba & Snorkel Adventures
SNORKELING

(☑340-474-9332; www.stthomasadventures.com; Hull Bay) Located at Hull Bay, the company rents paddleboards and kayaks (per hour US$30) and leads terrific night snorkel tours (per person US$45). It also offers a slew of other snorkeling, diving, kayaking and hiking jaunts around the island. Reservations required.

Tree Limin' Extreme
ADVENTURE

(☑340-777-9477; www.ziplinestthomas.com; 7406 Estate St Peter; 2½hr tour adult/child US$119/109) Guides whisk you through the jungle canopy via zip line. The ride is relatively tame and provides great views of the island-dotted seascape. Afterward stroll across the street and explore the free St Peter Mountain Great House Botanical Gardens. Tree Limin' operates via reservation only.

🎉 Festivals & Events

St Thomas Carnival
CARNIVAL

(www.vicarnival.com; ☺Apr) It's the second-largest carnival in the Caribbean (after the one at Port of Spain, Trinidad), with a full month of events at various locations.

🛏 Sleeping

Charlotte Amalie has more casual guest-houses than you'll find elsewhere around the island. The downside of staying here is it gets pretty deserted come nightfall.

★ Green Iguana
GUESTHOUSE $$

(☑340-776-7654; www.thegreeniguana.com; 1002 Blackbeard's Hill; r US$150-210; ❄🛜) Up the hill behind Blackbeard's Castle, this welcoming place is set in lush gardens and overlooks St Thomas Harbor. The nine rooms come in several configurations, but all have free wi-fi, satellite TV, a microwave and refrigerator; some also have a fully equipped kitchen and private balcony. It's more plain than luxurious, but good value if you don't mind the steep walk.

Miller Manor
GUESTHOUSE $$

(☑888-229-0762; www.millermanor.com; 2527 Prindsesse Gade; r US$120-170, with shared bath-room US$100; ❄🛜) A 160-year-old Danish manor house anchors this low-key, 19-room, hillside establishment, which has a groovy terrace and bar overlooking the harbor. Rooms range from singles with a shared bathroom to large rooms with water-view balconies. Continental breakfast is included. While the manor is in a safe neighborhood, the dicey Savan district lies between here and downtown. Take a taxi at night.

Crystal Palace
B&B $$

(☑340-777-2277; www.crystalpalaceusvi.com; 12 Crystal Gade; r US$139-169; ❄🛜) Ronnie Lockhart owns this five-room property in a colonial mansion that has been in his family for generations. It's a bit run-down, but full of character. Two rooms have private bathrooms; the other three share a bathroom. Antique West Indian decor pervades, and there's a view-tastic patio on which to eat the continental breakfast or swill a drink from the honor bar.

Best Western Emerald Beach Resort
HOTEL $$

(☑340-777-8800; www.emeraldbeach.com; 8070 Lindbergh Bay; r US$215-300; ❄@🛜⛱) Located near the airport, this property has 90 large, snazzy rooms with private balconies and flat-screen TVs. The main selling point: you're right on the beach at sheltered Lindbergh Bay. The trade-off: you're isolated from downtown Charlotte Amalie and will need a taxi to reach its shops and restaurants (though the resort does have a bar-restaurant on-site).

🍴 Eating

Downtown is good for breakfast and lunch, though dinner options are scarce as most places close by 5pm. Frenchtown holds several great restaurants that buzz in the evening. Havensight is touristy and chain-oriented but offers a fun, high-energy atmosphere.

★ Daylight Bakery & Diamond Barrel
CARIBBEAN $

(☑340-776-1414; 18 Norre Gade; items US$2-5; ☺6am-6pm Mon-Sat) It's mostly locals who visit this friendly spot at downtown's edge. If you can get past the guava tarts, sugar cakes and dum bread (flour sweetened with coconut and baked in a 'dum' oven), pans of okra, fish stew, fungi (semihard cornmeal pudding) and more island dishes await. Point to your choice behind the glass case, and servers heap it into a styrofoam clamshell.

MBW Cafe & Bakery
CAFE $

(☎340-715-2767; www.mbwcafeandbakery.com; Back St; sandwiches US$6-13; ☺7am-4pm) MBW is My Brother's Workshop, a nonprofit group that helps at-risk youth learn a trade. At the cheery cafe, teens bake the wares and run the place. The egg-filled breakfast sandwiches are a good deal, and the muffins and cake slices appease sugar addicts. Lots of locals hang out at the tables in back of the cafe.

Greengo's Cantina
MEXICAN $

(☎340-714-8282; www.greengoscantina.com; 34-35 Dronningens Gade; US$12-15; ☺11am-5pm, to 9pm Fri) Join the boisterous young expat crowd chowing down on Greengo's tacos, burritos and quesadillas and knocking back shots from the 150-strong tequila array.

Barefoot Buddha
CAFE $

(☎340-777-3668; www.barefootbuddhavi.com; 9715 Estate Thomas; US$8-11; ☺7am-6pm Mon-Sat, 8am-3pm Sun; ☎☞) The island's yoga-philes hang out at yin-yang decorated wood tables, tucking into healthy specials such as the blackened tofu wrap and the everyday list of toasted sandwiches (go for the hummus and rosemary goat's cheese). The Buddha is also popular for breakfast, thanks to the long list of organic coffee drinks and egg sandwiches. It's near Havensight's cruise dock.

Famous Delite Dairy Bar
ICE CREAM $

(☎340-777-6050; www.facebook.com/famousdelite; milkshakes US$5.50-7; ☺12:30-6:30pm Mon, from 10:30am Tue-Sat, from 11:30am Sun; ☞) A 15-minute (uphill) walk from Magens Bay, Famous Delite whips up awesome milkshakes. Adults can get their creamy goodness spiked with booze. Many locals still refer to this place by its former name, Udder Delite.

Nile Valley
VEGETARIAN $

(☎340-775-6453; 9a Norre Gade; small/large plates US$10/15; ☺10am-6pm Mon-Sat; ☞) ☙ Curried tofu stew, coconut rice, fried lentil patties and other vegetarian dishes are on the menu at this locally sourced Rasta cafe. Pick and mix a platter of daily specials from the glass case, perfect alongside a fresh mango or passionfruit juice. There are a few tables inside, or carry out and have a picnic at nearby Veteran's Memorial Park.

Bumpa's
CAFE $

(☎340-776-5674; 38a Waterfront Hwy; mains US$10-16; ☺8am-5pm Mon-Sat, to 3pm Sun) Climb the stairs to the 2nd floor, order at the counter, then carry your hearty oatmeal pancakes, pumpkin muffin, veggie burger, chicken *pate* or grilled fish wrap to the small patio overlooking the street.

★ Pie Whole
ITALIAN $$

(☎340-642-5074; www.piewholepizza.com; Frenchtown; mains US$17-24; ☺11am-3pm & 5-10pm Mon-Fri, 5-10pm Sat & Sun) Six tables and 10 barstools comprise this cozy eatery. The 13in, crisp-crusted, brick-oven pizzas are the claim to fame. Superfresh ingredients, eg spinach and ricotta or mozzarella and basil, top the white or wheat crust. Several housemade pastas and a robust beer list raise Pie Whole well beyond the norm.

★ Cuzzin's Caribbean Restaurant & Bar
CARIBBEAN $$

(☎340-777-4711; 7 Back St; mains US$13-22; ☺11am-4:30pm Mon-Sat) With exposed-brick walls, burnished wood furnishings and red-clothed tables, classy-but-casual Cuzzin's is a favorite stop for West Indian cuisine. Try the conch (a local shellfish) curried, buttered or Creole-style, or the catch of the day alongside fungi, fried plantains and a rum-laden cocktail.

Gladys' Cafe
CARIBBEAN $$

(☎340-774-6604; www.gladyscafe.com; 5600 Royal Dane Mall; mains US$13-22; ☺7am-5pm Mon-Sat, 8am-3pm Sun) With the stereo blaring beside her, Gladys belts out Tina Turner tunes while serving some of the best West Indian food around. Locals and tourists pile in for her callaloo, fungi, Ole Wife (triggerfish), fried plantains and sweet potatoes. Gladys' homemade hot sauces (for sale at the front) make a fine souvenir.

Hook, Line & Sinker
SEAFOOD $$

(☎340-776-9708; www.hooklineandsinkervi.com; Frenchtown; mains US$14-27; ☺11:30am-11pm Mon-Sat, 10am-2:30pm Sun) This open-air, mom-and-pop operation feels like a real sea shack, where you smell the salt water, feel the ocean breeze and see sailors unload their boats dockside. The menu mixes sandwiches, salads, pastas and seafood mains, such as the almond-crusted yellowtail, with plenty of beers to wash it down.

Old Stone Farmhouse
AMERICAN $$$

(☎340-777-6277; www.osfhvi.com; Mahogany Run Golf Course; mains US$29-42; ☺5-9:30pm Wed-Sat, 10am-2pm & 5-9:30pm Sun) The 200-year-old farmhouse – once the stable for a nearby sugar plantation – sits high on a hill overlooking St Thomas' only golf course. The rustic, low-lit room impresses with its arched stone walls and mahogany ceiling. The menu changes, but local fish (snapper, wahoo, mahi-mahi) are always available, as well as a vegetarian option.

🍷 Drinking & Nightlife

Frenchtown Brewing   MICROBREWERY
(☑ 340-642-2800; www.frenchtownbrewing.com; Frenchtown; ⊙ 5:30-7:30pm Wed & Fri, 1-5pm Sat) The brewery is indeed micro: it's only open a few days per week, it only brews a couple of beers and they're only on tap here. Beer buffs will want to seek it out for the Belgian-style Frenchie Farmhouse Saison and Hop Alley IPA. Tours are available; call to make an appointment if you want to visit outside regular hours.

Epernay Bistro & Wine Bar   WINE BAR
(☑ 340-774-5348; Frenchtown; ⊙ 5-11pm Mon-Thu, to midnight Sat & Sun) Guess what they pour here? Epernay is a popular hangout for St Thomian professionals and snowbirds. Friday-evening happy hour is the biggest scene.

Greenhouse   PUB
(☑ 340-774-7998; www.thegreenhouserestaurant. com; Waterfront Hwy; mains US$12-29; ⊙ 11am-9pm; 🛜) Cavernous, open-air Greenhouse overlooks the harbor and rocks hard during happy hour (4:30pm to 7pm, when drinks are two for the price of one). The cuisine is predictable American pub fare, but the menu is extensive, with burgers, pizzas and seafood. When everything else downtown closes by 5pm, Greenhouse is the one reliable place still open.

🛍 Shopping

Jewelry is the big deal in town. Brands like Rolex, Tag Heuer and Pandora are well represented, and there are diamond sellers galore. US citizens can leave with a whopping US$1600 in tax-free, duty-free goods.

Made in the Virgin Islands   GIFTS & SOUVENIRS
(☑ 340-776-7822; Drakes Passage; ⊙ 10am-4pm) The name doesn't lie: mini Cruzan Rum bottles, St John Brewers beer, Sunny Carib spices (from Tortola), jewelry from island artisans and other locally made goods fill the shelves of the small shop.

Camille Pissarro Gallery   ART
(☑ 340-774-4621; 14 Main St; ⊙ 10am-4pm Mon-Sat, to 1pm Sun) Located in Pissarro's boyhood home, the gallery sells a few reproductions of the famous impressionist's St Thomas scenes, but mostly focuses on works by contemporary artists.

Yacht Haven Grande   SHOPPING CENTER
Next door to Havensight is this marina and chic shop complex. Gucci and Louis Vuitton headline the tony roster, along with several waterfront bistros where you can sip cosmos and watch megayachts drift in to the dock. A **farmers market** (Yacht Haven Grande; ⊙ 10am-2pm, 1st & 3rd Sun) with produce and crafts sets up on the grounds every other Sunday.

AH Riise   MALL
(☑ 340-777-2222; www.ahriise.com; 37 Main St) This is the famous mall that most visitors beeline to, where you can buy everything from watches and jewels to tobacco and liquor.

ℹ Information

DANGERS & ANNOYANCES
Waterfront Hwy and Main St in the town center are fine at night, but move a few blocks away and the streets get deserted quickly. Avoid the Savan area, a red-light district that surrounds Main St west of Market Sq and north of the Windward Passage hotel. In general, travelers who take reasonable precautions should have no problems.

INTERNET ACCESS
Restaurants and bars at Havensight offer free wi-fi more so than in downtown Charlotte Amalie.

MONEY
FirstBank, Scotiabank, Banco Popular and other banks are on Waterfront Hwy.

POST
Main Post Office (☑ 340-774-3750; Norre Gade; ⊙ 7:30am-4:30pm Mon-Fri, to noon Sat) On the west side of Emancipation Garden.

TOURIST INFORMATION
There is no official tourist office downtown, but the free *St Thomas/St John This Week* magazine has maps and everything else you'll need.

ℹ Getting There & Away

AIR
Cyril E King Airport (p849) is located 3 miles west of Charlotte Amalie. Taxis (ie multipassenger vans) are readily available. The fare to downtown is US$7; it's US$15 to Red Hook. Luggage costs US$2 extra per piece.

The **Seaplane Terminal** (p820), where 20-minutes flights to St Croix depart, is downtown next to the Marine Terminal.

BOAT

The **Marine Terminal** (Waterfront Hwy) is a 10-minute walk west of downtown. It's a hub for ferries to Tortola and Virgin Gorda. A **ferry to St John** (1-way US$13; ⊙ 45min) departs downtown at the foot of Raadet's Gade at 10am, 1pm and 5:30pm daily; cash only.

Charlotte Amalie also has two cruise-ship terminals: Havensight (1.5 miles east of downtown) and Crown Bay (1.5 miles west of downtown).

BUS

'Dollar' buses (aka 'safaris') mosey along Waterfront Hwy. The fare is US$2. To get on, wave your hand to flag them down. To get off, press the buzzer when you reach your destination.

CAR

There's an Avis outlet at the Seaplane Terminal. Otherwise, most rental companies are at the main airport.

TAXI

Taxis huddle around the Vendors' Plaza. The following are the set, per-person rates from downtown:

Frenchtown US$4
Havensight US$6
Magens Bay US$10
Red Hook US$13

Red Hook & East End

The East End holds the bulk of the island's resorts. Red Hook is the only town to speak of, though it's small and built mostly around the St John ferry dock and American Yacht Harbor marina. Lovely beaches sprawl throughout the area, along with ace opportunities for diving, fishing and kayaking.

◉ Sights

Secret Harbour Beach

(🖼) Small and hammock-strewn, this west-facing beach in front of the eponymous resort could hardly be more tranquil. It's an excellent place to snorkel with equipment rented from the resort's water-sports operation. Kids like swimming out to the platform that floats in the bay. Bathrooms and food are available.

Sapphire Beach
BEACH

Sapphire is among St Thomas' prettiest white-sand beaches, and as such, it draws a big tourist crowd. Amenities include water-sports rentals (windsurfers, snorkel gear, kayaks), bathrooms and a bar-restaurant.

There's good snorkeling on the reef to the right of the beach.

Lindquist Beach
BEACH

(adult/child US$5/free) Part of protected Smith Bay Park, this narrow strand is a beauty all right: calm, true-blue water laps the soft white sand, while several cays shimmer in the distance. Hollywood has filmed several commercials here. There is a lifeguard, picnic tables and a bathhouse with showers, but no other amenities. It's low-key and lovely for a swim. Parking costs US$2. Cash only.

Coki Beach
BEACH

Coki is on a protected cove at the entrance to Coral World marine park. The snorkeling is excellent with lots of fish action, and you can dive from the shore with gear from the on-site dive shop. The narrow beach crowds with both locals and tourists enjoying the eateries, hair-braiding vendors and loud music. A festive scene results. However, Coki is the one beach on St Thomas with touts – as soon as you arrive someone will quickly become your 'friend'.

🏃 Activities

Diving & Snorkeling

St Thomas features several premier dive sites, and most resort hotels have a dive service on the property. Dive centers also rent snorkeling gear for US$10 to US$15 per day.

Red Hook Dive Center
DIVING

(☑ 340-777-3483; www.redhookdivecenter.com; American Yacht Harbor; 1-/2-tank dive US$90/$125; ⊙ 8am-5pm) Boat dives depart from here for all the fishy hot spots; lessons take place at nearby Sugar Bay Resort. There's a night dive every Wednesday.

Coki Dive Center
DIVING

(☑ 340-775-4220; www.cokidive.com; Coki Point; 1-tank beach dive US$60) Just steps from Coki Beach, it offers shore and night dives in addition to boat dives, plus Professional Association of Diving Instructors (PADI) courses.

Fishing

Troll for wahoo, or get the live bait ready for yellowfin tuna. Add blue marlin to the list from May through October. Most trips depart from American Yacht Harbor. Expect to pay about US$800 for a half-day excursion, and US$1450 for a full day.

Nate's Custom Charters

BOATING

(☏340-244-2497; www.stthomasboatcharters.com; 6300 Estate Frydenhoj, Compass Point Marina) Fishing, snorkeling, island-hopping: Nate's arranges a boat, captain and gear to do any or all. Prices vary by group size and destinations.

☞ Tours

★ Virgin Islands Ecotours

KAYAKING

(☏340-779-2155; www.viecotours.com; Mangrove Lagoon Marina; 2½hr tours adult/child US$69/39; ◷10am & 2pm; ⛵) The company offers guided kayak-and-snorkeling expeditions where you paddle through a mangrove lagoon to a coral-rubble beach and reef. There's also a three-hour tour that adds hiking to the mix. Bird, ghost and stand-up paddleboard trips are available, too. The location is just east of the intersection of Rtes 30 and 32.

☆ Festivals & Events

St Thomas International Regatta

SAILING

(www.stthomasinternationalregatta.com; ◷late Mar) World-class racing boats gather at St Thomas Yacht Club.

⛏ Sleeping

Resorts are the East End's primary option. Antilles Resorts (www.antillesresorts.com) manages several of the local properties. Many units are privately owned condos, and they vary widely in quality. Savvy visitors say they have better luck booking through home-sharing websites where they deal with the condo owners directly.

Rhoda's Guesthouse/Tillett Hostel

HOSTEL $

(☏340-998-5993; www.rhodasguesthouse.com; 4126 Anna's Retreat, Tillett Gardens; dm US$50; ❄🛜) Located in a colorful artists community within walking distance of Tutu Park Mall, this hostel is your spot for a local experience. There are two well-kept, eight-bed dorms (one for men, one for women), a communal TV room and kitchen, and a bar and stage for bands on the leafy grounds. It's on the 'safari' bus route, 15 minutes from Red Hook.

Two Sandals by the Sea Inn

B&B $$

(☏340-998-2394; www.twosandals.com; 6264 Estate Nazareth; r US$190-260; ❄🛜) Two Sandals offers a homey alternative to the East End's resorts. The rooms are nothing fancy but each is modern and spacious with a wood-beamed ceiling, crisp white linens, dark wood decor and a private bathroom. A pastry-laden continental breakfast on the sea-view balcony is included. Secret Harbour's beach is a five-minute walk, while Red Hook's restaurants are a 10-minute walk.

Bolongo Bay Beach Resort

RESORT $$$

(☏340-775-1800; www.bolongobay.com; 7150 Bolongo Bay; r US$275-440; ❄🛜🏊) Family-owned Bolongo is fun, casual and offers a full array of free water sports. The rooms won't win awards for size or decor, but who cares? You'll be outside. 'Ocean-view' rooms are on the 2nd and 3rd floors. 'Beachfront' rooms are on the 1st floor. All have sea views and private patios. The 'value' rooms are in a building across the street.

Secret Harbour Beach Resort

RESORT $$$

(☏340-775-6550; www.secretharbourvi.com; 6280 Estate Nazareth; ste US$350-650; ❄🛜🏊) Secret Harbour is a humble family favorite, with 48 suites filling four buildings right on the serene, palmy, same-named beach with water-sport opportunities. Suites come in three main sizes: studio (660 sq ft), one bedroom (935 sq ft) and two bedrooms (1360 sq ft). All have a kitchen and a balcony or patio prime for sunset views.

Point Pleasant Resort

RESORT $$$

(☏888-619-4010; www.pointpleasantresort.com; 6600 Estate Smith Bay; ste US$325-450; ❄🛜🏊) On a steep hill overlooking Water Bay, the resort has lots of charm though the decor is somewhat dated. The suites are in multiunit buildings tucked into the hillside forest. Each suite has a full kitchen, separate bedroom and large porch. The grounds have walking trails and three pools. It's about a half mile from Coki Beach.

Pavilions & Pools

RESORT $$$

(☏800-524-2001; www.pavilionsandpools.com; 6400 Estate Smith Bay; ste US$300-350; ❄🛜🏊) The cool thing about this small property is that each of the 25 suites has its own pool – yeah, you read that right. Suites have full kitchens and separate bedrooms with sliding doors that open to your own swimmin' hole. Each unit is individually owned, so quality can vary. Sapphire Beach is within walking distance.

✕ Eating

Iggie's Beach Bar & Grill

SEAFOOD $$

(☏340-693-2600; www.iggiesbeachbar.com; 7150 Bolongo Bay; mains US$15-28; ◷11am-11pm) Set in a large, open-air pavilion overlooking the broad shore at Bolongo Bay Beach Resort, festive Iggie's is beloved for its conch fritters with mango dipping sauce, grilled fish and rum-soaked Voodoo Juice served in a bucket. There's live music every evening, and ruthless beanbag-toss competitions. Wednesday is 'Carnival Night' with a limbo show and fire-eaters.

Latitude 18   CARIBBEAN $$

(☑340-777-4552; www.latitude18stt.com; Vessup Bay Marina; mains US$20-28; ⊙11am-1am) This funky sea ramblers' place is a patio protected by a roof of old sails and tarps. Locals rave about the flavorful dishes coming from the little kitchen, such as the Trinidad 'bake' sandwiches and shrimp creole. Most nights Latitude brings in fiddlin' bands that fire up the crowd.

Molly Malone's   PUB FOOD $$

(☑340-775-1270; American Yacht Harbor; mains US$15-30; ⊙7am-midnight) A re-creation of an Irish pub, Molly's has a huge menu, from omelets to shepherd's pie to veggie lasagna. Lots of boaters shuffle in to watch sports on overhead TVs and cool off with a brew and meal at the bar.

🍷 Drinking & Nightlife

★Cup-N-Kettle   TEAHOUSE

(☑340-998-7405; www.cupnkettle.com; 2ga Ridge Rd; ⊙7am-2pm) Gracious owner Evelyn has decorated her cute-as-a-button teahouse with pretty china from her worldly travels. Try local bush tea – three-tea tastings are a fine option – alongside a a coconut tart or slice of rum cake. Coffee and fruit smoothies are also available. Sip indoors in the cozy main room or outdoors in the storybook gazebo.

Duffy's Love Shack   BAR

(☑340-779-2080; www.duffysloveshack.com; 6500 Red Hook Plaza; ⊙11:30am-midnight) It may be a frame shack in the middle of a paved parking lot, but Duffy's creates its legendary, tiki-themed atmosphere with high-volume rock and crowds in shorts and tank tops. The people-watching is excellent and the cocktails are great fun, like the 64oz 'shark tank' or the flaming 'volcano.' The food is classic, burger-based pub fare. Cash only.

Tap & Still   BAR

(☑340-642-2337; American Yacht Harbor; mains $US6-10; ⊙11am-midnight) This beyond-the-norm sports bar lets you sip a decent beer selection and cheap bourbon drinks while munching juicy burgers and thick, hand-cut fries in view of boats bobbing in the harbor. Also on the menu: funnel cakes (sugar-topped fried dough), a vastly underrated booze accompaniment. There's another Tap & Still at Havensight.

❶ Getting There & Away

Red Hook's **ferry dock** bustles, with most traffic headed to St John; passenger ferries (US$7 one way, 20 minutes, cash only) to Cruz Bay depart on the hour. Ferries also go to Tortola's West End at least four times daily.

Taxis queue outside the marine terminal; it's US$13 to Charlotte Amalie. A taxi from Red Hook to the resorts runs about US$8 per person.

ST JOHN

Two-thirds of St John is a protected national park, with gnarled trees and spiky cacti spilling over its edges. There are no airports or cruise-ship docks, and the usual Caribbean resorts are few and far between. It's blissfully low-key compared to its island neighbors.

Hiking and snorkeling are the big to-dos. Trails wind by petroglyphs and sugar-mill ruins, and several drop out on to beaches prime for swimming with turtles and spotted eagle rays.

Two towns bookend the island: Cruz Bay, the ferry landing and main village that hosts a hell of a happy hour; and Coral Bay at the east end, the sleepy domain of folks who want to feel like they're living on a frontier.

❶ Getting There & Away

BOAT

All ferries arrive in Cruz Bay. Boats from St Thomas glide into the main ferry dock, while boats from the British Virgin Islands arrive at a smaller dock by the US Customs & Immigration building a short walk east.

BUS

Vitran (p850) operates air-con buses over the length of the island via Centerline Rd. Buses leave Cruz Bay in front of the ferry terminal at 6am and 7am, then every hour at 25 minutes after the hour until 7:25pm. They arrive at Coral Bay about 40 minutes later.

CAR

St John rentals are all via small, independent companies. Most provide 4WDs and SUVs to

MONGOOSES, DONKEYS & GOATS, OH MY!

Whether you are camping, hiking or driving on St John, it won't be long before you have a close encounter with the island's odd menagerie of feral animals. Hundreds of goats, donkeys, pigs and cats roam the island, descendants of domestic animals abandoned to the jungle eons ago. White-tailed deer and mongooses are two other introduced species that multiplied in unexpected numbers.

The donkeys are the big attention-grabbers. Often you'll see them on Centerline Rd, where they'll come right up to your car and stick their snout in any open window.

Do not tempt the animals by offering them food or leaving food or garbage where they can get at it. And do not approach them for petting or taking a snapshot. While most have a live-and-let-live attitude and don't mind you stepping around them on the trails, they are all capable of aggression if provoked.

handle the rugged terrain. Costs hover near US$90 per day. Companies typically have a three- to five-day minimum to reserve in advance. The other option – waiting to rent on the spot – is iffy. Most companies are in Cruz Bay and either walkable from the ferries or they'll meet you at the dock.

Courtesy Car Rental (☑ 340-776-6650; www.courtesycarrental.com)

St John Car Rental (☑ 340-776-6103; www.stjohncarrental.com)

Sunshine's Jeep Rental (☑ 340-690-1786; www.sunshinesjeeprental.com; Rte 10)

TAXI

Rates are set. From Cruz Bay it costs per person US$9 to Cinnamon Bay and US$16 to Coral Bay. Call the **St John Taxi Commission** (☑ 340-774-3130) for pickups.

Cruz Bay

Nicknamed 'Love City,' St John's main town indeed wafts a carefree, spring-break party vibe. Hippies, sea captains, American retirees and reggae worshippers hoist happy-hour drinks in equal measure, and everyone wears a silly grin at their great good fortune for being here. Cruz Bay is also the place to organize your hiking, snorkeling, kayaking and other activities, and to fuel up in the surprisingly good restaurant mix. Everything grooves within walking distance of the ferry docks.

👁 Sights

Virgin Islands National Park　　NATIONAL PARK
(☑ 340-776-6201, ex 238; www.nps.gov/viis; ☉ visitor center 8am-4:30pm) FREE VI National Park covers two-thirds of St John, plus 5650 acres underwater. It's a tremendous resource, offering miles of shoreline, pristine reefs and

20 hiking trails. The park visitors center sits on the dock across from the Mongoose Junction shopping arcade. It's an essential first stop to obtain free guides on hiking, bird-watching, petroglyph sites and ranger-led activities. Green iguanas, geckos, hawksbill turtles and wild donkeys roam the landscape. A couple of good trails leave from behind the center.

🏃 Activities & Tours

Hiking

Lind Point Trail　　HIKING
One of the most accessible trails, it departs from behind the national park visitors center and moseys for 1.1 miles through cactus and dry forest, past the occasional donkey and bananaquit, to Honeymoon Beach. A 0.4-mile upper track goes to Lind Battery, once a British gun emplacement, 160ft above the sea. The lower track goes directly to the beach.

Reef Bay Hike　　HIKING
(☑ 340-693-7275; www.friendsvinp.org/hike; per person US$40; ☉ 9am-3pm Mon & Thu year-round, plus Tue & Fri Dec-Apr) Rangers from VI National Park guide you on a 3-mile downhill trek through tropical forests, past petroglyphs and plantation ruins to a swimming beach at Reef Bay, where a boat runs you back to Cruz Bay (hence the fee). It's very popular, and the park recommends reserving at least two weeks in advance. Departure is from the park visitors center.

Water Sports

Arawak Expeditions　　KAYAKING
(☑ 340-693-8312; www.arawakexp.com; half-/full-day trips from US$75/110) Well-planned kayaking and stand-up paddleboarding trips depart out of Cruz Bay and glide around island

hot spots such as Hurricane Hole; snorkel gear costs extra (US$7).

Low Key Watersports
DIVING

(☎340-693-8999; www.divelowkey.com; One Bay St; 2-tank dive US$125; ☉8:30am-8pm Mon-Sat, to 6pm Sun) This is a great dive-training facility and has some of the most experienced instructors on the islands. It offers wreck dives to the RMS *Rhone*, as well as night dives and dive packages. It also has day-sail trips that go to either the Baths or Jost Van Dyke in the British Virgin Islands.

Cruz Bay Watersports
DIVING

(☎888-756-0631; www.cruzbaywatersports.com; 300a Chocolate Hole; 2-tank dive US$135; ☉8am-6pm) Located at the Westin Resort, this company goes out for daily dives and snorkel trips around St John. It also offers sunset cruises and sailing jaunts to the BVI's Baths and Jost Van Dyke.

✲✲ Festivals & Events

8 Tuff Miles
SPORTS

(www.8tuffmiles.com; ☉late Feb) Popular foot race from Cruz Bay to Coral Bay.

St John Carnival
CULTURAL

(www.stjohnfestival.org; ☉early Jul) The island's biggest celebration; surrounds Emancipation Day (July 3) and US Independence Day (July 4).

🛏 Sleeping

★ Hotel Cruz Bay
HOTEL $$

(☎340-642-1702; www.cruzbayhotel.com; King St; r US$235; ❇🏠) It's the closest lodging to the ferry dock, smack in the heart of Cruz Bay. The 10 tidy white rooms are located above two restaurants (one Italian, one Caribbean), and are good value for the island, which is why they book up fast. Free continental breakfast.

★ St John Inn
HOTEL $$

(☎340-693-8688; www.stjohninn.com; 277 Estate Enighed; r US$255-315; ❇🏠✷) The 10 rooms at the uberpopular inn are decked out with bright-hued walls, tiled floors and handcrafted wood furniture. A homey atmosphere pervades, and guests grill fresh fish on the communal barbecue, laze on the sun deck or dip in the small pool. Continental breakfast, evening rum punch and beach chairs are included. Located up the hill from the ferry dock.

Samuel Cottages
APARTMENT $$

(☎340-776-6643; www.samuelcottages.com; Centerline Rd; apt US$150; ❇) These three peach-colored cottages are a stiff 10-minute walk uphill from the ferry dock, but you'll be hard-pressed to beat the value. They are sort of like state-park cabins – nothing fancy, but clean and spacious enough, with a fully equipped kitchen and deck for sitting and contemplating how much cash you're saving.

HIKING ST JOHN

St John is the premier island for hiking. Virgin Islands National Park maintains 20 paths, and any reasonably fit hiker can walk them safely without a local guide. Download the free *Trail Guide for Safe Hiking* brochure from the park website (www.nps.gov/viis, then click Plan Your Trip, then Brochures). The **Friends of the Park Store** (p832) sells a terrific, more detailed map for US$3.

If you prefer guided jaunts, the park sponsors several free ones, including birding expeditions and shore hikes, but its best-known offering is the **Reef Bay Hike** (p829). Rangers lead the 3-mile trek that takes in petroglyphs and plantation ruins and ends with a swim at Reef Bay's beach. The tour fee covers a taxi to the trailhead (about 5 miles from Cruz Bay) and a boat ride back.

These other favorite trails are each less than 3 miles round-trip; all have identifying signs at the trailheads and small lots to park your car.

Ram Head (p834) Rocky, uphill slog to a worth-every-drop-of-sweat clifftop view.

Lind Point (p829) Departs from behind the park visitors center, past donkeys and bananaquits, to secluded Honeymoon Beach.

Leinster Bay (p833) Goes from the Annaberg sugar-mill ruins to fantastic snorkeling at Waterlemon Cay.

Cinnamon Bay (p833) Easy loop trail that swings through tropical forest and mill ruins.

Garden by the Sea B&B
B&B $$

(☑ 340-779-4731; www.gardenbythesea.com; 203 Enighed; r US$250-275; ❄ ☎) B&B-ers swoon over this place. The owners live on-site and have splashed the three rooms in bright hues of sea green, lavender and blueberry, each with a sturdy, four-post canopy bed and private bathroom. Solar panels provide the electricity. Cash or traveler's checks only. Three- to six-night minimum stay required.

Coconut Coast Villas
APARTMENT $$$

(☑ 340-693-9100; www.coconutcoast.com; 268 Estate Enighed; apt from US$329; ❄ ☎ ≋) The nine units in this compound – including single-room studios, two-bedroom suites and three-bedroom spreads when combined – stand right on the cobblestone beach at Turner Bay. Each apartment comes with local art, a kitchen, private deck and wi-fi. There's a communal swimming pool, hot tub and barbecue grill. Cruz Bay is a 10-minute walk over the hill. Five-night minimum stay required.

✗ Eating

⭐ Baked in the Sun
BAKERY $

(☑ 340-693-8786; Rte 104; sandwiches US$6-9; ⊙ 6am-3pm Mon-Fri, to 2pm Sat) This little bakery buzzes with locals munching butter croissants and meaty sandwiches on thick-cut house-made bread. Drool-inducing cakes, cookies and pastries tempt from the glass case. It's up the hill from the ferry dock.

Jake's
BREAKFAST $

(☑ 340-777-7115; www.jakesstjohn.com; Lumberyard; mains US$10-16; ⊙ 7:30am-2pm) Breakfast is Jake's forte, including well-stuffed omelets, crispy home fries and strong coffee. Ceiling fans whir, newspapers rustle and reggae drifts from the speakers – then the couple next to you orders a triple shot of Jack Daniel's to accompany their pancakes. This open-air cafe is that kind of place.

Starfish Market
SUPERMARKET $

(☑ 340-779-4949; www.starfishmarket.com; Marketplace Bldg; ⊙ 7:30am-9pm) Self-caterers can stock up at this full-service supermarket. Beer, wine and cheese are in a separate shop across the hall from the main market's front door. It's about a 15-minute walk northeast from the ferry dock.

Lime Inn
SEAFOOD $$

(☑ 340-776-6425; www.thelimeinn.com; King St; mains US$26-34; ⊙ 11:30am-3pm & 5:30-9:30pm Mon-Sat) Lime Inn is a travelers' favorite for quality cuisine and top-notch service

at moderate prices. Tables sit amid swaying ferns, gently spinning fans and pops of bright-green paint on the walls. The New England clam chowder, shrimp scampi and chocolatey desserts earn rave reviews. Reservations are a good idea.

Uncle Joe's BBQ
BARBECUE $$

(☑ 340-693-8806; North Shore Rd; mains US$16-18; ⊙ 11:30am-9pm) Locals and visitors go wild tearing into the barbecue chicken, ribs and corn on the cob at this open-air restaurant across from the post office. The chef grills the meats outside, perfuming the entire harbor-front with their tangy goodness. Cash only.

Rhumb Lines
FUSION $$

(☑ 340-776-0303; www.rhumblinesstjohn.com; Meada's Plaza; mains US$25-32; ⊙ 5-10pm Mon-Sat, 10am-2pm & 5-10pm Sun) Tucked in a lush courtyard and decorated in tropical South Seas style, this little restaurant brings on creative dishes melding Thai, Szechuan, Filipino and other Asian flavors. Try selections from the 'pu pu' menu, a mix of tapas-like treats. There's air-conditioned indoor seating, or outdoor seating under umbrellas and bamboo torches. Well-made cocktails accompany the food.

Da Livio
ITALIAN $$

(☑ 340-779-8900; www.dalivio.it; King St; mains US$22-41; ⊙ 5:30-9:30pm, closed Mon May-Nov) Fork into authentic Italian food lovingly cooked by a chef transplanted from the motherland. Staff makes all the pasta and gnocchi from scratch. The wood-fired, crisp-crust pizzas are a favorite, as are the hearty wines. Corks dot the ceiling, and the black-and-white decor gives the trattoria a sleek-casual ambience.

Morgan's Mango
CARIBBEAN $$$

(☑ 340-693-8141; www.morgansmango.com; by Mongoose Junction; mains US$30-40; ⊙ 5-10pm) Take in a view of the harbor while dining on imaginative Caribbean recipes for dishes such as Haitian voodoo snapper or Cuban citrus chicken. The owners often bring in live acoustic acts (usually Wednesday through Friday), making Morgan's a good choice for a fun or romantic night out.

🍷 Drinking & Nightlife

⭐ Tap Room
MICROBREWERY

(☑ 340-715-7775; www.stjohnbrewers.com; Mongoose Junction, 2nd fl; ⊙ 11am-midnight; ☎) St John Brewers makes its sunny, citrusy suds here. Join locals hanging off the barstools and sip a flagship Mango Pale Ale, or try the alcohol-free options, including house-made root beer, ginger beer and Green Flash energy drink. Sample-laden tours (US$12) take place at 4pm Monday, Wednesday and Friday. Sign up in the downstairs Brewtique, which has fun souvenirs for sale.

Joe's Rum Hut   BAR
(☑ 340-775-5200; www.joesrumhut.com; Wharfside Village; ⊙ 11am-1am) Around 11am, a bartender materializes with rum and a whopping bowl of limes at this beachfront boozer. After that, it's all about sitting at the open-air counter, clinking the ice in your mojito and watching the boats drift in the bay out front. Joe's is tucked in the Wharfside Village mall, on the 1st floor fronting the water.

Woody's Seafood Saloon   BAR
(☑ 340-779-4625; www.woodysseafood.com; Centerline Rd; ⊙ 11am-1am) St John's daily party starts here at 3pm, when the price on domestic beers drops precipitously (US$1 for a bottle of Coors). By 4pm the tanned crowd in the tiny place has spilled over on to the sidewalk. Bartenders pass beers out a streetside window. Woody's serves some reasonable noshes; try the shark bites (spiced fish pieces) or corn-crusted scallops.

🛍 Shopping

Friends of the Park Store   GIFTS & SOUVENIRS
(☑ 340-779-8700; www.friendsvinp.org; Mongoose Junction; ⊙ 9am-6pm) 🖊 Looking for paper made out of local donkey poo? Thought so. It's here, along with shelves of other ecofriendly wares and sea-glass jewelry. Proceeds go to the Virgin Islands National Park.

ℹ Information

There's a FirstBank branch with ATM near Woody's.

Connections (☑ 340-776-6922; www.connectionsstjohn.com; cnr Prince & King Sts; per 30min US$5; ⊙ 8:30am-5:30pm Mon-Fri, to 1:30pm Sat) An all-purpose communications center where you can use the internet terminals, print, send packages, etc.

Post Office (☑ 340-779-4227; King St) Across the street from the US Customs & Immigration building.

US Customs & Immigration (☑ 340-776-6741; ⊙ 8am-noon & 1-5pm) Adjoins the British Virgin Islands ferry dock. If you arrive on a ferry or on a yacht from the BVI, you must clear immigration here (typically a no-hassle process) before you head into town.

Visitors Center (⊙ 8am-4:30pm Mon-Fri) A small building next to the post office with brochures and whatnot.

ℹ Getting There & Away

BOAT

Boats from St Thomas arrive at the busy main **ferry dock**, while boats from the British Virgin Islands arrive by the US Customs & Immigration building. Check **Inter Island** (p850) for BVI schedules. Main routes:

Red Hook, St Thomas US$7 one-way, 20 minutes, hourly (big pieces of luggage cost US$4 extra)

Charlotte Amalie, St Thomas US$13 one-way, 45 minutes, three daily

West End, Tortola US$40 one-way, 30 minutes, four daily

Jost Van Dyke US$60 one-way, 45 minutes, two daily (except none Thursday)

BUS

Vitran (p850) buses pick up in front of the ferry terminal roughly once per hour. They stop along Centerline Rd en route to Coral Bay (a 40-minute trip).

CAR

Costs are around US$90 per day. Companies with reliable, rugged vehicles:

Courtesy Car Rental (p829)

St John Car Rental (p829)

Sunshine's Jeep Rental (p829)

TAXI

Taxis hang out by the ferry terminal. From downtown it costs per person US$8 to Trunk Bay, US$11 to Maho Bay and US$16 to Coral Bay.

North Shore

Life's a beach on the tranquil North Shore, where the national park's main attractions lie, including its most popular patches of sand and their swimming and hiking hot spots.

◎ Sights

Honeymoon Beach   BEACH
Honeymoon is a mile hike from the park visitors center along the Lind Point Trail. The handsome, white-sand strand is often empty and quiet – except on days when charter boats arrive between midmorning and midafternoon. A hut on-site sells snacks and rents chairs, hammocks, kayaks and other water-sports gear. Snorkeling is good off the west side, where psychedelic fish and turtles swarm over the coral reef.

Caneel Bay
BEACH

The shore in front of Caneel Bay resort actually has seven beaches, but this is the one it permits visitors to use. It's a lovely place, with fair snorkeling off the east point. You must sign in at the guardhouse when you enter the resort property, and pay US$20 if you're parking (though this is waived if you buy US$20 worth of food at the cafe).

Hawksnest Bay
BEACH

The bay here is a deep circular indentation between hills with a narrow ring of sand on the fringe. The beach is usually pretty quiet. Amenities include a bathroom, picnic shelter and barbecue grills.

Peace Hill
RUINS

Look for the Peace Hill sign as you're driving between Hawksnest and Jumbie Bays. Pull into the small parking lot, and if you're willing to walk 0.1 miles you'll be rewarded with moody ruins of an old windmill and pretty views out to sea. A statue of Jesus once lorded (pun!) over the hill, but Hurricane Marilyn in 1995 proved to be the stronger force. Look for the plaque marking his former post.

Jumbie Bay
BEACH

Jumbie is the word for ghost in the Creole dialect, and this secluded beach has a plethora of ghost stories. Look for the parking lot on North Shore Rd that holds only three cars. From here, take the wooden stairs and a short trail down to the sand.

Trunk Bay
BEACH

(adult/child US$5/free) This long, gently arching beach is the most popular strand on the island and the only one that charges a fee. The beach has lifeguards, showers, toilets, picnic facilities, snorkel rental, a snack bar and a taxi stand. No question, the sandy stretch is scenic, but it often gets packed. Everyone comes here to swim the underwater snorkeling trail, though experienced snorkelers will likely not be impressed by the murkiness or quality of what's on offer beneath the surface.

★ Cinnamon Bay
BEACH

(🚻) Mile-long Cinnamon Bay is St John's biggest beach and arguably its best. It has showers, toilets, a restaurant, grocery store, taxi stand, campground and – something you don't see at every beach – an archaeological museum of Taino relics. The Water Sports Center rents sailboats, windsurf boards, stand-up paddleboards and sea kayaks

(US$20 to US$35 per hour). It also offers lessons and leads guided paddling jaunts. Across the highway, a half-mile hiking trail winds by the ruins of an old sugar factory.

Maho Bay
BEACH

(🚻) The water is shallow and less choppy than elsewhere (good for snorkeling and kids) and it's a good bet you'll see green sea turtles in the early morning or late afternoon, and maybe a stingray or two. There's a parking lot and changing room, but no other facilities. Maho can get crowded (especially after 11am), but never overwhelmingly so.

Annaberg Sugar Mill Ruins
HISTORIC SITE

(www.nps.gov/viis; ⊘9am-4pm, demonstrations 10am-2pm Mon-Fri) FREE Part of the national park, these ruins near Leinster Bay are the most intact sugar-plantation ruins in the Virgin Islands. A 30-minute, self-directed walking tour leads you through the slave quarters, village, windmill, rum still and dungeon. The schooner drawings on the dungeon wall may date back more than 100 years.

When you're finished milling around, hop on the **Leinster Bay Trail** that starts near the picnic area and ends at, yep, Leinster Bay. It's 1.6 miles, round-trip.

Leinster Bay
BEACH

This bay adjoins the Annaberg mill ruins. Park in the plantation's lot and follow the trail along the water for 25 minutes. Some of St John's best snorkeling is at the bay's east end, offshore at Waterlemon Cay, where turtles, spotted eagle rays, barracudas and nurse sharks swim. Be aware that the current can be strong. There are no amenities and usually few people out here.

🏃 Activities & Tours

Snorkeling is the big to-do at the beaches. A couple of the larger strands rent gear onsite. For the others, it is best to rent gear from dive shops in Cruz Bay.

Virgin Islands Ecotours
KAYAKING

(☑340-779-2155; www.viecotours.com; Honeymoon Beach; 3hr tours adult/child US$89/59) This groovy company, which also operates on St Thomas, offers several guided jaunts that include kayaking, snorkeling and/or hiking. Some trips are kid-friendly (Caneel Bay), some are strenuous (Henley Cay). Most tours depart from Honeymoon Beach, but a few leave from the national-park visitor center (including the one to the Annaberg ruins and Leinster Bay).

🛏 Sleeping

Most of the North Shore is undeveloped. Aside from scattered private villas, there are only a few lodging options.

Cinnamon Bay Resort
& Campground   CAMPGROUND $

(☎ 669-999-8784; www.cinnamonbayresort.com; campsites US$45, platform tents US$75, cottages US$90-163; ⊘ closed Sep) There are four options, all on the gorgeous beach. Use your own tent; stay in a 10ft-by-14ft tent that sits on a wood platform and comes equipped with four cots and linens; or stay in a concrete cottage with electric lights, fans, a stove and dishware. Ecotents join the array in 2018; they're like soft-sided cabins with electricity, beds and a deck.

Caneel Bay Resort   RESORT $$$

(☎ 340-776-6111; www.caneelbay.com; r from US$575; ❄️@🛜⛵) It's the resort that started it all, back in 1955. Located 2 miles north of Cruz Bay, Caneel Bay is where folks such as Angelina Jolie, Denzel Washington and Harrison Ford come when they need seven beaches, 10 tennis courts, four restaurants and all-round elegance. There are no phones or TVs in rooms.

❶ Getting There & Away

A rental car is the easiest way to see the area via North Shore Rd (Rte 20) and Centerline Rd (Rte 10), but taxis will also drop you at the beaches. From Cruz Bay it costs US$9 per person to Cinnamon Bay and US$13 to Leinster Bay.

Coral Bay & East End

Coral Bay, St John's second town, is a slowpoke outpost. Located at the island's east end, the area is ripe for hiking and ecoglamping.

◉ Sights

Salt Pond Bay   BEACH

Salt Pond Bay provides decent snorkeling in calm water. Keep an eye out for turtles. Two dandy trails take off from the beach's south end: Ram Head Trail rises to a tall cliff jabbing out into the sea, and the Drunk Bay Trail leads to some crazy rock art. The beach is rarely crowded, perhaps because there are no facilities. It's located a few miles from Coral Bay town, down Rte 107 and a 10-minute walk from the parking lot.

🏃 Activities & Tours

★ Ram Head Trail   HIKING

This moderately difficult path climbs from Salt Pond Bay over switchbacks to the Ram Head, a promontory 200ft above the water at St John's southernmost tip, a grandly lonesome and windswept place. It is 2 miles round-trip and exposed, so bring sun protection. Try to go for sunset or at night during a full moon.

Drunk Bay Trail   HIKING

The easy footpath leaves Salt Pond Bay and follows the rim of the inland salt pond to a wild, rocky beach that faces east to the British Virgin Islands. The trade-wind-driven seas pile up on this shore, and the waves carry all manner of coral, fishing nets and other flotsam that locals sculpt into eye-popping artworks. It is 0.6 miles round-trip.

Hidden Reef Eco-Tours   KAYAKING

(☎ 877-529-2575; www.hiddenreefecotours.com; 2/3hr tours US$65/75) Guided kayak-and-snorkel tours depart from remote, unspoiled Haulover Bay. The shorter trip is a good one for beginners and kids.

🛏 Sleeping

★ Concordia Eco-Resort   TENTED CAMP $$

(☎ 340-715-0500; www.concordiaeco-resort.com; 20 Estate Concordia; tent/apt from US$220/315; @⛵) 🍃 The ecotents are wood-framed, soft-sided, 16ft-by-16ft units that sit amid foliage up the hillside – kind of like a tree house. Each has a 2nd-floor loft and a private bathroom, with composting toilet and solar-heated shower (still a bit chilly). A kitchen (small refrigerator and two-burner propane stove) and sea view complete the package. Concordia also offers traditional studio apartments with upgraded amenities.

The property has a cafe, activities center (for yoga and water sports), swimming pool and grocery store. It's all strung together by boardwalks and steps up the steep hillside. About 3.5 miles south of Coral Bay, Concordia is quiet and remote. You'll likely want a rental car, though patient souls can access it by public bus.

🍴 Eating

Easygoing, pub-style restaurants pop up around the bay along Rte 10 to the east and Rte 107 to the south.

Skinny Legs
BURGERS $

(☑ 340-779-4982; www.skinnylegsvi.com; Rte 10; mains US$10-14; ☺ 11am-9pm) Salty sailors, bikini-clad transients and east-end villa dwellers mix it up at this open-air grill just past the fire station. Overlooking a small boatyard, it's not about the view, but the jovial clientele and lively bar scene. Cheeseburgers win the most raves, so open wide for one, or try a grilled-fish sandwich. Live music and dancing rock weekend nights.

Cafe Concordia
CAFE $$

(☑ 340-693-5855; www.concordiaeco-resort.com; 20 Estate Concordia; mains US$20-28; ☺ 1-7:30pm Mon & Thu-Sat, from 4.30pm Sun) The casual, open-air restaurant at Concordia Eco-Resort is surprisingly ambitious in its dinner mains. The chef might whip up a rich-broth ramen bowl that wouldn't be out of place at a hipster noodle house, or a prettily plated appetizer of yogurt-stuffed baby red peppers. The menu changes often. The cocktails dazzle thanks to fresh juices and spices, especially the nutmeggy Painkiller.

Miss Lucy's
CARIBBEAN $$

(☑ 340-693-5244; Rte 107; mains US$18-30; ☺ 11am-5pm Mon-Sat, 10am-2pm Sun) Miss Lucy passed away in 2007 at age 91, but her restaurant lives on, as famous for its Sunday jazz brunch and piña colada pancakes as for its weekday conch chowder and johnny-cakes – all served at water's edge under the sea-grape trees as the occasional pet goat wanders by.

❶ Getting There & Away

Coral Bay is just over 8 miles from Cruz Bay, but it takes a good 30 minutes or so to drive it over the winding roads. The public bus also runs between the two towns. A taxi costs US$16.

ST CROIX

St Croix is the Virgins' big boy – it's more than twice the size of St Thomas – and it sports an exceptional topography spanning mountains, a spooky rainforest and a fertile coastal plain that, once upon a time, earned it the nickname 'Garden of the Antilles' for its sugarcane-growing prowess. Today the island is known for its scuba diving, rum making, marine sanctuary and 18th-century forts.

Perhaps because St Croix drifts by its lonesome 40 miles south of the other Virgins, the vibe here is different: it feels less touristy, less congested, and more 'lived in' by locals. It has two main towns: Christiansted, the largest, sits on the northeast shore. Frederiksted, its much quieter counterpart, resides on the west end, where an occasional cruise ship glides in and kicks up the pace.

❶ Getting There & Away

AIR

Henry E Rohlsen Airport (p849) is on St Croix' southwest side and handles flights from the US, many connecting via San Juan, Puerto Rico or St Thomas.

Seaborne Airlines flies seaplanes between St Thomas and St Croix – a sweet little ride (one way US$90, 20 minutes). They land in Christiansted's downtown harbor.

BOAT

The cruise-ship dock is in Frederiksted on the island's west end.

❶ Getting Around

BUS

Vitran (p850) buses travel along Centerline Rd between Christiansted and Frederiksted. The schedule is erratic; buses depart roughly every hour or two.

CAR

Rentals cost about US$55 per day. Many companies have branches at both the main airport and the seaplane dock.

Avis (☑ 340-778-9355; www.avis.com)

Budget (☑ 340-778-9636; www.budgetstcroix.com)

Centerline Car Rentals (☑ 888-288-8755; www.stxrentalcar.com)

Hertz (☑ 340-778-1402; www.rentacarstcroix.com)

Olympic (☑ 340-718-3000; www.olympicstcroix.com)

TAXI

Rates are set. It costs US$24 to go between Christiansted and Frederiksted.

Christiansted

Christiansted evokes a melancholy whiff of the past. Cannon-covered Fort Christiansvaern rises up on the waterfront. It abuts Kings Wharf, the commercial landing where, for more than 250 years, ships landed with slaves and set off with sugar or molasses. Today the wharf is fronted by a boardwalk of restaurants, dive shops and bars. It all comes together as a well-provisioned base from which to explore the island.

◉ Sights

Christiansted National Historic Site

HISTORIC SITE

(☑ 340-773-1460; www.nps.gov/chri; US$3; ☉ 8:30am-4:30pm) This historic site includes several structures. The most impressive is **Fort Christiansvaern** (1749), a four-point citadel occupying the deep-yellow buildings on the town's east side. Built out of Danish bricks (brought over as ships' ballast), the fort protected citizens from the onslaught of pirates, hurricanes and slave revolts. Cannons on the ramparts, an echoey claustrophobic dungeon and latrines with top-notch sea views await inside. The fort entrance has brochures for self-guided exploration of the other nearby historic buildings.

Protestant Cay

BEACH

(⛱) This small triangular cay, located less than 200yd from Kings Wharf, is a little oasis. It's the site of a mellow resort with a sandy beach and bar-restaurant that are open to the public. The water-sports center rents out snorkel gear, kayaks and windsurfers. There's a surprising amount of underwater life to see while snorkeling. It's also great for kids, with calm, shallow water. The ferry (US$5 round-trip, five minutes) departs from the wharf in front of the Avocado Pit cafe.

🏃 Activities & Tours

★ Tan Tan Jeep Tours

ADVENTURE

(☑ 340-773-7041; www.stxtantantours.com) Tan Tan goes four-wheeling to the Annaly Bay tide pools, deep into the rainforest and to other hard-to-reach destinations. Tours range from 2½ hours (US$100 per person) to eight hours (US$160 per person); the driver will pick you up. Book at least 48 hours in advance.

St Croix Water Sports Center

WATER SPORTS

(☑ 340-773-7060; www.facebook.com/stcroix watersports; ☉ 9am-4pm) Rents Jet Skis, snorkel gear, kayaks, pedal boats, windsurfers and more on the beach at Protestant Cay (p836).

Boating

Caribbean Sea Adventures

BOATING

(☑ 340-773-2628; www.caribbeanseaadventures. com; 59 Kings Wharf) Half-day trips to Buck Island are aboard a glass-bottom powerboat; full-day trips are on a catamaran. Half-/full-day trips cost US$75/95.

Big Beard's Adventures

BOATING

(☑ 340-773-4482; www.bigbeards.com; Queen Cross St, Caravelle Hotel) Makes trips to Buck Island aboard catamaran sailboats. Half-/full-day trips cost US$75/105.

DIVING ST CROIX

If you are a scuba enthusiast worth your sea salt, you'll be spending lots of time underwater in St Croix. It's a diver's mecca thanks to two unique features: one, it's surrounded by a massive barrier reef, so turtles, rays and other sea creatures are prevalent; and, two, a spectacular wall runs along the island's north shore, dropping at a 60-degree slope to a depth of more than 3200ft.

The best dives on the north shore are at Cane Bay Wall and North Star Wall. The top west island dives are at the Butler Bay shipwrecks (including the *Suffolk Maid* and *Rosaomaira*) and at Frederiksted Pier. While almost all dive operators offer boat dives, many of the most exciting dives, such as Cane Bay, involve beach entries with short swims to the reef.

The operators listed here go to the various sites around the island:

Cane Bay Dive Shop (p841) Across the highway from the beach and the Cane Bay Wall, and with shops in both Christiansted and Frederiksted.

Dive Experience (p837) This woman-owned shop has been around for 35-plus years and has a strong environmental commitment.

N2 The Blue (p842) Specializes in west-end wreck dives and Frederiksted Pier dives (including colorful night dives).

St Croix Ultimate Bluewater Adventures (p837) An ultraprofessional company that offers dives all over the island.

World Ocean School
BOATING

(☑ 340-626-7877; www.worldoceanschool.org; 2½hr tours adult/child US$45/35; ⊙4pm mid-Dec–late-Mar) Head out to sea aboard the sharp-looking, historic schooner *Roseway*. Added bonus: sailing with these folks supports their nonprofit group that teaches local students sailing and leadership skills. Departures are from Gallows Bay.

Buck Island Charters
BOATING

(☑ 340-773-3161; teroro@msn.com) A trimaran sailboat to Buck Island whose captain will entertain you completely; trips leave from Green Cay Marina, east of Christiansted. It's around US$75 per person for a half-day trip (including snorkeling), depending on the number of guests.

Diving

Dive Experience
DIVING

(☑ 340-773-3307; www.divexp.com; boardwalk at King's Alley; 2-tank dive US$115; ⊙7:30am-6pm) This woman-owned shop has been around for 35-plus years and has a strong environmental commitment. Boats go out most days around 9am for a half-day trip.

Cane Bay Dive Shop East
DIVING

(☑ 340-718-9913; www.canebayscuba.com; boardwalk at Pan Am Pavilion; 2-tank dive US$115) Specializes in dives at the spectacular Cane Bay Wall on the north shore and can arrange transportation there.

St Croix Ultimate Bluewater Adventures
DIVING

(☑ 877-567-136; www.stcroixscuba.com; 81 Queen Cross St; 2-tank dive US$125; ⊙7:30am-6pm) An ultraprofessional company that offers dives all over the island.

Hiking

Ay-Ay Eco-Hikes
HIKING

(☑ 340-772-4079; ayaytours@gmail.com; US$50-60) Naturalist Ras Lumumba offers tours to Maroon Ridge, Annaly Bay, Salt River Bay and more. Learn about the areas' trees, herbs, wildlife and history along the way. Hikes average between 2½ and four hours; some are strenuous.

St Croix Hiking Association
HIKING

(www.stcroixhiking.org) Sponsors a couple of guided hikes per month. They're in offbeat locales, moderately strenuous and take three to five hours. Cost is US$10.

St Croix Environmental Association
OUTDOORS

(☑ 340-773-1989; www.stxenvironmental.org) Offers two-hour hiking, birdwatching, kayaking and snorkeling trips a few times per month. Many are free; some cost US$10. Departure points vary.

✹✷ Festivals & Events

Jump Ups (music-filled street carnivals) take place four times per year, usually in February, April, June and November.

Art Thursday
ART

(www.facebook.com/artthursday; ⊙5-8pm, 3rd Thu of month Nov-May) Several painters, jewelry makers and photographers have galleries in town, and the third Thursday of the month from November through May they stay open late to party. Food and music are part of the hoppin' scene.

Cruzan Christmas Fiesta
CHRISTMAS

(www.vicarnivalschedule.com/stcroix/; ⊙early Dec–early Jan) It's a month of pageants, parades and calypso competitions, putting a West Indies spin on the Christmas holidays.

St Croix Agricultural Festival
CULTURAL

(www.viagrifest.org; ⊙mid-Feb) The three-day event features island crafters, food stalls with superb examples of West Indian and Puerto Rican cooking, bands and livestock contests.

Ironman 70.3 Triathlon St Croix
SPORTS

(www.ironman.com; ⊙early May) Participants strive for Ironman qualification in this half-triathlon.

🛏 Sleeping

Hotel on the Cay
HOTEL $$

(☑ 340-773-2035; www.hotelonthecay.com; r US$135-195; ✳@🛜🏊) The hotel sits offshore on its own little island called Protestant Cay, accessible by a five-minute ferry ride (free for guests). It's good value for the spacious rooms with full kitchenettes and bright furnishings, even if they're a bit faded. Private balconies let you take in cool breezes and sea views. Access to the island's small beach and pool is included.

King's Alley Hotel
HOTEL $$

(☑ 340-773-0103; King's Alley; d US$169; ✳🛜) King's Alley has 35 rooms above a gallery of shops and restaurants right on the harbor. The setup imitates a 19th-century Danish great house with colonial-style mahogany furniture and vaulted ceilings to match. The big, handsome rooms have French doors that open on to tiny but pretty balconies. It's the hotel many businesspeople use, though the wi-fi is sporadic.

Club Comanche Hotel St Croix HOTEL $$
(☏ 340-773-0210; www.clubcomanche.com; 1 Strand St; r US$150-250; ❋ 🛜 ⛱) This downtown property, set in a 250-year-old Danish mansion, gives off a boutique-hotel vibe. The 23 rooms have West Indian antique decor, comfy beds, flat-screen satellite TVs and decent wi-fi, plus there's a wine bar on the premises. It's in the heart of Christiansted's entertainment district, right by the boardwalk, though this means the area can be noisy. Breakfast included.

Caravelle Hotel HOTEL $$
(☏ 340-773-0687; www.hotelcaravelle.com; 44a Queen Cross St; r US$149-229; ❋ 🛜 ⛱) Located on the waterfront in a canary-yellow building, this recently renovated 42-room property is a bit more fancy than its wharfside hotel neighbors, complete with an on-site casino. All rooms have airy white decor and white tile floors; more expensive rooms have harbor views. You can also get a harbor view by heading out to the pool and sundeck.

✖ Eating

On one hand, you'll find imaginative, upscale dining at chic little bistros. On the other, you'll find local holes-in-the-wall that specialize in budget-priced West Indian fare (King St offers a good row of these between King Cross and Smith Sts). Casual bar-restaurants that fall somewhere in the middle line the waterfront. Many eateries close on Sunday and/or Monday.

★ Harvey's CARIBBEAN $
(☏ 340-773-3433; 11b Company St; mains US$11-16; ⏱ 11:30am-3pm Mon-Sat) At breezy, 10-table Harvey's, a classic tropical cafe, you half expect Humphrey Bogart from *Casablanca* to walk in and order a drink. Conch in butter sauce, grouper, sweet potato–based Cruzan stuffing, rice and peas and more West Indian dishes arrive heaped on plates. Look for the mural outside of NBA star Tim Duncan; he used to wait tables here.

Singh's Fast Food CARIBBEAN $
(☏ 340-773-7357; 23b King St; mains US$9-14; ⏱ 7am-8:30pm Mon-Sat; ✍) When the roti craving strikes – and it will – Singh's will satiate with its multiple meat and tofu varieties. The steamy, three-table joint also serves shrimp, conch, goat, turkey and tofu stews – all while island music ricochets off the pastel walls. Cash only. For dessert, walk across the street to the signless bakery for delicious cheap macadamia-nut cookies and coconut tarts.

Toast Diner BREAKFAST $
(☏ 340-692-0313; Pan Am Pavilion; mains US$10-15; ⏱ 8am-3pm; 🕾) It's hard not to love this teensy, bright-colored spot with all-day breakfast. Omelets and rum-cake French toast are specialties, as are *arepas* (South American corn pancakes) with fillings such as beets and goat's cheese, or chicken. The chalkboard menu splayed across the walls tells the story of these dishes and more.

Avocado Pit CAFE $
(☏ 340-773-9843; 59 Kings Wharf; mains US$7-14; ⏱ 7am-3pm) Young staff pour strong coffee and fruity smoothies at this wee cafe overlooking the fort and harbor. The granola-and-yogurt wins raves for breakfast, while the wraps (spicy tuna, tofu or avocado) make a delicious lunch or Buck Island picnic fare. Cash only.

★ Balter CARIBBEAN $$
(☏ 340-719-5896; www.balterstx.com; 39a Queen Cross St; mains US$27-34; ⏱ 11:30am-2pm & 6-10pm Mon-Sat) ✍ Balter puts a graceful modern spin on classic Crucian dishes. Callaloo speckled with pork belly, plantains with duck rillettes and tamarind-infused cocktails might pop up on the menu. The chef uses local, sustainably harvested ingredients, so the offerings change based on what's available. The long, open room charms with its wood-beam ceiling, fresh white walls and color-splashed paintings by island artists.

Ital in Paradise VEGETARIAN $$
(☏ 340-713-4825; 22-20b Queen Cross St; veg/fish platter US$15/18; ⏱ 11:30am-8pm Mon-Sat; ✍) The tiny Rasta eatery serves two daily platters: one vegetarian (usually with tofu) and the other a fish dish. They come with sides such as roasted cauliflower, coconut rice and kale salad. Portions are big and delicious. You can eat in at one of the four cramped tables but most people carry out. Cash only.

Savant INTERNATIONAL $$
(☏ 340-713-8666; www.savantstx.com; 4c Hospital St; mains US$20-34; ⏱ 6-10pm Mon-Sat; ✍)

HAMILTON, THE EARLY YEARS

For 250 years, no one cared much about Alexander Hamilton, the guy on the US$10 bill. That he grew up in Christiansted elicited yawns. Then the musical *Hamilton* hit the stage in 2015 and became a Broadway smash. It won Pulitzer, Tony and Grammy awards for telling the historic figure's story via hip-hop tunes. Now visitors want to know more about his early days.

Hamilton was born on the neighboring island of Nevis in 1755, but spent his formative years in Christiansted. His was a hard-knock life – born illegitimately, orphaned by age 12, impoverished – but he worked hard and impressed the local merchants, who sent him to school in New York.

He flourished in the US and became a major voice during the Revolutionary War. George Washington appointed him to be the architect of the new country's economic policies. In 1789 Hamilton became the first secretary of the treasury – which is what earned him the honor of being on the US currency.

Hamilton died infamously in a duel with Aaron Burr in 1804.

The entrance at Fort Christiansvaern has free brochures about Hamilton's time on St Croix, including a self-guided walking tour of places he frequented. Alas, most of the buildings from the era have been destroyed, so you'll have to use your imagination to see where young Alex lived and worked. One place that does still exist: the cell at Fort Christiansvaern where his mom Rachel was imprisoned for leaving her first husband.

Cozy, low-lit Savant serves upscale fusion cookery in a colonial town house. The ever-changing menu combines spicy Caribbean, Mexican and Thai recipes; sweat over them indoors in the air-conditioning or outdoors in the courtyard under twinkling lights. Reservations recommended.

🍷 Drinking & Nightlife

Places to pop in for a drink are all along the boardwalk. It's OK to carry drinks and sip in public.

⭐ **Brew STX** MICROBREWERY
(📞340-719-6339; www.facebook.com/brewstx; 55 King's Alley; ⊗11am-9pm; 🛜) Right on the boardwalk overlooking yachts bobbing in the sea, this open-air brewpub is primo for sampling the small-batch suds cooked up steps away from the taps. Build-your-own salads and wraps provide a healthful boost before you squander it on the saison or pale ale.

Tavern 1844 PUB
(📞340-773-1844; Company St; 11:30am-12:30am Tue-Sat) Lots of hop-heads line up at this cozy bar, where 75 different microbrews (mostly bottled) await. Fat burgers come with a pail of fries to help soak up the suds.

The Mill BAR
(boardwalk at Comanche Walk; ⊗11:30am-midnight) Set around an old windmill at the water's edge, this spot is hard to miss. It hosts a crowd of grizzled regulars in the afternoon, then morphs into a younger, clubbier scene at night. The windmill used to pump sea water to St Croix' first hotel pool. These days, the bar mostly pumps rum and beer.

🛍 Shopping

Riddims MUSIC
(📞340-719-1775; www.riddimsmusic.com; 3a Queen Cross St; ⊗10am-5pm Mon-Sat) Good source for reggae and *quelbe* music from the Virgin Islands, plus clothing, hats, incense and other Caribbean cultural items.

The shop also helps sponsor occasional reggae/dub festivals around the island. Ask staff for the lowdown on what's going on in the local scene.

ℹ Information

There are a couple of banks with ATMs on King St near Prince St.

ℹ Getting There & Away

AIR

Henry E Rohlsen Airport (p849) is 8 miles southwest of Christiansted. Taxis from the airport to Christiansted cost US$16 per person.

Seaborne Airlines (p835) seaplanes arrive in Christiansted's downtown harbor. It's less than a 10-minute walk to most hotels.

CAR

Rentals cost about US$55 per day. These companies are at or near the seaplane dock.

Avis (p835)

Budget (p835)

Centerline Car Rentals (p835)

TAXI

Rates are set. There's a taxi stand on King St near Church St. Rides between Christiansted and Frederiksted cost US$24.

Point Udall & East End

The scalloped coastline and steep hills of the East End beg for a drive. Rte 82 (aka East End Rd) unfurls along the beach-strewn northern shore, rolling all the way to Point Udall for sublime views and hikes to a turtle-inhabited nature preserve.

◉ Sights

Point Udall VIEWPOINT

(Rte 82) Point Udall is the easternmost geographic point in US territory. As you face into a 25-knot trade wind, the vista from the promontory high above the surf-strewn beaches is enough to make you hear symphonies. Hikers will like the challenge of taking the steep path down the hillside to isolated Isaac Bay, a nesting area for endangered sea turtles; look for the trailhead near the Millennium Monument.

Isaac Bay BEACH

This secluded beach offers no shade or facilities, and you'll have to hike about 20 minutes through scrub to reach it, but you'll be hard-pressed to find a more beautiful stretch of sand. The Nature Conservancy manages the area as part of a preserve for green and hawksbill turtles, which are active from July to December. Snorkeling on the coral reef here is good, though be careful of the strong current.

To get to the beach, take the trail down the hill from Point Udall. It starts just before the Millennium Monument. Isaac Bay is actually the second beach you come to on the trail (down the wood stairs). Head to the west end of Issac and the trail continues on to Jack Bay, which is also part of the nature preserve. Nudists sometimes hang out on the beaches.

⛏ Sleeping

Several big resorts – the kind with tennis courts and golf courses – dot the East End's shores.

Divi Carina Bay Beach Resort RESORT $$$

(✆877-773-9700; www.diviresorts.com; 25 Estate Turner Hole; r from US$500; ❄@☎☀) One of St Croix' splashiest resorts, it's located on the southeast shore and draws visitors and locals alike. The former come to stay at the 180 mod, wicker-furnished rooms. The latter

---

> **WORTH A TRIP**
>
> ### BUCK ISLAND REEF NATIONAL MONUMENT
>
> For such a small land mass – 1 mile long by 0.5 miles wide – Buck Island draws big crowds. It's not so much what's on top but what's underneath that fascinates: an 18,800-acre fish-frenzied coral-reef system surrounding the island, known as **Buck Island Reef National Monument** (www.nps.gov/buis).
>
> The sea gardens and a marked underwater trail create captivating **snorkeling** on the island's east side. On land at pretty **Turtle Beach**, endangered hawksbill and green sea turtles come ashore. A **hiking trail** circles the island's west end and leads to an impressive observation point.
>
> Most visitors glide here aboard tour boats departing from Kings Wharf in Christiansted, 5 miles to the west. Expect to pay US$75/105 (half/full-day) per person, including snorkeling gear. Note that in winter, the trade winds blow hard at Buck Island, which can result in rough water for newbies to the mask and fins. Recommended operators include the following:
>
> **Big Beard's Adventures** (p836) Trips are aboard catamaran sailboats.
>
> **Caribbean Sea Adventures** (p836) Half-day trips are aboard a glass-bottom power boat; full-day trips are on a catamaran.
>
> **Buck Island Charters** (p837) A trimaran sailboat whose captain will entertain you completely; trips leave from Green Cay Marina, east of Christiansted.

come to win big at the island's only casino. The resort is all-inclusive, so all meals and water sports are included.

✗ Eating

Cheeseburgers in Paradise   BURGERS $$
(☑340-718-1118; Rte 82; mains US$12-18; ⊙11am-9:30pm; ⊞) The setting is a roadside field with a small bar and kitchen building surrounded by a collection of open-air tables, all shaded under canopies. The ambience says 'picnic.' The menu revolves around beefy cheeseburgers, nachos and mahi Reuben sandwiches that taste best washed down with cold brews. There's a toy-filled play area for kids.

East End Pizza   PIZZA $$
(☑340-773-9700; 25 Estate Turner Hole; pizzas from US$15; ⊙5-10pm Wed-Sun) Located at Divi Carina Bay resort, this outdoor pizzeria bakes decent thin-crust pies that emerge cut into fat wedges. The jerk-chicken pizza provides a palate kick. Alas, the eatery gets crowded so orders can take a long time. But it's nothing a few icy Carib beers can't fix.

❶ Getting There & Away

Hospital Rd in Christiansted morphs into Rte 82 (aka East End Rd) a short distance beyond downtown. A taxi to Point Udall costs US$18 per person.

North Shore

Luminescent bays, Chris Columbus' landing pad and hot dive sites await along the north shore. Kayaking through the glowing water of Salt River Bay at night is a St Croix highlight.

◎ Sights

Hibiscus Beach   BEACH
Sand seekers hit palm-fringed Hibiscus Beach, with good snorkeling (at the beach's west end) but no amenities (the hotel and beach bar here are currently closed). It is located less than 2 miles west of Christiansted off Rte 75/Northside Rd.

Salt River Bay
National Historic Park   PARK
(www.nps.gov/sari) FREE About 4 miles west of Christiansted, Salt River Bay is the only documented place where Christopher Columbus landed on US soil. Don't expect bells and whistles; the site remains undeveloped

beach. The 700 acres surrounding the Salt River estuary is an ecological reserve filled with mangroves, egrets and bioluminescent life come nighttime.

Cane Bay   BEACH
A long, thin strand along Rte 80 about 9 miles west of Christiansted, Cane Bay is deservedly venerated. It provides easy access to some of the island's best dives, and it's also the gateway into the rainforest's steep hills. The beach has several small hotels, restaurants, bars and the Cane Bay Dive Shop.

🏃 Activities & Tours

Cane Bay Dive Shop   DIVING
(☑340-718-9913; www.canebayscuba.com; Cane Bay; 2-tank dive US$115) The largest shop on the island, located across the highway from the beach and the Cane Bay Wall, and with shops in both Christiansted and Frederiksted.

VI Bike & Trails   CYCLING
(☑340-277-2433; www.vibikeandtrails.com; 29 Little Fountain; 2½hr tours adult/child US$60/25) Pedal past sugar-plantation ruins, beaches and tide pools with a guide; more difficult rides bounce over rainforest trails. Bicycle rentals (per day US$35) are available for DIY adventures.

Kayaking

Virgin Kayak Tours   KAYAKING
(☑340-514-0062; www.virginkayaktours.com; Salt River Marina; 2hr tours US$50; ⊞) The company uses pedal-driven kayaks, so they are easy for novices to maneuver. By day, tours go through the mangrove estuary and stop on the beach where Columbus landed. By night, tours take in the bioluminescent bay. Call or reserve online.

Sea-Thru Kayaks VI   KAYAKING
(☑340-244-8696; www.seathrukayaksvi.com; Salt River Marina; 2hr tours US$60) It does its tours of bioluminescent Salt River Bay in ubercool clear kayaks so you can see what's gliding around and beneath you. Call for times and other details.

Caribbean Adventure Tours   KAYAKING
(☑340-778-1522; www.stcroixkayak.com; 7a Salt River Marina; 2hr tours US$50; ⊞) The sunset paddle through the bioluminescent bay is terrific. There's also a history-focused daytime paddle that goes through the mangrove forest.

🛏 Sleeping

Divers and beach lovers can choose from a smattering of cool little hotels and B&Bs to be near the action. Properties are more casual than glamorous.

★ Arawak Bay Inn at Salt River   B&B $$
(☏ 340-772-1684; www.arawakhotelstcroix.com; 62 Salt River Rd; r US$160-170; ❉@🅿🛜) The pick of the local litter for value, this peachy B&B has 14 bright rooms, each with different color schemes and decor. It's best to have a car for stays here, as the peaceful hillside property is not walking distance to the beaches and eateries (though Cane Bay and Christiansted are a quick drive away). A cooked breakfast is included.

Waves at Cane Bay   HOTEL $$
(☏ 340-718-1815; www.thewavescanebay.com; 112c Cane Bay; r US$170-200; ❉🛜🅿) The small, tidy Waves has pretty darn big rooms painted in tropical pastels. All 10 units have a balcony, kitchenette, cable TV and free (but spotty) wi-fi. Sure, they're a bit dated, but the Waves is really all about location: you can dive right off the rocks out front or lounge in the saltwater lagoon pool.

🍴 Eating

★ Rowdy Joe's
North Shore Eatery   INTERNATIONAL $$
(☏ 340-718-0055; North Shore Rd; mains US$13-24; ⊙ noon-9pm, closed Wed; 🛜) Sit on the porch, and order off the blackboard menu. The chef strives for 'good mood food' using ingredients from St Croix's farms and fishers. Dishes might include the Cubano pork sandwich, fish tacos or house-made pasta.

Eat@Cane Bay   AMERICAN $$
(☏ 340-718-0362; www.eatatcanebay.com; North Shore Rd; mains US$12-25; ⊙ 11am-9pm Mon-Fri, 9am-9pm Sat & Sun) Located across from Cane Bay beach, this place serves burgers that are a cut above the norm, along with wine and cold Caribbean beers. Weekend breakfast is popular for eggs Benedict and croissant French toast. Live music (often reggae) rocks the joint Monday, Wednesday and Friday nights and Sunday afternoons.

❶ Getting There & Away

King St in Christiansted turns into Northside Rd (Rte 75) at the town's western edge and heads toward the north shore. North Shore Rd (Rte 80) then splits off toward Salt River and Cane Bay. A taxi from Christiansted to Cane Bay costs US$24.

Frederiksted

St Croix' second-banana town is a motionless patch of colonial buildings snoring beside the teal-blue sea. Other than the occasional cruise ship of visitors, it'll be you and that lizard sunning itself who will have the gritty outpost to yourselves. With its out-of-the-mainstream, laissez-faire ambience, Frederiksted is the center for gay life on St Croix.

⊙ Sights

Frederiksted Pier & Waterfront   PIER
The palm-lined seafront has benches where you can sit and watch the cruise-ship scene. During quiet times (ie when cruise ships aren't here), snorkelers and divers gravitate to the pier's pilings, which attract an extensive collection of marine life, including schools of sea horses.

Fort Frederik   FORT
(adult/child US$5/free; ⊙ 8:30am-4pm Mon-Fri) The deep-red color of this fort at the foot of the pier is what most visitors remember about the little citadel. It's also where the island's slaves were emancipated in 1848. Exhibits inside explain the event.

🏃 Activities

N2 The Blue   DIVING
(☏ 340-772-3483; www.n2theblue.com; 202 Custom House St; ⊙ 8:30am-4:30pm) It specializes in west-end wreck dives and Frederiksted Pier dives (including colorful night dives).

Freedom City Surf Shop   SURFING
(☏ 340-227-0682; Frederiksted Beach; ⊙ 11am-8pm) The congenial owners rent beach chairs and snorkel gear, but their specialty is stand-up paddleboard rentals and lessons (US$30 per hour).

⭐ Festivals & Events

Sunset Jazz Festival   MUSIC
(Buddhoe Park; ⊙ 6pm 3rd Fri of month) Throngs of locals and visitors come to the waterfront with blankets and picnics in tow. The free concerts last about three hours.

🛏 Sleeping

Frederiksted is teeny, so it only holds a couple of options. Few visitors spend the night out here. Expect a subdued stay.

Inn on Strand Street HOTEL **$$**
(☑ 340-772-0500; www.innonstrandstreet.com; 442 Strand St; r US$100-150; ❋@☎) The bright-blue Inn sits right downtown. Four floors are built around a courtyard, and many rooms have patios overlooking the pier. The 32 units each have tiled floors and standard hotel-style furnishings, plus a refrigerator. The property is sparse, but that may change as new ownership is renovating it. Many people still call it by its old name: the Frederiksted Hotel.

Sand Castle on the Beach HOTEL **$$**
(☑ 340-772-1205; www.sandcastleonthebeach. com; 127 Estate Smithfield; r/ste from US$179/299; ❋☎≋) On the beach about a mile south of Frederiksted, 21-room Sand Castle is one of the few gay- and lesbian-oriented hotels in the Virgin Islands. The vibrant, tropical-themed rooms come with kitchenettes; most have sea views. There's a good cafe on-site for easy eats.

✖ Eating & Drinking

Mosey along Strand and King Sts downtown near Frederiksted Pier, and you'll find the bulk of the town's cafes, sandwich shops and Caribbean restaurants.

Freedom City Beach Bar BURGERS **$**
(☑ 340-713-5159; Frederiksted Beach; mains US$14-16; ⊙11am-8pm) This superfriendly enterprise whips up lovely burgers, tacos and black-bean and fish burritos right by the sea. The surf shop (p842) next door rents paddleboards and beach gear. Stay for sunset – the colors dazzle. Live bands play on occasion.

Polly's at the Pier CAFE **$**
(☑ 340-719-9434; 3 Strand St; mains US$6-11; ⊙8am-3pm Mon-Sat; ☎) Polly's serves coffee, tea, sandwiches, omelets, waffles and cocktails a stone's throw from the pier. Savor it in the cafe's open, airy, island-bohemian ambience. It's reliably open when many other places in town are not.

Rose's Dream Cuisine CARIBBEAN **$$**
(☑ 340-692-0341; 58a King St; mains US$13-19; ⊙11:30am-10pm Mon-Sat, from 11am Sun) Rose and her family deliver quintessential island hospitality. Yes, your order may take a while, but relax with a cold Carib beer at one of the unfussy, white-clothed tables. When your curried goat with red beans, conch in butter sauce or other home-style meal arrives, you won't remember the wait.

Turtles SANDWICHES **$$**
(☑ 340-772-3676; 37 Strand St; mains US$11-17; ⊙8:30am-10pm Mon-Sat) Chow hulking sandwiches on homemade bread or sip a fine cup of coffee at beachfront tables under seagrape trees. At night the action moves upstairs for burgers, callaloo soup, grilled lobster (especially on Fridays) and sunset views at Turtles After Dark. The deli is cash only.

Blue Moon CARIBBEAN **$$**
(☑ 340-772-2222; 7 Strand St; mains US$25-31; ⊙6-9pm Wed-Sat) Frederiksted's fine-dining hot spot dishes up Caribbean and Cajun cuisine in an atmospheric colonial warehouse. Fork into mango-butter-sauced jumbo shrimp or andouille sausage mixed with spicy pasta alfredo at candlelit tables. There's live jazz Wednesday and Friday nights.

Lost Dog Pub PUB
(☑ 340-772-3526; 14 King St; ⊙4pm-1am) Friendly expats hang out at the Dog to sip cold beer, chow pizza and rock out to the jukebox. Think of something clever to write on the wall before the night is done.

❶ Getting There & Away

Taxis huddle near Fort Frederik. It costs US$24 to go to Christiansted and takes 45 minutes or so.

Around Frederiksted

The area around Frederiksted has two distinct sides to its topography and character. First, there are the wild mountains and beaches of the rainforest area in the island's northwest pocket. Second, south of the mountains is the broad coastal plain that once hosted the majority of sugar plantations. Today, the area is largely a modern commercial and residential zone where much of St Croix' population lives. But sprinkled along the land bordering Centerline Rd are some remarkable heirlooms from the colonial era. Oh, and rum factories.

◉ Sights

Estate Whim Plantation Museum MUSEUM
(☑ 340-772-0598; www.stcroixlandmarks.com; Centerline Rd; adult/child US$10/5; ⊙10am-3pm Wed-Sat) Only a few of Whim Plantation's original 150 acres survive at the museum, but the grounds thoroughly evoke the colonial days when sugarcane ruled St Croix.

Guided tours leave every 30 minutes, or wander by the crumbling stone windmill and chimney on your own. Don't forget to ask for the Landmarks Society's map to other ruins around the island.

St George Village Botanical Garden
GARDENS

(☑340-692-2874; www.sgvbg.org; 127 George Rd; adult/child US$8/1; ⊙9am-5pm Mon-Sat) The pretty, 16-acre park is built over a colonial sugar plantation. More than 1500 native and exotic species grow on the grounds. Orchid lovers, in particular, are in for a treat.

★Cruzan Rum Distillery
DISTILLERY

(☑340-692-2280; www.cruzanrum.com; 3a Estate Diamond, Rte 64; tours US$8; ⊙9am-4pm Mon-Fri, 10am-2pm Sat & Sun) To find out how the islands' popular elixir gets made, stop by the historic distillery for a tour. The journey through gingerbread-smelling (from molasses and yeast), oak-barrel-stacked warehouses takes 20 minutes, after which you get to sip plenty of the good stuff. The Nelthropp family, Cruzan Rum's owners, have been perfecting the recipes since 1760. Cash not accepted; credit cards only.

Captain Morgan Rum Distillery
DISTILLERY

(☑340-713-5654; www.captainmorganvisitorcenter.com; Rte 66; adult/child US$10/3; ⊙tours 10am-3pm Mon-Fri) Captain Morgan opened its shiny new distillery on St Croix in 2010. The hour-long tour includes a multimedia film (the best part), a tram ride with a certain costumed pirate and, of course, samples of the Captain's happy juice.

☞ Tours

Ridge to Reef Farm
TOURS

(☑340-220-0466; www.ridge2reef.org; tour US$10-25; ⊙10am-4pm Mon-Wed, Fri & Sat) Tour an organic farm in St Croix' rainforest, either on your own (per person US$10) or with a guide (US$25 Tuesday and Friday only, advance reservations required). You can also work in the fields and stay overnight; lodging is provided from US$35 per day.

Paul & Jill's Equestrian Stables
HORSE RIDING

(☑340-772-2880; www.paulandjills.com; Rte 58; 1½hr tour US$99) The stables offer trail rides that lead through hidden plantation ruins and the rainforest to hilltop vistas. You'll also trot along the beach.

🛏 Sleeping

The area is more residential than touristy, so you won't find abundant options, but you will find a few special, ecologically minded ones.

Mt Victory Camp
CAMPGROUND $

(☑340-201-7983; www.mtvictorycamp.com; Rte 58; campsites US$30, equipped tents US$90, apt US$110; ⊛) 🍃 Pitch your own tent in the forest, or choose one of four bungalows (aka screened-in perma-tents on a wood platform, each with electricity and a kitchen with cold-water sink, propane stove and cooking utensils). Guests share the solar-heated bathhouse, pavilion with refrigerator and wi-fi, and sublime nature sounds. There's also an apartment (with en suite bathroom) carved from an old schoolhouse.

★Northside Valley
VILLA $$

(☑340-772-0558; www.northsidevalley.com; 2 Estate Northside; apt US$145-215; ⊛) 🍃 The property offers eight concrete-and-tile villas, each with two bedrooms and a fully equipped kitchen, set amid jungle like trees. It's wonderfully remote: no TV, air-con or wi-fi (though the latter is available in the common area). There is a one-week minimum stay in high season. It's near Butler Bay, across the road from the beach.

Ecofriendly features include solar panels and rainwater reuse.

🛍 Shopping

St Croix Leap
ARTS & CRAFTS

(☑340-772-0421; Rte 76; ⊙10am-5pm Mon-Sat) Woodworkers transform chunks of fallen mahogany trees into all manner of art and housewares at this open-air studio set deep in the rainforest. Be prepared for bats fluttering above! The opening hours can be erratic, but if someone is there you'll likely get a personal tour of the space. It's a wild road to reach it. Cash only.

ℹ Getting There & Away

The key sights lie south of Frederiksted around Centerline Rd (Rte 70). A taxi from Frederiksted costs US$10 or so. The main routes through the rainforest are Mahogany Rd (Rte 76) and Creque Dam Rd (Rte 58), both narrow and bumpy.

UNDERSTAND
US VIRGIN ISLANDS

History

Pirates & Power Brokering

Folks have been living on the islands from as early as 2000 BC. The Taínos ruled the roost for a while, but the ruthless, seafaring Caribs eventually wiped them out.

Around this time Christopher Columbus sailed up to St Croix' Salt River Bay during his second trip to the Caribbean. It was 1493, and he gave the islands their enduring name: Santa Ursula y Las Once Mil Vírgenes, in honor of a 4th-century princess and her 11,000 maidens. Mapmakers soon shortened the mouthful to 'The Virgins.'

The islands remained under Spanish control until the English defeated the Spanish Armada in 1588. England, France and Holland were quick to issue 'letters of marque,' which allowed privateers the rights to claim territory and protect those claims.

One king's privateer became every other king's pirate. Blackbeard (Edward Teach) operated in the Virgin Islands before 1720, with a collection of other rascals.

The Danes and English bickered over the islands, while each built vast sugar and tobacco plantations. The English held colonies on islands east of St John, while the Danes held St Thomas to the west. St John remained disputed territory. Finally, in 1717 the Danes sent a small but determined band of soldiers to St John and drove the British out. The Narrows, between St John and Tortola in the British Virgin Islands, became the border that has divided the eastern (first Danish, now US) Virgins from the British Virgins for more than 250 years.

Slavery & Liberation

The West Indies grew rich producing sugar and cotton for Europe. In pursuit of profits, the Danish West India and Guinea Company declared St Thomas a free port in 1724, and purchased St Croix from the French in 1733. By the end of the century, the number of African slaves on the islands exceeded 40,000.

Harsh living conditions and oppressive laws drove slaves to revolt. Meanwhile, sugar production in Europe and American tariffs

WORTH A TRIP

CALEDONIA RAIN FOREST

In the island's wet, mountainous northwest pocket, a thick forest of tall mahogany, silk cotton and white cedar trees grow. Technically, as only about 40in of rain fall here per year, the Caledonia Rain Forest is not a true 'rainforest.' No matter – it looks the part, with clouds, dripping trees and earthy aromas. Mahogany Rd (Rte 76) cuts through the spooky woods; it's twisty and potholed, so be careful.

on foreign sugar cut into the islands' profits. The deteriorating economy put everyone in a foul mood. Something had to give and it finally did in 1848, when Afro-Caribbeans on St Croix forced the legal end to slavery.

However, they remained in economic bondage. Life on the islands was dismal. A series of labor revolts left the plantation infrastructure in ruins.

USA Eyes the Prize

The USA, realizing the strategic value of the islands, negotiated with Denmark to buy its territories. The deal was almost done in 1867, but the US Congress choked at paying US$7.5 million (more than the US$7.2 million it had just paid for Alaska).

As WWI began in Europe, the USA grew concerned that German armies might invade Denmark and claim the Danish West Indies. Finally, the USA paid the Danes US$25 million in gold for the islands in 1917.

The US Navy then took control, which resulted in tensions with the local population. The USA tried to enforce Prohibition here, an unusual concept for an economy tied to the production, sale and distribution of rum. In 1931 President Herbert Hoover traveled to the Virgins. He stayed for less than six hours and left unimpressed.

In 1934, however, President Franklin Delano Roosevelt visited and saw the potential that Hoover had missed. Soon, the USA instituted programs to eradicate disease, drain swamps, build roads, improve education and create tourism infrastructure.

Islanders received the right to elect their own governor in 1970. Though local politics brought its share of nepotism, cronyism and other scandals, the next four decades also brought unprecedented growth in tourism and raised the standard of living. Hurricane Marilyn took a chunk out of the islands in 1995, but they got back to business quickly thereafter.

Every once in a while, USVI citizens get a bee in their bonnet and seek greater self-determination through a Virgin Islands Constitution. They've tried and failed to ratify it five times.

Culture

The US Virgin Islands are a territory of the USA, and the islands participate in the political process by sending an elected, nonvoting representative to the US House of Representatives. All citizens of the USVI are US citizens (and have been since 1927) with one exception: they cannot vote in presidential elections.

Though the USVI wears a veneer of mainstream American culture, with conveniences such as shopping malls and fast food, West African culture is a strong and respected presence.

Since 1970 the population of USVI has quadrupled, although current growth has plateaued. Economic opportunities draw immigrants from other parts of the West Indies, along with US mainlanders who come to escape the politics and busyness of American life, or to retire in the sun. Tourism accounts for 80% of GDP and employment, and many locals work as hoteliers, restaurant owners, taxi drivers and shopkeepers.

JUMP UP!

Reggae and calypso tunes blast from USVI vehicles and emanate from shops, restaurants and beach bars. *Quelbe* and fungi (*foon*-ghee, also an island food made of cornmeal) are two types of folk music. *Quelbe* blends jigs, quadrilles, military fife and African drum music with lyrics (often biting satire) from slave field songs. Fungi uses homemade percussion such as washboards, ribbed gourds and conch shells to accompany a singer. The best time to experience island music is during the 'jump up' parades and competitions associated with major festivals such as Carnival on St Thomas and St John, or at St Croix' Cruzan Christmas Fiesta.

Per the most recent census data, 76% of the population is black, 16% is white and the rest is a mix. About half the population was born in the USVI; another third hail from Latin America or elsewhere in the Caribbean, and about 15% were born in the US.

Landscape & Wildlife

The Land

The US Virgins consist of about 50 islands, 40 miles east of Puerto Rico. They are the northernmost islands in the Lesser Antilles chain and, along with the British Virgin Islands, form an irregular string of islands stretching west to east. The one exception to this string is the USVI's largest island, St Croix, which lies 40 miles south.

The mountain slopes are dense subtropical forests. All the timber is second or third growth; the islands were stripped for sugar, cotton and tobacco plantations in the colonial era. There are no rivers and very few freshwater streams. Coral reefs of all varieties grow in the shallow waters near the seashores.

Wildlife

Very few of the land mammals that make their home in the US Virgin Islands are natives; most mammal species have been accidentally or intentionally introduced over the centuries. St John has a feral population of donkeys and pigs, and all the islands have wild goats, white-tailed deer, cats and dogs. Other prevalent land mammals include mongooses and bats.

The islands are home to a few species of snake (none of which are poisonous), including the Virgin Island tree boa.

More than 200 bird species – including the official bird, the bananaquit – inhabit the islands.

Environmental Issues

The US Virgin Islands have long suffered from environmental problems, including deforestation, soil erosion, mangrove destruction and a lack of freshwater. During the 18th century, logging operations denuded many of the islands to make room for plantations. The demise of the agricultural economy in the late 19th century allowed the islands to reforest, and in recent years locals (especially on St John) have begun several forest-conservation projects.

But population growth and rapid urbanization continue to pose grave threats. If not for the desalination plants (which make freshwater out of seawater) the islands couldn't support even a quarter of their population, let alone visitors. When a hurricane strikes, power and desalination facilities shut down. Islanders with enough foresight and money keep rainwater cisterns for such emergencies, but folks without suffer.

Rising sea temperatures are another topic of concern, as they impact local reefs and cause coral bleaching. In 2005 a particularly 'hot' period killed about half of the USVI's coral. Another widespread bleaching event occurred in 2010.

Prior years of overfishing have put conch in a precarious situation. Currently, conch fishing is not allowed from July through October so stocks can replenish.

The past decade has seen an increase in the level of awareness, resources and action dedicated to conservation efforts. Friends of Virgin Islands National Park (www.friends-vinp.org) is one group working toward environmental preservation.

SURVIVAL GUIDE

ⓘ Directory A-Z

ACCOMMODATIONS

Guesthouses, hotels, private villas and condo resorts are abundant on all the islands. High season is mid-December through April, when rooms are costly and advance reservations essential. Three-night-minimum-stay requirements are common.

Be aware that while air-conditioning is widely available, it is not a standard amenity, even at top-end places. If you want it, be sure to ask about it when you book.

Accommodations Services

Carefree Getaways (☑340-779-4070; www.carefreegetaways.com) A St John-focused company that rents villas and condos around the island.

Caribbean Villas (☑800-338-0987; www.caribbeanvilla.com) This St John-focused company rents condos and villas around the island.

PRACTICALITIES

Newspapers The *VI Daily News* is the main paper. VI Source (www.visource.com) provides news online for free.

Magazines *St Thomas/St John This Week* and *St Croix This Week* are free and widely available monthly (despite the name!) magazines.

Radio WVGN (93.1FM) is the National Public Radio (NPR) affiliate, airing from St Thomas.

TV Local stations include channels 8 (ION) and 12 (PBS).

Smoking Banned in all restaurants, bars and other public venues.

Weights & Measures The islands use imperial weights and measurements. Distances are in feet and miles; gasoline is measured in gallons.

Catered To (☑340-776-6641; www.cateredto.com) This company rents villas and condos around St John.

CHILDREN
The islands are relatively child friendly. While baby-change facilities and smooth pavements for prams are not ubiquitous, calm beaches and comfortable lodgings for families are.

Specific beaches that are good for children, with shallow water and minimal waves, include Secret Harbour and Magens Bay (St Thomas), Maho Bay and Cinnamon Bay (St John), and Protestant Cay (St Croix). Magens and Cinnamon have large water-sports centers that rent kayaks, paddleboards and more, so teens groove on these beaches, too.

St Croix' cannon-clad forts are cool for youngsters. Teens like dipping a paddle on tours with St Thomas' **Virgin Islands Ecotours** (p827) and St Croix' **Virgin Kayak Tours** (p841); the latter uses easy-to-maneuver pedal-operated vessels.

All the islands offer villa and condominium rentals, which have lots of space and kitchens for DIY meals. Resorts offer similar amenities. St Thomas' East End is laden with such properties. **Caneel Bay Resort** (p834) on St John is another good option.

Even if most restaurants do not have a children's menu, they often serve burgers and pizza as part of their lineup. The ambience tends to be informal and relaxed wherever you go.

SLEEPING PRICE RANGES

The following price indicators refer to a double room with bathroom in peak season. Unless otherwise stated, breakfast is not included in the price, nor is tax (12.5%) or energy surcharge (often 8% to 15%).

$ less than US$100

$$ US$100–300

$$$ more than US$300

On St John, **Island Baby** (www.islandbabyvi.com) rents out gear such as high chairs (per week US$60), baby hiking backpacks (per week US$50), baby monitors and much more, which can lighten one's travel load considerably.

EMBASSIES & CONSULATES

Danish Consulate (☎340-776-0656; www.dkconsulateusvi.com; Scandinavian Center, Havensight Mall, Bldg 3)

Swedish Consulate (☎340-774-6845; charlotteamalie@consulateofsweden.org; 1340 Taarneberg; ⊗8:30am-5pm Mon-Fri)

EMERGENCY NUMBERS

Police	☎911
Fire	☎911
Ambulance	☎911

FOOD

Small, unadorned restaurants serving West Indian fare are common. Soups and stews are staples in local cooking. Meat dishes (chicken, pork and goat) are primarily curried or barbecued with tangy spices. All manner of fish and shellfish (especially conch) make it to island tables. Roots such as yam and cassava are boiled, mashed or steamed and served as side dishes. Plantains and mangoes are popular fruits.

Essential Food & Drink

Callaloo Spicy soup stirred with okra, various meats, greens and hot peppers.

Pate (pah-*tay*) Flaky fried dough pockets stuffed with spiced chicken, fish or other meat.

Fungi (*foon*-ghee) A polenta-like cornmeal cooked with okra, typically topped by fish and gravy.

Mango Pale Ale Fruit-tinged microbrew by St John Brewers.

Cruzan Rum St Croix' happy juice since 1760, from light white rum to banana, guava and other tropical flavors.

GLBT TRAVELERS

While a fair number of islanders are gay, you're not likely to meet many who are 'out,' nor are you likely to see public displays of affection among gay couples.

St Croix is the most gay friendly of the islands, with Frederiksted the center of gay life, but overall there aren't many structured outlets for meeting. One exception is **Sand Castle on the Beach** (p843), in Frederiksted.

HEALTH

Governor Juan F Luis Hospital (☎340-778-6311; www.jflusvi.org; ⊗24hr) is about 2 miles west of Christiansted via Centerline Rd.

Myrah Keating Smith Community Health Center (☎340-693-8900; Centerline Rd; ⊗8am-8pm Mon-Fri) About 2 miles east of Cruz Bay.

Roy Schneider Community Hospital (☎340-776-8311; www.rlshospital.org; 9048 Sugar Estate Rd; ⊗24hr) On the east side of Charlotte Amalie, this full-service hospital has an emergency room, recompression chamber and doctors in all major disciplines.

LEGAL MATTERS

The blood-alcohol limit in the USVI is 0.08%. Driving under the influence of alcohol is a serious offense, subject to stiff fines and even imprisonment.

Open-container laws do not exist here, so you can walk around with drinks on the streets.

MONEY

Currency is the US dollar (US$). ATMs in main towns on all three islands. Credit cards accepted in most hotels and restaurants.

Exchange Rates

AUSTRALIA	A$1	US$0.77
CANADA	C$1	US$0.76
EUROPE	€1	US$1.06
JAPAN	¥100	US$0.88
NZ	NZ$1	US$0.72
UK	UK£1	US$1.24

For current exchange rates, see www.xe.com.

Tipping

Hotels US$1 to US$2 per bag for bellhop; US$2 to US$5 per night for cleaning staff

Restaurants 15% to 20% of bill

Taxis 10% to 15% of fare

Dive/tour-boat operators 15% of fee is reasonable

PUBLIC HOLIDAYS

New Year's Day January 1

Three Kings Day (Feast of the Epiphany) January 6

Martin Luther King Jr's Birthday Third Monday in January

Presidents' Day Third Monday in February

Transfer Day March 31

Holy Thursday & Good Friday Before Easter Sunday (in March or April)

Easter Monday Day after Easter Sunday

Memorial Day Last Monday in May

Emancipation Day July 3

Independence Day (Fourth of July) July 4

Labor Day First Monday in September

Columbus Day Second Monday in October

Liberty Day November 1

Veterans' Day November 11

Thanksgiving Day Fourth Thursday in November

Christmas Day December 25

Boxing Day December 26

TAXES & REFUNDS

The islands have no sales tax on goods or services. The stated price on restaurant menus and in shops is what you pay.

TELEPHONE

Country code ☏1

Area code ☏340

Dialing USVI phone numbers consist of a three-digit area code, followed by a seven-digit local number. If you are calling from abroad, dial all 10 digits preceded by ☏1. If you are calling locally, just dial the seven-digit number.

TIME

The islands are on Atlantic Standard Time (GMT/UTC minus 4). Relative to New York, Miami and the eastern time zone: the Virgins are one hour ahead in winter, and in the same time zone in summer (due to daylight saving time).

TOURIST INFORMATION

See St John (www.seestjohn.com) An excellent resource with detailed hiking-trail directions and beach guides.

St Croix This Week (www.stcroixthisweek.com) A widely available free monthly magazine with maps and events listings.

USVI Department of Tourism (www.visitusvi.com) Official tourism site with a 'hot deals' link.

TRAVELERS WITH DISABILITIES

While the *Americans With Disabilities Act* holds sway in the USVI, facilities are not accessible to the same degree as they are in the US. On St

---

EATING PRICE RANGES

The following price indicators denote the cost of a main dish for dinner.

$ less than US$15

$$ US$15 to US$35

$$$ more than US$35

John, **Concordia Eco-Resort** (p834) provides well-regarded accessible lodging.

VOLUNTEERING

Friends of Virgin Islands National Park (www.friendsvinp.org) Volunteer for weekly trail or beach cleanups on St John.

St Croix Environmental Association (www.stxenvironmental.org) Help clean beaches where sea turtles nest.

Ridge to Reef Farm (www.ridge2reef.org) Stay on an organic farm in St Croix' rainforest and work in the fields.

ⓘ Getting There & Away

AIR

St Thomas has the main airport. St Croix' airport is smaller. Each facility has an ATM, food concessions, car rentals and taxis.

Cyril E King Airport (STT; www.viport.com) On St Thomas.

Henry E Rohlsen Airport (STX; ☏340-778-1012; www.viport.com) On St Croix.

American Airlines, Delta, JetBlue, Spirit Airlines and United Airlines all fly to the USVI. Hubs with nonstop flights include New York, Boston, Philadelphia and Atlanta. Many flights transit through Miami or San Juan, Puerto Rico.

Regional airlines serving the USVI from around the Caribbean include the following:

Air Sunshine (☏954-434-8900; www.airsunshine.com)

Cape Air (☏800-227-3247; www.capeair.com)

LIAT (www.liat.com)

Seaborne Airlines (☏787-946-7800; www.seaborneairlines.com)

SEA

Cruise Ship

Cruise ships are big business in the USVI, especially on St Thomas.

Ferry

Excellent ferry connections link St Thomas and St John with Tortola, Virgin Gorda and Jost Van Dyke. **VI Now** (www.vinow.com) has schedules. For trips between the USVI and BVI, a passport is required.

Ferries between the two territories run until about 5pm only. Watch out for scheduling issues if you're trying to get from one to the other at night.

Taxes are not included in the following fees. There is a US$10 port fee to leave the USVI, and a US$20 departure tax to leave the BVI. Luggage costs US$3 per bag. Arrive at least 30 minutes before departure time to buy tickets at the terminal.

Main companies and routes:

Inter Island (☏ 340-776-6597; www.inter islandboatservices.com)

Native Son (☏ 340-775-8685; www.native sonferry.com)

Road Town Fast Ferry (☏ 340-777-2800; www. roadtownfastferry.com)

Smith's Ferry/Tortola Fast Ferry (☏ 340-775-7292; www.bviferryservices.com)

Speedy's (☏ 284-495-5240; www.bviferries. com)

Ferries to/from Charlotte Amalie:

Road Town, Tortola direct 45 minutes, three daily, one way US$35; Road Town Fast Ferry

Road Town, Tortola via West End 60 minutes, several daily, one way US$35; Native Son and Smith's

Spanish Town, Virgin Gorda 90 minutes, three weekly (Tuesday, Thursday, Saturday), one way US$40; Speedy's

Ferries to/from Red Hook:

West End, Tortola 60 minutes, four daily, one way US$35; Native Son

Jost Van Dyke 75 minutes, two daily (except none Thursday), one way US$60; Inter Island

Ferries to/from Cruz Bay:

West End, Tortola 30 minutes, four daily, one way US$40; Inter Island

Jost Van Dyke 45 minutes, two daily (except none Thursday), one way US$60; Inter Island

Yacht

If arriving by yacht to the USVI from another country, it must be at one of the following ports, which have customs and immigration facilities:

St Thomas Charlotte Amalie Marine Terminal

St John Cruz Bay

St Croix Gallows Bay (near Christiansted)

❶ Getting Around

AIR

Seaborne Airlines (p849) operates sea-planes between the downtown harbors of St Thomas' Charlotte Amalie and St Croix' Christiansted. The flight takes 20 minutes and goes roughly once per hour. **Cape Air** (p849) goes between St Thomas' and St Croix' main airports.

BOAT

Frequent ferries run between the St Thomas and St John. They go hourly from between Red Hook and Cruz Bay (US$7 one way, 20 minutes), and three times daily between Charlotte Amalie and Cruz Bay (US$13 one way, 45 minutes). No ferries currently go to St Croix. Check **VI Now** (www.vinow.com) for updated schedules.

BUS

Vitran (fare US$1) operates air-conditioned public buses over the length of St Thomas, St John and St Croix. Buses run daily between 5:30am and 7:30pm (approximately one bus per hour). Service isn't very reliable. St Thomas also has 'safari' buses, ie open-air trucks outfitted with benches.

CAR & MOTORCYCLE

To rent a car in the USVI you need to be at least 25 years old, hold a valid driver's license and have a major credit card.

Cars start at around US$70 per day (higher on St John). If you're traveling in peak season, it's wise to reserve a couple of months in advance, as supplies are limited. Major international car-rental companies have branches at the airports and sometimes at ferry terminals.

Road Conditions

Be prepared for challenging road conditions, including steep, winding roads and copious pot-holes. Chickens, cows, goats and donkeys often dart in and out of the roadway, to boot.

Road Rules

➾ Rule number one: drive on the left-hand side of the road.

➾ Seat-belt use is compulsory; children under age five must be in a car seat.

➾ Driving while using a hand-held cell phone is illegal (but ear pieces are permitted).

TAXI

All the islands have taxis that are easily accessible in the main tourist areas. Most vehicles are vans that carry up to 12 passengers; sometimes they're open-air trucks with bench seats and awnings and room for 20 people. Taxis service multiple destinations and may stop to pick up passengers along the way, so rates are usually charged on a per-person basis. Rates are set, with prices listed in the free tourist magazines and at **VI Now** (www.vinow.com). Rates go down a bit if more than one person takes the taxi. Always confirm the price before getting in.

Survival Guide

Directory A–Z

Accommodations

The Caribbean offers almost any accommodations choice you could wish for. Advance booking is always a good idea, especially if you're planning to visit in high season or are staying in a resort.

Hotels These range from simple local outfits to the most luxurious boutique offerings available.

Villas Private villa rentals are popular in the Caribbean, especially for groups, and can be found for most budgets.

Resorts Room only or all-inclusive resorts are a classic Caribbean offering, and come in family-friendly or adult-only varieties.

Guesthouses Small family-run guesthouses are a great way to get a taste of the local culture.

All-Inclusive Resorts

Born in Jamaica and now prevalent across the Caribbean, all-inclusive resorts allow you to pay a set price and then nothing more once you arrive. You usually get a wristband that allows you free access to the hotel or resort's restaurants, bars and water-sports equip-ment. Many properties have jumped onto the 'all-inclusive' bandwagon, but don't necessarily supply the goods. Be sure to find out exactly what 'all-inclusive' includes.

➡ What is the variety and quality of food available?

➡ How many meals are included?

➡ Are all drinks included?

➡ Is 'free alcohol' limited to wine with dinner?

➡ Are there lots of extra-charge options at mealtimes (steaks etc), meaning that the regular food is uninspiring?

➡ What activities are included (an extra charge for snorkeling gear is a sign of stinginess)?

Booking Services

The following accommodations services can all book villas across the Caribbean:

Caribbean Way (www.caribbeanway.com)

CV Villas (☑in the UK 020-7401-1010; www.cvtravel.co.uk)

Villas of Distinction (www.villasofdistinction.com)

Wimco Villas (www.wimcovillas.com)

Camping

Camping is limited in the Caribbean, and on some islands freelance camping is either illegal or discouraged.

Guesthouses

The closest thing the Caribbean has to hostels, guesthouses are usually great value. Often in the middle of a town or village and rarely alongside a beach, they offer good opportunities for cultural immersion.

Hotels

Across the Caribbean, hotel rooms can range from humdrum to massive 1000-room resorts to glorious villas hovering over the sea.

Rental Accommodations

If you're traveling with your family or a large group, you might want to look into renting a condo or villa. Villas are great because you have room to stretch out, do your own cooking and enjoy plenty of privacy. Prices start at about US$700 per week and climb ever higher.

Seasonal Price Differences

During low season, May to mid-December, rates may be up to 40% less or the property may be closed.

Climate

Freeport/Lucaya

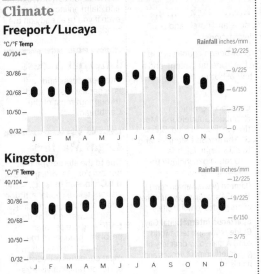

Kingston

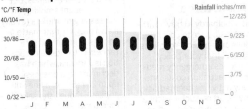

Port of Spain

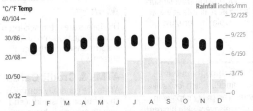

San Juan

Bargaining

You will likely have a chance to try out your bargaining skills at some point in the Caribbean, mostly with beach vendors and at tourist markets. Most shops and produce markets have fixed prices.

Embassies & Consulates

Nations such as Australia, Canada, New Zealand and the US have embassies and consulates in the largest Caribbean countries. See the destination chapters for details.

Etiquette

The Caribbean is famously laid-back, but it's also a place that insists on good manners.

Greetings Always greet people properly, and treat elders with extra respect. That said, don't be surprised at the directness of many conversations.

Dress Caribbean people dress smartly when they can (even more so when heading to a party or social event), and many government offices and banks have written dress codes on the door – beachwear should be confined to the beach.

Island time Even though locals may be relaxed about the clock, it's always wise to turn up to appointments at the stated hour (but be prepared to wait).

Food

You can eat almost anything in the Caribbean at any type of restaurant. You'll rarely need to do more than turn up or book on the day, though some top-end places require advance booking.

Restaurants Caribbean restaurants run from casual beach grills to fine dining.

Cafes & bars Cafes are good for a casual breakfast or lunch, or simply a cup of coffee. Bars often offer meals.

Hotels Many hotels have excellent restaurants open to nonguests. All-inclusives usually have a selection of restaurants, both buffet and à la carte.

Essential Food

These dishes can be found across the Caribbean.

Callaloo A creamy thick soup or stew blending a variety of vegetables (eg spinach, kale, onions, carrots, eggplant, garlic, okra) with coconut milk and sometimes crab or ham. The base can be spinachlike.

Roti Fiery chutney sets off the curried chicken, beef, conch or

PRACTICALITIES

Smoking Banned in public places and hotels and restaurants in many Caribbean destinations.

Weights & Measures Some Caribbean countries use the metric system, others use the imperial system, and a few use a confusing combination of both.

vegetable fillings in these burri-to-like flat-bread wraps.

Conch Look for farm-raised versions as conch in the wild are endangered. This large pink mollusk is cooked with onion and spices in a stew, fried up as fritters, or sliced raw and served with a lime marinade.

GLBT Travelers

Parts of the Caribbean are not particularly gay-friendly destinations and on many of the islands overt homophobia and machismo is prevalent.

Gay men and lesbians generally keep a low profile, and public hand-holding, kissing and other outward signs of affection are not commonplace. Homosexuality remains illegal in some countries, most notably Jamaica and Barbados.

Still, there are several niches for gay travelers. Particularly friendly islands include Aruba, Bonaire,

Curaçao, Dominican Republic, Guadeloupe, Martinique, Puerto Rico, Saba, St-Martin/Sint Maarten and the US Virgin Islands.

Useful links include the following:

Damron (www.damron.com) The USA's leading gay publisher offers guides to world cities.

Spartacus International Gay Guide (www.spartacusworld.com) A male-only directory of gay entertainment venues and hotels.

Insurance

It's foolhardy to travel without insurance to cover theft, loss and medical problems. Check that your policy includes emergency medical evacuation costs, and any activities deemed risky by insurers, such as scuba diving or other adventure sports.

Worldwide travel insurance is available at www.lonelyplanet.com/travel_

MANCHINEEL TREES

Manchineel trees grow on beaches throughout the Caribbean. The fruit of the manchineel, which looks like a small green apple, is poisonous. The milky sap given off by the fruit and leaves can cause severe skin blisters, similar to the reaction caused by poison oak. If the sap gets in your eyes, it can result in temporary blindness. Never take shelter under the trees during a rainstorm, as the sap can be washed off the tree and onto anyone sitting below.

Manchineel trees can grow as high as 40ft (12m), with branches that spread widely. The leaves are green, shiny and elliptical in shape. On some of the more visited beaches, trees will be marked with warning signs or bands of red paint. Manchineel is called *mancenillier* on the French islands.

services. You can buy, extend and claim online anytime – even if you're already on the road.

Internet Access

Internet access and wi-fi is generally easily found throughout most of the Caribbean.

Legal Matters

Due to the stereotype that pot-smoking is widespread in the Caribbean (it isn't), some visitors take a casual attitude about sampling island drugs.

Be forewarned that drug trafficking is a serious problem throughout the Caribbean and officials in most countries have little to no tolerance of visitors caught using. Penalties vary throughout the islands, but getting caught smoking or possessing marijuana (or any illegal drug for that matter) can result in stiff jail sentences. The notable exception is Jamaica, which has decriminalized possession of up to 2oz (56.7g; a fine still applies), though the sale of marijuana is not legal.

Money

US dollars are often accepted in lieu of local currency (and in some cases are the local currency).

ATMs & Credit Cards

ATMs are generally common on all but small islands (and increasingly available in Cuba). Many give out US dollars in addition to the local currency. Credit cards are widely accepted but watch for surcharges.

Cash

The US dollar is accepted almost everywhere, so it's not necessary to have local currency before you arrive. Carry smaller denominations to pay for taxis, street snacks or tips.

Taxes & Refunds

Value Added Tax is added on goods and services across the region. Rates vary from island to island. In some countries VAT is not included in menu prices, leading to unexpectedly inflated bills. Check whether quoted hotel rates include tax when booking.

It's sometimes possible for visitors to obtain VAT refunds on goods bought during a trip.

Tipping

Restaurants Varies in the region although 15% is average. Watch for service charges added to bills.

Taxis Not usually tipped.

Traveler's Checks

Traveler's checks are now uncommon and are inconvenient across the region.

Opening Hours

Opening hours vary across the region, although Sunday remains sacrosanct, with businesses and offices firmly shut throughout the Caribbean. Note that small and family-run businesses may close for a period between August and November.

Public Holidays

Regionwide public holidays:

New Year's Day January 1

Good Friday Late March/early April

Easter Monday Late March/early April

Whit Monday Eighth Monday after Easter

Christmas Day December 25

Boxing Day December 26

Safe Travel

In terms of individual safety and crime, the situation is quite varied in the Caribbean. Employ common sense.

TELEPHONE CODES

ISLAND	COUNTRY CODE
Anguilla	+264
Antigua & Barbuda	+268
Aruba	+297
The Bahamas	+242
Barbados	+248
Bonaire	+599
British Virgin Islands	+284
Cayman Islands	+345
Cuba	+53
Curaçao	+599
Dominica	+767
Dominican Republic	+809 or +829
Grenada	+473
Guadeloupe	+590
Haiti	+509
Jamaica	+876
Martinique	+596
Montserrat	+664
Puerto Rico	+787
Saba	+599
Sint Eustatius	+599
St-Barthélemy	+590
St Kitts & Nevis	+869
St Lucia	+758
St-Martin/Sint Maarten	+599
St Vincent & the Grenadines	+784
Trinidad & Tobago	+868
Turks & Caicos	+649
US Virgin Islands	+340

➡ In big cities and tourist areas, take taxis at night.

➡ Avoid flashing your wealth, whether jewelry or blindly following your smartphone.

➡ Exercise extra caution in urban areas such as Pointe-à-Pitre (Guadeloupe), Fort-de-France (Martinique), some areas of Kingston (Jamaica), Port-au-Prince (Haiti) and downtown Port of Spain (Trinidad).

Telephone

Cell Phones

Most cell phones work in the Caribbean; avoid roaming charges with easily bought local SIM cards. The biggest operators in the Caribbean are Digicel and Flow. Puerto Rico and US Virgin Islands are included in US plans.

ISLAND TIME

In the Caribbean life moves at a slow, loosely regimented pace. You'll often see signs in front of shops, bars and restaurants that say 'open all day, every day' and this can mean several things; the place could truly be open all day every day of the week, but don't count on it. If business is slow, a restaurant, shop or attraction might simply close. If a bar is hopping and the owner's having fun, it could stay open until the wee hours. If the rainy season is lasting too long, a hotel or restaurant might close for a month. In other words, hard and fast rules about opening times are hard to come by.

The only consistent rule is that Sundays are sacred and 'open every day' generally translates to 'open every day except Sunday.'

Time

Eastern Standard Time (EST; five hours behind GMT/UTC) Turks and Caicos, Jamaica, the Cayman Islands, the Dominican Republic

Atlantic Standard Time (AST; four hours behind GMT/UTC) All other islands

Only the Turks and Caicos observe daylight saving time.

Toilets

Except in major tourist areas there are usually few public toilets, and those that do exist are often best avoided. Most restaurants have restrooms, but may require you to make a purchase before you can use them.

Tourist Information

Travel information is often available by the kilo. Many free publications found in hotel lobbies are excellent and most islands have a tourist information center in the main town and offices at the airport.

Travelers with Disabilities

Travel in the Caribbean is not particularly easy for those with physical disabilities. Overall there is little or no awareness of the need for easier access onto planes, buses or rental vehicles. One exception is Puerto Rico, where good compliance with the Americans Disabilities Act (ADA) means many sights and hotels have wheelchair accessibility.

Visitors with special needs should inquire directly with prospective hotels for information on their facilities. The larger, more modern resorts are most likely to have the greatest accessibility, with elevators, wider doorways and wheelchair-accessible bathrooms.

While land travel may present some obstacles, cruises are often a good option for travelers with disabilities in the Caribbean. Many cruise lines can coordinate shore-based excursions in tour buses equipped for special needs.

The **Society for Accessible Travel & Hospitality** (www.sath.org) has useful information.

Download Lonely Planet's free Accessible Travel guide from http://lptravel.to/AccessibleTravel.

Visas

Requirements vary from island to island. Citizens of Canada, the EU and the US don't need visas for visits of under 90 days throughout the region.

Volunteering

Many volunteer programs in the Caribbean mix holiday fun with good intentions, and include themes such as 'learn to dive while saving the reef' (if only it were that easy). Some organizations don't provide a lot of value beyond the interesting experience for the traveler. Always ask hard questions of organizations as to who is really benefiting – the volunteer or the actual beneficiaries of the program. Note that most volunteer organizations levy charges to take part in their programs.

Volunteer programs include the following:

Gapforce (www.gapforce.org)

Global Volunteers (www.globalvolunteers.org)

Habitat for Humanity (www.habitat.org)

Women Travelers

Although the situation varies between islands, machismo is alive and well. Men can get aggressive, especially with women traveling alone. On many islands local men have few qualms about catcalling, hissing, whistling, sucking their teeth or making kissy sounds to attract female attention. While much of this is simply annoying, it can make women feel unsafe.

Like it or not, women will generally feel much safer if traveling with a male companion. Women traveling alone need to be sensible and careful: avoid walking alone after dark, heading off into the wilderness alone, hitchhiking or picking up male hitchhikers. Generally try to avoid any situation where you're isolated and vulnerable. Don't wear skimpy clothing when you're not on the beach – it will just garner you a lot of unwanted attention. Also note that 'harmless flirtation' at home can be misconstrued as a serious come-on in the Caribbean.

Work

The Caribbean has high unemployment rates and low wages, as well as strict immigration policies aimed at preventing foreign visitors from taking up work.

One good bet for working is to crew with a boat or yacht. As boat hands aren't usually working on any one island in particular, the work situation is more flexible and it's easier to avoid hassles with immigration. Marinas are a good place to look for jobs on yachts; check the bulletin-board notices, strike up conversations with skippers or ask around at the nearest bar. Marinas in Miami and Fort Lauderdale are considered good places to find jobs, as people sailing their boats down for the season stop here looking for crew.

You can also look for jobs with a crew-placement agency such as UK-based Crew Finders (www.crewfinders.com) or US-based Crew Seekers (www.crewseekers.net).

Transportation

GETTING THERE & AWAY

All US citizens traveling to the Caribbean will need a passport to reenter the US if traveling by air. If traveling by sea (eg on a cruise ship), you will need a passport or a passport card to reenter the US. The latter is essentially a wallet-sized US passport that is only good for land and sea travel between the US and Canada, Mexico and the Caribbean. In some circumstances you may only need a valid driver's license but confirm this carefully with the cruise line.

The law does not affect the US state territories of Puerto Rico and the US Virgin Islands, which will continue to allow established forms of identification like valid driver's licenses.

Flights, cars and tours can be booked online at lonelyplanet.com/bookings.

Entering the Region

Passport requirements vary from island to island, but visas aren't required for most nationalities.

Air

Flight options to the Caribbean will vary between islands.

Airports & Airlines

It doesn't matter which island you fly into, touching down on Caribbean land is always a thrilling experience. Some islands, such as Saba, Montserrat or Sint Eustatius, have tiny runways, where small regional planes miraculously land on airstrips that don't look much longer than Band-Aids. When you fly into the Bahamas you feel like you're surely going to land in the ocean. Other islands, such as Dominica, look like vague colonial outposts, surrounded by cane fields, dusty roads or mountains. Conversely, airports such as those in Barbados, Aruba and Sint Maarten are as big and modern as you could wish.

Major Caribbean islands have flights from North America, the only exceptions being ones with airports unable to handle jets. Larger islands also have service from the UK and Europe.

FROM NORTH AMERICA

Most major airlines in North America fly direct to the more popular islands in the Caribbean. In fact such service is so widespread that even places as tiny as Bonaire have nonstop service to major US cities. Generally, however, getting to the Caribbean from US cities without hub airports will involve changing planes somewhere. American Airlines has major hubs for its extensive

CLIMATE CHANGE & TRAVEL

Every form of transport that relies on carbon-based fuel generates CO_2, the main cause of human-induced climate change. Modern travel is dependent on airplanes which might use less fuel per kilometer per person than most cars but travel much greater distances. The altitude at which aircraft emit gases (including CO_2) and particles also contributes to their climate change impact. Many websites offer 'carbon calculators' that allow people to estimate the carbon emissions generated by their journey and, for those who wish to do so, to offset the impact of the greenhouse gases emitted with contributions to portfolios of climate-friendly initiatives throughout the world. Lonely Planet offsets the carbon footprint of all staff and author travel.

Caribbean service in Miami and San Juan, Puerto Rico.

Also note that service to the Caribbean is seasonal. An island that has, say, weekly nonstop flights from Chicago in January may have none at all in June.

FROM EUROPE

You can reach the Caribbean nonstop from Europe. Proving that old colonial ties linger, airlines from the UK serve former British colonies like Barbados and Antigua; French airlines serve the French-speaking islands; and Dutch carriers fly to Aruba, Bonaire, Curaçao and Sint Maarten. There are no direct flights to the Caribbean from Australia, New Zealand or Asia – travelers fly via Europe or the US.

CHARTERS

Charter flights from the US, Canada, the UK and Europe offer another option for getting to the islands. Fares are often cheaper than on regularly scheduled commercial airlines, but you usually have to depart and return on specific flights and you'll probably have no flexibility to extend your stay. Such flights also often come as part of packages that include stays in resorts.

Sea

The only way to reach the Caribbean by sea is on a cruise ship (or for a few lucky people, on a yacht).

GETTING AROUND

Air

The Caribbean has an extensive network of airlines serving even the smallest islands.

Bicycle

The popularity of cycling in the Caribbean depends on where you go. Several islands are prohibitively hilly, with narrow roads that make cycling difficult. On others, such as Cuba, cycling is a great way to get around. Many of the islands have bicycles for rent. Bike shops are becoming more common. Most ferries will let you bring bikes on board at no extra charge; regional airlines will likely charge a fee.

Boat

Getting around the islands by yacht is a fantasy for many. Charters are generally quite easy.

Ferries link some islands within the Caribbean, including the following:

➡ Anguilla, Saba, St-Martin/ Sint Maarten and St-Barthélemy

➡ British Virgin Islands and US Virgin Islands

➡ Dominica, Guadeloupe, Martinique and St Lucia

➡ Dominican Republic and Puerto Rico

Bus

Inexpensive bus service is available on most islands, although the word 'bus' has different meanings in different places. Some islands have full-size buses, while on others a 'bus' is simply a pickup truck with wooden benches in the back.

Whatever the vehicle, buses are a good environmental choice compared to rental cars and are an excellent way to meet locals. People are generally quite friendly and happy to talk to you about their island. Buses are also a good way to hear the most popular local music tracks, often at an amazingly loud volume.

Buses are often the primary means of commuting to work or school and thus are most frequent in the early mornings and from mid- to late afternoon. There's generally a good bus service on Saturday mornings, but Sunday service is often nonexistent.

Car & Motorcycle

Driving in the Caribbean islands can rock your world, rattle your brains and fray

THREE RULES OF FLYING

Our writers learned from experience three things you should remember:

➡ Try not to arrive on a regional flight in the afternoon when most of the North American and European flights arrive, swamping immigration and customs.

➡ Keep anything essential you might need for a few days with you. Luggage often somehow misses your flight – even if you see it waiting next to the plane as you board. It may take days – if ever – to catch up with you.

➡ Check in early. Bring a book and snack and hang out. We saw people with confirmed seats repeatedly bumped after flights checked in full and their alternative was days later. A two-hour wait is not bad if you're prepared for it. In many airports you can check in early and then go someplace else like the incredibly fun beach bars near the Sint Maarten airport runway.

DEPARTURE TAX

Some airports may charge a departure tax that is *not* included in the price of the ticket.

your nerves. At first. Soon, you'll get used to the often-poor road conditions, slow speeds and relaxed adherence to road rules and using your horn to punctuate any maneuver or passing thought on the road conditions.

Island Driving

Offer a lift It's common courtesy on many islands to slow down and offer pedestrians a lift (and is considered obligatory on some).

Beware of goats! Keep an eye out for stray dogs, iguanas, wild horses, chickens and goats, all of which meander aimlessly on the island roads.

Cede the right-of-way Drivers often stop to let others turn or pedestrians to cross even when you don't think its necessary.

Driver's Licences

You'll need your driver's license in order to rent a car, and frequently need to be over 21. On some of the former British islands, you may need to purchase a visitor's driver's license from your car-rental agent.

Rental

Car rentals are available on nearly all of the islands, with a few exceptions (usually because they lack roads). On most islands there are affiliates of the international chains, but local rental agencies may have better rates. Advance booking almost always attracts cheaper rates.

International rental agencies found across many islands in the Caribbean include **Avis** (www.avis.com), **Budget** (www.budget.com), **Dollar** (www.dollar.com), **Europca** (www.europcar.com)r and **Hertz** (www.hertz.com).

Road Rules

Road rules vary by island. In general, note that driving conditions may be more relaxed than you are used to.

Many Caribbean countries drive on the left, but what side of the road to drive on depends on the island: this can be confusing if you're island-hopping and renting cars on each island. Adding to the confusion, some cars have steering columns on the opposite side of where you'd expect.

Hitchhiking

Hitchhiking is an essential mode of travel on most islands, though the practice among foreign visitors is uncommon. Hitching is never entirely safe, and we don't recommend it. Travellers who hitch should understand that they are taking a small but potentially serious risk.

If you're driving a rental car, giving locals a lift can be a great form of cultural interaction and much appreciated by those trudging along the side of the road while – comparatively – affluent foreigners whiz past.

Health

Prevention is the key to remaining healthy while traveling abroad. Travelers who receive the recommended vaccinations for the destination and follow common-sense precautions usually come away with nothing more serious than a little diarrhea.

From a health point of view, the Caribbean is generally safe as long as you're reasonably careful about what you eat and drink. The most common travel-related diseases, such as dysentery and hepatitis, are acquired by consumption of contaminated food and water. Mosquito-borne illnesses aren't a significant concern on most of the islands, except during outbreaks of dengue fever.

Health standards in major resort islands, such as Barbados, Bermuda and the Cayman Islands, are high, and access to health care is good.

Before You Go

Insurance

If your health insurance does not cover you for medical expenses while abroad, consider supplemental insurance; travel agents and the internet are good places to start looking. Find out in advance if your insurance plan will make payments directly to providers or reimburse you later for overseas health expenditures.

Note that Cuba requires proof of medical insurance to enter the country. On remote islands, such as the Grenadines, you will require transport to more developed areas for any significant problem, so be sure your insurance covers medical transport and evacuation.

Recommended Vaccinations

At the time of writing there were no recommended vaccinations for the Caribbean, but check with your physician before travelling. If you are traveling away from major resort areas or going to places such as Haiti, however, it is vital that you consult a travel medical clinic at least three weeks before departure to check whether vaccinations are needed.

Medical Checklist

Bring medications in their original containers and clearly labeled. A signed, dated letter from your physician describing all medical conditions and medications, including generic names, is also a good idea. If carrying syringes or needles, be sure to have a physician's letter documenting their medical necessity.

Recommended items for a personal medical kit:

➡ acetaminophen/paracetamol (eg Tylenol) or aspirin

➡ antibacterial hand sanitizer (eg Purell)

➡ antibacterial ointment (eg Bactroban) for cuts and abrasions

➡ antihistamines (for hay fever and allergic reactions)

➡ anti-inflammatory drugs (eg ibuprofen/Advil)

➡ DEET-containing insect repellent

➡ steroid cream or cortisone (for allergic rashes)

➡ sunscreen.

Health Advisories

It's always a good idea to consult your government's travel-health website before departure, if one is available:

Australia (www.smartraveller.gov.au)

Canada/US (www.cdc.gov/travel)

UK (www.cdc.gov/travel)

In the Caribbean Islands

Availability & Cost of Health Care

Acceptable health care is available in most major cities throughout the Caribbean, but may be hard to locate in rural areas. To find a good local doctor, your best bet is to ask the management of the hotel where you are staying or contact your local embassy.

HAITI

Many of Haiti's challenges are health related, due in part to the introduction of cholera by UN peacekeepers and the country's poor infrastructure. Malaria is also seasonally present. A higher level of health vigilance is required in Haiti than in the rest of the Caribbean. Always check reliable travel-health resources before travel to Haiti.

Many doctors and hospitals expect payment in cash, regardless of whether you have travel-health insurance. If you develop a life-threatening medical problem, you'll probably want to be evacuated to a country with state-of-the-art medical care. Since this may cost tens of thousands of dollars, be sure you have insurance to cover this before you depart.

Many pharmacies are well supplied, but important medications may not be consistently available. Be sure to bring along adequate supplies of all your prescription drugs.

Infectious Diseases

You are unlikely to come down with an infectious disease in the Caribbean, especially if you are just visiting resorts and the more developed islands. Cruisers will find themselves sprayed with antibacterial hand sanitizer at every turn as the cruise lines seek to prevent mass viral outbreaks.

DENGUE FEVER

Dengue fever is a viral infection common throughout the Caribbean. Dengue is transmitted by *Aedes* mosquitoes, which bite mostly during the daytime and are usually found close to human habitations, often indoors. They breed primarily in artificial water containers, such as jars, barrels, cans, cisterns, metal drums, plastic containers and discarded tires. As a result, dengue is especially common in densely populated, urban environments.

Dengue usually causes flu-like symptoms, including fever, muscle aches, joint pains, headaches, nausea and vomiting, often followed by a rash. The body aches may be quite uncomfortable, but most cases resolve uneventfully in a few days. Severe cases usually occur in children aged under 15 who are experiencing their second dengue infection.

If you suspect you have dengue fever, seek out medical advice. There is no vaccine. The cornerstone of prevention is protection against insect bites.

HEPATITIS A

Hepatitis A is the second-most-common travel-related infection (after traveler's diarrhea). The illness occurs throughout the world, but the incidence is higher in developing nations. It occurs throughout the Caribbean, particularly in the northern islands.

Hepatitis A is a viral infection of the liver that is usually acquired by ingesting contaminated water, food or ice, though it may also be acquired by direct contact with infected persons. Symptoms may include fever, malaise, jaundice, nausea, vomiting and abdominal pain. Most cases resolve without complications, though hepatitis A occasionally causes severe liver damage. There is no treatment.

The vaccine for hepatitis A is extremely safe and highly effective. If you get a booster six to 12 months later, it lasts for at least 10 years. You should get it before you go to any developing nation. Because the safety of the hepatitis A vaccine

has not been established for pregnant women or children under the age of two, they should instead be given a gamma globulin injection, which temporarily boosts immunity.

SCHISTOSOMIASIS

A parasitic infection carried by snails and acquired by exposure of skin to contaminated freshwater, schistosomiasis has been reported in parts of the Dominican Republic, Guadeloupe, Martinique, Puerto Rico, Antigua and Barbuda, Montserrat and St Lucia. To find out whether or not schistosomiasis is present in the areas you'll be visiting, go to the World Health Organization's Global Schistosomiasis Atlas (www.who.int/schis tosomiasis/epidemiology/ global_atlas/en/).

Early symptoms may include fever, loss of appetite, weight loss, abdominal pain, weakness, headaches, joint and muscle pains, diarrhea, nausea and a cough, but most infections are asymptomatic at first.

When traveling in areas where schistosomiasis occurs, you should avoid swimming, wading, bathing or washing in bodies of freshwater, including lakes, ponds, streams and rivers. Toweling yourself dry after exposure to contaminated water may reduce your chance of getting infected, but does not eliminate it. Saltwater and chlorinated pools carry no risk of schistosomiasis.

TRAVELER'S DIARRHEA

In places where tap water is safe to drink – much of the Caribbean – your risk of diarrhea is not high. But in places where the tap water is suspect, take the usual precautions: eat fresh fruits or vegetables only if cooked or peeled; be wary of dairy products that might contain unpasteurized milk; and be highly selective when eating food from street vendors.

ZIKA

Zika is present in many parts of the Caribbean. The virus spreads through the bite of an infected *Aedes* mosquito. Common symptoms include fever, rash, joint pain and conjunctivitis. Most victims experience mild illness with symptoms that last for several days to a week. Since Zika may cause brain damage to a fetus in utero, pregnant women should avoid visiting a Zika hot spot. The virus may also be sexually transmitted by an infected partner. Since there is no vaccine or treatment, the cornerstone of prevention is protection against mosquito bites.

Environmental Hazards

A few things to watch out for:

Mosquito bites Caribbean mosquitoes and other biting/ stinging insects come in all shapes and sizes, and are quite common. The biggest concern here, outside the few areas with malaria, is simply discomfort and hassle. Make certain you have a good insect repellent with at least 25% DEET.

Rabies Some islands do have rabies, so do as you would at home and avoid touching or petting strays.

Sea stingers Spiny sea urchins and coelenterates (coral and jellyfish) are a hazard in some areas. If stung by a coelenterate,

WATER

Tap water is safe to drink on some of the islands, but not on others. Unless you're certain that the local water is safe, you shouldn't drink it.

Note: if tap water is safe to drink – as it is on the major destination islands except for Cuba – then avoiding bottled water reduces the significant environmental impact of plastic water containers.

apply diluted vinegar or baking soda. Remove tentacles carefully, but not with bare hands. If stung by a stinging fish, such as a stingray, immerse the limb in water at about 115°F (45°C).

Sunburn Wear sunscreen with a high SPF as the Caribbean sun is very strong and sunburn is common. Every day we see people who are as pink as lobsters and have their trips ruined because they didn't apply sunscreen, especially after time in the water.

Language

The rich language environment of the greater Caribbean is testament to the diverse array of people that have come to call it home.

From a colonial past that saw the dying out of virtually all traces of indigenous languages, there is the legacy of English, French, Spanish, Dutch and Portuguese. Outside these predominant languages, perhaps the most notable influences can be traced back to the slaves brought to the islands from West Africa. European tongues, creoles, patois, local accents and pidgins contribute to the particular linguistic mix of each island.

To find out who speaks what where, see the opening pages of each On the Road chapter.

FRENCH

The French used in the Caribbean is flatter in intonation, with less of the traditional French lilting cadence. Also, speakers of Creole pay less attention to gender; anything or anyone can be il (the French word for 'he').

There are nasal vowels (pronounced as if you're trying to force the sound through the nose) in French, indicated in our pronunciation guides with o or u followed by an almost inaudible nasal consonant sound m, n or ng. Note also that air is pronounced as in 'fair', eu as the 'u' in 'nurse', ew as ee with rounded lips, r is a throaty sound, and zh is pronounced as the 's' in 'pleasure'.

Basics

| Hello. | Bonjour. | bon·zhoor |

QUESTION WORDS – FRENCH

How?	Comment?	ko·mon
What?	Quoi?	kwa
When?	Quand?	kon
Where?	Où?	oo
Who?	Qui?	kee
Why?	Pourquoi?	poor·kwa

Goodbye.	Au revoir.	o·rer·vwa
Excuse me.	Excusez-moi.	ek·skew·zay·mwa
Sorry.	Pardon.	par·don
Please.	S'il vous plaît.	seel voo play
Thank you.	Merci.	mair·see
Yes.	Oui.	wee
No.	Non.	non

What's your name?
Comment vous appelez-vous? — ko·mon voo·za·play voo

My name is ...
Je m'appelle ... — zher ma·pel ...

Do you speak English?
Parlez-vous anglais? — par·lay·voo ong·glay

I don't understand.
Je ne comprends pas. — zher ner kom·pron pa

How much is it?
C'est combien? — say kom·byun

Accommodations

campsite	camping	kom·peeng
guesthouse	pension	pon·syon
hotel	hôtel	o·tel
youth hostel	auberge de jeunesse	o·berzh der zher·nes

Do you have a ... room?	Avez-vous une chambre ...?	a·vey·voo ewn shom·bre ...
single	à un lit	a un lee
double	avec un grand lit	a·vek ung gron lee

How much is it per ...?	Quel est le prix par ...?	kel ey le pree par ...
night	nuit	nwee
person	personne	pair·son

Eating & Drinking

What would you recommend?
Qu'est-ce que vous   kes·ker voo
conseillez?   kon·say·yay

Do you have vegetarian food?
Vous faites les repas   voo fet ley re·pa
végétariens?   vey·zhey·ta·ryun

I'll have ...	*Je prends ...*	zhe pron ...
Cheers!	*Santé!*	son·tay

I'd like the ...,	*Je voudrais ...,*	zhe voo·drey ...
please.	*s'il vous plaît.*	seel voo pley
bill	*l'addition*	la·dee·syon
menu	*la carte*	la kart

breakfast	*petit*	per·tee
	déjeuner	day·zher·nay
lunch	*déjeuner*	day·zher·nay
dinner	*dîner*	dee·nay

Emergencies

Help!
Au secours!   o skoor

Leave me alone!
Fichez-moi la paix!   fee·shay·mwa la pay

I'm lost.
Je suis perdu(e). (m/f)   zhe swee pair·dew

I'm ill.
Je suis malade.   zher swee ma·lad

Where are the toilets?
Où sont les toilettes?   oo son ley twa·let

Call ...!	*Appelez ...!*	a·play un ...
a doctor	*un médecin*	un mayd·sun
the police	*la police*	la po·lees

Transportation & Directions

Where's ...?
Où est ...?   oo ay ...

What's the address?
Quelle est l'adresse?   kel ay la·dres

Can you show me (on the map)?
Pouvez-vous m'indiquer   poo·vay·voo mun·dee·kay
(sur la carte)?   (sewr la kart)

One ... ticket	*Un billet*	um bee·yey
(to Bordeaux),	*... (pour*	... (poor
please.	*Bordeaux),*	bor·do)
	s'il vous plaît.	seel voo pley

NUMBERS – FRENCH

1	*un*	un
2	*deux*	der
3	*trois*	trwa
4	*quatre*	ka·trer
5	*cinq*	sungk
6	*six*	sees
7	*sept*	set
8	*huit*	weet
9	*neuf*	nerf
10	*dix*	dees

one-way	*simple*	sum·ple
return	*aller et retour*	a·ley ey re·toor

boat	*bateau*	ba·to
bus	*bus*	bews
plane	*avion*	a·vyon
train	*train*	trun

SPANISH

While Spanish in the Caribbean is mutually intelligible with European Spanish, there are some differences, as migration and indigenous languages have left their mark on local vocabulary and pronunciation.

Spanish vowels are generally pronounced short. Note that ow is pronounced as in 'how', kh as in the Scottish loch (harsh and guttural), rr is rolled and stronger than in English, and v is a soft 'b' (pronounced between the English 'v' and 'b' sounds).

Basics

Hello.	*Hola.*	o·la
Goodbye.	*Adiós.*	a·dyos
Excuse me.	*Perdón.*	per·don
Sorry.	*Lo siento.*	lo syen·to
Please.	*Por favor.*	por fa·vor
Thank you.	*Gracias.*	gra·syas
Yes.	*Sí.*	see

WANT MORE?

For in-depth language information and handy phrases, check out Lonely Planet's *Latin American Spanish*, *French*, and *Dutch Phrasebooks*. You'll find them at **shop. lonelyplanet.com**, or you can buy Lonely Planet's iPhone phrasebooks at the Apple App Store.

QUESTION WORDS – SPANISH

How?	¿Cómo?	ko·mo
What?	¿Qué?	ke
When?	¿Cuándo?	kwan·do
Where?	¿Dónde?	don·de
Who?	¿Quién?	kyen
Why?	¿Por qué?	por ke

| No. | No. | no |

What's your name?
¿Cómo se llama   ko·mo se ya·ma
Usted? (pol)   oo·ste
¿Cómo te llamas? (inf) ko·mo te ya·mas

My name is ...
Me llamo ...   me ya·mo ...

Do you speak English?
¿Habla/Hablas   a·bla/a·blas
inglés? (pol/inf)   een·gles

I don't understand.
Yo no entiendo.   yo no en·tyen·do

How much is it?
¿Cuánto cuesta?   kwan·to kwes·ta

Accommodations

campsite	terreno de camping	te·re·no de kam·peeng
guesthouse	pensión	pen·syon
hotel	hotel	o·tel
youth hostel	albergue juvenil	al·ber·ge khoo·ve·neel

| Do you have a ... room? | ¿Tiene una habitación ...? | tye·ne oo·na a·bee·ta·syon ... |
| single | individual | een·dee·vee·dw· |

NUMBERS – SPANISH

1	uno	oo·no
2	dos	dos
3	tres	tres
4	cuatro	kwa·tro
5	cinco	seen·ko
6	seis	seys
7	siete	sye·te
8	ocho	o·cho
9	nueve	nwe·ve
10	diez	dyes

KEY PATTERNS

To get by in Spanish, mix and match these simple patterns with words of your choice:

When's (the next flight)?
¿Cuándo sale   kwan·do sa·le
(el próximo vuelo)?   (el prok·see·mo vwe·lo)

Where's (the station)?
¿Dónde está   don·de es·ta
(la estación)?   (la es·ta·syon)

Where can I (buy a ticket)?
¿Dónde puedo   don·de pwe·do
(comprar un billete)?   (kom·prar oon bee·ye·te)

Do you have (a map)?
¿Tiene (un mapa)?   tye·ne (oon ma·pa)

Is there (a toilet)?
¿Hay (servicios)?   ai (ser·vee·syos)

I'd like (a coffee).
Quisiera (un café).   kee·sye·ra (oon ka·fe)

I'd like (to hire a car).
Quisiera (alquilar   kee·sye·ra (al·kee·lar
un coche).   oon ko·che)

Can I (enter)?
¿Se puede (entrar)?   se pwe·de (en·trar)

Could you please (help me)?
¿Puede (ayudarme),   pwe·de (a·yoo·dar·me)
por favor?   por fa·vor

Do I have to (get a visa)?
¿Necesito   ne·se·see·to
(obtener   (ob·te·ner
un visado)?   oon vee·sa·do)

al

| double | doble | do·ble |

How much is it per ...?	¿Cuánto cuesta por ...?	kwan·to kwes·ta por ...
night	noche	no·che
person	persona	per·so·na

Eating & Drinking

What would you recommend?
¿Qué recomienda?   ke re·ko·myen·da

Do you have vegetarian food?
¿Tienen comida   tye·nen ko·mee·da
vegetariana?   ve·khe·ta·rya·na

I'll have ...   Para mí ...   pa·ra mee ...

Cheers!   ¡Salud!   sa·loo

I'd like the ...,   Quisiera ...,   kee·sye·ra ...
please.   por favor.   por fa·vor

bill	la cuenta	la *kwen*·ta
menu	el menú	el me·*noo*
breakfast	desayuno	de·sa·*yoo*·no
lunch	comida	ko·*mee*·da
dinner	cena	se·na

Emergencies

Help!
¡Socorro! — so·*ko*·ro

Go away!
¡Vete! — ve·te

I'm lost.
Estoy perdido/a. (m/f) — es·*toy* per·dee·do/a

I'm ill.
Estoy enfermo/a. (m/f) — es·*toy* en·*fer*·mo/a

Where are the toilets?
¿Dónde están los servicios? — don·de es·*tan* los ser·*vee*·syos

Call ...!	¡Llame a ...!	*lya*·me a ...
a doctor	un médico	oon *me*·dee·ko
the police	la policía	la po·lee·*see*·a

Transportation & Directions

Where's ...?
¿Dónde está ...? — don·de es·*ta* ...

What's the address?
¿Cuál es la dirección? — kwal es la dee·rek·*syon*

Can you show me (on the map)?
¿Me lo puede indicar (en el mapa)? — me lo *pwe*·de een·dee·*kar* (en el *ma*·pa)

a ... ticket	un billete de ...	oon bee·*ye*·te ... de ...
one-way	ida	*ee*·da
return	de ida y vuelta	de *ee*·da ee *vwel*·ta
boat	barco	*bar*·ko
bus	autobús	ow·to·*boos*
plane	avión	a·*vyon*
train	tren	tren

DUTCH

While it isn't necessary to speak Dutch to get by on the islands of Saba, Sint Eustatius and Sint Maarten, these Dutch basics might help you make some new friends in the East Caribbean.

HAITIAN CREOLE

Here are a few basics to get you started in the predominant lingo of Haiti.

Good day.	Bonjou. (before noon)
Good evening.	Bonswa. (after 11am)
See you later.	Na wè pita.
Yes./No.	Wi./Non.
Please.	Silvouple.
Thank you.	Mèsi anpil.
Sorry./Excuse me.	Pàdon.
How are you?	Ki jan ou ye?
Not bad.	M pal pi mal.
I'm going OK.	M-ap kenbe.
What's your name?	Ki jan ou rele?
My name is ...	M rele ...
Do you speak English?	Eske ou ka pale angle?
I don't understand.	M pa konprann.
How much is it?	Konbyen?
I'm lost.	M pèdi.
Where is/are ... ?	Kote ... ?

Note that aw is pronounced as in 'saw', eu as the 'u' in 'nurse', ew as 'ee' with rounded lips, oh as the 'o' in 'note', öy as the '-er y-' in 'her year' (without the 'r'), uh as the 'a' in 'ago', kh as in the Scottish loch (harsh and guttural), and zh as the 's' in 'pleasure'.

Basics

Hello.	Goedendag.	khoo·duh·*dakh*
Goodbye.	Dag.	dakh
Excuse me.	Pardon.	par·*don*
Sorry.	Sorry.	so·ree
Please.	Alstublieft. (pol)	al·stew·*bleeft*
	Alsjeblieft. (inf)	a·shuh·*bleeft*
Thank you.	Dank u/je. (pol/inf)	dangk ew/yuh
Yes.	Ja.	yaa
No.	Nee.	ney

What's your name?
Hoe heet u/je? (pol/inf) — hoo heyt ew/yuh

My name is ...
Ik heet ... — ik heyt ...

GLOSSARY

ABCs – Aruba, Bonaire and Curaçao

accra – fried mixture of okra, black-eyed peas, pepper and salt

agouti – short-haired rabbitlike rodent resembling a guinea pig with long legs; it has a fondness for sugarcane

Arawak – linguistically related tribes that inhabited most of the Caribbean islands and northern South America

bake – sandwich made with fried bread and usually filled with fish

bareboat – sail-it-yourself charter yacht usually rented by the week or longer

beguine – Afro-French dance music with a bolero rhythm that originated in Martinique in the 1930s; also spelled 'biguine'

bomba – musical form and dance inspired by African rhythms and characterized by call-and-response dialogues between musicians and interpreted by dancers; often considered as a unit with *plena*, as in *bomba y plena*

breadfruit – large, round, green fruit; a Caribbean staple that's comparable to potatoes in its carbohydrate content and is prepared in much the same way

bush tea – tea made from the islands' leaves, roots and herbs; each tea cures a specific illness, such as gas, menstrual pain, colds or insomnia

BVI – British Virgin Islands

cabrito – goat meat

callaloo – spinachlike green, originally from Africa; also spelled 'kallaloo'

calypso – popular Caribbean music developed from slave songs; lyrics reflect political opinions, social views and commentary on current events

Carnival – major Caribbean festival; originated as a pre-Lenten festivity but is now observed at various times throughout the year on different islands; also spelled 'Carnaval'

casa particular – private house in Cuba that lets out rooms to foreigners

cassava – a root used since precolonial times as a staple of island diets, whether steamed, baked or grated into a flour for bread; also called 'yucca' or 'manioc'

cay – small island; comes from an Arawak word

cayo – coral key (Spanish)

chattel house – type of simple wooden dwelling placed upon cement or stone blocks so it can be easily moved

chutney – up-tempo, rhythmic music used in celebrations of various social situations in Trinidad's Indian communities

colombo – spicy, East Indian–influenced dish that resembles curry

conch – large gastropod that, due to overfishing, is endangered; its chewy meat is often prepared in a spicy *Creole*-style sauce; also called *lambi*

conkies – mixture of cornmeal, coconut, pumpkin, sweet potatoes, raisins and spice, steamed in a plantain leaf

cou-cou – creamy cornmeal and okra mash, commonly served with saltfish

Creole – person of European, or mixed black and European ancestry; local language predominantly a combination of French and African languages; cuisine characterized by spicy, full-flavored sauces and heavy use of green peppers and onions

dancehall – contemporary offshoot of reggae with faster, digital beats and an MC

dasheen – type of taro; the leaves are known as *callaloo*, while the starchy tuberous root is boiled and eaten like a potato

daube meat – pot roast seasoned with vinegar, native seasonings, onion, garlic, tomato, thyme, parsley and celery

dolphin – a marine mammal; also a common type of white-meat fish (dolphinfish; sometimes called *mahimahi*); the two

are not related, and 'dolphin' on any menu always refers to the fish

duppy – ghost or spirit; also called *jumbie*

flying fish – gray-meat fish named for its ability to skim above the water, particularly plentiful in Barbados

fungi – semihard cornmeal pudding similar to Italian polenta that's added to soups and used as a side dish; also a Creole name for the music made by local scratch bands; 'funchi' on Aruba, Bonaire and Curaçao

gade – street (Danish)

gîte – small cottages for rent (French)

goat water – spicy goat-meat stew often flavored with cloves and rum

gommier – large native gum tree found in Caribbean rainforests

green flash – Caribbean phenomenon where you can see a green flash as the sun sets into the ocean

guagua – local bus; *gua-gua* in Dominican Republic

I-tal – natural style of vegetarian cooking practised by Rastafarians

irie – all right; used to indicate that all is well

jambalaya – a Creole dish usually consisting of rice cooked with ham, chicken or shellfish, spices, tomatoes, onions and peppers

jintero/a – tout or prostitute; literally 'jockey'

johnnycake – corn-flour griddle cake

jug-jug – mixture of Guinea cornmeal, green peas and salted meat

jumbie – see *duppy*

jump-up – nighttime street party that usually involves dancing and plenty of rum drinking

lambi – see *conch*

limin' – hanging out, relaxing, chilling; also spelled 'liming'; from the Creole verb 'to lime'

mahimahi – see *dolphin*

mairie – town hall (French)

malecón – main street; literally 'sea wall'

manchineel – tree whose poisonous fruit sap can cause a severe skin rash; common on Caribbean beaches; called *man-cenillier* on the French islands, and *anjenelle* on Trinidad and Tobago

manicou – opossum

mas camp – workshop where artists create Carnival costumes; short for 'masquerade camp'

mento – folk *calypso* music

mojito – cocktail made from rum, mint, sugar, seltzer and fresh lime juice

mountain chicken – legs of the crapaud, a type of frog found in Dominica

négritude – Black Pride philosophical and political movement that emerged in Martinique in the 1930s

Obeah – system of ancestral worship related to *Vodou* and rooted in West African religions

oil down – mix of breadfruit, beef, pork, *callaloo* and coconut milk

out islands – islands or *cays* that lie across the water from the main islands of an island group

Painkiller – popular alcoholic drink made with two parts rum, one part orange juice, four parts pineapple juice, one part

coconut cream and a sprinkle of nutmeg and cinnamon

paladar – privately owned restaurant in Cuba serving reliable, inexpensive meals

panyards – place where steel pan is practiced in the months leading up to *Carnival*

parang – type of music sung in Spanish and accompanied by guitars and maracas; originated in Venezuela

pate – fried pastry of *cassava* or *plantain* dough stuffed with spiced goat, pork, chicken, *conch*, lobster or fish

pepperpot – spicy stew made with various meats, accompanied by peppers and cassareep

plantain – starchy fruit of the banana family; usually fried or grilled like a vegetable

playa – beach (Spanish)

público – collective taxis; *publique* in Haiti

quelbe – blend of jigs, quadrilles, military fife and African drum music

rapso – a fusion of *soca* and hip-hop

reggaeton – mixture of hip-hop, reggae and *dancehall*

roti – curry (often potatoes and chicken) rolled inside flat bread

rumba – Afro-Cuban dance form that originated among plantation slaves during the 19th century; during the 1920s and '30s, the term 'rumba' was adopted in North America and Europe for a ballroom dance in 4/4 time; in Cuba today, 'to rumba' means 'to party'

salsa – Cuban music based on *son*

Santería – Afro-Caribbean religion representing the syncretism of Catholic and African beliefs

snowbird – North American, usually retired, who comes to the Caribbean for its warm winters

soca – energetic offspring of *calypso*; it uses danceable rhythms and risqué lyrics to convey pointed social commentary

son – Cuba's basic form of popular music, with African and Spanish elements

souse – dish made out of pickled pig's head and belly, spices and a few vegetables; commonly served with a pig-blood sausage called 'pudding'

steel pan – instrument made from oil drums or the music it produces; also called 'steel drum' or 'steel band'

SVG – St Vincent and the Grenadines

Taíno – settled, Arawak-speaking tribe that inhabited much of the Caribbean prior to the Spanish conquest; the word itself means 'We the Good People'

taptap – local Haitian bus

timba – contemporary *salsa*

TnT – Trinidad and Tobago

USVI – US Virgin Islands

Vodou – religion practised in Haiti; a synthesis of West African animist spirit religions and residual rituals of the *Taíno*

zouk – popular French West Indies music that draws from the *beguine* and other French Caribbean folk forms

Behind the Scenes

SEND US YOUR FEEDBACK

We love to hear from travelers – your comments keep us on our toes and help make our books better. Our well-traveled team reads every word on what you loved or loathed about this book. Although we cannot reply individually to your submissions, we always guarantee that your feedback goes straight to the appropriate authors, in time for the next edition. Each person who sends us information is thanked in the next edition – the most useful submissions are rewarded with a selection of digital PDF chapters.

Visit **lonelyplanet.com/contact** to submit your updates and suggestions or to ask for help. Our award-winning website also features inspirational travel stories, news and discussions.

Note: We may edit, reproduce and incorporate your comments in Lonely Planet products such as guidebooks, websites and digital products, so let us know if you don't want your comments reproduced or your name acknowledged. For a copy of our privacy policy visit lonelyplanet.com/privacy.

OUR READERS

Many thanks to the travelers who used the last edition and wrote to us with helpful hints, useful advice and interesting anecdotes: Cameron Ewen, Claus Nelson, Gerardo Celis, Jared Rosenthal, John Malone, Katrin Flatscher, Mo Miller, Moriz Heyss, Rachel Edwards, Sofie Widén

WRITERS' THANKS

Mara Vorhees

For local insights, thanks to Ewald Muschenich at Beach House Aruba, as well as excellent staff at Scuba Lodge in Curaçao and Sunset Divers in Cayman. I am especially grateful to Bill and Suzie Mulvey for their wonderfully warm welcome in Bonaire, while Luigi Moxam showed off the very best of Cayman. As always, so much love and gratitude to Jerry Easter and Roy & Ruth Vorhees for making it possible for me to do what I love to do.

Paul Clammer

Thanks to all my co-authors for their valiant efforts, and destination editor Bailey Freeman for fielding a hundred questions. In Kingston, big thanks to Matthew Smith and Ishtar Govia, to David Scott, Joshua Chamberlain, Annie Paul, and everyone at LifeYard. In Ocho Rios, thanks to Shelly Ann Johnson. In Port Antonio, thanks to Charlene Bryden and Jim Sibthorpe. Grazie to Carla Gullotta in Drapers. At home, thanks and love as always to Robyn, especially for Monkey-wrangling while I was on the road.

Ashley Harrell

Thanks to: David Roth for hiking Pico Duartewith me. Vince DeGennaro and Grace Tilly for the hospitality. Kevin Raub, Bailey Freeman and Paul Clammer for their help and expertise. Soulouque for the wild ride. Caroline and Kaitlyn for the girl-time. Diane Pellerin for the dancing. Paul Guggenheim for the ideas and company. Sam Luok for existing. Tania Simonet for loving food like I do. Amy Benziger for the truest friendship I've ever known. And JC Taillandier, for just everything.

Liza Prado

Mil gracias to all the locals whose names I never learned but whose help was essential to me. Special thanks to my long lost *sanjuanero* friend Carlos Rivas, Kathy Gannett in Esperanza and Keishya Salko in Punta Santiago. Thank you to Mom, Dad, Joe, Elyse and Susan for all the kid help, and to Eva and Leo for waiting so patiently to play. And to Gary, my heart, thank you for your support and love; there's no way I could do what I do without you.

Brendan Sainsbury

Thanks to all my Cuban amigos, many of whom helped me immensely during this research (and have been doing so for years). Special thanks to Carlos Sarmiento, Luis Miguel, Maité & Idolka in Morón, Julio & Elsa Roque, Joel in Matanzas, Beny in Varadero, Ramberto on the Isla de la Juventud, and to my wife Liz and son Kieran for accompanying me on the road.

Alex Egerton

Firstly massive thanks to Chrystabel Sifflet for all the on the ground coordination, also thanks to Tonya Paul, Luc Weevers, Tabiah Regis, and Kent Warren for the island introductions. On the home front thanks as always to Olga Mosquera and Nicholas Kazu.

Anna Kaminski

A big thank you to Bailey for entrusting me with half of Jamaica, to fellow scribe Paul and to everyone who helped me along the way. In particular: Richard and Nicole in Falmouth/Santa Cruz/Accompong, Valerie and Leroy in MoBay, Ann and Lisa in Mandeville, Susan in Windsor, Allison in Black River, Captain Dennis in Treasure Beach, the brownie lady in Negril, Nancy and Lindsey in Kingston, and Elise and Darryl for the most memorable meal in Ochi.

Catherine Le Nevez

Merci mille fois/hartelijk bedankt first and foremost to Julian, and everyone on Anguilla, St Martin/Sint Maarten, St-Barthélemy, Saba, St Eustatius and throughout the Caribbean who provided insights, inspiration and great times. Huge thanks too to destination editor Bailey Freeman, my Leeward Islands co-author Andrea Schulte-Peevers and French Antilles co-author Tom Masters, and everyone at LP. As ever, a heartfelt *merci encore* to my parents, brother, *belle-sœur* and *neveu*.

Tom Masters

Many thanks to Rosemary Masters, Sylvain Delanoë, Gilbert Wass, Fabien Guyon, Héloïse Duchamp and Michel Brent for their assistance in Martinique and Guadeloupe.

Carolyn McCarthy

Heartfelt thanks to those who made my work in Cuba possible: from my host Luis Miguel in Havana to Domingo Cuza in Bayamo, the Muñoz family, Rafael in Camagüey, Nilson and Infotur. Brendan Sainsbury, Diego y Roy: *para su ayuda y buenos consejos, no hay suficiente Havana Club en el mundo para compensarles, pero intentamos!*

Hugh McNaughtan

I'd like to express thanks for the patience and support of Tasmin, Maise and Willa, the top-notch editorial and technical assistance of Bailey and the LP support team, and the kindness and generosity of so many in the Bahamas and Turks and Caicos.

Kevin Raub

Thanks to my wife, Adriana Schmidt Raub, who has to put up with me being gone more than being home (she might like it!). Bailey Freeman, Ashley Harrell and all my partners-in-crime at LP. On the road, Kim Beddall, Pierre and Monick Rouleau, Terry Baldi, Flora Tours, Paul and Audrey and all at the Dive Academy, Catherine DeLaura, Gill Thomas, Kate Wallace, Mael Moisan, Simon Suarez, Andria Mitsakos and Christina Little.

Andrea Schulte-Peevers

I'd like to thank the following people who went the extra mile in helping me with my research (in no particular order): Carol Ann Watson, Tom & Sharie Decherd, Iris Azoulay, Tim Antal, Alan Napier, Val Kempadoo, Lochton Grant, Julian Moore, David Lea, Clover Lea, Sunny Lea, Helen Marden, Troy Dixon and Jessica Foreman.

Polly Thomas

Thanks to Dexter, Aaron and Soleil Lewis for their patience and love during research; to Lynette, Dale, Gillian, Dean, Sion and all the Lewis clan for fabulous family times; to Skye Hernandez and Mampuru Stollmeyer for putting us up and putting up with us with such love; to Jillian Fourniller for stopping me from being hangry; to Gunda Busch-Harewood for a great road trip; and to Lara and Briony Baden-Semper and Sean Edghill for Port of Spain nightlife re-immersion.

Luke Waterson

Thank you Aurelio, Juan Julio and his stalwart JCB for rescuing me when my car came off the road and was teetering on the edge of a rather deep ravine. And, welcome as a piña colada on a sultry afternoon, was the assistance of Tamaris, José and Eddie in San Juan, Trevor in Isabela, Lisa in Rincón and Kurt in Jayuya. At LP, gratitude streams across the oceans to co-writer Liza and editor Bailey for helping bring this book together.

Karla Zimmerman

Thanks to fab pals Lisa Beran and Tamara Robinson for patience, good humor and invaluable assistance driving, snorkeling, drinking Painkillers and full moon partying. Thanks most to Eric Markowitz, partner-for-life supremo, who shoveled snow while I sat under palm trees. You top my Best List.

ACKNOWLEDGEMENTS

Climate map data adapted from Peel MC, Finlayson BL & McMahon TA (2007) 'Updated World Map of the Köppen-Geiger Climate Classification', *Hydrology and Earth System Sciences*, 11, pp1633–44.

Cover photograph: Yacht in Antigua, Aurora Photos / AWL ©s

THIS BOOK

This 7th edition of Lonely Planet's *Caribbean Islands* guidebook was researched and written by Mara Vorhees, Paul Clammer, Alex Egerton, Ashley Harrell, Catherine Le Nevez, Tom Masters, Hugh McNaughtan, Liza Prado, Brendan Sainsbury, Andrea Schulte-Peevers, Polly Thomas and Karla Zimmerman. The previous edition was written by Ryan Ver Berkmoes, Jean-Bernard Carillet, Nate Cavalieri, Paul Clammer, Michael Grosberg, Anna Kaminski, Beth Kohn, Adam Karlin, Tom Masters, Emily Matchar, Brandon Presser, Kevin Raub, Brendan Sainsbury, Andrea Schulte-Peevers, Polly Thomas, Luke Waterson and Karla Zimmerman. This guidebook was produced by the following:

Destination Editor Bailey Freeman

Product Editors Tracy Whitmey, Kate Mathews

Senior Cartographers Corey Hutchison, Alison Lyall

Book Designers Michael Buick, Wibowo Rusli

Assisting Editors Ronan Abayawickrema, William Allen, Janet Austin, Andrew Bain, Judith Bamber, Imogen Bannister, Michelle Bennett, Andrea Dobbin, Gabrielle Innes, Helen Koehne, Kellie Langdon, Jodie Martire, Kristin Odijk, Charlotte Orr, Chris Pitts, Sarah Reid, Ross Taylor, Saralinda Turner, Simor Williamson

Cover Researcher Naomi Parker

Thanks to Bruce Evans, Shona Gray, Liz Heynes, Elizabeth Jones, Sandie Kestell, Catherine Naghten, Lauren O'Connell, Rachel Rawling, Amanda Williamson

Index

NOTES

Map Legend

Sights

- Beach
- Bird Sanctuary
- Buddhist
- Castle/Palace
- Christian
- Confucian
- Hindu
- Islamic
- Jain
- Jewish
- Monument
- Museum/Gallery/Historic Building
- Ruin
- Shinto
- Sikh
- Taoist
- Winery/Vineyard
- Zoo/Wildlife Sanctuary
- Other Sight

Activities, Courses & Tours

- Bodysurfing
- Diving
- Canoeing/Kayaking
- Course/Tour
- Sento Hot Baths/Onsen
- Skiing
- Snorkelling
- Surfing
- Swimming/Pool
- Walking
- Windsurfing
- Other Activity

Sleeping

- Sleeping
- Camping

Eating

- Eating

Drinking & Nightlife

- Drinking & Nightlife
- Cafe

Entertainment

- Entertainment

Shopping

- Shopping

Information

- Bank
- Embassy/Consulate
- Hospital/Medical
- Internet
- Police
- Post Office
- Telephone
- Toilet
- Tourist Information
- Other Information

Geographic

- Beach
- Gate
- Hut/Shelter
- Lighthouse
- Lookout
- Mountain/Volcano
- Oasis
- Park
- Pass
- Picnic Area
- Waterfall

Population

- Capital (National)
- Capital (State/Province)
- City/Large Town
- Town/Village

Transport

- Airport
- Border crossing
- Bus
- Cable car/Funicular
- Cycling
- Ferry
- Metro station
- Monorail
- Parking
- Petrol station
- Subway station
- Taxi
- Train station/Railway
- Tram
- Underground station
- Other Transport

Note: Not all symbols displayed above appear on the maps in this book

Routes

- Tollway
- Freeway
- Primary
- Secondary
- Tertiary
- Lane
- Unsealed road
- Road under construction
- Plaza/Mall
- Steps
- Tunnel
- Pedestrian overpass
- Walking Tour
- Walking Tour detour
- Path/Walking Trail

Boundaries

- International
- State/Province
- Disputed
- Regional/Suburb
- Marine Park
- Cliff
- Wall

Hydrography

- River, Creek
- Intermittent River
- Canal
- Water
- Dry/Salt/Intermittent Lake
- Reef

Areas

- Airport/Runway
- Beach/Desert
- Cemetery (Christian)
- Cemetery (Other)
- Glacier
- Mudflat
- Park/Forest
- Sight (Building)
- Sportsground
- Swamp/Mangrove

Carolyn McCarthy

Cuba Carolyn specializes in travel, culture and adventure in the Americas. She has written for *National Geographic*, *Outside*, *BBC Magazine*, *Boston Globe* and other publications. A former Fulbright fellow and Banff Mountain Grant recipient, she has documented life in the most remote corners of Latin America. Carolyn gained her expertize by researching guidebooks in diverse destinations. She has contributed to more than 30 guidebooks for Lonely Planet, including *Colorado*, *USA*, *Argentina*, *Chile*, *Trekking in the Patagonian Andes*, *Panama*, *Peru* and *USA's National Parks*. For more information, visit www.carolynmccarthy.org or follow her Instagram travels at @masmerquen

Hugh McNaughtan

Bahamas, Turks & Caicos A former English lecturer, Hugh swapped grant applications for visa applications, and turned his love of travel into a full-time thing. Having done a bit of restaurant-reviewing in his home town (Melbourne), he's now eaten his way across four continents. He's never happier than when on the road with his two daughters. Except perhaps on the cricket field.

Kevin Raub

Dominican Republic Writer, Punta Cana & the Southeast, Península de Samaná, The Southwest & Península de Pedernales. Kevin Raub grew up in Atlanta and started his career as a music journalist in New York, working for *Men's Journal* and *Rolling Stone* magazines. He almost didn't accept this assignment, his third through the region, until he found out the road to Sabana de la Mar was finished – he just couldn't bear another go on the formerly tortuous, pothole-ridden road. Follow him on Twitter and Instagram (@RaubOnTheRoad).

Andrea Schulte-Peevers

Antigua & Barbuda, Dominica, Montserrat, St Kitts & Nevis Born and raised in Germany and educated in London and at UCLA, Andrea has traveled the distance to the moon and back in her visits to some 75 countries. She has earned her living as a professional travel writer for over two decades and authored or contributed to nearly 100 Lonely Planet titles as well as to newspapers, magazines and websites around the world. She also works as a travel consultant, translator and editor. Andrea's destination expertise is especially strong when it comes to Germany, Dubai and the UAE, Crete and the Caribbean Islands. She makes her home in Berlin.

Polly Thomas

Trinidad & Tobago Polly has been writing about the Caribbean for 20 years, authoring guide books to Jamaica, Antigua & Barbuda, St Lucia and Trinidad & Tobago. Having lived for five years in Port of Spain, Trinidad, she's now back in her hometown, London, seeking out good roti and doubles whenever she can.

Luke Waterson

Puerto Rico Raised in the remote Somerset countryside in Southwest England, Luke quickly became addicted to exploring out-of-the-way places. While completing a Creative Writing degree at the University of East Anglia, he shouldered his backpack and vowed to see as much of the world as possible. Fast-forward a few years and he has traveled the Americas from Alaska to Tierra del Fuego and developed an obsession for Soviet architecture and pre-Columbian ruins in equal measure. He divides his time between Wales and Slovakia, on which he keeps the world's leading English-language content site on Slovak travel and culture, www.englishmaninslovakia.co.uk.

Karla Zimmerman

British Virgin Islands, US Virgin Islands Karla lives in Chicago, where she eats doughnuts, yells at the Cubs, and writes stuff for books, magazines, and websites when she's not doing the first two things. She has contributed to 40-plus guidebooks and travel anthologies covering destinations in Europe, Asia, Africa, North America, and the Caribbean – all of which are a long way from the early days, when she wrote about gravel for a construction magazine and got to trek to places like Fredonia, Kansas. To learn more, follow her on Instagram and Twitter (@karlazimmerman).

Brendan Sainsbury

Cuba Born and raised in the UK in a town that never merits a mention in any guidebook (Andover, Hampshire), Brendan spent the holidays of his youth caravanning in the English Lake District and didn't leave Blighty until he was nineteen. Making up for lost time, he's since squeezed 70 countries into a sometimes precarious existence as a writer and professional vagabond. His rocking chair memories will probably include staging a performance of 'A Comedy of Errors' at a school in war-torn Angola, running 150 miles across the Sahara Desert in the Marathon des Sables, and hitchhiking from Cape Town to Kilimanjaro with an early, dog-eared copy of LP's *Africa on a Shoestring*. In the last 11 years he has written over 40 books for Lonely Planet, from Castro's Cuba to the canyons of Peru. When not scribbling research notes, Brendan likes partaking in ridiculous 'endurance' races, strumming old Clash songs on the guitar, and experiencing the pain and occasional pleasures of following Southampton Football Club.

Alex Egerton

Barbados, Grenada, St Lucia, St Vincent & the Grenadines A news journalist by trade, Alex has worked for magazines, newspapers and media outlets on five continents. Having had his fill of musty newsrooms and the insatiable corporate appetite for superficial news, Alex decided to leap into travel writing in order to escape the mundane. He spends most of his time on the road checking under mattresses, sampling suspicious street food and chatting with locals as part of the research process for travel articles and guidebooks. A keen adventurer, Alex has hiked through remote jungles in Colombia, explored isolated tributaries of the mighty Mekong and taken part in the first kayak descent of a number of remote waterways in Nicaragua. When not on the road, you'll find him at home amongst the colonial splendor of Popayán in southern Colombia.

Anna Kaminski

Jamaica Having majored in Caribbean and Latin American history at university and having lived in Kingston and worked in Jamaica's prisons and ghettos in 2006, Anna was thrilled to research Jamaica for Lonely Planet a second time. On this occasion, she drove the scenic and often gnarly back roads of west Jamaica, visited numerous plantation houses, hiked through rugged Cockpit Country, attended the Maroon Festival, attended the country's second-largest reggae gig and went to Boston Bay in search of Jamaica's best jerk pork. When not on the road for Lonely Planet, Anna calls London home.

Catherine Le Nevez

Anguilla, Saba, Sint Eustatius, St-Barthélemy, St-Martin/Sint Maarten Catherine's wanderlust kicked in when she roadtripped across Europe from her Parisian base aged four, and she's been hitting the road at every opportunity since, travelling to around 60 countries and completing her Doctorate of Creative Arts in Writing, Masters in Professional Writing, and postgrad qualifications in Editing and Publishing along the way. Over the past dozen-plus years she's written scores of Lonely Planet guides and articles covering Paris, France, Europe and far beyond. Her work has also appeared in numerous online and print publications. Topping Catherine's list of travel tips is to travel without any expectations.

Tom Masters

Guadeloupe, Martinique Dreaming since he could walk of going to the most obscure places on earth, Tom has always had a taste for the unknown. This has led to a writing career that has taken him all over the world, including North Korea, the Arctic, Congo and Siberia. Despite a brief spell living in the English countryside, Tom has always called London, Paris and Berlin home.

After graduating with a degree in Russian literature from the University of London, Tom went to work in Russia as a journalist at the *St Petersburg Times*. This first writing job took him on to work at the BBC World Service in London, and as a freelance contributor to newspapers and magazines around the world, as well as working in documentary production for UK and US television companies. Tom indulges his love of communist architecture by living on Karl-Marx-Allee in Berlin's Friedrichshain, but still returns regularly to the former Soviet Union for work. His most recent projects include guides to China, Central America and Venezuela. He can be found online at www.tommasters.net.

OUR STORY

A beat-up old car, a few dollars in the pocket and a sense of adventure. In 1972 that's all Tony and Maureen Wheeler needed for the trip of a lifetime – across Europe and Asia overland to Australia. It took several months, and at the end – broke but inspired – they sat at their kitchen table writing and stapling together their first travel guide, *Across Asia on the Cheap*. Within a week they'd sold 1500 copies. Lonely Planet was born.

Today, Lonely Planet has offices in Franklin, London, Melbourne, Oakland, Dublin, Beijing and Delhi, with more than 600 staff and writers. We share Tony's belief that 'a great guidebook should do three things: inform, educate and amuse'.

OUR WRITERS

Mara Vorhees

Aruba, Bonaire, Cayman Islands, Curaçao Mara Vorhees writes about food, travel and family fun around the world. Her work has been published by *BBC Travel*, *Boston Globe*, *Delta Sky*, *Vancouver Sun* and more. For Lonely Planet, she regularly writes about destinations in Central America and Eastern Europe, as well as New England, where she lives. She often travels with her twin boys in tow, earning her an expertise in family travel. Follow their adventures and misadventures at www.havetwinswilltravel.com.

Paul Clammer

Jamaica Paul Clammer has worked as a molecular biologist, tour leader and travel writer. Since 2003 he has worked as a guidebook author for Lonely Planet, contributing to over 25 LP titles, covering swathes of South and Central Asia, West and North Africa and the Caribbean. In recent years he's lived in Morocco, Jordan, Haiti and Fiji, as well as his native England. Find him online at paulclammer.com or on Twitter as @paulclammer. Paul also wrote the Plan and Survival Guide sections of this guidebook.

Ashley Harrell

Dominican Republic, Haiti After a brief stint selling day-spa coupons door-to-door in South Florida, Ashley decided she'd rather be a writer. She went to journalism grad school, convinced a newspaper to hire her, and starting covering wildlife, crime and tourism, sometimes all in the same story. She traveled widely and moved often, from a tiny NYC apartment to a vast California ranch to a jungle cabin in Costa Rica, where she started writing for Lonely Planet. From there her travels became more exotic and farther flung, and she still laughs when paychecks arrive.

Liza Prado

Puerto Rico Liza Prado has been a travel writer since 2003, when she made a move from corporate lawyering to travel writing (and never looked back). She's written dozens of guidebooks and articles as well as apps and blogs to destinations throughout the Americas. She takes decent photos too. Liza is a graduate of Brown University and Stanford Law School. She lives in Denver, Colorado, with her husband and fellow LP writer, Gary Chandler, and their two kids.

OVER PAGE MORE WRITERS

Published by Lonely Planet Global Limited
CRN 554153
7th edition – Nov 2017
ISBN 978 1 78657 650 7
© Lonely Planet 2017   Photographs © as indicated 2017
10 9 8 7 6 5 4 3 2 1
Printed in Singapore